CORPORATE FINANCE AND FINANCIAL STRATEGY

PEARSON

At Pearson, we have a simple mission: to help people
make more of their lives through learning

We combine innovative learning technology with
trusted content and educational expertise to provide
engaging and effective learning experiences
that serve people wherever and whenever
they are learning.

From classroom to boardroom, our curriculum
materials, digital learning tools
and testing programmes help to educate millions
of people worldwide - more
than any other private enterprise.

Every day our work helps learning flourish,
and wherever learning flourishes,
so do people.

To learn more please visit us at www.pearson.com/uk

CORPORATE FINANCE AND FINANCIAL STRATEGY

Optimising corporate and shareholder value

TONY DAVIES

and

IAN CRAWFORD

Harlow, England • London • New York • Boston • San Francisco • Toronto • Sydney • Auckland • Singapore • Hong Kong
Tokyo • Seoul • Taipei • New Delhi • Cape Town • São Paulo • Mexico City • Madrid • Amsterdam • Munich • Paris • Milan

PEARSON EDUCATION LIMITED
Edinburgh Gate
Harlow CM20 2JE
United Kingdom
Tel: +44 (0)1279 623623
Web: www.pearson.com/uk

First published 2014 (print and electronic)

ISBN: 978-0-273-77386-3 (print)
     978-0-273-77390-0 (ePub)
     978-0-273-78933-8 (eText)

British Library Cataloguing-in-Publication Data
A catalogue record for the print edition is available from the British Library

Library of Congress Cataloging-in-Publication Data
Davies, Tony.
  Corporate finance and financial strategy: optimising corporate and shareholder value / Tony Davies and Ian Crawford.
     pages cm
  ISBN 978-0-273-77386-3
  1. Corporations–Finance.   2. Strategic planning.   I. Crawford, Ian (Ian Peter)   II. Title.
  HG4026.D3784 2013
  658.15–dc23

                              2013012467

10 9 8 7 6 5 4 3 2 1
17 16 15 14 13

Print edition typeset in 9.5/12.5 pt Charter ITC Std by 71
Print edition printed and bound in Great Britain by Ashford Colour Press Ltd, Gosport, Hampshire

NOTE THAT ANY PAGE CROSS REFERENCES REFER TO THE PRINT EDITION

Brief contents

Contents

18 Reorganisations and restructuring   **805**

APPENDICES   **835**

Supporting resources

Visit **www.pearsoned.co.uk/daviestony** to find valuable online resources.

Companion website for students

- Multiple-choice questions to test your understanding
- Additional case studies
- Additional exercises
- Flashcards to test your understanding of key terms
- Links to relevant sites on the World Wide Web
- Author biographies

For instructors

Visit **www.pearsoned.co.uk/daviestony** to access a comprehensive suite of instructor resources, including an Instructor's Manual with:

- Teaching notes for each chapter
- Debriefs to all case studies in the book
- Additional case studies and debriefs
- Solutions to all chapter-end exercises
- Additional exercises and solutions
- PowerPoint presentations for each chapter, including all illustrations from the book
- Useful weblinks and an author Q&A.

Also, the Companion website provides the following features:

- Search tool to help locate specific items of content
- E-mail results and profile tools to send results of quizzes to instructors
- Online help and support to assist with website usage and troubleshooting

For more information please contact your local Pearson Education sales representative or visit **www.pearsoned.co.uk/daviestony**

Features

Case studies

Press extracts

Figures

This book is dedicated to
Frances Davies

Preface

Coverage of financial issues by the press and media increases almost daily in both volume and complexity. The importance and media coverage of these issues has escalated enormously since the beginning of the so-called 'credit crunch', the global financial crisis that began in 2008. This includes topics such as debt, interest rates, corporate financial fraud, stock market performance, investment and growth, mergers and acquisitions, venture capitalists and private equity, derivatives, and foreign currency exchange rates. Each of these topics is in some way concerned with the risks faced by government organisations and individuals, and by financial institutions, banks, manufacturing and service companies, and their shareholders and lenders, and the corresponding cash returns that they expect to receive in reward for acceptance of such risks.

Corporate finance is concerned with all these financial issues, which impact on us all in one way or another and are forever changing in their composition and focus. The discipline of corporate finance is about:

- the way in which financial resources are acquired
- how these resources are most effectively used
- the control of these activities.

The topicality and critical importance of these topics therefore makes their study exciting and very relevant to a better understanding of the performance of countries' economies and businesses, and the decisions and problems they face.

This new textbook is called *Corporate Finance and Financial Strategy* because it includes not only the theory and key areas of corporate finance and the range of techniques that may be used and applied in practice, but also the appropriate financial strategies that may be adopted in order to optimise the use of the scarce resource of money (or cash flow).

One of the main objectives in writing this book was to produce a clear and user-friendly text, which embraces both the core principles and practice of corporate finance and also financial strategy. This book uses a comprehensive set of learning features, illustrative worked examples and assessment material to support and reinforce your study. It is aimed primarily at students who are undertaking a degree or diploma in accounting, finance, economics or business management, which includes a course in corporate finance or financial strategy, or both. It is also aimed at students undertaking postgraduate finance and business masters degrees, MBA students, and students pursuing professional accounting and finance courses.

Content and structure

The content and structure of the text have been carefully researched to follow closely the typical requirements of most introductory corporate finance and financial strategy courses at both undergraduate and postgraduate levels. This text assumes no prior knowledge of the subject:

we start at square one and take you step-by-step through the concepts and application of techniques, with clear explanations and numerous examples.

The text comprises 18 chapters, and is structured into two parts: corporate finance, and financial strategy:

Corporate finance is broadly concerned with the effective acquisition and use of financial resources in creating corporate value, and its translation into shareholder value. It includes a wide range of strategic financial management techniques and decision-making relating to capital investment; capital structure; working capital; the management of financial risk; financial planning; international operations and investment. It also covers accountability of company directors and their relationships with shareholders and other stakeholders.

Financial strategy decisions in general relate to the levels of:

- investment in the assets of the business, and the choice of types of asset
- most appropriate methods of funding – debt or equity
- profit retention
- profit distribution
- gearing, or capital structure of the business
- management of financial risk,

with the aim of maximisation of shareholder wealth.

Financial strategy is concerned with the creation of corporate value, but also how this is then reflected in increased shareholder wealth through creation of shareholder value consistent with levels of perceived risk and the returns required by investors.

Each of these areas and their component chapters are outlined in the introductory section to each part of the text.

A further key objective in writing this text was to provide a flexible study resource. There is a linkage between each of the chapters, which follow a structure that has been designed to facilitate effective learning of the subject in a progressive way. However, each chapter may also be used on a standalone basis; equally, chapters may be excluded from study if they relate to subjects that are not essential for a specific course. Therefore, the text is intended to be suitable for modules of either one or two semesters' duration.

Each chapter aims to help students understand the broader context and relevance of corporate finance and financial strategy in the business environment, and how these may assist in improving both corporate value and shareholder value. To put each topic in context we have provided numerous examples and commentary on company activity within each chapter, including at least one extract from the press and financial media; companies featured include Nestlé, Tesco, Barclays Bank, Ericsson, Next, Punch Taverns and BT. In addition, the book includes extracts and analysis of the actual Report and Accounts 2012 of Johnson Matthey, a major UK plc.

Using this book

To support your study and reinforce the topics covered, we have included a comprehensive range of learning features and assessment material in each chapter, including:

- learning objectives
- introduction
- highlighted key terms

- mini cases about real companies
- fully worked examples
- integrated progress checks
- key points summary
- glossary of key terms
- questions
- discussion points
- exercises.

Within each chapter we have also included numerous diagrams and charts that illustrate and reinforce important concepts and ideas. The double-page Guided Tour that follows on pages xxvii–xxviii summarises the purpose of these learning features and the chapter-end assessment material. To gain maximum benefit from this text and to help you succeed in your study and exams, you are encouraged to familiarise yourself with these elements now, before you start the first chapter.

It is easy, but mistaken, to read on cruise control, highlighting the odd sentence and gliding through the worked examples, progress checks and chapter-end questions and exercises. Active learning needs to be interactive: if you haven't followed a topic or an example, go back and work through it again; try to think of other examples to which particular topics may be applied. The only way to check you have a comprehensive understanding of things is to attempt all the integrated progress checks and worked examples, and the chapter-end assessment material, and then to compare with the text and answers provided. Fully worked solutions are given immediately after each example, and solutions to around 45% of the chapter-end exercises (those with their numbers in colour) are provided in Appendix 2. Additional self-assessment material is available in the student centre of the book's accompanying website (see page xvi).

Case studies

Throughout the book there are six case studies that may be tackled either individually or as a team. The case studies are a little more weighty than the chapter-end exercises and integrate many of the topics covered in the book. Each case study therefore gives you an opportunity to apply the techniques and knowledge gained, and to develop these together with the analytical skills, judgement, and strategic approach required to deal with real-life business problems. Additional cases are provided on the accompanying website.

We hope this textbook will enhance your interest, understanding and skills. Above all, relax, learn and enjoy!

Guided tour

Learning objectives at the beginning of each chapter enable you to focus on what you should understand after using each section of the book.

Learning objectives

Completion of this chapter will enable you to:

- Explain financial planning as part of the strategic management process.
- Outline the purpose of financial planning.
- Describe the financial planning process.
- Use financial modelling to plan the long-term activities of a business.
- Identify the ways in which a company may use alternative forecasting methods.
- Prepare a cash flow forecast as part of the financial planning process to determine a company's funding requirements.
- Explain the ways in which a business may plan for its future growth.
- Consider the financing options that a company may use to fund its future growth.
- Outline the ways in which a company's performance may be measured against its plans.
- Explain the ways in which the balanced scorecard may be used to translate a company's strategic plans into operational terms.

The **Introduction** gives you a brief overview of the content and aims of each chapter, and how it links to the previous chapter.

Introduction

Many companies have started up with very good ideas and good intentions with regard to their development and future sales growth. However, the corporate graveyard is full of companies that have been unsuccessful in these endeavours because they have failed to plan for such growth in terms of its impact on costs and planned levels of investment and funding.

This chapter considers financial planning, which is an important part of the strategic management process, concerned not with the absolute detail but taking a look at the big picture of the company as a whole. Strategic financial planning is not short term, but is concerned with periods of more than one year, and looks at expected levels of a company's sales growth and how it may be financed.

In order to produce forecast long-term financial statements, financial plans are prepared based on the company's planned growth rate, and its financial ratios relating to costs, working capital, tax, dividends, and gearing. Forecasts are not plans or budgets but are predictions of what may happen in the future. There are a variety of techniques, both qualitative and quantitative, which are used to forecast growth rates. Quantitative methods include use of the statistical techniques of exponential smoothing and regression analysis.

Cash flow forecasting is one part of the financial planning process and is used to determine a company's future funding requirements on a monthly and yearly basis. The company may use its own resources of retained earnings to support its plans for future sales growth. In some circumstances, additional external funding is necessary for a company planning future growth.

Key terms are highlighted the first time they are introduced, alerting you to the core concepts and techniques in each chapter. A full explanation is given in the Glossary section at the end of the chapter.

purposes to influence improved business unit and departmental performance. Monitoring of actual performance against plans is used to provide feedback in order to take the appropriate action necessary to reach planned performance, and to revise plans in the light of changes.

The role of financial planning is crucial to any business and it is important to be as accurate as possible. As the Thomas Cook press extract below indicates, the impact of a failure to accurately **forecast** the costs of long-term projects can have serious consequences for a company's financial stability.

Currently, many companies are taking the view that the traditional planning and annual budgeting systems are unsuitable and irrelevant in rapidly changing markets. Further, they believe that budgets fail to deal with the most important drivers of shareholder value such as intangible assets like brands and knowledge. Some of these companies, like Volvo, Ikea, and Ericsson, have already revised their need for annual budgets as being an inefficient tool in an

Press extracts feature real company examples from the press, including commentary that highlights the practical application of corporate finance in the business environment.

Mature takeover target

Sadly, there is still plenty of action in Afghanistan. But for investors in Inmarsat – the UK satellite company that provides phones and internet services to ships, aircraft and soldiers in such remote places – some action in the boardroom would be welcome. Over the past year, the company's share price has fallen by two-fifths as a stalled shipping industry and cutbacks in military activity hurt business. Is this a perfect moment to make a bid?

Inmarsat's shares jumped 4 per cent yesterday on speculation that it may be a takeover target. EADS and General Electric have been aired as possible candidates. The Franco-German aerospace group bought Vizada, one of Inmarsat's main distributors, last year for €1bn and adding Inmarsat may open some prospect of synergies. Cost savings are less obvious for GE, though.

That said, Inmarsat's tepid medium-term outlook could be a turn-off for a publicly listed acquirer. Its earnings before interest, tax, depreciation and amortisation in 2012 are forecast to fall by 4 per cent and there is little prospect of growth in 2013. That perhaps opens the door for private equity. In a leveraged buy-out scenario, if a buyer paid, say, £2.5bn – or £5.54 per share, a 30 per cent premium to Inmarsat's undisturbed share price – funded half with debt, then even assuming no ebitda growth over five years, it could produce an internal rate of return of 12 per cent. Not bad.

Boosting Inmarsat's appeal is that its long-term future looks favourable. It has yet to materially tap into emerging markets and its new global broadband satellites could boost its military business revenues late next year. Current investors may be fed up with the lack of action but a private buyer with a longer-term perspective should be able to find value in the business. For Inmarsat's long-suffering shareholders, that would be a relief.

Source: Inmarsat, Lex column (2012), Financial Times, 9 February.
© The Financial Times Limited 2012. All Rights Reserved.

Numerous **Worked examples** throughout the book provide an application of the learning points and techniques included within each topic. By working through the step-by-step solutions, you have an opportunity to check your knowledge at frequent intervals

Worked example 11.6

Martin plc, a UK multinational company, has equity with a market value of £150m and debt capital with a market value of £100m. The company's current cost of equity is 12%, and its after-tax cost of debt is 7%.

Martin plc has secured a contract worth Aus$80m to supply and install plant and equipment for a company in Australia. The payment terms of the contract set by Martin plc, which are non-negotiable, are:

- Aus$20m payment to be made on completion of stage one of the contract at the end of year one
- Aus$24m payment to be made on completion of stage two of the contract at the end of year two
- Aus$36m payment to be made on completion of stage three of the contract at the end of year three

The estimated cost of the supply and installation of the plant and equipment is Aus$70m.

Project cash outflows in respect of the project are expected to involve three currencies – Aus$, £ sterling, and euro – and cash flows are estimated as follows:

Year	0	1	2	3
Inflows				
Aus$	0	20	24	36
Outflows				
Aus$	6	3	7	4
UK £	3	3	1	3
€	3	3	4	5

The current exchange rates at the start of the project are:

$$£ = \text{Aus}\$2.50$$
$$€ = \text{Aus}\$1.67$$

Progress checks allow you to check and apply your understanding of each key topic before you move on.

Progress check 11.7

Explain the significance of the choice of discount rate in international investment appraisal.

Mini case boxes provide a real-world context for key topics.

Mini case 17.2

One of the benefits of using a rights issue to fund an acquisition lies in the opportunity to maintain the same profile of shareholders after the funds have been raised without increasing the gearing of the company outside normal levels.

In September 2009 Balfour Beatty plc, a UK engineering and construction company, announced the acquisition of the US professional services business Parsons Brinckerhoff in a $626m (£380m) takeover.

Balfour Beatty plc offered a 3 for 7 rights issue at 180 pence per ordinary share (a discount of 48%) to raise approximately £353m, net of issue expenses. The outcome was that existing shareholders bought 97% of 199.5m new shares, with the remaining 6m shares bought by other investors.

After the acquisition, the overall spread of shareholders therefore altered only marginally, and the gearing ratio remained at a level acceptable to the company.

Balfour Beatty plc gearing 2006 to 2010

2010	2009	2008	2007	2006
115%	140%	104%	158%	160%

A **Summary of key points** features at the end of each chapter. This allows you to check that you understand all the main points covered before moving on to the next chapter.

Summary of key points

- Internationalisation, with regard to the increasing geographical dispersion of economic, cultural, social, educational, technological, and political activities across national borders, has an increasing impact on the role of the financial markets and the activities of international companies.
- The international financial marketplace is an interrelated network of buyers and sellers in which exchange activities occur in the pursuit of profit and reward, and has obvious significance for international companies.
- Companies may wish to undertake overseas operations for a variety of reasons, but particularly to gain access to overseas markets by enabling them to get closer to their customers.
- Companies may engage in various types of international operations, for example through exporting, use of agents, licensing, franchising, or the establishment of a branch, joint venture, or an overseas subsidiary.
- International companies may consider foreign direct investment (FDI) in terms of investments in new or expanded facilities overseas.
- There are additional, unique features associated with international investment appraisal in a multi-currency, overseas environment, compared with the appraisal of domestic investment projects, for example taxation, foreign currency cash flows, overseas interest rates, transfer prices, royalties, management fees, exchange controls, and country risk.
- The evaluation of international investment using NPV requires the choice of a suitable cost of capital as a discount rate, the most appropriate of which may be the required return specific to the individual investment.
- The choice of financing for international investments requires the consideration of currency risk, interest rate risk, taxation, gearing, and country risk.
- Country risk, which is also called political risk, is the exposure a company faces as a consequence of a change in government action, against which it may protect itself through, for example, insurance, negotiation, development of close relationships, establishment of a local presence, and the use of local financing.

At the end of each chapter a **Glossary of key terms** in alphabetical order provides full definitions of any key terms that have been introduced. The numbers of the pages on which key term definitions appear are high-lighted in the index.

Glossary of key terms

arbitrage This is the act of exploiting the price differences in financial instruments, or other assets, in different markets by simultaneously buying and selling the assets to make a profit from the price difference. It exists because there are market inefficiencies but it also provides a means of ensuring that prices do not remain different for long periods and that an equilibrium price is finally reached.

cost of debt The annual percentage rate of return required by long-term lenders to a company (loans and bonds), generally expressed net of tax as a cost to the company.

cost of equity The annual percentage rate of return required by the shareholders of a company.

dividend growth model (or Gordon growth model) A method of calculating cost of equity that assumes a direct link between the share price and expected future dividends and recognises the expected rate of dividend growth (G) achieved through reinvestment of retained earnings.

dividend model A method of calculating the cost of equity that divides the current dividend by the current share price, which is based on the notion that shareholders may value shares by the value of their expected dividends.

Short narrative-type **Questions** encourage you to review and check your understanding of all the key topics. There are typically 7 to 10 of these questions at the end of each chapter.

A **Discussion points** section typically includes 2 to 4 thought-provoking ideas and questions that encourage you to critically apply your understanding and/or further develop some of the topics introduced in each chapter, either individually or in group discussion.

Questions

Q17.1 Why is the method of financing important in M&As?

Q17.2 In what ways does a cash purchase of a business differ from a vendor placing?

Q17.3 How may eps be enhanced from a takeover?

Q17.4 Describe the various forms of equity restructuring that may be used by a target company to avoid its being taken over.

Q17.5 How may profit announcements, and changes in dividend policy, be used by target companies to provide defences after a takeover bid has been made?

Q17.6 Describe and explain the range of defence strategies used by companies facing a hostile takeover bid.

Q17.7 Outline the types of problem faced by employees and managers after their company has been taken over.

Discussion points

D17.1 'Takeovers merely satisfy the inflated egos of power-hungry company bosses.' Discuss.

D17.2 'The ways in which M&As are financed do not have any influence on their subsequent success.' Discuss.

D17.3 'There is no real defence against a takeover bid from a determined predator company.' Discuss.

D17.4 'The position of shareholders, managers, and employees in M&As is largely disregarded by both predator and target companies.' Discuss.

Exercises provide comprehensive examination-style questions which are graded by their level of difficulty, and also indicate the time typically required to complete them. They are designed to assess your knowledge and application of the principles and techniques covered in each chapter. Full solutions to the colour-highlighted exercise numbers are provided in Appendix 2 to allow you to self-asses your progress

Exercises

Solutions are provided in Appendix 2 to all exercise numbers highlighted in colour.

Level I

E2.1   *Time allowed – 15 minutes*

Identify the components of shareholder wealth and explain how the strategic financial decisions made by a company impact on each of them.

E2.2   *Time allowed – 15 minutes*

Explain what is meant by shareholder value and consider the value-creating alternatives. Outline three ways of measuring shareholder value.

E2.3   *Time allowed – 30 minutes*

Explain how alternative methods may be used to measure shareholder value and give your view as to which may be the most appropriate measure.

Level II

E2.4   *Time allowed – 30 minutes*

At a recent board meeting the managing director of Angel plc announced that the company's directors had been awarded substantial cash bonuses and share options, despite the company incurring substantial losses during the last financial year. Explain why the above represents an agency problem within a company between the directors and the shareholders, and the ways in which it may be resolved.

Acknowledgements

Author

Thank you to the university lecturers who were involved in the initial market research, and to those who provided useful review comments and technical checks of the draft chapters during the development phase of this project.

Thank you to CIMA (the Chartered Institute of Management Accountants) for their permission to include extracts from their Management Accounting Official Terminology 2005 edition.

Thank you also to Johnson Matthey Plc for permission to use extracts of their Report and Accounts 2012 as an excellent example of the information provided to shareholders by a major UK plc. The financial reporting and corporate governance and sustainability reporting by Johnson Matthey is truly world class.

Thank you to Katie Rowland, Gemma Doel, Kate Brewin for their support and encouragement in the writing of this book and the development of the website.

Publisher

We are grateful to the following for permission to reproduce copyright material:

Tables

Table 11.1 from 'Foreign Direct Investment flows by region in 2010', UNCTAD World Investment report 2011, United Nations Publication ISBN 978-92-1-1 112828-4 © United Nations 2011.

Text

Extract on p. 23 from 'Revenues up but restructuring programme pushes McBride into loss', *Manchester Evening News,* 19/2/2012 (James McBride), Manchester Evening News; Extract on p. 36 from ISA 200 (International Standard on Auditing 200) the International Standards on Auditing 2011, 2011 International Federation of Accountants. This text is an extract from ISA 200 of the Handbook of International Quality Control, Auditing, Review, Other Assurance, and Related Services Pronouncements, published by the International Federation of Accountants (IFAC) in July 2012 and is used with permission of IFAC; Extract on p. 60 from 'Astra-Zeneca chief quits with derision ringing in his ears', *The Times,* 27/04/2012 (Andrew Clarke), The Times; Extract on p. 135 from The Cadbury Committee from Committee's Code of Best Practice 1992 incorporated in latest revision under the title of the UK Corporate Governance Code issued by the FRC in June 2010, FRC (Financial Reporting Council); Extract on p. 139

from Financial Reporting Council; Extract on p. 145 from EU definition of Corporate Social Responsibility (CSR), http://ec.europa.eu/enterprise/policies/sustainable-business/corporate-social-responsibility European Commission; Article on pp. 157–8 from 'The small cases that will have a big influence on the way we work; Gary Slapper reflects on the deaths that have led to changes in the corporate manslaughter law', *The Times,* 11/07/2009 (Gary Slapper), The Times/News International Syndication; Article on p. 229 from 'Finance chiefs aim to raise debt', *Financial Times,* 11/10/2010 (Emma Saunders), © The Financial Times Limited. All Rights Reserved.; Article on p. 283 from 'Call to MPs to put party politics aside and join Bombardier fight', *Derby Evening Telegraph,* 3/9/2011 (Robin Johnson), Derby Evening Telegraph; Article on pp. 344–5 from 'There is some good to be seen in the death of flotations', *Financial Times,* 12/5/2011 (David Blackwell), © The Financial Times Limited. All Rights Reserved; Article on pp. 348–9 from 'Islamic bonds stage a comeback from crisis slump', *Financial Times,* 29/3/2012 (Robin Wigglesworth and Camilla Hall), © The Financial Times Limited. All Rights Reserved; Article on p. 384 from 'Farewell then . . . floppy discs', *Daily Mail,* 28/4/2010 (Chris Beanland), Solo Syndication, credit Daily Mail ; Article on p. 394 from 'Firms forced to 'rob Peter to pay Paul' in late-payments circle', *The Western Mail,* 11/4/2012 (Siôn Barry), ©Mirrorpix ; Extract on p. 446 from 'Thomas Cook to close stores and slash jobs to cut losses', *The Telegraph,* 19/12/2011 (Graham Ruddick and Alistair Osborne), copyright © Telegraph Media Group Limited 2012/2011; Case Study 9.1 from Next plc, Quarterly Management Statement, issued 2 May, 2012; Article on p. 498 from 'Gm halts Volt output as slow sales create overhang', *Financial Times,* 03/3/2012 (Ed Crooks), © The Financial Times Limited. All Rights Reserved;

Article on pp. 552–3 from 'Reconnaissance mission unearths new markets; diversification leads to major expansion for Midlands company', *The Times,* 23/4/2012 (Alan Copps), NI Syndication; Article on p. 611 from 'Barclays accused over Libor fix rate', *The Daily Telegraph,* 25/4/2012 (Harry Wilson), The Telegraph Media Group Ltd, copyright © Telegraph Media Group Limited 2012/2011; Article on pp. 612–3 from 'Heads or Tails? Just Don't Bet On It', *Financial Times,* 16/6/2012 (Tim Harford), © The Financial Times Limited. All Rights Reserved; Article on pp. 655–6 from 'Desire for dividends outweighs financial growth', *Financial Times,* 19/05/2011 (David Blackwell), © The Financial Times Limited. All Rights Reserved; Article on pp. 667–9 from 'In search of outside inspiration', from Business Life section, *Financial Times,* 13/03/2012, © The Financial Times Limited. All Rights Reserved; Article on pp. 683–4 from 'NMC's flotation raises £117m', *Financial Times,* 2/4/2012 (Robin Wigglesworth), © The Financial Times Limited. All Rights Reserved; Case Study 14.1 from Annual report on the business angel market in the United Kingdom: 2009/10 Ref 11/P116 Department for Business Innovation and Skills; Article on p. 713 from 'Mature Takeover Target', Inmarsat,Lex column, *Financial Times,* 9/2/2012 © The Financial Times Limited. All Rights Reserved; Article on pp. 739–41 from 'Corporate Transactions & Financing: Keeping an eye on M&A activity', Commercial reports section, *Sunday Business Post,* 04/12/2011, Post Publications Ltd; Article on p. 795 from 'Minerva overrides shareholders by reinstating chairman', *Financial Times,* 5/12/2009 (Daniel Thomas), © The Financial Times Limited. All Rights Reserved; Article on pp. 797–8 from 'Rio Tinto ups bid for Hathor to trump offer from Cameco', *The Independent,* 19/11/2011 (Tom Bawden); Article on pp. 790–1 from 'Illumina moves to fend off hostile Roche bid', *Financial Times,* 27/1/2012 (Alan Rappaport, Helen Thomas and Andrew Jack), © The Financial Times Limited. All Rights Reserved; Article on p. 813 from 'Time Warner makes approach for Endemol', *Financial Times,* 5/11/2011 (Andrew Edgecliffe-Johnson, AnoushaSakoui and Ben Fenton), © The Financial Times Limited. All Rights Reserved; Article on p. 820 from 'CPA set to seal £440m buy-out', *Financial Times,* 25/1/2010 (Martin Arnold), © The Financial Times Limited. All Rights Reserved; Article on p. 827 from 'Wasps will be saved by former player

Ken Moss – provided they avoid relegation from Premiership', *The Daily Telegraph,* 27/4/2012 (Gavin Mairs), Telegraph Media Group Ltd, © Telegraph Media Group Limited 2012/2011; Article on pp. 814–5 from 'Punch Taverns tries to gauge extent of coverage after group is split', *Financial Times,* 2/5/2011 (Rose Jacobs), © The Financial Times Limited. All Rights Reserved; Article on pp. 815–6 from 'Pfizer talks to banks about unit's $3bn part-flotation', *Financial Times,* 20/2/2012 (AnoushaSakoui and Helen Thomas), © The Financial Times Limited. All Rights Reserved; Article on pp. 810–11 from 'Citic Bank surprises with cheaply priced rights issue', *Euroweek,* 30/6/2011, Euromoney Institutional Investor PLC; Article on pp. 811–12 from 'Banks mop up Pendragon rights issue', *The Daily Telegraph,* 18/08/2011 (Ben Harrington), © Telegraph Media Group Limited 2012/2011; General displayed text on pp. 88–132 and 374–7 from Annual report 2012, pp. 76–117 and pp. 120–1. Johnson Matthey Plc, extracts from their 2012 Annual Report and Accounts, courtesy of Johnson Matthey Plc.

In some instances we have been unable to trace the owners of copyright material, and we would appreciate any information that would enable us to do so.

Part I

CORPORATE FINANCE

Introduction to Part I

Part I of this book is about corporate finance, which is concerned with the effective use of financial resources in creating corporate value. It looks at the financial environment in which businesses operate, their financial aims and objectives, and includes a wide range of financial management techniques related to financial decision-making. These include, for example, capital investment, capital structure, working capital, the management of financial risk, financial planning, and international operations and investment. It also considers the ways in which compliance with various corporate governance guidelines broadly supports the achievement of business objectives in determining the responsibilities and accountability of company directors and their relationships with shareholders and other stakeholders.

In Chapter 1, Figure 1.1 provides the framework of strategic corporate finance on which this book is based. The topics included in each of the shaded areas in Figure 1.1 are covered in Chapters 1 to 12, except for financial strategy, which is covered in Chapters 13 to 18 in Part II of this book.

Part I is concerned primarily with the creation of corporate value and its translation into shareholder value. Part II of this book is about the use of appropriate financial strategies, as distinct from business strategies. This looks at what companies may do to ensure not only the creation of corporate value, but also that the performance of the business is reflected in the maximisation of shareholder value. Companies may do all the right things in terms of creating value from investments in value-creating projects. However, if this performance is not translated into and reflected in optimal shareholder value through dividend growth and an increasing share price then the primary objective of the business – maximisation of shareholder wealth – is not being achieved.

The providers of the capital for a business, its shareholders and lenders, require appropriate returns on their investments from dividends, interest, and share price increases, commensurate with the levels of risk they are prepared to accept associated with the type of businesses and industrial sectors in which they invest. The directors or managers of a company have the responsibility for pursuit of the objective of shareholder wealth maximisation. Faced with different types and levels of risk at each stage in a company's development, directors' responsibilities therefore include not only ensuring that value is added to the business, that is corporate value, through making 'real' investments in projects that return the highest possible positive net present values of cash flows, but also ensuring that appropriate financial strategies are adopted that reflect this in the value created for shareholders, that is shareholder wealth.

These 'real' investment types of decision and their financing are dealt with in Part I. Part II looks at how companies are exposed to varying levels of financial risk at each of the different stages in their development, and in response to these how they may apply the techniques dealt with in Part I. Part II also considers how the creation of corporate value by companies at each stage of their development may then be reflected in increased shareholder value through the use of appropriate financial strategies and exploitation of market imperfections. We will explore how different financial strategies may apply at different stages in the development of a company. Shareholder value is provided in two ways: from increases in the price of shares; and the payment of dividends on those shares.

In Part II we look at the ways in which strategic financial decisions may be made relating to the levels of:

- investment in the assets of the business, and the types of assets
- most appropriate methods of funding – debt or equity
- profit retention
- profit distribution
- gearing, or capital structure of the business,

with the aim of maximisation of shareholder wealth through creation of shareholder value consistent with levels of perceived risk and returns required by investors and lenders.

To provide a framework for Part II in which to consider these decisions we will use a simplified, theoretical 'business life cycle' model, the BLC, which describes the stages through which businesses may typically progress from their initial start-up through to their ultimate decline and possible demise. The financial parameters particular to each stage of this simplified business life cycle will be identified and appropriate financial strategies will be discussed that may be used to exploit the specific circumstances in order to create shareholder value.

Chapter 1 looks at the financial environment in which businesses operate and their financial aims and objectives. This chapter provides the framework of corporate finance.

Chapter 2 considers the objectives of businesses. A business raises money from shareholders and lenders to invest in assets, which are used to increase the wealth of the business and its owners. The underlying fundamental economic objective of a company is to maximise shareholder wealth.

In Chapter 3 we provide an introduction to corporate governance. This topic has become increasingly important, particularly since 2008 and the unacceptable behaviour of banks and other financial institutions, and as the responsibilities of directors continue to increase. We look at the ways in which compliance with the various corporate governance guidelines broadly supports the achievement of the aims and objectives of companies in determining the responsibilities and accountability of company directors and their relationships with shareholders and other stakeholders. The burden lies with management to run businesses in strict compliance with statutory, regulatory, and accounting requirements, so it is crucial that directors are aware of the rules and codes of practice that are in place to regulate the behaviour of directors of limited companies.

Chapter 4 examines the relationship between risk and return and how diversification may be used to mitigate and reduce risk. It considers the impact of diversification and looks at the portfolio theory developed by Markowitz.

Chapter 5 considers the way in which a company's average cost of capital may be determined from the costs of its various types of capital financing. The average cost of a company's capital is an important factor in determining the value of a business. In theory the minimisation of the combined cost of equity, debt, and retained earnings used by a company to finance its business should increase its value. The average cost of a company's capital may also be used as the discount rate with which to evaluate proposed investments in new capital projects. Chapter 5 considers whether an optimal capital structure is of fundamental importance to its average cost of capital and looks at the various approaches taken to determine this.

Chapter 6 considers how businesses make decisions about potential investments that may be made in order to ensure that the wealth of the business will be increased. This is an important area of decision-making that usually involves a great deal of money and relatively long-term commitments. It therefore requires appropriate techniques to ensure that the financial objectives of the company are in line with the interests of the shareholders.

Chapter 7 deals primarily with long-term, external sources of business finance available for investment in businesses. This relates to the various types of funding available to a business, including the raising of funds from the owners of the business (the shareholders) and from lenders external to the business. Chapter 7 closes with an introduction to the fast-growing area of Islamic banking and Islamic finance.

Chapter 8 is headed *Financial analysis*. The three main financial statements provide information about business performance. Much more may be gleaned about the performance of a business through further analysis of the financial statements, using financial ratios and other techniques, for example trend analysis, industrial and inter-company analysis. Chapter 8 looks at the analysis and interpretation of the published accounts of a business. It uses the Report and Accounts for the year ended 31 March 2012 of Johnson Matthey Plc to illustrate the type of financial and non-financial information provided by a major UK public company. The chapter closes with a look at some of the measures that approximate to cash flow, for example earnings before interest, tax, depreciation, and amortisation (EBITDA), and economic value added (EVA), that may be used to evaluate company performance.

Chapter 9 deals with the way in which businesses, as part of their strategic management process, translate their long-term objectives into financial plans. This chapter includes consideration of the role of forecasting, financial modelling, and planning for growth.

In Chapter 10 we look at one of the sources of finance internal to a business, its working capital, and the impact that its effective management has on cash flow, profitability, and return on capital. Working capital comprises the short-term assets of the business, inventories, trade receivables, and cash, and claims on the business – trade payables. This chapter deals with how these important items may be more effectively managed. We are now living in a global economy in which businesses trade internationally, and may also have a presence in a number of overseas countries.

In Chapter 11 the implications of internationalisation are discussed with regard to companies' involvement in overseas operations, directly and indirectly, and it considers the appraisal and financing of international investments.

Chapter 12 looks at financial risk faced by businesses resulting from the variation in interest rates, and currency exchange rates, from one period to another. We consider the different ways in which these risks may be approached by companies, and the techniques that may be used to manage such risks. We consider the development of derivatives and look at examples of their use by companies (and their misuse, which we have seen over the past ten years or so). Finally, we explore the relatively newly developed topic of behavioural finance that aims to understand and explain the sometimes seemingly irrational behaviour of investors.

1

The financial environment

Chapter contents

Learning objectives

Completion of this chapter will enable you to:

- Outline the framework of corporate finance and its link with financial strategy.
- Illustrate the different types of business entity: sole traders, partnerships, private limited companies, public limited companies.
- Explain the role of the finance function within a business organisational structure.
- Explain the nature and purpose of financial statements.
- Consider the issues of accountability and financial reporting.
- Describe what is meant by accounting and corporate finance.
- Outline how the corporate finance function is managed to meet business objectives.
- Explain the underlying principles of corporate finance.

Introduction

This chapter explains why finance is such a key element of business life. For aspiring finance directors, finance managers, and accountants, and those of you who may not continue to study finance and accounting, the underlying principles of finance are important topics. A broad appreciation will be useful not only in dealing with the subsequent text, but also in the context of the day-to-day management of a business.

The chapter begins by explaining how the discipline of corporate finance was established and developed. It provides the framework on which each of the subsequent chapters is based. It also explains the links between corporate finance and strategy, and how the financial models and techniques covered in the first part of the book are used in the adoption of appropriate financial strategies by companies at different stages in their development.

The owners or shareholders of the range of business entities may be assumed to have the primary objective of maximisation of their wealth. Directors of the business manage the resources of the business to meet shareholders' objectives. Directors and managers are responsible for running businesses, and their accountability to shareholders is maintained through their regular reporting on the activities of the business.

The finance function plays a crucially important part in all organisations. Its responsibilities include both accounting and corporate finance, the latter relating to the management and control of the financial resources at its disposal. The effective management of corporate finance is essential in ensuring that the business meets its primary objective of maximisation of shareholder wealth. This chapter introduces the fundamental concepts and principles of corporate finance.

A large number of financial terms are used throughout this book, the definitions of which may be found in the glossaries of key terms at the end of each chapter.

Corporate finance and financial strategy

The business environment comprises companies that have just started up or are in various stages of their development. Each has its own reason for being in business and each has its own financing requirements. In the early part of the 20th century when new industries and technologies were emerging there was a growing requirement for new financing, particularly from external sources. This requirement saw increasing interest in various types of securities, particularly equity shares, and also led to the establishment of finance as a discipline separate from economics, in which it had its origins.

The growth in equity shareholdings increased (and has continued to increase up to the present day) but confidence was drastically dented during the economic depression and as a result of the financial scandals of the 1930s. As bankruptcy became a real possibility more attention began to be focused on companies' liquidity and financial structure, and there was a need for increased disclosure of financial information and its analysis. The 1940s saw an increase in financial analysis of cash flow, planning, and methods of control. In the 1950s capital budgeting emerged together with the financial management of assets, and an awareness of how financial decision-making impacted on the value of businesses. This all led to the establishment of the discipline of corporate finance in the early 1960s supported by the publication of a number of academic papers on topics such as the capital markets and share prices, which had previously been considered only in the areas of economics and statistics.

Corporate finance continues to be developed from its beginnings at the start of the 20th century, as do the techniques used in the management of corporate finance, and with an increasing emphasis on international aspects of trade, investment and financing. This book covers all the main areas of corporate finance and its management (financial management).

Let's consider each of the elements of the chart in Figure 1.1, which provides the framework on which this book is based. It is not strictly a flow chart but contains the topics, roles, and techniques covered in this book (and the relationships between them), which are represented by the elements of the chart that are shaded.

Corporate objectives (see Chapter 2) are formulated by a business, in alignment with its underlying mission and company policy, and may include for example profit maximisation, or market share maximisation. Its mission is the company's general sense of purpose or underlying belief. Its policy is a long-lasting, usually unquantified, statement of guidance about the way in which the company seeks to behave in relation to its stakeholders. A company normally has social and environmental responsibilities, responsibilities to its employees, and responsibilities to all its other stakeholders. However, this should not be inconsistent with its primary responsibility to its shareholders. We are assuming that the aim of a business is to add value for its shareholders with the primary objective of maximising shareholder wealth. Shareholder wealth comprises the dividends paid to shareholders on the shares they hold, and the gains achieved from the increase in the market price of their shares.

The directors of a business are appointed by the shareholders to manage the business on their behalf. The directors are responsible for developing appropriate strategies that determine *what* the company is going to do to achieve its objectives, with the primary aim of maximising shareholder wealth. A strategy is a course of action that includes a specification of resources required to achieve a specific objective; it is *what* the company needs to do long term to achieve its objectives, but it does not include *how* to achieve them.

A company's strategy includes its business strategy, which establishes the type of business, its location, its products and services, its markets, its use of resources, and its growth objectives. These areas are assessed with regard to the risks associated with them for which

Figure 1.1   The framework of corporate finance and financial management

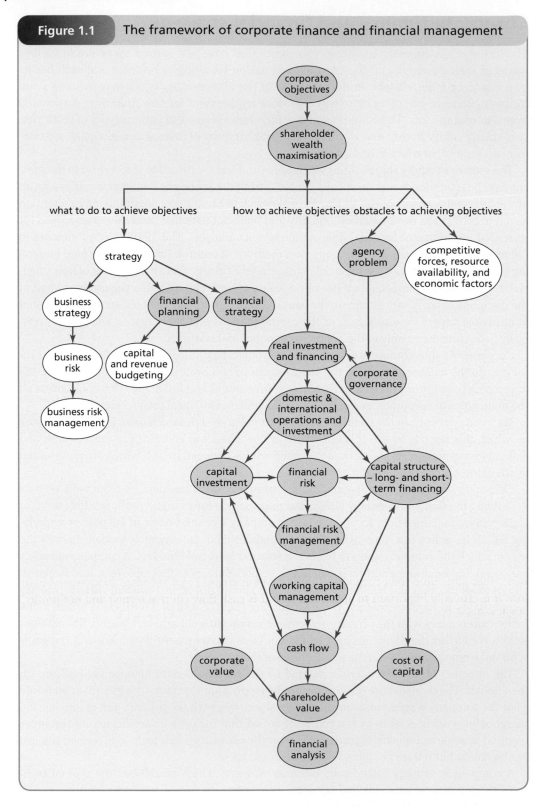

appropriate risk management techniques may be put in place. The company's business strategy is quantified for the long term (typically three years, five years, or ten years) through its financial planning function (see Chapter 9). The short term is quantified in the company's six-monthly or yearly budgets.

A company's strategy also includes financial strategy. This book links corporate finance and financial management with financial strategy. Chapters 1 to 12 discuss the various aspects, models, and hypotheses relating to the discipline of corporate finance, and the techniques and methods used in the financial management of a business. Chapters 13 to 18 deal with the various stages of development of a business, and each chapter considers the most appropriate financial strategies that may be adopted by companies with regard to their current stage of development. 'Most appropriate financial strategies' means those financial strategies that result in the optimisation of the value of the business, with the aim of maximising shareholder wealth. An example of such a strategy is a company that may buy insurance to cover the risks relating to the achievement of its commercial objectives. The high cost of the insurance premiums means that the short-term profits of the company are reduced, but the long-term value of the business to the shareholders will be increased because of the removal of uncertainty about the company's future earnings.

At the heart of corporate finance are two broad areas that deal with *how* the company will achieve its objectives, and specifically its financial objective of maximisation of shareholder wealth. The first area relates to the allocation and use of financial resources for real capital investment (see Chapter 6) in, for example, new product development, land and buildings, and plant and equipment (as distinct from the popular meaning of investment in securities, stocks and shares). The second area relates to the financing of such investments, which may be internal to the company from the retained earnings of the business or from improvements in its management of working capital (see Chapter 10) or from external financing. External financing broadly comprises loans and equity share capital provided to companies by investors and which may be acquired and traded in capital markets like, for example, the London Stock Exchange (see Chapter 7).

Capital investments may be made by companies in their own domestic countries, but companies are also now becoming increasingly involved in international operations and investment (see Chapter 11), and international financing (see Chapter 7). Domestic and international investment, and domestic and international financing, all face various types of risk (see Chapter 4), including financial risk, the management of which is discussed in Chapter 12.

If good decisions are made by a company's managers and directors, which result in investments that add value then corporate value will be increased and reflected in increased cash flow. It is crucially important to appreciate that it is cash flow (in real terms) and not profits, which reflects the true value of a business. If good decisions are made with regard to financing then the capital structure of the company will result in the cost of capital of the company being at a level that will also enhance its corporate value (see Chapter 5). However, an increase in corporate value may not necessarily result in an increase in shareholder value. That will depend partly on how much of the cash flow that has been generated has been used to pay out dividends (or retained for future investment), and partly in the increase (or not) in the share price. The share price will depend on the market's perception of the financial health of the business, and the demand for and level of trading in the company's shares. The analysis of the financial performance and the financial position of a business is considered in Chapter 8.

In theory, the creation of value through adoption of appropriate strategies, and making the right decisions, looks simple and straightforward. In practice, there are of course many obstacles in the way to prevent a company from achieving its objectives. There are competitive forces in most markets from existing companies, from new entrants to the market, and from substitute and alternative products and services. There may be pressures on revenues, costs, and profitability from powerful customers or groups of customers who may demand lower selling prices, or higher levels of quality or service for the same price. There may be pressures on costs and profitability from suppliers or groups of suppliers who may increase prices or control the supply of materials, components, or services. There may be constraints in terms of market demand, availability of materials and people, knowledge, technology, legislation, taxation, import tariffs, social and environmental responsibilities, and media and political pressure.

In addition to the predominantly external obstacles to achieving corporate objectives outlined above, there may also be a major internal obstacle, which is called the agency problem (see Chapter 2). As we have said, the shareholders appoint the directors to manage the company on their behalf. The primary role of the directors is to make decisions and manage the business consistent with the objective of maximisation of shareholder wealth. The agency problem is concerned mainly with situations in which there is a lack of goal congruence between the directors and shareholders of a company, and the decisions of the directors are not aligned with the requirements of the shareholders. The most serious examples of this have been seen in the numerous cases of fraud and corporate excesses over the past 30 years, which have been extensively reported in the financial press. In the UK, the USA, and many other countries throughout the world the concern about financial reporting and accountability and the effect of such financial scandals resulted in the development of various codes of corporate governance (see Chapter 3). Corporate governance is broadly the system by which companies are directed and controlled, and how directors report on the activities and progress of companies to their shareholders.

In the section above we have been talking about businesses and companies in general with regard to corporate finance and financial strategy. Many of the financial techniques covered in this book relate primarily, although not exclusively, to medium-sized and large limited companies. However, it is useful to consider all the various types of business entity that exist and exactly what we mean by a **private limited company (Ltd)** and a **public limited company (plc)**, which is all discussed in the next section.

Types of business entity

Business entities are involved in manufacturing (for example, food and automotive components), or exploration, extraction and production (for example oil, gas, and precious metals), or in providing services (for example, retailing, hospitals, and television broadcasting). Such entities include profit-making and not-for-profit organisations, and charities. The main types of entity and the environments in which they operate are represented in Figure 1.2. The four main types of profit-making organisations are explained in the sections that follow.

The variety of business entities can be seen to range from quangos (quasi-autonomous non-government organisations), to partnerships, to limited companies.

Sole traders

A sole trader entity is applicable for most types of small business. It is owned and financed by one individual, who receives all the profit made by the business, even though more than one person may work in the business.

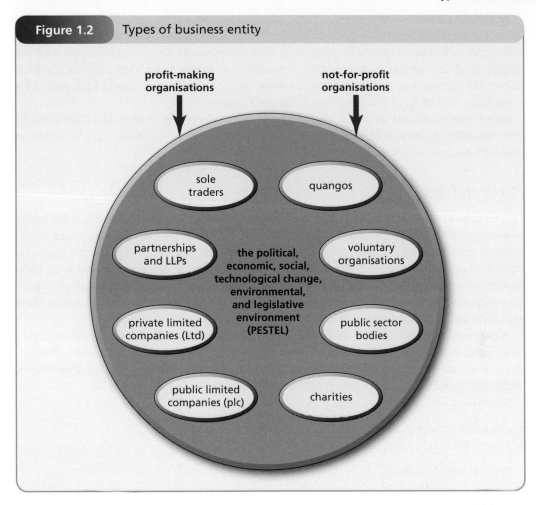

Figure 1.2   Types of business entity

The individual sole trader has complete flexibility regarding:

- the type of (legal) activities in which the business may be engaged
- when to start up or cease the business
- the way in which business is conducted.

The individual sole trader also has responsibility for:

- financing the business
- risk-taking
- decision-making
- employing staff
- any debts or loans that the business may have (the responsibility for which is unlimited, and cases of financial difficulty may result in personal property being used to repay debts).

A sole trader business is simple and cheap to set up. There are no legal or administrative set-up costs as the business does not have to be registered since it is not a legal entity separate from its owner. As we shall see, this is unlike the legal position of owners, or shareholders, of limited companies who are recognised as separate legal entities from the businesses they own.

Accounting records are needed to be kept by sole traders for the day-to-day management of the business and to provide an account of profit made during each tax year. Unlike limited companies, sole traders are not required to file a formal report and accounts each year with the **Registrar of Companies**. However, UK sole traders must prepare accounts on an annual basis to provide the appropriate financial information for inclusion in their annual tax return for submission to HMRC (Her Majesty's Revenue and Customs).

Sole traders normally remain quite small businesses, which may be seen as a disadvantage. The breadth of business skills is likely to be lacking since there are no co-owners with whom to share the management and development of the business.

Partnerships

Partnerships are similar to sole traders except that the ownership of the business is in the hands of two or more persons. The main differences are in respect of how much money each of the partners puts into the business, who is responsible for what, and how the profits are to be shared. These factors are normally set out in formal partnership agreements, and if the partnership agreement is not specific then the provisions of the Partnership Act 1890 apply. There is usually a written partnership agreement (but this is not absolutely necessary) and so there are initial legal costs of setting up the business.

A partnership is called a firm and is usually a small business, although there are some very large partnerships, for example firms of accountants like PricewaterhouseCoopers. Partnerships are formed by two or more persons and, apart from certain professions like accountants, architects, and solicitors, the number of persons in a partnership is limited to 20.

A partnership:

- can carry out any legal activities agreed by all the partners
- is not a legal entity separate from its partners.

The partners in a firm:

- can all be involved in running the business
- all share the profits made by the firm
- are all jointly and severally liable for the debts of the firm
- all have unlimited liability for the debts of the firm (and cases of financial difficulty may result in personal property being used to repay debts)
- are each liable for the actions of the other partners.

Accounting records are needed to be kept by partnerships for the day-to-day management of the business and to provide an account of profit made during each tax year. Unlike limited companies, partnership firms are not required to file a formal report and accounts each year with the Registrar of Companies, but partners must submit annual returns for tax purposes to HMRC.

A new type of legal entity was established in 2001, the limited liability partnership (LLP). This is a variation on the traditional partnership, and the maximum number of partners is unlimited. It has a separate legal identity from the partners, which therefore protects them from personal bankruptcy.

One of the main benefits of a partnership is that derived from its broader base of business skills than that of a sole trader. A partnership is also able to share risk-taking, decision-making, and the general management of the firm.

Limited companies

A limited company is a legal entity separate from the owners of the business, which may enter into contracts, own property, and take or receive legal action. The owners limit their obligations to the amount of finance they have put into the company by way of the share of the company they have paid for. Normally, the maximum that may be claimed from shareholders is no more than they have paid for their shares, regardless of what happens to the company. Equally, there is no certainty that shareholders may recover their original investment if they wish to dispose of their shares or if the business is wound up, for whatever reason.

A company with unlimited liability does not give the owners (or shareholders) of the company the protection of limited liability. If the business were to fail, the members would be liable, without limitation, for all the debts of the business.

A further class of company is a company limited by guarantee, which is normally incorporated for non-profit-making functions. The company has no share capital and has members rather than shareholders. The members of the company guarantee to contribute a predetermined sum to the liabilities of the company, which becomes due in the event of the company being wound up.

The legal requirements relating to the registration and operation of limited companies is contained within the Companies Act 2006. Limited companies are required to be registered with the Registrar of Companies as either a private limited company (Ltd) or a public limited company (plc).

Private limited companies (Ltd)

A private limited company is designated as Ltd. There are legal formalities involved in setting up a Ltd company which result in costs for the company. These formalities include the drafting of the company's Memorandum and Articles of Association (M and A) that describe what the company is and what it is allowed to do, the registration of the company and its director(s) with the Registrar of Companies, and the registration of the name of the company.

The shareholders provide the financing of the business in the form of share capital, of which there is no minimum requirement, and are therefore the owners of the business. The shareholders must appoint at least one director of the company, who may also be the company secretary, who carries out the day-to-day management of the business. A Ltd company may only carry out the activities included in its M and A.

Limited companies must regularly produce annual accounts for their shareholders and file a copy with the Registrar of Companies (at Companies House), and therefore the general public may have access to this information. A Ltd company's accounts must be audited by a suitably **qualified accountant**, unless it has a small company exemption from this requirement, currently (with effect from 6 April 2008) by having annual sales revenue of less than £6.5m and a **balance sheet** total of less than £3.26m. The exemption is not compulsory and having no audit may be a disadvantage: banks, financial institutions, customers, and suppliers may rely on information from Companies House to assess creditworthiness, and they are usually reassured by an independent audit. Ltd companies must also provide copies of their annual accounts to HMRC and also generally provide a separate computation of their profit on which corporation tax is payable. The accounting profit of a Ltd company is adjusted for:

- various expenses that may not be allowable in computing taxable profit
- tax allowances that may be deducted in computing taxable profit.

Limited companies tend to be family businesses and smaller businesses with the ownership split among a few shareholders, although there have been many examples of very large private limited companies. The shares of Ltd companies may be bought and sold but they may not be offered for sale to the general public. Since ownership is usually with family and friends there is rarely a ready market for the shares and so their sale usually requires a valuation of the business.

Progress check 1.1

Which features of a limited company are similar to those of a sole trader?

Public limited companies (plc)

A public limited company is designated as plc. A plc usually starts its life as a Ltd company and then becomes a public limited company by applying for registration as a plc and a listing of its shares on the Stock Exchange or the **Alternative Investment Market (AIM)**, and making a public offer for sale of shares in the company. Plcs must have a minimum issued share capital of (currently) £50,000. The offer for sale, dealt with by a financial institution and the company's legal representatives, is very costly. The formalities also include the redrafting of the company's M and A, reflecting its status as a plc, registering the company and its director(s) with the Registrar of Companies, and registering the name of the plc.

The shareholders must appoint at least two directors of the company, who carry out the day-to-day management of the business, and a suitably qualified company secretary to ensure the plc's compliance with company law. A plc may only carry out the activities included in its M and A.

Plcs must regularly produce annual accounts, a copy of which they must send to all their shareholders. They must also file a copy with the Registrar of Companies, and therefore the general public may have access to this information. The larger plcs usually provide printed glossy annual reports and accounts which they distribute to their shareholders and other interested parties. A plc's accounts must be audited by a suitably qualified accountant, unless it is exempt as a small company as noted above. The same drawback applies to having no audit as applies with a Ltd company. Plcs must also provide copies of their annual accounts to HMRC and also generally provide a separate computation of their profit on which corporation tax is payable. The accounting profit of a plc is adjusted for:

- various expenses that may not be allowable in computing taxable profit
- tax allowances that may be deducted in computing taxable profit.

The shareholders provide the financing of the plc in the form of share capital and are therefore the owners of the business. The ownership of a plc can therefore be seen to be spread among many shareholders (individuals, and institutions like insurance companies and pension funds), and the shares may be freely traded and bought and sold by the general public.

Progress check 1.2

What are the different types of business entity? Can you think of some examples of each?

Worked example 1.1

Ike Andoowit is in the process of planning the setting up of a new residential training centre. Ike has discussed with a number of his friends the question of registering the business as a limited company, or being a sole trader. Most of Ike's friends have highlighted the advantages of limiting his liability to the original share capital that he would need to put into the company to finance the business. Ike feels a bit uneasy about the whole question and decides to obtain the advice of a professional accountant to find out:

- the main disadvantages of setting up a limited company as opposed to a sole trader
- if Ike's friends are correct about the advantage of limiting one's liability
- what other advantages there are to registering the business as a limited company.

The accountant may answer Ike's questions as follows:

Setting up as a sole trader is a lot simpler and cheaper than setting up a limited company. A limited company is bound by the provisions of the Companies Act 2006, and, for example, may be required to have an independent annual audit. A limited company is required to be much more open about its affairs.

The financial structure of a limited company is more complicated than that of a sole trader. There are also additional costs involved in the setting up, and in the administrative functions of a limited company.

Running a business as a limited company requires registration of the business with the Registrar of Companies.

As Ike's friends have pointed out, the financial obligations of a shareholder in a limited company are generally restricted to the amount he, or she, has paid for their shares. In addition, the number of shareholders is potentially unlimited, which widens the scope for raising additional capital.

It should also be noted that:

- a limited company is restricted in its choice of business name
- if any director or 10% of the shareholders request it, a limited company is required to hold a general meeting at any time
- any additional finance provided for a company by a bank is likely to require a personal guarantee from one or more shareholders.

Progress check 1.3

There are some differences between those businesses that have been established as sole traders and those established as partnerships, and there are also differences between private limited companies and public limited companies. What are these differences, and what are the similarities?

Throughout this book, when we talk about companies we are generally referring to limited companies, as distinct from sole traders and partnerships (or firms – although this term is frequently wrongly used to refer to companies). As we have discussed, limited liability companies have an identity separate from their owners, the shareholders, and the liability of shareholders is limited to the amount of money they have invested in the company, that is their shares in the company.

Ownership of a business is separated from its stewardship, or management, by the shareholders' assignment to a board of directors the responsibility for running the company. The directors of the company are accountable to the shareholders, and both parties must play their part in making that accountability effective.

Business organisational structures

The board of directors of a limited company includes its chairman, a managing director (or CEO – chief executive officer), and a number of functional executive directors that may include one or more professionally qualified accountants, one of whom may be the finance director. The directors of the company necessarily delegate to middle managers and junior managers the responsibility for the day-to-day management of the business. It is certainly likely that this body of managers, who report to the board of directors, will include a further one or more qualified accountants responsible for managing the finance function.

The traditional structure of the finance function in a medium- to large-sized company (see Figure 1.3) splits responsibilities broadly between accounting and finance, both being the responsibility of the finance director (or CFO – chief financial officer). Accounting is

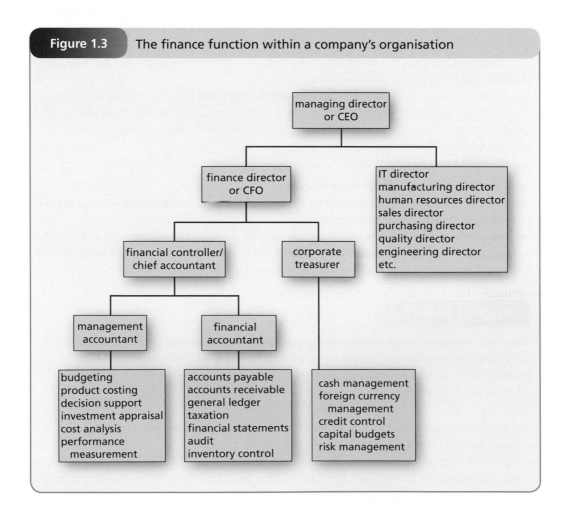

Figure 1.3   The finance function within a company's organisation

managed by the financial controller (or chief accountant), and cash and corporate finance may be managed by a corporate treasurer (or financial manager), and they both report to the finance director. Historically, the IT function (information technology or data processing) has also been the responsibility of the finance director in the majority of companies. This is because the accounting function was the first major user of computers for payroll and then accounting ledgers, financial reporting, budgeting, financial information, etc. In most large companies the IT function, including communications generally, has become a separate responsibility under an IT director. In the same way, the responsibility for the payroll function has moved away from the finance function to being the responsibility of the HR (human resources) director.

Accounting

The original, basic purposes of **accounting** were to classify and record monetary transactions and present the financial results of the activities of an entity, in other words the scorecard that shows how the business is doing. As the business and economic environment has become more complex the accounting profession has evolved, and accounting techniques have been developed for use in a much broader business context. To look at the current nature of accounting and the broad purposes of accounting systems we need to consider the three questions these days generally answered by accounting information:

- how are we doing, and are we doing well or badly?   **a scorecard (like scoring a game of cricket, for example)**

- which problems should be looked at?   **attention-directing**
- which is the best alternative for doing a job?   **problem-solving**

Although accountants and the accounting profession have retained their fundamental roles they have grown into various branches of the profession, which have developed their own specialisms and responsibilities.

The accounting system is a part of the information system within an organisation. Accounting also exists as a service function, which ensures that the financial information that is presented meets the needs of the users of financial information. To achieve this, accountants must not only ensure that information is accurate, reliable and timely, but also that it is relevant for the purpose for which it is being provided, consistent for comparability, and easily understood (see Figure 1.4).

In order to be useful to the users of financial information, the accounting data from which it is prepared, together with its analysis and presentation, must be:

- accurate – free from error of content or principle
- reliable – representing the information that users believe it represents
- timely – available in time to support decision-making
- relevant – applicable to the purpose required, for example a decision regarding a future event or to support an explanation of what has already happened
- consistent – the same methods and standards of measurement of data and presentation of information to allow like-for-like comparison
- clear – capable of being understood by those for whom the information has been prepared.

Progress check 1.4

What are the main purposes of accounting?

Figure 1.4	Features of useful financial information

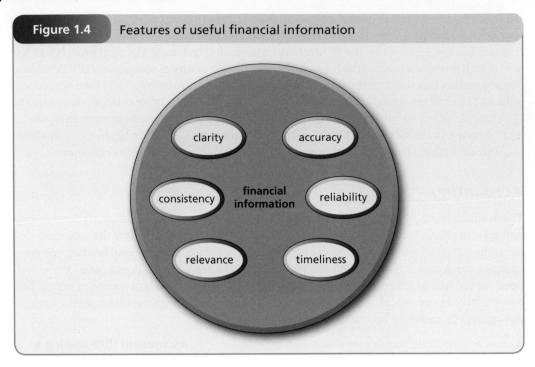

The provision of a great deal of financial information is mandatory; it is needed to comply with, for example, the requirements of Acts of Parliament and HMRC. However, there is a cost of providing information that has all the features that have been described, which therefore renders it potentially useful information. The benefits from producing information, in addition to mandatory information, should therefore be considered and compared with the cost of producing that information to decide on which information is 'really' required.

Accountants may be employed by accounting firms, which provide a range of accounting-related services to individuals, companies, public services, and other organisations. Alternatively, accountants may be employed within companies, public services, and other organisations. Accounting firms may specialise in **audit**, corporate taxation, personal taxation, value added tax (VAT), or consultancy (see the right-hand column of Figure 1.5). Accountants within businesses, public service organisations etc., may be employed in the main functions of **financial accounting**, **management accounting**, and **treasury management** (see the left-hand column of Figure 1.5), and also in general management. Accounting skills may also be required in the area of **financial management** (or the management of corporate finance), which may also include treasury management. Within companies this may include responsibility for investments, and the management of cash and interest and foreign currency risk. External to companies this may include advice relating to mergers and acquisitions, and stock exchange **flotations**, or initial public offerings (IPOs).

Progress check 1.5

Does all accounting data provide useful financial information?

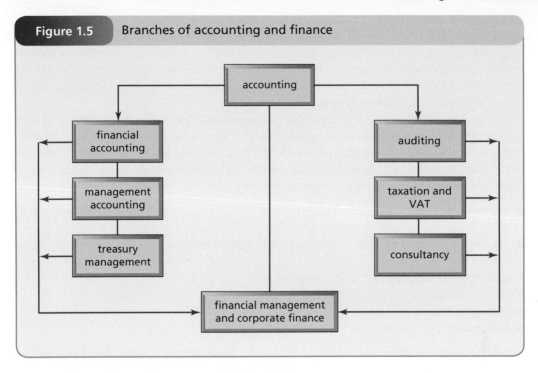

Figure 1.5   Branches of accounting and finance

Financial accounting is primarily concerned with the first question answered by accounting information, the scorecard function. Taking a car-driving analogy, financial accounting makes greater use of the rear-view mirror than the windscreen; financial accounting is primarily concerned with historical information.

Financial accounting is the function responsible in general for the reporting of financial information to the owners of a business, and specifically for preparation of the periodic external reporting of financial information, statutorily required, for shareholders. It also provides similar information as required for government and other interested third parties, such as potential investors, employees, lenders, suppliers, customers, and financial analysts. Financial accounting is concerned with the three key **financial statements**: the balance sheet; **income statement**; **statement of cash flows**. It assists in ensuring that financial statements are included in published reports and accounts in a way that provides ease of analysis and interpretation of company performance.

The role of financial accounting is therefore concerned with maintaining the scorecard for the entity. Financial accounting is concerned with the classification and recording of the monetary transactions of an entity in accordance with established **accounting concepts**, principles, **accounting standards**, and legal requirements. These transactions are presented and reported in income statements, balance sheets, and statements of cash flow, during and at the end of an **accounting period**. Within most companies, the financial accounting role usually involves much more than the preparation of the three main financial statements. A great deal of analysis is required to support such statements and to prepare information both for internal management and in preparation for the annual audit by the company's external **auditor**. This includes sales revenue analyses, bank reconciliations, and analyses of various types of expenditure.

A typical finance department in a medium- to large-sized company has the following additional functions within the financial accounting role: control of **accounts payable** to suppliers

⟱ (the purchase ledger); control of **accounts receivable** from customers (the sales ledger). The financial accounting role also includes the responsibility for the control of non-current assets, inventory control, and traditionally included responsibility for payroll, whether processed internally or by an external agency. However, most companies these days elect to transfer the responsibility for payroll to the personnel, or human resources department (bringing with it
⟱ the possibility of loss of **internal control**).

The breadth of functions involved in financial accounting can require the processing of high volumes of data relating to purchase invoices, supplier payments, sales invoices, receipts from customers, other cash transactions, petty cash, employee expense claims, and payroll data. The control and monitoring of these functions therefore additionally requires a large number of reports generated by the accounting systems, for example:

- analysis of accounts receivable: those customers who owe money to the company – by age of debt
- analysis of accounts payable: those suppliers to whom the company owes money – by age of invoice
- sales revenue analyses
- cheque and electronic payments
- records of non-current assets
- invoice lists.

Past performance is never a totally reliable basis for predicting the future. However, the vast amount of data required for the preparation of financial statements, and maintenance of the further subsidiary accounting functions, provides an indispensable source of data for use in another branch of accounting, namely management accounting. Management accounting is primarily concerned with the provision of information to managers within the organisation for product costing, planning and control, and decision-making, and is to a lesser extent involved in providing information for external reporting.

The functions of management accounting are wide and varied. Whereas financial accounting is primarily concerned with past performance, management accounting makes use of historical data, but focuses almost entirely on the present and the future. Management accounting is involved with the scorecard role of accounting, but in addition is particularly concerned with the other two areas of accounting, namely problem-solving and attention-directing. These include cost analysis, decision-making, sales pricing, forecasting, and planning and budgeting.

Progress check 1.6

What roles are included within the accounting function?

Financial management

The discipline of corporate finance has its roots in economics, although it also uses many of the techniques used in accounting. Financial management (or the management of corporate finance) is broadly defined as the management of all the processes associated with the efficient acquisition and deployment of both short- and long-term financial resources. The financial management role assists an organisation's operations management to reach its financial objectives.

This includes, for example, evaluation of investment opportunities, responsibility for treasury management, which is concerned with the management and control of cash, relationships with banks and other financial institutions, the management of interest rate and foreign currency exchange rate risk, and credit control. The cashier function includes responsibility for cash payments, cash receipts, managers' expenses, petty cash, etc.

The management of an organisation generally involves the three overlapping and interlinking roles of strategic management, risk management, and operations management. Financial management supports these roles to enable management to achieve the financial objectives of the shareholders. The corporate finance function assists in the way that financial results are reported to the users of financial information, for example shareholders, lenders, and employees.

The responsibility of the finance function for managing corporate finance includes the setting up and running of reporting and control systems, raising and managing funds, investment, the management of relationships with financial institutions, and the use of information and analysis to advise management regarding planning, policy, and capital investment. The overriding requirement of the corporate finance function is to ensure that the financial objectives of the company are in line with the interests of the shareholders, the primary objective being to maximise shareholder wealth.

The finance function therefore includes both accounting and corporate finance, which inevitably overlap in some areas. Financial management includes the management and control of corporate funds, in line with company policy. This includes the management of banking relationships, borrowings, and investment. Treasury management may also include the use of the various financial instruments, which may be used to hedge the risk to the business of changes in interest rates and foreign currency exchange rates, and advising on how company strategy may be developed to benefit from changes in the economic environment and the market in which the business operates.

Progress check 1.7

In what way does corporate finance and the financial management function use accounting information?

Worked example 1.2

A friend of yours is thinking about pursuing a career in finance and would like some views on the major differences between accounting and the management of corporate finance (financial management).

The following notes provide a summary that identifies the key differences.

Accounting: The financial accounting function deals with the recording of past and current transactions, usually with the aid of computerised accounting systems. Of the various reports prepared, the key reports for external users include the income statement, balance sheet, and statement of cash flows. In a plc, such reports must be prepared at least every six months, and must comply with current legal, accounting, and reporting requirements.

The management accounting function works alongside the financial accounting function, using a number of the day-to-day financial accounting reports from the accounting system. Management accounting is concerned largely with looking at current issues and problems, and the future in terms of decision-making and forecasting, for example the consideration of 'what if' scenarios during the course of preparation of plans and budgets. Management accounting outputs are mainly for internal users, with much confidential reporting, for example to the directors of the company.

Financial management: The financial management function includes responsibility for corporate finance and the treasury function. Corporate finance includes the management and control of corporate funds, within parameters specified by the board of directors. The role includes the management of company borrowings, investment of surplus funds, the management of both interest rate and foreign currency exchange rate risk, and giving advice on economic and market changes and the exploitation of opportunities. This function is not necessarily staffed by accountants. Plcs report on the treasury activities of the company in their periodic reporting and financial review.

The press extract below, which appeared in the *Manchester Evening News*, relates to Manchester-based McBride plc, a leading supplier of private label household and personal care products. Falling operating profits linked to increasing raw material prices together with a weakened euro triggered a restructuring programme. The elements of the programme were supply chain restructuring and renegotiation of long-term contracts allied with 'operational excellence' initiatives, which by early 2012 had already generated £1m savings through implementing lean manufacturing processes at five sites across Europe.

There are inevitably extra costs associated with restructuring programmes, but once the cost savings begin to take effect the improvements justify the exceptional costs. McBride's restructuring programme illustrates some of the important applications of financial management, which include:

- planning activities
- negotiations with key suppliers
- evaluation of investments in new future prospects
- review of current market trends and costs.

Progress check 1.8

What are the main differences between accounting and corporate finance?

Financial statements

Limited companies produce financial statements for each accounting period to provide information about how the company has been doing. There are three main financial statements – balance sheet, income statement, and statement of cash flows. Companies are obliged to provide financial statements at each year end to provide information for their shareholders, HMRC, and the Registrar of Companies.

Financial management in action

Sales at shampoo to mouthwash maker McBride grew by four per cent in the six months to December 31 but one-off costs pushed it into a £400,000 pre-tax loss. Revenues for the period were up to £423.1m from £407.9m.

The firm, which specialises in making private label products for supermarkets, was hit by a £6.3m exceptional charge following a supply chain restructuring programme. McBride said its margins had remained under pressure from high raw materials costs, but a restructuring, including the closure of its Burnley factory, would create savings of around £5m in the current year.

That closure will see 12 production lines relocated to its factories in Middleton, Greater Manchester and Bradford, which was on track to be completed by the end of March. McBride's Middleton factory produced record volumes in December, which chief executive Chris Bull said would continue to grow. He said: 'The restructuring is all about reducing costs, not capacity. We have seen the development of the private label market across Europe, particularly in the household goods sector. Once consumers try private label, they stick with it. Consumers are looking for value, and retailers are getting behind their own products as they look to differentiate themselves.'

Revenues were boosted by three per cent growth in UK sales to £163.5m, with four per cent growth in western Europe to £211.4m and five per cent in eastern Europe to £71.3m. McBride, which supplies retailers across Europe, has its UK headquarters and main factory in Middleton, Greater Manchester. McBride said all of its three European divisions had achieved growth in the first six months of its financial year and that raw material prices had stabilised since the middle of 2011.

A key focus for the business is new product development, and it was working closely with retailers on that. Mr Bull said: 'By investing in product innovation and improving our competitiveness, we expect to be able to continue to take market share.'

McBride will maintain an interim dividend of 2p per share. Its shares were up 3.75p, or 3.09 per cent, to 125.25p on the news.

Analyst Nicola Mallard, of Investec Securities, said: 'Operational changes in the group's factories have produced savings. Market share growth should help support underlying revenue growth for McBride.'

Source: **Revenues up but restructuring programme pushes McBride into loss,** by James Ferguson © *Manchester Evening News*, 10 February 2012

Balance sheet

The balance sheet (or statement of financial position) summarises the financial position of the business; it is a financial snapshot at a moment in time. It may be compared to looking at a DVD movie in 'pause' mode. In 'play' mode the DVD movie is showing what is happening as time goes by, second by second. If you press 'pause' the DVD stops on a picture. The picture does not tell you what has happened over the period of time up to the pause (or what is going to happen after the pause). The balance sheet is the financial position of the company at the 'pause' position, and the consequence of everything that has happened up to that time. It does not explain how the company got to that position. It just shows the results of financial impacts of events and decisions up to the balance sheet date. The year end may be 31 December, but other dates may be chosen. A company's year-end date is (normally) the same date each year.

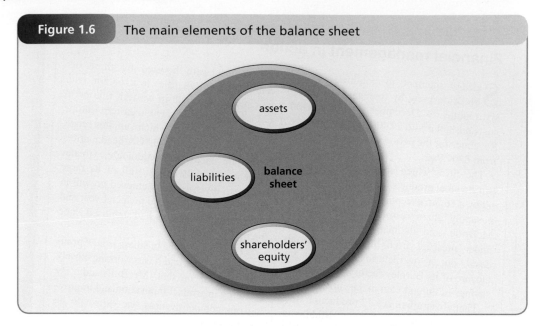

Figure 1.6   The main elements of the balance sheet

The balance sheet comprises a number of categories, within the three main elements (see Figure 1.6), which are labelled **assets**, **liabilities**, and shareholders' equity (usually referred to as just **equity**). The balance sheet is always in balance so that:

total assets (TA) = equity (E) + total liabilities (TL)

The balance sheet is a summary of all the accounts of the business in which the total assets equal the shareholders' equity plus total liabilities. Figure 8.3 in Chapter 8 shows an example of a typical balance sheet for Flatco plc as at 31 December 2012.

Whereas the balance sheet is the financial snapshot at a moment in time – the 'pause' on the DVD movie – the two other financial statements, the income statement and statement of cash flows, are the equivalent of what is going on throughout the accounting period – the 'play' mode on the DVD movie.

Valuation of assets

The question of valuation of assets at a specific balance sheet date arises in respect of choosing the most accurate methods relating to non-current assets, inventories and receivables (and similarly payables), which support the fundamental requirement to give a true and fair view. Companies must be very careful to ensure that their assets are valued in a way that realistically reflects their ability to generate future cash flows. This applies to both current assets such as inventories, and non-current assets such as land and buildings. The balance sheets of companies rarely reflect either the current market values of non-current assets, or their future earnings potential, since they are based on historical costs.

Mini case 1.1

During 2008 the house building market suffered greatly as property prices fell and the demand for new housing diminished. We saw several house builders failing or being the subject of takeover bids. One of the UK's largest house builders, Persimmon, recorded a loss of £780m in 2008. However, in 2009 they reported a profit of £77.8m.

In 2008 Persimmon had written down the value of the land they held by £664.1m, which largely explained the huge loss for that year. In 2009, following a review of the value of the company's land, the directors decided to reverse £74.8m of these write-offs, which was added back to profit. Directors of companies must take care in such valuation increases that reflect the impact of property price inflation, which may not be sustained, and which ignore the future earning potential of the assets. The effect on Persimmon was that the shareholders, and the market, were delighted at the tremendous reversal in fortunes in the year, particularly as rival house builder Taylor Wimpey reported a £640m pre-tax loss in 2009.

Differences between the methods chosen to value various assets (and liabilities) at the end of accounting periods may have a significant impact on the results reported in the income statement for those periods. Examples of this may be seen in:

- non-current assets and depreciation
- inventories valuations and cost of sales
- valuations of trade payables and trade receivables denominated in foreign currencies
- provisions for doubtful debts.

The rules applicable to the valuation of balance sheet items are laid down in the international accounting standards and UK financial reporting standards (IASs, IFRSs, and FRSs). These rules require companies to prepare their financial statements under the historical cost convention (the gross value of the asset being the purchase price or production cost), or alternative conventions of historical cost modified to include certain assets at a revalued amount or current cost.

Under alternative conventions, the gross value of the asset is either the market value at the most recent valuation date or its current cost: tangible non-current assets should be valued at market value or at current cost; investments (non-current assets) are valued at market value or at any value considered appropriate by the directors; short-term investments are valued at current cost; inventories are valued at current cost. If a reduction in value of any non-current assets is expected to be permanent then provision for this must be made. The same applies to investments even if the reduction is not expected to be permanent.

Non-current assets with finite lives are subject to depreciation charges. Current assets must be written down to the amount for which they could be disposed of (their **net realisable value**), if that value is lower than cost or an alternative valuation. It should be noted that provisions for reductions in value no longer considered necessary must be written back to the profit and loss account.

There is an element of choice between alternative valuation methods that may be adopted by businesses. Because of this, difficulties may arise in trying to provide consistent comparisons of the performance of companies even within the same industrial sectors. If changes in accounting policies have been introduced, further inconsistencies arise in trying to provide a realistic comparison of just one company's performance between one accounting period and another.

Income statement

The income statement (or statement of financial performance) is a financial statement that summarises the total of all the accounts included within the profit and loss account section of the general ledger. Profit (or loss) may be considered in two ways, which both give the same result.

The income statement is an indication of the change in the book wealth of the business over a period. The book wealth of the business is the amount it is worth to the owners, the shareholders. The accumulation of the total change in wealth since the business began, up to a particular point in time, is reflected within the equity section of the balance sheet under the heading 'retained earnings'. Retained earnings are the accumulated profits of the business minus amount deducted in respect of dividends. Using the DVD analogy, the income statement measures the change in the balance sheet from one 'pause' to another. An increase in equity is a profit and a decrease in equity is a loss.

The income statement is more usually considered in its measurement of the trading performance of the business (see Figure 1.7). The income statement calculates whether or not the company has made a profit or loss on its operations during the period, through producing and selling its goods or services. The result, the earnings, net income or **profit** (or loss), is derived from deducting expenses incurred from revenues derived throughout the period between two 'pauses'. Retained earnings for the period is net profit for the period, less dividends.

The profit and loss account comprises the total of the expenses (debits) accounts and revenues (credits) accounts within the general ledger. The total of these may be a net debit or a net credit. A net debit represents a loss and a net credit represents a profit. The profit or loss, net of dividends, is reflected in the balance sheet of the business under the heading retained earnings, which is part of shareholders' equity. All the other accounts within the general ledger, other than expenses and revenues, may be summarised into various other non-profit and loss account categories and these represent all the other balances that complete the overall balance sheet of the business.

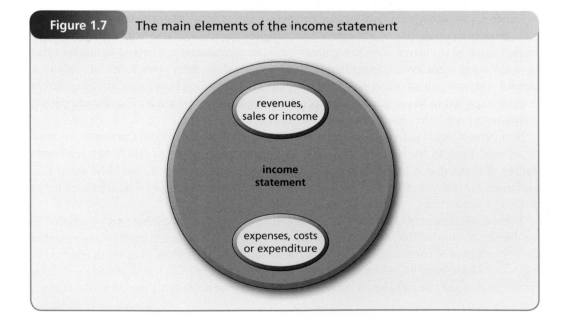

| Figure 1.7 | The main elements of the income statement |

revenues, sales or income

income statement

expenses, costs or expenditure

Figure 8.4 in Chapter 8 shows an example of a typical income statement for Flatco plc for the year ended 31 December 2012.

There are three main points to consider regarding the income statement and how it differs from the statement of cash flows. First, revenues (or sales revenues, or income) and expenses (or costs, or expenditure) are not necessarily accounted for at the same time as when cash is paid or received. Sales revenues are normally accounted for when goods or services are delivered and accepted by the customer. Cash will rarely be received immediately from the customer, except in businesses like high-street retailers and supermarkets; it is normally received weeks or months later.

Second, the income statement does not take into account all the events that impact on the financial position of the company. For example, an issue of new **shares** in the company, or a loan to the company, will increase cash but they are neither revenue nor expenses.

Third, non-cash flow items, for example depreciation and provisions for doubtful debts, reduce the profit, or increase the loss, of the company but do not represent outflows of cash.

Therefore it can be seen that net profit is not the same as cash flow. A company may get into financial difficulties if it suffers a severe **cash** shortage even though it may have positive net earnings (profit).

Statement of cash flows

Between them, the balance sheet and income statement show a company's financial position at the beginning and at the end of an accounting period and how the profit or loss has been achieved during that period.

The balance sheet and income statement do not show or directly analyse some of the key changes that have taken place in the company's financial position, for example:

- how much capital expenditure (for example, equipment, machinery and buildings) has the company made, and how did it fund the expenditure?
- what was the extent of new borrowing and how much **debt** was repaid?
- how much did the company need to fund new **working capital** (which includes, for exam- ple, an increase in trade receivables and **inventories** as a result of increased business activity)?
- how much of the company's funding was met by funds generated from its trading activities, and how much by new external funding (for example, from banks and other lenders, or new shareholders)?

The income statement and the statement of cash flows are the two 'DVD movies' which are running in parallel between the two 'pauses' – the balance sheets at the start and the finish of an accounting period. However, the statement of cash flows goes further in answering the questions like those shown above. The aim of the statement of cash flows is to summarise the cash inflows and outflows and calculate the net change in the cash position of the company throughout the period between two 'pauses'.

Figure 1.8 shows the main elements of a statement of cash flows, and Figures 8.6 and 8.7 in Chapter 8 are examples of a typical statement of cash generated from operations and a statement of cash flows for Flatco plc for the year ended 31 December 2012.

Figure 1.8   The main elements of the statement of cash flows

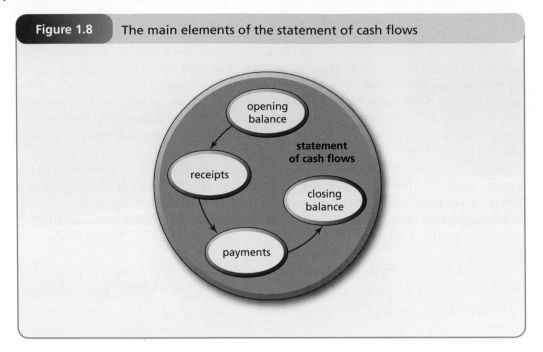

Worked example 1.3

Fred Osborne, a graduate trainee in the finance department of a large engineering group, pursued his finance studies with enthusiasm. Although Fred was more interested in business planning and getting involved with new development projects, his job and his studies required him to become totally familiar with, and to be able to prepare, the financial statements of a company. Fred was explaining the subject of financial statements and what they involve to a friend of his, Jack, another graduate trainee in human resources.

Fred explained the subject of financial statements to Jack, bearing in mind that he is very much a non-financial person.

Limited companies are required to produce three main financial statements for each accounting period with information about company performance for:

- shareholders
- HMRC
- banks
- City analysts
- investing institutions
- the public in general.

The three key financial statements are the:

(a)   balance sheet
(b)   income statement
(c)   statement of cash flows.

(a) **Balance sheet:** a financial snapshot at a moment in time, or the financial position of the company comparable with pressing the 'pause' button on a DVD player. The DVD movie in 'play' mode shows what is happening as time goes on second by second, but when you press 'pause' the DVD stops on a picture; the picture does not tell you what has happened over the period of time up to the pause (or what is going to happen after the pause). The balance sheet is the consequence of everything that has happened up to the balance sheet date. It does not explain how the company got to that position.

(b) **Income statement:** this is like a DVD movie in 'play' mode. It is used to calculate whether or not the company has made a gain or deficit on its operations during the period, its financial performance, through producing and selling its goods or services. Net earnings or net profit is calculated from revenues derived throughout the period between two 'pauses', minus costs incurred in deriving those revenues.

(c) **Statement of cash flows:** this is the DVD movie again in 'play' mode, but net earnings is not the same as cash flow, since revenues and costs are not necessarily accounted for when cash transfers occur. Sales are accounted for when goods or services are delivered and accepted by the customer but cash may not be received until some time later. The income statement does not reflect non-trading events like an issue of shares or a loan that will increase cash but are not revenues or costs. The statement of cash flows summarises cash inflows and cash outflows and calculates the net change in the cash position for the company throughout the period between two 'pauses'.

The reporting of financial information

The information provided by plcs in particular is frequently used by City analysts, investing institutions, and the public in general. After each year end, plcs prepare their **annual report and accounts** for their shareholders. Copies of the annual report and accounts are filed with the Registrar of Companies and copies are available to other interested parties such as financial institutions, major suppliers, and other investors. In addition to the income statement and statement of cash flows for the year and the balance sheet as at the year-end date, the annual report and accounts includes notes to the accounts, **accounting policies**, and much more financial and non-financial information such as company policies, financial indicators, corporate governance compliance, directors' remuneration, employee numbers, business analysis, and segmental analysis. The annual report also includes the chief executive's review of the business, a report by the auditors of the company, and the chairman's statement.

The auditors' report states compliance or otherwise with accounting and financial reporting standards and that the accounts are free from material misstatement, and that they give a true and fair view prepared on the assumption that the company is a going concern. The chairman's statement offers an opportunity for the chairman of the company to report in unquantified and unaudited terms on the performance of the company during the past financial period and on likely future developments. However, the auditors would object if there was anything in the chairman's statement that was inconsistent with the audited accounts.

In theory, the balance sheet of a private limited company or a plc should tell us all about the company's financial structure and liquidity – the extent to which its assets and liabilities are held in cash or in a near cash form (for example, bank accounts and deposits). It should also tell us about the assets held by the company, the proportion of current assets, and the extent to which they may be used to meet current obligations. However, an element of caution should be noted in analysing balance sheet information. The balance sheet is a historical document. It may have looked entirely different six months or a year ago, or even one week ago. There is not always consistency between the information included in one company's balance sheet and that of another company. Two companies even within the same industry are usually very difficult to compare. Added to that, different analysts very often use alternative calculations for financial ratios or use them in different ways. In addition to the wide choice of valuation methods, the information in a typical published balance sheet does not tell us anything about the quality of the assets, their real value in money terms or their value to the business.

The audit report provided by external auditors in a company's annual report and accounts normally states that they represent a **true and fair view** of the business. For a number of reasons, which we will discuss in Chapter 3, companies' reports and accounts may not in fact represent a true and fair view and may hide fraudulent activities or may have been subjected to some **creative accounting**, such as **off balance sheet financing** and **window dressing**. Off balance sheet financing relates to the funding of operations in such a way that the relevant assets and liabilities are not disclosed in the balance sheet of the company concerned. Window dressing is a practice in which changes in short-term funding have the effect of disguising or improving the reported liquidity (cash and near cash) position of the reporting organisation. The auditors of WorldCom and Enron stated that their reports and accounts provided a true and fair view of those businesses. The reality was somewhat different, as we can see from Mini cases 1.2 and 1.3.

Mini case 1.2

WorldCom was one of the world's largest telecommunications companies with 20 million consumer customers, thousands of corporate clients and 80,000 employees. During 2001/2002 WorldCom improperly recorded US$3.8bn as capital expenditure instead of operating expenditure, which distorted its reported cash flow and profit. In reality, World-Com should have reported a loss instead of US$1.4bn net income in 2002. WorldCom's accounting irregularities were thought to have begun in 2000. Instead of accounting for expenses when they were incurred, WorldCom hid the expenses by pushing them into the future, giving the appearance of spending less and therefore making more profit.

This apparent profitability obviously pleased Wall Street analysts and investors, which was reflected in increases in the WorldCom share price up until the accounting irregularities were discovered. WorldCom filed for bankruptcy, and many of the directors and employees subsequently received custodial sentences for fraud.

Mini case 1.3

The story of Enron, which was guilty of using off balance sheet financing, is complex. Enron began life as a natural gas company started up by Kenneth Lay. He saw an opportunity to profit from the deregulation of the gas industry, for which the core business was established. In its early days Enron did the right things for the right reasons and gained substantial credibility on Wall Street.

In its latter years successful operations were replaced with the illusion of successful operations. The business started to use its substantial credibility to sustain operations through loans to acquire companies on a global basis. In the course of acquiring companies the enterprise recruited a team of financial market experts whose original function was to manage operational risks that the company faced. This team became involved in market speculation and either by luck or perhaps by deception apparently made a lot of money.

The directors of the enterprise that became Enron thought that the profits being made were dependable. They therefore retained the team of experts, who were then called market traders, as an integral part of the company. However, the company also tried to disguise the nature of the operations of the team. After some initial successes the traders began to have some financial failures and Enron was no longer really making a profit. The market traders were really only people who were gambling or speculating for very high stakes, and became no longer a source of profits for the business but a source of huge losses.

The company, with the assistance of its bankers and its auditors Arthur Andersen, covered up its losses in a number of ways relating to a manipulation of the rules relating to the accounting for securities. The company covered its funding shortfalls by borrowing money in such a way that it was not disclosed in the company's balance sheet.

The company grew enormously from both domestic and international ventures and at the same time so did cases of excessive management spending of corporate funds on unnecessary luxury items. In the years prior to its bankruptcy Enron executives paid for such luxuries out of company borrowing because it had no real profits, which was therefore at the expense of lenders to the company.

Enron eventually went bankrupt. In 2004, Enron's two key executives, Kenneth Lay and Jeff Skilling, were tried for fraud and convicted in 2006. Kenneth Lay, before his imprisonment, died at the age of 64.

Corporate fraud is by no means confined to the West or to developed economies. There have also been many examples in developing economies as illustrated in Mini case 1.4 below.

Mini case 1.4

In January 2009 there was considerable surprise when a US$1bn fraud at one of India's largest outsourcing companies, Satyam Computer Services, was revealed. The company, whose name ironically means 'truth' in Sanskrit, provided a wide range of services from handling databases to running payrolls for over one third of the Fortune 500 companies. From a small operation founded in 1987 the company had grown by 2009 to over 53,000 employees and operated in 66 countries.

Perhaps more surprising was the way in which the fraud was revealed. Although in the previous year analysts had voiced concerns over some of the aspects of the management of the company, there was no suggestion of accounting irregularities until the chairman, Ramalingam Raju, wrote a letter to the Securities & Exchange Board of India explaining that 50.4bn rupees, or US$1.04bn, of the 53.6bn rupees in cash and bank loans that the company had listed as assets were in fact non-existent. He also admitted inflating sales revenues by 76% and profits by 97%. In the letter, Mr Raju explained that 'what started as a marginal gap between actual operating profit and the one reflected in the books of account continued to grow over the years. It has attained unmanageable proportions as the size of company operations grew.' The fraud had been running since 2004 and had gone undetected by auditors who were subsequently fined US$7.5m.

After two years and eight months in prison Mr Raju, along with his brother B Rama Raju and Satyam's former chief financial officer, Vadlamani Srinivas, left prison on bail in November 2011.

Progress check 1.9

What are the three main financial statements reported by a business? How are business transactions ultimately reflected in financial statements?

Users of financial information

Financial information is important to a wide range of groups both internal and external to the organisation. Such information is required, for example, by individuals outside the organisation to make decisions about whether or not to invest in one company or another, or by potential suppliers who wish to assess the reliability and financial strength of the organisation. It is also required by managers within the organisation as an aid to decision-making. The main users of financial information are shown in Figure 1.9, and are discussed in Worked example 1.4.

Worked example 1.4

Kevin Green, a trainee accountant, has recently joined the finance department of a newly formed public limited company. Kevin has been asked to work with the company's auditors who have been commissioned to prepare some alternative formats for the company's annual report.

As part of his preparation for this, Kevin's manager has asked him to prepare a draft report about who is likely to use the information contained in the annual report, and how they might use such information.

Kevin's preparatory notes for his report included the following:

- **Competitors** as part of their industry competitive analysis studies, to look at market share and financial strength
- **Customers** to determine the ability to provide a regular, reliable supply of goods and services, and to assess customer dependence
- **Employees** to assess the potential for providing continued employment and assess levels of remuneration
- **General public** to assess general employment opportunities, social, political and environmental issues, and to consider potential for investment
- **Government** corporate taxation and **value added tax (VAT)**, government statistics, grants and financial assistance, monopolies and mergers

- **Investment analysts** investment potential for individuals and institutions with regard to past and future performance, strength of management, risk versus reward
- **Lenders** the capacity and the ability of the company to service debt and repay capital
- **Managers/directors** to a certain extent an aid to decision-making, but such relevant information should already have been available internally
- **Shareholders/investors** a tool of accountability to maintain a check on how effectively the directors/managers are running the business, and to assess the financial strength and future developments
- **Suppliers** to assess the long-term viability and whether the company is able to meet its obligations and pay suppliers on an ongoing basis.

Progress check 1.10

How many users of financial information can you think of and in what ways do you think they may use this information?

Figure 1.9   Users of financial and accounting information

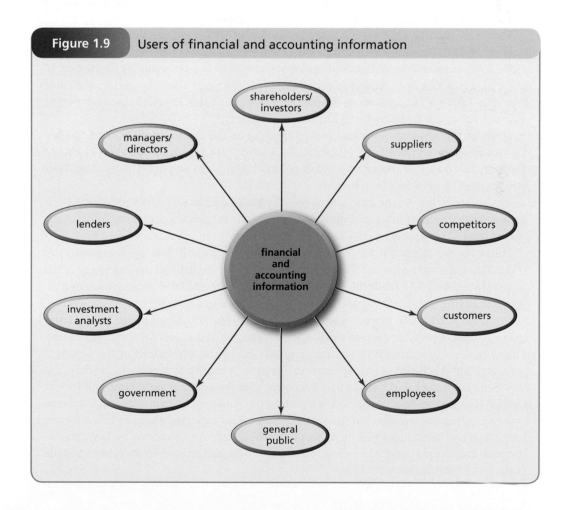

Accountability and financial reporting

The directors of a company are appointed by the shareholders to manage the business on their behalf. The accountability of the directors is maintained by reporting on the financial performance and the financial position of the company to shareholders on both a yearly and an interim (half-yearly) basis. The reporting made in the form of the financial statements includes the balance sheet, income statement, and statement of cash flows.

Mini case 1.5

Corporate executives may seek to deceive the public and shareholders for a number of reasons. The longer the deception continues the more extreme their responses may become to keep the truth hidden and potentially the greater the impact when the facts become known.

In October 2011, Japanese camera and medical equipment manufacturer Olympus lost two presidents, saw its share price plummet by almost 75%, and came under investigation from regulators and enforcement agencies. The cause was the company's CEO and president Michael Woodford who raised the issue of irregular payments and poor investments surrounding four acquisitions of start-up companies made in 2006 and 2008.

The value of three companies acquired for a total of US$773m had been written down to a mere US$187m in 2009. The majority of the purchase money went to Cayman Islands-based companies that were dissolved or closed down shortly after receiving the money. In the final acquisition of a UK medical company, Gyrus, Olympus allegedly paid US$687m in fees to two advisory companies on the purchase worth US$2bn. On this value an expected advisory fee would be around US$40m.

News of these transactions had been picked up by the Japanese media and this led Mr Woodford to carry out an investigation. In October 2011 he advised Olympus chairman Tsuyoshi Kikukawa to resign as a result of the dealings. In response, three days later Mr Woodford was sacked from his post.

The company line on the dismissal as given by Mr Kikukawa was that Mr Woodford was removed from his post in a unanimous vote due to cultural clashes, and an inability on the part of the CEO to appreciate the subtle nuances of Japanese business.

Following his dismissal Mr Woodford assessed the overall loss to shareholders at US$1.2bn and told reporters, 'The whole board is contaminated and that company needs to be cleaned out. The whole board have had discussions and vote unanimously and no one asks anything. It's just complete and utter obedience to Kikukawa.'

In January 2012, the company absolved the external auditors of any blame in the matter but suggested there were deficiencies in the performance of the internal audit procedures. Meanwhile, the on-going investigations engendered by the revelations of the Japanese press and Mr Woodford led prosecutors in Tokyo in February to arrest the, by then, ex-President Tsuyoshi Kikukawa, former Executive Vice President Hisashi Mori and former auditor Hideo Yamada on suspicion of violating the Financial Instruments and Exchange Law. Following the arrests, the *Independent* newspaper reported that the three former executives had been identified by an investigative panel, commissioned by Olympus, as the main culprits in the fraud, seeking to delay the reckoning from risky investments made in the late 1980s economic bubble.

There are guidelines, or standards, which have been developed by the accountancy profession to ensure truth, fairness and consistency in the preparation and presentation of financial information.

A number of bodies have been established to draft accounting policy, set accounting standards, and to monitor compliance with standards and the provisions of the Companies Act. The **Financial Reporting Council (FRC)**, whose chairman and deputy chairman are appointed by the Secretary of State for Business, Innovation and Skills, develops accounting standards policy and gives guidance on issues of public concern.

The FRC is divided into two committees: the Codes and Standards Committee (CSC); and the Conduct Committee. The CSC comprises three Councils: Accounting, Actuarial, and Audit and Assurance, of which the **Accounting Council** is responsible for consideration and advice to the FRC on the development of draft codes and standards and changes to existing codes and standards.

The accounting standards are called **Financial Reporting Standards (FRSs)**. Up to 1990 the accounting standards were known as **Statements of Standard Accounting Practice (SSAPs)**, and were issued by the Accounting Standards Committee (ASC). The ASC was replaced by the **Accounting Standards Board (ASB)** and this board was subsequently replaced by the Accounting Council on 2 July 2012. Although some SSAPs have now been withdrawn there are, in addition to the new FRSs, a large number of SSAPs that are still in force.

The Accounting Council also deals with any urgent issues relating to accounting standards when there are conflicts with new practice or events occur which render current standards insufficient to comply with EU legislation or emerging business practices. The Accounting Council took over this role on its formation from the so-called Urgent Issues Task Force (UITF) which had dealt with such matters since 1990. It was announced that a new committee would be formed to handle such matters but at the time of writing this book this committee had not yet been set up.

The Conduct Committee comprises two other committees: the Monitoring Committee; the Case Management Committee. The Monitoring Committee, as part of its duties, is responsible for the Financial Reporting Review Panel (FRRP), which reviews comments and complaints from users of financial information. It enquires into the annual accounts of companies where it appears that the requirements of the Companies Act, including the requirement that annual accounts shall show a true and fair view, might have been breached. The Stock Exchange rules covering financial disclosure of publicly quoted companies require such companies to comply with accounting standards and reasons for non-compliance must be disclosed.

Pressure groups, organisations and individuals may also have influence on the provisions of the Companies Act and FRSs (and SSAPs). These may include some UK Government departments (for example HMRC and the Office of Fair Trading) in addition to the Department for Business, Innovation and Skills (BIS) and employer organisations such as the Confederation of British Industry (CBI), and professional bodies like the Law Society, Institute of Directors, and the Chartered Management Institute.

There are therefore many diverse influences on the form and content of company accounts. In addition to legislation, standards are continually being refined, updated and replaced and further enhanced by various codes of best practice. As a response to this the UK Generally Accepted Accounting Practices (UK GAAP), first published in 1989, includes all practices that are considered to be permissible or legitimate, either through support by statute, accounting standard or official pronouncement, or through consistency with the needs of users and of meeting the fundamental requirement to present a true and fair view, or even simply through authoritative support in the accounting literature. UK GAAP is therefore a dynamic concept, which changes in response to changing circumstances.

Within the scope of current legislation, best practice, and accounting and financial reporting standards, each company needs to develop its own specific accounting policies. Accounting policies are the specific accounting bases selected and consistently followed by an entity as being, in the opinion of the management, appropriate to its circumstances and best suited to present fairly its results and financial position. Examples are the various alternative methods of valuing inventories of materials, or charging the cost of a machine over its useful life, that is, its depreciation.

You may question why all the accounting and financial reporting regulation that we have discussed in the earlier sections of this chapter is necessary at all. Well, there are a number of arguments in favour of such regulation:

- It is very important that the credibility of financial statement reporting is maintained so that actual and potential investors are protected as far as possible against inappropriate accounting practices.
- Generally, being able to distinguish between the good and not-so-good companies also provides some stability in the financial markets.
- The auditors of companies must have some rules on which to base their true and fair view of financial position and financial performance, which they give to the shareholders and other users of the financial statements.

External auditors are appointed by, and report independently to, the shareholders. They are professionally qualified accountants who are required to provide objective verification to shareholders and other users that the financial statements have been prepared properly and in accordance with legislative and regulatory requirements; that they present the information truthfully and fairly; and that they conform to the best accounting practice in their treatment of the various measurements and valuations. The purpose of the audit is defined in ISA 200 (International Standard on Auditing 200) in the **International Standards on Auditing (ISAs)** as 'to enhance the degree of confidence of intended users in the financial statements. This is achieved by the expression of an opinion by the auditor on whether the financial statements are prepared, in all material respects, in accordance with an applicable financial reporting framework'.

The financial reporting of the company includes preparation of the financial statements, notes and reports, which are audited and given an opinion on by the external auditors. A regulatory framework exists to see fair play, the responsibility for which is held jointly by the government and the private sector, including the accountancy profession and the Stock Exchange.

The UK Government exercises influence through bodies such as the Department of Business, Innovation and Skills (BIS) and through Parliament by the enactment of legislation, for example the Companies Act. Such legal regulation began with the Joint Stock Companies Act 1844. Subsequent statutes exerted greater influence on company reporting: the Companies Acts 1948, 1967, and 1981. The provisions included in these Acts were consolidated into the Companies Act 2006. The Companies Act 2006 contains the overall current legal framework.

The **International Accounting Standards Committee (IASC)** set up in 1973, which is supported by each of the major professional accounting bodies, fosters the harmonisation of accounting standards internationally. To this end each UK FRS includes a section explaining its relationship to any relevant international accounting standard.

There are wide variations in the accounting practices that have been developed in different countries. These reflect the purposes for which financial information is required by the different users of that information, in each of those countries. There is a different focus on the type of information and the relative importance of each of the users of financial information in each country. This is because each country may differ in terms of:

- who finances the businesses – individual equity shareholders, institutional equity shareholders, debenture holders, banks, etc.
- tax systems, either aligned with or separate from accounting rules
- the level of government control and regulation
- the degree of transparency of information.

The increase in international trade and globalisation has led to a need for convergence, or harmonisation, of accounting rules and practices. The IASC was created in order to develop international accounting standards, but these have been slow in appearing because of the difficulties in bringing together differences in accounting procedures. Until 2000 these standards were called **International Accounting Standards (IASs)**. The successor to the IASC, the **International Accounting Standards Board (IASB)** was set up in April 2001 to make finan- cial statements more comparable on a worldwide basis. The IASB publishes its standards in a series of pronouncements called **International Financial Reporting Standards (IFRSs)**. It has also adopted the body of standards issued by the IASC, which continue to be designated IASs.

The former chairman of the IASB, Sir David Tweedie, has said that 'the aim of the globalisation of accounting standards is to simplify accounting practices and to make it easier for investors to compare the financial statements of companies worldwide'. He also said that 'this will break down barriers to investment and trade and ultimately reduce the cost of capital and stimulate growth' (*Business Week*, 7 June 2004).

On 1 January 2005 there was convergence in the mandatory application of the IFRSs by listed companies within each of the European Union member states. The impact of this should be negligible with regard to the topics covered in this book, since UK accounting standards have already moved close to international standards. The reason for this is that the UK Statement of Principles (SOP) was drawn up using the 1989 IASB conceptual framework for guidance.

At the time of writing this book, major disagreements between the EU and accountants worldwide over the influence of the EU on the process of developing International Accounting Standards are causing concern that the dream of the globalisation of accounting standards may not be possible.

It may be argued that the increasing amount of accounting regulation itself stifles responses to changes in economic and business environments, and discourages the development of improved financial reporting. We have already seen that the development of various conceptual frameworks indicates that there is wide disagreement about what constitutes accounting best practice. The resistance to acceptance of international accounting standards may be for political reasons, the rules perhaps reflecting the requirements of specific interest groups or countries.

It is also true that despite increasing accounting regulation there have been an increasing number of well-publicised financial scandals in the USA in particular, where the accounting systems are very much 'rule-based', as well as in the UK, Italy, and Japan. However, these scandals have usually been the result of fraudulent activity. This leads to another question as to why the auditors of such companies did not detect or prevent such fraud. The answer is that, despite the widespread perception of the general public to the contrary, auditors are not appointed to detect or prevent fraud. Rather, they are appointed by the shareholders to give their opinion as to whether the financial statements show a true and fair view and comply with statutory, regulatory, and accounting and financial reporting standards requirements.

Progress check 1.11

In what ways may the reliability of financial reporting be ensured?

Worked example 1.5

You are thinking of changing jobs (within marketing) and moving from a local, well-established retailer that has been in business for over 20 years. You have been asked to attend an interview at a new plc that started up around two years ago. The plc is a retailer via the Internet. Your family has suggested that you investigate the company thoroughly before your interview, paying particular attention to its financial resources. There is a chance the plc may not be a going concern if its business plan does not succeed.

You will certainly want to include the following questions at your interview.

(a) Are any published accounts available for review?
(b) What is the share capital of the company (for example, is it £50,000 or £1,000,000)?
(c) Is the company profitable?
(d) Does the company have loan commitments?
(e) Is the company working within its bank overdraft facilities?
(f) Are any press analyses of the company available?
(g) What is the current customer base?

The answers may suggest whether the company can continue trading for the foreseeable future.

Managing corporate finance

The finance function, or more specifically the finance director of a business, has the responsibility for managing the financial resources of the business to meet the objectives of the business.

The finance director's corporate finance responsibilities involve:

■ raising and controlling the provision of funds for the business
■ deciding on the deployment of these funds – the assets, new projects, and operational expenditure required to increase the value of the business
■ controlling the resources of the business to ensure that they are being managed effectively
■ managing financial risks such as exposures relating to movements in interest rates and foreign currency exchange rates.

The finance director is also responsible for the accounting function of the business, but it is a separate and different discipline to corporate finance. The management of corporate finance, or financial management, draws on the techniques of both financial accounting and management accounting, relating to decision-making and financial reporting. However, corporate finance is concerned with the future and relates to the management of the financial resources of the business in order to optimise the returns to investors in the business. In this context the finance directors must decide on:

- what level of assets should the company have?
- how should investment projects be chosen and how should they be funded?
- in what proportions should the company's funding be regarding shareholders' equity and borrowings?
- what proportions of profit after tax should be paid out in dividends or retained for future investment?

Accounting may assist in these decisions, for example capital investment appraisal (management accounting) and the impact on financial statement reporting (financial accounting). Therefore, although corporate finance and accounting are both the responsibility of the finance director, they are separate disciplines with the former very much supported by the latter.

Progress check 1.12

What are the key responsibilities of the finance director with regard to the financial management of a business?

Underlying principles of corporate finance

We have seen that corporate finance is about obtaining and managing the financial resources of a business in order to achieve the objectives of the business. The primary objective of the business is the maximisation of shareholder wealth, and there are a number of principles that underpin the decision-making of financial managers in pursuit of this objective.

Shareholder wealth maximisation

The maximisation of shareholder wealth is the prime objective of the majority of companies. The reason why investors put funds into a business is to receive returns that are better than the returns that they may receive from alternative investments. It is the responsibility of the directors of the company to make the optimum use of these funds to ensure that shareholder returns are maximised. But how do they do this and what is shareholder wealth?

Shareholder wealth is derived by shareholders from two sources:

- dividends paid on their equity, or ordinary, shares
- capital appreciation from the increase in the price of their ordinary shares.

As illustrated in Mini case 1.6, dividends do not have to be paid by a company. Dividends are paid out of the profits of the company available for distribution after interest and corporation tax have been paid, and assuming that the company has sufficient cash for their payment. The increase in share price is uncertain and depends generally on the demand for the company's shares and the volume of dealing activity in those shares.

Mini case 1.6

In March 2012, Rentokil Initial, a company specialising in pest control and hygiene services, announced a dividend for the first time in 3 years.

The accounting year end for Rentokil Initial is 31 December and final dividends are announced at the beginning of March.

The table below shows the full dividend for the year, the eps (earnings per share), and share price at the date of the announcement of the final dividend.

	2007	**2008**	**2009**	**2010**	**2011**
Dividend per 1p share (p)	7.38	0.65	0.00	0.00	1.33
eps (p)	36.20	1.04	2.63	−1.29	−3.84
Share price at announcement (p)	83.00	45.50	128.00	134.80	89.00
P/E ratio	2	44	49	−104	−23

From the table above we can see that the announcement of a dividend may have a favourable or adverse impact on share price.

A company's shares may be in demand because prospective share buyers believe that there are good prospects of future share price increases and/or increased dividend payments. The reason for such optimism may be that the company has demonstrated its success in investing in value-creating projects ('real' investment) and its ongoing intention of making even greater value-adding investments. The success of such investments in cash terms will provide the future cash flow for the payment of dividends and sustained future investment in new projects.

Cash flow

It is the success of investments in new projects that provides the key to future growth in both dividends and the company's share price (see Chapter 6). In this context, by success we mean returns in cash terms over and above the cost of the funds used for those investments and above the average returns in that particular market. It is cash flow from investments and not profit that is important here. Profit is an accounting term, which is subjective and open to many interpretations. Cash is a matter of fact and its measurement is completely objective – you either have it or you don't. Real funds can be seen in cash but not in accounting profit. Interest charges become payable as soon as money is made available, for example, from a lender to a borrower, not when an agreement is made or when a contract is signed. Therefore, in corporate finance it is cash flow that is important rather than profit.

Worked example 1.6

Cox Ltd is a local electrical retailer with retail outlets throughout the north of England. The company is currently considering opening a new temporary retail outlet, and is considering three alternative development options. As the company's financial adviser, you have been asked to evaluate the financial aspects of each of the options and advise which option the company should select, from a purely cash flow perspective (ignoring the time value of money, which is discussed in the next section).

The following financial information has been made available:

Year	Option 1 £000	Option 2 £000	Option 3 £000
	Investment		
0	12,000	12,000	12,000
	Cash receipts		
1	9,500	3,000	6,000
2	8,500	4,500	6,000
3	3,500	8,000	6,000
4	2,500	8,500	6,000

In cash flow terms all three options provide the same net cash flow, but the timings of the cash flow receipts differ significantly. Given that the future is invariably uncertain, it is likely that from a purely cash flow perspective, the rational choice would be to maximise the cash flows derived earlier rather than later, in which case the selection would be Option 1.

Time value of money

It is not only the cash flows themselves from investments that are important in terms of their size but also when they are received. The timing of cash flows, and their certainty of being received at all are also risks relating to cash flows. This has not been considered at all in Worked example 1.6.

A receipt of £100 today has greater value than receipt of £100 in one year's time. Its value changes over time primarily because:

■ the money could have been alternatively invested to receive interest
■ purchasing power will have been lost over a year due to inflation.

The percentage rate by which the value of money may be eroded over one year is called the discount rate, and the amount by which the value of money is eroded over one year is calculated by dividing it by what is called the discount factor [1/(1 + discount rate %)]. The value of money continues to be reduced by application of the discount factor (or using the appropriate discount factor if the discount rate has changed); its value therefore normally becomes less and less. Using this method, a discount factor may be applied to future cash flows to calculate today's value of future cash flows. This technique is called discounted cash flow (DCF). It is today's value of cash flows, their present values, which are the relevant cash flows with regard to investments. We will return to DCF in more detail in Chapter 6.

Risk

Increases in shareholder wealth comprise dividends and capital gains from share price increases, which together are termed returns to shareholders. Interest paid on loans to companies is called the return to debt holders, or lenders. The returns from 'real' investments in new assets and projects are the present values of the cash flows derived from the profits from such investments. Whichever return we are considering, we are talking specifically about future expected cash flows from investments. There is a close correlation between the returns and the level of risk relating to these investments.

An actual return on an investment will never be exactly what was expected – it will be either higher or lower, better or worse. Risk relates to the possibility that an actual return will be different from an expected return. The more risky an investment, the greater is the possibility that the return will be different from that expected. The higher the risk of an investment, the higher will be the expected return; the lower the risk of an investment, the lower will be the expected return. Throughout this book we will return to risk many times in:

- Chapter 5 when we look at the cost of capital – the funds used for investments
- Chapter 6 when we look at capital investment decisions
- Chapter 7 when we look at the type of funds used by companies – equity or loans
- Chapter 9 when we look at financial planning
- Chapter 11 when we look at international operations and investment
- Chapter 12 when we look at financial risk management
- Part II when we look at financial strategy.

Progress check 1.13

What is meant by shareholder wealth maximisation?

Summary of key points

- The four main types of profit-making businesses in the UK are sole traders, partnerships, limited companies (Ltd), and public limited companies (plc).
- The finance function has an important position within an organisation, and includes responsibility for accounting and corporate finance.
- Accountability of directors is maintained by reporting on the financial performance and the financial position of the company to shareholders on both a yearly and a half-yearly basis, and the audit function.
- Financial statements are produced by companies for each accounting period to provide information about how the business has been doing.
- The three main financial statements that appear within a business's annual report and accounts, together with the chairman's statement, directors' report, and auditors' report, are the balance sheet, income statement, and statement of cash flows.
- Corporate finance and accounting are both the responsibility of the finance director, and although they are separate disciplines corporate finance is very much supported by the accounting function.
- The effective management of corporate finance impacts greatly on how well the company is able to achieve its primary objective of maximisation of shareholder wealth.
- The underlying principles of corporate finance include cash flow (rather than profit), the time value of money, and the risk and uncertainty relating to future cash flows.

Glossary of key terms

accounting The classification and recording of monetary transactions, the presentation and interpretation of the results of those transactions in order to assess performance over a period and the financial position at a given date, and the monetary projection of future activities arising from alternative planned courses of action.

accounting concepts The principles underpinning the preparation of accounting information. Fundamental accounting concepts are the broad basic assumptions that underlie the periodic financial accounts of business enterprises.

Accounting Council A UK standard-setting body set up in July 2012 with responsibility for advising the FRC Board on financial codes and standards to ensure that a high-quality, effective and proportionate approach is taken and to provide advice on proposed developments in relation to international codes and standards and regulations. It is a part of the Codes and Standards Committee of the FRC (see below).

accounting period The time period covered by the accounting statements of an entity.

accounting policies The specific accounting bases selected and consistently followed by an entity as being, in the opinion of the management, appropriate to its circumstances and best suited to present fairly its results and financial position (FRS 18, Companies Act and IAS 8).

accounting standards Authoritative statements of how particular types of transaction and other events should be reflected in financial statements. Compliance with accounting standards will normally be necessary for financial statements to give a true and fair view.

Accounting Standards Board (ASB) A UK standard-setting body set up in 1990 to develop, issue and withdraw accounting standards. Its aims are to 'establish and improve standards of financial accounting and reporting, for the benefit of users, preparers and auditors of financial information'.

accounts payable The money owed by entities to suppliers for goods and services.

accounts receivable The money owed to entities by customers.

Alternative Investment Market (AIM) A securities market designed primarily for small companies, regulated by the Stock Exchange but with less demanding rules than apply to the Stock Exchange official list of companies.

annual report and accounts A set of statements which may comprise a management report (in the case of companies, a directors' report), an auditors' report, and the financial statements of the entity.

asset A right or other access to future economic benefits which can be measured reliably and are controlled by an entity as a result of past transactions or events (IAS 16).

audit A systematic examination of the activities and status of an entity, based primarily on investigation and analysis of its systems, controls, and records. A statutory annual audit of a company is defined by International Standard on Auditing 200 as the expression of an opinion by the auditor on whether the financial statements are prepared, in all material respects, in accordance with an applicable financial reporting framework.

auditor A professionally qualified accountant who is appointed by, and reports independently to, the shareholders, providing an objective verification to shareholders and other users that the financial statements have been prepared properly and in accordance with legislative and regulatory requirements; that they present the information truthfully and fairly, and that they conform to the best accounting practice in their treatment of the various measurements and valuations.

balance sheet A statement of the financial position of an entity at a given date disclosing the assets, liabilities, and accumulated funds such as shareholders' contributions and reserves, prepared to give a true and fair view of the financial state of the entity at that date.

cash (and cash equivalents) Cash and cash equivalents comprise cash on hand and demand deposits, together with short-term, highly liquid investments that are readily convertible to a known amount of cash (IAS 7).

creative accounting A form of accounting which, while complying with all regulations, nevertheless gives a biased (generally favourable) impression of a company's performance.

debt One of the alternative sources of capital for a company, also called long-term debt or loans.

equity The total investment of the shareholders in the company – the total value of book wealth. Equity comprises share capital, share premiums, and retained earnings.

financial accounting The accounting function responsible for the periodic external reporting, statutorily required, for shareholders. It also provides such similar information as required for government and other interested third parties, such as potential investors, employees, lenders, suppliers, customers, and financial analysts.

financial management (or management of corporate finance) The management of all the processes associated with the efficient acquisition and deployment of both short- and long-term financial resources. Within an organisation financial management assists operations management to reach their financial objectives.

Financial Reporting Council (FRC) The UK body responsible for:

(i) promoting high standards of corporate governance
(ii) setting standards for corporate reporting and actuarial practice and monitoring and enforcing accounting and auditing standards
(iii) overseeing the regulatory activities of the actuarial profession and the professional accountancy bodies.

Financial Reporting Standards (FRSs) The accounting standards of practice published by the Accounting Standards Board between August 1990 and July 2012, and by the Accounting Council from July 2012, and which are gradually replacing the Standard Statements of Accounting Practice (SSAPs), which were published by the Accounting Standards Committee up to August 1990.

financial statements Summaries of accounts, whether to internal or external parties, to provide information for interested parties. The three key financial statements are: income statement; balance sheet; statement of cash flows. Other financial statements are: report of the auditors; reconciliation of movements in shareholders' funds.

flotation A flotation, or initial public offering (IPO), is the obtaining of a listing by a company on a stock exchange, through the offering of its shares to the general public, financial institutions, or private sector businesses.

income statement The statement of financial performance that measures and reports whether or not the company has made a profit or loss on its operations during the period, through producing and selling its goods or services.

internal control As defined in the Cadbury Report, it is the whole system of controls, financial or otherwise, established in order to provide reasonable assurance of:

(i) effective and efficient operation
(ii) internal financial control
(iii) compliance with laws and regulations.

International Accounting Standards (IASs) The international financial reporting standards issued by the IASC, which are very similar to the SSAPs and FRSs, which are used in the UK.

International Accounting Standards Board (IASB) The IASB is the body that is responsible for setting and publishing International Financial Reporting Standards (IFRSs). It was formed on 1 April 2001 and succeeded the International Accounting Standards Committee (IASC) which had been formed in 1973. The parent body of the IASB is the International Accounting Standards Committee Foundation, which was incorporated in the USA in March 2001, and was also responsible for issuing International Accounting Standards (IASs).

International Accounting Standards Committee (IASC) A committee supported by many national accounting bodies worldwide, whose objectives are:

(i)   to facilitate and publish, in the public interest, accounting standards to be observed in the presentation of financial statements, and to promote their worldwide acceptance and observance.

(ii) to work generally for the improvement of harmonisation of regulations, accounting standards, and procedures relating to the presentation of financial statements.

International Financial Reporting Standards (IFRSs) The international financial reporting standards issued by the IASB, which incorporate the IASs, issued by the IASC.

International Standards on Auditing (ISAs) A set of professional standards that deals with the independent auditor's responsibilities when conducting an audit of financial statements.

inventories Inventories, according to IAS 2, comprise:

- assets held for sale in the ordinary course of business (finished goods)
- assets in the production process for sale in the ordinary course of business (work in progress) and
- materials and supplies that are consumed in production (raw materials).

liabilities An entity's obligations to transfer economic benefits as a result of past transactions or events (IAS 37).

management accounting The application of the principles of accounting and financial management to create, protect, preserve and increase value so as to deliver that value to the stakeholders of profit and not-for-profit enterprises, both public and private. Management accounting is an integral part of management, requiring the identification, generation, presentation, interpretation and use of information relevant to:

- formulating business strategy
- planning and controlling activities
- decision-making
- efficient resource usage
- performance improvement and value enhancement
- safeguarding tangible and intangible assets, corporate governance and internal control.

net realisable value The amount for which an asset could be disposed, less any direct selling costs (SSAP 9 and IAS 2).

off balance sheet financing The funding of operations in such a way that the relevant assets and liabilities are not disclosed in the balance sheet of the company concerned.

private limited company (Ltd) A company in which the liability of members for the company's debts is limited to the amount paid and, if any, unpaid on the shares taken up by them.

profit (or profit after tax or profit for the year) Profit before tax (PBT) less corporation tax.

public limited company (plc) A company limited by shares or by guarantee, with a share capital, whose memorandum states that it is public and that it has complied with the registration procedures for such a company. A public company is distinguished from a private company in the following ways: a minimum issued share capital of £50,000; public limited company, or plc, at the end of the name; public company clause in the memorandum; freedom to offer securities to the public.

qualified accountant A member of the accountancy profession, and in the UK a member of one of the six professional accountancy bodies: CIMA; ICAEW; ICAS; ICAI; ACCA; CIPFA, and internationally the CGMA (amalgamation of CIMA and the American AICPA).

Registrar of Companies Government official agency that is responsible for initial registration of new companies and for collecting and arranging public access to the annual reports of all limited companies.

share A fixed identifiable unit of capital which has a fixed nominal or face value, which may be quite different from the market value of the share.

statement of cash flows A statement that summarises the inflows and outflows of cash for a period, classified under the following standard headings (IAS 7):

- operating activities
- investing activities
- financing activities.

The statement of cash flows is one of the three key financial statements.

Statements of Standard Accounting Practice (SSAPs) The accounting standards of practice published by the Accounting Standards Committee up to 1 August 1990.

subsidiary A subsidiary company, defined by IAS 27, is a company for which another company (the parent company) owns more than half the voting shares or has power:

- over more than one half of the voting rights by virtue of an agreement with other investors or
- to govern the financial and operating policies of the entity under a statue or an agreement or
- to appoint or remove the majority of the members of the board of directors or
- to cast the majority of votes at a meeting of the board of directors.

treasury management The corporate handling of all financial matters, the generation of external and internal funds for business, the management of currencies and cash flows, and the complex strategies, policies, and procedures of corporate finance.

true and fair view The requirement for financial statements prepared in compliance with the Companies Act to 'give a true and fair view' overrides any other requirements. Although not precisely defined in the Companies Act, this is generally accepted to mean that accounts show a true and fair view if they are unlikely to mislead a user of financial information by giving a false impression of the company.

window dressing A creative accounting practice in which changes in short-term funding have the effect of disguising or improving the reported liquidity position of the reporting organisation.

working capital Also called net current assets, working capital is the capital available for conducting day-to-day operations of an organisation: normally the excess of current assets over current liabilities.

Assessment material

Questions

Q1.1   What are the different types of business entity and what are the fundamental differences between them?

Q1.2   (i)   Why is financial information produced?
(ii)   Who is it produced for and what do they use it for?

Q1.3   Outline the responsibilities of the finance director of a large public limited company (plc).

Q1.4   Which are the three key financial statements that are used to provide information to shareholders and others about the company's financial position and financial performance, and what are their limitations?

Q1.5   (i)   What information does a balance sheet provide?
(ii)   What information does an income statement provide?
(iii)   What information does a statement of cash flows provide?

Q1.6   How do financial statements ensure that accountability for the reporting of timely and accurate information to shareholders is maintained?

Q1.7   (i)   What is corporate finance?
(ii)   How does corporate finance relate to accounting and perhaps other disciplines?

Q1.8   Describe the main corporate finance responsibilities of the finance director of a large public limited company (plc).

Q1.9   Explain the key principles that underpin the discipline of corporate finance.

Discussion points

D1.1   The managing director of a large public limited company stated: 'I've built up my business over the past 15 years from a one-man band to a large plc. As we grew we seemed to spend more and more money on accountants, financial managers, and auditors. During the next few months we are restructuring to go back to being a private limited company. This will be much simpler and we can save a fortune on finance departments and auditing costs.' Discuss. (Hint: You may wish to research Richard Branson's Virgin Group on the Internet to provide some background for this discussion.)

D1.2   'So long that, as a company, we continue to report profits each year then the shareholders will have no reason to complain.' Discuss.

Exercises

Solutions are provided in Appendix 2 to all exercise numbers highlighted in colour.

Level I

E1.1   *Time allowed – 30 minutes*
At a recent meeting of the local branch of the Women's Institute they had a discussion about what sort of organisation they were. The discussion broadened into a general debate about all types of organisation, and someone brought up the term 'business entity'. Although there were many opinions, there was little sound knowledge about what business entities are. Jane Cross said that her husband was an accountant and she was sure he would not mind spending an hour one evening to enlighten them on the subject. Chris Cross fished out his textbooks to refresh his knowledge of the subject and came up with a schedule of all the different business entities he could think of together with the detail of their defining features and key points of difference and similarity.

> **Prepare the sort of schedule that Chris might have drafted for his talk and identify the category that the Women's Institute might fall into.**

E1.2   *Time allowed – 30 minutes*
Mary Andrews was a finance manager but is now semi-retired. She has been asked by her local comprehensive school careers officer to give a talk entitled: 'What is corporate finance and what is financial management?'

> **Prepare a list of bullet points that covers everything necessary for Mary to give a comprehensive and easy-to-understand presentation to a group of sixth-formers at the school.**

E1.3   *Time allowed – 30 minutes*
It is sometimes said that the only user of financial information is the accountant.

> **Outline the range of other users of financial information.**

Level II

E1.4   *Time allowed – 30 minutes*
Financial statements are produced each year by businesses, using prescribed formats.

> **Should major plcs be allowed to reflect their individuality in the formats in which their own financial statements are presented?**

E1.5   *Time allowed – 45 minutes*

Professionals in the UK, for example, doctors, solicitors, accountants, etc., normally work within partnerships. Many tradesmen, such as plumbers, car mechanics, carpenters, etc., operate as sole traders. Software engineers seem to work for corporations and limited companies.

> Consider the size of operation, range of products, financing, the marketplace, and the geographical area served, to discuss why companies like Microsoft and Yahoo! should operate as plcs.

E1.6   *Time allowed – 60 minutes*

Bill Walsh has just been appointed finance director of a medium-sized engineering company, Nutsan Ltd, which has a high level of exports and is very sensitive to economic changes throughout the UK and the rest of the world. One of the tasks on Bill's action list is a review of the accounting and finance function.

> What are the senior financial roles that Bill would expect to be in place and what are the important functions for which they should be responsible?

E1.7   *Time allowed – 60 minutes*

The Olympic Games held in London in August 2012 was originally budgeted in 2006 to cost £2.35bn, but by the beginning of 2007 this estimate had risen to £9.3bn. By the start of the Games in July 2012 the estimated cost was over £12bn. The centrepiece Olympic Stadium in east London alone cost £537m. Work on the stadium began in 2007 and yet by December 2008 the UK Government had allocated a further £29m to the project. In December 2011 the UK Government admitted that even the estimated cost of £40m for the opening ceremonies for the Olympic and Paralympic Games was only half of the amount that would be needed. In short, projections were way short of the actual costs – much to the concern of the media and taxpayers alike.

> You are required to research into the 2012 Olympic Games budget and the progress of the costs using the BBC, the *Financial Times*, other serious newspapers, and the Internet, and summarise the financial aspects of the project that you gather. You should focus on the attitudes expressed by the general public and Government ministers and consider examples of bias, non-timeliness, and lack of transparency.

2

Corporate objectives

Chapter contents

Learning objectives

Completion of this chapter will enable you to:

- Outline the strategic management process with regard to mission, corporate objectives, corporate appraisal, and strategic choice.
- Explain why the maximisation of shareholder wealth is the primary corporate objective.
- Consider the secondary, or surrogate, objectives of a company.
- Appreciate the importance of how companies may adopt appropriate financial strategies to create shareholder value.
- Explain the efficient market hypothesis and its place in corporate financial theory.
- Describe the concept of shareholder value.
- Outline the key strategic financial decisions faced by companies.
- Explain agency theory and what is meant by the agency problem.
- Describe the range of alternative incentive schemes that may be used to overcome the agency problem.

Introduction

This chapter begins by looking generally at the strategic management process. It puts the corporate objectives of the company into context and how they are linked to shareholder value and financial strategy. We will consider the range of corporate objectives of a business, and in particular the primary objective of maximisation of shareholder wealth. Other objectives, which are considered secondary to the main objective, are often described as substitute or surrogate objectives. These may exist in support of the primary objective, or because of the diverse interests of the other stakeholders in a business apart from the shareholders, for example employees, the general public, suppliers, and customers. This chapter deals with what is meant by shareholder value and its relationship with corporate value, and the key financial decisions faced by businesses in their endeavours to achieve their primary objective. An introduction to the subject of financial strategy will indicate how the appropriate financial strategy may be used to increase value. The chapter closes with a look at why the objective of maximisation of shareholder wealth may not always be aligned with the goals of the managers of a business because of the agency problem. The ways in which the agency problem may be dealt with are expanded on in Chapter 3 when we discuss corporate governance.

Strategic management

The origins of strategy are in military campaigns and manoeuvring. Strategy is fundamentally long term. It is concerned with the long-term 'whats' of the company rather than the 'hows', for example what it wants to do, what it wants the organisation to be, and where it wants the organisation to go, including the specification of resources required to achieve specific objectives. Strategy is not the 'how' to achieve those things. Tactics are the short-term plans for achieving the objectives of the organisation. They are the shorter-term 'hows'.

The **strategic management** process includes making decisions on:

- the objectives of the organisation
- changes in these objectives
- the resources used to attain these objectives
- the policies that govern the acquisition, use, and disposition of these resources.

It is incorrect to assume that strategic management, which includes strategic planning, is just an extension of budgeting. But there is a close relationship between these processes. A strategic plan (see Chapter 9) looks at the long term, which is defined as more than one year and typically five or ten years. A budget is a short-term (less than one year) quantified statement, for a defined period of time, which may include planned investments, revenues, expenses, assets, liabilities, and cash flows. A budget provides a focus for the organisation, aids the co-ordination of activities, and facilitates control.

The way in which a typical strategic management process may be carried out in an organisation is illustrated in the flow chart in Figure 2.1. The flow chart shows particularly how analysis is used to develop strategies and actions.

It is fundamental for every company to have a **mission** developed from a vision of what it would like to achieve. The mission statement may be a summary of goals and policies, which does not have to be in writing, but is generally a sense of purpose or underlying belief of the company. A mission includes four elements, defined in the Ashridge Mission Model developed by Andrew Campbell and Sally Yeung in 1991: purpose; values; strategies; behaviour standards. In addition it should answer the strategic question 'what do we do?' by defining the scope of the business in terms of markets and products (Campbell, A and Yeung, S 'Creating a sense of mission' *Long Range Planning*, Volume 24 Number 4, pages 10–20 (1991)). The most important thing about a company's mission is that it should be understood and believed in by every employee in the business.

Strategic decisions cannot generally be collated by a company into some sort of total decision matrix to arrive at an optimum overall strategy. Life is never as simple as this because there are

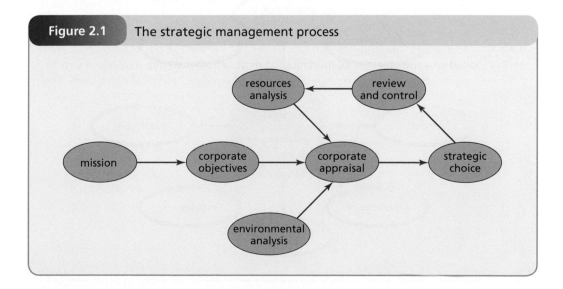

Figure 2.1   The strategic management process

too many variables, which are changing constantly, and also limitations with regard to knowledge and processes. In practice, strategy tends to emerge and develop in an incremental way in order to maintain a strategic fit between corporate goals and resources and changing market opportunities.

An organisation's policy is the framework expressing the limits within which actions should occur. Whereas policy is a long-lasting, usually unquantified, statement of guidance about the way in which an organisation seeks to behave in relation to its stakeholders, corporate **objectives** are the visionary statements set out by the company before it starts its detailed planning.

Corporate objectives

A company is owned by its shareholders who have invested money in the business in order to increase the value of, and maximise the return from, their investment. The primary objective of a business is therefore assumed to be the maximisation of shareholder wealth. A company is managed by its directors on behalf of its shareholders. Directors are appointed by shareholders and are charged with the primary aim of achievement of the shareholder wealth maximisation objective. An increase in shareholder wealth is derived from cash received by shareholders from the receipt of dividends and from capital gains from increases in the market price of their shares.

The shareholders are not the only stakeholders in a business; there are many others, as shown in Figure 2.2. Their aims and objectives do not necessarily coincide with the objectives of the shareholders.

| Figure 2.2 | The stakeholders of a business |

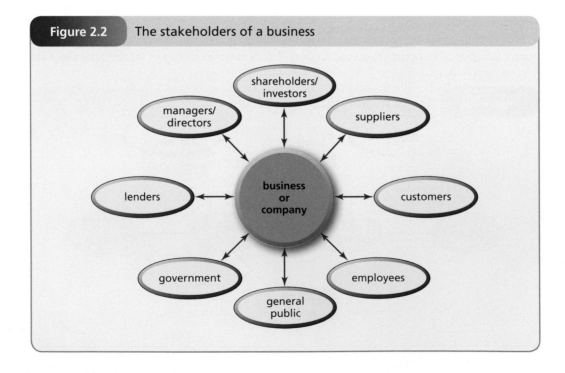

Surrogate objectives

Although we are assuming throughout this book that the primary objective of a company is the maximisation of shareholder wealth, there are many other objectives including business objectives, operational objectives, and individual objectives that should be formalised and in writing. Other aims and objectives of the business, which must be secondary to the primary objective, are called surrogate, or alternative objectives (see Figure 2.3), and may include:

- profit maximisation
- market share maximisation
- earnings per share (eps) growth
- social responsibility
- sales maximisation
- survival
- dividend growth,

and may include non-financial objectives such as customer satisfaction and delivery reliability. There are a number of problems associated with these **surrogate objectives**:

- the choice of timescale applicable to profit maximisation may be long or short term
- the measurement of profit is very subjective
- a profit-maximising strategy is not without risk
- with a sales maximisation strategy there is sometimes a danger of overtrading, in which there is a lack of adequate working capital to support such increases in levels of business
- survival, while an important objective, cannot be a long-term objective of a business
- a business cannot exist merely to meet its social responsibility, for example to please its employees, the local community, etc.
- surrogate or secondary objectives may actually be contrary to or may undermine the primary objective of shareholder wealth maximisation.

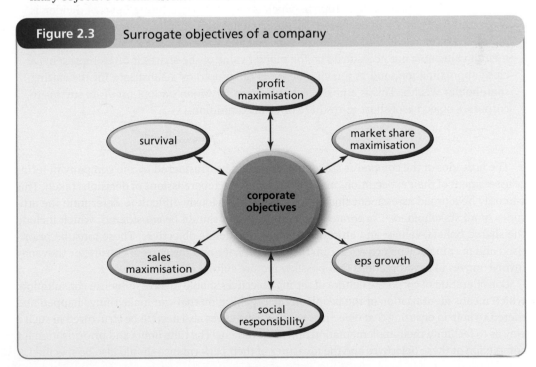

Figure 2.3   Surrogate objectives of a company

Why is maximisation of shareholder wealth a company's primary objective?

The relationships between the objectives of a company should ensure that there is no conflict. Their importance should also be assigned by ranking priorities. Objectives are set in order to support the planning process and to assign responsibility to individuals. They should aim to integrate each area of the company so that they are all moving in the same direction in alignment with the company's mission and shareholders' requirements. Objectives are also used to motivate employees and to enable performance evaluation of individuals, departments, business units, and companies.

Worked example 2.1

During a discussion at a recent board meeting the finance director of Moon plc explained that traditional financial theory suggests that companies should pursue a primary objective of long-term shareholder wealth maximisation. He went on to explain that most companies also pursue one or more surrogate corporate objectives, and that Moon plc should pursue an objective of short-term share price maximisation.

How can the adoption of such a surrogate corporate objective be justified?

Maximisation of shareholder wealth may be considered in terms of maximisation of shareholder returns. Shareholder returns are derived from two sources – a regular flow of dividends and capital growth from an increase in share price. A shareholder will invariably demand a required rate of return, which is the anticipated future flows of dividends expressed in today's values, based on the shareholder's required rate of return. This method is often used to determine the fundamental value of a share. While this fundamental value may not necessarily be the market value of the shares it often represents a close approximation, and as a consequence is often used as a substitute for measuring shareholder wealth. This is a possible justification for Moon's adoption of its surrogate corporate objective of short-term share price maximisation.

The attitudes of the company's stakeholders should be considered by the company in terms of assessment of their expectations and reactions and the repercussions of decisions taken. This can only be a broad assessment since in practice it is obviously difficult to determine the attitudes of all stakeholders. Corporate and cultural power should be considered, which include the shared beliefs, values, and attitudes that serve to define objectives. These must be prioritised and may include objectives within the current scope and the current culture, or they may involve moves in new directions that possibly require culture changes.

Consideration of corporate culture in setting objectives should involve influence consultation, which means identification of the people in the organisation that can make things happen and therefore help in ensuring that objectives are met. Objectives also need to be structured in such a way as to facilitate their implementation and achievement. The time limits and prioritisation for completion of these objectives and the measures of their performance should also be specified.

Corporate appraisal

Having established its objectives, a company's strategic management process continues to consider many ideas and options and 'what-ifs'. The purpose of this is to try and provide the best 'fit' between the company and its environment, to enable it to focus on its most important objectives, and to assist in determining how the company may achieve its objectives. The first part of the process involves a corporate appraisal, which includes a review of the business in terms of external factors (**environmental analysis**) and internal factors (**resources analysis**, or position audit) to assess the possibility of attaining objectives, and considers the basis of the company's competitive advantage – Porter's generic strategy (Porter, ME (1980) *Competitive Strategy: Techniques for Analyzing Industries and Competitors*, New York: The Free Press).

Environmental analysis of the company includes consideration of, for example:

- the nature of the company's environment, whether it is complex or simple, and whether the company is slow or dynamic in reacting to what is going on in the environment
- analysis of PESTEL (political, economic, social, technological change, environmental, and legistative) factors
- external elements of a SWOT (strengths, weaknesses, opportunities, threats) analysis – the part of the SWOT analysis (see an example in Chapter 8) that looks at major external threats to the company and how these may be avoided, turned round, or exploited along with all other opportunities
- structural analysis of the competitive environment (Porter), which looks at the competitive reactions of current and potential competitors in the industry and how they may compete, and considers:
    - analysis of the market characteristics of supply and demand
    - forecasting (see Chapter 9) and the use of databases and a range of information sources.

The position audit or resources analysis of the company considers things like, for example:

- availability and control of the 5Ms – the resources of people (men), materials, plant and equipment (machines), cash flow (money), and markets
- the company's industrial sectors and its products
- internal elements of a SWOT analysis (see an example in Chapter 8) that look at the major internal weaknesses of the company and how these may be eliminated and how the company may capitalise on its strengths
- portfolio analysis of the company – product life cycle (PLC) and the Boston Consulting Group (BCG) matrix (see Chapter 13)
- gap analysis, which looks at gaps that may exist between the company and the best in the industry and considers areas such as levels of productivity, quality, distribution, and service efficiency
- skills and flexibility analysis – the human resources analysis of the strengths, knowledge and experience of all employees and their ability to work in teams
- financial analysis (see Chapter 8)
- comparative analysis of historical performance and industry norms, using benchmarking and the company's own records
- the learning curve with regard to new employees, new products, and new processes.

Porter's generic strategy describes the way in which a business may derive a competitive advantage through either cost leadership, or differentiation of its products and services from its competitors on the basis of, for example, technology, quality, service, or branding. Having chosen cost leadership or differentiation, the company may then focus on either broad markets or narrow markets of specific products and customers.

Strategic choice

The next step in the company's strategic management process considers **strategic choice**, which uses the information provided from the corporate appraisal to evaluate the suitability, feasibility, and acceptability of the development of alternative strategies through:

- screening options, using ranking, decision trees, scenario analysis, and simulation
- financial analysis using, for example, cost–benefit analysis, break-even analysis, return on capital employed (see Chapter 8), payback, and DCF (see Chapter 6)
- risk analysis (see Chapter 12),

and strategic method, which deals with the ways in which a company may develop and grow.

Corporate development and growth may be either through internal organic development or through acquisitions, mergers, or joint ventures. Organic growth is achieved from investment by the company in value-adding projects (see Chapter 6), and the development of new products and services, processes, and markets.

Strategic method may use techniques such as the Ansoff growth matrix analysis, which considers gaps in the market, and the products and markets in which the business wishes to compete. The company may adopt a strategy of doing nothing, withdrawing from a market, penetrating and developing a market, consolidating the company's position by developing products, or diversifying. The Ansoff diversification model (Ansoff, HI 'Strategies for diversification' *Harvard Business Review* 25(5), pages 113–25 (1957)) considers the various methods of diversification, which may be related (horizontal, or vertical backward and forward) or unrelated to the company's current areas of business through conglomerate growth involving acquisitions (see Chapter 16).

Implementation of strategy requires consideration of the planning and allocation of resources, development of an appropriate organisational structure and the people and systems within the corporate environment. It also requires consideration of how strategies will be managed as they are rolled out and systems put in place for their review and control. The outcomes of review and control systems are usually fed back into a company's systems of resources analysis in order that refinements or changes may be made to strategy as necessary.

Worked example 2.2

We are required to identify a policy, a strategy, and tactics for Mediatrix plc, which is a designer and manufacturer of hi-tech consumer products, and which wants to develop a specific multi-media product that is number one in the marketplace.

The policy for Mediatrix may be to aim for a product that is technically superior to the competition.

The strategy for Mediatrix may involve planning to spend 15% of its sales revenue on research and development.

A tactic for Mediatrix may be to set up a cross-functional new product development (NPD) team.

A further level below the tactical level is operational control. In the case of Mediatrix this may involve the monitoring of feedback from the cross-functional NPD team.

Progress check 2.2

What is strategy?

Financial strategy

We have seen that the development of **business strategy** is concerned with plans relating to markets, product planning, the competitive position of the business, and so on. This book is more concerned with **financial strategy** and its role in the selection of appropriate methods of funding a business, and how those funds are most effectively used for wealth creation in terms of returns on investment in new projects, and the distribution of those returns to the investors in the business.

Individual shareholders and others, for example pension funds and other financial institutions, invest in companies to achieve **shareholder value** (or investor value). Here we are talking about the popular meaning of investment – the purchase of shares in a company. Shareholder value may be reflected in the expected returns of the capital markets mirrored in the value placed on the company's shares by the markets. This may be the market value of the shares of the business, or it may be a value of the business derived from using a range of other methods (which we will discuss in Chapter 16 when we look at mergers and acquisitions).

Companies invest in a range of projects with an aim of spreading risk and creating corporate value in order to try and provide value for the shareholders. Here we are talking about 'real' investments by companies in strategies and projects to provide growth and make them better businesses. The expected future returns are valued at a discount rate appropriate to the business. **Corporate value** is defined as the value today of the expected future returns from current business strategies and future investment projects, valued at an appropriate discount rate (see Chapter 6). Sometimes companies may invest in a combination of projects to spread the risk, but the result may not be a reduction in overall risk. Very often overall risk may be increased, without any corresponding increase in value and although eps (earnings per share) may be increased, shareholder value may actually be destroyed. Examples of this may be seen in conglomerates which have acquired a business in which they have no real expertise, or if too high a price has been paid for the acquisition of a company, or if the method of financing an acquisition is not cost-effective.

The AstraZeneca press extract below illustrates how inappropriate financial strategies resulted in the destruction of shareholder value. Dissatisfaction with the company's performance peaked with the CEO, David Brennan, resigning hours before the start of the annual shareholders' meeting in April 2012. Although the Anglo-Swedish drug-maker had appeared outwardly healthy in recent years, this was due to the distribution of ever larger dividends and the launching of share buy-backs with its cash generated from revenues from existing medicines. However, behind this lay the failure of a number of acquisitions and lack of progress in research projects which led to a decline in share price. Analysis of the share price over a longer period may provide even more convincing support for the argument that shareholder value may be destroyed through use of an inappropriate financial strategy.

How an inappropriate financial strategy can destroy shareholder value

The outgoing chief executive of Astra-Zeneca is set to walk away with at least £38 million for his six-year tenure despite deep unease in the City over the company's future.

A chorus of shareholder anger surrounded David Brennan's decision yesterday to stand down in June, a resignation that the company insisted was entirely voluntary. Mr Brennan, 59, said that he was retiring for 'personal' reasons: 'I've been very busy with my job. I'm looking forward to spending time with my family.'

He will be replaced on an interim basis by the chief financial officer, Simon Lowth. The company's chairman, Louis Schweitzer, is standing down ahead of schedule to allow his successor, the former Volvo boss Leif Johansson, to preside over the choice of a new chief executive. Mr Schweitzer said: 'David felt it was time for him to change his lifestyle and the board accepted his decision.'

Mr Brennan's departure was announced alongside a profit warning as AstraZeneca revealed that the loss of patent protection on several key drugs had blown a hole in its quarterly revenue, which fell by 11 per cent to $7.3 billion. Shares in the company fell 6.1 per cent to £26.76. He will receive a payoff of at least £5.4 million, although the figure could rise to as much as £12 million if AstraZeneca allows him to keep share awards that are due to mature up to 2018.

This golden parachute will come on top of his accumulated earnings of £32.4 million since he was appointed chief executive in 2006, and a pension fund of £985,000 accrued over 36 years at the company.

Institutional investors have been clamouring for change at AstraZeneca, alarmed by a slide in revenues and by the failure of key medicines in clinical trials. At the company's annual meeting at a hotel near Tower Bridge, small shareholders queued to berate the board, whose members include John Varley, the former Barclays chief executive, who chairs the remuneration committee.

One investor, John Farmer, accused the company of overpaying its senior executives and of under-performing rivals such as Glaxo SmithKline and Bristol Myers-Squibb. 'A lot is being paid for a little, by which I mean this paltry shareholder return,' he said. Another thundered 'shame on you, shame on you' at the stony-faced leadership team, adding: 'Mr Brennan may have shortcomings, but the blame for all this lies with the board.'

AstraZeneca's difficulties are largely caused by the looming expiry of exclusive ten-year patents on its biggest-selling drugs, including a cholesterol-lowering medicine, Crestor, an antidepressant, Seroquel, and Nexium, a treatment for heartburn.

When patents expire, the price of medicines drops by as much as 90 per cent as generic manufacturers make cheap copies. AstraZeneca's efforts to develop new drugs to make up the shortfall have largely failed.

Thousands of jobs have been lost under Mr Brennan's leadership as AstraZeneca wielded the axe in an attempt to maintain its profits. The company recently announced 7,300 redundancies, including a withdrawal from neurology research, on top of 21,000 job losses over the preceding five years. A spate of recent deals has underlined the company's need for new medicines, including the $1.26 billion (£780 million) takeover this week of a US developer of an unproven treatment for gout.

Mike Mitchell, a pharmaceuticals analyst at Seymour Pierce, said that AstraZeneca faced a long-term battle to maintain its independence: 'It looks like a business that has been flailing desperately for some kind of lifeline.'

Source: **AstraZeneca chief quits with derision ringing in his ears,** by Andrew Clarke © *The Times*, 27 April 2012

Mini case 2.1

An example of destruction of shareholder value was seen in the Eurotunnel project. The world's biggest privately funded project (at that time) began in 1987, but by 2004 Euro-tunnel's share price had dropped by 90% to under 20p. By 2005 it had fallen even further to around 17p, but recovered a little to around 25p during 2006.

Eurotunnel incurred huge losses and debts counted in billions of £ sterling, which it could not afford to service or repay. At the outset Eurotunnel had been extremely over-optimistic in its forecasts. It actually attracted around 35% of the original prediction of 16 million passengers per year, and only around 25% of its initial forecast of an annual 7 million tonnes of freight business. The initial costs of the project were greatly exceeded, with the cost of building the tunnel at £10bn instead of an estimated £6bn. That problem was further exacerbated by their high loan interest rates in the early 1990s of between 11% and 17%, which subsequently fell to between 5% and 7%. Eurotunnel was also hit by an economic downturn, which resulted in a fall in numbers of people travelling, and increased price competition from the cross-Channel ferries, and discount airlines such as easyJet and Ryanair. Eurotunnel's fate was blamed by some on the fact that when Margaret Thatcher, and former French premier François Mitterrand, gave the final go-ahead for the tunnel in 1987, Mrs Thatcher insisted that the project should be completely privately funded, and with no subsequent government help.

In a perfectly competitive market it may be argued that the return from a portfolio (or spread) of investments exactly matches the return demanded by shareholders and other investors and so no (additional) value is created. Financial strategy is to do with decisions related to the financing of the business or individual projects, using debt or equity. The appraisal of the individual 'real' investment project opportunities available to a business, which is discussed in Chapter 6, is used to determine if they are viable and will add value to the business. Financial strategy is also to do with decisions about capital structure, and how much profit should be paid in interest or dividends and how much should be retained for investment in new projects. It is also to do with decisions about the choice of which type of loan may be most appropriate, the management of financial risk, the use of derivatives, and mergers and acquisitions.

Imagine the following hypothetical scenario:

- all information about companies and their markets is fully known by all investors
- all companies' capital is homogenous and debt is the same as equity in terms of its risk and cost
- dividends are not paid
- all investment projects have the same risk and returns
- there is no corporation tax
- companies' share prices reflect the book values of their net assets.

Clearly in the above scenario financial strategy has little significance. In such a perfectly competitive market all investors would receive the same returns and no additional value would be created, and investors would have no financial reason to invest in one company rather than another. It is because each of the above hypothetical situations do not apply in practice, and because companies and investors do not have access to, or do not know all relevant information, that opportunities arise which enable financial strategies to be adopted that provide value over and above market expectations.

In reality, capital is not homogeneous in terms of its characteristics, risks and returns, and different costs. In addition, different returns may exist for the same type of loan, for example, in different sectors of the same market or in alternative markets. A company has a choice as to whether or not it pays a dividend to its shareholders. The appropriate financial strategy will be one that selects the required type of capital at the lowest cost and adopts a corresponding dividend policy, which together result in an optimisation of corporate value and shareholder value.

Actual investment projects vary considerably with regard to their risks and returns. Their actual returns will also differ from their expected returns because of variations in original investment costs, the timings and values of future cash flows, and variations in the cost of capital. Financial strategy with regard to 'real' investment relates to the use of appropriate capital investment evaluation methods, use of relevant discount rates, and the assessment and management of risk that result in an optimisation of corporate value.

Corporation tax is normally payable by companies in the UK. The levels of tax incurred by a company will depend on the financial measures taken by the company to avoid and mitigate its corporation tax payable, with the aim of optimisation of corporate value.

If a company makes all the 'right' decisions, which result in the optimisation of its level of corporate value, this may not necessarily be reflected in the maximisation of shareholder wealth in terms of dividends and the market price of its shares. To achieve this a company must therefore also adopt the 'right' financial strategies relating to, for example, levels of gearing and dividend policy. It must also pursue other strategies that have an impact on the share price, which may include:

- creation of competitive advantages and barriers to market entry, through for example, effective marketing, establishment of strong brand names, and economies of scale
- employment of a strong management team with the credibility that inspires confidence among investors, City analysts, and potential investors
- development of efficient communication channels and public relations that emphasise company achievements and awareness of future plans
- actions that reduce risk to the level commensurate with returns required by the shareholders, for example insurance, and the hedging of interest rate and foreign currency exchange rate risk (see Chapter 12).

Progress check 2.3

What is meant by corporate value and how is it different from shareholder value?

Financial strategy is therefore broadly concerned with corporate value and shareholder value, and the courses of action required to achieve the specific objective of creating shareholder value above the average returns expected for that specific type of company in that particular market. The use of appropriate financial strategies by a company will depend on its stage of development and also the behaviour of the financial markets in which it operates. Companies may benefit from the adoption of financial strategies that exploit imperfections and inefficiencies in the markets relating to each of the factors we have discussed, which we will explore in more detail throughout this book. The following section looks broadly at what is meant by market efficiency and inefficiency with regard to the capital or financial markets.

Efficient market hypothesis

The **efficient market hypothesis** states that stock markets respond immediately to all available information. An individual investor cannot therefore, in the long run, expect greater than average returns from a diversified portfolio of shares. Efficient market hypothesis research evidence suggests that accounting tricks and manipulations employed by companies do not increase company value, because the market is able to see through them. However, we may question whether in practice any market can respond immediately to all available information. As we have seen over the past few years, many creative techniques have been used to disguise presumably widely understood accounting transactions, for example WorldCom and Enron (see Chapter 1).

There are three types of market efficiency:

■ pricing efficiency, which refers to the notion or understanding that prices rapidly reflect all available information in an unbiased way
■ operational efficiency, which refers to the level of costs of carrying out transactions in capital markets in the most cost-effective way
■ allocational efficiency, which refers to the extent to which capital is allocated to the most profitable enterprise, and should be a product of pricing efficiency.

There are three forms of market efficiency, which are subsets of pricing efficiency:

■ weak form efficiency, which is seen in a market in which security prices instantaneously reflect all information on past price and volume changes in the market
■ semi-strong form efficiency, which is seen in a market in which security prices reflect all publicly available information
■ strong form efficiency, which is seen in a market in which security prices reflect instantaneously all information available to investors, whether publicly available or not.

In terms of financial markets the term efficiency generally refers to pricing efficiency. In the financial markets, like other markets in general, the price of a financial asset or a currency will be an equilibrium price between rational, well-informed, profit-seeking buyers and sellers. All information available in the public domain will be discounted into the price of a financial asset or currency.

A perfect market has the following characteristics:

■ information is freely available to everyone in the market
■ there is a large number of buyers and sellers who may freely enter and leave the market
■ there is no taxation
■ there are no transaction costs
■ there is perfect competition and no single buyer or seller dominates the market
■ everyone in the market will be aware of any creative accounting and window dressing of the financial information contained in companies' reports and accounts
■ financial assets are infinitely divisible
■ bankruptcies may occur but are without any cost.

Perfect markets imply efficient markets. However, efficient markets are not required to be perfect markets. Market efficiency promotes:

■ investor trust in the market and thus encourages capital investment
■ allocational efficiency,

and improves market information and therefore the choice of investments.

Substantial research has been carried out with regard to each form of efficiency to test how efficient security markets, equity markets, and currency markets really are, for example:

- weak form efficiency – Beechley, M, Gruen, D, and Vickery, J 'The efficient market hypothesis: a survey' *Research Paper Reserve Bank of Australia* (2000); Fama, EF 'The behaviour of stock market prices' *Journal of Business*, pages 34–106 (January, 1965); Roberts, HV 'Stock market patterns and financial analysis: methodological suggestions' *Journal of Finance* 1–10 (March, 1959)
- semi-strong form efficiency – Ball, R and Brown, P 'An empirical evaluation of accounting income numbers' *Journal of Accounting Research*, pages 159–78 (Autumn, 1968); Fama, EF, Fisher, L, Jensen, MC, and Roll, R 'The adjustment of stock prices to new information' *International Economic Review* 10(1), pages 1–21 (February, 1969)
- strong form efficiency – Jensen, MC 'The performance of mutual funds in the period 1945–1964' *Journal of Finance*, pages 389–416 (May, 1968).

In general, these tests are categorised as:

- weak form efficiency tests
- semi-strong form efficiency tests
- strong form efficiency tests,

and they have sought to evaluate the relative efficiency of such markets.

Weak form efficiency tests have sought to test the theory that prices follow patterns that can be used to predict future prices. This means that all prices fully reflect information contained in past price movements. Such studies have found no discernible pattern that can be used to predict future prices, but have indicated that prices follow a random walk, which means that:

- prices have no memory
- yesterday's prices cannot predict tomorrow's prices

and therefore

- only new information causes price changes.

The random walk theory suggests that share price movements are independent of each other and that today's share price cannot be used to predict tomorrow's share price. Therefore, the movement of a share price follows no predictable pattern, but moves in a random fashion with no discernible trend. This notion of random variability in the pricing of shares originates from the work of Kendall, M 'The analysis of economic time-series prices' *Journal of the Royal Statistical Society* 96, pages 11–25 (1953), in which he examined security and commodity price movements over a period of time. He was looking for regular price cycles, but was unable to identify any. Essentially, Kendall's theory states that the random walk occurs because, at any point in time, a share price will reflect all information available about the share and the company, and will only change as new information becomes available. However, because the next piece of information to arrive will be independent of the last piece of information to arrive, share prices react and move in an unpredictable fashion.

Semi-strong form efficiency tests have sought to test the theory that security prices fully reflect all information in the public domain. This means that all prices fully reflect all relevant publicly available information. These studies have also not produced any conclusive evidence that exceptional returns can be earned from information widely available in the public domain.

Strong form efficiency tests have sought to test the theory that security prices reflect all information, including insider information. This means that all prices fully reflect all relevant information including information that is privately held. Such studies have shown that insiders can make exceptional returns over and above those available from information in the public domain, usually only for a short period.

The implications of the efficiency tests described above may be summarised by saying that in efficient markets there is no bargain today, there is no memory of yesterday, and there is no knowledge of tomorrow. From this it may be concluded that markets generally follow a weak form efficiency, which means that pricing is generally regarded as inefficient.

Progress check 2.4

What is the efficient market hypothesis?

Worked example 2.3 illustrates the efficient market hypothesis and how information may impact on a company's share price.

Worked example 2.3

Predator plc has issued share capital of 24,000,000 shares, and Target plc has issued share capital of 8,000,000 shares. The following details relate to the time period days one to ten.

Day 1   The market value per share is Target plc £4 and Predator plc £6.

Day 3   The directors of Predator plc decide at a private and confidential meeting to make a cash bid for Target plc at a price of £6 per share with a settlement day of day 16. The takeover will result in large operating savings with a present value of £21 million.

Day 7   Predator plc publicly announces an unconditional offer to purchase all the shares in Target plc at a price of £6 per share. Details of the large operating savings are not announced and are not public knowledge.

Day 10   Predator plc makes a public announcement of the operating savings that will be realised from the takeover, and the share price increases to £6.21.

Let's assume semi-strong efficiency of the market, and consider the values of Predator plc and Target plc on days 1, 3, 7, and 10.

Days 1 and 3

Market value of Predator 24m × £6 = £144m
Market value of Target 8m × £4 = £32m

Day 7

Cost to Predator of offer for Target = [(8m × £6) − (8m × £4)] = £16m
Market value of Predator = 24m × £6 = £144m less £16m price offered for Target = £128m
Share price of Predator = £128m/24m = £5.33 per share

Day 10

Market value of Predator = 24m × £6.21 = £149m

If the market has the semi-strong form of efficiency then in theory the prices on days 1, 3, 7, and 10 should be as follows:

	Target £	Predator £
Days 1 and 3	4.00	6.00
Day 7	6.00	5.33
Day 10	6.00	6.21

The decision made on day 3 will have no impact on the share prices of Predator or Target, unless there has been a leak of information.

On day 7, following the announcement of the cash offer by Predator plc of £6 per share for Target plc the market price of Target's shares should increase from £4 to the bid price of £6. The value of Predator is likely to be reduced from £144m to £128m (£144m – £16m) or £5.33 per share. The share price was likely to fall because there did not appear to be any benefits from the acquisition.

On day 10, following the announcement of the benefit of operating savings with a present value of £21m (three days after the initial offer announcement), the share price of Predator plc increases to £6.21 per share and therefore its market value increases to £149m (24m × £6.21).

In reality, the share prices may not react in this way because there are many other factors that impact on share price movements.

Worked example 2.4

A colleague of yours has recently attended a series of finance seminars run by a local university. During one of the seminars your colleague recollects the speaker suggesting that 'an efficient market is good for all profit-orientated organisations', and has asked you to explain why that is the case.

There are a number of points that should be considered, the main ones being that an efficient market:

- promotes investor confidence
- reduces risk and uncertainty
- increases degrees of predictability
- reduces market costs
- reduces the need for excessive regulation
- reduces the need for proactive monitoring
- reduces costs of regulation.

In the financial markets the complicating role of governments and their central banks to influence the market operations of other institutional organisations and international companies as they constantly battle for the right to maximise potential financial rewards is of major importance. While imperfections may exist within the market, such imperfections may not necessarily exist due to problems in the supply and demand of information. They may be the direct consequence of political protectionism rather than a product of economic supply and demand.

The concept of the efficient market is the basis of many of the ideas of traditional corporate financial theory and its implications are, for example:

- that the market will have already discounted any manipulation of accounting information in share prices
- it is not possible to obtain any information that will result in better than average returns
- share prices reflect only investors' required returns for perceived levels of risk
- shares are never under-priced
- that it is not possible to achieve better than average stock market returns.

Although the UK stock market and other capital markets apparently respond relatively efficiently to new information as soon as it becomes available, the assumptions of efficient markets may be open to debate. The efficient market hypothesis is a theoretical, analytical framework. In a perfectly efficient market investors would receive their required returns dependent on the level of risk they are prepared to take, and no additional shareholder value would be created. In the real world markets are not perfectly efficient. Additional shareholder value may be created by companies using appropriate financial strategies to exploit the different perceptions of the market, which are called market imperfections. These imperfections include, for example, the information asymmetry that exists with regard to each of the stakeholders in companies. For example, managers, directors, lenders, and shareholders each have different levels and aspects of information about companies and their assets. There may also be significant periods of time between when important information is revealed or acquired by each of the different stakeholders.

Shareholder value

Value is a function of the relationship between perceived risk and the return required by shareholders and other key stakeholders. The higher the risk that is associated with a particular security, the higher is the required rate of return (see Figure 2.4). For the borrower, short-term debt (such as an overdraft) is riskier than long-term debt. There are a number of reasons for this:

- an overdraft is repayable on demand
- a short-term debt or an overdraft may not be renewed, or if they are re-negotiated then the terms may be less favourable
- interest rates are more volatile in the short term, particularly for overdrafts which have variable interest rates.

The difference between the interest rate paid on, for example, UK Government securities, which is effectively risk-free, and the interest rate that a company pays on loans is called the risk premium. Shareholders' equity is even riskier than shorter-term corporate debt (for example, a loan made to a company). Therefore, the earnings of the company need to be at a level such

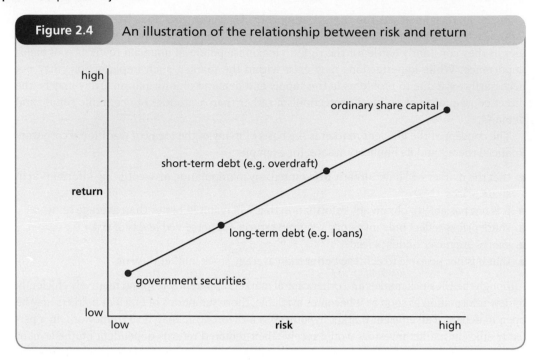

Figure 2.4 An illustration of the relationship between risk and return

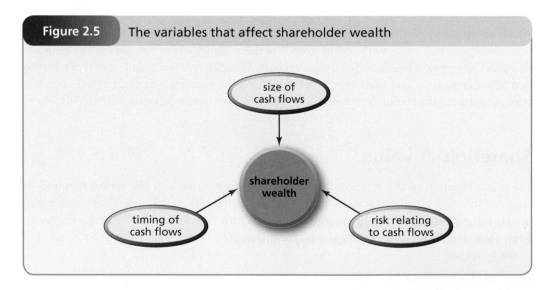

Figure 2.5 The variables that affect shareholder wealth

that the shareholders get a return in line with their level of risk. This should be the return on UK Government securities plus a risk premium, which is even higher than the risk premium payable on the corporate debt.

An increase in shareholders' wealth is derived from cash received by shareholders through dividends and capital gains from the increased market price of shares held. There are three variables that directly affect shareholders' wealth (see Figure 2.5):

■ the size of the company's cash flows – cash flows are considered rather than profit, which is subjective and involves problems in its measurement

- the time value of cash flows – £100 cash received today is generally worth more than £100 cash received in one year's time
- the risk associated with cash flows – risk impacts on the rate of return earned on the investment in the business, and therefore the cost of capital that affects today's value of cash received in the future.

Providing value means being better than the market, by providing better than expectation.

This can be compared to a perfect market, in which all investors would in theory receive their risk-adjusted required rates of return. A perfect market rarely exists because:

- information and knowledge may not always be freely and equally shared by all the players in the market
- entry and exit into and out of markets is generally not without cost
- all players may not act rationally, and they may have different expectations
- markets are usually dominated by a small number of players because of their buying power, possession of scarce resources, unique knowledge, technologies, or skills
- taxes and costs of transacting act as barriers to selling and buying.

Many financial theorists currently believe that the use of financial strategies and techniques by companies does not create and increase value, on the basis that today's financial markets are efficient and can easily and quickly identify and allow for the above factors. In theory this may be the case, but in practice financial managers actually do employ financial strategies that result in providing value over and above market expectation.

It is argued by some that markets are efficient but more volatile due to technological advances. It is true that markets are perhaps becoming more efficient as information becomes more freely and widely available, and the speed and cost of transactions are reduced (for example, through the use of electronic transactions and the Internet). However, the future cannot be forecast with certainty and so the market value of a business may rarely reflect the present value of its expected future cash flows. Also, investors' returns are related to the perceived risks of their investments, but this relationship may not be the same for all investors.

It may therefore be argued that markets are still not totally efficient. Therefore, shareholder value may be increased by exploitation of market imperfections, even though such imperfections may only be temporary. This may relate to exploitation of business competitive advantages, and the use of appropriate financial strategies that result in an increase in shareholder wealth. This includes, for example:

- cost reduction and profit improvement measures
- an optimal mix of products, services, and businesses
- investment in only those projects that provide increased cash flows in real terms
- minimisation of the company's after-tax cost of capital
- establishment of an optimal financial structure for the business
- appropriate use of debt financing
- the use of appropriate financial instruments, including derivatives
- appropriate dividend policy.

Progress check 2.5

Describe the variables that directly affect maximisation of shareholder wealth.

Shareholder value may be measured using two approaches, either book value (using accounting-based measures) or market value (using measures based on share price), and include the following performance indicators:

IIII➡ ■ **residual income (RI)**
IIII➡ ■ **shareholder value added (SVA)**
IIII➡ ■ **economic value added (EVA™)**
      ■ shareholder return

which are considered in the four sections that follow.

Residual income (RI)

Residual income (RI) may be calculated by deducting a notional interest charge for capital invested from profit before tax, and is therefore a measure of performance and an absolute measure of value added.

If

Profit before tax $=$ PBT
Capital invested $=$ I
Interest on capital invested $= i$

then

$$RI = PBT - (i \times I)$$

Worked example 2.5

Let's consider two divisions, A and B, within a company that have an opportunity to invest in projects that both have an initial cost of £10m, and have expected profits before tax of £2m and £1.3m respectively. The notional cost of capital for the company is 15% per annum.

The expected operating profits from each investment are shown below:

	Company A	Company B
Expected profit before tax	£2.0m	£1.3m
Cost of capital charge (15% of £10m)	£1.5m	£1.5m
Residual income (loss)	£0.5m	−£0.2m

Shareholder value added (SVA)

Alfred Rappaport (Rappaport, A (1998) *Creating Shareholder Value*, London: Free Press) considered that there were seven drivers of shareholder value. The first five drivers:

■ sales growth
■ operating profit margin
■ the cash tax rate
■ incremental capital expenditure investment
■ investment in working capital,

are used to determine forecast 'free cash flows' relating to the sixth driver

- a time period of competitive advantage, the planning horizon, and using the seventh driver
- the cost of capital,

to discount the cash flows to present values (today's values) to provide an enterprise value.

Shareholder value added (SVA) is a measure of enterprise value and Worked example 2.6 shows how SVA may be calculated in practice.

Worked example 2.6

Flag plc is a UK company whose shareholders require an annual return of 8%. The calculation of Flag plc's free cash flow for the current year highlights Rappaport's first five drivers of shareholder value:

		£m
sales growth	Sales revenue	5.0
	Operating costs	(3.0)
operating profit margin	Operating profit	2.0
cash tax rate	Income tax expense	(0.5)
	Profit for the year	1.5
	add back: Depreciation	0.4
		1.9
capital investment	less: Capital expenditure	(0.6)
investment in working capital	less: Additional working capital	(0.3)
	Free cash flow	1.0

In addition, Flag plc has estimated its free cash flow for the next five years as: £1.5m; £1.8m; £2.2m; £2.4m; £2.8m. Flag plc's planning horizon is six years and its estimated net asset value at the end of the planning horizon is £2.9m.

Let's calculate Flag's shareholder value added (SVA).

The value in perpetuity of the estimated net assets at the end of year six is:

$$£2.9.m/8\% = £36.25m$$

We can use the 'in perpetuity' value of Flag plc's net assets plus the free cash flows for years one to six to calculate the company's shareholder value added (SVA).

Year	Free cash flow £m	Discount factor at 8% p.a.	Present value £m
1	1.0	0.93	0.93
2	1.5	0.86	1.29
3	1.8	0.79	1.42
4	2.2	0.74	1.63
5	2.4	0.68	1.63
6	2.8	0.63	1.76
6	36.25	0.63	22.84
		SVA	31.50

The enterprise value of Flag plc, its shareholder value added (SVA), is therefore £31.5m.

Economic value added (EVA™)

A variation on RI is economic value added (EVA™), which aims to provide a measure that is highly correlated with shareholder wealth as well as financial performance.

Maximisation of shareholder wealth continues to be the prime objective with which managers of companies are charged. The extent to which success in particular performance measures aligns with shareholder wealth maximisation is particularly relevant. Equally important are the ways in which managers are motivated to maximise shareholder wealth. In most organisations managerial remuneration provides the link between the measures of financial performance and shareholder value.

Financial performance measures such as a company's share price are commonly used to indicate how well the company is doing. However, it may be questioned as to how directly the share price reflects decisions that have been taken by management. In the context of managers' performance against budget targets (and the company's overall financial performance) we may question the merits and otherwise of other performance measures such as profit after tax, earnings per share, dividends, return on capital employed, and cash flow, etc. Each has its limitations, but measures based on cash flow are now becoming accepted as perhaps better indicators than profit-related measures.

During the mid-1980s, Rappaport developed shareholder value analysis, from which the American firm Stern Stewart Management Services evolved economic value added (EVA) and **market value added (MVA)**. Through EVA, Stern Stewart attempted to reconcile the need for a performance measure correlated with shareholder wealth that was also responsive to actions taken by managers. By the mid-1990s over 200 global companies had been in discussion with Stern Stewart with regard to adoption of EVA; Lucas Varity in the UK and Coca-Cola in the USA were already successful users of EVA.

If we assume that the organisation's objective is to maximise shareholder wealth then this will be achieved if new projects are taken on and existing projects are allowed to continue only if they create value. Investment in capital projects may be made only on the basis of choosing those with a positive net present value (NPV). However, NPV cannot be applied to remuneration schemes because it is a summary measure based on projected cash flows and not realised performance.

Companies usually turn to company earnings and cash flow (which are termed flow measures) for management remuneration schemes. EVA supports the same sort of recommendations that NPV provides at the project level, but also provides a better measure of management performance because it rewards for earnings generated, while also including charges for the amount of capital employed to create those earnings.

If

Profit after tax $=$ PAT
Weighted average cost of capital $=$ WACC
Adjusted book value of net assets $=$ NA

then

$$\text{EVA} = \text{PAT} - (\text{WACC} \times \text{NA})$$

It should be noted that to calculate EVA the PAT should be adjusted by adding back interest paid. Profit before interest paid is therefore used to calculate EVA to avoid double counting because a charge for financing is being made by deducting WACC in the calculation.

Shareholder return

Residual income and EVA are both measures of the surplus of profit after allowing in some way for a cost of capital. However, they are really more measures of performance than measures of value, but they can show value created in a single period. SVA is a measure that relates to the life of a business or a project, but cannot be used to consider value added during a single period. These are all essentially 'internal' measures made by a company.

Total shareholder return (TSR) is a measure of how value is created for shareholders, and it is a measure that can be made external to the business. The total returns received by a shareholder in a period include the increase in their share price plus the dividends they have received. However, as a measure of value it also has disadvantages. Although there may be a correlation between dividends and how well the company is performing, the share price may be depressed because of, for example, rumours that the CEO may be resigning, even though the company may actually be performing very well. Equally, a company's share price may be artificially high because of, for example, possible takeover interest, or the patenting of a new 'miracle' drug, even though the company may actually be performing poorly.

If

Share price at the beginning of the year $= S1$
Share price at the end of the year $= S2$
Dividends paid during the year $= v$

then

$$TSR = S2 - S1 + v$$

Progress check 2.6

In what ways may shareholder value be measured?

Strategic financial decisions

We have looked at a few measures of shareholder value. RI, SVA, and EVA are measures that are based on factors 'within' the business, such as sales revenue, profit, capital employed, and the cost of capital. TSR return is a measure that is based on factors 'external' to the business: the gains from share price increases. It has many shortcomings as a measure, primarily because to a large extent it is outside the control of the company. A company's share price may rise or fall for reasons completely unrelated to its economic performance, being more closely related to market expectations. Despite its shortcomings, TSR is perhaps the most useful measure of shareholder value because dividends and gains from increases in share price are what shareholders actually receive, and which they may monitor on a continual basis. Let's look at the underlying decisions that a company, or rather its directors are required to make to achieve value.

A business uses its assets, through 'real' investment, to generate profits. Profits may be used for dividends paid to shareholders, or profits may be retained to finance future growth, which is an alternative to increasing debt or equity. The profit available for dividends is dependent on how much is left after interest has been deducted from pre-tax profit. Actual dividends are then an appropriation of post-tax profit. A company's level of interest payments is dependent on the level of its debt. High debt means paying high levels of interest, and so less profit is available for dividends and for further investment.

The decisions relating to the types and levels of investment, levels of debt, levels of retained earnings, and levels of dividends are all concerned with financial strategy. The directors of a company, therefore, broadly have four key decisions to make concerning financial strategy, which are all very closely linked:

■ how large should the company's asset base be? – the capital budgeting or investment decisions relating to the level of 'real' investment to be made by the business
■ what proportions of the company's financing should be debt or equity? – its capital structure, or gearing; if a company has a target ratio of debt to equity, then in theory an increase in its equity means that it can take on more debt
■ should the company issue new equity or new debt? – for expansion of the company's funding
■ how much profit should be paid out in dividends, and how much retained? – dividend policy.

> ### Progress check 2.7
>
> Outline the strategic financial decisions faced by companies.

In Part II of this book we will look at a number of ways in which the use of appropriate financial strategies at the relevant stages in the development of a business may be used to derive shareholder value.

The agency problem

We have talked about shareholder wealth maximisation as the primary objective of a business. But can we assume that the managers and directors of the business are making decisions and taking actions that are consistent with the objective of maximising shareholder wealth? Certainly managers and directors should make decisions consistent with the objective of shareholder wealth maximisation, because that is what they are appointed to do by the shareholders. In practice, this may not actually happen, because their goals may be different and they may be seeking to enhance their status, secure their positions, or maximise their own wealth rather than that of the shareholders.

The **agency problem** occurs when directors and managers are not acting in the best interests of shareholders. Directors and managers of a company run the business day-to-day and have access to internal management accounting information and financial reports, but shareholders only see the external annual and six-monthly reports. Annual and interim reporting may also, of course, be subject to manipulation by management.

The agency problem of directors not acting in the best interests of shareholders may be seen in, for example:

■ a high retention of profits and cash by directors to provide a cushion for easier day-to-day management of operations, rather than for investment in new projects
■ an unwillingness by directors to invest in risky projects in line with shareholders' required returns, because of fear of failure and possibly losing their jobs, particularly if they are close to retirement age and wish to protect their pension benefits

- receipt of high salaries, benefits, and perks by directors and chief executives, regardless of how well, or not, the business has performed
- participation by directors and managers in profit- or eps-related bonus and incentive schemes, which encourage short-term profit maximisation rather than creation of shareholder value.

Why should the agency problem exist? Well, it is management who are in the position, and who have the opportunity, to pursue the maximisation of their own wealth without detection by the owners of the business. Additionally, both financial analysts and managers and directors of companies have an obsession with eps as a measure of financial performance. This is despite the fact that profit is a totally subjective measure and that it is future cash flows and not short-term profit from which the real value of a business is determined.

A growth in profit does not necessarily translate into a sustained increase in shareholder value. For example, diversified multinational companies, conglomerates, have in the past acquired many businesses to effectively 'buy' additional profits. This has invariably not resulted in an increase in the share prices of such conglomerates. An example of this is shown in the performance of Tomkins plc illustrated in Mini case 2.2 below.

Mini case 2.2

Tomkins plc was a multinational conglomerate, which during the 1990s had grown enormously through acquisitions. Tomkins plc's eps increased consistently each year from around 12 pence in 1991 to around 28 pence in 2000, an average increase of 9.8% per annum. However, its share price averaged around £2.50 during the same period, although it briefly reached a high of £3.75 in early 1998, and then gradually fell again to around £1.50 by the beginning of 2000.

The agency problem manifests itself through a conflict of interest. There may be different views about risks and returns, for example. The shareholders may be interested in the long term, whereas the rewards paid to managers, for example, may be based on short-term performance. To address the agency problem between agents and principals – managers and shareholders – a number of initiatives may be implemented to encourage the achievement of goal congruence:

- audit of results
- reporting of manager performance
- work shadowing of managers and directors
- the use of external analysts.

Progress check 2.8

What are the conflicts that may arise between the managers and the shareholders of a business?

In addition to the agency problem relating to the directors and shareholders of a company, there may be a conflict between shareholders and the lenders to a company. The shareholders may exploit their relationship with lenders. The agency problem here is that shareholders may prefer the use of debt for investments by the company in new high-risk projects. Shareholders then subsequently benefit from the rewards gained from the success of such investments, but it is the debt-holders (lenders) who bear the risk. Debt-holders may protect their interests by having security over specific assets or the assets in general of the company. They may also include restrictive covenants in their loan agreements with the company, for example with regard to decision-making, and levels of debt taken on by the company.

There has been an increasing influence of institutional investors in the UK, which to some degree has helped in dealing with the agency problem. Institutional shareholders like banks, pension funds, and fund management companies have been getting tougher with companies that do not comply with the appropriate standards of behaviour, and in particular with the appropriate **corporate governance** requirements.

Mini case 2.3

In the mid-1990s one of the UK's largest life assurers, Standard Life, provided an example of financial institutions' 'get tough' policy on lax corporate governance. Standard Life expressed its concern about protecting its customers by focusing on directors' contracts and their remuneration, and the importance of non-executive directors. Standard Life also registered their opposition to shareholder returns (dividends plus share price increases) as a measure of management performance because they said that they had little to do with management success.

Corporate governance has become a major topic from both the practical and academic perspectives over the past 30 years, largely because of the increasing numbers of corporate financial scandals that have been revealed through the media.

In the 1990s:

- Polly Peck 1990 (Asil Nadir was found guilty in August 2012 and given a 10-year prison sentence)
- Robert Maxwell companies 1991
- Barings Bank 1995
- Versailles 1999.

In the 2000s:

- Enron 2001
- WorldCom 2002
- Tyco International 2002
- Parmalat 2004
- Nortel's executive pay scandals from 2001 to 2008
- Lehman Brothers 2008
- Bernard Madoff 2009.

Corporate governance is concerned with the relationship between company management, its directors, and its owners, the shareholders. It is the structure and the mechanisms by which the owners of the business 'govern' the management or the directors of the business. Its importance has been highlighted as a result of the increasing concern about the conduct of companies, following a spate of financial scandals, but also by concerns about senior executive remuneration. Such conduct has promoted a new area of study concerned with the psychology and drivers of financial decision-making and understanding the rationality, or otherwise, of economic agents such as managers and directors of companies, shareholders, and providers of loan finance. This area of research is commonly referred to as **behavioural finance**.

Behavioural finance suggests that:

- unpredicted share price movements
- inexplicably high dividend yields
- low ratios of companies' book values compared with their market capitalisation
- poor price performance of shares which have 'high expectations',

can and often do result from irrational behaviour of economic agents, and is largely psychologically based. There is a growing number of behavioural finance-related models that offer plausible explanations for market inefficiencies and share price volatility (see, for example, the *Journal of Behavioral Finance* at *www.journalofbehavioralfinance.org/journals/journals_main.html* and the *International Journal of Behavioural Accounting and Finance* at *www.inderscience.com/ijbaf*). It is a discipline that is taking time to achieve widespread acceptance within mainstream financial management, but it is a subject to which we will return in Chapter 12.

In the UK in 1991, a committee was set up by the Financial Reporting Council (FRC), the London Stock Exchange, and the accounting profession, which was chaired by Sir Adrian Cadbury. The aim of the committee was to address the concerns about company conduct and to make recommendations on best practice. The framework for establishing good corporate governance and accountability set up by the **Cadbury Committee** was formulated as the Committee's Code of Best Practice, published in December 1992. This provided a benchmark against which to assess compliance. The Cadbury Code was updated in 1998 by the **Hampel Committee**, in order to include their own Committee's work, and the Greenbury Committee report on directors' remuneration (published July 1995). In September 1999 the Turnbull Committee report on *Internal Control: Guidance for Directors on the Combined Code of Practice* was published by the Institute of Chartered Accountants in England and Wales (ICAEW).

In May 2000, the original Cadbury Code and subsequent reports were all consolidated by the Committee on Corporate Governance and published in the **Combined Code of Practice**. Following the consolidation two additional reports were commissioned with a view to strengthening the guidelines elaborated in the Combined Code of Practice. These additional reports were:

- Audit Committees Combined Code Guidance, a report and proposed guidance by an FRC-appointed group chaired by Sir Robert Smith published in 2003

  and

- a review of the role and effectiveness of non-executive directors by Sir Derek Higgs also published in 2003.

The guidance from these subsequent reports was, in turn, incorporated into the Combined Code of Practice when it was revised in July 2003 under the title of the **Combined Code on Corporate Governance**. Subsequent reviews and revisions of the Code took place in 2006 and 2008 leading to the latest revision under the title of the **UK Corporate Governance Code** issued by the FRC in June 2010. We will look at the UK Corporate Governance Code in more detail in Chapter 3.

Worked example 2.7

Directors of companies are concerned with the important issues of agency-related problems and their impact. What is the basis of discussions they may have to consider what actions they may implement to try and minimise the impact of such problems?

Their discussion may include the following:

The agency problem emerges when managers make decisions that are inconsistent with the objective of shareholder wealth maximisation. There are a number of alternative approaches a company can adopt to minimise the possible impact of such a problem, and while these would differ from company to company, in general such approaches would range between:

- the encouragement of goal congruence between shareholders and managers through the monitoring of managerial behaviour and the assessment of management decision outcomes

and

- the enforcement of goal congruence between shareholders and managers through the incorporation of formalised obligations and conditions of employment into management contracts.

Any such approach would invariably be associated with some form of remuneration package to include an incentive scheme to reward managers, such as performance-related pay, or executive share options.

Progress check 2.9

Outline how the agency problem may occur between the shareholders, directors, and lenders of a business.

We have seen that agency problems may exist not only between directors and shareholders but also between any of the stakeholders of the business: its employees; managers; shareholders; lenders; suppliers; customers. However, it is the agency problems arising between directors and shareholders with which we are primarily concerned in the current chapter, and in the next section we will look at how incentive schemes may be used to try and address such problems.

Incentive schemes

A big part of the corporate governance framework is concerned with directors' remuneration. Many different types of pay schemes have been developed to try and overcome the agency problem between managers and shareholders. For example, performance-related pay schemes may use performance measures like profit, and return on capital employed (ROCE) to compare against pre-agreed targets for the calculation of additional remuneration such as bonuses. As we have already seen, there are problems with these measures relating to their accuracy and the fact that they are open to manipulation. Perhaps even more importantly, these measures are not necessarily indicators of shareholder wealth.

Executive share option schemes have become increasingly popular because of the problems associated with performance-related pay schemes. Managers become potential shareholders and so they should have the same aims. Therefore the achievement of goal congruence is seen as a big benefit of such schemes. There are many examples of company directors participating in some extremely lucrative share option schemes.

Mini case 2.4

In 1985 the co-founder of Apple Computers, Steve Jobs, was forced to resign when company performance took a downturn. He left owning 7m Apple shares worth US$120m and went on to form Pixar, which went public in 1995, and in which his 80% stake was worth US$1.1bn. In 1997, Apple re-hired Jobs as CEO and in 2000 the board of directors of Apple granted Jobs share options worth US$200m (plus US$90m for the purchase and maintenance of a Gulfstream V jet). In May 2006, Disney paid US$8.06bn for Pixar, which resulted in Steve Jobs becoming the Disney Corporation's largest shareholder.

However, executive share option schemes do have disadvantages. There are many external impacts on share price that are outside the influence or the control of managers. Therefore, there is not a completely direct link between managers' performance and their rewards. There may be disagreement and discontent arising out of the decision as to which managers are chosen to participate in executive share option schemes. This may therefore be de-motivational and have a negative impact on the achievement of goal congruence.

Regardless of the disadvantages, executive share option schemes (rather like the company car used to be) are regarded as a 'must have' benefit. But are they a 'one-sided bet' for the managers? If the shares go down in price then the managers receive no penalty. However, share options do tend to be longer term and so there may be no reward if the managers leave the company. There has also been an increase in the popularity of eps-growth-based management incentives. Here, there are still potential problems concerned with accuracy and manipulation of the numbers, and as we saw in the Tomkins example an increase in eps does not necessarily result in an increase in shareholder value.

Progress check 2.10

How may directors' bonus incentive schemes be used to deal with the agency problem?

Summary of key points

- A company's strategic management process begins by defining its mission, its underlying belief, and continues with the establishment of corporate objectives, corporate appraisal analyses, and then development of its strategies and plans.
- The maximisation of shareholder wealth is the primary financial objective of companies.

- There may be a number of secondary or surrogate objectives of a company, for example profit maximisation, sales revenue maximisation, and survival.

- It is important that companies adopt appropriate financial strategies in pursuit of the objective of maximisation of shareholder wealth.

- The efficient market hypothesis is an important corporate finance theory, but in practice capital markets are generally regarded as inefficient.

- Shareholder wealth is derived from dividends and capital gains from the increase in share price.

- The key strategic financial decisions faced by companies are concerned with levels of 'real' investment and gearing, and dividend policy.

- Agency theory considers why the goals and aims of the various stakeholders of a company are not always aligned, particularly with regard to a company's managers and its shareholders.

- Incentive schemes may be used by companies to overcome the agency problem with regard to their directors and shareholders.

Glossary of key terms

agency problem Agency theory is a hypothesis that attempts to explain elements of organisational behaviour through an understanding of the relationships between principals (such as shareholders) and agents (such as company managers). The agency problem manifests itself in a conflict that may exist between the actions undertaken by agents in furtherance of their own self-interest and those required to promote the interests of the principals. Within the hierarchy of companies, the same lack of goal congruence may occur when divisional managers promote their own self-interest over those of other divisions and of the company generally.

behavioural finance An area of study concerned with the psychology of financial decision-making and understanding the rationality or otherwise of economic agents such as managers and directors of companies, shareholders, and providers of loan finance.

business strategy Strategy is the 'what' we want the organisation to be, what we want to do, and where we want the organisation to go, rather than the 'how' to achieve those things. Business strategy is concerned with these 'whats' in terms of plans relating to markets, product planning, the competitive position of the business.

Cadbury Committee The report of the Cadbury Committee (December 1992) on the Financial Aspects of Corporate Governance was set up to consider issues in relation to financial reporting and accountability, and to make recommendations on good practice, relating to:

- responsibilities of executive and non-executive directors
- establishment of company audit committees
- responsibility of auditors
- links between shareholders, directors, and auditors
- any other relevant matters.

The report established a Cadbury Code of Best Practice, which was succeeded by the Combined Code of Practice in 2000, which was itself succeeded by the Combined Code on Corporate Governance in 2003 and then the UK Corporate Governance Code in 2010.

Combined Code on Corporate Governance A code, which replaced, but was built upon, the Combined Code of Practice by including a review of the role and effectiveness of non-executive directors by Derek Higgs and the Smith review of audit committees.

Combined Code of Practice The successor to the Cadbury Code of Best Practice and issued by the Hampel Committee. The code consisted of a set of principles of corporate governance and detailed code provisions embracing the work of the Cadbury, Greenbury, and Hampel Committees. Section 1 of the code contained the principles and provisions applicable to UK-listed companies, while section 2 contained the principles and provisions applicable to institutional shareholders in their relationships with companies. The Combined Code of Practice was succeeded by the Combined Code on Corporate Governance, which was subsequently succeeded by the UK Corporate Governance Code.

corporate governance The system by which companies are directed and controlled. Boards of directors are responsible for the governance of their companies. The shareholders' role in governance is to appoint the directors and the auditors and to satisfy themselves that an appropriate governance structure is in place.

corporate value The present value of the returns expected from the range of 'real' investments made and business strategies pursued by a company.

economic value added (EVA™) Profit after tax adjusted for distortions in operating performance (such as goodwill, extraordinary losses, and operating leases) less a charge for the amount of capital employed to create that profit (calculated from the adjusted book value of net assets multiplied by the company's weighted average cost of capital).

efficient market hypothesis A hypothesis that the stock market responds immediately to all available information, with the effect that an individual investor cannot, in the long run, expect to obtain greater than average returns from a diversified portfolio of shares. There are three forms:

- weak form, which is a market in which security prices instantaneously reflect all information on past price and volume changes in the market
- semi-strong form, which is a market in which security prices reflect all publicly available information
- strong form, which is a market in which security prices reflect instantaneously all information available to investors, whether publicly available or not.

environmental analysis A part of corporate appraisal, which includes a review of the business in terms of its external factors.

financial strategy Financial strategy is concerned with investor value, and the courses of action required to achieve the specific objective of creating shareholder value above the returns expected for the specific type of investment and market. Financial strategy is to do with decisions related to the financing of the business, investments in individual projects, the use of debt or equity, and decisions about how much profit should be paid in dividends and how much should be retained for investment in new projects.

Hampel Committee The 1998 report of the Hampel Committee on Corporate Governance was set up to conduct a review of the Cadbury Code and its implications, and considered:

- a review of the role of directors
- matters arising from the Greenbury Study Group on directors' remuneration

- the role of shareholders and auditors
- other relevant matters.

The Hampel Committee was responsible for publication of the corporate governance Combined Code of Practice.

market value added (MVA) The difference between the market value of the company and the adjusted book value of its assets.

mission A summary of goals and policies, which does not have to be in writing, but is generally a sense of purpose or underlying belief of the organisation.

objectives Objectives are the visionary statements set out by the company before it starts its detailed planning, its primary financial objective being the maximisation of shareholder wealth.

residual income (RI) Profit before tax less an imputed interest charge for invested capital, which may be used to assess the performance of a division or a branch of a business.

resources analysis A part of corporate appraisal, which includes a review of the business in terms of its internal factors.

shareholder value (or investor value) The required returns from a company expected by the market, reflected in the value of its securities.

shareholder value added (SVA) A measure of shareholder value derived from cash forecasts over the specific time period of a company's competitive advantage using its sales growth, operating profit, tax rate, and investments in capital expenditure and working capital, discounted to present day values using the company's cost of capital.

strategic choice Strategic choice uses the information provided from the corporate appraisal (resources analysis and environmental analysis) to evaluate the suitability, feasibility, and acceptability of the development of alternative strategies through screening options, financial analysis, risk analysis, and strategic method, which deals with the ways in which a company may develop and grow.

strategic management The strategic management process, which includes strategic planning, is involved with making decisions on the objectives of the organisation, changes in these objectives, the resources used to attain these objectives, the policies that are to govern the acquisition, and the use and disposition of resources.

surrogate objectives The primary objective of a company is the maximisation of shareholder wealth but there are many other objectives in support of, but considered secondary to, the main objective that are described as substitute or surrogate objectives. These may include profit maximisation, share price maximisation, market share maximisation, earnings per share growth, sales maximisation, survival, dividend growth, social responsibility, nonfinancial objectives (like customer satisfaction and delivery reliability).

UK Corporate Governance Code The corporate governance code applicable to listed companies, issued by the Financial Reporting Council (FRC) in June 2010, and described as a 'guide only in general terms to principles, structure and processes'.

Assessment material

Questions

Q2.1 Outline the primary objective of a company, the maximisation of shareholder wealth, and how it may be achieved.

Q2.2 What are some of the surrogate objectives that a business may have and what is their relevance?

Q2.3 Outline the efficient market hypothesis with regard to corporate financial theory.

Q2.4 Explain the ways in which shareholder value may be measured.

Q2.5 What is financial strategy, and how does it differ from business strategy?

Q2.6 In what ways may strategic financial decisions impact on shareholder value?

Q2.7 Outline the agency problem and the ways in which it may manifest itself.

Q2.8 How may incentive schemes help deal with the agency problem?

Discussion points

D2.1 The CEO of a diversified multinational company said: 'So long as I continue to report an increase in eps for the business each year then I am doing my job and the shareholders should be pleased.' Discuss.

D2.2 Can the goal of maximisation of the value of the company conflict with other goals, such as avoiding unethical or illegal behaviour? Do the goals of, for example, customer and employee safety, the environment, and the general good of society fit within this framework, or are they essentially ignored?

D2.3 Company ownership varies around the world. Historically, individuals have owned the majority of shares in public companies in the United States. In Germany and Japan, however, banks, other large financial institutions, and other companies own most of the shares in public companies. Discuss whether agency problems are likely to be more or less severe in Germany and Japan than in the United States and why.

D2.4 In recent years, large financial institutions such as mutual funds and pension funds have increasingly become the owners of shares in the United States, and these institutions are becoming more active in corporate affairs. Discuss what the implications of this trend may be with regard to agency problems.

D2.5 Discuss the increasing popularity of share option schemes as an important element of executive remuneration.

D2.6 Why do you think there may have been such a proliferation of financial scandals in the USA, UK, and Europe during the 1990s and 2000s?

Exercises

Solutions are provided in Appendix 2 to all excercise numbers highlighted in colour.

Level I

E2.1   *Time allowed – 15 minutes*

Identify the components of shareholder wealth and explain how the strategic finan-cial decisions made by a company impact on each of them.

E2.2   *Time allowed – 15 minutes*

Explain what is meant by shareholder value and consider the value-creating alterna-tives. Outline three ways of measuring shareholder value.

E2.3   *Time allowed – 30 minutes*

Explain how alternative methods may be used to measure shareholder value and give your view as to which may be the most appropriate measure.

Level II

E2.4   *Time allowed – 30 minutes*

At a recent board meeting the managing director of Angel plc announced that the company's directors had been awarded substantial cash bonuses and share options, despite the company incurring substantial losses during the last financial year. Explain why the above represents an agency problem within a company between the directors and the shareholders, and the ways in which it may be rcsolved.

E2.5   *Time allowed – 30 minutes*

In 2012 Chancer Ltd announced that to finance the development of a new head office in the centre of London, the company would need to borrow £30m secured against the company's existing assets. As a result, the company's gearing ratio would rise from 20% to 85%. Outline the agency problems that may exist with regard to managers, shareholders, and lenders of the company, and suggest ways in which these agency problems may be reduced.

E2.6   *Time allowed – 30 minutes*

Research evidence suggests a large amount of support for the efficient market hypoth-esis. Examine the reasons why the movements in the share prices of companies may not be consistent with this theory.

E2.7   *Time allowed – 30 minutes*

> At a recent press briefing at the London Stock Exchange, a senior manager was quoted as saying 'an efficient market is a good market, which is good for the market, good for business, and good for profit'. Discuss what the senior manager meant and whether the statement is correct.

E2.8   *Time allowed – 30 minutes*

> Crosby plc has a stock market valuation of £25m, and Nash plc has a stock market valuation of £18m (the market valuation equals number of shares in issue multiplied by the share price).

Both companies have similar profit profiles, as follows:

	Crosby plc £m	Nash plc £m
2007	1.3	1.8
2008	1.7	1.2
2009	1.2	2.3
2010	1.5	1.5
2011	2.3	1.8
2012	2.0	1.4

Explain the reasons why shareholders may regard Crosby plc as being worth £7m more than Nash, despite their having had the same total profits over the past six years.

E2.9   *Time allowed – 30 minutes*

> In the context of the efficient markets hypothesis, distinguish between pricing efficiency, allocational efficiency, and operational efficiency.

E2.10   *Time allowed – 30 minutes*

> Briefly explain the implications of the efficient markets hypothesis for the financial managers of a medium-sized company that is seeking a public stock market listing.

E2.11   *Time allowed – 30 minutes*

> Explain the range of remuneration incentive schemes and how they may be used to encourage managers of companies to make decisions that are consistent with the objective of maximisation of shareholder wealth.

3

Corporate governance

Chapter contents

Managing
our business
in the
right way

Governance

This section introduces our board of directors and details the corporate governance structures that are in place to ensure we manage our business in a responsible and transparent way.

Delivering **Value**

→ **Supporting Our Strategy in Fine Chemicals**

People around the world are living longer. As a result, many will suffer from chronic diseases and will require more long term drug therapy. This, together with increasing demand from doctors and patients for efficient pain management and continued economic development in Asia, will further drive demand for pharmaceutical products.

Johnson Matthey holds a strong position in opiate based active pharmaceutical ingredients (APIs), which are used to relieve pain, and in other niche controlled APIs, in particular amphetamines used in the treatment of attention deficit hyperactivity disorder (ADHD). Its API Manufacturing businesses, based in the UK and USA, delivered strong growth this year, increasing their sales and growing market share.

This performance was supported by the businesses' Riverside manufacturing facility, located in Conshohocken, USA, which was acquired by Johnson Matthey in November 2010. This new plant, which more than doubles our manufacturing capacity in North America, has been successfully integrated with the businesses' other operations and is enabling us to manufacture products more efficiently, support growth and capitalise on new market opportunities.

- Clean room facilities at Riverside for the production of highly potent APIs.

- The Riverside facility more than doubles Johnson Matthey's API manufacturing capacity in North America.

Contents

78 **Johnson Matthey** Annual Report & Accounts 2012
Report of the Directors – Governance
Governance

Governance
Letter from the Chairman

Tim Stevenson
Chairman

"I am pleased to present the Governance section of the annual report, including the Corporate Governance Report for the year ended 31st March 2012."

Dear Shareholder

Good governance is a cornerstone of a successful and sustainable company. The group has a well established framework of policies, processes and management systems to support its governance and sustainability efforts, which apply to all group operations worldwide. These are described on pages 79 to 81.

The UK Corporate Governance Code

The formal Corporate Governance Report is set out on pages 84 to 99. The company is reporting against the UK Corporate Governance Code (the Code), which was introduced in June 2010. Although based on the Combined Code on Corporate Governance (the Combined Code) which it replaced, the Code contains a number of substantive changes to the Combined Code's main principles and provisions. In the main, these place greater emphasis on board behaviour. As in previous years, the company is reporting on how it has applied the main principles and whether it has complied with the relevant provisions. Under the Code, companies must explain their business model and strategies for delivering objectives. Explanations of our business model and strategy are contained in the Business Review on pages 4 to 75. The Responsibility of Directors statement is set out on page 120.

Board Role and Effectiveness

The preface to the Code encourages chairmen to report in their annual statement how they have ensured that the Code principles concerning leadership and board effectiveness have been applied during the year. I refer to this briefly in my Chairman's Statement on pages 6 and 7 and more fully in the Corporate Governance Report. In preparing these, account has been taken of the Guidance on Board Effectiveness issued by the Financial Reporting Council in March 2011, which is aimed at assisting boards in applying these Code principles.

Board and Committee Evaluation

We report on pages 96 and 97 on the board and committee evaluation process carried out following my appointment as Chairman Designate in March 2011. For the first time, the evaluation was externally facilitated by an independent consultant experienced in board evaluation. The evaluation process was ongoing at the date of publication of the 2011 annual report and has since been concluded. We report on the methodology used and the outcome. The board is conducting an internal review process this year and we describe the process being used. I propose to present the outcome of the evaluation, which is not complete at the date of publication of this annual report, to the meeting of the board in July 2012. I will report fully in the 2013 annual report.

Boardroom Diversity and Succession Planning

Boardroom diversity and succession planning are key issues for all boards. Descriptions of our approaches to these topics are set out on pages 92 and 93.

UK Corporate Governance Code Compliance Statement

Our statement of compliance with the provisions of the Code is set out on page 85. I am pleased to report that except in one limited respect, the company has complied with all relevant provisions of the Code throughout the year ended 31st March 2012 and from that date up to the date of publication of this annual report.

Tim Stevenson
Chairman

Governance and Sustainability

Introduction

The group has well established policies, processes and management systems to support its governance and sustainability efforts, which apply to all group operations worldwide. These encompass the key areas of:

- Business integrity and ethics
- Supply chain management
- Environment, health and safety (EHS)
- Human resources.

Together they provide the framework for managing environmental, social and governance matters. Brief summaries are set out in this section. Further details, together with information about progress and developments over the year to 31st March 2012, can be found on the company's website.

 Read more at www.matthey.com/sustainability.

Compliance with applicable legal requirements is a minimum standard for group operations and employees. In many cases we set standards which are in advance of those.

Employment contracts, handbooks and policies specify acceptable business practices and the group's position on ethical issues. The Group Control Manual, which is distributed to all group operations, and security manuals provide further operational guidelines to reinforce these.

The Corporate Governance Report on pages 84 to 99 describes the role of the board, the Audit Committee and other committees in risk management and internal control.

The board of directors is ultimately responsible for social, environmental and ethical matters. These matters are embedded into the group's risk management processes and reviewed annually by the board. The Audit Committee monitors performance and reviews the business risks associated with corporate social responsibility (CSR) at least once a year. Policies are set and approved by the Chief Executive's Committee (CEC).

The CEC also addresses risk and control issues and reviews key EHS, social and governance issues. The CSR Compliance Committee, a sub-committee of the CEC, has specific executive responsibility for the identification and monitoring of risks in these areas. It sets and oversees compliance with group standards through the dissemination, adoption and implementation of appropriate group policies and other operational measures.

Every business is required to include sustainability in its annual budget setting process and define the nature of programmes and projects to be undertaken together with capital expenditure requirements and value generated over a three year business cycle. Plans are discussed with the CEC and are formally approved by the board. As part of the process, progress against the Sustainability 2017 targets is assessed on a group basis to establish if additional management action is required.

We have a formal system of site and functional reviews to drive improved performance in sustainability. In 2011/12, 12 site reviews and six sustainability training sessions were undertaken.

The group's sustainability strategy (as detailed in the section on Our Strategy on pages 13 and 14) was defined following an assessment of the risks, major impacts and future commercial opportunities open to the business. The long term targets within it address the issues which could potentially have a material effect on the group's future performance. The group's materiality map outlines the key material issues and the targets in place to address and monitor them.

 View the materiality map online at www.matthey.com/sustainability.

The area of sustainability continues to develop rapidly and we continually monitor emerging issues, regulation, legislation, standards and good practice. Developments are proactively managed through reviewing the external landscape to understand the material issues that may negatively impact the group or present real business opportunities. Responsibility for identifying and assessing these issues lies with the group sustainability team and the CSR Compliance Committee.

During the year a gap analysis and peer review study against the ISO 26000 guidelines on social responsibility were conducted to ensure the group remains abreast of best practice developments in sustainability. We continued to develop our understanding of life cycle assessment (LCA) and completed the first full quantitative LCA of our automotive emission control catalysts (see page 29). In addition, a project to understand potential implications of water stress to our operations was carried out as described on page 74.

Governance continued

Business Integrity and Ethics

Johnson Matthey strives to maintain the highest standards of ethical conduct and corporate responsibility worldwide to ensure we act with integrity, transparency and care for the rights of the individual wherever we do business. The group's ethical principles and standards are set out in its Business Integrity and Ethics Policy which applies to all the group's employees.

 View the policy online at
www.matthey.com/sustainability.

The board and its committees, the Chairman, the Chief Executive and the other individual directors all play key roles, together with management, in the promotion and monitoring of ethical behaviour and the safeguarding of the group's reputation.

Compliance training is provided to employees to support their understanding of, and commitment to, group policies in order to protect and enhance the company's reputation. The training educates managers in their responsibilities for employees, commercial contracts and company assets and is delivered globally via online learning programmes, face to face seminars and individual training. Online compliance training for employees addresses the bribery and corruption, money laundering and competition risks faced by the group.

All facilities have established policies and procedures for employees to raise employment related issues for consideration and resolution.

A confidential, secure, externally-run 'whistleblowing' website and telephone helpline are also in place to give all employees additional means to raise any issue of concern. The website offers multilingual access and allows for written or telephone reports. The site is publicised via site notice boards and the company's corporate intranet site. Reports received through the website and helpline (as well as any received through other media, such as email, telephone or letter) are appropriately investigated in accordance with the Group Human Resources Policy on Whistleblowing. Responses and outcomes are posted on the website, or are communicated to employees via other internal media, such as site notices or briefings. For the group as a whole, there was a total of eight new whistleblowing reports in the calendar year 2011 and all but two have been resolved as at the date of publication of this annual report.

Supply Chain Management

Management of supply chain and contractor activities is a core component of the ISO 9000 and ISO 14000 series of standards. Supply chain and contractor management questionnaires are a requirement for achieving and maintaining registration and, as such, ISO registered Johnson Matthey operations require the completion of appropriate questionnaires. For those operations without ISO registration, the group EHS management system provides policy and guidance on supply chain management and contractor control.

The group's Ethical and Sustainable Procurement Policy provides clear guidance on various topics including those relating to the selection of suppliers, auditing against standards and ethical conduct with suppliers.

 View the policy online at
www.matthey.com/sustainability.

Johnson Matthey is confident of the human rights performance of its own operations but recognises that business practices in the supply chain are not always transparent and represent a risk that must be managed. Every effort is made to ensure the issues are managed effectively. We support the principles defined within the United Nations Universal Declaration of Human Rights and the International Labour Organisation Core Conventions including the conventions in relation to child labour, forced labour, non-discrimination, freedom of association and collective bargaining. Compliance with and respect for these core principles are integrated within the risk assessment procedures and impact assessments which are undertaken when entering into business in a new territory and within the due diligence processes when making an acquisition or entering a joint venture.

Johnson Matthey's North American businesses have developed a Conflict Free Minerals Policy in response to US legislative moves to address reports on the role of conflict minerals in financing human rights violations in the Democratic Republic of the Congo. The policy was published in March 2011. In January 2012, these businesses also issued a Slavery and Human Trafficking Policy in response to the California Transparency in Supply Chains Act 2010. Both policies are available on the company's website.

View the policies online at
www.matthey.com/sustainability.

Environment, Health and Safety

Johnson Matthey is committed to providing the highest level of protection to the environment and to safeguarding the health, safety and wellbeing of its employees, customers, communities and other stakeholders. This is supported by policies, a comprehensive management system, governance, careful risk assessment, auditing and training which promote continuous improvement and ensure that high standards are achieved at sites worldwide. In addition, all facilities have developed local policies to meet international, national, local and corporate requirements.

The Environment, Health and Safety Policy is a written statement, formulated and agreed by the CEC. Signed by the Chief Executive, it is available at all sites and forms the basis of the group EHS management system.

View the policy online at
www.matthey.com/sustainability.

The group EHS management system is available to all employees via the group intranet. It is regularly reviewed and, together with the corporate policies and objectives, it defines accountability and sets the standards against which conformance audits are assessed.

EHS compliance audits are conducted to maintain continuous improvement and all Johnson Matthey operated manufacturing and research and development facilities are included in the audit programme. Audit frequency for each facility is determined by the scale, inherent risk and past performance of the operation. Audits are carried out by experienced ISO qualified EHS professionals and controlled by the Group EHS Assurance Director. Health management reviews are undertaken every three to four years at all operational sites. They are conducted by the Director of Group Health who provides consulting advice to support the prioritisation and planning of programmes to optimise workplace health and promote workforce sustainability. In addition, all businesses undertake annual health management improvement planning to adjust health programmes to meet changing business needs.

At each board meeting, the board reviews group EHS performance reports for the prior months. These reports set out the group's EHS performance in terms of accident and incidence rates, lost work days and the rolling all lost time accident rate. The reports also contain information

• Development of new products for automotive glass applications at our Colour Technologies business' technology centre in Maastricht, the Netherlands.

• Sustainability initiatives at Johnson Matthey's sites around the world are focused on improving resource efficiency and developing more sustainable products.

from the businesses across the group on lost time accidents, as well as details of any contractor incidents, occupational illness, sickness absence and any regulatory action. The board reviews EHS strategy and reviews the EHS assurance process on an annual basis.

All EHS audit reports, including health management reviews, are reviewed by the CSR Compliance Committee and appropriate follow up actions are taken on outstanding issues. During 2011/12 a total of 26 detailed compliance audits and 19 one day audit action reviews were completed. Health management reviews were conducted at 16 facilities.

A variety of training programmes are in place to support continuous improvement in EHS performance and regular meetings are held in Europe, North America and Asia to enable the group's EHS professionals to network, share best practice and discuss the impact of future EHS legislation.

Human Resources

The group's human resources standards are progressive, consistent and aimed at bringing out the best in our people.

Group policies are supported by detailed regional and individual business procedures which are regularly updated to reflect both regional best practice and local legislation. Site specific human resources policies and procedures are communicated to staff at inductions and through staff handbooks. Human resources policies and risks are examined by the CEC and the CSR Compliance Committee.

The group's policies on equal opportunities and training are published on the company's website and are also detailed below.

View the policies online at www.matthey.com/sustainability.

In line with our Equal Opportunities Policy, we recruit, train and develop employees who meet the requirements of the job role regardless of gender, ethnic origin, age, religion, sexual orientation or disability. The policy recognises that people with disabilities can often be denied a fair chance at work because of misconceptions about their capabilities and seeks to enhance the opportunities available by attempting, wherever possible, to overcome obstacles, such as the need to modify equipment, restructure jobs or to improve access to premises, provided such action does not compromise health and safety standards.

Similarly, employees who become disabled during their employment will be offered employment opportunities consistent with their capabilities. We value the diversity of our people as a core component of a sustainable business and employment applications are welcomed and encouraged from all sections of the community including minority groups.

The Management Development and Remuneration Committee takes a special interest in ensuring compliance with the Training and Development Policy objectives in order to:

• Ensure highest standards in the recruitment of employees

• Assess training needs in the light of job requirements

• Ensure relevance of training and link with business goals

• Employ and evaluate effective and efficient training methods

• Promote from within, from high potential pools of talent

• Understand employees' aspirations

• Provide development opportunities to meet employees' potential and aspirations.

View the policy online at www.matthey.com/sustainability.

Following the development last year of a ten year human resources strategy to support business growth over the next decade, the focus now is on significant recruitment in our operations in Asia as our businesses in the region continue to expand.

82 **Johnson Matthey** Annual Report & Accounts 2012
Report of the Directors – Governance
Governance

Board of Directors

1. **Tim Stevenson OBE**
   Chairman, age 64; joined Johnson Matthey as Chairman Designate in March 2011; appointed Chairman in July 2011. Has been Chairman of The Morgan Crucible Company plc since December 2006 and was Chairman of Travis Perkins plc from November 2001 to May 2010. From 1975 to 2000 he held a variety of senior management positions at Burmah Castrol plc, including Chief Executive from 1998 to 2000. He is a qualified barrister and is Lord Lieutenant of Oxfordshire. M, N

2. **Neil Carson BSc**
   Chief Executive, age 55; joined Johnson Matthey in 1980; appointed Division Director, Catalytic Systems in 1997 after having held senior management positions in the Precious Metals Division as well as Catalytic Systems in both the UK and the US. Appointed to the board as Managing Director, Catalysts & Chemicals in August 1999 and additionally assumed board level responsibility for Precious Metals Division in August 2002. Appointed Chief Executive in July 2004. Currently a non-executive director of AMEC plc.

3. **Robert MacLeod**
   Group Finance Director, age 48; joined Johnson Matthey as Group Finance Director Designate in June 2009 and assumed his current role in September 2009. Previously he was Group Finance Director of WS Atkins plc and worked in a variety of senior financial roles at Enterprise Oil plc. He is currently a non-executive director of Aggreko plc. He is a Chartered Accountant.

4. **Michael Roney**
   Senior Independent Director and Chairman of the Management Development and Remuneration Committee, age 57; appointed a non-executive director in June 2007. Currently Chief Executive of Bunzl plc. Joined Bunzl plc as a non-executive director in 2003. Prior to becoming Chief Executive of Bunzl he was the Chief Executive Officer of Goodyear Dunlop Tires Europe BV and had an extensive career with the Goodyear Tire and Rubber Co holding a number of senior management positions with responsibilities in Latin America, Asia, Eastern Europe, the Middle East and Africa. A, M, N

5. **Alan Ferguson**
   Chairman of the Audit Committee, age 54; appointed a non-executive director in January 2011. Currently a non-executive director of Croda International Plc and The Weir Group PLC (where he is chairman of their respective audit committees). He was previously Chief Financial Officer and a Director of Lonmin Plc. He left Lonmin in December 2010. Prior to joining Lonmin, he was Group Finance Director of The BOC Group until late 2006 when the Linde Group acquired BOC. Before joining BOC in 2005, he worked for Inchcape plc for 22 years in a variety of roles including Group Finance Director from 1999 until his departure. He is a Chartered Accountant. A, M, N

6. **Sir Thomas Harris KBE CMG**
   Age 67; appointed a non-executive director in April 2009. Currently Vice Chairman of Standard Chartered Bank, a non-executive director of SC First Bank (Korea), City UK and the UK India Business Council. Until 2004, he was Director General of Trade & Investment USA responsible for British business and technology promotion throughout the United States. He served previously as British Ambassador to the Republic of Korea in Seoul, Deputy High Commissioner in Lagos, Nigeria and Commercial Counsellor in the British Embassy in Washington DC. A, M, N

7. **Dorothy Thompson**
   Age 51; appointed a non-executive director in September 2007. Currently Chief Executive of Drax Group plc. Joined the board of Drax Group plc as Chief Executive in 2005. Prior to joining Drax she was head of the European business of the global power generation firm, InterGen. First starting her career in banking she has had senior management roles in the UK, Asia and Africa. A, M, N

8. **Larry Pentz BS ChE, MBA**
   Executive Director, Environmental Technologies, age 57; joined Johnson Matthey in 1984; appointed Division Director, Process Catalysts and Technologies in 2001 after having held a series of senior management positions within Catalysts Division in the US. Appointed Executive Director, Process Catalysts and Technologies in August 2003, Executive Director, Emission Control Technologies in July 2004 and to his current position in April 2009. Currently a non-executive director of Victrex plc.

9. **Bill Sandford BA**
   Executive Director, Precious Metal Products, age 59; joined Johnson Matthey in 1977; appointed Division Director, Precious Metal Products in 2001 after holding a series of senior management positions within the division. Appointed Executive Director, Precious Metal Products in July 2009.

Committees of the Board
A   Audit Committee
M   Management Development and Remuneration Committee
N   Nomination Committee

Simon Farrant
Company Secretary; joined Johnson Matthey from corporate legal practice in 1994. Appointed Company Secretary in 1999 and Group Legal Director in 2007. He is a Solicitor and Attorney & Counselor-at-Law (State of New York).

84 **Johnson Matthey** Annual Report & Accounts 2012
Report of the Directors – Governance
Governance

Corporate Governance Report

→ ## Contents

This section of the annual report discusses the company's corporate governance structures and processes.

The UK Corporate Governance Code

The UK Corporate Governance Code (the Code), issued by the Financial Reporting Council (FRC) in June 2010, contains broad principles together with more specific provisions which set out standards of good practice in relation to board leadership and effectiveness, remuneration, accountability and relations with shareholders. Listed companies, such as Johnson Matthey, are required to report on how they have applied the main principles of good governance set out in the Code and either to confirm that they have complied with the Code's provisions or to provide an explanation where they have not. The Code replaced the previous Combined Code on Corporate Governance and applied to the company throughout the year ended 31st March 2012.

In his statement on pages 6 and 7, the Chairman comments on how the Code principles relating to the role and effectiveness of the board (in Sections A (Leadership) and B (Effectiveness) of the Code) have been applied throughout the year ended 31st March 2012.

This Corporate Governance Report, together with the Nomination Committee Report on page 105, the Audit Committee Report on pages 106 and 107 and the Remuneration Report on pages 108 to 117, describes how the company has complied with the provisions of the Code and applied the main principles set out in the Code during the year ended 31st March 2012.

Statement of Compliance with the Provisions of the Code

Except as referred to below, the company has complied with all relevant provisions of the Code throughout the year ended 31st March 2012 and from that date up to the date of publication of this annual report.

The company has not complied with part of Code provision E.1.1, which provides that *"the senior independent director should attend sufficient meetings with a range of major shareholders to listen to their views in order to help develop a balanced understanding of the issues and concerns of major shareholders"*. The board considers that there are appropriate mechanisms for the views of shareholders to be listened to and communicated to the board as a whole, without it being necessary for the Senior Independent Director to attend meetings with major shareholders. The Senior Independent Director is, however, available to attend such meetings if requested by shareholders. The board believes that its practices in this respect are both consistent with the relevant main principle of the Code concerning dialogue with shareholders, to which the Code provision relates, and consistent with good governance. More information on relations with shareholders is set out on pages 98 and 99.

Leadership

The Role of the Board

The names and biographical details of all the members of the board including details of their relevant experience and other significant commitments are set out on page 83.

The board's role is to provide leadership of the company and direction for management. It is collectively responsible and accountable to the company's shareholders for the long term success of the group and for ensuring the appropriate management and responsible operation of the group in pursuit of its objectives. The board reviews management performance and the operating and financial performance of the group as a whole. The board is responsible for ensuring that the necessary resources are provided for the company to meet those objectives.

The board sets, and is collectively responsible to the company's shareholders for the achievement of, the group's strategic objectives and it determines the nature and extent of the significant risks it is willing to take in order to achieve those objectives. Strategy is discussed in detail on pages 12 to 15. The process for the consideration of risk is discussed on pages 20 to 21.

The board approves the group's governance structures and reviews the group's internal control and risk management framework to ensure that they are prudent and effective and that risk is able to be assessed, monitored and managed. The board is collectively responsible to the company's shareholders for the group's system of corporate governance and is ultimately accountable for the group's activities, strategy, risk management and financial performance, for stewardship of the group's resources and for social, environmental and ethical matters.

Key matters for board decision include approval of the annual group operating and capital expenditure budgets and annual group three year plan, as well as the group strategy. The board also approves announcements of the group's results, the Annual Report and Accounts, the declaration of the interim dividend and recommendation of the final dividend. The board is responsible for considering and approving major capital projects, major acquisitions and major disposals of assets or operations in excess of defined thresholds.

In discharging its responsibilities the board seeks to set, promote and demonstrate adherence to clear values and ethical standards for the group. The board also remains cognisant of the need to observe the duties owed by directors in law, including the overriding duty for each director to act in the way he or she considers, in good faith, will be most likely to promote the success of the company for the benefit of its members as a whole, whilst balancing the interests of stakeholders (the company's shareholders, the group's employees, suppliers and customers and the broader community).

The board determines the structure, size and composition of the board, appointments to the board, selection of the Chairman and the Chief Executive, appointment of the Senior Independent Director and membership and chairmanship of board committees. The board has overall responsibility for succession planning for the Chief Executive and the other executive and non-executive directors and is involved in succession planning for senior management. Further information on the succession planning process is set out on page 92.

Certain types of decision are taken by the board and others are delegated by the board to executive management. A formal schedule of matters specifically reserved for board decision has been adopted by the board. This is set out in full in the Investor Relations / Corporate Governance section of the company's website.

86   **Johnson Matthey**   Annual Report & Accounts 2012
Report of the Directors – Governance
Governance

Corporate Governance Report continued

The board discharges its responsibilities through an annual programme of board and other meetings. Through a planned programme of board agendas, referred to further under 'The Role of the Chairman' below, the board ensures that all necessary matters are discussed. The board is afforded sufficient time for debate and challenge, particularly in respect of strategy and risk, including risk appetite. The board also seeks to allow sufficient opportunity for the review of past decisions where necessary. At board meetings, the board receives and considers papers and presentations from management in respect of matters under review. Effective review and decision making is supported by provision to the board of high quality, accurate, clear and timely information and the obtaining by the board of expert and independent opinion, analysis and advice where necessary (see 'Information and Support' on page 94). The board's processes in respect of conflicts of interest are dealt with under 'Directors' Conflicts of Interest' on pages 95 and 96. The board delegates certain specific responsibilities to board committees, as described under 'Board Committees' on page 88.

The Roles of the Chairman and the Chief Executive and Division of Responsibilities

Tim Stevenson was appointed Chairman with effect from the close of the 2011 Annual General Meeting on 19th July 2011, having been appointed to the board on 29th March 2011. Mr Stevenson's biographical details including details of his relevant experience and other significant commitments are set out on page 83.

Neil Carson was appointed Chief Executive in July 2004. Mr Carson's biographical details including details of his relevant experience and other significant commitments are set out on page 83.

There is a clear division of responsibilities between the running of the board and the executive responsibility for the running of the company's business. No one individual has unfettered powers of decision. The roles of Chairman and Chief Executive are separate and the division of responsibilities between these roles is clearly established in a written statement adopted by the board on 28th April 2005. This is set out in full in the Investor Relations / Corporate Governance section of the company's website.

The Role of the Chairman

The Chairman leads the board. He is responsible for creating the conditions for, and for ensuring, an effective board and effective contributions from individual directors, particularly non-executive directors, based on a culture of mutual respect, openness, debate and constructive challenge. To achieve this it is necessary for the Chairman to facilitate and encourage open communication and constructive working relations between the executive and non-executive directors. The Chairman seeks to ensure that the executive directors are open and responsive to constructive challenge by the non-executive directors of executive proposals. The Chairman is in frequent contact with the Chief Executive, meeting face to face or by telephone at least once each week. The Chairman also keeps the non-executive directors up to date with significant developments between board meetings. The Chairman is also responsible for ensuring effective communication with shareholders and this is discussed further under 'Relations with Shareholders' on pages 98 and 99.

The Chairman sets the board's agenda and ensures that adequate time is dedicated for discussion of all agenda items, particularly strategic issues and risk appetite. Since his appointment as Chairman in July 2011, Mr Stevenson has led a detailed process of board agenda review and planning, working with the Company Secretary, the chairmen of the board committees and the Chief Executive. During the year, the board approved an annual agenda plan designed to ensure that all necessary matters are reserved for board decision and are afforded adequate time for discussion throughout the year. Particular attention has been paid to ensuring that sufficient time is made available for the discussion of strategy in order to allow the opportunity for the non-executive directors to challenge and help develop strategy proposals. Strategy is discussed in detail on pages 12 to 15. The Chairman monitors, with assistance from the Company Secretary, the information distributed to the board to ensure that it is of high quality, accurate, clear and timely.

During the year ended 31st March 2012, the Chairman met with the non-executive directors without the executives being present in order to review executive director performance.

The Role of the Chief Executive

The Chief Executive has day to day management responsibility for the running of the group's operations, for the application of group policies and for the implementation of group strategy and policies agreed by the board. The board has given the Chief Executive broad authority to operate the business of the group and he is accountable for, and reports to the board on, the performance of the business. The Chief Executive also has a key role in the process for the setting and review of strategy. More broadly, the Chief Executive promotes the company's culture and standards, including appropriate governance standards, throughout the group. In addition, he ensures that the views of the executive directors on business issues and, as appropriate, employees' views on relevant issues are communicated to the board in a balanced way.

In carrying out his responsibilities, the Chief Executive is supported by the Group Finance Director who, together with the Chief Executive, is responsible amongst other things for ensuring that high quality information is provided to the board on the company's financial performance.

The Role of the Executive Directors

The biographical details of the executive directors and details of their relevant experience and other significant commitments are set out on page 83.

The executive directors have specific executive responsibilities but as directors their duties extend to the whole of the group's operations and activities and are not confined to the parts of the business encompassed by their specific executive roles.

The Role of the Non-Executive Directors

The biographical details of the non-executive directors including details of their relevant experience and other significant commitments are set out on page 83.

The role of the non-executive directors is to scrutinise the performance of management in meeting agreed goals and objectives and to monitor the reporting of performance. Their role is also to satisfy themselves on the integrity of financial information and that financial and non-financial controls and systems of risk management are robust and defensible.

As members of the board, the non-executive directors have a key role in constructively challenging in all areas and this is vital to the independence and objectivity of the board's deliberations and decision making. This is particularly important in helping develop proposals on strategy. The Chief Executive and the other executive directors are open and responsive to constructive challenge by the non-executive directors of executive proposals. Non-executive directors also have an important part to play in supporting the Chairman and the executive directors in instilling the company's culture, values and standards within the board and more broadly within the group.

As chairmen of the board committees (Michael Roney of the Management Development and Remuneration Committee and Alan Ferguson of the Audit Committee), the non-executive directors fulfill important leadership roles. The non-executive directors are also responsible for determining appropriate levels of remuneration for the executive directors and have a prime role in appointing and, where necessary, removing executive directors, and in succession planning. Further information on succession planning is set out on page 92.

The Role of the Senior Independent Director

Michael Roney was appointed by the board as the Senior Independent Director with effect from the close of the 2011 Annual General Meeting on 19th July 2011.

The role of a Senior Independent Director is to provide a sounding board for the Chairman, to serve as a focal point and intermediary for the concerns of the other non-executive directors when necessary and to ensure that any key issues not being addressed by the Chairman or the executive management are taken up. While no such circumstances have arisen in respect of the company, the board and the Senior Independent Director recognise that the Senior Independent Director may, if circumstances dictate, be required to work with the Chairman or others or to intervene to resolve any significant issues arising which threaten the stability of the company or the board.

The Senior Independent Director is available to shareholders should they have concerns which contact through the normal channels of Chairman, Chief Executive or other executive directors has failed to resolve or for which such contact may be inappropriate. He is available to attend meetings with major shareholders to listen to their views in order to help develop a balanced understanding of their issues and concerns.

The Senior Independent Director plays an important role in respect of succession to the group chairmanship by ensuring there is an orderly succession process. Alan Thomson, the then Senior Independent Director, led the work of the Nomination Committee in selecting and appointing a successor to Sir John Banham as Chairman of the board.

The Senior Independent Director is responsible for leading the annual appraisal of the Chairman's performance and this is discussed further under 'Review of the Chairman's Performance' on page 97.

The Role of the Company Secretary

Simon Farrant was appointed Company Secretary on 1st May 1999. He is secretary to the board and all of its committees. Mr Farrant's biographical details are set out on page 83.

The Company Secretary reports to the Chairman on board governance matters. Together with the Chairman he keeps the efficacy of the company's and the board's governance processes under review and considers improvements. He is also responsible to the board in respect of compliance with board procedures. He is responsible, through the Chairman, for advising and keeping the board up to date on all legislative, regulatory and governance matters and developments. Under the direction of the Chairman, the Company Secretary's responsibilities include ensuring good information flows within the board and its committees and between senior management and non-executive directors, as well as facilitating induction and assisting with professional development as required. The advice, services and support of the Company Secretary are available to all individual directors.

Board Meetings

The board meets regularly throughout the year in order to effectively discharge its duties.

During the year ended 31st March 2012 the board met seven times. The board met once between 31st March 2012 and the date of publication of this annual report.

At its meeting on 29th September 2011, the board reviewed and approved the board agenda plan for 2012/13 and for subsequent years. The board agreed that the business usually conducted at the meeting held in early May each year could be conducted at other meetings during the year and that such a meeting was not, therefore, required or necessary. Accordingly, the board has agreed to reduce the number of meetings it holds each year to six by eliminating its meeting in early May. The board will keep the efficacy of this change under review.

During the year ended 31st March 2012, the board met outside the UK on one occasion, in September 2011, in Philadelphia, USA when it visited Fine Chemicals' active pharmaceutical ingredients (API) manufacturing facility at Riverside, Conshohocken, Pennsylvania.

88   **Johnson Matthey**   Annual Report & Accounts 2012
Report of the Directors – Governance
Governance

Corporate Governance Report continued

Board Committees

The board has established the following committees:

• The Nomination Committee

• The Audit Committee

• The Management Development and Remuneration Committee (MDRC).

The Nomination Committee Report is on page 105, the Audit Committee Report is on pages 106 and 107 and the Remuneration Report, which describes the work of the MDRC, is on pages 108 to 117.

The reporting framework of the board committees and of the Chief Executive's Committee and its sub-committees is shown below.

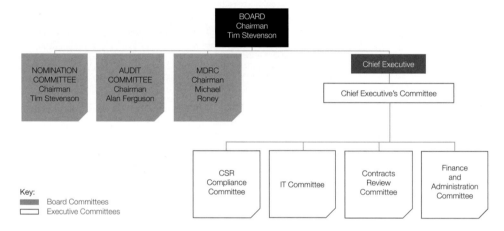

Key:
- Board Committees
- Executive Committees

The board ensures that its committees are provided with sufficient resources to undertake their duties, including access to the services of the Company Secretary as required. Each board committee has the authority to seek any information that it requires from any officer or employee of the company or its subsidiaries. In connection with its duties, each committee is authorised by the board to take such independent advice (including legal or other professional advice), at the company's expense, as it considers necessary. Each committee may request information from, or commission investigations by, external advisers.

The board committees formally report to the board on their proceedings after each meeting and generally on all matters and activities for which they are responsible through the committee chairmen and via committee minutes.

Board Committee Membership

Each independent non-executive director is a member of each board committee. No one other than the board committee chairmen and members is entitled to be present at a meeting of the Nomination Committee, the Audit Committee or the MDRC. Others may attend, however, at the invitation of the board committee. Executive directors are not members of the board committees. The Company Secretary is secretary to each of the board committees.

Alan Ferguson was appointed as Chairman of the Audit Committee with effect from the close of the 2011 Annual General Meeting, having been appointed as a non-executive director on 13th January 2011. Michael Roney took over the chairmanship of the Management Development and Remuneration Committee, also with effect from the close of the 2011 Annual General Meeting.

The current membership of the board committees is shown below:

	Nomination Committee	Audit Committee	MDRC
Tim Stevenson	Chairman	Invited to attend	Member
Neil Carson	Invited to attend	Invited to attend	Invited to attend
Alan Ferguson	Member	Chairman	Member
Sir Thomas Harris	Member	Member	Member
Robert MacLeod	–	Invited to attend	–
Larry Pentz	–	–	–
Michael Roney	Member	Member	Chairman
Bill Sandford	–	–	–
Dorothy Thompson	Member	Member	Member

The board takes into account the value of ensuring that board committee membership is refreshed when deciding chairmanship and membership of the committees, and in doing so seeks to ensure that undue reliance is not placed on particular individuals.

Board Committee Terms of Reference

Each board committee has written terms of reference which have been approved by the board and are reviewed periodically to ensure that they comply with the latest legal and regulatory requirements and reflect developments in best practice. The terms of reference of the Audit Committee were reviewed in detail during the year ended 31st March 2012 in order, in part, to reflect the recommendations of the Code. Its amended terms were adopted by resolution of the board on 22nd November 2011.

The terms of reference of each board committee can be found in the Investor Relations / Corporate Governance section of the company's website, or may be obtained from the Company Secretary. The following is a summary of the terms of reference of each board committee:

NOMINATION COMMITTEE

Responsibilities	Advising the board and making recommendations to the board on the appointment and, if necessary, the removal of executive and non-executive directors
Membership	All the independent non-executive directors and the group Chairman
Chairman	The group Chairman, Tim Stevenson (the group Chairman may not chair the committee when it is dealing with the matter of succession to the chairmanship of the company)
Attending by invitation	The Chief Executive, the Group Director, Human Resources and Environment, Health and Safety and external advisers when appropriate
Quorum	Two members, each of whom must be independent non-executive directors
Number of meetings per year	As required
Committee report	Page 105

AUDIT COMMITTEE

Responsibilities

Financial Reporting
- Monitoring the integrity of the group's reported financial information and reviewing significant financial reporting issues and judgments which they contain

Internal Control and Risk Management Systems
- Keeping under review the adequacy and effectiveness of the group's internal financial controls and internal control and risk management systems
- Reviewing the company's procedures for handling allegations from whistleblowers

Internal Audit
- Monitoring and reviewing the effectiveness of the group's internal audit function and approving the appointment and removal of the head of the internal audit function
- Considering and approving the remit of the internal audit function
- Reviewing and approving the annual internal audit plan
- Reviewing internal audit reports

External Audit
- Considering and making recommendations to the board, to be put to shareholders for approval at the annual general meeting, in relation to the appointment, reappointment and removal of the external auditor
- Overseeing the relationship with the external auditor including approving its fee for audit services and its terms of engagement, assessing annually the effectiveness of the audit process and the independence and objectivity of the external auditor, taking into account the provision of any non-audit services
- Developing and implementing a policy on the supply of non-audit services by the external auditor and keeping this policy and any fees paid to the external auditor in respect of the supply of non-audit services under review
- Meeting regularly with the external auditor, including at least once a year, without management being present, to discuss its remit and any issues arising from the audit
- Reviewing and approving the annual external audit plan and reviewing the findings of the audit with the external auditor

Corporate Governance Report continued

Board Committee Terms of Reference (continued)

AUDIT COMMITTEE (continued)

Membership	All the independent non-executive directors, at least one of whom is required to have recent and relevant financial experience. The group Chairman is not a member
Chairman	Alan Ferguson. The chairman is required to be an independent non-executive director
Attending by invitation	The group Chairman, the Chief Executive, the Group Finance Director, the Head of Internal Audit and Risk and representatives from finance and other group functions as and when appropriate and necessary. The external auditor is invited to attend on a regular basis. The chairman of the committee may request the attendance of others at meetings including external advisers and, if so requested, executive directors will also make themselves available
Quorum	Two members
Number of meetings per year	At least four per year at appropriate times in the reporting and audit cycle and otherwise as required
Committee report	Pages 106 and 107

THE MANAGEMENT DEVELOPMENT AND REMUNERATION COMMITTEE (MDRC)

Responsibilities	• Determining on behalf of the board fair remuneration for the Chief Executive, the executive directors and the group Chairman, which, while set in the context of what the company can reasonably afford, recognises their individual contributions to the company's overall performance
	• Assisting the board in ensuring that the current and future senior management of the group are recruited, developed and remunerated in appropriate fashion
	• Determining the remuneration and terms and conditions of employment (including in respect of pension entitlement) of the Chief Executive and the executive directors and the remuneration and terms of appointment of the group Chairman
	• Reviewing the proposals of the executive for recommendation to the board on share option schemes, executive bonus / incentive schemes and employee share participation schemes
	• Reviewing training, development and succession plans for senior management of the company
	• Reviewing the disclosure to be made of directors' remuneration in the annual report
Membership	All the independent non-executive directors and the group Chairman
Chairman	Michael Roney. The chairman of the committee is required to be an independent non-executive director
Attending by invitation	The Chief Executive, the Group Director, Human Resources and Environment, Health and Safety (except when their own performance and remuneration are discussed) and external advisers when appropriate
Quorum	Two members
Number of meetings per year	At least two per year and at such other times as the chairman of the committee requires
Committee report	Remuneration Report on pages 108 to 117

Board and Committee Attendance

The attendance of members at board and board committee meetings in the year ended 31st March 2012 was as follows:

	Board		Nomination Committee		Audit Committee		MDRC	
Director	Eligible to attend	Attended	Eligible to attend	Attended	Eligible to attend	Attended	Eligible to attend	Attended
Tim Stevenson	7	6[2]	2	1[2]	–	4[1]	4	3[2]
Sir John Banham	3	3	1	1	–	2[1]	2	2
Neil Carson	7	7	–	2[1]	–	4[1]	–	–
Alan Ferguson	7	7	2	2	4	4	4	4
Sir Thomas Harris	7	7	2	1[3]	4	4	4	4
Robert MacLeod	7	7	–	–	–	4[1]	–	–
Larry Pentz	7	7	–	–	–	–	–	–
Michael Roney	7	6[4]	2	2	4	3[4]	4	3[4]
Bill Sandford	7	7	–	–	–	–	–	–
Dorothy Thompson	7	7	2	2	4	4	4	4
Alan Thomson	3	3	1	1	2	2	2	2
Robert Walvis	3	3	1	1	2	2	2	2

Notes

(1) Includes meetings attended by invitation for all or part of meeting.

(2) Tim Stevenson was unable to attend the board meeting and the meetings of the Nomination Committee and the MDRC on 10th May 2011 as the date coincided with the annual general meeting of The Morgan Crucible Company plc of which he is Chairman.

(3) Sir Thomas Harris did not attend the meeting of the Nomination Committee on 29th March 2012, at which the matter of the appointment of an additional non-executive director following his prospective retirement from the board was discussed.

(4) Michael Roney was unable to attend the board meeting on 19th July 2011, the 2011 Annual General Meeting held later that day or the meetings of the Audit Committee and the MDRC held on the previous day because of coinciding commitments at Bunzl plc, where he is Chief Executive.

Where directors are unable to attend a board or board committee meeting, they communicate their comments and observations on the matter to be considered in advance of the meeting via the group Chairman, the Senior Independent Director or the relevant board committee chairman for raising as appropriate at the meeting.

Individuals' attendance at board and board committee meetings is considered, as necessary, during the one to one meetings conducted by the Chairman with directors as part of the formal annual review of their performance. Further information on performance evaluation is given under 'Evaluation of the Board, Board Committees and Directors' on pages 96 and 97.

The Chief Executive's Committee

In discharging his responsibilities, the Chief Executive is assisted by the Chief Executive's Committee (CEC). The CEC is a management committee chaired by the Chief Executive. It is responsible for the recommendation to the board of strategic and operating plans and on making recommendations on matters reserved to the board where appropriate. It is responsible for the executive management of the group's businesses.

During the year ended 31st March 2012 the CEC comprised the Chief Executive; the Group Finance Director; the two other executive directors; the division directors who do not sit on the board; the Group

Director, Corporate and Strategic Development; the Group Director, Human Resources and Environment, Health and Safety; and the Company Secretary and Group Legal Director.

During the year ended 31st March 2012, the CEC met eight times. In order to more effectively use the time of its members, the CEC no longer meets formally every month (except in August) and after September 2011 moved to a programme of meeting formally every other month and informally on such other occasions as may be necessary.

The CEC has a number of sub-committees as referred to further on page 88.

Effectiveness

The Composition of the Board

The board comprises the Chairman (Tim Stevenson), the Chief Executive (Neil Carson), three other executive directors (Robert MacLeod, Larry Pentz and Bill Sandford), and four independent non-executive directors (Alan Ferguson, Sir Thomas Harris, Michael Roney and Dorothy Thompson).

The board seeks to ensure that both it and its committees have the appropriate range and balance of skills, experience, knowledge and independence to enable them to discharge their respective duties and

responsibilities effectively. Further information on board and committee appointments is set out on page 92 under 'Appointments to the Board and its Committees' and in the Nomination Committee Report on page 105.

The board is of the view that it is of a size such that the requirements of the business can be met, that changes to the board's composition and that of its committees can be managed without undue disruption, and that it is not so large as to be unwieldy. The board is also of the view that it includes an appropriate combination of executive and non-executive directors (and, in particular, independent non-executive directors). The size of the board, as well as its composition, is kept under review by the Nomination Committee.

Throughout the year ended 31st March 2012, and from that date up to the publication of this annual report, at least half the board members, excluding the Chairman, were non-executive directors determined by the board to be independent (as referred to further on page 93).

As announced on 22nd May 2012, Sir Thomas Harris will be retiring from the board at the close of the 2012 Annual General Meeting on 25th July 2012. Following his retirement there will be a majority of executive directors on the board pending the appointment of an additional independent non-executive director. As described in the Nomination Committee Report on page 105, the process for the appointment of an additional non-executive director has commenced.

92   **Johnson Matthey**   Annual Report & Accounts 2012
Report of the Directors – Governance
Governance

Corporate Governance Report continued

Appointments to the Board and its Committees

The board, through the Nomination Committee, follows a formal, rigorous and transparent procedure for the selection and appointment of new directors to the board. The processes are similar for the appointment of executive and of non-executive directors.

The Nomination Committee leads the process for board appointments and makes recommendations to the board. Further information on the Nomination Committee and its work is set out in the Nomination Committee Report on page 105.

In considering board composition, the Nomination Committee assesses the range and balance of skills, experience, knowledge and independence on the board, identifies any gaps or issues, and considers any need to refresh the board. If it is determined in light of such evaluation that it is necessary to appoint a new non-executive director, the Committee prepares a description of the role and of the capabilities required for the appointment and sets objective selection criteria accordingly. In doing so it has regard for the benefits of diversity on the board, including gender diversity. This is discussed more fully under 'Boardroom Diversity' below.

The Committee considers any proposed recruitment in the context of the company's strategic priorities, plans and objectives as well as the prevailing business environment. The Committee also takes into account succession plans in place (and this is discussed further under 'Succession Planning' below). The Committee seeks prospective board members who can make positive contributions to the board and its committees, including the capability to challenge on such matters on strategy. This is balanced with the desire to maintain board cohesiveness.

The Committee uses external search consultancies to assist in the appointment process. Appointments are ultimately made on merit against the agreed selection criteria.

The board recognises the importance of developing internal talent for board appointments as well as recruiting externally. In this regard, the company has in place various mentoring arrangements and various types and levels of management development programmes.

The board also recognises the importance of recruiting non-executive directors with the necessary technical skills and knowledge relevant to the work of its committees and who have the potential to take over as committee chairmen.

Succession Planning

The board, through the MDRC, is actively engaged in ongoing succession planning in order to ensure that plans are in place for the orderly and progressive refreshing of the board and for the identification and development of senior management with potential for board and CEC positions.

Each division and corporate function across the group prepares and maintains succession plans with the assistance of divisional and group Human Resources. The CEC rigorously reviews these plans in detail annually, with a focus on ensuring an appropriate pipeline of talented and capable individuals to fill senior roles. A key aim is to ensure broad experience and encourage cross fertilisation across the group's divisions. The CEC also considers the identification and development of high potential individuals. The review of the plans by the CEC generally leads to further refinement and changes, resulting in the final plans which are submitted to the MDRC. The MDRC reviews succession policy, the succession plan and the management development and succession planning process each year.

Boardroom Diversity

The board believes that diversity is important for board effectiveness. The board has followed carefully the debate regarding the representation of women in the boardroom following the publication of Lord Davies' report, 'Women on Boards', in February 2011 (the Davies Report).

Statement on Board Diversity

In response to the Davies Report, on 28th November 2011 the board published the following statement on board diversity. It is set out in the Investor Relations / Corporate Governance section of the company's website.

"The board of Johnson Matthey has followed the important debate around the recommendations of Lord Davies' review on Women on Boards and the question of boardroom diversity. We do not think quotas, for the proportion of women on the board or otherwise, are appropriate for a number of reasons. We believe all appointments should be made on merit rather than through positive discrimination. We are clear, however, that maintaining an appropriate balance around our board table through a diverse mix of skills, experience, knowledge and background is of paramount importance. Gender diversity is a significant element of this.

At present the board has one woman member in a board of nine. When we next make an appointment to the board, our brief to search consultants in the selection process as regards external candidates will be to review candidates from a variety of backgrounds and perspectives. The consultants will be asked to work to a specification which will include the strong desirability of producing a long-list of possible candidates which fully reflects the benefits of diversity, including gender diversity. Any appointment of an internal candidate, while similarly based on merit, will also take into account the benefits of diversity, including gender diversity.

Looking beyond the board to our wider workforce, we recognise the importance of diversity, including gender diversity, and the benefits this can bring to our organisation. With regard to gender diversity specifically, Johnson Matthey faces challenges similar to those faced by other organisations in the chemical, technology and manufacturing sectors. To address these, we have policies and processes in place which are designed to support gender diversity in employee recruitment, development and promotion and we are committed to ensuring that women have an equal chance with men of developing their careers within our business. Finally, we encourage gender diversity at the early career stage by working outside Johnson Matthey to encourage women to enter scientific and industrial fields."

Gender Diversity Statistics

	Number	Proportion
The board	1 woman on the board as at the date of publication of this annual report	11% of board membership
Senior management	32 women out of 196 total as at 31st March 2012	16% of senior management
Graduate intake	–	30% of graduate intake
The group	2,205 women employees as at 31st March 2012	22% of group employees

The company has taken, and continues to take, several steps to promote diversity, including gender diversity, at senior management level and in the boardroom. The basis of these measures is in developing policies and processes that prevent bias in relation to recruitment and promotion, but the key to progress is in actively promoting diversity, ensuring that other positive measures are taken. These include requesting balanced shortlists when recruiting, looking at diversity mix in company events and conferences, actively discussing diversity in succession planning, promoting industrial and scientific careers to young women and developing family friendly and flexible employment policies. There are challenges to overcome, particularly in respect of gender diversity, given the sector within which the group operates but the group is making good progress.

Boardroom Diversity Policy

Following the publication of the Davies Report, in October 2011 the FRC confirmed its intention to include revisions in the next version of the amended Code to be published in 2012 in order to accommodate the Davies Report recommendation in respect of diversity policy. These revisions will require companies to include in the section of the annual report describing the work of the nomination committee a description of the board's policy on diversity, including gender, any measurable objectives that it has set for implementing the policy and progress on achieving the objectives. The changes will formally apply to companies with a financial year commencing on or after 1st October 2012, and so for Johnson Matthey's year ending 31st March 2014.

The board is in the process of reviewing the broad question of diversity within the group and is considering a policy for diversity.

Board Evaluation Process

The FRC also announced in October 2011 that a new supporting principle would be included in the Code to the effect that evaluation of the board should consider the balance of skills, experience, independence and knowledge of the company on the board, its diversity, including gender, how the board works together as a unit and other factors relevant to its effectiveness. Again, this change will be incorporated in an updated version of the Code to be published in 2012. The board is following this principle in its board and committee evaluation process which is underway as at the date of publication of this annual report.

Further information is set out under '2011/12 Evaluation Process' on pages 96 and 97.

Appointments to the Board

As described under 'Appointments to the Board and its Committees' on page 92, the search for board candidates is conducted, and appointments made, on merit, against objective selection criteria having due regard for the benefits of diversity on the board, including gender. Further information on diversity in the context of board appointments is contained in the Nomination Committee Report on page 105.

Board Balance – Independence of the Non-Executive Directors and of the Chairman

The question of the independence of the non-executive directors is relevant to board balance.

Director independence was reviewed by the board at its meeting on 29th March 2012. In making its determination of independence in respect of a director, the board considers all relevant relationships and circumstances, including those set out in the Code. The board considers, for example, whether the director has, or has had within the last three years, a material business relationship with the company, holds cross directorships or has significant links with other directors through involvement in other companies or bodies, or represents or has a material connection to a controlling or significant shareholder or is nominated by a shareholder.

The board considers that there are no business or other relationships or circumstances which are likely to affect,

or may appear to affect, the judgment of any non-executive director and each non-executive director was determined by the board to be independent in character and judgment.

There are no cross directorships or reciprocal directorships among the directors; no two directors are also directors of another company.

Tim Stevenson was considered by the board to meet the independence criteria set out in the Code on his appointment as a non-executive director and Chairman Designate in March 2011 and on his appointment as Chairman in July 2011. Sir John Banham, who retired as Chairman at the close of the 2011 Annual General Meeting in July 2011, was not involved in the selection or appointment of Mr Stevenson as Chairman.

Information on the company's procedures for authorising potential conflicts of interest is set out under 'Directors' Conflicts of Interest' on page 95.

Corporate Governance Report continued

Time Commitment of the Chairman and of the Non-Executive Directors

The board recognises that it is vital that all directors should be able to dedicate sufficient time to the company to effectively discharge their responsibilities.

The time commitment required by the company is considered by the board and by individual directors on appointment. The letters of appointment of the Chairman and of each non-executive director set out the expected minimum time commitment for their roles. Each undertake that they will have sufficient time to meet what is expected of them for the proper performance of their duties and acknowledge that there may, on occasion, be a need for additional time commitment. The minimum time commitment considered by the board to be necessary for a non-executive director and provided in the letters of appointment is two days per month following induction. In his letter of appointment, the Chairman undertook to devote such time to the affairs of the company as is required by his duties as Chairman.

The other significant commitments of the Chairman and of each non-executive director are disclosed to the board before appointment, with an indication of the time commitment involved. The board requires to be, and is, informed of subsequent changes as they arise.

Details of Tim Stevenson's other significant commitments are set out on page 83. There were no changes to these during the year ended 31st March 2012. On 8th May 2012 it was announced by The Morgan Crucible Company plc that Mr Stevenson would be retiring as chairman of that company on 31st July 2012.

Details of the non-executive directors' other significant commitments are set out on page 83. Alan Ferguson has, since his appointment to the board, been appointed as a non-executive director of Croda International Plc (in July 2011), where he has chaired the audit committee since August 2011. He was also appointed as a non-executive director of The Weir Group PLC in December 2011 and has chaired its audit committee since May 2012. These appointments were reported to the board as they arose. The board assessed the impact of these appointments and believes that Mr Ferguson continues to be able to manage his time commitments and allocate sufficient time to the company to discharge his responsibilities effectively, including his responsibilities as Chairman of the Audit Committee.

Terms of Appointment of the Non-Executive Directors

The non-executive directors are appointed for specified terms subject to annual election and to the provisions of the Companies Act 2006 (the 2006 Act) relating to the removal of a director.

Any term beyond six years for a non-executive director is subject to particularly rigorous review and takes into account the need for progressive refreshing of the board. No non-executive director who will be proposed for re-election at the 2012 Annual General Meeting on 25th July 2012 will then have served longer than six years.

The terms and conditions of appointment of the non-executive directors and the contracts of service of the executive directors with the company are available to be inspected by any person at the registered office of the company during normal business hours. They are also available for inspection at the annual general meeting of the company prior to the meeting and during the meeting. Accordingly, they will be available for inspection at Merchant Taylors' Hall, 30 Threadneedle Street, London EC2R 8JB from 10.00 am on Wednesday 25th July 2012 until the conclusion of the 2012 Annual General Meeting.

Annual Re-Election of Directors

The company's Articles of Association require one third of the board to retire by rotation at each annual general meeting. However, the Code provides that all directors of FTSE 350 companies should be subject to re-election by their shareholders every year subject to continued satisfactory performance. In accordance with this provision, the board has decided that all directors will retire at each annual general meeting and offer themselves for re-election by shareholders.

Each director stood for re-election at the 2011 Annual General Meeting. All directors will be offering themselves for re-election at the 2012 Annual General Meeting except for Sir Thomas Harris, who will be retiring from the board at the close of that meeting.

Biographical details of each of the directors, including details of their other directorships and responsibilities and relevant previous positions held, together with any further relevant factors including details of their skills and experience and contributions to the board, are set out in the circular to shareholders in respect of the 2012 Annual General Meeting. This is to assist shareholders to take an informed decision on the resolutions for their re-election.

The circular sets out to shareholders why the board believes each director should be re-elected based on continued satisfactory performance in the role. In the circular, the Chairman confirms to shareholders that, following formal performance evaluation, the performance of each non-executive director proposed for re-election continues to be effective and to demonstrate commitment to the role (including commitment of time for board and board committee meetings). Further information on performance evaluation is given under 'Evaluation of the Board, Board Committees and Directors' on page 96.

Information and Support

The board has in place processes to ensure that it is supplied in a timely manner with information in a form and of a quality appropriate to enable it to discharge its duties. The Chairman, through the Company Secretary and with the support of the executive directors and management, ensures that this information is of high quality in terms of its accuracy, clarity, appropriateness, comprehensiveness and currency.

Directors are able to seek clarification or amplification from management where necessary.

The role of the Company Secretary in providing support and information is set out on page 87.

Independent Professional Advice

The non-executive and the executive directors have access to independent external professional advice (such as legal and financial advice) at the company's expense where they judge this necessary to discharge their responsibilities as directors.

Director Induction, Familiarisation, Training and Development

Induction

The company puts in place full, formal and tailored induction programmes for all new directors on joining the board. While this takes into account the directors' different backgrounds and experience, the induction is aimed to be a broad introduction to the group's businesses and its areas of significant risk. Key elements of the induction process are meeting the executive directors and senior and middle management individually and collectively and visiting the group's major operating sites.

95

Since their appointments Tim Stevenson and Alan Ferguson have undergone tailored induction programmes facilitated by the Company Secretary. These programmes included meetings with the Chief Executive, the executive directors and senior management in order to be briefed on group strategy and on individual businesses, briefing sessions with key group functions and visits to the principal UK sites. The programmes also allowed Mr Stevenson and Mr Ferguson to familiarise themselves with any issues arising from service on, or chairmanship of, board committees. As part of his induction programme, Tim Stevenson had separate meetings with several major shareholders.

Familiarisation, Training and Development
To ensure the effective fulfilment of the roles of the directors on the board and on the board committees and to ensure that their contributions remain informed and relevant, various steps are taken to ensure that all directors are able to gain and to continually update and refresh their knowledge and skills. The intention is that all directors have familiarity with, and appropriate knowledge of, the company and gain access to its operations and employees. The board ensures that the company provides the necessary resources to allow this to happen.

Each board meeting includes one or more business or strategy presentations from senior managers. To ensure that the board is kept up to date on important matters, including environmental, legal, governance and regulatory developments, presentations are also made to the board by both external and internal advisers.

The board also holds at least one board meeting per year at one of the group's operational sites and takes the opportunity to tour the site and discuss business issues, risks and strategy with local management. During the year ended 31st March 2012, the board visited Fine Chemicals' API manufacturing facility at Riverside, Conshohocken, Pennsylvania, USA in September 2011 and Precious Metal Products' Catalysts and Chemicals manufacturing facility at Royston, Hertfordshire in the UK in March 2012. The board toured these sites and received presentations from management on the recently acquired facility at Riverside and on Catalyst and Chemicals' new products respectively. Individual non-executive directors also undertake site visits.

Such presentations, meetings and site visits assist the non-executive directors in familiarising themselves with, and gaining a greater insight into, the group's businesses and help to give a balanced overview of the group. They enable the non-executive directors to continue to develop and refresh their knowledge and understanding of the group's businesses, the markets in which it operates and its key relationships. They are also important for building links with the group's employees.

As part of the annual performance review process referred to under 'Evaluation of the Board, Board Committees and Directors' on page 96, the Chairman meets with each director annually on a one to one basis to review and agree their individual training and development requirements.

Indemnification of Directors and Insurance

Under Deed Polls dated 20th July 2005 the company granted indemnities in favour of each director of the company in respect of any liability that he or she may incur to a third party in relation to the affairs of the company or any group member. Such indemnities were in force during the year ended 31st March 2012 for the benefit of all persons who were directors of the company at any time during the year and remain in force for the benefit of all persons who are directors of the company as at the date when this Report of the Directors was approved and from that date up to the date of publication of this annual report.

Under Deed Polls also dated 20th July 2005 the company granted indemnities in favour of each director of its subsidiaries in respect of any liability that he or she may incur to a third party in relation to the affairs of any group member. Such indemnities were in force during the year ended 31st March 2012 for the benefit of all persons who were directors of the subsidiaries at any time during the year and remain in force for the benefit of all persons who are directors of the subsidiaries as at the date when this Report of the Directors was approved and from that date up to the date of publication of this annual report.

The company has in place appropriate directors and officers liability insurance cover in respect of legal action against, amongst others, its executive and non-executive directors.

Copies of the Deed Polls and the company's Articles of Association are available to be inspected by any person at the registered office of the company during normal business hours. They are also available for inspection at the annual general meeting of the company prior to the meeting and during the meeting. Accordingly, they will be available for inspection at Merchant Taylors' Hall, 30 Threadneedle Street, London EC2R 8JB from 10.00 am on Wednesday 25th July 2012 until the conclusion of that meeting.

Neither the company nor any subsidiary has indemnified any director of the company or a subsidiary in respect of any liability that he or she may incur to a third party in relation to a relevant occupational pension scheme.

Directors' Conflicts of Interest

Under the Companies Act 2006 (the 2006 Act), a director must avoid situations in which he or she has, or can have, a direct or indirect interest that conflicts with, or may conflict with, the interests of the company. This covers, in particular, the exploitation of property, information or opportunity and it applies whether or not the company is in a position to take advantage of it. There is no breach of this duty if authorisation of the conflict situation has been given by the independent directors. The company's Articles of Association give power to the independent directors to give such authorisation but board authorisation is not permitted in respect of the acceptance of benefits from third parties. Directors also have a duty under the 2006 Act to make prior declaration to the other directors of the nature and extent of any direct or indirect interest in a proposed transaction or arrangement with the company. Additionally, directors must declare the nature and extent of any direct or indirect interest in an existing transaction or arrangement entered into by the company, to the extent that the interest has not been declared under the duty in respect of proposed transactions or arrangements.

96 Johnson Matthey   Annual Report & Accounts 2012
Report of the Directors – Governance
Governance

Corporate Governance Report continued

Established procedures in accordance with the company's Articles of Association are in place to ensure compliance with the directors' conflicts of interest duties under the 2006 Act and for dealing with conflict of interest situations. The company has complied with these procedures during the year ended 31st March 2012 and from that date up to the date of publication of this annual report. During the year, details of any new conflicts or potential conflict matters were submitted to the board for consideration and, where appropriate, these were approved.

In March 2012, the board undertook an annual review of the register of previously approved conflict or potential conflict matters and, to the extent that these were still relevant, agreed that they should continue to be authorised on the terms previously set out. In each case, the review was undertaken by directors who were genuinely independent of the conflict matter. Authorised conflict or potential conflict matters will continue to be reviewed by the board on an annual basis.

The board confirms that the company complies with its procedures in place to authorise conflict situations and is satisfied that its powers to authorise conflict situations are being exercised properly and effectively and in accordance with the company's Articles of Association.

Evaluation of the Board, Board Committees and Directors

With the aim of improving effectiveness, the board undertakes a formal annual evaluation of its own performance and that of its committees and individual directors. The evaluation, which is led by the Chairman, aims to be as rigorous and objective as possible.

The process for evaluation of the board considers its strengths and weaknesses, the range and balance of skills, experience, independence and knowledge of the company on the board, its diversity, including gender diversity, how the board works together as a unit and any other factors considered relevant to its effectiveness. Individual evaluation aims to show whether each director continues to contribute effectively and to demonstrate commitment to the role (including time commitment). The Chairman acts on the results of the performance evaluation. The strengths are recognised and any weaknesses addressed.

2010/11 Evaluation Process

Following the appointment of Tim Stevenson as Chairman Designate in March 2011, the board instigated a formal evaluation of its performance and that of its committees and individual directors. This evaluation was led by Tim Stevenson and was externally facilitated by an independent consultant experienced in board evaluation. This was the first time that the board had undertaken an externally facilitated evaluation process. The external facilitator had no other connection with the company and was not subject to any conflict of interest. The evaluation was designed, in particular, to allow Tim Stevenson to gain an objective overview and evaluation of the workings of the board and its committees, of strengths and weaknesses, of areas for further improvement and of the contributions of individual directors. The review was intended to build on the internal board review carried out by the Company Secretary in 2009/10.

The methodology of the evaluation included a series of detailed one to one meetings with each director and the Company Secretary in order to gather views and feedback. The external evaluator also attended one full board meeting as an observer. The review covered the following main areas, which were determined by the Chairman and the external evaluator to be of most importance or value to the board:

- Overall board working and efficiency;
- Board composition and balance;
- Succession planning;
- Strategy process;
- Financial and non-financial monitoring;
- Risk management and risk management systems; and
- Board development (including training and site visits).

The full evaluation process was not complete at the date of publication of the 2011 annual report and has since been concluded. Overall feedback from the evaluation was provided in the form of a presentation by the external evaluator at a meeting of the board in May 2011, which then debated the findings. The board also discussed the evaluation process itself and agreed that the external evaluation was broadly effective. The external evaluator also provided a comprehensive written report to the Chairman, feedback to the board committee chairmen and individual feedback for the Chief Executive.

Good progress was noted across all the areas of review, building on initiatives and action developed as a result of prior effectiveness reviews. Certain suggestions were made to ensure continuing progress. The evaluation process gave assurance that each director continued to contribute effectively and demonstrated commitment to the role.

The Chairman agreed with the board that no actions or changes to board or committee practice were required in the immediate term following the review but that the output would be considered further following his appointment as Chairman in July 2011 and in the course of the review for 2011/12 to ensure continuing improvement.

2011/12 Evaluation Process

As the 2010/11 review process had been externally facilitated, the board decided to conduct an internal review process during 2012. The evaluation of the performance and effectiveness of the board and its committees and individual directors is being conducted by the Chairman in collaboration with the board committee chairmen. The evaluation is not complete at the date of publication of this annual report.

The evaluation process has included one to one interviews by the Chairman with each director and the Company Secretary. The topics being discussed, which were determined by the Chairman to be the principal areas of focus following the externally facilitated review in the previous year, include:

- Strategy and strategy focus;
- Monitoring financial and non-financial performance;
- Stakeholder relationships;
- Risk and uncertainties;
- Executive remuneration; and
- Key themes for discussion focus in 2012/13.

In carrying out the evaluation, the board is following the new supporting principle to be included in the Code, as announced by the FRC in October 2011, to the effect that evaluation of the board should consider, amongst other things, the board's diversity, including gender diversity. Further information is set out under 'Board Evaluation Process' on page 93.

The Chairman proposes to report the outcome of the evaluation process to the board meeting in July 2012. The board will debate the findings and any lessons to be learned and will agree any follow up actions and responsibilities as appropriate. The key outcomes of the evaluation processes and the steps the board intends to take to address any issues will be reported in the 2013 annual report.

Future Reviews

The board intends to undertake an externally facilitated evaluation process at least every three years. In the intervening years, the review will be facilitated by the Chairman supported by the Senior Independent Director and the Company Secretary.

Review of the Chairman's Performance

The non-executive directors recognise that the Chairman's effectiveness is vital to that of the board. Led by the Senior Independent Director, the non-executive directors are responsible for performance evaluation of the Chairman and for providing a fair and balanced assessment to shareholders.

In view of the change in the chairmanship of the company with the appointment of Tim Stevenson as Chairman on 19th July 2011, a separate formal review of the Chairman's performance was not undertaken during the year ended 31st March 2011 but feedback on the Chairman's performance was reflected in the externally facilitated evaluation referred to on page 96. A review of the Chairman's performance was, however, undertaken in the year ended 31st March 2012. On 28th March 2012, the non-executive directors, led by the Senior Independent Director, met separately, without the Chairman being present, to discuss the Chairman's performance. In doing so they took into account the views of executive directors. The results were subsequently reported by the Senior Independent Director to the board. They considered that the Chairman demonstrated effective leadership and that his performance and contribution were strong.

Accountability

The Audit Committee

The membership of the Audit Committee is set on page 90.

The terms of reference of the Audit Committee are summarised on pages 89 and 90. The terms of reference can be found in the Investor Relations / Corporate Governance section of the company's website or may be obtained from the Company Secretary.

The Audit Committee Report, which describes the work of the Audit Committee in discharging its responsibilities, is set out on pages 106 and 107.

Financial Experience

The board is satisfied that at least one member of the Audit Committee, Alan Ferguson, has recent and relevant financial experience. His biographical details are set out page 83.

Financial and Business Reporting

In its reporting to shareholders the board recognises its responsibility to present a fair, balanced and understandable assessment of the group's position and prospects. This responsibility covers the Annual Report and Accounts and extends to interim and other price sensitive public reports and reports to regulators as well as to information required to be presented by statutory requirements.

The Business Review on pages 4 to 75 sets out explanations of the basis on which the company generates or preserves value over the longer term (the business model) and the strategy for delivering the objectives of the company. This annual report is intended to provide the information necessary to enable an assessment of the company's performance, the business model and its strategy.

The group's organisational structure is focused on its three divisions. These are all separately managed but report to the board through a board director. The CEC receives and reviews monthly summaries of financial results from each division through a standardised reporting process. Forecasts are prepared monthly throughout the year. The group has in place a comprehensive annual budgeting and planning process including plans for the following two years. Budgets are approved by the board. Variances from budget are closely monitored. In addition to the annual budgeting process, there is a ten year strategy review process as referred to on page 12.

Directors' and Auditor's Responsibility

A statement of the directors' responsibility for preparing the Annual Report and Accounts is set out on page 120. A statement by the auditor, KPMG Audit Plc about its reporting responsibilities is set out on page 121.

Risk Management and Internal Control

The board is ultimately responsible for maintaining sound risk management and internal control systems (including financial controls, controls in respect of the financial reporting process and controls of an operational and compliance nature).

As the company is the parent company of a group, its internal control systems are on a groupwide basis and the review of their effectiveness is implemented and reported from a groupwide perspective. The directors' review of the effectiveness of internal control systems and the application of the Revised Guidance for Directors on the Combined Code issued by the FRC in October 2005 (Revised Turnbull Guidance) extends to the company and its subsidiaries.

The group's risk management systems and internal control systems are designed to meet the group's needs and manage the risks to which it is exposed, including the risk of failure to achieve business objectives, but such risks cannot be eliminated. Such systems can only provide reasonable, but not absolute, assurance against a failure to meet business objectives or against the risk of material misstatement or loss. They can never completely protect against such factors as unforeseeable events, human fallibility or fraud.

The board confirms that there is a framework of continuous and ongoing processes (established in accordance with the Revised Turnbull Guidance) in place for identifying, evaluating and managing the significant risks faced by the group. These processes are regularly reviewed by the board and the Audit Committee as appropriate and have been in place during the year ended 31st March 2012 and up to the date of approval of this annual report.

The board is responsible for determining the nature and extent of the significant risks it is willing to take in achieving its strategic objectives. The board's view of the group's key strategic and operating risks and how the company seeks to manage those risks is set out on pages 20 to 23.

98   Johnson Matthey   Annual Report & Accounts 2012
                         Report of the Directors – Governance
                         Governance

Corporate Governance Report continued

The Risk Management and Internal Control Systems

The group's risk management and internal control systems comprise group policies, procedures and practices covering a range of areas including the appropriate authorisation and approval of transactions, the application of financial reporting standards and the review of financial performance and significant judgments.

The Group Control Manual, which is distributed to all group operations, clearly sets out the composition, responsibilities and authority limits of the various board and executive committees and also specifies what may be decided without central approval. It is supplemented by other specialist policy and procedures manuals issued by the group, divisions and individual businesses or departments.

Review of Effectiveness of the Group's Risk Management and Internal Control Systems

A key responsibility of the board is for reviewing, assessing and confirming the adequacy and effectiveness of the group's risk management and internal control systems (including financial controls, controls in respect of the financial reporting process and controls of an operational and compliance nature). The board has delegated part of this responsibility to the Audit Committee. In addition to determining risk appetite, the board specifically reviews EHS strategy, performance and assurance processes as well as the performance of group HR and IT. The Audit Committee reviews other key risk areas and the assurance processes in respect of the management of risk.

The board, through setting its own annual agenda plan and in approving that of the Audit Committee, defines the process to be undertaken for the review, including the scope and frequency of assurance reports received throughout the year. The board and Audit Committee agenda plans are designed to ensure that all significant areas of risk are reported on and considered during the course of the year.

The Audit Committee receives and considers regular reports and presentations from management, from the heads of group corporate functions such as group treasury and from internal audit. These identify and provide assessments of areas of significant risk either for the businesses or the group as a whole and of the effectiveness of the control systems in managing those risks. Any significant issues are highlighted and discussed. The Audit Committee is thus able to focus on the key risk areas and effectively assess how they have been identified, evaluated and managed. In assessing the effectiveness of the control systems, the Audit Committee considers

carefully the impact of any weaknesses, whether necessary actions are being taken promptly and whether more extensive monitoring is needed. Amongst other matters, the Audit Committee reviews the group's credit control procedures and risks, controls over precious metals, IT controls and the group's whistleblowing procedures. The Audit Committee also reviews the performance of both the internal and external auditors. The Audit Committee also considers observations by the external auditor in relation to internal financial control.

The group's internal audit function plays an important part in the assessment of the risks facing the group and is responsible for independently monitoring and assessing the adequacy and effectiveness of the group's systems of internal financial control. Internal audit reports on control effectiveness to the Audit Committee in line with the agreed audit plan and Audit Committee agenda plan. The internal audit function is a unified, groupwide function under the leadership of the Head of Internal Audit and Risk. The global nature of the function allows for more holistic assurance and consistency in approach. The Head of Internal Audit and Risk has a dual reporting line to the Group Finance Director and to the Chairman of the Audit Committee. The Audit Committee approves the plans for internal audit reviews and receives the reports produced by the internal audit function on a regular basis. Plans for corrective action and control improvement are agreed with management to address any issues, non-compliance or control deficiencies identified by internal audits. Internal audit follows up the implementation of its recommendations, including any recommendations to improve internal controls, and reports the outcome to senior management and to the Audit Committee.

Each year businesses are required to formally review their financial and non-financial controls and their compliance with group policies and statutory and regulatory obligations and to provide assurance on these. The results of these reviews are collated and summarised by the internal audit function and a report is made annually to the Audit Committee.

The Audit Committee conducts an annual assessment of effectiveness on behalf of the board in order for the board to report on effectiveness in the annual report. The Audit Committee reports to the board on the operation and effectiveness of the risk management and internal control systems and such reports are considered by the board in forming its view of their effectiveness. A report from the Audit Committee on its activities and on the work of internal audit is given on pages 106 and 107.

The board, in part through the Audit Committee, has conducted an overarching review of the effectiveness of the company's risk management and internal control systems, covering all material controls, including financial, operational and compliance controls, for the year ended 31st March 2012 and up to the date of its approval of this annual report on 6th June 2012. The review process accords with the Revised Turnbull Guidance. Following this review, the group is enhancing and standardising the stock take procedures across its gold and silver refineries.

Remuneration

The board has established a remuneration committee, the Management Development and Remuneration Committee (MDRC).

The membership of the MDRC is set on page 90.

The terms of reference of the MDRC are summarised on page 90. The terms of reference can be found in the Investor Relations / Corporate Governance section of the company's website or may be obtained from the Company Secretary.

The Remuneration Report, which describes the work of the MDRC, is set out on pages 108 to 117.

Relations with Shareholders

Dialogue with Shareholders

The board welcomes the opportunity to openly engage with shareholders as it recognises the importance of a continuing effective dialogue (whether with major institutional investors, private or employee shareholders) based on the mutual understanding of respective objectives. The board as a whole takes responsibility for ensuring that such dialogue takes place.

Reporting of Results, Interim Management Statements and the Investor Day

The company reports formally to shareholders when its full year results are published in June and its half year results are published in November. The company's results are posted on the Investor Relations / Results Centre section of the company's website. The full year results are included in the company's annual report.

At the same time as publication of the results, executive directors give presentations on the half year and full year results in face to face meetings with institutional investors, analysts and the media in London. Live webcasts of these results presentations are available on the company's website.

The company's first quarter and third quarter Interim Management Statements (issued respectively on the day of the annual general meeting in July and in early February each year) are also made available on the Investor Relations / Results Centre section of the company's website.

The company also holds an annual 'Investor Day' for its institutional investors and analysts. At the 2012 Investor Day held in London on 1st February, the company gave a presentation in respect of its Precious Metal Products Division. This was designed to provide a deeper understanding of the division, its strategy and drivers and to highlight why the division is such an intrinsic part of the group. The presentation also outlined the group's role in the global platinum group metals market and the dynamics of the division's businesses. It also explained the role of R&D in adding value and providing future growth opportunities. A live webcast of the Investor Day presentations is made available on the company's website. A copy of the Investor Day presentation is posted on the Investor Relations / Presentations section of the company's website.

Shareholder Contact

While the Chairman takes overall responsibility for ensuring that the views of shareholders are communicated to the board as a whole and that all directors are made aware of major shareholders' issues and concerns, contact with major shareholders is principally maintained by the Chief Executive and the Group Finance Director. They maintain a continual dialogue with institutional shareholders throughout the year on performance, plans and objectives through a programme of regular one to one and group meetings and they ensure that shareholder views are communicated to the board. The group's Investor Relations Department acts as a focal point for contact with investors throughout the year.

The Chairman is available to meet with institutional investors to hear their views and discuss any issues or concerns, including on governance and strategy. The Senior Independent Director and the other non-executive directors are also available to meet with major shareholders if requested. Other than meetings held with shareholders by Tim Stevenson as part of his induction programme, no such meetings were held or requested during the year ended 31st March 2012 or from that date to the date of publication of this annual report.

The board believes that appropriate steps have been taken during the year to ensure that the members of the board, and in particular the non-executive directors, develop an understanding of the views of major shareholders about the company. Such steps have included, for example, analysts' and brokers' briefings, consideration by the board of monthly brokers' reports and of feedback from shareholder meetings on a six-monthly basis. The canvassing of major shareholders' views for the board in a detailed investor survey is usually conducted every two years by external consultants. At its meeting in November 2011, the board considered a perception analysis report prepared for the company by Smith's Corporate Advisory dated October 2011. The purpose of this was to ascertain the views and opinions of a broad range of both shareholders and non-shareholders.

Also, as reported in the Remuneration Report in the 2011 annual report, a selection of major institutional shareholders and institutional investor bodies were consulted in detail by the MDRC during 2010/11 in a collective consultation exercise as part of its comprehensive review of executive director and senior management remuneration arrangements within the group.

The board takes the view that these methods, taken together, are a practical and efficient way for the board, including the Senior Independent Director, to keep in touch with shareholder opinion and views and to reach a balanced understanding of major shareholders' objectives, issues and concerns.

Annual General Meetings

An important part of effective communication with shareholders is the Annual General Meeting.

The company's annual general meeting takes place in London. Notice of the meeting and any related papers are sent to shareholders at least 20 working days before the meeting and are also published on the Investor Relations / Shareholder Centre / Annual General Meeting section of the company's website. The circular sent to shareholders with the notice of meeting aims to set out a balanced and clear explanation of each resolution to be proposed.

All directors, including the chairmen of the Nomination Committee, the Audit Committee and the MDRC, who are able to attend the annual general meetings do so. The entire board was in attendance at the company's 2011 Annual General Meeting, except for Michael Roney who was unable to attend the meeting because of coinciding commitments at Bunzl plc, where he is Chief Executive.

In order to better communicate with shareholders a business presentation is made by the Chief Executive at the annual general meeting. Shareholder participation at the meeting is encouraged. All directors in attendance are available to answer questions in their capacity as directors or as committee chairmen, formally through the Chairman during the meeting and informally afterwards.

At the meetings, the company proposes separate resolutions on each substantially separate issue, including on the Annual Report and Accounts. For each resolution, shareholders have the option through the proxy appointment forms provided to direct their proxy to vote either for or against the resolution or to withhold their vote. The proxy form itself and the announcement of the results of a vote make it clear that a 'vote withheld' is not legally a vote and is not counted in the calculation of the proportion of the votes cast for and against the resolution. All valid proxy appointments received are properly recorded and counted.

All resolutions at the annual general meeting are decided on a poll as required by the company's Articles of Association (rather than on a show of hands) and poll voting is carried out by electronic means.

The results of the poll are announced to the market as soon as possible and posted on the Investor Relations / Shareholder Centre / Annual General Meeting section of the company's website. The announcement shows votes for and against as well as votes withheld.

Details of the annual general meeting to be held on 25th July 2012 are set out in the circular to shareholders accompanying this annual report and the resolutions to be proposed are summarised under '2012 Annual General Meeting' on page 100.

100 **Johnson Matthey** Annual Report & Accounts 2012
Report of the Directors – Governance
Governance

Other Statutory Information

→ | Contents

2012 Annual General Meeting

The 2012 Annual General Meeting of the company will be held at 11.00 am on Wednesday 25th July 2012 at Merchant Taylors' Hall, 30 Threadneedle Street, London EC2R 8JB.

The notice of the 2012 Annual General Meeting is contained in the circular to shareholders accompanying this annual report, together with an explanation of the resolutions to be considered at the meeting. The notice of the 2012 Annual General Meeting will be published on the Investor Relations / Shareholder Centre / Annual General Meeting section of the company's website.

The business to be transacted at the meeting will include:

- To receive the company's annual accounts for the year ended 31st March 2012 together with the Report of the Directors and the auditor's report on those accounts

- To receive and approve the directors' remuneration report for the year ended 31st March 2012 and the auditor's report on the auditable part of the directors' remuneration report

- To declare a final dividend per ordinary share in respect of the year ended 31st March 2012

- To declare a special dividend per ordinary share and to effect a share consolidation

- To re-elect all directors retiring at the meeting who are seeking reappointment

- To reappoint KPMG Audit Plc as auditor of the company and to authorise the directors to determine its remuneration

- To authorise the company (and all companies which are subsidiaries of the company) in aggregate to make political donations to political parties or independent election candidates, to make political donations to political organisations other than political parties and to incur political expenditure, provided that the combined aggregate amount of donations made and expenditure incurred does not exceed £50,000

- To authorise the directors to exercise all the powers of the company to allot shares in the company and to grant rights to subscribe for, or to convert any security into, shares in the company up to certain limits

- To empower the directors to dis-apply pre-emption rights when allotting equity securities for cash, subject to certain limits

- To authorise the company to make market purchases of its own ordinary shares, subject to certain limits and conditions

- To permit a general meeting of the company, other than an annual general meeting, to be called on not less than 14 clear days' notice.

A member entitled to attend and vote at the meeting is entitled to appoint a proxy to exercise all or any of his or her rights to attend and to speak and vote on his or her behalf at the meeting. A member may appoint more than one proxy in relation to the meeting provided that each proxy is appointed to exercise the rights attached to a different share or shares held by that member. A proxy need not be a member of the company.

Dividends

The interim dividend of 15.0 pence per share (2011 12.5 pence) was paid in February 2012.

The directors recommend a final dividend of 40.0 pence per share in respect of the year ended 31st March 2012 (2011 33.5 pence), making a total for the year of 55.0 pence per share (2011 46.0 pence), payable on 17th August 2012 to shareholders on the register at the close of business on 3rd August 2012.

At the 2012 Annual General Meeting a resolution will be proposed to declare a special dividend of 100.0 pence per share and to approve a share consolidation. Full information on the proposed special dividend and share consolidation is contained in the circular to shareholders in respect of the 2012 Annual General Meeting accompanying this annual report.

Other than as referred to under 'Employee Share Schemes' on page 102, during the year ended 31st March 2012 and from that date up to the date of publication of this annual report there were no arrangements under which a shareholder has waived or agreed to waive any dividends nor any agreement by a shareholder to waive future dividends.

Dividend Payments and DRIP

Dividends can be paid directly into shareholders' bank accounts. A Dividend Reinvestment Plan (DRIP) is also available. This allows shareholders to purchase additional shares in the company with their dividend payment. Further information and a mandate can be obtained from the company's registrars, Equiniti, whose details are set out on page 175 and on the Investor Relations section of the company's website.

Share Capital and Control

Capital Structure

The issued share capital of the company at 31st March 2012 was 214,675,736 ordinary shares of £1.00 each (excluding treasury shares). The company did not allot any shares during the year ended 31st March 2012.

As at 31st March 2012, the company held 5,997,877 treasury shares. There were no purchases, sales or transfers of treasury shares during the year ended 31st March 2012.

Purchase by the Company of its Own Shares

At the 2011 Annual General Meeting, shareholders renewed the company's authority to make market purchases of up to 21,467,573 ordinary shares representing 10% of the issued share capital of the company (excluding treasury shares) as at 1st June 2011. This authority subsisted at 31st March 2012.

During the year ended 31st March 2012 and from that date up to the date of publication of this annual report, the company did not make any purchases of its own shares or propose to purchase its own shares (either through the market or by an offer made to all shareholders or otherwise), nor did the company acquire any of its own shares other than by purchase. Since 31st March 2012 the company has not effected any purchases of its own shares, entered into any options to purchase its own shares or entered into any contracts to make such purchases (including transactions made through the market or by an offer made to all shareholders or otherwise).

At the 2012 Annual General Meeting the board will again seek shareholders' approval to renew the annual authority for the company to make purchases of its own shares through the market.

Rights and Obligations Attaching to Shares

The holders of ordinary shares in the company are entitled to receive dividends when declared, to receive the company's annual report, to attend and speak at general meetings of the company, to appoint proxies and to exercise voting rights.

As at 31st March 2012 and as at the date of publication of this annual report, except as referred to below, there are no restrictions on the transfer of ordinary shares in the company, no limitations on the holding of securities and no requirements to obtain the approval of the company, or of other holders of securities in the company, for a transfer of securities.

The directors may, in certain circumstances, refuse to register the transfer of a share in certificated form which is not fully paid up, where the instrument of transfer does not comply with the requirements of the company's Articles of Association, or if entitled to do so under the Uncertificated Securities Regulations 2001. The directors may also refuse to register a transfer of ordinary shares in certificated form, which represent 0.25% or more of the issued share capital of the company, following the failure by the member or any other person appearing to be interested in the shares to provide the company with information requested under section 793 of the Companies Act 2006 (the 2006 Act).

No person holds securities in the company carrying any special rights with regard to control of the company. There are no restrictions on voting rights (including any limitations on voting rights of holders of a given percentage or number of votes or deadlines for exercising voting rights) except that a shareholder has no right to vote in respect of a share unless all sums due in respect of that share are fully paid. There are no arrangements by which, with the company's cooperation, financial rights carried by shares in the company are held by a person other than the holder of the shares. As at 31st March 2012 and as at the date of publication of this annual report, there are no agreements known to the company between holders of securities that may result in restrictions on the transfer of securities or on voting rights.

Nominees and Liens

During the year ended 31st March 2012 and from that date up to the date of publication of this annual report:

- No shares in the company were acquired by the company's nominee, or by a person with financial assistance from the company, where the company has a beneficial interest in the shares (and there was no person who acquired shares in the company in a previous financial year in its capacity as the company's nominee or with financial assistance from the company); and

- The company did not obtain or hold a lien or other charge over its own shares.

Allotment of Securities for Cash and Placing of Equity Securities

During the year ended 31st March 2012 and from that date up to the date of publication of this annual report, the company has not allotted, nor has any major subsidiary undertaking of the company allotted, equity securities for cash (other than pursuant to an open offer, a rights issue or any issue specifically authorised by shareholders or otherwise). During the year ended 31st March 2012 and from that date up to the date of publication of this annual report the company has not participated in any placing of equity securities.

Listing of the Company's Shares

The company's shares have Premium Listing on the London Stock Exchange and trade as part of the FTSE 100 index under the symbol JMAT.

American Depositary Receipt Programme

The company has a sponsored Level 1 American Depositary Receipt (ADR) programme which BNY Mellon administers and for which it acts as Depositary. Each ADR represents two ordinary shares of the company. The ADRs trade on the US over-the-counter market under the symbol JMPLY. When dividends are paid to shareholders, the Depositary converts such dividends into US dollars, net of fees and expenses, and distributes the net amount to ADR holders. Contact details for BNY Mellon are set out on page 175.

102 **Johnson Matthey** Annual Report & Accounts 2012
Report of the Directors – Governance
Governance

Other Statutory Information continued

Employee Share Schemes

At 31st March 2012, 4,485 current and former employees, representing approximately 45% of employees worldwide, were shareholders in the company through the group's employee share schemes. Through these schemes, current and former employees held 3,803,914 ordinary shares (1.77% of issued share capital, excluding treasury shares). As at 31st March 2012, 282 current and former employees held options over 758,867 ordinary shares through the company's executive share option schemes. Also as at 31st March 2012, 2,676,241 ordinary shares had been allocated but had not yet vested under the company's long term incentive plan to 1,007 current and former employees.

Shares acquired by employees through the company's employee share schemes rank equally with the other shares in issue and have no special rights. Voting rights in respect of shares held through the company's employee share schemes are not exercisable directly by employees. However, employees can direct the trustee of the schemes to exercise voting rights on their behalf. The trustees of the company's employee share ownership trust (ESOT) have waived their rights to dividends on shares held by the ESOT which have not yet vested unconditionally in employees.

Interests in Voting Rights

The UK Financial Services Authority's (FSA) Disclosure and Transparency Rules (DTRs)

set out certain notification requirements in respect of voting rights in listed companies. In summary, a person must notify the issuer of securities of the percentage of its voting rights he or she holds as shareholder (or holds or is deemed to hold through his or her direct or indirect holding of certain financial instruments) if, as a result of an acquisition or disposal of shares in the company or financial instruments, the percentage of those voting rights reaches, exceeds or falls below certain thresholds. In respect of the company, the threshold is 3% (and each 1% threshold above 3%, up to 100%).

Information provided to the company pursuant to the FSA's DTRs is published on a Regulatory Information Service and on the Media / News / Regulatory News section of the company's website.

The following information had been disclosed to the company under the FSA's DTRs in respect of notifiable interests in the voting rights in the company's issued share capital exceeding the 3% notification threshold:

	Nature of holding [1]	Total voting rights	% of total voting rights [2]
As at 31st March 2012:			
BlackRock, Inc.	Indirect	21,440,270	9.99%
	Financial Instrument (CFD)	25,683	0.01%
Ameriprise Financial, Inc.	Direct	264,202	0.12%
	Indirect	10,512,731	4.89%
Lloyds Banking Group plc	Indirect	10,731,602	4.99%
FIL Limited	Indirect	10,516,934	4.89%
	Financial Instrument (CFD)	43,890	0.02%
Legal & General Group Plc	Direct	8,581,762	3.99%
From 31st March 2012 to 31st May 2012:			
BlackRock, Inc.	Indirect	21,262,792	9.90%
	Financial Instrument (CFD)	269,490	0.13%

(1) A person has an 'Indirect' holding of securities if they are held on its behalf or it is able to secure that rights carried by them are exercised in accordance with its instructions.

(2) Total voting rights attaching to the issued ordinary share capital of the company (excluding treasury shares) at the date of disclosure as notified to the company.

Other than as stated above, as far as the company is aware, there is no person with a significant direct or indirect holding of securities in the company.

Contracts with Controlling Shareholders

There were no contracts of significance (as defined in the FSA's Listing Rules) subsisting during the year ended 31st March 2012 or from that date up to the date of publication of this annual report between any group undertaking and a controlling shareholder. There were no contracts for the provision of services to any group undertaking by a controlling shareholder subsisting during the year ended 31st March 2012 or from that date up to the date of publication of this annual report.

Directors

The following served as directors during the year ended 31st March 2012:

- Tim Stevenson
- Sir John Banham (retired 19th July 2011)
- Neil Carson
- Alan Ferguson
- Sir Thomas Harris
- Robert MacLeod
- Larry Pentz
- Michael Roney
- Bill Sandford
- Dorothy Thompson
- Alan Thomson (retired 19th July 2011)
- Robert Walvis (retired 19th July 2011).

The biographical details of all the directors serving at 31st March 2012, including details of their relevant experience and other significant commitments, are shown on page 83.

As announced on 22nd May 2012, Sir Thomas Harris will be retiring from the board at the close of the 2012 Annual General Meeting on 25th July 2012.

Appointment and Replacement of Directors

The rules about the appointment and replacement of directors are contained in the company's Articles of Association. The Articles of Association provide that the number of directors is not subject to any maximum but must not be less than six, unless otherwise determined by the company by ordinary resolution. Directors may be appointed by an ordinary resolution of the members or by a resolution of the directors.

Under the Articles of Association, a director appointed by the directors must retire at the next following annual general meeting and is not taken into account in determining the directors who are to retire by rotation at the meeting. Also under the company's Articles of Association, at least one third of the board must retire by rotation at each annual general meeting. Notwithstanding these provisions, the board has agreed that all directors will seek re-election at each annual general meeting in accordance with the Code. Accordingly, all directors (other than Sir Thomas Harris) will be offering themselves for re-election at the 2012 Annual General Meeting.

A director may be removed by a special resolution of the company. In addition, a director must automatically cease to be a director if (i) he or she ceases to be a director by virtue of any provision of the 2006 Act or he or she becomes prohibited by law from being a director, or (ii) he or she becomes bankrupt or makes any arrangement or composition with his or her creditors generally, or (iii) he or she is suffering from a mental disorder, or (iv) he or she resigns from his or her office by notice in writing to the company or, in the case of an executive director, the appointment is terminated or expires and the directors resolve that his or her office be vacated, or (v) he or she is absent for more than six consecutive months without permission of the directors from meetings of the directors and the directors resolve that his or her office be vacated, or (vi) he or she is requested in writing, or by electronic form, by all the other directors to resign.

The Company's Articles of Association

The company's Articles of Association are available on the Investor Relations / Corporate Governance section of the company's website. The company's Articles of Association may only be amended by a special resolution at a general meeting of the company.

Powers of the Directors

The powers of the directors are determined by the company's Articles of Association, UK legislation including the 2006 Act and any directions given by the company in general meeting.

The directors have been authorised by the company's Articles of Association to issue and allot ordinary shares and to make market purchases of its own shares. These powers are referred to shareholders for renewal at each annual general meeting. Any shares so purchased by the company may be cancelled or held as treasury shares. Further information is set out under 'Purchase by the Company of its Own Shares' on page 101.

The Interests of Directors in the Company's Shares

The interests of persons who were directors of the company at 31st March 2012, and their connected persons, in the issued shares of the company (or in derivatives or other financial instruments relating to such shares) as at that date notified or notifiable to the company under the FSA's DTRs are given in the Remuneration Report on pages 116 and 117. The Remuneration Report also sets out details of any changes in those interests between 31st March 2012 and 31st May 2012.

Directors' Interests in Contracts

Other than service contracts, no director had any interest in any material contract with any group company at any time during the year ended 31st March 2012 or from that date up to the date of publication of this annual report. There were no contracts of significance (as defined in the FSA's Listing Rules) subsisting during the year ended 31st March 2012 or from that date up to the date of publication of this annual report to which any group undertaking was a party and in which a director of the company is or was materially interested.

Change of Control

During the year ended 31st March 2012 and from that date up to the date of publication of this annual report there were no significant agreements to which the company or any subsidiary was or is a party that take effect, alter or terminate on a change of control of the company following a takeover bid.

However, the company and its subsidiaries were, during this period, and are, as at the date of publication of this annual report, party to a number of commercial agreements that may allow the counterparties to alter or terminate the agreements on a change of control of the company following a takeover bid.

Other than the matters referred to below, these are not deemed by the company to be significant in terms of their potential effect on the group as a whole.

The group has a number of loan notes and borrowing facilities which may require prepayment of principal and payment of accrued interest and breakage costs if there is change of control of the company. The group has also entered into a series of financial instruments to hedge its currency, interest rate and metal price exposures which provide for termination or alteration if a change of control of the company materially weakens the creditworthiness of the group.

The company is party to a marketing agreement with a subsidiary of Anglo American Platinum Limited, originally entered into in 1992, under which the company was appointed as sales and marketing agent for refined platinum group metals worldwide excluding the US and the company agreed to provide certain marketing services. The agreement contains provisions under which the counterparty may have the right to terminate the agreement on a change of control of the company.

The executive directors' service contracts each contain a provision to the effect that if the contract is terminated by the company within one year after a change of control of the company, the company will pay to the director as liquidated damages an amount equivalent to one year's gross basic salary and other contractual benefits less the period of any notice given by the company to the director.

The rules of the company's employee share schemes set out the consequences of a change of control of the company on participants' rights under the schemes. Generally such rights will vest and become exercisable on a change of control subject to the satisfaction of relevant performance conditions.

During the year ended 31st March 2012 and from that date up to the date of publication of this annual report there were no other agreements between the company or any subsidiary and its or their directors or employees providing for compensation for loss of office or employment (whether through resignation, purported redundancy or otherwise) that occurs because of a takeover bid.

Other Statutory Information continued

Disabled Persons

A description of the company's policy applied during the year ended 31st March 2012 and from that date up to the date of publication of this annual report relating to the recruitment, employment and training of disabled employees can be found on page 81.

Employee Involvement

A description of the action taken by the company during the year ended 31st March 2012 and from that date up to the date of publication of this annual report relating to employee involvement can be found on pages 48 to 59.

Use of Financial Instruments

Information on the group's financial risk management objectives and policies and its exposure to credit risk, liquidity risk, interest rate risk and foreign currency risk can be found on pages 155 to 160.

Branches

The company and its subsidiaries have established branches in a number of different countries in which they operate.

Policy on Payment of Commercial Debts

The group's policy in relation to the payment of all suppliers and persons who may become suppliers is set out in its Group Control Manual, which is distributed to all group operations. The group's policy is that payment should be made within the credit terms agreed with the supplier, subject to the supplier having performed its obligations under the relevant contract. It is not the group's policy to follow any other specific code or standard on payment practice in respect of its suppliers.

At 31st March 2012, the company's aggregate level of 'creditor days' amounted to 5 days. Creditor days are calculated by dividing the aggregate of the amounts which were outstanding as trade payables at 31st March 2012 by the aggregate of the amounts the company was invoiced by suppliers during the year ended 31st March 2012 and multiplying by 365 to express the ratio as a number of days.

Charitable Donations

During the year ended 31st March 2012 the group donated £645,000 (2011 £517,000) to charitable organisations worldwide, of which £378,000 (2011 £320,000) was in the UK. Further information on donations made by the group worldwide are given on page 58.

Political Donations and Expenditure

It is the policy of the group not to make political donations or incur political expenditure.

Under applicable UK legislation (the 2006 Act), political donations by the company to any political parties, other political organisations or independent election candidates or the incurring by the company of political expenditure are prohibited unless authorised by shareholders in advance. Under the legislation, the terms political donation, political party, political organisation and political expenditure are capable of wide interpretation. Sponsorship, subscriptions, payment of expenses, paid leave for employees fulfilling public duties and support for bodies representing the business community in policy review or reform may fall within these definitions.

During the year ended 31st March 2012:

- No political donations were made by the company or its subsidiaries to any EU political party, to any other EU political organisation or to any EU independent election candidate (2011 £ nil);

- No EU political expenditure was incurred by the company or its subsidiaries (2011 £ nil); and

- No contributions were made by the company or any subsidiary to any non-EU political party within the meaning of the 2006 Act (2011 £ nil).

The term 'EU' as used above applies to parties, organisations and independent election candidates that seek public office in any EU Member State and to expenditure incurred in their support or in relation to any referendum held under the laws of an EU Member State. 'Non-EU political party' means any political party which carries on, or proposes to carry on, its activities wholly outside EU Member States.

The company has no intention either now or in the future of making any political donation or incurring any political expenditure in respect of any political party, political organisation or independent election candidate. However, to avoid inadvertently contravening the 2006 Act, the board is proposing at the 2012 Annual General Meeting to renew the authority, first granted by shareholders at the annual general meeting in 2004, and renewed at each subsequent annual general meeting, for the company to make political donations and to incur political expenditure. The proposed

authority will be subject to an overall aggregate limit on donations and expenditure of £50,000. As permitted under the 2006 Act, the resolution will extend to political donations made, or political expenditure incurred, by any subsidiaries of the company.

Financial Assistance Received from Government

The group received no financial assistance from government during the year.

Auditors and Disclosure of Information

In accordance with section 489 of the 2006 Act, resolutions are to be proposed at the 2012 Annual General Meeting for the reappointment of KPMG Audit Plc as auditor of the company and to authorise the directors to determine its remuneration.

So far as each person serving as a director of the company at the date this Report of the Directors was approved by the board is aware, there is no relevant audit information (that is information needed by the auditor in connection with preparing its report) of which the company's auditor is unaware. Each such director hereby confirms that he or she has taken all the steps that he or she ought to have taken as a director in order to make himself or herself aware of any relevant audit information and to establish that the company's auditor is aware of that information.

Management Report

The Report of the Directors is the "management report" for the purposes of the Financial Services Authority's Disclosure and Transparency Rules (DTR 4.1.8R).

The Report of the Directors was approved by the board on 6th June 2012 and is signed on its behalf by:

S. Farrant

Simon Farrant
Company Secretary

Nomination Committee Report

Tim Stevenson
Chairman of the Nomination
Committee

"I am pleased to present
the Report of the
Nomination Committee
for 2012."

Role

The terms of reference of the Nomination
Committee are summarised on page 89.
The terms of reference can be found in the
Investor Relations / Corporate Governance
section of the company's website or may
be obtained from the Company Secretary.

Composition

The Nomination Committee comprises all
the independent non-executive directors
together with the group Chairman. The
quorum necessary for the transaction of
business is two, each of whom must be
an independent non-executive director.
Biographical details of the independent
non-executive directors and the group
Chairman are set out on page 83. Their
remuneration is set out on page 114.

The group Chairman acts as the
Chairman of the Nomination Committee,
although he does not chair the Committee
when it is dealing with the matter of
succession to the chairmanship of the
company. A non-executive director may not
chair the Committee when it is dealing with a
matter relating to that non-executive director.

Only members of the Committee have
the right to attend committee meetings.
However, the Chief Executive, the Group
Director, Human Resources and Environment,
Health and Safety, external advisers and
others may be invited to attend for all or part
of any meeting as and when appropriate.

The Company Secretary is secretary
to the Nomination Committee.

The Committee has the authority to
seek any information that it requires from
any officer or employee of the company or
its subsidiaries. In connection with its duties,
the Committee is also authorised by the
board to take such independent advice
(including legal or other professional advice,
at the company's expense) as it considers
necessary. This includes requesting
information from, or commissioning
investigations by, external advisers.

Meeting Frequency

Meetings are held on an ad hoc basis,
usually immediately after a board meeting,
but on such other occasions as may be
needed.

Main Activities in the Year

The Nomination Committee met twice during the year ended 31st March 2012, on the following dates, and it conducted the following business:

Meeting date	Main activities
10th May 2011	• Agreed to recommend to the board the appointment of Michael Roney as Senior Independent Director and as Chairman of the Management Development and Remuneration Committee (MDRC) with effect from the close of the annual general meeting in July 2011 following the retirements of Alan Thomson and Robert Walvis respectively
29th March 2012	• Reviewed board size, structure and composition. The Chairman reported that Sir Thomas Harris would be retiring from the board at the close of the 2012 Annual General Meeting
	• Considered the process for the search for a new non-executive director, including the appointment of external search consultants
	• Discussed the selection criteria for the proposed appointment of a new non-executive director

Since 31st March 2012, the Nomination Committee met once, on the following date, and it conducted the following business:

Meeting date	Main activities
31st May 2012	• Reviewed progress in respect of the search for a new non-executive director, including the appointment of external search consultants

Boardroom Diversity

The search for board candidates is
conducted, and appointments made, on
merit, against objective selection criteria
having due regard, amongst other things,
to the benefits of diversity on the board,
including gender. Diversity is considered by
the Nomination Committee on behalf of the
board in considering board composition and
in its process for making board appointments,

including in setting selection criteria. This is
referred to further in the board's statement
on board diversity dated 28th November
2011 which is published in the Investor
Relations / Corporate Governance section
of the company's website and is set out on
page 92.

In respect of the proposed recruitment
of a new non-executive director, at its
meeting on 29th March 2012 the Committee

considered a specification which set out
certain essential characteristics for the role,
while stating the desirability of diversity.

On behalf of the Nomination Committee:

Tim Stevenson

Tim Stevenson
Chairman of the Nomination Committee

Audit Committee Report

Alan Ferguson
Chairman of the Audit
Committee

"I am pleased to
present the Report
of the Audit Committee
for 2012."

Role

The terms of reference of the Audit Committee, which were updated during the financial year, are summarised on pages 89 and 90. The terms of reference can be found in the Investor Relations / Corporate Governance section of the company's website or may be obtained from the Company Secretary.

Composition

The Audit Committee comprises all the independent non-executive directors. Biographical details of the independent non-executive directors are set out on page 83. Their remuneration is set out on page 114.

Alan Ferguson replaced Alan Thomson as Chairman of the Audit Committee in July 2011 on his retirement from the board. Details of Alan Ferguson's previous roles, experience and qualifications are set out on page 83.

The group Chairman, the Chief Executive, the Group Finance Director, the Head of Internal Audit and Risk and the external auditor attend Audit Committee meetings by invitation. The Committee also meets separately with the Head of Internal Audit and Risk and with the external auditor without management being present.

The Company Secretary is secretary to the Audit Committee.

Main Activities in the Year

The Audit Committee met four times during the year ended 31st March 2012, on the following dates, and it conducted the following business:

Meeting date	Main activities
26th May 2011	• Reviewed the group's preliminary announcement, draft report and accounts for the financial year
	• Reviewed papers on key accounting judgments, on credit control and credit risk and on litigation affecting the group
	• Considered reports from the external auditor on its audit and its review of the accounts including accounting policies and areas of judgment, and its comments on risk management and control matters
	• Met with both internal audit and the external auditor without management being present
18th July 2011	• Reviewed the group's interim management statement for the first quarter of the financial year
	• Considered reports on internal controls from the internal auditors
	• Reviewed the proposed external audit fees and audit scope for the financial year
	• Assessed the performance of the external auditor. The review of the external auditor was used to confirm the appropriateness of its reappointment and included assessment of its independence, qualification, expertise and resources, and effectiveness of the audit process
	• Recommended to the board the reappointment of KPMG Audit Plc as auditor
	• Considered reports on IT strategy and risks from the Group Director, Information Technology
21st November 2011	• Reviewed the group's half year results and announcement and the external auditor's review
	• Reviewed papers on key accounting judgments, on credit control and credit risk and on litigation affecting the group
	• Considered reports on the group's treasury activities from the Group Treasurer
	• Considered reports on internal controls from the internal auditors and group security
	• Recommended to the board the approval of revised terms of reference for the Committee
	• Assessed the performance of the internal auditors

Main Activities in the Year (continued)

Meeting date	Main activities
31st January 2012	• Reviewed the group's interim management statement for the third quarter of the financial year
	• Reviewed the group's risk register, reports on controls from the internal auditors and group security and reports from management on the effectiveness of the group's systems for internal financial control and risk management
	• Considered internal audit and security resource requirements and approved the internal audit and group security plans for 2012/13
	• Reviewed metal trading limits and controls
	• Received an update from the external auditor on accounting, reporting and governance developments
	• Reviewed non-audit services provided by the external auditor during the financial year to date and the associated authorisation policy
	• Reviewed the group's whistleblowing procedures and the matters raised during the year
	• Approved changes to the Group Control Manual, including changes to the group authority levels
	• Received and considered a presentation on the risks facing the Process Technologies business from its finance director

Since 31st March 2012, the Audit Committee has met once, on the following date, and it conducted the following business:

Meeting date	Main activities
31st May 2012	• Reviewed the group's preliminary announcement, draft report and accounts for the financial year and the group's assessment of going concern
	• Considered the reappointment of the external auditor for the following year
	• Considered reports on internal controls from the internal auditors and group security
	• Met with both internal audit and the external auditor without management being present

Independence of External Auditor

Both the board and the external auditor have for many years had safeguards in place to avoid the possibility that the auditor's objectivity and independence could be compromised. The issue of auditor independence is taken very seriously and is reviewed annually. This year some changes have been made to the senior audit team. A second partner has been introduced partly to provide greater senior level coverage but also to provide some continuity when the signing partner rotates in 2013.

Our policy in respect of services provided by the external auditor is as follows:

• Audit related services – the external auditor is invited to provide services which, in its position as auditor, it must or is best placed to undertake. This includes formalities relating to borrowings, shareholder and other circulars, various other regulatory reports and work in respect of acquisitions and disposals

• Tax compliance and advice – the auditor may provide such services where it is best suited, but otherwise such work is put out to tender

• Other services – these may not be provided where precluded by ethical standards or where we believe it would compromise audit independence and objectivity.

To the extent consistent with the above policy, services likely to cost less than £25,000 may be approved by the Group Finance Director. Services above this amount must be approved by the Chairman of the Audit Committee, unless they are likely to be in excess of £100,000, when they must be approved by the Audit Committee.

The split between audit and non-audit fees for the year ended 31st March 2012 and information on the nature of non-audit fees appear in note 5 on the accounts.

Internal Audit

Internal audit independently reviews the risks and control processes operated by management. It carries out independent audits in accordance with an internal audit plan which is agreed with the Audit Committee before the start of the financial year. As part of this process the Committee looks at the resources devoted to the function to ensure they are adequate to deliver the plan.

The plan provides a high degree of financial and geographical coverage and devotes significant effort to the review of the risk management framework surrounding the major business risks.

Internal audit reports include recommendations to improve internal controls together with agreed management action plans to resolve the issues raised. Internal audit follows up the implementation of recommendations and reports progress to senior management and the Audit Committee.

The Audit Committee reviews the findings of the internal audits completed during the year.

The effectiveness of the internal audit function is reviewed and discussed on an annual basis.

On behalf of the Audit Committee:

Alan Ferguson
Chairman of the Audit Committee

Remuneration Report

Remuneration Report to Shareholders for the
year ended 31st March 2012

Michael Roney
Chairman of the Management
Development and
Remuneration Committee

→ Contents

Introduction to the Remuneration Report

The overriding responsibility of a remuneration committee is to create
the remuneration policies and practices that achieve the best value for
shareholders. Pay and incentives have to be set at the right level to
attract and retain good management and to fully incentivise outstanding
management performance, but at levels that are in line with the sector in
general, and that provide a fair return to shareholders.

This year, we recognise that the remuneration of senior executives is
under more scrutiny than ever before and we are mindful of the
principles of remuneration published by stakeholder representatives
such as the Association of British Insurers (ABI) and of the potential
revisions to governance outlined by the Department of Business,
Innovation and Skills. This report seeks to be open and transparent in
reporting on remuneration and on the basis for remuneration, both
historically and going forward.

The remuneration committee is also charged with ensuring that the
long term interests of the company and shareholders are taken fully into
account, both in remuneration structure and in ensuring that good
processes exist for management development and succession planning.
This is particularly important in a high technology company where R&D
investment is required many years before those ideas come to
commercial fruition. Therefore we aim to build remuneration policies and
structures that reward performance over the long term and that
encourage directors and employees to develop long term careers with
the company.

I believe that the consistent results over the last decade, the
consistency and success of a largely internally developed management
team and the very strong year we have experienced in 2011/12 indicate
that we have good policies and practices in place. However, we will
continue to review all aspects of remuneration, management
development and succession planning to ensure that shareholders'
interests continue to be fully represented.

Michael J. Roney

Michael Roney

Terms of Reference and Constitution of the Management Development and Remuneration Committee (MDRC)

The Management Development and
Remuneration Committee is a committee
of the board and comprises all the
independent non-executive directors of the
company as set out on page 83 and the
group Chairman. The Chairman of the
Committee was Robert Walvis until his
retirement on 19th July 2011, after which
Michael Roney took over the role.

The Committee's terms of reference
include determination on behalf of the board
of fair remuneration for the Chief Executive,
the other executive directors and the group
Chairman (in which case the group
Chairman does not participate).

Non-executive directors' remuneration
is determined by the board, within the limits
prescribed by the company's Articles of
Association. The remuneration consists of
fees, which are set following advice taken
from independent consultants and are
reviewed at regular intervals.

In addition, the Committee assists the
board in ensuring that the company has well
developed plans for management
succession, including the recruitment and
development of senior management, along
with appropriate remuneration policies to
ensure that management are retained and
motivated.

The Group Director, Human Resources
and Environment, Health and Safety
(HR and EHS) acts as secretary to the
Committee. The full terms of reference
of the Committee are available on the
company's website at www.matthey.com
in the Investor Relations / Corporate
Governance section.

Activities of the MDRC

The Committee meets at least three times per year. The principal activities are set out in the terms of reference and the timetable for specific reviews and approval processes is set out below. In 2011/12 the committee met on four occasions.

Table of Remuneration Committee Activities

Meeting	Annual agenda items	Other agenda items
May	Review of CEC and senior managers' salary increases Review of executive directors' salary and bonus Review of pay within the group Approval of the Remuneration Report	
May or July	Approval of executive directors' salary and bonus Approval of LTIP allocation Approval of LTIP vesting Review of other senior managers' salary increases and bonus payments	Chairman's fees (every three years)
November	Management development and succession planning Review of the share incentive plan Update on remuneration issues Review of remuneration policy	
March	Approval of bonus scheme rules Review of the share incentive plan	Major review of structure of executive remuneration (every three years)

Johnson Matthey – Executive Remuneration Policy

Key Goals of Policy and Balance Between Fixed and Variable Remuneration

The key goal of the remuneration policy remains to obtain the best value for shareholders. This requires that the pay and benefits structure is competitive within the sector, whilst simultaneously providing stretching targets that require significant outperformance to maximise incentive payments.

Basic salaries are the primary element of remuneration and the general policy is to set basic salaries at the level required to retain and motivate, taking into account individual performance, the complexity and scale of the director's duties, length of time in post and taking due cognisance of market levels in the appropriate sector. The Committee recognises that there is a competitive market for successful executives and therefore benchmark data are regarded as relevant background information. However, it is not the policy of the Committee to set salaries directly in line with that data, or in line with benchmarks mathematically derived from that data.

With regard to variable pay, the Committee believes that the provision of appropriate rewards for superior performance is vital to the continued growth of the business.

Further incentives in variable pay are therefore to be structured in a way that provides the incentives for effective short and long term management and creates the opportunity for enhanced remuneration but only for outstanding performance.

The details of the structures devised for short term bonuses and long term incentives are described in the subsequent section of this Remuneration Report.

The Committee further considers the balance between fixed elements of remuneration, such as basic salaries, and the performance related aspects of the remuneration package and seeks to ensure that any earnings beyond basic salaries are fully reflected in increased shareholder value through higher profit and earnings per share.

It is also an element of the policy that executive directors are encouraged to build up over time, and hold, a shareholding in the company equal to at least their basic salary with a view to ensuring that their interests remain fully aligned with those of the shareholders. Details of directors' shareholdings are set out on page 116.

Global Pay and Employment Policies Across the Group

The remuneration policy of the group remains consistent in all countries and at all levels of the company with the overriding consideration being to pay competitive salaries in line with the appropriate country and sector and to provide opportunities to increase earnings to higher levels through superior performance. Almost all Johnson Matthey employees are able to earn bonuses based on business performance and around 900 employees are able to earn bonuses based on individual, team and business performance. Around 900 employees globally are eligible to participate in the Johnson Matthey Long Term Incentive Plan (LTIP).

Executive Pay in the Context of General Earnings Across the Group

In setting executive directors' basic salaries, annual bonus awards and LTIP allocations, the Committee is made aware of comparative data relating to the pay and benefits of other group employees. International data provided by the Hay Group is also utilised in considering and determining local settlements.

Policy with Regard to Remuneration Advisers

In determining the remuneration structure, the Committee appoints and receives advice from independent remuneration consultants on the pay and incentive arrangements prevailing in comparably sized industrial companies in each country in which Johnson Matthey has operations. During the year, such advice was received from the Hay Group, which also provided advice on job evaluation, and PricewaterhouseCoopers LLP. PricewaterhouseCoopers LLP also provided expatriate tax advice and other tax advice, tax audit work, completion of overseas tax returns, advice on set up of new overseas operations, some overseas payroll services and a review of some financial controls.

A statement regarding the use of remuneration consultants for the year ended 31st March 2012 is available on the company's website at www.matthey.com in the Investor Relations / Corporate Governance section.

Remuneration Report continued

The Committee also receives recommendations from the Chief Executive on the remuneration of those reporting to him as well as advice from the Group Director, HR and EHS.

This is the general remuneration policy of the Committee and the details of the exact remuneration structure are given in the subsequent section of this report.

Executive Remuneration Practices and Rules 2011/12

In 2010/11 a full review of remuneration was carried out, followed by a shareholder consultation in early 2011. The new practices and rules were described in last year's annual report and are now used in the calculation of variable pay and bonuses for the executive directors.

Remuneration Basis with Effect from 1st April 2011: the Rules as they Stand

Executive directors' remuneration consists of three principal elements: these being basic pay, annual bonus and a long term incentive plan. The details of these are set out below. Information on pension arrangements for the executive directors is also included in this section.

Basic Salary

The general policy regarding basic salaries has been set out on page 109, indicating that there are a number of determinants in arriving at the basic salary award. These key determinants are described in more detail below.

The first determinant is the performance of the individual executive. Performance is considered against a broad set of parameters including financial, environmental, social and governance issues.

The second factor taken into account is the length of time that the executive director has been in post. For example, where promotion has taken place, the salary may initially be set at a lower level than the outgoing director. This can then give rise to higher than normal salary increases while the director gathers experience and moves towards the job norm.

The third factor is a judgment as to whether the level of basic pay remains competitive and appropriate in the relevant comparator group. For the purposes of benchmarking, the remuneration comparator used by the Committee during 2011/12 for executive directors was drawn from FTSE 100 and 250 industrial and service companies (excluding the oil and financial sectors) with market capitalisation of around £4.8 billion and with over 40% of revenue coming from overseas. Further independent benchmark data was sourced from the Hay Group. Benchmark data are regarded as relevant background information for the Committee, but it is not its policy to set salaries directly in line with that data, or with benchmarks mathematically derived from that data. Basic salary is normally reviewed on 1st August each year.

LTIP

The LTIP is designed to incentivise above average performance and growth over the longer term. Shares allocated under the terms of the LTIP (which also applies to the group's 900 senior and middle managers) are released on the third anniversary of the allocation date with the release being subject to targets based on compound annual growth in the company's earnings per share (EPS). Current rules require that to achieve the maximum release of allocated shares, a compound annual growth in underlying EPS of 15% must be achieved over the three year period. The Committee strongly believes that EPS remains the best overall measure of the performance of the group across all strategic goals. The Committee has considered setting broader targets for LTIP in areas such as sustainability and new product development, but is satisfied that the full total of successful and long term focused company activities are best encapsulated in the simple and transparent measure of compound annual growth in EPS over a longer period.

Prior to 2011, the bases for share allocations were 150% of basic annual salary for the Chief Executive and 120% for executive directors. In 2011, in accordance with the review published in the 2011 annual report, share allocations of 175% of basic annual salary for the Chief Executive and 140% of annual salary for executive directors were made. These allocations remain within the LTIP rules, as approved by shareholders at the 2007 Annual General Meeting, which allow for share allocations of up to a maximum of 200% of basic annual salary each year, allowing the Committee to take account of evolution of market practice if required.

The minimum release, of 15% of the allocated shares, requires underlying EPS growth of 6% compound per annum over the three year period. For the maximum release of 100% of the allocation, underlying EPS must have grown by at least 15% compound per annum over the three year performance period. The number of allocated shares released will vary on a straight line basis between these points. There is no retesting of the performance target and so allocations will lapse if underlying EPS growth is less than 6% compound per annum over the three year performance period.

In 2009, following consultation with major shareholders, the Committee approved an adjustment to the performance targets for one year only to reflect the market conditions prevailing at the time of allocation. For the 2009 allocation only, the minimum release, of 15% of the allocation, requires underlying EPS growth of 3% compound per annum over the three year period, with no retesting of the performance target. For the maximum release of 100% of the allocation, underlying EPS must have grown by at least 10% compound per annum over the three year performance period. As a result of this adjustment, the level of award was reduced to 120% of basic annual salary for the Chief Executive and 100% for executive directors for that year. Also in 2009, there was a one-off allocation of 170% of basic salary to the then newly appointed Group Finance Director to ensure close alignment of his objectives with those of shareholders.

Although growth in underlying EPS is the primary financial measure, it is also a key objective of the company to achieve earnings growth only in the context of a good performance on return on invested capital (ROIC). Accordingly, the Committee is required to make an assessment of the group's ROIC over the performance period to ensure underlying EPS growth has been achieved with ROIC in line with the group's planned expectations. The Committee may scale back vesting to the extent that ROIC has not developed appropriately.

Annual Bonus

The annual bonus is complementary to the longer term LTIP award and provides a strong incentive for a short term delivery of budget in the relevant year. Whilst the LTIP target encourages business managers and the executive directors to set ambitious three year targets, the annual bonus allows the board to ensure that those plans are properly reflected in stretching but achievable annual budgets. The annual bonus is then based strictly on performance against budget, requiring that the group's budgeted underlying profit before tax (PBT) is exceeded by 10% to release the maximum payment.

The maximum bonus is set as a percentage of basic salary under the terms of the company's Executive Compensation Plan. As with the LTIP, this plan applies not only to the executive directors, but to around 200 of the group's most senior executives.

Annual Bonus Rules

	Bonus awarded at threshold (95% of budget) (% of salary)	Bonus awarded at target (% of salary)	Bonus awarded at 110% of budget (maximum award) (% of salary)	% of awarded bonus deferred
Chief Executive	15%	75%	150%	33.3%
Other executive directors	15%	62.5%	125%	20%

Setting the Annual Bonus Target

In order for the annual bonus to provide a strong short term performance incentive, it is key that the budgeted profitability is set at an achievable but demanding target. The board is responsible for agreeing the targeted performance and takes into account the detailed business climate for each operating division of the group. Commercial sensitivity prevents the advance publication of targets, but further information regarding historical performance is available in the following table.

Retrospective Data on Annual Budget Targets

Year	Budgeted underlying PBT (£ million)	Actual underlying PBT (£ million)	% of budget	Chief Executive's bonus (% of salary)	Executive directors' bonus (% of salary)	Vara consensus* (£ million)	Actual underlying PBT growth
2011/12	406.0	426.0	104.9%	111.75%	93.13%	382	23%

* The Vara consensus referred to is the published data regarding industry analysts' performance expectations for Johnson Matthey, as expressed at the start of the budget year in question. For example, the consensus for 2011/12 is that published in March 2011.

An annual bonus payment of 75% of basic salary (prevailing at 31st March) is paid to the Chief Executive and 62.5% of basic salary is paid to executive directors if the group meets the annual budget. This bonus may rise on a straight line basis to a maximum 150% of basic salary for the Chief Executive and 125% for executive directors if 110% of budgeted underlying PBT is achieved. Underlying PBT must reach 95% of budget for a minimum bonus of 15% of salary to be payable.

For the Chief Executive, 33.3% of the bonus payable is awarded as shares and deferred for a period of three years. For other executive directors, 20% of the bonus payable is awarded as shares and deferred for three years. The Committee is entitled to claw back the deferred element in cases of misstatement or misconduct or other relevant reason as determined by the Committee.

The Committee retains discretion in awarding annual bonuses and seeks to ensure that the incentive structure for senior management does not raise environmental, social and governance risks by inadvertently motivating irresponsible behaviour. The Committee is fully prepared to utilise this discretion where management has failed to properly address such risks.

Other Benefits

The other benefits available to the executive directors are private medical insurance, a company car and membership of the group's employee share incentive plans which are open to all employees in the countries in which the group operates such plans.

Service Contracts

The executive directors are employed on contracts subject to one year's notice at any time. On early termination of their contracts the directors would normally be entitled to 12 months' salary and benefits. The contracts of service of the executive directors and the terms and conditions of appointment of the non-executive directors are available for inspection at the company's registered office during normal business hours and at the forthcoming annual general meeting.

Pensions – General Description of Arrangements

The company provides executive directors with membership of its UK HM Revenue & Customs registered occupational pension scheme – the Johnson Matthey Employees Pension Scheme (JMEPS). The benefits provided to executive directors through JMEPS are the same as for all other UK employees, namely a defined benefit retirement pension, dependents' and life assurance benefits plus a top-up defined contribution account. There have been no significant changes to the JMEPS rules during 2011/12.

The pension earned in respect of service up to 31st March 2010 is based on a member's final salary at the point of retirement, or earlier date of withdrawal from employment. Pension earned in respect of service from 1st April 2010 is based on the member's career average revalued earnings. Members are not required to pay contributions to receive these defined benefits. However members may pay voluntary contributions to a supplemental defined contribution account and the

company will match any contribution made up to 3% of pensionable pay each year.

Under the provisions of the Finance Act 2004 benefits from a registered pension scheme that exceed the Annual Allowance or Lifetime Allowance will be subject to a tax charge. The Annual Allowance and Lifetime Allowance were reduced to £50,000 and £1.5 million respectively with effect from 6th April 2011. On reaching these thresholds members, including executive directors, are given the option to limit their benefits in JMEPS and receive a cash supplement in lieu of the pension benefit forgone, or to continue accruing benefits in the scheme and pay the tax charge. Any tax liability due is the responsibility of the individual not the company.

Neil Carson and Bill Sandford withdrew from pensionable service on 31st March 2006 and Robert MacLeod withdrew on 31st March 2011. No pensionable service in JMEPS has been accrued by these directors since then and all have received a cash supplement of 25% of basic salary in lieu of the pension benefit forgone. The increase in accrued pension for Messrs Carson and Sandford in the table on page 115 is attributable solely to the effect of the increase in their basic salary in 2011/12 on their pension earned before 1st April 2006.

During the year Larry Pentz accrued pension in JMEPS up to the Annual Allowance and elected to cease pension accrual for the remainder of the year in return for a cash supplement of 21% of basic salary.

The supplemental payments received by all executive directors are reflected in the table on page 114.

Remuneration Report continued

Outcomes – Actual Remuneration for 2011/12

This section provides details of the actual payments and awards to directors in 2011/12. Full numerical details are provided in the tables on pages 113 to 117.

In order to fully illustrate the relationships between actual payments, on target payments and stretch (maximum) payments, graphs of the relevant data are shown below for each of the four executive directors. This does not include share option exercises from awards made in prior years. See pages 116 and 117 for further details.

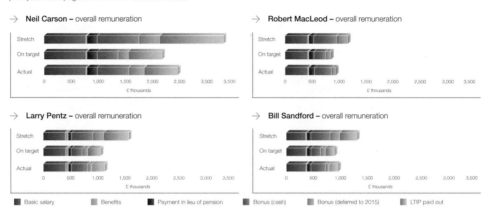

Basic Salary 2011/12

The changes in basic salary for each of the directors are illustrated in the table below.

Name	Basic salary at 1st August 2010 (£)	Basic salary at 1st August 2011 (£)	Increase (%)
Neil Carson	760,000	776,250	3.5
Robert MacLeod	406,600	421,000	3.5
Larry Pentz	390,000	403,650	3.5
Bill Sandford	345,000	357,100	3.5

Comparison to Other Pay Awards in Johnson Matthey

Pay awards throughout Johnson Matthey's global operations have generally ranged between 0% and 10% in the last year, depending on local pay conditions and on local business and economic conditions. Pay awards in the UK have generally been around the 3% level with some local variations dependent on business conditions.

113

LTIP Vesting in 2011/12 and Historical Information

The 2008 share allocation vested in July 2011. The performance condition was met to the extent that 52.42% of the allocated shares were released.

Details of LTIP awards, performance and vesting details are provided below.

	Year of allocation	Year of vesting	% salary awarded	Shares awarded	Compound annual growth in underlying EPS in the period	Shares released	Value at time of release (£)
Neil Carson							
	2007	2010	150	56,704	1.68%	0	0
	2008	2011	150	56,239	9.96%	29,480	614,233
	2009	2012	120	71,611	19.60%	71,611	Vesting July 2012
	2010	2013	150	72,393	n/a		
	2011	2014	175	69,096	n/a		
Robert MacLeod							
	2007	2010	n/a	0	1.68%	0	0
	2008	2011	n/a	0	9.96%	0	0
	2009	2012	170*	55,072	19.60%	55,072	Vesting July 2012
	2010	2013	120	31,397	n/a		
	2011	2014	140	29,979	n/a		
Larry Pentz							
	2007	2010	120	22,327	1.68%	0	0
	2008	2011	120	21,853	9.96%	11,455	238,672
	2009	2012	100	31,116	19.60%	31,116	Vesting July 2012
	2010	2013	120	30,115	n/a		
	2011	2014	140	28,744	n/a		
Bill Sandford							
	2007	2010	120	15,268	1.68%	0	0
	2008	2011	120	15,318	9.96%	8,029	167,289
	2009	2012	100	25,575	19.60%	25,575	Vesting July 2012
	2010	2013	120	26,640	n/a		
	2011	2014	140	25,429	n/a		

* See page 110.

114 **Johnson Matthey**   Annual Report & Accounts 2012
Report of the Directors – Governance
Governance

Remuneration Report continued

Summary Statement of Directors' Emoluments 2011/12

	Date of service agreement	Date of appointment	Basic salary £'000	Payment in lieu of pension[1] £'000	Annual cash bonus £'000	Annual deferred bonus[2] £'000	Benefits £'000	Total excluding pension £'000	Total prior year excluding pension £'000
Executive									
Neil Carson [3]	1.8.99	1.8.99	768	192	578	289	22	1,849	1,687
Robert MacLeod [4]	3.2.09	22.6.09	416	104	314	78	19	931	822
Larry Pentz [5]	1.1.06	1.8.03	399	57	301	75	59	891	810
Bill Sandford	21.7.09	21.7.09	353	88	266	67	17	791	774
Total			1,936	441	1,459	509	117	4,462	4,093

	Date of letter of appointment	Date of appointment	Fees £'000	Total excluding pension £'000	Total prior year excluding pension £'000
Non-executive [6]					
Sir John Banham (Chairman) [7]	10.12.05	1.1.06	91	91	293
Alan Ferguson	10.1.11	13.1.11	57[9]	57	11
Sir Thomas Harris	22.1.09	1.4.09	50	50	50
Michael Roney	29.3.07	1.6.07	56[10]	56	50
Tim Stevenson (Chairman Designate) [8]	10.1.11	29.3.11	225	225	–
Dorothy Thompson	22.5.07	1.9.07	50	50	50
Alan Thomson [7]	1.8.02	24.9.02	18[9]	18	60
Robert Walvis [7]	1.8.02	24.9.02	18[10]	18	58
Total			565	565	572

The aggregate amount of remuneration receivable by directors and non-executive directors totalled £5,027,000 (2011 £4,665,000).

Notes

[1]   Neil Carson, Bill Sandford and Robert MacLeod no longer accrue pensionable service in the Johnson Matthey Employees Pension Scheme. Messrs Carson and Sandford ceased to accrue with effect from 31st March 2006 and Mr MacLeod ceased to accrue with effect from 31st March 2011. They now receive an annual cash payment in lieu of pension equal to 25% of basic salary. Larry Pentz accrued pension during the year up to the Annual Allowance and received a cash supplement of 21% of basic salary thereafter. These payments are taxable under the PAYE system.

[2]   This is the element of the annual bonus which is payable as shares but is deferred for three years.

[3]   Neil Carson is a non-executive director of AMEC plc. His fees for the year in respect of this non-executive directorship were £54,375. This amount is excluded from the table above and retained by him.

[4]   Robert MacLeod is a non-executive director of Aggreko plc. His fees for the year in respect of this non-executive directorship were £61,750. This amount is excluded from the table above and retained by him.

[5]   Larry Pentz is a non-executive director of Victrex plc. His fees for the year in respect of this non-executive directorship were £48,000. This amount is excluded from the table above and retained by him.

[6]   Non-executive fees (other than for the Chairman) were reviewed on 1st April 2010 for the period from 1st April 2010 to 31st March 2013. The fees are £50,000 per annum, with the fee for chairmanship of the Audit Committee being £10,000 per annum and the Management Development and Remuneration Committee being £8,000 per annum. Sir John Banham's fees were reviewed on 1st August 2010 for the period 1st August 2010 to 19th July 2011 (the date of his retirement). The Chairman and the non-executive directors do not receive any pension benefits, LTIP allocations, share option grants or bonus payments.

[7]   Sir John Banham, Alan Thomson and Robert Walvis retired on 19th July 2011.

[8]   Tim Stevenson was Chairman Designate until Sir John Banham's retirement on 19th July 2011, after which he became Chairman.

[9]   Includes £10,000 per annum for chairmanship of the Audit Committee. Alan Ferguson was appointed Chairman of the Audit Committee on 19th July 2011. Alan Thomson previously carried out this role and retired on 19th July 2011.

[10]   Includes £8,000 per annum for chairmanship of the Management Development and Remuneration Committee. Michael Roney was appointed Chairman of the Management Development and Remuneration Committee on 19th July 2011. Robert Walvis previously carried out this role and retired on 19th July 2011.

Pension Benefits

Disclosure of directors' pension benefits has been made under the requirements of the Financial Services Authority's Listing Rules and in accordance with the Companies Act 2006. The information below sets out the disclosures under the two sets of requirements.

	Age as at 31st March 2012	Total accrued pension as at 31st March 2011[1] £'000 pa	Total accrued pension as at 31st March 2012[1] £'000 pa	Change in accrued pension after allowing for inflation £'000 pa	Transfer value as at 31st March 2011[2] £'000	Transfer value as at 31st March 2012[2] £'000	Directors' contributions[3] £'000	Change in transfer value less directors' contributions £'000
Neil Carson	54	353	365	(6)	6,402	7,655	–	1,253
Robert MacLeod	47	9	9	–	81	106	–	25
Larry Pentz [4]	56	111	116	2	1,371	1,702	–	331
Bill Sandford	58	179	185	(3)	3,779	4,390	–	611

Notes

[1]   The total accrued pension represents the pension which would be paid annually on normal retirement, based on pensionable service to 31st March 2012 (except in the case of Neil Carson and Bill Sandford whose pensionable service ceased on 31st March 2006 and Robert MacLeod whose pensionable service ceased on 31st March 2011). The element of the pension earned before 31st March 2010 would be subject to an actuarial reduction if retirement precedes age 60, and the element of the pension earned from 1st April 2010 will be reduced if taken before age 65.

[2]   The transfer values have been calculated in accordance with GN11 issued by the actuarial profession. For UK based pension benefits the assumptions used are the same as those in the calculation of cash equivalent transfers from JMEPS. For US based pension benefits the assumptions used are the same as those used for accounting disclosure. No allowance has been made in the transfer values for any discretionary benefits that have been or may be awarded.

[3]   Members are not required to pay contributions towards their pension benefits. Any voluntary contributions paid by executive directors are not shown except where these are matched by the company. Larry Pentz paid voluntary contributions into the supplemental defined contribution account amounting to 3% of his April 2011 salary, this contribution was matched by the company.

[4]   Larry Pentz is a US citizen but became a member of JMEPS on 1st January 2006. Prior to that he was a member of the Johnson Matthey Inc. Salaried Employees Pension Plan (a non-contributory defined benefit arrangement) and also of a US savings plan (401k). He also has benefits in a Supplemental Executive Retirement Plan (SERP). The pension values reported above are the aggregate for his separate membership of the UK and US pension schemes and the SERP. The total accrued pension as 31st March 2011 has been restated to include all of his pension benefits. US entitlements have been converted to sterling by reference to exchange rates on 31st March 2011 and 31st March 2012. Mr Pentz's US pension was fixed on 31st December 2005. The sterling equivalent of it has fluctuated over the year as a result of exchange rate movements. Of the change in the accrued benefit and the transfer value £300 and £3,020, respectively, is due to currency movements.

Other Historical and Statutory Information

Johnson Matthey and FTSE 100 Total Shareholder Return Rebased to 100

The following graph charts total cumulative shareholder return of the company for the five year period from 31st March 2007 to 31st March 2012 against the FTSE 100 as the most appropriate comparator group, rebased to 100 at 1st April 2007. The graph shows significant outperformance by Johnson Matthey against the FTSE 100 group over the five year period.

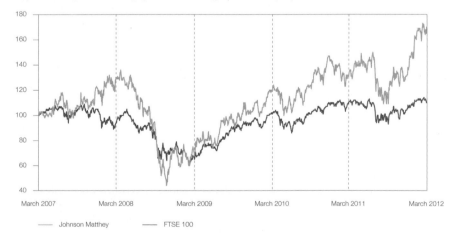

As at 31st March 2012, Johnson Matthey was ranked 60th by market capitalisation in the FTSE 100.

Remuneration Report continued

Share Options

The LTIP is now the company's single means for the provision of long term awards and from 2007 replaced the granting of share options under the Johnson Matthey 2001 Share Option Scheme (the 2001 Scheme). From 2001 to 2006 options were granted each year under the 2001 Scheme. There have been no option grants since 2006. Options were granted at the market value of the company's shares at the time of grant and were subject to performance targets over a three year period. Options may be exercised upon satisfaction of the relevant performance targets. Approximately 800 employees were granted options under the 2001 Scheme each year.

Options granted from 2004 to 2006

Grants made in 2004, 2005 and 2006 were subject to a three year performance target of EPS growth of UK RPI plus 3% per annum. If the performance target was not met at the end of the three year performance period, the options lapsed as there was no retesting of the performance target. In addition, to reduce the cost calculated under the International Financial Reporting Standard 2 – 'Share-based Payment', gains made on the exercise of options are capped at 100% of the grant price.

The Committee had the discretion to award grants greater than 100% of basic annual salary. Grants which were made above this threshold were, however, subject to increasingly stretching performance targets. Grants between 100% and 125% of basic annual salary were subject to EPS growth of UK RPI plus 4% per annum and grants between 125% and 150% of basic

annual salary were subject to EPS growth of UK RPI plus 5% per annum. The executive directors were granted options equal to 150% of basic annual salary. All the options, other than those granted in 2006 which were subject to EPS growth of UK RPI plus 5% per annum, have met their performance targets. The 2006 options which did not meet their performance targets have lapsed.

Options granted prior to 2004

Prior to 2004, options granted to the executive directors under the 2001 Scheme were up to a maximum of 100% of basic annual salary each year. Such options were subject to a performance target of EPS growth of UK RPI plus 4% per annum over any three consecutive years during the life of the option. The performance target was subject to annual retesting until the lapse of the options on the tenth anniversary of grant. All of these options have met their performance targets.

Directors' Interests

The interests (in respect of which transactions are notifiable to the company under the Financial Services Authority's Disclosure and Transparency Rules) of the directors as at 31st March 2012 in the shares of the company were:

1. Ordinary Shares

	31st March 2012	31st March 2011
Tim Stevenson	5,500	5,500*
Neil Carson	188,804	174,374
Alan Ferguson	1,000	1,000
Sir Thomas Harris	1,807	1,807
Robert MacLeod	3,604	3,388
Larry Pentz	25,789	25,383
Michael Roney	3,000	3,000
Bill Sandford	9,165	5,091
Dorothy Thompson	9,721	9,721

* Shares acquired on 3rd March 2011, not disclosed in the 2011 annual report.

All of the above interests were beneficial. The executive directors are also deemed to be interested in shares held by an employee share ownership trust (see note 30 on page 162).

Directors' interests as at 31st May 2012 were unchanged from those listed above, other than that the trustees of the Johnson Matthey Share Incentive Plan have purchased on behalf of Neil Carson, Robert MacLeod, Larry Pentz and Bill Sandford a further 33 shares each.

2. Share Options

As at 31st March 2012, individual holdings by the directors under the company's executive share option schemes were as set out below. Options are not granted to non-executive directors.

	Date of grant	Ordinary shares under option	Exercise price (pence)	Date from which exercisable	Expiry date	Total number of ordinary shares under option
Neil Carson	17.7.03	33,407	898	17.7.06	17.7.13	
	26.7.06	59,481	1,282	26.7.09	26.7.16	92,888
						(2011 218,282)
Larry Pentz	17.7.03	17,185	898	17.7.06	17.7.13	
	26.7.06	28,765	1,282	26.7.09	26.7.16	45,950
						(2011 101,530)
Bill Sandford	26.7.06	3,774	1,282	26.7.09	26.7.16	3,774
						(2011 18,868)

117

Between 1st April 2011 and 31st March 2012 the following options were exercised by directors:

	Date of grant	Date of exercise	Options exercised	Exercise price (pence)	Market price on exercise (pence)
Neil Carson	18.7.01	3.6.11	2,770	1,083	2,038
	18.7.01	3.6.11	16,621	1,083	2,034
	20.7.05	1.2.12	77,102	1,070	2,140
	17.7.02	14.2.12	28,901	865	2,281
Larry Pentz	17.7.02	11.1.12	17,730	865	1,998
	20.7.05	1.2.12	37,850	1,070	2,140
Bill Sandford	26.7.06	1.12.11	15,094	1,282	1,874

Gains made on exercise of options by the directors during the year totalled £2,113,928 (2011 £88,138).

The closing market price of the company's shares at 30th March 2012 was 2,359 pence. The highest and lowest closing market prices during the year ended 31st March 2012 were 2,403 pence and 1,523 pence respectively.

3. **LTIP Allocations**
    Number of allocated shares:

	As at 31st March 2011	Allocations during the year	Market price at date of allocation (pence)	Released during the year	Lapsed during the year	As at 31st March 2012
Neil Carson	200,243	69,096	1,966	29,480	26,759	**213,100**
Robert MacLeod	86,469	29,979	1,966	–	–	**116,448**
Larry Pentz	83,084	28,744	1,966	11,455	10,398	**89,975**
Bill Sandford	67,533	25,429	1,966	8,029	7,289	**77,644**

On 25th July 2011 shares allocated in 2008 under the LTIP were released to participants. The compound annual growth in the company's underlying EPS over the three year performance period, commencing in the year of allocation, resulted in a release of 52.42% of the allocated shares and the following gains:

	Number of shares released	Share price when released (pence)	Gain (£)
Neil Carson	29,480	2,084	614,233
Larry Pentz	11,455	2,084	238,672
Bill Sandford	8,029	2,084	167,289

The Remuneration Report was approved by the Board of Directors on 6th June 2012 and signed on its behalf by:

Michael Roney
Chairman of the Management Development and Remuneration Committee

Responsibility of Directors

Statement of Directors' Responsibilities in Respect of the Annual Report and Accounts

The directors are responsible for preparing the annual report and the group and parent company accounts in accordance with applicable law and regulations.

Company law requires the directors to prepare group and parent company accounts for each financial year. Under that law they are required to prepare the group accounts in accordance with International Financial Reporting Standards (IFRS) as adopted by the European Union (EU) and applicable law and have elected to prepare the parent company accounts on the same basis.

Under company law the directors must not approve the accounts unless they are satisfied that they give a true and fair view of the state of affairs of the group and parent company and of their profit or loss for that period. In preparing each of the group and parent company accounts, the directors are required to:

- select suitable accounting policies and then apply them consistently;
- make judgments and estimates that are reasonable and prudent;
- state whether they have been prepared in accordance with IFRS as adopted by the EU; and
- prepare the accounts on the going concern basis unless it is inappropriate to presume that the group and the parent company will continue in business.

The directors are responsible for keeping adequate accounting records that are sufficient to show and explain the parent company's transactions and disclose with reasonable accuracy at any time the financial position of the parent company and enable them to ensure that its accounts comply with the Companies Act 2006. They have general responsibility for taking such steps as are reasonably open to them to safeguard the assets of the group and to prevent and detect fraud and other irregularities.

Under applicable law and regulations the directors are also responsible for preparing a directors' report, directors' Remuneration Report and Corporate Governance statement that comply with that law and those regulations.

The directors are responsible for the maintenance and integrity of the corporate and financial information included on the company's website. Legislation in the UK governing the preparation and dissemination of accounts may differ from legislation in other jurisdictions.

Responsibility Statement of the Directors in Respect of the Annual Report and Accounts

Each of the directors as at the date of the Annual Report and Accounts, whose names and functions are set out on page 83, states that to the best of his or her knowledge:

- the group and parent company accounts, prepared in accordance with the applicable set of accounting standards, give a true and fair view of the assets, liabilities, financial position and profit or loss of the company and the undertakings included in the consolidation taken as a whole; and
- the management report (which comprises the Report of the Directors) includes a fair review of the development and performance of the business and the position of the company and the undertakings included in the consolidation taken as a whole, together with a description of the principal risks and uncertainties that they face.

This responsibility statement was approved by the board on 6th June 2012 and is signed on its behalf by:

Tim Stevenson
Chairman

Independent Auditor's Report
to the members of Johnson Matthey Public Limited Company

We have audited the group and parent company accounts of Johnson Matthey Plc for the year ended 31st March 2012 which comprise the Consolidated Income Statement, the Consolidated Statement of Total Comprehensive Income, the Consolidated and Parent Company Balance Sheets, the Consolidated and Parent Company Cash Flow Statements, the Consolidated Statement of Changes in Equity, the Parent Company Statement of Changes in Equity and the related notes. The financial reporting framework that has been applied in their preparation is applicable law and International Financial Reporting Standards (IFRS) as adopted by the EU and, as regards the parent company accounts, as applied in accordance with the provisions of the Companies Act 2006.

This report is made solely to the company's members, as a body, in accordance with Chapter 3 of Part 16 of the Companies Act 2006. Our audit work has been undertaken so that we might state to the company's members those matters we are required to state to them in an auditor's report and for no other purpose. To the fullest extent permitted by law, we do not accept or assume responsibility to anyone other than the company and the company's members, as a body, for our audit work, for this report, or for the opinions we have formed.

Respective Responsibilities of Directors and Auditor

As explained more fully in the directors' responsibilities statement set out on page 120, the directors are responsible for the preparation of the accounts and for being satisfied that they give a true and fair view. Our responsibility is to audit, and express an opinion on, the accounts in accordance with applicable law and International Standards on Auditing (UK and Ireland). Those standards require us to comply with the Auditing Practices Board's (APB's) Ethical Standards for Auditors.

Scope of the Audit of the Accounts

A description of the scope of an audit of accounts is provided on the APB's website at www.frc.org.uk/apb/scope/private.cfm.

Opinion on Accounts

In our opinion:

- the accounts give a true and fair view of the state of the group's and of the parent company's affairs as at 31st March 2012 and of the group's profit for the year then ended;
- the group accounts have been properly prepared in accordance with IFRS as adopted by the EU;
- the parent company accounts have been properly prepared in accordance with IFRS as adopted by the EU and as applied in accordance with the provisions of the Companies Act 2006; and
- the accounts have been prepared in accordance with the requirements of the Companies Act 2006 and, as regards the group accounts, Article 4 of the IAS Regulation.

Opinion on Other Matters Prescribed by the Companies Act 2006

In our opinion:

- the part of the directors' Remuneration Report to be audited has been properly prepared in accordance with the Companies Act 2006; and
- the information given in the directors' report for the financial year for which the accounts are prepared is consistent with the accounts.

Matters on Which we are Required to Report by Exception

We have nothing to report in respect of the following:

Under the Companies Act 2006 we are required to report to you if, in our opinion:

- adequate accounting records have not been kept by the parent company, or returns adequate for our audit have not been received from branches not visited by us; or
- the parent company accounts and the part of the directors' Remuneration Report to be audited are not in agreement with the accounting records and returns; or
- certain disclosures of directors' remuneration specified by law are not made; or
- we have not received all the information and explanations we require for our audit.

Under the Listing Rules we are required to review:

- the directors' statement, set out on page 47, in relation to going concern; and
- the part of the Corporate Governance statement on page 85 relating to the company's compliance with the nine provisions of the UK Corporate Governance Code specified for our review; and
- certain elements of the report to shareholders by the board on directors' remuneration.

D V Matthews (Senior Statutory Auditor)
for and on behalf of KPMG Audit Plc, Statutory Auditor
Chartered Accountants
15 Canada Square, London E14 5GL

6th June 2012

Five Year Record – Non-Financial Data

		2007[1]	2009[2]	2010[2]	2011[2]	**2012[2]**
Social						
Average employee numbers		8,013	8,742	8,575	9,388	**9,914**
Total employee turnover[3]	%	9.9	12.7	10.0	8.5	**11.7**
Voluntary employee turnover[3]	%	7.6	6.4	5.4	5.6	**6.4**
Employee gender (female)	%	22[4]	22[5]	21[5]	22[5]	**22[5]**
New recruits gender (female)	%	25	29	25	23	**25**
Trade union representation	%	34	34	33	38	**35**
Training days per employee		3.9	2.6	2.3	2.6	**3.1**
Training spend per employee[6]	£	327	346	291	390	**335**
Internal promotions	% of all recruitment in year	29	38	35	33	**35**
Attendance	days lost per employee	5.2	5.3	5.2	5.2	**5.0**
Sickness absence rate	%	2.1	2.2	2.1	2.1	**2.0**
Charitable donations	£ thousands	415[2]	495	458	517	**645**
Health and Safety						
Greater than three day accidents	per 1,000 employees	3.04	5.09	2.48	2.99[7]	**2.07**
Total lost time accidents		78	95	60[7]	74[7]	**55**
Total accident rate	per 1,000 employees	9.36	10.83	7.11	7.89[7]	**5.69**
Total lost time accident incident rate	per 100,000 hours worked	0.50	0.53	0.36	0.40[7]	**0.28**
Total days lost	per 1,000 employees	85	124	64	102	**90**
Occupational illness cases	per 1,000 employees	5.8	5.5	5.2	3.5	**3.5**
Environment						
Energy consumption	thousands GJ	3,787	4,070	4,001	4,749	**4,726**
Total global warming potential	thousands tonnes CO_2 equivalent	390	372	377	415	**417**
Total acid gas emissions	tonnes SO_2 equivalent	416	334	335	318	**444**
Total NOx emissions	tonnes	448	439	434	393	**566**
Total SO_2 emissions	tonnes	31.8	25.8	31.0	43.0	**47.5**
Total VOC emissions	tonnes	207.1	209.1	180.8	185.7	**189.8**
Total waste	tonnes	98,764	96,287	90,308	113,671	**120,363**
Total waste to landfill	tonnes	20,977	5,535	5,071	6,165	**10,708**
Packaging waste recycled – steel	tonnes	*	2,084	1,863	1,847	**2,314**
Packaging waste recycled – paper	tonnes	*	486	250	258	**704**
Packaging waste recycled – plastic	tonnes	*	648	396	439	**1,148**
Packaging waste recycled – wood	tonnes	*	1,811	828	896	**3,003**
Water consumption	thousands m[3]	2,048	1,951	1,750	2,076	**2,201**
Emissions to water	tonnes	360	376	236	251	**260**

[1] Calendar year (unless otherwise stated).

[2] Financial year (unless otherwise stated).

[3] Calculated by reference to the total number of leavers during the year expressed as a percentage of the average number of people employed during the year. Does not include agency workers not directly employed by Johnson Matthey.

[4] At 31st December.

[5] At 31st March.

[6] Does not include the cost of in house training or the cost of employees' wages during training.

[7] Restated.

* Not measured.

Learning objectives

Completion of this chapter will enable you to:

- Describe how the framework for establishing good corporate governance and accountability has been established in a UK Corporate Governance Code, developed from the work of the Cadbury, Greenbury, Hampel, and Turnbull Committees.

- Outline the corporate governance codes that have been developed in other countries, for example throughout Europe, China, and the Middle East, and including the USA's Sarbanes–Oxley Act 2002.

- Appreciate the importance of sustainability and corporate social responsibility (CSR) reporting by companies.

- Outline the various approaches to dealing with the agency problem, including corporate governance frameworks but also with consideration to the ethical dimension.

- Explain the statutory requirement for the audit of limited companies, the election by shareholders of suitably qualified, independent auditors, and the role of the auditors.

- Outline directors' specific responsibility to shareholders and responsibilities to society in general, for the management and conduct of companies.

- Recognise the fiduciary duties that directors have to the company, and their duty of care to all stakeholders and to the community at large, particularly with regard to the Companies Act 2006, Health and Safety at Work Act 1974, Health and Safety (Offences) Act 2008, and Financial Services Act 1986.

- Explain the implications for companies and their directors that may arise from the UK Corporate Manslaughter & Corporate Homicide Act 2007.

- Appreciate the importance of directors' duties regarding insolvency, the Insolvency Act 1986, and the Enterprise Act 2002.

- Consider the implications for directors of wrongful trading, and recognise the difference between this and the offence of fraudulent trading, and the possibility of criminal penalties.

- Outline the implication for directors of the Company Directors Disqualification Act 1986 and the Enterprise Act 2002.

- Explain the actions that directors of companies should take to ensure compliance with their obligations and responsibilities, and to protect themselves against possible non-compliance.

Introduction

In Chapter 3 we will see that a large part of Johnson Matthey Plc's report and accounts 2012 is devoted to the subject of corporate governance, the systems by which companies are directed and controlled. Before the start of this chapter you will have already seen pages 76 to 117, pages 120 to 121, and page 171 of Johnson Matthey's report and accounts 2012 (reproduced on pages 88 to 132 of this book). This chapter will refer to these extracts when it turns to the statutory and non-statutory rules that surround the financial reporting by limited companies.

The reports and accounts of public limited companies now increasingly include large sections that report on their systems of corporate governance. Corporate governance relates to the policies, procedures, and rules governing the relationships between the shareholders and the **directors** of a company. This chapter looks at how these have been developed in the UK, the USA, and many other countries in response to worldwide concerns about the ways companies are run following a spate of financial scandals over the past 30 years or so. Corporate governance codes offer guidance as to how the relationship between the various stakeholders of the business should be managed, and particularly the relationship between directors and shareholders.

In Chapter 1 we discussed the way in which the limited company exists in perpetuity as a legal entity, separate from the lives of those individuals who own and manage it. The limited company has many rights, responsibilities, and liabilities in the same way as individual people. As a separate legal entity the company is responsible for its own liabilities. These are not the obligations of the shareholders, their payment for their shares being the limit of their obligations to the company. The management and regulation of a company as a separate legal entity lies with the directors and the auditors. The directors are within, and part of, the company, and the auditors are external to, and not part of, the company. This chapter examines the roles and responsibilities of directors and auditors. It will also consider the obligations of directors, particularly with regard to the UK Corporate Governance Code and the many Acts that are now in place to regulate the behaviour of directors of limited companies. The chapter closes with a look at some of the steps that directors may take to protect themselves against possible non-compliance.

Corporate governance codes of practice

Concerns about financial reporting and accountability, and the impact on the business community (see Figure 3.1), grew during the 1980s following increasing numbers of company failures and financial scandals.

During the 1980s and 1990s there was further huge disquiet within the business community following the financial scandals surrounding, for example, Polly Peck (1990), the Robert Maxwell companies (1991), BCCI (1991), and Barings Bank–Nick Leeson (1995).

The concerns increased as in the 2000s we saw even larger scandals involving companies such as Enron (2001), Marconi (2001), WorldCom (2002), and Parmalat (2004), and in particular the involvement of the consulting arms of major accounting firms like Arthur Andersen. These concerns resulted in a growing lack of confidence in financial reporting, and in shareholders and others being unable to rely on auditors to provide the necessary safeguards for their reliance on company annual reports.

The main factors underlying the lack of confidence in financial reporting were:

- loose accounting standards, which allowed considerable latitude (an example in the past has been the treatment of extraordinary items in financial reporting)
- the lack of a clear framework to ensure directors were able to continuously review business controls

Figure 3.1   The business community

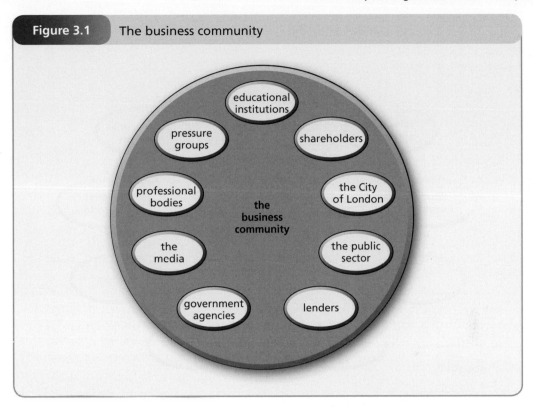

- competitive pressure within companies and on auditors, making it difficult for auditors to maintain independence from demanding boards
- a lack of apparent accountability regarding directors' remuneration and compensation for loss of office.

The Cadbury Committee, chaired by Sir Adrian Cadbury, was set up in May 1991 by the Financial Reporting Council, the London Stock Exchange, and the accounting profession, to address these concerns and make recommendations on good practice.

The Cadbury Committee defined corporate governance (see Figure 3.2) as:

> the system by which companies are directed and controlled. Boards of directors are responsible for the governance of their companies. The shareholders' role in governance is to appoint the directors and the auditors and to satisfy themselves that an appropriate governance structure is in place. The responsibilities of the board include setting the company's strategic aims, providing the leadership to put them into effect, supervising the management of the business and reporting to shareholders on their stewardship. The board's actions are subject to laws, regulations and the shareholders in general meeting.

Source: © Financial Reporting Council (FRC). Adapted and reproduced with the kind permission of the Financial Reporting Council. All rights reserved. For further information, please visit www.frc.org.uk or call +44 (0)20 7492 2300.

The financial aspects within the framework described by Cadbury are the ways in which the company's board sets financial policy and oversees its implementation, the use of financial controls, and how the board reports on activities and progress of the company to shareholders.

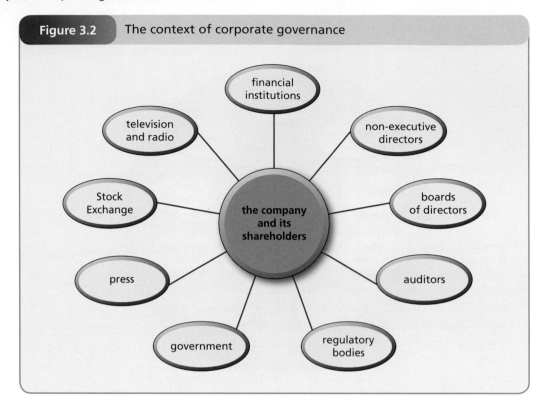

Figure 3.2 The context of corporate governance

The framework for establishing good corporate governance and accountability set up by the Cadbury Committee was formulated as the Committee's Code of Best Practice, published in December 1992. The main proposals and recommendations of the code were as follows:

- executive directors' service contracts should not exceed three years
- non-executive directors should be appointed to companies' boards of directors for specified terms
- the majority of non-executive directors should be independent of management and free from any business or other relationship
- executive remuneration should be subject to the recommendations of a Remuneration Committee made up entirely, or mainly, of non-executive directors
- an Audit Committee, comprising at least three non-executives, should be established.

The Cadbury Committee's Code of Best Practice provided a benchmark against which to assess compliance. The Greenbury Committee's findings on directors' remuneration were published in the Greenbury Report in July 1995. It incorporated a Code of Best Practice on Director's Remuneration, which dealt with four main issues:

- the role of a Remuneration Committee in setting the remuneration packages for the CEO and other directors
- the required level of disclosure needed by shareholders regarding details of directors' remuneration, and whether there is the need to obtain shareholder approval
- specific guidelines for determining a remuneration policy for directors
- service contracts and provisions binding the company to pay compensation to a director, particularly in the event of dismissal for unsatisfactory performance.

The Cadbury Code was updated in 1998 by the Hampel Committee, to include its own work, and the Greenbury Committee report on directors' remuneration (published July 1995). The

Hampel Committee was established in 1996 to review and revise the earlier recommendations of the Cadbury and Greenbury Committees. The Hampel Report emphasised the need for good governance rather than explicit rules in order to reduce the regulatory burden on companies. In particular, the Hampel Report recommended:

- greater shareholder involvement in company affairs
- the need for a sound system of internal control
- the need for executives to be accountable for all aspects of risk management.

In September 1999 the Turnbull Committee report on *Internal Control: Guidance for Directors on the Combined Code* was published by the ICAEW. The aim of the report was to provide guidance to ensure that all companies trading on the London Stock Exchange (LSE) have in place an adequate system of internal control in order to facilitate the management of business risk. The report was based on the adoption of a risk-based approach in establishing a sound system of internal control. It required companies to develop ongoing processes and procedures for:

- identifying, evaluating, and managing significant business risks
- reviewing the effectiveness of the system of internal control
- ensuring adequate procedures exist for the management and disclosure of internal control problems and issues.

The Turnbull Report provided that in assessing internal controls consideration should be given to:

- the nature and extent of the risks facing the organisation
- the extent and categories of risk which are regarded as acceptable
- the likelihood of the risks concerned materialising
- the company's ability to reduce the incidence and impact on the organisation of risks that materialise.

The Turnbull Report also suggested that internal controls should be:

- embedded in the operation of the organisation and form part of its culture
- capable of responding quickly to evolving risks,

and procedures should be included for reporting any significant control failings immediately to appropriate levels of management.

In May 2000 the original Cadbury Code and subsequent reports were all consolidated by the Committee on Corporate Governance and published in the Combined Code of Practice.

The underlying principles of the Code were:

- openness
- integrity
- accountability.

The effect of the three principles of the Combined Code had to be dealt with by directors within the context of the business environments in which they conducted their business.

Openness

Openness from companies was seen to be constrained within the limits of their competitive position but formed the basis for the confidence that needed to exist between a business and all those who have a stake in its success. Openness in disclosure was seen to add to the effectiveness of the market economy and it forced boards to take action and allow shareholders and others to look more closely and thoroughly into companies.

Integrity

Integrity means straightforward dealing and completeness. Financial reporting should be honest and present a balanced view of the state of a company's affairs. The integrity of a company's reports depends on the integrity of the people responsible for preparing and presenting them.

The corporate governance section of a company's annual report and accounts may contain details under the following headings:

- directors' biographies
- board responsibilities
- board composition and function
- board committees:
  - audit committee
  - nomination committee
  - remuneration committee
  - IT committee
  - capital expenditure committee
  - **non-executive directors**' committee
- directors' remuneration
- relations with shareholders
- internal financial control
- incentive compensation
- directors' pensions
- corporate strategy.

This may not be a complete list but it gives a broad indication of the areas of compliance which were laid down by the Combined Code and which are standard in corporate governance reports of most UK companies.

Accountability

Accountability of boards of directors to their shareholders required the commitment from both to make the accountability effective. Boards of directors need to play their part by ensuring the quality of information that is provided to shareholders. Shareholders need to exercise their responsibilities as owners of the business. The major investing institutions (for example, pension funds and insurance companies) are in regular contact with the directors of UK plcs to discuss past, current, and future performance.

Subsequent to 2000, further reviews of various aspects of corporate governance were set up:

- the *Review of the role and effectiveness of non-executive directors*, by Sir Derek Higgs and published January 2003
- the *Audit Committees Combined Code guidance*, by a group led by Sir Robert Smith and also published January 2003.

The Higgs Review examined the role, independence, and recruitment of non-executive directors, and outlined a series of tests of independence such as length of service, associations with executive management, financial interests, and significant shareholdings. With regard to recruitment, Higgs recommended stronger provisions governing nomination committees, and called for all listed companies to establish a nomination committee, chaired by an independent non-executive director (not the chairman) and comprising a majority of independent non-executive directors.

Other important recommendations of the Higgs Review included:

- the board of directors should review its own performance, the performance of its committees, and that of individual directors at least once a year
- the company secretary should be accountable to the board of directors through the chairman on all governance matters
- the terms of reference of the remuneration committee should be published.

The Higgs and Smith reviews were undertaken during a period in which investor confidence had been badly shaken both by lapses in corporate governance and by the high-profile failure of some corporate strategies, the latter two being very much in response to these events. The reviews were reflected in a revision to the 2000 Combined Code of Practice, which was published by the Financial Reporting Council (FRC) in July 2003 – the Combined Code on Corporate Governance.

The spirit of the 2003 Code on Corporate Governance was largely prescriptive. Founded on the previous decade's body of work, the Code on Corporate Governance, which largely incorporated the guidance of the Turnbull Committee, and the Higgs and Smith reviews, sought to guide directors' activities based on the established principles of openness, integrity, and accountability which had been clarified in the 2000 Combined Code of Practice.

The Code on Corporate Governance, however, made clear that while the Code was designed to promote partnership and trust based on mutual understanding between shareholders and boards, it cautioned that shareholders should not be too critical if boards failed to comply at all times. Shareholders needed to be mindful of the size and complexity of the company and the nature of the risks and challenges that it faced. The Code on Corporate Governance expressed for the first time the 'comply or explain' principle, which was based on ideas raised in the Cadbury Report and placed the onus on boards to comply with the Code, but if they do not they should explain their reasons.

The Code on Corporate Governance was revised by the FRC several times up to June 2008. Following an extensive consultation process, in June 2010 the FRC issued a new code of corporate governance entitled the UK Corporate Governance Code. This Code was to be effective for the financial years beginning after 29 June 2010. The consultation was prompted by the worldwide financial crisis. The FRC, while they acknowledge the quality of the 2003 Code, highlighted an increasing problem within organisations in that 'it seems that there is almost a belief that complying with the Code in itself constitutes good governance'. The FRC, therefore, insisted that to 'follow the spirit of the Code to good effect, boards must think deeply, thoroughly and on a continuing basis, about their overall tasks and the implications of these for the roles of their individual members'.* The new Code then follows the 'comply or explain' approach to corporate governance, and concentrates on developing sound mechanisms, which the FRC believe to be central to effectively following the five key principles of corporate governance. These five key principles, on which all listed companies must report to shareholders as to how they have applied them, are: leadership; effectiveness; accountability; remuneration; relations with shareholders.

Companies listed on the London Stock Exchange are requested to comply with the Code, but other companies may also benefit from compliance. It is not compulsory for any company, but rather a recommended target of best practice to aim for. The 'comply or explain' principle means that companies listed on the London Stock Exchange are required to include in their annual

---

* © Financial Reporting Council (FRC). Adapted and reproduced with the kind permission of the Financial Reporting Council. All rights reserved. For further information, please visit www.frc.org.uk or call +44 (0)20 7492 2300.

report and accounts a statement to confirm that they have complied with the Code's provisions throughout the accounting period, or to provide an explanation if that is not the case.

In February 2012, *World Finance* magazine named HSBC as UK winner of its corporate governance award. Each year the magazine names a company from each of 53 countries, which have achieved excellent levels of corporate governance serving the best interests of their shareholders with maximum transparency. The extracts below, from the extensive corporate governance coverage on HSBC's governance webpages, show clearly how the company endorses the UK Corporate Governance Code and the guidance available for directors to enable them to carry out their governance duties effectively. The section on codes of governance demonstrates clearly the 'comply or explain' principle in action.

It is not only the UK that has introduced codes of corporate governance. On a worldwide basis many countries are continuing to develop their own approaches to the issue. The HSBC

HSBC codes of governance

We are committed to high standards of corporate governance. We have complied throughout the year with the applicable code provisions of The UK Corporate Governance Code issued by the Financial Reporting Council and the Code on Corporate Governance Practices in Appendix 14 to the Rules Governing the Listing of Securities on The Stock Exchange of Hong Kong Limited, save that the Group Risk Committee (all the members of which are independent non-executive Directors), which was established in accordance with the recommendations of the Report on Governance in UK banks and other financial industry entities, is responsible for the oversight of internal controls (other than internal controls over financial reporting) and risk management systems (Code on Corporate Governance Practices provision C.3.3 paragraphs (f), (g) and (h)). If there were no Group Risk Committee, these matters would be the responsibility of the Group Audit Committee. The UK Corporate Governance Code is available at *www.frc.org.uk* and the Code on Corporate Governance Practices is available at *www.hkex.com.hk*

HSBC internal control

The Directors are responsible for internal control in HSBC and for reviewing its effectiveness. Procedures have been designed for safeguarding assets against unauthorised use or disposal; for maintaining proper accounting records; and for the reliability and usefulness of financial information used within the business or for publication. Such procedures are designed to manage and mitigate the risk of failure to achieve business objectives and can only provide reasonable and not absolute assurance against material misstatement, errors, losses or fraud. The procedures also enable HSBC Holdings to discharge its obligations under the *Handbook of Rules and Guidance* issued by the FSA, HSBC's lead regulator.

The key procedures that the Directors have established are designed to provide effective internal control within HSBC and accord with the *Internal Control: Revised Guidance for Directors on the Combined Code* on corporate governance issued by the Financial Reporting Council. Such procedures for the on-going identification, evaluation and management of the significant risks faced by HSBC have been in place throughout the year and up to 27 February 2012, the date of approval of the *Annual Report and Accounts 2011*. In the case of companies acquired during the year, the internal controls in place are being reviewed against HSBC's benchmarks and integrated into HSBC's processes.

summary of its corporate governance principles also makes similar comments with regard to their endorsement of the corporate governance principles adopted in Hong Kong and the USA. Further information about HSBC's corporate governance codes may be found at *www.hsbc. com/1/2/investor-relations/governance/codes*.

The USA's response to concerns about major corporate financial scandals, including Enron, Tyco International, and WorldCom (now trading as MCI), resulted in the passing of a United States federal law on 30 July 2002, called the Sarbanes–Oxley Act. This Act is also known as the Public Company Accounting Reform and Investor Protection Act of 2002, and is generally referred to as SOX or SARBOX. It was named after its sponsors, Senator Paul Sarbanes and Representative Michael G Oxley.

The Sarbanes–Oxley Act established new wide-ranging standards for all US public companies covering issues such as auditor independence, corporate governance, corporate responsibilities, and financial disclosure. The main provisions of the Sarbanes–Oxley Act include:

- the creation of the Public Company Accounting Oversight Board
- a requirement for public companies to evaluate and disclose the effectiveness of their internal controls as they relate to financial reporting
- the certification of financial reports by chief executive officers and chief financial officers
- a requirement for auditor independence
- a requirement that companies listed on stock exchanges must possess fully independent audit committees to oversee the relationship between the company and its auditor
- a prohibition on most personal loans to any executive officer or director
- a requirement for accelerated reporting of insider trading
- enhanced criminal and civil penalties for violations of US securities law
- the imposition of significantly longer maximum jail sentences and larger fines for corporate executives who knowingly and wilfully mis-state financial statements.

For non-compliance with SOX requirements, penalties range from fines of up to US$5m and/ or imprisonment for up to 20 years. The Sarbanes–Oxley Act 2002 covers similar areas to those within UK corporate governance requirements. In addition, the SOX requirements increasingly have a wide-ranging impact on corporate governance and issues associated with managerial control and accountability on a worldwide basis.

The development of corporate governance systems in specific countries is related very much to each country's particular business environment and the diverse range of problems faced by them. The importance of corporate governance has gathered pace in the GCC (Gulf Cooperation Council) countries (Bahrain, Kuwait, Oman, Qatar, Saudi Arabia, and United Arab Emirates) over the past few years. In October 2006 the outcome of the first corporate governance survey of GCC countries by the Institute of International Finance (IIF) and Hawkamah (the Institute of Corporate Governance) was reported. It found that in general, corporate governance in GCC countries lagged significantly behind international corporate governance best practices among emerging markets.

The IIF and Hawkamah survey report was part of a co-ordinated strategy towards the harmonisation of corporate governance standards in the GCC and their alignment with international best practices. However, the survey also found a great degree of variation between corporate governance frameworks in the six countries. Oman was the only country in the GCC that had a code of corporate governance and had the strongest corporate governance framework complying with about 70% of IIF guidelines. This was followed by Kuwait and Saudi Arabia with about 50% compliance, and Bahrain and UAE with 40% compliance with IIF guidelines. The greatest room for improvement was found in Qatar where corporate governance requirements complied with only 35% of IIF guidelines. Improvements were expected as the authorities were taking steps to improve governance practices in listed companies. The study identified three key factors that were driving the introduction of improved governance practices in the GCC:

- policy makers' reaction to the volatility in the prices of securities
- the importance of IPOs (initial public offerings) in the growth of GCC equity markets
- foreign direct investment (FDI).

The study also observed that efforts were being made to strengthen corporate governance in the region.

A different set of problems faced the development of corporate governance in China, which has also gathered momentum over the past few years. The state policy of maintaining a full or controlling ownership interest in enterprises in several business sectors creates a dilemma. The state wants enterprises to be run efficiently, but not necessarily with the objective of maximisation of shareholder wealth. The state may have alternative objectives, for example in areas of employment levels and control of sensitive industries. This means that objectives cannot easily be measured, which therefore creates monitoring difficulties. Continuing state involvement results in a conflict of interest between the state as controlling shareholder, and other shareholders. In this way the state uses its control for purposes other than shareholder wealth maximisation, and therefore exploits the other minority shareholders who have no other way to benefit from their investment.

Progress check 3.1

What is corporate governance and how is it implemented?

Johnson Matthey Plc has always treated corporate governance as extremely important and fundamental to the success of the group. Corporate governance is now a very substantial part of Johnson Matthey's reporting as we can see from its report and accounts. Pages 76 to 117 and pages 120 to 121 of their report and accounts 2012 (reproduced on pages 88 to 131 of this book). This section includes the corporate governance report itself, details of the board of directors, other statutory information, and the nomination committee report, audit committee report, remuneration report, the responsibility of directors, and the independent auditor's report.

The Johnson Matthey Plc 2012 Corporate Governance section begins with a letter from the Chairman, Tim Stevenson, which he starts by saying: 'Good governance is a cornerstone of a successful and sustainable company.' This is something with which we agree wholeheartedly, and are values that Johnson Matthey continually reinforces throughout its report.

Worked example 3.1

What are the basic problems that may be encountered by new shareholders with small shareholdings as they enter a relationship with the company they effectively part-own?

Most major UK plcs are owned by both individual and institutional shareholders. Some shareholders have large shareholdings, and some have small shareholdings, the analysis of which can be found in their companies' annual reports and accounts.

Usually within a very short time of acquiring their shares, most new small shareholders realise they have neither influence nor power.

As plcs have increasingly engaged in wider ranges of activities and become global businesses, so their directors have become more and more distanced from their shareholders. Compare the large multinational banks, for example, with locally based building societies.

During the move towards growth and expansion by companies, particularly throughout the 1980s, considerable disquiet regarding accountability emerged in the business community. In response to this the UK Government appointed the Committee on the Financial Aspects of Corporate Governance (Cadbury Committee), which produced its report in December 1992.

At the same time, there was also a great deal of unease regarding remuneration, bonus schemes, option schemes, and contracts. Various other committees on corporate governance, subsequent to Cadbury, such as the Greenbury, Hampel and Turnbull Committees, have reviewed each of these areas.

The UK Corporate Governance Code and Johnson Matthey's compliance with its provisions are set out on page 85 of its report and accounts 2012. On pages 86 to 90 of its Corporate Governance report, Johnson Matthey outlines the roles of the chairman, chief executive, executive directors, and non-executive directors, and explains the roles and composition of each of the corporate governance committees. Non-executive directors are represented on all Johnson Matthey's main committees, except the chief executive's committee:

- the Chief Executive's Committee (CEC) is responsible for recommending strategic and operating plans to the board of directors, and is chaired by the chief executive and comprises all the executive directors and non-board divisional directors and directors responsible for strategic development, human resources, legal, health and safety, and the company secretary, and has four sub-committees responsible for:
  - **corporate social responsibility (CSR)** compliance
  - information technology (IT)
  - contracts review
  - finance and administration
- the Nomination Committee is a sub-committee of the board of directors responsible for advising the board and making recommendations on the appointment, and if necessary, the removal of executive and non-executive directors, and is chaired by the company chairman and comprises all non-executive directors
- the Audit Committee is a sub-committee of the board of directors and is responsible for the monitoring and review of the systems of financial reporting, internal control and risk management, internal audit, and external audit, and is chaired by a non-executive director and comprises all non-executive directors, one of whom must have recent financial experience
- the Management Development and Remuneration Committee is a sub-committee of the board of directors and determines the remuneration of executive directors and senior management on behalf of the board of directors, including pension entitlements, share and bonus schemes, training, development and succession planning of senior management, and remuneration disclosure, and is chaired by a non-executive director and comprises all non-executive directors, and the company chairman.

The importance of CSR and sustainability is emphasised throughout Johnson Matthey's report and accounts 2012. Sustainability and CSR is outlined in the Governance and Sustainability report on pages 79 to 81 of the report (reproduced in this book on pages 91 to 93).

Sustainability and corporate social responsibility (CSR) reporting

Throughout the past 15 years or so companies have started to show greater interest in their position with regard to environmental and social issues. General corporate awareness has increased with regard to the adverse and favourable social and environmental effects that may result from the adoption of particular policies. Environmental issues naturally focus on our inability to sustain our use of non-renewable resources, the disappearance of the ozone layer, de-forestation, pollution, and waste treatment. Social issues may include problems associated with race, gender, disability, sexual orientation, and age, and the way that companies manage bullying, the incidence of accidents, employee welfare, training and development.

The increase in awareness of environmental and social issues has followed the concern that the focus of traditional reporting has been weighted too heavily towards the requirements of shareholders, with too little regard for the other stakeholders. That led to an over-emphasis on the financial performance, particularly the profitability, of the business. The accountancy profession and other interested parties have given thought to the widening of the annual report and accounts to meet the requirements of all stakeholders, and not just the shareholders of the business.

In March 2000, the UK Government appointed a Minister for Corporate Social Responsibility, and subsequently produced two reports on CSR:

- Business and Society, developing corporate social responsibility in the UK (2001)
- Business and Society – corporate social responsibility report (2002).

The UK Government, prior to May 2010, viewed CSR as the business contribution to sustainable development goals. It regarded CSR as essentially about how a business takes account of its economic, social, and environmental impacts in the way it operates – maximising the benefits and minimising the downsides. Indeed, the role played by businesses was clearly put at the centre of the Government's vision for the development of sustainable CSR, which saw 'UK businesses taking account of their economic, social, and environmental impacts, and acting to address the key sustainable development challenges based on their core competencies wherever they operate – locally, regionally, and internationally'. However, following the May 2010 general election change of government, the UK has been without a minister for CSR, thus putting the responsibility to continue its development firmly with businesses in the private sector.

CSR is about companies moving beyond a base of legal compliance to integrating socially responsible behaviour into their core values, and in recognition of the sound business benefits in doing so. In principle, CSR applies to SMEs as well as to large companies.

There is currently no consensus of 'best practice' in the area of social and environmental reporting. Nor is there a compulsory requirement for companies to include such statements in their annual reports and accounts. The UK Government's approach has been to encourage the adoption and reporting of CSR through best practice guidance, including development of a Corporate Responsibility Index and, where appropriate, intelligent regulation and fiscal incentives. Most large companies have reacted positively to the need for such reporting, although the quality, style and content, and the motives for inclusion, may vary from company to company. Motives may range from a genuine wish to contribute to the goal of sustainable development to simple reassurance, or attempts to mould and change opinion, and political lobbying.

While CSR does not currently appear to be one of the UK Government's top priorities, the European Union remains strongly supportive of CSR initiatives. The EU defines CSR as 'a concept whereby companies integrate social and environmental concerns in their business operations and in their interaction with their stakeholders on a voluntary basis'. EU material on CSR may be viewed on its website at: *http://ec.europa.eu/enterprise/policies/sustianable-business/corporate-social-responsibility.*

CSR performance reporting is still in its infancy. Although there has not been a great deal of work on what really constitutes best practice in CSR reporting some research has suggested that the higher standards of quality in CSR reporting are to be found in large companies which have the potential for greater impact on the environment. Companies engaged in CSR may benefit from improvements in their image and reputation, and in the longer term perhaps their profitability. As the focus on standardisation of targets, indicators, and audit of social and environmental performance increases, then the pressure for wider reporting may increase, and perhaps may be supported by a CSR financial reporting standard.

In Johnson Matthey's 2012 Governance and Sustainability report it states that the board of directors is ultimately responsible for social, environmental, and ethical matters. These matters are embedded into the group's risk management processes and reviewed annually by the board. The Audit Committee monitors performance and reviews the business risks associated with corporate social responsibility (CSR) at least once a year. Policies are set and approved by the Chief Executive's Committee (CEC). The CEC also addresses risk and control issues and reviews key environment, health and safety (EHS), social and governance issues. The CSR Compliance Committee, a sub-committee of the CEC, has specific executive responsibility for the identification and monitoring of risk in these areas. It sets and oversees compliance with group standards through the dissemination, adoption and implementation of appropriate group policies and other operational measures.

Every business within the Johnson Matthey group is required to include sustainability in its annual budget-setting process and define the nature of programmes and projects to be undertaken together with capital expenditure requirements and value generated over a three-year business cycle. Plans are discussed with the CEC and are formally approved by the board. As part of the process, progress against the Sustainability 2017 targets (see page 172 of Johnson Matthey's report and accounts 2012 for the international standardisation basis for these goals) is assessed on a group basis to establish if additional management action is required. The group has a formal system of site and functional reviews to drive improved performance in sustainability.

Companies that include CSR reporting in their annual reports and accounts now endeavour to go beyond a simple outline of their environmental and social policies. Many companies include reports expanding on these policies in qualitative ways that explain the performance of the business in its compliance with national and international standards. Some companies (for example Johnson Matthey Plc) have taken the next step to provide detailed quantitative reports of targets, performance, and the financial impact of social and environmental issues. Non-financial reporting may include data relating to, for example, energy consumption, water consumption, and total waste. A wide range of social, health and safety, and environment measures are included on page 171 of Johnson Matthey's report and accounts 2012 (reproduced on page 132.

In addition to CSR reporting, the CSR process itself is vitally important to a company's image, and ultimately its financial performance. Mini case 3.1 below provides examples of this by considering the contrasting approaches of Mattel and Toyota in dealing with some product quality issues.

A vital component of a company's CSR procedures is the speed and quality of its response to unexpected events. While CSR may be seen in this context like an insurance policy, which a company would rather not cash in, the effect of untoward events can have a serious impact on a company's reputation.

In 2007, American toy manufacturer Mattel recalled 20 million toys made in China over concerns with the lead content of paint and potentially loose, and therefore dangerous, components in some of their toys. A situation that could have been highly damaging to Mattel's reputation was handled swiftly by the company. They advertised the problem across major Internet sites and directed customers' attention to detailed instructions on Mattel's website on how to return products. In addition, Mattel's CEO took immediate responsibility, issuing a public apology and assuring customers that steps were being taken to prevent a similar incident.

A robust set of procedures can mitigate potentially harmful impacts on the reputation of major brands. A product recall is a damaging event but the problem can be compounded by the way in which the company reacts.

In 2010, Toyota announced that it was recalling vehicles as a result of a sticking accelerator pedal. In total, over 4 million cars were recalled to garages for repairs. However, events that had raised the alarm had begun in late 2009 and Toyota were seriously criticised for their slow response to the problem. In addition, it was alleged that the company had been applying the fix to cars in production a week before they went public with the problem and it was two weeks after recalls began that the company president made a public announcement. A damaging event was made worse by the company's inability to react decisively, therefore damaging corporate reputation.

The audit and the role of auditors

The annual audit of the accounts is a statutory requirement for most limited companies. However, for accounting periods starting on or after 6 April 2008, companies satisfying at least two of the following three limits qualify for the small company annual audit requirement exemption: an annual sales revenue of less than £6.5m; a balance sheet total of less than £3.26m; number of employees less than 50 (refer to the Department of Business Innovation and Skills website *www.bis.gov.uk* for changes to these limits). The shareholders of a limited company are responsible for appointing suitably qualified, independent persons, either individually or as a firm, to act as auditors. The external auditors are not part of the company but are responsible to the shareholders, with a main duty of objectively reporting to shareholders and others as to whether, in their opinion, the financial statements show a true and fair view, and comply with statutory, regulatory and financial and accounting standards requirements. Such an opinion is referred to as an unqualified opinion.

The report of the auditors is usually very short, and additionally includes:

- reference to the directors' responsibility for preparation of the annual report and accounts
- reference to the responsibility as auditors being established by
  - UK statute

  - the **Audit and Assurance Council**
  - the Listing Rules of the Financial Services Authority
  - the accountancy profession's ethical guidance.

The auditors are required to explain the basis of the audit, and report if, in their opinion:

- the directors' report is not consistent with the accounts
- the company has not kept proper accounting records
- they have not received all the information and explanations required for the audit
- information specified by law, or the Listing Rules regarding directors' remuneration and transactions with the company, is not disclosed
- company policies are appropriate and consistently applied and adequately disclosed
- all information and explanations considered necessary provide sufficient evidence to give reasonable assurance that the accounts are free from material mis-statement
- the overall presentation of information in the accounts is adequate.

There may very occasionally be circumstances when the financial statements may be affected by an inherent and fundamental uncertainty. In such cases the auditors are obliged to draw attention to the fundamental uncertainty. If the fundamental uncertainty is adequately accounted for and disclosed in the financial statements then the opinion of the auditors may remain unqualified. If there is inadequate disclosure about the fundamental uncertainty then the auditors must give what is termed a qualified opinion. A qualified **audit report** is something that may destroy company credibility and create uncertainty, and is obviously something to be avoided.

In addition to their reporting on the financial statements of the company, auditors' reports now include a statement of the company's corporate governance compliance with the provisions of the UK Corporate Governance Code (prior to 29 June 2010 the Combined Code on Corporate Governance). This review is in accordance with guidelines issued by the Audit and Assurance Council. The auditors are not required to:

- consider whether the statements by the directors on internal control cover all risks and controls
- form an opinion on the effectiveness of the company's corporate governance procedures or its risk management and internal control procedures
- form an opinion on the ability of the company to continue in operational existence.

The audit and the perceived role of auditors have been the subject of much criticism over the years. The responsibility of the auditors does not include guarantees that:

- the financial statements are correct
- the company will not fail
- there has been no fraud.

This gap, 'the expectations gap', between public expectation and what the audit actually provides is understandable in the light of the numerous examples of company failures and financial scandals from the 1980s to date. This has led to a lack of confidence of the business community in financial reporting, and in shareholders being unable to rely on safeguards that they assumed would be provided by their auditors.

The problem is that 'correctness' of financial statements is an unachievable result. We have seen this from our consideration of both the balance sheet and income statement because of inconsistencies in asset valuation and the level of subjective judgement required in their preparation. Directors are required to prepare, and auditors give an opinion on, accounts that give a true and fair view rather than accounts that are deemed 'correct'.

Companies increasingly face a greater diversity and level of risk:

- financial risk
- commercial risk
- operational risk,

and the increasing possibility of corporate failure is very real. Although the financial statements of companies are based on the going concern concept, the directors and auditors cannot realistically give any assurance that those businesses will not fail.

An area of risk that is of increasing concern to companies is fraud. This is perhaps due to the:

- increasing pace of change
- widespread use of computer systems
- ease and speed of communications and transfer of funds
- use of the Internet
- increase in staff mobility
- increasing dependence on specific knowledge (for example, Nick Leeson and Barings, and dot.com companies' IT experts).

Fraud is perhaps something on which auditors may arguably be expected to give an opinion. This is not something that is currently required from an external audit. It is something for which an **internal audit** department may be responsible. In the same way, external auditors could be requested to report on the adequacy or otherwise of systems of internal control.

Internal auditors are employees of the company. They are responsible and normally accountable to a non-executive director's audit committee within the company and independent of any functional activity or procedure within the company. The primary functions of an internal auditor are to:

- examine and evaluate how the company is managing its operational or strategic risks
- provide the company (audit committee or the board of directors) with information about whether risks have been identified, and how well such risks are being managed
- offer an independent opinion on the effectiveness and efficiency of internal controls (current operation protocols, policies, and procedures)
- review accounting information systems development to ensure that appropriate internal controls policies and procedures are maintained
- provide consultancy services and undertake special reviews at the request of management.

The role of an internal auditor includes:

- appraisal of the efficiency of the operational activities of the company
- assessment of the effectiveness of internal administrative and accounting controls
- evaluation of conformance with managerial procedures and policies,

and generally involves undertaking a wide range of audits, examinations, and reviews, including:

- systems-based audits
- internal control evaluations
- risk appraisals
- governance reviews
- security audits, particularly of computer-based information systems.

Major corporate fraud is now increasingly associated with communications and IT systems. The use of internal (or external) audit for the:

- detection of fraud
- minimisation of fraud
- elimination of fraud

therefore tends to be specialised and is something for which the costs and benefits must be carefully evaluated.

Progress check 3.2

What is an external audit and to whom are the auditors responsible, and for what?

The report of the independent auditors to the shareholders of Johnson Matthey Plc is included on page 121 of the report and accounts 2012 (reproduced on page 131 of this book). It can be seen to have complied with the standard audit reporting requirements outlined above. It may be interesting to compare the auditors' report for say 1982 with the same report for the year 2012, in which so many more areas are covered, and to appreciate the importance of corporate governance.

Worked example 3.2

The audit is the objective review (or sometimes the detailed examination) of business systems of internal control, risk management, and corporate governance, and the company's financial transactions. A business may engage internal and external auditors. The latter are considered the more independent, although both are paid by the business. External auditors are appointed by, and report to, the shareholders, whereas the internal auditors are employed by the company and report to the company's audit committee.

(i)   Why should the external auditors of a plc report directly to the shareholders and not to the chairman of the company?
(ii) Why should the internal auditors of a plc report to the audit committee and not to the finance director?
(iii) In what ways may the independence of a company's audit committee be demonstrated?

Suggested answers to these questions are:

(i)   The external auditors are appointed by and are responsible to the shareholders. The annual general meeting (AGM) is the formal meeting of directors, shareholders, and auditors. Conceivably, the chairman could shelve the report, with shareholders unaware of the contents. The law is quite strict on auditors' right to communicate directly with shareholders.
(ii) The finance director is responsible for the system of recording transactions. The finance director could prevent vital information from the internal auditors being distributed to others in the organisation.
(iii) The audit committee may request the non-executive directors to review specific areas, for example, the output from the internal auditors. The audit committee meets many times during the year and it offers a degree of objectivity. The careers of its members do not depend on the continuance of their directorship.

The directors of a company may not be accountants and they very rarely have any hands-on involvement with the actual putting together of a set of accounts for the company. However, directors of companies must make it their business to be fully conversant with the content of the accounts of their companies. Directors are responsible for ensuring that proper accounting records are maintained, and for ensuring reasonably accurate reporting of the financial position of their company, and ensuring their compliance with the Companies Act 2006. Immediately following the Remuneration Committee report, Johnson Matthey Plc's report and accounts 2012 includes on page 120 a section headed Responsibility of Directors (reproduced on page 130 of this book), which details the responsibilities of its directors in the preparation of its accounts.

We will now consider the role of directors and their responsibilities in more detail, and with regard to the UK Corporate Governance Code. We will also look at some of the circumstances in which directors of limited companies are particularly vulnerable, and how these may lead to disqualification of directors.

The fact that a corporate governance code exists or even that the appropriate corporate governance committees have been established is not necessarily a guarantee of effective corporate governance. There have been many examples of companies that have had corporate governance committees in place relating to directors and their remuneration, relations with shareholders, accountability, and audit. Nevertheless, some of these companies have given cause for great concern from shareholders following much-publicised revelations about financial scandals and apparent loosely-adhered-to corporate governance practices.

Such examples have been by no means confined to the UK. In 2009 Bernie Madoff, founder and principal of Bernard L Madoff Investment Securities, had traded on Wall Street for 40 years, where he was described as a 'legend'. He seemed to epitomise probity and honesty in the sometimes murky world of financial dealings. Madoff's investment fund consistently outperformed similar funds and demonstrated remarkably little volatility of returns irrespective of market conditions. With his apparent astute financial skills and quiet authority there was no shortage of investors eager to increase their savings in Madoff's fund. The bad news was that Madoff's fund was a US$65bn fraud, a Ponzi scheme which paid returns to investors from their own investments or from the money from other investors.

The USA Securities and Exchange Commission (SEC) defined a Ponzi scheme as an investment fraud that involves the payment of purported returns to existing investors from funds contributed by new investors. Ponzi scheme organisers often solicit new investors by promising to invest funds in opportunities claimed to generate high returns with little or no risk. In many Ponzi schemes, the fraudsters focus on attracting new money to make promised payments to earlier-stage investors and use for personal expenses, instead of engaging in any legitimate investment activity. The SEC further stated that:

> the schemes are named after Charles Ponzi, who duped thousands of New England residents into investing in a postage stamp speculation scheme back in the 1920s. At a time when the annual interest rate for bank accounts was five percent per annum, Ponzi promised investors that he could provide a 50 per cent return in just 90 days.

Bernie Madoff was sentenced to 150 years in prison in June 2009 for his part in what is probably the biggest financial fraud ever perpetrated. However, it is most unlikely that much of the investors' money embezzled will ever be recovered.

Directors' responsibilities

The board of directors of a limited company is appointed by, and is responsible to, the shareholders for the management of the company, maintained through their regular reporting on the activities of the business. Some directors may be senior managers employed within the business. Other directors may be non-executive directors who are not employed by the company. As we saw in Chapter 1 from the organisation chart in Figure 1.3, in addition to a chairman, the board of directors includes a chief executive (or managing director), and may include non-executive directors and executive directors responsible for each of the key areas of the business, for example:

- research and development
- sales and marketing
- human resources
- purchasing
- quality
- engineering
- manufacturing
- logistics
- information technology
- finance and accounting.

From Johnson Matthey's report and accounts 2012 we can see on page 83 (reproduced on page 95 in this book) that its board of directors comprises a chairman, chief executive, four executive directors, and four non-executive directors. There is also a company secretary who reports to the board.

Even though each director may have specific functional responsibilities, they also have general responsibilities as agents of the shareholders to manage the business in accordance with the objectives of the shareholders. The responsibilities of directors, however, are wider than to just the shareholders. They are also responsible for acting correctly towards their employees, suppliers, customers, and the public at large.

Agency and the ethical dimension

In Chapter 2 we introduced agency theory and saw how directors and managers of a company may not always act in the best interests of the shareholders. The agency problem manifests itself in a number of ways, for example through improper behaviour by managers and directors, such as:

- fraudulent activity
- misuse of company assets
- empire building
- awarding themselves excessive salaries, benefits, and perks.

The agency problem may also manifest itself in poor decision-making by managers and directors resulting in:

- a lack of investment in high-risk, value-adding projects investments – managers may prefer 'safer' options that do not put their jobs at risk
- investment in projects that generate negative NPVs (net present values) – managers may use inappropriate investment appraisal techniques
- a focus on earnings per share (eps) maximisation (which may be the basis of directors' remuneration incentive schemes), instead of shareholder wealth maximisation.

Jensen and Meckling (Jensen, MC and Meckling, WH 'Theory of the firm: managerial behaviour, agency costs, and ownership structure' *Journal of Financial Economics*, pages 305–60 (3 October, 1976)) identified alternative approaches to try and ensure that managers' and directors' objectives are aligned with shareholders' objectives. Their first approach considered how managers' and directors' behaviour may be monitored by shareholders by obtaining reports on their performance, work shadowing, and independent audits and analysis. This approach may be costly compared with the benefits derived from the alignment of managers' behaviour. It may also be impossible to spread such costs between all shareholders, and so the burden may fall on a few major shareholders, but with any resultant benefits being received by all shareholders.

Jensen and Meckling's alternative approach to achievement of goal congruence was to try and induce managers and directors on a contractual basis. Service contracts for directors and senior managers may include incentives to motivate goal congruence such as performance-related pay and share option schemes, as discussed in Chapter 2. Both approaches therefore incur agency costs of monitoring or inducement. Regardless of whichever approach has been adopted by companies, there have been obvious failures, which is apparent from the number of corporate financial scandals that have occurred.

We have seen how, in the wake of all these financial scandals, corporate governance guidelines have been developed on a worldwide basis essentially to try and deal with the agency problem relating to directors and shareholders. However, it may also be useful to consider the ethical dimension of agency rather than just the governance framework.

We made the assumption at the start of this book that maximisation of shareholder wealth is the primary objective of companies. Should we believe that in the real world the majority of company directors and managers act with integrity, and that they are law-abiding, honest, and conscientious in their efforts to maximise shareholder wealth? Alternatively, should we believe that the majority of company directors are greedy individuals who act purely in their own self-interest rather than looking after the interests of the shareholders? It has been suggested that perhaps managers should not be required to act in the best interests of shareholders. There is a body of opinion that argues that managers and directors of companies should actually look after themselves rather than the interests of the shareholders.

However, there may not actually be a conflict between the shareholder value-adding objective and acting with integrity and honesty. At the outset, in order to create any wealth at all directors and managers must ensure that the business is run on a cost-effective basis and satisfies its customers by providing goods and services at the quality and price they require. To achieve this, managers and directors will generally observe the unwritten rules and codes of good business behaviour. They do this because such codes have stood the test of time and generally work in everyone's interest. Directors and managers of companies are also aware that the credibility and good name of their businesses are key assets, and therefore their honesty, integrity, and trustworthiness are paramount.

In the area of corporate finance the reputation of a business is particularly important because there is not always absolute certainty about the product being bought and sold. For example, there is a big difference between buying a security and buying a refrigerator with regard to information asymmetry. When you buy a refrigerator you probably know as much about the product as the seller, which is unlikely to be the case when you buy a security. The businesses of financial institutions and banks should be built on establishing unblemished reputations for honesty, integrity, and square dealing. Anything that dents that reputation will be regarded as unacceptable and may cost them dearly.

Even if we assume that managers and directors of businesses generally act with honesty and integrity it is not always clear what is and what is not ethical behaviour. There are many grey areas and many not so grey areas of what may be considered unethical, for example:

- importing of clothing, footwear, and consumer goods from countries which exploit employment of children and other low-cost labour
- supply of cosmetics and pharmaceuticals which have been developed using testing on animals
- manufacture and sale of tobacco products

- manufacture and sale of alcohol
- a company's employment of men and women with the same experience and qualifications at different salary levels
- the sale of car fuel at different prices in different areas of the country
- a bank's issue of an identical loan at one rate of interest to one company and another rate of interest to another company.

Whether or not companies rely on:

- performance monitoring of managers and directors, or
- contractual inducements, or
- unwritten codes of good business behaviour, or
- corporate governance systems,

the 'good' management of a business is really dependent on individuals' personal values and ethical standards. Perhaps unethical people (for example Bernie Madoff) will always find ways of getting round the system, whereas people with integrity will not.

Directors' obligations

The responsibilities of directors, in terms of the UK Corporate Governance Code, can be seen to be important and far-reaching. It has been said that being a director is easy, but being a responsible director is not. It is important for all directors to develop an understanding and awareness of their ever-increasing legal obligations and responsibilities to avoid the potential personal liabilities, and even disqualification, which are imposed if those obligations are ignored.

It can be seen that the aims of most of the codes of practice and legislation have been to promote better standards of management in companies. This has also meant penalising irresponsible directors, the effect of which has been to create an increasingly heavy burden on directors regardless of the size or nature of the business they manage. The UK Government is actively banning offending directors.

Directors' duties are mainly embodied in the:

- Companies Act 2006
- Insolvency Act 1986 (as amended by the Enterprise Act 2002)
- Company Directors Disqualification Act 1986 (as amended by the Enterprise Act 2002)
- Enterprise Act 2002
- Health and Safety at Work Act 1974
- Health and Safety (Offences) Act 1986
- Financial Services Act 1986
- Corporate Manslaughter and Corporate Homicide Act 2007.

In addition, it should be noted that further statutory provisions giving rise to vicarious liability of directors for corporate offences are included in Acts of Parliament, which currently number well over 200! Directors can be:

- forced to pay a company's losses
- fined
- prevented from running businesses
- imprisoned.

The Directors' Remuneration Report Regulations 2002 (Statutory Instrument 2002 No. 1986) are now in force and require the directors of a company to prepare a remuneration report that is clear, transparent, and understandable to shareholders. Many smaller companies without continuous legal advice are unaware about how much the rules have tightened. It is usually not until there is wide publicity surrounding high-profile business problems that boards of directors are alerted to the demands and penalties to which they may be subjected if things go wrong.

Mini case 3.2

At the end of 1999, accounting irregularities caused trading in engineering company Trans-Tec shares to be suspended, with Arthur Andersen called in as administrative receiver. The case was fuelled by the revelation by former TransTec chief accountant Max Ayris that nearly £500,000 of a total of £1.3m in grants from the then Department of Trade and Industry (now re-designated as the BIS) was obtained fraudulently. TransTec, founded by former Government Minister Geoffrey Robinson, collapsed in December 1999, after the accounting irregularities were discovered, with debts of more than £70m. Following the collapse of the company the role of the auditors to the company, PricewaterhouseCoopers, was also to be examined by the Joint Disciplinary Scheme, the accountancy profession's senior watchdog.

Also during 1999, the trade finance group Versailles discovered that there had been some double counting of transactions, which also prompted the then DTI to take a close interest in its affairs.

Non-executive directors are legally expected to know as much as executive directors about what is going on in the company. Ignorance is not a defence. Directors must be aware of what is going on and have knowledge of the law relating to their duties and responsibilities. Fundamentally, directors must:

- use their common sense
- be careful in what they do
- look after shareholders
- look after creditors
- look after employees.

Progress check 3.3

What are the main responsibilities of directors with regard to the accounting and financial reporting of their companies?

Duty of care

It is the duty of a director to exercise his or her powers in the best interests of the company, which includes not acting for his or her personal benefit, or for an improper use of the company's assets. In the year 2000, Greg Hutchings, the then chairman of a major plc, Tomkins, was criticised for alleged excessive perks, unauthorised donations, improper use of the company's assets, and inclusion of members of his family and household staff on the company payroll, without proper disclosure. Investors' concern over corporate governance practices at the group had been triggered by a fall in the share price of over 50% in two years. The resignation of the chairman followed an initial investigation. The new chairman very quickly launched a full inquiry into executive perks within the group, overseen by him personally.

Duty of care means doing the job with the skill and care that somebody with the necessary knowledge and experience would exercise if they were acting on their own behalf. Delegation of directors' power must be 'properly and sensibly done'. If a director of a company does not choose the right people or supervise them properly, all the directors may be liable for the misdeeds and mistakes of the people they have appointed.

When a company fails and is found to be insolvent, the **receiver** appointed will leave no stone unturned to identify whether any money may be recovered in order to pay off creditors. This will include checking for any oversights by directors for items they should have spotted 'if they had exercised their proper level of skill'.

> **Progress check 3.4**
>
> What is a director's duty of care?

Fiduciary duty

Directors have a **fiduciary duty**, which means that they must act in the best interests of the company. Courts will support directors who act honestly and in good faith. Acting in the best interests of the company includes not making personal profit at the company's expense, not letting personal interest interfere with the proper running of the business, or doing business which favours directors or their close associates. In the late 1990s and early 2000s there were several business failures within the dot.com sector, where directors did act in the best interests of the company although their business plans may not have been commercially successful (for example, *www.breathe.com*).

> **Progress check 3.5**
>
> What is a director's fiduciary duty?

Corporate manslaughter

There is an offence of **corporate manslaughter**, of which a company may be guilty if a failure by its management is the cause of a person's death, and their failure is because their conduct is well below what can be reasonably expected. Before 1999 there were only five prosecutions in the UK for corporate manslaughter, resulting in two convictions. The risk for companies and their directors is remote but very real, and should therefore be managed in terms of awareness, training, preventative measures, and liability insurance.

In earlier years companies were outside the criminal law. As one judge put it, 'a company had a soul to damn and no body to kick'. What he meant was that because a company did not have an actual existence it could not be guilty of a crime because it could not have a guilty will. In 1965 a case established the validity of the indictment of a company for manslaughter. Since then over 19,000 people have been killed as a result of corporate activity, but no company stood trial for manslaughter, apart from P&O European Ferries (Dover) Ltd after the capsize and sinking of the *Herald of Free Enterprise* off Zeebrugge in 1987. The directors of P&O Ferries did stand trial, but were acquitted because the trial collapsed halfway through. To succeed in a case of corporate manslaughter against a company there was a need to prove gross negligence and to prove that at least one sufficiently senior official was guilty of that same gross negligence.

Although each year hundreds of people are killed at work or in commercially related activity, if companies were prosecuted at all they were charged under the Health and Safety at Work Act (1974) and other regulatory legislation. Many of the companies implicated in work fatalities and public transport disasters operated with diffuse management systems and much delegated power. Such systems that appeared to have no 'controlling mind' made it difficult to meet the requirement of the law because of the difficulty in identifying the individual(s) who may possess the mental element for the crime.

Mini case 3.3

A case that was successfully prosecuted involved a small company, OLL Ltd, which organised a canoe expedition at Lyme Bay in 1993, in which four teenage schoolchildren died. In 1994 the jury in the case found OLL Ltd guilty of manslaughter – a historic decision. Peter Kite, the managing director of the activity centre responsible for the canoeing disaster, was jailed for three years for manslaughter, and OLL Ltd was fined £60,000. OLL Ltd was the first company in the UK ever to be found guilty of manslaughter, in a decision that swept away 400 years of legal history.

The Lyme Bay case was atypical of corporate homicide incidents. The company was small, so it was relatively easy to discover the 'controlling mind'; the risks to which the schoolchildren were exposed were serious and obvious and, critically, they were not technical or esoteric in any way. However, in the case of a large corporation with many levels of management it is virtually impossible to identify a controlling mind.

Great Western Trains was fined £1.5m over the Southall (1997) rail crash in which seven people were killed, following a Health and Safety Executive (HSE) prosecution. But no individual within the company was charged with manslaughter.

The Paddington (1999) rail crash case that resulted in 31 people killed and over 400 injured was a case again brought by the HSE. The company, Thames Trains, was fined £2m in April 2004, but even though the HSE said its enquiries had revealed 'serious failing in management', there was no prosecution for corporate manslaughter.

A few years ago the legal profession considered that the promised review of the Law Commission's recommendation for an involuntary homicide Act 'could result in company directors being made personally responsible for safety and therefore potentially liable in cases of avoidable accidents'. The Corporate Manslaughter and Corporate Homicide Act (2007) replaces the concept of the 'controlling mind' with a consideration of the way in which an organisation's activities were managed or organised. The Act puts emphasis on examining management systems and practices across the organisation to establish whether an adequate standard of care was applied to the fatal situation. In 2011, the first attempted prosecution under the rules of the new Act was being tried in the courts, following several adjournments. The importance of this landmark case is illustrated in the press extract below.

Progress check 3.6

Why should companies be aware of the risk of corporate manslaughter?

A new chapter in English law on corporate manslaughter?

In law, small cases often mark major milestones. When the prosecution of Cotswold Geotechnical Holdings begins next week at Stroud Magistrates' Court, a new chapter in English law will begin. It will be the first case brought under the Corporate Manslaughter and Corporate Homicide Act 2007 and it signifies a new approach to prosecuting companies for alleged crimes.

The case concerns the death of Alexander Wright, 27, a geologist, who was taking soil samples from a pit that had been excavated as part of a site survey when the sides collapsed, crushing him.

The first chapter of corporate manslaughter law began on February 2, 1965, but it was rather an empty one. The Times reported what was then an innovation in English law: a company had stood trial for manslaughter. Glanville Evans, a 27-year-old welder, had been killed when the bridge at Boughrood that he was demolishing collapsed and he fell into the River Wye. The company had evidently been reckless in instructing him to work in a perilous way but an attempt to convict it for manslaughter at Glamorgan Assizes failed on the evidence.

Nonetheless, the court accepted that a company could be prosecuted for manslaughter. A new crime was recognised. Since then more than 40,000 people have been killed at work or in commercial disasters, such as those involving ferries and trains, while prosecutions for corporate manslaughter have totalled just 38.

The old common law made it very difficult to prosecute companies because the doctrine of identification required the prosecution to pin all the blame on at least one director whose will was identified as the 'mind' of the company. As companies commonly had responsibility for safety matters distributed across more than one directorial portfolio, pinning all the blame on one person was difficult. Various directors claimed to know only a fragment of the lethal danger that materialised. It was not permissible to incriminate the company by aggregating the fragmented faults of several directors.

The new law aims to criminalise corporate killing without the need to find all the blame in one individual. The offence is committed where an organisation owes a duty to take reasonable care for a person's safety but the way in which its business has been 'managed or organised' amounts to a gross breach of that duty and causes death.

The law says that, for a conviction, a 'substantial element' of the gross negligence must come from 'senior management' (as opposed to a maverick worker) but any company trying to evade the law by not making safety the responsibility of a senior manager would, by virtue of that very stratagem, be open to legal attack.

Companies convicted of manslaughter can be made to publicise their wrongdoing in the national press and are subject to an unlimited fine. The Sentencing Advisory Panel has suggested a level of fine of between 2.5 and 10 per cent of a convicted company's average annual turnover [revenue] during the three years before the offence. This is a dramatic change. Most large companies convicted of fatal safety crimes are now fined at a level that is less than one 700th of annual turnover.

Directors can be prosecuted for safety offences alongside a corporate manslaughter prosecution and the Health and Safety (Offences) Act 2008 has widened the range of offences for which prison is a possible punishment.

The new corporate manslaughter law obliges the jury to consider whether a company is guilty by looking at what happened in the context of general safety law. Jurors are also invited to consider how far the evidence shows that there were 'attitudes, policies, systems or accepted practices within the organisation' that were likely to have encouraged the safety failures that resulted in death.

Historically, the law was chiselled to govern individuals accused of homicide and it could not properly be adapted to prosecute corporations. That became more problematic once companies became so powerful

– of the world's 100 largest economic entities today, 49 are countries and 51 are companies. Having corporate citizens that are
more powerful than governments is a challenge for good social governance.

Globally, more people are killed each
year at work or through commercial enterprise – more than two million – than die in

wars. If the Act works well in the United
Kingdom it will be a good template to be
adopted in other countries, and that would
confer a substantial social benefit.

Source: **The small cases that will have a big
influence on the way we work**; Gary Slapper reflects
on the deaths that have led to changes in corporate
manslaughter law © *The Times*, 11 July 2009

The defendant in the above case was found guilty on 15 February 2011. The Corporate
Manslaughter and Corporate Homicide Act 2007 is now expected to dramatically increase
the level of directors' accountability to ensure the provision of safe work environments for
their employees.

Progress check 3.7

What impact is the Corporate Manslaughter and Corporate Homicide Act 2007 likely to have
on directors' management practice?

Other responsibilities

Directors do not owe a direct duty to shareholders, but to the company itself. Directors have no
contractual or fiduciary duty to outsiders and are generally not liable unless they have acted in
breach of their authority. Directors must have regard to the interests of employees but this is
enforceable against directors only by the company and not by the employees.

Insolvency

 Insolvency, or when a company becomes insolvent, is when the company is unable to pay
creditors' debts in full after realisation of all the assets of the business. The penalties imposed
on directors of companies continuing to trade while insolvent may be disqualification and personal liability. Many directors have lost their houses (as well as their businesses) as a result of
being successfully pursued by the receivers appointed to their insolvent companies.

The Insolvency Act 1986 (as amended by the Enterprise Act 2002) provides guidance on
matters to be considered by liquidators and receivers in the reports that they are required to
prepare on the conduct of directors. These matters include:

- breaches of fiduciary and other duties to the company
- misapplication or retention of monies or other property of the company
- causing the company to enter into transactions which defrauded the creditors
- failure to keep proper accounting and statutory records
- failure to make annual returns to the Registrar of Companies and prepare and file annual
  accounts.

If a company is insolvent, the courts assess the directors' responsibility for:

- the cause of the company becoming insolvent
- the company's failure to supply goods or services which had been paid for
- the company entering into fraudulent transactions or giving preference to particular creditors
- failure of the company to adhere to the rules regarding creditors' meetings in a creditors' **voluntary winding-up**
- failure to provide a **statement of affairs** or to deliver up any proper books or information regarding the company.

Mini case 3.4

In March 2012, following an investigation by The Insolvency Service's Company Investigations Team, Paul William Sharpley, a director of Property 360 Limited in Suffolk, was disqualified from acting as a company director or from managing or in any way controlling a company for seven years.

Mr Sharpley, whose company provided marketing services to estate agents, was accused of failing to ensure the company maintained, preserved or delivered up adequate accounting records.

The National Insolvency Service reported that it had been unable to establish the financial position, income and expenditure, or the use of company funds at any point during its trading. It was also unable to explain why the computerised bank report showed £76,098 as a bank balance at 2 March 2010 when in fact the balance was only £22. The National Insolvency Service reported that at the time of the company's liquidation it could not verify how much the company owed HMRC in unpaid VAT.

It is not only the directors who may be prosecuted. If a company employs a disqualified director it too is liable for prosecution. Scottish businessman Craig Whyte acquired the controlling interest in Glasgow Rangers FC in May 2011 while he was still under a seven-year ban. Rangers went into administration in February 2012 and on discovery of Mr Whyte's ban in the same month Rangers were fined £50,000 by the London-based PLUS Stock Exchange which also suspended trading in the company's shares.

Progress check 3.8

How does insolvency impact on directors and what are their responsibilities in this regard?

Wrongful trading

A major innovation of the Insolvency Act 1986 was to create the statutory tort (civil wrong) of **wrongful trading**. It occurs where a director knows or ought to have known before the commencement of winding up that there was no reasonable prospect of the company avoiding insolvency and he or she does not take every step to minimise loss to creditors. If the court is satisfied of this it may:

- order the director to contribute to the assets of the business,

  and

- disqualify him or her from further involvement in corporate management for a specified period.

A director will not be liable for wrongful trading if he or she can show that from the relevant time he or she 'took every step with a view to minimising the potential loss to the company's creditors as (assuming him or her to have known that there was no reasonable prospect that the company would avoid going into insolvent liquidation) he or she ought to have taken'. A company goes into insolvent liquidation, for this purpose, if it does so at a time when its assets are insufficient for the payment of its debts and other liabilities and the costs of a winding-up.

Both subjective tests and objective tests are made with regard to directors. A director who is responsible, for example, for manufacturing, quality, purchasing, or human resources, is likely to have less skill and knowledge regarding the financial affairs of the company than the **finance director**, unless otherwise fully briefed. Directors with financial or legal experience will certainly be expected to bear a greater responsibility than other directors because of their specialist knowledge.

Progress check 3.9

What is wrongful trading?

Fraudulent trading

Fraudulent trading is an offence committed by persons who are knowingly party to the continuance of a company trading in circumstances where creditors are defrauded, or for other fraudulent purposes. Generally, this means that the company incurs more debts at a time when it is known that those debts will not be met. Persons responsible for acting in this way are personally liable without limitation for the debts of the company. The offence also carries criminal penalties.

The offence of fraudulent trading may apply at any time, not just in or after a winding-up. If a company is wound up and fraudulent trading has taken place, an additional civil liability arises in respect of any person who was knowingly a party to it.

Progress check 3.10

Are there any differences between wrongful trading and fraudulent trading? If so, what are they?

Disqualification of directors

Disqualification means that a person cannot be, for a specified period of time, a director or manager of any company without the permission of the courts. Disqualification is governed under the Company Directors (Disqualification) Act 1986, and may result from breaches under:

■ the Companies Act 2006 – from cases of fraud or other breaches of duty by a director
■ the Insolvency Act 1986 (as amended by the Enterprise Act 2002) – if the courts consider that the conduct of a director makes him or her unfit to be concerned in the future management of a company.

While there are serious implications for directors of companies under the Company Directors (Disqualification) Act 1986, it should be noted that the Act is not restricted to company directors. Over one half of the liabilities fall on 'any persons' as well as company directors. 'Any persons' in this context potentially includes any employee within the organisation.

The following offences, and their penalties, under the Act relate to any persons:

- being convicted of an indictable offence – disqualification from company directorships for up to five years, and possibly for up to 15 years
- fraud in a winding-up – disqualification from company directorships for up to 15 years
- participation in fraudulent or wrongful trading – disqualification from company directorships for up to 15 years
- acting as a director while an undischarged bankrupt, and failure to make payments under a county court administration order – imprisonment for up to two years, or a fine, or both
- personal liability for a company's debts where the person acts while disqualified – civil personal liability.

The following offences, and their penalties, under the Act relate to directors (but in some instances include other managers or officers of the company):

- persistent breaches of company legislation – disqualification from company directorships for up to five years
- convictions for not less than three default orders in respect of a failure to comply with any provisions of companies' legislation requiring a return, account or other document to be filed, delivered, sent, etc., to the Registrar of Companies (whether or not it is a failure of the company or the director) – disqualification from company directorships for up to five years
- finding of unfitness to run a company in the event of the company's insolvency – disqualification from company directorships for a period of between two years and 15 years
- if after investigation of a company the conduct of a director makes him or her unfit to manage a company – disqualification from company directorships for up to 15 years
- attribution of offences by the company to others if such persons consent, connive or are negligent – imprisonment for up to two years, or a fine, or both, or possibly imprisonment for not more than six months, or a fine.

Mini case 3.5

In February 2010 it was reported that five former directors of a timeshare company, Worldwide International UK Limited, had been disqualified for a total of 32 years following an investigation by the Companies Investigation Branch (CIB). Mr Bruce Goss, the controlling director of the family firm, was disqualified for 8 years after the CIB investigation found that the company, which marketed timeshare and holiday products, was run with a 'serious lack of commercial probity', leading to several complaints to trading standards. The CIB suggested he caused the company to trade while insolvent and was responsible for 'intermingling' the accounts of several different companies. There was also a failure to keep proper accounts and a failure to pay debts. In addition, it was claimed that the family had a 'propensity' to transfer surplus funds to their own accounts. In the judgment disqualifying Mr Goss, the High Court Registrar said, 'I am therefore satisfied that the allegations made against Mr Goss disclose persistent and serious dishonesty. Even when the company's financial situation was clearly hopeless he allowed it to continue to take money from customers and those customers who sought explanations were lied to and deceived'.

Let's look at the important implications of the above case and the way in which the law protects society from the actions of unscrupulous directors. There are some fundamental reasons why it is necessary for society to ban certain individuals from becoming directors of limited companies.

- The limited liability company is a very efficient means of conducting business, but if used by unscrupulous persons then innocent people can lose money, through no fault of their own.
- The limited liability company can offer a financial shield to protect employees and investors if things go wrong and the company ceases trading, and is unable to pay its creditors.

UK law is now quite strict and will attack an obviously unscrupulous person who takes advantage of the protection of the limited liability company and leaves various creditors out of pocket.

The UK Government is now banning an increasing number of persons from becoming directors, as well as publishing their names in the public domain (for example, on the Internet). Almost certainly the current, recently-introduced regime is showing its teeth and punishing guilty directors in a most practical manner.

In some circumstances directors may be disqualified automatically. Automatic disqualification occurs in the case of an individual who revokes a county court administration order, and in the case of an undischarged bankrupt unless **leave of the court** is obtained. In all other situations the right to act as a director may be withdrawn only by an order of the court, unless a company, through its Articles of Association, provides for specific circumstances in which a director's appointment may be terminated. The City of London has seen a major toughening of the circumstances where persons have found themselves unemployable (for example, the fallout from the Barings Bank debacle in the mid-1990s).

> ### Progress check 3.11
>
> In what circumstances may a director be disqualified?

Summary of directors' obligations and responsibilities

In summary, the following may serve as a useful checklist of the board of executive and non-executive directors' obligations and responsibilities:

- both executive and non-executive directors must act with care, look after the finances of the business, and act within their powers, and look after employees
- directors are responsible for keeping proper books of account and presenting shareholders with accounts, and failure to do so can result in disqualification
- directors should understand the accounts and be able to interpret them
- the board of directors is responsible for filing accounts with the Registrar of Companies and must also notify changes to the board of directors and changes to the registered address
- shareholders must appoint auditors
- the directors are responsible for calling and holding annual general meetings, and ensuring minutes of all meetings are appropriately recorded
- directors are responsible for ensuring that the company complies with its memorandum and articls of association
- if a company continues to trade while technically insolvent and goes into receivership a director may be forced to contribute personally to repaying creditors
- a director trading fraudulently is liable to be called on for money
- any director who knew or ought to have known that insolvency was unavoidable without minimising loss to the creditors becomes liable
- directors can be disqualified for paying themselves too much
- inadequate attention paid to the financial affairs of the company can result in disqualification
- directors are required to prepare a remuneration report.

We have seen the onerous burden of responsibility placed on directors of limited companies in terms of compliance with guidelines and legislation. The obligations of directors continue to grow with the increase in government regulation and legislation. Sixteen new directives were introduced in the UK during the two years to 2001, relating to such issues as employee working conditions, health and safety and, for example, administration of a minimum wage policy.

How can directors make sure that they comply and cover themselves in the event of things going wrong?

Actions to ensure compliance

Directors of companies need to be aware of the dividing line between the commission of a criminal offence and the commission of technical offences of the Companies Act. Directors should take the necessary actions to ensure compliance with their obligations and responsibilities, and to protect themselves against possible non-compliance:

- directors may delegate their responsibilities within or outside the company and in such circumstances they must ensure that the work is being done by competent, able and honest people
- directors of small companies in particular should get professional help to ensure compliance with statutory responsibilities
- directors must ensure that they are kept fully informed about the affairs of the company by having regular meetings and recording minutes and material decisions
- directors should ensure they have service contracts that cover the company's duties, rights, obligations and directors' benefits
- directors must ensure that detailed, timely management accounts are prepared, and, if necessary, professional help sought to provide, for example, monthly reporting systems and assistance with interpretation of information produced and actions required.

It is essential that directors carefully watch for warning signs of any decline in the company's position, for example:

- falling sales or market share
- over-dependence on one product or customer or supplier
- overtrading (see Chapter 16)
- pressure on bank borrowings
- increases in trade payables
- requirements for cash paid in advance
- increasing inventories levels
- poor financial controls.

The protection that directors may obtain is extremely limited. All directors should certainly take out individual professional liability insurance. But above all it is probably more important that all directors clearly understand their obligations and responsibilities, closely watch company performance, and take immediate, appropriate action as necessary, to ensure compliance and minimise their exposure to the type of personal risks we have discussed above.

Progress check 3.12

What actions should directors take to ensure they meet their obligations, and to protect themselves should things go wrong?

Summary of key points

- The framework for establishing good corporate governance and accountability has been established in a UK Corporate Governance Code, developed from the work of the Cadbury, Greenbury, Hampel, and Turnbull Committees.

- Corporate governance codes are increasingly being developed in many other countries, for example throughout Europe, China, and the Middle East, and including the USA's Sarbanes–Oxley Act 2002.

- Sustainability and corporate social responsibility (CSR) reporting by companies is becoming increasingly important and includes areas such as environmental and social issues, global warming, waste management, and the efficient use of resources such as water and energy.

- There are various approaches to dealing with the agency problem, including monitoring performance and offering incentives to company managers and directors, and development of corporate governance systems, but consideration should also be given to the ethical dimension.

- There is a statutory requirement for the audit of the accounts of limited companies, except for smaller limited companies which may be exempted.

- The election of suitably qualified, independent auditors is the responsibility of the shareholders, to whom they are responsible.

- Directors of limited companies have a specific responsibility to shareholders, and general responsibilities to all stakeholders and the community, for the management and conduct of companies. (Note the continued activities of pressure groups such as Greenpeace and Friends of the Earth.)

- Directors of limited companies have a fiduciary duty to act in the best interests of the company, and a duty of care to all stakeholders and to the community at large, particularly with regard to the Companies Act 2006, Health and Safety at Work Act 1974, Health and Safety (Offences) Act 2008, Financial Services Act 1986, Insolvency Act 1986, and Enterprise Act 2002.

- The risk for companies and their directors from the Corporate Manslaughter and Homicide Act 2007 has become very real, and should therefore be managed in terms of awareness, training, preventative measures and liability insurance.

- The implications for directors of wrongful trading may be to contribute to the assets of the business, and disqualification from further involvement in corporate management for a specified period.

- The implications for directors of fraudulent trading may be to contribute to the assets of the business without limit, disqualification, and possible criminal and civil penalties.

- The implications of the Company Directors (Disqualification) Act 1986 (as amended by the Enterprise Act 2002) apply not only to company directors, and over 50% of the provisions relate to any persons.

- Directors of limited companies, in addition to taking out individual professional liability insurance, must ensure that they clearly understand their obligations and responsibilities.

Glossary of key terms

Audit and Assurance Council The body which considers and advises the FRC Board and the Codes and Standards Committee on audit and assurance matters. Its work includes preparation of standards and guidance for auditors and development of ethical standards and guidance for auditors' and reporting accountants' integrity, objectivity and independence.

audit report An objective verification to shareholders and other users that the financial statements have been prepared properly and in accordance with legislative and regulatory requirements; that they present the information truthfully and fairly; and that they conform to the best accounting practice in their treatment of the various measurements and valuations.

corporate manslaughter An offence for which a company may be guilty if a failure by its management is the cause of a person's death, and their failure is because their conduct is well below what can be reasonably expected. This is covered by the Corporate Manslaughter and Homicide Act 2007.

corporate social responsibility (CSR) CSR is the decision-making and implementation process that guides all company activities in the protection and promotion of international human rights, labour and environmental standards, and compliance with legal requirements within its operations and in its relations to the societies and communities where it operates. CSR involves a commitment to contribute to the economic, environmental, and social sustainability of communities through the ongoing engagement of stakeholders, the active participation of communities impacted by company activities, and the public reporting of company policies and performance in the economic, environmental and social arenas (*www.bench-marks.org*).

director A person elected under the company's articles of association to be responsible for the overall direction of the company's affairs. Directors usually act collectively as a board and carry out such functions as are specified in the articles of association or the Companies Acts, but they may also act individually in an executive capacity.

duty of care A duty of care means doing the job with the skill and care that somebody with the necessary knowledge and experience would exercise if they were acting on their own behalf, and if a director of a company does not choose the right people or supervise them properly, all the directors may be liable for the misdeeds and mistakes of the people they have appointed.

fiduciary duty A duty of directors to act in the best interests of the company, and with a duty of care to all stakeholders and to the community at large, particularly with regard to the Companies Act 2006, Health and Safety at Work Act 1974, Health and Safety (Offences) Act 2008, Financial Services Act 1986, Insolvency Act 1986, and Enterprise Act 2002.

finance director The finance director of an organisation is actively involved in broad strategic and policy-making activities involving financial considerations. The finance director provides the board of directors with advice on financing, capital expenditure, acquisitions, dividends, the implications of changes in the economic environment, and the financial aspects of legislation. The finance director is responsible for the planning and control functions, the financial systems, financial reporting, and the management of funds.

fraudulent trading An offence committed by persons who are knowingly party to the continuance of a company trading in circumstances where creditors are defrauded or for other fraudulent purposes. Generally, this means that the company incurs more debts at a time when it is known that those debts will not be met. Persons responsible for so acting are personally liable without limitation for the debts of the company. The offence also carries criminal penalties.

insolvency The inability of a company, partnership, or individual to pay creditors' debts in full after realisation of all the assets of the business.

internal audit An independent appraisal function established within an organisation to examine and evaluate its activities as a service to the organisation. The objective of internal auditing is to assist members of the organisation in the effective discharge of their responsibilities. To this end, internal auditing furnishes them with analyses, appraisals, recommendations, counsel, and information concerning the activities reviewed (Chartered Institute of Internal Auditors – UK).

leave of the court This is where the court will make a decision after hearing all the relevant information.

non-executive director A director who does not have an executive function to perform within the company's management. The usual involvement is to attend board meetings and chair and attend corporate governance committee meetings.

receiver A person appointed by secured creditors or by the court to take control of company property, usually following the failure of the company to pay principal sums or interest due to debenture holders whose debt is secured by fixed or floating charges over the assets of the company. The receiver takes control of the charged assets and may operate the company's business with a view to selling it as a going concern. In practice, receivership is usually closely followed by liquidation.

statement of affairs Details submitted to the receiver during the winding-up of a company identifying the assets and liabilities of the company. The details are prepared by the company directors, or other persons specified by the receiver, and must be submitted within 14 days of the winding-up order or the appointment of a provisional liquidator.

voluntary winding-up A voluntary winding-up of a company occurs where the company passes a resolution that it shall liquidate and the court is not involved in the process. A voluntary winding-up may be made by the members (the shareholders) of the company or by its creditors, if the company has failed to declare its solvency.

wrongful trading Wrongful trading occurs where a director knows or ought to have known before the commencement of winding-up that there was no reasonable prospect of the company avoiding insolvency and he or she does not take every step to minimise loss to creditors. If the court is satisfied of this it may (i) order the director to contribute to the assets of the business, and (ii) disqualify him or her from further involvement in corporate management for a specified period (Insolvency Act 1986).

Assessment material

Questions

Q3.1 (i) How was the UK Corporate Governance Code developed?
(ii) Why was it considered necessary?

Q3.2 Refer to the Johnson Matthey Plc section on corporate governance in its annual report and accounts 2012, shown on pages 88 to 130, and illustrate their areas of compliance (or not) under the UK Corporate Governance Code (as distinct from the previous Combined Code of Practice).

Q3.3 (i) Which areas of the business do auditors' opinions cover?
(ii) What happens if there is any fundamental uncertainty as to compliance?

Q3.4 Explain the implications of the 'expectation gap' with regard to external auditors.

Q3.5 Explain the obligations of directors of limited companies in terms of their duty of care, their fiduciary duty, and the Corporate Manslaughter and Corporate Homicide Act (2007).

Q3.6 If the severity of the penalty is determined by the seriousness of the offence, describe the half dozen or so most serious offences under the Company Directors (Disqualification) Act 1986 (as amended by the Enterprise Act 2002), which relate to directors of limited companies.

Q3.7 Outline the general responsibilities of a director of a limited company with regard to the company, its shareholders, and other stakeholders.

Q3.8 What are the key actions that a director of a limited company may take to ensure compliance with his or her obligations and responsibilities?

Discussion points

D3.1 Discuss, and illustrate with some examples, how far you think the UK Corporate Governance Code goes to preventing the kind of corporate excesses we have seen in the recent past.

D3.2 'I pay my auditors a fortune in audit fees. I look upon this almost as another insurance premium to make sure that I'm protected against every kind of financial risk.' Discuss.

D3.3 'Everyone who embarks on a career in industry or commerce aspires to becoming a director of their organisation, because then all their troubles are over! Directors just make a few decisions, swan around in their company cars, and pick up a fat cheque at the end of each month for doing virtually nothing.' Discuss.

D3.4 In an age of increasingly sophisticated computer systems, is the traditional role of the auditor coming to an end?

Exercises

Solutions are provided in Appendix 2 to all exercise numbers highlighted in colour.

Level I

E3.1   *Time allowed – 15 minutes*

> What role does accounting information play in corporate governance?

E3.2   *Time allowed – 30 minutes*

> Identify the major participants within the corporate financial environment and explain how they contribute to effective corporate governance.

E3.3   *Time allowed – 30 minutes*

> Discuss why users of financial statements should have information on awards to directors of share options, allowing them to subscribe to shares at fixed prices in the future.

E3.4   *Time allowed – 30 minutes*

> Outline the basic reasons why there should be openness regarding directors' benefits and 'perks'.

E3.5   *Time allowed – 30 minutes*

> Can you think of any reasons why directors of UK plcs found that their contracts were no longer to be open-ended under the UK Corporate Governance Code?

E3.6   *Time allowed – 60 minutes*

> William Mason is the managing director of Classical Gas plc, a recently formed manufacturing company in the chemical industry, and he has asked you as finance director to prepare a report that covers the topics, together with a brief explanation, to be included in a section on corporate governance in their forthcoming annual report and accounts.

Level II

E3.7   *Time allowed – 60 minutes*

After the birth of her twins Vimla Shah decided to take a couple of years away from her career as a company lawyer. During one of her coffee mornings with Joan Turnbull, Joan confided in her that although she was delighted at her husband Ronnie's promotion to commercial director of his company, which was a large UK plc in the food industry, she had heard many horror stories about problems that company directors had encountered, seemingly through no fault of their own. She was worried about the implications of these obligations and responsibilities (whatever they were) that Ronnie had taken on. Vimla said she would write some notes about what being a director of a plc meant, and provide some guidelines as to the type of things that Ronnie should be aware of, and to include some ways in which Ronnie might protect himself, that may all offer some reassurance to Joan.

Prepare a draft of what you think Vimla's notes for Joan may have included.

E3.8   *Time allowed – 60 minutes*

Li Nan has recently been appointed managing director of Pingers plc, which is a company that supplies table tennis equipment to clubs and individuals throughout the UK and Europe. Li Nan is surprised at the high figure that appeared in last year's accounts under audit fees.

Li Nan is not completely familiar with UK business practices and has requested you to prepare a detailed report on what the audit fees cover, and to include the general responsibilities of directors with regard to the external audit.

E3.9   *Time allowed – 60 minutes*

Use the following information, extracted from Tomkins plc report and accounts as a basis for discussing the needs of users of financial information for information on directors' remuneration.

	Basic salary	Benefits in kind	Bonuses
G Hutchings, executive director	£975,000	£45,000	£443,000
G Gates (USA), non-executive director	nil, but has a US$ 250,000 consultancy agreement		
R Holland, non-executive director	£23,000	Nil	Nil

E3.10   *Time allowed – 60 minutes*

Explain what is meant by insolvency and outline the responsibilities of receivers appointed to insolvent companies.

4

Risk, return, and portfolio theory

Chapter contents

Learning objectives

Completion of this chapter will enable you to:

- Explain the relationship between risk and return.
- Outline investor attitudes to risk.
- Describe what is meant by business risk and financial risk.
- Consider the impact of risk on financing.
- Describe what is meant by systematic and unsystematic risk.
- Explain the role of diversification in the mitigation of unsystematic risk.
- Explain portfolio theory.
- Appreciate the significance of risk-free investments, investors' preferences, and the capital market line (CML).

Introduction

This chapter looks at the uncertainty and risk surrounding decisions made by both the shareholders and managers and directors of businesses and how these relate to the returns or paybacks achieved following such decisions.

The fundamental objective of a business is to maximise the wealth of the shareholders, or the owners of the business. The increase in the wealth of shareholders, or total share-holder return, is derived from dividends and increases in the market prices of their shares. The ability of a company to pay dividends is ultimately determined by its decision-making success with regard to its 'real' investment in value-creating projects. The market price of a company's shares is determined by the demand for its shares, which in turn depends on the market perception of the business and its ability to generate future cash flows.

When an investor buys shares there is uncertainty with regard to the level of future dividends that may be received. There is also uncertainty with regard to how much the share price may increase, or decrease. The level of total shareholder returns is therefore uncertain and some shares are more uncertain or riskier than others. For example, the expected returns from an investment in the shares of a hi-tech company will generally be far riskier than the expected returns from an investment in the shares of a food manufacturer.

When the directors of a business make 'real' investments in new projects there is uncertainty not only with regard to each of the factors relating to a project like its investment cost, its cost of capital etc., but particularly with regard to the expected returns on the investments. The level of returns from 'real' investments is therefore uncertain, and some projects are more uncertain or riskier than others.

This chapter will consider the relationship between the risks and returns from both investments in shares and investments in 'real' projects. We will consider the way in which approaches to risk are different from one individual to another, and how risk may be mitigated or reduced by investing in a range or portfolio of shares or projects.

The chapter examines Markowitz's portfolio theory, which deals with the way in which investors are able to diversify risk by holding combinations of different securities. This chapter closes with a look at investors' preferences with regard to investments in risk-free and market risk securities and the proportions of both which may be shown on the capital market line (CML).

The relationship between risk and return

There is a fundamental relationship that exists between risk and return. We will consider this relationship, and also investor attitudes to risk, the different types of risk and their impact on the business, its cost of capital, and its strategies.

Decision-making relates to alternative outcomes that may occur as a result of whichever decision is taken. The likelihood of a particular outcome occurring is never certain. The return or payback resulting from a particular decision may be more or less than expected. The level of uncertainty relating to the expected outcome that may be quantified is the level of the risk of that outcome not occurring. Generally, the higher the level of risk the higher will be the expected return. The lower the level of risk, the lower will be the expected return. As we have seen in earlier chapters, the directors of businesses make decisions to invest in new projects only if they are expected to provide value added to the business in real terms.

Worked example 4.1

Eryl Ltd is considering investing surplus cash in one of the following companies:

Company	Expected return %	Risk %
AB plc	10	12
CD plc	10	24
EF plc	20	24
GH plc	20	28

We are required to advise Eryl Ltd which investment should be selected.

If Eryl Ltd is a rational and risk-averse investor, then it would invest in AB plc (minimum investment risk). If Eryl Ltd is a rational but risk-taking investor, then it would invest in EF plc (maximum return).

Neither CD plc, nor GH plc should be selected since CD plc has the same return as AB plc but higher risk, and GH plc has the same return as EF plc but a higher risk.

Let's consider a company, which has a risk/return profile represented by the line YXZ in Figure 4.1. This means that the company will maintain the same level of value wherever it may position itself along line YXZ in terms of combinations of risk and return.

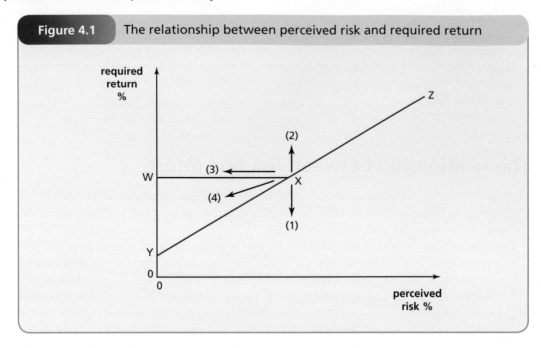

Figure 4.1 The relationship between perceived risk and required return

If the company is assumed to be at point X in terms of its perceived risk and required return from current projects we can consider the impact of any strategic move by the company from point X, along the line YXZ, and to either above or below line YXZ. Increasing value is not just about increasing return or reducing risk, but it is to do with the level of increased required return compared with the increased perception of risk. A move down the line XY reduces risk but proportionately reduces returns, and a move up the line XZ increases returns but proportionately increases risk. Either way, value is neither created nor destroyed.

Any strategic move (1) to below line YXZ will destroy existing value, because risk is disproportionately higher for any increased returns when compared against the current risk/return profile YXZ.

Any strategic move above line YXZ will create shareholder value. A move (2) above the line WXZ will increase returns for any given reduction in risk and by proportionately more than any increase in risk. We can clearly see that a move (3) along the line XW will reduce risk, while at the same time maintaining the same level of return. However, a move (4) to within the triangle WXY will reduce risk but by proportionately less than any increase in required return, but it is still value adding. An example of this may be seen when a company decides to pay out large insurance premiums to cover specific risks faced by the company. This has the effect of reducing profit, but it also reduces risk and therefore protects the company's future cash flows and so increases the value of the business.

There is also a degree of risk involved whenever any investment is made in a company's securities. The total actual return on investment in ordinary (equity) shares may be better or worse than hoped for. Unless the investor settles for risk-free securities a certain element of risk is unavoidable.

Progress check 4.1

What is the relationship between risk and return?

However, investors in companies or in projects can diversify their investments in a suitably wide portfolio. Some investments may do better and some worse than expected. In this way, average returns should turn out much as expected. Risk that is possible to be diversified away in this way is referred to as **unsystematic risk**.

Some investments are by their very nature more risky than others. This is nothing to do with chance variations in actual compared with expected returns. It is inherent risk that cannot be diversified away. This type of risk is referred to as **systematic risk** or market risk, as distinct from unsystematic risk (risk that is unique to a specific company). The investor must therefore accept systematic risk, unless they invest entirely in risk-free investments. In return for accepting systematic risk an investor will expect to earn a return that is higher than the return on risk-free investment.

The two broad components of systematic risk are **business risk** and **financial risk**. The amount of systematic risk depends, for example, on the industry or the type of project. If an investor has a completely balanced portfolio of shares they may incur exactly the same systematic risk as the average systematic risk of the stock market as a whole. The capital asset pricing model (CAPM), which we will discuss further in Chapter 5, is mainly concerned with how systematic risk is measured and how systematic risk affects required returns and share prices. It was first formulated for investments in shares on the stock exchange, but is now also used for company investments in capital projects.

Systematic risk is measured using what is known as a **beta factor (β)**. A beta factor is the measure of the volatility of a share in terms of market risk. The CAPM is a statement of the principles outlined above. An investor can use the beta factor in such a way that a high factor will automatically suggest a share may be avoided because of its considerably high risk in the past.

Mini case 4.1

Consider the possible impact in January 2001 on the beta factor of Iceland plc caused by the resignation from the board of the major shareholder, Malcolm Walker, together with the issue of a profits warning by the company. Given that Iceland was plunged into a £120m loss after an amazing £145m of exceptional items, it is very likely that Iceland's beta factor increased significantly because there would have been a great deal of volatility in the trading of its shares. Many senior managers were forced to leave the company in 2002, at which time the company was also renamed The Big Food Group. The Big Food Group's sales revenue levels, profits, and share price continued to fluctuate with a downward trend over the subsequent few years during which time it is likely that the company's beta value remained fairly high. In 2005 The Big Food Group's shareholders accepted an offer for the business by a consortium led by Baugur, an investment group based coincidentally in Iceland! After 21 years on the stock market, Iceland (Big Food Group) became a private company once more, with shareholders receiving only a fraction of the value that the group had enjoyed at its peak. The business was subsequently split into its main component parts and Iceland placed under the management of Malcolm Walker and other senior executives who had been ejected in 2001.

Mini case 4.2

Recent research suggests that the least risky industry sectors are food, textiles and clothing. The relative riskiness of companies' shares can be seen from the list below of the beta factors of 10 major UK companies in diverse sectors listed on the London Stock Exchange's FTSE 100. It comes as no surprise that companies active in speculative activities such as mining, real estate and banking have the higher beta values.

Company	Sector	Beta at 18 May 2012
Barclays	Banking	1.86
Bunzl	Support services	0.54
Hammerson	Real estate investment trusts	1.21
Imperial Tobacco	Tobacco	0.46
Marks and Spencer	General retailers	0.74
Pearson	Media	0.66
Reckitt Benckiser	Household goods	0.33
Rio Tinto	Mining	1.42
Tesco	Food and drug retailers	0.74
Vodafone	Mobile telecommunications	0.62

Source: Thomson One

Progress check 4.2

Describe what is meant by systematic risk and unsystematic risk.

Investor attitudes to risk

There is a potential conflict between the risk and return perceptions of managers and investors. They may generally display one of three attitudes to risk. These may be:

- risk-taking, in which case they have a preference for a high return in exchange for taking a high level of risk
- risk-neutral, in which case they are indifferent to the level of risk faced
- risk-averse, in which case they have a preference for low-risk, low-return investments.

Attitudes to risk may also be considered with regard to their impact on an individual's level of utility. A risk-taker and a risk-averse person may both take on the same risk, but the risk-averse person would require a higher potential return than the risk-taker before making an investment. For example, one person might be willing to bet on a horse in a race if odds of 2 to 1 were offered, while another person might only bet on the same horse in the same race if they could be offered better odds of say 4 to 1. The risk-taker accepts a potentially lower return for the same level of risk as the risk-averse person who would expect a higher return. If the risk-averse person cannot obtain the return (or odds) that they require then they will not invest (or bet). This is also situationally specific in that on another occasion roles might be reversed as their perspectives of the risk involved might change.

Investors also display different attitudes to risk. While equity shareholders are generally risk-takers, providers of debt capital are generally risk-averse. There may also be conflicts. For example, risk-loving venture capitalists may have aims that may clash with the aims of the risk-averse senior managers of a business. As a consequence, the company may not go ahead with high-risk investments necessary to provide the high returns expected by venture capitalists.

Progress check 4.3

What is meant by an individual's attitude to risk?

Business risk and financial risk

One part of systematic or market risk is business risk. Business risk is due to the variability of a company's operating profits or cash flows given the line of business in which the company is operating. These are risks to the company's operating results that are dependent on the industry in which the company is operating.

The wide range of factors relating to business risk is shown in Figure 4.2, relating to each of the main elements of cost, price, demand, growth, business environment, and financial factors that impact on the level of a company's operating profits and cash flows.

Figure 4.2	Factors relating to business risk

COST
Number of suppliers
Suppliers' financial stability
Reliance on specific materials
Operating gearing
Committed costs

PRICE
Marketing mix
Economic conditions
Price competition
Substitute products
Complementary products

DEMAND
Marketing mix
Fashion and taste
Competition
Shorter product life cycle

GROWTH
New product development
Management skills
Production facilities
Location

BUSINESS ENVIRONMENT
PESTEL factors
Environmental issues
Industrial factors

FINANCIAL
Interest rate changes
Foreign currency exposure
Working capital requirements

Progress check 4.4

What is business risk?

Financial risk comprises the other element of systematic risk: credit risk, currency risk, liquidity risk, and interest rate risk which arises from fluctuations in interest rates causing reductions in a company's after-tax earnings and hence its ability to pay dividends. Financial risk can be measured by using a gearing ratio (the relationship between a company's debt and equity), since it is a risk inherent in the company's choice of financial structure. The financial risk is seen in the sensitivity of the company's cash flows to changes in the interest payments it has to make on its debt. Financial risk increases as gearing increases.

Figure 4.3 illustrates the ways in which financial risk may impact on the lenders (providers of debt), equity shareholders, and on the company. For example, it can be seen that while

Figure 4.3	Levels of financial risk for the investor and the company

DEBT

Low financial risk for the investor	Interest must be paid contractually according to the loan agreement
and	The loan must be repaid contractually on the agreed date
High financial risk for the company	A loan is usually secured on company assets and assets may be repossessed

EQUITY

High financial risk for the investor	It is the company's choice to pay dividends and dividends do not have to be paid
and	Equity capital does not have to be repaid under normal circumstances
Low financial risk for the company	Capital growth from expected share price increases may not happen

equity capital represents high financial risk for the investor, it represents low financial risk for the company.

Progress check 4.5

What is financial risk?

The impact of risk on financing

The premium required for business risk is an increase in the required rate of return due to uncertainty about the company's future prospects.

The premium for financial risk relates to the danger of high gearing (an increasing level of debt compared with equity capital). The higher the gearing, the greater the financial risk to ordinary shareholders, reflected in a higher risk premium and therefore higher cost of capital.

Business risk and financial risk are the two elements of non-diversifiable systematic risk, or market risk. Systematic risk may not be diversified away by investors through holding a portfolio of shares in different companies because it relates to macroeconomic factors such as interest rates, exchange rates, and taxation, which affect all companies.

Progress check 4.6

How is financial risk related to a company's financial gearing?

Systematic and unsystematic risk

The total risk in a security that is faced by investors may be separated into unsystematic risk and systematic risk. Systematic risk represents, for example, how investment returns are affected by business cycles, trade tariffs, and the possibilities of war, etc. It is inherent risk that cannot be diversified away. Some investments are by their very nature more risky than others; this is nothing to do with chance variations in actual compared with expected returns. Systematic risk represents the relative effect on the returns of an individual security of changes in the market as a whole. Systematic risk may be measured using what are called β factors (see earlier in this chapter). β is a measure of the volatility of the return on a share relative to the market. The β factor for the market as a whole is 1. If a share were to rise in price at double the market rate then it would have a β factor of 2.

It is generally assumed that on average systematic risk accounts for about 30% of the total risk attached to an individual share. Bruno Solnik (Solnik, B 'Why not diversify internationally rather than domestically?' *Financial Analysts Journal*, January/February 1995, reprinted from July/August 1974), suggested that for shares in the UK systematic risk is approximately 34% of the total risk of a share. Unsystematic risk is therefore generally assumed on average to account for about 70% of the total risk attached to an individual share.

Unsystematic risk is unique risk specific to a company. It is the risk of the company performing badly, or the risk of it going into liquidation. Unsystematic risk can therefore be diversified away by spreading money over a portfolio of investments. Although the proportion of total risk attached to an individual share relating to unsystematic risk is high at around 70%, an investor may progressively reduce this type of risk by maintaining a diversified portfolio of projects or securities.

Worked example 4.2

A colleague of yours has recently applied for the post of assistant finance officer of Flag plc, a medium-sized investment company. As part of the interview process she was asked to make a 15-minute presentation on risk, and in particular about the different types of risk an investment company like Flag plc may face.

We will consider the main points that she would have included in her presentation.

First, she may have given a broad definition of risk. Risk can be defined as 'the chance or possibility of loss or bad consequence', which arises from a past, present, or future hazard or group of hazards about which some uncertainty exists regarding possible effects or consequences.

Whereas a hazard or a group of hazards is a source of danger, risk is the likelihood of such a hazard or group of hazards causing actual adverse consequences or effects. In this context, uncertainty relates to the measure of variability in possible outcomes – the variability (qualitatively rather than quantitatively) of the possible impact and consequences or effects of such hazards. While such uncertainty can arise as a result of a whole host of complex and often interrelated reasons, in the corporate context in particular it more often than not arises as a result of a lack of knowledge or a lack of information and understanding.

Second, what are the types of risk? As with the never-ending variety that is symptomatic of modernity, there are many types and definitions of risk, many of which overlap in terms of definition and context, for example:

- social risk – the possibility that intervention (whether socio-cultural, political, or institutional) will create, fortify, or reinforce inequity and promote social conflict
- political risk – the possibility that changes in government policies will have an adverse and negative impact on the role and functioning of institutions and individuals
- economic risk – the risk that events (both national and international) will impact on a country's business environment and adversely affect the profit and other goals of particular companies and other business-related enterprises
- market risk – the risk of a decline in the price of a security due to general adverse market conditions, also called systematic risk
- financial risk – the possibility that a given investment or loan will fail to provide a return and may result in a loss of the original investment or loan
- business risk – the risk associated with the uncertainty of realising expected future returns of the business.

Diversification

 As we have discussed, unsystematic risk (or non-market risk) is diversifiable. Businesses that have reached a mature stage of their development sometime use **diversification** as a strategy to mitigate unsystematic risk. However, it should be noted that diversification by its very nature also increases the risk of the unknown!

Companies may diversify their activities by buying businesses engaged in providing products and services in different business sectors to the ones in which they currently operate. They may also diversify by investing in new projects for new products and services in different markets and different geographical areas.

Individual investors may also diversify by effectively creating a portfolio of investments that include their own mixes of growing and maturing companies in a variety of market sectors in order to mitigate risk.

The diversification by companies into unrelated markets is illustrated in the press extract below which shows how a long-established company, Fujifilm, decided in 2011 that it had to further diversify its portfolio of activities into new markets and new products to mitigate unsystematic risk.

In diversified groups, or conglomerates, the signalling given by such groups to the financial markets via their dividend or gearing policy is not as clear as in a one-product company. Conglomerates may, in theory, be evaluated using a minimum weighted average price/earnings ratio of the component businesses. The excess of the market value over this minimum, in theory, represents value created by the conglomerate. In reality, the share value of most conglomerates is below this minimum, which is why most such groups have increasingly been broken up in recent years. We will look further at diversification in Part II of this book when we discuss mergers and acquisitions in Chapters 16 and 17.

Diversify to give a clearer picture

People want to look good in photographs, so perhaps it makes sense for one of the world's largest camera and photographic film producers to launch a line of cosmetics.

Fujifilm will do just that in the new year, when it launches 12 anti-ageing skincare products in Britain to be sold under its Astalift brand.

While this may appear to be one of the stranger examples of diversification, the Japanese company argues that it is logical. Its scientists understand collagen, a main component of photographic film as well as the main protein in human skin, and makes sunlight-resistant photographs using antioxidants, which are essential to prevent skin ageing. The group is also an expert in nano-technology, which is used in skin creams.

Fujifilm's move into cosmetics is in direct response to the decline in its traditional photo business, which it started in 1934. Film sales peaked in 2000 at about 2.5 billion rolls and the company decided to diversify in anticipation of falling demand because of the advent of digital cameras.

First it opted for the obvious routes, including digital cameras and cameras for smartphones, reproducing documents for businesses and medical imaging equipment. But, by 2006, Fujifilm's board decided to try cosmetics, launching a range in Japan the following year.

It has diversified so far that traditional photo film represents only 1 per cent of its £18 billion in annual sales. 'We don't have a choice, we have to diversify, new markets, new products', David Honey, a director of Fujifilm UK, said.

The company will launch Astalift in Britain in its first crack at the highly competitive European cosmetics market and will follow in France, Germany and Spain in the spring.

Despite a recognisable brand name, the group decided to name the cosmetic range after astaxanthin, the antioxidant agent derived from seaweed used in the products because it feared customers may not have wanted to buy skincare products from a camera company.

Source: **Try our cream, because the camera doesn't lie,** by Peter Stiff © *The Times*, 5 December 2011

Progress check 4.7

What is meant by diversification?

Risk measurement

Risk is as important a factor with regard to investor preferences as it is to the 'real' investment decisions taken by the directors of companies. It may be measured in a number of ways, for instance using probability distributions. For example, although the outcomes of a decision to buy a particular security may be uncertain, probabilities may be assigned to the various alternative outcomes. Estimates of probabilities are likely to be obtained from an analysis of previous experience or of similar scenarios. Probabilities are used to measure the likelihood that an event will occur, and a probability distribution lists all possible outcomes for an event and the probability that each will occur.

Worked example 4.3

Imagine you are contemplating buying shares in company A or B, and you have been given the following estimates about whether the share prices are likely to move up or down.

Outcome x	Share A probability p	Share B probability p
Share price will increase	0.90	0.60
Share price will fall	0.10	0.40
	1.00	1.00

Which share appears to be more risky?

The table above is a probability distribution that tells us that share A appears less risky than share B because it is less likely to fall in price and consequently more likely to increase in price. Probability distributions provide more meaningful information than stating the most likely outcome, for example that both shares are more likely to increase and less likely to fall in price.

Instead of presenting probability distributions for each alternative, summary measures of risk measurement may be used, for example:

- expected value (EV)
- standard deviation (σ).

Expected value

The expected value is the weighted average of the possible outcomes (x) of a decision, and it represents the long-run average outcome if the decision were to be repeated many times.

$$\text{EV} = \text{the sum of } (p \times x)$$

Worked example 4.4

The estimated price of a share is shown in the following table, and the probability has been estimated of it being one price or another.

Probability p	£ estimated share price x
0.40	2.00
0.35	3.00
0.25	5.00
1.00	

What is the expected value of the share price?

Expected value of the share price:

Probability	£ estimated share price	EV
p	x	p × x
0.40	2.00	£0.80
0.35	3.00	£1.05
0.25	5.00	£1.25
		£3.10

The expected value of the share price is the average expected price, except as we can see, £3.10 is not a specific share price that may actually be expected.

Expected values may give an indication with regard to a decision based on the limited amount of information available. There is a distinction between the two types of information, perfect information and imperfect information. Perfect information is information that predicts what will happen with certainty and when, which in practice does not exist. Imperfect information adds to what the investor, for example, already knows, but the information cannot be relied on with certainty, and the information may be wrong. Most information, in practice, for example forecast economic outlooks and expected share price movements, is imperfect. However, a decision-maker may obtain more information before making a decision about buying a particular share and the cost of that information should be quantified to be justified by potential benefits. There are no potential benefits unless the extra information might make the investor choose a different decision option. Let's look at an example of this.

Worked example 4.5

An investment of £10,000 in the shares of each of three companies is expected to generate gains from share price increases over the next year, depending on the state of the stock market. Probabilities of each market state occurring have been estimated as I: 0.5 II: 0.2 III: 0.3.

The following is a payoff table that includes the likely gain from each share for each market state.

Share	Market state		
	I	II	III
	£	£	£
A	750	200	50
B	450	800	550
C	350	600	900

Assuming that the share with the highest EV should be chosen, which share should be chosen?

How would that choice change if information about the likely state of the market could be purchased for £150?

We first need to calculate expected values of each share and each market state to determine this, by multiplying probabilities by likely gains.

Market state	Probability	Expected values		
		A £	**B** £	**C** £
I	0.50	375	225	175
II	0.20	40	160	120
III	0.30	15	165	270
EV of gains		430	550	565

The shares in company C should be purchased because that choice provides the highest EV, which is an average of £565.

Let's consider the situation if information about the likely state of the market could be purchased for £150 from a broker who has specialist knowledge. With perfect information about the future state of the market the choice of share will be the one giving the highest expected gain for the market state which the perfect information predicts will occur.

If state I is forecast, share A would be chosen, to gain £750.
If state II is forecast, share B would be chosen, to gain £800.
If state III is forecast, share C would be chosen, to gain £900.

We can then calculate the EVs of gains given perfect information about the market:

Market state	Share choice	Gain £	Probability	EV £
I	A	750	0.50	375
II	B	800	0.20	160
III	C	900	0.30	270
EV of gain with perfect information				805

Choosing share C with no information about the likely state of the market gives an EV = £565
The value of the benefit from information about the market is £805 − £565 = £240

Therefore, it would be worth buying the information from the broker for £150.

Standard deviation

A standard deviation measures the risk of the possible variations, the dispersion, around an expected value.

$$\text{variance } \sigma^2 = \text{ the sum of } p(x - EV)^2$$

The standard deviation is the square root of the statistical variance:

$$\text{standard deviation } \sigma = \sqrt{\text{variance}}$$

Use of the standard deviation is appropriate for comparison if EVs are the same – the higher the standard deviation the higher the risk.

Worked example 4.6

Shares in companies Q and R have the following estimated share prices (x), probabilities of occurring (p), and expected values (EV) over the next month.

	Probability p	Estimated share price £	EV £
Company Q	0.30	2.00	0.60
	0.40	3.00	1.20
	0.30	4.00	1.20
			3.00
Company R	0.20	1.00	0.20
	0.20	2.00	0.40
	0.20	3.00	0.60
	0.20	4.00	0.80
	0.20	5.00	1.00
			3.00

Both companies have the same share price expected value. How should an investor choose which is the best share to buy?

Since the expected value of the share price is the same for both companies the share chosen should be the one with the smallest risk, the one with the lowest standard deviation.

	Probability p	Share price – EV (x – EV)	Variance p(x – EV)²	σ = √variance
Company Q	0.30	−1.00	0.30	
	0.40	0.00	0.00	
	0.30	+1.00	0.30	
			0.60	$\sigma = \sqrt{0.6} = 0.775$
Company R	0.20	−2.00	0.80	
	0.20	−1.00	0.20	
	0.20	0.00	0.00	
	0.20	+1.00	0.20	
	0.20	+2.00	0.80	
			2.00	$\sigma = \sqrt{2.0} = 1.414$

A risk-averse investor would choose to invest in company Q. Its forecast share price has the smallest standard deviation and therefore the lowest risk.

Portfolio risks and returns

Investors may be companies, individuals, or institutions that make investments on behalf of private individuals. While short-term investments should certainly hold their original value and be capable of being converted into cash at short notice, funds are generally invested to make the highest return at an acceptable level of risk. If all funds are put into an investment in one type of project or one type of security then there is a risk that if the investment performs badly, there will be a total loss. A more prudent approach may be to spread investments over several types of project or security, so that losses on some may be offset by gains on others.

The use of portfolios of different investments may relate to 'real' investments in capital projects or investments in stocks and shares. The major factors relating to the choice of investments are cash flow, and the time value of money, together with the return expected by the investor and the perceived risk associated with that investment. The time value of money (usually) means that money received or paid today has greater value than receipt or payment at a future date (see Chapter 6).

If an investor has a portfolio of securities, then it will be expected that the portfolio itself will provide a certain return on investment. The expected return from the portfolio is the weighted average of the expected returns of the investments in the portfolio, weighted by the proportion of total funds invested in each. If W_S is the percentage of the portfolio that relates to an investment S that is expected to yield $s\%$ and W_T is the percentage of the portfolio that relates to an investment T that is expected to yield $t\%$, the portfolio's expected return is:

$$(W_S \times s) + (W_T \times t)$$

For example, if 60% of the portfolio relates to an investment that is expected to yield 8% and 40% to an investment that is expected to yield 10%, the portfolio's expected return is:

$$(60\% \times 8\%) + (40\% \times 10\%) = 8.8\%$$

The risk associated with either an investment or a portfolio of investments is that the actual return will not be the same as the expected return. The actual return may be higher or it may be lower than the expected return. It is rarely likely to equal the expected return. A prudent investor will want to avoid as much risk as possible so that actual returns may be as close as possible to expected returns. The risk associated with a single investment or in a portfolio of investments may be measured by the standard deviation of expected returns using estimated probabilities of actual returns.

Worked example 4.7

A single investment has the following probabilities of earning alternative expected returns:

Return %	Probability	Expected value
x	p	$p \times x$
10	0.30	3.00
15	0.40	6.00
20	0.20	4.00
25	0.20	_5.00_
		18.00

We are required to calculate the standard deviation and therefore the risk of the investment.

The expected value of returns is 18% and may be denoted as EV_x, and the standard deviation of the expected value can be calculated as follows:

Return x %	x − EV_x %	p	p(x − EV)^2
10	−8.00	0.30	19.20
15	−3.00	0.40	3.60
20	2.00	0.20	0.80
25	7.00	0.20	9.80
			Variance 33.40

The standard deviation is the square root of the variance $\sqrt{33.4}$ which equals 5.78%, and so the expected return of the investment is 18% with a risk of 5.78%.

The risk of an investment might be high or low, depending on the nature of the investment.

There is a positive correlation between risk and return so that in general low-risk investments usually provide low returns, and high-risk investments usually provide high returns.

Within a portfolio, the individual investments should not only be looked at in terms of their own risks and returns. In a portfolio the relationships between the return from one investment and the return from other investments are very important. The relationship between two investments can be one of three types:

- positive correlation – if one investment does well or badly it is likely that the other investment will perform likewise, so you would expect an investment in a company making umbrellas and in another which sells raincoats both to do badly in dry weather
- negative correlation – if one investment does well the other will do badly, and *vice versa*, so you would expect an investment in a company making umbrellas to do badly in dry weather and well in wet weather, and you would expect an investment in a company which sells ice cream to do well in dry weather and badly in wet weather – the weather will affect each company differently
- zero correlation, where the performance of one investment will be independent of how the other performs, so you would not expect there to be any relationship between the returns from an investment in a pharmaceutical company and an investment in a communications company.

An example of correlation is shown in Mini case 4.3 below.

Mini case 4.3

In May 2012, Indian policy research organisation PHD Chamber of Commerce and Industry issued data showing that following the global debt crisis (which began in 2008) the significant strengthening of the US$ against the euro was directly proportional to the volatility in the behaviour of the rupee.

They compared the US$/euro exchange rate with the US$/rupee exchange rate for each month January 2011 to May 2012. The data revealed a correlation coefficient of the euro and the rupee at 0.89. This, they suggested gave a clear indication of the impact on the behaviour of the rupee. They said that the US$/rupee exchange rate was severely affected by the global economic slowdown, especially in the eurozone economies.

Monthly US$/euro exchange rates compared with US$/rupee exchange rates January 2011 to May 2012

Month	US$/euro exchange rate	US$/rupee exchange rate
Jan-31-2011	0.73	45.90
Feb-28-2011	0.72	45.27
Mar-31-2011	0.70	44.63
Apr-29-2011	0.67	44.30
May-31-2011	0.70	45.06
Jun-30-2011	0.69	44.68
Jul-29-2011	0.70	44.19
Aug-31-2011	0.69	45.95
Sep-30-2011	0.74	49.01
Oct-31-2011	0.72	48.74
Nov-30-2011	0.74	52.17
Dec-30-2011	0.77	53.07
Jan-31-2012	0.75	49.43
Feb-29-2012	0.74	48.95
Mar-30-2012	0.74	50.94
Apr-30-2012	0.75	52.70
May-16-2012	0.78	54.49
Correlation coefficient	**0.89**	

This relationship between the returns from different investments is measured by the **correlation coefficient**. A correlation coefficient that approaches $+1$ indicates a high positive correlation, and a correlation coefficient that approaches -1 indicates a high negative correlation. Zero indicates no correlation at all. If alternative investments show a high negative correlation, then overall risk may be reduced by combining them in a portfolio. Risk may also be reduced by combining investments that have no correlation at all in a portfolio.

Worked example 4.8

Shares in two companies S and T have the following expected returns:

Probability p	Company S return %	Company T return %
0.20	10%	5%
0.60	20%	25%
0.20	30%	45%

Let's calculate the expected returns and risks of each company.

Let's also calculate the risks assuming that an investor acquires a portfolio P consisting of 50% shares in company S and 50% shares in company T, with perfect positive correlation, perfect negative correlation, and zero correlation.

The expected return from each security is as follows:

	Company S		Company T	
Probability	**Return s**	EV_S	**Return t**	EV_T
p	**%**	**%**	**%**	**%**
0.20	10	2	5	1
0.60	20	12	25	15
0.20	30	6	45	9
	Expected return EV_S = 20		Expected return EV_T = 25	

The variance of the expected return for each company is the sum of each $p(s - EV_S)^2$ and $p(t - EV_T)^2$

Probability	Company S			Company T		
	Return			**Return**		
p	**s**	$(s - EV_S)$	$p(s - EV_S)^2$	**t**	$(t - EV_T)$	$p(t - EV_T)^2$
0.20	10	(10)	20	5	(20)	80
0.60	20	0	0	25	0	0
0.20	30	10	20	45	20	80
	EV_S = 20	Variance = 40		EV_T = 25	Variance = 160	

The standard deviation is the square root of the variances.

$$\text{Company S risk} = \sqrt{40} = 6.32\%$$
$$\text{Company T risk} = \sqrt{160} = 12.65\%$$

Company T therefore offers a higher return than company S, but at a greater risk.

Let's now assume that an investor acquires a portfolio P consisting of 50% shares in company S and 50% shares in company T.

The expected return from the portfolio (EV_P) will be

$$(0.5 \times 20\%) + (0.5 \times 25\%) = 22.5\%$$

This is less than the expected return from company T alone, but more than that from company S. The combined portfolio should be less risky than an investment in company T alone (although in this example of just a two-investment portfolio, it will be more risky than an investment in company S alone except when returns are not at all correlated).

We can calculate the standard deviation of the expected return if there is:

■ perfect positive correlation between the returns from each security, so that if S gives a return of 10%, then T will give a return of 5%; if S gives a return of 20%, then T will give a return of 25%; if S gives a return of 30%, then T will give a return of 45%

- perfect negative correlation between the returns from each security, so that if S gives a return of 10%, T will yield 45%; if S gives a return of 30%, T will yield 5%; if S gives a return of 20%, T will yield 25%
- no correlation between returns, for which the probability distribution of returns is as follows:

S %	T %		p
10	5	(0.2 × 0.2)	0.04
10	25	(0.2 × 0.6)	0.12
10	45	(0.2 × 0.2)	0.04
20	5	(0.6 × 0.2)	0.12
20	25	(0.6 × 0.6)	0.36
20	45	(0.6 × 0.2)	0.12
30	5	(0.2 × 0.2)	0.04
30	25	(0.2 × 0.6)	0.12
30	45	(0.2 × 0.2)	0.04
			1.00

Perfect positive correlation

Given an expected return EV_P of 22.5%, the standard deviation of the portfolio is as follows:

Probability	Return from 50% S	Return from 50% T	Combined portfolio return		
p	%	%	p%	$(p - EV_P)$	$p(p - EV_P)^2$
0.20	5	2.50	7.50	(15)	45
0.60	10	12.50	22.50	0	0
0.20	15	22.50	37.50	15	45
				Variance =	90

The standard deviation or risk is $\sqrt{90} = 9.49\%$

Perfect negative correlation

Given an expected return EV_P of 22.5%, the standard deviation of the portfolio is as follows:

Probability	Return from 50% S	Return from 50% T	Combined portfolio return		
p	%	%	p%	$(p - EV_P)$	$p(p - EV_P)^2$
0.20	5	22.50	27.50	5	5
0.60	10	12.50	22.50	0	0
0.20	15	2.50	17.50	(5)	5
				Variance =	10

The standard deviation or risk is $\sqrt{10} = 3.16\%$

Zero correlation

Given an expected return EV_P of 22.5%, the standard deviation of the portfolio is as follows:

Probability	Return from 50% S	Return from 50% T	Combined portfolio return		
p	%	%	p%	$(p - EV_P)$	$p(p - EV_P)^2$
0.04	5	2.50	7.50	(15)	9
0.12	5	12.50	17.50	(5)	3
0.04	5	22.50	27.50	5	1
0.12	10	2.50	12.50	(10)	12
0.36	10	12.50	22.50	0	0
0.12	10	22.50	32.50	10	12
0.04	15	2.50	17.50	(5)	1
0.12	15	12.50	27.50	5	3
0.04	15	22.50	37.50	15	9
				Variance =	50

The standard deviation is $\sqrt{50} = 7.07\%$

Therefore, for the same expected return of 22.5% the risk expressed in the standard deviation is:

- highest at 9.49% when there is perfect positive correlation between the returns of the individual securities in the portfolio
- lowest at 3.16% when there is perfect negative correlation – the risk is then less than for either individual security taken on its own
- low at 7.07% when there is no correlation.

An alternative way of calculating the standard deviation of a portfolio of two investments is to use the formula:

$$\sigma_P = \sqrt{(\alpha_S^2 \times \sigma_S^2) + (\alpha_T^2 \times \sigma_T^2) + (2 \times \alpha_S \times \alpha_T \times r \times \sigma_S \times \sigma_T)}$$

where

σ_P is the standard deviation of a portfolio of the two investments, S and T
σ_S is the standard deviation of the returns from investment S
σ_T is the standard deviation of the returns from investment T
σ_S^2, σ_T^2 are the variances of returns from investment S and T (the squares of the standard deviations)
α_S is the weighting or proportion of investment S in the portfolio
α_T is the weighting or proportion of investment T in the portfolio
r is the correlation coefficient of returns from investment S and T, which is

$$r = \frac{\text{covariance of investments S and T}}{\sigma_S \times \sigma_T}$$

and the covariance is the sum of:

$$\text{probability} \times (\text{return}_S - EV_S) \times (\text{return}_T - EV_T)$$

Worked example 4.9

We can use the data from Worked example 4.8 for a portfolio of a 50% investment in company S and a 50% investment in company T to illustrate the alternative way of calculating the standard deviation of a portfolio of two investments.

When there is perfect positive correlation between the returns from S and T, $r = 1$.

$$
\begin{aligned}
\sigma_P^2 &= (\alpha_S^2 \times \sigma_S^2) + (\alpha_T^2 \times \sigma_T^2) + (2 \times \alpha_S \times \alpha_T \times r \times \sigma_S \times \sigma_T) \\
&= (0.5^2 \times 40) + (0.5^2 \times 160) + (2 \times 0.5 \times 0.5 \times 1 \times \sqrt{40} \times \sqrt{160}) \\
&= 10 + 40 + (0.5 \times 6.325 \times 12.649) \\
&= 90
\end{aligned}
$$

The standard deviation or risk of the portfolio is $\sqrt{90} = 9.49\%$
When there is perfect negative correlation between returns S and T, $r = -1$.

$$
\begin{aligned}
\sigma_P^2 &= (0.5^2 \times 40) + (0.5^2 \times 160) + (2 \times 0.5 \times 0.5 \times -1 \times \sqrt{40} \times \sqrt{160}) \\
&= 10 + 40 - (0.5 \times 6.325 \times 12.649) \\
&= 10
\end{aligned}
$$

The standard deviation or risk of the portfolio is $\sqrt{10} = 3.16\%$
When there is zero correlation between returns S and T, $r = 0$.

$$
\begin{aligned}
\sigma_P^2 &= (0.5^2 \times 40) + (0.5^2 \times 160) + (2 \times 0.5 \times 0.5 \times 0 \times \sqrt{40} \times \sqrt{160}) \\
&= 10 + 40 + 0 \\
&= 50
\end{aligned}
$$

The standard deviation or risk of the portfolio is $\sqrt{50} = 7.07\%$
The above are exactly the same standard deviations that we calculated in Worked example 4.8.

Worked example 4.10 is an illustration of how the correlation between two investments may be calculated.

Worked example 4.10

PLT plc is considering investing in two companies CHT plc and HGT plc, for which the following information is available:

Probability p	CHT plc return RC	HGT plc return RH
0.25	24%	28%
0.50	12%	12%
0.25	0%	4%
Expected return e	12%	14%
Variance σ^2	72	76
Standard deviation σ	8.49	8.72

We are required to calculate the correlation coefficient of the above companies, and advise PLT plc what this means with regard to their decision to invest.

The relationship or correlation between the two investments can be calculated as follows:

The covariance of CHT and HGT = the sum of the probability
$\times$ (return − expected return from investment CHT)
$\times$ (return − expected return from investment HGT)

or

$$\text{cov}(RC \times RH) = \Sigma p \times (RC - e_C) \times (RH - e_H)$$
$$\text{cov}(RC \times RH) = 0.25 \times (24 - 12) \times (28 - 14) + 0.50$$
$$\times (12 - 12) \times (12 - 14) + 0.25 \times (0 - 12) \times (4 - 14)$$
$$= 42 + 0 + 30$$
$$= 72$$

Since correlation

$$r = \frac{\text{cov}(RC \times RH)}{\sigma_C \times \sigma_H}$$
$$r = 72/(8.49 \times 8.72)$$
$$r = 0.97$$

Because the correlation coefficient r is positive and very close to 1 this means that the returns on the two investments are almost perfectly positively correlated. However, based on the information given, PLT plc cannot make a decision as to which is the best investment without first obtaining further information.

Markowitz's portfolio theory

We will use Worked example 4.11 to illustrate Markowitz's **portfolio theory** (Markowitz, H ◀▥ 'Portfolio selection' *Journal of Finance* 6, pages 815–33 (1952)). This theory deals with the way in which investors can diversify away unsystematic risk through investing in portfolios of shares in different companies. It considers sets of investors' portfolio choices of different combinations of risky investments.

Worked example 4.11

Let's look at a portfolio of two investments with different risks and returns. We can assume that the two investments may be combined in any proportions with an infinite number of possible combinations of risk and return. We will consider whether one individual investment is the 'best' option or whether some combination of proportions of the two investments is a 'better' option.

The two investments are K and L and their expected returns and risks are as follows:

Investment	Return expected %	Risk (standard deviation) %
K	11	6.7
L	14	7.5

The correlation coefficient of KL is −0.3
The covariance KL is therefore −0.3 × 6.7 × 7.5 = −15.075

We can use the formulae shown on pages 186 and 191 to calculate the weighted average returns expected from six different risk/return combinations of proportions of the two investments and their corresponding risks (standard deviations), as follows:

K %	L %	Return expected %	Risk (standard deviation) %
100	0	11.0	6.7
80	20	11.6	5.1
60	40	12.2	4.2
40	60	12.8	4.5
20	80	13.4	5.7
0	100	14.0	7.5

At the outset, if we were totally risk-averse we may invest exclusively in K because it has a lower standard deviation, and therefore risk, than L. Alternatively, if we chose to combine proportions of K and L we can see that as the proportion of K reduces and the proportion of L increases then the standard deviation, or risk, of the portfolio reduces and the combined expected return increases. The combined risk continues to reduce as the proportion of L increases until a point is reached, as we can see in the table above, where the impact of the higher risk of L becomes greater than the benefit of negative correlation and the combined risk starts to increase. In this example, this is shown at around point C, which we can see from the ABC section of the graph illustrated in Figure 4.4.

As proportions of L continue to be increased, and proportions of K reduce, we can see from the CDEF section of the graph that the combined expected return continues to increase but risk also increases. However, it can also be seen from the graph that any

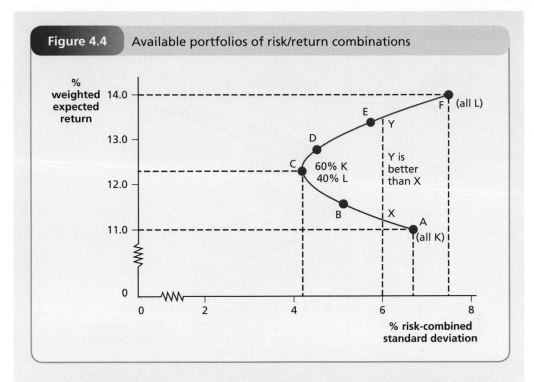

Figure 4.4   Available portfolios of risk/return combinations

point on section CF is better than any point on section AC because a greater combined return may be obtained for the same level of risk. See, for example, combination Y, which gives a greater return than combination X for the same level of risk. The individual portfolios of combinations of investments that lie along the CF section of the graph are called efficient portfolios and the line itself is called the **efficient frontier**.

We may conclude that:

- we cannot identify the 'best' investment option
- an investor wishing to minimise total risk would choose combination C (60% K, 40% L)
- an investor wishing to maximise return would choose F (100% L)
- any portfolio chosen by an investor along the CF line depends on the level of the investor's risk aversion – the amount of extra return they require to compensate for a particular level of extra risk.

The choice of combinations of investments all depends on an investor's attitude to risk. If we could quantify an investor's risk aversion and determine the premium they require on their return for a specific amount of additional risk then we may identify their 'best' portfolio. We will consider this later in this chapter when we look at investors' preferences.

Worked example 4.11 considered possible combinations of just two investments to provide portfolios with different combinations of risk and return. If we include another possible investment M into the choice of portfolios then unsystematic risk may be further diversified (see Figure 4.5).

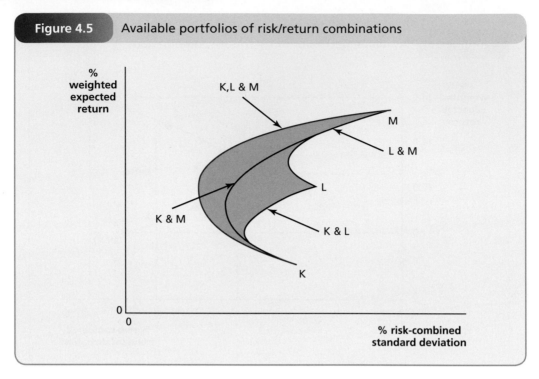

Figure 4.5 Available portfolios of risk/return combinations

An investor may consider each of K, L, or M alone as an individual investment, or may consider the following portfolios:

- K and L
- L and M
- K and M
- K, L, and M,

which may provide a huge number of combinations of combined risk and return.

'Better' portfolios may be obtained by combining all three investments. The coloured line KM in Figure 4.5 represents all combinations of K, L, and M, which gives the investor a wider range rather than the two-investment portfolio combinations of K and L, L and M, or K and M.

Further investments may be included to give even greater opportunities to diversify away unsystematic risk. This is the basis of the portfolio theory developed by Markowitz, in which investor choice includes all risky investments. As we saw from the two-investment portfolio, identification of the optimum portfolio is dependent on investor attitude to risk, and this also applies to multi-investment portfolios together with our ability to quantify the premium required for specific levels of additional risk.

Markowitz's theory considers a large number of portfolio choices of risky investments available to investors. The shaded area KML that we saw in Figure 4.5 is called the envelope curve and represents the range of combinations of returns and risks of risky investments (in that case relating to three investments). Figure 4.6 shows a similar curve relating to five risky investments for illustration, but which actually may be any number. Here, the shaded area KONML is the envelope curve.

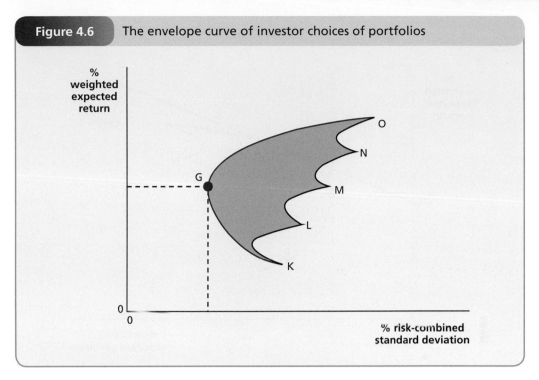

Figure 4.6 The envelope curve of investor choices of portfolios

All the possible investment combinations available to an investor are the range portfolios within the envelope curve. We saw in Figure 4.4 that at point C the higher risk started to outweigh the benefit of negative correlation. The same effect occurs in Figure 4.6 at point G. The efficient portfolios therefore lie along the line GO and GO is the efficient frontier. In the same way as in Figure 4.4, in Figure 4.6 investors will rationally invest only in portfolios along the coloured line GO. This is because they are better than all the other portfolios within the rest of the envelope curve, providing either the best return for a specific level of risk or the lowest risk for a specific return.

Risk-free investments

All the portfolios we have looked at carry some degree of risk. So far, we have considered investor choices concerned only with risky investments. But some investments are risk-free. We know that investors may actually also lend and borrow at a virtually risk-free rate of return. It is extremely unlikely that the UK Government would default on any payment of interest and capital on its loan stocks, and therefore Government loans are generally assumed to be risk-free investments.

As investors lend and borrow at higher rates of return then the corresponding levels of risk will also be higher. For the market as a whole we may assume a linear relationship between risk and return. We have superimposed a market risk/return line onto the graph in Figure 4.6, which is shown in Figure 4.7. It has been assumed that the risk-free rate of return R_f is known. The line has been drawn by starting at R_f and pivoting the line until it is tangential to the

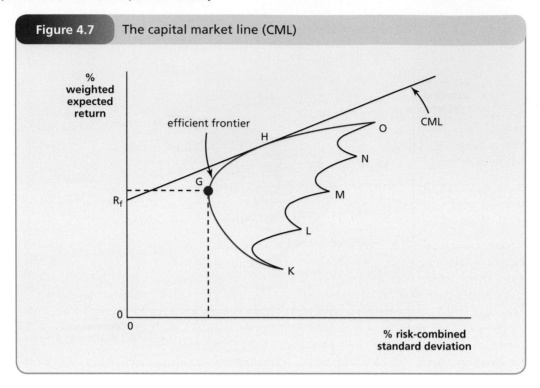

Figure 4.7   The capital market line (CML)

efficient frontier. This line is called the **capital market line (CML)** and the point of tangency H is known as the market portfolio, which is the optimal combination of risky investments, on the assumption that a risk-free rate of return exists.

Capital market line (CML)

The capital market line represents a combination of risk-free securities and the market portfolio of securities, and is drawn along the efficient frontier starting from the risk-free rate of return. It is an expression of the relationship between risk and return for a fully diversified investor. This means that if an investor is able to identify and invest in the market portfolio, and borrow or lend at the risk-free rate of return, then the possible risk/return combinations for the investor would lie along a straight line, the capital market line (CML).

Assuming the existence of a risk-free rate of return, rational investors will always choose a portfolio that lies on the CML rather than the efficient frontier GO because the portfolios on the CML are better than those on GO. Point H, the market portfolio, is of course the same on both the CML and the efficient frontier. Risk-taking investors will choose portfolios lying on the CML to the right of point H – the further to the right, the higher risk-taking they are. Risk-averse investors will choose portfolios lying on the CML to the left of point H – the further to the left towards Rf, the more highly risk-averse they are. Investors who put all their investments into a market portfolio will choose point H.

The particular portfolio on the CML chosen by an investor will depend on their choice of maximum return for an acceptable level of risk. It is therefore dependent on investor preference.

Investors' preferences

Investors should rationally choose a portfolio of investments, which gives them a satisfactory balance between:

- expected returns from the portfolio
- risk that the actual returns from the portfolio will be higher or lower than expected, some portfolios being more risky than others.

Rational investors wish to maximise return and minimise risk. If two portfolios have the same element of risk like V and R in Figure 4.8, the rational investor will choose V, the one yielding *b* more return for the same level of risk. If two portfolios offer the same return, like S and R, the rational investor will select the portfolio with the lower risk, which is S. Portfolio S offers the same return as R, but with less risk amounting to *a*.

Therefore, portfolio V will be preferred to portfolio R because it offers a higher expected return for the same level of risk, and portfolio S will be preferred to portfolio R because it offers the same expected return for lower risk. But whether an investor chooses portfolio V or portfolio S will depend on the individual's attitude to risk – whether they wish to accept a greater risk for a greater expected return.

In Figure 4.8 the choice of portfolio S, T, U, V, or W will depend on the individual investor's attitude to risk. Curve A is called the investor's **indifference curve** or utility curve. An investor

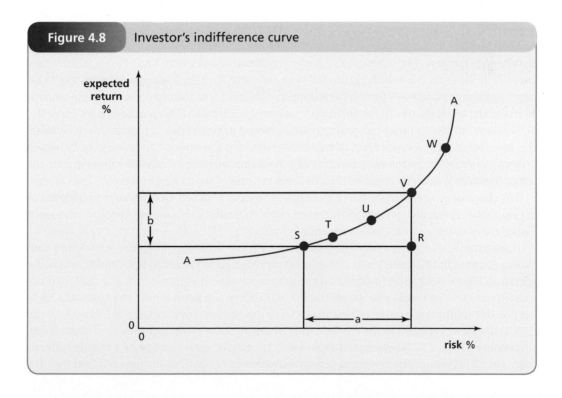

Figure 4.8   Investor's indifference curve

Figure 4.9	Indifference curve comparison

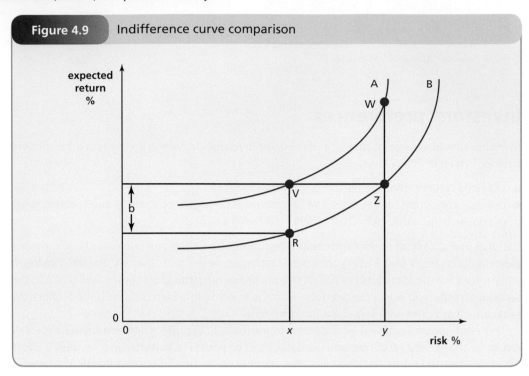

is generally indifferent between the portfolios that give a mix of risk and expected return which lie on this curve. To the investor, the portfolios S, T, U, V, or W are all just as good as each other, and each of them is better than portfolio R.

Portfolio R lies on a separate indifference curve of return/risk combinations B (see Figure 4.9), all of which may be equally acceptable to the investor, but their choice is dependent on their attitude to risk. However, these portfolios are all less acceptable than the portfolios on indifference curve A. The investor will prefer combinations of return and risk on indifference curve A to those on curve B in Figure 4.9 because curve A offers higher returns for the same degree of risk (and less risk for the same expected returns). For example, for the same amount of risk x, the expected return for portfolio V on curve A is b more than portfolio R on curve B.

Similarly, an investor may move from point Z, having a level of risk y, to point V which offers the same returns for a lower level of risk x. Alternatively, the investor may move to W, which offers a higher return for the same level of risk y. A rational investor will always move either to the left or upwards in order to optimise their position in terms of return and acceptable level of risk.

The shape of an indifference curve indicates the extent to which an investor is a risk taker or is risk-averse. A steeply inclined indifference curve indicates a risk-averse investor, whereas a flatter curve indicates a risk-taking investor.

If we assume that an investor has indifference curves shaped as in Figure 4.9 we can consider a range of indifference levels (or utilities) represented by curves A, B, C, and D, which are shown in Figure 4.10 superimposed on the graphs we saw in Figure 4.7. If the CML had not existed the investor would choose portfolio J, which is at the point where the investor's highest possible indifference curve (C) is tangential to the efficient frontier GO. In Figure 4.10 the CML is drawn at a tangent to the efficient frontier and cuts the y axis at the point of the risk-free investment's return R_f. As we saw in Figure 4.7, because of the existence of a risk-free investment the CML (capital market line or securities market line) becomes the new efficient frontier.

Figure 4.10   Indifference curves and the CML

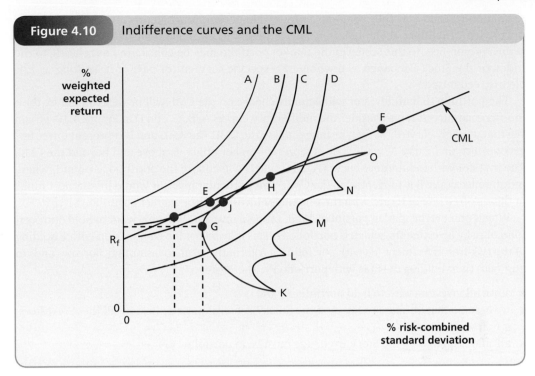

More risk-averse investors will choose points on the CML closer to R_f, which means investing in a large proportion of risk-free investments. Risk-taking investors will choose points on the CML approaching point H, investing a higher proportion of their funds in the market portfolio. Portfolio H in Figure 4.10 is the same as point H in Figure 4.7. It is the efficient portfolio that will appeal most to the risk-taking investor, ignoring risk-free investments. The only portfolio that consists entirely of risky investments, which a rational investor should want to hold, is portfolio H.

Progress check 4.9

What are investors' indifference curves?

As with the curved efficient frontier line, one portfolio on the CML line is as attractive as another to a rational investor. One investor may wish to hold portfolio E, which lies between risk-free investment R_f and portfolio H.

Another investor may wish to hold portfolio F, which entails putting all their funds in portfolio H and borrowing money at the risk-free rate to acquire more of portfolio H. This investor, in order to meet their individual risk/return requirement, therefore uses a process of first selecting the market portfolio and then, second, combining the optimal portfolio of risky investments with borrowing (or lending) at the risk-free rate. This two-stage process is known as the **separation theorem** (Tobin, J 'Liquidity preference as behaviour toward risk' *Review of Economic Studies* No. 25, February, pages 65–86 (1958)). The separation theorem deals with the way that investors identify the market portfolio, which all rational investors should prefer, and how they combine a proportion of their funds in this together with either borrowing or lending at the risk-free rate of return to optimise their own individual risk/return preference. In this scenario the market portfolio may be considered as relating to the index of the Stock Exchange as a whole or a specific segment or part of it, so long as it is clearly recognised.

The portfolio that an investor will actually choose on the CML will be determined by their indifference curves. If we consider the indifference curves A, B, C, and D in Figure 4.10 we can see that it is only curve B that can be tangential to the CML. Curves C and D represent lower levels of utility, and curve A, while it does represent higher utility, is above and beyond the CML. The investor with indifference curves A, B, C, and D will choose the portfolio at point I, where indifference curve B is tangential to the CML. This particular investor would invest most funds at the risk-free rate of return with the remainder invested in the market portfolio.

Why is point H the market portfolio? Well, rational investors will only want to hold one portfolio of risky investments, which is portfolio H. This may be held in conjunction with a holding of the risk-free investment (as with portfolio E). Alternatively, an investor may borrow funds to augment their holding of H (as with portfolio F). Therefore:

- since all investors wish to hold portfolio H, and
- we assume that all shares quoted on the Stock Exchange must be held by all these investors, it follows that
- all shares quoted on the Stock Exchange must be in portfolio H.

Portfolio H is the 'market portfolio' and each investor's portfolio will contain a proportion of it. (Although in the real world, investors do not hold every quoted security in their portfolio, in practice a well-diversified portfolio should reflect the whole market in terms of weightings given to particular sectors, high income and high capital growth securities, and so on.)

Actually, investors may be able to build up a small portfolio of shares that does better than the market, or they may end up with portfolios that perform worse than the market. Let's look at a worked example to illustrate this.

Worked example 4.12

The following data relate to four different portfolios of shares:

Portfolio	Expected rate of return	Standard deviation or risk of the portfolio
	%	%
A	10	6
B	15	7
C	12	4
D	18	11

The expected rate of return on the market portfolio is 7% with a standard deviation of 2%. The risk-free rate is 4% (R_f).

Let's consider which of these portfolios is better or worse than the market.

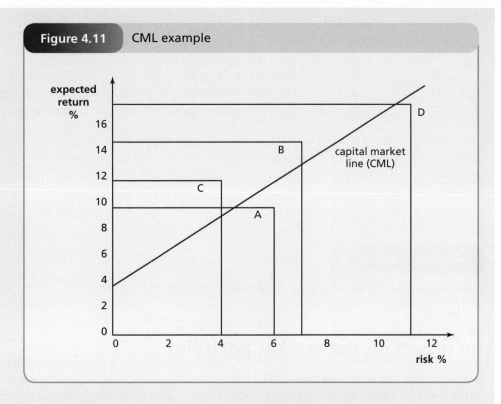

Figure 4.11   CML example

We can identify which of these portfolios may be regarded as better than the market (efficient) or worse than the market (inefficient) by drawing a CML (see Figure 4.11). When risk is zero the return is 4, and when risk is 2 the return is 7, so these points can be plotted and joined up, and the line can be extended to produce the CML.

The individual portfolios A, B, C, and D can also be plotted on the same chart and any portfolio which is above the CML is said to be efficient and any portfolio which is below the CML is inefficient.

Portfolio C is very efficient, and portfolio B is also efficient, but portfolios A and D are both inefficient.

We can approach this in an alternative way, numerically instead of using graphs, by calculating the formula for the CML, assuming the standard deviation of a portfolio to be x, and the return from a portfolio to be y.

The CML formula is $y = R_f + bx$, and b is the slope of the line,

where R_f is the risk-free rate of return, which in this example is 4.

If $x = 2$ then $y = 7$, and if $x = 0$ then $y = 4$

Therefore $b = \dfrac{7 - 4}{2 - 0} = \dfrac{3}{2} = 1.5$

The CML therefore is $y = 4 + 1.5x$

Portfolio	Standard deviation	CML return		Expected return	Portfolio type
	x	y	%	%	
A	6	$(4 + 1.5 \times 6) = 13.0$		10	Inefficient

Portfolio	Standard deviation	CML return		Expected return	Portfolio type
	x	y	%	%	
B	7	$(4 + 1.5 \times 7) = 14.5$		15	Efficient
C	4	$(4 + 1.5 \times 4) = 10.0$		12	Very efficient
D	11	$(4 + 1.5 \times 11) = 20.5$		18	Inefficient

If the expected return exceeds the CML return for the given amount of risk, the portfolio is efficient. In this example B is efficient (15% > 14.5%) and C is even more efficient (12% > 10%), but D is inefficient (18% < 20.5%) and A even more inefficient (10% < 13%).

Progress check 4.10

When may a portfolio be considered as inefficient with regard to the CML?

The return on the market portfolio

The expected returns from a portfolio will be higher than the return from risk-free investments because investors expect a greater return for accepting a degree of investment risk. The size of the risk premium will increase as the risk of the portfolio increases, and we can show this with an analysis of the capital market line (Figure 4.12).

Let's assume that:

R_f is the risk-free rate of return
R_m is the return from the market portfolio X
R_p is the return on portfolio P, which is a mixture of investments in portfolio X and risk-free investments
σ_m is the risk (standard deviation) of returns from the market portfolio X
σ_p is the risk (standard deviation) of returns from portfolio P

The slope of the CML

$$b = \frac{(R_m - R_f)}{\sigma_m}$$

which represents the extent to which the investor's required returns from the portfolio should exceed the risk-free rate of return in compensation for the risk.

We can use the formula for the CML which was expressed in the $y = a + bx$ format in the previous worked example (where a is the risk-free rate of return R_f and bx represents the increase in the return as the risk increases). We know that when $y = R_p$, then $x = \sigma_p$ and so if we substitute $(R_m - R_f)/\sigma_m$ for b, the equation of the CML can be expressed as:

$$R_p = R_f + \frac{(R_m - R_f)}{\sigma_m}\sigma_p$$

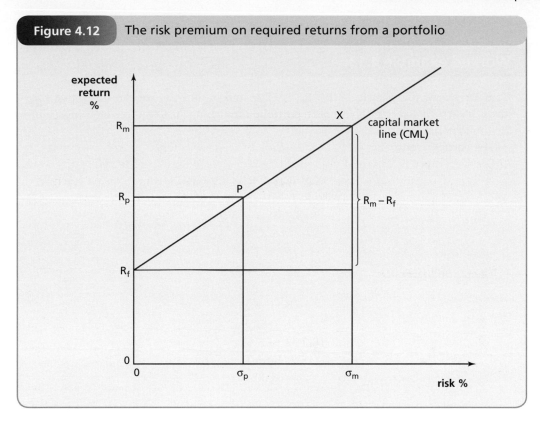

Figure 4.12   The risk premium on required returns from a portfolio

where the expression

$$\frac{(R_m - R_f)}{\sigma_m} \sigma_p$$

is actually the risk premium that the investor should require as compensation for accepting the risk of the portfolio σ_p.

The portfolio risk σ_p may be determined by rearranging the formula above:

$$\sigma_p = \frac{R_p - R_f}{(R_m - R_f)} \times \sigma_m$$

The expected return of a portfolio lying on the CML can be written as:

$$R_p = (X \times R_m) + R_f \times (1 - X)$$

where X is the proportion invested in the market portfolio, and $(1-X)$ is the proportion invested in risk-free securities.

Let's look at a worked example.

Worked example 4.13

If an investor is told that R_f is 6%, R_m is 15%, and σ_m is 24%, we can determine the investor's return and risk if they hold a portfolio comprising 75% risk-free securities, and 25% market risk securities.

The portfolio return is:

$$
\begin{aligned}
R_p &= (X \times R_m) + R_f \times (1 - X) \\
&= (25\% \times 15\%) + (6\% \times 75\%) \\
&= 3.75\% + 4.5\% \\
&= 8.25\%
\end{aligned}
$$

The portfolio risk is:

$$
\begin{aligned}
\sigma_p &= \frac{(R_p - R_f)}{(R_m - R_f)} \times \sigma_m \\
&= \frac{(8.25\% - 6\%)}{(15\% - 6\%)} \times 24\% \\
&= 6.00\%
\end{aligned}
$$

We can also re-calculate to determine what the investor's return would be if they held a portfolio comprising 50% risk-free securities, and 50% market risk securities, and also 25% risk-free securities, and 75% market risk securities.

Portfolio type	Portfolio return %	Portfolio risk %
75% risk-free securities, and 25% market risk securities	8.25	6
50% risk-free securities, and 50% market risk securities	10.50	12
25% risk-free securities, and 75% market risk securities	12.75	18

The results are summarised in the table above and show that as the proportion of risk-free securities is reduced the overall risk to the investor is increased and the overall return to the investor is also increased.

We derived the equation for the CML which was expressed as (see page 204):

$$
R_p = R_f + \frac{(R_m - R_f)}{\sigma_m} \sigma_p
$$

In the above relationship σ_p/σ_m represents the beta factor (β). We have discussed the beta factor (β) as a measure of the volatility of a share, or a security, in terms of market risk and we illustrated βs for a number of leading companies (see pages 175 to 176).

We can see that by replacing σ_p/σ_m with β in the CML equation above then an investor's required expected return from a portfolio (R_p) can be stated as:

$$R_p = R_f + \beta \times (R_m - R_f)$$

This is a representation of the **capital asset pricing model (CAPM)**, and may be used when attempting Exercises E4.3 and E4.4 at the end of this chapter. The derivation of β is central to this concept, and we will return to this in Chapter 5 when we further consider portfolio risks and returns and take a more detailed look at CAPM.

Summary of key points

- There is a positive correlation between risk and return – the higher the risk the higher the return, and the lower the risk the lower the return.
- Individuals display different attitudes to risk, and they may be risk-taking, risk-averse, or indifferent to risk.
- Companies face both business risk and financial risk.
- Business risk comprises the general risks of companies not achieving satisfactory levels of operating profit.
- Financial risk arises from the level of debt or loans held by companies and their ability to pay interest and repay the debt.
- Business risk and financial risk together comprise systematic or market risk.
- Systematic risk is inherent risk and cannot be diversified away.
- Unsystematic risk is unique risk specific to a company or project, which may be mitigated through diversification.
- Markowitz's portfolio theory deals with the mitigation or reduction of unsystematic risk through holding a range or a portfolio of investments.
- Different investors have different preferences with regard to perceived risk and expected returns and their choices with regard to investments in risk-free and market risk securities and the proportions of both are shown on the capital market line (CML).

Glossary of key terms

beta factor (β) The measure of the volatility of the return on a share relative to the market. If a share price were to rise or fall at double the market rate, it would have a beta factor of 2. Conversely, if the share price moved at half the market rate, the beta factor would be 0.5.

business risk Risk is a condition in which there exists a quantifiable dispersion in the outcomes from an activity. Business risk relates to activities carried out within an entity, arising from structure, systems, people, products, or processes.

capital asset pricing model (CAPM) A theory which predicts that the expected risk premium for an individual share will be proportional to its beta, such that the expected risk premium on a share equals beta multiplied by the expected risk premium in the market. The risk premium is defined as the expected incremental return for making a risky investment rather than a safe one.

capital market line (CML) A graphical representation of the linear relationship of the optimal risk/return trade-off of all rational investors' portfolios (i.e. the whole market) in which their funds are spread between the market portfolio and risk-free investments.

correlation coefficient A statistical measure that shows how one variable is linked with another variable, for example a measure of how closely the returns from two investments move in the same direction as each other.

diversification The 'real' or financial investment in more than one asset, or in more than one product group or industrial sector, such that the returns are not perfectly correlated, in order to reduce exposure to unsystematic risk.

efficient frontier The range of optimum portfolios determined from the complete set of risk/return combinations of specific investments available to an investor.

financial risk Financial risk relates to the financial operation of an entity and includes:

- credit risk – the possibility that a loss may occur from the failure of another party to perform according to the terms of a contract
- currency risk – the risk that a value of a financial instrument will fluctuate due to changes in foreign exchange rates (IAS 32)
- interest rate risk – the risk that interest rate changes will affect the financial well-being of an entity
- liquidity risk – the risk that an entity will encounter difficulty in realising assets or otherwise raising funds to meet commitments associated with financial instruments (also known as funding risk).

indifference curve A graph which represents combinations of risk and return that provide equal utility or indifference for an investor.

portfolio theory A theory relating to risk and return developed by Markowitz in 1952, which considers how investors can diversify away from unsystematic risk by holding portfolios of different shares.

separation theorem The two-stage process in which unsystematic risk is diversified away by an investor by choosing the appropriate market portfolio of risky securities and then combining this with borrowing or lending at the risk-free rate in order to meet their particular risk/return requirement.

systematic risk (or market risk) Some investments are by their very nature more risky than others. This is nothing to do with chance variations in actual compared with expected returns; it is inherent risk that cannot be diversified away.

unsystematic risk Risk that can be diversified away.

Assessment material

Questions

Q4.1 Describe the relationship between the return required by an investor and the perceived risk of the investment.

Q4.2 How may different individual attitudes to risk result in conflict?

Q4.3 Describe the types of risk that comprise systematic risk.

Q4.4 What are the main differences between systematic risk and unsystematic risk and what are their implications for an investor?

Q4.5 What is financial risk and what are its implications for highly geared companies?

Q4.6 How may a company, and how may an investor reduce the impacts of unsystematic risk?

Q4.7 Explain what is meant by the efficient frontier.

Q4.8 What is a capital market line (CML)?

Q4.9 What do indifference curves tell us about investors' choices of the various risk/return combinations relating to a portfolio of investments?

Discussion points

D4.1 'It is not practical for individual investors to apply Markowitz's portfolio theory to their stock market investments.' Discuss the validity of this statement and whether or not and how Markowitz's portfolio theory may be applied by individual investors.

D4.2 'Inappropriate management of financial risk may result in a company going out of business.' Discuss.

Exercises

Solutions are provided in Appendix 2 to all exercise numbers highlighted in colour.

Level I

E4.1   *Time allowed – 15 minutes*
The level of risk for a market portfolio is 3% and the expected market return is 12%. The risk-free rate of return is 4%.

> **You are required to plot the capital market line (CML) from the above data.**

E4.2   *Time allowed – 30 minutes*
The data in the table below relates to a portfolio of 30% of shares in Caldey plc and 70% of shares in Tenby plc.

Probability	Forecast return Caldey plc %	Forecast return Tenby plc %
0.20	10	12
0.60	12	18
0.20	14	24

The way in which returns from investments in portfolios of two or more securities vary together determines the riskiness of the portfolio. Ignoring the possibility of a zero correlation between the returns of Caldey plc and Tenby plc, you are required to calculate the portfolio returns and the risk of each if there is:

(i)   perfect positive correlation
(ii) perfect negative correlation.

E4.3   *Time allowed – 30 minutes*

The following data relates to four share portfolios A, B, C, and D.

Portfolio	Expected return	Standard deviation
A	10%	4%
B	10%	7%
C	15%	3%
D	25%	5%

Required:

(i)   Explain what is meant by the term efficient portfolio.
(ii)   Use the graph from Exercise E4.1 to plot the position of share portfolios A, B, C, and D, and state whether each portfolio is efficient or inefficient.
(iii) Assuming that an investor is using risk measurement to identify suitable shares in which to invest, use the CAPM equation to calculate what beta coefficient an investor would look for if they required a return of 11% on their investment.
(iv)   Calculate what rate of return a share should yield if it has a beta coefficient of 1.3.

Level II

E4.4   *Time allowed – 30 minutes*

French plc and Saunders plc are considering a variety of investment projects in a range of different industries, which are each expected to last for one year. The net cash flows and beta values of each project are shown in the table below:

Project	Beta factor	French plc net cash flow £000	Saunders plc net cash flow £000
I	1.3	300	
II	1.4		100
III	1.4		100
IV	0.8		200

The risk-free rate of return is 3% and the market rate of return is 8%.

Required:

(i) Calculate the present values of each of the projects being considered by French plc and Saunders plc.

(ii) What will be the total beta factor of Saunders plc on the basis of all projects II, III, and IV going ahead?

(iii) Which company is likely to be valued most highly based on the above information, French or Saunders?

E4.5   *Time allowed – 30 minutes*

Describe the characteristics of an efficiently diversified portfolio of equities and explain the reasons why diversification is used to reduce investor risk.

E4.6   *Time allowed – 45 minutes*

Abdul is an investor who has invested one quarter of his funds at the risk-free rate, which is 7%, and he has invested the remainder of his funds in a market portfolio of equities. The expected total return on his portfolio is 12% with a risk of 8%. Said is another investor who holds a similar market portfolio of equities to Abdul and his expected total return on his portfolio is 18%. Both investors can lend and borrow at the risk-free rate, and both of their portfolios lie on the capital market line (CML).

Required:

(i) Provide calculations that illustrate the composition of the expected returns of Abdul's and Said's portfolios in terms of equity returns and fixed interest.

(ii) Draw the capital market line (CML) and show the position of both Adbul's and Said's portfolio.

(iii) Assume that Abdul wants to keep his portfolio on the CML and calculate the standard deviation he would have to accept in order to increase his expected return to 13% and show how the composition of his portfolio will change.

E4.7   *Time allowed – 45 minutes*

Bill Brownbridge is a UK-based investor who is currently considering making an investment in one or both of two listed companies, X plc and Y plc. Information relating to expected returns from the two companies and the probabilities of their occurrence is shown below:

	Possible rates of return %	Probability of occurrence
X plc	30	0.3
	25	0.4
	20	0.3
Y plc	50	0.2
	30	0.6
	10	0.2

You may assume that there is no correlation between the expected rates of return from the companies within the portfolio, and that Bill Brownbridge is a risk-averse investor.

Required:

(i)   Calculate the expected return for each security separately and for the portfolio comprising 60% X plc shares and 40% Y plc shares.

(ii)   Using the standard deviation of returns from the expected rate of return as a measure of risk, calculate the risk of each share separately and of the portfolio as defined in (i) above.

(iii) Briefly outline the objectives of portfolio diversification and explain in general terms why the risk of individual securities may differ from that of the portfolio as a whole.

5

Capital structure and the cost of capital

Chapter contents

Learning objectives

Completion of this chapter will enable you to:

- Outline the capital asset pricing model (CAPM) and the importance of the β factor.
- Consider arbitrage pricing theory (APT) as an alternative to CAPM.
- Evaluate the cost of equity of a company using CAPM, and using the simple dividend growth model.
- Evaluate the cost of debt of a company.
- Calculate a company's weighted average cost of capital (WACC).
- Explain capital structure (or financial structure) and the concept of gearing or leverage of a company.
- Consider whether or not there may be an optimal capital structure.
- Explain the traditional approach, the Miller and Modigliani approaches, pecking order theory, and the WACC approach to capital structure.

Introduction

In Chapter 4 we saw how risk impacts on the returns from 'real' investments in value creating projects and also financial investments in shares. We also looked at how risk may be reduced through investment in a range, or portfolio, of diversified investments. We introduced CAPM and how β factors may be used to measure the volatility of the return of a share relative to the market. This chapter looks further at CAPM and how it may be used as a method of calculating cost of equity.

We will also look at other methods of calculating the cost of equity and cost of debt capital. A company's cost of equity and cost of debt may then be used to calculate its weighted average cost of capital, its WACC.

The proportion of debt in a company's total capital (total debt plus equity) is called its capital structure, or financial structure. This chapter considers how a company's capital structure, its gearing or leverage, is measured. Any discussion about capital structure usually prompts the question 'What is a company's best (or optimal) capital structure?' The chapter closes with a review of a number of approaches to answering this question, including those proposed by Miller and Modigliani.

Capital asset pricing model (CAPM)

We saw in Chapter 4 that the risk premium that an investor should require as compensation for accepting the risk of a portfolio σ_p is:

$$\frac{(R_m - R_f)}{\sigma_m} \sigma_p$$

This risk premium may be rearranged into:

$$\frac{\sigma_p}{\sigma_m} \times (R_m - R_f)$$

and the expression $\frac{\sigma_p}{\sigma_m}$ is referred to as the beta factor (β).

Therefore, an investor's required return from a portfolio:

$$R_p = R_f + \frac{(R_m - R_f)}{\sigma_m}\sigma_p$$

can be re-stated as:

$$\text{Portfolio return } R_p = R_f + \beta \times (R_m - R_f)$$

The beta factor, β, can be used to measure the extent to which a portfolio's return (or an individual security's return) should exceed the risk-free rate of return. The beta factor is multiplied by the difference between the average return on market securities R_m and the risk-free return R_f to derive a portfolio or security risk premium. The risk premium includes both a business risk and a financial risk element. This equation forms the basis of the capital asset pricing model (CAPM).

CAPM considers the market return, and also the risk-free return and volatility of a share. Shareholders expect returns that are in terms of dividends and capital growth. However, actual shareholder returns may be higher or lower than expected, because of risk.

As we have already seen in Chapter 4, diversified portfolios of investments may eliminate some unsystematic risk. Some companies may perform badly while others do well. But some risk cannot be diversified away – systematic risk. Systematic risk includes business or operating risks, for example those resulting from economic changes. Systematic risk also includes the financial risk in geared companies because of interest payable.

The return on risk-free investments (R_f), like UK Government securities, should be exceeded by the returns on other investments. Some investments have larger market (systematic) risk and some lower than the average market risk and so expected returns vary more or less than average. The relationship between the expected return on a company's shares, its **cost of equity** (K_e), and the average market return (R_m) may be measured by β (note that $\beta = 1$ for the stock market as a whole).

Investors can measure the beta factor of their portfolios by obtaining information about the beta factors of individual securities. β factors may be calculated using data collected in respect of periodic returns of market and individual company data using regression analysis. β values are also obtainable from a variety of sources such as investment analysts who specialise in the charting of the volatility of shares and markets, and their findings may regularly be found in the UK financial press. β values are also published quarterly by the London Business School's Financial Services in their publication entitled *Risk Measurement Service*.

It should be noted that CAPM recognises 'chance' returns and share price variations due to market risk. CAPM measures the β of individual shares by reliable statistical measures, but it does not take unsystematic risk into account, although it may be significant for an undiversified investor or a company with few products. But an investor may reduce or eliminate unsystematic risk through diversification.

CAPM may therefore be used to calculate the return on a company's shares while making some allowance for the systematic risk relating to that company. CAPM can be stated as follows:

> **the expected return from a security = the risk-free rate of return, plus a premium for market risk, adjusted by a measure of the volatility of the security**

If

R_s	is the expected return from an individual security
β	is the beta factor for the individual security
R_f	is the risk-free rate of return
R_m	is the return from the market as a whole
$(R_m - R_f)$	is the market risk premium

then

$$R_s = R_f + \{\beta \times (R_m - R_f)\}$$

A variation of the above β relationship may be used to establish an equity cost of capital for use in project appraisal. The cost of equity K_e equates to the expected return from an individual security R_s, and the beta value for the company's equity capital β_e equates to the beta factor for the individual security β.

So, the returns expected by ordinary shareholders, or the cost of equity to the company, is equal to the risk-free rate of return plus a premium for market risk adjusted by a measure of the volatility of the ordinary shares of the company.

Therefore:

$$K_e = R_f + \{\beta_e \times (R_m - R_f)\}$$

as represented in Figure 5.1.

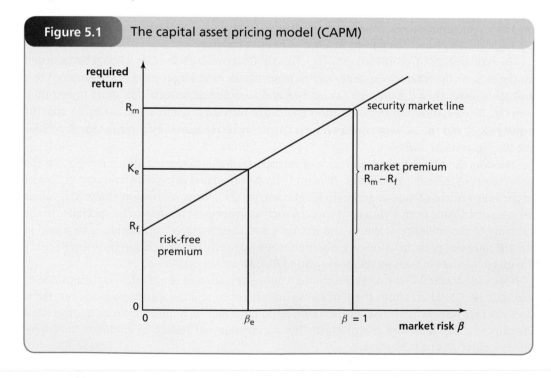

Figure 5.1 The capital asset pricing model (CAPM)

In Figure 5.1 it should be noted that the linear relationship between risk and return is represented by the **security market line (SML)**. Whereas the capital market line (CML) that we discussed in Chapter 4 represents the linear risk and return trade-off for investors in a portfolio of risky market-based assets and other risk-free assets, the SML represents the relationship between systematic risk (measured by β) and the required rate of return on capital assets.

CAPM assumes that the relationship between the return from a share and the average return for the whole market is a linear relationship. It should also be remembered that the CAPM considers systematic risk only. CAPM is a market equilibrium theory that was developed relating to the prices of shares and their risks.

As we discussed in Chapter 4, just as an individual security or share has a beta factor, so too does a portfolio of securities. A portfolio consisting of a weighted proportion of all the securities on the stock market, excluding risk-free securities, will have an expected return equal to the expected return for the market as a whole, and so a β factor of 1. A portfolio consisting entirely of risk-free securities will have a β factor of zero.

Worked example 5.1

The beta factor of an investor's portfolio (β_p) is the weighted average of the β factors of the securities in the portfolio, as illustrated in the following portfolio:

Security	Percentage of portfolio	β factor of security %	Weighted average
V	25	0.8	0.200
W	20	1.4	0.280
X	10	1.2	0.120
Y	15	1.3	0.195
Z	30	0.6	0.180
	100	Portfolio β_p =	0.975

We are also told that the risk-free rate of return is 8% and the average market portfolio return is 15%.

Let's calculate the expected return from the portfolio.

Using:

$$R_p = R_f + \beta_p(R_m - R_f)$$

the expected return from the portfolio is:

$$8\% + 0.975 \times (15\% - 8\%) = 14.825\%$$

The calculation could alternatively have been made as follows where $R_m = 15\%$, and $R_f = 8\%$:

Security	Beta factor	Expected return $[R_f + \beta (R_m - R_f)]$	Weighting	Weighted return
		%	%	%
V	0.8	13.6	25	3.400
W	1.4	17.8	20	3.560
X	1.2	16.4	10	1.640
Y	1.3	17.1	15	2.565
Z	0.6	12.2	30	3.660
			100	14.825

What are the practical implications of CAPM theory for portfolio management? Well, the conclusions we can draw from CAPM theory are that the investor should:

■ decide on what β factor they would like to have for their portfolio – they may prefer a portfolio beta factor of greater than 1 in expectation of above-average returns when market returns are high, and lower-than-average returns if market returns are low, or alternatively they may prefer a portfolio β factor below 1
■ seek to invest in shares with a low β factor in a bear market, when average market returns are falling, and also sell shares with a high beta factor
■ seek to invest in shares with a high β factor in a bull market, when average market returns are rising.

Limitations of CAPM

There are a number of limitations to the CAPM, including:

■ it is a single-factor model
■ the model makes unrealistic assumptions, for example that the cost of insolvency is zero and that markets are efficient
■ the parameters of the model cannot be estimated precisely, for example those used in determining the risk-free rate of return and beta values
■ the model assumes a linear relationship between its variables.

The CAPM is generally only usable where shares are traded on the open market. While the CAPM may be used to determine the value of a share, or determine the risk of a portfolio of shares, increasing doubt was expressed by Fama and French (Fama, EF and French, K 'The cross-section of expected stock returns' *Journal of Finance* 47, June, pages 427–65 (1992)) as to whether the SML exists, and whether beta has any impact on the level of returns earned on shares. We may question the validity of the CAPM. The model is difficult to test because the Stock Exchange indices that are used to approximate market return may be poor surrogates:

■ they do not include all tradable shares
■ they exclude un-tradable shares and other financial and non-financial assets like bonds, property, land, etc.

Arbitrage pricing theory (APT)

Tests of the CAPM have shown it not to be a perfect explanation of the relationship between the level of risk and the expected risk premium. This led to the development of other approaches. The arbitrage pricing theory (APT) model developed by Stephen Ross (Ross, SA 'The Arbitrage Theory of Capital Asset Pricing' *Journal of Economic Theory*, Volume 13, pages 341–60 (1976)) deserves a mention even though interest in this model has waned in recent years.

The APT model includes four macroeconomic factors, for example industrial output and inflation levels, that impact on risk that cannot be eliminated by diversification. APT assumes that there is not just one unique explanation of the risk premium relationship, as with the CAPM, but a number of factors. The APT model says that the expected return (K_e) of a stock or share depends on the risk associated with each factor and the sensitivity to each of the factors.

CAPM says that

$$K_e = R_f + \{\beta_e \times (R_m - R_f)\}$$

If we denote the average market risk premium ($R_m - R_f$) by λ then

$$K_e = R_f + \lambda\beta_e$$

APT says that

$$K_e = R_f + \lambda_1\beta_1 + \lambda_2\beta_2 + \lambda_3\beta_3 + \lambda_4\beta_4$$

where λ_1, λ_2, λ_3, and λ_4 are the average risk premiums for each of the four factors in the model and β_1, β_2, β_3, and β_4 are measures of the sensitivities of the particular stock or share to each of the four factors.

In the 1980s the *Journal of Finance* included many reports on empirical tests on the APT model. The tests seemed to show that it was robust and it worked and indicated its apparent superiority to the CAPM model in explaining historical returns on stock and shares. But because the APT model relates to four factors (which may not all be clearly defined) rather than the one-factor market portfolio in CAPM, its practical usefulness may be even more questionable than the use of CAPM. APT does not currently appear to be used in practice to any significant extent. CAPM may be less than perfect but its broad approach is useful in deriving an appropriate discount rate for investment decision-making.

Cost of equity

In Chapter 4 we introduced the concept of risk and its correlation with returns on investments. The relationship between risk and return is also one of the key concepts relating to determination of the **cost of debt** and cost of equity capital. It is an important concept and so we will briefly explore risk a little further, with regard to investments in companies. We will discuss the cost of debt based on future income flows to the lender – interest payments. We shall similarly discuss the cost of equity based on future income flows to the shareholder – dividends. Dividends and dividend policy will be considered in more detail in Chapters 13 and 15.

The cost of equity to a company may be determined by considering its expected future cash flows. In the case of equity or ordinary shares these future cash flows are dividends. One difference between this method and the method applied to debt is that there is no tax relief for dividend payments.

The value of an ordinary share may be simply expressed as the present value of its expected future dividend flows:

$$S = v_1/(1 + K_e) + v_2/(1 + K_e)^2 + v_3/(1 + K_e)^3 + \ldots + v_n/(1 + K_e)^n$$

Where

$$K_e = \text{cost of equity capital}$$
$$v_1 \ldots v_n = \text{expected future dividends for each of 1 to } n \text{ years}$$
$$S = \text{the current market value of the share}$$

If dividends are expected to remain level over a period of time the formula may be simplified to:

$$S = \frac{v_1}{K_e}$$

Therefore, the cost of equity to the company would be:

$$K_e = \frac{v_1}{S}$$

This simple **dividend model** is based on the notion that shareholders value shares based on the value of their expected dividends. A disadvantage of the simple dividend model is that it assumes that shareholders are rational and consistent in their long-term dividend expectations.

Simple dividend growth model

A big assumption made in using the simple dividend model is that capital growth in share price is ignored because the share price at any time reflects expectations of future dividends at that time. Dividends payable on a particular share rarely stay constant from year to year. However, dividends may grow at a regular rate.

The so-called **dividend growth model** (or Gordon growth model) approach to cost of equity may be developed by revising the simple dividend model formula. The dividend growth model assumes a direct link between share price and expected future dividends and recognises the expected rate of dividend growth (G) achieved through reinvestment of retained earnings.

If

$$K_e = \text{cost of equity capital}$$
$$v = \text{current dividend}$$
$$S = \text{the current market value of the share}$$

then

$$S = v/(1 + K_e) + v(1 + G)/(1 + K_e)^2 + v(1 + G)^2/(1 + K_e)^3 + \ldots + v(1 + G)^{n-1}/(1 + K_e)^n$$

If it is assumed that the share is held for an indefinite period then n can be assumed to tend towards infinity and if G is assumed to be constant the equation may be rewritten as:

$$\text{Current share price S} = \frac{v(1 + G)}{(K_e - G)}$$

Therefore

$$\text{Cost of equity } K_e = \frac{v(1 + G)}{S} + G$$

If the first year dividend v_1 is assumed to have grown at a rate of G so that $v(1 + G) = v_1$ then the cost of equity may be restated as:

$$K_e = \frac{v_1}{S} + G$$

Worked example 5.2

Cher Alike plc has 3m ordinary shares in issue that currently have a market price (S) of £2.71. The board have already recommended next year's dividend (v_1) at 17p per share. The chairman, Sonny Daze, is forecasting that dividends will continue to grow (G) at 4.2% per annum for the foreseeable future.

What is Cher Alike plc's cost of equity?

$$K_e = \text{cost of equity capital}$$
$$= \frac{v_1}{S} + G$$
$$= \frac{0.17}{2.71} + 4.2\%$$
$$= 0.063 + 0.042$$
$$= 10.5\%$$

Progress check 5.1

In what ways may a company's cost of equity be calculated?

Cost of debt

The interest rate paid on a loan is known almost with certainty. Even if the debt carries a floating or variable interest rate then that is far easier to estimate than expected dividend flows on ordinary shares. Debt comprises debentures, loans etc., and may be corporate or government debt. Their levels of risk are different, and some debt may be secured on specific assets or the assets of a company in general. The cost of debt is generally based on the current market rate for debt, having a specific level of risk.

Two of the main differences between the cost of equity and the cost of debt are:

- the different levels of risk between debt and equity
- a **tax shield** is applicable to interest paid on debt, but not to equity dividends paid.

The cost of servicing debt capital is the yearly or half-yearly interest payment, which is an allowable expense for tax purposes. The cost of repayment of a loan, or debt, depends on the type of loan. Loan capital, a debenture for example, may be irredeemable and traded, with a market value, or redeemable at a specific date. We will look at the calculation of the cost to a company of a redeemable loan and also the cost of an irredeemable loan.

If

K_d = cost of debt
i = annual loan interest rate
L = the current market value of the loan as a percentage of its nominal value

if the loan is redeemable, and if R is the loan value at redemption after n years, then:

$$L = i/(1 + K_d) + i/(1 + K_d)^2 + i/(1 + K_d)^3 + \ldots + (i + R)/(1 + K_d)^n$$

The cost of debt in the above equation can be calculated by trial and error, by interpolation, or using the appropriate Excel function.

For an irredeemable loan the interest is payable in perpetuity (for ever), so:

$$L = i/(1 + K_d) + i/(1 + K_d)^2 + i/(1 + K_d)^3 + \ldots \text{ to infinity}$$

therefore:

$$L = i/K_d$$

Because interest payable on loans is an allowable deduction for corporation tax the cost of debt is normally calculated by adjusting the interest rate by the percentage of corporation tax to provide an after-tax rate of interest.

Therefore, if t = the rate of corporation tax then

$$K_d = i \times \frac{(1 - t)}{L}$$

The expression $(1 - t)$ is called the tax shield.

By rearranging the formula it can be seen that market value of the debt is dependent on the level of future returns, the interest rate paid, which is determined by the level of risk associated with the investment, and the rate of corporation tax:

$$L = i \times \frac{(1 - t)}{K_d}$$

Worked example 5.3

Owen Cash plc pays 12% interest (i) per annum on an irredeemable debt of £1m, with a nominal value of £100. The corporation tax rate (t) is currently 50%. The market value of the debt (L) is currently £90.

What is Owen Cash plc's cost of debt?

K_d = cost of debt capital

$$K_d = \frac{i \times (1 - t)}{L} = \frac{12\% \times (1 - 50\%)}{90\%}$$

$$= \frac{12\% \times 50\%}{90\%} = 6.7\% \text{ after tax}$$

What would be the cost of debt if instead this loan were redeemable at par (R) after three years? If K_d is the cost of debt of the redeemable loan then

$$L = i/(1 + K_d) + i/(1 + K_d)^2 + i/(1 + K_d)^3 + \ldots + (i + R)/(1 + K_d)^n$$
$$90 = 6/(1 + K_d) + 6/(1 + K_d)^2 + (6 + 100)/(1 + K_d)^3$$

Solving this equation gives

$$K_d = 10.0\%, \text{ or } 5\% \text{ after tax}$$

Alternatively by interpolation, using a discount rate of 12% the NPV = −£4.59, and using a discount rate of 8% the NPV = £4.48.

The difference between the two is £9.07, and therefore

$$K_d = 8\% + (£4.48 \times 4)/£9.07 = 9.98 \text{ or } 10\%, \text{ or } 5\% \text{ after tax}$$

Progress check 5.2

How can the cost of debt be determined?

Weighted average cost of capital (WACC)

Weighted average cost of capital (WACC) is the weighted cost of financing a company ◀▥ (equity, debentures, bank loans) weighted according to the proportion of each, based on their market valuations. Once the company's cost of debt (K_d) and cost of equity (K_e) have been calculated the individual costs of finance can then be weighted by the relative proportions of debt (D) and equity (E) within the existing capital structure to calculate its WACC.

The weighted average cost of capital (WACC) may be defined as the average cost of the total financial resources of a company, i.e. the shareholders' equity and the net financial debt. WACC may also be calculated on a marginal basis for additional incremental finance packages comprising debt or equity.

In practice, conditions within a company may change daily and so calculations of the cost of equity and the cost of debt may not be totally accurate. As the relative proportions of a company's equity and debt, its **gearing**, change, the returns required by investors and the levels of perceived risk may also change. It should be noted that the terms of a debt may require interest to be paid at a floating rate rather than a fixed rate, in which case an equivalent 'fixed' rate then has to be estimated.

If we represent shareholders' equity as E and net financial debt as D then the relative proportions of equity and debt in the company's total financing are:

$$\frac{E}{E + D} \quad \text{and} \quad \frac{D}{E + D}$$

The cost of equity is the expected return on equity, the return the shareholders expect from their investment. If we represent the cost of shareholders' equity as K_e and the cost of financial debt as K_d, and t is the rate of corporation tax, then we can derive the formula to calculate WACC.

$$\text{WACC} = \left\{ \frac{E}{E + D} \times K_e \right\} + \left\{ \frac{D}{E + D} \times K_d \times (1 - t) \right\}$$

Interest on debt capital is an allowable deduction for purposes of corporate taxation and so the cost of share capital and the cost of debt capital are not properly comparable costs. Therefore this tax relief on debt interest ought to be recognised in any discounted cash flow calculations. One way would be to include the tax savings due to interest payments in the cash flows of every project. A simpler method, and the one normally used, is to allow for the tax relief in computing the cost of debt capital, to arrive at an after-tax cost of debt. Therefore, in order to calculate WACC, the cost of debt (K_d) must be adjusted for corporation tax (t), by $(1 - t)$ the tax shield.

Worked example 5.4

Fleet Ltd has the following financial structure:

$K_e = 15\%$ return on equity (this may be taken as given for the purpose of this example)

$K_d = 10\%$ lower risk, so lower than the return on equity

$t = 30\%$ rate of corporation tax

$\dfrac{E}{E + D} = 60\%$ equity to equity plus debt ratio

$\dfrac{D}{E + D} = 40\%$ debt to equity plus debt ratio

We can calculate the WACC for Fleet Ltd, and also evaluate the impact on WACC of a change in capital structure to equity 40% and debt 60%.

Calculation of WACC for Fleet Ltd with the current financial structure:

$$\text{WACC} = \left\{ \frac{E}{E + D} \times K_e \right\} + \left\{ \frac{D}{E + D} \times K_d \times (1 - t) \right\}$$

$$\text{WACC} = (60\% \times 15\%) + \{40\% \times 10\%(1 - 30\%)\} = 11.8\%$$

If the company decides to change its financial structure so that equity is 40% and debt is 60% of total financing, then WACC becomes:

$$(40\% \times 15\%) + \{60\% \times 10\%(1 - 30\%)\} = 10.2\%$$

So it appears that the company has reduced its WACC by increasing the relative weighting from 40% to 60% of the cheapest financial resource, debt, in its total financing. However, this may not happen in practice because as the debt/equity ratio of the company increased from 0.67 (40/60) to 1.50 (60/40) the company's financial risk has also increased. There is a well-established correlation between risk and return; as financial risk has increased then the providers of the financial resources will require a higher return on their investment. So, it is probably not correct to calculate the WACC using the same returns on equity and debt, as both may have increased. This is one of the problems of trying to calculate an accurate WACC for a company, which is based on its relative proportions and costs of debt and equity capital.

As an alternative to the two dividend models we have seen, the cost of equity of a company may be calculated by making an allowance for risk using the CAPM. This cost of capital may then be used to calculate a company's WACC.

Progress check 5.3

How is the weighted average cost of capital (WACC) calculated?

The uses of WACC

The market value of a company may be determined by evaluating its future cash flows discounted to present values by using its WACC. The lower the WACC then the higher the net present values of its future cash flows and therefore the higher its market value. The determination of the optimum D/E (debt/equity) ratio is one of the most difficult tasks facing the finance director. The risks and costs associated with debt capital and equity capital are different and subject to continual change, and may vary from industry to industry and between different types of business. Measurement of the D/E ratio may therefore not be a straightforward task, particularly for diversified groups of companies. Companies in different markets and indeed diversified companies that have trading divisions operating within different markets and producing different products face different levels of risk. If division A operates with a higher risk than division B then the required rate of return of A's investments should be higher than the hurdle rate (see Chapter 6 section about discounted cash flow) of return of B's investments. The difference is 'paying' for the difference in risk. This is an important principle but very difficult to implement in practice.

Mini case 5.1

Regulated industries are subject to a number of performance measures, one of which is a post-tax WACC set by the regulating authority. This target is regularly reviewed and there is some variation between industries. Water regulator Ofwat set a new WACC target of 4.5% in their 2011 Regulatory Compliance document, reducing it from their previous 5.1% set in 2004. The regulator's decision can have serious ramifications for the public utility companies which then have to ensure the stringent requirements are met in coming years.

Examples of WACC and some year-on-year variations can be seen in the table below:

Industry	Year of review	Post-tax WACC
Water	1994	5.7%
Water	1999	4.1%
Water	2004	5.1%
Water	2011	4.5%
London airports	1996	6.0%
London airports	2002	5.0%
Electricity distribution	1999	4.6%
Railtrack	2000	5.6%

There are many arguments for and against the use of WACC for investment appraisal. Its use is argued on the basis that:

- new investments must be financed by new sources of funds – retained earnings, new share issues, new loans, and so on
- the cost of capital to be applied to new project evaluation must reflect the cost of new capital
- the WACC reflects the company's long-term future capital structure, and capital costs; if this were not so, the current WACC would become irrelevant because eventually it would not relate to any actual cost of capital.

It is sometimes argued that the current WACC should be used to evaluate projects, because a company's capital structure changes only very slowly over time; therefore, the marginal cost of new capital will be roughly equal to the WACC. If this view is correct, then by undertaking investments that offer a return in excess of the WACC, a company will increase the market value of its ordinary shares in the long run. This is because the excess returns would provide surplus profits and dividends for the shareholders.

The arguments against the use of WACC are based on the criticisms of the assumptions made that justify the use of WACC:

- new investments have different risk characteristics from the company's existing operations; therefore the return required by investors may go up or down if the investments are made, because their business risk is perceived to be higher or lower
- finance raised to fund a new investment:
    - may substantially change the capital structure and perceived risk of investing in the company
    - may determine the extent to which either debt or equity used to finance the project will change the perceived risk of the entire company, which must be taken into account in the investment appraisal

■ many companies raise floating rate debt capital as well as fixed rate debt capital, having a variable rate that changes in line with current market rates; this is difficult to include in a WACC calculation, the best compromise being to substitute an 'equivalent' fixed debt rate in place of the floating rate.

Worked example 5.5

Bittaboth plc has ordinary shares in issue with a market value four times the value of its debt capital. The interest paid on debt (i) of 11% before tax is also considered to be the risk-free rate of interest (R_f). The beta value of Bittaboth's equity capital has been estimated at 0.9 (β_e) and the average market return on equity capital is 17% (R_m). Corporation tax is at 50% (t).

Let's use CAPM to calculate Bittaboth plc's cost of equity and its WACC.

$$K_e = \text{cost of equity capital}$$
$$K_e = R_f + \{\beta_e \times (R_m - R_f)\}$$
$$= 11\% + \{0.9 \times (17\% - 11\%)\}$$
$$= 0.11 + (0.9 \times 0.06)$$
$$= 0.164 \text{ or } 16.4\%$$

$$K_d = \text{cost of debt capital}$$

which after tax

$$K_d = i \times (1 - t) \text{ or } 11\% \times 50\%$$
$$= 5.5\%$$

Any capital projects that Bittaboth may wish to consider may be evaluated using its WACC, which may be calculated as:

$$(4/5 \times 16.4\%) + (1/5 \times 5.5\%) = 14.2\%$$

14.2% is Bittaboth's weighted average cost of capital (WACC).

Progress check 5.4

What are some of the reasons why WACC is so important to companies?

Capital structure

We have already discussed the importance of the level of a company's debt with regard to its strategic financial decision-making. It is also very important with regard to its gearing, or financial (capital) structure. Strategic financing decisions on the appropriate levels of debt and equity at the lowest cost to the company have a big impact on shareholder wealth.

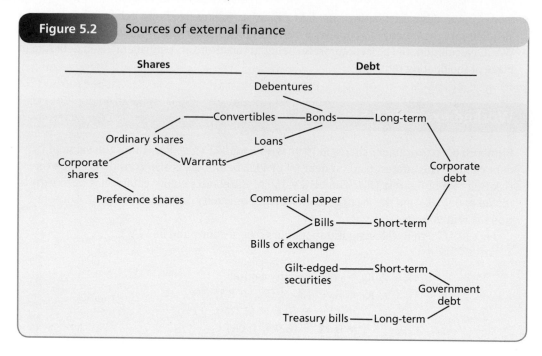

Figure 5.2 Sources of external finance

The financial structure of a company comprises both internal and external finance. If we first consider internal financing, then we can see that the aim of optimal investment in non-current assets results in profits that may be distributed in the form of dividends or retained for future investment. If the non-current assets are the engine of the business then working capital is the oil needed to lubricate it and enable it to run efficiently. The effective management of working capital is a further source of internal finance that supports the investment in non-current assets (see Chapter 10).

External finance broadly comprises debt (loans, debentures, etc.) and equity (ordinary shares). Examples of the broad range of different types of debt and equity are shown in Figure 5.2, each of which will be discussed in detail in Chapter 7.

Gearing – debt and equity

Gearing is the relationship between debt and equity capital that represents the capital structure or financial structure of an organisation. The relationship between the two sources of finance, loans and ordinary shares, or debt and equity, gives a measure of the gearing of the company. A company with a high proportion of debt capital to share capital is highly geared, and it is low geared if it has a high proportion of share capital to debt capital. We will consider the importance of gearing to companies and then consider worked examples that compare the impact of the use of debt capital compared with ordinary share capital.

Gearing (leverage, or debt/equity) has important implications for the long-term stability of a company because of, as we have seen, its impact on financial risk. The level of a company's gearing, its capital or financial structure, is also very important with regard to its dividend policy. A company that is very low geared has a relatively high proportion of equity capital and may potentially have to pay out a high level of dividends. On the other hand, since its level of debt is relatively low then its level of interest payments will also be relatively low. A consequence of this is that it will also have a low tax shield relating to its interest payments.

A company that is very highly geared has a relatively low proportion of equity capital and therefore a low level of potential dividend payments. Consequently, since its level of debt is relatively high then its level of interest payments will also be relatively high. This will mean that it will also have a high tax shield relating to its interest payments. Specific dividend policies relating to companies at different stages in the life cycle are discussed in more detail in Chapters 13 and 15.

Companies closely monitor their gearing ratios to ensure that their capital structure aligns with their financial strategy. Finance directors will make appropriate adjustments to their companies' gearing in order to balance capital structure as is clearly demonstrated by the press extract below.

Companies ignore the risk of high gearing at their peril

Finance directors of Britain's biggest companies are increasingly aiming to raise debt levels relative to equity, in spite of declining optimism for the future. More finance chiefs believe UK corporate balance sheets are under rather than over-leveraged, though the majority view remains that levels are about right, according to a survey by Deloitte, the professional services firm. This represents a significant shift since last quarter and is the first time finance directors have, on balance, thought companies under-leveraged since the survey began in 2007.

When asked about their capital structure plans, a growing number of finance chiefs said they aimed to increase gearing in the next 12 months. They were fairly equally divided between those in favour of raising, holding and reducing. While the net balance remained slightly in favour of reducing leverage, the survey has not reported such enthusiasm for debt relative to equity since before the collapse of Lehman Brothers in 2008.

Ian Stewart, chief economist at Deloitte, said: 'Corporates are finding it much easier to raise credit and there has been a remarkable improvement in perceptions of bank credit availability.' Companies with higher leverage – a higher ratio of debt to equity capital – are typically considered riskier, as cash flow is committed in advance to pay creditors. The more leveraged a company is, the greater the risk that it will struggle to repay or refinance its debt.

As such, it might seem strange that financial directors, who remain cautious, should want to ramp up their debt. Three-quarters of them said that now was a bad time to be taking on greater risk and yet three-quarters said that now was a good time to issue corporate bonds, the favoured approach to funding. The disconnect is probably explained by the rising availability and falling cost of credit for large companies. Credit is, on balance, considered readily available for the first time, and cheaper than at any time, since the survey began.

Finance directors tempted to raise debt cheaply are well aware of the risks – and not just because the financial crisis is such recent history. A record 14 per cent of them consider government bonds 'very overvalued' with a further 39 per cent concluding they are 'somewhat overvalued'.

Source: Saunders, E. (2010) Finance chiefs aim to raise debt, *Financial Times*, 11 October. © The Financial Times Limited 2012. All Rights Reserved.

Various alternative actions may be taken by companies, as necessary, to adjust their capital structures by increasing or decreasing their respective levels of debt and equity. An example of one of the ways in which this may be achieved is to return cash to shareholders. In May 2004 Marshalls plc, the paving stone specialist that supplied the flagstones for the pedestrianised Trafalgar Square in London, announced that they were planning to return £75m to shareholders through a capital reorganisation. The reason the company gave for this was that it expected a more efficient capital structure as a result. The company was geared at only 6%, and had generated a £5.3m cash surplus in its previous financial year, after dividends and £40m capital expenditure, which its chairman said had reflected its success in growing shareholder value and generating cash.

The extent to which the debt/equity ratio is high or low geared has an effect on the earnings per share (eps) of the company:

- if profits are increasing, then higher gearing is preferable to benefit from the lower cost of debt and the tax shield
- if profits are decreasing, then lower gearing or no gearing is preferred to avoid the commitment to paying high levels of interest and because dividends do not have to be paid.

Similarly, the argument applies to the riskiness attached to capital repayments. If a company goes into receivership or liquidation, lenders have priority over shareholders with regard to capital repayment. So, the more highly geared the company the less chance there is of ordinary shareholders being repaid in full.

Progress check 5.5

What is gearing?

The many types of short- and long-term capital available to companies leads to complexity, but also the expectation that overall financial risks may be reduced through improved matching of funding with operational needs. The gearing position of the company may be considered in many ways depending on whether the long-term capital structure or the overall financial structure is being analysed. It may also be analysed by concentrating on the income position rather than purely on the capital structure.

The two financial ratios that follow are the two most commonly used (see also Chapter 8). Both ratios relate to financial gearing, which is the relationship between a company's borrowings, which includes both prior charge capital and long-term debt, and shareholders' funds (share capital plus reserves).

$$\text{gearing} = \frac{\text{long-term debt}}{\text{equity} + \text{long-term debt}}$$

$$\text{debt equity ratio, or leverage} = \frac{\text{long-term debt}}{\text{equity}}$$

Worked example 5.6 illustrates the calculation of both ratios.

Worked example 5.6

Two companies have different gearing. Company A is financed totally by 20,000 £1 ordinary shares, while company B is financed partly by 10,000 £1 ordinary shares and a £10,000 loan on which they pay 10% per year. In all other respects the companies are the same. They both have assets of £20,000 and both make the same profit before interest and tax (PBIT).

We can calculate their gearing and debt/equity ratios.

➡

	A	B
	£	£
Assets	20,000	20,000
less 10% loan	–	(10,000)
	20,000	10,000
Ordinary shares	20,000	10,000

$$\text{gearing} = \frac{\text{long-term debt}}{\text{equity} + \text{long-term debt}} = \frac{0}{20,000 + 0} = 0\% \quad \frac{10,000}{10,000 + 10,000} = 50\%$$

$$\text{debt equity ratio} = \frac{\text{long-term debt}}{\text{equity}} = \frac{0}{20,000} = 0\% \quad \frac{10,000}{10,000} = 100\%$$

Company B must make a profit before interest of at least £1,000 to cover the cost of interest payable on the 10% loan. Company A does not have any minimum PBIT requirement to cover interest payable because it has no debt. Company A is lower geared and considered less risky in terms of profitability than company B which is a more highly geared company. This is because the PBIT of a lower geared company is more likely to be sufficiently high to cover interest charges and make a profit for its shareholders.

Gearing calculations can be made in a number of ways, and may also relate to earnings/interest relationships in addition to capital values. For example:

$$\text{dividend cover (times)} = \frac{\text{earnings per share (eps)}}{\text{dividend per share}}$$

This ratio indicates the number of times the profits attributable to the equity shareholders covers the actual dividends paid and payable for the period. Financial analysts usually adjust their calculations for any exceptional items of which they may be aware.

$$\text{interest cover (times)} = \frac{\text{profit before interest and tax}}{\text{interest payable}}$$

This ratio calculates the number of times the interest payable is covered by profits available for such payments. It is particularly important for lenders to determine the vulnerability of interest payments to a drop in profit. The following ratio determines the same vulnerability in cash terms.

$$\text{cash interest cover} = \frac{\text{net cash inflow from operations} + \text{interest received}}{\text{interest paid}}$$

Progress check 5.6

Outline some of the ways in which gearing may be calculated.

Worked example 5.7

Swell Guys plc is a growing company that manufactures equipment for fitting out small cruiser boats. Its planned expansion involves investing in a new factory project costing £4m. Chief executive, Guy Rope, expects the 12-year project to add £0.5m to profit before interest and tax each year. Next year's operating profit is forecast at £5m, and dividends per share are forecast at the same level as last year. Tax is not expected to be payable over the next few years due to tax losses that have been carried forward.

Swell Guys' last two years' results are as follows:

	Last year £m	Previous year £m
Income statement for the year ended 31 December		
Revenue	18	15
Operating costs	16	11
Operating profit	2	4
Finance costs	1	1
Profit before tax	1	3
Income tax expense	0	0
Profit after tax	1	3
Dividends	1	1
Retained profit	0	2
Balance sheet as at 31 December		
Non-current assets	8	9
Current assets		
Inventories	7	4
Trade and other receivables	4	3
Cash and cash equivalents	1	2
Total current assets	12	9
Total assets	20	18
Current liabilities		
Borrowings and finance leases	4	2
Trade and other payables	5	5
Total current liabilities	9	7
Non-current liabilities		
Loan	6	6
Total liabilities	15	13
Net assets	5	5
Equity		
Share capital (25p ordinary shares)	2	2
Retained earnings	3	3
Total equity	5	5

Swell Guys is considering two alternative financing options for the new project:

(a) Issue of £4m 15% loan stock repayable in five years' time.
(b) Rights issue of 4m 25p ordinary shares at £1 per share after expenses.

For each of the options the directors would like to see:

(i)   how the retained earnings will look for next year
(ii) how earnings per share will look for next year
(iii) how the equity will look at the end of next year
(iv) how long-term loans will look at the end of next year
(v)   how gearing will look at the end of next year.

(i)   **Swell Guys plc forecast income statement for next year ended 31 December**
      Operating profit £5m + £0.5m from the new project

		New debt £m	New equity £m
Operating profit		5.5	5.5
Interest payable	[1.0 + 0.6]	1.6	1.0
Profit before tax		3.9	4.5
Income tax expense		0.0	0.0
Profit after tax		3.9	4.5
Dividends		1.0	1.5
Retained profit		2.9	3.0

(ii) **Earnings per share**

$$\frac{\text{profit available for ordinary shareholders}}{\text{number of ordinary shares}} \quad \frac{£3.9m}{8m} = 48.75p \quad \frac{£4.5m}{12m} = 37.5p$$

(iii) **Equity**

		£m		£m
Share capital (25p ordinary shares)	(8m shares)	2.0	(12m shares)	3.0
Share premium account		0.0		3.0
Retained earnings		5.9		6.0
Total equity		7.9		12.0

(iv) **Loan**   [6 + 4]   10.0   6.0
(v)   **Gearing**

$$\frac{\text{long-term debt}}{\text{equity + long-term debt}} = \frac{£6m + £4m}{£7.9m + £6m + £4m} = 55.9\% \quad \frac{£6m}{£12m + £6m} = 33.3\%$$

Progress check 5.7

Explain how a high interest cover ratio can reassure a prospective lender.

Return on equity (ROE) may be considered as a function of financial structure (debt/equity ratio) and return on assets (ROA).

If

$$D = \text{debt capital}$$
$$E = \text{equity capital}$$
$$t = \text{corporation tax rate}$$
$$i = \text{interest rate on debt}$$
$$\text{ROA} = \text{return on assets}$$

then

$$\text{ROE} = \{\text{ROA} \times (1 - t)\} + \{(\text{ROA} - i) \times (1 - t) \times D/E\}$$

In general, when ROA is greater than i then the higher the D/E, the higher the ROE; when ROA is less than i then the higher the D/E, the lower the ROE. These relationships are important with regard to a company's performance and its level of gearing. This should be of interest to shareholders and analysts, and particularly bankers who may not be too happy to allow the debt/equity ratio to continue to increase even if profitability (ROA) exceeds interest.

Progress check 5.8

Why may a company not increase its debt/equity ratio indefinitely?

Optimal capital structure

A shareholder's return may be seen as comprising the return from a risk-free investment plus a return for the risk associated with that particular business. As the debt level of the business increases shareholders also require an additional premium for the financial risk relating to interest paid on debt. At high levels of gearing when debt levels are very high, shareholders will require a further additional premium to compensate for the risk of bankruptcy.

The debt-holder's return, or cost of debt, does not vary as levels of profit may vary, or generally as levels of gearing change. However, at very high levels of gearing when debt levels are very high, debt-holders may require an additional premium to compensate for some risk of bankruptcy, although perhaps not at the level of return demanded by shareholders.

We will consider whether or not an optimal capital structure exists and look at a number of approaches to the capital structure of a company including:

- the traditional approach
- the Miller and Modigliani (I) net income approach
- the Miller and Modigliani (II) market imperfections approach
- the Miller corporate and personal taxation approach
- pecking order theory
- the weighted average cost of capital (WACC) approach.

Traditional approach to capital structure (or financial structure)

The traditional approach to capital structure is based on a number of assumptions:

- taxation is ignored
- debt and equity can be simultaneously changed
- all earnings are paid out in dividends
- the business risk for the company is constant
- earnings and dividends do not grow over time.

If we assume that a company starts with no debt and 100 per cent equity capital (see point U in Figure 5.3). At that point the cost of capital is the risk-free rate of return plus a premium for the business risk of the company. If debt is increased in steps, the cost of equity (see the K_e line) increases steadily because of the additional premium required due to the financial risk arising from the increase in debt. The cost of equity continues to rise steadily until high levels of gearing are reached when it begins to rise steeply due to bankruptcy risk.

As levels of debt are increased in steps the cost of debt (see the K_d line) remains unchanged. However, at high levels of gearing the cost of debt also begins to rise, in the same way as the cost of equity, due to bankruptcy risk.

The WACC of the company is based on the cost of equity and the cost of debt. If the company increases its level of low-cost debt and reduces its level of equity its WACC can be seen to decrease (see the WACC line). WACC gradually drops as gearing increases to an optimal point V, after which WACC begins to slowly increase as the benefit of the low cost of debt is outweighed by an increase in the cost of equity. WACC increases sharply at very high levels of gearing (W) as the impact of higher costs of both equity and debt are felt, due to the risk of bankruptcy.

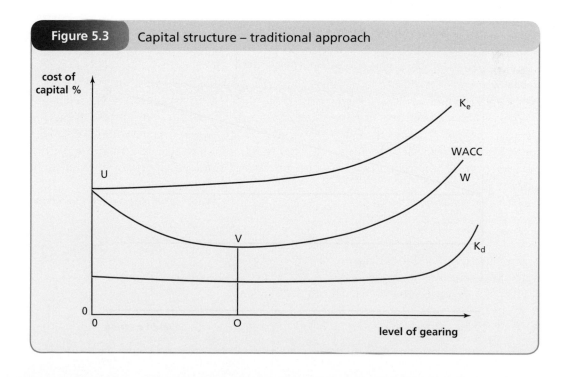

Figure 5.3 Capital structure – traditional approach

The traditional approach to capital structure is that there is an optimal point at the bottom of the WACC curve, the lowest cost of capital to the company. The company will aim for levels of equity and debt that give the level of gearing at point O to achieve its lowest average cost of capital.

Miller and Modigliani (I) net income approach to capital structure

In 1958 Miller and Modigliani (MM) developed their first approach to capital structure (Modigliani, F and Miller, MH 'The cost of capital, corporate finance and the theory of investment' *American Economic Review* 48, pages 261–97 (1958)). Their approach assumed that there was no tax and that the capital markets were perfect so that there were no bankruptcy costs and therefore the cost of debt was constant at all levels of gearing (see the K_d line in Figure 5.4). As the company increases its level of gearing, with equity being replaced by an equal amount of debt, the increased cost of equity (see the K_e line) is exactly offset by the increased total cost of debt and therefore the company's WACC remains constant (see the WACC line) at all levels of gearing.

MM therefore implied that there was no optimal capital structure in proposing that a company's WACC remains unchanged at all levels of gearing. This theory assumed that the cost of debt remains unchanged as gearing rises, but the cost of equity rises in such a way as to keep WACC constant.

MM defended their approach basing it on the behavioural proposition that investors would use **arbitrage** to keep WACC constant when gearing changed. Generally, arbitrage excludes the possibility of perfect substitutes selling at different prices in the same market. MM argued that companies that were identical (apart from their gearing levels) should not have different costs of capital. Therefore, the valuations of these companies should also be the same.

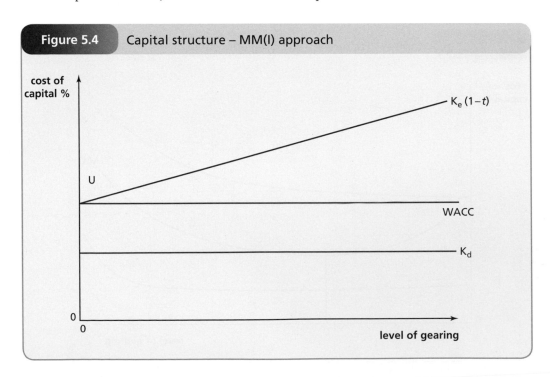

Figure 5.4 Capital structure – MM(I) approach

Miller and Modigliani (II) market imperfections approach to capital structure

In 1963 MM revised their thinking and amended their earlier model by recognising the existence of corporation tax (a market imperfection) and its impact on the cost of debt (Modigliani, F and Miller, MH 'Corporate income taxes and the cost of capital: a correction' *American Economic Review* 53, pages 433–43 (1963)). Interest payable on debt is an allowable expense in computing the company's taxable profit. The tax deductibility of debt interest implied that the greater the debt the more the company would shield its profits from corporation tax.

The so-called tax shield is illustrated in Worked example 5.8.

Worked example 5.8

A company pays interest on its loan at 10% per annum. The company pays corporation tax at a rate of 30% on its profits.

$$\text{Cost of debt, interest payable} = 10\% \text{ per annum}$$
$$\text{Actual cost of debt} = 10\% \times (1 - 30\%)$$
$$= 10\% \times 70\%$$
$$= 7\%$$

The $(1 - 30\%)$ in this example is referred to as the tax shield.

In Figure 5.5 we can see that the cost of equity (see line K_e) increases as gearing increases. The cost of debt is constant at all levels of gearing but at a lower cost, which allows for the tax

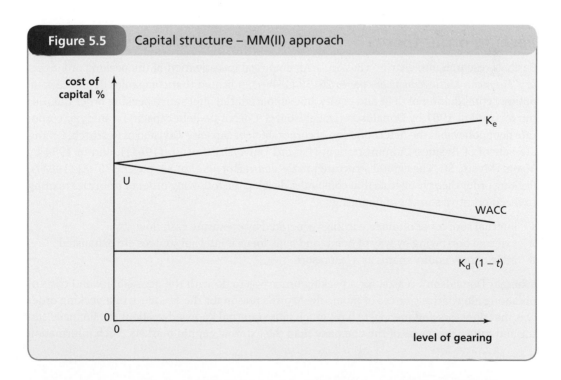

Figure 5.5   Capital structure – MM(II) approach

shield – see the $K_d(1 - t)$ line on the graph. However, the more debt the company takes on the greater the tax shield benefit and so WACC continues to decrease (see the WACC line on the graph).

The conclusion is that the optimal capital structure is therefore 100% debt since WACC will continue to decrease as gearing increases. In practice, of course, such a structure would be impossible since all companies have a legal requirement to issue a minimum number of equity shares.

Further approaches to capital structure

Miller approach to capital structure

Around 15 years later in 1977 Miller revised the MM(II) model to take account of not only corporate tax, but to include the impact of personal taxation with regard to debt and equity, and also the levels of equity and debt that were available to investors (Miller, MH 'Debt and taxes' *Journal of Finance* 32, pages 261–75 (1977)). Put very simply, Miller's model said that investors will choose to invest in either the equity or debt of companies to suit their individual personal tax situations. Their choice will depend on their personal income tax and capital gains tax positions and the timings of such payments. Companies may prefer a higher level of gearing to take advantage of the tax shield relating to interest payments. This involves encouraging investors to move from equity investment to debt investment, which may result in a less favourable personal tax position. Investors may be induced to switch from equity to debt by companies offering a higher interest rate. Miller argued that the higher interest rate would be mitigated by the tax shield and the weighted average cost of capital would remain the same. The result is a horizontal WACC line, the same as in the MM(I) model shown in Figure 5.4. Since Miller did not make any allowance for bankruptcy costs which may occur at very high levels of debt, then the WACC line remained horizontal at all levels of gearing. If bankruptcy costs were allowed for then the WACC line would curve upwards at the highest levels of gearing.

Pecking order theory

Baskin's research into gearing (Baskin, J 'An empirical investigation of the pecking order theory' *Financial Management* 18, pages 26–35 (1989)) indicated that companies do not seek an optimal combination of debt and equity, but supported the alternative pecking order theories put forward in 1961 by Donaldson (Donaldson, G 'Corporate debt capacity: a study of corporate debt policy and the determination of corporate debt capacity' Division of Research, Graduate School of Business Administration, Harvard University, Boston (1961)), and in 1984 by Myers (Myers, SC 'The capital structure puzzle' *Journal of Finance* 34, pages 575–92 (1984)). Pecking order theory suggests that companies develop the following order of priorities relating to the alternative sources of financing:

1 internal sources of retained earnings generated by operating cash flow
2 external borrowing by way of bonds and bank loans if internal sources are exhausted
3 issue of new equity shares as a last resort.

Whereas Donaldson's reason for a pecking order was to do with the accessibility and costs of obtaining alternative sources of financing, Myers's reason for the existence of a pecking order was that directors and managers have much more internal knowledge about the financial status and future prospects of the company than the external capital markets. Such information asymmetry means that managers may have a more realistic view of the value of the business than the markets. Therefore, managers will only want to issue new shares if they believe that the market has overvalued the company. Managers will not want to issue new shares if they believe that the market has undervalued the company, and so will first consider retained earnings to finance a new project, and then choose debt finance if there are not sufficient earnings. A further disadvantage of a share issue by a company is that it may sometimes be seen as a signal that the shares are overvalued, which then results in a share price mark-down and therefore an increase in the company's cost of equity.

Is there an optimal capital structure?

We have seen that the MM(I), Miller, and pecking order theories suggest that an optimal capital structure does not exist for companies. However, the traditional approach to capital structure and the MM(II) model suggest that it does exist. The WACC approach to capital structure considers the market imperfections of personal tax, corporation tax, and bankruptcy and agency costs, and may lead us to accept the existence of an optimal capital structure. There may be an agency problem because at high levels of gearing the shareholders have a lower stake in the business and they prefer high-risk projects, to provide a high return, and because they have less to lose. Debt-holders on the other hand are generally risk-averse.

The traditional approach to capital structure that we looked at earlier gave us the theoretical WACC line shown in Figure 5.3 and this is reproduced in Figure 5.6. In practice, companies may increase debt to sensible levels to enjoy the tax advantages and reduce WACC, so long as levels are not reached that cause investor concern about agency risk and possible bankruptcy. However, an optimal capital structure (O) obtained from a particular combination of debt and equity is unlikely. In reality, it is more likely that there is a range of capital structures within which a company can minimise its WACC (between N and P on the WACC in practice line in the graph in Figure 5.6) and so in practice the WACC graph is likely to be much flatter than the traditional graph.

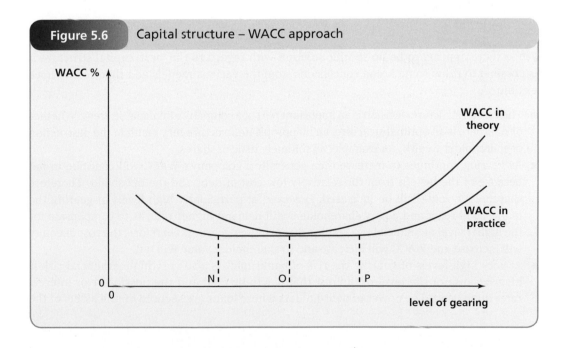

Figure 5.6   Capital structure – WACC approach

Mini case 5.2

The debate on optimal capital structure has continued for many years. An article published in the *Journal of Financial and Strategic Decisions* back in 1994 suggested an overall finding that the relationship between a company's debt level and that of its industry does not appear to be of concern to the market. We can move on 17 years to an article by van Binsbergen, Graham, and Yang in the *Journal of Applied Corporate Finance,* which notes that, despite all the research, a consensus on optimal capital structure has yet to emerge. As a consequence, in many cases it is difficult to make a specific recommendation about how much debt a company should have.

The lack of consensus, however, does not stop companies publishing acknowledgements in their annual reports that an optimal capital structure is achievable. A review of annual reports noted in the London Stock Exchange Aggregated Regulatory News Service (ARNS) for April 2012 showed 13 companies indicating they had strategies for optimising their capital structure.

The following extract from the 2011 annual report of Anpario plc, a food additives company, is typical of many:

'The Group's objectives when managing capital are to safeguard the Group's ability to continue as a going concern in order to provide returns for shareholders and benefits for other stakeholders and to maintain an optimal capital structure to reduce the cost of capital. In order to maintain or adjust the capital structure, the Group may adjust the amount of dividends payable to shareholders, return capital to shareholders, issue new shares or sell assets to reduce debt.'

Sources: Hatfield, G, Cheng, L, and Davidson, W 'The Determination of Optimal Capital Structure: The Effect of Firm and Industry Debt Ratios on Market Value', *Journal of Financial and Strategic Decisions*, Volume 7, Number 3 (1994).

Van Binsbergen, J, Graham, J, and Yang, J 'An Empirical Model of Optimal Capital Structure', *Journal of Applied Corporate Finance*, Volume 23, Issue 4 (2011).

While there appears to be no specific solution with regard to the 'best' capital structure it is possible to draw some broad conclusions from the various models and theories we have examined:

- The capital structure decision is an important part of a company's financial strategy. Whether or not there is an optimal structure, an inappropriate structure may result in the destruction of shareholder wealth; for example, an untimely issue of shares.
- As gearing continues to increase then generally a company's WACC will continue to fall because of the benefit from the relatively low cost of debt and the tax shield. Therefore shareholder value will be increased. However, at particularly high levels of gearing the market will react and equity shareholders will demand higher returns to compensate for the higher level of financial risk resulting from higher gearing. Therefore, the cost of equity will increase and WACC will increase and so shareholder value will fall.
- At very high levels of gearing the risk of bankruptcy is also very high. Financial risk is high because of the level of interest that has to be paid and the possibility of interest rates increasing. The power of debt-holders whose loans are secured on the assets of the

company is such that they may force the company to cease trading, and sell its assets to repay the debt.

- The tax benefits from borrowing are very real but this should not be the primary reason for borrowing. Tax benefits may be obtained in alternative ways, which therefore avoid the risk associated with high levels of gearing.
- Many companies adopt the financial strategy of increasing debt to finance new investments to obtain tax benefits and reduce WACC, even though they may have cash surpluses. The decision to increase debt impacts on a company in a number of important ways, each of which should not be considered in isolation:
  - financial risk – is future profitability sufficient to service and repay debt?
  - dividends – can satisfactory levels of dividends be maintained at high levels of debt?
  - WACC – at what point will an increase in gearing result in an increase in WACC?
  - future interest rates – at what level will interest rates have a significant impact on profitability?
  - banking relationships – it may be impractical and financially unfavourable to negotiate with and maintain relationships with a large number of banks.

Progress check 5.9

Outline the various approaches that have tried to answer the question 'Does a company have an optimal capital structure?'

Summary of key points

- The capital asset pricing model (CAPM) was developed from Markowitz's portfolio theory and considers systematic risk in order to establish a fair price for a security or a business.
- Arbitrage pricing theory (APT) may be considered as an alternative to the CAPM.
- Gearing, or the debt/equity ratio, is the relationship between the two sources of finance, debt and equity – a company having more debt capital than equity capital is highly geared, and a company having more equity capital than debt capital is low geared.
- The weighted average cost of capital (WACC) is the average cost of the total financial resources of a company, i.e. the shareholders' equity and the net financial debt, that may be used as the discount rate to evaluate investment projects, a measure of company performance, and to provide a valuation of the company.
- Both the cost of debt and the cost of equity are based on future income flows, and the risk associated with such returns.
- The cost of equity and cost of debt are both dependent on their levels of risk, which therefore also impact on the overall cost of a company's financing.
- A certain element of risk is unavoidable whenever any investment is made, and unless a market investor settles for risk-free securities, the actual return on investment in equity (or debt) capital may be better or worse than hoped for.

- Systematic risk may be measured using the capital asset pricing model (CAPM), and the β factor, in terms of its effect on required returns and share prices.

- The return on equity may be considered as a function of the gearing, or financial structure of the company.

- There are many approaches, for example the Miller and Modigliani approaches, which consider whether or not there may be an optimal capital structure for companies.

- Consideration of the WACC approach to capital structure suggests that perhaps a company's optimal capital structure may exist somewhere within a range of combinations of debt and equity.

Glossary of key terms

arbitrage This is the act of exploiting the price differences in financial instruments, or other assets, in different markets by simultaneously buying and selling the assets to make a profit from the price difference. It exists because there are market inefficiencies but it also provides a means of ensuring that prices do not remain different for long periods and that an equilibrium price is finally reached.

cost of debt The annual percentage rate of return required by long-term lenders to a company (loans and bonds), generally expressed net of tax as a cost to the company.

cost of equity The annual percentage rate of return required by the shareholders of a company.

dividend growth model (or Gordon growth model) A method of calculating cost of equity that assumes a direct link between the share price and expected future dividends and recognises the expected rate of dividend growth (G) achieved through reinvestment of retained earnings.

dividend model A method of calculating the cost of equity that divides the current dividend by the current share price, which is based on the notion that shareholders may value shares by the value of their expected dividends.

gearing Gearing calculations can be made in a number of ways. Financial gearing (or leverage) is generally seen as the relationship between a company's borrowings, which include both prior charge capital (capital having a right of interest or preference shares having fixed dividends) and long-term debt, and its ordinary shareholders' funds (share capital plus reserves).

security market line (SML) A linear graphical relationship between a security's return and its systematic risk, in an efficient market, measured by the company's beta, as defined in the capital asset pricing model (CAPM). It is effectively the capital market line (CML) adjusted for systematic risk.

tax shield A reduction in corporation tax payable due to the use of tax-allowable deductions against taxable income.

weighted average cost of capital (WACC) The average cost of the capital or financial resources of a company, which is its shareholders' equity plus its debt (debentures, bank loans, etc.) weighted according to the proportion each element bears to the total pool of capital. Weighting is usually based on market valuations, current yields, and costs after tax.

Assessment material

Questions

Q5.1 Explain the capital asset pricing model (CAPM).

Q5.2 Describe the ways in which the cost of debt and cost of equity capital may be ascertained.

Q5.3 How does risk impact on the cost of debt and cost of equity?

Q5.4 What are the advantages and disadvantages for a company in using WACC as a discount factor to evaluate capital projects?

Q5.5 What is the β factor, and how may it be related to WACC?

Q5.6 What are the implications for a company of different levels of gearing?

Q5.7 How may a company's return on equity (ROE) be related to its financial structure?

Q5.8 Is there an optimal capital structure?

Q5.9 Explain the Miller and Modigliani I and II approaches to capital structure.

Q5.10 What is the WACC approach to capital structure?

Discussion points

D5.1 'In the real world the CAPM does not appear to be valid, therefore it is not a useful tool for dealing with required returns and systematic risk.' Discuss.

D5.2 The marketing manager of a large UK subsidiary of a multinational plc said, 'Surely the interest rate that we should use to discount cash flows in our appraisal of new capital investment projects should be our bank overdraft interest rate. I don't really see the relevance of the weighted average cost of capital (WACC) to this type of exercise.' Discuss.

D5.3 In the long run does it really matter whether a company is financed predominantly by ordinary shares or predominantly by loans? What's the difference?

Exercises

Solutions are provided in Appendix 2 to all exercise numbers highlighted in colour.

Level I

E5.1 *Time allowed – 30 minutes*
A critically important factor required by a company to make financial decisions, for example the evaluation of investment proposals and the financing of new projects, is its cost of capital. One of the elements included in the calculation of a company's cost of capital is the cost of equity. ➡

(i) Explain in simple terms what is meant by the cost of equity capital for a company.

The relevant data for Normal plc and the market in general is given below.

Normal plc

Current price per share on the London Stock Exchange	£1.20
Current annual dividend per share	£0.10
Expected average annual growth rate of dividends	7%
β coefficient for Normal plc's shares	0.5

The market

Expected rate of return on risk-free securities	8%
Expected return on the market portfolio	12%

(ii) Calculate the cost of equity capital for Normal plc, using two alternative methods:
  (a) capital asset pricing model (CAPM)
  (b) a dividend growth model of your choice.

E5.2   *Time allowed – 30 minutes*

Normal plc pays £20,000 a year interest on an irredeemable debenture, which has a nominal value of £200,000 and a market value of £160,000. The rate of corporation tax is 30%.

You are required to:

(i) calculate the cost of the debt for Normal plc
(ii) calculate the weighted average cost of capital for Normal plc using the two costs of equity calculated in Exercise E5.1 (ii) if Normal plc has share capital of 300,000 £1 shares
(iii) comment on the impact on a company's cost of capital of changes in the rate of corporation tax
(iv) calculate Normal plc's WACC if the rate of corporation tax were increased to 50%.

Level II

E5.3   *Time allowed – 45 minutes*

Adam plc is a publicly listed fashion retail company. The current market price of the company's shares is £25 (*ex dividend*), per share. The current dividend yield of the company's shares is 5%, and the current price/earnings ratio of the company's shares is 10.

Based on recently released information about the company and its future growth prospects, market dealers expect Adam plc to achieve a constant dividend growth rate of 3% per annum for the foreseeable future. We may assume that:

- the average return on the stock market is 10%
- the risk-free rate of return is 4%
- the β coefficient of Adam plc's shares is currently 1.25.

Required:

(i)   Calculate the proportion of earnings paid out as dividends by the company.

(ii) Using the dividend growth model calculate the expected rate of return on the shares of Adam plc.

(iii) Using your results from requirement (ii) above, calculate by how much the share appears to be over- or under-valued according to the capital asset pricing model (CAPM).

(iv) Briefly explain why a difference may exist between using the dividend growth model share price and the share price calculated using CAPM.

(v)   Evaluate the principal assumptions of the CAPM, and the limitations of such assumptions in using the CAPM to value equities.

E5.4   *Time allowed – 30 minutes*

Lucky Jim plc has the opportunity to manufacture a particular type of self-tapping screw, for a client company, that would become indispensable in a particular niche market in the engineering field.

Development of the product requires an initial investment of £200,000 in the project. It has been estimated that the project will yield cash returns before interest of £35,000 per annum in perpetuity.

Lucky Jim plc is financed by equity and loans, which are always maintained as two thirds and one third of the total capital respectively. The cost of equity is 18% and the pre-tax cost of debt is 12%. The corporation tax rate is 40%.

If Lucky Jim plc's WACC is used as the cost of capital to appraise the project, should the project be undertaken?

E5.5   *Time allowed – 30 minutes*

Abey plc has a WACC of 16%. It is financed partly by equity (cost 18% per annum) and partly by debt capital (cost 10% per annum). The company is considering a new project which would cost £5,000,000 and would yield annual profits of £850,000 before interest charges.

It would be financed by a loan at 10%. As a consequence, the cost of equity would rise to 20%. The company pays out all its profits in dividends, which are currently £2,250,000 a year. You may assume that Abey plc has a traditional view of WACC and gearing.

Required:

(i)   Calculate the effect on the value of equity of undertaking the project.

(ii) Consider the extent to which the increase or decrease in equity value may be analysed into two causes:

   (a)   the net present value of the project at the current WACC
   (b)   the effect of the method of financing.

E5.6   *Time allowed – 45 minutes*

The following financial information has been taken from the financial statements of Homeslore plc, a large national electrical equipment retailer.

All figures in £000s

Summary of profits and dividends for the years ended 31 December 2006 to 2012

	2006	2007	2008	2009	2010	2011	2012
Profit before tax	1,600	1,800	1,800	2,000	1,900	1,800	2,300
Income tax expense	(550)	(600)	(600)	(750)	(550)	(620)	(980)
Profit for the year	1,050	1,200	1,200	1,250	1,350	1,180	1,320
Dividends	(570)	(600)	(600)	(700)	(800)	(850)	(900)
Retained profit	480	600	600	550	550	330	420

Balance sheet as at 31 December 2012

Non-current assets	10,200
Investments	3,500
Current assets	4,500
Income tax payable	(1,000)
Other current liabilities	(2,000)
Total assets less current liabilities	15,200
5% debentures	4,000
Net assets	11,200
Equity	
Share capital £1 ordinary shares issued	4,500
Reserves	6,700
Total equity	11,200

On 31 December 2012 the market value of Homeslore plc's ordinary shares was £4.60 per share *cum dividend*. Shortly after that date an annual dividend of £900,000 was due to be paid. The debentures are redeemable at par in five years' time. Their current market value at 31 December 2012 was £90. Annual interest has just been paid on the debentures. The company's capital structure has remained unchanged for the past seven years and there have been no issues or redemption of ordinary share capital or debentures during that period. You may assume the rate of corporation tax is 30% and that no changes have been made to the system of taxation or the rates of tax during the past seven years.

Required:

(i) Calculate Homeslore plc's cost of equity.
(ii) Calculate Homeslore plc's cost of debt.
(iii) Calculate (to the nearest whole percentage) the weighted average cost of capital that Homeslore plc may use as a discount rate in the evaluation of new investment opportunities.

E5.7   *Time allowed – 45 minutes*

An opportunity has arisen for Homeslore plc (see Exercise E5.6) to acquire inventories of special-ised materials from an overseas supplier. The cost of the specialised inventories will be £700,000.

The sales manager of Homeslore plc has suggested that the net revenues from the sale of these inventories will be influenced by a number of factors originating from outside the company, and has provided the following additional information:

	Possible sales revenues	Probability
	£	%
Year 1	440,000	50
	200,000	40
	460,000	10
Year 2	600,000	60
	580,000	20
	350,000	20

The estimates for year two are independent of the estimates of year one.

> **Required:**
>
> (i)   Use the company's weighted average cost of capital (calculated in Exercise E5.6) to calculate the expected sales revenues for each year, and the net present value of the project.
>
> (ii) Briefly comment on the validity of the company using its weighted average cost of capital as a discount rate for the evaluation of investment opportunities.

E5.8   *Time allowed – 60 minutes*

Yor plc is a fast growing, hi-tech business. Its income statement for the year ended 30 September 2012 and its balance sheet as at 30 September 2012 are shown below. The company has the opportunity to take on a major project that will significantly improve its profitability in the forthcoming year and for the foreseeable future. The cost of the project is £10m, which will result in large increases in sales revenue, which will increase profit before interest and tax by £4m per annum. The directors of Yor plc have two alternative options to finance the project: the issue of £10m of 4% debentures at par; or a rights issue of 4m ordinary shares at a premium of £1.50 per share (after expenses).

Regardless of how the new project is financed, the directors will recommend a 10% increase in the dividend for 2012/2013. You may assume that the effective corporation tax rate is the same for 2012/2013 as for 2011/2012.

Income statement for the year ended 30 September 2012

	£m
PBIT	11.6
Finance cost	(1.2)
Profit before tax	10.4
Income tax expense	(2.6)
Profit for the year	7.8
Retained earnings 1 October 2011	5.8
	13.6
Dividends	(3.0)
Retained earnings at 30 September 2012	10.6

Balance sheet as at 30 September 2012

	£m
Non-current assets	28.8
Current assets	
Inventories	11.2
Trade and other receivables	13.8
Cash and cash equivalents	0.7
Total current assets	25.7
Current liabilities	
Trade and other payables	9.7
Dividends	1.6
Taxation	2.6
Total current liabilities	13.9
Net current assets	11.8
Total assets less current liabilities	40.6
Less	
Non-current liabilities	
6% loan	20.0
Net assets	20.6
Equity	
Share capital (£1 ordinary shares)	10.0
Retained earnings	10.6
Total equity	20.6

The directors of Yor plc would like to see your estimated income statement for 2012/2013, and a summary of total equity at 30 September 2013, assuming:

(i)　the new project is financed by an issue of the debentures
(ii)　the new project is financed by the issue of new ordinary shares.

To assist in clarification of the figures, you should show your calculations of:

(iii)　eps for 2011/2012
(iv)　eps for 2012/2013, reflecting both methods of financing the new project
(v)　dividend per share for 2011/2012
(vi)　dividend per share for 2012/2013, reflecting both methods of financing the new project.

Use the information you have provided in (i) and (ii) above to:

(vii)　calculate Yor plc's gearing, reflecting both methods of financing the new project, and compare with its gearing at 30 September 2012
(viii)　summarise the results for 2012/2013, recommend which method of financing Yor plc should adopt, and explain the implications of both on its financial structure.

E5.9 *Time allowed – 60 minutes*
Sparks plc is a large electronics company that produces components for MP4s and iPods. It is close to the current year end and Sparks is forecasting a profit after tax at £60m. ➡

The following two years' post-tax profits are each expected to increase by another £15m in each year, and years four and five by another £10m each year.

The forecast balance sheet for Sparks plc as at 31 December is as follows:

	£m
Non-current assets	500
Current assets	
Inventories	120
Trade and other receivables	160
Total current assets	280
Current liabilities	
Borrowings and finance leases	75
Trade and other payables	75
Total current liabilities	150
Net current assets	130
Total assets less current liabilities	630
less	
Non-current liabilities	
Long-term loan	150
Net assets	480
Equity	
Share capital (£1 ordinary shares)	220
Share premium account	10
Retained earnings	250
Total equity	480

Sparks plc has a large overdraft of £75m on which it pays a high rate of interest at 15%. The board would like to pay off the overdraft and obtain cheaper financing. Sparks also has loan capital of £150m on which it pays interest at 9% per annum. Despite its high level of debt Sparks is a profitable organisation. However, the board is currently planning a number of new projects for the next year, which will cost £75m. These projects are expected to produce profits after tax of £8m in the first year and £15m a year ongoing for future years.

The board has discussed a number of financing options and settled on two of them for further consideration:

(1) a 1 for 4 rights issue at £3.00 a share to raise £150m from the issue of 50m £1 shares
(2) a convertible £150m debenture issue at 12% (pre tax) that may be converted into 45m ordinary shares in two years' time.

Sparks plc's ordinary shares are currently at a market price of £3.37. Gearing of companies in the same industry as Sparks plc ranges between 25% and 45%. In two years' time it is expected that all Sparks' debenture holders will convert to shares or none will convert.

The rate of corporation tax is 50%.

Repayment of the overdraft will save interest of £5.625m a year after tax.

The board of Sparks plc requires analysis of the numbers to compare against the current position:

(i)   if they make the rights issue
(ii)   if they issue debentures
(iii) if the debentures are converted.

The analysis should show:

(a)   the impact on the balance sheet
(b)   the impact on the profit for the year after tax
(c)   earnings per share
(d)   gearing
(e)   which option should be recommended to the board and why.

6

Capital investment decisions

Chapter contents

Learning objectives

Completion of this chapter will enable you to:

- Explain what is meant by an investment.
- Outline the key principles underlying investment selection criteria.
- Calculate simple and compound interest, annuities, and perpetuities.
- Outline the strengths and weaknesses of the five investment appraisal criteria.
- Explain what is meant by discounted cash flow (DCF).
- Consider investment selection using the appraisal criteria of net present value (NPV) and internal rate of return (IRR).
- Explain the effects of inflation, working capital requirements, length and timing of projects, taxation, and risk and uncertainty on investment criteria calculations.
- Evaluate the impact of risk and uncertainty and the use of sensitivity analysis, scenario analysis, and simulation in decision-making.
- Use capital budgeting techniques, including the profitability index (PI) for single-period capital rationing.
- Consider the ways in which capital projects may be controlled and reviewed.
- Appreciate the importance of the project post-completion audit.

Introduction

This chapter looks at the specific area of decision-making that relates to investment. Such decisions may relate to whether or not to invest in a project, or choices between investments in alternative projects, which are competing for resources.

We will begin by looking at exactly what an investment is, and outlining the techniques used to decide on whether or not to invest, and how to choose between alternative investments.

We shall evaluate the advantages and disadvantages of the five main investment appraisal criteria used by companies and consider examples that illustrate their use. The most important of these are the discounted cash flow methods of net present value (NPV), and internal rate of return (IRR). The technique of discounted cash flow (DCF) will be fully explained.

In addition to the initial costs of an investment and the returns expected from it, a number of other factors usually need to be taken into account in investment decision-making. These include, for example, inflation, the need for working capital, taxation, and the length and timing of the project. We will consider the possible impact of these factors and how the effects of risk and uncertainty on the appraisal of investments may be quantified using sensitivity analysis, scenario analysis, and simulation.

Capital budgeting is a process that assists managers to make optimal investment decisions with the aim of maximisation of shareholder wealth. Capital budgeting may be required where the level of funds available is rationed for one period or for successive future periods – single-period and multiple-period capital rationing. This chapter considers the use of the profitability index (PI) method for single period capital rationing.

Appraisal of an investment is more than an accounting exercise. An investment decision is a crucially significant and important decision for a business. It is usually a highly politically charged area in the management of an organisation, which if mismanaged is capable of destroying shareholder value. Once an investment decision has been made the project may then be planned and implemented. This chapter closes with an introduction to the ways in which capital investment projects may be controlled and reviewed.

What is an investment?

For the accountant an **investment** appears within the assets section of the balance sheet under non-current assets. For the finance director an investment is any decision that implies expenditure today with the expectation that it will generate cash inflows tomorrow.

Investment decisions are extremely important because they are invariably concerned with the future survival, prosperity, and growth of the organisation. The organisation's primary objective of maximisation of shareholder wealth is a basic assumption that continues to hold true. Investments must be made not only to maintain shareholder wealth but more importantly to increase it. To meet the shareholder wealth maximisation objective it is crucial that those managing the organisation make optimal decisions that are based on the best information available and use of the most appropriate appraisal techniques.

At the corporate level, investment (in shares) relates to the amount that shareholders are willing to invest in the equity of a company in the expectation of future cash flows in the form of dividends and enhancement of share price. The level of future dividends and share price enhancement are in turn dependent on the extent to which the company is able to optimise returns on 'real' investment (investment in companies, plant, machinery, working capital) in new products, projects, new business, and so on. There is a great deal of pressure on chief executives to ensure that profitable 'real' investments are made to provide sustained dividend growth and increasing share prices.

Investment decisions faced by companies are therefore financially driven, and so if performance is deemed inadequate or unlikely to meet shareholder expectations, then the pressure becomes even greater to identify alternative, more profitable projects. Decisions are made by managers and not by the management accountant. Levels of authority within the management hierarchy are determined by company policy. Companies normally establish limits at each management level for each type of decision, and the level of expenditure allowed. The approval of one or more directors is normally required for all capital expenditure and for major projects.

Investment may appear in the balance sheet within non-current assets in line with the accountants' definition, for example land, buildings, plant, machinery, etc. It may also appear in the income statement in terms of, for example, advertising, public relations, employee training and development, and research and development. In some cases the amount of money gained as a result of making an investment is relatively easy to measure, such as cost savings, capacity increases, etc. In other cases, it may be impossible to measure the gains – company image, knowledge, and so on. The amount of spend may be relatively easy to forecast, for example the costs of computerisation of a process to reduce the production of non-quality products. In other projects, such as research and development, costs and benefits may be more uncertain.

Regardless, an investment decision is required before spending shareholders' and lenders' funds. The decision made needs to be one that shareholders and lenders would be happy with;

it is one that is expected to provide anticipated gains in real terms that greatly exceed the funds spent today, in other words a good return on the money invested. Otherwise the investment should not be made.

Investments in new projects selected by a company invariably have different levels of risks associated with them, some being more risky and some less risky than others. The use of a company's cost of capital to evaluate such an investment may over- or under-state its net present value (NPV). This is because the company's cost of capital only represents an average discount rate appropriate for use with average or normal risk investments. Such a situation may be avoided by using a risk-adjusted discount rate to compensate for the additional risk and uncertainty that may exist regarding the timing and value of a project's cash flows.

In general, financial managers should use a discount rate higher than the company's cost of capital where an investment project is considered to be of a higher than average risk, and perhaps a discount rate lower than the company's cost of capital where a project is considered to be of a lower than average risk.

Determination of an appropriate risk-adjusted discount rate (RADR) for each investment project can be problematic. A common approach is to use investment project risk classes to assign a different discount rate to each class of risk. For example, a company may take a certainty approach to classifying investment projects by certainty or uncertainty of demand – a higher discount rate may be assigned to those projects of greater uncertainty. Such uncertainty may be estimated using historical data to calculate the coefficient of variation of various investment projects to determine their relative uncertainty, or an actual discount rate may be estimated using either:

■ simulation, scenario analysis, or sensitivity analysis to estimate an appropriate cost of capital, which we will consider later in this chapter
■ the capital asset pricing model (CAPM), to estimate a risk-adjusted cost of capital, which was covered in Chapter 5.

Progress check 6.1

Describe what is meant by investment.

Future values, present values, perpetuities, and annuities

Simple interest is interest that is calculated over successive periods based only on the principal amount of a loan. Compound interest is calculated over successive periods based on the principal loan plus interest, which has accrued to date.

Worked example 6.1

A company has a short-term cash surplus of £250,000, which it may transfer to a savings account that pays simple interest of 6% per annum. Alternatively, the £250,000 may be transferred to a deposit account paying compound interest at 6% per annum. However, the deposit account commits the company to leaving its cash in the account for five years.

What is the gain in interest income to the company over five years should it decide to place its cash in the deposit account?

➡

Savings account paying annual simple interest £250,000 $\times$ 6% $\times$ 5
$$= £15,000 \times 5$$
$$= £75,000 \text{ interest received for five years}$$
Deposit account paying compound interest value after five years $= £250,000 \times (1 + 0.06)^5$
$$= £250,000 \times 1.338$$
$$= £334,500$$

Value after five years $-$ principal $=$ interest received for five years
£334,500 $-$ £250,000 $=$ £84,500 interest received for five years

The company's commitment to placing its cash in the deposit account for five years is worth an extra £9,500 (£84,500 $-$ £75,000) in interest income.

Future values and present values

A future value (FV) is the amount to which a sum of money will grow over a number of successive periods after earning interest, which is compounded each period. If I is the initial loan, i is the annual interest rate, and t is the number of years, then

$$FV = I \times (1 + i)^t$$

Worked example 6.2

We can calculate the future value of £1,000 if interest is compounded annually at a rate of 4% for 10 years.

$$FV = I \times (1 + i)^t$$
$$FV = £1,000 \times (1 + 0.04)^{10}$$
$$FV = £1,480.24$$

Mini case 6.1

An often-quoted example of compound interest and future value is the purchase of Manhattan Island, New York. Peter Minuit of the Dutch West India Company legitimised the claim of Dutch settlers by allegedly buying this land from local Indians for 60 guilders in the year 1626. At the time, that was equivalent to around US$24, and we can calculate the FV to see what US$24 is worth in 2012 if it is compounded at say 8% per annum.

$$FV = 24 \, US\$ \times (1 + 0.08)^{386} = US\$191.329 \text{trillion}$$

Was this a good deal or not in 1626?

Well possibly, although the value of Manhattan Island was perhaps considerably less than US$191trillion in 2012.

However, 8% may be an unrealistically high average interest rate to use over the 386 years.

A present value is the cash equivalent now of a sum receivable or payable at a future date. It is the value today of a future cash flow. The principle is effectively the same as using compound interest to calculate a future value, but in reverse. If PV is the present value and i is the interest rate for the period, then:

$$PV = \frac{FV \text{ after } t \text{ periods}}{(1 + i)^t}$$

Worked example 6.3

Assume that you are buying a new car for £30,000, for which payment is due in two years' time, interest free. If you can earn 6% per annum on your money, how much money should you set aside today (the PV) in order to make the payment when due in two years?

$$PV = \frac{FV}{(1 + i)^t}$$

$$PV = \frac{£30,000}{(1 + 0.06)^2}$$

$$PV = £26,700$$

You need to set aside £26,700 now, which will earn 6% per annum compounded over two years to become £30,000 with which to pay for the car.

The present value of a future payment of £1, US$1, 1 riyal, or any other currency is called a discount factor. The rate (r), used to calculate a present value (PV) of future cash flows over a number of successive periods (t) is called a discount rate rather than an interest rate (and which may also be referred to as the cost of capital). The discount factor (DF) of £1 or US$1 for t periods is:

$$DF = \frac{1}{(1 + r)^t}$$

A discount factor can be used to calculate the present value of a cash flow occurring at any time in the future. A discount factor may also be used to calculate the present value (PV) of any number of future cash flows C_1, C_2, C_3 etc. occurring in successive future periods:

$$PV = \frac{C_1}{(1 + r)^1} + \frac{C_2}{(1 + r)^2} + \frac{C_3}{(1 + r)^3} + \cdots$$

where C_1, C_2 etc. represent the cash flows in each future period, 1, 2, 3 and so on, and r is the discount rate.

Worked example 6.4

Lovely Laptops Ltd has offered you alterative ways to pay for a new laptop computer. You may pay £2,000 cash immediately, or make three payments: £1,000 immediately, and £600 at the end of the next two years. If the interest rate is 7% per annum, which is your cheapest option?

Immediate payment		= £1,000.00
PV of £600 next year	$\dfrac{£600}{(1 + 0.07)^1} =$	£560.75
PV of £600 following year	$\dfrac{£600}{(1 + 0.07)^2} =$	£524.06
Total PV		= £2,084.81

The instalment plan total cost of £2,084.81 is more expensive than the £2,000 cash purchase and so outright purchase appears to be the preferred option.

When decisions need to be made regarding investment in new capital projects some appraisal techniques use an extension of the method shown in Worked example 6.4 to calculate the present value of future project cash flows. The principles underlying this method are cash flow (as opposed to profit), and the time value of money. The method is called **discounted cash flow (DCF)**, which is used to discount projected future net cash flows to ascertain their present values, using an appropriate discount rate, or cost of capital. This will be discussed in more detail later in this chapter when we look at net present value.

Perpetuities and annuities

A **perpetuity** is a periodic payment continuing for a limitless period – a stream of level cash payments that never ends. The present value (PV) of a perpetuity, where C is the annual cash payment and r the per annum discount rate is:

$$PV = \frac{C}{r}$$

Worked example 6.5

Suppose that an individual wishes to set aside a sum of money (an endowment), which pays £150,000 per year forever. We can calculate how much money must be set aside today if the rate of interest is 6% per annum. In other words, we need to calculate the present value of £150,000 a year in perpetuity at 6% per annum.

$$PV = \frac{C}{r} = \frac{£150,000}{0.06} = £2,500,000$$

Alternatively, if it is decided that the first £150,000 payment should not be received until five years from today, we can calculate the different sum of money that needs to be set aside today.

$$PV = \frac{2,500,000}{(1 + 0.06)^5} = £1,868,145$$

An **annuity** comprises an equally spaced level stream of cash flows for a limited period of time. The present value (PV) of an annuity, where C is the annual cash payment, r is the per annum discount rate, and t is the number of years each cash payment is received is:

$$PV = C \times \left\{ \frac{1}{r} - \frac{1}{r(1 + r)^t} \right\}$$

where $\left\{ \dfrac{1}{r} - \dfrac{1}{r(1 + r)^t} \right\}$

is described as the present value annuity factor (PVAF), which is the present value of £1 a year for each of t years, and therefore:

$$PV = C \times PVAF$$

Worked example 6.6

Let's assume that you are planning to purchase a car, which requires payment by four annual instalments of £6,000 per year. We can calculate the real total cost you will incur for purchase of the car, assuming a rate of interest of 6% (in other words the PV).

$$PV = C \times \left\{ \frac{1}{r} - \frac{1}{r(1 + r)^t} \right\}$$

$$PV = £6,000 \times \left\{ \frac{1}{0.06} - \frac{1}{0.06(1 + 0.06)^4} \right\}$$

$$\text{Real total cost } PV = £20,794$$

This is obviously considerably lower than the total of the actual cash payments for the four years, which is £24,000 (4 × £6,000).

As we discussed earlier in this chapter, the relationship between present value and future value is:

$$PV = \frac{FV}{(1 + r)^t}$$

and therefore

$$FV = PV \times (1 + r)^t$$

We also saw that:

$$PV = C \times PVAF$$

Therefore, by combining each of the above two equations, we can see that the future value (FV) of equal annual payments over t periods is:

$$FV = (C \times PVAF) \times (1 + r)^t$$

Worked example 6.7

Let's assume that you plan to save £7,000 every year for 30 years and then retire, and the rate of interest is 5% per annum. We can calculate the future value (FV) of your retirement fund as follows:

$$FV = (C \times PVAF) \times (1 + r)^t$$

or

$$FV = C \times \left\{ \frac{1}{r} - \frac{1}{r(1 + r)^t} \right\} \times (1 + r)^t$$

$$FV = £7,000 \times \left\{ \frac{1}{0.05} - \frac{1}{0.05(1 + 0.05)^{30}} \right\} \times (1 + 0.05)^{30}$$

Value of fund at retirement FV = £465,072

Investment appraisal methods

The five main methods used in investment appraisal are shown in Figure 6.1:

- the **accounting rate of return (ARR)** for appraising capital investment projects is based on profits and the costs of investment; it takes no account of cash flows or the time value of money
- the **payback** method for appraising capital investment projects is based on cash flows (or possibly profits), but also ignores the time value of money
- **net present value (NPV)** is one of the two most widely used investment decision criteria that are based on cash flow and the time value of money
- **internal rate of return (IRR)** is the second of the two most widely used investment decision criteria that are based on cash flow and the time value of money
- the **discounted payback** appraisal method is also based on cash flow and the time value of money.

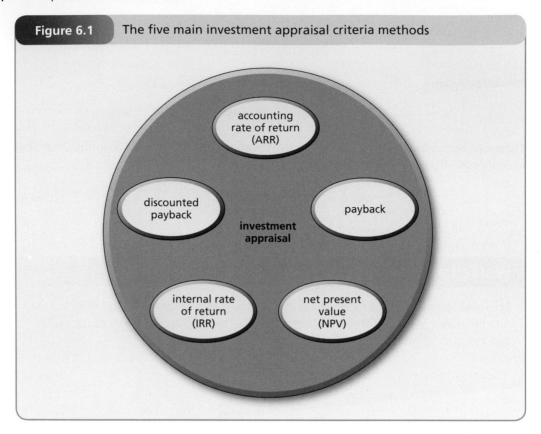

Figure 6.1   The five main investment appraisal criteria methods

We will look at examples of each of the five appraisal criteria and the advantages and disadvantages of using each of them.

Accounting rate of return (ARR)

ARR is a simple measure that may be used for investment appraisal. It is a form of return on capital employed, based on profits rather than cash flows, and ignores the time value of money.

ARR may be calculated using:

$$\frac{\textbf{average accounting profit over the life of the project}}{\textbf{initial investment}} \times \textbf{100\%}$$

There are alternative ways of calculating ARR. For example, total profit may be used instead of average profit, or average investment may be used instead of initial investment. It should be noted that in such a case if, for example, a machine originally cost £800,000 (the initial investment) and its final scrap value was £50,000 (investment at end of project) then the average investment is £850,000/2, or £425,000.

It should also be noted that the method of calculation of ARR that is selected must be used consistently. However, ARR, although simple to use, is not recommended as a primary appraisal method. The method can provide an overview of a new project but it lacks the sophistication of other methods. The impact of cash flows and time on the value of money really should be considered in investment appraisal, which we will discuss in a later section about key principles underlying investment selection criteria.

Worked example 6.8

Alpha Engineering Ltd is a company that has recently implemented an investment appraisal system. Its investment authorisation policy usually allows it to go ahead with a capital project if the accounting rate of return is greater than 25%. A project has been submitted for appraisal with the following data:

	£000
Initial investment	100 (residual scrap value zero)

Per annum profit over the life of the project:

Year	Profit
	£000
1	25
2	35
3	35
4	25

The capital project may be evaluated using ARR.

$$\text{Average profit over the life of the project} = \frac{£25{,}000 + £35{,}000 + £35{,}000 + £25{,}000}{4}$$

$$= £30{,}000$$

$$\text{Accounting rate of return} = \frac{£30{,}000}{£100{,}000} \times 100\% = 30\%$$

which is higher than 25% and so acceptance of the project may be recommended.

Progress check 6.2

What is the accounting rate of return (ARR) and how is it calculated?

Payback

Payback is defined as the number of years it takes the cash inflows from a capital investment project to equal the cash outflows. An organisation may have a target payback period, above which projects are rejected. It is useful and sometimes used as an initial screening process in evaluating two mutually exclusive projects. The project that pays back in the shortest time may on the face of it be the one to accept.

Worked example 6.9

Beta Engineering Ltd's investment authorisation policy requires all capital projects to pay back within three years, and views projects with shorter payback periods as even more desirable. Two mutually exclusive projects are currently being considered with the following data:

	Project 1 **£000**	**Project 2** **£000**	
Initial investment	200	200	(residual scrap values zero)

Per annum cash inflows over the life of each project:

Year	**Project 1**		**Project 2**	
	Yearly cash inflow £000	Cumulative cash inflow £000	Yearly cash inflow £000	Cumulative cash inflow £000
1	60	60	100	100
2	80	140	150	250
3	80	220	30	280
4	90	310	10	290

The projects may be evaluated by considering their payback periods.

- Project 1 derives total cash inflows of £310,000 over the life of the project and pays back the initial £200,000 investment three quarters of the way into year three, when the cumulative cash inflows reach £200,000 [£60,000 + £80,000 + £60,000 (75% of £80,000)].
- Project 2 derives total cash inflows of £290,000 over the life of the project and pays back the initial £200,000 investment two thirds of the way into year two, when the cumulative cash inflows reach £200,000 [£100,000 + £100,000 (67% of £150,000)].
- Both projects meet Beta Engineering Ltd's three-year payback criterion.
- Project 2 pays back within two years and so is the preferred project, using Beta's investment guidelines.

Worked example 6.9 shows how payback may be used to compare projects. However, in practice the total returns from a project should also be considered, in addition to the timing of the cash flows and their value in real terms. As with ARR, although from experience the use of payback appears to be widespread among companies, it is not recommended as the main method. This method can also provide an overview but should not be the primary appraisal method used in larger companies or with regard to large projects because it ignores the time value of money.

Progress check 6.3

What is payback and how is it calculated?

Key principles underlying investment selection criteria: cash flow, the time value of money, and discounted cash flow (DCF)

The first two appraisal criteria we have considered are simple methods that have limitations in their usefulness in making optimal capital investment decisions. The three further appraisal criteria are NPV, IRR, and discounted payback. Whichever of these three methods is used, three basic principles apply: *cash is king, time value of money*, and *discounted cash flow (DCF)*.

Cash is king

- Real funds can be seen in cash but not in accounting profit.
- Interest charges become payable as soon as money is made available, for example from a lender to a borrower, not when an agreement is made or when a contract is signed.

Time value of money

Receipt of £100 today has greater value than receipt of £100 in one year's time. There are three reasons for this:

- The money could have been invested alternatively in, for example, risk-free UK Government gilt-edged securities.
- Purchasing power will have been lost over a year due to inflation.
- The risk of non-receipt in one year's time.

Discounted cash flow (DCF)

Whichever of the three methods of appraisal is used:

- NPV
- IRR
- discounted payback,

a technique of discounting the projected cash flows of a project is used to ascertain its **present value**. Such methods are called discounted cash flow or DCF techniques. They require the use of a discount rate to carry out the appropriate calculation.

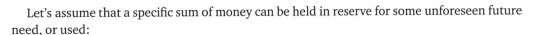

Let's assume that a specific sum of money can be held in reserve for some unforeseen future need, or used:

- to earn interest in a bank or building society account over the following year
- to buy some bottles of champagne (for example) at today's price
- to buy some bottles of champagne at the price in one year's time, which we may assume will be at a higher price because of inflation.

We may also assume that the bank or building society interest earned for one year, or the amount by which the price of champagne goes up due to inflation over one year is, say, 5%. Then we can see that £100 would be worth £105 if left in the building society for one year, and £100 spent on champagne today would actually buy just over £95 worth of champagne in one year's time because of its price increase.

The percentage rate by which the value of money may be eroded over one year is called the discount rate. The amount by which the value of, say, £100 is eroded over one year is calculated by multiplying it by what is called the discount factor:

$$£100 \times \frac{1}{(1 + \text{discount rate \%})}$$

So, for example, we could buy champagne in one year's time worth:

$$£100/(1 + 5\%) \text{ or } £100/1.05 = £95.24$$

If the £95.24 were left for another year, and assuming that prices continued to increase at 5% per annum, we could buy champagne after a further year worth:

$$£95.24/(1 + 5\%) \text{ or } £95.24/1.05 = £90.70$$

The yearly buying power continues to be reduced by application of the discount factor (or using the appropriate discount factor if the discount rate has changed). If the money is not used either to earn interest or to buy something, its value therefore normally becomes less and less. The discount factor for each year obviously depends on the discount rate. The successive year-by-year impact on £100 using an unchanging discount rate of 5% per annum may be illustrated using a simple graph showing its value from the start until the end of 10 years. The graph shown in Figure 6.2 illustrates the concept of the time value of money.

Whichever of the three discounted cash flow methods of appraisal is used, NPV, IRR, or discounted payback, a technique of discounting the projected cash flows of a project is used to ascertain its present value. They require the use of a discount rate to carry out the appropriate calculation.

If we consider a simple company balance sheet:

$$\text{net assets} = \text{equity} + \text{financial debt}$$

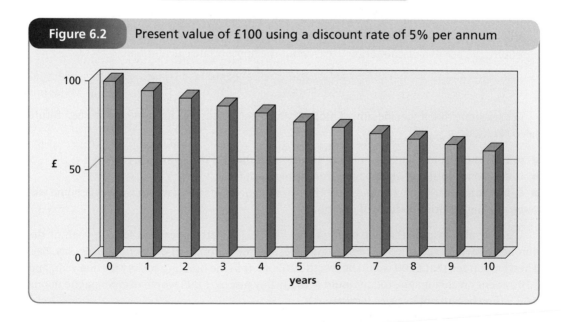

Figure 6.2 Present value of £100 using a discount rate of 5% per annum

we can see that an investment is an additional asset that may be financed by equity or debt or by both.

Shareholders and lenders each require a return on their investment that is high enough to pay for the risk they are taking in funding the company and its assets. The expected return on equity will be higher than the cost of debt because the shareholders take a higher risk than the lenders (see Chapter 5 in which we discussed the cost of various types of capital and their associated levels of risk). The average cost of these financial resources provided to the company is called the weighted average cost of capital (WACC). An important rule is that the return generated by a new investment undertaken by a company must be higher than the WACC, which reflects the discount rate – the rate of financing the investment. If, say, a company's WACC is 10%, an investment may be accepted if the expected rate of return is 15% or 16%. The importance of WACC and the significance of the debt and equity financial structure of a business was considered in detail in Chapter 5.

Other discount rates may be used, such as a borrowing interest rate or even the accounting rate of return. However, the company's cost of capital, its WACC, is usually a more suitable hurdle rate, the opportunity cost of funds with which to evaluate new investments.

A hurdle rate may be defined as a rate of return that must be achieved by a proposed capital project if it is to be accepted. There are many alternative rates a company may use as a hurdle rate (see Arnold, G and Hatzopoulos, PD 'The theory practice gap in capital budgeting: evidence from the United Kingdom' *Journal of Business Finance and Accounting* 27(5) and 27(6), pages 603–26 (June/July 2000)), for example:

- the cost of equity (using CAPM)
- interest payable on debt capital (where debt financing is used)
- dividend yield on shares plus an estimated capital growth in share price
- earnings yield on shares
- an arbitrarily chosen figure.

Companies use WACC (to which they may sometimes add a risk premium) as a hurdle rate to ensure that only those projects that offer a return in excess of WACC will be accepted. This therefore ensures that these projects will contribute to the overall funds of the company. However, methods of calculating WACC may differ greatly between companies.

Arnold and Hatzopoulos found that only 41% of small companies, 63% of medium-sized companies, and 61% of large companies used WACC as a hurdle rate. Although specific reasons are difficult to establish in general, the main reason why many companies continue to use a hurdle rate other than a WACC-based hurdle rate appeared to be a lack of understanding of WACC. It is perhaps worth noting that Francis and Minchington (Francis, G and Minchington, C 'Value-based metrics as divisional performance measures' in Arnold, G and Davis, M (2000) *Value Based Management*, London: Wiley) found that in large divisional-based companies approximately 24% of companies used a divisional cost of capital that only reflected the cost of debt rather than WACC, with 69% of such companies failing to use a risk-adjusted rate for different divisions to reflect different levels of risk.

In the earlier section about future values and present values we saw how present values may be determined using interest rates. The same calculation may be applied using discount rates. If r represents the discount rate (cost of capital), and n is the number of periods (for example years), these can be used to derive a present value discount factor:

$$\text{discount factor} = \frac{1}{(1 + r)^n}$$

where n may have a value from 0 to infinity.

(Note the similarity between this and the way we calculated the present values of £100 illustrated in Figure 6.2).

If we consider a project where the initial investment in year 0 is I, and each subsequent year's net cash flows are C_1, C_2, C_3, C_4 and so on for n years up to C_n, and the cost of capital is r, then the

---

Present value of the cash flows $= -I + C_1/(1 + r) + C_2/(1 + r)^2 + \cdots + C_n/(1 + r)^n$

The present value of the cash flows using an appropriate cost of capital, or discount rate, is called the net present value or NPV.

Progress check 6.4

What do we mean by discounted cash flow (DCF) and what are the principles on which it is based?

Net present value (NPV)

NPV is today's value of the difference between cash inflows and outflows projected at future dates, attributable to capital investments or long-term projects. The value now of these net cash flows is obtained by using the discounted cash flow method with a specified discount rate.

Worked example 6.10

An investment of £5,000 is made in year 0. For the purpose of NPV, year 0 is regarded as being today. The investment generates subsequent yearly cash flows of £1,000, £3,000, £3,000, and £2,000. The cost of capital is 10%. We will evaluate the investment using an NPV approach.

$$NPV = -I + C_1/(1 + r) + C_2/(1 + r)^2 + \cdots + C_n/(1 + r)^n$$
$$NPV = -£5,000 + £1,000/1.1 + £3,000/1.1^2 + £3,000/1.1^3 + £2,000/1.1^4$$
$$NPV = -£5,000 + (£1,000 \times 0.91) + (£3,000 \times 0.83) + (£3,000 \times 0.75)$$
$$+ (£2,000 \times 0.68)$$
$$NPV = -£5,000 + £910 + £2,490 + £2,250 + £1,360$$
$$NPV = +£2,010 \text{ which is greater than 0, and being positive the}$$
$$\text{investment should probably be made.}$$

Such an analysis is more usefully presented in tabular form. The discount rates for each year: $1/1.1$, $1/1.1^2$, $1/1.1^3$, $1/1.1^4$, may be shown in the table as discount factor values which are calculated, or alternatively obtained from present value tables (see the extract below from the present value table in Appendix 1 at the end of this book).

Rate r %	1	2	3	4	5	6	7	8	9	10	11	12
After n years %												
1	0.99	0.98	0.97	0.96	0.95	0.94	0.93	0.93	0.92	**0.91**	0.90	0.89
2	0.98	0.96	0.94	0.92	0.91	0.89	0.87	0.86	0.84	**0.83**	0.81	0.80
3	0.97	0.94	0.92	0.89	0.86	0.84	0.82	0.79	0.77	**0.75**	0.73	0.71
4	0.96	0.92	0.89	0.85	0.82	0.79	0.76	0.74	0.71	**0.68**	0.66	0.64
5	0.95	0.91	0.86	0.82	0.78	0.75	0.71	0.68	0.65	0.62	0.59	0.57

Tabular format of NPV analysis

Year	Cash outflows £	Cash inflows £	Net cash flow £	Discount factor at 10%	Present values £
0	−5,000		−5,000	1.00	−5,000
1		1,000	1,000	0.91	910
2		3,000	3,000	0.83	2,490
3		3,000	3,000	0.75	2,250
4		2,000	2,000	0.68	1,360
				NPV	+2,010

Progress check 6.5

What is net present value (NPV) and how is it calculated?

Internal rate of return (IRR)

The NPV of a capital investment project is calculated by:

- discounting, using a rate of return, discount rate, or cost of capital, to obtain
- the difference in present values between cash inflows and cash outflows.

The internal rate of return (IRR) method calculates:

- the rate of return

where

- the difference between the present values of cash inflows and outflows, the NPV, is zero.

We saw earlier that

$$NPV = -I + C_1/(1 + r) + C_2/(1 + r)^2 + \cdots + C_n/(1 + r)^n$$

Therefore if NPV = 0

$$0 = -I + C_1/(1 + r) + C_2/(1 + r)^2 + \cdots + C_n/(1 + r)^n$$

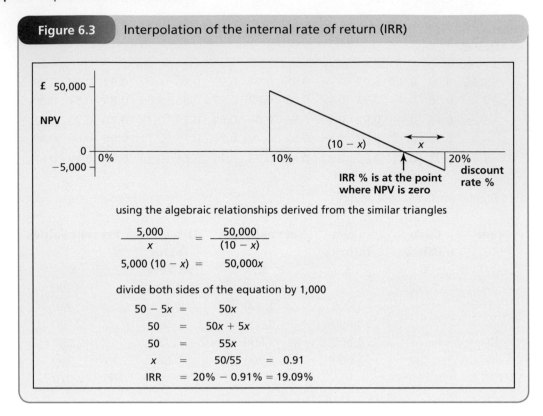

Figure 6.3   Interpolation of the internal rate of return (IRR)

using the algebraic relationships derived from the similar triangles

$$\frac{5,000}{x} = \frac{50,000}{(10-x)}$$

$$5,000\,(10-x) = 50,000x$$

divide both sides of the equation by 1,000

$$50 - 5x = 50x$$
$$50 = 50x + 5x$$
$$50 = 55x$$
$$x = 50/55 = 0.91$$
$$\text{IRR} = 20\% - 0.91\% = 19.09\%$$

By solving this equation r is the internal rate of return (IRR), the exact rate of return that the project is expected to achieve. An organisation would then undertake the project if the expected rate of return, the IRR, exceeds its target rate of return.

Solving the above equation mathematically is difficult. IRR may be determined more easily graphically and by using a little trigonometry and algebra and through interpolation. This assumes a linear relationship between the NPVs of a capital investment project derived using different discount rates. If, for example, a project generates a positive NPV of £50,000 using a discount rate of 10% and a negative NPV of £5,000 using a discount rate of 20%, then the IRR (at which point NPV is zero) must be somewhere between 10% and 20%. The exact rate may be determined by interpolation as illustrated in Figure 6.3.

A similar approach may be adopted if both NPVs are positive. Consider a different project, which generates a positive NPV of £50,000 using a discount rate of 10% and a positive NPV of £20,000 using a discount rate of 15%, then the IRR (at which point NPV is zero) may be extrapolated as shown in Figure 6.4.

As an alternative to the graphical approach, the calculation of IRR can be carried out manually using a trial and error process, which is a quite laborious task. This may be overcome since IRR can also be determined using the appropriate spreadsheet function in Excel, for example. However, there are a couple of further serious difficulties with the use of IRR.

Discount rates may change over the life of a project because of changes in the general level of interest rates. The IRR calculated for a project may therefore be greater than expected rates of return in some years and less in other years, which makes a decision on the project very difficult to make. Alternatively, the NPV approach may use different discount rates for each year of a project.

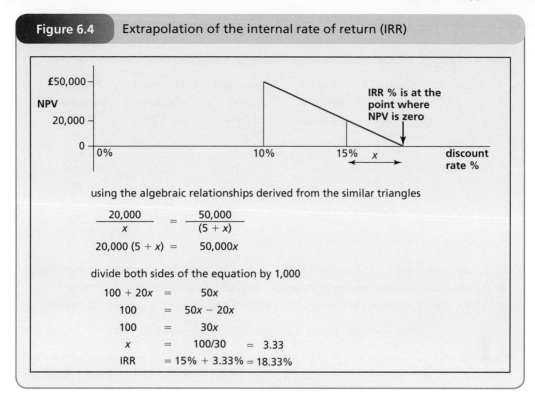

Figure 6.4 Extrapolation of the internal rate of return (IRR)

using the algebraic relationships derived from the similar triangles

$$\frac{20,000}{x} = \frac{50,000}{(5 + x)}$$

$$20,000 (5 + x) = 50,000x$$

divide both sides of the equation by 1,000

$$100 + 20x = 50x$$

$$100 = 50x - 20x$$

$$100 = 30x$$

$$x = 100/30 = 3.33$$

$$IRR = 15\% + 3.33\% = 18.33\%$$

The cash flows of projects do not normally fall into the simple pattern of an outflow at the start of the project followed by positive cash flows during each successive year. Project cash flows may be positive at the start, or may vary between negative and positive throughout the life of a project. Such irregular cash flow sequences throughout each period may lead to a project having no IRR or multiple IRRs. Multiple IRRs make it impossible to use IRR for decision-making.

Progress check 6.6

What is the internal rate of return (IRR) and how is it calculated?

Worked example 6.11 illustrates the use of both NPV and IRR, using conventional cash flows.

Worked example 6.11

Gamma plc is a diversified multinational group that wishes to acquire a computer system costing £600,000, which is expected to generate cash gains of £170,000 per year over five years. The computer system will have a residual value of zero after five years. The suggested cost of capital is 12%. For this example we may ignore taxation. Gamma has a target IRR of 15%. We will evaluate Gamma plc's computer system investment by considering its IRR.

					£
Yearly cash gains					170,000

Year	Cash outflows £000	Cash inflows £000	Net cash flow £000	Discount factor at 12%	Present values £000
0	−600		−600	1.00	−600.0
1		170	170	0.89	151.3
2		170	170	0.80	136.0
3		170	170	0.71	120.7
4		170	170	0.64	108.8
5		170	170	0.57	96.9
				NPV	+13.7

Alternatively, because the cash inflow is the same for each of the five years at £170,000, we may use the cumulative present values in the present value tables in Appendix 1. The five-year cumulative present value, or discount factor of £1 at 12% is £3.61, therefore:

$$\text{NPV} = -£600{,}000 + (£170{,}000 \times 3.61) = +£13{,}700$$

The project gives a positive NPV of £13,700 over five years. If Gamma plc used NPV to appraise capital projects then acceptance of this project may be recommended because NPV is positive.

The IRR is the rate of return that would give an NPV of zero. The interpolation technique shown in Figure 6.3 may be used to derive the internal rate of return of the project.

If we assume a discount rate of 20%, the five-year cumulative discount factor is 2.99 (from the cumulative present value of £1 in the present value tables in Appendix 1).

The new NPV would be:

$$-£600{,}000 + (£170{,}000 \times 2.99) = -£91{,}700$$

(Note that if Gamma plc used NPV to appraise capital projects then acceptance of this project would not be recommended at a cost of capital of 20% because it is negative.)

We have already calculated the positive NPV of £13,700 using a cost of capital of 12%. The IRR must be at some point between 20% and 12% (difference 8%). Using a similar calculation to that used in Figure 6.3:

$$\frac{£91{,}700}{x} = \frac{£13{,}700}{(8-x)}$$

$$£91{,}700\,(8-x) = £13{,}700x$$

$$(£91{,}700 \times 8) - £91{,}700x = £13{,}700x$$

$$£733{,}600 - £91{,}700x = £13{,}700x$$

$$£733{,}600 = £13{,}700x + £91{,}700x$$

$$£733{,}600 = £105{,}400x$$

$$x = \frac{£733{,}600}{£105{,}400}$$

$$x = 7.0$$

Therefore, interpolation gives us an IRR of 20% less 7%, which is 13%.

If the Gamma group uses IRR to appraise capital projects then this project may be rejected as the target rate is 15%. Because of the NPV to discount rate linearity assumption discussed above, the 13% IRR is an approximation.

NPV or IRR?

We have looked at the two main capital appraisal methods, which use the DCF technique. Which method should an organisation adopt for the appraisal of capital investment projects? Which is the better method?

IRR is relatively easy to understand, particularly for non-financial managers. It can be stated in terms that do not include financial jargon, for example 'a project will cost £1m and will return 20% per annum, which is better than the company's target of 15%'. Whereas, NPV is not quite so clear, for example 'a project will cost £1,000,000 and have an NPV of £250,000 using the company's weighted average cost of capital of 12%'. But there are major disadvantages with the use of IRR:

- IRR is very difficult to use for decision-making where expected rates of return may change over the life of a project
- if project cash flows do not follow the usual 'outflow at the start of the project followed by inflows over the life of the project' the result may be no IRR, or two or more IRRs, which can lead to uncertainties and difficulties in interpretation
- IRR should not be used to decide between mutually exclusive projects because of its inability to allow for the relative size of investments.

IRR ignores the size of investment projects, because it is a percentage measure of a return of a project rather than an absolute cash return value. Two projects, one with a large initial investment and one with a small initial investment, may have the same IRR, but one project may return many times the cash flow returned by the other project. So, if the projects were judged solely on IRR they would seem to rank equally.

We have already discussed the use of hurdle rates by companies to evaluate proposed investments. While their use by companies is widespread they may lead to sub-optimal decisions being made because otherwise good, value-adding projects may be rejected because they return just below the required hurdle rate.

If mutually exclusive projects need to be compared then the following rules for acceptance generally apply:

- is the IRR greater than the hurdle rate (usually the WACC)?

    If so

- the project with the highest NPV should be chosen assuming the NPV is greater than zero.

A company may be considering a number of projects in which it may invest. If there is a limited amount of funds available then **capital rationing** is required (see later in this chapter). This method requires ranking the competing projects in terms of NPV per each £ of investment in each project. Investment funds may then be allocated according to NPV rankings, given the assumption that the investments are infinitely divisible.

Progress check 6.7

What are the disadvantages in the use of internal rate of return (IRR) in the support of capital investment appraisal decisions?

Despite the apparent advantages of using NPV and the disadvantages with using IRR as an appraisal method, many companies appear to prefer IRR. As a consequence, IRR is sometimes used in a slightly different way in order to adjust IRR to bring it in line with the reinvestment assumption of the NPV approach. This is referred to as the **modified internal rate of return (MIRR)**.

Modified internal rate of return (MIRR)

As with IRR, the modified internal rate of return (MIRR) is the rate of return that gives an NPV of zero. However, with MIRR it is the rate of return when the initial investment is compared with the terminal value of the project's net cash flows reinvested at the cost of capital. Therefore, it is necessary to calculate the terminal value of the investment by compounding, using the cost of capital, all cash flows through to the end of the project. The MIRR is then the return at which the terminal value equals the initial cost.

Worked example 6.12

Dancer Ltd is considering a £35,000 investment in a manufacturing process improvement. The savings resulting from the investment are expected to result in cash flows of £17,000 in each of the first two years of the project and £13,000 in the third and fourth years. The company's cost of capital is 15% per annum. The IRR has been calculated at 23.9%, but the company wishes to determine the MIRR of the project.

Year	Cash flows	Future value factor	Terminal value
	£	@ 15%	£
1	17,000	$(1.15)^3$	25,855
2	17,000	$(1.15)^2$	22,483
3	13,000	$(1.15)^1$	14,950
4	13,000	$(1.15)^0$	13,000
			76,288

We can now find the discount rate that gives the present value discount factor obtained by dividing the initial investment by the terminal value of the cash flows because

$$PV = \frac{FV}{(1 + r)^t}$$

$1/(1 + r)^t$ is the present value discount factor

therefore

$$present\ value\ discount\ factor = \frac{PV}{FV}$$

$$present\ value\ discount\ factor = \frac{£35,000}{£76,288} = 0.46$$

From the present value table in Appendix 1 at the end of this book, we can see that for a four-year project this value relates to a discount rate of approximately 21.5% per annum. The MIRR is therefore 21.5%, compared with the IRR of 23.9%.

Discounted payback

The discounted payback appraisal method requires a discount rate to be chosen to calculate the present values of cash inflows and then the payback is the number of years required to repay the original investment.

Worked example 6.13

A new leisure facility project is being considered by Denton City Council. It will cost £600,000 and is expected to generate the following cash inflows over six years:

Year	£
1	40,000
2	100,000
3	200,000
4	350,000
5	400,000
6	50,000

The cost of capital is 10% per annum.

Denton City Council evaluates projects using discounted payback, so let's evaulate the project.

Year	Net cash flow £000	Cumulative net cash flow £000	Discount factor at 10%	Present values £000	Cumulative present values £000
0	−600	−600	1.00	−600.0	−600.0
1	40	−560	0.91	36.4	−563.6
2	100	−460	0.83	83.0	−480.6
3	200	−260	0.75	150.0	−330.6

4	350	90	0.68	238.0	−92.6
5	400	490	0.62	248.0	155.4
6	_50_	540	0.56	_28.0_	183.4
	_540_		NPV	_+183.4_	

Taking a simple payback approach we can see that the project starts to pay back at nearly three quarters of the way through year four. The discounted payback approach shows that with a cost of capital of 10% the project does not really start to pay back until just over a third of the way into year five. This method also highlights the large difference between the total real value of the project of £183,400 in discounted cash flow terms, and the total value of actual cash flows of £540,000.

Progress check 6.8

What is discounted payback and how is it calculated?

Advantages and disadvantages of the five investment appraisal methods

We have discussed the five capital investment methods and seen examples of their application. The table in Figure 6.5 summarises each of the methods and the advantages and disadvantages of their practical use in investment appraisal.

It is interesting to note that even as recently as ten years ago payback still seemed to be the most popular appraisal method within UK companies. This was closely followed by IRR and NPV, and discounted payback and ARR appeared to be equal third, sharing around the same level of popularity (see Drury, C, Braund, S, Osborne, P, and Tayles, M 'A Survey of Management Accounting Practices in UK Companies', *Chartered Association of Certified Accountants*, London (1993)). In a more recent study of Australian companies published in 2011, Kalyebara and Ahmad surveyed the investment appraisal practices of the top 500 companies listed on the Australian Stock Exchange (Kalyebara, B and Ahmed, A 'Determination and use of a hurdle rate in the capital budgeting process: evidence from listed Australian companies' *IUP Journal of Applied Finance*, Volume 17, Number 2, pages 59–76 (2011)). The researchers gained responses from 41% of the companies. As the table below indicates (see Figure 6.6), the profile of methods used by major companies to evaluate capital investments has shifted to NPV and IRR methods from previously more popular payback and accounting-based measures.

It should be emphasised that the whole area of capital investment appraisal is one that requires a great deal of expertise and experience. In real-life decision-making situations these types of appraisal are generally carried out by the accountant or the finance director. These sorts of longer-term decisions are concerned primarily with the maximisation of shareholder wealth, but they also impact on issues relating to the health and future development of the business. Therefore, such decisions are normally based on qualitative as well as quantitative factors.

Figure 6.5   Advantages and disadvantages of the five investment appraisal methods

	definition	advantages	disadvantages
accounting rate of return (ARR)	average accounting profit over the life of the project divided by the initial or average investment	quick and easy to calculate and simple to use	based on accounting profit rather than cash flows
		the concept of a % return is a familiar one	a relative measure and so no account is taken of the size of the project
		very similar to ROCE	Ignores timing of cash flows and the cost of capital
payback	the point where the cumulative value of a project's profits or cash flows becomes positive	easily understood	ignores the timing of cash flows
		considers liquidity	ignores profits or cash flows that occur after the payback point
		looks only at relevant cash flows	ignores the cost of capital, i.e. the time value of money
net present value (NPV)	the total present values of each of a project's cash flows, using a present value discount factor	uses relevant cash flows	its use requires an estimate of the cost of capital
		allows for the time value of money	
		absolute measure and therefore useful, for example, for comparison of the change in corporate value	
		it is additive which means that if the cash flow is doubled then the NPV is doubled	
internal rate of return (IRR)	the discount factor at which the NPV of a project becomes zero	does not need an estimate of the cost of capital	it is a relative rate of return and so no account is taken of the size of the project
		because the result is stated as a % it is easily understood	its use may rank projects incorrectly
			as cash flows change signs −ve to +ve or vice versa throughout the project there may be more than one IRR
			it is difficult to use if changes in the cost of capital are forecast
discounted payback	the point where the cumulative value of a project's discounted cash flows becomes positive	easily understood	its use requires an estimate of the cost of capital
		considers liquidity	ignores cash flows that occur after the payback point
		looks only at relevant cash flows	
		allows for the value of money	

Figure 6.6	Australian companies' capital budgeting evaluation techniques in 2011

Capital Budgeting Evaluation Techniques	Frequency	%
NPV	66	32
IRR	55	27
Payback	53	26
ARR	18	9
Others	8	4
Profitability index	4	2

Source: Kalyebara, Baliira: Ahmed, Abdullahi D, *Determination and Use of a Hurdle Rate in the Capital Budgeting Process: Evidence from Listed Australian Companies, IUP Journal of Applied Finance,* Vol. 17, Issue 2, 2011.

Non-financial factors are now increasingly as important, if not more important, to businesses in their appraisal of new projects. These may include, for example:

- customer relationships
- employee welfare
- the fit with general business strategy
- competition
- availability of scarce resources such as skills and specialised knowledge.

In addition, there are a number of other important quantitative factors, which are discussed in the next section, which should also be considered in new project appraisal. The impact of taxation, for example, is sometimes forgotten with regard to the allowances against tax on the purchase of capital items and tax payable on profits, and therefore cash flows, resulting from a capital project. The uncertainty surrounding future expectations and the sensitivity of the outcome of a project to changes affecting the various elements of an appraisal calculation, are factors that also require measured assessment.

Progress check 6.9

Which technique do you think is the most appropriate to use in capital investment appraisal, and why?

Other factors affecting investment decisions

A number of further factors may have an additional impact on investment criteria calculations:

- the effect of inflation on the cost of capital, or on future cash flows
- whether additional working capital is required for the project
- taxation
- the length of the project
- risk and uncertainty.

Inflation

As we saw earlier in Figure 6.2 we used a discount rate of 5%. But exactly what type of discount rate is it?

Actual interest rates, costs of capital, or rates of return, are often referred to as real rates, whereas money rates adjusted for inflation are referred to as money interest rates, costs of capital, or rates of return, and can be calculated as follows:

$$1 + \text{money interest rate} = (1 + \text{real interest rate}) \times (1 + \text{inflation rate})$$

or

$$1 + \text{real interest rate} = \frac{1 + \text{money interest rate}}{1 + \text{inflation rate}}$$

Alternatively, an approximate money rate value may be calculated as follows:

$$\text{money interest rate} = \text{real interest rate} + \text{inflation rate}$$

This equation applies equally to inflation-adjusted interest rates or discount rates.

$$1 + \text{money discount rate} = (1 + \text{real discount rate}) \times (1 + \text{inflation rate})$$

If r is the real discount rate or cost of capital and the inflation rate is f, then the money discount rate or cost of capital, a may be denoted as follows:

$$(1 + a) = (1 + r) \times (1 + f)$$

Therefore

$$\text{money discount rate } a = (1 + r) \times (1 + f) - 1$$

Worked example 6.14

Bruce plc is considering an investment and uses a discount rate of 10%. Inflation is expected to remain at a constant rate of 2.5% for the foreseeable future. What is Bruce plc's money discount rate?

$$
\begin{aligned}
1 + \text{money discount rate} &= (1 + \text{real discount rate}) \times (1 + \text{inflation rate}) \\
&= (1 + 10\%) \times (1 + 2.5\%) \\
\text{money discount rate} &= 1.1275 - 1 \\
&= 0.1275 \\
&= 12.75\%
\end{aligned}
$$

Alternatively the money discount rate may be approximated:

$$
\begin{aligned}
\text{money discount rate} &= \text{real discount rate} + \text{inflation rate} \\
&= 10\% + 2.5\% \\
&= 12.5\%
\end{aligned}
$$

Both calculations give a money discount rate of between 12% and 13%.

Discounting real cash flows using inflation-adjusted discount rates actually gives the same result as discounting inflation-adjusted cash flows using real discount rates. Most financial analysts find it more convenient to use inflation-adjusted cash flows and real discount rates.

Worked example 6.15

What is a company's real cost of capital if its money cost of capital is 11% and inflation is running at 2%?

Real cost of capital

$$r = \frac{(1 + a)}{(1 + f)} - 1$$

$$r = \frac{1.11}{1.02} - 1$$

$$r = 0.088 \text{ or } 8.8\%$$

This would normally then be rounded to say 9% and forecast money cash flows that have been adjusted for inflation may then be discounted using this real cost of capital. Alternatively, if forecast cash flows have not been adjusted for inflation, then these real cash flows would be discounted using the company's money cost of capital of 11%. The result is approximately the same using either method.

Working capital

In addition to capital investments, any increases in working capital required for a project need to be shown as cash outflows as necessary in one or more years, offset by cash inflows to bring the total to zero by the end of the project, at which time it is assumed that all working capital will have been liquidated.

Worked example 6.16

Delta Precision plc, a manufacturing company, has the opportunity to invest in a machine costing £110,000 that will generate net cash inflows from the investment of £30,000 for five years, after which time the machine will be worth nothing. Cost of capital is 10% per annum. We may ignore inflation and taxation in our evaluation of the project using NPV.

Year	Cash outflows £000	Cash inflows £000	Net cash flow £000	Discount factor at 10%	Present values £000
0	−110		−110	1.00	−110.0
1		30	30	0.91	27.3
2		30	30	0.83	24.9
3		30	30	0.75	22.5

4		30	30	0.68	20.4
5		30	30	0.62	18.6
				NPV	+3.7

The positive NPV of £3,700 would indicate acceptance of this investment.
Let's consider that in addition to the above factors, for this project Delta required:

- £20,000 working capital in year one
- £40,000 working capital in year two, but then
- zero working capital in years three, four and five.

The revised cash flows would become:

Year	0 £000	1 £000	2 £000	3 £000	4 £000	5 £000	Total £000
Investment	−110						−110
Cash inflows		30	30	30	30	30	150
Working {		−20		20			0
Capital {			−40	40			0
Total	−110	10	−10	90	30	30	40

The total cash flow of the project is still the same at £40,000, but the timings of the cash flows are different.

Year	Net cash flows £000	Discount factor at 10%	Present values £000
0	−110	1.00	−110.0
1	10	0.91	9.1
2	−10	0.83	−8.3
3	90	0.75	67.5
4	30	0.68	20.4
5	30	0.62	18.6
		NPV	−2.7

The need for, and the timing of, working capital gives a negative NPV of £2,700 which would now indicate rejection of this investment.

Taxation

In practice, tax must always be allowed for in any capital investment appraisal calculations. The following two examples provide an introduction to this topic.

Worked example 6.17

Epsilon Ltd is a company that manufactures and distributes consumer products. It is currently considering the acquisition of a machine costing £2,700,000 to market a new product.

The machine will be worth nothing after 10 years but is expected to produce 10,000 units of a product per year during that period, with variable costs of £35 per unit.

The product can be sold for £120 per unit.

Fixed costs directly attributed to this product will be £300,000 per year.

The company's cost of capital is 10% per annum.

We may assume that all costs and revenues are paid and received during each year.

We may further assume that corporation tax is paid in the year that profit is made and calculated at 40% of profit, and that for tax purposes each year's depreciation is equal to capital allowances.

We will evaluates the acquisition of the machine using NPV.

	£000	
Sales revenue	1,200	[10,000 ×£120]
Variable costs	(350)	[10,000 × £35]
Depreciation	(270)	[2,700,000 over 10-year life]
Fixed costs	(300)	
Taxable profit	280	
Corporation tax at 40%	(112)	[based on taxable profit plus depreciation less capital allowances]
Profit after tax	168	
Add back depreciation	270	[non-cash flow]
Yearly cash flow	438	

Using the cumulative present value tables (see Appendix 1) the present value factor for £1 at 10% over 10 years is 6.15, therefore:

$$\text{NPV} = -£2,700,000 + (£438,000 \times 6.15) = -£6,300$$

The NPV is less than 0 and the project may therefore not be recommended.

Corporation tax is normally payable by a company in the year following the year in which profit is earned. If a project lasts for, say, four years then cash flow in respect of tax must also be shown in the fifth year. The length of the project is then effectively five years. Tax payable in respect of operating profit must be shown separately from cash flows in respect of capital allowances. The first investment year is normally shown as year 0 and the first tax allowance year is therefore year one.

Worked example 6.18 uses a UK tax scenario to illustrate the importance of the timing of the tax cash flows in investment appraisal.

Worked example 6.18

Zeta plc has the opportunity to invest in a machine costing £100,000 that will generate cash profits of £30,000 per year for the next four years after which the machine would be sold for £10,000. The company's after-tax cost of capital is 8% per annum.

We may assume:

- corporation tax at 30%
- annual writing down allowances in each year are on the investment reducing balance at 25%
- there will be a balancing charge or allowance on disposal of the machine.

We can consider whether the investment should be made, using an NPV approach.

Capital allowances:

Year	Opening balance £	Capital allowance at 25% £	Balancing allowance £	Closing balance £
0	100,000	25,000		75,000
1	75,000	18,750		56,250
2	56,250	14,063		42,187
3	42,187	10,547		31,640
4	31,640	7,910		23,730
	23,730		13,730	10,000
Proceeds				−10,000
Total		76,270	13,730	–

Note that the totals of the capital allowances and balancing allowance equal £90,000, the net cost of the machine £100,000 less the £10,000 estimated disposal value.

Next, we can calculate the taxable profit and the tax payable.

Year	0 £	1 £	2 £	3 £	4 £
Profit		30,000	30,000	30,000	30,000
Capital allowances	25,000	18,750	14,063	10,547	21,640
Taxable profit	−25,000	11,250	15,937	19,453	8,360
Tax receivable/ (payable) at 30%	7,500	−3,375	−4,781	−5,836	−2,508

Because profits are cash profits we can use these to calculate the net cash flows and the present values of the project:

Year	Investment	Cash profit	Tax	Net cash flow	Discount factor at	Present value
	£	£	£	£	8% pa	£
0	−100,000			−100,000	1.00	−100,000
1		30,000	7,500	37,500	0.93	34,875
2		30,000	−3,375	26,625	0.86	22,897
3		30,000	−4,781	25,219	0.79	19,923
4	10,000	30,000	−5,836	34,164	0.74	25,281
5			−2,508	−2,508	0.68	−1,705
					NPV	+1,271

The positive NPV of £1,271 would indicate acceptance of this investment.

Progress check 6.10

Why and how should inflation and working capital be allowed for in making capital investment decisions?

Capital investment decisions take on a wider dimension for international corporations with the consideration of a further factor, the uncertainty associated with foreign currency exchange rate fluctuations. For UK-based companies this has had a particular significance over recent years with the uncertainty surrounding the UK's adoption of the euro.

Back in 2001, Nissan's decision to build its new Micra car in Sunderland in the UK illustrated the importance of some of the additional factors that influence investment appraisal decisions. The strength of the £ sterling against the euro had damaged Sunderland's chances of winning the contract. But the level of Government support and the flexibility of the Sunderland workforce were factors that impacted favourably on the Nissan decision, in addition to their positive initial financial appraisal of the investment.

As we can see from the press extract below the cheaper costs of manufacturing abroad (and not just in the Far East but also now in the eurozone) put pressure on UK companies which cannot match tender offers. In terms of cost, Peugeot Citroën preferred Europe to the UK, which led it to close its UK manufacturing plant in 2006 and transfer production to Slovakia. Alongside Kia Motors, Ford, Hyundai, and Volkswagen it is helping to turn Slovakia into the European car manufacturing hub. Traditional UK industries are in decline as a result of cheaper manufacturing tenders from abroad as the press extract illustrates.

Foreign currency exchange rate risk is not discussed in detail in this chapter but is an important topic that we will return to in Chapters 11 and 12.

The impact of high UK costs on investments by large foreign companies

A Derby MP has written to hundreds of his colleagues in Westminster calling on them to unite in the fight to save the UK's rail industry.

Chris Williamson has written to 265 Conservative and 49 Lib Dem MPs asking for their support. He wants them to join the campaign to overturn the Government's decision not to award the Thameslink rail contract to Derby train maker Bombardier. The campaign has already received cross-party support at Derby City Council as well as backing from several Labour MPs and local Conservative MPs.

But Mr Williamson is keen to get more MPs from every political party on board ahead of a protest that will take place at the Houses of Parliament on Wednesday. In his letters, the Derby North MP spells out the gravity of the situation facing Bombardier and the UK rail industry. In June, the Department for Transport announced that German manufacturer Siemens had been selected as the preferred bidder for the £1.4 billion contract. The firm will build the 1,200 carriages in Germany.

In his letter, Mr Williamson writes: 'If the Department for Transport concludes the Thameslink contract with Siemens, Bombardier could pull out of the UK altogether leading to the collapse of the British train building industry. Such an outcome would be disastrous for Derby, a major blow to British manufacturing and undermine the Government's attempts to rebalance the economy. The campaign to save the British train-making industry has united my city and the wider county of Derbyshire and is gaining support from all over the country. Politicians of every persuasion, business leaders, trade unionists, community groups, young people and old are calling on the Government to intervene before it is too late. Your support is vital in securing a rethink. Please do join us.'

The campaign to get the Thameslink decision overturned has already attracted support from MPs up and down the country. An Early Day Motion tabled by Mr Williamson has attracted the signatures of 44 MPs. The parliamentary petition has been signed by 40 Labour MPs, along with three Lib Dems and one Green Party MP. No Conservative MPs, including those who represent Derbyshire constituencies, have added their names.

Mr Williamson said: 'My hope is that both Conservative and Lib Dem MPs will put party politics to one side and support this campaign. I haven't sent the letters out to members of the Cabinet or the Government Whips because they should already be fully aware of the situation. But I have sent a copy to West Derbyshire MP Patrick McLoughlin, who is Chief Whip – and the other four local Tory MPs Pauline Latham, Jessica Lee, Nigel Mills and Heather Wheeler, as a matter of courtesy. I've also sent out more bespoke letters to those MPs who have previously held positions that are relevant to the topic.'

Bombardier's Litchurch Lane site had been relying on Thameslink to secure its long-term future.

Since missing out on the deal it has shed 1,400 jobs and is also carrying out a full review of its UK operations. It has not ruled out closing its Derby factory. This would result in more jobs being lost and many more in the supply chain. It would also spell the end of the UK's last remaining train-building factory.

So far, the Government has refused to review the decision – despite arguments about previous corruption charges against Siemens that could have disqualified it from the bidding process and its ability to deliver the technology for the project. The Government said it chose Siemens because it offered the best value for money for taxpayers.

Source: **Call to MPs to put party politics aside and join Bombardier fight**, by Robin Johnson © *Derby Evening Telegraph*, 3 September 2011

Risk and uncertainty and decision-making – sensitivity analysis

The decision-making process includes a comparison of actual results following implementation of the decision with the expected outcome. Our own experience tells us that actual outcomes usually differ considerably from expected outcomes. In terms of investments in projects, the greater the timescale of the project the more time there is for more things to go wrong; the larger the investment, the greater may be the impact.

As a final step in evaluation of the investment in a project it is prudent to carry out some sort of **sensitivity analysis**. Sensitivity analysis may be used to assess the risk associated with a capital investment project. A project having a positive NPV may on the face of it seem viable. It is useful to calculate how much the NPV may change should there be changes to the factors used in the appraisal exercise. These factors are shown in Figure 6.7.

Sensitivity may be illustrated graphically:

- NPV is plotted on the *y* vertical axis
- the percentage change in the variable factors, used in the appraisal, is plotted on the *x* horizontal axis.

This process is then carried out for each variable, for example:

- sales
- cost savings
- investment
- scrap value,

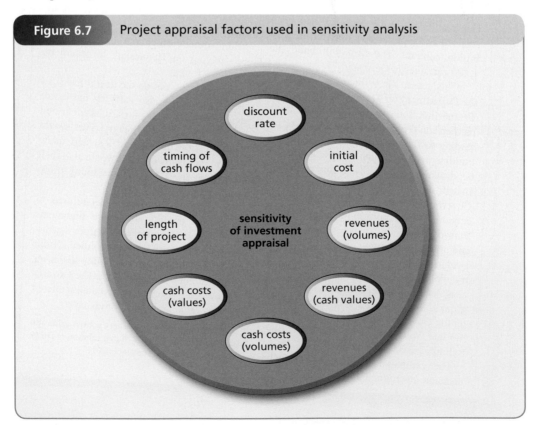

Figure 6.7 Project appraisal factors used in sensitivity analysis

and the most sensitive variable is the one with the steepest gradient.

Sensitivity may also be evaluated through numerical analysis, which is illustrated in Worked examples 6.19 to 6.23.

Worked example 6.19

Theta Ltd has the opportunity to invest in a project with an initial cost of £100,000 that will generate estimated net cash flows of £35,000 at the end of each year for five years. The company's cost of capital is 12% per annum. For simplicity we can ignore the effects of tax and inflation.

The sensitivity of the initial investment in the project can be evaluated using an NPV approach.

The cumulative present value tables show us that the annuity factor over five years at 12% per annum is 3.61 (see Appendix 1). Therefore the NPV of the project:

$$= -£100,000 + (£35,000 \times 3.61)$$
$$= -£100,000 + £126,350$$
$$NPV = +£26,350$$

The positive NPV of £26,350 would indicate going ahead with the investment in this project.

We will consider the sensitivity analysis of the project to changes in the initial investment.

Initial investment

The NPV of the project is £26,350. If the initial investment rose by £26,350 to £126,350 (£100,000 + £26,350) the NPV would become zero and it would not be worth taking on the project. This represents an increase of 26.4% on the initial investment.

Worked example 6.20

Using the data from Worked example 6.19 we can evaluate the sensitivity of the project to changes in the annual cash flows from the project, using an NPV approach.

Annual cash flow

If we again consider what needs to happen to bring the NPV to zero then:

$$NPV = 0 = -£100,000 + (c \times 3.61)$$

where c is the annual cash flow
therefore

$$c = £100,000/3.61$$
$$c = £27,700$$

which is a reduction of 20.9% from the original per annum cash flow of £35,000.

Worked example 6.21

Using the data from Worked example 6.19 we can evaluate the sensitivity of the project to changes in the cost of capital of the project for Theta Ltd, using an NPV approach.

Cost of capital

When the NPV is zero the internal rate of return (IRR) is equal to the cost of capital. If the cost of capital is greater than the IRR then the project should be rejected.

In this case, therefore, we first need to calculate the cumulative discount factor at which the NPV is zero.

$$NPV = 0 = -£100,000 + (£35,000 \times d)$$

where d is the cumulative discount factor for five years
therefore
$$d = £100,000/£35,000$$
$$d = 2.857$$

The cumulative present value tables show us that the annuity factor over five years of 2.86 represents a discount rate of 22%. The IRR is therefore approximately 22%, which is an 83.3% increase over the cost of capital of 12%.

Worked example 6.22

Using the data from Worked example 6.19 we can evaluate the sensitivity to changes in the length of the project for Theta Ltd, using an NPV approach.

Length of project

The original project was five years for which we calculated the NPV at £26,350. We may consider what would be the effect if the project ended after say four years or three years. If the project was four years, the cumulative discount factor (from the tables) is 3.04 so the NPV of the project:

$$= -£100,000 + (£35,000 \times 3.04)$$
$$= -£100,000 + £106,400$$
$$NPV = +£6,400$$

The positive NPV of £6,400 still indicates going ahead with the investment in this project.

If the project was three years the cumulative discount factor (from the tables) is 2.40 so the NPV of the project:

$$= -£100,000 + (£35,000 \times 2.40)$$
$$= -£100,000 + £84,000$$
$$\text{NPV} = -£16,000$$

The negative NPV of £16,000 indicates not going ahead with the investment in this project if the length of the project drops below four years, which is the year in which NPV becomes negative.

This is a change of 20% (that is a drop from five years to four years).

Worked example 6.23

Each of the sensitivities that have been calculated in Worked examples 6.19 to 6.22 may be summarised and we can draw some conclusions about the sensitivity of the project that are apparent from the summary.

The sensitivity analysis that we have carried out is more usefully summarised for each of the factors we have considered, to show:

- the values used in the original appraisal
- the critical values of those factors
- the percentage change over the original values that they represent.

Factor	Original value	Critical value	% change
Initial investment	£100,000	£126,350	+26.4
Annual cash flow	£35,000	£27,700	−20.9
Cost of capital	12%	22%	+83.3
Length of project	5 years	4 years	−20.0

We may draw the following conclusions from our sensitivity analysis:

- none of the factors used in the appraisal was critical, their critical values all being +/−20%
- cost of capital is the least critical factor at 83.3%, which is useful to know since the accuracy of the calculation of cost of capital may not always be totally reliable.

The same technique of sensitivity analysis may be used as an early warning system before a project begins to show a loss. It can be seen from the factors outlined in this section that a board of directors should request a sensitivity analysis on all major projects. However, there are limitations to the use of sensitivity analysis. In the worked examples we have considered we have looked at the effect of changes to individual factors in isolation. In reality two or more factors may change simultaneously. The impact of such changes may be assessed using the more sophisticated technique of linear programming. A further limitation may be the absence of clear rules governing acceptance or rejection of the project and the need for the subjective judgement of management.

Simulation analysis

The risk associated with an investment project may also be considered by using a probability simulation. Worked example 6.24 uses the weighting of cash flows of a project by the probabilities of their occurrence in order to calculate an expected NPV.

Worked example 6.24

Kappa plc has the opportunity of engaging in a two-year project for a specific client. It would require an initial investment in a machine costing £200,000. The machine is capable of running three separate processes. The process used will depend on the level of demand from the client's final customers. Each process will therefore generate different yearly net cash flows, each with a different likelihood of occurrence. The company's cost of capital is 15% per annum.

The forecast probabilities and net cash flows for each year are:

Process	Probability of occurrence	Per annum cash flow
Process 1	0.5	£150,000
Process 2	0.1	£15,000
Process 3	0.4	£90,000
	1.0	

The total of the probabilities is 1.0, which indicates that one of the options is certain to occur.

Even though only one process will definitely be used should Kappa take on the project?

We first need to use the probabilities to calculate the weighted average of the expected outcomes for each year.

Process	Cash flow £	Probability	Expected cash flow £
1	150,000	0.5	75,000
2	15,000	0.1	1,500
3	90,000	0.4	36,000
Expected per annum cash flows			112,500

To calculate the expected NPV of the project we need to discount the expected annual cash flows using the discount rate of 15% per annum.

Process	Expected cash flow £	Discount rate at 15%	Expected present value £
1	112,500	0.87	97,875
2	112,500	0.76	85,500
Total	225,000		183,375
Initial investment (year 0)			200,000
Expected NPV			−16,625

The negative expected NPV of £16,625 indicates that Kappa plc should reject investment in this project.

Although the technique of expected net present value is a clear decision rule with a single numerical outcome there are caveats:

- this technique uses an average number which in the above example is not actually capable of occurrence
- use of an average number may cloud the issue if the underlying risk of outcomes worse than the average is ignored.

Consider, for example, the impact on Kappa in Worked example 6.24 if the expected per annum cash flow from Process 1 had been £300,000 and the expected NPV had been positive, but that the client then actually required the use of Process 2.

An example of a simulation model using Excel is included on the website that accompanies this book.

Progress check 6.11

Risk and uncertainty increasingly impact on investment decisions. What are these risk factors, and how may we evaluate their impact?

Scenario analysis

The examples of the sensitivity analysis techniques we have considered only deal with changing each variable or key factor one at a time. These techniques don't consider, for example, questions like 'What would be the outcome if the worst happens?' or 'What is the best outcome?' Uncertainty analysis (as distinct from risk analysis) is an unquantified approach that takes the view that just how much actual outcomes may be worse or better than rational estimates can't be quantified. Uncertainty in terms of worst, best, and likely outcomes may be considered using the technique of scenario analysis. Risk analysis is a quantified approach about how future outcomes may vary expressed as probabilities. Risk analysis techniques include simulation analysis using probabilities, which is an extension of scenario analysis.

Monte Carlo simulation

The probability simulation we used in Worked example 6.24 is a simple example that considers probabilities of only a very small number of outcomes. In real-life situations there may be many variables subject to random variation. Also, the number of likely combinations of events may be massive, and therefore it may be very difficult to calculate a solution. The simulation of a large number of events may be carried out using what is called a Monte Carlo simulation, which employs a random device for what happens at a given point in a situation.

Because of the large amount of data, Monte Carlo simulation is necessarily a computerised technique. The computer uses random numbers to generate thousands of possible combinations of variables according to a pre-specified probability distribution. The Monte Carlo simulation applied to investment analysis provides an NPV outcome from each scenario and the NPVs of each scenario provide a probability distribution of outcomes. Companies may therefore use the Monte Carlo method, and other simulation techniques that use probabilities, to assess risk relating to future cash flows of investments. However, these techniques do not provide any help with regard to the selection of an appropriate discount rate.

Mini case 6.2

Many companies employ Monte Carlo simulations to gauge potential risks.

American multinational company 3M outlined its use of simulation in the notes to its 2011 annual report. A Monte Carlo simulation technique was used to test the company's exposure to changes in currency and interest rates and assess the risk of loss or benefit in after-tax earnings of financial instruments, derivatives and underlying exposures outstanding at 31 December 2011.

Cenkos Securities plc (an institutional securities company) use a Monte Carlo simulation to value investments. They outline their methodology in the notes to their 2011 financial statements. Trading investments include options over securities, which have been received as consideration for corporate finance services rendered. The fair value of these investments was calculated with reference to a Monte Carlo simulation model. Inputs into the model were based on management's best estimates of appropriate volatility, the discount rate and share price growth. The volatility input was calculated based on the volatility of historical share price movements.

Real options

It should be noted that the techniques of both sensitivity analysis and Monte Carlo simulation do not recognise the ability to change projects. The various options that may be considered in order to modify projects use what are called **real options**. A real option is particularly useful in investment appraisal if:

- there is a great deal of uncertainty surrounding the project
- the project requires a high level of flexibility
- the NPV analysis provides a borderline result.

There are four main types of real options applicable to investment decisions:

- expansion options, using, for example, decision trees to evaluate alternatives, which identify opportunities to invest and expand on the success of the original investment

■ abandonment options, which enable the company to get out of or shrink a project if cash flows are below expectations, and therefore enable it to recover some of the costs of plant and equipment and any other project assets

■ timing options provide the options of waiting and learning before going ahead with investment in a project even if it has a positive NPV – a company may want to go ahead with an investment immediately to take advantage of market opportunities, or it may prefer to wait if there are market uncertainties

■ strategic production options, which give companies the flexibility to vary the inputs or outputs of the production process – this may relate to the use in a capital project of, for example, alternative sources of energy like gas or oil, dependent on price and availability.

Real options in practice may relate to advantages of projects that may be perceived as being intangible, but which may be fundamental to the investment decision.

An example of how an option to abandon a project may be evaluated can be seen in the Worked example below.

Worked example 6.25

Horizon Ltd has invested £700,000 in a new capital project. Horizon has the option to abandon the project and sell it for £550,000 at the end of year one. Horizon's cost of capital is 10% per annum and its finance director has estimated future cash flows together with their probabilities for the first two years of the project as shown below:

Year 1		Year 2	
Probability	Cash flow £000	Probability	Cash flow £000
		0.3	200
0.3	300	0.4	350
		0.3	450
		0.4	400
0.3	500	0.3	550
		0.3	600
		0.3	700
0.4	800	0.4	900
		0.3	1,000

Based on the cash flows and their probabilities we can use the real options technique to assess the best course of action at the end of year one.

Using the estimated cash flows and their corresponding probabilities we can calculate the expected net present value of the project were it to continue to the end of year two by discounting at 10% per annum the cash flows under each condition by the appropriate discount factor and then multiplying the present value by the probability.

Cash flows		Discount factor		Present value (PV)			Probability	Year 1
Year 1	Year 2	Year 1	Year 2	Year 1	Year 2	Year 1 + year 2 PV	year 1 and year 2	and year 2 PV × joint probability
£000	£000			£000	£000	£000		£000
300	200	0.91	0.83	273	166	439	(0.3 × 0.3) = 0.09	40
300	350	0.91	0.83	273	291	564	(0.3 × 0.4) = 0.12	68
300	450	0.91	0.83	273	374	647	(0.3 × 0.3) = 0.09	58
500	400	0.91	0.83	455	332	787	(0.3 × 0.4) = 0.12	94
500	550	0.91	0.83	455	457	912	(0.3 × 0.3) = 0.09	82
500	600	0.91	0.83	455	498	953	(0.3 × 0.3) = 0.09	86
800	700	0.91	0.83	728	581	1,309	(0.4 × 0.3) = 0.12	157
800	900	0.91	0.83	728	747	1,475	(0.4 × 0.4) = 0.16	236
800	1,000	0.91	0.83	728	830	1,558	(0.4 × 0.3) = 0.12	187
							Expected PV	1,008
							Less capital investment	700
							Expected NPV	308

The project would therefore give an expected net present value of £308,000 if there were no option to abandon at the end of year one.

With the option to abandon the project at the end of year one, we can evaluate the decision based on the three possible outcomes of year one once they are known.

First outcome – year one cash flow is £300,000

The expected cash flows for year two in £000 would be

$$(200 \times 0.3) + (350 \times 0.4) + (450 \times 0.3)$$
$$= 60 + 140 + 135$$
$$= 335$$

The expected PV after year one would be

$$335/1.10 = 304.55 \text{ or } £304,550$$

Since this is less than the value of £550,000 at which Horizon could sell the project, it would abandon the project.
The NPV of the project would be

$$(300 + 550)/1.10 - 700$$
$$= 72.73$$

Second outcome – year one cash flow is £500,000

The expected cash flows for year two in £000 would be

$$(400 \times 0.4) + (550 \times 0.3) + (600 \times 0.3)$$
$$= 160 + 165 + 180$$
$$= 505$$

The expected PV after year one would be

$$505/1.10$$
$$= 459.09 \text{ or } £459,090$$

Since this is less than the value of £550,000 at which Horizon could sell the project, it would abandon the project.

The NPV of the project would be

$$(500 + 550)/1.10 - 700$$
$$= 254.55$$

Third outcome – year one cash flow is £800,000

The expected cash flows for year two in £000 would be

$$(700 \times 0.3) + (900 \times 0.4) + (1,000 \times 0.3)$$
$$= 210 + 360 + 300$$
$$= 870$$

The expected PV after year one would be

$$870/1.10$$
$$= 790.91 \text{ or } £790,910$$

Since this is more than the value of £550,000 at which Horizon could sell the project, they would continue with the project.

The NPV of the project would be

$$(800/1.10) + (870/1.10^2) - 700$$
$$= 746.27$$

Since we know the probabilities of each of the three possible year one outcomes, we can calculate the expected NPV of the project.

$$\text{Expected NPV} = (72.73 \times 0.3) + (254.55 \times 0.3) + (746.27 \times 0.4)$$
$$= 21.82 + 76.37 + 298.51$$
$$= 396.70 \text{ or } £396,700$$

The expected NPV with the option to abandon is greater than the expected NPV without the option to abandon. We can therefore calculate the value of the option to abandon as £396,700 − £308,000 = £88,700.

Equivalent annual cost (EAC)

The calculation of a net present value (NPV) takes the cash flows of future periods and converts them into one sum which represents their value expressed in today's US$, £ sterling, riyals, dirhams, euros, or any other currency. It is possible to carry out this calculation in reverse by taking the total of today's original investment and converting it into a stream of equivalent future cash flows. These equivalent future cash flows are called **equivalent annual costs (EACs)**. EAC is a particularly useful financial tool, which we have illustrated in Worked example 6.26.

Worked example 6.26

A water company in the Middle East required a significant capital investment in order to upgrade its desalination plants. This prompted the question 'How much would the price of water have to be increased following this investment?' It was estimated that an upgrade of a desalination plant would require the company to invest 5 billion dirhams. The company's money (inflation-adjusted) cost of capital is 5% and the new equipment will last for 20 years. The desalination plant's total clean water production will be 4.5 million litres a year. For simplicity it may be assumed that the upgrade will not require any additional materials or changes to operating costs. The company needed to know how many dirhams per litre it would have to charge to recover the investment cost. We will use EAC to answer that question and ignoring taxation, which is not payable in this Middle Eastern country.

To calculate how much additional income the desalination plant would need for each of the 20 years to cover the 5 billion dirhams investment we need to calculate the 20 year annuity (see the earlier section about annuities) with a present value of 5 billion dirhams.

$$\text{present value of an annuity} = \text{annuity payment} \times \text{annuity factor}$$

therefore

$$\text{annuity payment} = \frac{\text{present value of an annuity}}{\text{annuity factor}}$$

Using a cost of capital or 5% per annum the 20 year annuity factor (see page 258):

$$= \left\{ \frac{1}{r} - \frac{1}{r(1 + r)^t} \right\}$$

$$= \left\{ \frac{1}{0.05} - \frac{1}{0.05 \times 1.05^{20}} \right\}$$

$$= 12.46$$

$$\text{annuity payment} = \frac{5,000,000 \text{ dirhams}}{12.46}$$

$$= 401,284 \text{ dirhams per annum}$$

The amount per litre is

$$\frac{401,284 \text{ dirhams}}{4,500,000 \text{ litres}} = 0.0892 \text{ dirhams per litre}$$

Progress check 6.12

With regard to investment appraisal what is an equivalent annual cost (EAC)?

Capital budgeting

Investment appraisal techniques are just one part of the capital investment process. They may be used in one form or another as part of a company's capital budgeting process. Capital budgeting should be an incremental decision-making process involving many departments within a business, and not just the finance department, or the accountant, or financial analyst.

Capital budgeting is a process with a distinct number of stages. The capital investment procedures in companies must be designed to allow managers to make optimal investments with the aim of maximisation of shareholder wealth. The main aim of capital budgeting is to ensure that resources are made available to implement capital projects that are value-adding and are aligned with corporate goals. Good investment ideas should not be held back and poor investment ideas rejected or further refined. The steps in the capital budgeting process are:

- determination of the budget
- the search for and development of new investment projects
- evaluation of alternative investment projects
- obtaining approval for new projects
- monitoring and controlling projects.

Capital rationing – the profitability index (PI)

A company may be considering a number of projects in which it may invest. If the business has limited funds available for investment then capital rationing is required. Capital rationing is a restriction on an organisation's ability to invest capital funds and comprises two types: soft capital rationing and hard capital rationing:

- soft capital rationing is a restriction that is caused by an internal budget ceiling being imposed on capital expenditure by senior management, for example via departmental or company capital budgets
- hard capital rationing is as a result of external limitations being applied to the organisation, for example when additional borrowed funds cannot be obtained.

A company may impose a restriction on the amount of funds available to individual divisional heads in order to direct investment funds into particular areas or activities of the company to maximise its returns. Such a restriction would be an example of soft capital rationing. However, where such a restriction exists because of external constraints it would be an example of hard capital rationing. Examples of this may be seen where a company may not be able to raise funds because of a lack of security or collateral, or where restrictions are imposed by existing lenders (for example to limit the level of the company's gearing).

If capital rationing exists, how should a company choose between alternative investment opportunities? One widely used technique is the profitability index, which is an attempt to identify the relationship between the costs and benefits of a proposed project through the use of a ratio. The profitability index ratio is:

$$PI = \frac{\text{present value of future cash flows}}{\text{initial investment}}$$

A ratio of one is the lowest acceptable measure of the index since any value lower than one would indicate that the project's present value of future cash flows is less than the initial investment required to generate the cash flows. Consequently, as the value of the profitability index increases, so does the financial attractiveness of a proposed project. Where there is no restriction on investment capital, all projects with a profitability ratio greater than 1 may be accepted.

It should be noted that the profitability index is only useful where single-period capital rationing exists. This relates to situations where there is a limit on the availability of finance for positive NPV projects for one year only. Where multi-period capital rationing exists there is a limit on the availability of finance for projects with a positive NPV for more than one year, and therefore in that situation the profitability index cannot be used.

Appraisal of investments in single-period capital rationing situations requires the evaluation of competing projects. This uses the profitability index technique, which some companies refer to as DPI (dollar per investment). The PI method requires the ranking of competing projects in terms of their NPVs achieved from each dollar of investment in each project. Of course the PI technique is not just restricted to the US$ and relates to the ranking of competing investments denominated in any currency. Competing investment funds may then be allocated according to the NPV rankings of each investment. Funds should then be allocated for investment in the project with the highest PI, and then funds allocated for investment in the next highest ranked project PI and so on. In this way, the company continues to allocate funds for investment in the 'best' projects up to the total of the capital investment budget that has been set either through soft or hard capital rationing.

Worked example 6.27

A company is considering two projects A and B, with the following estimates of investment cost, present values of future cash flows, and NPVs.

Project	Investment	Present values of future cash flows	NPV
	£	£	£
A	400,000	460,000	60,000
B	800,000	880,000	80,000

Let's consider these projects in terms of capital rationing.

Both projects have an NPV greater than zero and may therefore be accepted. If the projects are mutually exclusive then the company will choose project B because it has a higher NPV than project A.

If the company has capital rationing with a constraint on the amount of funds available for investment then it should consider a PI approach.

$$\text{Project A} \quad PI = \frac{\pounds460{,}000}{\pounds400{,}000} = 1.15$$

$$\text{Project B} \quad PI = \frac{\pounds880{,}000}{\pounds800{,}000} = 1.1$$

Project A has a higher PI than project B, which means that it will return more NPV per £ invested than project B, a return of 15% compared with 10%. Therefore, if the company uses PI criteria then it will choose project A. Assume that there are a number of projects with the same investment and NPV as project A and the maximum funding available for investment is £800,000. The company could invest in two projects type A which will produce a total NPV of 2 × £60,000 = £120,000, compared with an £80,000 NPV from project B.

The PI approach gives the right decision in a single-period capital rationing situation as we have seen in Worked example 6.27, if the total amount of funds available can be used. If there is more than one period then the PI approach will not work. If capital rationing is expected to continue from the current period into future periods then the timing of future cash flows must be considered. For multiple-period capital rationing the NPV per amount available for investment (the limiting factor) must still be maximised but on the assumption that projects may be divisible, and then an optimal solution may be found using linear programming.

Worked example 6.28

Stu VW Ltd is considering five potential new projects, which will involve a capital outlay in 2012 and will then run over the three years 2013, 2014 and 2015. The company's cost of capital is 11% per annum. The capital outlays and expected net cash inflows from each of the projects are as shown below:

Year Project	2012 £000	2013 £000	2014 £000	2015 £000
S	−40	10	30	25
T	0	5	5	5
U	−60	35	40	10
V	−80	30	50	30
W	−30	20	15	20

Each project has the capacity to be reduced to the level of available capital, which means that part investment in projects is allowed in 2012.

Capital for all projects must be paid out in 2012, but Stu VW Ltd has only £120,000 available to apply to projects in 2012 although there are no constraints on capital in subsequent years.

We will consider how Stu VW Ltd may use the limited capital available to maximise corporate value.

First we need to calculate the NPVs of each of the projects. We can then calculate the profitability index (PI) of each of the projects.

$$PI = \frac{NPV}{\text{initial investment}}$$

We have a constraint on the amount of capital available and so we need to rank the projects by their PIs. The rule is that the higher the PI then the higher the ranking of the project.

Project T has no capital outlay and so this project will be undertaken regardless, so long as it returns a positive NPV. The capital constraint will be divided among the other projects according to their ranking.

The NPVs of each project and their PIs have been calculated as follows:

Year	2012	2013	2014	2015		
Discount factor @ 11%	1.00	0.90	0.81	0.73		
					NPV	**PI**
Project	£000	£000	£000	£000	£000	
S	−40.00	9.00	24.30	18.25	11.55	0.289
T	0.00	4.50	4.05	3.65	12.20	
U	−60.00	31.50	32.40	7.30	11.20	0.187
V	−80.00	27.00	40.50	21.90	9.40	0.118
W	−30.00	18.00	12.15	14.60	14.75	0.492

Each project may be ranked according to their PIs:

Ranking	1	2	3	4	5
Project	T	W	S	U	V

Finally we can apply the capital to the projects based on the constraint of £120,000 available:

Project	£000	
T	0	full project
W	30	full project
S	40	full project
U	50	5/6 of project
V	0	no project
Total	120	

Control of capital investment projects

Once a project has been appraised and a sensitivity analysis carried out and the approval has been given at the relevant level in the organisation, project controls must be established and then post-project completion audits carried out. The project controls should cover the three main areas of:

- capital spend – note the number of subjective areas where things can go wrong
- project-timing – delays appear to be 'routine' in many major projects as evidenced almost daily in the financial press (note the new Wembley Stadium project)
- benefits – evidenced almost as frequently in the financial press, this is another area where things may not turn out as planned.

Capital spending limits are usually put in place by most organisations with levels of spend requiring authorisation at the appropriate managerial level. Capital expenditure proposals should be documented to show:

- project details, including costs, benefits, and the life of the project
- appraisal calculations and comparisons with the organisation's targets assumptions
- names of the project manager and the project team
- name(s) and signature(s) of the manager(s) authorising the project
- the period(s) during which expenditure should take place.

Material delays in capital spend or in the progress of the project should prompt a re-submitted proposal together with the reasons for delay. A good project manager with the appropriate level of responsibility and authority should ensure that projects run to plan.

Benefits from projects are not easy to control because they are usually derived over many years. The importance of having a good project manager in place cannot be over-emphasised. The project manager should ensure that expected benefits actually materialise and are as large in value as anticipated. The project manager should also ensure that costs are kept in line with expectation.

Post-implementation audits should be carried out for all projects if possible. Although after the event corrective action cannot usually be taken, variances may be analysed to use the project as an information and learning tool:

- to appraise manager performance
- to identify strengths and weaknesses in the company's forecasting and estimating techniques
- to identify areas of improvement in the capital investment process
- to advertise the fact that both project and manager performance are being monitored.

Progress check 6.13

In what ways can we ensure that capital investment projects are adequately controlled?

Summary of key points

- An investment requires expenditure on something today that is expected to provide a benefit in the future.

- The decision to make an investment is extremely important because it implies the expectation that expenditure today will generate future cash gains in real terms that greatly exceed the funds spent today.

- '£1 received today is worth more than £1 received in a year's time' is an expression of what is meant by the time value of money.

- The present value of a perpetuity may be calculated for a stream of level cash payments that continues indefinitely. The present value of an annuity may be calculated for an equally spaced level stream of cash flows for a limited period of time.

- The principles underlying the investment appraisal techniques that use the discounted cash flow (DCF) method are cash flow (as opposed to profit), and the time value of money.

- Five main criteria are used to appraise investments: accounting rate of return (ARR); payback; net present value (NPV); internal rate of return (IRR); and discounted payback – the latter three being DCF techniques.

- The technique of discounted cash flow discounts the projected net cash flows of a capital project to ascertain its present value using an appropriate discount rate, or cost of capital.

- Additional factors impacting on investment criteria calculations are: the effect of inflation on cash flows and the cost of capital; working capital requirements; length of project; taxation; risk and uncertainty.

- There may be a number of risks associated with each of the variables included in a capital investment appraisal decision: estimates of initial costs; uncertainty about the timing and values of future cash revenues and costs; the length of project; variations in the discount rate.

- Sensitivity analysis, scenario analysis, and simulation may be used to assess the risk and uncertainty associated with a capital investment project.

- To establish the appropriate levels of control, the appointment of a good project manager with the appropriate level of responsibility and authority, together with regular project reviews, are absolute essentials to ensure that projects run to plan.

- The techniques of capital investment appraisal require a great deal of expertise and experience, and specialised training is essential in order to use them in real-life decision-making situations.

Glossary of key terms

accounting rate of return (ARR) Annual profit divided by investment. It is a form of return on capital employed. Unlike NPV and IRR, it is based on profits, not cash flows.

annuity A fixed periodic payment which continues either for a specified time, or until the occurrence of a specified event.

capital rationing This is a restriction on an organisation's ability to invest capital funds, caused by an internal budget ceiling being imposed on such expenditure by management (soft capital rationing), or by external limitations being applied to the organisation, for example when additional borrowed funds cannot be obtained (hard capital rationing).

discounted cash flow (DCF) The discounting of the projected net cash flows of a capital project to ascertain its present value, using a yield or internal rate of return (IRR), net present value (NPV) or discounted payback.

discounted payback The number of years required to repay an original investment using a specified discount rate.

equivalent annual cost (EAC) The yearly annuity payments (or the annual cash flows) sufficient to recover a capital investment, including the cost of capital for that investment, over the investment's economic life.

internal rate of return (IRR) The annual percentage return achieved by a project, at which the sum of the discounted cash inflows over the life of the project is equal to the sum of the discounted cash outflows, that is, when NPV equals zero.

investment Any application of funds which is intended to provide a return by way of interest, dividend, or capital appreciation.

modified internal rate of return (MIRR) The annual percentage return achieved by a project when the initial investment is compared with the terminal value of the project's net cash flows reinvested at the cost of capital. The MIRR is then the return at which the terminal value equals the initial cost.

net present value (NPV) The difference between the sums of the projected discounted cash inflows and outflows attributable to a capital investment or other long-term project.

payback The number of years it takes the cash inflows from a capital investment project to equal the cash outflows. An organisation may have a target payback period, above which projects are rejected.

perpetuity A periodic payment continuing for a limitless period.

present value The cash equivalent now of a sum receivable or payable at a future date.

real option The right to undertake certain business alternatives such as abandoning, expanding, reducing or continuing unchanged a business activity. In general terms the use of real options refers to the appraisal of the cash flow impacts of the various options and making decisions on the basis of those appraisals.

sensitivity analysis A modelling and risk assessment technique in which changes are made to significant variables in order to determine the effect of these changes on the planned outcome. Particular attention is thereafter paid to variables identified as being of special significance.

Assessment material

Questions

Q6.1 (i) What is capital investment?
(ii) Why are capital investment decisions so important to companies?

Q6.2 Outline the five main investment appraisal methods.

Q6.3 Describe the two key principles underlying DCF investment selection methods.

Q6.4 What are the advantages in the use of NPV over IRR in investment appraisal?

Q6.5 What are the factors that impact on capital investment decisions?

Q6.6 (i) What is meant by risk with regard to investment decisions?
(ii) How does sensitivity analysis help?

Q6.7 Describe how capital investment projects may be controlled and reviewed.

Discussion points

D6.1 'I know that cash and profit are not always the same thing but surely eventually they end up being equal. Therefore, surely we should look at the likely ultimate profit from a capital investment before deciding whether or not to invest?' Discuss.

D6.2 'This discounted cash flow business seems like just a bit more work for the accountants to me. Cash is cash whenever it's received or paid. I say let's keep capital investment appraisal simple.' Discuss.

D6.3 'If you don't take a risk you will not make any money.' Discuss.

Exercises

Solutions are provided in Appendix 2 to all exercise numbers highlighted in colour.

Level I

E6.1 Time allowed – 30 minutes

Global Sights & Sounds Ltd (GSS) sells multi-media equipment and software through its retail outlets. GSS is considering investing in some major refurbishment of one of its outlets to enable it to provide improved customer service, until the lease expires at the end of four years. GSS is currently talking to two contractors, Smith Ltd and Jones Ltd. Whichever contractor is used, the improved customer service has been estimated to generate increased net cash inflows as follows:

Year	£
1	75,000
2	190,000
3	190,000
4	225,000

Smith:
The capital costs will be £125,000 at the start of the project, and £175,000 at the end of each of years 1 and 2.

Jones:

The capital costs will be the same in total, but payment to the contractor can be delayed.

Capital payments will be £50,000 at the start of the project, £75,000 at the end of each of years 1, 2 and 3, and the balance of the capital cost at the end of year 4. In return for the delayed payments the contractor will receive a 20% share of the cash inflows generated from the improved services, payable at the end of each year. In the interim period, the unutilised funds will be invested in a short-term project in another department store, generating a cash inflow of £60,000 at the end of each of years 1, 2 and 3.

It may be assumed that all cash flows occur at the end of each year.

The effects of taxation and inflation may be ignored.

> **You are required to advise GSS Ltd on whether to select Smith or Jones, ignoring the time value of money, using the appraisal basis of:**
>
> (i)   accounting rate of return (ARR), and
> (ii) comment on the appraisal method you have used.

E6.2   *Time allowed – 30 minutes*

> **Using the information on Global Sights & Sounds Ltd from Exercise E6.1, you are required to advise GSS Ltd on whether to select Smith or Jones, ignoring the time value of money, using the appraisal basis of:**
>
> (i)   payback, and
> (ii) comment on the appraisal method you have used.

E6.3   *Time allowed – 60 minutes*

Rainbow plc's business is organised into divisions. For operating purposes, each division is regarded as an investment centre, with divisional managers enjoying substantial autonomy in their selection of investment projects. Divisional managers are rewarded via a remuneration package, which is linked to a return on investment (ROI) performance measure. The ROI calculation is based on the net book value of assets at the beginning of the year. Although there is a high degree of autonomy in investment selection, approval to go ahead has to be obtained from group management at the head office in order to release the finance.

Red Division is currently investigating three independent investment proposals. If they appear acceptable, it wishes to assign each a priority in the event that funds may not be available to cover all three. The WACC (weighted average cost of capital) for the company is the hurdle rate used for new investments and is estimated at 15% per annum.

The details of the three proposals are as follows:

	Project A £000	Project B £000	Project C £000
Initial cash outlay on non-current assets	60	60	60
Net cash inflow in year 1	21	25	10
Net cash inflow in year 2	21	20	20
Net cash inflow in year 3	21	20	30
Net cash inflow in year 4	21	15	40

Taxation and the residual values of the non-current assets may be ignored.
Depreciation is straight line over the asset life, which is four years in each case.

You are required to:

(i) give an appraisal of the three investment proposals with regard to divisional performance, using return on investment (ROI) and residual income (RI)

(ii) give an appraisal of the three investment proposals with regard to company performance, using a DCF approach

(iii) explain any divergence between the two points of view, expressed in (i) and (ii) above, and outline how the views of the division and the company can be brought into line with each other.

Level II

E6.4 Time allowed – 30 minutes

Using the information on Global Sights & Sounds Ltd from Exercise E6.1, you are required to:

(i) advise GSS Ltd on whether to select Smith or Jones, using the appraisal basis of net present value (NPV), using a cost of capital of 12% per annum to discount the cash flows to their present value

(ii) comment on the appraisal method you have used.

E6.5 *Time allowed – 30 minutes*

Using the information on Global Sights & Sounds Ltd from Exercise E6.1, you are required to:

(i) advise GSS Ltd on whether to select Smith or Jones, using the appraisal basis of discounted payback, using a cost of capital of 12% per annum to discount the cash flows to their present value

(ii) comment on the appraisal method you have used.

E6.6 *Time allowed – 45 minutes*

Using the information on Global Sights & Sounds Ltd from Exercise E6.1, you are required to:

(i) advise GSS Ltd on whether to select Smith or Jones, using the appraisal basis of internal rate of return (IRR)

(ii) comment on the appraisal method you have used.

E6.7 *Time allowed – 45 minutes*

In Exercise E6.1 we are told that a 20% share of the improved cash inflow has been agreed with Jones Ltd.

You are required to:

(i) calculate the percentage share at which GSS Ltd would be indifferent, on a financial basis, as to which of the contractors Smith or Jones should carry out the work

(ii) outline the other factors, in addition to your financial analyses in (i), that should be considered in making the choice between Smith and Jones.

E6.8 Time allowed – 60 minutes

Alive & Kicking Ltd (AAK) owns a disused warehouse in which a promoter runs regular small gigs.

There are currently no facilities to provide drinks. The owners of AAK intend to provide such facilities and can obtain funding to cover capital costs. This would have to be repaid over five years at an annual interest rate of 10%.

The capital costs are estimated at £120,000 for equipment that will have a life of five years and no residual value. To provide drinks, the running costs of staff, etc., will be £40,000 in the first year, increasing by £4,000 in each subsequent year. AAK proposes to charge £10,000 per annum for lighting, heating, and other property expenses, and wants a nominal £5,000 per annum to cover any unforeseen contingencies. Apart from this, AAK is not looking for any profit as such from the provision of these facilities, because it believes that there may be additional future benefits from increased use of the facility.

It is proposed that costs will be recovered by setting drinks prices at double the direct costs.

It is not expected that the full sales revenue level will be reached until year 3. The proportions of that level estimated to be reached in years 1 and 2 are 40% and 70% respectively.

You are required to:

(i) calculate the sales revenue that needs to be achieved in each of the five years to meet the proposed targets

(ii) comment briefly on four aspects of the proposals that you consider merit further investigation.

You may ignore the possible effects of taxation and inflation.

E6.9 Time allowed – 90 minutes

Lew Rolls plc is an international group that manufactures and distributes bathroom fittings to major building supply retailers and DIY chains. The board of Lew Rolls plc is currently considering four projects to work with four different customers to develop new bathroom ranges (toilet, bidet, bath, basin, and shower).

Rolls has a limit on funds for investment for the current year of £24m. The four projects represent levels of 'luxury' bathrooms. The product ranges are aimed at different markets. The lengths of time to bring to market, lives of product, and timings of cash flows are different for each product range.

The Super bathroom project will cost £3m and generate £5m net cash flows spread equally over five years.

The Superluxury bathroom project will cost £7m and generate £10m net cash flows spread equally over five years.

The Executive bathroom project will take a long time to start paying back. It will cost £12m and generate £21m net cash flows, zero for the first two years and then £7m for each of the next three years.

The Excelsior bathroom project will cost £15m and generate £10m net cash flows for two years. For ease of calculation it may be assumed that all cash flows occur on the last day of each year.

Projects may be undertaken in part or in total in the current year, and next year there will be no restriction on investment. Lew Rolls plc's cost of capital is 10%.

You are required to:

(i)   calculate the NPV for each project
(ii)   calculate the approximate IRR for each project
(iii) advise on the acceptance of these projects on the basis of NPV or IRR or any other method of ranking the projects
(iv)   list the advantages of the appraisal method you have adopted for Lew Rolls plc
(v)   comment on what other factors should be used in the final evaluations before the recommendations are implemented.

E6.10   Time allowed – 90 minutes

A UK subsidiary of a large multinational is considering investment in four mutually exclusive projects. The managing director, Indira Patel, is anxious to choose a combination of projects that will maximise shareholder wealth. At the current time the company can embark on projects up to a maximum total of £230m. The four projects require the following initial investments:

£20m in project Doh
£195m in project Ray
£35m in project Mee
£80m in project Fah.

The projects are expected to generate the following net cash flows over the three years following each investment. No project will last longer than three years.

Project Year	Doh £m	Ray £m	Mee £m	Fah £m
1	15	45	15	20
2	30	75	25	25
3		180	60	100

The company's WACC is 12% per annum, which is used to evaluate investments in new projects. The impact of tax and inflation may be ignored.

Advise Indira with regard to the projects in which the company should invest on the basis of maximisation of corporate value, given the limiting factor of the total funds currently available for investment.

7

Sources of finance and the capital markets

Chapter contents

Learning objectives

Completion of this chapter will enable you to:

- Identify the different sources of external finance available to an organisation and the internal sources, such as retained earnings, trade credit, and gains from more effective management of working capital.

- Compare the company's use of external short-term finance with long-term finance.

- Describe the unique characteristics and rights of equity (ordinary share) finance and debt (loan) finance.

- Outline the importance of dividends, rights issues, scrip (bonus) issues, share splits, scrip dividends, and share buy-backs to companies and investors.

- Explain the use of preference shares as a source of long-term share capital.

- Appreciate the range of debt finance available to companies, for example, loans, debentures, and bonds.

- Evaluate the difference between a redeemable debenture and an irredeemable loan.

- Outline the growing importance of international debt finance and the use of Eurobonds.

- Explain what is meant by hybrid finance, which includes convertible preference shares, convertible bonds, warrants, and mezzanine debt.

- Consider how companies may use leasing as a source of medium- and short-term finance.

- Outline the way in which companies may benefit from UK Government and European sources of finance.

- Explain what is meant by the primary and secondary capital markets, and their importance to companies and investors.

- Outline the various ways in which a company may issue new equity finance, and their advantages and disadvantages.

- Describe the role of the Stock Exchange and the Alternative Investment Market (AIM).

- Outline the roles of financial institutions, such as banks, merchant banks, pension funds, and insurance companies.

- Recognise the increasing growth of Islamic banking and Islamic finance in the UK and worldwide, as an alternative to traditional Western-style banking.

- Appreciate the impact of the global financial crisis that started in 2008, who it affects, and how it happened.

Introduction

This chapter begins with an outline of the types of finance available to businesses. Organisations require finance for short-, medium-, and long-term requirements and the types of financing should usually be matched with the funding requirement. Longer-term finance (longer than one year) is usually used to fund capital investment in non-current assets and other longer-term projects. Short-term finance (shorter than one year) is usually used to fund an organisation's requirement for working capital.

Financing may be internal or external to the organisation, and either short or long term. One of the sources of internal financing is derived from the more effective management of working capital, which is discussed in Chapter 10.

In Chapter 6 we dealt with decisions related to capital investment appraisal – the investment decision. This chapter will consider a number of alternative ways in which company investment may be financed – the financing decision – and includes leasing and Government grants, but will focus on the main sources of long-term external finance available to an organisation: loans (or debt) and ordinary shares (or equity). We will also consider the various ways in which the different types of finance are raised. One of the fundamental differences between equity and debt financing is the risk associated with each, which has an impact on their cost, the determination of which we looked at in Chapter 5.

There are a number of sources of finance that are neither purely equity nor purely debt, but have characteristics that put them somewhere between the two. These are referred to as hybrid finance, and include, for example, convertible loans.

This chapter looks at the markets in which long-term financial securities are traded, and which are called the capital markets. Primary capital markets are the markets in which investors, both private individuals and financial institutions, provide funds for companies, which require new long-term finance by way of equity or debt. The secondary capital markets are the markets in which investors may sell and buy their securities, which are also a source of financial information for current and potential investors and for pricing information with regard to the primary markets. The main secondary markets are stock exchanges, the most important in the UK being the London Stock Exchange.

The chapter closes with a look at the range of financial institutions used by organisations and the roles they fulfil in corporate financing, and provides an introduction to the growing area of Islamic finance and Islamic banking.

Sources of finance internal to the business

The sources of finance available to a company may be regarded very broadly as being provided from within the company or provided from sources external to the company. These two sources are called internal finance and external finance.

Internal finance may be provided from retained earnings (or retained profit), extended trade credit, and cash improvements gained from the more effective management of working capital (see Figure 7.1).

Retained earnings

Retained earnings (retained profit) is reported in a company's balance sheet as the residual profit for the year that remains after all costs, net interest charges, and corporation tax charges have been deducted, and ordinary share dividends payable and minority interests have been accounted for. This is the amount of profit that is added to the equity of the company in the balance sheet under the heading retained earnings. The accumulated retained earnings of the company are increased by the net profit for the year less any dividends payable; they are part of the shareholders' funds and therefore appear on the balance sheet within the equity of the company. Similarly, losses will reduce the equity of the company.

The profit earned in a year is not the same as the cash flow for the year, because profit includes non-cash items like depreciation. It is also because the transactions from which profit is derived are generally not all realised in cash when they occur. These are the differences relating

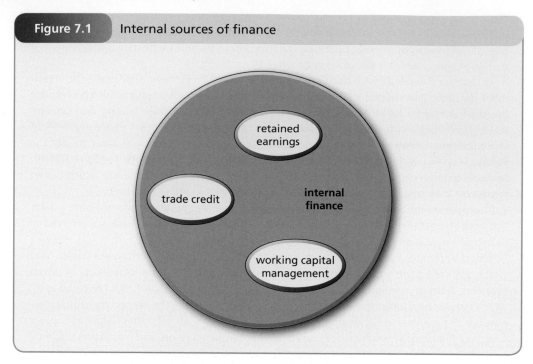

Figure 7.1 Internal sources of finance

to changes in the working capital requirement of inventories plus trade receivables minus trade payables. In addition, profit does not include items like purchases of non-current assets or funds received from loans or new share issues.

Cash flow is represented by the movements in and out of cash (notes and coins), bank accounts, and bank deposits, the balances of which are shown as assets in the balance sheet. If cash is borrowed either by bank overdraft or bank loans then these are shown as liabilities in the balance sheet.

The retained earnings shown in a company's balance sheet as a part of shareholders' equity is not totally represented by the cash and bank balances (less any loans and overdrafts) also shown in the balance sheet as assets (and liabilities). Retained earnings includes sales revenue and is the surplus after deductions for:

- the operational costs of running the business
- net interest payable
- corporation tax payable
- dividends payable,

but all sales revenues may not yet have been received in cash and all operational costs, interest, tax, and dividends may not yet have been paid out of cash. In addition, retained profit does not include:

- cash paid to increase or replace non-current assets
- cash received from loans or the issue of shares,

which are both items that are not related to the operational activities of the business.

It is the operational cash flow (minus interest, tax, and dividends actually paid) that is the real internal source of finance rather than retained earnings. Companies may have high levels of retained profits and earnings per share, but little or no cash or borrowings. It is cash not profit that is required for investment.

There is statistical evidence that shows that through the 1990s the majority of capital funding of UK companies continued to be derived from internal sources of finance. Retained earnings is the primary source of internal finance, and there are a number of reasons for this:

- it is the shareholders who approve at the annual general meeting (AGM) how much of the company's earnings will be distributed to shareholders as dividends, the balance being held as retained earnings and reinvested in the business
- unlike with an issue of additional ordinary shares or loan stock, there are no administrative or legal costs, and no dilution of control
- unlike with an increase in debt, there is no increase in risk to the company arising from security required from charges over its assets
- retained earnings are immediately available and easily accessible provided the company has sufficient cash.

Trade credit

Trade payables are often seen as a 'free' source of internal finance. This really is not the case, and extended payment terms that may be negotiated with suppliers inevitably include a cost. Extended credit terms will usually mean that a cost of this additional financing will already have been factored into the price charged for the product or service. When discounts are offered by suppliers for early settlement, for example 1% discount for payment one month early (12% per annum), it immediately becomes apparent that the supplier's selling price must have included some allowance for finance charges. Therefore trade payables are a source of finance but it is not free.

Large companies may employ the unethical policy of delaying payment to their suppliers, particularly small businesses or 'unimportant' suppliers, to enhance cash flow. While delay of payments may occasionally be required to alleviate a short-term cash problem it really should be considered only as a last resort and regarded as a temporary measure. It is not only unethical, but it is not conducive to the development of good supplier relationships.

Working capital management

The more effective management of the company's operating cycle or working capital requirement as an additional source of internal finance is discussed in Chapter 10.

The choice between the use of external and internal finance by companies, for growth, new investment projects, and expansion of their operations, involves major policy decisions. The use of retained earnings as a means of internal financing, while immediately accessible, is not free. The cost of shareholders' equity is a reflection of the level of dividends paid to shareholders, which is usually dependent on how well the company has performed during the year. The profit or net earnings generated from the operations of the company belongs to the shareholders of the company. There is a cost, an opportunity cost, which is the best alternative return that shareholders could obtain on these funds elsewhere in the financial markets. The amount of earnings retained is dependent on a company's dividend and profit retention policy. A company which maintains a low level of dividend cover (earnings per share divided by dividend per share) is likely to require a lower proportion of external funding than a company with a high dividend cover.

In general, companies may have sufficient cash flow from their normal operations to be able to use retained earnings for small investments or, for example, for replacement of furniture and equipment. If companies do not have sufficient cash flow from operations, or if they are considering large new investment projects, then it is more likely that they will require a larger proportion of external finance in the form of debt or equity.

Regardless of whether external finance is in the form of debt or equity, issue costs will inevitably be incurred. While dividends do not have to be paid by the company, interest payment is a commitment for the company and this increases the level of financial risk faced by the company.

> ## Progress check 7.1
>
> What are the differences between the three main sources of internal finance available to a company?

Short-term external sources of finance

The decision by companies on the use of either short-term or long-term funding should really be made with regard to the uses for which the funding is required. The risk and return profiles of the uses of the funding should be matched with risk and return profiles of the funding. The financing of the acquisition of long-term, or non-current, assets should be provided from long-term funding. The financing of the acquisition of short-term assets, or net current assets or working capital requirements, should normally be provided from short-term funding. At a personal level, for example, it would not make economic sense to finance the purchase of one's house with short-term finance such as a bank overdraft, which is repayable on demand. House purchase is normally funded with a long-term mortgage.

The level of working capital requirement comprises inventories and trade receivables less trade payables, which are all constantly changing. The funding of an investment in the working capital requirement therefore needs to be flexible in line with its changing levels. Short-term financial debt includes the elements of overdrafts, loans, and leases that are repayable within one year of the balance sheet date. Short-term finance tends to be more expensive, but more flexible than long-term debt and usually does not require any security. Short-term debt is therefore normally matched to finance the fluctuations in levels of the company's net current assets, its working capital.

Short-term finance generally incurs a higher interest rate than long-term finance, and it represents a higher level of risk for the borrower. Interest rates can be volatile, and an overdraft, for example, is technically repayable on demand. The company may finance its operations by taking on further short-term debt, as levels of working capital increase. Because of the higher risk associated with short-term debt, many companies adopting a conservative funding policy may accept a reduction in profitability and use long-term debt to finance not only non-current assets, but also a proportion of the company's working capital. Less risk-averse companies may use short-term debt to finance both working capital and non-current assets; such debt may be attractive because there is no commitment to pay a fixed level of interest over an extended period.

The main sources of external short-term finance are overdrafts, short-term loans, and leasing (see Figure 7.2).

Overdrafts

A bank overdraft is borrowing from a bank on a current account, which is repayable on demand. The maximum overdraft allowed is normally negotiated and agreed with the bank prior to the facility being made available. Interest, which is calculated on a daily basis, is charged on the

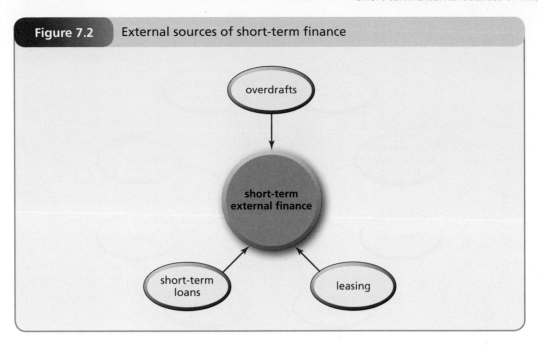

Figure 7.2 External sources of short-term finance

amount borrowed, and not on the agreed maximum borrowing facility. In addition to overdraft interest, banks normally charge an initial fee for setting up an overdraft facility and an annual fee for its re-negotiation and administration.

Most businesses are regularly financed to some extent by overdrafts. They are flexible but are risky in terms of their being immediately repayable on demand by the bank. This may represent a problem to companies that are using overdrafts to finance other than working capital requirements but may be unable to easily obtain longer-term financing.

Short-term loans and leasing

Companies may occasionally obtain loans from banks or others, which are repayable within one year, in which case they are called short-term loans. However, loans and financial leases are generally sources of long-term finance (see the section on long-term external sources of finance below). The reason for including these topics in this section on short-term finance is to explain their appearance in the current liabilities section of company balance sheets.

In the *liabilities* part of a company's balance, within the section *current* (or short-term) *liabilities*, the heading *borrowings and finance leases* includes the elements of overdrafts, loans and leases that are payable within one year of the balance sheet date. An overdraft is technically repayable within one year of the balance sheet date and so only appears within *borrowings and finance leases* within the section *current liabilities*. The heading *borrowings and finance leases* also appears in the *liabilities* part of a company's balance sheet, within the section *non-current liabilities*. This includes the long-term elements of loans and leases that are expected to be payable after one year of the balance sheet date.

Progress check 7.2

Why do companies have overdrafts?

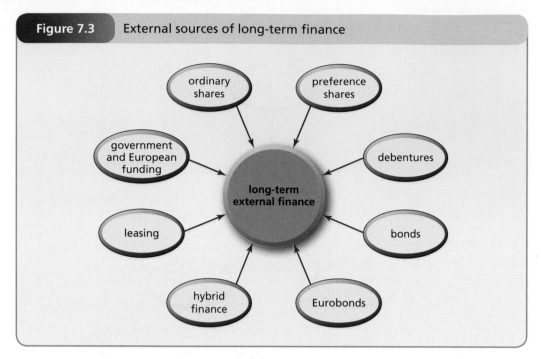

Figure 7.3 External sources of long-term finance

Long-term external sources of finance

As we have discussed above, in matching the risk and return profiles of funding with the risk and return profiles of the uses of that funding, long-term funding should be used for the acquisition of long-term non-current assets. Non-current assets include land, buildings, machinery, and equipment. External sources of long-term finance (see Figure 7.3) include:

- **ordinary shares** (or equity shares)
- **preference shares**
- loan capital (financial debt that includes bank loans, **debentures**, and other loans)
- **bonds**
- **Eurobonds**
- **hybrid finance** (**convertible bonds**, **warrants**, and **mezzanine debt**)
- leasing
- UK Government funding
- European funding.

The two main primary sources of long-term finance available to a company, which are both external, are broadly:

- equity share capital (ordinary shares)
- debt (long-term loans),

and each has a unique set of characteristics and rights. The main ones are shown in the table in Figure 7.4.

The choice by a company of which of the various types of long-term external sources of finance to use depends on a number of factors, which include, for example:

- the type of company (plc or Ltd)
- the company's financial status

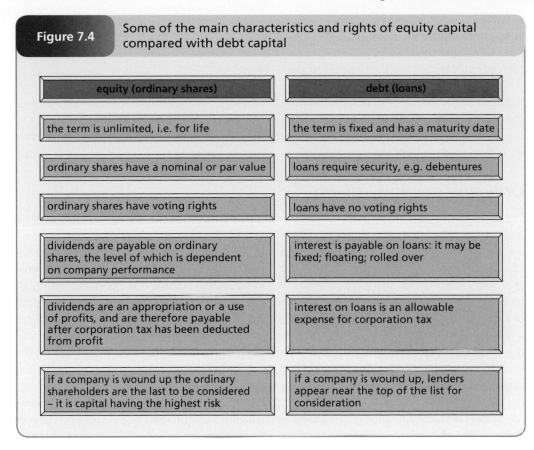

Figure 7.4 Some of the main characteristics and rights of equity capital compared with debt capital

equity (ordinary shares)	debt (loans)
the term is unlimited, i.e. for life	the term is fixed and has a maturity date
ordinary shares have a nominal or par value	loans require security, e.g. debentures
ordinary shares have voting rights	loans have no voting rights
dividends are payable on ordinary shares, the level of which is dependent on company performance	interest is payable on loans: it may be fixed; floating; rolled over
dividends are an appropriation or a use of profits, and are therefore payable after corporation tax has been deducted from profit	interest on loans is an allowable expense for corporation tax
if a company is wound up the ordinary shareholders are the last to be considered – it is capital having the highest risk	if a company is wound up, lenders appear near the top of the list for consideration

■ the company's ability to provide security
■ the cost of the individual source of finance
■ the company's existing capital structure (which we discussed in Chapter 5).

Each of the factors influencing a company's choice of financing is likely to depend on the stage it has reached in its development. For example, a start-up company is unlikely to be making profits or generating high levels of operating cash flow. The original investors in a start-up company are usually unlikely to be able to provide all the cash required in the early years to cover start-up costs, research and development, investment, and operational requirements. Therefore, outside investors are usually sought. These may perhaps be venture capitalists who provide developing companies with either equity or debt capital for a relatively short period after which time they withdraw, having usually received a very high return on their capital.

Growth companies, which have emerged from the start-up phase and established themselves in their particular markets, are likely to be making modest profits and have sufficient cash flows for operational requirements. However, they are still likely to have additional cash requirements for investment in future growth. This may be acquired from debt or equity, or a combination of the two, or from leasing for example. The choice will depend on the company's individual circumstances, its growth prospects, and how it is perceived by potential investors.

Mature companies will be well established in their particular markets. They are likely to be generating significant profits and cash flows, but with limited growth prospects. Shareholders in mature companies will expect high levels of dividends because there may be no scope for share price growth. Since the level of new, 'real', risky investment by a mature company may be low, it is unlikely to require additional equity financing. On the other hand, it may seek debt financing in order to reduce its WACC in order to increase shareholder value and deter hostile takeover bids by making the business too expensive.

The choice of financing will be considered in more detail in Chapters 14 and 15, when we will look at the financial strategies that may be adopted during each of the above stages in a company's life cycle, and in Chapters 16 and 17, which deal with mergers and acquisitions. The role of venture capitalists is considered in more detail in Chapter 14, and in Chapter 18 when we look at management buy-outs (MBOs).

Ordinary, or equity shares

The equity of a company includes its share capital and accumulated earnings retained to date and since the business commenced trading. Share capital comprises ordinary shares and preference shares (see below). Ordinary shares entitle the shareholders to the profits remaining after all other prior charges, including interest on loans, corporate taxation, and for example preference share dividends, have been met. When a business is formed the maximum number of shares that the company is ever likely to need is determined at the outset in its memorandum of association and this level is called its authorised share capital. The number of shares actually in issue at any point in time is normally at a level for the company to meet its foreseeable requirements. These shares are called the company's issued share capital which, when all the shareholders have paid for them, are referred to as fully paid-up issued share capital. Issued ordinary share capital represents the long-term capital provided by the owners of a company.

Ordinary shares have a nominal value (or par value) of, for example, 25p or £1 or US$1 or 10 riyals. The nominal value of the shares is decided when the level of authorised shares is decided. The shares cannot then be issued to shareholders for less than their nominal value. When shares are issued to shareholders they are usually issued at a premium. For example, 10,000 £1 shares may be issued for a total value of funds raised of £25,000. This means that share capital is raised amounting to £10,000 (nominal value) in addition to a share premium of £15,000. Both amounts are shown within the equity section of the company's balance sheet but under two separate headings: *ordinary shares*; and the *share premium account*.

After shares have been issued they may be bought and sold by investors between each other in the case of a private (Ltd) company, or via a stock exchange in the case of a public (plc) company. The subsequent sale and purchase of ordinary shares after the initial issue of shares provides no further funds for the company and has no impact on its balance sheet. The level of activity in the selling and buying of shares is a factor of their demand and depends on the view taken by investors of their future returns by way of an increase in share price and future dividend flows.

Ordinary shareholders receive a dividend at a level determined usually by company performance and not as a specific entitlement. The level of dividends is usually based on the underlying profitability of the company (Tesco plc actually advised their shareholders of this relationship in the late 1990s). In addition, ordinary shareholders normally have voting rights (whereas lenders and preference shareholders do not).

Ordinary shareholders have voting rights attached to their shares, which allow them to vote at the annual general meeting (AGM). There is an additional class of shares called non-voting shares, which have no voting rights.

When a company goes into receivership an administrator is appointed who draws up a list of creditors to which the company owes money including the government, suppliers, employees, lenders, and ordinary shareholders. The ordinary shareholders are always last on the list to be repaid. Ordinary shareholders are paid out of the balance of funds that remains after all other creditors have been repaid. As ordinary shares therefore represent capital of the highest risk to investors, then ordinary shareholders expect the highest returns compared with the returns from other investments.

Additional equity capital may be raised through issuing additional shares up to the level of authorised share capital. A company may increase its number of shares through making **scrip** **issues** and **rights issues**. A scrip issue (or **bonus issue**) increases the number of shares with the additional shares going to existing shareholders, in proportion to their holdings, through capitalisation of the reserves, or retained earnings, of the company. In a scrip issue no cash is called for from the shareholders. In a rights issue, the right to subscribe for new shares (or loans) issued by the company is given to existing shareholders, and additional cash is raised by the company.

Dividends

The return expected by investors in the highest-risk securities, ordinary shares, comprises capital appreciation in the form of share price increases and income in the form of dividends. The dividend decision, or earnings retention decision, is strategically very important to a company with regard to five key areas:

- the views and expectations of shareholders
- the level of profits being made by the company
- the use of retained earnings for financing new investment
- the level of the company's cash resources
- the way in which surplus funds should be used should suitable investment opportunities be unavailable.

After a company has paid all its expenses, costs, interest, and corporate taxes, what is left is the net profit that effectively belongs to the shareholders. With regard to the five points above, a level of dividends may be proposed by the directors and declared for cash payment by the company in the UK usually every six months (in the USA usually every three months), with reference to its level of profitability. In the UK an interim dividend is paid halfway through the company's financial year, and the final dividend is paid after the end of the financial year. It is paid after the year end because the shareholders need to approve the final dividend at the company's annual general meeting (AGM).

In general, a company must be making profits in order to declare a dividend and it must have the cash available in order to pay a dividend. Profits may include those for the current year and past profits so that according to the Companies Act 2006 dividends may be paid out of accumulated net realised profits. A dividend is not an expense but an appropriation of profit and as such is not an allowable deduction for corporation tax. Income tax is normally paid by shareholders on the dividends they receive.

The level of a company's financial gearing, its proportion of debt compared with equity capital, has an effect on the level of dividends it may pay. If the company is highly geared then it has a comparatively high proportion of debt and therefore a commitment to paying high levels of interest. A high level of interest payments means a lower level of profit and cash with which to pay dividends. The company's decision to pay dividends is also affected by its requirement for the funding of new capital investment projects. The cost of using its retained earnings may be cheaper for the company, and so that cost should be compared with that of external sources of finance (see the sections in Chapter 5 about cost of capital).

Before considering the use of retained earnings for new investment by paying a lower level of dividends to shareholders the company must also consider the effect that this may have on shareholders and the share price.

The declaration of a dividend has an impact on a company's share price. The share price may change immediately a dividend is announced and is called a *cum dividend* share price. The share price remains *cum dividend* during a period when whoever holds the shares will receive the dividend. At a given date the entitlement to the dividend ceases and the share price becomes *ex dividend*. Everything being equal, the difference between the *cum dividend* share price and *ex dividend* share price will be the amount of dividend per share.

We will further consider the effect of dividends on share prices in more detail in Chapter 15 when we look at the theories of dividend relevance and irrelevance.

Rights issues

Companies have a legal obligation to first offer any new shares that they decide to issue to their existing shareholders. The term rights issues is used to describe such issues of new shares, which are normally for multiples of the shares held, for example two new shares for every one share held.

The 'rights' to buy the new shares are usually fixed at a price discounted by around 10% to 20% below the current market price. A shareholder not wishing to take up a rights issue may sell the rights. Discounts are offered in order to attract existing shareholders. The announcement of the offer of a rights issue by a company may immediately change the share price of the company, which is then called the *cum rights* share price. The *cum rights* share price will initially increase to reflect the right to apply for new shares at a price less than the market price. The share price remains *cum rights* for the period up to when the rights issue offer closes, during which time whoever holds the shares will have the right to receive or sell their rights. At the offer close date the entitlement to the rights ceases and the share price becomes *ex rights*. Everything being equal, the *ex rights* share price will then drop.

The amount of discount on the current share price that is offered to existing shareholders is chosen by the company at a level that makes the rights issue attractive to investors. However, the resultant rights issue share price will have an impact on the earnings per share of the company (see Worked example 7.1).

Worked example 7.1

A company that achieves a profit after tax of 10% on capital employed has the following capital structure:

2,000,000 ordinary shares of £1	£2,000,000
Retained earnings	£500,000

In order to invest in some new profitable projects the company wishes to raise £780,000 from a rights issue. The company's current ordinary share price is £1.50.

The company would like to know the number of shares that must be issued if the rights price is: £1.30; £1.25; £1.20.

Capital employed is £2.5m [£2m + £0.5m]
Current earnings are 10% of £2.5m = £250,000

$$\text{Therefore, earnings per share (eps)} = \frac{£250,000}{2,000,000}$$
$$= 12.50p$$

After the rights issue, earnings will be:

10% of £3.28m [£2m + £0.5m + £0.78m] = £328,000

Rights price £	Number of new shares £780,000 divided by the rights price	Total shares after rights issue new plus old shares	eps £328,000 divided by total shares pence
1.30	600,000	2,600,000	12.62
1.25	624,000	2,624,000	12.50
1.20	650,000	2,650,000	12.38

We can see that at a high rights issue share price the eps are increased. At lower issue prices eps are diluted. The 'break-even point', with no dilution, is where the rights share price equals the current capital employed per share £2.5m/2m = £1.25.

A rights issue may also have an impact on shareholder wealth. If existing shareholders fully take up their rights entitlement and either hold the shares or sell them, in any proportion, their wealth position will be unaffected (see Worked example 7.2). If existing shareholders do not exercise their rights the number of shares they hold will be unchanged but their wealth will have reduced because the *ex rights* share price is likely to be lower than the *cum rights* share price.

Worked example 7.2

A company has 1,000,000 £1 ordinary shares in issue with a market price of £2.10 on 1 June. The company wished to raise new equity capital by a one-for-four share rights issue at a price of £1.50. Immediately the company announced the rights issue the price fell to £1.95 on 2 June. Just before the issue was due to be made the share price had recovered to £2 per share, the *cum rights* price.

The company may calculate the *ex rights* price, the theoretical new market price as a consequence of an adjustment to allow for the discount price of the new issue.

The market price will theoretically fall after the issue, as follows:

1,000,000 shares × the *cum rights* price of £2	£2,000,000
250,000 shares × the issue price of £1.50	£375,000
Theoretical value of 1,250,000 shares	£2,375,000

Therefore, the theoretical *ex rights* price is	$\dfrac{£2,375,000}{1,250,000} = £1.90$ per share

Or to put it another way

Four shares at the *cum rights* value of £2	£8.00
One new share issued at £1.50	£1.50
	£9.50
Therefore, the theoretical *ex rights* price is	$\dfrac{£9.50}{5} = £1.90$ per share

Generally the costs of a rights issue are lower than any other method of issuing shares to the public. If all the rights are taken up by the existing shareholders then there is no dilution of their current shareholdings. However, if they do not take up all their rights then their holdings will be diluted. Existing shareholders may not have sufficient funds to take up all their rights if the issue is very large. For this reason, rights issues may be the most appropriate method for relatively small share issues.

Scrip, or bonus issues

We have discussed the way in which retained earnings may be used as a source of funding by a company. Retained earnings may also be converted into share capital and issued at no cost to existing shareholders on a *pro rata* basis. Such issues of new shares are called scrip issues, or bonus issues, and no cash is required from shareholders. The number of issued shares increases but the total equity of the company remains unchanged; it is merely its composition that changes. Scrip issues may be made by companies whose share price is relatively high and therefore a trading constraint. However, the share price may fall because of earnings dilution.

Share splits

When a company makes a share split it increases the number of shares in issue but correspondingly reduces the nominal value of the shares. This is done in such a way that the total nominal value of ordinary shares in the balance sheet remains as it was before the share split.

The possible reasons for their use are similar for both scrip issues and share splits:

- a share reconstruction may signal confidence in the investments that profit retention has been used to fund
- a reduction in the value of each share may put them into a more marketable price range and theoretically increase their liquidity – an idea contradicted by some academic research because of higher transaction costs and lower trading volumes
- shareholders may feel that a share reconstruction has in some way increased their wealth and while some research has disputed this, other research has given some credibility to the idea of share splits giving the perception by shareholders of a favourable impact regarding the company's greater capacity to pay dividends in the future.

Scrip dividends

A scrip dividend, or share dividend, is yet another way in which a company may issue new equity without raising additional finance. A company may give more shares in the company to existing shareholders, either partially or totally, instead of paying cash dividends. As a result of the company paying a scrip dividend the share price should not fall. However, scrip dividends are taxed in the same way as cash dividends, unless the shareholder is exempt from paying tax.

Scrip dividends have some impact on the company, the big benefit obviously being that no cash is required to pay out scrip dividends, and they may be issued at very little cost. The company's financial gearing may decrease slightly, because of the increase in shares, which may or may not be to the company's advantage.

Share buy-backs

In the UK, a company may buy back its shares from its shareholders so long as they have given their permission for this at a general meeting of the company. This may be made by the company via the market or by a tender to all its shareholders. It is a method of returning cash to shareholders, which is an alternative to paying dividends. However, the company may usually only pay for the shares it buys back out of distributable profit. The exception to this is a share buy-back that may be permitted from a fresh issue of shares (Companies Act 2006).

There are a number of possible reasons why a company may want to buy back its own shares:

- It is a method of returning capital to shareholders.
- It is a method of increasing gearing.
- If gearing is increased with little increase in financial risk the share price should increase, and so the re-purchase by the company of its shares is now a tactic used quite widely in the UK as a defence against a hostile takeover.
- The number of shares is reduced and so earnings per share will be increased.
- Capital employed is reduced and therefore the return on capital employed will be increased.

A **share re-purchase** (or **share buy-back**) is an alternative method to dividends of returning value to shareholders. Share buy-backs benefit shareholders because the return of their funds enables them to reinvest or use their capital in a more effective way. The value per share of the reduced number of shares is also increased, and the market share price should also increase.

A company may use a share buy-back as a method of managing its capital structure and its weighted average cost of capital (WACC). This may therefore provide the opportunity for investments in projects that may otherwise have been rejected because of inadequate net present values. A disadvantage may be the increase in gearing of the company. However, the main advantages to the company are that eps and ROCE will be increased.

Share buy-backs can therefore be seen to be very closely linked with dividend policy, which is discussed in more detail in Chapters 13 and 15.

Progress check 7.3

What are ordinary shares and what are their distinguishing features?

Preference shares

Preference shares receive a dividend at a level that is fixed and, subject to the conditions of issue of the shares, they have a prior claim to any company profits available for distribution. No ordinary share dividends may be paid until all preference share dividends have been fully paid. Preference shareholders may also have a prior claim over ordinary shareholders to the repayment of capital in the event of the company being wound up.

Preference shares are part of a company's share capital and the cost to the company of issuing preference shares is similar to the cost of issuing ordinary shares, but whereas ordinary shares have voting rights, preference shares do not. They do bear some risk for investors. Preference shares risk is higher than that of debt capital, but at a far lower level than that of ordinary shares. Debt capital has a lower risk than preference shares because:

■ loan interest must be paid before preference dividends are paid
■ debt-holders have a prior claim over preference shareholders to the repayment of capital in the event of the company being wound up
■ debt capital normally has security based on one or more of a company's assets, whereas preference shares have no security.

Preference shares are normally cumulative preference shares that entitle the shareholders to a fixed rate of dividend and include the right to have any arrears of dividend paid out of future profits with priority over any distribution of profits to the holders of ordinary share capital. There are a further five classes of preference shares:

■ participating preference shares entitle their holders to a fixed dividend and, in addition, the right to participate in any surplus earnings after payment of agreed levels of dividends to ordinary shareholders has been made
■ zero dividend rate preference shares receive no dividends throughout the life of the shares
■ variable dividend rate preference shares have their dividend agreed at a fixed percentage plus, for example, LIBOR (London Interbank Offered Rate of interest), rather than receiving a fixed level of dividend, or they may have a variable dividend which is set at regular intervals to a market rate by means of an auction process between investors known as AMPS (auction market preferred stock) – auction market securities are money market financial instruments, created in 1984, which reset dividends at a rate that is fixed until the next auction date, when the securities adjust with a new yield to reflect market conditions
■ redeemable preference shares are issued on terms which require them to be bought back by the issuer at some future date, in compliance with the conditions of the Companies Act 2006, either at the discretion of the issuer or of the shareholder
■ convertible preference shares have terms and conditions agreed at the outset, which provide the shareholder with the option to convert their preference shares into ordinary shares at a later date.

There are advantages and disadvantages in the use of preference shares by companies and investors. As with ordinary shares, the company does not have to pay dividends on preference shares if there are insufficient profits, and for this reason preference shareholders may expect higher returns. However, if preference shares are cumulative, then dividends will eventually have to be paid. In the same way as ordinary share dividends, preference share dividends are not allowable for corporation tax. A disadvantage for the company is that because preference shares bear a higher risk than debt capital, and they have no tax shield, then the cost of preference share capital is likely to be higher than debt capital.

The use of preference shares has been particularly popular in situations where venture capitalists (VCs) are involved, for example in new business start-ups and management buy-outs (MBOs). We will discuss the way in which this may operate in Chapter 18. VCs may also consider convertible preference shares, which may be converted into ordinary shares at a later date, as a means of further benefiting from a successful new venture.

Progress check 7.4

In what ways do preference shares differ from ordinary shares?

Long-term loans

Generally, companies should try and match their longer-term financing with the purpose for which it is required, and the type of assets requiring to be financed which include:

■ non-current assets
■ long-term projects.

Long-term debt is normally matched to finance the acquisition of non-current assets, which are long-term assets from which the company expects to derive benefits over several future periods. It is usually more expensive and less flexible than short-term debt but has, to some extent, less risk for the investor than short-term debt.

Whereas dividends paid on shares are an appropriation of profit and therefore paid out of the company's after tax profit, interest payable on long-term loans (and short-term loans and overdrafts) is an expense. Loan interest and overdraft interest is therefore deducted from profit before tax, and therefore the effective cost of interest is reduced by the amount of the corporation tax rate. For example, if corporation tax were at 30% per annum, a loan on which interest is payable at 10% per annum would actually cost the company 7%, that is {10% − (10% × 30%)}. The amount by which the interest is reduced because of the effect of corporation tax is called the tax shield.

Long-term financial debts are the elements of loans and leases that are payable after one year of the balance sheet date. Debt capital may take many forms: loans, debentures, mortgages, etc. Each type of long-term debt requires interest payments and capital repayment of the loan and, in addition, security or collateral is usually required. Loan interest is a fixed commitment, which is usually payable once or twice a year. But although debt capital is burdened with a fixed commitment of interest payable, it is a tax-efficient method of financing because interest payments are an allowable deduction for corporation tax whereas dividends are not.

Debentures

Debentures and other long-term loans are long-term debt, which have a nominal, or par value of normally £100 in the UK. They may also have a market price, which is determined by their market demand related to their level of risk, interest rate, and period of issue. Debentures, long-term loans, and bonds are terms that are often taken to mean the same thing and may be for periods of between 10 and 20 years or more. Long-term loans may be either unsecured, or secured on some or all of the assets of the company. Lenders to a company receive interest, payable yearly or half-yearly, at a rate called the coupon rate, which may vary with market conditions. A debenture, which is a type of bond, more specifically refers to the written acknowledgement of a debt by a company, usually given under its seal, and normally containing provisions as to payment of interest and the terms of repayment of the principal. A debenture may be secured on some or all of the assets of the company or its subsidiaries. Other long-term loans are usually unsecured.

The debenture trust deed includes details that relate to:

- period of the loan
- security for the loan
- power to appoint a receiver
- interest rate and payment terms
- financial reporting requirements
- redemption procedures
- restrictive covenants.

Security for a debenture may be by way of a floating charge, without attachment to specific assets, on the whole of the business's assets. A floating charge is a form of protection given to secured creditors, which relates to the assets of the company, which are changing in nature. Often current assets like trade receivables or inventories are the subject of this type of charge. In the event of default on repayment, in which the company is not able to meet its obligations, the lender may take steps to enforce the floating charge so that it crystallises and becomes attached to current assets like trade receivables or inventories. Floating charges rank after certain other prior claims if a company goes into liquidation.

Security for a debenture may alternatively, at the outset, take the form of a fixed charge on specific assets like land and buildings. A fixed charge is a form of protection given to secured creditors, which relates to specific assets of the company. The charge grants the lender the right of enforcement against the identified asset, in the event of default on payment, so that the lender may realise the asset to meet the debt owed. Fixed charges rank first in order of priority if a company goes into liquidation.

Debentures are relatively low-risk investments for investors, and therefore returns will be much lower than those demanded by equity shareholders. They are a tax-efficient method of corporate financing, which means that interest payable on such loans is an allowable deduction in the computation of taxable profit. The cost of long-term financial debt to companies therefore tends to be relatively low. However, the higher the proportion of debt that a company has, the higher the level of financial risk it faces, as a result of its having to pay interest and the possibility that debt-holders may force the company to cease trading and realise its assets should it have difficulty in servicing (or repaying) the loan.

A company may buy back its debentures on the open market, whether they are redeemable or irredeemable, which may be an advantageous method of cancelling their debt if the market price is below its par value. However, if they are redeemable debentures then sufficient cash must be found by the company for their repayment at the due dates. The consequences of a company not being able to meet its redemption commitments may result in lenders exercising their right to call a creditors meeting and appoint a receiver. A company may try and ease the burden of redemption in a number of ways:

- inclusion in the trust deed of the option of early redemption by the company at any time up to the redemption date rather than on the redemption date, with or without compensation to the debt-holders
- re-financing through replacement of the redeemable debt with a new debt issue having a later redemption date, using what is called a rollover bond
- creation of a sinking fund, in which money is put aside periodically and invested in perhaps a bond to provide a return which together with the principal will produce the required sum at the redemption date.

Lenders may try and protect themselves from the consequences of the company failing to meet its interest and capital repayment commitments, by preventing changes to the company's risk profile, through the inclusion of restrictive covenants in the debenture trust deed, for example:

- a minimum current ratio (current assets divided by current liabilities) or quick ratio (current assets minus inventories, divided by current liabilities) reflected in the company's balance sheet
- conditions relating to the disposal of non-current assets
- restrictions on taking on additional debt and/or equity and maintenance of a specific level of financial gearing
- restrictions on amounts of dividends payable and if the company does not fulfil the covenant conditions, then the trust deed will provide lenders with the right to seek immediate repayment in full.

Interest – fixed and floating rates

Loans may be taken by companies, which require payment of interest at either fixed or floating rates. A floating interest rate is generally linked to LIBOR (London Interbank Offer Rate of interest); for example, interest may be payable at LIBOR plus 2%. If a company expects that interest rates in the future may rise then it may try and protect itself with a loan that has a fixed interest rate. However, if future interest rates actually fall then there is an opportunity cost to the company, which could have been paying lower interest charges had it not committed to a fixed rate loan. If the company expects that interest rates in the future may fall then it may try and protect itself with a loan that has a floating interest rate, so that it may take advantage of lower future market rates.

However, if lenders fear that future interest rates may fall then they may prefer a loan with a fixed interest rate. If lenders expect that future interest rates may rise then they may prefer the flexibility of a loan with a floating interest rate, to be in line with market rates.

Progress check 7.5

What is long-term debt and what are its distinguishing features?

Bonds – medium-term and long-term debt capital

There are many different types of debt instruments, of which the bond is perhaps the most popular. It is defined as a debt instrument, normally offering a fixed rate of interest (coupon) over a fixed period of time, and with a fixed redemption value (par). A debenture is often referred to as a bond.

The level of the risk relating to bonds, in terms of future interest payments and principal repayment, is measured by a number of organisations with reference to a standard risk index. Companies like Standard & Poor's and Moody's carry out detailed financial analyses of specific companies, which have issued bonds regarding their forecast financial performances, and also general economic analyses and analysis of the financial markets. The resultant ratings for such bonds are indicated by letters assigned to them that denote their level of quality and risk. For example, Moody's highest rating for a particular bond is Aaa and its lowest rating is C. The rating, and perhaps more importantly any rating downgrading of a bond is likely to have a serious negative impact on its market value.

A bond is a negotiable debt instrument of which there are broadly three varieties:

- domestic bond
- foreign bond
- Eurobond.

A domestic bond is a bond issued in the country in which the borrower is domiciled. It is a negotiable debt instrument denominated in the home country currency and essentially available for domestic distribution only.

A foreign bond is a bond issued in the country other than that in which the borrower is domiciled. It is a negotiable debt instrument denominated in the local currency of the issuer, but available for international distribution.

A Eurobond is a bond issued outside the country of its currency (see the next section below). Such bonds may be issued by borrowers domiciled in almost any country, and may also be acquired by investors domiciled in almost any country.

Bonds and loans may be irredeemable or redeemable debt in which case the principal, the original sum borrowed, will need to be repaid on a specific date. Irredeemable bonds are not particularly common and so most bonds are redeemable. Irredeemable bonds are perpetual bonds and have no redemption date. The value of an irredeemable bond (V_0) may be calculated (see Worked example 7.3) in the same way as one would value a perpetuity, by dividing the annual amount of interest payable on the debt (i) by the market rate of return on debt expected by investors (R_d):

$$V_0 = \frac{i}{R_d}$$

The value of redeemable debt (V_0) may be found (see Worked example 7.4) by using the DCF method to calculate the present value of future interest plus the present value of the future redemption value of the debt after n years (V_n), which is usually its par value, using the market rate of return on debt expected by investors (R_d):

$$V_0 = i/(1 + R_d) + i/(1 + R_d)^2 + i/(1 + R_d)^3 + \cdots + (i + V_n)/(1 + R_d)^n$$

There is a wide range of types of bond, some of which we have already described, the most popular being:

- fixed rate bonds
- zero coupon bonds
- floating rate bonds – bonds, issued at a deep discount on their par value, on which no interest is payable and which are attractive to investors seeking capital gains rather than income from interest
- sinking fund bonds
- rollover bonds
- convertible bonds – debts which are convertible to equities at a later date.

Worked example 7.3

A Government stock, which has a par value of £100, offers a fixed annual income of £5, but there is no obligation to repay the capital. The market return on debt expected by investors is 5.5%.

We are required to calculate the market value of this irredeemable debt.

$$i = £5 \qquad R_d = 5.5\%$$

Using

$$V_0 = \frac{i}{R_d} \text{ the market value of the debt} = \frac{£5}{0.055} = £90.91$$

The market value is less than, or at a discount to, the par value of the debt, because the loan stock is paying less than the expected market rate.

Worked example 7.4

A bond has a par value of £100 and pays 7% per annum and is redeemable at par in three years' time. The return expected by investors in this particular bond market is 6.5% per annum. We are required to calculate the market value of this redeemable bond.

$$i = £7 \qquad R_d = 6.5\% \qquad n = 3 \text{ years} \qquad V_n = £100$$

Using

$$V_0 = i/(1 + R_d) + i/(1 + R_d)^2 + i/(1 + R_d)^3 + \cdots + (i + V_n)/(1 + R_d)^n$$

The market value of the bond is

$$
\begin{aligned}
&= 7/(1.065) + 7/(1.065)^2 + (7 + 100)/(1.065)^3 \\
&= £6.57 + £6.17 + £88.58 \\
&= £101.32
\end{aligned}
$$

The market value is more than, or at a premium to, the par value of the bond, because the bond is paying more than the expected market rate.

International debt finance and Eurobonds

As global trade and the need for international finance increases, the use of international debt instruments, and in particular debt instruments such as bonds, is an area of growing importance to international financial managers. A company may have a subsidiary company in a foreign country; it may finance its subsidiary by borrowing in the subsidiary's local currency or in some other currency if it feels that its lower interest rate gains outweigh any risk of losses through exchange rate fluctuations. A Eurobond is long-term debt that facilitates such foreign borrowing.

The Eurocurrency market is described by Buckley (Buckley, A (2004) *Multinational Finance*, London: FT/Prentice Hall) as a market in which 'Eurobanks accept deposits and make loans denominated in currencies other than that of the country in which the banks are located'. A Eurobond is a type of bearer bond, issued in a Eurocurrency, usually US$, with maturities of 5 to 15 years. A bearer bond is a negotiable bond or security whose ownership is not registered by the issuer, but is presumed to lie with whoever has physical possession of the bond. A Eurobond is denominated in a currency other than that in the country in which the bond is issued. It is therefore outside the control of that country and may be bought and sold in different countries by governments and companies.

For the past 25 years or so, Eurobonds have become increasingly more attractive to lenders and borrowers for a number of reasons:

- existence of few regulatory requirements in the Eurobond markets
- increasing flexibility of such instruments
- relative ease with which such bonds may be raised.

As a consequence, the Eurobond market has grown substantially in size over the same period. The advantages of the Eurobond market for both borrowers and lenders arise because of the substantial size of the market, its ability to absorb frequent issues, and its now established institutional framework. Such advantages include the following:

- lower borrowing costs inherent in the Eurobond market
- higher deposit rates inherent in the Eurobond market
- the increased convertibility of Eurobonds
- the existence of not only a primary market but also an active secondary market for both lenders and borrowers (see the later sections in this chapter about capital markets).

Mini case 7.1

In recent years Eurobonds have become increasingly popular in emerging markets and especially in Eastern Europe, despite the Eurozone crisis. The popularity of the Eurobond in Eastern Europe continued to surge in early 2012.

At the beginning of April 2012, the Bulgarian cabinet gave a mandate to finance minister, Simeon Dyankov, to start a procedure for placing euro-denominated government securities on the international markets. The value of the issue was to be €950m and would be used to finance the maturing of €818.5m of debt plus interest in early 2013. Just prior to this, Hungary's debt management agency AKK announced that it was considering coming to the Eurobond market to fund all or part of its €4.6bn refinancing needs for the year and only days before state-owned Russian Railways raised 25m roubles with a seven-year Eurobond. The attractiveness of the market to Russia was apparent when in May Gazprombank intimated that it was about to issue US$ Eurobonds with a five-year maturity on the Irish stock exchange. This came only weeks after the bank sold a US$500m Eurobond with a yield of 7.25% on 27 April 2012.

The Eurobond market, which trades in bonds issued in Eurocurrencies, needs to be distinguished from the new Euro Bond which was mooted in 2012. The new Euro Bond is a bond issued by a sovereign state, for example Greece, but whose coupon payments and principal payments are underwritten by all EU states. This bond is therefore a collective debt, making bonds issued by financially weaker EU states more attractive to investors as the bonds are backed collectively by the stronger EU states.

The key factors that an international company should consider when exploring the possibility of raising international debt capital and determining a debt policy are the same as many of the factors relevant to a domestic company. However, these factors and the different types of debt capital available should be considered in an international context.

The key factors a company needs to take into account when developing a borrowing strategy or a debt policy can be divided into two groups:

- external factors, or factors related to external perceptions of the company
- internal factors, or factors related to the internal policy-making structure within the company.

The emphasis placed on the above external and internal factors will depend on the nature, level, and composition of borrowing the company is considering, and whether it is:

- short-term – less than one year
- medium-term – between one year and 10 years
- long-term – over 10 years,

or a combination of each of these.

Generally, the external factors include:

- the overall business risk profile of the company
- the debt-servicing ability of the company
- the borrowing constraints imposed on the company or industrial sector by lenders, or government regulation and legislation
- the perceived gearing norm for the particular industrial sector.

Factors which are more internal to the company would include:

- the maturity profile of the company's existing debt
- the impact of additional debt on its financial gearing
- the interest rate mix of existing debt and new debt
- the availability of security for additional debt
- the potential impact of interest rate changes and exchange rate changes on both existing debt and new debt.

When seeking to reconcile the conflicting pressures of all the above internal and external factors, the company should seek to ensure that:

- the debt maturity profile of its existing debt matches its asset maturity profile
- where possible it maintains a balanced combination of fixed and floating rate debt
- where possible debt maturity is overlapped to avoid excessive outflows of cash or near cash resources and any associated liquidity problems.

Progress check 7.6

Explain the use of Eurobonds as long-term debt.

Hybrid finance – convertibles, warrants, and mezzanine debt

Loans may sometimes be required by companies particularly as they progress through a period of growth, their growth phase. These loans are usually required by companies to finance specific asset acquisitions or projects. Some of the disadvantages of the use of loans rather than equity are:

- the increase in financial risk resulting from a reduction in the amount of equity compared with debt
- the commitment to fixed interest payments over a number of years
- the requirement of an accumulation of cash with which to repay the loan on maturity.

Alternatively, if an increase in equity is used for this type of funding, eps (earnings per share) may be immediately 'diluted'.

However, some financing is neither totally debt nor equity, but has the characteristics of both. Such hybrid finance, as it is called, includes financial instruments like convertible loans (and convertible preference shares which we mentioned earlier in the section about preference shares).

Convertible loans

A convertible loan is a 'two stage' financial instrument. It may be a fixed interest debt, which can be converted into ordinary shares of the company at the option of the lender. Eps will therefore not be diluted until a later date. The right to convert may usually be exercised each year at a pre-determined conversion rate up until a specified date, at which time the loan must be redeemed if it has not been converted. The conversion rate may be stated as:

- a conversion price (the amount of the loan that can be converted into one ordinary share)

or

- a conversion ratio (the number of ordinary shares that can be converted from one unit of the loan).

The conversion price or ratio will be specified at the outset and may change during the term of the loan. The conversion value equals the conversion price multiplied by the conversion ratio and is the market value of the ordinary shares into which the loan may be converted. Conversion values are below the issue values of loans when they are issued, and as the conversion date approaches they should increase if the ordinary share price has increased so that investors will want to convert. The difference between the conversion value and the market price of the loan is called the conversion premium. The market price of the loan, and therefore the market premium are determined by the:

- likelihood of investors converting according to market expectation
- current and expected conversion values
- amount of time left to conversion.

There are two aspects to the valuation of a convertible bond:

- the conversion value of a convertible bond after n years (V_n) must be at a level which makes conversion attractive to investors, and its value depends on an estimate of what the ordinary share price (S) will be at the conversion date
- the current value of a convertible bond (V_0) depends on its future conversion value.

If the expected annual percentage growth rate of the share price is g and the number of ordinary shares that will be received on conversion is N, then the conversion value of the convertible bond (V_n) may be calculated as:

$$V_n = S \times (1 + g)^n \times N$$

The current market value of the convertible bond (V_0) may be found (see Worked example 7.5) by using the DCF method to calculate the present value of future annual interest (i) plus the present value of the bond's conversion value after n years (V_n), using the market rate of return on bonds expected by investors (R_d):

$$V_0 = i/(1 + R_d) + i/(1 + R_d)^2 + i/(1 + R_d)^3 + \cdots + (i + V_n)/(1 + R_d)^n$$

When convertible debt is first issued its market value will be the same as its redemption value. The conversion value will initially be less than the redemption value, but as the ordinary share price increases over time the conversion value will become increasingly greater than the redemption value. During the period up to conversion, the market value of the debt will be greater than the conversion value, because investors will expect that the share price will increase even further in the future, but it converges towards the conversion value at the conversion date.

Worked example 7.5

A convertible bond with a par value of £100 pays 6% per annum and on the redemption date in three years' time may be converted into 50 ordinary shares or redeemed at par. The current share price is £2 and it is expected to grow by 7% per annum. An investor requires a return of 6.5% per annum and we are required to advise the maximum price that they should be prepared to pay currently for the bond.

$$S = £2 \qquad g = 7\% \qquad N = 50$$

Using

$$V_n = S \times (1 + g)^n \times N$$

the conversion value of the bond is

$$V_n = £2 \times (1.07)^3 \times 50 = £122.50$$

The conversion value is higher than the par value of £100 and so an investor would choose to convert.

The present values of the future cash flows can then be calculated to determine the current market value of the bond V_0.

$$R_d = 6.5\% \qquad i = £6 \qquad V_n = £122.50$$

Using

$$V_0 = i/(1 + R_d) + i/(1 + R_d)^2 + i/(1 + R_d)^3 + \cdots + (i + V_n)/(1 + R_d)^n$$

the current market value of the bond is

$$V_0 = 6/(1.065) + 6/(1.065)^2 + (6 + 122.50)/(1.065)^3$$
$$V_0 = £5.63 + £5.29 + £106.38$$
$$V_0 = £117.30$$

The maximum price that should be paid currently for the bond is therefore £117.30.

Loans and bonds are generally lower-risk investments for investors than ordinary shares.

Therefore, an advantage for investors in convertible bonds is that initially they may make a lower-risk investment in a company and monitor its performance over a period of time before deciding to convert their bonds at a later date into higher-risk ordinary shares. If the company's performance has not been particularly good and the share price has not risen sufficiently then investors may decide not to convert. This may be a disadvantage for the company if the convertible bonds then run their term to their maturity at which time the company will have to redeem them for cash. If the company's performance has been good and the share price has increased then at the conversion date the convertible bondholders have the choice of deciding to convert their bonds into ordinary shares.

The big advantage for companies of convertible bonds compared with straight loans is that under normal circumstances they do not have to be redeemed with cash. Convertibles increase the company's gearing to a higher level than investors may wish, but this may be acceptable since they know that gearing will again be reduced to an acceptable level when conversion takes place.

Although convertible bonds may eventually be converted into equity capital, until that time the company has the use of capital by paying interest at a lower cost than the cost of equity and which is allowable for corporation tax, which lowers its effective cost of capital even further. If the company feels that at the time it is looking to raise new capital its shares are under-priced and the company is undervalued, then convertible bonds may be an ideal alternative to an issue of equity.

Convertibles tend to pay a lower rate of interest than straight loans, which is effectively charging lenders for the right to convert to ordinary shares. They also pay a fixed rate of interest. Therefore, they provide benefits in terms of the company's cash flow as well as cost of financing, and facilitate accurate forecasting of interest payments. However, any increase in the debt of a company increases gearing and interest payments, which reduce profits, and therefore reduces earnings per share. The increase in gearing also increases the level of financial risk faced by the company during the period up to when conversion takes place. Dilution of earnings per share and the level of control of the existing ordinary shareholders will also occur on conversion.

Progress check 7.7

What makes convertible loans attractive sources of finance to both investors and companies?

Warrants

Bond issues are sometimes made that include what are called warrants, or the rights to buy new ordinary shares in the company at a later date at a fixed share price called the exercise price. A warrant is defined as a financial instrument that requires the issuer to issue shares (whether contingently or not) and contains no obligation for the issuer to transfer economic benefits (FRS 25 and IAS 32).

The warrant itself may be considered separately from the bond and traded. The reason for the inclusion of warrants in bond issues is to try and make the issue even more attractive to investors, who may then be able to reduce the cost of their investments by selling off the warrants. Therefore, for investors a bond issue with warrants provides a cost-effective investment that is also less risky than ordinary shares.

An advantage gained by companies from the issue of bonds with warrants is that the interest rate will normally be lower than that paid on straight loans. The level of additional ordinary shares as a result of exercising the warrants will normally be less than with convertible bonds, which means less impact on gearing and earnings per share. Making the bond issue more attractive to investors by including warrants should make the issue successful. This may be the case even if the company is unable to provide the levels of security that may normally be required for similar straight loans.

The calculation of what is called the intrinsic value of a warrant (V_W) is the current price of the ordinary shares (S), minus the exercise price (E), multiplied by the number shares (N) provided by each warrant:

$$V_W = (S - E) \times N$$

The market value of a warrant is actually higher than its intrinsic value by what is called its time value, because of possible growth in the share price:

$$\text{intrinsic value} + \text{time value} = \text{market value of warrant}$$

Warrants also possess gearing, which relates to the relationship between the movement in warrant value and the movement in share price. This is best illustrated with a worked example.

Worked example 7.6

A company's loan stock has warrants attached to it, which entitle their holders to purchase 10 ordinary shares at an exercise price of £3 per share. The current share price is £4. We will calculate the intrinsic value of the warrant and evaluate the gearing effects of a share price increase and decrease over a year to £5 and £3 respectively.

Using

$$V_W = (S - E) \times N$$

the intrinsic value of the warrant is

$$V_W = (£4 - £3) \times 10 = £10$$

If the share price rises to £5, the intrinsic value of the warrant becomes

$$V_W = (£5 - £3) \times 10 = £20$$

So a 25% increase in share price results in a 100% increase in warrant value. The gain from buying and holding the warrant is proportionately greater than the gain from buying and holding ordinary shares.

If the share price falls to £3, the intrinsic value of the warrant becomes

$$V_W = (£3 - £3) \times 10 = £0$$

So a 25% decrease in share price results in a 100% decrease in warrant value to zero. The loss from buying and holding the warrant is proportionately greater than the loss from buying and holding ordinary shares.

Mezzanine debt

Another type of hybrid finance is called mezzanine finance. Mezzanine finance is unsecured debt finance but its risk/return profile is somewhere between debt and equity. Its level of risk is higher than that of loans with security, but lower than ordinary shares, and it is lower on the list of priority payments than straight debt, should the company go into receivership or liquidation. Because of this the interest rate for mezzanine debt is relatively high, typically at around 5% or more plus LIBOR. Mezzanine debt is usually provided by banks and normally may be convertible into ordinary shares or includes warrants for the option to buy new shares.

Mezzanine debt is often used to finance company takeovers, and also MBOs (management buy-outs). The reason for this is that it gives investors the opportunity of capital gains from exercising warrants or convertibles if the buy-out successfully results in high performance and an increase in share price. However, the downside risk of mezzanine finance is faced by both the company and investors.

Leasing

Leases are contracts between a lessor and lessee for the hire of a specific asset. Why then is leasing seen as a source of long-term financing? There are two types of leases, the **operating lease** and the **finance lease**, and the answer to the question lies in the accounting treatment of the latter. Under both types of leasing contract the lessor retains the ownership of the asset but gives the lessee the right to use the asset over an agreed period in return for specified rental payments in accordance with IAS 17 (International Accounting Standard 17: Leases). The lease term is the period for which the lessee has contracted to lease the asset and any further terms for which the lessee has the option to continue to lease the asset with or without further payment; which option the lessee will exercise is reasonably certain at the inception of the lease (see IAS 17).

An operating lease is any lease other than a finance lease. It is a rental agreement for an asset, which may be leased by one lessee for a period, and then another lessee for a another period, and so on. The lease period is normally less than the economic life of the asset, and the lease rentals are charged as a cost in the income statement of the lessee as they occur. The leased asset does not appear in the lessee's balance sheet, and so an operating lease is a method of off balance sheet financing. IAS 17 requires a company to disclose in its balance sheet only the lease payments due to be paid in the next accounting period. The lessor is responsible for maintenance and regular service of assets like photocopiers, cars, and personal computers. The lessor therefore retains most of the risks and rewards of ownership.

A finance lease is a non-cancellable agreement between a lessor and a lessee and it relates to an asset where the present value of the lease rentals payable amounts to at least 90% of its fair market value at the start of the lease. The lessee is usually responsible for all service and maintenance of the asset. The term of a finance lease usually matches the expected economic life of the asset. The primary period of a finance lease relates to the main period of the lease during which the lessor recovers the capital cost of the asset, plus a return, from the lease payments made by the lessee. During the secondary period of a finance lease the lessee may continue to lease the asset for a nominal sum, which is called a peppercorn rent.

Under a finance lease the legal title to the asset remains with the lessor, but the difference in accounting treatment, as defined by IAS 17, is that a finance lease is capitalised in the balance sheet of the lessee. A value of the finance lease is shown under non-current assets, based on a calculation of the present value of the capital part (excluding finance charges) of the future lease rentals payable. The future lease rentals are also shown in the balance sheet as long- and short-term creditors. A lessee in a finance lease, although not the legal owner, therefore has substantially all the risks and rewards of ownership of the asset transferred to him by the lessor.

The main differences between an operating lease and a finance lease are:

- an operating lease is for the rental of an asset for a specific purpose over a short period of time, but a finance lease covers the economic life of the asset

- an operating lease can easily be terminated but a finance lease is non-cancellable
- obsolescence risk is borne by the lessor in an operating lease, but by the lessee in a finance lease
- an operating lease is typically more expensive than a finance lease.

In the UK prior to the mid-1980s the main factor in the growth in popularity of leasing was the benefit derived from its treatment for taxation. Before 1984 there was no distinction between a finance lease and an operating lease and both were seen as off balance sheet financing. In 1984 the taxation incentives were reduced but leasing continued to grow in popularity for other reasons. In April 1984 SSAP 21 distinguished more clearly between operating and finance leases, requiring finance leases to be capitalised in companies' balance sheets. This point was also made in IAS 17, which was issued in 1997.

Both operating and finance leases provide a source of finance if a company has a liquidity shortage because it means that the company does not have to provide the whole of the funding for the purchase of an asset at the outset. Even if borrowing is an option, some companies, and particularly start-up companies, may lack assets of sufficient quality to provide security for borrowing. Leasing may also still provide taxation benefits if the tax situations of the lessee and lessor are different.

In addition to being a source of funding, leasing may also be used by a company to increase cash or alleviate a cash flow problem. Assets may be sold by a company to a leasing company and then leased back from them. In 2001 the international law firm Denton Wilde Sapte advised the board of Marks & Spencer plc on the structured sale and leaseback of 78 stores across the UK for a cash consideration of £348m to Topland Group Holdings Ltd, a privately owned real estate investment group. Under this deal, Topland would lease the stores back to Marks & Spencer over the next 26 years for £24.6m per year at an annual rental increase of 1.95%.

An operating lease may be an answer to the obsolescence problem because assets like personal computers may be leased for periods of, say, up to one year and then exchanged for the latest models and acquired under a new operating lease. An operating lease still remains off balance sheet with regard to there being no requirement for the asset and the liability to be disclosed in a company's balance sheet.

A company may buy an asset outright for cash. The alternatives are to borrow funds for the purchase, or to lease. The decision to invest in the acquisition of an asset is one decision, the investment decision; the borrowing or leasing as a source of finance is a separate decision, the financing decision.

The investment decision and the financing decision may be made separately in either order or they may form a combined decision, and should take account of a number of factors:

- the asset purchase price and its residual value
- the lease rental amounts and the timing of their payments
- service and maintenance payments
- tax:
  - capital allowances for purchased non-current assets
  - tax-allowable lease rental expenses
- VAT (relating to the asset purchase and the lease rentals)
- interest rates (the general level of rates of competing financing options).

The leasing decision evaluation process involves appraisal of the investment in the asset itself, its outright purchase or lease, and an evaluation of leasing as the method of financing, and in order to achieve an optimal result the decision may be considered in three ways:

- first make the investment decision, then find the optimal financing method – but in this case an investment may be rejected which would otherwise have been accepted if low-cost financing had been considered

- evaluate both the investment and the financing method together – involving very advanced investment and financing appraisal techniques
- first make the financing decision, then evaluate the investment – the two decisions are separate and so to evaluate the financing it may be assumed that the investment decision has already been made and then leasing and borrowing may be compared using DCF, the appropriate discount rate being the lessee's cost of borrowing.

In the following worked example it has been assumed that the decision to invest has already been made. The example looks at the comparison between borrowing and lending as the method of financing the investment.

Worked example 7.7

Bollees Ltd intends to buy a machine on 14 May 2009, when it would be 'qualifying plant and machinery' for a 40% first-year capital allowance against UK corporation tax. Bollees expected the machine to have a useful economic life of five years. The cost of the machine is £100,000.

Bollees Ltd does not have surplus cash available and so it will have to borrow funds for outright purchase at 10% per annum, and since it would own the machine it would also have to pay maintenance costs of £1,500 per annum.

Alternatively, the machine could be leased using an operating lease. The lease payments would be £25,000 per annum for five years, which are allowable for tax, and are payable at the beginning of each year, and maintenance costs would be borne by the lessor.

Bollees pays corporation tax on its taxable profits for each year, payable in each of the following years, at 30% per annum. It may claim 40% of the cost as a capital allowance in the first year and then 25% per annum on a reducing balance basis.

It is assumed that an appropriate capital investment appraisal has been made and that this is a viable investment for the company.

We will evaluate each of the options to determine whether Bollees Ltd should borrow to buy, or lease the machine.

The two alternatives for the company are leasing and borrowing, and so the relevant cash flows of the two alternatives can be compared using Bollees Ltd's after-tax cost of borrowing, which is 10% $\times$ (1 − 0.30), or 7%.

The capital allowances on the machine over five years are:

Year		
1	£100,000 $\times$ 0.4 =	£40,000
2	£60,000 $\times$ 0.25 =	£15,000
3	£45,000 $\times$ 0.25 =	£11,250
4	£33,750 $\times$ 0.25 =	£ 8,437
5	balancing allowance	£25,313
		£100,000

Bollees Ltd's deductions allowed for tax are the capital allowances and the maintenance costs.

Year	Capital allowances £	Maintenance costs £	Total deductions £	30% tax relief £	Year tax relief taken
1	40,000	1,500	41,500	12,450	2
2	15,000	1,500	16,500	4,950	3
3	11,250	1,500	12,750	3,825	4
4	8,437	1,500	9,937	2,981	5
5	25,313	1,500	26,813	8,044	6

The present values of the costs of leasing and of borrowing can now be compared.

Cost of borrowing present value

Year	Loan £	Maintenance costs £	30% tax relief £	Net cash flow £	Discount factor at 7%	Present value £
0	(100,000)			(100,000)	1.00	(100,000)
1		(1,500)		(1,500)	0.93	(1,395)
2		(1,500)	12,450	10,950	0.87	9,527
3		(1,500)	4,950	3,450	0.82	2,829
4		(1,500)	3,825	2,325	0.76	1,767
5		(1,500)	2,981	1,481	0.71	1,052
6			8,044	8,044	0.67	5,389
						(80,831)

Cost of leasing present value

Year		Cash flow £	Discount factor at 7%	Present value £
0–4	lease payments	25,000	4.39	(109,750)
2–6	30% tax relief	7,500	3.83	28,725
				(81,025)

We can see that the cost of leasing present value of £81,025 is greater than the cost of borrowing present value of £80,831, and so on a DCF basis Bollees Ltd should borrow funds for purchase rather than lease.

Other factors should be considered, such as the impact of borrowing on Bollees Ltd's financial gearing and its cost of capital. If the investment were to be reappraised using a revised cost of capital then on a DCF basis it may be rejected.

> ### Progress check 7.8
>
> In what ways may a company use leasing as a source of finance?

UK Government and European Union funding

Businesses involved in certain industries or located in specific geographical areas of the UK may from time to time be eligible for assistance with financing. This may be by way of grants, loan guarantees, and subsidised consultancy. Funding may be on a national or a regional basis from various UK Government or European Union sources.

By their very nature, such financing initiatives are continually changing in format and their areas of focus. In the UK, for example, funding assistance has been available in one form or another for SMEs, the agriculture industry, tourism, former coal and steel producing areas, and parts of Wales.

This type of funding may include support for the following:

- business start-ups
- new factories
- new plant and machinery
- research and development
- IT development.

There are many examples of funding schemes that currently operate in the UK. For example, the Government, via the Department for Business, Innovation and Skills (BIS), can provide guarantees for loans from banks and other financial institutions for small businesses that may be unable to provide the security for conventional loans. Via the various regional development agencies, they may also provide discretionary selective financial assistance in the form of grants or loans for businesses that are willing to invest in 'assisted areas'. The BIS and Government Business Link websites, *www.bis.gov.uk* and *www.businesslink.gov.uk*, provide up-to-date information of all current funding initiatives.

The Welsh Assembly's use of European Structural Funds (ESFs) assists businesses in regenerating Welsh communities. For example, through a scheme called match funding, depending on the type of business activity and its location, ESFs can contribute up to 50% of a project's funding. The balance of the funding is provided from the business's own resources or other public or private sector funding. Websites like the Welsh European Funding Office website, *www.wefo.wales.gov.uk*, provide information on this type of funding initiative.

The capital markets

In principle, in the same way as estate agents bring together buyers and sellers in the property markets, the capital markets provide the means by which investors and companies, and national and local governments requiring long-term finance are brought together. This long-term finance may be debt (loans, debentures, bonds, Government securities) or equity (ordinary shares). The information available in the capital markets includes companies' announcements and press statements relating to, for example, dividends and profit forecasts, companies' interim and year-end reports and accounts, and general economic and financial information relating to, for example, inflation rates, current and forecast interest rates, and market indices.

The capital market in which new equity and debt capital is initially raised by companies from investors is called the primary capital market. The issue of shares by a company to obtain a listing on a stock exchange is done through what is called an **initial public offering (IPO)**. Investors include private individuals and financial institutions like pension funds and insurance companies.

There are five other methods used in the UK (see the section on new share issues below) by which funds may be raised through the issue of ordinary shares:

- **placings**, and **intermediary offers**
- **offers for sale**, and **issues by tender**
- **introductions**.

The capital markets also provide the means by which equity or debt may be transferred between one investor and another. The secondary markets include stock exchanges and stock markets on a worldwide basis, which provide the marketplace in which local and international securities may be traded. Stock exchanges have a primary market role as well as a secondary market role.

In small, private companies with few shareholders, the mechanism by which shareholders are able to sell or dispose of their shares is quite cumbersome. They first need to find a buyer for their shares – an existing shareholder, or a relative or friend. They next need to obtain a valuation of the business in order to calculate a share price. This usually means that such shares are not easily transferable and this difficulty is usually reflected in a lower share price than if the shares had been easily transferable.

For larger companies with many shareholders this would obviously be impractical, and companies themselves do not hold reserves of cash in order to redeem investors' securities. The secondary market is therefore essential for investors to be able to readily sell their investments, and also for investors to buy additional investments to add to their holdings. This means that securities listed on a stock exchange therefore have a high degree of liquidity, which is reflected in their value. The secondary market also provides a marketplace of investors in which organisations may raise additional long-term finance.

The most important long-term securities, which are traded in the capital markets, were discussed in earlier sections of this chapter, and include:

- ordinary, or equity shares
- preference shares
- long-term loans
- debentures
- bonds
- Eurobonds
- convertible bonds.

Government securities, like gilt-edged securities and UK Treasury bills, are also traded in the capital markets.

Ideally the capital markets should reflect perfectly fair prices of securities; they should aim to be markets that are perfectly efficient. Market efficiency is measured in terms of the amount and quality of market data available to investors and potential investors and their impact on market prices. We discussed the various forms of market efficiency (weak, semi-strong, and strong forms) and the efficient market hypothesis in Chapter 4.

New issues

Initial public offerings (IPOs)

In start-up businesses the ordinary shares are usually owned by the founder(s) of the business, and by family and friends, or possibly by other investors (maybe venture capitalists, seeking a gain in their value as the business develops). As a company grows it may need to make important decisions with regard to:

- raising further equity share capital, in order to finance its growth, at levels much higher than the founders of the business or their friends and family are willing or able to afford

or

- offering its shares for sale by making them publicly available and freely traded, to realise gains in their value for the founders or other investors.

The way in which a business may action these decisions is to go from being an unquoted company to become a quoted company. It does this by 'going public' – by making an initial public offering (IPO) of shares in the company. This means that shares are offered for sale to the general public and to financial institutions which are then listed and traded on stock exchanges – in the UK, the London Stock Exchange (LSE) or the Alternative Investment Market (AIM – see below). The Public Offer of Securities Regulations 1995 governs the new issue of shares of unlisted companies in the UK.

A company seeking an IPO requires an adviser, sponsor, or broker, for example a merchant bank, to manage the listing process. The responsibilities of the sponsor or broker (which in practice may be the same organisation) include:

- advice regarding the offer price of the shares
- the timing of the issue
- preparing and issuing a prospectus
- liaising with the stock exchange
- marketing the share issue to individual and institutional investors.

There is no guarantee that 'going public' with a new share issue will be successful. It very much depends on the current state of the financial markets but also on the company's past record of sales and profitability, and its growth potential, and the credibility and experience of its managers and directors. A company seeking a full listing on the LSE must comply with a number of important criteria, which are included in what's called its Purple Book, the main ones being:

- an issue of a prospectus that includes financial performance forecasts and other information required by prospective investors
- a minimum of 25% of the shares must be owned by the public after the listing
- any controlling shareholder must not interfere with the company's independent decision-making and operations
- the company must have made sales for at least three years up to the listing date from an independent business activity
- there should not have been any significant changes in directors and senior managers of the business over the previous three years
- a minimum market capitalisation of £700,000
- audited accounts of the company must be provided for the past three years.

Placings and intermediary offers

A company may offer to issue its shares to selected institutional investors like insurance companies and pension funds using a placing. The institutions are approached by the company's sponsor, a merchant bank or stockbroker, prior to the issue taking place when the shares are offered at a fixed price. The company's sponsor underwrites the issue and therefore takes up any unplaced shares. This method also has the advantage of lower costs than other issue methods.

Other institutional and individual investors and the general public are not able to buy shares that have been placed until after the listing and official dealing takes place. Placings are therefore used specifically by companies as a method of issuing their shares to institutions and so the spread of shareholding is initially narrower than with other share issue methods.

An intermediary offer is effectively the same as a placing, but in this case the shares are placed with financial intermediaries like stockbrokers. The brokers other than the ones advising the company may then receive an allocation of the shares, which they can then distribute to their clients. This method therefore enables a wider spread of the shareholding than a placing.

Offers for sale and issues by tender

If a company is seeking a listing for the first time and it is a large share issue then the issue method used is usually an offer for sale. It is the method that must be used for share issues worth £30m or more. The company's broker and sponsor advise the company about the issue price, which is fixed prior to the offer and needs to be at a level that will attract investors but also at a level sufficient to raise the level of funds required for a given number of shares. The shares are initially sold to the company's sponsor, which is an issuing house like a merchant bank, which also underwrites the issue. This means that they will take up any shares that may not be taken up by institutions and individual investors. The issuing house may also arrange for sub-underwriting of the issue with other financial institutions to ensure that the company receives the funds it requires and to avoid any risk of the issuing house having to take up large numbers of shares itself.

The shares are offered for sale at a fixed price by the issuing house to institutions and individual investors by sending out a prospectus and share application forms. In the UK the prospectus must be published in the national press and must include details of the company's past performance and future expectations and full details about the company as required by the LSE's rules according to the Yellow Book.

An issue by tender is a variation on an offer for sale and may be used as an alternative to an offer for sale. In this case there is no prior fixed share price. Potential investors comprising the general public and institutional investors are invited to bid for shares at any price of their choosing, which is above the minimum share price set and underwritten by the issuing house. A resultant **striking price** is the price at which the shares are then sold, which is determined by the volume of applications at various prices. The shares on offer are allocated to all the investors who have bid the striking price or higher in order to ensure that all the shares that have been offered are sold. Refunds are paid to those investors whose bids were higher than the striking price.

Issues by tender may be used if it is difficult to establish an appropriate share issue price. However, an issue by tender is the most expensive method of share issue.

Introductions

If a company has a very large and widely spread share ownership where the amount of shares held by the general public is more than 25% (and remains so after the flotation) then a listing may be obtained by a Stock Exchange introduction. No new finance is raised and no new shares in the company are sold. Therefore, an introduction is a method of obtaining a Stock Exchange listing rather than a method of issuing new shares.

The reasons for a company using a Stock Exchange introduction for a listing are to:

■ gain access to the capital markets
■ ascertain a market value for its shares
■ increase and widen the marketability of the shares.

With a Stock Exchange introduction the shares do not have to be marketed, and do not need to be underwritten. An introduction is therefore the least expensive Stock Exchange listing method.

Bond issues

There are a number of ways in which debt finance may be raised by companies. Bonds may be issued directly to financial institutions and the public by advertising in the financial press. Alternatively, they may be sold as new issues in the primary market through a merchant bank acting as an issuing house. The company may also request that the bank uses placings (as with equity capital) by allocating bonds with a number of its larger institutional customers prior to the date of issue.

Progress check 7.9

What are the ways in which a company may make a new issue of equity or debt?

The Stock Exchange

A stock exchange is a registered capital market for dealing in securities; it is where the securities of plcs may be bought and sold. The Financial Services Authority (FSA), in its role as the competent authority for listing securities, is referred to as the UK Listing Authority (UKLA), which regulates the London Stock Exchange (LSE) under the Financial Services and Markets Act 2000. The UKLA is responsible for regulating sponsors for new issues and for the listing of all securities and maintaining the Official List. It may also, in exceptional circumstances, suspend listings.

The numbers of new issues of securities (securities being offered for sale by companies for the first time) on the LSE increased again throughout 2005, 2006, and 2007 after a slowdown between 2001 and 2004. However in 2008, the year that saw the start of the global financial crisis, numbers dropped again, but they recovered somewhat in 2011. The levels of further issues of securities also fell between 2001 and 2004 and after increases during 2005 to 2007 they also fell back for similar reasons to new issues from 2008, but again recovered in 2011 (see Figures 7.5 and 7.6, source: London Stock Exchange).

Members of the public and institutions may buy and sell securities, but they may only do so through a member of the LSE. Members of the LSE are firms of stockbrokers, comprising brokers and jobbers, who up to the 1980s conducted transactions face-to-face on the 'floor' of the LSE. Since that time dealing has now become computerised, where the same dealing process takes place using the Stock Exchange Automated Quotations (SEAQ) system that enables securities prices to be displayed by members, which are updated continuously.

Figure 7.5	London Stock Exchange new issues of securities on the Main Market 2000 to 2011

Year	Public & International Offerings	Placings	Placings & Open Offers	Total
2000	35	89	3	127
2001	6	44	2	52
2002	7	18	0	25
2003	5	7	0	12
2004	17	15	0	32
2005	25	24	1	50
2006	28	28	1	57
2007	35	28	1	64
2008	12	8	0	20
2009	1	3	1	5
2010	3	9	15	27
2011	8	12	25	45

Figure 7.6	London Stock Exchange selected further issues on the Main Market 2000 to 2011

Year	Public & International Offerings	Placings	Rights	Options	Total
2000	10	68	36	151	265
2001	8	27	27	88	150
2002	2	4	27	132	165
2003	4	6	21	88	119
2004	6	21	19	176	222
2005	4	16	19	298	337
2006	1	61	12	280	354
2007	1	94	7	246	348
2008	1	74	16	139	230
2009	5	83	50	65	203
2010	2	84	7	87	180
2011	1	248	8	82	339

The Alternative Investment Market (AIM)

An alternative to the LSE and operated by the LSE is the Alternative Investment Market (AIM). Since 1995 the AIM has been in existence for small companies, with a market capitalisation of less than £100m and typically around £20m, to obtain a listing. The AIM is both a primary and secondary capital market for an organisation's securities. Its advantage is that when companies apply for a listing on the AIM they do not have to have 25% or more shares held in public hands and do not have to report on three or more years' trading performance.

The number of flotations on the AIM may fluctuate in response to economic conditions. As the press extract below illustrates, a reduction in the number of flotations in 2011 saw more intense competition between the accountancy firms that assist companies with their listings. This resulted in lower flotation costs for companies that do decide to go public on the AIM.

The AIM can be a robust source from which to raise further funds for companies already listed on the market. However, listing can be a gamble and plans may go awry with companies unable to raise the levels of required funding. As we can see from the same press extract, Wine Investors (a managed fund set up to invest in fine wines) had great difficulty in raising its required £30m to invest in some high-quality Bordeaux wines. In December 2010 we saw a further example of this problem when PeerTV, an Israeli Internet television specialist, joined the AIM. When it announced its intention to float in October 2010, it was planning to raise up to £6m but investors were so unimpressed by the company that it finally raised less than £2m when it floated.

Floating on the AIM

The amount of money being raised on AIM for new companies is showing no signs of recovery.

The latest statistics from the London Stock Exchange show that only £9.73m of new money was raised last month, taking the total so far this year to £87.1m, well down on the £322.9m raised in the first four months of last year. The figure looks even worse when set against the final four months of 2010, when £671m of new money was raised in a spate of flotations that spurred hopes of a renaissance this year.

However, every cloud has a silver lining. The scarcity of flotations is intensifying competition among the nominated advisers, or nomads, and keeping costs down. A survey from UHY Hacker Young, the accountancy firm, has found that last year the cost of listing on London's junior market rose at the slowest rate for more than five years.

Back in 2006 the average cost of an initial public offering (IPO) was 6.2 per cent of the funds raised. The percentage rose rapidly to 7.24 per cent in the years to 2009, when the number of IPOs tumbled. But in spite of the signs of recovery late last year, costs as a percentage of total funds raised only edged up to 7.29 per cent.

Costs rose sharply after the AIM regulatory environment was tightened in 2005. 'Although most would agree that those changes have been for the best, at the same time they have increased the extent of due diligence undertaken on candidates for AIM, driving up the cost,' says Laurence Sacker, a partner at the firm. But the trend of increasing levels of due diligence work has levelled off. Mr Sacker believes that 'investment banks and broking firms are once again competing for market share in AIM IPO work. So they are being slightly more flexible on fees.'

Mr Sacker is not alone among AIM professionals in believing that there are a number of companies in the pipeline waiting for the right conditions to float. However, the statistics show that the total number of new companies arriving on AIM, including those from overseas, was 22 in the first four months, three fewer than in the corresponding period last year.

Even candidates with a good story to tell have found the going tough. Wine Investors announced in January plans to raise £30m through a placing at 100p to invest in the fine wines of Bordeaux, including Château Lafite and Château Margaux. Andrew della Casa, a founding director, believes the top wines are an unbeatable asset class. Demand from the wealthy is constant for a supply that both diminishes through consumption and improves in quality with age. Yet the company is still working on raising the money.

What looked like a straightforward reverse takeover of Bidtimes ran into a hitch at the end of last month, postponing its arrival on the market. Bidtimes, which has been on AIM since 2000 in various guises, will change its name to PowerHouse Energy and specialise in converting waste into clean energy. But unexpectedly a dispute emerged over PowerHouse's rights in Australia to a patented technology.

So perhaps it is not surprising that potential candidates are holding back from a nervous and fragile market. Private companies outside the retail sector may be trading well, and seeing their quoted competitors and customers performing strongly. But – and this column is probably guilty – the news tends to focus on the downside and companies suffering under a heavy debt burden grab the attention.

A further deterrent is that smaller companies are undervalued. Look at OpSec Security, the AIM-quoted anti-counterfeiting specialist, which is under offer from Orca Holdings at a 117 per cent premium. 'We have consistently said publicly we think our share price is understated,' says Mike Angus, OpSec's finance director. The offer document says the downturn 'has impacted on investor appetite for AIM and small-cap stocks, which has limited OpSec's ability to access the equity markets for funding'.

But that is not the case for many AIM companies, which have been able to raise further funds relatively easily. The secondary market is proving strong, with £2bn raised in the first four months, twice as much as at this time last year.

While the lack of flotations may be disappointing, AIM is doing its job for many of the companies that already have a quote. Perhaps the last word should be left to one of the City's most experienced small-cap fund managers, Andrew Buchanan of Octopus Investments. 'The market is in much better health than a cursory glance at the headlines would suggest,' he says.

Source: Blackwell, D. (2011) There is something to be seen in dearth of floatations, *Financial Times*, 12 May. © The Financial Times. All Rights Reserved.

The fact that a company may not have been able to obtain a full listing on the LSE may imply for potential investors that such an investment may be more risky than an investment in a company with a full listing. However, the AIM has proved to be very successful for small, growing businesses, which were typically family-owned or MBOs (management buy-outs), to raise finance and create a market for their shares. The costs of obtaining a listing on the AIM is cheaper than an LSE listing and it provides a means for investors like venture capitalists to realise their investments (see Chapter 18).

Progress check 7.10

What are the roles of the London Stock Exchange and the Alternative Investment Market (AIM) and how do the two institutions differ?

Financial institutions

We have already discussed a number of financial institutions when we looked at the various sources of finance and new issues of debt and equity. The range of financial institutions is illustrated in Figure 7.7.

Banks in the UK are part of the clearing system, which they use to clear cheques for payment and ensure that they are paid out of the payer's account and received by the payee's account. The UK banks provide one or more branches in most towns and cities for a range of banking services, including receiving cheques and cash into current accounts and interest-bearing deposit

Figure 7.7	The range of financial institutions

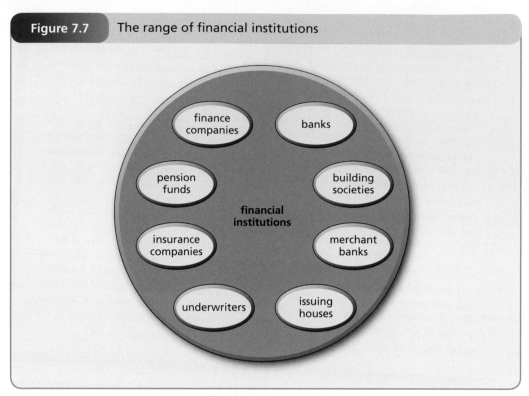

accounts, and making payments by cash, electronic transfer, mail transfer, Internet etc., or by whatever other means the customer requires.

A company must have a bank account in order to process its financial transactions. Few businesses use only one bank and most companies use the services of many banks. Large, multinational companies will have a large number of different banks, not just because of their size but because of their diversity of transactions and dealings. While this may be a necessity and good business practice it does impose an additional burden on the company having to manage such a large number of relationships.

Banks provide a wide range of services for companies, including overdraft facilities, long-term loans, interest and foreign exchange dealing facilities, but also advice and support. Banks do not like surprises and so it is important that good banking relationships are maintained by both small and large businesses. For the development of strong banking relationships it is necessary for the company to be completely open and honest with its bank managers. This requires regular face-to-face meetings and the provision of a regular supply of financial and non-financial information regarding the company's:

■ financial performance
■ financial position
■ strategic plans
■ budgets
■ new investment
■ progress of new projects
■ risks.

It is important to provide regular information to the bank about bad news as well as good news. It is only from a position of trust that a bank can feel able to give help as necessary to a company should it perhaps encounter a temporary slowdown or a period of continuing recession.

When companies wish to raise new capital through equity or debt then, as we have seen, various financial institutions may need to become involved. Loans may be made by banks with security, or without. Small companies in the UK, for example, are able to obtain unsecured bank loans from banks with Government help in the form of loan guarantees. The main areas of lending by the UK high street retail banks are overdrafts, loans, and mortgages. Over recent years they have taken a large part of the mortgage lending business away from building societies, which were the institutions traditionally used for borrowing for property purchases, in addition to their role as borrowers to provide investors with building society savings accounts. Following deregulation of the financial services sector, many building societies also now increasingly provide most of the services provided by banks and so the distinction between themselves and banks is slowly disappearing.

We discussed earlier how issuing houses arrange new issues of equity or debt for companies. Issuing houses are normally merchant banks. Merchant banks are part of the wholesale banking sector and are members of the Issuing Houses Association, which is responsible for Stock Exchange flotations. A merchant bank's role in new issues of equity and debt extends beyond that of acting as an issuing house, by also acting as a broker or adviser to a company in a new issue.

Merchant banks have other roles in addition to their responsibilities in new corporate financing. They are also increasingly active in developing derivatives like options and swaps (see Chapter 12), and providing advice in mergers and acquisitions (M&As) and corporate reorganisations and restructuring, and advice regarding strategic defences against hostile M&As (see Chapters 16, 17, and 18). Merchant banks also have a fund management role in managing the portfolios of investments of other financial institutions like, for example, insurance companies, investment and unit trusts, pension funds, and also some charities. A unit trust is a syndicate established under a trust deed, which pools investors' funds into an investment portfolio, and whose spread of buying and selling price reflects the value of the securities in the portfolio. An investment trust is usually a publicly quoted limited company, which invests in securities, whose share price reflects both the value of the portfolio of securities and the demand for its shares, and which is usually lower than the net asset values.

If a company's new issue is not successful in raising the funds the company requires, then the company may be left with unsold shares. This would be bad news for the company, not only because it will have raised insufficient funds, but because its credibility will have been dented and any subsequent issue will be even more difficult and more expensive. Companies therefore appoint underwriters to take up any shares, or debt, that are not sold during the new issue. A company is therefore guaranteed to raise the funds required. An underwriter of new issues may be a merchant bank but is more likely to be a pension fund or insurance company.

The growth in the popularity of leasing in the UK up to the mid-1980s saw an increase in the establishment of finance companies, which specialise in various forms of leasing and hire purchase. As we have seen, leases provide the use of assets by lessees over varying periods of time where ownership of the assets remains with the lessor. With a hire purchase agreement legal title passes when the final instalment has been paid. Finance companies also provide a popular means of financing in the retail sector, for example for cars, computers, televisions and DVD recorders, and white goods. The finance companies themselves are generally specialist subsidiaries of banks.

Progress check 7.11

Explain the range of financial institutions that may be used by companies.

Islamic banking and Islamic finance

Over the past few years in the UK and worldwide there has been an increase in the use of **Islamic banking**, which is broadly based on the teachings of the Qur'an and forbids the charging of interest and engaging in businesses like alcohol and gambling. The first Islamic bank was opened in the early 1960s in Egypt and was called the Savings Bank of Mit Ghmar. In 1970, in the United Arab Emirates, the Dubai Islamic Bank was opened, which is one of the biggest and longest-established Islamic banks. Since then, Islamic banks have been established in many other countries with the main centres being Saudi Arabia, Bahrain, Pakistan, and Malaysia.

Many Western banks now provide Islamic banking facilities within their own countries and overseas. Benefits of the Islamic financing system may be seen from its being less dependent on conventional company accounts than traditional systems, and in having a lower volume of documentation with less complexity. The UK's HSBC Amanah, HSBC's Islamic finance division, was launched in 1998. In July 2003 it introduced UK customers to the high street's first Shari'a home purchase scheme and current account. Since that time, HSBC has seen the UK Islamic banking market grow from strength to strength.

Despite the start of the global financial crisis in 2008, there has been an increase in the potential opportunities for Islamic financing. Ernst & Young's World Islamic Banking Competitiveness Report of 2011 estimated that Islamic banks worldwide would be managing assets worth US$1.1trn by the end of 2012, representing a 33% increase from their 2010 level of US$826bn. Further evidence of this can be seen in the press extract below, particularly with regards to the *sukuk* (see the later section about *sukuks*). A report at the same time by Deutsche Bank indicated that as the global crisis pushes institutions to seek alternatives to traditional lending methods there could be an increase of assets managed under Islamic financing to US$1.8trn by 2016.

The growth of Islamic financing

Islamic bonds have staged a comeback, after several gloomy years in which even Muslim bankers and clerics questioned the debt instruments' religious credentials and issuance dipped precipitously. The bonds, known as sukuks, are structured to comply with Muslim law, or Sharia, and pay a profit rate rather than interest, which is banned in Islam.

Clerical doubts over prominent structures, Dubai's debt crisis and the global financial crisis had combined to send issuance tumbling. However, sukuk sales rebounded strongly in 2011, hitting a record $32.6bn, according to Dealogic. Issuance has continued at a robust pace this year as borrowers have sought to capitalise on the relative health of Islamic banks, which cannot invest in conventional debt instruments. There have been $10.4bn of sukuk sales in 2012, the strongest start to a year on record

and more than twice the amount issued over the same period last year. 'We chose to issue a sukuk because of strong demand from Islamic regional accounts,' says Daniele Vecchi, head of group treasury at Majid Al-Futtaim, a Dubai-based mall group that sold a debut $400m Islamic bond in February. 'Pricing also compared well with conventional paper.'

Indeed, after years of often pricing and trading at a slight discount to conventional bonds, the strong demand for Islamic bonds and a 'captive' buyer base have sent yields tumbling, with some sukuk trading at a tighter spread than comparable conventional bonds. The yield of HSBC-Nasdaq Dubai's sukuk index has declined to 3.65 per cent this year, not far off the record low touched in August last year. Yields move inversely to prices. 'I think that that trend is going to continue through this year as long as global market conditions are relatively stable,' says Abdul Kadir Hussain, chief executive officer of Mashreq Capital, an investment bank and asset manager.

While the main buyers of sukuk remain in the Gulf and Malaysia, the spectrum of issuers has broadened in recent years. More maiden issuers from new markets are expected in 2012. South Africa and Nigeria have recently voiced interest in selling sukuk. Countries including Australia, Turkey and Hong Kong have announced plans to make their laws more conducive to domestic sukuk issuance, with National Australia Bank already considering an inaugural sale.

Perhaps the most significant new member of the 'sukuk club' is Saudi Arabia. Although several Saudi companies have sold Islamic bonds, the oil-rich kingdom this year sold its first sovereign-guaranteed sukuk , a SR15bn ($4bn) offering to finance an airport expansion. By setting a sovereign sukuk curve that other companies can use as a pricing benchmark, this could set the stage for bigger issuance. Saudi Arabia remains a small part of the global sukuk market, but many bankers and investors say this might change.

Despite the sukuk market's resurgence, many issues surrounding the instrument highlighted by the financial crisis remain unresolved – not least how the instruments are treated in a bankruptcy. Dubai managed to avoid defaulting on one of its Islamic bonds in late 2009 thanks to aid from Abu Dhabi, but the legal uncertainties it brought to light remain. Indeed, the outcome of the restructuring of a prominent $650m sukuk in Saudi Arabia remains murky, several years after it went into default.

The global sukuk market also remains relatively narrow, despite the issuance from new companies and countries. The vast preponderance of issuance remains from Malaysia, despite Saudi Arabia's $4bn sukuk skewing the statistics towards the Gulf this year. Moreover, there are still some industry insiders who worry that the constant evolution of the Islamic bond market means that it risks eroding its credibility with devout investors if it strays too far from its roots.

A warning from one scholar in 2008 that some structures had diverged from Islamic principles contributed to the market's post-financial crisis slowdown. Goldman Sach's plans to sell a sukuk have also been clouded by uncertainty over its structure. 'There is a conflict between the demands of the market – both from the borrowers and lenders – and what Sharia demands,' says Khalid Howladar, a senior analyst at Moody's. 'There's always an issue that certain instruments evolve into something too similar to conventional bonds defeating the purpose of Islamic finance.'

The growing importance of Islamic financing is also reflected in the fact that the ACCA (Association of Chartered Certified Accountants) have now included Islamic Finance in their F9 Financial Management examination syllabus, the topics of which are covered throughout this section.

The objective of traditional economics is the efficient allocation of resources while the objective of Islamic economics is the elimination of poverty. This is an important fundamental principle and must be considered whenever a new financial instrument is introduced to justify its existence. Islamic banking is based on economic legislation within the Shari'a, which represents the rules of God that came as a revelation from God to the prophet Mohamed. The sources of the Shari'a are the Qur'an (the Holy Book of Islam), the Sunnah (Ways of the Prophet), and Ijmaa (matters agreed by Islamic scholars), with the Qur'an being the primary influence. Since Islam represents universality, the ideology of Islamic banking and financial institutions makes them universal institutions with no restrictions regarding locality and nationality. **Islamic finance** is founded on the following bases:

■ wealth must be created from legitimate trade and asset-based investment
■ investments should have wider social and ethical benefits
■ risk should be shared
■ all activities that Shari'a law considers harmful (*haram*) must be avoided.

This, therefore, prohibits usury and investments in businesses that are involved with for example alcohol, gambling, pornography, drugs and speculation.

The requirements of Shari'a compliant financing also prevent investments in companies which are highly geared (usually defined as having debt in excess of 33% of the company's stock market value over the previous 12 months) and in situations where uncertainty of extreme risk exist. Speculation in futures and options markets and the selling of something that one does not own is also therefore prohibited. This creates difficulties when, for example, contracting to manufacture a product for a customer, because at that time the product does not exist and therefore cannot be owned. However, as we shall see there are financing instruments which make this possible. But the focus of Islamic finance is the forbidding of usury and interest. It does this without undermining or contradicting other religions, cultures, economic and financial systems, and prevents injustice by separately identifying what is lawful from what is prohibited.

The Shari'a requires a redistribution of wealth and income to provide every Muslim with a guaranteed fair standard of living. This is achieved from a levy of an Islamic tax called a *zakat*, which each Muslim should calculate individually. The payment of a *zakat* is obligatory on every mentally stable, free, and financially able adult male and female Muslim, to support Muslims who are poor or in need. It is currently interpreted as a 2.5% levy on most valuables and savings held for a full lunar year, provided that the total value is more than a basic minimum known as *nisab* (3 ounces, or 87.48 grams of gold). Islamic banks maintain a *zakat* fund for collecting tax and distributing it to the people that need it either directly or through religious institutions.

The central theme of Islamic economics is the prohibition of *riba*, or interest. This is not dissimilar to the Christian and Jewish faiths that were also against usury, and many leading philosophers, like Aristotle, also rejected usury. Interest has harmful social implications because it encourages the accumulation of more and more money for its own sake rather than to support trade or real investment. Usury is absolutely forbidden by the Islamic faith.

The traditional properties of money are that it is:

■ a unit of measurement
■ a medium of exchange
■ a store of value.

Islamic economists accept the first two properties but do not think of money as a store of value. Islamic economics says that money itself doesn't have a value, but holding it just enables purchases at some time in the future. The Islamic system identifies a number of implications with regard to the charging of interest:

■ interest does not reflect real wealth creation and only increases money capital without a similar increase in the supply of goods – Islamic economics requires new capital to come from real commercial activities rather than simply monetary transactions
■ interest interferes with market forces
■ prohibition of interest means that non-commercial borrowing is eliminated because lenders have no incentive to lend money

- if the financing of non-commercial activities is eliminated, inflationary pressures are reduced resulting in less volatility and more stability in the value of money
- since public sector borrowing is considered both unjustified and unethical unless it is to acquire physical assets, then current expenditure must be held within available national resources
- if governments are prohibited from borrowing unlimited funds to meet current expenditure then deficit financing is prevented (in theory)
- if financing is only backed by the assets of commercial transactions then it does not create a debt burden for future generations because assets may be liquidated to repay debt.

In the Islamic economic system, returns are generated through the trading of assets from commercial activities, and are normally shared on a predetermined basis between parties. While Islamic banks aim to safeguard the assets of their clients and maximise investment returns, they are under no obligation to pay fixed returns on deposits or charge clients fixed costs of borrowing. Their primary objectives are:

- attracting funds by providing competitive returns on investment
- promoting economic growth by directing funds to production and commercial activities
- ensuring that investments result in an equitable distribution of wealth, through the provision of ethical and just financial support, and technological and management expertise for value-creating opportunities
- encouraging the emergence and development of entrepreneurs through the requirement of technical expertise instead of security as the basis for financing, resulting in employment, wealth creation, and growth, but also eliminating the need for large conglomerates
- efficiently providing other banking services to clients that conform with Islamic Shari'a.

Traditional banks exploit market imperfections to maximise shareholder wealth. Islamic banks are only intermediaries, and they provide a balance between the interests of shareholders, depositors, borrowers, and society in general. Islamic banks carry out trust and advisory functions and their client funds are all fiduciary, except for demand deposits. Because of their relationship with their depositors, Islamic banks are relatively less risky than traditional banks for a number of reasons:

- deposits other than demand deposits do not count as bank liabilities, therefore they are lower geared than traditional banks
- there is no guarantee of repayment of a loan principal plus a profit
- clients who deposit funds are closely involved in its operations, so if there is an economic downturn the bank is unlikely to experience a run on deposits
- direct lending does not take place – loans are made in the form of prepayments and so there is no impact on debt to equity and debt to assets ratios.

This is all very different from traditional banking systems, which normally have the following disadvantages:

- Constraints are placed on customers because of their liabilities and gearing levels.
- Bank reserves are not always sufficient to avoid a run on a bank because its liabilities are short term, whereas a large proportion of its assets are longer term.
- Repayment of a loan principal plus a return is guaranteed at a future date, which are both therefore liabilities of the bank, and therefore the lender takes a risk that the bank's assets will provide sufficient value to make repayment at the maturity date.

Islamic banks are organised and operate in line with all appropriate company legislation that applies wherever they are operational. They are organised with a board of directors to which the chief executive and management committee report, but also an audit committee and a religious board, which is the ultimate authority. Each operation, documentation, product, and service is submitted to the Shari'a board by the bank's management for approval before they may be used or offered to clients. The religious board therefore has mandatory power to ensure that all operations, products, services, and documentation comply fully with Islamic Shari'a.

Because Islamic banks prohibit interest, they are expected to undertake activities only on the basis of various types of profit- and loss-sharing arrangement. The following financial instruments principally comprise two of the main pillars of Islamic banking:

Mudaraba (trust financing)

This is an agreement made between two parties: one provides 100% of the capital for the project and another party, known as the *modarib*, manages the project using his entrepreneurial skills. Profits arising from the project are distributed according to a pre-determined ratio but are not guaranteed. Any losses are borne by the provider of capital, who has no control over the management of the project.

Musharaka (partnership financing)

This is a financing technique involving a partnership between two parties who both provide capital towards the financing of a project. Both parties share profits based on a pre-agreed ratio, but losses are shared on the basis of equity participation. Management of the project may be carried out by both of the parties or by just one party. This is a very flexible partnership arrangement where the sharing of the profits and management can be negotiated and pre-agreed by all parties.

The *mudaraba* concept has been expanded in practice to include three parties:

- the depositor as financier
- the bank as an intermediary
- the entrepreneur who requires funds.

When the bank receives funds from depositors it acts as an entrepreneur. When the bank provides funds to entrepreneurs it acts as financier. The bank therefore operates a two-tier system in which it acts with regard to both savings and the investment portfolio. For the depositors, an Islamic bank manages their funds to generate profits subject to the rules of *mudaraba*. The bank may then use the depositors' funds on a *mudaraba* basis in addition to other methods of financing, including mark-up, lease purchase, and benevolent loans (see below).

Both the *mudaraba* and *musharaka* comply fully with Islamic principles and are the main ways in which funds flow out of the banks. However, there are other important methods of uses of funds applied by Islamic banks, which include the eight methods that follow.

Istisna'a (manufacturing)

Istisna'a is a contract for the purchase of goods by specification or order, where the price is paid progressively in accordance with the progress of completion of a job. It is used, for example, for the purchases of houses to be constructed where the payments made to the developer or builder are based on the stage of work completed. In the case of *bai al salam* (described below) the full payment is made in advance to the seller before delivery of goods.

Bai al salam

Bai al salam is a contract for the purchase of goods, where the price is paid in advance and the goods are delivered in the future.

Murabaha (mark-up or cost-plus financing)

This is a contract of sale for a profit- and loss-sharing arrangement between the bank and its client for the sale of goods at a price that includes a profit margin agreed by both parties. As a financing technique it involves the purchase of goods by the bank as requested by its client. The goods are sold to the client with a mark-up. Repayment, usually in instalments, is specified in the contract.

Worked example 7.8

A company wishes to acquire a printing machine, which can be bought from a supplier for £50,000. They could go to a non-Islamic bank and obtain a loan for £50,000 repayable after three years and pay 8% interest per annum. The agreement for the finance would not need to specify the item to be acquired and the bank would advance the money to the company for them to make the acquisition. In total the company would repay £50,000 principal and £12,000 interest.

An alternative would be to acquire the machine under a *murabaha* agreement.

In the case of a *murabaha* agreement the bank would acquire the machine on behalf of the company and sell it to the company on a cost-plus sale agreement. The bank would buy the machine for £50,000 and sell it to the company for £50,000 plus say a £12,000 arrangement fee, a total of £62,000. An agreement is then arranged for the company to pay the bank £62,000 over three years.

In terms of the numbers, the company pays the same amount of money, but no *riba* (or interest) is charged. There are, nonetheless, some other fundamental differences.

In the first case the company is borrowing money from the bank without specifying the purpose (although it is to buy a machine).

In the second case the company is not borrowing money but buying a specific asset from the bank. For the transaction to be Shari'a compliant: the item that is the subject of the transaction must exist at the time of the contract; the item must be in the ownership of the bank at the time of the contract; the item must have value and that value must be certain at the time of the contract; the item must not be used for non-Islamic purposes.

Unlike an interest-bearing loan, if the company is late on its payments under the *murabaha* contract, the bank cannot charge penalties as this would amount to charging interest.

Bai bithaman ajil

This contract refers to the sale of goods on a deferred payment basis. Equipment or goods that have been requested by a client, are bought by the bank, which subsequently sells the goods to the client at an agreed price that includes the bank's mark-up (profit). The client may be allowed to settle by instalments within a pre-agreed period, or in a lump sum. *Bai bithaman ajil* is a credit sale and similar to a *murabaha* contract.

Qard ul hasan (a benevolent or good loan)

Qard ul hasan is an interest-free, benevolent loan that is given either for welfare purposes or for bridging short-term funding requirements. The borrower is required to pay back only the amount borrowed.

Ijara (leasing)

Ijara is a contract under which the bank buys and then leases equipment to a client for an agreed rental and for an agreed duration. Ownership of the equipment remains in the hands of the bank.

Ijara wa-iqtina (lease/hire purchase)

Ijara wa-iqtina is very similar to *ijara*, except that it is agreed in advance that the client commits to buy the equipment from the bank at an agreed price at the end of the lease period. The rental fees that have been paid constitute part of the price.

Sukuk

One of the most widely used Islamic financial instruments is the *sukuk*, which is effectively the Islamic equivalent of a traditional bond.

Sukuks are securities that comply with the Shari'a and its investment principles, which prohibits the charging, or paying of interest. Shari'a requires that financing should only be raised for trading in, or construction of, specific and identifiable assets. Trading in 'indebtedness' is prohibited and so the issue of traditional fixed-income, interest-bearing bonds would not be compliant.

Originally, *sukuk* referred to any document representing a contract or conveyance of rights, obligations or monies done in conformity with Shari'a. It is believed that the *sukuk* was extensively used during medieval Islam for the transferring of financial obligations originating from trade and other commercial activities. In today's Islamic finance, the essence of the *sukuk* is in the concept of asset monetisation, or securitisation achieved through the process of issuing a *sukuk*. *Sukuks* are structured in parallel with the acquisition of a physical asset. Revenue streams from, for example, roads, airports, seaports, utilities, new buildings, power plants, and oil facilities are used to pay a profit on the *sukuk*. All *sukuk* returns and cash flows are linked to assets purchased or those generated from an asset once constructed and not simply considered as income that is interest based. A *sukuk* may be issued on existing assets as well as assets that may become available at a future date.

Shari'a-compliant products must be approved by a Shari'a scholar certified for issuing a *fatwa* (Islamic decree). There are currently apparently fewer than 20 scholars with such skills worldwide, which therefore increases the time taken to approve products like *sukuks*. Currently most *sukuks* are bought and held, and so to date there has tended not to be an active secondary market.

There has been some considerable debate recently about whether Western banks should be permitted to engage in Islamic finance particularly as many Western banks are now issuing Islamic finance instruments. In addition to HSBC, Deutsche Bank, Barclays Capital and Citi are all involved in Islamic finance as the Mini case below illustrates.

According to Standard & Poor's, London – as one of the major financial hubs to handle Islamic transactions – has become the sole non-Muslim competitor of natural Islamic markets in Dubai, Kuala Lumpur, and Bahrain. The UK Government demonstrated its commitment in the Finance Act of 2007 by introducing new measures for *sukuks*, enabling them to be issued, held and traded in the same way as corporate bonds.

Mini case 7.2

Many banks and investment houses are appreciating the need to develop Shari'a-compliant financial packages in order to attract new business and to develop markets with Islamic clients. The market for Islamic financing instruments is an extremely viable alternative to Western financing methods and the volume of Islamic *sukuks* in early 2012 was clear evidence of the strength of the market.

A traditional market for Islamic finance has been the aviation sector, which is growing strongly in the Middle East. The Dubai-based Emirates Airlines raised US$265m in Islamic financing to pay for two Boeing jets delivered in 2011. The transaction involved 12-year leases for the Boeing 777-300ER aircraft. Boeing Capital (the wholly owned financing subsidiary of the Boeing aircraft corporation) announced in late 2011 that it was exploring opportunities for Islamic finance in the aviation sector. It was looking at the possibility of using the Islamic *sukuk* market for aircraft financing in which an aircraft finance portfolio would be secured by an instrument known as an Enhanced Equipment Trust Certificate. The company estimated that the Middle East airlines would need 2,520 new aircraft over the next 20 years for fleet renewal and growth, and as a consequence the development of Islamic financing packages could be extremely advantageous for Boeing. In January 2012, the Saudi General Authority of Civil Aviation raised 15bn Saudi riyals (US$4bn) – one of the largest *sukuks* on record.

The airline industry is not the only business sector in which Islamic financial instruments are gaining a strong position. The issuing of *sukuks* is developing at an exceptional rate in the lucrative infrastructure industry. On 28 March 2012 the Saudi British Bank, the local arm of HSBC, raised 1.5bn Saudi riyals (US$400m) from a private placement of Islamic bonds and the day previously the state-owned Saudi Electricity Company had raised a US$1.75bn dual-tranche *sukuk* issue, comprising a US$500m *sukuk* with a five-year maturity and a US$1.25bn *sukuk* with a 10-year maturity. These have helped Saudi Arabia to become the biggest *sukuk* issuer in the Gulf region for the first quarter of 2012 with total issues amounting to US$6.4bn (15% of world *sukuk* issues).

By April 2012, the total global *sukuk* issuance for both government and corporate sectors was estimated at US$44bn for the year. Malaysia easily held on to top spot in the world rankings with 71 per cent or close to US$31bn. This was in comparison with the total global issuance of *sukuks* in 2011 of US$26.5bn.

The Islamic financial instruments we have looked at above are contracts on which commercial transactions may be based. International transactions normally use letters of credit, as do traditional banks. The difference is that the Islamic banks own the goods until full payment is received from the importer during which time the importer is given rights for the clearing of goods or products as agreed in the contract. Islamic banks actually deal with the goods whereas traditional banks only deal with documents. In cases of default, Islamic banks are in a much better legal position to recover losses since title has not yet passed on to the importer so they are better able to control credit. In traditional banking, legal title to goods would have been passed to the importer, and so recovery of losses would depend on security or insurance cover.

Islamic banks have their own capital and rely on two main sources of funds:

- transaction deposits, which are free of risk but yield no return
- investment deposits, which carry the risks of capital loss in exchange for the promise of variable returns.

There are four main types of Islamic bank account:

- current accounts – depositors are guaranteed repayment of their funds, but they do not receive a return because the funds will not be used for profit- and loss-sharing ventures as these funds can only be used to balance the liquidity needs of the bank
- savings accounts – depositors earn an income, which is a premium paid by the bank at its discretion, dependent on the bank's financial results
- investment accounts – the provider of the funds, the *mudarib* or active partner, has absolute freedom in the management of the investment. Investment accounts are different from savings accounts because:
  - they have a higher fixed minimum amount of deposit
  - they have a longer duration of deposit

  and most importantly

  - the depositor may lose some of or all their funds should the bank make losses
- special investment accounts – the depositors are usually large investors or institutions, and the accounts operate under the *mudaraba* principle. The differences between these accounts and investment accounts are that:
  - the funds are related to specific projects
  - investors have the choice to invest directly in projects carried out by the bank.

Because the relationship with their depositors is based on profit sharing, Islamic banks need to have fuller financial disclosure than traditional banks. The development of accounting standards for Islamic banks has therefore been of paramount importance. In the early 1990s a set of published accounting guidelines was established by the Accounting and Auditing Organisation for Islamic Financial Institutions (AAOIFI), which has up until 2012 issued 85 standards on accounting, auditing, governance, ethics, and Shari'a compliance, including a statement on capital adequacy. These standards are either mandatory or used as a guideline by the regulators in countries like Bahrain, Sudan, Jordan, Malaysia, Qatar, Saudi Arabia, United Arab Emirates, Lebanon, and Syria, and their widespread use continues to increase.

An important aspect of a bank's management of Shari'a-compliant products is the Shari'a board. The board is responsible for ensuring that all products and services offered are in accordance with Shari'a law. The board comprises a committee of Islamic scholars and in addition to the oversight of all products offered the board will also make judgements on all cases referred to it for example ensuring that a potential customer's business proposals are in accordance with Shari'a law. The decisions of the bank's board are issued in the form of *fatwas*. Moreover, the activities of the bank's Shari'a boards are in turn supervised by the International Association of Islamic Bankers and its Supreme Religious Board reviews the *fatwas* issued by bank boards to determine whether they do conform with Shari'a law.

We have seen that there are a number of advantages and benefits provided by Islamic banking. However, it should be noted that there are also a number of issues and challenges faced by the Islamic banking system because it has:

- no lender of last resort
- highly liquid positions maintained by most banks
- no secondary capital market
- no conventional money markets
- little product innovation
- no pricing benchmark other than LIBOR or its local equivalent (which is used only as an indicator rather than an interest rate).

Progress check 7.12

What are the major differences between traditional banking and Islamic banking, and what are their similarities?

The global financial crisis

The current global financial crisis started in the USA in the early 2000s and then spread to the UK and many other parts of the world. The global financial crisis or 'credit crunch' is a subject that has generated a plethora of opinions about its causes and possible solutions. It came to a head in 2008 and we are still many years later facing global financial problems on a massive scale.

The global financial crisis is something which all of us, and particularly those working in corporate finance roles need to understand, and is the reason that this topic is included in this book by introducing the basic issues surrounding the crisis. But who is affected by this crisis and how did it happen?

The initial financial crisis developed from the relationship between two groups of people: house-owners and investors. House-owners borrow money, mortgages, to buy houses. Investors, large financial institutions like pension funds, sovereign (government-backed) funds, mutual funds, and insurance companies have money they wish to invest. These groups were brought together through the financial system, the banks and brokers comprising Wall Street in the USA and the City of London in the UK. These banks were closely connected to the housing market.

If we look at the USA in the years up to 2007/2008 (when the crisis began) institutional investors generally had vast sums of money to invest and obtain the best possible returns. Traditionally these investors went to the USA Federal Reserve where they invested in Treasury bills, believed to be the safest investment (AAA-rated) for a reasonable return on their money.

However, a couple of things happened in the early 2000s that dramatically changed America's economic climate: the dot.com bubble burst; the World Trade Center was destroyed by terrorists on 11 September 2001. These events had a huge detrimental effect on the USA economy. In the wake of this, the then Federal Reserve chairman Alan Greenspan lowered interest rates to just 1% to try and re-generate the USA economy. At the same time as all this was happening in the USA, other economies like China and the Middle East were generating large surpluses, which also resulted in a reduction of interest rates. All these factors together gave rise to a global abundance of cheap credit.

Even though the reduction in interest rates in the USA led to low 1% returns on Treasury bills which investors were not happy to accept, it also meant that the Wall Street banks could borrow from the Federal Reserve at 1%. The cost of borrowing was so low and credit was so easily available that it was very easy for banks to borrow money very cheaply, which they did on a massive scale. This high degree of leverage, or borrowing, at such low rates of interest enabled the banks to hugely multiply the amount of business they could transact and therefore hugely multiply the amount of money well over and above what they would normally make.

How did they use leverage to do this? Well, if you take an example of a normal deal where someone with £10 buys an item for £10 and then sells it to someone else for £11, they make a fair profit of £1. However, if someone with £10 borrows a further £990 they then have £1,000 to buy 100 items for £10 each. They then sell these 100 items to someone else for £11 each for a total of £1,100. After paying back the £990 borrowed plus interest of say £10, and deducting their original £10, they are left with a profit of £90. Leverage has increased their profit from £10 to £90.

This is a major way in which banks make their money. In the low interest and easy credit scenario we have described, Wall Street banks were able to take on massive credit and borrow sums of money on an unprecedented scale to finance deals that were making them tremendously wealthy.

Investors saw what was going on and they also wanted a piece of the action. This gave Wall Street the idea of connecting investors to the house-ownership market through mortgages on which they considered they could make good returns. If you consider a family that wants to buy a house they usually save for a down payment and then contact a mortgage broker (who gets paid a commission) who connects them to a mortgage lender who gives them a loan, a mortgage. The family then buys a house and become house-owners. This made sense because house prices had always been rising in the past.

In the low-interest scenario, Wall Street and investors saw mortgages as an opportunity for a good return, so investment bankers wanted to buy mortgages from the mortgage lenders, who sold them for a fee. The investment bankers borrowed vast sums of money and bought thousands more mortgages. Every month the investment bankers received cash in from payments from all the house-owners' mortgages.

The investment bankers then packaged the mortgages and cut the package into the slices: the top slice was safe mortgages; the middle slice was average-risk mortgages; the bottom slice was high-risk mortgages, where there was risk of default. The investment bankers then repackaged the slices and called them a **collateralised debt obligation (CDO)**.

CDOs are products developed by financial institutions to package together unrelated debt instruments, such as bonds and mortgages, and then portions of that package are sold to investors. Up until the 2007/2008 financial crisis, billions of dollars and pounds worth of mortgage-backed securities were bundled together into highly complex CDOs, producing massive profits for banks.

A CDO works like three cascading 'trays'. As money comes in from house-owners paying their mortgages it first fills the top tray, safe mortgages, and then it spills over into the middle tray, average-risk mortgages, and whatever is left spills into the bottom tray, high-risk mortgages. If some house-owners don't pay and default on their mortgages then less money comes in and the bottom tray may not get filled. To compensate for the higher risk the bottom tray receives a higher rate of return, say 10%, while the top tray receives a lower, say 4%, reasonable return. The middle tray receives say 7%. To make the top tray even safer the banks may insure it for a small fee, say 1%, called a **credit default swap**, bringing the net return down to say 3%. Credit default swaps are a form of credit insurance in which one party pays another party to protect it from the risk of default on a particular debt instrument. If that debt instrument (for example a mortgage) defaults, the insurer compensates the insured for his loss.

The investment banks assigned different rates of return to the three levels of risk and the credit rating agencies rated the top tray AAA, an investment as safe as can be, and the highest safest rating there is. The average-risk middle tray was rated BBB and still quite good. The high-risk tray was unrated. Because of the AAA rating the investment bankers could sell the safe CDOs to investors who only want safe investments, the average-risk CDOs to other banks, and the high-risk CDOs to hedge funds and other risk-takers. The investment bankers made many millions of dollars in this way, and the investors were very happy, having found a good investment that provided returns much better than the 1% Treasury bills.

As this situation continued, investors were so pleased that they wanted more CDOs, so the investment bankers tried to buy even more mortgages from the mortgage lenders. In turn, the mortgage lenders tried to get more mortgages from the mortgage brokers. But the situation had reached the point where the mortgage brokers couldn't find any new mortgages – everyone that qualified for a mortgage already had one. This gave the mortgage lenders an idea: when house-owners default on a mortgage the lender gets the house and houses are always increasing in value; because they are covered, if a house-owner defaults then mortgage lenders should be able to add risk to new mortgages by not requiring a down payment, and not requiring any proof of income. So that is exactly what the mortgage lenders did. They started to lend to less responsible borrowers using so-called sub-prime mortgages (as distinct from so-called prime mortgages to responsible house-owners).

This was the turning point. What happened in the USA was that mortgage brokers connected less responsible families with mortgage lenders, who again made their commission. These families obtained mortgages and were able to buy big houses. The increase in mortgage lending in the sub-prime category came not from banks but from non-bank mortgage lenders, companies that provide mortgages but are not registered banks. These non-banks, usually private lenders and finance companies, target residential mortgage business and because they operate in areas outside normal banking they are often seen as a source of mortgages for people who cannot get financing from a bank.

As before, the mortgage lenders sold the mortgages to the investment bankers who turned them into CDOs and sold slices to investors and others. It worked out well for everyone and made them all very wealthy. No-one worried about if the house-owners defaulted because as soon as each institution sold a mortgage to the next institution then it became their problem, and they were all making millions. This was a 'time-bomb' waiting to explode. Unfortunately, the confidence in the new CDOs was over-inflated by the property speculation boom and household debt levels began to reach unsustainable levels, as shown in Figure 7.8, not only in the USA but also the UK and Europe.

Ben S Bernanke, the then chairman of the Federal Reserve, noted the trend in sub-prime mortgage failures. In a speech at a conference in May 2007, he identified the difficulties becoming apparent in the sub-prime market and gave an early warning of what was to come. By the end of 2007 the sub-prime mortgage market had grown to unprecedented levels. Many of these mortgages had floating, or flexible interest rates and in 2006 rates had begun to rise. As many borrowers were struggling to maintain or continue their mortgage payments a rash of mortgage defaults resulted in the USA as we can see from Figure 7.9.

It could hardly have been a surprise when the less responsible house-owners started to default on their mortgages, which at that time were owned by the bankers and other investors in the form of CDOs. However, the bankers could foreclose on the house-owners and their monthly payments were turned into houses. Initially this was not seen as a problem because the bankers could put the houses up for sale. However, more and more of the bankers' monthly

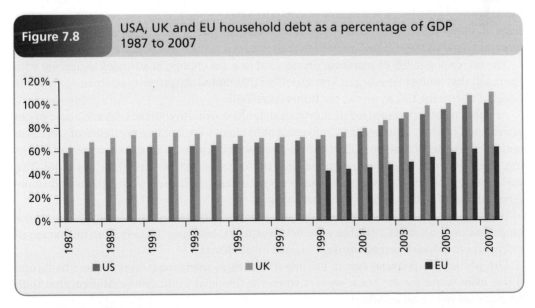

Figure 7.8   USA, UK and EU household debt as a percentage of GDP 1987 to 2007

Source: The Turner Review.

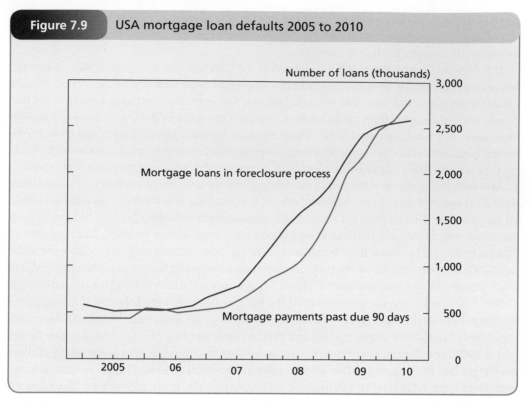

Figure 7.9 USA mortgage loan defaults 2005 to 2010

Source: Bank of England.

payments turned into houses. So many houses came up for sale that a market was created where there was more supply than demand, so that house prices not only stopped rising but in fact fell sharply. This created an interesting problem for many house-owners who were still paying their mortgages. As all the houses in their neighbourhood went up for sale following foreclosure, the value of their houses went down so they wondered 'Why are we paying back our US$250,000 mortgage when the house is now only worth US$75,000?' Even though they could afford to pay, huge numbers of house-owners decided that it did not make sense to continue to pay off their mortgages and so they walked away from their houses leaving them with the banks.

The increasing levels of mortgage defaults led to a sea change in attitudes to lending with the result that house prices began a rapid decline that ended the property boom not only in the USA but also in the UK, as we can see from Figure 7.10.

As house prices continued to fall, mortgage defaults swept through the USA and house prices plummeted further. This meant that investment bankers were holding portfolios of worthless houses. They tried to sell their CDOs but investors were by then obviously not interested in buying. They knew that the stream of money into the 'trays' wasn't even a dribble any more. This was a huge problem for investment bankers because they had borrowed millions and sometimes billions of dollars to fund these transactions.

Investment bankers were not the only ones in trouble. Investors had already bought thousands and thousands of CDOs that were now worthless. Mortgage lenders were unable to sell mortgages to banks. Mortgage brokers became unemployed.

The whole USA financial system became frozen as so many businesses became bankrupt. It was even worse for the house-owners when the financial institutions told them that their investments were also worthless.

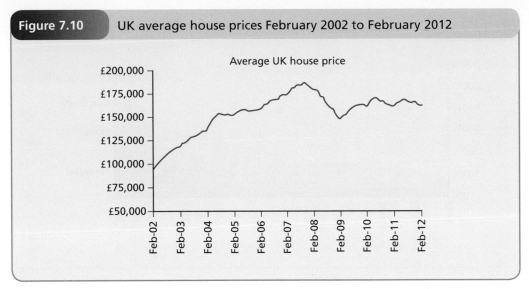

Figure 7.10   UK average house prices February 2002 to February 2012

Average UK house price

Source: Nationwide Building Society.

From the cycle we have described above we can see how the financial crisis developed. Two major, private organisations sponsored by the USA government to facilitate mortgages, Freddie Mac and Fannie Mae, had to be bailed out by the government in 2008 resulting in 80% government ownership. However, it was probably the 2008 collapse of Lehman Brothers that sparked off the worldwide financial crisis. Following that, between December 2008 and February 2011, 35 USA banks collapsed that had been supervised by the Federal Reserve.

But of course the USA financial system does not operate in isolation. Banks, investment banks, and other financial institutions are global businesses that operate worldwide. The spread of this crisis was seen in the subsequent collapse of major banks in the UK and Europe. In the UK in 2008, for example, Northern Rock bank was nationalised by the UK Government due to financial problems caused by the sub-prime mortgage crisis (the Virgin group subsequently finalised a deal to buy the bank in January 2012). The Royal Bank of Scotland and Lloyds TSB bank had to be bailed out by the UK Government and still remain heavily supported. The crisis had also spread to Europe with major financial problems in Greece, Spain, Italy, Portugal, and Ireland.

In March 2009, the Turner Review was published in the UK, having been commissioned in October 2008 to review the causes of the financial crisis. It indicated that the vast majority of the losses that arose were not in the books of end investors intending to hold the assets to maturity, but on the books of highly leveraged banks and bank-like institutions. The impact was seen not only in an increase in household debt; it was seen also in massively over-leveraged financial institutions which had been buying the newly developed financial instruments using debt, to then sell them on to other institutions which were also buying them with debt. As Figure 7.11 shows, there was a considerable growth in the relative size of the financial sectors in both the USA and the UK in the period leading up to the financial crisis along with a massive increase in debt in financial institutions.

Many valuable lessons should have been learned from the current global financial crisis and while many blame the failure as being an issue of inadequate regulation, the Turner Review heads its list of recommendations with strong warnings about capital inadequacy in the banking and non-banking system and the dangers of over-leveraging.

The banking system worldwide and the extensive use of debt (leveraging) have certainly been at the heart of the global financial crisis.

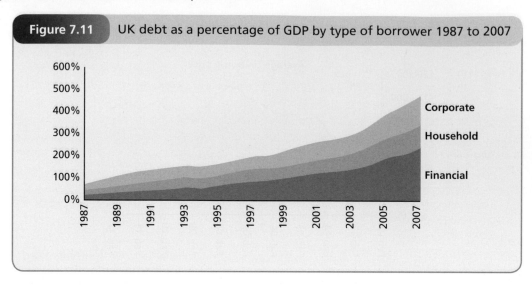

Figure 7.11 UK debt as a percentage of GDP by type of borrower 1987 to 2007

Source: The Turner Review.

Inadequate regulation, and the lowering of banking standards, and a culture in which there was a lack of ethical standards, and the lack of a moral compass have been very influencial factors. Bankers are certainly now held in the lowest esteem by the general public and the business community. As Mark Twain is alleged to have said 'a banker is a fellow who lends you his umbrella when the sun is shining, but wants it back the minute it begins to rain'. During the period since 2008, bankers have added fuel to the fire by triggering the huge escalation of the bonus culture (which will hopefully not continue), with bankers and the financial sector as the winners. The losers have been manufacturing, retailing, and service businesses, the general public and economies in general. Also, on 28 June 2012, BBC News reported that major banks were being investigated for interest rate fixing. Barclays Bank, which had been indirectly bailed out during the crisis, was the first bank to be fined (a total of £290m) for this practice in the USA and UK. Between 2005 and 2008, Barclays staff who submitted estimates of their own inter-bank lending, LIBOR, rates were frequently lobbied by their derivatives traders to put in numbers which would benefit their trading positions, in order to produce a profit for the bank (profits on which bonuses would be paid). Between 2007 and 2009, during the height of the global financial crisis, Barclays employees put in artificially low numbers, to avoid the suspicion that the bank was under financial stress and thus having to borrow at noticeably higher rates than its competitors.

Many financial commentators recommend that the tightening of regulation of the banking system is crucial to try and avoid a future financial crisis. Regulation may also ensure that banks (and all other organisations) establish an equitable and transparent top to bottom pay structure and eliminate the bonus culture. They further recommend a reform of the banking system through a splitting of the banking sector into traditional retail and investment banking.

Businesses are dependent on banks as a primary source of finance as debt has increasingly become the key source of new capital for business expansion. While leveraging, or an increasing proportion of debt taken on by an organisation, certainly magnifies potential rewards, it also increases financial risk, and this risk was un-hedged when the property bubble burst in 2007/2008, leaving banks with insufficient capital or liquidity that led to their failure.

But why do businesses use debt to finance expansion? As we saw in Chapter 4, it is because debt is relatively cheap and loan interest is allowable for tax, and therefore, as the level of a company's debt increases the company's average cost of capital may be reduced. But, the apparent higher net returns on investment projects may not perhaps have allowed for the risk of non-payment of the interest, or the risk of a failure to repay the loans themselves that supported such investments. Loans are relatively easily accessible and may be obtained quite quickly. Therefore, new investment projects can get started and completed quicker than by waiting longer for alternative funding, thereby satisfying the short-termist shareholders' aim of quick returns. Developed economies have therefore become totally reliant on debt and the current banking system, along with its high financial risk.

Many economists believe that an emphasis on equity funding for business expansion from banks, other financial institutions, and individuals, could perhaps reduce business reliance on high debt, which would reduce financial risk, and the risk of bankruptcy. This may be achieved through, for example, tax incentives related to equity financing and dividends, and perhaps retained earnings, and to encourage wider business ownership by employees, perhaps along the lines of the John Lewis Partnership.

The moral and ethical perspectives are more difficult to deal with and are largely down to individual behaviour.

The strengthening of, and giving teeth to, the corporate governance practices of developed economies could have a huge impact on avoiding future financial crises. In the UK, for example, it is possible that the UK Corporate Governance Code 2010 may be reinforced through legislation to further protect shareholder and employee interests. Perhaps the independence and powers of non-executive directors have not been what was originally intended by the Cadbury Committee? Maybe a more effective structure like the German two-tier board system could provide supervisory boards that may include persons with a specific interest, for example employee, shareholder, bank, and lender representatives. These would have the power of veto over executive board decisions, and be able to stand up to the Fred Goodwins and Robert Maxwells of this world.

In summary, it is our view that the underlying issues of the global financial crisis are:

- developed economies' dependence on the housing market
- too much reliance on debt, or leverage
- low interest rates
- cheap and easy credit
- lowering of banking standards
- lack of ethical and moral standards
- newly developed financial instruments.

The recent growth in popularity of Islamic banking may be partly as a result of the desire for financing that is subject to more coherent regulation than many of the products marketed by traditional Western banks.

Summary of key points

- Sources of finance internal to a company are its retained earnings, extended credit from suppliers, and the benefits gained from the more effective management of its working capital.
- Short-term, external sources of finance include overdrafts and short-term loans, which are used primarily to fund companies' working capital requirements.
- The main sources of long-term, external finance available to a company are equity (ordinary shares), preference shares, and debt (loans).
- Long-term finance is used to fund new businesses, companies that wish to 'go public', and to fund the acquisition of long-term non-current assets and new investment projects.

- Equity (ordinary shares) and debt (loans) have a number of unique characteristics and rights. For example, ordinary shares receive dividends and votes at the AGM, and loans receive interest and have no votes at the AGM.

- Dividends form part of the wealth of shareholders and are an important method of giving money back to shareholders, as are rights issues and share buy-backs.

- There is a range of debt finance available to companies, for example, loans, debentures, and bonds, which may be redeemable at a specific date, or irredeemable and never have to be repaid.

- As internationalisation increases there is a growing importance of international debt finance and the use of Eurobonds.

- Hybrid finance is neither purely debt nor equity, and includes convertible preference shares, convertible bonds, warrants, and mezzanine debt.

- Other sources of long-term, external finance available to UK companies include leasing, which companies may use as a source of long- and short-term finance, and UK Government and European Union funding.

- The primary capital markets are markets in which new equity and debt capital is initially raised by companies from investors.

- There are many methods that companies may use to issue new equity and debt finance.

- Stock exchanges, and in the UK the London Stock Exchange and the Alternative Investment Market (AIM), comprise the secondary capital markets.

- Financial institutions: banks; merchant banks; pension funds; insurance companies; finance companies, each play an important role in corporate financing.

- Islamic banking, as an alternative to traditional Western-style banking, is a fast-growing element of the financial sector, and Western banks have now established Islamic banking facilities within their own countries and overseas.

- The global financial crisis that started in the USA in 2008 and spread to the rest of the world is still with us many years later.

Glossary of key terms

bond A debt instrument, normally offering a fixed rate of interest (coupon) over a fixed period of time, and with a fixed redemption value (par).

bonus issue See scrip issue.

collateralised debt obligation (CDO) A product developed by financial institutions to package together unrelated debt instruments, such as bonds and mortgages, and then sell portions of that package to investors.

convertible bond A loan which gives the holder the right to convert to other securities, normally ordinary shares, and at a predetermined price and time.

credit default swap A form of credit insurance contract in which one party pays another party to protect it from the risk of default on a particular debt instrument. If that debt instrument (for example a mortgage) defaults, the insurer compensates the insured for his loss.

debenture The written acknowledgement of a debt by a company, usually given under its seal, and normally containing provisions as to payment of interest and the terms of repayment of the principal. A debenture may be secured on some or all of the assets of the company or its subsidiaries.

Eurobond A Eurobond is a type of bearer bond, which is a negotiable bond whose ownership is not registered by the issuer, but is presumed to lie with whoever has the physical possession of the bond. Specifically, a Eurobond is issued in a currency other than the currency of its country of issue, usually Eurodollars.

finance lease A lease is a contract between a lessor and a lessee for the hire of a specific asset. The lessor retains ownership of the asset but gives the right to the use of the asset to the lessee for an agreed period in return for the payment of specified rentals (SSAP 21 and IAS 17). A finance lease transfers substantially all the risks and rewards of ownership of the asset to the lessee.

hybrid finance A financial instrument that has the characteristics of both debt and equity.

initial public offering (IPO) The process by which a company may obtain a listing on a stock exchange. An IPO is a company's first public sale of its shares. Shares offered in an IPO are often, but not always, those of young, small companies seeking outside equity capital and a public market for their shares. Investors purchasing shares in IPOs generally must be prepared to accept considerable risks for the possibility of large gains.

intermediary offer An intermediary offer is effectively the same as a placing (see below), but in this case the shares are placed with financial intermediaries like stockbrokers.

introduction A Stock Exchange introduction may be used to obtain a listing, rather than issue new shares, if a company has a very large and widely spread share ownership where the amount of shares held by the general public is more than 25% (and remains so after the flotation).

Islamic banking A banking system based on economic legislation within the Shari'a, which represents the rules of God that came as a revelation from God to the prophet Mohamed.

Islamic finance Islamic finance focuses on the forbidding of usury and interest. It also excludes the areas forbidden by Islamic economic teaching, for example: usury; gambling; speculation; deception; monopoly; extortion.

issue by tender An issue by tender is a variation and alternative to an offer for sale (see below), where there is no prior fixed share price. The general public and institutional investors are invited to bid for shares at any price above the minimum share price set and underwritten by the issuing house. The shares on offer are then allocated at the striking price, which is determined by volume of applications at various prices, to all investors who have bid the striking price or higher ensuring that all shares that have been offered are sold.

mezzanine debt A non-traded debt which has risk and return characteristics somewhere between debt and equity, and attracts a high rate of interest. It is unsecured debt finance with a higher level of risk than that of loans with security, but lower than ordinary shares, and lower on the list of priority payments than straight debt.

offer for sale An invitation by a party other than the company itself to apply for shares in the company based on information contained in a prospectus.

operating lease A lease is a contract between a lessor and a lessee for the hire of a specific asset. The lessor retains ownership of the asset but gives the right to the use of the asset to the lessee for an agreed period in return for the payment of specified rentals (SSAP 21 and IAS 17). An operating lease is a lease other than a finance lease, where the lessor retains most of the risks and rewards of ownership.

ordinary share Shares which entitle the holders to the remaining divisible profits (and, in a liquidation, the assets) after prior interests, for example creditors and prior charge capital, have been satisfied.

placing A method of raising capital in which there is no public issue of the shares or bonds. Instead they are issued in 'blocks' to individual investors or institutions who have previously agreed to purchase at a predetermined price.

preference share Shares carrying a fixed rate of dividend, the holders of which, subject to the conditions of issue, have a prior claim to any company profits available for distribution. Preference shares may also have a prior claim to the repayment of capital in the event of a winding up.

rights issue The raising of new capital by giving existing shareholders the right to subscribe to new shares or debentures in proportion to their current holdings. These shares are usually issued at a discount to the market price. A shareholder not wishing to take up a rights issue may sell the rights.

scrip issue (or **bonus issue**) The capitalisation of the reserves of a company by the issue of additional shares to existing shareholders, in proportion to their holdings. Such shares are normally fully paid-up with no cash called for from the shareholders.

share re-purchase (or **share buy-back**) An arrangement where a company buys its own shares on the stock market. UK companies may purchase their own shares so long as the shareholders have given permission in a general meeting of the company. It is a way of returning cash to shareholders. The number of shares in issue decreases and so the earnings per share increase as does the value of the shares.

striking price See issue by tender above.

warrant A financial instrument that requires the issuer to issue shares (whether contingently or not) and contains no obligation for the issuer to transfer economic benefits (FRS 25 and IAS 32).

Assessment material

Questions

Q7.1 What are retained earnings and why are they an important source of corporate internal finance?

Q7.2 (i) What are the main sources of long-term, external finance available to an organisation?
(ii) What are their advantages and disadvantages?

Q7.3 Describe the key characteristics of ordinary share capital and the rights of ordinary shareholders.

Q7.4 Explain the various types of preference shares and their uses.

Q7.5 Describe the key characteristics of debt capital and the rights of debt holders.

Q7.6 Why in recent years have Eurobonds become an important source of international finance?

Q7.7 What are the advantages and disadvantages of convertible loans and warrants to companies and investors?

Q7.8 Why may leasing be considered as a long-term source of finance?

Q7.9 Why may the shareholders of a private limited company seek a listing on the Stock Exchange, and in what circumstances should they consider the AIM as an alternative?

Q7.10 Explain the various roles of merchant banks in the areas of corporate finance and fund management.

Discussion points

D7.1 The ex-owner/manager of a private limited company recently acquired by a large plc, of which he is now a board member, said: 'This company has grown very quickly over the past few years so that our sales revenue is now over £20m per annum. Even though we expect our revenue to grow further and double in the next two years I cannot see why we need to change our existing financing arrangements. I know we need to make some large investments in new machinery over the next two years but in the past we've always operated successfully using our existing overdraft facility, which has been increased as required, particularly when we've needed new equipment. I don't really see the need for all this talk about additional share capital and long-term loans.' Discuss.

D7.2 'The growth in the use of various forms of hybrid finance has complicated the financing process, and has provided no real benefit to companies or investors.' Discuss.

D7.3 'The only gain I can see from the use of leasing for our company is that it is a method of off balance sheet financing.' Discuss.

D7.4 Discuss the factors that an international company should consider in the raising of international debt capital and in determining its debt policy.

D7.5 'All banks operate using the same rules and regulations.' Discuss.

D7.6 'The cause of the 2008 global financial crisis was unethical banking.' Discuss.

D7.7 'The cause of the 2008 global financial crisis was excessive borrowing'. Discuss.

D7.8 'The cause of the 2008 global financial crisis was the USA housing market.' Discuss.

Exercises

Solutions are provided in Appendix 2 to all exercise numbers highlighted in colour.

Level I

E7.1   *Time allowed – 30 minutes*

Vine plc is a UK retail company that has been trading successfully for a number of years. The management of the company has, however, become increasingly concerned because there has been a substantial reduction in the company's bank balance for the year ending 31 December 2012, even though the company has continued to generate profits.

The Vine plc financial statements for 2011 and 2012 are as follows:

Income statement as at 31 December

	2011 £000	2012 £000
Revenue	7,000	9,000
Cost of sales	(3,500)	(4,200)
Gross profit	3,500	4,800
Operating expenses	(1,400)	(2,100)
Profit before tax	2,100	2,700
Income tax expense	(1,000)	(1,000)

(continued)

Profit for the year	1,100	1,700
Dividends	(600)	(700)
Retained profit for the year	500	1,000

Balance sheet as at 31 December

	2011 £000	2012 £000
Non-current assets	3,800	6,500
less Depreciation	(1,700)	(2,000)
	2,100	4,500
Current assets		
Inventories	3,200	4,200
Trade receivables	2,800	5,100
Other receivables	900	500
Cash and cash equivalents	1,500	100
	8,400	9,900
Current liabilities		
Trade payables	2,000	3,000
Other payables	500	500
Income tax payable	1,000	1,000
Dividends payable	600	700
	4,100	5,200
Non-current liabilities		
Debentures	2,000	3,200
Net assets	4,400	6,000
Equity		
Share capital	2,000	2,600
Retained earnings	2,400	3,400
Total equity	4,400	6,000

Required:

Vine plc's retained earnings have increased in 2012 compared with 2011 but to what extent has the business generated sufficient retained earnings to provide the financing it may require for the internal funding of new investment projects in the near future?

Provide the appropriate analysis to support your explanation about the retained earnings of the company.

E7.2   *Time allowed – 30 minutes*

Lamarr plc is an established UK-based manufacturing company, which currently generates profits of 16% on shareholders' funds. The company's current capital structure is as follows:

	£
Ordinary shares (£1)	400,000
Share premium account	175,000
Retained earnings	225,000
	800,000

The company is currently expanding its European operations and is considering raising £200,000 from a rights issue to fund a new investment project. As a result of its investment the company expects its return on total shareholders' funds to increase to an average of 16.5%. The current *ex-dividend* market price of Lamarr plc's shares is £2.20. The finance director of Lamarr plc has suggested three alternative prices for the rights issue:

$$£2.00$$
$$£1.80$$
$$£1.60$$

Required:

Which rights issue share price should Lamarr plc use if the company wishes to maximise its eps?

Level II

E7.3   *Time allowed – 45 minutes*
The directors of Emlyn plc are considering three methods of raising external finance of £5.5m by issuing either:

(a)   6% unsecured bonds at par
(b)   new ordinary shares by a one-for-four rights issue at an issue price of £2.20 per share
(c)   7% preference shares of £1 at par.

The current share price at 18 December 2012 is £2.50. The income statement for the year to 30 September 2012 and balance sheet as at 30 September 2012 are shown below.

Income statement for the year ended 30 September 2012

	£m
Revenue	45.5
Cost of sales	(29.6)
Gross profit	15.9
Distribution costs	3.1
Administrative expenses	1.4
Operating profit	11.4
Net finance costs	2.0
Profit before tax	9.4
Income tax expense	(3.3)
Profit for the year	6.1
Dividends	3.8
Retained profit for the year	2.3

Balance sheet as at 30 September 2012

	£m
Non-current assets	26.7
Current assets	29.9
Current liabilities	
Borrowings	6.3
Trade and other payables	13.2
Total current liabilities	19.5
Net current assets	10.4
Total assets less current liabilities	37.1
less	
Non-current liabilities	
4% debentures	13.5
Net assets	23.6
Equity	
Ordinary shares (50p)	5.0
Share premium account	3.9
Retained earnings	14.7
Total equity	23.6

Required:

Evaluate each of the sources of external finance that are being considered by Emlyn plc and recommend which should be used by the company, ignoring issue costs. You should clearly state any assumptions that you make.

E7.4 *Time allowed – 45 minutes*

Globe plc has issued share capital of 500,000 £1 ordinary shares, and the current share price is £3.80, in a market in which there is currently a general upward movement in share prices. Globe plc's eps have been increasing at a relatively stable rate and were reported at 50p in the most recent annual report and accounts. Globe plc is planning to redeem £400,000 5% redeemable bonds by making a one-for-four rights issue of ordinary shares. However, the company does not want to dilute its eps by more than 12%. The company also wants the rights issue shares to be priced around 10% below the current share price. The company's rate of corporation tax is 35%.

Required:

(i) How many shares would be required and what is the lowest market price at which the company would consider making the issue?

(ii) In theory what would be the resultant *ex rights* price of the shares, and the corresponding P/E (price earnings) ratio?

(iii) Outline the reasons generally why a company may prefer to make a rights issue of ordinary shares as a way of raising new capital rather than issue long-term debt, and explain whether there are circumstances in which a resulting dilution of earnings per share would be acceptable to shareholders.

E7.5   *Time allowed – 45 minutes*

Recently Wiltel plc issued £5m of convertible 8% debenture. The debentures have a nominal value of £100 and a current market value of £106. An interest payment was recently made. The debentures will be convertible into equity shares in three years' time at a rate of four shares for every £10 debenture. The shares are expected to have a market value of £3.50 each at that time, and all the debenture holders are expected to convert their debentures.

You may assume that Wiltel plc pays an average rate of corporation tax of 25%, and tax savings occur in the same year as the interest payments.

Required:

Calculate the cost of capital of the convertible debenture.

E7.6   *Time allowed – 45 minutes*

(i)   **Distinguish between the nature and functions of the primary and secondary capital markets, and illustrate with examples.**

(ii)   **Comment briefly on the suggestion that there is not enough new investment generally in industry because funds are otherwise used for speculation in secondary markets.**

(iii) **Explain the role of financial intermediaries as the financial institutions that help overcome the problems in ensuring that funds are put into economically desirable projects, by explaining the nature of the problems, the ways in which financial institutions help to overcome them, and why the large size of such financial institutions may be so beneficial.**

E7.7   *Time allowed – 45 minutes*

The board of Nimrod plc, a medium-sized UK-based retail company, is seeking to raise additional equity finance. They are not sure about in which market they should seek a listing – the London Stock Exchange or the Alternative Investment Market (AIM).

Required:

Explain the advantages and disadvantages of a market listing, and the differences between a listing on the London Stock Exchange and a listing on the AIM.

E7.8   *Time allowed – 45 minutes*

Curtis E Carr & Co specialises in hiring out executive cars. It is expanding its operations and is currently seeking to acquire a new fleet of four new cars. Purchase of the fleet of cars would cost the company £150,000. Alternatively, leasing the cars would cost the company £30,000 per annum for seven years. If the fleet of cars is purchased it is estimated that the net residual value after seven years would be £5,000 each. Curtis E Carr & Co currently has a cost of capital of 10% per annum.

Required:

(i)   **Calculate and compare the costs of purchase and leasing.**

(ii)   **Advise Curtis E Carr & Co with regard to lease or purchase and identify the additional factors that should be considered and their potential impact on this decision.**

E7.9 *Time allowed – 45 minutes*

Corston Carpentry is a medium-sized company that makes bespoke staircases for newly built houses. The company wishes to acquire some new equipment, which it estimates will cost £300,000. The managing director, Brian Wood, had intended to ask the company's bank for a medium-term loan. However, the finance director, John Cash, suggests that as the bank is now offering a suite of Islamic financing products they might consider this as an option.

Required:

Suggest what Shari'a-compliant financial products might be suitable for the acquisition of the new carpentry equipment and explain what is unique about these products.

8

Financial analysis

Chapter contents

Consolidated Income Statement

for the year ended 31st March 2012

	Notes	2012 £ million	2011 restated £ million
Revenue	1,2	**12,023.2**	9,984.8
Cost of sales		**(11,270.2)**	(9,337.2)
Gross profit		**753.0**	647.6
Distribution costs		**(119.8)**	(112.2)
Administrative expenses		**(183.1)**	(169.2)
Major impairment and restructuring charges	3	**–**	(71.8)
Amortisation of acquired intangibles	4	**(16.7)**	(14.5)
Operating profit	1,6	**433.4**	279.9
Finance costs	7	**(35.4)**	(33.1)
Finance income	8	**11.3**	12.4
Dissolution of associate		**–**	0.1
Profit before tax		**409.3**	259.3
Income tax expense	9	**(93.9)**	(75.5)
Profit for the year from continuing operations		**315.4**	183.8
Loss for the year from discontinued operations	40	**–**	(1.9)
Profit for the year		**315.4**	181.9
Attributable to:			
Owners of the parent company		**315.9**	181.5
Non-controlling interests		**(0.5)**	0.4
		315.4	181.9
		pence	pence
Earnings per ordinary share attributable to the equity holders of the parent company			
Continuing operations			
Basic	11	**148.7**	86.1
Diluted	11	**146.9**	85.6
Total			
Basic	11	**148.7**	85.2
Diluted	11	**146.9**	84.7

Consolidated Statement of Total Comprehensive Income

for the year ended 31st March 2012

	Notes	2012 £ million	2011 restated £ million
Profit for the year		**315.4**	181.9
Other comprehensive income:			
Currency translation differences	31	**(53.7)**	(8.9)
Cash flow hedges	31	**6.1**	3.7
Fair value gains on net investment hedges		**23.7**	2.2
Actuarial (loss) / gain on post-employment benefits assets and liabilities	14	**(70.6)**	85.4
Tax on above items taken directly to or transferred from equity	32	**18.7**	(30.0)
Other comprehensive (expense) / income for the year		**(75.8)**	52.4
Total comprehensive income for the year		**239.6**	234.3
Attributable to:			
Owners of the parent company		**240.1**	233.9
Non-controlling interests		**(0.5)**	0.4
		239.6	234.3

The notes on pages 131 to 167 form an integral part of the accounts.

Notes on the Accounts
for the year ended 31st March 2012

1 Segmental information

For management purposes, the group is organised into three operating divisions – Environmental Technologies, Precious Metal Products and Fine Chemicals and each division is represented by a director on the Board of Directors. These operating divisions represent the group's segments. Their principal activities are described on pages 26 to 42. The performance of the divisions is assessed by the Board of Directors on underlying operating profit, which is before amortisation of acquired intangibles, major impairment and restructuring charges and profit or loss on disposal of businesses. Each division is also assessed on sales excluding precious metals including inter-segment sales. Sales between segments are made at market prices, taking into account the volumes involved.

Year ended 31st March 2012

	Environmental Technologies £ million	Precious Metal Products £ million	Fine Chemicals £ million	Eliminations £ million	Total £ million
Revenue from external customers	3,123.6	8,609.4	290.2	–	12,023.2
Inter-segment revenue	131.0	1,232.0	2.2	(1,365.2)	–
Total revenue	3,254.6	9,841.4	292.4	(1,365.2)	12,023.2
External sales excluding the value of precious metals	1,861.9	534.3	282.4	–	2,678.6
Inter-segment sales	13.8	47.7	2.3	(63.8)	–
Sales excluding the value of precious metals	1,875.7	582.0	284.7	(63.8)	2,678.6
Segmental underlying operating profit	211.8	200.8	69.7	–	482.3
Unallocated corporate expenses					(32.2)
Underlying operating profit					450.1
Amortisation of acquired intangibles (note 4)					(16.7)
Operating profit					433.4
Net finance costs					(24.1)
Profit before tax					409.3
Segmental net assets	1,448.6	324.6	418.8	–	2,192.0
Net debt					(454.2)
Post-employment benefits net assets and liabilities					(169.4)
Deferred income tax assets and liabilities					(28.0)
Provisions and non-current other payables					(67.1)
Unallocated corporate net assets					58.5
Total net assets					1,531.8
Segmental capital expenditure	97.1	31.6	15.8	–	144.5
Other additions to non-current assets (excluding financial assets, deferred tax assets and post-employment benefits net assets)	0.3	–	–	(0.3)	–
Segmental total additions to non-current assets	97.4	31.6	15.8	(0.3)	144.5
Corporate capital expenditure					5.1
Total additions to non-current assets					149.6
Segment depreciation and amortisation	82.8	22.6	17.4	–	122.8
Corporate depreciation					3.3
Amortisation of acquired intangibles (note 4)					16.7
Total depreciation and amortisation					142.8

Notes on the Accounts

for the year ended 31st March 2012

1 Segmental information (continued)

Year ended 31st March 2011 (restated)

	Environmental Technologies £ million	Precious Metal Products £ million	Fine Chemicals £ million	Eliminations £ million	Total £ million
Revenue from external customers	2,703.4	7,028.3	253.1	–	9,984.8
Inter-segment revenue	4.6	1,241.3	1.9	(1,247.8)	–
Total revenue	2,708.0	8,269.6	255.0	(1,247.8)	9,984.8
External sales excluding the value of precious metals	1,561.3	475.4	243.6	–	2,280.3
Inter-segment sales	4.5	65.8	1.8	(72.1)	–
Sales excluding the value of precious metals	1,565.8	541.2	245.4	(72.1)	2,280.3
Segmental underlying operating profit	164.7	172.9	56.2	–	393.8
Unallocated corporate expenses					(27.6)
Underlying operating profit					366.2
Major impairment and restructuring charges (note 3)					(71.8)
Amortisation of acquired intangibles (note 4)					(14.5)
Operating profit					279.9
Net finance costs					(20.7)
Dissolution of associate					0.1
Profit before tax					259.3
Segmental net assets	1,534.9	357.3	417.5	–	2,309.7
Net debt					(639.4)
Post-employment benefits net assets and liabilities					(130.4)
Deferred income tax assets and liabilities					(19.8)
Provisions and non-current other payables					(89.1)
Unallocated corporate net assets					(27.2)
Total net assets					1,403.8
Segmental capital expenditure	90.1	26.1	16.0	–	132.2
Other additions to non-current assets (excluding financial assets, deferred tax assets and post-employment benefits net assets)	62.8	2.1	10.9	(0.3)	75.5
Segmental total additions to non-current assets	152.9	28.2	26.9	(0.3)	207.7
Corporate capital expenditure					5.7
Total additions to non-current assets					213.4
Segment depreciation and amortisation	78.8	24.3	17.2	–	120.3
Corporate depreciation					2.9
Amortisation of acquired intangibles (note 4)					13.6
Total depreciation and amortisation					136.8

The group received £1,690.0 million of revenue from one external customer (2011 £1,196.8 million) which is 14% (2011 12%) of the group's revenue from external customers. The revenue is reported in Precious Metal Products as it is generated by the group's platinum marketing and distribution activities and so has a very low return on sales.

Notes on the Accounts
for the year ended 31st March 2012

1 Segmental information (continued)

The group's country of domicile is the UK. Revenue from external customers is based on the customer's location. Non-current assets are based on the location of the assets and exclude financial assets, deferred tax assets and post-employment benefits net assets.

	Revenue from external customers		Non-current assets	
	2012	2011	2012	2011 restated
	£ million	£ million	£ million	£ million
UK	3,534.4	2,442.0	665.3	665.0
Germany	869.4	762.1	227.9	242.8
Rest of Europe	1,379.7	1,242.3	97.2	105.4
USA	2,896.9	2,690.5	343.3	350.4
Rest of North America	126.8	105.0	16.0	14.2
China (including Hong Kong)	1,497.4	1,197.9	51.8	53.1
Rest of Asia	1,027.4	965.1	123.8	118.6
Rest of World	691.2	579.9	34.3	42.7
Total	12,023.2	9,984.8	1,559.6	1,592.2

2 Revenue

	2012 £ million	2011 £ million
Sale of goods	11,771.9	9,801.1
Rendering of services	193.1	145.0
Royalties and licence income	58.2	38.7
Total revenue	12,023.2	9,984.8

3 Major impairment and restructuring charges

During the year ended 31st March 2011 the group closed its Haverton manufacturing site in Billingham, UK. This gave rise to a pre-tax impairment and restructuring charge of £14.8 million in that year, which was excluded from underlying operating profit.

During the year ended 31st March 2011 the group announced it was starting consultation with the Works Council about the closure of its autocatalyst facility in Brussels. The plant ceased production in July 2011, the closure of the site then commenced and is expected to be completed during the year ending 31st March 2013. This gave rise to a pre-tax impairment and restructuring charge in the year ended 31st March 2011 of £57.0 million, which was excluded from underlying operating profit. There is no impact in the consolidated income statement in the year ended 31st March 2012.

4 Amortisation of acquired intangibles

The amortisation of intangible assets which arise on the acquisition of businesses, together with any subsequent impairment of these intangible assets, is shown separately on the face of the income statement. It is excluded from underlying operating profit.

Learning objectives

Completion of this chapter will enable you to:

- Carry out a performance review of a business, including the use of SWOT analysis.
- Identify the limitations of the performance review process.
- Differentiate between divisional manager performance measurement and economic performance measurement.
- Analyse business performance through the use of ratio analysis of profitability; efficiency; liquidity; investment; financial structure.
- Use both profit and cash flow in the measurement of business performance.
- Identify the relationship between return on equity (ROE), return on assets (ROA), and gearing, using the Du Pont system of ratios.
- Carry out a horizontal analysis of the income statement and the balance sheet.
- Carry out a vertical analysis of the income statement and the balance sheet.
- Interpret the information provided by segmental reporting.
- Compare the use of cash flow versus profit as the best measure in the evaluation of financial performance.
- Use earnings before interest, tax, depreciation, and amortisation (EBITDA) as a close approximation of a cash flow performance measure.
- Explain the use of economic value added (EVA™) and market value added (MVA) as performance measures.
- Outline some of the multivariate discriminant analysis (MDA) methods of predicting corporate financial failure.

Introduction

Before the start of this chapter you will have already seen pages 122, and 131 to 133 of Johnson Matthey's report and accounts 2012 (reproduced on pages 374 to 377 of this book).

This chapter is concerned with how the performance of a business may be reviewed through analysis and evaluation of the balance sheet, the income statement, and the statement of cash flows. Business performance may be considered from outside or within the business for a variety of reasons. The performance review process provides an understanding of the business which, together with an analysis of all the relevant information, enables interpretation and evaluation of its financial performance during successive accounting periods and its financial position at the end of those accounting periods.

The chapter begins with an outline of the steps involved in the performance review process and also considers the limitations of such a process. The main body of this chapter is concerned with ratio analysis. Financial ratio analysis looks at the detailed use of profitability, efficiency, liquidity, investment, and financial structure ratios in the evaluation of financial performance. We also look at three further tools of analysis. Horizontal analysis, or common size analysis, provides a line-by-line comparison of the accounts of a company (income statement and balance sheet) with those of the previous year. Vertical analysis considers each item in the income statement and balance sheet, which are expressed as a percentage of, for example, total sales revenue and net assets (or total equity). Segmental reporting by large companies discloses information by each class of business, and by geographical region. Segmental analysis provides users of financial information with much more meaningful financial analysis of companies, which comprise diverse businesses supplying different products and services, rather than being engaged in a single type of business.

There is an ongoing debate as to whether cash flow or profit represents the best basis for financial performance measurement. The use of earnings per share (eps) and cash flow in performance measurement are discussed along with the measurement of earnings before interest, tax, depreciation, and amortisation (EBITDA) as an approximation of cash flow. Economic value added (EVA™) has become increasingly important in its use by companies as a performance measure, being an even closer approximation of cash flow. The chapter closes with an outline of some of the methods of multivariate discriminant analysis (MDA) that have been developed to try and predict corporate financial failure.

The performance review process

The availability of accurate and timely accounting and financial information is very important in support of the corporate finance function. Analyses of accounting and financial information is of interest to the various stakeholders of companies, both internal and external to the organisation, and for a variety of reasons. For example, shareholders, lenders, suppliers, customers, and banks are interested in analysing a company's financial performance and position from the perspective of safeguarding their interests and ensuring that objectives are being met with regard to their own particular requirements.

At the strategic level, a company will be interested in analysing:

- its own financial performance
- the performance of other companies.

Companies' annual and interim reports and accounts, which include their financial statements, provide a wealth of financial and non-financial information. The reasons for the analysis by a company of the performance of other companies may be to determine:

- the financial stability of potential new suppliers
- the financial health of customers
- the financial policies and cost structures of competitors
- identification of possible takeover targets
- valuation of shares of Ltd companies
- valuation of companies in mergers and acquisitions,

and banks and other financial institutions will be particularly interested in using financial analysis to try and predict corporate failure and identify companies that may represent a poor lending risk.

A performance review and analysis by the company of it own accounting, financial, and non-financial information may be undertaken for a number of reasons, for example to:

- support the planning and budgeting process
- assist in investment decisions
- monitor manager performance against targets
- monitor company performance against standards

- identify areas where there is room for improvement
- assist in the management of working capital
- support the cash management and treasury function.

The main aim of a performance review is to provide an understanding of the business and, together with an analysis of all the relevant information, provide an interpretation of the results. A performance review is generally undertaken using a standard format and methodology. The most effective performance review is provided from a balanced view of each of the activities of the organisation, which necessarily involves the close co-operation of each role: marketing; research and development; design; engineering; manufacturing; sales; logistics; finance; human resources management.

The performance review process begins with a **SWOT analysis** and works through a number of steps to the conclusions, as outlined in Figure 8.1. A SWOT analysis includes an internal analysis of the company, and an analysis of the company's position with regard to its external environment.

1. SWOT analysis

SWOT is shorthand for strengths, weaknesses, opportunities, and threats. The first look at a company's performance usually involves listing the key features of the company by looking internally at its particular strengths and weaknesses, and externally at risks or threats to the company and opportunities that it may be able to exploit. The SWOT analysis may

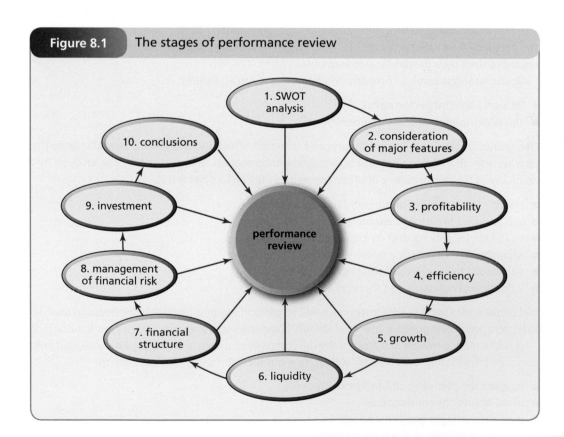

Figure 8.1 The stages of performance review

give some indication of, for example, the strength of the company's management team, how well it is doing on product quality, and areas as yet untapped within its marketplace. To keep the analysis focused, a cruciform chart may be used for SWOT analysis. An example is shown in Figure 8.2, relating to the position in 2010 of the low-budget airline, Ryanair.

Figure 8.2   **An example of a SWOT analysis – Ryanair 2010**

Strengths	**Weaknesses**
Firm operating strategy Robust route network Strong fleet operations	Declining profitability Legal proceedings Unfunded employee post-retirement benefits
Opportunities	**Threats**

Accelerating UK airlines industry
Positive outlook for the European online
  travel market
Growing global travel and tourism industry
	Intense competition and price discounting
	EU regulations on denied boarding
	  compensation

---

2. Consideration of major features

The increasing amount of information currently provided in published financial statements enables the analyst to look in detail at the various industrial and geographical sectors of any business, the trends within these and the business in general. Further background information may be extracted from the accounting policies, the auditors' report, chairman's report and details of any significant events that have been highlighted.

3. Profitability

A number of financial indicators and ratios may be considered to assess the profitability of the company, which may include:

- gross profit (or gross margin) compared with sales revenue
- return on sales (ROS)
- **return on capital employed (ROCE)**, or **return on investment (ROI)**.

4. Efficiency

The efficiency of the company may be considered in terms of its:

- operating cycle – its receivables **collection days**, **payables days**, and **inventories days**
- asset turnover
- operational gearing (see Chapter 13)
- **vertical analysis** of its income statement.

In a vertical analysis of the income statement (which may also be applied to the balance sheet) each item is expressed as a percentage of sales revenue. The vertical analysis provides evidence of structural changes in the accounts such as increased profitability through more efficient production.

5. Growth

Growth of the organisation may relate to sales revenue growth and gross profit growth. **Horizontal analysis** (or common size analysis) of the income statement provides a line-by-line analysis of the numbers in the financial statements compared with those of the previous year. It may provide a trend of changes showing either growth or decline in these numbers over a number of years by calculation of annual percentage growth rates in profits, sales revenues, inventories or any other item.

6. Liquidity

Liquidity is concerned with the short-term solvency of the company. It is assessed by looking at a number of key solvency ratios, for example:

- **current ratio**
- **quick ratio** (or acid test)
- **defensive interval**
- cash ROCE
- **cash interest cover**.

7. Financial structure

How the company is financed relates to the long-term solvency of the company. It is assessed by looking at a number of further key solvency ratios, for example:

- **gearing** – the proportion of capital employed financed by lenders rather than shareholders, expressed in a number of ways, for example the **debt/equity ratio** (long-term loans and preference shares/ordinary shareholders' funds)
- **dividend cover** (eps/dividend per share)
- **interest cover** (profit before interest and tax (PBIT)/interest payable)
- various forms of off balance sheet financing.

Off balance sheet financing is defined as the funding or refinancing of a company's operations in such a way that, under legal requirements and existing accounting conventions, some or all of the finance may not be disclosed in its balance sheet. The International Accounting Standards Board (IASB) has tried (and indeed continues to try) to introduce regulations forcing the exclusion of this type of financing.

8. Management of financial risk

The global market is here. Companies increasingly trade globally with greater levels of sophistication in products, operations, and financing. Risk assessment and the management of risk are therefore now assuming increasing importance. The main areas of financial risk are in investment, foreign currency exchange rates and interest rates, and levels of trade credit.

9. Investment

Investment ratios examine whether or not the company is undertaking sufficient investment to ensure its future profitability. These ratios include, for example:

- earnings per share (eps)
- **price/earnings ratio (P/E)**
- capital expenditure/sales revenue
- capital expenditure/gross non-current assets
- **dividend yield**.

10. Conclusions

The conclusions of the performance review will include consideration of the company's SWOT analysis and the main performance features. It will consider: growth and profitability, and whether or not these are maintainable; levels of finance and investment, and whether there is sufficient cash flow; the future plans of the business.

All performance reviews must use some sort of benchmark. Comparisons may be made against past periods and against budget; comparisons may also be made with other companies and using general data relating to the industry within which the company operates. Later in this chapter we will look in more detail at the use of profitability, efficiency, liquidity, and investment ratios, and ratios relating to financial structure.

> **Progress check 8.1**
>
> Describe each of the stages in a business performance review process.

Limitations of the performance review process

There are many obvious limitations to the above approach. In comparing performance against other companies (and sometimes within the company in comparing past periods), or looking at industrial data, it should be borne in mind that:

- there may be a lack of uniformity in accounting definitions and techniques
- the balance sheet is only a snapshot in time, and only represents a single estimate of the company's position
- there may actually be no standards for comparison
- changes in the environment and changes in money values, together with short-term fluctuations, may have a significant impact
- the past should really not be relied on as a good predictor of the future.

The speed of change in the computer peripherals market is well known to manufacturers. Some components may have been large revenue generators for many years yet even they finally cease to have a market. Sony had sold 3.5 inch floppy disks since 1983 and in 2002 sold 47 million of them in Japan. Inevitably, new technologies eventually superseded the floppy disk, leading to its decline in sales revenues (see the press extract below). Even a product that currently provides a strong income stream will not do so indefinitely.

The past is not a good predictor of the future

They were once the stalwarts of the technological era. But the humble floppy disk is about to bite the dust once and for all. The unwieldy storage devices have been shown the door by their biggest manufacturer, Sony, which has announced that production will cease next year.

The plastic storage 'disks' have been usurped by smaller USB drives, which have more space for data and are far easier to transport. To tell the truth, we thought sales of floppy disks had nose-dived years ago. Yet, incredibly, Sony still sold 12 million floppy disks last year in Japan.

The first floppy was invented by IBM in 1971 and was eight wobbly inches wide. And while most people thought the floppiness of the whole thing gave the product its name, it was actually the circular magnetic disk inside that was technically the 'floppy' bit. This pioneering technology allowed information to be passed between computers – but heaven forbid you forgot to slap a brightly coloured sticky label on your anonymous-looking disk to remind you of the contents.

Later, the more common 3.5in disks weren't floppy at all, but the name stuck – though some show-offs called them 'diskettes'. Hundreds of millions of floppy disks have been sold since 1971 – until now.

But although computers don't have built in floppy drives any more, the floppy's legacy will live on – we still click on a little icon of one to save a document when we're using most computer software today.

Source: **Farewell then … floppy disks**, by Chris Beanland © *Daily Mail*, 28 April 2010

Diversified companies present a different set of problems. Such companies by their very nature comprise companies engaged in various industrial sectors, each having different market conditions, financial structures, and expectations of performance. The notes to the accounts, which appear in each company's annual report and accounts, invariably present a less than comprehensive picture of the company's position.

Progress check 8.2

What are the main limitations encountered in carrying out the performance review of a business?

As time goes by, and accounting and financial standards and legislation get tighter and tighter, the number of loopholes which allow any sort of window dressing of a company's results are reduced. Inevitably, however, there will always remain the possibility of the company's position being presented in ways that may not always represent the 'truth'. We will now look at the type of information that may be used and the important financial ratios and their meaning and relevance.

Economic performance measurement

Most large organisations are divided into separate divisions or business units in which their individual managers have autonomy and total responsibility for investment and profit. Within each business unit there is usually a functional structure comprising many departments. Divisionalisation is more appropriate for companies with diversified activities. The performance of the managers of each division may be measured in a number of ways, for example return on investment (ROI) and residual income (RI).

The relationships between divisions should be regulated so that no division, by seeking to increase its own profit, can reduce the profitability of the company as a whole. Therefore, there are strong arguments for producing two broad types of performance measure. One type of measure is used to evaluate managerial performance and the other type of measure is used to evaluate economic performance. In this chapter we are primarily concerned with the performance of the organisation as a whole. We will look at ratios that measure economic performance, which focus not only on profit and profitability, but on a range of other areas of performance that include, for example, cash and working capital.

Ratio analysis

The reasons for a performance review may be wide and varied. Generally, it is required to shed light on the extent to which the objectives of the company are being achieved. These objectives may be:

- to earn a satisfactory return on capital employed (ROCE)
- to maintain and enhance the financial position of the business with reference to the management of working capital, non-current assets, and bank borrowings
- to achieve cost targets and other business targets such as improvements in labour productivity.

Ratio analysis is an important area of performance review. It is far more useful than merely considering absolute numbers, which on their own may have little meaning. Ratios may be used:

- for a subjective assessment of the company or its constituent parts
- for a more objective way to aid decision-making
- to provide **cross-sectional analysis** and **inter-company comparison**
- to establish models for loan and credit ratings
- to provide equity valuation models to value businesses
- to analyse and identify under-priced shares and takeover targets
- to predict company failure – there are various prediction models such as those developed by John Argenti and also Edward Altman (see the later section about predicting corporate financial failure).

As we saw in our examination of the performance review process, the key ratios include the following categories:

- profitability
- efficiency
- liquidity
- investment
- financial structure.

We will use the financial statements of Flatco plc, an engineering company, shown in Figures 8.3 to 8.8, to illustrate the calculation of the key financial ratios. The income statement and statement of cash flows are for the year ended 31 December 2012 and the balance sheet is as at 31 December 2012. Comparative figures are shown for 2011.

| Figure 8.3 | Flatco plc balance sheets as at 31 December 2011 and 2012 |

Flatco plc
Balance sheet as at 31 December 2012

	2012 £000	2011 £000
Assets		
Non-current assets		
Tangible	1,884	1,921
Intangible	416	425
Investments	248	248
Total non-current assets	2,548	2,594
Current assets		
Inventories	311	268
Trade and other receivables	1,162	1,134
Cash and cash equivalents	327	17
Total current assets	1,800	1,419
Total assets	4,348	4,013
Liabilities		
Current liabilities		
Borrowings and finance leases	50	679
Trade and other payables	553	461
Current tax liabilities	50	44
Dividends payable	70	67
Provisions	82	49
Total current liabilities	805	1,300
Non-current liabilities		
Borrowings and finance leases	173	–
Trade and other payables	154	167
Deferred tax liabilities	–	–
Provisions	222	222
Total non-current liabilities	549	389
Total liabilities	1,354	1,689
Net assets	2,994	2,324
Equity		
Share capital	1,200	1,000
Share premium account	200	200
Retained earnings	1,594	1,124
Total equity	2,994	2,324

Profitability ratios

It is generally accepted that the primary objective for the managers of a business is to maximise the wealth of the owners of the business. To this end there are a number of other objectives, subsidiary to the main objective. These include, for example:

- survival
- stability
- growth
- maximisation of market share
- maximisation of sales revenues
- maximisation of profit
- maximisation of return on capital.

Figure 8.4

Flatco plc income statements for the years ended 31 December 2011 and 2012

Flatco plc
Income statement for the year ended 31 December 2012

	2012 £000	2011 £000
Revenue	3,500	3,250
Cost of sales	(2,500)	(2,400)
Gross profit	1,000	850
Distribution costs	(300)	(330)
Administrative expenses	(250)	(160)
Other income	100	90
Operating profit	550	450
Finance income	111	80
Finance costs	(71)	(100)
Profit before tax	590	430
Income tax expense	(50)	(44)
Profit for the year from continuing operations	540	386
Profit for the year from discontinued operations	–	–
Profit for the year	540	386

Figure 8.5

Flatco plc additional information to the financial statements 2012

Additional information

Administrative expenses for 2012 include an exceptional item of £95,000 redundancy costs.

Dividends were £70,000 for 2012 (2011: £67,000) and retained earnings were £470,000 (2011: £319,000).

Authorised and issued share capital 31 December 2012 was 1,200,000 £1 ordinary shares (2011: 1,000,000).

Total assets less current liabilities 31 December 2010 were £2,406,000.

Trade receivables 31 December 2012 were £573,000 (2011: £517,000; 2010: £440,000).
Other receivables (prepayments) 31 December 2012 were £589,000 (2011: £617,000).
The market value of ordinary shares in Flatco plc on 31 December 2012 was £2.75 (2011: £3.00).

During the year 2012 tangible non-current assets were acquired at a cost of £286,000 (2011: £170,000), and intangible non-current assets were acquired at a cost of £34,000. During 2012, intangible non-current assets were sold for £21,000, generating neither a profit nor a loss.

Tangible non-current assets depreciation provision at 31 December 2012 was £1,102,000 (2011: £779,000)

Current liabilities: Provisions for 2012 include Accruals £82,000, and for 2011 include Accruals £49,000. Trade and other payables for 2012 include Trade payables £553,000 and other payables zero, and for 2011 include Trade payables £461,000 and other payables zero.

Figure 8.6	Flatco plc cash generated from operations for the years ended 31 December 2011 and 2012

Flatco plc
Cash generated from operations for the year ended 31 December 2012

	2012 £000	2011 £000
Profit before tax	590	430
Depreciation and amortisation charges	345	293
Adjust finance (income)/costs	(40)	20
Increase in inventories	(43)	(32)
Increase in trade and other receivables [1,134 − 1,162]	(28)	(25)
Increase in trade and other payables, and provisions		
[461 − 553 + 49 − 82 + 167 − 154]	112	97
Cash generated from operations	936	783

Figure 8.7	Flatco plc statement of cash flows for the years ended 31 December 2011 and 2012

Flatco plc
Statement of cash flows for the year ended 31 December 2012

	2012 £000	2011 £000
Cash flows from operating activities		
Cash generated from operations	936	783
Interest paid	(71)	(100)
Income tax paid	(44)	(40)
Net cash generated from operating activities	821	643
Cash flows from investing activities		
Purchases of tangible assets	(286)	(170)
Proceeds from sales of intangible assets	21	–
Purchases of intangible assets	(34)	–
Interest received	11	–
Dividends received	100	80
Net cash outflow from investing activities	(188)	(90)
Cash flows from financing activities		
Proceeds from issue of ordinary shares	200	290
Proceeds from borrowings	173	–
Dividends paid to equity shareholders	(67)	(56)
Net cash inflow from financing activities	306	234
Net increase in cash and cash equivalents in the year	939	787
Cash and cash equivalents and bank overdrafts at beginning of year	(662)	(1,449)
Cash and cash equivalents and bank overdrafts at end of year	277	(662)

Figure 8.8	Flatco plc analysis of cash and cash equivalents and bank overdrafts as at 31 December 2011 and 2012

Flatco plc
Analysis of cash and cash equivalents and bank overdrafts as at 31 December 2012

	At 1 January 2012 £000	At 31 December 2012 £000
Cash and cash equivalents	17	327
Bank overdrafts	(679)	(50)
Cash and cash equivalents and bank overdrafts	(662)	277

	At 1 January 2011 £000	At 31 December 2011 £000
Cash and cash equivalents	–	17
Bank overdrafts	(1,449)	(679)
Cash and cash equivalents and bank overdrafts	(1,449)	(662)

Each group of financial ratios is concerned to some extent with survival, stability, growth, and maximisation of shareholder wealth. We will first consider ratios in the broad area of profitability (see Figure 8.9), which give an indication of how successful the business has been in its financial performance objectives.

Figure 8.9	Profitability ratios

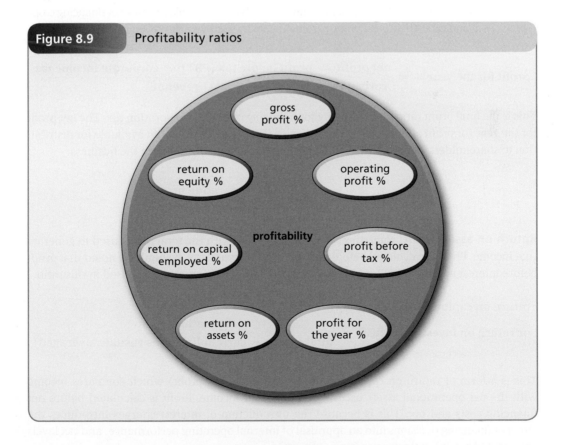

$$\text{gross profit \%} = \frac{\text{gross profit}}{\text{revenue}} = \frac{\text{revenue} - \text{cost of sales (COS)}}{\text{revenue}}$$

This ratio is used to gain an insight into the relationship between production and purchasing costs and sales revenue. The gross profit (or gross margin) needs to be high enough to cover all other costs incurred by the company, and leave an amount for profit. If the gross profit percentage is too low then sales prices may be too low, or the purchase costs of materials or production costs may be too high.

$$\text{operating profit \%} = \frac{\text{operating profit}}{\text{revenue}}$$
$$= \frac{\text{revenue} - \text{COS} - \text{other operating expenses}}{\text{revenue}}$$

The operating profit ratio (or profit before interest and tax (PBIT) excluding other operating income) is a key ratio that shows the profitability of the business before incurring financing costs. If the numerator is not multiplied by 100 to give a percentage, it shows the profit generated from each £1 of sales revenue.

$$\text{profit before tax (PBT) \%} = \frac{\text{profit before tax}}{\text{revenue}} = \frac{\text{operating profit} +/- \text{net interest}}{\text{revenue}}$$

This is the profit ratio that uses profit after financing costs, having allowed for interest payable and interest receivable. It should be remembered that profit before tax (PBT) is a profit measure that goes further than dealing with the trading performance of the business, in allowing for net financing costs. It provides an indication of pre-tax profit-earning capability from the sales revenue for the period.

$$\text{profit for the year \%} = \frac{\text{net profit}}{\text{revenue}} = \frac{\text{profit before tax (PBT)} - \text{corporate income tax}}{\text{revenue}}$$

This is the final profit ratio after allowing for financing costs and corporation tax. The net profit for the year (or profit after tax) or return on sales (ROS) ratio is the profit available for distribution to shareholders in the form of dividends and/or future investment in the business.

$$\text{return on assets (ROA) \%} = \frac{\text{operating profit}}{\text{total assets}}$$

Return on assets (ROA) compares operational income with the total assets used to generate that income. Profit is calculated before net financing costs and tax. It should be noted that profit before interest and tax (PBIT) or profit after tax (PAT) may alternatively be used in this ratio.

$$\text{return on capital employed (ROCE)}$$
$$\text{or return on investment (ROI)} = \frac{\text{operating profit}}{\text{total assets} - \text{current liabilities (usually averaged)}}$$

This is a form of return on capital employed (using pre-tax profit) which compares income with the net operational assets used to generate that income. Profit is calculated before net financing costs and tax. This is because the introduction of interest charges introduces the effect of financing decisions into an appraisal of internal operating performance, and tax levels are decided by external agencies (governments).

The average cost of a company's finance (equity, debentures, loans), weighted according to the proportion each element bears to the total pool of capital, is called the weighted average cost of capital (WACC). The difference between a company's ROI and its WACC is an important measure of the extent to which the organisation is endeavouring to optimise its use of financial resources. In its 2009 annual report, Sainsbury's plc reported on the improvement in their ROCE versus WACC gap, stating that 'the pre-tax return on average capital employed continued to improve significantly, increasing by 85 basis points in the year to 11.0 per cent, around 70 basis points above the company's weighted average cost of capital'.

A company manages its ROCE through monitoring its operating profit as a percentage of its capital employed. A company manages its WACC by planning the proportions of its financing through either equity (ordinary shares) or debt (loans), with regard to the relative costs of each, based on dividends and interest.

WACC is an important measure when companies are considering acquisitions. This is emphasised by the Rio Tinto Group plc in their 2009 annual report, where the company identified how WACC is used in determining the potential future benefits that may be derived from investments:

> Forecast cash flows are discounted to present values using Rio Tinto's weighted average cost of capital with appropriate adjustment for the risks associated with the relevant cash flows, to the extent that such risks are not reflected in the forecast cash flows. For final feasibility studies and ore reserve estimation, internal hurdle rates are used which are generally higher than the weighted average cost of capital.

This refers to the importance of WACC as a factor used in the evaluation of investment in projects undertaken (or not) by a business (see Chapters 5 and 7).

$$\text{return on equity (ROE)} = \frac{\text{net profit}}{\text{equity}}$$

Another form of return on capital employed, **return on equity (ROE)**, measures the return to the owners on the book value of their investment in a company. The return is measured as the residual profit after all expenses and charges have been made, and after corporate income tax has been deducted. The equity comprises share capital, retained earnings and reserves.

The profitability performance measures discussed above consider the general performance of organisations as a whole. It is also important for managers to be aware of particular areas of revenue or expenditure that may have significant importance with regard to their own company and that have a critical impact on the net profit of the business. Companies may, for example:

- suffer large warranty claim costs
- have to pay high royalty fees
- receive high volumes of customer debit notes (invoices) for a variety of product or service problems deemed to be their fault.

All managers should fully appreciate such key items of cost specific to their own company and be innovative and proactive in identifying ways that these costs may be reduced and minimised.

Managers should also be aware of the general range of costs for which they may have no direct responsibility, but nevertheless may be able to reduce significantly by:

- improved communication
- involvement
- generation of ideas for waste reduction, increased effectiveness, and cost reduction.

Such costs may include:

- the cost of the operating cycle
- costs of warehouse space
- project costs
- costs of holding inventories
- depreciation (as a result of capital expenditure)
- warranty costs
- repairs and maintenance
- stationery costs
- communications costs
- printing costs.

The relative importance of these costs through their impact on profitability will of course vary from company to company.

Worked example 8.1

We will calculate the profitability ratios for Flatco plc for 2012 and the comparative ratios for 2011, and comment on the profitability of Flatco plc.

Gross profit

$$\text{gross profit \% 2012} = \frac{\text{gross profit}}{\text{revenue}} = \frac{£1,000 \times 100\%}{£3,500} = 28.6\%$$

$$\text{gross profit \% 2011} = \frac{£850 \times 100\%}{£3,250} = 26.2\%$$

Profit before interest and tax, PBIT (PBIT is operating profit plus finance income)

$$\text{PBIT \% 2012} = \frac{\text{PBIT}}{\text{revenue}} = \frac{£661 \times 100\%}{£3,500} = 18.9\%$$

$$\text{PBIT \% 2011} = \frac{£530 \times 100\%}{£3,250} = 16.3\%$$

Profit for the year (or profit after tax PAT), or return on sales (ROS)

$$\text{PAT \% 2012} = \frac{\text{net profit}}{\text{revenue}} = \frac{£540 \times 100\%}{£3,500} = 15.4\%$$

$$\text{PAT \% 2011} = \frac{£386 \times 100\%}{£3,250} = 11.9\%$$

Return on assets, ROA

$$\text{ROA \% 2012} = \frac{\text{operating profit}}{\text{total assets}} = \frac{£550 \times 100\%}{£4,348} = 12.6\%$$

$$\text{ROA \% 2011} = \frac{£450 \times 100\%}{£4,013} = 11.2\%$$

Return on capital employed, ROCE (or return on investment, ROI)

$$\text{ROCE \% 2012} = \frac{\text{operating profit}}{\text{total assets} - \text{current liabilities (average capital employed)}}$$

$$= \frac{£550 \times 100\%}{(£3,543 + £2,713)/2} = \frac{£550 \times 100\%}{£3,128} = 17.6\%$$

$$\text{ROCE \% 2011} = \frac{£450 \times 100\%}{(£2,713 + £2,406)/2} = \frac{£450 \times 100\%}{£2,559.5} = 17.6\%$$

Return on equity, ROE

$$\text{ROE \% 2012} = \frac{\text{PAT}}{\text{equity}} = \frac{£540 \times 100\%}{£2,994} = 18.0\%$$

$$\text{ROE \% 2011} = \frac{£386 \times 100\%}{£2,324} = 16.6\%$$

Report on the profitability of Flatco plc

Sales revenue for the year 2012 increased by 7.7% over the previous year, partly through increased volumes and partly through higher selling prices.

Gross profit improved from 26.2% to 28.6% of sales revenue, as a result of increased selling prices but also lower costs of production.

PBIT improved from 16.3% to 18.9% of sales revenue (and operating profit, which is calculated as operating profit × 100/sales revenue, improved from 13.8% to 15.7%). If the one-off costs of redundancy of £95,000 had not been incurred in the year 2012 operating profit would have been £645,000 (£550,000 + £95,000) and the operating profit ratio would have been 18.4% of sales revenue, an increase of 4.6% over 2011. The underlying improvement in operating profit performance (excluding the one-off redundancy costs) was achieved from the improvement in gross profit and from the benefits of lower distribution costs and administrative expenses.

ROA increased from 11.2% to 12.6%. This was because although the total assets of the company had increased by 8.3%, operating profit had increased by 22.2% in 2012 compared with 2011.

ROCE was static at 17.6% because the increase in capital employed as a result of additional share capital of £200,000 and long-term loans of £173,000 was matched by a similar increase in operating profit.

Return on equity increased from 16.6% to 18%, despite the increase in ordinary share capital. This was because of improved profit after tax (up 3.5% to 15.4%) arising from increased income from non-current asset investments and lower costs of finance. Corporation tax was only marginally higher than the previous year despite higher pre-tax profits.

Progress check 8.3

How may financial ratio analysis be used as part of the process of review of business performance?

Efficiency ratios

The regular monitoring of efficiency ratios by companies is crucial because they relate directly to how effectively business transactions are being converted into cash. For example, if companies are not regularly paid in accordance with their terms of trading:

- their profit margins may be eroded by the financing costs of funding overdue accounts
- cash flow shortfalls may put pressure on their ability to meet their day-to-day obligations to pay employees, replenish inventory, etc.

Despite the introduction of legislation to combat slow payment of suppliers, the general situation is still poor in the UK. As a result the UK Government announced in 2011 that it would implement the EU Directive on late payments in the first half of 2012, instead of in 2013 as originally planned. The basic principle of the Directive is that it sets 30 days as standard terms for public and private entities to pay invoices. This may be extended to 60 days when suppliers have specifically agreed to give customers a grace period. Additionally, small companies may also charge 8% interest on

Companies that fail to pay suppliers on time

Businesses across Wales are trapped on a late payment merry-go-round as they try to reconcile time spent maintaining a healthy cash flow with fighting the ongoing downturn, according to new research from Bibby Financial Services. According to the study, almost half of Welsh businesses (49%) surveyed reported that they had been forced to accept extended payment terms from customers during the past 12 months. As a result, businesses are in turn squeezing their own suppliers to bridge the resulting cash flow gap with 53% asking suppliers to wait longer for their invoices to be settled. However, with the delayed European late payment directive due to come into force on March 16, 2013, Welsh businesses have just under a year to clean up their act and get payments under control in line with the new regulations.

Designed to protect businesses by capping maximum contractual payment periods at 60 days, firms that have agreed longer terms with suppliers to offset the delay in customer payments are in danger of non-compliance as they struggle to bring payment cycles within the legal requirements. The research found when it comes to payment cycles, a significant 88% offer payment terms beyond 60 days on their invoices as a matter of course. And with 35% typically having to wait at least a month beyond agreed payment terms to get paid, businesses in Wales are putting themselves under real pressure when it comes to balancing the books.

Terry Wolfendale, spokesman for Bibby Financial Services Wales, said: 'Over and above the need to clean up their act with the late payment directive on the horizon, taking a 'rob Peter to pay Paul' approach to late payment is not good business practice when it comes to managing cash flow. Despite 65% of the businesses we spoke to agreeing that extended payment terms have had a negative effect on their cash flow management, unfortunately, many firms feel they have no choice but to join the late payment merry-go-round as they struggle to keep customers happy and treat suppliers fairly.'

Interestingly, there appears to be a clear north/south divide in dealing with the late payment problem between firms in the north forced to extend payment terms from customers over the last year, and those in the south who have continued with the same agreements. However, unfortunately it is businesses in Wales that have been the most widely affected by the late payment issue, with almost one in two (49%) having payment terms extended over the last 12 months, compared to just 23% in the South West of England.

Source: **Firms forced to 'rob Peter to pay Paul' in late-payments circle,** by Siôn Barry © *The Western Mail*, 11 April 2012

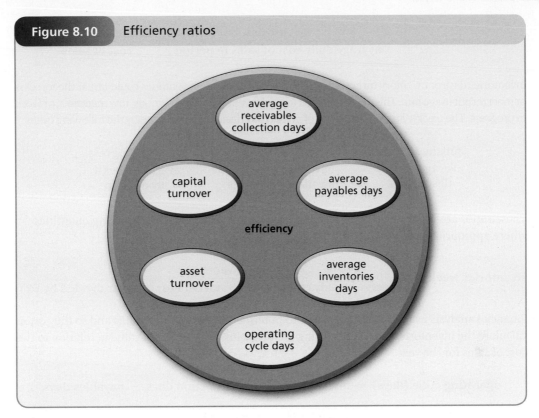

Figure 8.10   Efficiency ratios

overdue invoices in addition to a £35 fee to cover costs. However, some companies are finding it difficult to realise the benefits from this Directive as illustrated in the press extract above.

The range of efficiency ratios is illustrated in Figure 8.10.

Efficiency generally relates to the maximisation of output from resources devoted to an activity or the output required from a minimum input of resources. Efficiency ratios measure the efficiency with which such resources have been used.

$$\text{collection days} = \frac{\text{trade receivables} \times 365}{\text{revenue}}$$

Collection days indicate the average time taken, in calendar days, to receive payment from credit customers. Adjustment is needed if the ratio is materially distorted by VAT (or other taxes). This is because sales invoices to customers, and therefore trade receivables, may include the net sales value plus VAT. However, sales revenue is reported net of VAT. To provide a more accurate ratio, VAT may be eliminated from the trade receivables numbers as appropriate. (Note: for example, export and zero-rated sales invoices, which may be included in trade receivables, do not include VAT and so an adjustment to total trade receivables by the standard percentage rate for VAT may not be accurate.)

$$\text{payables days} = \frac{\text{trade payables} \times 365}{\text{cost of sales (or purchases)}}$$

Payables days indicate the average time taken, in calendar days, to pay for supplies received on credit. For the same reason, as in the calculation of collection days, adjustment is needed if the ratio is materially distorted by VAT or other taxes.

$$\text{inventories days} = \frac{\text{inventories}}{\text{average daily cost of sales in period}} \text{ or } \frac{\text{inventories} \times 365}{\text{cost of sales}}$$

Inventories days or inventory turnover is the number of days that inventories could last at the forecast or most recent usage rate. This may be applied to total inventory, finished goods, raw materials, or work in progress. The weekly internal efficiency of inventory utilisation is indicated by the following ratios:

$$\frac{\text{finished goods}}{\substack{\text{average weekly} \\ \text{despatches}}} \qquad \frac{\text{raw materials}}{\substack{\text{average weekly} \\ \text{raw material usage}}} \qquad \frac{\text{work in progress}}{\substack{\text{average weekly} \\ \text{production}}}$$

These ratios are usually calculated using values but may also be calculated using quantities where appropriate.

$$\text{inventories weeks} = \frac{\text{inventories}}{\text{average weekly cost of sales (total COS for the year divided by 52)}}$$

Financial analysts usually only have access to published reports and accounts and so they often calculate the inventories weeks ratio using the total closing inventories value in relation to the cost of sales for the year.

$$\text{operating cycle (days)} = \text{inventories days} + \text{collection days} - \text{payables days}$$

The operating cycle, or working capital cycle, is the period of time that elapses between the point at which cash begins to be expended on the production of a product or service, and the collection of cash from the customer.

$$\text{operating cycle \%} = \frac{\substack{\textit{working capital requirement} \\ (\text{inventories} + \text{trade receivables} - \text{trade payables})}}{\text{revenue}}$$

The operating cycle may alternatively be calculated as a percentage.

$$\text{asset turnover (times)} = \frac{\text{revenue}}{\text{total assets}}$$

Asset turnover measures the performance of the company in generating sales revenue from the assets under its control. The denominator may alternatively be average net total assets.

$$\text{capital turnover} = \frac{\text{revenue}}{\text{average capital employed in year}}$$

The capital turnover expresses the number of times that capital employed is turned over in the year, or alternatively the sales revenue generated by each £1 of capital employed. This ratio will be affected by changes to the company's capital that may have taken place throughout a period but that may not have impacted materially on the performance for that period. Further analysis may be required to determine the underlying performance.

Worked example 8.2

We will calculate the efficiency ratios for Flatco plc for 2012 and the comparative ratios for 2011, and comment on the efficiency of Flatco plc.

Receivables collection days

$$\text{collection days 2012} = \frac{\text{trade receivables} \times 365}{\text{revenue}} = \frac{£573 \times 365}{£3,500} = 60 \text{ days}$$

$$\text{collection days 2011} = \frac{£517 \times 365}{£3,250} = 58 \text{ days}$$

Payables days

$$\text{payables days 2012} = \frac{\text{trade payables} \times 365}{\text{cost of sales}} = \frac{£553 \times 365}{£2,500} = 81 \text{ days}$$

$$\text{payables days 2011} = \frac{£461 \times 365}{£2,400} = 70 \text{ days}$$

Inventories days (or inventory turnover)

$$\text{inventories days 2012} = \frac{\text{inventories}}{\text{average daily cost of sales in period}} = \frac{£311}{£2,500/365}$$

$$= 45 \text{ days (6.4 weeks)}$$

$$\text{inventories days 2011} = \frac{£268}{£2,400/365} = 41 \text{ days (5.9 weeks)}$$

Operating cycle days

$$\text{operating cycle 2012} = \text{inventories days} + \text{collection days} - \text{payables days}$$
$$= 45 + 60 - 81 = 24 \text{ days}$$
$$\text{operating cycle 2011} = 41 + 58 - 70 = 29 \text{ days}$$

Operating cycle %

$$\text{operating cycle \% 2012} = \frac{\text{working capital requirement}}{\text{revenue}}$$

$$\frac{(£311 + £573 - £553) \times 100}{£3,500} = 9.5\%$$

$$\text{operating cycle \% 2011} = \frac{(£268 + £517 - £461) \times 100\%}{£3,250} = 10.0\%$$

Asset turnover

$$\text{asset turnover 2012} = \frac{\text{revenue}}{\text{total assets}} = \frac{£3,500}{£4,348} = 0.80 \text{ times}$$

$$\text{asset turnover 2011} = \frac{£3,250}{£4,013} = 0.81 \text{ times}$$

Capital turnover

$$\text{capital turnover 2012} = \frac{\text{revenue}}{\text{average capital employed in year}} = \frac{£3,500}{£3,128} = 1.1 \text{ times}$$

$$\text{capital turnover 2011} = \frac{£3,250}{£2,559.5} = 1.3 \text{ times}$$

Report on the efficiency of Flatco plc

A major cash improvement programme was introduced by the company late in the year 2012, which began with the implementation of new cash collection procedures and a reinforced credit control department. This was not introduced early enough to see an improvement in the collection days for the year 2012. Average receivables collection days actually worsened from 58 to 60 days.

The purchasing department negotiated terms of 90 days with a number of key large suppliers. This had the effect of improving the average payables period from 70 to 81 days.

A change in product mix during the latter part of the year 2012 resulted in a worsening of the average inventory turnover period from 41 to 45 days. This is expected to be a temporary situation. An improved **just in time (JIT)** system and the use of **vendor managed inventory (VMI)** with two main suppliers in the year 2013 are expected to generate significant improvements in inventory turnover.

Despite the poor inventory turnover, the operating cycle improved from 29 days to 24 days (operating cycle % from 10.0% to 9.5%). Operating cycle days are expected to be zero or better by the end of year 2013.

Asset turnover dropped from 0.81 in 2011 to 0.80 times in the year 2012. New capital was introduced into the company in 2012 to finance major new projects which are expected to result in significant increases in sales levels over the next few years which will result in improvements in asset turnover over and above 2011 levels.

Capital turnover for 2012 dropped to 1.1 times from 1.3 times in 2011. As with asset turnover, the new capital introduced into the company in the year 2012 to finance major new projects is expected to result in significant increases in sales revenue levels over the next few years, which will be reflected in improvements in capital turnover over and above 2011 levels.

Progress check 8.4

What do the profitability and efficiency ratios tell us about the performance of a business?

Liquidity ratios

The degree to which assets are held in cash or near-cash is determined by the level of obligations that need to be met by the business. Liquidity ratios (see Figure 8.11) reflect the health or otherwise of the cash position of the business and its ability to meet its short-term obligations.

$$\text{current ratio (times)} = \frac{\text{current assets}}{\text{current liabilities}}$$

The current ratio is an overall measure of the liquidity of the business. It should be appreciated that this ratio will be different for different types of business. For example, an automotive manufacturer may have a higher ratio because of its relatively high level of inventories (mainly work in progress) compared with a supermarket retailer, which holds a very high percentage of fast-moving inventories.

$$\text{quick ratio (times)} = \frac{\text{current assets} - \text{inventories}}{\text{current liabilities}}$$

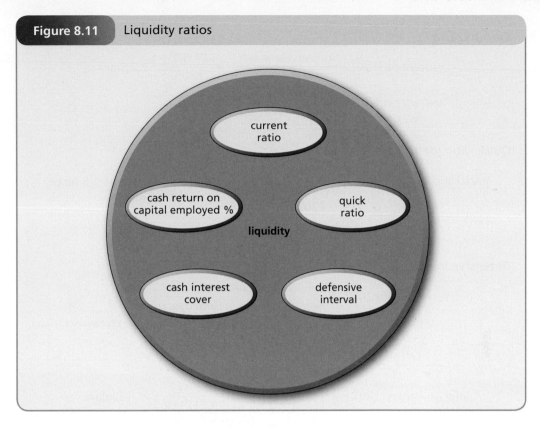

Figure 8.11   Liquidity ratios

The quick ratio (or acid test ratio) excludes inventories from current assets. While trade receivables and trade payables are just one step away from being converted into cash, inventories are two or more steps away from being converted into cash; they need to be worked on and processed to produce products, which are then sold to customers. Therefore, the quick ratio indicates the ability of the company to pay its trade payables out of its trade receivables in the short term. This ratio may not be particularly meaningful for supermarket retailers because they don't generally sell on credit and therefore have no trade receivables.

$$\text{defensive interval (days)} = \frac{\text{quick assets (current assets } - \text{ inventories)}}{\substack{\textbf{average daily cash from operations} \\ \textit{opening receivables + revenue} - \textit{closing receivables}}}$$

The defensive interval shows how many days a company could survive at its present level of operating activity if no inflow of cash were received from sales revenue or other sources.

We will consider the other two ratios outlined in Figure 8.11 later in this chapter.

Worked example 8.3

We will calculate the liquidity ratios for Flatco plc for 2012 and the comparative ratios for 2011, and comment on the liquidity of Flatco plc.

Current ratio

$$\text{current ratio 2012} = \frac{\text{current assets}}{\text{current liabilities}} = \frac{£1,800}{£805} = 2.2 \text{ times}$$

$$\text{current ratio 2011} = \frac{£1,419}{£1,300} = 1.1 \text{ times}$$

Quick ratio (or acid test)

$$\text{quick ratio 2012} = \frac{\text{current assets} - \text{inventories}}{\text{current liabilities}} = \frac{£1,800 - £311}{£805} = 1.8 \text{ times}$$

$$\text{quick ratio 2011} = \frac{£1,419 - £268}{£1,300} = 0.9 \text{ times}$$

Defensive interval

$$\text{defensive interval 2012} = \frac{\text{quick assets}}{\text{average daily cash from operations}}$$

$$(opening\ trade\ receivables + sales\ revenue - closing\ trade\ receivables)/365$$

$$\frac{£1,800 - £311}{(£517 + £3,500 - £573)/365} = 158 \text{ days}$$

$$\text{defensive interval 2011} = \frac{£1,419 - £268}{(£440 + £3,250 - £517)/365} = 132 \text{ days}$$

Report on the liquidity of Flatco plc

From the statement of cash flows we can see that cash generated from operations improved from £783,000 in 2011 to £936,000 in 2012. Investments in non-current assets were more than covered by increases in long-term financing in both years. Operational cash flow improvement was reflected in the increase in net cash flow of £939,000 from £787,000 in 2011.

The improved cash flow is reflected in increases in the current ratio (1.1 to 2.2 times) and the quick ratio (0.9 to 1.8 times). The increase in the defensive interval from 132 to 158 days has strengthened the position of the company against the threat of a possible downturn in activity.

Although there has been a significant improvement in cash flow, the increase in investment in working capital is a cause for concern. Three key actions have already been taken since the year end 31 December 2012 to try and maximise the return on investment: reduction in inventories levels (noted above); further reductions in trade receivables; investment of surplus cash in longer-term investments.

Progress check 8.5

What are liquidity ratios and why are they so important?

Figure 8.12   Investment ratios

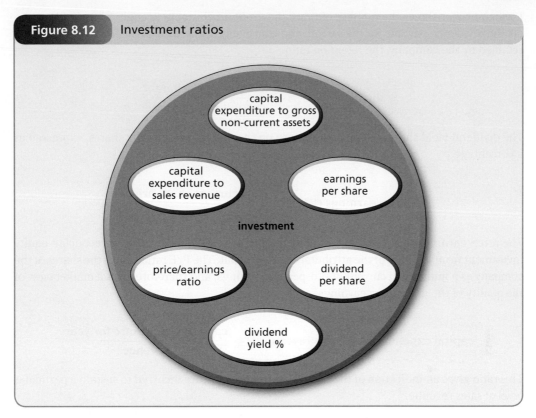

Investment ratios

Investment ratios (see Figure 8.12) generally indicate the extent to which the business is undertaking capital expenditure to ensure its survival and stability, and its ability to sustain current revenue and generate future increased revenue.

$$\text{earnings per share (or eps)} = \frac{\text{profit for the year} - \text{preference share dividends}}{\text{number of ordinary shares in issue}}$$

Earnings per share, or eps, measures the return per share of profit available to shareholders. The eps of quoted companies may be found in the financial pages sections of the daily press.

$$\text{dividend per share} = \frac{\text{total dividends paid to ordinary shareholders}}{\text{number of ordinary shares in issue}}$$

Dividend per share is the total amount declared as dividends per each ordinary share in issue. It is the dividend per share actually paid in respect of the financial year. The amount must be adjusted if additional equity shares are issued during the financial year.

$$\text{dividend cover} = \frac{\text{earnings per share}}{\text{dividend per share}}$$

Dividend cover shows the number of times the profit attributable to equity shareholders covers the dividends payable for the period, and conversely also indicates the level of profit being retained by the company, the retention ratio.

$$\text{dividend yield \%} = \frac{\text{dividend per share}}{\text{current share price}}$$

The dividend yield shows the dividend return on the market value of the shares, expressed as a percentage.

$$\text{price/earnings (P/E) ratio} = \frac{\text{current share price}}{\text{eps}}$$

The price/earnings or P/E ratio shows the number of years it would take to recoup an equity investment from its share of the attributable equity profit. The P/E ratio values the shares of the company as a multiple of current or prospective earnings, and therefore gives a market view of the quality of the underlying earnings.

$$\text{capital expenditure to sales revenue \%} = \frac{\text{capital expenditure for year}}{\text{revenue}}$$

This ratio gives an indication of the level of capital expenditure incurred to sustain a particular level of sales revenue.

$$\text{capital expenditure to gross non-current assets \%} = \frac{\text{capital expenditure for year}}{\text{gross value of tangible non-current assets}}$$

This is a very good ratio for giving an indication of the replacement rate of new for old non-current assets.

Worked example 8.4

We will calculate the investment ratios for Flatco plc for 2012 and the comparative ratios for 2011, and comment on the investment performance of Flatco plc.

Earnings per share, eps

$$\text{eps 2012} = \frac{\text{profit for the year} - \text{preference share dividends}}{\text{number of ordinary shares in issue}} = \frac{£540,000}{1,200,000} = 45\text{p}$$

$$\text{eps 2011} = \frac{£386,000}{1,000,000} = 38.6\text{p}$$

Dividend per share

$$\text{dividend per share 2012} = \frac{\text{total dividends paid to ordinary shareholders}}{\text{number of ordinary shares in issue}}$$

$$\frac{£70,000}{1,200,000} = 5.8\text{p per share}$$

$$\text{dividend per share 2011} = \frac{£67,000}{1,000,000} = 6.7\text{p per share}$$

Dividend cover

$$\text{dividend cover 2012} = \frac{\text{earnings per share}}{\text{dividend per share}}$$

$$\frac{45\text{p}}{5.8\text{p}} = 7.8\text{ times}$$

$$\text{dividend cover 2011} = \frac{38.6\text{p}}{6.7\text{p}} = 5.8\text{ times}$$

Dividend yield %

$$\text{dividend yield 2012} = \frac{\text{dividend per share}}{\text{share price}}$$

$$= \frac{5.8\text{p} \times 100\%}{£2.75} = 2.11\%$$

$$\text{dividend yield 2011} = \frac{6.7\text{p} \times 100\%}{£3.00} = 2.23\%$$

Price/earnings ratio, P/E

$$\text{P/E ratio 2012} = \frac{\text{current share price}}{\text{eps}} = \frac{£2.75}{45\text{p}} = 6.1\text{ times}$$

$$\text{P/E ratio 2011} = \frac{£3.00}{38.6\text{p}} = 7.8\text{ times}$$

Capital expenditure to sales revenue %

$$\text{capital expenditure to sales revenue 2012} = \frac{\text{capital expenditure for year}}{\text{revenue}}$$

$$= \frac{£286 \times 100\%}{£3,500} = 8.2\%$$

$$\text{capital expenditure to sales revenue 2011} = \frac{£170 \times 100\%}{£3,250} = 5.2\%$$

Capital expenditure to gross non-current assets %

capital expenditure to gross non-current assets 2012 =

$$\frac{\text{capital expenditure for year}}{\text{gross value of tangible non-current assets}} = \frac{£286 \times 100\%}{(£1,884 + £1,102)} = 9.6\%$$

(net book value + cumulative depreciation provision)

$$\text{capital expenditure to gross non-current assets 2011} = \frac{£170 \times 100\%}{(£1,921 + £779)} = 6.3\%$$

Report on the investment performance of Flatco plc

The improved profit performance in 2012 compared with 2011 was reflected in improved earnings per share from 38.6p to 45p.

The price/earnings ratio dropped from 7.8 to 6.1 times, indicating that an investment in the company's shares may be recovered in 6.1 years from its current level of net profit.

The board of directors reduced the dividend for the year to 5.8p per share from 6.7p per share in 2011, establishing a dividend cover, or profit retention ratio, of 7.8 times. The increased profit retention provided internal financing in addition to its external financing to fund the company's increase in capital expenditure.

The increase in the capital expenditure to sales revenue ratio from 5.2% to 8.2% indicates the company's ability to both sustain and improve upon current sales revenue levels.

The increase in the capital expenditure to gross non-current assets ratio from 6.3% to 9.6% illustrates Flatco's policy of ongoing replacement of old assets for new in order to keep ahead of the technology in which the business is engaged.

Each of the above five ratios indicate that Flatco is a growth company, from which increased sales revenues and profits may be expected in future years.

The dividend yield reduced from 2.23% at 31 December 2011 to 2.11% at 31 December 2012.

Progress check 8.6

What are investment ratios and what is their purpose?

Financial ratios

Financial ratios (see Figure 8.13) are generally concerned with the relationship between debt and equity capital, the financial structure of an organisation. This relationship is called gearing. Gearing was discussed in detail in Chapter 5.

The ratios that follow are the two most commonly used. Both ratios relate to financial gearing, which is the relationship between a company's borrowings, which includes both prior charge capital and long-term debt, and its shareholders' funds (share capital plus reserves).

$$\text{gearing} = \frac{\text{long-term debt}}{\text{equity} + \text{long-term debt}}$$

and

$$\text{debt/equity ratio (D/E or leverage)} = \frac{\text{long-term debt}}{\text{equity}}$$

These ratios are both equally acceptable in describing the relative proportions of debt and equity used to finance a business. Gearing calculations can be made in other ways, and in addition to those based on capital values may also be based on earnings/interest relationships, for example:

$$\text{dividend cover (times)} = \frac{\text{earnings per share (eps)}}{\text{dividend per share}}$$

Figure 8.13 Financial ratios

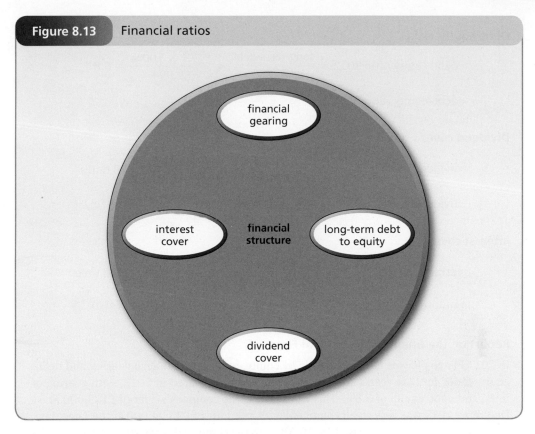

This ratio indicates the number of times the profits attributable to the equity shareholders cover the actual dividends paid and payable for the period. Financial analysts usually adjust their calculations for any exceptional or extraordinary items of which they may be aware.

$$\text{interest cover (times)} = \frac{\text{profit before interest and tax}}{\text{interest payable}}$$

This ratio calculates the number of times the interest payable is covered by profits available for such payments. It is particularly important for lenders to determine the vulnerability of interest payments to a fall in profit.

Worked example 8.5

We will calculate the financial ratios for Flatco plc for 2012 and the comparative ratios for 2011, and comment on the financial structure of Flatco plc.

Gearing

$$\text{gearing 2012} = \frac{\text{long-term debt}}{\text{equity + long-term debt}} = \frac{£173 \times 100\%}{(£2,994 + £173)} = 5.5\%$$

$$\text{gearing 2011} = \frac{£0 \times 100\%}{(£2,324 + £0)} = 0\%$$

Debt/equity ratio

$$\text{debt/equity ratio 2012} = \frac{\text{long-term debt}}{\text{equity}} = \frac{£173 \times 100\%}{£2,994} = 5.8\%$$

$$\text{debt/equity ratio 2011} = \frac{£0 \times 100\%}{£2,324} = 0\%$$

Dividend cover

$$\text{dividend cover 2012} = \frac{\text{earnings per share (eps)}}{\text{dividend per share}} = \frac{45p}{5.8p} = 7.8 \text{ times}$$

$$\text{dividend cover 2011} = \frac{38.6p}{6.7p} = 5.8 \text{ times}$$

Interest cover

$$\text{interest cover 2012} = \frac{\text{profit before interest and tax}}{\text{interest payable}} = \frac{£661}{£71} = 9.3 \text{ times}$$

$$\text{interest cover 2011} = \frac{£530}{£100} = 5.3 \text{ times}$$

Report on the financial structure of Flatco plc

In 2011 Flatco plc was financed totally by equity, reflected in its zero gearing and debt/equity ratios for that year. Flatco plc was still very low geared in 2012, with gearing of 5.5% and debt/equity of 5.8%. This was because the company's debt of £173,000 at 31 December 2012 was very small compared with its equity of £2,994,000 at the same date.

Earnings per share increased by 16.6% in 2012 compared with 2011. However, the board of directors reduced the dividend, at 5.8p per share for 2012, by 13.4% from 6.7p per share in 2011. This provided an increase in retained earnings (retained profit), shown by the increase in dividend cover from 5.8 times in 2011 to 7.8 times in 2012.

Interest payable was reduced by £29,000 in 2012 from the previous year, but PBIT was increased by £120,000 year on year. The result was that interest cover nearly doubled from 5.3 times in 2011 to 9.3 times in 2012. This ratio may drop again in 2013 as a result of an increase in interest payable in 2013 because of the loan taken by the company late in 2012.

Progress check 8.7

What are financial ratios and how may they be used to comment on the financial structure of an organisation?

Return on equity (ROE), return on assets (ROA), and the Du Pont system

Some companies and analysts like to link profitability, efficiency, and gearing ratios. This is illustrated in a number of relationships known as the Du Pont system of ratios. The first of these relationships considers another form of return on capital employed, return on assets (ROA):

$$\text{return on assets (ROA)} = \frac{\text{PBIT}}{\text{total assets}}$$

You should note that this is slightly different to the operating profit version of ROA, which we used earlier in this chapter. ROA may be rewritten as:

$$\text{ROA} = \underbrace{\frac{\text{PBIT}}{\text{total assets}}}_{} = \underbrace{\frac{\text{revenue}}{\text{total assets}}}_{\substack{\text{asset turnover} \\ \text{ratio}}} \times \underbrace{\frac{\text{PBIT}}{\text{revenue}}}_{\substack{\text{profit margin} \\ \text{ratio}}}$$

Asset turnover is an efficiency ratio, which is used to measure the performance of the company in generating sales revenues from the assets under its control. The ability of a company to earn a higher return on assets is limited by competition. The profit margin ratio is a profitability ratio, and there is also a trade-off between the sales revenue/assets ratio and profit margin. Companies in different industries may have the same level of ROA but different relationships between their asset turnover and profit margins. For example, a hotel chain may have a low asset turnover, which is compensated for by a high margin, whereas a fast food chain may have a high asset turnover but a lower margin.

We looked at return on equity (ROE) as a form of return on capital employed in the profitability ratios section earlier in this chapter.

$$\text{return on equity (ROE)} = \frac{\text{profit after tax (PAT)}}{\text{equity}}$$

The second Du Pont relationship is derived from an expanded version of the ROE equation above, which may be re-written as:

$$\text{ROE} = \underbrace{\frac{\text{total assets}}{\text{equity}}}_{\substack{\text{equity multiplier} \\ \text{(a gearing ratio)}}} \times \underbrace{\frac{\text{revenue}}{\text{total assets}}}_{\substack{\text{asset turnover} \\ \text{ratio}}} \times \underbrace{\frac{\text{PBIT}}{\text{revenue}}}_{\substack{\text{profit margin} \\ \text{ratio}}} \times \underbrace{\frac{\text{PBT}}{\text{PBIT}}}_{\substack{\text{interest} \\ \text{burden}}} \times \underbrace{\frac{\text{PAT}}{\text{PBT}}}_{\substack{\text{tax} \\ \text{burden}}}$$

The second and third terms are the efficiency ratio and profitability ratio that combined represent the company's ROA, which is dependent on operations and marketing skills and not on the financial structure of the company. The first and fourth terms are dependent on the financial structure of the business. The fifth term represents the extent of tax payable on profit before tax.

The equity multiplier is a gearing ratio, which is a way of examining the extent to which a company uses debt or equity to finance its assets. This ratio shows a company's total assets per £ (or unit of any other currency) of shareholders' equity. A high equity multiplier indicates that the company is relying on a relatively low level of equity to finance its assets, and *vice versa* if the equity multiplier is low. The interest burden is a measure of the extent to which the cost of interest reduces profits. If a company is financed totally by equity then terms one and four would both be 1. ROE would therefore equal ROA multiplied by the tax burden. If a company is geared then the first term would be greater than 1, because total assets are greater than equity; the fourth term would be less than 1, because the numerator now includes interest payable.

Worked example 8.6

We will calculate and comment on the Du Pont ratios for Flatco plc for 2012 and the comparative ratios for 2011.

Return on assets (ROA)

$$\text{ROA \% 2012} = \frac{\text{PBIT}}{\text{total assets}} = \frac{\text{revenue}}{\text{total assets}} \times \frac{\text{PBIT}}{\text{revenue}}$$

$$= \frac{£661}{£4,348} = \frac{£3,500}{£4,348} \times \frac{£661}{£3,500}$$

$$= 15.2\% = 0.80 \text{ times} \times 18.9\%$$

$$\qquad ROA \qquad\qquad asset\ turnover \qquad profit\ margin$$
$$\qquad\qquad\qquad\qquad ratio \qquad\qquad\qquad ratio$$

$$\text{ROA \% 2011} = \frac{£530}{£4,013} = \frac{£3,250}{£4,013} \times \frac{£530}{£3,250}$$

$$= 13.2\% = 0.81 \text{ times} \times 16.3\%$$

$$\qquad ROA \qquad\qquad asset\ turnover \qquad profit\ margin$$
$$\qquad\qquad\qquad\qquad ratio \qquad\qquad\qquad ratio$$

Return on equity (ROE)

$$\text{ROE \% 2012} = \frac{\text{PAT}}{\text{equity}} = \frac{£540}{£2,994} = 18.0\%$$

$$= \frac{\text{total assets}}{\text{equity}} \times \frac{\text{revenue}}{\text{total assets}} \times \frac{\text{PBIT}}{\text{revenue}} \times \frac{\text{PBT}}{\text{PBIT}} \times \frac{\text{PAT}}{\text{PBT}}$$

$$= \frac{£4,348}{£2,994} \times \frac{£3,500}{£4,348} \times \frac{£661}{£3,500} \times \frac{£590}{£661} \times \frac{£540}{£590}$$

$$= 1.45 \text{ times} \times 0.80 \text{ times} \times 18.9\% \times 0.89 \text{ times} \times 0.92 \text{ time}$$

$$\quad equity\ multiplier \quad\text{---}\quad ROA \quad\text{---}\quad interest\ burden \quad tax\ burden$$

$$\text{ROE \% 2011} = \frac{£386}{£2,324} = 16.6\%$$

$$= \frac{£4,013}{£2,324} \times \frac{£3,250}{£4,013} \times \frac{£530}{£3,250} \times \frac{£430}{£530} \times \frac{£386}{£430}$$

$$= 1.73 \text{ times} \times 0.81 \text{ times} \times 16.3\% \times 0.81 \text{ times} \times 0.90 \text{ times}$$

$$\quad equity\ multiplier \quad\text{---}\quad ROA \quad\text{---}\quad interest\ burden \quad tax\ burden$$

Report on the Du Pont ratios for Flatco plc

ROA has increased from 13.2% in 2011 to 15.2% in 2012. This shows an improvement, which was not apparent from the unchanged ROCE from 2011 to 2012. This was because the additional funding received in 2012 had not all been spent on new assets until 2013.

Asset turnover remained at 0.81 in 2011 and 2012. The new capital introduced into the company in 2012 to finance major new projects is expected to result in significant increases in sales revenue levels over the next few years, which will see improvements in asset turnover over and above 2012 levels.

Return on equity increased from 16.6% to 18%, despite the increase in ordinary share capital. This was because of improved profit after tax (up 3.5% to 15.4% of sales revenue) arising from increased income from non-current asset investments and lower costs of finance. Corporation tax was marginally lower in 2012 than in 2011.

The interest burden of 0.89 times in 2012 increased from 0.81 in 2011, reflecting increased gearing and therefore the requirement to pay additional interest in future years. This resulted from the borrowing of £173,000 in 2012. The drop in the equity multiplier from 1.73 to 1.45 in 2012 indicated that the company had increased its equity financing of its assets, despite its increased gearing.

We have seen how the level of gearing has the effect of either increasing or reducing ROE. We will examine this further by looking at another equation that represents the relationship between ROE and ROA, which can be determined by rearranging the company's cost of capital formula. We may assume that the company's cost of capital approximates to its ROA, adjusted for the tax shield. If E is the proportion of equity capital, D is the proportion of debt capital, i is the interest rate paid on debt, and t is the corporation tax rate:

$$\text{ROA } (1 - t) = \frac{E \times \text{ROE}}{E + D} + \frac{D \times i \times (1 - t)}{E + D}$$

$$\{\text{ROA} \times E \times (1 - t)\} + \{\text{ROA} \times D \times (1 - t)\} = (E \times \text{ROE}) + \{D \times i \times (1 - t)\}$$

$$\text{ROA} \times E \times (1 - t) + \text{ROA} \times D \times (1 - t) - D \times i \times (1 - t) = (E \times \text{ROE})$$

$$\text{ROA} \times E \times (1 - t) + (\text{ROA} - i) \times D \times (1 - t) = (E \times \text{ROE})$$

Therefore, dividing both sides of the equation by E:

$$\text{ROE} = \{\text{ROA} \times (1 - t)\} + \{(\text{ROA} - i) \times (1 - t) \times D/E\}$$

which shows return on equity (ROE) as a function of return on assets (ROA) and the financial structure, leverage, or gearing of the company.

Worked example 8.7 illustrates the use of this relationship and also provides a general rule derived from it.

Worked example 8.7

A hospital equipment manufacturing company, Nilby Mouth plc, makes an operating profit (PBIT) of £12m on sales revenue of £100m and with a total investment of £60m. The total assets are £60m, financed by equity (E) of £40m and debt (D) of £20m with an interest rate (i) of 10%. Assume the corporation tax rate (t) is 30%.

We will calculate:

(i)   the current return on equity (ROE)
(ii)   the ROE if financing were changed so that debt was £40m and equity was £20m
(iii) the current ROE if PBIT was reduced to £4m
(iv)   the ROE if PBIT was reduced to £4m and if financing was changed so that debt was £40m and equity was £20m.

Figures in £m

(i) **Calculation of return on equity (ROE) if PBIT is £12m, and debt is £20m and equity is £40m**

Profit before interest and tax, or operating profit PBIT $= 12$

PBT $= 12 - (20 \times 10\%) = 10$
Tax $= 10 \times 30\% = 3$
PBIT $-$ tax $= 12 - 3 = 9$
Return on assets ROA $= 9/60 = 15\%$
Debt/equity ratio D/E $= 20/40 = 50\%$
ROE $=$ ROA $\times (1 - t) + \{(\text{ROA} - i) \times (1 - t) \times \text{D/E}\}$
Return on equity ROE $= \{15\% \times (1 - 30\%)\} + \{(15\% - 10\%) \times (1 - 30\%) \times 50\%\}$
$\qquad\qquad = 12.25\%$

ROA is 15%, i is 10%, debt/equity is 50%, and ROE is 12.25%.

(ii) **Calculation of ROE if PBIT is £12m, and debt is £40m and equity is £20m**

PBIT $= 12$; PBT $= 12 - (40 \times 10\%) = 8$; Tax $= 8 \times 30\% = 2.4$; PBIT $-$ tax $= 12 - 2.4 = 9.6$
Return on assets ROA $= 9.6/60 = 16\%$
Debt/equity ratio D/E $= 40/20 = 200\%$
ROE $=$ ROA $\times (1 - t) + \{(\text{ROA} - i) \times (1 - t) \times \text{D/E}\}$
Return on equity ROE $= \{16\% \times (1 - 30\%)\} + \{(16\% - 10\%) \times (1 - 30\%) \times 200\%\}$
$\qquad\qquad = 19.60\%$
ROA is greater than i, debt/equity ratio has increased, and ROE has increased,

16% > 10%   50% to 200%   12.25% to 19.60%

(iii) **Calculation of ROE if PBIT was reduced to £4m, and debt is £20m and equity is £40m**

PBIT $=$ PBT $= 4 - (20 \times 10\%) = 2$; Tax $= 2 \times 30\% = 0.6$; PBIT $-$ tax $= 4 - 0.6 = 3.4$
Return on assets ROA $= 3.4/60 = 5.67\%$
Debt/equity ratio D/E $= 20/40 = 50\%$
ROE $=$ ROA $\times (1 - t) + \{(\text{ROA} - i) \times (1 - t) \times \text{D/E}\}$
Return on equity ROE $= \{5.67\% \times (1 - 30\%)\} + \{(5.67\% - 10\%) \times (1 - 30\%) \times 50\%\}$
$\qquad\qquad = 2.45\%$
ROA is less than i, the debt/equity ratio is still 50%, and ROE has decreased,
5.67% < 10%   12.25% to 2.45%

(iv) **Calculation of ROE if PBIT is £4m, and debt is £40m and equity is £20m**

PBIT $= 4$; PBT $= 4 - (40 \times 10\%) = 0$; Tax $= 0 \times 30\% = 0$; PBIT $-$ tax $= 4 - 0 = 4$
Return on assets ROA $= 4/60 = 6.67\%$
Debt/equity ratio D/E $= 40/20 = 200\%$

$$\text{ROE} = \text{ROA} \times (1 - t) + \{(\text{ROA} - i) \times (1 - t) \times \text{D/E}\}$$

Return on equity ROE $= \{6.67\% \times (1 - 30\%)\} + \{(6.67\% - 10\%) \times (1 - 30\%) \times 200\%\}$

$= 0.007\%$

ROA is less than i, the debt/equity ratio has increased, and ROE has decreased,

| 6.67% < 10% | 50% to 200% | 2.45% to 0.007% |

The general rule apparent from the relationships derived from the calculations in Worked example 8.7 is:

- when ROA is greater than i the higher the D/E, the higher the ROE
- when ROA is less than i the higher the D/E, the lower the ROE.

However, even if ROA is greater than debt interest the company's bankers may not automatically allow the D/E to increase indefinitely. The company's risk increases as the D/E ratio increases, in terms of its commitment to high levels of interest payments, and bankers will not tolerate too high a level of risk; they will also be inclined to increase the debt interest rate as D/E increases. Shareholders will have the same reaction; they are happy with an increase in ROE but realise that they also have to face a higher risk, and will therefore demand a higher return.

When a plc is seen to embark on a policy of increased borrowings and increasing its gearing ratio and thereby increasing its ROE, the financial press is usually quick to alert its readership to the increased financial risk. Plcs are usually prepared and ready for such comments in order to respond with their defence of such a policy.

Progress check 8.8

Discuss why bankers may refuse additional lending to a company as its debt/equity ratio increases.

Horizontal analysis

Growth of a company, which may be considered in terms of sales revenue or gross profit, may be looked at using an income statement horizontal analysis, which presents all numbers in the income statement as a percentage using a base year, which is 100, for year-on-year comparison. Financial commentators usually begin articles on the performance of plcs by comparing the current year performance with the previous year, and then attempt a forecast of future performance. This is an example of a basic horizontal analysis that focuses on sales revenue and profits. In practice, only a few companies actually succeed in growing year on year over an extended period (for example, 10 years).

Horizontal analysis, or common size analysis, of the income statement allows a line-by-line analysis of each element compared with those of the previous year. It may provide a trend of changes over a number of years showing either growth or decline in these elements of the income statement through calculation of annual percentage growth rates in profits, sales revenues, cost of sales, or any other item.

Mini case 8.1 illustrates the technique applied to a summary of the Johnson Matthey Plc income statement for the years to 31 March 2012 and 31 March 2011 (see the consolidated income statement of the Johnson Matthey group from page 122 of its Annual Report and Accounts 2012, shown on page 374).

Mini case 8.1

We can prepare a horizontal analysis using a summary of the income statement results for Johnson Matthey Plc for 2011 and 2012, using 2011 as the base year.

(You may note that a part of the income statement refers to profit for the year from **continuing operations**, as distinct from **discontinued operations,** which are defined in the glossary at the end of this chapter.)

Johnson Matthey Plc
Consolidated income statement for the year ended 31 March 2012

	2012 £m	2011 £m
Revenue	12,023.2	9,984.8
Cost of sales	(11,270.2)	(9,337.2)
Gross profit	753.0	647.6
Distribution costs	(119.8)	(112.2)
Administrative expenses	(183.1)	(169.2)
Major impairment and restructuring charges	–	(71.8)
Amortisation of acquired intangibles	(16.7)	(14.5)
Operating profit	433.4	279.9
Finance costs	(35.4)	(33.1)
Finance income	11.3	12.4
Dissolution of associate	–	0.1
Profit before tax	409.3	259.3
Income tax expense	(93.9)	(75.5)
Profit for the year from continuing operations	315.4	183.8
Profit for the year from discontinued operations	–	(1.9)
Profit for the year	315.4	181.9
Attributable to:		
Equity holders of the parent company	315.9	181.5
Minority interests	(0.5)	0.4
	315.4	181.9

Mini case 8.1 considers only two years, and has used 2011 as the base year 100. This means, for example that:

if revenue for 2011 of £9,984.8m = 100

then

$$\text{revenue for 2012 of £12,023.2m} = \frac{£12,023.2m \times 100}{£9,984.8m} = 120.4$$

Johnson Matthey Plc
Consolidated income statement for the year ended 31 March 2012

Horizontal analysis	2011	2012
Revenue	100.0	120.4
Cost of sales	100.0	120.7
Gross profit	100.0	116.3

(continued)

Distribution costs	100.0	106.8
Administrative expenses	100.0	108.2
Major impairment and restructuring charges	100.0	–
Amortisation of acquired intangibles	100.0	115.2
Operating profit	100.0	154.8
Finance costs	100.0	106.9
Finance income	100.0	–
Dissolution of associate	100.0	–
Profit before tax	100.0	157.8
Income tax expense	100.0	124.4
Profit for the year from continuing operations	100.0	171.6
Profit for the year from discontinued operations	100.0	–
Profit for the year	100.0	173.4
Attributable to:		
Equity holders of the parent company	100.0	174.0
Minority interests	100.0	–

We can see from the above horizontal analysis how the profit for the year has been derived compared with that for 2011. Sales revenue in 2012 increased by 20.4% over 2011, and operating profit for 2012 increased by 54.8% over 2011. Corporation tax in 2012 was 24.4% higher than 2011, and profit for the year was 73.4% higher than the previous year.

Subsequent years may be compared with 2011 as base 100, using the same sort of calculation.

The horizontal analysis technique is particularly useful to make a line-by-line comparison of a company's financial statements for each accounting period over, say, five or 10 years, using the first year as the base year. When we look at financial statements that cover successive periods we may by observation automatically carry out this process of assessing percentage changes in performance over time. However, presentation of the information in tabular form, for a number of years, gives a much clearer picture of trends in performance in each area of activity and may provide the basis for further analysis.

Progress check 8.9

What can a horizontal analysis of the information contained in the financial statements of a company add to that provided from ratio analysis?

Vertical analysis

A company's financial performance (and financial position) may also be considered by looking at a vertical analysis of its income statement (and balance sheet). In a vertical analysis of the income statement (or balance sheet) each item is expressed as a percentage of the total sales revenue (or total assets). The vertical analysis provides evidence of structural changes in the company's performance such as increased profitability through more efficient production. Mini case 8.2 uses total sales revenue as the basis for calculation, and the analysis confirms some of the conclusions drawn from the horizontal analysis in Mini case 8.1.

Mini case 8.2

We can prepare a vertical analysis using the summary of the consolidated income statement for Johnson Matthey Plc for 2011 and 2012, shown in Mini case 8.1.

Johnson Matthey Plc
Consolidated income statement for the year ended 31 March 2012

Vertical analysis	2011	2012
Revenue	100.0	100.0
Cost of sales	(93.5)	(93.7)
Gross profit	6.5	6.3
Distribution costs	(1.1)	(1.0)
Administrative expenses	(1.7)	(1.5)
Major impairment and restructuring charges	(0.7)	–
Amortisation of acquired intangibles	(0.2)	(0.2)
Operating profit	2.8	3.6
Finance costs	(0.3)	(0.3)
Finance income	0.1	0.1
Dissolution of associate	–	–
Profit before tax	2.6	3.4
Income tax expense	(0.8)	(0.8)
Profit for the year from continuing operations	1.8	2.6
Profit for the year from discontinued operations	–	–
Profit for the year	1.8	2.6
Attributable to:		
Equity holders of the parent company	1.8	2.6
Minority interests	–	–

Operating profit increased from 2.8% of sales revenue in 2011 to 3.6% in 2012. Profit before tax increased from 2.6% of sales revenue in 2011 to 3.4% in 2012. Profit for the year increased from 1.8% of sales revenue in 2011 to 2.6% in 2012.

Progress check 8.10

What can a vertical analysis of the information contained in the financial statements of a company add to the information provided from a horizontal analysis and a ratio analysis?

Segmental reporting

The section headed 'Notes on the Accounts' in the annual report and accounts of companies contains information that must be reported additional to, and in support of, the financial statements. This includes segmental information, which is analysis by business and geographical area relating primarily to sales revenue, profit, and assets. The first note in the notes on the accounts in Johnson Matthey's report and accounts for 2012 is headed segmental information. International Financial Reporting Standard IFRS 8, Operating Segments, requires large companies to disclose segmental information by each operating segment, which could be a type of activity, a class of product or service or a geographical region. **Segmental reporting** is required in order that users of financial information may carry out more meaningful financial analysis.

Most large companies usually comprise diverse businesses supplying different products and services, rather than being engaged in a single type of business. Each type of business activity may have:

■ a different structure
■ different levels of profitability
■ different levels of growth potential
■ different levels of risk exposure.

The financial statements of such diversified companies are consolidated to include all business activities, which is a potential problem for the users of financial information. For analysis and interpretation of financial performance, aggregate numbers are not particularly useful for the following reasons:

■ difficulties in evaluation of performance of a business which has interests that are diverse from the aggregated financial information
■ difficulties of comparison of trends over time and comparison between companies because the various activities undertaken by the company are likely to differ in size and range in comparison with other businesses
■ differences in conditions between different geographical markets, in terms of levels of risk, profitability, and growth
■ differences in conditions between different geographical markets, in terms of political and social factors, environmental factors, currencies, and inflation rates.

Segmental reporting analysis enables:

■ the further analysis of segmental performance to determine more accurately the likely growth prospects for the business as a whole
■ evaluation of the impact on the company of changes in conditions relating to particular activities
■ improvements in internal management performance, because it may be monitored through disclosure of segmental information to shareholders
■ evaluation of the acquisition and disposal performance of the company.

Mini case 8.3

The information in the table below relates to global sales revenue of Nestlé SA, the Swiss nutrition and foods giant, for the years 2009 and 2008.

Figures in Swiss francs (CHF) millions

	Europe	Americas	Asia and Africa	Europe	Americas	Asia and Africa
	2009	**2009**	**2009**	**2008**	**2008**	**2008**
Beverages	5,362	3,746	5,331	5,072	3,830	5,576
Milk products	3,147	9,884	5,228	2,708	9,698	5,013
Prepared dishes	7,243	5,291	2,565	6,288	5,414	2,680

(continued) ➡

Confectionery	5,416	4,632	1,850	4,686	4,831	1,852
Pet care	3,930	7,804	733	3,774	8,395	770
Total sales	25,098	31,357	15,707	22,528	32,168	15,891

(i) Using the information provided we may prepare a simple table that compares the sales revenue for 2009 with the sales revenue for the year 2008.

(ii) We can also consider how a simple sales revenue analysis can provide an investor with information that is more useful than just global sales revenue for the year.

(i)

Beverages	5,362	+5.72%	5,072	3,746	−2.19%	3,830	5,331	−4.39%	5,576
Milk products	3,147	+16.21%	2,708	9,884	+1.92%	9,698	5,228	+4.29%	5,013
Prepared dishes	7,243	+15.19%	6,288	5,291	−2.27%	5,414	2,565	−4.29%	2,680
Confectionery	5,416	+15.58%	4,686	4,632	−4.12%	4,831	1,850	−0.01%	1,852
Pet care	3,930	+4.13%	3,774	7,804	−7.04%	8,395	733	−4.81%	770
Total sales	25,098	+11.41%	22,528	31,357	−2.52%	32,168	15,707	−1.16%	15,891

(ii) Numbers that are blandly presented in a global format do not usually reveal trends. Analysis of information year-on-year by area and by percentage, for example, may reveal trends and may illustrate the impact of new policies or the changes in specific economic environments. The analysis of the Nestlé SA sales revenue for the two years shows:

- in which geographical area sales revenues have increased or decreased
- which products' sales revenues have increased or decreased.

Analysis of the results over several years is usually needed to provide meaningful trend information as a basis for investigation into the reasons for increases and decreases.

An operating segment is a component of a company that engages in business activities from which it earns revenues and incurs expenses and for which discrete financial information is available.

For each operating segment of a company, IFRS 8 requires information to be provided about

- how the business identifies its operating segments
- the types of products and services from which it earns revenues in each operating segment
- the reported profit or loss of each segment.

Also required is an analysis of revenues and non-current assets by geographical area irrespective of the identification of operating segments and a requirement to disclose information about transactions with major customers.

Let's take a look at Johnson Matthey's segmental reporting (see pages 375 to 377). This may be used to provide even more useful information through horizontal and vertical analysis of the numbers. Such an analysis over a five- or 10-year period would be particularly useful to identify trends in performance, and changes that may have taken place in the activities of the business and the areas of the world in which the company has operated.

Mini case 8.4

If we refer to note 1 in the Johnson Matthey Plc notes on the accounts in their annual report and accounts 2012 we can identify total sales revenue for each global division for 2012 and 2011. We can use this to present the data in both pie chart format (see Figure 8.14 and Figure 8.15) and bar chart format (see Figure 8.16) and more clearly explain JM's sales results for 2012 and 2011.

The pie charts give a broad indication of sales revenue by type of business, and show that for both years precious metals provide over two thirds of the sales revenue and it is increasing, and environmental technologies provide over one quarter of sales revenue. Fine chemicals is the smallest sector that provides the balance.

The bar chart is probably more useful in showing more clearly that sales revenue from the largest sector has increased in 2012 over 2011, that the next largest sector has decreased, and the smallest sector has remained at around the same volume.

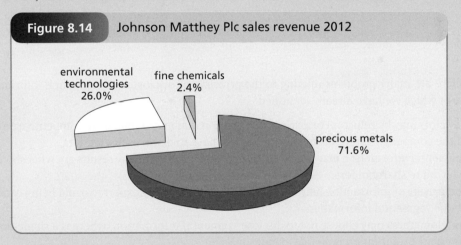

Figure 8.14 Johnson Matthey Plc sales revenue 2012

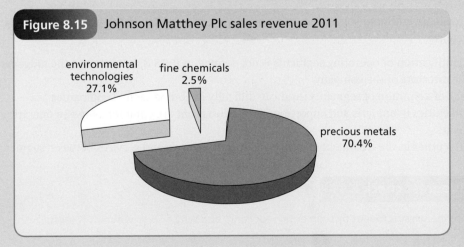

Figure 8.15 Johnson Matthey Plc sales revenue 2011

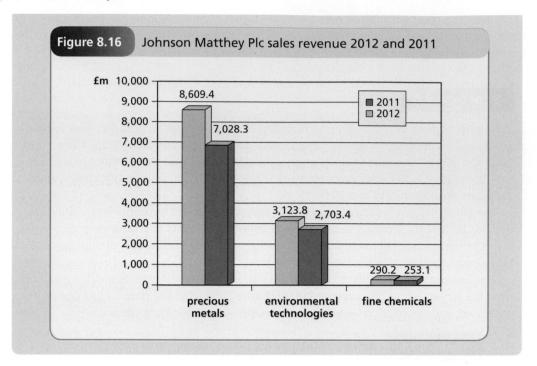

Figure 8.16 Johnson Matthey Plc sales revenue 2012 and 2011

There are many problems relating to the principle of disclosure of segmental information, some of which we have already identified:

- directors may be reluctant to disclose information that may damage the competitive position of the company – foreign competitors may not have to disclose similar data
- segmental information may not be useful since the total company results are what should be relevant to shareholders
- some users of information may not be sufficiently financially expert to avoid being confused by the segmental information
- conglomerates may choose not to disclose segmental information, whereas a single-activity company by definition is unable to hide anything.

There are, in addition, some accounting problems concerned with the preparation of segmental reports:

- identification of operating segments is not defined in IFRS 8, but is left to the judgement of the directors of the company
- lack of definition of segments results in difficulty in comparison of companies
- difficulties in analysis and apportionment of costs that are common between operating segments
- difficulties in the treatment of costs of transfers of goods and services between segments.

Progress check 8.11

Describe what is meant by segmental reporting, and why and to whom it is useful.

In this chapter we have looked at most of the key ratios and techniques for review of company performance, and their meaning and relevance. However, the limitations we have already identified generally relating to performance review must always be borne in mind. In addition, it should be noted that the calculations used in business ratio analysis are based on past performance. These may not, therefore, reflect the current or future performance of an organisation. Performance ratio analyses can also sometimes be misleading if their interpretation does not also consider other factors that may not always be easily quantifiable, and may include non-financial information, for example customer satisfaction, and delivery performance. There may be inconsistencies in some of the measures used in ratio analysis. For example, sales revenues and costs are reported net of VAT, but trade receivables and trade payables normally include VAT. Extreme care should therefore be taken in any performance review to avoid reaching conclusions that may perhaps be erroneous.

If all the financial literature were thoroughly researched the number of different ratios that may be discovered would run into hundreds. It is most helpful to use a limited set of ratios and to fully understand their meaning. The ratios will certainly help with an understanding of the company but do not in themselves represent the complete picture.

Calculation of the ratios for one company for one year is also very limited. It is more relevant to compare companies operating in the same market and to analyse how a company has changed over the years. However, difficulties inevitably arise because it is sometimes impossible to find another company that is strictly comparable with the company being analysed. In addition, the company itself may have changed so much over recent years as to render meaningless any conclusions drawn from changes in ratios.

Cash versus profit, and EBITDA, EVA™, and MVA

The use of cash flow versus profit (or earnings per share) as a measure of company performance has become increasingly important. The advantages and disadvantages in the use of each are shown in Figures 8.17 and 8.18.

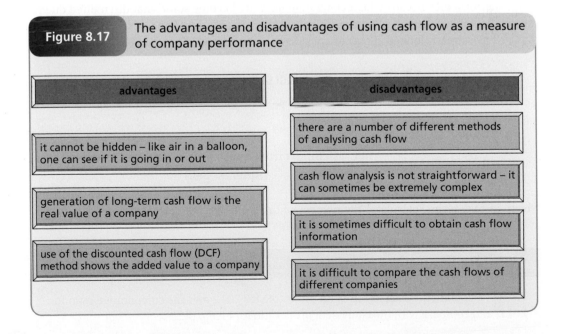

Figure 8.17 The advantages and disadvantages of using cash flow as a measure of company performance

advantages

it cannot be hidden – like air in a balloon, one can see if it is going in or out

generation of long-term cash flow is the real value of a company

use of the discounted cash flow (DCF) method shows the added value to a company

disadvantages

there are a number of different methods of analysing cash flow

cash flow analysis is not straightforward – it can sometimes be extremely complex

it is sometimes difficult to obtain cash flow information

it is difficult to compare the cash flows of different companies

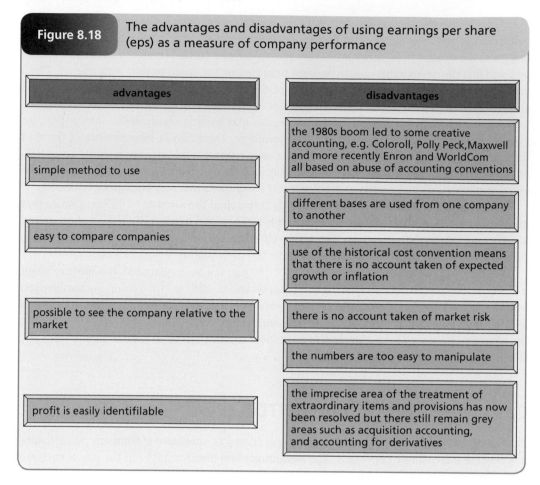

Figure 8.18 The advantages and disadvantages of using earnings per share (eps) as a measure of company performance

advantages	disadvantages
	the 1980s boom led to some creative accounting, e.g. Coloroll, Polly Peck, Maxwell and more recently Enron and WorldCom all based on abuse of accounting conventions
simple method to use	different bases are used from one company to another
easy to compare companies	use of the historical cost convention means that there is no account taken of expected growth or inflation
possible to see the company relative to the market	there is no account taken of market risk
	the numbers are too easy to manipulate
profit is easily identifilable	the imprecise area of the treatment of extraordinary items and provisions has now been resolved but there still remain grey areas such as acquisition accounting, and accounting for derivatives

Cash flow reporting has become increasingly important and has gained popularity as a measure of performance because the income statement has become somewhat discredited due to the unacceptable degree of subjectivity involved in its preparation. Some of the financial ratios that we have already looked at may be considered in cash terms, for example:

$$\text{cash ROCE \%} = \frac{\text{net cash flow from operations}}{\text{average capital employed}}$$

and

$$\text{cash interest cover} = \frac{\text{net cash inflow from operations + interest received}}{\text{interest paid}}$$

which, in cash terms, calculates the number of times the interest payable is covered by cash available for such payments.

Worked example 8.8

We will calculate the cash ROCE % for Flatco plc for 2012 and the comparative ratio for 2011, and compare with the equivalent profit ratio for Flatco plc.

Cash ROCE %

$$\text{cash ROCE \% 2012} = \frac{\text{net cash flow from operations}}{\text{average capital employed}} = \frac{£936 \times 100\%}{(£3,543 + £2,713)/2}$$

$$= \frac{£936 \times 100\%}{£3,128} = 29.9\%$$

$$\text{cash ROCE \% 2011} = \frac{£783 \times 100\%}{(£2,713 + £2,406)/2} = \frac{£783 \times 100\%}{£2,559.5} = 30.6\%$$

Report on the cash and profit ROCE of Flatco plc

While the profit ROCE % was static at 17.6% for 2011 and 2012, the cash ROCE % decreased from 30.6% to 29.9%. Operating cash flow for 2012 increased by only 19.5% over 2011, despite the fact that operating profit for 2012 increased by 22.2% over 2011.

Operating profit before depreciation (EBITDA) was £895,000 [£550,000+£345,000] for 2012, which was an increase of 20.5% over 2011 [£450,000+£293,000=£743,000]. If pre-depreciation operating profit had been used to calculate ROCE, it would have been 28.6% for 2012 compared with 29.0% for 2011, a reduction of 0.4% and more in line with the picture shown by the cash ROCE.

The chairman of Flatco plc expects that ROCE will be improved in 2013 as a result of:

- increased profitability resulting from higher sales revenues generated from the investments in new projects
- reduction in levels of working capital, with more efficient use of company resources.

Progress check 8.12

What are the benefits of using cash flow instead of profit to measure financial performance? What are the disadvantages of using cash flow?

The increasing importance of cash flow as a measure of performance has led to new methods of measurement:

- the Rappaport method, which uses DCF looking 10 years ahead as a method of valuing a company
- the economic value added (EVA™) method
- enterprise value, a very similar method to EVA but which excludes the peripheral activities of the company.

A profit-based measure of financial performance **EBITDA**, or earnings before interest, tax, depreciation, and amortisation, is used by some companies as an approximation to operational cash flow. Amortisation, in the same way as depreciation applies to tangible non-current assets, is the systematic write-off of the cost of an intangible asset. The way in which EBITDA may be used has been illustrated in the Flatco plc Worked example 8.8.

Graphs showing BT plc's EBITDA and free cash flows derived from EDITDA for the years 2006 to 2010, which were included in the group's annual report for the year 2010, are shown in Figure 8.19.

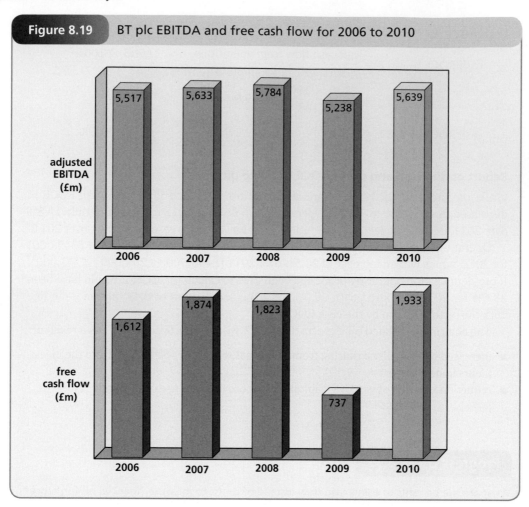

Figure 8.19 BT plc EBITDA and free cash flow for 2006 to 2010

In its 2010 annual report and accounts, BT plc commented on its use of EBITDA as a performance measure:

> EBITDA is a common measure used by investors and analysts to evaluate the operating financial performance of companies, particularly in the telecommunications sector. We consider EBITDA to be a useful measure of our operating performance because it reflects the underlying operating cash costs, by eliminating depreciation and amortisation. EBITDA is not a direct measure of our liquidity, which is shown by our statement of cash flows, and it needs to be considered in the context of our financial commitments.

We have seen that the method of performance measurement is not a clear-cut cash or profit choice. It is generally useful to use both. However, many analysts and the financial press in general continue to depend heavily on profit performance measures with a strong emphasis on earnings per share (eps) and the price/earnings ratio (P/E). Maximisation of shareholder wealth continues to be the prime objective with which managers of companies are charged. The extent to which success in particular performance measures aligns with shareholder wealth is particularly relevant. Equally important are the ways in which managers are motivated to maximise shareholder wealth, and in most organisations managerial remuneration provides the link between the measures of financial performance and shareholder value.

Financial performance measures such as a company's share price are commonly used to indicate how well the company is doing. However, it may be questioned as to how directly the share price reflects decisions that have been taken by management. In the context of managers' performance against budget targets, and the company's overall financial performance, we have previously discussed the merits and otherwise of performance measures such as profit after tax, earnings per share, dividends, return on capital employed, and cash flow, etc. Each has its limitations, but cash flow-based measures are now becoming accepted as perhaps better indicators than profit related measures.

If we assume that the organisation's objective is to maximise shareholder wealth then this should ultimately be achieved if new projects are taken on and existing projects are allowed to continue only if they create value. Investment in capital projects should be made only on the basis of choosing those with a positive net present value (NPV). However, NPV cannot be applied to remuneration schemes because it is a summary measure based on projected cash flows and not on realised performance. Companies usually turn to company earnings and cash flow (which are termed flow measures) for management remuneration schemes. We were introduced to the alternative measure of EVA™ in Chapter 2, and how it may be used to support NPV project recommendations aligned with a better measure of management performance on which to base manager remuneration. In Chapter 2 we saw that:

$$EVA = PAT - (WACC \times NA)$$

Worked example 8.9 illustrates the calculation of EVA and its relationship with NPV.

Worked example 8.9

A manager has to choose between three mutually exclusive projects. The company may invest:

£50,000 in project A, or
£110,000 in project B, or
£240,000 in project C

Project A is expected to generate incremental profits after tax (PAT) of £50,000 in year one, £40,000 in year two (total £90,000), after which the project is terminated.

Project B is expected to generate incremental PATs of £45,000 in year one, £70,000 in year two, £70,000 in year three (total £185,000), after which the project is terminated.

Project C is expected to generate incremental PATs of £55,000 in year one, £75,000 in year two, £80,000 in year three (total £210,000), after which the project is terminated.

The company's WACC is 10% per annum. Asset levels may be assumed to be maintained throughout the life of each project. That is, each year's new capital expenditure equals depreciation in that year. Assets are sold at their book value in the final year of each project so free cash flow (operating cash flow less capital expenditure) will be equal to PAT each year except the final year when the capital investment costs are recovered.

We will assess which project the manager will choose if his or her remuneration is:

(i)   tied to the NPV of the project
(ii)   based on IRR
(iii) based on project earnings
(iv)   based on EVA.

Using a discount rate of WACC at 10% per annum, we first calculate the NPVs of each project.

Year	Cash outflows £000	Cash inflows £000	Net cash flow £000	Discount factor at 10%	Present values £000
Project A					
0	−50		−50	1.00	−50.0
1		50	50	0.91	45.5
2		90 [40 + 50]	90	0.83	74.7
3		0	0	0.75	0.0
Total	−50	140	90	NPV	+70.2
Project B					
0	−110		−110	1.00	−110.0
1		45	45	0.91	40.9
2		70	70	0.83	58.1
3		180 [70 + 110]	180	0.75	135.0
Total	−110	295	185	NPV	+124.0
Project C					
0	−240		−240	1.00	−240.0
1		55	55	0.91	50.0
2		75	75	0.83	62.3
3		320 [80 + 240]	320	0.75	240.0
Total	−240	450	210	NPV	+112.3

The IRR is the rate of return that would give an NPV of zero.

Interpolation or extrapolation techniques, which we covered in Chapter 6, may be used to derive the internal rate of return of each project.

For project C, if we assume a discount rate of 30%, we may calculate a revised NPV as follows:

Year	Cash outflows £000	Cash inflows £000	Net cash flow £000	Discount factor at 30%	Present values £000
0	−240		−240	1.00	−240.0
1		55	55	0.77	42.4
2		75	75	0.59	44.3
3		320	320	0.46	147.2
Total	−240	450	210	NPV	−6.1

We have already calculated the positive NPV for project C of £112,300 using a cost of capital of 10%. The IRR of project C must be at some point between 30% and 10% (difference 20%).

Using a similar calculation to that used in Figure 6.3 (Chapter 6):

$$\frac{£6,100}{x} = \frac{£112,300}{(20 - x)}$$

$$(£6,100 \times 20) - £6,100x = £112,300x$$
$$£122,000 = £118,400x$$
$$x = \frac{£122,000}{£118,400}$$
$$x = 1.03$$

Therefore, interpolation gives us an IRR of 30% less 1.03%, which equals 28.97% and may be rounded up to 29%.

The IRRs of projects A and B may be calculated in the same way.

The cash flows, NPVs and IRRs of the three projects may be summarised as:

Project	PAT			Cash out	Cash in			Total cash flow	IRR	NPV
	Year 1 £000	Year 2 £000	Year 3 £000	£000	Year 1 £000	Year 2 £000	Year 3 £000	£000	%	£000
A	50	40		−50	50	90 [40+50]		90	93	70.2
B	45	70	70	−110	45	70	180 [70+110]	185	53	124.0
C	55	75	80	−240	55	75	320 [80+240]	210	29	112.3

(i)   Based on the highest NPV, project B at £124,000 is best for the company shareholders.

(ii) But if the manager's remuneration is based on IRR then he or she will choose project A at 93%.

(iii) If the manager is remunerated on total project earnings then he or she will choose project C at £210,000.

(iv) We can calculate the EVA for each project, which equals profit after tax for each period, less capital employed at the start of each period multiplied by the weighted average cost of capital.

Year	Project A		Project B		Project C	
	£000	EVA £000	£000	EVA £000	£000	EVA £000
1	50 − (50 × 10%)	45	45 − (110 × 10%)	34	55 − (240 × 10%)	31
2	40 − (50 × 10%)	35	70 − (110 × 10%)	59	75 − (240 × 10%)	51
3		___	70 − (110 × 10%)	59	80 − (240 × 10%)	56
Total		80		152		138

If the manager's remuneration is based on EVA then project B would be chosen at £152,000.

We may also calculate the NPV of the EVAs of each project:

Year	Discount factor at 10%	Project A		Project B		Project C	
		EVA £000	NPV £000	EVA £000	NPV £000	EVA £000	NPV £000
1	0.91	45	41.0	34	30.9	31	28.2
2	0.83	35	29.1	59	49.0	51	42.3
3	0.75	___	___	59	44.2	56	42.0
Total		80	+70.1	152	+124.1	138	+112.5

This above table shows that the NPVs of the EVAs are the same as the NPVs of each project based on cash flows. The small differences between the totals calculated for project A and project C are as a result of rounding differences.

If the manager is remunerated based on EVA it will be consistent with maximising NPV, which is best for shareholders. EVA is therefore the best measure on which to base manager remuneration because it also maximises corporate value.

We have seen from Worked example 8.9 that earnings-based remuneration schemes (profit or cash flow) may result in the creation of lower than optimal levels of corporate value. The use of EVA as a basis for management remuneration takes account of the fact that the use of net assets is charged for by applying a WACC percentage. Additionally, at the project level, the present value of the EVAs gives the same result as NPVs derived from free cash flows – compare the results in the project NPV tables with the NPVs of the EVAs of each project in Worked example 8.9.

Although the free cash flow NPVs give the same result as the present values of the EVAs, EVA is more appropriate for remuneration schemes because, as well as being fundamentally related to corporate value and therefore shareholder value, it is a flow measure of performance. The reason that flow measures of performance are needed for periodic remuneration is because remuneration is designed to provide a flow of rewards. EVA and cash flow are both flow mea-

Worked example 8.10

We will compute the EVA for 2010, 2011 and 2012 for a major plc from the following information.

Group cost of capital 5%

		£m
Adjusted net assets	2012	750
	2011	715
	2010	631
Profit for year	2012	550
	2011	526
	2010	498
Total equity	2012	100
	2011	48
	2010	115
Net debt	2012	800
	2011	802
	2010	546

Year	Profit after tax £m	Adjusted net assets £m	5% cost of capital × net assets £m	EVA £m	EVA % of net profit
2012	550	750	37.50	512.50	93
2011	526	715	35.75	490.25	93
2010	498	631	31.55	466.45	94

Note how the profits are being earned using borrowed funds to finance the group. The plc can earn a very high EVA by using borrowed funds.

sures, but EVA is a better basis for manager remuneration than cash flow because it takes into account the cost of capital invested in the project.

We have talked about EVA with regard to projects, and that the present value of future EVAs equals the NPVs derived from future free cash flows. At a company level, the present value of EVAs equals the **market value added (MVA)** of a business. This is defined as the difference between the market value of the company and the adjusted book values of its assets.

EVA is a good financial performance measure because it answers the question of how well the company has performed in generating profits over a period, given the amount of assets used to generate those profits. However, the asset base is a difficult element to estimate in calculating EVA. The total net assets value on a balance sheet is not an accurate representation of either the liquidation value or the replacement cost value of the business. Stern Stewart consider more than 250 possible accounting adjustments to a balance sheet to arrive at a valuation of the company's assets. In practice most organisations find that no more than a dozen or so adjustments are truly significant, for example adding back interest to profit, and those relating to inventory valuations, depreciation calculations, goodwill and impairment, doubtful debt provisions, leasing, deferred tax, and closure costs.

Further information about EVA may be obtained from the Stern Stewart weblink *www.sternstewart.co/index.php?content=main*.

Worked example 8.11

We will compute the MVA for 2011 and 2012 from the following extracts from the annual report and accounts of a major plc, using the adjusted value of its net assets.

	2012	**2011**
Number of shares (5p)	950.2m	948.9m
Share price	278p	268p
Net assets	£1,097m	£1,437m
Market value	£2,641m	£2,543m
MVA	£1,544m	£1,106m

Progress check 8.13

What is economic value added (EVA) and what is it used for?

EVA probably does not change or add anything to the conclusions reached on the basis of conventional cash flow-based valuation analysis. EVA is primarily a behavioural tool that corrects possible distortions. However, along with most other financial measures, it fails to measure on an *ex post* basis. EVA is undoubtedly a very useful concept for measuring and evaluating management and company performance. It is not a cure for poor management and poor investment decisions but it does raise the profile and the awareness of the costs of capital involved in undertaking projects and in running the business.

Predicting corporate financial failure

One of the uses of ratio analysis is in the area of trying to predict corporate failure. The various groups of corporate stakeholders have an obvious interest in such predictions, for example:

- shareholders would like to know how risky their investments are
- employees would like to know how secure their jobs are
- suppliers would like to be sure that they will be paid
- lenders would like to be reassured that interest and loan repayments will be made.

If stakeholders are able to determine which companies are riskier than others then they may make better informed decisions. There has been a great deal of research that has resulted in the development of various **multivariate discriminant analysis (MDA)** models that are used to try and predict corporate financial failure, such as those developed by:

- Edward Altman
- Datastream
- Richard Taffler
- John Argenti.

Edward Altman's original model (Altman, EI 'Financial ratios, discriminant analysis and the prediction of corporate bankruptcy' *Journal of Finance*, Volume 23, Issue 4, pages 589–609 (September, 1968)) was based on a sample of 66 publicly traded manufacturing companies, 33 of which failed and 33 of which did not, matched by size and industry and selected on a stratified random basis. Altman then examined several common financial ratios based on data retrieved from annual financial reports. After linearly combining these ratios, Altman arrived at an empirical equation for a *Z-Score* (Z for Zeta) that predicted the risk of corporate failure within two years with an accuracy of 72%, and false positives at 6%. The five ratios are:

- working capital/total assets
- retained earnings/total assets
- earnings (profit) before interest and tax/total assets
- market value of equity/total liabilities
- sales revenue/total assets,

each of which is multiplied by constant factors 1.2, 1.4, 3.3, 0.6, and 0.998 respectively.

For convenience, in practice the 0.998 was usually rounded up to 1.0 and Altman's model could be used for prediction of corporate failure by calculating his *Z-Score* for a public industrial company based on the equation where *Z* equals:

$$1.2 \times \frac{\text{working capital}}{\text{total assets}} + 1.4 \times \frac{\text{retained earnings}}{\text{total assets}} + 3.3 \times \frac{\text{PBIT}}{\text{total assets}}$$
$$+ 0.6 \times \frac{\text{market value of equity}}{\text{total liabilities}} + 1.0 \times \frac{\text{sales revenue}}{\text{total assets}}$$

The market value of equity is the market value of all tradable shares in issue.

Altman's model predicted that public industrial companies with a *Z-Score*:

- less than 1.88 were highly likely to become insolvent
- between 1.80 and 2.70 were likely to become insolvent within two years
- between 2.77 and 2.99 indicated that caution was required
- over 2.99 were considered to be financially sound.

Altman also tested the above equation against companies not in the initial sample, which predicted insolvency to a high degree of accuracy.

More recently, Altman published a working paper in 2000 entitled 'Predicting financial distress of companies: Revisiting the Z-Score and Zeta® models', which can be found on the Stern School of Business website at *http://pages.stern.nyu.edu/~ealtman/Zscores.pdf*. In this paper Altman provided a *Z-Score* equation for private industrial companies, Z_1. This equation uses different multiplying constant factors but the same ratios as for Z except that the book value of equity is used instead of the market value of equity. For a private industrial company Z_1 equals:

$$0.717 \times \frac{\text{working capital}}{\text{total assets}} + 0.847 \times \frac{\text{retained earnings}}{\text{total assets}} + 3.107 \times \frac{\text{PBIT}}{\text{total assets}} + 0.42 \times \frac{\text{book value of equity}}{\text{total liabilities}} + 0.998 \times \frac{\text{sales revenue}}{\text{total assets}}$$

The book value of equity is the total shareholders' equity as shown in the balance sheet.

Altman's model predicted that private industrial companies with a Z_1-*Score*:

- less than 1.23 were highly likely to become insolvent
- over 2.90 were considered to be financially sound.

In the same 2000 paper Altman also provided a *Z-Score* equation for non-manufacturing companies, Z_2. This equation uses further different multiplying constant factors and four of the same ratios as for the Z_1. For a non-manufacturing company Z_2 equals:

$$1.2 \times \frac{\text{working capital}}{\text{total assets}} + 1.4 \times \frac{\text{retained earnings}}{\text{total assets}} + 3.3 \times \frac{\text{PBIT}}{\text{total assets}} + 0.6 \times \frac{\text{book value of equity}}{\text{total liabilities}}$$

Altman's model predicted that non-manufacturing companies with a Z_2-*Score*:

- less than 1.10 were highly likely to become insolvent
- over 2.60 were considered to be financially sound.

Worked example 8.12

From its balance sheet and income statement shown in Figures 8.3 and 8.4 we can calculate the Altman *Z-Score* for Flatco plc for 2012.

$$Z = \frac{1.2 \times 995}{4,348} + \frac{1.4 \times 1,594}{4,348} + \frac{3.3 \times 661}{4,348} + \frac{0.6 \times 3,300}{1,354} + \frac{1.0 \times 3,500}{4,348}$$
$$= 0.275 + 0.513 + 0.502 + 1.462 + 0.805$$
$$= 3.557$$

So with an Altman *Z-Score* greater than 2.99, Flatco plc may be considered to have a sound financial position.

Datastream is a commercial company, which provides a range of statistical and economic information, including *Z-Scores*, for selected companies based on their own model developed by Marais (Marais, DAJ *A Method of Quantifying Companies' Relative Financial Strength*, Bank of England Discussion Paper No. 4 (1979)). The model is based on a sample of 100 UK companies, 50 of which failed and 50 of which did not, and is based on four independent measures of company performance:

- profitability
- liquidity
- gearing
- inventory turnover.

Yet another *Z-Score* provided by Taffler (Taffler, RJ 'Forecasting company failure in the UK using discriminant analysis and financial ratio data', *Journal of Royal Statistical Society*, (A) 145, Part 3, pages 342–58 (1982), and 'The use of the Z-Score approach in practice', City University Business School Working Paper 95/1 (1995)) is based on the four ratios:

- profit before tax/current liabilities
- current assets/total liabilities
- current liabilities/total assets
- liquid current assets/daily cash operating expenses,

each of which is multiplied by constant factors.

Taffler's *Z-Scores* range between negative (higher risk) and positive (lower risk); the higher or lower the *Z-Scores* indicate the level of potential failure or survival.

As we can see, Altman's work in the 1960s led to the development and refinement over subsequent years of quantitatively based methodologies to determine indicators of corporate collapse based on an analysis of reported financial numbers. John Argenti (Argenti, J (1976) *Corporate Collapse: The Causes and Symptoms*, London: McGraw-Hill) on the other hand believed that a qualitative approach would give a broader appreciation of the factors which in themselves create failed companies by seeking to identify patterns of managerial failure (a key cause of corporate collapse); the numbers reported in the financial statements are the products of managerial actions.

Argenti's methodology identified three trajectories of corporate collapse. The first trajectory relates to newly formed organisations which fail within two to eight years. The new company begins with poor management which leads to poor accounting, high gearing, negative cash flows, crisis action such as price reductions, insufficient profits, and ultimate business failure.

Trajectory two relates dramatically to young organisations failing over a period of between four and 14 years. Such organisations have poor but arrogant management who will not take advice.

Trajectory three is the agonising death of a large, formerly successful, corporation; a company which was successful in the past but over time loses touch with its customers and employees. It is a company that has grown too used to success to adapt to its environment, and has created the myth of immortality. Management seek to take the company forward with ill-judged projects which prove to be loss-making, as gearing increases and profits fall.

The essence of Argenti's approach is that there are typical corporate failure patterns which are the product of identifiable managerial activities. In a later work Argenti (Argenti, J 'Predicting corporate failure', *Account Digest* No. 138 (1983)) takes his model a stage further by creating a more quantitative model; this relates to Argenti's *A-Score*. He argues that the initial defects that initiate the corporate collapse can be divided into management weaknesses and accounting deficiencies and that they can be ascribed a score if these conditions exist and a zero if they do not, as follows:

- Management weaknesses
  autocratic chief executive (8)

failure to separate role of chairman and chief executive (4)

passive board of directors (2)

lack of balance of skills in management team – financial, legal, marketing, etc. (4)

weak finance director (2)

lack of 'management in depth' (1)

poor response to change (15).

- Accounting deficiencies

  no budgetary control (3)

  no cash flow plans (3)

  no costing system (3).

The total for both categories combined is 45, and according to Argenti if a company's score is less than 10, then this is classed as satisfactory. In the logical sequence of corporate decline managerial weakness leads to mistakes being made and Argenti identifies three key mistakes and scores them also. These are:

- high gearing (15)
- overtrading (15)
- the 'big project', the failure of which would destroy the company (15).

According to the *A-Score* paradigm the maximum allowable score on this category is 15; Argenti allows management one mistake. These mistakes however will ultimately lead to clearly visible symptoms of failure classified as follows:

- financial signs (4)
- creative accounting (4)
- non-financial signs, for example frozen management salaries, delayed capital expenditure, falling market share, rising employee turnover (3)
- terminal signs when the company is so far in decline its imminent collapse is obvious (1).

Argenti's *A-Score* method suggests that companies scoring overall above 25 are exhibiting the signs that precede failure and are therefore at risk. If a company scores less than 25 overall but scores (for example) over 10 on the first category, there may be cause for concern as the management and accounting within the company are clearly weak and this may lead to future problems. Usually, companies not at risk have fairly low scores (0 to 18 being common), whereas those at risk usually score well above 25 (often 35 to 70).

The issues raised in Argenti's models are very much related to the corporate governance issues we have already discussed in Chapter 3 and the financial strategies and corporate finance decisions we will consider in Chapters 13 to 18 when we look at the development of businesses throughout their various stages of start-up, growth, maturity, and decline.

The many refinements to Altman's *Z-Score*, which are used by banks and by companies to assess creditworthiness, are kept highly secret because a successful method gives a business a significant competitive advantage in being able to identify good and bad borrowers and suppliers. For example, the ability of banks to accurately identify good and bad credit risks has a big impact on their level of bad debt write-offs, and therefore their profitability. In 2006 the Royal Bank of Scotland reported an increase in its bad debts of 4.7% over the previous year to £887m. Compare that with the 50% and 20% increases for Barclays Bank and Lloyds TSB Bank respectively for the same period.

Caution should be exercised in the use of financial failure prediction models for a number of reasons. Such models are inevitably based on past data, business structures, and economic environments. For example, the 1990s and prior would not have included the significant presence of the 'hi-tech' and dot.com companies that we have in the 2000s.

The use of MDA models may be augmented by statistical analyses of financial data and ratios to further assist in this area of prediction of corporate failure using, for example, time series and line of business analyses. However, the use of any financial analysis is not an exact science because of the alternative application of financial standards and accounting policies adopted by companies.

We have assumed that the financial failure of a business means insolvency, but failure may have wider implications than the liquidation of a company. Although models to predict financial failure are used extensively by banks, credit rating organisations, and financial analysts, and there has been much research into the development of the MDA models themselves, there has been less research and analysis into the validity and reliability of these models in practice.

Progress check 8.14

Who are the main users of *Z-Scores* and how do they use them?

Summary of key points

- The main aims of a business performance review are to provide an understanding of the business and provide an interpretation of results.

- Care must be taken in reviewing business performance, primarily because of lack of consistency in definitions, and changes in economic conditions.

- An important area of business performance review is the use of ratio analysis looking at profitability, efficiency, liquidity, investment and growth, and financial structure.

- The Du Pont system of ratios can be used to identify the relationship between return on equity (ROE), return on assets (ROA), and gearing.

- Horizontal analysis of the income statement (which may also be applied to the balance sheet) for two or more years starts with a base year 100 and shows each item, line-by-line, indexed against the base year, and is particularly useful in looking at performance trends over a number of years.

- Vertical analysis of the income statement (which may also be applied to the balance sheet) shows every item as a percentage of sales revenue (balance sheet: percentage of total assets), and is also particularly useful in looking at performance trends over a number of years.

- Segmental reporting provides a further dimension to the financial statements through analysis of sales revenue, profit, and assets, by business class and geographical segments.

- Cash flow and cash ratios are becoming increasingly as important as profit and profitability ratios in the measurement of business performance.

- There is no best way of evaluating financial performance and there are advantages and disadvantages in using both earnings per share and cash flow as the basis of measurement.

- EBITDA (earnings before interest, tax, depreciation, and amortisation) is commonly used as a close approximation of a cash flow performance measure.

- Economic value added (EVA™) is becoming widely used by companies as a performance measure that is very close to cash flow, and as a value creation incentive basis for remuneration.

- There are a number of multivariate discriminant analysis (MDA) methods of predicting corporate financial failure used by banks, credit agencies, and financial institutions; the most well-known are the various versions of the *Z-Score* analyses developed by Taffler, Marais (Datastream), and Altman.

Glossary of key terms

cash interest cover Net cash inflow from operations plus interest received, divided by interest paid, calculates the number of times the interest payable is covered by cash flow available for such payments.

collection days Average trade receivables divided by average daily sales revenue on credit terms indicates the average time taken, in calendar days, to receive payment from credit customers.

continuing operations Operations not satisfying all the conditions relating to discontinued operations (see below).

cross-sectional analysis Cross-sectional analysis provides a means of providing a standard against which performance can be measured and uses ratios to compare different businesses at the same points in time (see **inter-company comparison**).

current ratio Current assets divided by current liabilities is an overall measure of liquidity.

debt/equity ratio A gearing ratio that relates to financial gearing, which is the relationship between a company's borrowings, which includes both prior charge capital and long-term debt, and its ordinary shareholders' funds (share capital plus reserves).

defensive interval Quick assets (current assets excluding inventories) divided by average daily cash from operations shows how many days a business could survive at its present level of operating activity if no inflow of cash was received from sales or other sources.

discontinued operations Components of an entity that have either been disposed of or are classified as held for sale and:

- represent, or are part of a single plan to dispose of, separate major lines of business or geographical areas of operations; or
- are subsidiaries acquired exclusively with a view to resale (IFRS 5).

dividend cover Earnings per share divided by dividend per share indicates the number of times the profits attributable to the equity shareholders cover the actual dividends payable for the period.

dividend yield Dividend return on the market value of a share shown as a percentage.

EBITDA Earnings before interest, tax, depreciation, and amortisation.

gearing Financial gearing calculations can be made in a number of ways. Gearing is generally seen as the relationship between a company's borrowings, which include both prior charge capital (capital having a right of interest or preference shares having fixed dividends), and long-term debt plus ordinary shareholders' funds (share capital plus reserves).

horizontal analysis (or common size analysis) An analysis of the income statement (or balance sheet) that allows a line-by-line analysis of the accounts with those of the previous year. It may provide a trend of changes over a number of years showing either growth or decline in these elements of the accounts through calculation of annual percentage growth rates in profit, sales revenue, inventory, or any other item.

interest cover Profit before interest and tax divided by interest payable, calculates the number of times the interest payable is covered by profits available for such payments. It is particularly important for lenders to determine the vulnerability of interest payments to a drop in profit.

inter-company comparison Systematic and detailed comparison of the performance of different companies generally operating in a common industry. Normally the information distributed by the scheme administrator (to participating companies only) is in the form of ratios, or in a format that prevents the identity of individual scheme members from being identified.

inventories days Inventories value divided by average daily cost of sales, which measures the number of days' inventories at the current usage rate. Inventories are goods held for future use comprising:

- goods or other assets purchased for resale
- consumable stores
- raw materials and components purchased for incorporation into products for sale
- products and services, in intermediate stages of completion (work in progress)
- long-term contracts
- finished goods.

just in time (JIT) The management philosophy that incorporates a 'pull' system of producing or purchasing components and products in response to customer demand, which contrasts with a 'push' system where inventories act as buffers between each process within and between purchasing, manufacturing, and sales.

market value added (MVA) The difference between the market value of the company and the adjusted book values of its assets.

multivariate discriminant analysis (MDA) MDA is a statistical technique which has been used to develop models that try to predict financial failure by: classifying samples of companies into two similar groups (one group in which all companies are predicted to survive and the other group in which all companies are predicted to fail) using a discriminant prediction equation of financial ratios; testing the theory by observing whether the companies are classified as predicted; investigating differences between or among the groups of companies; determining the optimum combination of discriminator ratios (for example a *Z-Score*) to best distinguish between the two groups of companies.

payables days Average trade payables divided by average daily purchases on credit terms indicates the average time taken, in calendar days, to pay for supplies received on credit.

price/earnings ratio (P/E) The market price per ordinary share divided by earnings per share shows the number of years it would take to recoup an equity investment from its share of the attributable equity profit.

quick ratio (or acid test) Quick assets (current assets excluding inventories) divided by current liabilities measures the ability of the business to pay accounts payable in the short term.

return on assets (ROA) Return on assets compares operational profit with the total assets used to generate that profit. Profit is calculated before net finance costs and corporation tax.

return on capital employed (ROCE) ROCE, or return on investment (ROI), is the profit before interest and tax divided by average capital employed. It indicates the profit-generating capacity of capital employed.

return on equity (ROE) A form of return on capital employed which measures the return to the owners on their investment in a company. The return is measured as the residual profit after all charges and appropriations other than to ordinary shareholders have been made, and the equity is ordinary share capital plus reserves.

return on investment (ROI) See return on capital employed (ROCE).

segmental reporting The inclusion in a company's report and accounts of analysis of sales revenue, profit, and net assets by class of business and by geographical segments (Companies Act 2006 and IFRS 8).

SWOT analysis Performing a SWOT analysis is a means of gaining a clear picture of the Strengths, Weaknesses, Opportunities, and Threats, which made the organisation what it is.

SWOT analysis can apply across diverse management functions and activities, but is particularly appropriate to the early stages of formulating strategy.

vendor managed inventory (VMI) The management of inventories on behalf of a customer by the supplier, the supplier taking responsibility for the management of inventories within a framework that is mutually agreed by both parties. Examples are seen in separate supermarket racks maintained and stocked by merchandising groups for such items as spices, and car parts distributors topping up the shelves of dealers and garages, where the management of the inventories, racking, and shelves is carried out by the merchandising group or distributor.

vertical analysis An analysis of the income statement (or balance sheet) in which each item is expressed as a percentage of the total. The vertical analysis provides evidence of structural changes in the business such as increased profitability through more efficient production.

Assessment material

Questions

Q8.1   (i)   Who is likely to carry out a business performance review?
   (ii)   Describe what may be required from such reviews giving some examples from different industries and differing perspectives.

Q8.2   (i)   Outline how the business performance review process may be used to evaluate the position of a dot.com company like Amazon UK.
   (ii)   What are the limitations to the approach that you have outlined?

Q8.3   How is ratio analysis, in terms of profitability ratios, efficiency ratios, liquidity ratios, investment ratios, and financial structure ratios used to support the business review process?

Q8.4   Why should we be so careful when we try to compare the income statement of a plc with a similar business in the same industry?

Q8.5   (i)   Why does profit continue to be the preferred basis for evaluation of the financial performance of a business?
   (ii)   In what ways can cash flow provide a better basis for performance evaluation, and how may cash flow be approximated?

Q8.6   In what way is company growth of such interest to shareholders?

Q8.7   Business performance may be evaluated to determine ways in which it can be improved upon. If managers are capable of delivering improved performance how can EVA™ be used to support this?

Q8.8   Explain how models that have been developed to predict corporate financial failure may be used in practice.

Discussion points

D8.1   In what ways may the performance review process be used to anticipate and react to change?

D8.2   'Lies, damned lies, and statistics.' In which of these categories do you think ratio analysis sits, if at all?

D8.3   'Economic value added (EVA™) is nothing more than just flavour of the month.' Discuss.

Exercises

Solutions are provided in Appendix 2 to all exercise numbers highlighted in colour.

Level I

E8.1 *Time allowed – 30 minutes*

The information below relates to Priory Products plc's actual results for 2011 and 2012 and their budget for the year 2013.

	2011 £000	2012 £000	2013 £000
Cash at bank	100	0	0
Overdraft	0	50	200
Loans	200	200	600
Ordinary shares	100	200	400
Profit and loss account	200	300	400

You are required to calculate the following financial ratios for Priory Products for 2011, 2012, and 2013:

(i) debt/equity ratio (net debt to equity)
(ii) gearing (long-term loans to equity and long-term loans).

E8.2 *Time allowed – 60 minutes*

From the financial statements of Freshco plc, a Lancashire-based grocery and general supplies chain supplying hotels and caterers, for the year ended 30 June 2012, prepare a report on performance using appropriate profitability ratios for comparison with the previous year.

Freshco plc
Balance sheet as at 30 June 2012

	2012 £m	2011 £m
Non-current assets	146	149
Current assets		
Inventories	124	100
Trade receivables	70	80
Cash and cash equivalents	14	11
Total current assets	208	191
Total assets	354	340
Current liabilities		
Trade payables	76	74
Dividends payable	20	13
Income tax payable	25	20
Total current liabilities	121	107
Non-current liabilities		
Debenture loan	20	67
Total liabilities	141	174
Net assets	213	166

(continued)

Equity

	2012	2011
Share capital	111	100
General reserve	14	9
Retained earnings	88	57
Total equity	213	166

Freshco plc
Income statement for the year ended 30 June 2012

	2012 £m	2011 £m
Revenue	894	747
Cost of sales	(690)	(581)
Gross profit	204	166
Distribution costs and administrative expenses	(121)	(84)
Operating profit	83	82
Net finance costs	(2)	(8)
Profit before tax	81	74
Income tax expense	(25)	(20)
Profit for the year	56	54
Retained profit brought forward	57	16
	113	70
Dividends for the year	(20)	(13)
	93	57
Transfer to general reserve	(5)	–
Retained profit carried forward	88	57

Additional information:

(i)   Authorised and issued share capital 30 June 2012, £222m £0.50 ordinary shares (£200m, 2011).

(ii)   Total assets less current liabilities 30 June 2010, £219m. Trade receivables 30 June 2010, £60m.

(iii)   Market value of ordinary shares in Freshco plc 30 June 2012, £3.93 (£2.85, 2011).

(iv)   Non-current assets depreciation provision 30 June 2012, £57m (£44m, 2011).

(v)   Depreciation charge for the year to 30 June 2012, £13m (£10m, 2011).

Freshco plc
Cash generated from operations for the year ended 30 June 2012

	2012 £m	2011 £m
Profit before tax	81	74
Depreciation charge	13	10
Adjust finance costs	2	8
Increase in inventories	(24)	(4)
Decrease/(increase) in trade receivables	10	(20)
Increase in trade payables	2	9
Cash generated from operations	84	77

Freshco plc
Statement of cash flows for the year ended 30 June 2012

	2012 £m	2011 £m
Cash flows from operating activities		
Cash generated from operations	84	77
Interest paid	(2)	(8)
Income tax paid	(20)	(15)
Net cash generated from operating activities	62	54
Cash flows from investing activities		
Purchases of tangible assets	(10)	(40)
Net cash outflow from investing activities	(10)	(40)
Cash flows from financing activities		
Proceeds from issue of ordinary shares	11	0
Proceeds from borrowings	0	7
Repayments of borrowings	(47)	0
Dividends paid to equity shareholders	(13)	(11)
Net cash outflow from financing activities	(49)	(4)
Increase in cash and cash equivalents in the year	3	10

E8.3   *Time allowed – 60 minutes*

Using the financial statements of Freshco plc from Exercise E8.2, for the year ended 30 June 2012, prepare a report on performance using appropriate efficiency ratios for comparison with the previous year.

E8.4   *Time allowed – 60 minutes*

Using the financial statements of Freshco plc from Exercise E8.2, for the year ended 30 June 2012, prepare a report on performance using appropriate liquidity ratios for comparison with the previous year.

E8.5   *Time allowed – 60 minutes*

Using the financial statements of Freshco plc from Exercise E8.2, for the year ended 30 June 2012, prepare a report on performance using appropriate investment ratios for comparison with the previous year.

E8.6   *Time allowed – 60 minutes*

Using the financial statements of Freshco plc from Exercise E8.2, for the year ended 30 June 2012, prepare a report on performance using appropriate financial structure ratios for comparison with the previous year.

Level II

E8.7 *Time allowed – 30 minutes*

You are required to compute the MVA for 2010, 2011, and 2012 from the estimated information for a large supermarket group shown below.

	2012	2011	2010
Number of shares	6.823m	6.823m	6.776m
Share price	261p	169p	177p
Adjusted net assets	£5,000m	£4,769m	£4,377m

E8.8 *Time allowed – 60 minutes*

The summarised income statement for the years ended 31 March 2011 and 2012 and balance sheets as at 31 March 2011 and 31 March 2012 for Boxer plc are shown below:

Boxer plc
Income statement for the year ended 31 March

	2011	2012
	£000	£000
Revenue	5,200	5,600
Cost of sales	(3,200)	(3,400)
Gross profit	2,000	2,200
Expenses	(1,480)	(1,560)
Profit before tax	520	640

Boxer plc
Balance sheet as at 31 March

	2011	2012
	£000	£000
Non-current assets	4,520	5,840
Current assets		
Inventories	1,080	1,360
Trade receivables	680	960
Cash and cash equivalents	240	–
Total current assets	2,000	2,320
Total assets	6,520	8,160
Current liabilities		
Borrowings and finance leases	–	160
Trade payables	360	520
Income tax payable	240	120
Dividends payable	280	384
Total current liabilities	880	1,184
Non-current liabilities		
Debenture loan	1,200	1,200

(continued)

Total liabilities	2,080	2,384
Net assets	4,440	5,776
Equity		
Ordinary share capital	4,000	5,200
Retained earnings	440	576
Total equity	4,440	5,776

Required:

(i) Calculate the following ratios for the years 2011 and 2012:
   (a) gross profit percentage of sales revenue
   (b) profit before tax percentage of sales revenue
   (c) return on capital employed
   (d) collection days
   (e) payables days
   (f) inventory turnover
   (g) current ratio
   (h) quick ratio.

(ii) Comment on Boxer plc's financial performance over the two years and explain the importance of effective management of working capital (net current assets).

E8.9   *Time allowed – 90 minutes*

The chief executive of Laurel plc, Al Chub, wants to know the financial strength of Laurel's main competitor, Hardy plc. He has asked you to write a report that evaluates the financial performance of Hardy plc using its financial statements for the past three years, and to include:

(i) a ratio analysis that looks at profitability, efficiency, and liquidity
(ii) an identification of the top five areas which should be investigated further
(iii) details of information that has not been provided, but if it were available would improve your analysis of Hardy's performance.

Hardy plc
Balance sheet as at 31 March

	2010	2011	2012
	£m	£m	£m
Non-current assets	106	123	132
Current assets			
Inventories	118	152	147
Trade receivables	53	70	80
Cash and cash equivalents	26	29	26
Total current assets	197	251	253
Total assets	303	374	385
Current liabilities			
Trade payables	26	38	38

(continued)

	2010	2011	2012
Other payables	40	52	55
Total current liabilities	66	90	93
Non-current liabilities			
Debenture loan	38	69	69
Total non-current liabilities	38	69	69
Total liabilities	104	159	162
Net assets	199	215	223
Equity			
Share capital	50	50	50
Retained earnings	149	165	173
Total equity	199	215	223

Hardy plc
Income statement for the year ended 31 March

	2010 £m	2011 £m	2012 £m
Revenue	420	491	456
Cost of sales	(277)	(323)	(295)
Gross profit	143	168	161
Distribution costs and administrative expenses	(93)	(107)	(109)
Operating profit	50	61	52
Net interest	(3)	(7)	(9)
Profit before tax	47	54	43
Income tax expense	(22)	(26)	(23)
Profit for the year	25	28	20
Dividends	(12)	(12)	(12)
Retained profit for the year	13	16	8

E8.10 *Time allowed – 90 minutes*

The following are the summarised financial statements of Dandy plc, a UK manufacturing company. The company has been operating successfully for a number of years. Whilst over recent years, market opportunities have resulted in an expansion in manufacturing operations, recent sales revenues and profits have nevertheless fallen over the past three years. The company has had severe cash problems resulting in an increase in overall debt.

Dandy plc
Income statement for the year ended 30 November

	2010 £000	2011 £000	2012 £000
Revenue	11,200	8,000	6,000
Cost of sales	(5,600)	(3,000)	(2,800)
Gross profit	5,600	5,000	3,200
Operating expenses	(4,000)	(2,600)	(2,000)
Profit before tax	1,600	2,400	1,200
Income tax expense	(600)	(1,100)	(550)
Profit for the year	1,000	1,300	650
Dividends	(600)	(200)	(300)
Retained profit for the year	400	1,100	350
Market price of shares at 30 November	£0.80	£0.90	£0.45

Dandy plc
Balance sheet as at 30 November 2012

	2010 £000	2011 £000	2012 £000
Non-current assets	3,600	2,700	6,500
Less: depreciation	(1,000)	(700)	(1,400)
	2,600	2,000	5,100
Current assets			
Inventories	1,700	1,800	2,200
Trade receivables	2,900	5,550	5,000
Other receivables	300	1,800	500
Cash and cash equivalents	400	50	400
	5,300	9,200	8,100
Current liabilities			
Trade payables	1,300	1,200	1,000
Other payables	1,000	1,000	1,500
Income tax payable	600	1,100	550
Dividends payable	600	200	300
	3,500	3,500	3,350
Total assets less current liabilities	4,400	7,700	9,850
less			
Non-current liabilities			
Debenture loan	(1,000)	(3,000)	(4,500)
Net assets	3,400	4,700	5,350
Equity			
Share capital (£1 ordinary shares)	2,000	2,200	2,500
Retained earnings	1,400	2,500	2,850
Total equity	3,400	4,700	5,350

Required:

(i) Using the information provided, and stating all the assumptions you have made, evaluate the past performance of Dandy plc and the future potential of the company.

(ii) Which other performance evaluation techniques (other than financial ratios) could be used to measure the performance of Dandy plc?

E8.11 *Time allowed – 120 minutes*

Locate the website for HSBC Bank plc on the Internet. Use their most recent annual report and accounts to prepare a report that evaluates their financial performance, financial position, and future prospects. Your report should include calculations of the appropriate ratios for comparison with the previous year.

E8.12 *Time allowed – 120 minutes*

Locate the websites for Tesco plc and Morrison Supermarkets plc on the Internet. Use their most recent annual report and accounts to prepare a report that evaluates and compares their financial performance, and financial position. Your report should include calculations of the appropriate ratios for comparing the two groups, and an explanation of their differences and similarities.

9

Financial planning

Chapter contents

Learning objectives

Completion of this chapter will enable you to:

- Explain financial planning as part of the strategic management process.
- Outline the purpose of financial planning.
- Describe the financial planning process.
- Use financial modelling to plan the long-term activities of a business.
- Identify the ways in which a company may use alternative forecasting methods.
- Prepare a cash flow forecast as part of the financial planning process to determine a company's funding requirements.
- Explain the ways in which a business may plan for its future growth.
- Consider the financing options that a company may use to fund its future growth.
- Outline the ways in which a company's performance may be measured against its plans.
- Explain the ways in which the balanced scorecard may be used to translate a company's strategic plans into operational terms.

Introduction

Many companies have started up with very good ideas and good intentions with regard to their development and future sales growth. However, the corporate graveyard is full of companies that have been unsuccessful in these endeavours because they have failed to plan for such growth in terms of its impact on costs and planned levels of investment and funding.

This chapter considers financial planning, which is an important part of the strategic management process, concerned not with the absolute detail but taking a look at the big picture of the company as a whole. Strategic financial planning is not short term, but is concerned with periods of more than one year, and looks at expected levels of a company's sales growth and how it may be financed.

In order to produce forecast long-term financial statements, financial plans are prepared based on the company's planned growth rate, and its financial ratios relating to costs, working capital, tax, dividends, and gearing. Forecasts are not plans or budgets but are predictions of what may happen in the future. There are a variety of techniques, both qualitative and quantitative, which are used to forecast growth rates. Quantitative methods include use of the statistical techniques of exponential smoothing and regression analysis.

Cash flow forecasting is one part of the financial planning process and is used to determine a company's future funding requirements on a monthly and yearly basis. The company may use its own resources of retained earnings to support its plans for future sales growth. In some circumstances, additional external funding is necessary for a company planning future growth.

This chapter looks at how this additional funding may be acquired using debt and equity. Two of the most widely used measures to compare companies' actual against planned performance are return on capital employed (ROCE) and earnings per share (eps). However, companies are now increasingly using non-financial measures in addition to financial measures to measure performance. This chapter closes with a look at such a technique, the balanced scorecard, which is a method used to link companies' long-term strategies into operational targets using key performance indicators (KPIs).

The strategic view

The whole area of financial **planning** was questioned in an article printed in *Accountancy Age* in June 2004 (Schlesinger, L 'How realistic are financial plans?') which emphasised the time spans over which financial plans may be realistic and therefore useful. This article, based on a survey of 258 finance directors, considered whether plans for large projects like the Olympics can be realistic when they are prepared so many years ahead of the events. Indeed, 79% of the finance directors interviewed believed it was unrealistic for the 2012 London Olympics finance team to draw up budget plans eight years in advance of the event taking place.

There are clearly different views as to whether or not the plans and budgets are effective and essential business tools. However, the majority of the world's most successful companies have attributed a large part of their success to their reliance on traditional formal planning systems. The strategic (long-term) and **budget** (short-term) planning processes are core management tasks that are critically important to the future survival and success of the business. The strategic plan and the budget prepared for planning purposes, as part of the strategic management process, are the quantitative plans of management's belief of what the business's costs and revenues will be over a specific future period. The budget prepared for control purposes, even though it may have been based on standards that may not be reached, is used for motivational purposes to influence improved business unit and departmental performance. Monitoring of actual performance against plans is used to provide feedback in order to take the appropriate action necessary to reach planned performance, and to revise plans in the light of changes.

The role of financial planning is crucial to any business and it is important to be as accurate as possible. As the Thomas Cook press extract below indicates, the impact of a failure to accurately **forecast** the costs of long-term projects can have serious consequences for a company's financial stability.

Currently, many companies are taking the view that the traditional planning and annual budgeting systems are unsuitable and irrelevant in rapidly changing markets. Further, they believe that budgets fail to deal with the most important drivers of shareholder value such as intangible assets like brands and knowledge. Some of these companies, like Volvo, Ikea, and Ericsson, have already revised their need for annual budgets as being an inefficient tool in an increasingly changing business environment. Volvo abandoned the annual budget 10 years ago. Instead, they provide three-month forecasts and monthly board reports, which include financial and non-financial indicators. These forecasts and reports are supplemented with a two-year rolling forecast, updated quarterly, and four- and 10-year strategic plans updated yearly. It should also be noted that many of the dot.com companies that failed during the 1990s and early 2000s also felt that traditional budget methods were a little old-fashioned and irrelevant.

How realistic are financial plans?

Thomas Cook is to close up to 200 stores and cut up to 1,000 jobs as it battles to turn around its struggling UK business. The holiday company – shares in which fell 75pc in a day last month after admitting to a £100m cash shortfall – confirmed the closures as it posted an annual pre-tax loss of £398m against a £41.7m profit last time. Thomas Cook will initially close 125 stores, putting at risk 660 jobs, but is planning to close 200 loss-making stores in total over the next two years as leases expire.

The cuts are a pivotal part of Thomas Cook's plan to save £110m per year from its UK business, alongside reducing its fleet of aircraft from 41 to 35. However, it is another setback for Britain's high streets, where more than one in 10 shops is empty. The loss for Thomas Cook in the year to September 30 emerged from £573m of write-downs, primarily because of reduced future prospects for British, Canadian and French businesses. However, this also includes an £86.3m write-down on an IT project that was launched in 2006 under former chief executive Manny Fontenla-Novoa.

The new IT system was intended to modernise Thomas Cook's reservation system on to a single platform, but has been abandoned because it is running over budget, is heavily delayed and is not working properly. The spiralling costs of the programme are understood to have been behind the collapse of technology group BlueSky Technologies in 2009, which sparked a legal row between the company's former employees and Thomas Cook.

Sam Weihagen, interim chief executive, said it has been a 'very challenging year' for Thomas Cook. He has instigated a strategic review that will consider the sale of every Thomas Cook business as the company seeks to reduce its £891m debt mountain by up to £500m.

Source: **Thomas Cook to close stores and slash jobs to cut losses,** by Graham Ruddick and Alistair Osborne © *The Telegraph*, 19 December 2011

The broad purposes of budgeting include:

- planning and control, through
    - exception reporting of financial and non-financial indicators, which
    - economises on managerial time, and
    - maximises efficiency
- co-ordination, which
     - assists **goal congruence**
- communication, through
    - the feedback process, which should
    - reduce or prevent sub-optimal performance
- motivation and alignment of individual and corporate goals, through
    - participation of many people in the budget-setting process
- evaluation of performance, to facilitate control.

As a planning tool the budget is used to reflect the short-term outcomes from the use of a company's resources in line with its strategy. Planning is the establishment of objectives and the formulation, evaluation, and selection of the policies, strategies, tactics, and actions required to achieve them. Planning comprises long-term **strategic planning** and short-term operational planning. The latter usually refers to a period of one year. With regard to a new retail product, the strategic (long-term) plan of the business, for example, may include the aim to become profitable, and to

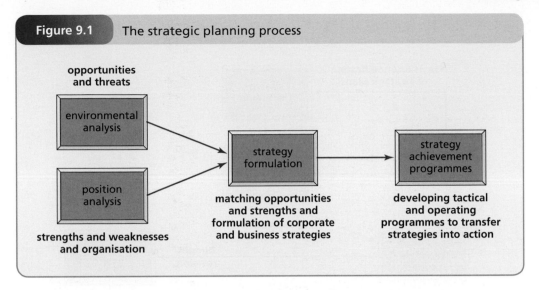

Figure 9.1 The strategic planning process

opportunities and threats

environmental analysis

position analysis

strengths and weaknesses and organisation

strategy formulation

matching opportunities and strengths and formulation of corporate and business strategies

strategy achievement programmes

developing tactical and operating programmes to transfer strategies into action

become a market leader within three years. The short-term operational plan may be, for example, to get the product stocked by at least one leading supermarket group within 12 months.

Strategic planning is the process of deciding on:

- the objectives of the organisation
- changes in these objectives
- the resources used to attain these objectives
- the policies that are to govern the acquisition, use, and disposition of these resources.

The way in which a typical strategic planning process may be carried out in an organisation is illustrated in the flow charts in Figures 9.1 and 9.2. Strategic planning involves many ideas and options and lots of 'what-if' analysis. Its purpose is to try and provide a 'fit' between the company and its environment, and a focus on its main goals, and to assist in reaching those goals.

The chart in Figure 9.1 shows how analysis is linked to the development of strategies and actions. The environmental analysis includes the opportunities and threats elements of a SWOT analysis of the business. It provides an audit of the company's external environment by considering political, economic, social, technological, environmental, and legal factors. It also considers the nature of the organisation's environment and its level of complexity. Environmental analysis provides a structural analysis of the competitive environment, and the company's competitive position and its market position.

Resources analysis looks within the organisation by considering the strengths and weaknesses elements of a SWOT analysis of the business. It uses value stream analysis, and an audit of its resources of people, materials, machinery and equipment, cash flow, and markets. Resources analysis includes financial analysis, and a comparative analysis of historical performance, industry norms, and the company's experience curve. It also includes an analysis of the company's levels of skills and flexibility, and an analysis of its various products and the stages in their product life cycles.

It is not correct to assume that planning is just an extension of budgeting, but there is a close relationship between these processes. A strategic plan is a long-term plan, which spans more than one year and is normally three, five years, or 10 years or more. The chart in Figure 9.2 shows the sequence of each step in the process and the relationship between strategic planning and budgeting.

Figure 9.2   The strategic planning relationship with budgeting

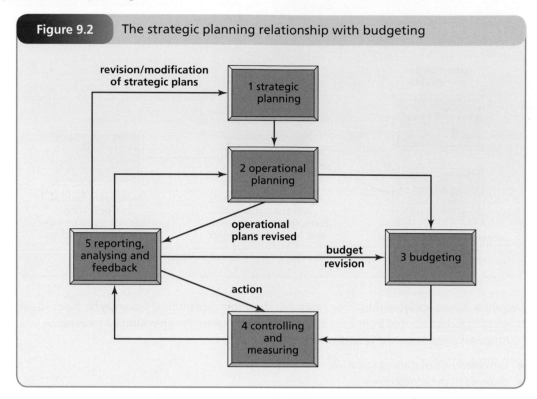

A budget is a quantified statement for a defined period of time of no more than one year, based on operational plans, which may include planned revenues, expenses, assets, liabilities, and cash flows. Strategy is expressed in broad conceptual terms, and for budgeting purposes it needs to be operationalised or translated into more detailed tactical and operational plans that can be understood at the functional level within the company. It must be translated into specific plans for functional areas such as:

- marketing
- research and development
- purchasing
- sales
- production
- human resources
- information systems.

Important aspects of this operationalisation are:

- identification of required resources
- development of appropriate performance criteria
- implementation of appropriate control systems
- development of relevant operational budgets.

A budget provides a focus for the organisation, aids the co-ordination of activities, and facilitates control. To enable control of operations, actual performance may be compared with the budget. Differences between actual and budget are reported, and analysed, and then feedback is used:

- to provide information for appropriate remedial action to rectify 'out of control' operations
- to enable necessary revisions of future short-term operational plans
- to revise or modify long-term strategic plans, if necessary.

Financial planning is a part of the strategic planning process and includes:

- assessment of investment opportunities that will add value to the business
- consideration of the various alternative methods of financing new investment
- identification of the risks associated with alternative investment options
- ranking of alternative investment and financing options to optimise decisions
- measurement of performance of the financial planning process.

Although new capital investments may be proposed by a company's operational and administrative managers, the co-ordination of the total investment by the company is made by the directors of the business in line with their strategic objectives. In order to create corporate value it is essential that investments are made which return positive net present values (NPVs).

Investments that the company must ensure return positive NPVs include new projects or profit improvement projects within the business, or they may include acquisitions of other companies. The performance of subsidiary companies not meeting this criterion should be critically reviewed and, where appropriate, sold off or liquidated.

Financial planning at the company level is effectively capital budgeting at the top level dealing with each business sector rather than the detail of cost centre and revenue centre capital budgeting. It will include the five- or 10-year proposed financial plans submitted at departmental level consolidated to consider the growth expectations of the business as a whole and a consideration of the financial implications should the company not meet its growth expectations. Such plans will include proposed capital expenditure and its alternative methods of financing. It will also consider working capital requirements, and the impacts of inflation and taxation.

The purpose of financial planning

There are a number of reasons why companies devote considerable resources to the development of financial plans. They would not do this unless they anticipate that the benefits may be equally considerable.

Mini case 9.1

It is standard practice for listed companies to issue interim management statements that forecast performance for the following quarter and to extrapolate to the year end. On 2 May 2012, Next plc issued their quarterly management statement forecasting their expected full year profit. Part of their statement is reproduced below and it clearly indicates the basis upon which the company made their predictions.

First half outlook to July 2012

The second quarter's retail comparatives are much less demanding than the first's, as exceptionally warm weather and the Royal Wedding boosted last year's first quarter sales. We remain confident that Next brand sales for the first half will remain within our +1% to +4% guidance range and we are forecasting that profit for the first half will be ahead of last year.

> **Full year guidance to January 2013**
>
> We now believe that the profit scenarios given in March represent a reasonable guidance range for the full year. To reiterate, we believe that if sales were up between +1% and +4% for the full year, then profits would be between £560m and £610m. This is in line with market expectations and the majority of analyst forecasts fall within this range.

There are differences between forecasts, budgets, and long-term financial plans. Forecasts look at what is likely to happen, and that information is used in budget preparation. Strategic financial plans consider what events may occur, but also look at potential problems that may arise, and their reasons and impact. Sensitivities may be looked at using scenario analysis and simulations to determine the impact on financial plans of various 'what-if' questions. For example, what would be the impact on a financial plan if costs were 10% higher, or if sales revenues were 10% lower? Having determined the impact of possible deviations from the plan, the company may then include appropriate contingencies in the plan.

Financial plans should consider not only opportunities that the company may have which add value by providing a positive NPV, but also include other opportunities presented to the company which are of more strategic interest. These include opportunities for developing new products or new markets in ways that provide options for the company to make appropriate capital investments or not at some time in the future.

A company's financial plan should reflect its expected growth and how this may be financed. Growth may be financed internally through reinvestment of retained earnings. Alternatively, its capital investment for growth may require further external funding through either additional equity or additional debt. The plan itself will provide consistency in ensuring that growth is matched by whatever level of additional finance is required by the company.

The financial plan also provides consistency between the various corporate objectives. For example, a company may be planning levels of profit, sales revenue, and costs; it is only by looking at the big picture of a financial plan that embraces all these objectives that it can be seen if these are consistent and mutually achievable. This applies to any corporate objectives that are in terms that relate to accounting ratios like, for example, return on capital employed and return on sales. Such ratios that are stated as objectives must also consider the strategic decisions that need to be made to achieve them – for example, levels of investment, sales volumes, selling prices, and costs – and must be reflected in the financial plan.

> ### Progress check 9.1
>
> Explain the overall strategic planning process and the relationships between forecasting, budgeting, and planning.

The financial planning process

A company may have a number of alternative strategies, and these need to be translated into financial plans in order that they may be realistically compared. A simple model includes an income statement plan of sales revenues and costs, and a balance sheet plan of assets, debt,

| Figure 9.3 | Financial planning income statement flow diagram |

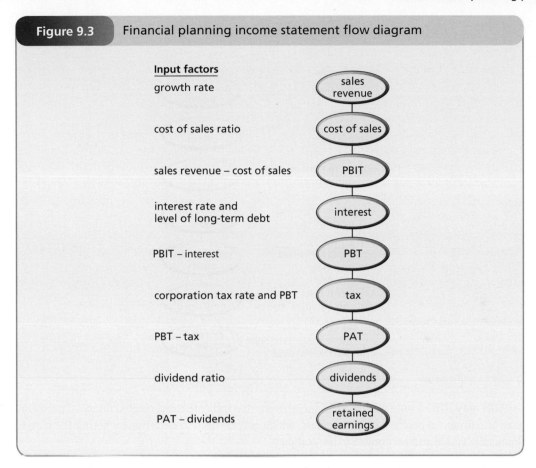

Input factors

growth rate	sales revenue
cost of sales ratio	cost of sales
sales revenue – cost of sales	PBIT
interest rate and level of long-term debt	interest
PBIT – interest	PBT
corporation tax rate and PBT	tax
PBT – tax	PAT
dividend ratio	dividends
PAT – dividends	retained earnings

and equity. More sophisticated models include a far greater number of variables and the relationships between them. These models are necessarily computerised, using spreadsheets such as Excel. There are three main elements in the financial planning process:

- input factors
- the financial model
- output factors.

The inputs are the company's financial statements and assumptions made about the future period to which the financial plan relates. The assumptions relate to, for example, estimated sales revenues and levels of sales growth, costs to sales relationships, investment levels, and working capital ratios. The financial statements include the income statement, balance sheet, and statement of cash flows.

Figure 9.3 shows a financial planning income statement flow diagram and the input factors that the financial model may include. Figure 9.4 shows a financial planning balance sheet flow diagram and the input factors that the financial model may include. The financial model comprises the relationships between each of the input factors, and the ways in which outputs are calculated and the consequences of changes to any of the inputs.

The outputs are the planned future financial statements based on the inputs and assumptions, and calculated by the financial model. These are referred to as *pro forma* financial statements.

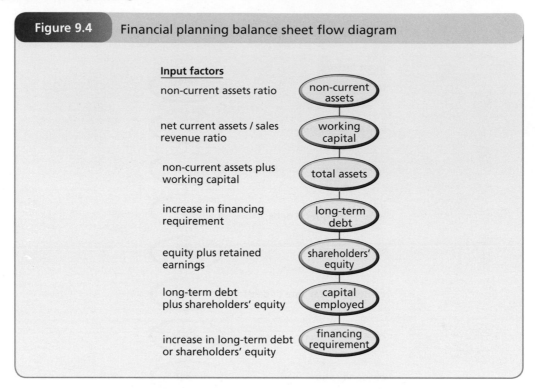

Figure 9.4   Financial planning balance sheet flow diagram

Input factors

non-current assets ratio	non-current assets
net current assets / sales revenue ratio	working capital
non-current assets plus working capital	total assets
increase in financing requirement	long-term debt
equity plus retained earnings	shareholders' equity
long-term debt plus shareholders' equity	capital employed
increase in long-term debt or shareholders' equity	financing requirement

Outputs may also include a range of financial ratios that indicate the projected financial performance and financial position of the business, which may be used to determine whether the plan is financially viable and acceptable to the company.

Financial modelling

Using the flow diagrams shown in Figures 9.3 and 9.4 as the basis, we will illustrate the development of a company's financial planning model in the worked examples that follow.

Worked example 9.1

Supportex Ltd's income statement for year one and its balance sheet at the end of year one are shown in Figure 9.5.

Supportex has assumed that its total costs will vary directly in line with changes in its levels of sales revenue. It has also planned to maintain its debt/equity ratio at 10%.

Let's consider what will happen if in year two sales revenue is increased by 20%.

Because costs vary with sales revenue then costs will also increase by 20%. If we assume that Supportex has no spare capacity then for year two then total assets also need to be increased by 20% to support the increased sales revenue. We may also assume that the increased assets level is financed by a similar 20% increase in

Figure 9.5   Supportex year 1 simple income statement and balance sheet

	A	B	C
1	**Income statement**	**Year 1**	
2	**Figures in £000s**		
3	Total sales revenue	800	
4	Total costs	(600)	Costs are assumed to vary in line with sales
5	Net profit	200	
6			
7	**Balance sheet**	**End Year 1**	
8	Total assets	1,100	
9	Debt	(100)	10% debt/equity ratio
10		1,000	
11			
12	Equity	1,000	

Figure 9.6   Supportex year 1 and year 2 simple income statement and balance sheet

	A	B	C
1	**Income statement**	**Year 1**	**Year 2 dividend £40k**
2	**Figures in £000s**		
3	Total sales revenue	800	960
4	Total costs	(600)	(720)
5	Net profit	200	240
6			
7	**Balance sheet**	**End Year 1**	
8	Total assets	1,100	1,320
9	Debt	(100)	(120)
10		1,000	1,200
11			
12	Equity	1,000	1,200

long-term debt, and maintains the debt/equity ratio at 10%. The income statement and balance sheet for year two will appear as shown in Figure 9.6 (year one is shown for comparison).

We can see that equity has increased from £1m to £1.2m, an increase of £200,000. However, the income statement shows net profit for year two as £240,000 and not £200,000. Therefore, £40,000 dividends must have been paid out of net profit, leaving retained earnings of £200,000 which has been added to equity. The planned sales revenue growth of 20% and the decision by the company to maintain its debt/equity ratio of 10% have effectively determined the dividend level as a consequence of these decisions. Supportex's increase in total assets of £220,000 is financed by an increase in retained earnings of £200,000 and an increase in debt of £20,000.

Worked example 9.2

Let's consider what would happen in Worked example 9.1 if Supportex chose to pay £60,000 in dividends in year two instead of £40,000.

Retained earnings would then be £180,000 and equity would become £1.18m. The increase of £20,000 in dividends may be financed out of additional debt of £20,000. The level of gearing would therefore increase from 10% to 11.9% (£140/£1,180). Supportex's increase in total assets of £220,000 is financed by an increase in retained earnings of £180,000 and an increase in debt of £40,000. In such a model the level of debt can be seen to be the balancing item on the balance sheet.

Alternatively, if Supportex required its debt to be held at £120,000, then new equity of £20,000 would need to be issued to fund the additional dividends, which would maintain its debt/equity ratio at 10%. Supportex's increase in total assets of £220,000 is then financed by an increase in retained earnings of £180,000, an increase in equity of £20,000, and an increase in debt of £20,000 (see Figure 9.7).

Figure 9.7	Supportex year 1 and year 2 simple income statement and balance sheet, with additional funding

	A	B	C	D
1	**Income statement**	**Year 1**	**Year 2 dividend £60k (debt increase)**	**Year 2 dividend £60k (equity increase)**
2	**Figures in £000s**			
3	Total sales revenue	800	960	960
4	Total costs	(600)	(720)	(720)
5	Net profit	200	240	240
6				
7	**Balance sheet**			
8	Total assets	1,100	1,320	1,320
9	Debt	(100)	(140)	(120)
10		1,000	1,180	1,200
11				
12	Equity	1,000	1,180	1,200

The models shown in Worked examples 9.1 and 9.2 show the ways in which the sales revenue growth of the business may be financed by combinations of retained earnings and increases in debt and equity. The models do not tell us which is the best option. Dividend policy depends on a number of factors as we shall see in Chapter 15, and may be interpreted by shareholders in many different ways. Although these models do not provide answers to these issues they do show us the impact on the balance sheet of the various options.

Worked example 9.3 takes things a step further by looking at Supportex's financial statements in a little more detail. Worked examples 9.3 and 9.4 illustrate a step-by step approach to Supportex Ltd's five-year planning process.

Worked example 9.3

The financial statements for Supportex shown in Figure 9.8 identify the various elements of cost in the income statement, and in the balance sheet separate total assets into non-current assets and working capital.

The income statement shows sales revenue and costs for year one and the balance sheet shows the financial position of Supportex at the start of year one and the end of year one, and states the assumptions which identify the relationships between the numbers.

With regard to Supportex's operating activities we can see that its cost of sales is 62.5% of sales revenue and therefore its profit before interest and tax (PBIT) is 37.5% of sales revenue. Its tax rate is 31% of profit before tax (PBT). Its working capital is 50% of sales revenue. For modelling purposes it is reasonable to assume that these percentages will remain constant as sales revenue levels change.

Supportex Ltd is currently financed by both debt and equity. Its interest payment is 10% of the debt balance at the start of the year. However, we cannot assume that the debt/equity ratio of 10% will remain constant as levels of sales revenue change. The company may decide on various different levels of gearing (through issues of debt or equity), regardless of its operational activities.

Figure 9.8	Supportex year 1 detailed income statement and balance sheet

	A	B	C	D
1	**Income statement**		**Year 1**	**Assumptions**
2	**Figures in £000s**			
3	Total sales revenue		800	
4	Cost of sales		(500)	62.5% of sales
5	Profit before interest and tax		300	total sales less cost of sales
6	Interest		(10)	10% of debt at start of year
7	Profit before tax		290	PBIT less interest
8	Tax		(90)	31% of profit before tax
9	Net profit		200	PBT less tax
10	Dividends		(30)	15% dividend payout ratio
11	Retained earnings		170	85% profit retention ratio
12				
13	**Balance sheet**	**Start Year 1**	**End Year 1**	**Assumptions**
14	**Figures in £000s**			
15	Non-current assets		700	87.5% of sales revenue
16	Working capital		400	50% of sales revenue
17	Total assets		1,100	
18	Debt	(100)	(100)	
19			1,000	
20				
21	Equity	830	1,000	

The company has forecast that in year two sales revenue will increase by 20%. It has also decided that the dividend payout and profit retention ratio will be maintained at 15% and 85% respectively, and has assumed that the interest rate of 10% will not change. It is assumed that non-current assets and working capital will increase at the same rate to support the 20% increase in sales revenue.

Let's prepare a planned income statement and balance sheet for year 2.

We can see from Figure 9.9 that, based on the above assumptions, net profit for year two is £241,000, and retained earnings are £205,000, which has been added to the equity from year one. We can see from the balance sheet at the end of year two that, in order for net assets to be equal to equity, additional financing of £15,000 was required for the balance sheet to be in balance. This has been assumed to have been provided from an increase in debt, shown in the increase in debt from £100,000 to £115,000 (debt/equity ratio 9.5%).

Alternatively, the additional external financing could have comprised debt or equity or a combination of both equity and debt. If new equity of £15,000 had been issued instead of debt, then equity would be increased to £1,220,000 and debt would remain at £100,000 (debt/equity ratio 8.2%). If an increase in both debt and equity had been made, for example £10,000 debt and £5,000 equity, this would result in totals of £110,000 debt and £1,210,000 equity, resulting in gearing of 9.1%, which would be closer to the original 10%.

Figure 9.9	Supportex year 1 and year 2 detailed income statement and balance sheet

	A	B	C	D
1	**Income statement**		**Year 1**	**Year 2**
2	**Figures in £000s**			
3	Total sales revenue		800	960
4	Cost of sales		(500)	(600)
5	Profit before interest and tax		300	360
6	Interest		(10)	(10)
7	Profit before tax		290	350
8	Tax		(90)	(109)
9	Net profit		200	241
10	Dividends		(30)	(36)
11	Retained earnings		170	205
12				
13	**Balance sheet**	**Start Year 1**	**End Year 1**	**End Year 2**
14	**Figures in £000s**			
15	Non-current assets		700	840
16	Working capital		400	480
17	Total assets		1,100	1,320
18	Debt	(100)	(100)	(115)
19			1,000	1,205
20				
21	Equity	830	1,000	1,205
22				
23	Additional financing required			15

Worked example 9.4

We will use the year one financial statements from Worked example 9.3 to calculate a five-year plan for Supportex Ltd. The five-year plan is based on sales revenue growth of 20% per annum for each year. For planning purposes the model will use the assumptions shown in Worked example 9.3 and will also assume that any additional financing is obtained by increasing debt.

The results are shown in Figure. 9.10, and the numbers have been rounded to the nearest thousand.

The 20% growth in sales revenue for each year has also resulted in an increase in total assets of 20% for each year. The increases in total assets in each year of £220,000, £264,000, £317,000 and £380,000 have been financed by increases in retained earnings of £205,000, £247,000, £296,000 and £356,000, and increases in debt of £15,000, £17,000, £21,000 and £24,000 for years two to five. This has resulted from the dividend payout policy of 15% of net profit each year. Each year the debt/equity ratio has been reduced from 10% at the end of year one to 9.5%, 9.1%, 8.8%, and 8.4% at the end of years two to five.

The model is also represented in the Excel spreadsheet shown in Figure 9.11, which incorporates the forecast assumptions in columns A and B. The cell formulae for the calculations

| Figure 9.10 | Supportex five-year plan income statement and balance sheet |

	A	B	C	D	E	F	G
1	**Income statement**		**Year 1**	**Year 2**	**Year 3**	**Year 4**	**Year 5**
2	**Figures in £000s**						
3	Total sales revenue		800	960	1,152	1,382	1,659
4	Cost of sales		(500)	(600)	(720)	(864)	(1,037)
5	Profit before interest and tax		300	360	432	518	622
6	Interest		(10)	(10)	(12)	(13)	(15)
7	Profit before tax		290	350	420	505	607
8	Tax		(90)	(109)	(130)	(157)	(188)
9	Net profit		200	241	290	348	419
10	Dividends		(30)	(36)	(43)	(52)	(63)
11	Retained earnings		170	205	247	296	356
12							
13	**Balance sheet**	**Start Year 1**	**End Year 1**	**End Year 2**	**End Year 3**	**End Year 4**	**End Year 5**
14	**Figures in £000s**						
15	Non-current assets		700	840	1,008	1,210	1,452
16	Working capital		400	480	576	691	829
17	Total assets		1,100	1,320	1,584	1,901	2,281
18	Debt	(100)	(100)	(115)	(132)	(153)	(177)
19			1,000	1,205	1,452	1,748	2,104
20							
21	Equity	830	1,000	1,205	1,452	1,748	2,104
22							
23	Additional financing			15	17	21	24

for year four in column I (which also apply to columns G, H, and K) are shown in column K. Setting up a planning model in a spreadsheet makes it a simple task to change the forecast growth rate and then review the impacts on both the income statement and balance sheet. The consequences may also be assessed for changes in financial strategy, for example dividend and gearing levels. They may also be assessed for changes in interest rates and tax rates and changes in strategy relating to investments in non-current assets and working capital.

Using the spreadsheet in Figure 9.11 if we change the growth rate in cell B6 to 30% per annum the model will calculate different additional financing requirements, and therefore different debt/equity ratios for each year. We can summarise the results of changing the forecast growth rate for a range of values, for example 0% to 30%, which is shown in Figure 9.12.

Figure 9.11	**Excel five-year planning model for Supportex**

	A	B	C	D	E	F	G	H	I	J	K
1	Model assumptions		Income statement			Year 1	Year 2	Year 3	Year 4	Year 5	Column I formulae
2			Figures in £000								
3	Growth	20.0%	Total sales revenue			800.0	960.0	1,152.0	1,382.4	1,658.9	+H3+$B3*H3
4	% sales revenue	62.5%	Cost of sales			(500.0)	(600.0)	(720.0)	(864.0)	(1,036.8)	−I3*$B$4
5	% sales revenue	37.5%	PBIT			300.0	360.0	432.0	518.4	622.1	+I3+I4
6	% of debt	10.0%	Interest			(10.0)	(10.0)	(11.5)	(13.2)	(15.3)	−H18*$B$6
7			PBT			290.0	350.0	420.5	505.2	606.8	+I5+I6
8	% of PBT	31.0%	Tax			(89.9)	(108.5)	(130.4)	(156.6)	(188.1)	−I7*$B$8
9			Net profit			200.1	241.5	290.2	348.6	418.7	+I7+I8
10	% of net profit	15.0%	Dividends			(30.0)	(36.2)	(43.5)	(52.3)	(62.8)	−I9*$B$10
11	% of net profit	85.0%	Retained earnings			170.1	205.3	246.6	296.3	355.9	+I9+I10
12											
13			Balance sheet								
14			Figures in £000								
15	Growth	20.0%	Non-current assets			700.0	840.0	1,008.0	1,209.6	1,451.5	+H15+$B15*H15
16	% of sales	50.0%	Working capital			400.0	480.0	576.0	691.2	829.4	+I3*$B$16
17			Total assets			1,100.0	1,320.0	1,584.0	1,900.8	2,281.0	+I15+I16
18			Debt	(100.0)		(100.0)	(114.7)	(132.1)	(152.6)	(176.9)	+H18−I23
19						1,000.0	1,205.3	1,451.9	1,748.2	2,104.1	+I17+I18
20											
21			Equity			1,000.0	1,205.3	1,451.9	1,748.2	2,104.1	+H21+I11
22											
23			Additional financing required				14.7	17.4	20.5	24.3	+I17−H17−I11

Figure 9.12	**Supportex five-year plan external funding requirement and debt/equity ratios**

	A	B	C
1	Sales revenue growth rate per annum %	Additional funding requirement Years 2 to 5 £000	Debt/equity %
2	0.0	−742.6	0.0
3	10.0	−394.7	0.0
4	20.0	76.9	8.4
5	30.0	696.9	34.0

The role of forecasting

A forecast is not a plan or a budget but a prediction of future environments, events, and outcomes. Forecasting is required in order to prepare plans and budgets. This should start with projected sales prices, sales volumes and market share of current and new products. Examples of forecasts by product, or sector, can be found regularly in the press, for example car sales and mobile telephone sales.

Large companies need to be very sensitive to trends and developments within their forecasting process as mistakes can prove very expensive. For example, before Easter one year a major UK chocolate manufacturer made too many eggs, which did not sell; its forecasts and therefore its financial plans were proved to be very wide of the mark, and the impact on the business was extremely costly.

Forecasting usually relies on the analysis of past data to identify patterns used to describe it. Patterns may then be extrapolated into the future to prepare a forecast. There are many different methods of both **qualitative forecasting** and **quantitative forecasting**, and there is no one best model.

Qualitative techniques

Qualitative forecasting techniques do not use numbers or probabilities but use non-numeric information and consider trends in demand and behaviour. The following are examples of these techniques:

- the Delphi method – use of a panel of recognised experts, a group of wise men
- consumer market surveys – using questionnaires, surveys, etc.
- sales force estimates – the views of the people who may be closest to the customers and the market
- executive opinion – expert views of professionals in specific areas
- technological comparisons – independent forecasters predicting changes in one area by monitoring changes in another area
- subjective curve-fitting – using demand curves of similar products that have been launched in the past, for example similar product life cycles for similar products like CD players and DVD players.

Quantitative techniques

Quantitative forecasting techniques use numerical data and probabilities, and use historical data to try to predict the future. These techniques rely heavily on statistical analysis to project, for example, sales demand and relationships between the factors impacting on sales. Qualitative forecasting includes both univariate time series models and causal models. The following are examples of both these techniques.

Univariate time series models:
- moving averages
- exponential smoothing
- trend projections.

Causal models:
- regression analysis
- multiple regression.

Causal models involve the use of the identification of other variables related to the variable being predicted. For example, linear regression may be used to forecast sales, using the independent variables of sales price, advertising expenditure, and competitors' prices. Major retailers may be seen to be highly proactive in revising their sales prices and their advertising activities (and expenditure) as a result of changes in the marketplace.

The use of such statistical models is usually a question of fitting the pattern of historical data to whichever model best fits. It could be argued that it is easier to forecast the volume of ice-cream sales than it is to forecast the number of Internet music downloads by a new band. Apparently, the major music-based companies have also found this a mystery over the years. Whichever method is used it is important that the basis and the methodology of the forecasting are understood. All assumptions made and the parameters of time, availability of past data, costs, accuracy required, and ease of use must be clearly stated to maintain any sort of confidence in the forecasts.

> ### Progress check 9.2
>
> What is the role of forecasting and what are qualitative and quantitative techniques?

Cash flow forecasting and planning

Cash flow forecasting and planning is an area which, in practice, may use a number of methods of calculation. It is an important part of financial planning because in addition to the funding requirements projected on an annual basis, the company also needs to consider its monthly cash requirements. A company may have healthy year-by-year projected cash positions, which indicate that it requires no additional funding. However, because the sales and operational activities of the business may not be spread evenly over each year, then monthly phasing of the planned cash flow may reveal that additional funding within each year may be required.

The statement of cash flows reported in a company's annual report and accounts uses a technique called the indirect cash flow method to determine operating cash flow. The indirect cash flow method starts with the company's operating profit and then adds back depreciation, which is not a cash outflow, and then adjusts for changes in working capital, and the result is operating cash flow. The working capital adjustment is required because profit is rarely realised in cash at the same time that transactions take place: inventory is not used immediately it is acquired; suppliers are not paid immediately goods or services are provided; customers do not pay immediately sales are made. Cash generated from operations is then used as the basis from which to calculate the company's total cash flow, which is shown in a statement of cash flows like the example shown in Figure 8.7, which we saw in Chapter 8.

Planning and forecasting of cash requirements may also be made using the indirect method described above. However, it is usually prepared to validate and support the results of monthly cash plans that have been prepared using the direct cash flow method. An actual direct statement of cash flows for the year details the actual receipts from customers and payments to suppliers, employees, and others. The same technique may be used for month-by-month cash planning. The advantage of this is that it may benefit from the experience of the finance director or financial planner preparing the plan.

Let's look at an example that for simplicity just considers the first three months of the first year of the financial plan of a business.

Worked example 9.5

Dubai Dreams is a retailing outfit that has prepared a financial plan for its operations over the next five years. The company's finance director expects the next three months from January to March to demand some cash requirements beyond the normal operational outflows.

A monthly cash forecast must therefore be prepared from the following information, which has been made available by the company:

1 Dubai Dreams has a cash balance of (dirhams) Dhs28.7m at the end of December and a balance of at least Dhs20,000 must be available at the end of each month.
2 Sales revenue forecasts are: December Dhs180m; January Dhs240m; February Dhs200m; March Dhs240m. The company has recently introduced a credit card system, which applies to 40% of the sales revenue for each month and which is received in cash by the middle of the following month.
3 Cost of goods sold averages 75% of sales revenue. Inventories purchased during each month are at a level that ensures that inventories of 1.5 times the value of the next month's cost of sales is held at the end of each month. The value of inventories on hand on 31 December amounted to Dhs270m, Dhs200m having been purchased during December. Inventories are purchased consistently over each month and suppliers are paid in the month following purchase.
4 Operating expenses are forecast as follows:

(a) Salaries and wages at 12% of sales revenue, are paid in the month of sale.
(b) Other expenses at an average 10% of sales revenue, are paid in the month of sale.
(c) Cash receipts expected from the repayment of a loan to a director of Dhs6m is due in March.
(d) Repayment of a short-term loan of Dhs3m is due in February.
(e) Repayments of a long-term loan are due at Dhs4m each in January and March.
(f) New equipment was purchased for Dhs48m and four payments of Dhs12m each are due in February, March, April and May.
(g) Depreciation of all equipment is charged to the profit and loss account at the rate of Dhs5m per month.
(h) Interest received from an investment of Dhs4.9m per month is expected.
(i) Bonuses totalling Dhs52m are due to be paid to staff in January.
(j) A company tax payment of Dhs14m is due to be paid in March.

We can prepare a cash forecast for each month from the beginning of January to the end of March in order to identify possible cash needs for each month up to the end of March.

The cash forecast for January to March is shown in Figure 9.13 below.

This example shows that Dubai Dreams requires short-term funding over the three months totalling 95.2m dirhams. We can see from Figure 9.13 that the levels of funding requirement are different for each of the three months. In practice, the company would expand this phased forecast to cover the five years of the plan to determine the level and pattern of the funding required throughout the entire period of the plan. The forecast would also in practice be updated on a monthly basis, six months or perhaps one year ahead.

Figure 9.13	Dubai Dreams three-month cash forecast

	A	B	C	D	E	F
1	**Cash forecast January to March**					
2	**Dirhams millions**	**January**	**February**	**March**		**Total**
3	**CASH RECEIPTS**					
4	Cash sales	144.0	120.0	144.0		408.0
5	Credit card sales	72.0	96.0	80.0		248.0
6	Loan repayment			6.0		6.0
7	Investment income	4.9	4.9	4.9		14.7
8	**Total receipts**	**220.9**	**220.9**	**234.9**		**676.7**
9	**CASH PAYMENTS**					
10	Supplier	200.0	135.0	195.0		530.0
11	Salaries	28.8	24.0	28.8		81.6
12	Other expenses	24.0	20.0	24.0		68.0
13	Short-term loan repayment		3.0			3.0
14	Long-term loan repayment	4.0		4.0		8.0
15	Equipment payment		12.0	12.0		24.0
16	Staff bonuses	52.0				52.0
17	Company tax			14.0		14.0
18	**Total payments**	**308.8**	**194.0**	**277.8**		**780.6**
19	Month net cash flow	−87.9	26.9	−42.9		−103.9
20	Start month cash balance	28.7	−59.2	−32.3		28.7
21	End month cash balance	−59.2	−32.3	−75.2		−75.2
22	End month minimum cash balance	20.0	20.0	20.0		20.0
23	**Month funding required/(surplus)**	79.2	−26.9	42.9		
24	**Cumulative funding required**	79.2	52.3	95.2		95.2
25	New end month cash balance	**20.0**	**20.0**	**20.0**		**20.0**

Planning for growth

We have looked at fairly fundamental financial planning models. In practice, such models will necessarily be a little more sophisticated and allow for depreciation of non-current assets, and the interrelationship of variables like levels of debt, interest, working capital, and retained earnings. A more sophisticated model may allow for changes to many variables at one time and provide options with regard to their impact.

In the models we have considered we have assumed percentage changes that apply over each of the years in the plan. A more complex model will allow for different percentages to be applied to each year. It will also allow for changes in capital investment and working capital requirements resulting from the additional capacity requirements should particular sales levels be reached. However, it is also important to keep strategic financial plans as simple as possible so that a focus on the long-term objectives of the business is maintained.

The key relationship for a business that is planning for growth is the relationship between its growth, its internal funding, and its external funding requirements. The amount available from internal funding from retained earnings will depend on the company's dividend policy. It is possible to derive relationships that may determine how the company's growth may be achieved.

A company's ratio of its sales revenue to its total assets (non-current assets plus working capital) tells us how much sales revenue is currently being derived from each £, US$, etc., of assets at its disposal. If the reciprocal of this ratio is multiplied by the company's planned sales increase, the result will therefore be the total amount of funding required for such growth. Therefore:

$$\text{funding requirement} = \text{planned sales revenue increase} \times \frac{\text{assets}}{\text{sales revenue}}$$

The funding may come from internal retained earnings or it may come from external sources.

If we assume that the planned sales revenue increase is at the same rate as the required increase in investment in assets, then

$$\text{planned sales revenue growth rate} = \frac{\text{planned sales revenue increase}}{\text{sales revenue}}$$

$$= \frac{\text{required new investment in assets}}{\text{assets}}$$

Therefore:

$$\text{required new investment in assets} = \text{planned sales revenue growth rate} \times \text{assets}$$

and

$$\text{required new investment in assets} = \text{funding requirement}$$

and

$$\text{required new investment in assets}$$
$$= \text{new external funding} + \text{funding from retained earnings}$$

If a company plans no growth at all there will be no requirement for additional capital and so any profits that have been retained are surplus to current requirements. As a company increases its projected growth rates then it will gradually use more and more of its retained earnings to fund this growth. At a particular level of planned growth the company will, in addition, require external funding. The growth rate where retained earnings are fully utilised and no external funding is required is the company's sales growth rate from internal funding.

This may be expressed as:

$$\text{sales revenue growth rate from internal funding} = \frac{\text{funding from retained earnings}}{\text{assets}}$$

Therefore it can be seen that if a company has a high earnings retention ratio then it can achieve a high rate of sales revenue growth without needing additional external funding.

This ratio may be expanded into:

$$\text{sales growth rate from internal funding} = \frac{\text{funding from retained earnings}}{\text{net profit}}$$
$$\times \frac{\text{net profit}}{\text{equity}} \times \frac{\text{equity}}{\text{assets}}$$

or

$$\text{sales growth rate from internal funding} = \text{retention ratio} \times \text{ROE} \times \frac{\text{equity}}{\text{assets}}$$

From this relationship we can see that high sales revenue growth may be achieved if the company pays a low level of dividends (high retention ratio), earns a high ROE, and has a high equity to assets ratio, or a low debt to assets ratio.

Financing growth

Companies may be very interested in how much growth they can achieve without taking on any additional external funding, by way of either debt or equity. They may also be interested in how much growth they can achieve by using retained earnings, plus additional equity but by not increasing debt; or, by using retained earnings, plus additional debt but by not increasing equity. These two scenarios will reflect the gearing level or financial structure that the company has targeted in its financial plan.

If we consider the relationship

$$\text{sales growth rate from internal funding} = \text{retention ratio} \times \text{ROE} \times \frac{\text{equity}}{\text{assets}}$$

we can see that the maximum growth rate that the company can sustain if its gearing is not increased is

$$\text{sales growth rate from internal funding} = \text{retention ratio} \times \text{ROE}$$

which is dependent only on its retention ratio and its ROE.

Worked example 9.6

In Worked example 9.3 we saw that Supportex had a profit retention ratio of 85%, and was projecting an annual sales revenue growth rate of 20% per year. The company has reported that its equity and debt at the start of year one were £0.83m and £0.1m respectively, and its assets were £0.93m. Its net profit for year one was £0.2m.

We can calculate the maximum growth rate for Supportex assuming that it maintains its total assets growth (non-current assets plus working capital) in line with its planned sales revenue growth, and does not want to take on any additional external funding.

$$\text{ROE} = \pounds 0.2m/\pounds 0.83m = 24.1\%$$
$$\text{equity/assets} = \pounds 0.83m/\pounds 0.93m = 89.2\%$$

$$\text{sales growth rate from internal funding} = \text{retention ratio} \times \text{ROE} \times \frac{\text{equity}}{\text{assets}}$$

$$= 0.85 \times 0.241 \times 0.892$$
$$= 0.18273 \text{ or } 18.3\%$$

This is lower than the company's planned growth rate of 20%. It can only achieve the higher growth rate by obtaining external funding. If Supportex was additionally prepared to maintain its gearing ratio of 12% (£0.1m/£0.83m) then using

$$\text{sales revenue growth rate from internal funding} = \text{retention ratio} \times \text{ROE}$$
$$= 0.85 \times 0.241$$
$$= 0.20485 \text{ or } 20.5\%$$

we can see that the company could achieve a better growth rate of 20.5%, which is about in line with its financial plan.

If Supportex's sales revenue growth from internal funding had been less than its planned growth rate then the company would either have to reduce its planned growth rate, or take on additional debt and increase its debt/equity ratio (gearing) in order to achieve its planned growth rate. In those circumstances, it is likely that the company would also eventually need to increase its level of equity.

A company's final, agreed financial plan should not be accepted until the projected financial position of the business has been reviewed in terms of the adequacy, or otherwise, of funding. In the determination of requirements for additional funding, and to safeguard the future of the business, risk analysis and risk assessment are essential to be carried out with regard to each of the uncertain areas of the plan.

Short-term additional funding may be obtained through extended overdraft facilities, but longer-term funding will be from loans, or bonds, or the issue of additional share capital. The appropriate funding decision should be made and matched with the type of activity for which funding is required. For example, major capital expenditure projects would not normally be funded by an overdraft; the type of longer-term funding generally depends on the nature of the project.

Strategic performance assessment

A company may measure financial performance against its long-term financial plan in many different ways. Each year of the financial plan may be translated into short-term budgets, which may be used for both planning and control. Performance may be considered using return on capital employed (ROCE) or earnings per share (eps). Such short-term performance measures focus only on the performance for that specific period.

ROCE is calculated as a percentage by dividing operating profit (pre-tax) by capital employed (total assets less current liabilities), which is usually averaged for the year. It is therefore a relative measure of profitability rather than an absolute measure of profitability. Eps is calculated by dividing profit after tax by the number of ordinary shares in issue, and is therefore an absolute measure.

Worked example 9.7

Consider two companies, A and B, which have reported the following results for 2012:

	A	B
Operating profit	£1m	£2m
Average net assets	£4m	£20m

The ROCE for company A is 25% and for company B is 10%.
Company B earns higher profits but A is more profitable.

Chief executive officers (CEOs) may, for example, be rewarded via a remuneration package, which is linked to a ROCE performance measure. Since ROCE tends to be low in the early stages of a company's business life cycle, CEOs may take a short-term view in appraising new investment proposals because they will be anxious to maintain their level of remuneration. CEOs may therefore reject proposals for such investments even though they may provide a satisfactorily high ROCE over the longer term. The owners of the business, the shareholders, will of course be more interested in the longer-term ROCE of the business.

The divergence between the two points of view may occur because CEOs and shareholders are each using different assessment criteria. The views of CEOs and the shareholders may be brought into line if they both used the same criteria. This would mean abandoning the practice of linking a CEO's remuneration directly to short-term ROCE because it is likely to encourage short-term thinking. An alternative performance measure to ROCE, residual income (RI), is illustrated in Worked examples 9.8 and 9.9 below.

Worked example 9.8

Let's consider two companies within a group, X and Y, which have an opportunity to invest in projects that both have an initial cost of £10m. The overall cost of capital for the group is 15% per annum. The expected operating profits from each investment and the current returns earned by the companies are shown below:

Company	X	Y
Investment cost	£10m	£10m
Expected operating profit	£2m	£1.3m
Current ROCE	25%	9%

The expected returns from each proposed project are 20% (£2m/£10m) for company X and 13% (£1.3m/£10m) for company Y. On a ROCE basis, the CEO of company X would not be motivated to invest in the new project because 20% is less than the current ROCE. The CEO of company Y would be motivated to invest in the project because 13% is greater than the current ROCE. However, both decisions would be incorrect for the benefit of the group as a whole. This is because the company Y project returns 2% less, and the company X project returns 5% more, than the average cost of capital for the group of 15%.

Worked example 9.9

Let's again consider the same two companies X and Y, in Worked example 9.8, which have an opportunity to invest in projects that both have an initial cost of £10m. The overall cost of capital for the group is 15% per annum. The expected operating profits and residual income from each investment are shown below:

Company	X	Y
Proposed investment	£10m	£10m
Expected operating profit	£2.0m	£1.3m
Cost of capital charge (15%)	£1.5m	£1.5m
(RI) residual income (deficit)	£0.5m	£(0.2)m

On an RI basis, the CEO of company X will be motivated to invest and the CEO of company Y will not be motivated to invest. Both decisions would be correct for the benefit of the group as a whole, because the company X project is adding value but the company Y project is not adding value.

It is sometimes claimed that eps as a measure is more likely to encourage goal congruence, but a similar lack of goal congruence to that resulting from the use of ROCE may occur if a CEO's performance is measured using eps. If performance is based on eps then a CEO may decide to replace old equipment (resulting in lower ROCE and worsened cash flow) to increase profit and therefore increase eps. The reduction in ROCE may therefore result in a sub-optimisation decision for the company as a whole. Alternatively, if CEOs' performances are based on ROCE then they may decide to make do with old equipment, resulting in a higher ROCE and improved cash flow, but which may result in a reduced eps. There have been many cases of UK manufacturers whose plant was much older than that used by overseas competitors, which may have been as a direct result of the type of performance measure being used.

If a great deal of pressure is placed on CEOs to meet short-term performance measurement targets, there is a danger that they will take action that will improve short-term performance but will not maximise long-term profits. For example, by skimping on expenditure on advertising, customer services, maintenance, and training and staff development costs, it is possible to improve short-term performance. However, such actions may not maximise long-term profits.

It is probably impossible to design performance measures that will ensure that maximising short-term performance will also maximise long-term performance. Some steps, however, can be taken to improve the short-term performance measures so that they minimise the potential conflict. For example, during times of rising prices, short-term performance measures can be distorted if no attempt is made to adjust for the changing price levels.

The use of ROCE as a performance measure has a number of deficiencies. For example, it encourages CEOs to accept only those investments that are in excess of their current ROCE, leading to the rejection of profitable projects. Such actions may be reduced by replacing ROCE with eps as the performance measure. However, as we have seen, merely changing from ROCE to eps may not eliminate the short-term versus long-term conflicts.

Ideally, performance measures ought to be based on future results that can be expected from a CEO's actions during a period. This would involve a comparison of the present value of future cash flows at the start and end of the period, and a CEO's performance would be based on the increase in present value during the period. Such a system may not be totally feasible, given the difficulty in predicting and measuring future outcomes from current actions. Economic value added (EVA™)

aims to provide a performance measure that is highly correlated with both shareholder wealth and divisional performance. As we have already seen, EVA (which is similar to RI) is calculated by deducting from profit after tax a financial charge for the use of the company's net assets. The net assets number reported in the balance sheet is usually adjusted (in a variety of different ways) to reflect as realistic a valuation as possible of the company's net assets. The basis for the financial charge is usually the average cost of the capital used by the company (see Chapter 8).

ROCE and eps represent single summary measures of performance. It is virtually impossible to capture in summary financial measures all the variables that measure the success of a company. It is therefore important that financial managers broaden their reporting systems to include additional non-financial measures of performance that give indications of future outcomes from current actions. This may include, for example, obtaining feedback from customers regarding the quality of service that encourages managers not to skimp on reducing the quality of service in order to save costs in the short term. Other suggestions have focused on refining the financial measures so that they will reduce the potential for conflict between actions that improve short-term performance at the expense of long-term performance.

As part of their strategic management process many companies now link their financial (and non-financial) plans with operations by using techniques like the **balanced scorecard** (Kaplan, RS and Norton, DP 'The Balanced Scorecard: measures that drive performance', *Harvard Business Review* Volume 70, Issue 1, pages 71–9 (Jan/Feb, 1992)). In 1990, David Norton and Robert Kaplan were involved in a study of a dozen companies that covered manufacturing and services, heavy industry, and high technology to develop a new performance measurement model. The findings of this study were published in the *Harvard Business Review* in January 1992 and gave birth to an improved measurement system, the balanced scorecard.

Mini case 9.2

You know when an idea or concept has become popular when there is an award for it. The Palladium Group Inc (founded by David Norton and Robert Kaplan), a global management consultancy, introduced the Balanced Scorecard Hall of Fame to honour organisations that have achieved extraordinary performance results through the use of the Kaplan–Norton Balanced Scorecard.

The most recent awards for the Europe, Middle East and Africa region were held in Bahrain in June 2011 at which Bahrain company, YK Almoayyed and Sons, won the Hall of Fame award. As managing director Mona Almoayyed pointed out, 'Companies that concentrate only on profits tend to decline over time because they are not investing and focusing on the future. Since adopting the Balanced Scorecard, we have experienced significant growth.'

The balanced scorecard concept had evolved by 1996 from a measurement system to a core management system. *The Balanced Scorecard* published by Kaplan and Norton in 1996 illustrated the importance of both financial and non-financial measures being incorporated into companies' management systems; these are included not on an *ad hoc* basis but are derived from a top-down process driven by the company's mission and its strategy.

An example of a balanced scorecard is shown in Figure 9.14. It provides a framework for translating a strategy into operational terms. The balanced scorecard includes headings covering the following four key elements:

- financial
- internal business processes

- learning and growth
- customer.

The four perspectives provide both a framework for measuring a company's activities in terms of its vision and strategies, and a measurement tool to give managers a comprehensive view of the performance of a business.

The financial perspective is concerned with measures that reflect the financial performance of a company. This is its ability to create wealth, and may be reflected in key performance indicators that include, for example:

- level of working capital
- cash flow
- sales revenue growth
- profitability
- ROCE.

The emphasis placed on such financial indicators would depend on the position of the company within its business life cycle.

The internal business processes perspective is concerned with measures that reflect the performance of key activities, for example:

- the time spent prospecting new customers
- the cost of product processing
- number of units that require re-working.

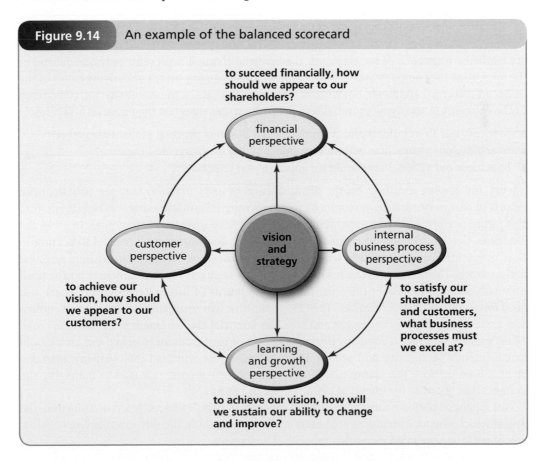

Figure 9.14   An example of the balanced scorecard

Such measurements are designed to provide managers with an understanding of how well their parts of the business are running, and whether products and services conform to customer requirements.

The learning and growth perspective includes measures that describe the company's learning curve, and is concerned with indicators related to both individual and corporate self-improvement, for example:

■ the number of employee suggestions received
■ the total hours spent on staff development.

The customer perspective is concerned with measures that consider issues having a direct impact on customer satisfaction, for example:

■ time taken to deliver the products or services
■ results of customer surveys
■ number of customer complaints received
■ the company's competitive rankings.

If customers are not satisfied, then they will find other companies with which to do business. Consequently, poor performance from this perspective is generally considered a leading indicator of future decline, even though the current financial position of a company may be good. From Figure 9.14 it can be seen that although

■ objectives
■ measures
■ targets
■ initiatives,

are implied within each of the elements, the financial element represents only one quarter of the total. How the company appears to its shareholders is an important underlying factor of the balanced scorecard approach, but it is interesting to see that the measures that are considered by the company in satisfying shareholders go much further than just the financial measures:

■ To satisfy our shareholders and customers, what business processes must we excel at?
■ To achieve our vision, how will we sustain our ability to change and improve?
■ To achieve our vision, how should we appear to our customers?

Norton and Kaplan comment on the dissatisfaction of investors who may see only financial reports of past performance. Investors increasingly want information that will help them forecast future performance of companies in which they have invested their capital. In 1994 the American Certified Public Accountants (CPA) Special Committee on Financial Reporting in New York reinforced this concern with reliance on financial reporting for measuring business performance. 'Users focus on the future while today's business reporting focuses on the past. Although information about the past is a useful indicator of future performance, users also need forward-looking information.' The CPA committee was concerned with how well companies are creating value for the future and how non-financial measurement must play a key role. 'Many users want to see a company through the eyes of management to help them understand management's perspective and predict where management will lead the company. Management should disclose the financial and non-financial measurements it uses in managing the business that quantify the effects of key activities and events.'

Non-financial performance measures and concepts like the balanced scorecard illustrate the way in which financial measures are becoming less dominant in the measurement and evaluation of performance in an increasing number of businesses.

Progress check 9.3

Describe the framework of the balanced scorecard approach and explain the ways in which this provides links with the financial plans of a company.

Summary of key points

- Financial planning is an integral part of a company's strategic management process.

- The main purpose of financial planning is to consider the big picture of a company's activities over the long term, five, 10 years or more, with regard to its growth and how that growth may be financed.

- A company's financial planning process includes the development of a planning model that will produce long-term forecasts of its three main financial statements, which are based on input of the company's parameters and variables relating to its planned growth rate, and key financial ratios.

- Financial models may be used to plan the long-term impacts of a planned growth in the sales revenue of a business.

- Forecasts are not plans or budgets but are predictions of future environments, events, and outcomes, and may be derived using both qualitative and quantitative techniques.

- Cash flow forecasts are part of the financial planning process and are used to determine a company's future funding requirements on a monthly and yearly basis.

- A company may plan for its future growth without necessarily using any additional external funding, but to use its own resources of retained earnings.

- A company that is planning future growth may require funding in addition to retained earnings, and may consider the financing options of debt and equity to fund such future growth.

- A company's performance may be measured against its financial plans using a range of financial ratios (see Chapter 8), with return on capital employed (ROCE) and earnings per share (eps) being the most widely used.

- Residual income (RI) and economic value added (EVA) are performance measures that may be used as alternatives to ROCE.

- Many companies, on a worldwide basis, have now adopted the balanced scorecard as a method of linking their long-term strategies into operational targets and key performance indicators.

Glossary of key terms

balanced scorecard An approach to the provision of information to management to assist strategic policy formulation and achievement. It emphasises the need to provide the user with a set of information which addresses all relevant areas of performance in an objective and unbiased fashion. The information provided may include both financial and non-financial elements, and cover areas such as profitability, customer satisfaction, internal efficiency, and innovation.

budget A quantified statement, for a defined period of time not more than one year, which may include planned revenues, expenses, assets, liabilities, and cash flows.

forecast A prediction of future events and their quantification for planning purposes.

goal congruence The state which leads individuals or groups to take actions which are in their self-interest and also in the best interest of the company. Goal incongruence exists when the interests of individuals or of groups associated with a company are not in harmony.

planning The establishment of objectives, and the formulation, evaluation, and selection of the policies, strategies, tactics, and action required to achieve them. Planning comprises long-term strategic planning and short-term operational planning, the latter being usually for a period of up to one year.

qualitative forecasting Forecasting in terms that are not expressed numerically.

quantitative forecasting Forecasting in terms that are expressed numerically.

strategic planning A process of deciding on the objectives of an organisation, the resources used to attain these objectives, and on the policies that are to govern the acquisition, use, and disposition of these resources. The results of this process may be expressed in a strategic plan, which is a statement of long-term goals along with a definition of the strategies and policies, which will ensure achievement of those goals.

Assessment material

Questions

Q9.1 (i) Why do businesses need to prepare financial plans?
(ii) What are they used for?

Q9.2 (i) Give some examples of the ways in which forecasting techniques may be used to assess a company's future sales revenue growth rates.
(ii) What are the advantages and disadvantages in using each of these forecasting techniques?

Q9.3 Use diagrams to illustrate how the financial planning process may be used to produce long-term forecast financial statements.

Q9.4 Explain and illustrate the ways in which a business may plan for its future growth.

Q9.5 How may a business use a financial model to assess the levels of internal and external funding required to support its long-term growth?

Q9.6 What are the various financing options that a company may use to fund its planned future growth, and how may their levels be determined?

Q9.7 (i) How may a company's performance be measured and compared with its strategic financial plan?
(ii) What are the advantages and disadvantages of these measures?

Q9.8 Outline the way in which the balanced scorecard links a company's strategy with its operational activities.

Discussion points

D9.1 'Financial plans are not accurate because in general they do not differentiate between the behaviour of variable and fixed costs.' Discuss.

D9.2 'The area of financial planning is a minefield of potential problems and conflicts.' How should these problems and conflicts be approached to ensure that the performance of the business is aligned with its primary objective of shareholder wealth maximisation?

D9.3 'It is impossible to make accurate predictions about a company's activities even over a short-term period of say six months, therefore strategic financial plans of five and 10 years have no value at all.' Discuss.

Exercises

Solutions are provided in Appendix 2 to all exercise numbers highlighted in colour.

Level I

E9.1 *Time allowed – 15 minutes*

Hearbuy plc is a growth business, which assembles and sells mobile phones. They make and sell one model only and expect to sell 2,684,000 units during the next four years. The volume for each year is expected to be 20% above the preceding year. The selling price is £50 each, and the cost of sales is expected to be 70% of the selling price. Hearbuy plc have prepared an estimated balance sheet as at the end of year one as follows:

	£m	£m
Non-current assets	13.50	
Inventories	10.47	
Trade receivables	4.01	
Cash and cash equivalents	3.55	31.53
Trade receivables	3.03	
Loans	4.50	
Equity	24.00	31.53

Interest is paid at 10% each year on the balance of its loans outstanding at the start of each year. The loans at the start of year one were £4.5m. Dividends are planned to continue each year at 60% of profit after tax. The company's corporation tax rate is expected to be 35%. The growth in investment in non-current assets is expected to be the same level as the growth in sales revenue. Working capital is planned at 60% of sales revenue.

> Use an Excel spreadsheet to prepare a sales plan for Hearbuy plc in units and £m values for years one to four.

E9.2 *Time allowed – 30 minutes*

> From the data in E9.1 use an Excel spreadsheet to prepare an income statement for Hearbuy plc for year one.

Level II
E9.3   *Time allowed – 30 minutes*

From the data in E9.1 and E9.2 use an Excel spreadsheet to prepare an income statement and balance sheet for Hearbuy plc for years one to four, which show the levels of additional funding required, if any, by the company for each year.

E9.4   *Time allowed – 30 minutes*

From the income statement and balance sheet for Hearbuy plc from E9.3, identify and discuss the actions the company may take to eliminate the need for the additional funding in each year.

E9.5   *Time allowed – 30 minutes*

Using the income statement for year one from E9.3, and the relevant balance sheet data at the start of year one, determine the level of growth that Hearbuy plc may achieve if it took on no additional external funding in years two to four, assuming that the growth in total assets each year is expected to be at the same level as the planned growth in sales revenue (that is, the ratio of total assets to sales revenue remains constant).

E9.6   *Time allowed – 30 minutes*

Using the income statement for year one from E9.3, and the relevant balance sheet data at the start of year one, determine the level of growth that Hearbuy plc may achieve if its growth in total assets each year is expected to be at the same level as the planned growth in sales revenue (that is, the ratio of total assets to sales remains constant), and if it maintained its gearing ratio at the start of year one level for years one to four.

E9.7   *Time allowed – 30 minutes*
An extract of the financial results for 2012 for three of the companies in the Marx Group plc is shown below:

	Company		
	Chico	**Groucho**	**Harpo**
Average net operating assets	£7.5m	£17.5m	£12.5m
Operating profit	£1.5m	£1.4m	£2.0m
Administrative expenses	£0.8m	£0.3m	£0.65m
Cost of capital per annum	7%	5%	10%

Required:

(i)   Calculate the ROCE for each company for 2012.
(ii)   Calculate the EVA each company for 2012.

(iii) **Which measure provides the best performance measure for each company and why?**

(iv) **If each company is presented with an investment opportunity that is expected to yield a return of 9%**

    (a) **which company(s) would accept and which company(s) would reject the investment opportunity if their performance is measured by ROCE, and why?**

    (b) **which company(s) would accept and which company(s) would reject the investment opportunity if their performance is measured by EVA, and why?**

E9.8 *Time allowed – 45 minutes*

Ros Burns intends opening a new retail business on 1 October 2012, and intends investing £25,000 of her own capital in the business on 1 October 2012. The business, which will trade under the name of Arby Ltd, will sell fashion accessories.

The company intends purchasing non-current assets costing £80,000. These will be purchased in November 2012. They are estimated to have, on average, a five-year useful economic life with a residual value of zero. They will be paid for in two equal instalments, one instalment due in December 2012, and one instalment due in February 2013. Forecast sales revenues from October 2012 to March 2013 are expected to be:

	£
October	200,000
November	205,000
December	180,000
January	200,000
February	205,000
March	200,000

30% of total sales revenue is expected to be paid in cash in the month of sale, the remaining 70% being sold on credit terms of one month. Bad debts are estimated to be 5% of credit sales. Wages costs are expected to be as follows:

	£
October	90,000
November	105,000
December	90,000
January	85,000
February	90,000
March	100,000

Materials costs are expected to be as follows:

	£
October	60,000
November	70,000
December	65,000
January	70,000
February	55,000
March	70,000

           ➡

Wages will be paid in the month they are incurred, but materials will be purchased on the following basis:

- 50% of the material costs will be paid for one month following the month of purchase
- 50% of the material costs will be paid for two months following the month of purchase.

Overheads expenses, which are payable in the month in which they are incurred, are expected to be £35,000 each month.

Required:

(i) Prepare a monthly cash budget for Arby Ltd for the six-month period ending 31 March 2013. It should show the net cash flow for each month and the cumulative budgeted cash position at the end of each month to determine the level of additional financing required, if any.

(ii) Prepare a brief report for Ros advising her of the possible alternative sources of short-term and long-term finance available to the company, together with your recommendations, with reasons, of which types of financing she should consider using.

Case Study I: Gegin Ltd

Gegin is a UK-based high-quality kitchen units manufacturer, which was launched in the late 1980s by Tim Imber. The business started its operations from one shop in Chester and grew substantially so that by 2011 the business operated from a total of 48 shops, located all around the UK. In addition, in 2008, a seven-year contract with a national chain of leading builders' merchants was signed which gave Gegin wider market access in return for a flat fee and a percentage share of profits.

Originally, Tim Imber was the only full-time employee of Gegin. He was responsible for the design, construction, and marketing of the business's products as well as the day-to-day management of the company. The business, which required £190,000 to start, was funded 50% by Tim and 50% of the required capital was provided by Tim's brother-in-law, Len Graham. Len was an accountant by profession and acted in a part-time capacity as the company accountant and assisted Tim in certain aspects of management.

The company quickly expanded and problems emerged as supply could not keep pace with demand. It became necessary, therefore, to employ someone else to assist Tim in the construction of the furniture. As the business continued to grow, more people joined Gegin, so that as early as 1995, 25 people were employed by the company. At the same time, further shops were opened and a separate workshop and warehouse was established. Gegin's expansion was funded by a combination of re-investing profits and medium-term bank loans.

The result of all these changes was that by 1995, Tim Imber's time was almost exclusively given over to the management of the business. The following year the decision was made that Gegin would become a private limited company (Ltd), and it was at this point that Len Graham joined full-time employment as finance director. One of the first changes that Len brought about was the direct sourcing of the core materials used in Gegin's products. The timber now used was directly imported from Canada and Scandinavia.

On 31 March 2012 after 24 years of trading, the financial statements of the company showed sales revenue of £60m, and a pre-tax profit of £14m. The following financial statements relate to Gegin Ltd for the years 2010 to 2012:

Balance sheet as at 31 March

	2010 £m	2011 £m	2012 £m
Non-current assets	36	27	55
less			
Depreciation	(10)	(7)	(14)
	26	20	41
Current assets			
Inventories	16	16	22
Trade receivables	28	27	20
Other receivables	3	16	5
Cash and cash equivalents	5	7	8
	52	66	55

(continued)

Current liabilities

Trade payables	18	15	10
Other payables	15	7	16
Income tax payables	6	9	7
Dividends payable	3	4	2
	42	35	35
Total assets less current liabilities	36	51	61
less			
Non-current liabilities			
Debentures	(2)	(4)	(6)
	34	47	55
Equity			
Share capital (£1 ordinary shares)	20	22	25
Retained earnings	14	25	30
Total equity	34	47	55

Income statement for the year ending 31 March

	2010	2011	2012
	£m	£m	£m
Revenue	40	80	60
Cost of sales	(12)	(30)	(28)
Gross profit	28	50	32
Operating expenses	(10)	(26)	(18)
Profit before tax	18	24	14
Income tax expense	(6)	(9)	(7)
Profit for the year	12	15	7
Dividends	(6)	(4)	(2)
Retained profit for the year	6	11	5

Strategic review

In 2011, external consultants were asked to identify the strategic options open to Gegin. The review found that, although the middle to upper end of the fitted kitchen market was becoming increasingly competitive, there was still room for significant growth. Despite numerous shop openings, Gegin was still very much a regional operator. Expansion of the market was predicted to continue for many years, although Gegin's product and strategic positioning left the business vulnerable to changes in the business cycle. The company had been affected quite significantly by a fall in sales revenue by the late 1990s. The consultants identified these issues and suggested a number of options for Gegin.

Option 1 – additional new shops

Initial investment cost	£86m
Potential annual income	£16m p.a.

The first option was for more shops to be opened, particularly in the south of England, where the company had little presence. This option had implications for the management and organisational structure of the company as at least two additional workshops, a warehouse, and distribution centres would be necessary to provide the required infrastructure. Such a centre was opened in the latter part of 2004, as a programme of shop openings had already been an idea that the management had been considering for some time. The company had previously considered franchising as a way to achieve this growth, and the company had already in 2008 entered into a seven-year contract that was signed with a large UK-based builders' merchant chain. However, subsequent market and business research regarding the UK market had suggested that franchising would not be a profitable proposition for a company like Gegin Ltd, and as a consequence the policy was abandoned.

Option 2 – diversification

Initial investment cost £23m
Potential annual income £6m p.a.

The second option was diversification, because the company's significant experience of the import of quality timber from North America and Northern Europe was, the consultants suggested, not being exploited. The wholesaling of timber was therefore recommended. This had the added advantage of producing economies of scale, which would have the effect of reducing unit costs. Tim and Len together with their senior managers had not previously considered this proposal and felt that so long as they were not supplying major competitors this was a proposition that could and should be pursued.

Option 3 – lifestyle concept

Initial investment cost £57m
Potential annual income £10m p.a. rising to £15m p.a. in four years

The consultants suggested, as their third option, the development of the 'lifestyle concept' store format–shops that not only sold kitchen units, but also related accessories (such as kitchen furnishings and equipment) in a themed environment. Such shops had started to develop at the lower end of the market, but this format had not yet been rolled out in the market that Gegin Ltd occupied. This proposal found immediate favour with the directors of the company, although the size of each of the existing shops would not easily accommodate such a change. The movement to larger retail outlets, or the opening of new additional shops that could accommodate this format would be necessary, but costly.

Option 4 – move into the Asian market

Initial investment cost £46m
Potential annual income £6m p.a. rising to £14m p.a. in six years

The demand for English-designed quality kitchens had always been popular in Asia. The region as a whole was becoming potentially a more significant market and the consultants argued that a gradual move into this market would in time reduce Gegin Ltd's dependence on UK demand. The consultants, concerned about the risk associated with this option, felt that expansion in this way should be by way of a joint venture. This idea was one with which Tim, Len, and their senior managers readily agreed.

The proposal suggested that, in the long term, furniture should be manufactured in Asia using designs and templates from the UK. In the short and medium term, however, in order to establish the viability of the market, furniture should be exported – a practice that the consultants suggested should continue until the market was sufficiently mature – for approximately five years.

Despite their caution, Tim and Len were very interested in each of the options identified by the external consultants. The question was how this growth should be financed. The consultants suggested the following alternative methods of funding:

1 The company may obtain a 'listing' as a public limited company (plc). This, the consultants suggested, would raise £40m from additional equity shares. The balance of any additional investment required could be provided from taking on additional debt capital, which was assumed would cost 10% per annum in interest.

2 Any new investment may be funded totally by taking on additional new debt, which was assumed would cost 10% per annum in interest.

It was assumed that Gegin Ltd's sales revenue and profit performance for 2013 would be identical to 2012 if no new investment were undertaken. If one of the new investment options were to be undertaken then, regardless of which option, taxation as a percentage of profit before tax would be the same as 2012 and dividends as a percentage of profit after tax would be the same as 2012.

> **Required:**
> **Prepare a report which:**
>
> (i)   considers
>   - Gegin Ltd's financial status, and possible reasons for it
>   - the company's objectives
>   - why the company's directors may have engaged external consultants to carry out a strategic review of its activities
>
> (ii)   provides a short-term evaluation of the options suggested by the external consultants, assuming that one option is taken up by the company at the start of April 2012, showing:
>
>   (a)   a summarised income statement and retained earnings for the year ended 31 March 2013
>   (b)   total equity at 31 March 2013
>   (c)   medium- and long-term loans at 31 March 2013
>   (d)   gearing ratio at 31 March 2013
>   (e)   earnings per share for the year ended 31 March 2013
>
>   for each option, and comparing the two funding options: a stock exchange listing and possible partial debt funding; total debt funding
>
> (iii) advises the board which option the company should select, based on the information available, stating your assumptions, and giving appropriate reasons for the conclusions you have reached, and the recommendations you make.

> Your report should identify some of the possible constraints the company may face, and give some consideration to non-financial factors that may affect the company, with regard to each option and in particular with regard to your proposed recommendation if implemented by the company.
>
> (Note: a discounted cash flow approach is not required for this case study.)

10

Management of working capital

Chapter contents

Learning objectives

Completion of this chapter will enable you to:

- Explain what is meant by working capital and the operating cycle.
- Describe the management and control of the working capital requirement.
- Explain the use of working capital management as a strategic tool, and its impact on profitability, ROCE, ROE, and liquidity.
- Outline how good working capital management releases resources that can be used to provide the internal finance to fund value-adding projects, or repay debt and reduce the interest payable.
- Outline some of the working capital policies that may be adopted by companies.
- Implement the systems and techniques that may be used for the management and control of inventories and optimisation of inventory levels.
- Outline a system of credit management and the control of accounts receivable.
- Consider the management of accounts payable as an additional source of finance.
- Use the operating cycle to evaluate a company's working capital requirement performance.
- Action the appropriate techniques to achieve short-term and long-term cash flow improvement.
- Evaluate how the use of cash management models such as those developed by Baumol and by Miller and Orr assist financial managers to manage their companies' cash flows.

Introduction

Strategy is a course of action that includes a specification of resources required to achieve a specific objective. The overall strategy of a company is *what* the company needs to do long term to achieve its objectives, and is primarily focused on maximisation of shareholder wealth. Working capital and its financing are important elements of these resources.

In previous chapters we have looked at the longer-term resources of capital investments in assets and projects, and the alternative sources of funds to finance them. This chapter considers the shorter-term elements of the balance sheet, the net current assets (current assets less current liabilities) or working capital, which is normally financed with short-term funding, for example bank overdrafts. The chapter begins by considering what is really meant by working capital, with an overview of its nature and its purposes.

Regular evaluation of the working capital cycle, or cash operating cycle, may be used to monitor a company's effectiveness in the management of its working capital requirement (WCR). Minimisation of working capital is an objective that reduces the extent to which external financing of working capital is required. However, there is a fine balance between minimising the costs of finance and ensuring that sufficient working capital is available to adequately support the company's operations.

An emphasis is placed on optimisation rather than minimisation and on the importance of good management of the working capital requirement for the sustained success of companies. The techniques that may be used to improve the management of inventories, accounts receivable, and accounts payable are explored in detail.

This chapter will close by linking working capital to the effective management of cash and by considering some of the ways that both long-term and short-term cash flow may be improved.

Working capital and working capital requirement

The balance sheet is sometimes presented showing all the assets in one part of the balance sheet and all the liabilities in another part of the balance sheet. This may be said to be a little unsatisfactory since the various categories within the assets section and within the liabilities heading are very different in nature. Cash, for example, is a financial asset and has very different characteristics to non-current assets and to inventories.

If we consider the following relationship:

$$\text{assets} = \text{equity} + \text{liabilities}$$

it may be rewritten as

$$\text{non-current assets} + \text{inventories} + \text{trade receivables} + \text{prepayments} + \text{cash}$$
$$=$$
$$\text{equity} + \text{financial debt} + \text{trade payables} + \text{accruals}$$

This may be further rewritten to show homogeneous items on each side of the = sign as follows:

$$\text{equity} + \text{financial debt} - \text{cash}$$
$$=$$
$$\text{non-current assets} + \text{inventories} + \text{trade receivables} - \text{trade payables}$$
$$- \text{accruals} + \text{prepayments}$$

Therefore

$$\textbf{equity}$$
$$=$$
$$\textbf{non-current assets} + \textbf{inventories} + \textbf{trade receivables} - \textbf{trade payables}$$
$$- \textbf{accruals} + \textbf{prepayments} - \textbf{financial debt} + \textbf{cash}$$

Financial debt comprises two parts:

- long-term debt (loans repayable after one year, in accounting terms)
- short-term debt (overdrafts and loans repayable within one year, in accounting terms),

and so from substitution and rearranging the equation above we can see that:

$$
\text{equity} + \text{long-term debt}
$$
$$
=
$$
$$
\text{non-current assets} + \text{inventories} + \text{trade receivables} - \text{trade payables} - \text{accruals}
$$
$$
+ \text{prepayments} - \text{short-term debt} + \text{cash}
$$

or

$$
\textbf{equity} + \textbf{long-term debt} = \textbf{non-current assets} + \textbf{working capital}
$$

Therefore, equity plus long-term financial debt is represented by non-current assets plus working capital (WC) and so

$$
\textbf{WC} = \textbf{inventories} + \textbf{trade receivables} - \textbf{trade payables} - \textbf{accruals} + \textbf{prepayments}
$$
$$
- \textbf{short-term financial debt} + \textbf{cash}
$$

Inventories, of course, comprise raw materials, finished products, and work in progress (including their share of allocated and apportioned production overheads).

Progress check 10.1

Explain briefly the main components of working capital, using an example of a UK plc.

The need for working capital – the operating cycle

The interrelationship of each of the elements within working capital may be represented in the cash operating cycle (Figure 10.1).

The operating cycle includes:

- acquisition of raw materials and packaging, which are at first stored in warehouses prior to use, are invoiced by suppliers and recorded by the company in accounts payable, and then normally paid for at a later date
- use of materials and packaging in the manufacturing process to create partly completed finished goods, work in progress, stored as inventories in the company's warehouses
- use of materials, packaging, and work in progress to complete finished goods, which are also stored as inventories in the company's warehouses
- despatch of finished goods from the warehouses and delivery to customers, who accept the products for which they will pay
- recording as sales by the company its deliveries to customers, which are included in its accounts receivable, and normally paid for by customers at a later date
- use of cash resources to pay overheads, wages, and salaries
- use of cash resources to pay suppliers (trade payables) for production overheads and other expenses
- use of cash resources to pay suppliers (trade payables) for raw materials.

Figure 10.1   The cash operating cycle

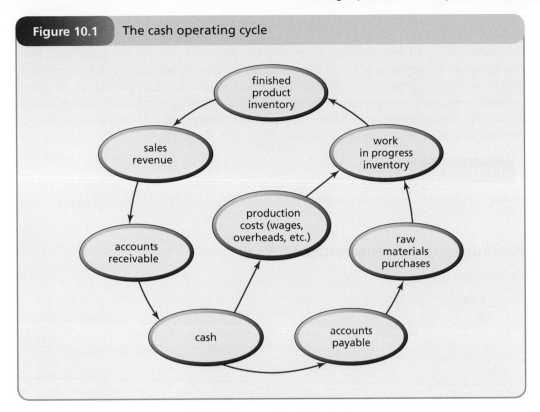

Worked example 10.1

We can identify which of the following categories may be included within a company's cash operating cycle:

- plant and machinery
- accounts payable
- investments in subsidiaries
- cash
- work in progress
- patents
- accounts receivable
- fixtures and fittings.

Non-current assets are not renewed within the operating cycle. The following items extracted from the above list relate to non-current assets:

plant and machinery   patents
investments in subsidiaries   fixtures and fittings

The remaining categories therefore relate to the operating cycle, as follows:

accounts payable   cash
work in progress   accounts receivable

A company with a low number of operating cycle days is likely to have a better operating cash position than a similar company with a high number of operating cycle days. The company therefore uses these funds to finance its inventories, through the manufacturing process, from raw materials to finished goods, and also the time lag between delivery of the finished goods or services and the payments by customers of accounts receivable. Short-term funds, for example bank overdrafts, are needed to finance the working capital the company requires as represented in the operating cycle. Many companies use the flexibility of the bank overdraft to finance fluctuating levels of working capital.

Progress check 10.2

How is a company's need for investment in operations explained by the operating cycle?

Working capital requirement (WCR)

We have seen that

$$
\text{equity} + \text{long-term debt}
$$
$$
=
$$
$$
\text{non-current assets} + \text{inventories} + \text{trade receivables} - \text{trade payables} - \text{accruals}
$$
$$
+ \text{prepayments} - \text{short-term debt} + \text{cash}
$$

and so

$$
\textbf{equity} + \textbf{long-term debt} + \textbf{short-term debt} - \textbf{cash}
$$
$$
=
$$
$$
\textbf{non-current assets} + \textbf{inventories} + \textbf{trade receivables} - \textbf{trade payables} - \textbf{accruals}
$$
$$
+ \textbf{prepayments}
$$

From this equation we can see that the total financial resources of the company are equity plus long- and short-term financial debt minus cash. This represents the total money invested in the company, and is called the total investment. Therefore

$$
\textbf{total investment}
$$
$$
=
$$
$$
\textbf{non-current assets} + \textbf{inventories} + \textbf{trade receivables} - \textbf{trade payables} - \textbf{accruals}
$$
$$
+ \textbf{prepayments}
$$

The total investment in the company can therefore be seen to comprise broadly two elements:

- investment in non-current assets
- investment in operations

where the investment in operations is

$$
\textbf{inventories} + \textbf{trade receivables} - \textbf{trade payables} - \textbf{accruals} + \textbf{prepayments}
$$

which is called the working capital requirement (WCR).

Stated in words, the WCR is telling us something very important: the company has to raise and use some of its financial resources, which have a cost, to invest in its operating cycle. These financial resources are specifically for the company to purchase and create inventories, while it waits for payments from its customers. The impact of this is decreased by the fact that suppliers also have to wait to be paid. Added to this is the net effect of accruals and prepayments. Prepayments may be greater than accruals (requiring the use of funds) or accruals may be greater than prepayments (which is a source of funds).

In most manufacturing companies the WCR is positive. The smaller the WCR, the smaller are the total financial resources needed, and the more liquid is the company. Some businesses, for example supermarkets, may have limited inventories and zero accounts receivable, but high accounts payable. In such cases WCR may be negative and these companies are effectively able to fund the acquisition of non-current assets with the credit they receive from their suppliers.

Throughout this chapter we will use the balance sheet and income statement of Flatco plc, an engineering company, shown in Figures 8.3 and 8.4 in Chapter 8, to illustrate the calculation of the key working capital ratios. The income statement is for the year ended 31 December 2012 and the balance sheet is as at 31 December 2012. Comparative numbers are shown for 2011.

Worked Example 10.2

From the balance sheet of Flatco plc for 2012 and the comparatives for 2011 (see Figures 8.3 and 8.5 in Chapter 8) we may calculate the working capital requirement for 2012 and the working capital requirement for 2011.

Figures in £000

Working capital requirement:

WCR = inventories + trade receivables − trade payables − accruals + prepayments
WCR for 2012 = 311 + 573 − 553 − 82 + 589 − 838
WCR for 2011 = 268 + 517 − 461 − 49 + 617 = 892

Progress check 10.3

What is meant by the working capital requirement (WCR)?

Working capital (WC)

Working capital (WC) is normally defined as:

current assets − current liabilities

or

WC = inventories + trade receivables − trade payables − accruals + prepayments − short-term debt + cash

Therefore

WC = WCR − short-term debt + cash

The difference between WC and WCR can be seen to be cash less short-term financial debt.

The financial analyst considers the definitions of long- and short-term in a different way to the accountant, thinking of long-term as 'permanent' or 'stable' and so will consider WC in an alternative way by calculating the difference between the stable financial resources of the company and its long-term use of funds, its non-current assets.

Since

$$\text{equity} + \text{short-term debt} + \text{long-term debt} - \text{cash}$$
$$=$$
$$\text{non-current assets} + \text{inventories} + \text{trade receivables} - \text{trade payables}$$
$$- \text{accruals} + \text{prepayments}$$

and

$$\text{WC} = \text{inventories} + \text{trade receivables} - \text{trade payables} - \text{accruals} + \text{prepayments}$$
$$- \text{short-term financial debt} + \text{cash}$$

an alternative representation of working capital is

$$\textbf{WC} = \textbf{equity} + \textbf{long-term debt} - \textbf{non-current assets}$$

As a general rule, except in certain commercial circumstances, WC should always be positive in the long run because if it were negative then the company would be financing its (long-term) non-current assets with short-term debt. Renewal of such debt represents a major liquidity risk. It is the same thing as, say, financing one's house purchase with an overdraft. Since WC has to be positive and the aim should be for WCR to be as small as possible, or even negative, there is a dilemma as to the acceptability of either positive or negative cash. The answer really depends on the quality of the WCR.

If net cash is negative then short-term debt is higher than the cash balance and so WCR is financed partly with short-term debt. So the question may be asked 'will the company suffer the same liquidity risk as with a negative WC?' If inventories are of high-quality champagne, the value of which will probably rise year by year, or if the trade receivables are, say, blue chip companies with no credit risk, then a bank is likely to finance such WCR with no restrictions. If the quality of the WCR is poor the bank is unlikely to finance the WCR with short-term debt. The management and control of each of the elements of WCR: inventories; trade receivables; trade payables, must be considered in terms of both their quality and their level. We will look at each of these elements in the sections that follow.

Progress check 10.4

What is meant by working capital (WC)? How may it differ in a manufacturing company compared with a supermarket retailer?

Working capital management as a strategic tool

In Chapter 6 we saw how strategically important capital investment decisions are to companies for their survival and growth in the future value of the business. We also saw that in addition to initial capital investment costs it is essential to include investments in working capital requirements in the appraisal of new projects. To ignore working capital requirements in the appraisal of an investment project is likely to result in subsequent under-funding and possibly a failure to provide an increase in corporate value.

Capital investment decisions are usually long-term strategic decisions, and in Chapter 7 we saw the various choices of long-term sources of finance that may be used by companies to fund such investments. The long-term sources of external finance include loans, bonds, and new equity. However, capital investment projects may also be financed internally, which may be cheaper and more easily accessible than external finance. In Chapter 7 we considered retained earnings as an internal source of finance and how good management of working capital may augment this.

There are conflicting objectives in the management of working capital with regard to a company's profitability and liquidity. Increased profitability is required in support of the company's primary objective of maximisation of shareholder wealth. The net current assets (working capital) of the company are a part of its capital employed; a company's capital employed comprises its non-current assets plus its net current assets. If we consider the company's return on capital employed (ROCE) as profit before interest and tax (PBIT) divided by capital employed (see page 390, Chapter 8) we can see that the lower the denominator, the higher will be the ROCE. Therefore, as the level of working capital is reduced the level of ROCE is increased.

Further to this, a reduction in working capital means reductions in either or both accounts receivable and inventories levels, and increases in levels of accounts payable. This results in the requirement for lower levels of short-term financing (for example, overdrafts or short-term loans), which result in lower levels of interest payable. A reduction in levels of interest payable results in an increase in profit after tax (PAT). Therefore, since one of our definitions of ROCE is:

$$\text{return on capital employed, ROCE} = \frac{\text{PAT}}{\text{capital employed}}$$

the level of ROCE is further increased as a result of a reduction in working capital. Also, since

$$\text{return on equity, ROE} = \frac{\text{PAT}}{\text{equity}}$$

then the level of ROE is also increased as a result of a reduction in working capital.

A reduction in the level of working capital and an increase in profit after tax may therefore release resources that can be used to provide the internal funds to finance further investments in productive assets (generating returns greater than the cost of capital), or repay debt, both of which reduce the burden of interest payable and add value to the business.

From the above we can see that the lower the level of working capital and the higher the return obtained from the increase in funds that creates, the greater will be the increase in corporate value.

In addition to the objective of increased profitability, appropriate levels of liquidity are required for the company to meet its operational cash requirements and to stay in business. The higher the level of cash, and therefore the higher the level of working capital, the more comfortable the company's managers will feel in meeting their day-to-day cash requirements, and the more able they will be to meet any unforeseen cash requirements. However, a high level of cash held by the company, while a comfort to managers, is not good news for shareholders. At worst, cash held as cash will earn no returns at all. At best, cash held in a bank deposit account may earn some interest, which will increase both profit and cash flow to some extent. But bank deposit interest is unlikely to be anywhere near the returns from the type of investment projects that will generate value at the levels expected by shareholders.

In addition to higher levels of cash, a higher level of working capital also means increases in either or both accounts receivable and inventories levels, and reductions in levels of accounts payable. These result in the requirement for higher levels of short-term financing (for example, overdrafts or short-term loans), which result in higher levels of interest payable. An increase in levels of interest payable results in a reduction in profit after tax (PAT). Therefore, since

$$ROCE = \frac{PAT}{\text{capital employed}}$$

the level of ROCE is reduced as a result of an increase in working capital. Also, since

$$\text{return on equity, ROE} = \frac{PAT}{\text{equity}}$$

then the level of ROE is also reduced as a result of an increase in working capital.

Worked example 10.3

The financial statements for Supportex Ltd shown in Figure 10.2 for years one, two and three are an extract from the five-year plan model in Figure 9.10 in Chapter 9. The

| Figure 10.2 | Supportex working capital 50% of sales revenue |

	A	B	C	D	E
1	**Income statement**	**Year 1**	**Year 2**	**Year 3**	**Assumptions**
2	**Figures in £000s**				
3	Sales revenue	800	960	1,152	20% growth
4	Cost of sales	(500)	(600)	(720)	62.5% of sales revenue
5	Profit before interest and tax	300	360	432	sales revenue less cost of sales
6	Interest	(10)	(10)	(12)	10% of debt at start of year
7	Profit before tax	290	350	420	PBIT less interest
8	Tax	(90)	(109)	(130)	31% of profit before tax
9	Profit for the year	200	241	290	PBT less tax
10	Dividends	(30)	(36)	(43)	15% dividend payout ratio
11	Retained earnings	170	205	247	85% profit retention ratio
12					
13	**Balance sheet**	**End Year 1**	**End Year 2**	**End Year 3**	**Assumptions**
14	**Figures in £000s**				
15	Non-current assets	700	840	1,008	87.5% of sales
16	Working capital	400	480	576	50% of sales
17	Total assets	1,100	1,320	1,584	
18	Debt	(100)	(115)	(132)	
19	Net assets	1,000	1,205	1,452	
20					
21	Equity	1,000	1,205	1,452	
22	ROCE	18.2% (200/1,100)	18.3% (241/1,320)	18.2% (290/1,584)	
23	ROE	20.0% (200/1,000)	20.0% (241/1,205)	20.0% (290/1,452)	

income statement shows sales revenue and costs for each year and the balance sheet shows the financial position of Supportex at the end of each year. The assumptions are stated, which identify the relationships between the numbers. The company's level of working capital is assumed to be 50% of sales revenue. ROCE and ROE are 18.2% and 20.0% respectively.

Let's consider what happens if working capital is reduced to 30% of sales revenue (see Figure 10.3).

In Figure 10.3 we can see the consequences for Supportex Ltd of a reduction in working capital from 50% of sales revenue to 30% of sales revenue. These are summarised in Figure 10.4.

We can see from Figure 10.4 that the reduction in the level of working capital has resulted in an improved cash position for Supportex, enabling it to repay its debt in year

Figure 10.3 Supportex working capital 30% of sales revenue

	A	B	C	D	E
1	**Income statement**	**Year 1**	**Year 2**	**Year 3**	**Assumptions**
2	**Figures in £000s**				
3	Sales revenue	800	960	1,152	20% growth
4	Cost of sales	(500)	(600)	(720)	62.5% of sales revenue
5	Profit before interest and tax	300	360	432	sales revenue less cost of sales
6	Interest	(10)	–	–	10% of debt at start of year
7	Profit before tax	290	360	432	PBIT less interest
8	Tax	(90)	(112)	(134)	31% of profit before tax
9	Profit for the year	200	248	298	PBT less tax
10	Dividends	(30)	(37)	(45)	15% dividend payout ratio
11	Retained earnings	170	211	253	85% profit retention ratio
12					
13	**Balance sheet**	**End Year 1**	**End Year 2**	**End Year 3**	**Assumptions**
14	**Figures in £000s**				
15	Non-current assets	700	840	1,008	87.5% of sales
16	Cash surplus	60	83	111	
17	Working capital	240	288	345	
18	Total assets	1,000	1,211	1,464	30% of sales
19	Debt	–	–	–	
20	Net assets	1,000	1,211	1,464	
21					
22	Equity	1,000	1,211	1,464	
23	ROCE	20.0% (200/1,000)	20.5% (248/1,211)	20.4% (298/1,464)	
24	ROE	20.0% (200/1,000)	20.5% (248/1,211)	20.4% (298/1,464)	

Figure 10.4	Consequences of Supportex's working capital reduction to 30% of sales revenue

	A	B	C	D
1		Year 1	Year 2	Year 3
2	**Figures in £000s**			
3				
4	Working capital has been reduced for each year by	160	192	231
5	Therefore it has been possible to repay the debt of			
6	£100,000 and provide a cash surplus for each year of	60	83	111
7	The profit for Year 1 remains the same, but			
8	for Years 2 and 3 there is no interest and so			
9	Profit before tax is increased to		360	432
10	Tax is increased to		(112)	(134)
11	Profit for the year is increased to		248	298
12	Dividends are increased to		(37)	(45)
13	Retained earnings are increased to		211	253
14	Therefore			
15	Debt has been reduced to zero and			
16	Equity has been increased by retained earnings to		1,211	1,464

one and generate a cash surplus in years one, two and three. (It should be noted that the cash surpluses should strictly speaking be included as part of working capital – they have been separately identified here for illustration purposes.) In practice, the company would invest the cash surpluses either on deposit to earn interest or in new investment projects to earn returns. The benefits of such investments have not been included in this model. Even so, the company is showing increased profitability because of its reduction in interest because of its debt repayment. This is reflected in increased dividends and also in retained earnings, which have consequently increased the total equity of the company.

In this example, because we have not included any returns on investments from the cash surpluses the improvement profitability is small. Nevertheless, as a result of the reduction in working capital from 50% to 30% of sales revenue ROCE and ROE have both increased from 20.0% in year one to 20.4% in year three.

Worked example 10.4

Let's use the same financial statements for Supportex Ltd used in Worked example 10.3 and consider what happens if working capital is increased from 50% to 70% of sales revenue (see Figure 10.5).

In Figure 10.5 we can see the consequences for Supportex Ltd of an increase in working capital from 50% of sales revenue to 70% of sales revenue. These are summarised in Figure 10.6.

We can see from Figure 10.6 that the increase in the level of working capital has resulted in a worsened cash position for Supportex requiring it to increase its debt in years one, two and three. The company is also showing reduced profitability because of its increase in interest resulting from its increase in debt. This is reflected in lower dividends and retained earnings, which have consequently reduced the total equity of the company. As a result of the increase in working capital from 50% to 70% of sales revenue both ROCE and ROE have decreased from 15.9% and 20.0% in year one to 15.2% and 19.3% respectively in year three.

Figure 10.5 Supportex working capital 70% of sales revenue

	A	B	C	D	E
1	**Income statement**	**Year 1**	**Year 2**	**Year 3**	**Assumptions**
2	**Figures in £000s**				
3	Sales revenue	800	960	1,152	20% growth
4	Cost of sales	(500)	(600)	(720)	62.5% of sales revenue
5	Profit before interest and tax	300	360	432	sales revenue less cost of sales
6	Interest	(10)	(26)	(32)	10% of debt at start of year
7	Profit before tax	290	334	400	PBIT less interest
8	Tax	(90)	(103)	(124)	31% of profit before tax
9	Profit for the year	200	231	276	PBT less tax
10	Dividends	(30)	(35)	(41)	15% dividend payout ratio
11	Retained earnings	170	196	235	85% profit retention ratio
12					
13	**Balance sheet**	**End Year 1**	**End Year 2**	**End Year 3**	**Assumptions**
14	**Figures in £000s**				
15	Non-current assets	700	840	1,008	87.5% of sales
16	Working capital	560	672	806	70% of sales
17	Total assets	1,260	1,512	1,814	
18	Debt	(260)	(316)	(383)	
19	Net assets	1,000	1,196	1,431	
20					
21	Equity	1,000	1,196	1,431	
22	ROCE	15.9% (200/1,260)	15.3% (231/1,512)	15.2% (276/1,814)	
23	ROE	20.0% (200/1,000)	19.3% (231/1,196)	19.3% (276/1,431)	

Figure 10.6	Consequences of Supportex's working capital increase to 70% of sales revenue

	A	B	C	D
1		Year 1	Year 2	Year 3
2	**Figures in £000s**			
3				
4	Working capital has been increased for each year by	160	192	230
5	Therefore debt has been increased each year by	160	201	251
6	As a consequence, interest has been increased by		16	20
7	The profit for Year 1 remains the same, but			
8	for Years 2 and 3 because of the increase in interest			
9	Profit before tax is reduced to		334	400
10	Tax is reduced to		(103)	(124)
11	Profit for the year is reduced to		231	276
12	Dividends are reduced to		(35)	(41)
13	Retained earnings are reduced to		196	235
14	Therefore			
15	Debt has been increased and			
16	Equity, because of reduced retained earnings, is		1,196	1,431

Working capital policy

As we saw in Chapter 7, companies should ideally adopt a policy of matching financing with the type of investment being made in new assets and projects. Such a policy finances the long-term investment in non-current assets with long-term funding such as loans, bonds, equity, and retained earnings. The financing of its investment in operations, its short-term working capital requirement (WCR), offers a number of options to a company. Choices may be made between internal and external finance. The external financing of the WCR is usually provided by bank overdraft. This is because of its flexibility in accommodating the fluctuating nature of net current assets. However, this incurs a relatively high cost – short-term interest rates are normally higher than long-term interest rates.

The servicing costs of bank overdrafts, and other short-term funding, are not insignificant and so it is of obvious benefit for companies to maintain their overdraft facility requirements at minimum levels. Such requirements may be reduced by the adoption of appropriate policies with regard to the level of investment in working capital that a company chooses to operate.

The working capital policy adopted will be dependent on individual company objectives that may be influenced by the type of business and the commercial or industrial sector in which it operates. The choice of policy inevitably presents a conflict between the goals of profitability and liquidity, and there is a range of working capital policies that may be chosen that lie somewhere between the following two approaches:

- aggressive
- conservative.

If the company adopts an aggressive working capital policy then for a given level of activity it will aim to operate with low levels of inventories and cash. This type of policy is adopted in order to increase profitability. However, it is a high-risk strategy that provides little flexibility for the company, and may result in:

- an inability to meet customer demand because of stock-outs
- poor customer relationships or loss of customers because of tight credit terms
- an inability to meet current commitments or pay suppliers because of cash shortages, and therefore a danger of interrupted supply of materials or services.

If the company adopts a conservative working capital policy then for a given level of activity it will aim to operate with higher levels of inventories and cash. This type of policy is adopted in order to increase liquidity. It is a policy that provides greater flexibility, but its higher levels of inventories and cash will result in reduced profitability because of:

- the high costs of holding inventories (see the later section about inventory management)
- extended credit terms, meaning that cash is received from customers later and therefore has to be funded by short-term overdraft, which incurs high interest costs
- the opportunity cost of holding cash, which is the return that could otherwise have been earned from investment in profitable projects (which may be mitigated to some extent with interest earned from short-term lending of cash surplus to immediate requirements).

A conservative working capital policy presents lower levels of risk for the company because of:

- customer demand being easier to meet with less likelihood of stock-outs
- good customer relationships and customer retention because of favourable credit terms
- the ability to meet current commitments and pay suppliers and therefore avoiding interrupted supply of materials or services.

Any working capital policy adopted that lies between the two extremes of conservative and aggressive may be tailored to suit the requirements of the business and its particular market. A company cannot determine the 'right' working capital policy with absolute precision. However, it may benchmark similar companies in its particular industrial sector.

For example, companies like automotive manufacturers, house builders (Taylor Wimpey plc), and retailers of fashion items and non-perishable goods will inevitably need to hold relatively high levels of materials, work in progress and finished products, and will therefore have relatively higher levels of working capital (see Figure 10.7). On the other hand, companies like supermarkets, food companies, and retailers of fast-moving and perishable goods will have a much higher turnover of inventories and therefore lower levels of working capital. Additionally, supermarkets have only cash customers and therefore zero trade receivables, and are also able to extend their credit with suppliers, and so their working capital tends to be extremely low or negative, or even highly negative (Morrison Supermarkets plc). Somewhere between these extremes are companies like Croda International plc, a manufacturer of speciality and industrial chemical used in cosmetics, food supplements, plastic bags, and motor vehicles.

Figure 10.7	Illustrations of the range of working capital ratios in the construction, chemical, and supermarket industrial sectors

	2011 £m	2010 £m
Taylor Wimpey plc		
Revenue	1,808	1,768
Working capital	2,073 (114.7% of revenue)	2,668 (150.9% of revenue)
Croda International plc		
Revenue	1,068	1,002
Working capital	155 (14.5% of revenue)	160 (16.0% of revenue)
Morrison Supermarkets plc		
Revenue	16,479	15,410
Working capital	−948 (−5.6% of revenue)	−1,060 (−6.9% of revenue)

Working capital is the 'lubricant' of the investment in a company's operations, enabling the 'engine' of the business, its investment in non-current assets, to be most effectively exploited. An under-utilisation of non-current assets can result in higher inventory levels, which increase the working capital requirement and therefore the requirement for additional short-term financing and its associated costs. Reductions in levels of the WCR reduce the requirement for financing and its associated costs. Maintenance of optimal, and therefore more manageable levels of the WCR increase levels of **efficiency** and **effectiveness** and, as we have seen above, additionally contribute to increased profitability and a reduction in the requirement for external financing.

Regardless of the policies adopted, the improved management of working capital may have a significant impact on the level of requirement for external and internal financing. Good management of their working capital requirement by companies can therefore be seen to be crucially important to both their short- and long-term success.

Progress check 10.5

Why is the good management of the working capital requirement (WCR) crucial to company success?

Inventories management

A lean enterprise uses less of everything to provide more, which results from the control and elimination of waste in all its forms. The Japanese quality guru Taiichi Ohno (Ohno, T (1988) *The Toyota Production System*, Portland, Oregon, USA: Productivity Press) identified seven main areas of waste (called *muda* by Ohno), which relate to inventories to a large extent in terms of their handling, their movement and their storage, in addition to the levels held and the proportion of defective and obsolete inventories. These areas of waste emphasise the importance for companies to identify and take the appropriate action for improvement in this aspect of the management of working capital.

Overproduction

Overproduction is the most serious area of waste, which discourages the smooth flow of goods and services and inhibits quality, productivity, and communication, and causes increases in inventories and

- leads to excessive lead and storage times
- leads to a lack of early detection of defects
- results in product deterioration
- creates artificial work rate pressures
- causes excessive work in progress
- leads to dislocation of operations and poorer communications
- encourages the push of unwanted goods through the system, for example, through the use of bonus systems.

Pull systems and **kanban** provide opportunities to overcome overproduction.

Waiting

Waiting waste occurs when there is no moving or work taking place and

- affects materials, products, and people
- should be used for training, maintenance or **kaizen** but not overproduction.

Transportation

Transportation waste is incurred from unnecessary movement and double-handling and

- may result in damage and deterioration – for example, in 1999 and 2000 the UK car manufacturers Rover and Vauxhall found themselves with unsold or excess inventories of vehicles being stored for too long in the open air, and were then forced to cut back production because of storage and damage problems
- increased distance means slower communication or feedback of poor quality, therefore slower corrective action.

Inappropriate processing

Inappropriate processing waste often results from complex solutions to simple procedures, such as

- the use of large inflexible machines instead of small flexible ones, which encourages overproduction to recoup the investment in them
- poor layout leading to excessive transportation and poor communications – the ideal is to use the smallest machine for the required quality located next to the preceding and succeeding operations
- the lack of sufficient safeguards, for example, **poka yoke** and **jidoka**, leading to poor quality.

Unnecessary inventories

The holding of unnecessary inventories is a waste that leads to increased lead times, the need for more space, and therefore higher storage costs and

- prevents rapid identification of problems
- discourages communication,

which all lead to hidden problems that can be identified only by reducing inventories.

Unnecessary motion

 Unnecessary motion waste refers to the importance of **ergonomics** for quality and productivity.

Quality and productivity are ultimately affected by operators stretching unnecessarily, bending, and picking up, leading to undue exertion and tiredness.

Product defects

Product defects waste is a direct money cost and provides an opportunity to improve performance. It is an area that is therefore a target for immediate *kaizen* activity. An example of the significant and widespread impact of overproduction resulting in excessive inventories can be seen from the General Motors press extract below. Its immediate effect is to increase the length of the operating cycle and in manufacturing companies results in further production being curtailed or even stopped. The further effect of high inventory levels is the downward impact on profit from the cost of increased waste in the ways we have examined above.

The problem of too much inventory

General Motors has suspended production of its electric Chevrolet Volt for five weeks to work off a backlog of vehicles created by disappointing sales. About 1,300 workers from the Volt plant in Detroit will be sent home on paid leave while production is halted, from late March to late April.

Volt sales, which had already been falling short of GM's hopes, dropped sharply in January following a wave of negative publicity when US regulators found the cars' battery packs had caught fire in three separate test crashes. The Volt has now been modified with additional shielding around the battery to protect it in side-impact collisions. After peaking at 1,529 in December, Volt sales dropped to 603 in January, recovering only to 1,023 in January. GM said there were about 3,600 Volts on dealers' forecourts – more than three months of demand at February's rate of sales – plus more in transit, and it wanted to halt production to work off the excess inventory.

In 2010, GM had an objective of making 45,000 Volts in 2012 – an average of 3,750 per month – but now says it is not setting a target. The company said: 'We continue to advertise and market the Volt. We are just going to concentrate on creating demand for a revolutionary vehicle, and will build accordingly.'

GM hopes that economic recovery, the rising price of petrol, and recent support from California, where some Volts with lone drivers will be allowed in carpool lanes, will boost sales.

The result of General Motors' overestimation of demand for the all-electric Chevrolet Volt in early 2012 led to temporary cessation of production. This was a public relations disaster for GM. Research suggested that since the US Government had subsidised the company by about US$3bn, it was costing US$250,000 of taxpayers' money for every Volt sold. The impact on GM in terms of share price and future subsidies is possibly appreciable.

Inventory levels should be optimised so that neither too little is held to meet orders nor too much is held so that waste occurs. The forecasting of inventory requirements must be a part of the management process. In addition, inventory level optimisation requires the following:

- establishment of robust inventories purchase procedures
- appropriate location and storage of inventories
- accurate and timely systems for the recording, control and physical checks of inventories
- monitoring of inventory turnover performance
- implementation of effective inventories management and reorder systems.

Progress check 10.6

Briefly explain how **electronic point of sales (EPOS)** provides a system of monitoring inventory turnover performance.

Inventory purchase

For cash flow (and operational efficiency) purposes it is crucial that efficient and effective sales order, materials procurement and inventory control systems are in place and operated by highly trained staff. Authority levels for the appropriate purchasing and logistics managers must be established for both price and quantities, for initial orders and reorders.

Inventory location

A variety of options exist for the location of inventories and the ways in which they may be stored. Related items of inventories may be grouped together, or they may be located by part number, or by frequency of pick, or located based on their size or weight.

Inventory recording and physical checks

Ideally, all inventory transactions should be recorded simultaneously with their physical movement. Inventory turnover must be regularly reviewed so that damaged, obsolete and slow-moving inventory may be disposed of, possibly at discounted sales prices or for some scrap value.

In cash terms, holding on to unsaleable inventories is a 'waste' of the highest order. It uses up valuable space and time and needs people to manage it. It clogs up the system and reduces efficient order fulfilment and represents money tied up in assets of little or no value. Businesses need to move on and dispose of old, obsolete and slow-moving inventories.

Progress check 10.7

What are the ways in which improvements in a company's management of inventories may contribute to achievement of optimisation of its level of working capital requirement (WCR)?

It is inevitable that inventories will be required to be physically counted from time to time, to provide a check against inventory records. This may be by way of a complete physical count two or three times a year, with one count taking place at the end of the company's financial year. Alternatively, physical **cycle counts** may take place continuously throughout the year. This system selects groups of inventories to be counted and checked with inventory records in such a way that all inventories are checked two, three, four or more times up to maybe 12 times a year, dependent on such criteria as value or frequency of usage.

Inventory ratios

You may refer to the section in Chapter 8 about efficiency ratios that includes inventory turnover ratios to monitor inventories levels. Inventories days (or inventory turnover) is the number of days that inventories could last at a forecast usage rate or the most recent usage rate. This may be applied to total inventories, or individually, for example, to finished goods, raw materials, or work in progress. Financial analysts usually only have access to published accounts and so they often calculate the inventory days or weeks ratios using the total closing inventories value in relation to the cost of sales for the year.

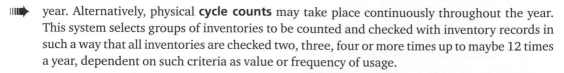

Worked example 10.5

From Flatco plc's balance sheet and income statement for 2012 and the comparatives for 2011 (see Figures 8.3 and 8.4 in Chapter 8), we may calculate the inventories days (inventory turnover) for 2012 and 2011.

$$\text{inventories days 2012} = \frac{\text{inventories value}}{\text{average daily cost of sales in period}} = \frac{£311}{£2,500/365}$$

$$= 45 \text{ days (6.4 weeks)}$$

$$\text{inventories days 2011} = \frac{£268}{£2,400/365} = 41 \text{ days (5.9 weeks)}$$

The performance for 2011, 2012 and future years may be more clearly presented in a trend analysis. If 2011 was the first year in the series, then 41 days may be expressed as the base of 100. The 45 days for the year 2012 is then expressed as 110 [45 × 100/41], and so on for subsequent years. Comparison of 110 with 100 more clearly shows its significance than the presentation of the absolute numbers 45 and 41.

ABC and VIN analysis

The appropriate level of control of inventories may be determined through assessment of the costs of control against the accuracy required and the potential benefits. Use of a **Pareto analysis** (80/20 analysis) allows selective levels of control of inventories through their categorisation into A items, B items and C items. The ABC method uses Pareto to multiply the usage of each inventory item by its value, ranking from the highest to the lowest and then calculating the cumulative result at each level in the ranking.

A items, for example, may be chosen so that the top five inventory items make up 60% of the total value. Such items would then be continuously monitored for unit-by-unit replenishment. B items, for example, may be chosen from say 60% to 80% of the total value. Such items would be subject to automated systematic control using cycle counts, with levels of inventories replenished using economic order quantities (see below). C items, for example, may be identified as the 20% of inventories remaining – 'the trivial many' in financial terms. These inventories may be checked by sample counting; because of their low value, more than adequate levels may be held.

Other important factors impact on the choice of inventory levels. Total acquisition costs must be considered rather than simply the unit purchase price. There may be requirements to provide items of inventory using a just in time approach (see the section dealing with JIT later in this chapter). The cost of not having a particular item in inventory, even though it may itself have a low cost, may be significant if it is an integral part within a process. Consequently, in addition to ABC categories, inventories are usually allocated vital/important/nice to have (VIN) categories, indicating whether they are:

- vital (V) – out of inventory would be a disaster
- important (I) – out of inventory would give significant operational problems or costs
- nice to have (N) – out of inventory would present only an insignificant problem.

Progress check 10.8

Describe how inventory turnover may be regularly monitored.

Economic order quantity (EOQ)

A simplistic model called the **economic order quantity (EOQ)** model, aims to reconcile the problem of the possible loss to a business through interruption of production, or failure to meet orders, with the cost of holding inventories levels large enough to give security against such loss. EOQ may be defined as the most economic inventory replenishment order size that minimises the sum of inventory ordering costs and inventory holding costs. EOQ is used in an optimising inventory control system.

If

P = the £ cost per purchase order

Q = order quantity of each order in units

N = annual units usage

S = annual £ cost of holding one unit

then

> the annual cost of purchasing
> = cost per purchase order $\times$ the number of orders to be placed in a year
> (which is the annual usage divided by quantity ordered per purchase)

or

$$P \times N/Q$$

or

$$PN/Q$$

> annual cost of holding inventory
> = annual cost of holding one unit in inventory $\times$ average number of units held in inventory
> = $0.5Q \times S$ or $QS/2$

The minimum total cost occurs when the annual purchasing cost equals the annual holding cost, or

$$PN/Q = QS/2$$

Cross-multiplication gives

$$2PN = Q^2/S$$

or

$$Q^2 = 2PN/S$$

Therefore when the quantity ordered is the economic order quantity:

$$EOQ = \sqrt{2PN/S}$$

Let's look at a simple example.

Worked example 10.6

E.C.O. Nomic & Sons, the greengrocers, buy cases of potatoes at £20 per case.

£ cost of one purchase order	P = £5 per order
Number of cases turned over in a year	N = 1,000 cases (units)
Annual £ cost of holding one case	S = 20% of purchase price

What is the economic order quantity?

The economic order quantity

$$EOQ = \sqrt{2PN/S} = \sqrt{2 \times 5 \times 1,000/4}$$
$$EOQ = \sqrt{2,500}$$
$$EOQ = 50 \text{ cases of potatoes per order}$$

EOQ illustrates the principle of inventory ordering and inventory holding optimisation but it is extremely limited. In practice, significant divergences from the EOQ may result in only minor cost increases:

- the optimum order quantity decision may more usually be dependent on other factors like storage space, storage facilities, purchasing department resources, logistical efficiency, etc.
- costs of purchasing and holding inventories may be difficult to quantify accurately so the resultant EOQ calculation may be inaccurate
- in periods of changing prices, interest rates, foreign currency exchange rates, etc., continual recalculation is required that necessitates constant updates of all purchasing department and warehouse records of purchases and inventories – computerised systems can assist in

providing the answers to some of the financial 'what-ifs' presented by changes in the business environment.

Outline the basic conflict that might arise between the marketing department and the finance department when discussing the practical application of an economic order quantity (EOQ) system.

The emphasis over the past three decades on inventory minimisation or inventory elimination systems through the implementation of, for example, JIT, *kanban*, and vendor managed inventory (VMI) has reinforced the disadvantages of holding large inventories. High inventory levels reduce the risk of disappointing customers, but it is a costly process, not only in the inherent cost of the inventory itself but in the cost resulting from the wastes identified by Ohno that we discussed earlier in this chapter.

Just in time (JIT), materials requirement planning (MRP), and optimised production technology (OPT)

Just in time (JIT)

Just in time (JIT) is sometimes incorrectly referred to as an inventory reduction or a zero inventory system. JIT is a philosophy that is a response to two key factors: the reduction in product life cycles and the increase in levels of quality required from demanding customers.

JIT is a management philosophy that incorporates a 'pull' system of producing or purchasing components and products in response to customer demand. In a JIT system products are pulled through the system from customer demand back down through the supply chain to the level of materials and components. The consumer buys, and the processes manufacture the products to meet this demand. The consumer therefore determines the schedule.

The JIT system contrasts with a 'push' system where levels of buffer inventories are built up between each process within and between purchasing, manufacturing, and sales. In a push system, products are produced to schedule, and the schedule may be based on:

■ a 'best guess' of demand
■ last year's sales
■ intuition.

Some of the key principles and techniques of waste elimination, which in turn support improved inventory management, are embraced within the implementation of the JIT process:

■ total quality control (TQC), which embraces a culture of waste elimination and 'right first time'
■ *kanban* which is a system of signals used to control inventories levels and smooth the rate of production, for example using cards to prompt top-up of materials or components driven by demand from the next process

- set-up time reduction for reduced manufacturing batch sizes
- *heijunka*, which is the smoothing of production through levelling of day-to-day variations in schedules in line with longer-term demand
- *jidoka*, or autonomation, where operators are empowered to stop the line if a quality problem arises, avoiding poor-quality production and demanding immediate resolution of the problem
- improved production layout
- *poka yoke* (mistake-proofing) fail-safe devices, supporting *jidoka* by preventing parts being fitted in the wrong way, so that poor quality is not passed to the next stage in the production process
- employee involvement including self-quality and operator first-line maintenance
- multi-skilling of employees for increased flexibility
- supplier development for higher quality and greater reliability of supply – in the UK, M&S, for example, has publicised its adoption of this practice.

Two other approaches to inventory management:

- **materials requirement planning (MRP or MRPI)**, its development into **manufacturing resource planning (MRPII)** ,

and

- **optimised production technology (OPT)**

are sometimes seen as alternatives to JIT, but in fact may be used to complement JIT systems.

> ### Progress check 10.10
>
> Explain briefly what benefits might be gained by both supplier (manufacturer) and customer (national retailer) if they work jointly on optimisation of inventories levels and higher quality levels.

Materials requirement planning (MRP)

MRP is a set of techniques, which uses the bill of materials (BOM), inventory data and the **master production schedule** to calculate future requirements for materials. It essentially makes recommendations to release material to the production system. MRP is a 'push' approach that starts with forecasts of customer demand and then calculates and reconciles materials requirements using basic mathematics. MRP relies on accurate BOMs and scheduling **algorithms**, EOQ analyses and allowances for wastage and shrinkage.

Optimised production technology (OPT)

OPT is a philosophy, combined with a computerised system of shop-floor scheduling and capacity planning, that differs from a traditional approach of balancing capacity as near to 100% as possible and then maintaining flow. It aims to balance flow rather than capacity. Like JIT, it aims at improvement of the production process and is a philosophy that focuses on factors such as:

- manufacture to order
- quality

- lead times
- batch sizes
- set-up times,

and has important implications for purchasing efficiency, inventory control, and resource allocation.

OPT is based on the concept of **throughput accounting (TA)**, developed by Eli Goldratt and vividly portrayed in his book (Goldratt, E (1984) *The Goal*, Aldershot, UK: Gower). The aim of OPT is to make money, defined in terms of three criteria: throughput (which it aims to increase), and inventory and operating expense, which should at the same time both be reduced. It does this by making better use of limited capacity through tightly controlled finite scheduling of bottleneck operations, and use of increased process batch sizes, which means producing more of a high-priority part once it has been set up on a bottleneck machine.

Progress check 10.11

In the UK there are several low-volume car manufacturers, for example the Morgan Motor Company of Malvern and Ascari Motor Company of Crewkerne. How would you relate the optimised production technology (OPT) philosophy to their operations?

Factory scheduling is at the root of OPT and the critical factor in OPT scheduling is identification and elimination or management of bottlenecks. OPT highlights the slowest function. This is crucially important in OPT: if one machine is slowing down the whole line then the value of that machine at that time is equivalent to the value of the whole production line. Conversely, attention paid to improving the productivity of a non-bottleneck machine will merely increase inventories.

Progress check 10.12

What are some of the systems and techniques that may be used to optimise the levels of inventories held by a manufacturing company?

Trade receivables and credit management

All companies that sell on credit to their customers should maintain some sort of system of credit control. Improved collections from customers is invariably an area that produces significant, immediate cash flow benefits from the reduction of trade receivable balances. It is therefore an area to which time and resources may be profitably devoted.

Cash flow is greatly affected by the policies established by a company with regard to the:

- choice of customers
- way in which sales are made
- sales invoicing system
- speedy correction of errors and resolution of disputes
- means of settlement
- monitoring of customer settlement performance
- overdue accounts collection system.

These are all areas that can delay the important objective of turning a sale into an account receivable and an account receivable into cash in the shortest possible time. Each area of policy involves a cost. Such costs must be weighed against the levels of risk being taken.

Customers and trading terms

Salespersons are enthusiastic to make sales. It is important that they are also aware of the need to assess customer risk of the likelihood of slow payment or non-payment. If risks are to be taken then this must be with prior approval of the company and with an estimate of the cost of the risk included within the selling price. Similar limits and authorisations must be in place to cover credit periods, sales discounts, and the issue of credit notes.

Credit checks should always be made prior to allowing any level of credit to a potential new customer. Selling on credit with little hope of collection is a way of running out of cash very quickly and invariably resulting in business failure. The procedure for opening a new account must be a formal process that shows the potential customer that it is something that the organisation takes seriously. Many risky customers may thus be avoided.

Before it is agreed to open a new customer account, at least three references should be obtained: one from the customer's bank and two from high-profile suppliers with whom the customer regularly does business. It is important that references are followed up in writing with requests as to whether there are any reasons why credit should not be granted. A credit limit should be agreed that represents minimum risk, but at a level that the customer can service. It should also be at a level within which the customer's business may operate effectively.

A copy of the latest annual and interim accounts of a potential customer should be requested from the Registrar of Companies. These will indicate the legal status of the company, who the owners are, and its financial strength. These accounts are by their nature historical. If large volumes of business are envisaged then details of future operations and funding may need to be discussed in more detail with the potential customer. If such large contracts involve special purchases then advance payments should be requested to reduce any element of risk.

Having established relationships with creditworthy customers a number of steps may be taken to further minimise risk associated with ongoing trading:

- sale of goods with reservation of title (**Romalpa clause**) – the goods remain in the ownership of the selling company until they are paid for, and may be recovered should the customer go into liquidation
- credit insurance cover in respect of customers going into liquidation and export risk
- passing of invoices to a factoring company for settlement; the factoring company settles the invoices, less a fee for the service, which therefore provides a type of insurance cover against non-payment – a factoring company can be used as a source of finance, enabling short-term funds to be raised on the value of invoices issued to customers.

The measures adopted should be even more rigorous in their application to the supply of goods or services to businesses abroad. This is because of the inevitable distance, different trading conditions, regulations, currencies, and legislation.

Progress check 10.13

What are the ways in which improvements in the management of trade receivables and credit management may contribute to achievement of optimal levels of working capital requirement (WCR)?

Settlement methods

Payment collection methods should be agreed with all customers at the outset. The use of cheques, though still popular, is becoming a costly and ineffective collection method. Cash, credit card receipts and automated electronic transfers are the main methods used by retailers and regular speedy banking is the cornerstone of efficient use of funds. Bankers' drafts are the next best thing to cash but should be avoided because of the risk involved through their potential for accidental or fraudulent loss. Electronic mail transfers are frequently used for settlement by overseas companies. These tend to be costly and have been known to 'get lost' in the banking systems. **Letters of credit** together with sight drafts are frequently used for payments against large contracts.

Extreme care needs to be taken with letters of credit, which are a minefield of potential problems for non-settlement. Letters of credit must be completed providing full details and with the requisite numbers of copies of all supporting documentation. The conditions stipulated must be fully complied with and particularly regarding delivery of goods at the right time at the right location and in the quantity, quality and condition specified.

The use of electronic collection methods continues to increase on a massive scale. Direct debit payments are an option where settlement may be made on presentation of agreed sales invoices to the bank. Personal banking via the Internet has grown significantly. As its use and level of sophistication continues to be developed, corporate banking transactions conducted through the Internet are inevitably taking the place of paper transactions. Absolute control is required over both receivables and payables transactions, and all businesses benefit from the strict adherence to administrative routines by the employees involved. Successful control of cash and cheques requires well-thought-out procedures. Examples may be seen in the formal recording that takes place in the systems adopted in high-volume businesses.

One of the most acceptable methods is payment through **BACS (bankers' automated clearing services)**. The BACS method requires customers to register as BACS users and to specify the type of payment pattern they wish to adopt for settlement of their suppliers' accounts or payroll. Every week, or two weeks or every month, companies supply details of payments to be made – names of payees and amounts. These are then settled by BACS exactly on the day specified and with only one payment transaction appearing on the bank statement. This means that the problems of cost of individual cheques and the uncertainty of not knowing when each payment will be cleared are avoided.

Cash sales must be strictly controlled in terms of a log and the issue of receipts. Regular physical counts must be carried out and cash banked twice daily or at least once daily. Cheques may be lost in the mail, or bear wrong dates, or wrong amounts, or the customer may have forgotten to sign. Specific company employees should be nominated to receive and bank cash and cheques. Separate persons should manage accounts receivable in order to maintain internal control.

Sales invoices

The sales invoicing system must ensure that prompt, accurate invoices are submitted to customers for all goods and services that are provided. A control system needs to be implemented to prevent supply without a subsequent sales invoice being issued. An invoicing delay of just one day may result in one month's delay in payment. Incorrect pricing, VAT calculations, invoice totalling, and customer names and addresses may all result in delay. A customer is unlikely to point out an undercharged invoice.

Sales invoices may be routinely followed up with statements of outstanding balances. The credit period offered to customers should obviously be as short as possible. Care should be taken in offering cash discounts for immediate or early payment. This is invariably a disadvantage. Many customers will take the discount but continue to take the extended credit. This is something that may not even be spotted by employees responsible for checking and processing receipts from customers, which effectively results in an unauthorised cost being incurred by the business.

Trade receivables ratios

Please refer to the relevant section in Chapter 8 about efficiency ratios that relates to trade receivables collection days, which is a measure used to monitor customer settlement performance. Collection days indicate the average time taken, in calendar days, to receive payment from credit customers. Adjustment is needed if the ratio is materially distorted by VAT or other taxes.

Worked example 10.7

From the balance sheet and income statement of Flatco plc for 2012, and the comparatives for 2011 (see Figures 8.3 and 8.4 in Chapter 8), we may calculate the collection days for 2012 and the collection days for 2011.

$$\text{collection days 2012} = \frac{\text{trade receivables} \times 365}{\text{sales revenue}} = \frac{\pounds573 \times 365}{\pounds3,500} = 60 \text{ days}$$

$$\text{collection days 2011} = \frac{\pounds517 \times 365}{\pounds3,250} = 58 \text{ days}$$

A similar trend analysis to that described in Worked example 10.5 may be used for greater clarification of performance. If in 2011, 58 days = 100, then the year 2012 collection days would = 103.

Progress check 10.14

Describe how customer settlement performance may be regularly monitored.

Collection policy

As a great many experienced businessmen may confirm, perhaps the key factor underlying sustained, successful collection of customer accounts is identification of 'the person' within the customer organisation who actually makes things happen and who can usually speed up the processing of a payment through the company's systems. Payments are usually authorised by the finance director or managing director or the accountant. However, 'the person' is the one who prepares payments and pushes them under the nose of the appropriate manager for signature. Cultivation of a good relationship with 'the person' within each customer organisation is an investment that usually pays massive dividends.

The benefit of issue of regular monthly statements of account to customers may be questioned. Most companies pay on invoice and so a brief telephone call to confirm that all invoices have been received, to check on the balance being processed for payment, and the payment date, usually results in settlement. Issue of a statement is usually of greater benefit as an *ad hoc* exercise to resolve queries or when large numbers of transactions are involved.

A routine should be established for when settlement of invoices becomes overdue. This process should include having employees who have the specific responsibility for chasing overdue accounts – credit controllers. Chasing overdue accounts by telephone is usually the most effective method. It allows development of good working relationships with customers to enable problems to be quickly resolved and settled.

It is absolutely essential that accurate accounts receivable information is available, up-to-date in terms of inclusion of all invoices that have been issued and allowing for all cash received, before calling a customer to chase payment. It is also imperative that immediately errors are identified, for example errors in invoicing, they are corrected without delay. These are two of the commonest areas used by customers to stall payment and yet the remedy is within the hands of the company!

An indispensable information tool to be used by the credit controller should be an up-to-date **aged accounts receivable report** giving full details of all outstanding invoices (see Figure 10.8). This shows the totals of accounts receivable from all customers at a given date and also an analysis of the outstanding invoices in terms of the time between the date of the report and the dates on which the invoices were issued.

Figure 10.8 Example of an aged accounts receivable report

Hannagan plc
Aged Accounts Receivable as at 30 September 2012

Customer name	total balance	up to 30 days	over 30, up to 60 days	over 60, up to 90 days	over 90 days
	£	£	£	£	£
Alpha Chemicals Ltd	16,827	7,443	8,352	635	397
Brown Manufacturing plc	75,821	23,875	42,398	6,327	3,221
Caramel Ltd	350,797	324,776	23,464	2,145	412
.	.	.	.	.	.
.	.	.	.	.	.
.	.	.	.	.	.
.	.	.	.	.	.
Zeta Ltd	104,112	56,436	43,565	3,654	457
Total	**4,133,714**	**2,354,377**	**1,575,477**	**184,387**	**19,473**
% ageing		**56.96%**	**38.11%**	**4.46%**	**0.47%**

In addition, it is useful to have available the full details of each customer's payment record showing exactly what has been paid and when, going back perhaps one year. To provide a historical analysis and assist in resolving possible customer disputes, computerised systems may hold customer data going back many years, for future retrieval. The friendly agreement of the facts on a customer account on the telephone usually goes a very long way towards obtaining settlement in accordance with agreed terms.

Perhaps one of the most effective methods of extracting payment from a customer with an overdue account is a threat to stop supply of goods or services. If a debt continues to be unpaid then the next step may be a chasing letter that shows that the organisation means business and will be prepared to follow up with legal action. Prior to sending any such letter the facts should be checked and double-checked – people and computers make mistakes! This letter should clearly explain what is expected and what the implications may be for non-compliance with agreed terms. A solicitor's letter should probably not be considered, as a rule of thumb, before an invoice is, say, 90 days overdue from its expected settlement date.

The last resort is to instruct a solicitor to take action against a customer for non-payment. Small debts in the UK may be recovered through the small claims court. The costs are low and the services of a solicitor are not necessarily required. Large debts may be recovered by suing the customer for non-payment. This is an expensive and very time-consuming business. The use of the last resort measures that have been outlined should be kept to a minimum. Their use may be avoided through a great deal of preliminary attention being paid to the recruitment of excellent staff, and the establishment of excellent systems, robust internal controls, and a formal credit control system.

Progress check 10.15

What are some of the ways in which the settlement of accounts receivable from customers may be speeded up?

Trade payables management

The balance sheet category of trade and other payables that are payable within one year comprises taxes, employee taxes, VAT, etc. and accounts payable to suppliers of materials, goods and services provided to the company. Payments to the UK Government are normally required to be made promptly.

Trade payables are sometimes considered a 'free' source of finance because if a company has not paid a supplier then it is able to hold onto and use that cash. However, this really is not the case and unpaid trade payables are not a free way to borrow money. A supplier is likely to charge a higher price for a product if it is paid 90 days after delivery than if it is paid 30 days after delivery. The following worked example illustrates this point.

Worked example 10.8

A supplier may offer Justin Time Ltd payment terms of 90 days from delivery date. If Justin Time Ltd alternatively proposes to the supplier payment terms of 60 days from delivery date the supplier may, for example, offer 1% (or 2%) discount for settlement 30 days earlier.

Annual cost of discount:

$$\text{at 1\% discount} \quad \frac{365 \times 1\%}{30} = 12.2\% \text{ per annum}$$

$$\text{at 2\% discount} \quad \frac{365 \times 2\%}{30} = 24.3\% \text{ per annum}$$

A discount of 1% for settlement one month early is equivalent to over 12% per annum (and a discount of 2% is over 24% per annum). Consequently, it becomes apparent that the supplier's selling price must have included some allowance for financial charges; accounts payable are therefore not a free debt.

Many companies habitually delay payments to suppliers, in order to improve cash flow, either to the point just before relationships break down or until suppliers refuse further supply. Trade payables may be paid more slowly than the agreed terms to gain a short-term cash advantage, but even as a short-term measure this should only be regarded as temporary. It is very short-term thinking and obviously not a strategy that creates an atmosphere conducive to the development of good supplier relationships. A more systematic approach to the whole purchasing and payables system is the more ethical and professional means of providing greater and sustainable benefits. This approach was supported by changes in UK legislation that were introduced during 1999/2000, but despite this the situation in the UK is still unacceptable. This is why, as we saw in Chapter 8, the UK Government announced in 2011 that it would implement the EU Directive on late payments in the first half of 2012.

With regard to suppliers, overall business effectiveness and improved control over cash flow may be better served by establishment of policies, in much the same way as was suggested should apply to customers, with regard to:

- choice of suppliers
- the way in which purchases are made
- the purchase invoicing system
- speedy correction of errors and resolution of disputes
- means of settlement
- the monitoring of supplier payment performance.

Progress check 10.16

Explain whether or not trade payables are a 'free' or even a cheap source of finance for a company, and why.

Suppliers and trading terms

New suppliers should be evaluated perhaps even more rigorously than customers with particular regard to quality of product, quality and reliability of distribution, sustainability of supply, and financial stability. Appropriate controls must be established to give the necessary purchasing authority to only the minimum number of managers. This requires highly skilled buyers who are able to source the right quality product for the job at the best total acquisition price (the base price, allowing for delivery costs, currency risk, etc.), in the delivery quantities and frequencies required and at the best possible terms. Their authority must be accompanied by rules governing:

- which suppliers may be dealt with
- acceptable ranges of product
- purchase volumes
- price negotiation
- discounts
- credit terms
- transaction currencies
- invoicing
- payment methods
- payment terms.

Terms of trading must be in writing. Most companies print their agreed terms on their purchase orders.

Payment methods

Traditional supplier payment methods include:

- cash – very little used now by large businesses, because of its impracticality and issues of security and fraud
- bill of exchange – a negotiable instrument drawn by a supplier on the company, who by accepting (signing) the bill acknowledges the debt, which may be payable immediately (sight draft) or at a future date (time draft), is a method of guaranteed payment and an instrument which may be discounted to raise cash
- cheque – a common form of payment, which is a bill of exchange drawn on a banker and payable on demand
- sight draft – a bill of exchange payable on presentation to a bank.

However, electronic payment methods have now become the most commonly used methods of payment used by companies. Electronic funds transfer (EFT) is a system used by banks and other financial institutions for the movement of funds between accounts and for the provision of information. EFT is an electronic method used by the banks for relatively low-value, high-volume automated payments. An early form of EFT adopted by the UK banking system was BACS (discussed earlier), which has been used by companies for transactions such as payroll and supplier payments. There are significant supply chain benefits of EFT, for example global activity 24 hours a day, 365 days a year, and control over cash flow through being able to determine exactly when payments will be cleared through the banking system. Potential risks arise from the use of EFT if EDI (electronic systems interchange) systems are unable to guarantee the transmission of complete and accurate transmission of data together with verification of its authenticity. It is essential the EFT users ensure appropriate procedures for limiting authorised access to the systems.

Payments to suppliers should be made in line with terms of trading, but advantages may be gained from cheaper payment methods and providing better control than through the issue of cheques. For example, the payables system may automatically prepare weekly payment schedules and trigger automated electronic payments directly through the bank.

Alternatively, submission of correct supplier invoices directly to the company's bank may also be used to support automatic payment in line with agreed terms. Provided that adequate controls are put in place to check and monitor such transactions these methods provide a cost-effective method of controlling cash outflows and may be an invaluable aid to cash planning.

International trade

For international trade there is a range of methods that may be used for international payments that includes:

- payment in advance
- irrevocable letter of credit
- counter-trade
- documentary collection
- open account payment
- payment on consignment,

and each of the payment strategies that may be adopted by companies trading internationally has its own advantages and disadvantages and varying types and level of risk. The decision on which method of payment to use will often depend on a range of interrelated issues, for example:

- perceived risk associated with the transaction
- terms generally on offer within the marketplace for similar products and services
- terms offered by competitors
- requirements of the supplier.

Payment in advance

With payment in advance, payment is expected by the supplier in full before goods are shipped. This method is normally used where a supplier has serious doubts about the company's ability to pay, or where the supplier's bank will not finance the transaction or extend existing credit arrangements. The advantage of this method of payment is that it eliminates the risk of payment default. However, the disadvantage is it may have a negative impact on the overall demand for a company's goods or services, especially where competitors offer more favourable terms of payment.

Irrevocable letter of credit

An irrevocable letter of credit may be used as an alternative to payment in advance. However, because the associated bank charges of a letter of credit can be high, its use is often restricted to transactions of a substantial nature. A letter of credit is an internationally accepted financial instrument generally issued in the form of an undertaking by the issuing bank (the importer's bank) to an exporter, through an advising bank (normally in the exporter's country). The undertaking is that the issuing bank will pay on presentation of documents, provided that the terms of the credit are strictly complied with. A second assurance of payment (usually by a bank) prevents surprises and means that the issuing bank has been deemed acceptable by the confirming bank.

There are various types of letters of credit of which the confirmed irrevocable credit is the most secure. The advantages of using letters of credit are:

- the contract is with the bank
- the responsibility for ensuring all conditions on both sides are complied with rests with the bank
- they provide a contract of sale during manufacture
- they provide certainty of sale, making the possibility of arranging borrowing easier for the exporter.

A disadvantage of using letters of credit is that they are usually legally and administratively complex. They are also expensive to arrange, which imposes extra cost on the supplier.

Counter-trade

Counter-trade can take many forms, some of the more popular being:

- counter-purchase – an agreement where the exporter undertakes to purchase goods and services from the country concerned (very common in Eastern Europe and developing countries)
- barter or compensation trade – the direct exchange of goods without any exchange of funds
- buy-back – an agreement where the exporter receives payment for the future output of goods or services supplied
- offset – the incorporation of components, materials etc., from the importing country into the exporter's finished product
- switch trading – an agreement where an importer utilises credit surpluses accumulated in another country to finance exports from a third country
- evidence accounts – the exporter maintains accounts which demonstrate matching counter-purchases from a particular market in which it has a continuing involvement.

The relative advantages and disadvantages of counter-trade really depend on the precise nature of the counter-trade agreement.

Documentary collection

Documentary bank collection is less secure than a letter of credit and involves sending shipping documents through the banking system to a bank in the buyer's country. These documents are only released to the buyer upon payment or acceptance of a bill of exchange, depending on the terms agreed in the sales contract.

The advantage of a documentary collection is that it minimises the risk of payment default. However, a disadvantage is that the bank charges for handling a bill of exchange can be fairly high, especially in some EU countries.

Open account payment

This is the international version of most domestic transactions where companies generally offer 30, 60, or 90 days to pay, and invoice the customer accordingly. In an open account arrangement the customer is trusted to ensure payment is made by the agreed method on or before the agreed date. Open account payment should be used only when the supplier is sufficiently confident that the company can be trusted to make full payment by an agreed date, and so the integrity of the company must therefore be beyond question or else the supplier has no security against non-payment.

An advantage of open account payment is that it is simple, and administratively cost-effective to use. The big disadvantage is the high level of trust required between the supplying company and the purchasing company; the risk and therefore cost of payment default can be high.

Payment on consignment

Payment on consignment is in principle the same as payment on open account, but ownership of the goods remains with the supplier until the payment is made. The advantage of consignment payment is that it is often easier to repossess the goods in the event of non-payment.

International trade risk

The risks involved in international trade may be divided into three main types:

- **country risk** (or **political risk**)
- **property risk**
- credit and commercial risk.

Country risk

The country risk, or political risk, associated with international trade can be considerable. While such risks can develop in a number of different ways, they are generally related to government actions and policies that seek to:

- expropriate company assets and profits
- impose foreign exchange currency controls
- impose price intervention policies that discriminate between domestic and non-domestic companies
- impose tax laws that offer preferential treatment to domestic companies
- impose social or work-related regulations that offer preferential treatment of domestic companies
- impose regulations that restrict access to local finance
- restrict the movement of company assets and resources.

The impact of such policies on a company's ability to undertake commercial activities, generate profits, and repatriate or reinvest such profits for future growth can be substantial. Therefore the recognition, assessment, and management of such risk is an important aspect of a company's international trading activities. However, given that international competitive advantage can only be attained by trading off higher levels of risk for higher overall returns, in general, companies tend to adopt management strategies and policies that seek to minimise company risk rather than eliminate it altogether. Such policies include:

- obtaining insurance against the possibility of expropriation of assets
- negotiating overseas government concessions or guarantees to minimise the possibility of creditor default or the expropriation of company assets
- structuring the company's financial and operating policies to ensure they are acceptable to, and consistent with regulatory requirements
- developing close social and political relationships with overseas country institutions
- integrating international production of products to include the overseas country and home country companies to ensure that overseas country companies are dependent on home country companies.

Property risk

Property risk relates to the risks involved in the transit of goods and services and the possibility that, during the transfer, loss or damage may occur before the completion of the sales contract. To minimise such risks it is important that a company involved in international trade should ensure:

- agreed protocols are in place
- agreed procedures and documentation are followed and completed and such trade protocols and procedures may include agreement on the following:
  - responsibility for the transport of the goods and services
  - responsibility for obtaining customs clearance
  - the requirement for insurance
  - the requirement for letters of credit
  - the currency of payment
  - the requirement for documentary evidence of receipt and collection
  - the nature and timing of payment.

There may also be a need to establish the import requirements of a particular country well before date of shipment to ensure the required documentation, for example number of copies of invoices, bills of lading, and certificates of origin. Procedures and documents may include use of the following:

- transport documents, including bills of lading, or airway bills
- commercial documents, including invoices, packing lists, and inspection certificates
- government documents, including certificates of origin, export and import licences, and health certificates.

Credit and commercial risk

Credit and commercial risk relates to the risks associated with payment default by the buyer as a consequence of solvency problems or liquidation. The management of this risk, regardless of whether trade is domestic or international, should always commence at the quotation stage of the trade agreement or contract and continue through to the contract for sale. Such procedures underpin the whole export transaction from receipt of the order to final settlement, and can include the following:

- credit assessment of the buyer prior to agreement to trade
- regular revision of the level of trade contracts with the buyer
- regular updating of credit arrangements.

Companies can also try and minimise credit and commercial risk by insuring against non-payment, or using letters of credit, or bank drafts, to help secure payment for the goods and service supplied.

Purchase invoices

Integrated purchase order, inventory control, and payables systems, preferably computerised, should be used to control approval of new suppliers, trading terms, prices, etc. When supplier invoices are received by the organisation they must match completely with goods or services received and also be matched with an official order. An efficient recording system should allow incorrect deliveries or incorrect invoices to be quickly identified, queried, and rectified. The recording system should verify the credit terms for each invoice.

Progress check 10.17

What are some of the ways in which payments to suppliers may be improved to the mutual benefit of the company and its suppliers?

Trade payables ratios

Please refer to the relevant section in Chapter 8 about efficiency ratios that relates to payables days, which is a measure used to monitor supplier payment performance. Payables days indicate the average time taken, in calendar days, to pay for supplies received on credit. Adjustment is needed if the ratio is materially distorted by VAT, other taxes, or unusual trading terms.

Worked example 10.9

From the balance sheet and income statement for Flatco plc for 2012, and the comparatives for 2011 (see Figures 8.3 and 8.4 in Chapter 8), we may calculate the payables days for 2012 and the payables days for 2011.

$$\text{payables days 2012} = \frac{\text{trade payables}}{\text{cost of sales}} \times 365 = \frac{£553 \times 365}{£2,500} = 81 \text{ days}$$

$$\text{payables days 2011} = \frac{£461 \times 365}{£2,400} = 70 \text{ days}$$

A trend analysis may also be calculated in the same way as discussed in Worked examples 10.5 and 10.7.

Payment policy

The priority for the accounts payable manager must be to maintain the level of payables and cash outflows in line with company policy, but at all times ensuring absolutely no interruption to any manufacturing processes or any other operations of the business. Fundamental to this is the development of good working relationships with suppliers so that problems may be quickly resolved and settled, thus avoiding any threats to supply.

The accounts payable manager must have accurate accounts payable information that is up to date in terms of all invoices received, invoices awaited, and payments made. In the same way that the credit controller deals with customer queries it is also imperative that the accounts payable manager requests corrections of invoice errors, immediately errors are identified. The accounts payable manager should have access to an up-to-date **aged accounts payable report** (see Figure 10.9). This shows the totals of accounts payable to all suppliers at a given date and also an analysis of the balances in terms of the time between the date of the report and the dates of the invoices from suppliers.

Figure 10.9	Example of an aged accounts payable report

Hannagan plc
Aged Accounts Payable as at 31 December 2012

――――――――――――― ageing ―――――――――――――

Supplier name	total balance	up to 30 days	over 30, up to 60 days	over 60, up to 90 days	over 90 days
	£	£	£	£	£
Ark Packaging plc	9,800	4,355	2,555	445	2,435
Beta Plastics plc	45,337	32,535	12,445	144	213
Crown Cases Ltd	233,536	231,213	2,323	.	.
.	.	.	.	.	.
.	.	.	.	.	.
.	.	.	.	.	.
.	.	.	.	.	.
Zonkers Ltd	89,319	23,213	21,332	12,321	32,453
Total	**3,520,811**	**2,132,133**	**1,142,144**	**123,213**	**123,321**
% ageing		**60.56%**	**32.44%**	**3.50%**	**3.50%**

The accounts payable manager should also have available detailed reports of all unpaid invoices on each account, and full details of each supplier's payment record showing exactly what has been paid and when, going back perhaps one year. The availability for use of correct, up-to-date information goes a long way to ensuring the avoidance of the build-up of any potential disputes.

Progress check 10.18

Describe how supplier payment performance may be regularly monitored.

Operating cycle performance

The cash operating cycle, or working capital cycle, which was illustrated in Figure 10.1, is the period of time that elapses between the point at which cash begins to be expended on the production of a product and the collection of cash from the customer. It determines the short-term financing requirements of the business. For a business that purchases and sells on credit the cash operating cycle may be calculated by deducting the average payment period for suppliers from the average inventory turnover period and the average customer settlement period.

operating cycle (days) = inventories days + collection days − payables days

The operating cycle may alternatively be calculated as a percentage:

$$\text{operating cycle } \% = \frac{\text{working capital requirement (inventories } + \text{ trade receivables } - \text{ trade payables)}}{\text{sales revenue}}$$

Worked example 10.10

From the working capital requirement calculated in Worked example 10.2 and the inventories days, receivables days, and payables days calculated in Worked examples 10.5, 10.7, and 10.9, we may calculate the operating cycle in days and % for Flatco plc for 2012 and 2011.

Operating cycle days:

$$\text{operating cycle 2012} = \text{inventories days} + \text{collection days} - \text{payables days}$$
$$= 45 + 60 - 81 = 24 \text{ days}$$
$$\text{operating cycle 2011} = 41 + 58 - 70 = 29 \text{ days}$$

Operating cycle %:

$$\text{operating cycle \% 2012} = \frac{\text{working capital requirement}}{\text{sales revenue}}$$

$$= \frac{(£311 + £573 - £553) \times 100\%}{£3,500} = 9.5\%$$

$$\text{operating cycle \% 2011} = \frac{(£268 + £517 - £461) \times 100\%}{£3,250} = 10.0\%$$

From this example we can see that Flatco plc's operating cycle has improved by five days from 2011 to 2012, an improvement of 0.5%. The deterioration in collection days and inventory turnover in this example has been more than offset by the increase in payables days. Despite the overall improvement, this must be a cause for concern for the company which should therefore set targets for improvement and action plans to reduce its average customer collection period and reduce its number of inventories days.

Overtrading

We have seen just how important its good management of WCR is to a company. Personal judgement is required regarding choice of optimal levels of working capital appropriate to the individual company and its circumstances. This generally leads to the quest for ever-reducing levels of working capital. However, there is a situation called overtrading which occurs if the company tries to support too great a volume of trade from too small a working capital base.

Overtrading occurs when a business enters into commitments in excess of its available short-term resources. This can arise even if the company is trading profitably, and is typically caused by financing strains imposed by a lengthy operating cycle or production cycle. Overtrading is not inevitable. If it does occur then there are several strategies that may be adopted to deal with it, including for example:

- reduction in business activity to consolidate and give some breathing space
- introduction of new equity capital rather than debt, to ease the strain on short-term resources
- drastically improve the management of working capital in the ways which we have outlined.

This chapter has dealt with working capital and the working capital requirement (WCR). We have looked specifically at management of the WCR. The appreciation by managers of how working capital operates, and its effective management, is fundamental to the survival and success of the company. Cash and short-term debt are important parts of working capital, the management of which we shall consider in the section that follows.

Progress check 10.19

How may a company's investment in operations, its operating cycle, be minimised? What are the potential risks to the company in pursuing an objective of minimisation?

Cash improvement techniques

We have already discussed how profit and cash flow do not mean the same thing. Cash flow does not equal profit. However, all elements of profit may have been or will be at some time reflected in cash flow. It is a question of timing and also the quality of each of the components of profit:

- day-to-day expenses are usually immediately reflected in the cash book as an outflow of cash
- non-current assets may have been acquired with an immediate outflow of cash, but the cost of these assets is reflected in the profit and loss account through depreciation which is spread over the life of the assets
- sales of products or services are reflected as sales revenue in the profit and loss account even though cash receipts by way of settlement of sales invoices may not take place for another month or two, or more
- some sales invoices may not be paid at all even though the sales revenue has been recognised and so will subsequently be written off as a bad debts cost in the profit and loss account
- purchases of materials are taken into inventories and are not reflected in the profit and loss account until they are used, and that may be before or some time after cash has been paid to the suppliers of the materials.

Cash flow is therefore importantly linked to business performance, or profit, which may fluctuate from period to period. There is also a significant impact from non-profit items, which may have a more permanent effect on cash resources.

The non-profit and loss account items that affect short-term and long-term cash flow may be identified within each of the areas of the balance sheet (see Figure 10.10). The short-term cash position of a business can be improved by:

- reducing current assets
- increasing current liabilities.

The long-term cash position of a business can be improved by:

- increasing equity
- increasing non-current liabilities
- reducing the net outflow on non-current assets.

We shall consider each of these actions for improvement in the cash position of the business.

Progress check 10.20

Profit and cash do not always mean the same thing. Why is operating profit different from operating cash flow?

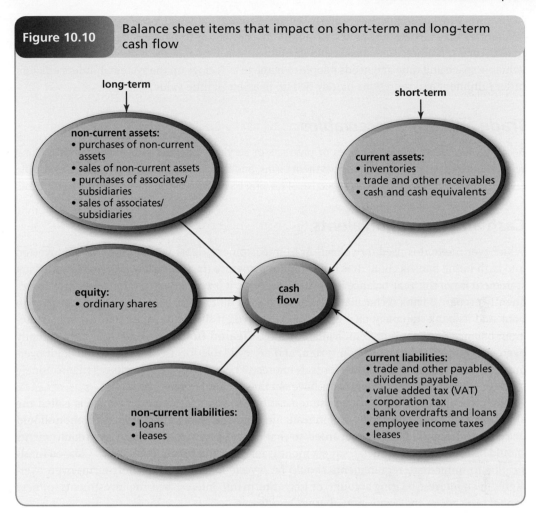

Figure 10.10 Balance sheet items that impact on short-term and long-term cash flow

Short-term cash flow improvement

Inventories levels

Inventories levels should be optimised so that neither too little is held to meet production schedules and sales orders, nor too much is held so that waste occurs. It is a fine balance that requires planning, control, and honesty. Many companies either hide or are prepared to turn a blind eye to inventory errors, over-ordering or over-stocking because managers do not like to admit their mistakes, and in any case the higher the inventory then the higher the reported profit!

For cash flow (and operational efficiency) purposes it is crucial to put in place:

- efficient sales order systems
- materials procurement systems
- inventory control systems,

operated by highly trained employees.

Inventory turnover must be regularly reviewed so that damaged, obsolete and slow-moving inventories may be disposed of at discounted sales prices or for some scrap value if possible. In cash terms, holding on to unsaleable inventories is a 'waste' of the highest order. It uses up valuable space and time and needs people to manage it. It clogs up the system, hinders efficient order fulfilment and represents money tied up in assets of little value.

Trade and other receivables

Accounts receivable arise from sales of products or services. The methods employed in making sales, the sales invoicing system, the payment terms, and the cash collection system, are all possible areas that can delay the important objective of turning a sale into cash in the shortest possible time.

Cash and cash equivalents

Whichever method is used for collection from customers, debts will ultimately be converted into cash in the bank account. It is important to recognise that the balance shown on the bank statement is not the 'real' balance in the bank account. It is very important for a company to frequently prepare a bank reconciliation that details the differences between the company's cash book and its bank statement on a given date. However, it should be noted that the bank statement balance does not represent available funds. **Cleared funds** are funds that have actually been cleared through the banking system and are available for use. It is this balance, if overdrawn, which is used to calculate overdraft interest. There are software packages that routinely monitor bank charges and many users have obtained refunds from their banks.

The difference between the bank statement balance and the cleared balance is called the 'float' and this can very often be a significant amount. The cleared balance information should be received from the bank and recorded so that it can be monitored daily. Cash requirements should be forecast in some detail say six months forward and regularly updated. Cleared funds surplus to immediate requirements should be invested. This may be short-term, even overnight, in an interest-bearing account, or longer-term into interest-bearing investments, or new capital projects, or the acquisition of other businesses.

Trade and other payables

Ordering anything from a third party by any individual within the organisation is a commitment to cash leaking out at some time in the future. Tight controls must be in place to give such authority to only the absolute minimum of employees. This authority must be accompanied by rules governing:

- which suppliers may be dealt with
- acceptable ranges of product
- purchase volumes
- price negotiation
- discounts
- credit terms
- transaction currencies
- invoicing
- payment methods
- payment terms.

A tightly controlled and computerised system of:

- integrated purchase order
- inventory control
- payables,

must also include countersigned approval of, for example:

- new suppliers
- terms
- price ranges.

When supplier invoices are received by the organisation they must match absolutely with goods or services received and be matched with an official order. The recording system should verify the credit terms for each invoice. If payments are made by cheque, then the cheques should always bear two signatures as part of the company's control system.

Cash improvements may be gained from the purchasing and accounts payables system in a number of ways. The starting point must be a highly skilled buyer or buyers who are able to source the right quality product for the job at the best total acquisition price (base price plus delivery costs plus allowance for currency risk, for example), in the delivery quantities and frequencies required and at the best possible terms.

Further gains may be achieved from efficient recording systems that allow incorrect deliveries or incorrect invoices to be quickly identified, queried, and rectified. Payments should be made in line with terms but advantages may be gained from less costly payment methods and better control than the issue of cheques. For example, the payables system may automatically prepare weekly payment schedules and trigger automated electronic payments directly through the bank.

Alternatively, submission of correct supplier invoices directly to the company's bank may also be used to support automatic payment in line with agreed terms. Provided that adequate controls are put in place to check and monitor such transactions they provide a cost-effective method of controlling cash outflows and cash planning.

Bank overdrafts and loans

If a bank overdraft facility is required by a company, then the lowest possible interest rate should be negotiated. As with the purchase of any service, it pays to shop around to obtain the best deal. Bank interest charges should be checked in detail and challenged if they look incorrect – all banks make mistakes. Computer software packages are available to routinely monitor bank charges.

A bank statement should be received routinely by the company weekly, or daily, and should always be thoroughly checked. A detailed monthly schedule of bank charges should be requested from the bank and checked very carefully. These charges should be strictly in line with the tariff of charges agreed at the outset with the bank. In the same way as interest charges, bank charges should be challenged if they look incorrect.

At all times minimisation of both bank interest and bank charges must be a priority. This can be achieved by cash flow planning and optimisation of the methods of receipts into and payments out of the bank account. If several bank accounts are held they should be seriously reviewed and closed unless they are really essential and add value to the business.

Corporation tax

Taxation on corporate profit is a complicated and constantly changing area. Tax experts may be engaged to identify the most tax-efficient ways of running a business. At the end of the day, if a business is making profits then tax will become payable. Obvious cash gains may be made from knowing when the tax payment dates are and ensuring they are adhered to. Penalties and interest charges for late and non-payment are something to avoid.

Value added tax (VAT)

Value added tax (VAT) is probably an area that is even more complicated than corporate taxation. VAT does not impact on the profit of the business. Businesses are unpaid collectors of VAT. If a business is registered for VAT (currently mandatory for businesses with sales revenue of £77,000 or more) it is required to charge VAT at the appropriate rate on all goods and services that are vatable. Accurate records must be maintained to account for all such VAT. Such VAT output tax, as it is called, must be paid over to HMRC every three months or every month, whichever has been agreed.

VAT charged by suppliers, or input tax, may be offset against output tax so that the net is paid over monthly or quarterly. If input tax exceeds output tax, the VAT is refunded by HMRC. It is important to note that VAT offices look very carefully at trends on VAT returns. A return that is materially different to the trend will usually result in a visit from a VAT inspector who will carry out an extremely rigorous audit of all accounting records.

It may benefit an organisation to choose to account either monthly or quarterly for VAT. In the same way as for corporate taxation, great care must be taken to submit correct VAT returns, and pay VAT on the correct date to avoid any penalties or interest charges.

Employee income taxes

In the UK, taxes are collected by companies and paid to the Government on behalf of employees. Such taxes include Pay As You Earn (PAYE) taxation and National Insurance (NI) contributions, which must be deducted at source by UK companies from payments to employees. Salaries net of PAYE and NI are paid to employees, and the PAYE and NI and a further contribution for employer's NI are then paid to HMRC. Employees may be paid weekly or monthly and then PAYE and NI are paid over to the HMRC on a fixed date of the following month. In exceptional circumstances HMRC may allow an odd day's delay. However, as with all other taxes, payment on the due date without fail is the best advice to avoid unnecessary outflows of cash in penalties and interest for non-compliance.

Dividends payable

Dividends are payable to shareholders by companies as a share of the profits. They are not a cost nor a charge against profits but are a distribution of profits. There are some factors for consideration regarding cash flow. The timing of dividend payments is within the control of the company. Dividends may therefore be paid on dates that are most convenient in terms of cash flow and it is important to remember to include these in cash planning.

Progress check 10.21

Which areas within the income statement and the balance sheet may be considered to identify improvements to the short-term cash position of a company?

Worked example 10.11

An extract from Flatco plc's balance sheet as at 31 December 2012 and 2011 is shown below. From it we can see that trade receivables at 31 December 2011 were £517,000. Sales revenue was £3,250,000 and so collection days for 2011 were 58 days. Trade receivables at 31 December 2012 were £573,000. Sales revenue was £3,500,000 and collection days for 2012 had worsened to 60 days. Although new cash collection procedures and a reinforced credit control department were introduced in the latter part of 2012, it was too early to see an improvement by December 2012.

A report published on the industry for 2011 indicated that the average time customers took to pay was 35 days, with the best-performing companies achieving 25 days.

We will calculate the range of savings that Flatco would expect if it were to implement the appropriate measures to achieve average performance, or if it improved enough to match the best performers. We may assume that sales revenue is more or less evenly spread throughout the year. Flatco's profit before tax for 2011 was £430,000. The average bank interest paid or earned by Flatco plc was 9% per annum.

Flatco plc
Extract of the balance sheet as at 31 December 2012

Current assets	2012	2011
	£000	£000
Inventories	311	268
Trade receivables	573	517
Prepayments	589	617
Cash and cash equivalents	327	17
	1,800	1,419

➡

	Flatco 2011		Average (derived)		Best (derived)
Trade receivables	£517,000		£312,000		£223,000
Revenue	£3,250,000		£3,250,000		£3,250,000
Collection days	58		35		25
Gain per annum		[517 – 312]	£205,000	[517 – 223]	294,000
Interest saved or earned at 9% per annum			£18,450		£26,460
Improvement to profit before tax		$\dfrac{£18,450 \times 100}{£430,000} = +4.3\%$		$\dfrac{£26,460 \times 100}{430,000} = +6.2\%$	

Assuming that Flatco plc's new credit control procedures become effective, at current trading levels it should result in a profit improvement of between 4.3% and 6.2% per annum.

Long-term cash flow improvement

Equity

Shareholders' equity has many advantages in providing a means of improving long-term cash flow. Provision of additional equity by the shareholders immediately strengthens the balance sheet. It also indirectly strengthens the profit position because equity (ordinary shares) does not bear a commitment to pay interest. Additional equity is an investment in future business, which will ultimately result in dividends payable from successful trading.

When owners of the organisation provide additional equity, a personal cost is imposed on them in that the funding is from their own capital. It also may dilute their own stake or percentage of the business. Private equity firms or venture capitalists may be another source of equity. This carries the same advantages but also the expectation of rewards is generally much higher than the cost of interest-bearing loans.

Loans

Long-term loans that may bear a fixed or variable rate have certain advantages, particularly for the acquisition of non-current assets, even though they carry a commitment to regular interest payments. The period of the loan may be matched with the life of the asset and the agreed repayment schedule may be included in the cash flow plan with reasonable certainty.

Borrowing is always a big decision regardless of the amount. It has a cost and always has to be repaid. The ability to service any borrowing and the ability to repay must be assessed before making the decision to borrow. The real payback on borrowing for investment in non-current assets and working capital should be calculated and cheaper alternatives, such as:

- re-use of equipment
- renovation of equipment
- renegotiated terms of trading,

fully explored before borrowing.

A disadvantage of long-term loans is that they are invariably secured by lenders on the company's existing non-current assets or those to be acquired, or on other long-term or short-term assets. This requirement for security may limit the company's flexibility with regard to its future short-term or long-term borrowing requirements.

If a company needs to acquire land and buildings in order to trade it has a choice of purchasing leasehold or freehold, or renting. Purchase of premises additionally takes an organisation immediately into the property business. While property prices are rising, this speculation may appear attractive. However, it does represent some risk to the organisation – property speculation has proved disastrous to many companies in the past – and it may result in a lack of flexibility. If a company needs to expand or relocate it may not be able to achieve this quickly and may be hampered by the fixed cost of owning a property.

Renting or short leases may present lower risk and greater opportunities in terms of location and flexibility and with regular payments that may be included in the cash flow plan. It also gives the organisation further financing opportunities, by not having a fixed liability of a loan secured on property.

Leasing

Leasing may be used for financing acquisitions of non-current assets. A lease may be an operating lease (short-term) or a finance lease (long-term). An operating lease requires the payment of lease rentals, which are treated as an operating cost. A finance lease incurs interest charges on the capital amount of the lease, and depreciation on the asset, which are charged against profits. The term of a finance lease is matched with the expected life of the asset acquired. Cash flow may be planned in advance whichever method is chosen.

Purchases of non-current assets

The acquisition of non-current assets may represent an immediate outflow of cash. Cash-rich organisations may see advantages in outright purchases. However, the majority of organisations generally need to seek alternative funding. The sources of such funding may be from shares, loans or leasing, either within the UK or overseas.

The use of an overdraft facility is not usually appropriate for acquisition of non-current assets. Non-current assets by definition have a long life and may be permanent in nature. An overdraft is repayable on demand, which is suitable for working capital requirements but represents a risk if used to finance, for example, some machinery which may have an expected life of say 15 years.

Sales of non-current assets

Sales of non-current assets are an obvious means of raising funds. However, the opportunity cost of disposal of an asset must be considered prior to disposal and this should be evaluated in real terms using discounted cash flows with some allowance for inflation and taxation. An alternative may be to consider the sale of the asset to a leasing company, which then leases it back to the company.

Cash management

The Baumol cash management model

The similarity between cash and inventories was recognised in the Baumol cash management model (Baumol, WJ 'The transactions demand for cash', *Quarterly Journal of Economics* 66 (4), pages 545–56 (1952)). Cash may be regarded as a type of inventory, a minimum level of which is required for a business to operate. This is particularly true for the control and management of bank balances which are drawn on and replenished (as with inventories in the EOQ model we saw earlier), and where surpluses are invested for interest in the short term. The EOQ model may be applied to the transaction costs incurred in selling short-term investments in securities in order to replenish and maintain cash balances.

In this case if

P = the £ cost for a sale of one security
N = annual cash payments
S = the cost of holding cash, or the annual interest rate

then, using $EOQ = \sqrt{2PN/S}$

---

economic amount of cash to be transferred

$= \sqrt{2 \times \text{cost of the sale of a security} \times \text{annual cash payments/annual interest rate}}$

Let's look at a simple example.

Worked example 10.12

The finance director of Nina plc regularly invests surplus funds very short term in organisations that pay interest averaging 8% per annum. The transaction cost every time an investment is sold is £40. The cash payments for each month total £900,000, or £10.8m for the year.

We can use the Baumol cash management model to calculate the most economic amount to transfer to the bank account each time and how often these transfers should be made.

£ cost of the sale of one investment	P = £40 per order
Annual cash payments	N = £10.8m
Annual £ cost of holding cash	S = 8% interest rate

$$EOQ = \sqrt{2PN/S} = \sqrt{2 \times £40 \times £10,800,000/0.08} = £103,923$$

The most economic amount of cash to be transferred to the bank account is say £104,000. The finance director should transfer cash £10.8m/£104,000, or 104 times a year, which is twice a week.

The Baumol model may be relevant if the pattern of a company's cash flows and the transfers from its bank accounts are fairly consistent. Irregular cash flow patterns are more usual in most companies. The cash Miller–Orr management model (Miller, MM and Orr, D 'A model of the demand for money by firms', *Quarterly Journal of Economics,* 80, pages 413–35 (1966)) suggests that daily bank balances cannot be predicted and regular cash payments should not be assumed.

The Miller-Orr cash management model

The Baumol cash management model may be used to determine the frequency with which cash transfers should be made if cash flow patterns are regular. However, the Miller-Orr cash management model is based on the assumption that irregular or random cash flow patterns are usually the norm in most companies. This model suggests upper and lower limits that prompt cash transfers by selling short-term investments, which maintain the balance at a pre-determined return point.

The Miller-Orr model deals with the setting of the upper and lower limits and the position of the return point. If a company's daily cash flows fluctuate widely then the upper and lower limits will be wider apart (compared with if cash flows were less variable) and short-term interest will be lower and transaction costs higher.

If

R = the range between the upper and lower limits
P = the £ cost for a sale of one security
V = statistical variance of daily cash flows
S = the daily interest rate cost of holding cash
RP = return point
LL = lower limit

then the Miller-Orr model sets the range between the upper and limits as:

$$R = 3 \times (0.75 \times P \times V/S)^{1/3}$$

and the return point as:

$$RP = LL + R/3$$

We can see that the return point is not halfway between the upper and lower limits, but at a point somewhere below that, which means that the average cash balance on which interest is charged is therefore lower.

Let's look at a simple example.

Worked example 10.13

Let's assume that the cash flows of Nina plc (see Worked example 10.12) have become extremely irregular and unpredictable. The finance director of Nina plc has determined that the minimum cash balance required by the company is £75,000, and the variance of daily cash flows on a historical basis is £12.25m (£3,500 standard deviation). The company continues to make regular short-term investments of surplus funds, which now pay interest averaging at 9.125% per annum. The transaction cost every time an investment is sold is now £30.

We can use the Miller-Orr cash management model to determine the cash return point and how the finance director may manage this.

$$\text{Range} = 3 \times (0.75 \times 30 \times 12{,}250{,}000/0.00025)^{1/3}$$
$$= £30{,}992$$

Since the lower limit is £75,000 then the upper limit
$$= £75{,}000 + \text{range } £30{,}992 = £105{,}992$$

Return point
$$= \text{LL} + \text{R}/3$$
$$= £75{,}000 + £30{,}992/3$$
$$= £85{,}330$$

Once the cash balance drops to the lower limit of £75,000 the finance director should sell investments amounting to £10,330 to return the cash to £85,330. As soon as the cash balance gets up to the upper limit of £105,992 the finance director should buy investments amounting to £20,662 to return the cash to £85,330.

Whether it is assumed that a company's cash flows are predictable (the Baumol cash management model) or unpredictable (the Miller-Orr cash management model), in practice the finance director or treasurer of a company should be able to determine the minimum and maximum cash balances that the company requires to operate, from experience and through the use of continuously updated cash plans and forecasts.

Cash management in practice

Any cash improvement exercise should include the factors we have discussed, and the cash position should also be regularly reviewed. However, in order to maintain control over cash flow it is crucial that a cash flow plan or statement is prepared on a month-by-month or week-by-week basis for, say, six months ahead.

The phased cash flow plan should be updated weekly or monthly. It may be continually reviewed and revised in the light of actual performance, and for advantage to be taken of opportunities for improvement through savings and re-phasing as a result of consideration of the factors we have discussed above.

The recruitment of honest and reliable employees to deal with the control of cash and working capital is extremely important. Insufficient attention to this point together with a lack of frequent, appropriate training in credit control and cash management is a common occurrence, much to the cost of many companies. Many customers may detect a weak system of credit control and take advantage, resulting in considerable delays in payment of invoices.

Effective, integrated, computerised purchasing, inventory control, order processing and sales invoicing systems are the tools necessary for trained and motivated employees to optimise the use of cash resources and safeguard the company's assets. It should be appreciated that until a customer has paid an invoice it remains an asset, which is effectively under the direct control of another business.

Progress check 10.22

Which areas within the income statement and the balance sheet may be considered to identify improvements to the long-term cash position of a company?

Cash shortage is a common reason for business failure. However, businesses that are cash-rich may also fail to take full advantage of opportunities to maximise the return on capital employed in the business. Such opportunities may include:

- acquisition of new businesses
- investment in research and development
- investment in new products
- lending to gain the most tax-efficient returns.

All investments should, as a matter of company policy, be appraised using one of the recognised discounted cash flow techniques. A realistic company cost of capital should be used to determine whether each project is likely to pay back an acceptable return.

If surplus funds are to be invested for short-term returns, the most tax-efficient investments should be sought. An understanding of the relationship between risk and reward is a prerequisite. High-risk investment strategies should only be undertaken if the downside risk is fully understood, and the consequences are what the business could bear and survive should the worst happen. In both the UK and USA there have been some high-profile failures of deposit-takers, resulting in massive losses by the depositors (note the collapse of BCCI in the UK).

Companies should endeavour to maintain good relationships with their bankers at all times, with regular meetings and the provision of up-to-date information on company performance, plans and new initiatives. The bank should ensure that bank statements, daily cleared bank balance positions, and detailed financial information relating to loans, interest and bank charges are provided to the company as frequently as required. The company's finance department should regularly and thoroughly check their accuracy, and challenge the bank with regard to incorrect bank charges and interest. All slow-moving or inactive accounts, particularly, for example, old currency accounts opened for one-off contracts, should be closed to avoid incurring continuing account maintenance charges.

Summary of key points

- The cash operating cycle of working capital (WC), the net of current assets less current liabilities, is the period of time which elapses between the point at which cash begins to be expended on the production of a product or service, and the collection of cash from the customer.

- The difference between working capital (WC) and working capital requirement (WCR) is cash less short-term financial debt (bank overdrafts and short-term loans).

- The working capital requirement is normally financed by bank overdraft because of its flexibility in accommodating the fluctuating nature of net current assets.

- The cost of short-term borrowing is relatively higher than long-term borrowing.

- Effective management and control of inventories requires its appropriate location and storage, establishment of robust inventory purchase procedures and reorder systems, and accurate and timely systems for recording, control, and physical checks of inventories.

- Effective management and control of trade receivables requires establishment of appropriate policies covering choice of the way in which sales are made, the sales invoicing system, the means of settlement, and the implementation of a credit management and overdue accounts collection system.

- Although not free, trade payables provide the company with an additional source of finance.

- Effective management and control of trade payables requires the establishment of appropriate policies covering choice of suppliers, the way in which purchases are made, the purchase invoicing system, and the means of settlement.

- Regular measurement of the cash operating cycle, which determines the short-term financing requirements of the business, enables the company to monitor its working capital performance against targets and identify areas for improvement.

- The short-term cash position of an organisation may be improved by reducing current assets, and increasing current liabilities.

- The long-term cash position of an organisation may be improved by increasing equity, increasing long-term liabilities, and reducing the net outflow on non-current assets.

- Cash management models (for example Baumol and Miller-Orr) have been developed to try and optimise the levels of cash held by companies, but in practice it is usually the experience and expertise of financial managers using continuously updated cash plans and forecasts that enable businesses to effectively manage their cash flows.

Glossary of key terms

aged accounts payable report The amount owed to suppliers (accounts payable), classified by age of debt.

aged accounts receivable report The amount owed by customers (accounts receivable), classified by age of debt.

algorithm A process or set of rules used for a mathematical calculation.

BACS (bankers' automated clearing services) An electronic bulk clearing system generally used by banks and building societies for low-value and repetitive items such as standing orders, direct debits, and automated credits such as salary payments.

cleared funds Cleared funds are funds that have actually been cleared through the banking system and are available for use. It is the cleared funds balance, if overdrawn, which is used to calculate overdraft interest.

country risk (or **political risk**) The risk associated with undertaking transactions with, or holding assets in, a particular country. Sources of risk might be political, economic, or regulatory instability affecting overseas taxation, repatriation of profits, nationalisation, currency instability, etc.

cycle count The process of counting and valuing selected stock items at different times, on a rotating basis, so that all stocks are counted two, three, four or more times each year.

economic order quantity (EOQ) The most economic inventory replenishment order size, which minimises the sum of inventories ordering costs and inventory-holding costs. EOQ is used in an 'optimising' inventory control system.

effectiveness The utilisation of resources such that the output of the activity achieves the desired result. In other words, efficiency alone is not enough – efficiency in areas that optimise output is what is required to be effective (to avoid being a 'busy fool').

efficiency The achievement of either maximum useful output from the resources devoted to an activity, or the required output from the minimum resource input.

electronic point of sale (EPOS) EPOS systems process sales transactions electronically and scan and capture real-time product information at the point of sale. The systems range from networked cash registers in retail and wholesale outlets with links to business computer systems, to larger systems that link point-of-sale information with warehousing, suppliers' ordering systems, customer databases and online web stores.

ergonomics The study of the efficiency of persons in their working environment.

heijunka The smoothing of production through the levelling of schedules. This is done by sequencing orders in a repetitive pattern and smoothing the day-to-day variations in total orders to correspond with longer-term demand.

jidoka Autonomation, which increases productivity through eliminating the non-value adding need for operators to watch machines, thus freeing them for more productive work, for example quality assurance.

kaizen An 'umbrella' concept covering most of the 'uniquely Japanese' practices, it is a technique used for continuous improvement in all aspects of performance, at every level within the organisation.

kanban A signal, for example a card used in JIT production, to prompt top up of materials or components driven by demand from the next process.

letter of credit A document issued by a bank on behalf of a customer authorising a third party to draw funds to a specified amount from its branches or correspondents, usually in another country, when the conditions set out in the document have been met.

manufacturing resource planning (MRPII) An expansion of material requirements planning (MRPI) to give a broader approach than MRPI to the planning and scheduling of resources, embracing areas such as finance, logistics, engineering, and marketing.

master production schedule A time-phased statement (usually computerised) of how many items are to be produced in a given period (like a giant timetable), based on customer orders and demand forecasts.

materials requirement planning (MRP or MRPI) A system that converts a production schedule into a listing of the materials and components required to meet that schedule, so that adequate inventory levels are maintained and items are available when needed.

optimised production technology (OPT) OPT is a manufacturing philosophy combined with a computerised system of shop-floor scheduling and capacity planning. It is a philosophy that focuses on factors such as manufacture to order, quality, lead times, batch sizes, and set-up times, and differs from a traditional approach of balancing capacity as near to 100% as possible and then maintaining flow. The aim of OPT is to balance flow rather than capacity. The goal of OPT is to make money by increasing throughput and reducing inventories and operating expenses, by making better use of limited capacity by tightly controlled finite scheduling of bottleneck operations.

Pareto analysis This is a statistical technique (also known as the 80/20 rule) which enables concentration on the key tasks or issues which produce the greatest overall impact. In quality improvement a large majority of problems (80%) are produced by a few key causes (20%). This is also known as the vital few and the trivial many.

poka yoke Failsafe devices that support *jidoka* by preventing parts being mounted or fitted in the wrong way and alerting operators by flashing lights, ringing buzzers – it is a method of spotting defects, identifying, repairing, and avoiding further defects.

political risk See country risk.

property risk The risk of loss or damage occurring in the transit of goods and services before the completion of the sales contract.

pull system A system whose objective is to produce or procure products or components as they are required for use by internal and external customers, rather than for inventories. This contrasts with a 'push' system, in which inventories act as buffers between processes within production, and between production, purchasing, and sales.

Romalpa clause A contractual clause, named after a case in which its effect was litigated in 1976, by which the ownership of goods is to remain with the seller until they have been paid for. This can provide a useful protection for the seller in the event of the buyer's insolvency. Its value may be questionable if the goods are mixed with other goods in a manufacturing process or if they are resold to a third party.

throughput accounting (TA) A method of performance measurement which relates production and other costs to throughput. Throughput accounting product costs relate to usage of key resources by various products.

Assessment material

Questions

Q10.1 Describe how a company's financing of its investment in operations may be different from its financing of its investment in non-current assets.

Q10.2 (i) Explain the differences between working capital (WC) and working capital requirement (WCR).
(ii) What are the implications for companies having either negative or positive WCs or WCRs?

Q10.3 Outline the policy options available to a company to finance its working capital requirement (WCR).

Q10.4 Outline the processes and techniques that may be used by a company to optimise its inventories levels.

Q10.5 (i) Explain what is meant by economic order quantity (EOQ).
(ii) Describe some of the more sophisticated inventory management systems that the EOQ technique may support.

Q10.6 Describe the areas of policy relating to the management of its customers on which a company needs to focus in order to minimise the amount of time for turning sales into cash.

Q10.7 Outline the processes involved in an effective collections and credit management system.

Q10.8 Describe the policies and procedures that a company may implement for effective management of its suppliers.

Q10.9 (i) What is meant by overtrading?
(ii) What steps may be taken by a company to avoid the condition of overtrading?

Q10.10 Describe

(i) a review of the cash operating cycle, and
(ii) an appropriate action plan that may be implemented to improve the short-term cash position of a business.

Q10.11 (i) For what reasons may some companies require increases in long-term cash resources?
(ii) What sources are available to these companies?

Discussion points

D10.1 If working capital is the 'lubricant', a company's investment in its operations, that enables 'the engine', its investment in non-current assets, to be most effectively exploited, how does the company choose the best method of lubrication and how often should this oil be changed?

D10.2 'Management of working capital is simply a question of forcing suppliers to hold as much inventory as we require for order and delivery at short notice, and extending payment as far as possible to the point just before they refuse to supply, and putting as much pressure as possible on customers by whatever means to make sure they pay within 30 days.' Discuss.

D10.3 'A manufacturing company that adopts a policy of minimising its operating cycle may achieve short-term gains in profitability and cash flow but may suffer longer-term losses resulting from the impact on its customer base and its ability to avoid disruption to its production processes.' Discuss.

Exercises

Solutions are provided in Appendix 2 to all exercise numbers highlighted in colour.

Level I

E10.1 *Time allowed – 30 minutes*

Oliver Ltd's sales revenue budget for 2012 is £5,300,000. Oliver Ltd manufactures components for television sets and its production costs as a percentage of sales revenue are:

	%
Raw materials	40
Direct labour	25
Overheads	10

Raw materials, which are added at the start of production, are carried in inventory for four days and finished goods are held in inventory before sale for seven days. Work in progress is held at levels where products are assumed to be 25% complete in terms of labour and overheads.

The production cycle is 14 days and production takes place evenly through the year. Oliver Ltd receives 30 days' credit from suppliers and grants 60 days' credit to its customers. Overheads are incurred evenly throughout the year.

> **What is Oliver Ltd's total working capital requirement?**

E10.2 *Time allowed – 45 minutes*

Coventon plc's income statement for the year ended 30 June 2012, and its balance sheet as at 30 June 2012 are shown below. The chief executive of Coventon has set targets for the year to 30 June 2013, which he believes will result in an increase in PBT for the year. The marketing director has forecast that targeted collection days of 60 would result in a reduction in sales of 5% from 2012 but also a £30,000 reduction in bad debts for the year. The same gross profit percentage is expected in 2013 as 2012 but inventories days will be reduced by 4 days. The CEO has set further targets for 2013: savings on administrative expenses and distribution costs of £15,000 ➡

for the year; payables days to be rigidly adhered to at 30 days in 2013. One third of the loan was due to be repaid on 1 July 2012, resulting in a proportionate saving in interest payable.

Coventon plc
Income statement for the year ended 30 June 2012

	£000
Revenue	2,125
Cost of sales	(1,250)
Gross profit	875
Distribution and administrative costs	(300)
Operating profit	575
Finance costs	(15)
Profit before tax	560
Income tax expense	(125)
Profit for the year	435
Retained profit 1 July 2011	515
	950
Dividends	(125)
Retained profit 30 June 2012	825

Coventon plc
Balance sheet as at 30 June 2012

	£000
Non-current assets	
Intangible	100
Tangible	1,875
Total non-current assets	1,975
Current assets	
Inventories	125
Trade receivables	425
Prepayments	50
Cash and cash equivalents	50
Total current assets	650
Total assets	2,625
Current liabilities	
Borrowings and finance leases	50
Trade payables	100
Accruals	150
Dividends payable	125
Income tax payable	125
Total current liabilities	550
Non-current liabilities	
Loan	250
Total liabilities	800
Net assets	1,825
Equity	
Share capital	1,000
Retained earnings	825
Total equity	1,825

You are required to calculate the following:

(i)   operating cycle days for 2011/2012
(ii) operating cycle days for 2012/2013
(iii) the expected value of inventories plus trade receivables less trade payables as at 30 June 2013
(iv) the PBT for 2012/2013.

(Hint: use cost of sales for 2012 in the inventories days calculation rather than the average daily cost of sales in the period.)

E10.3   *Time allowed – 45 minutes*

Trumper Ltd has recently appointed a new managing director who would like to implement major improvements to the company's management of working capital. Trumper's customers should pay by the end of the second month following delivery. Despite this they take on average 75 days to settle their accounts. Trumper's sales revenue for the current year is estimated at £32m, and the company expects bad debts to be £320,000.

The managing director has suggested an early settlement discount of 2% for customers paying within 60 days. His meetings with all the company's major customers have indicated that 30% would take the discount and pay within 60 days; 70% of the customers would continue to pay within 75 days on average. However, the finance director has calculated that bad debts may reduce by £100,000 for the year, together with savings of £20,000 on administrative costs.

Trumper Ltd has a bank overdraft facility to finance its working capital on which it pays interest at 12% per annum.

The managing director would like to know how Trumper may gain from introducing early settlement discounts, if it is assumed that sales revenue levels would remain unchanged. The managing director would also like suggestions as to how the company may reduce its reliance on its bank overdraft, perhaps through better management of its trade receivables, and whether the bank overdraft is the best method of financing its working capital.

Level II

E10.4   *Time allowed – 45 minutes*

Josef Ryan Ltd has experienced difficulties in getting its customers to pay on time. It is considering the offer of a discount for payment within 14 days to its customers, who currently pay after 60 days. It is estimated that only 50% of credit customers would take the discount, although administrative cost savings of £10,000 per annum would be gained. The marketing director believes that sales would be unaffected by the discount. Sales revenue for 2013 has been budgeted at £10m. The cost of short-term finance for Ryan is 15% per annum.

What is the maximum discount that Josef Ryan Ltd may realistically offer?

E10.5   *Time allowed – 45 minutes*

Worrall plc's sales revenue for 2012 was £8m. Costs of sales were 80% of sales revenue. Bad debts were 2% of sales. Cost of sales variable costs were 90% and fixed costs were 10%. Worrall's cost of finance is 10% per annum. Worrall plc allows its customers 60 days' credit, but is now considering increasing this to 90 days' credit because it believes that this will increase sales. Worrall plc's sales manager estimated that if customers were granted 90 days' credit, sales revenue may be increased by 20%, but that bad debts would increase from 2% to 3%. The finance director calculated that such a change in policy would not increase fixed costs, and neither would it result in changes to trade payables and inventories.

> **Would you recommend that Worrall plc should increase customer credit to 90 days?**

E10.6   *Time allowed – 45 minutes*

Chapman Engineering plc has annual sales revenue of £39m achieved evenly throughout the year. At present the company has a bank overdraft facility on which its bank charges 9% per annum interest.

Chapman Engineering plc currently allows its customers 45 days' credit. One third of the customers pay on time, in terms of total sales revenue. The other two thirds pay on average after 60 days. Chapman believes that the offer of a cash discount of 1% to its customers would induce them to pay within 45 days. Chapman also believes that two thirds of the customers who now take 60 days to pay would pay within 45 days. The other third would still take an average of 60 days. Chapman estimates that this action would also result in bad debts being reduced by £25,000 a year.

> (i)   **What is the current value of trade receivables?**
>
> (ii) **What would the level of trade receivables be if terms were changed and 1% discount was offered to reduce collection days from 60 days to 45 days?**
>
> (iii) **What is the net annual cost to the company of granting this discount?**
>
> (iv) **Would you recommend that the company should introduce the offer of an early settlement discount?**
>
> (v)   **What other factors should Chapman consider before implementing this change?**
>
> (vi) **Are there other controls and procedures that Chapman could introduce to better manage its trade receivables?**

E10.7   *Time allowed – 60 minutes*

Sarnico Ltd, a UK subsidiary of a food manufacturing multinational group, makes sandwiches for sale by supermarkets. The group managing director, Emanuel Recount, is particularly concerned with Sarnico's cash position. The financial statements for 2012 are as follows:

Income statement for the year ended 30 September 2012

	£m	£m
Revenue		49
less: Cost of sales		
Opening inventories	7	
add: Purchases	40	
	47	
less: Closing inventories	10	37
Gross profit		12
Expenses		(13)
Loss for the year		(1)

Balance sheet as at 30 September 2012

	£m
Non-current assets	15
Current assets	
Inventories	10
Trade receivables	6
Total current assets	16
Total assets	31
Current liabilities	
Bank overdraft	11
Trade payables	4
Total current liabilities	15
Non-current liabilities	
Loans	8
Total liabilities	23
Net assets	8
Equity	
Ordinary share capital	3
Retained earnings	5
Total equity	8

You may assume that trade receivables and trade payables were maintained at a constant level throughout the year.

(i)   Why should Emanuel Recount be concerned about Sarnico's liquidity?

(ii) Describe what is meant by the cash operating cycle?

(iii) Why is the operating cycle important with regard to the financial management of Sarnico?

(iv) Calculate the operating cycle for Sarnico Ltd.

(v)   What actions may Sarnico Ltd take to improve its operating cycle performance?

E10.8 *Time allowed – 60 minutes*

The balance sheet for Flatco plc as at 31 December 2012, and its income statement for the year to 31 December 2012 are shown in Figures 8.3 and 8.4 in Chapter 8.

A benchmarking exercise that looked at competing companies within the industry revealed that on average collection days for 2012 were 33 days, average payables days were 85 days, and average inventories days were 32 days. The exercise also indicated that in the best-performing companies in the industry the time that customers took to pay was 24 days, with payables days at 90 days and inventories days at 18 days.

You are required to calculate the range of values of savings that Flatco may achieve in 2013 (assuming the same activity levels as 2012) if it were to implement the appropriate measures to achieve average performance or if it improved enough to match the best performers.

You may assume that sales revenue is evenly spread throughout the year. The average bank interest paid and earned by Flatco plc is 9% per annum.

11

International operations and investment

Chapter contents

Learning objectives

Completion of this chapter will enable you to:

■ Appreciate the nature of internationalisation and the importance of international markets.

■ Explain what comprises the international financial marketplace, and its significance for international companies.

■ Outline why it is that companies may wish to undertake overseas operations.

■ Describe the various types of international operation that international companies may engage in.

■ Explain foreign direct investment (FDI) in terms of an international company's investment in new or expanded facilities overseas.

■ Compare the unique features of investment appraisal in a multi-currency, overseas environment with the appraisal of domestic investment projects.

■ Evaluate international investment projects based on multi-currency cash flow forecasts.

■ Describe the factors that may influence the taxation strategy of multinational companies.

■ Describe the use of transfer pricing by multinational companies, and the impact of exchange controls.

■ Consider the alternative discount rate options that may be used in international investment appraisal.

■ Describe the main sources of finance for international investment.

■ Explain what is meant by country risk (or political risk) and outline the strategies that international companies may adopt to mitigate the impact of such risk.

Introduction

In Chapter 6 we looked at investment appraisal and decisions relating to whether or not to invest in a project, and choices between investments in alternative projects, which are competing for resources. These investments were fundamentally related to projects undertaken by companies in their own home countries. In this chapter we will consider the appraisal of investments that companies may undertake in overseas countries.

Before looking specifically at international investment we set the scene by looking at internationalisation in the broader context. We will begin by looking at the meaning of internationalisation, and in particular how it relates to the activities of international companies, and how the international financial marketplace operates.

Companies engage in overseas operations for a variety of reasons and they may enter international markets in a number of ways. Companies may start with a basic export operation and then develop this through further options, which may ultimately result in the establishment of an overseas presence in the form of an overseas subsidiary company.

The appraisal of international investments such as an overseas subsidiary may be a little more complex than the appraisal of domestic investments, with a greater number of variables to consider, for example the volatility of foreign currency exchange rates and cash flows, and local taxation systems. When international investments are evaluated using net present value (NPV) there is inevitably a wider choice of cost of capital that may be used as a discount rate.

The choice of financing for international investments also requires the consideration of additional factors in comparison with domestic financing. These factors relate to the quality and types of relationship that the home country parent company has with its overseas contacts as well as the financial considerations of foreign currency and interest rate risks, taxation, and gearing. They also relate to the risk in general of engaging in business overseas.

The chapter closes with a section about country risk (or political risk) and the ways in which companies may adopt strategies to reduce or eliminate such risk. This topic is also explored further in Chapter 12, where we look at specific techniques for dealing with risks arising from international operations.

Internationalisation

Internationalisation means many different things, for example, in the context of business, education, training, IT, and finance. Internationalisation refers basically to the act of bringing something under international control and relates to the increasing geographical dispersion of economic, as well as cultural, social, educational, technological, and political activities across national borders. The economic phenomenon of internationalisation has an increasing impact on:

- the role of the financial markets
- the activities of international companies.

Financial and commodity markets are increasingly concerned with issues related to the growing impact of international market pressures on:

- local cultures
- traditional political boundaries
- market structures.

These pressures affect the social, political, and economic framework within which international companies operate. They are at the root of many of the international financial management issues of concern to international companies, and also responsible for the continually changing nature of the international financial marketplace.

The world in the 21st century is a complex place in which the interrelationships and interdependencies of the emerging new world orders are often dominated by the politics of competition, and the economics of the marketplace. Such increasing interrelationships and interdependencies may possibly reflect divergence into the development of separate economic, social, and political systems, or they may reflect convergence into the development of a 'single' world system, having the same sort of economic structures, and social and institutional environments. On the other hand, these interrelationships and interdependencies may reflect the rejection of traditional systems and a complete change through the development of a postmodern economic, social, and political system.

There are important issues relating to internationalisation and many theories of internationalisation that are concerned with international finance and the increasing global mobility of capital within and between differing geographical sovereign territories. It is also important to consider areas other than, for example, economic rationality, corporate financial objectives, and shareholder returns, such as, for example, internationalisation in the social, cultural, and political context. Social, cultural, and political factors contribute greatly to the creation of the interconnections and interrelationships that are increasingly essential to the survival of the international company. They also act as counterbalances against the potential excesses of the international financial marketplace, and potentially act as protective mechanisms against the possible exploitation of third world countries.

Progress check 11.1

What does internationalisation mean with regard to a company's international operations?

The international financial marketplace

The international financial marketplace is basically like any other market. It is an interrelated network of buyers and sellers in which exchange activities occur in the pursuit of profit and reward, and may be:

- open to the public with unrestricted access
- private and semi-closed with access restricted to particular organisations
- private and semi-closed with access restricted to transactions related to particular commodities or assets.

Whichever it is, the international financial marketplace is a place where the legal title of an asset, commodity, or currency is exchanged for either:

- the legal title of another asset, commodity, or currency

or

- the legal promise that such an agreed exchange will take place at an agreed time and at an agreed place in the future.

There is a growing significance and increasing level of efficiency of international financial markets and their participants, which also have an increasing social, political, and economic influence on the day-to-day transactions within the domestic marketplace.

There are a number of important characteristics unique to the international financial marketplace:

- It is one of the largest global markets in operation, and it comprises an interrelated but geographically dispersed network of many different and unrelated buyers and sellers.
- In the absence of any politically imposed regulatory requirements, there is generally freedom of entry to, and freedom of exit from, the international financial marketplace.
- Information regarding commodities, assets, and currencies available on the international financial marketplace is widely available to most of the buyers and sellers, many of whom undertake both buying and selling activities.
- The majority of activities in the international financial marketplace take place between commercial banks.

There is a diversity of buyers and sellers in the international financial marketplace, who may in general be assumed to be:

- rational
- predominantly profit driven, their primary motive being profit maximisation

- well informed
- able to access relevant and useful information
- risk-takers.

The international financial marketplace is an interconnected network of key participants of either individuals or groups (see Figure 11.1), and the key interrelating transactions between them all are the buying and selling of securities, currencies, and other financial assets.

As an interconnected network of buyers and sellers, the foreign exchange market exists as a collection of geographically dispersed trading centres located around the world. From London to New York, Paris to Hong Kong, Tokyo to Dubai, each of these markets has grown considerably through the latter part of the 20th century and into the 21st century. As they continue to grow at an increasing rate, the importance of the international financial marketplace is beyond doubt. Even the most minor fluctuations in the international financial markets now have a significant impact on companies and individuals worldwide, whether they are investors or not.

While the activities of any of the participants in the international financial marketplace affect the supply and demand of tradable commodities, assets, and currencies within the marketplace, by far the most influential group are the central banks. The reasons for their influence may be:

- politically motivated and therefore structural in consequence
- economically motivated and therefore transactional or market-based in consequence.

Structural intervention is concerned with the establishment of exchange rate systems with:

- fixed exchange rates
- floating exchange rates

Figure 11.1   The international financial marketplace

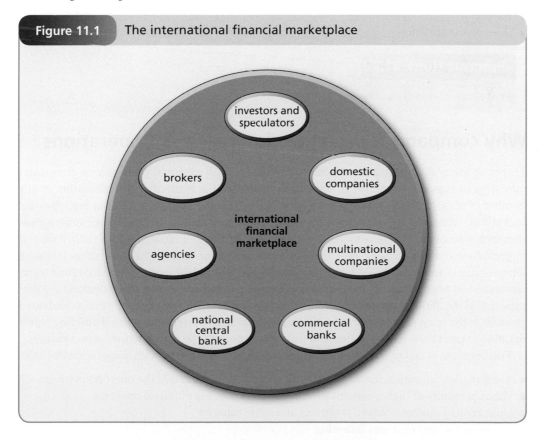

- managed exchange rates
- pegged exchange rates.

Transactional or market-based intervention is concerned with the need to protect or stabilise currency exchange rate movements relative to other currencies. The motivation for this is generally economic, but there may also be political reasons for intervention to protect or support a specific country's currency.

Modern sophisticated markets often exhibit some inefficiencies. However, the international financial markets are generally regarded as being fairly efficient. This is important because efficient markets promote:

- increased volumes of transactions
- greater mobility of funds
- the involvement of a greater number of participants
- a more efficient allocation of resources.

The implication of such efficiency is that while in the short term market outsiders may earn profits higher than the market average because of luck or chance, it is unlikely that over the longer term market outsiders may consistently outperform the market. Therefore, it may be argued that abnormal gains are generally unlikely to be made by rational, and honest, participants in the international marketplace. The relevance of such an argument is beyond doubt with regard to an economically driven market that functions primarily on the mechanics of supply and demand. The appropriateness of such an argument may be questioned. There may be a number of powerful participants driven by motives that are other than economic, for example politically based motives, which may have a substantial impact on:

- the overall market mechanisms – the availability of market assets, commodities, and currencies
- the activities of other market participants as part of the supply and demand mechanism.

Progress check 11.2

What is the international financial marketplace?

Why companies undertake international operations

There are many diverse economic, political, strategic, and personal reasons why companies may wish to engage themselves in operations overseas. It is likely that a combination of any number of reasons, rather than just one, stimulates companies' involvement in international operations. What may be strategically the most important reason is that such involvement gives companies access to overseas markets by enabling them to get closer to both their final and intermediate customers. Note how the world's major motor vehicle manufacturers (through joint ventures) started to build plants in China in the 1990s, before even the basic road infrastructure had been constructed. This was in anticipation of the tremendous demand for cars expected in the 2000s by the whole Chinese population, following the country's unprecedented growth. At the same time, motor vehicle component manufacturers also started building plants in China to meet their expected demand from the motor vehicle manufacturer joint ventures.

Further motives and reasons why companies may undertake international operations include:

- home market saturation, leaving development of overseas markets as the only option for growth
- the opportunity of higher returns for shareholders possibly obtained overseas
- utilisation of underemployed resources and spare capacity
- access to cheaper overseas financing

- keeping up with competitors
- exploitation of emerging and growing economies
- access to overseas government help with financing, grants, and development
- diversification of economic risk by trying to smooth out the boom–bust cycle relating to overseas countries' differing levels of economic growth
- lower overseas production costs, for example labour, plant, and machinery
- access to specialist overseas know-how and expertise
- economies of scale
- increasing and widening the exposure of companies' brand names and global strategies.

Companies undertake international operations in a variety of ways, and in some circumstances the route chosen may be related to the specific reason or reasons for their endeavours.

> ### Progress check 11.3
>
> Outline the reasons why companies may wish to develop international operations.

Types of international operation

When companies first begin to explore international markets they are faced with so many new situations and uncertainties. Initial forays into such unknown territories are usually on a small scale rather than making large-scale investments at the outset. Internationalisation by companies may be either through indirect means or by establishing a direct presence in the foreign country, and may take place in a number of ways, as shown in Figure 11.2.

Figure 11.2 Types of international operation

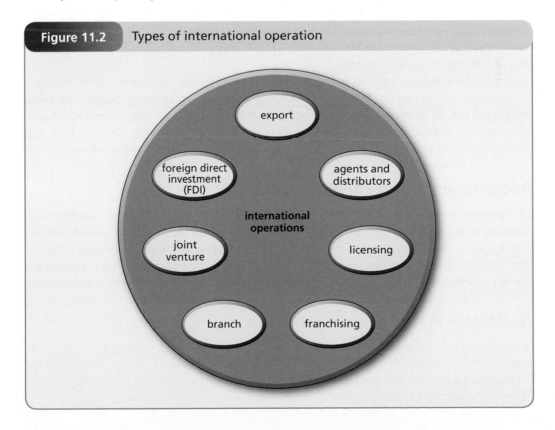

Types of indirect international operations include:

- exporting
- appointment of an agent or distributor
- trademark licensing
- franchising.

Alternatively, a company may have a direct presence in a foreign country through:

- establishing a branch operation
- a **joint venture**
- **foreign direct investment (FDI)** – an outward investment in an overseas subsidiary by the domestic company.

Risk will be present whichever internationalisation strategy is adopted. Whether a business is a large, well-established multinational or a small business entering an international market for the first time, most companies will initially try to keep risk to a minimum and usually start with a small export operation. Buckley's incremental model of internationalisation (Buckley, A (2004) *Multinational Finance*, 5th edition, London: FT/Prentice Hall) describes the route to establishing an overseas subsidiary as usually taking place incrementally, which may include all or some of the indirect and direct types of operation outlined above. This gradual exposure to a new international market is a process of risk-minimisation, familiarisation, and learning.

Exporting

Export activities offer a relatively low-risk entry into the international marketplace. Exporting allows a company to expand its markets and its output, and at the same time most of the value-adding activities are maintained within the home country. Home market saturation may be the reason for expansion into new overseas markets, or it may be that higher shareholder returns may be achieved from such ventures.

Returns from exports need to be higher than those from domestic activities because distribution and selling costs will be higher. Although export activities do not require the initial investment that an overseas subsidiary requires, there will be the learning curve cost of familiarisation with the new market, the development and growth of the foreign customer base, and possible barriers to trade.

Appointment of an agent or distributor

The appointment of a local agent may be the answer to some of the difficulties involved with direct exporting by the home country company. This may require the services of an independent overseas agent or distributor who operates in a similar market and with an existing customer base that may also be accessed. Alternatively, a sole agent may be appointed for that specific country whose function it is to promote and sell only the home company's products and services.

Trademark licensing

In marketing-led businesses it may be beneficial for a home country company to allow its brand-named products to be sold by overseas companies. A trademark licence may assign the manufacturing and selling rights for a product to an overseas company in return for payment of royalties. Licensing provides a means of:

- avoiding trade barriers that may be encountered with direct exporting activities
- overcoming possible problems of remitting profits to the parent company
- accessing rapidly expanding overseas markets without the need for an initial investment, and in circumstances where sufficient investment resources may not be available.

While licensing does not involve the cost of an initial investment, there are costs of negotiating, agreeing, and granting licences, and ongoing costs of monitoring their use and ensuring correct receipts of royalties. The granting of licences to overseas licensee companies may provide these companies with the opportunity to subsequently copy and compete with the home country company's products and steal customers and market share. The fact that they are based in foreign countries may make it difficult or impossible to enforce any non-competition agreements that may have been made.

Franchising

Companies may exercise a degree of control over an overseas company's use of its brands and trademarks through franchising. In this way the company licenses a complete business – for example, the McDonald's and KFC chains. As with trademark licensing, franchising involves similar administrative costs of set-up and monitoring. However, the threat of competition from overseas franchisees setting up on their own may be less than that posed by a company with a trademark licence.

Progress check 11.4

Outline the indirect ways in which a company may operate internationally.

Branch operation

A further low-cost step up from exporting may be the establishment of an overseas branch in a foreign country that may be run by local employees of that country, and possibly with some expatriate staff. An overseas branch provides a local presence overseas without requiring the large investment required to set up a subsidiary. However, any funding that is required must be provided by the parent company.

Joint venture

A home country company's involvement in a joint venture allows it an even greater level of control over operations than the granting of trademark licences or franchises. In general, a joint venture is a project undertaken by two or more persons or entities joining together with a view to profit, often in connection with a single operation. More specifically, a joint venture is defined as an organisation in which one entity holds an interest on a long-term basis and is jointly controlled by that entity and one or more other entities under a contractual arrangement.

In practice, the participants in a joint venture will each provide specific attributes and resources. In an overseas joint venture these may be, for example, knowledge of the particular country and markets, technical knowledge and expertise, financial resources, local connections and contacts such as customers, suppliers of materials, and distribution channels. Local partners in joint ventures may also be important in political lobbying, and providing the know-how with regard to finding the way through bureaucratic red tape, and dealing with legal and governmental regulation.

However, the advantages of joint ventures must be weighed against their disadvantages, which revolve around the issue of control and goal congruence. The joint venture may have too much flexibility and a lack of control, or it may be too inflexible and unable to adapt or change. A home country company, which has set up an overseas joint venture, may not be able to exercise an appropriate degree of direct control. It may also find that the attributes and resources promised by the other participants may not be at the levels expected.

The agency problem (see Chapters 2 and 3) is likely to manifest itself in a joint venture through a lack of goal congruence. The joint venture may originally have been set up with specific policies relating to, for example, investment, choice of markets and customers, choice of suppliers, and levels of dividend. However, each of the participants in the joint venture may have different individual priorities. The levels of payment of royalties and management fees to the separate parent companies may also be a problem area, as may be the (transfer) prices paid for goods and services provided by each company that has invested in the joint venture (see the sections below about profit repatriation, transfer pricing, and royalties and management fees).

In some countries a joint venture is the only way of establishing an investment in a subsidiary or related company within a foreign country. For example, for many years this was pretty much the only method of investing in China, and investment regulations were heavily weighted in favour of local Chinese partners. That was because the Chinese government was keen to ensure that not too much control was left in the hands of foreign investors (even though it was keen to attract foreign money). More recently, the Chinese investment environment has changed significantly and most foreign investment is now in the form of wholly foreign-owned enterprises. However, in some cases it may still be necessary or advantageous for investments in China to take the form of joint ventures.

Investment in an overseas subsidiary

Foreign direct investment (FDI) may be inward (domestic investment by overseas companies) or outward (overseas investment by domestic companies). Here we are talking about outward FDI with regard to the establishment of new overseas facilities or the expansion of existing overseas facilities by a home country investor. It is a financial interest in perpetuity by an organisation in an overseas company in which it has effective control over its day-to-day management. The importance of global FDI can be seen from Mini case 11.1 below.

Mini case 11.1

The financial importance of international trade is made very clear by statistics issued by the United Nations Conference on Trade and Development (UNCTAD). The table below sourced from their published statistics shows the vast sums of foreign direct investment in US$m flowing between the developed and developing worlds. The significance of the Asian developing markets as both a destination of investment and as a source of funding is apparent from the numbers.

Foreign Direct Investment flows by region in 2010

	Inflows US$m	Outflows US$m
Developed economies		
Europe	313,100	475,763
North America	251,662	367,490

(continued)

Other developed economies	37,144	91,937
Developing economies		
Africa	55,040	6,636
Latin America & Caribbean	159,171	76,273
Asia & Oceania	359,357	244,656
South-East Europe & CIS (Commonwealth of	68,197	60,584
Independent States – the former Soviet Republics)		
World Totals	1,243,671	1,323,339

Source: UNCTAD World Investment Report 2011.

An investment in an overseas subsidiary is different from an investment in a non-related overseas business. The latter is what is called portfolio investment and relates to an organisation's acquisition of shares or loans in an unrelated overseas company, in which it has no control over day-to-day management.

An investment in an overseas subsidiary is also different from an investment in a home country subsidiary. Differences are due to problems arising out of, for example, movements in foreign currency exchange rates, exchange controls, differences in taxation systems, and transfer pricing (see the relevant sections below in which we discuss each of these issues).

The reasons for a direct investment in an overseas subsidiary may be summarised as:

- a possible means of ensuring maximisation of shareholder wealth
- natural progression from initial international involvement through exporting, use of agents, licensing, and franchising
- progression from a branch activity or a joint venture
- tax benefits
- alternative to unsatisfactory agency, licensing, or franchise arrangements
- requirements of local supply by overseas manufacturers
- lower distribution and transportation costs
- shorter supply chain and avoidance of time delays
- lower production costs
- intellectual property rights and patents protection
- after-sales customer service requirements
- the personal ambitions of individuals who wish to establish a business in a particular country.

Compared with exporting, an overseas subsidiary will derive obvious benefits from being closer to the customers, and through reduced distribution and selling costs, and the avoidance of bureaucratic inconvenience, import tariffs, and exchange controls (see the section on exchange controls below). After-sales service requirements will be better catered for by the local employees of an overseas subsidiary and so it is more likely to enhance the reputation and reliability of the product and achieve growth from repeat business and recommendation. This is illustrated in the press extract below which describes MIRA, a UK-based independent vehicle engineering consultancy, which has progressed its overseas expansion along an incremental development path from trading links to a full trading operation in China. This progress allows the company to consolidate its activities at each stage before committing further capital to its expansion programme.

From trading links to direct overseas presence

The MACE 2 is a squat, ungainly looking robot vehicle. Clad in camouflage, it climbs nimbly over a series of obstacles in the Warwickshire countryside, in sharp contrast to the sleek Lamborghini roaring round the adjacent test track. Yet this unmanned ground vehicle (UGV), already deployed in Afghanistan in place of troops risking their lives on reconnaissance and other missions, is a useful symbol of the way its developer, MIRA, has changed over the past few years.

MIRA was set up with government funding in 1953 as the Motor Industry Research Association (a title it no longer uses because its activities have diversified). It became an independent, commercial enterprise in the 1970s, supported by the motor industry, and built up an international reputation for its consultancy, research and development, engineering and test facilities outside Nuneaton.

Now it has launched an ambitious programme to update those facilities within a spectacular new technology park, to expand its activities overseas and to extend farther into areas such as aerospace, rail and defence, as exemplified by the UGV. Revenues have already increased from £28 million in 2009 to £41.7 million last year and are continuing to grow, with a target of £75 million by 2015. The developments are expected to generate 2,000 new jobs over the next decade. 'When I arrived here in 2009, things were really tough; the motor industry had been knocked really hard,' says Dr George Gillespie, MIRA's chief executive. 'But the only way out of that kind of crisis is through developing new products. Fortunately, many of our clients, premium manufacturers such as Jaguar Land Rover and Nissan, are big spenders on research and development. As a result we have now seen two years of strong growth.'

Another part of the strategy was to increase overseas activities. There were existing links with manufacturers in Japan, Korea and elsewhere, but in the past few years the company has set up a joint venture in India for engineering and computer services, launched a MIRA subsidiary in Brazil and upgraded its Chinese operation to a full trading organ-

isation. 'China and India already have test assets, but what they need, and what we can provide, is the ability to analyse test data and provide engineering solutions,' Gillespie says.

A third thrust was to identify areas for expansion. 'MIRA decided to diversify about ten years ago, applying its special vehicle engineering systems to the defence field,' Gillespie adds. 'But this has grown dramatically in the past three or four years and now represents about 30 per cent of our revenues. It is not just about the UGV technology; we are carrying out a lot of testing for the large defence suppliers and directly for the Ministry of Defence.'

There has been a similar expansion in work on electric and other low-carbon vehicles as manufacturers have upped the pace of innovation in that field and in intelligent transport systems. 'That means smart cars that talk to each other or talk to the infrastructure; providing integrated journey management by road, rail and air; and dealing with congestion,' Gillespie says. A lot of this work has been funded by government and EU research grants, but as manufacturers produce advanced 'driver assistance systems', MIRA has helped to pioneer the testing and certification of this technology.

Essential to MIRA's business model is its independence from manufacturers and its ability to work confidentially on development for individual companies. So to fund its development plans, MIRA is looking for an investor and Gillespie is confident that the money will soon be in place. Last week, MIRA took possession of the first building for the £300 million technology park that will eventually cover 1.5 million square feet of its 850-acre site, which has been declared an enterprise zone. This will house the 30 member companies who already have on-site offices and others who are on a waiting list. The 1950s offices will be demolished and state-of-the-art laboratories and test areas will be built. Of the 2,000 new jobs, 500 will be directly for MIRA, doubling the workforce. The rest will be for clients and support facilities, including a 100-bed hotel.

Five things MIRA got right

- Looking at its strengths in engineering services and aiming to expand on the back of them, at home and overseas.
- Setting up joint ventures, subsidiary companies, etc, to manage growth and secure finance through regional development funds and private equity.
- Making sure the right people with the right skills are in place at board level, to expand into areas such as defence, and to ensure high standards of corporate governance.
- Exploiting assets such as the land available for the technology park, which has been designated an enterprise zone.
- Maintaining a strong customer base by a commitment to provide clients and member companies with on-site facilities within the new development.

Source: **Reconnaissance mission unearths new markets; diversification leads to major expansion for Midlands company**, by Alan Copps © *The Times*, 23 April 2012

There are advantages in establishing an overseas subsidiary compared with a branch. As we have discussed above, branch funding is provided by the parent company, whereas an overseas subsidiary may be financed by debt or equity in its local currency. The parent company may also gain a tax advantage if the overseas subsidiary (rather than overseas branch) is in a relatively low corporate tax area. When overseas branch profits are remitted to a parent company they are normally taxed at the home country's tax rate, because a branch is not a legal entity separate from the parent company.

Setting up a new overseas subsidiary from scratch will obviously incur similar costs to the setting up of a domestic subsidiary. An advantage is that the business can be established exactly as the parent company wishes, without any costs of, for example, rationalisation and re-training of employees that may arise from the acquisition of an existing business. However, the acquisition of an existing reputable overseas company may incur such post-acquisition costs, but may also offer distinct advantages, such as an established supplier and customer base, and distribution network.

An overseas subsidiary may be set up in order to satisfy some personal requirements or ambitions of a parent company's chief executive or chairman, rather than the primary objective of maximisation of shareholder wealth. We discussed the possibility of the agency problem arising with an overseas joint venture, and this may also arise with an overseas subsidiary. We have already seen many examples in Chapter 3 of the serious impact of a lack of goal congruence and how company directors may pursue their own rather than shareholders' objectives. At an overseas subsidiary level the opportunities for this may be even greater because of distance, possible remoteness, and less direct control.

Progress check 11.5

Outline the direct ways in which a company may operate internationally.

International investment appraisal

Corporate investment appraisal is an area of corporate finance that is complex and sometimes controversial, and is particularly so with regard to international investment appraisal. The evaluation of an international investment may be considered from two perspectives:

- appraisal within the foreign country of the investment in that country's currency
- home country appraisal of the foreign investment by the parent company.

The perspective chosen will require a different treatment of the cash flows and other factors related to the international investment. Appraisal of a foreign investment within the context of the foreign country itself requires consideration of the following:

■ initial investment
■ additional working capital requirement (WCR)
■ values of future cash flows
■ timing of future cash flows
■ profit repatriation
■ local taxation
■ **transfer prices**
■ residual assets values.

Appraisal of a foreign investment from the home country's perspective by the parent company requires consideration of the following additional factors:

■ forecasts of currency exchange rates and assessment of the impact of their changes
■ differences between project cash flows and holding company cash flows due to the imposition of exchange controls
■ differences in the tax systems and tax rates between the country of investment and the home country of the parent company
■ the consequences of imposed royalties and management fees
■ differences between project cash flows and holding company cash flows as a consequence of country risk (or political risk).

There may also be legal, ethical, environmental, and social constraints, for example pollution laws, and weekends occurring on a Thursday and Friday as in Muslim countries. Particular customs and practices may relate to specific countries, for example working practices, the rights of women, and perhaps the prohibition of alcohol. We will consider some of the factors outlined above relating to international investment appraisal, together with a discussion about how international transfer pricing may be used in the mitigation of exchange controls, and the influence of various different international taxation scenarios on international investment strategies. An overview of country risk and the strategies that international companies may use to minimise their impact is discussed in the final section of this chapter.

Initial investment

An estimate of the cost of an initial investment is likely to be no more accurate for an international investment than for a domestic investment. In fact, because of the greater number of variables involved it is likely to be less accurate, particularly where such expenditure may be made in a foreign currency (see the section about forecast currency exchange rates below). An overseas subsidiary's investment in non-current assets of land, buildings, plant, and equipment, may be provided by local debt or equity or may be provided by the parent company's own funds, or from debt or equity. Non-current assets may also be transferred to the overseas subsidiary by the home country parent company, which should be valued at their opportunity cost.

Working capital requirement

The working capital requirement of an overseas subsidiary will be ongoing throughout its life. It arises in the normal course of manufacturing and trading through accounts receivable, inventories of materials, work in progress, and finished products, and accounts payable. Materials and inventories may be acquired locally, and some may be provided by the parent company at agreed transfer prices (see the section about transfer pricing below).

Future cash flows

The estimation of future cash flows is likely to be even more precarious and subject to greater margins of error than estimates of initial investment costs. The further into the future one tries to estimate, the less accurate is the forecast. With future cash flows from an overseas investment there are the added complications of dealing with a foreign currency and the possible impact of overseas taxation.

The investment in an overseas subsidiary may be evaluated using the cash flows within the foreign country of the investment in that country's currency. On that basis, the investment appraisal may result in a positive net present value indicating an increase in corporate value. This may or may not be truly accurate and is dependent on which particular cost of capital has been used in the calculation. Further to that, corporate value is determined by the value added to the parent company and therefore the home country appraisal of the foreign investment by the parent company may be more relevant. The net present value of the investment in the overseas subsidiary should be calculated using the initial investment by the parent company and the future cash flows transferred to it, which may be restricted (see profit repatriation below).

Profit repatriation

If an overseas subsidiary has been financed by its parent company then the parent company will expect to receive dividends and possibly loan interest and loan repayments. In certain countries profit repatriation may be restricted by the government so that funds have to be retained for future investment in that country. Some countries possibly impose such constraints to limit any action by another country that may weaken their currencies, or to promote action themselves that may strengthen their currencies.

Worked example 11.1

Wood Inc. is a company in the USA that is proposing to invest US$1.5m in a project in Spain. The project would be managed by Rono SA, a wholly owned Spanish subsidiary of Wood Inc. We will assume that:

- taxes will not be payable in either the USA or Spain
- foreign exchange rates will not change over the period of the project
- cash remittances from Spain are limited to 32% of the original investment in any one year.

The investment has the following expected cash flow profile:

Year	0	1	2	3
Project cash flows US$000	(1,500)	800	800	800

The project remittances to the holding company are limited to 32% of US$1.5m p.a.:

Year	0	1	2	3	4	5
Receipts remitted US$000	0	480	480	480	480	480

We will consider whether the project should be accepted if Wood Inc. requires a 20% return on investments made in Europe.

For Rono SA, using a discount rate of 20% the project will have the following net present value:

Year	0	1	2	3		
Project cash flows US$000	(1,500)	800	800	800		
Discount factor	1.0	0.83	0.69	0.58		
Present value US$000	(1,500)	664	552	464		NPV +180

The NPV of the project is + US$180,000, therefore from the subsidiary's point of view the project is wealth-creating.

For Wood Inc. the project will have the following net present value:

Year	0	1	2	3	4	5	
Project cash flows US$000	(1,500)	480	480	480	480	480	
Discount factor	1.0	0.83	0.69	0.58	0.48	0.40	
Present value US$000	(1,500)	398	331	278	230	192	NPV −71

The NPV of the project is −US$71,000, therefore from the holding company point of view the project is not wealth-creating, and clearly Wood Inc. should not undertake the project.

How should Wood Inc. resolve this apparent dilemma? If Wood Inc. is still keen to invest in the project then it may investigate a number of courses of action:

- review the project cash flows
- try and identify ways to reduce the initial investment
- attempt to re-negotiate the level of remitted cash flows from Spain.

Forecast currency exchange rates

The estimation of initial investments in a foreign currency, and the forecasting of cash flow values and timings in a country and currency that is not the home currency may be difficult because of different practices, behavioural patterns, and expectations within that country. If currency cash flows require translation into the home country's currency of the parent company, not only do the future foreign currency cash flows need to be forecast but so do the future expected exchange rates ruling at the appropriate future dates. In a perfect market the movement in exchange rates would not be a problem because in theory the purchasing power of the two currencies varies in the same proportion as exchange rate movements (see the exchange rate equivalency model which is discussed in Chapter 12). In practice, this may not be so and the risk of exposure to foreign currency exchange rate movements presents a very real problem to companies that have invested in overseas subsidiaries. Some of the methods used to address this problem are also discussed in Chapter 12.

Worked example 11.2

Dale plc is a UK retail company, which is planning to invest £2m in a project in Germany that would potentially lead to the creation of a Europe-wide retail chain. As a result of investing in the project Dale plc will receive a single one-off payment of €3.5m at the end of year four of the project.

The current exchange rate (and the agreed exchange rate for the proposed investment) is £1 = €1.34. The management of Dale plc expects that over the next few years the euro will strengthen against the £ sterling. The company expects that the £/€ exchange rate at the end of year four will be between £1 = €1.05 and £1 = €1.12. The company requires a return of 12% on European investments.

We will ignore taxation and assume there are no exchange controls between the UK and Germany, and consider whether Dale plc should undertake the project.

At an expected rate of return of 12% the equivalent value of £2m in four years would be:

$$\text{£2m} \times (1.12)^4 = \text{£2m} \times 1.5735 = \text{£3,147,039}$$

This means that in order to break even the project should generate an equivalent cash flow at the end of year four of £3,147,039.

If the expected receipt at the end of year four is €3,500,000, then the exchange rate would need to be 3,500,000/3,147,039 or £1 = €1.11. This exchange rate of £1 = €1.11 is within the range expected by the company and as a result Dale plc may accept the project.

However, the range of exchange rates has been based on forecasts, and Dale plc may be a little concerned about their reliability. If Dale plc took out a euro loan at 12% per annum to cover the original investment, the loan would be for £2m at the current exchange rate of £1 = €1.34, which equals €2.68m. The total cost of the loan including repayment of the principal would be:

$$\text{€2.68m} \times (1.12)^4 = \text{€2.68m} \times 1.5735 = \text{€4,216,980}$$

which means a cash cost of €3.5m − €4.22m, or €0.72m to the company.

In practice, such a hedge is a logical option but in this particular case the cost of €0.72m may be prohibitive.

Exchange controls

Exchange controls are a major concern for many companies trading and investing internationally. Exchange controls can have serious consequences because they can prevent the movement and restrict adequate management of assets and resources.

There are many types of exchange control that an international company may face and, in response, multinational companies have developed a range of techniques to mitigate some of their adverse impacts. Exchange controls relate to a wide range of regulations that may impact on both residents and non-residents of a country, and which prevent or restrict:

- possession of assets denominated in a foreign currency
- engagement in foreign currency transactions
- acquisition, retention, and disposal of assets and liabilities located outside the country
- acquisition, retention, and disposal of assets and liabilities denominated in a foreign currency.

The above restrictions are usually imposed by national central banks to contain or restrict the convertibility of foreign currency where a shortage of such a foreign currency may exist, and seek to restrict, prevent, or control economic activity. Such economic activity can include, for example, imports, exports, access to financial markets, the possession of foreign assets and foreign currencies, and repatriation of profits or cash flows.

Exchange controls that affect imports generally attempt to restrict imports to a level significantly less than that under free market conditions, because when a currency depreciates or devalues then imports increase. Exchange controls generally require resident overseas subsidiary companies to obtain strictly controlled licences for the importation of goods and services. The licences are then used to enforce import restrictions and to restrict access to the foreign currency forward exchange market to their holders.

On the other hand, exchange controls that affect exports not only attempt to promote and encourage export activities, but more importantly seek to attract premium foreign currency exchange rates. However, these exchange controls may:

- impose controls on payments related to exports
- restrict export activities by the use of export licensing regulations
- impose restrictions that limit access to foreign currency exchange markets.

With regard to borrowing, exchange controls may on the one hand seek to discourage or even prohibit local borrowing by non-residents, while on the other hand they may encourage overseas borrowing by residents by seeking to control loan terms and conditions of borrowing. Exchange controls may also seek to restrict possession of, and access to, foreign assets by subjecting the ownership and acquisition of such assets to national central bank permission. These exchange controls may also apply not only to the establishment and operation of foreign bank accounts, but also to the possession of foreign currencies.

While the above types of exchange control are very important, it is the imposition of exchange controls with regard to profit repatriation that may affect the movement of a company's cash flows, which is perhaps the most critical type. Many developed countries may allow free repatriation of investment capital and profit. However, other countries may impose severe restrictions on the repatriation of profit. These exchange controls are often complex, usually politically motivated, and frequently changed. Such restrictions may impose:

- limits on the movement of all profits generated within a country
- percentage restrictions on the level of profits available for repatriation
- time limits on the repatriation of profits.

Companies may seek assurances on the imposition of such exchange controls but changes of government, particularly in politically unstable countries, often render such agreements worthless. Nevertheless, there are various means by which companies may release profits, which would otherwise be restricted by the imposition of exchange controls. Such methods include:

- use of transfer pricing
- establishment of fee and royalty agreements
- use of leading and lagging
- payment of dividends
- payment of management fees
- use of research and development fees
- use of currency invoicing
- use of parallel loans
- establishment of counter trade deals and agreements.

Worked example 11.3

Gretchen AG is a German company that is considering investing €12.5m in a project in France. The company intends undertaking the project through Bondi SA, a partly owned French subsidiary. It has been assumed that:

- taxes are not payable in either Germany or France
- foreign currency exchange rates will not change over the period of the project
- no exchange controls exist between France and Germany to prevent the remittance of investment cash flows.

The investment has the following cash flow profile:

Year	0	1	2	3	4
Project cash flows €000	(12,500)	6,500	3,500	4,800	1,500

Because the project is to be managed through Bondi SA, a management fee of 10% on all project cash flows will be paid by Gretchen AG.

We will appraise the investment on the basis that Gretchen AG requires a 10% return on investments made in France.

Year	0	1	2	3	4	
Project cash flows €000	(12,500)	6,500	3,500	4,800	1,500	
Discount factor @ 10%	1.0	0.909	0.826	0.751	0.683	
Present value €000	(12,500)	5,908	2,891	3,605	1,024	NPV + 928

The NPV of the project is + €928,000, and therefore the project is value-creating. However, we should also consider the impact that the management fees have on the net present value of the project. If we deduct 10% from the cash flows in years one to four, we have the following cash flows and revised net present value:

Year	0	1	2	3	4	
Project cash flows €000	(12,500)	5,850	3,150	4,320	1,350	
Discount factor @ 10%	1.0	0.909	0.826	0.751	0.683	
Present value €000	(12,500)	5,318	2,602	3,244	922	NPV − 414

The revised NPV of the project is −€414,000, and therefore incurring the management fees results in the project being non-value-creating. Under the current arrangements, Gretchen AG should reject the project. However, since this project is basically value-creating then negotiation regarding the level of management fees would clearly benefit both companies. If Bondi SA were to reduce its management fees by 4% to 6% then the revised cash flows and net present value would be as follows:

Year	0	1	2	3	4	
Project cash flows €000	(12,500)	6,110	3,290	4,512	1,410	
Discount factor @ 10%	1.0	0.909	0.826	0.751	0.683	
Present value €000	(12,500)	5,554	2,718	3,388	963	NPV + 123

The NPV of the project would then be + €123,000, and therefore acceptable to Gretchen AG. It would also mean that Bondi SA would receive 6% × €16.3m (the total project cash flows) = €978,000 as opposed to nothing at all if Gretchen AG rejected the investment project.

Taxation

Taxation is political in origin, while its effect is economic. It is as a consequence of such origins that international differences in rates of tax and schemes of assessment continue to exist, resulting in significant problems for international companies seeking to operate and invest internationally.

If a company seeks to maximise the wealth of its shareholders, a company operating and investing internationally will not only seek to:

- minimise the impact and consequences of domestic and foreign taxes but also to
- legitimate the means through which these taxes can be reduced.

An international company has a responsibility to its shareholders to try and minimise its global tax burden on its domestic and international profits, provided that such a strategy does not impact on its other business activities. One way of achieving this involves the use of tax havens, of which there are a number of types. They may be, for example, countries where no income or capital gains taxes are levied at all, or countries where tax rates are very low. They also include countries that do not tax foreign income as a means of trying to attract inward capital investment. For a tax haven to be acceptable to international companies the country would normally be required to have a:

- stable political and economic structure
- well-balanced social structure
- structured and well-managed financial services sector
- good communications network
- stable long-term economic outlook.

Where possible, tax treaties should exist between the company's home country and potential tax haven countries, and few if any exchange controls should be in operation. The tax haven country should also levy low taxes on domestically generated income.

There are a number of problems and risks associated with companies' use of tax havens to minimise overall tax, which generally arise from changes in:

- internal political structure of the country due to social or political unrest
- economic alliances of the country due to negotiated trade agreements
- tax changes due to changes to or the global harmonisation of taxation systems.

The various taxation schemes used in overseas countries may have an impact on international investment because of their different tax rates. They may also have an impact because of the availability or not of investment incentives, and whether or not overseas tax paid may be offset against domestic corporation tax through double taxation agreements. The following worked example considers some of these issues.

Worked example 11.4

Dennis Ltd is a UK company, which is planning to invest in a project in Spain that is expected to generate the following net cash flows (and profits) over the three years of the project:

Year 1	€5m
Year 2	€4m
Year 3	€3m

Spanish corporation tax is expected to be:

Year 1	24%
Year 2	25%
Year 3	26%

Withholding tax is payable on all foreign dividends remitted to the UK at the following estimated rates:

Year 1	15%
Year 2	15%
Year 3	20%

UK corporation tax is currently paid at 35%, and full tax credits are available for taxes paid in Spain.

It is assumed that foreign exchange rates will not change over the life of the investment, and that there are no exchange controls between the UK, Spain, and France to prevent the remittance of investment cash flows.

We will calculate the after-tax cash flows for each of the following scenarios:

- all project profits remitted to the UK
- all project profits reinvested in Spain
- the investment is managed by a wholly owned French subsidiary with the dividends remitted to France for further investment outside the UK.

All project profits remitted to the UK

Figures in €000

Year	1	2	3
Cash flow/profit	5,000	4,000	3,000
Spanish corporation tax	1,200	1,000	780
at	24%	25%	26%
Dividend	3,800	3,000	2,220
Withholding tax	570	450	444
(% of dividend)	15%	15%	20%
Net dividend received	3,230	2,550	1,776
UK corporation tax (35% of profit)	1,750	1,400	1,050
Foreign tax credit (Spanish corporation tax plus withholding tax)	1,770	1,450	1,224
Residual tax (UK corporation tax less the tax credit, which is limited to the amount of UK corporation tax)	–	–	–
Net profit after tax (net dividend less residual tax)	3,230	2,550	1,776

Total cash flow/profit after tax over the life of the project is €7.556m.

All project profits reinvested in Spain

Figures in €000

Year	1	2	3
Cash flow/profit	5,000	4,000	3,000
Spanish corporation tax	1,200	1,000	780
at	24%	25%	26%
Dividend	3,800	3,000	2,220

Total profit after tax over the life of the project is €9.02m.

The investment is managed by a wholly owned French subsidiary with the dividends remitted to France for further investment outside the UK

Figures in €000

Year	1	2	3
Cash flow/profit	5,000	4,000	3,000
Spanish corporation tax	1,200	1,000	780
at	24%	25%	26%
Dividend	3,800	3,000	2,220
Withholding tax	570	450	444
(% of dividend)	15%	15%	20%
Net cash flow/profit after tax	3,230	2,550	1,776

Total profit after tax over the life of the project is €7.556m.

Transfer pricing

A transfer price is the price at which goods or services are transferred between different units of the same company. If those units are located within different countries then it is referred to as international transfer pricing.

The extent to which the transfer price covers costs and contributes to profit is a matter of policy. A transfer price may be, for example, based on marginal cost, full cost, or market price, or determined through negotiation. Where the transferred products cross national boundaries, then transfer prices used may have to be agreed with the governments of the countries concerned.

It can be seen that the whole issue of transfer pricing is potentially full of difficulties and conflicts, particularly in the area of international transfer pricing. Transfer pricing is a technique used by many multinational companies operating in a range of overseas countries, with an obvious potential for profit manipulation, tax avoidance and tax evasion through the creative application of transfer pricing policies. The tax issues can be clearly seen from Mini case 11.2 below.

Mini case 11.2

The difficulties encountered by transfer pricing and its role in tax avoidance were thrown into high relief by the publication in July 2010 of 'Transfer Pricing Guidelines for Multinational Enterprises and Tax Administrations' issued by the Organisation for Economic Co-operation and Development (OECD).

The document aims to provide guidance on the application of the 'arm's length principle' for the valuation, for tax purposes, of cross-border transactions between associated enterprises.

The impact of the OECD publication was a flurry of new legislation in the member countries across the world bringing the new principles into national company law. The UK introduced the principles into the Finance Act 2011.

One not totally unexpected outcome of the changes in legislation was noted in the *Irish Examiner* on 19 December 2011 where it was reported that research had found the pay of tax specialists increased by an average 15.6% in 2011. This was in large part attributed to the adoption of the OECD guidelines making tax specialists who were experts in the new rules even more sought after.

For a multinational company operating in a large number of countries there are factors that may influence the use of transfer pricing and determination of transfer pricing strategies and policies. Transfers of goods and services between companies may take place for a variety of reasons, for example transfer of:

- raw materials and components to assist in the production process
- sales and distribution facilities
- other services.

A multinational company may use transfer prices to:

- protect corporate funds
- minimise taxes
- minimise tariffs
- avoid exchange controls and quotas
- minimise exchange risk
- maximise profit
- optimise areas of inadequate financial performance.

In general, companies will set a transfer price at a minimum of the sum of the additional cost per unit incurred to the point of transfer plus the opportunity costs per unit to the company as a whole. However, a wide range of factors may influence the actual level of transfer prices used by a company, for example:

- size of the company
- organisation structure
- managerial behaviour
- legal requirements
- social and cultural influences
- national and international fiscal requirements
- international pressures.

While each of the above factors are important influences their impact will ultimately be determined by:

- corporate objectives, the overriding objective being the maximisation of shareholder wealth
- the competitive position of the company
- government influence on the company's activities
- the profit distribution/retention policy of the company.

Royalties and management fees

Some international companies impose 'management fees' on their subsidiaries for services provided by senior managers and technical personnel, and may also make royalty charges on patents used by their subsidiaries. This is an area that is usually very carefully monitored by tax authorities as such transfers of funds have often been a source of tax evasion.

The impact of charges made between companies within the same group, such as royalties and management fees, resulting from a company investing overseas may result in a value creating project being rejected. This sort of issue is best dealt with by first establishing the viability of the proposal as a standalone investment project. The project may then be evaluated by calculating the impact of any additional fees and costs to determine its acceptability or not. Let's look at a worked example of this.

Worked example 11.5

Hill Street Inc is a company based in Chicago, USA, which has the opportunity to invest US$20m in a project in Australia. The project would be managed by Everage Ltd, which is a subsidiary company based in Australia.

The estimated cash flows of the investment project are:

Figures in US$m

Year	Cash flow
0	(20.0)
1	13.0
2	9.0
3	10.5
4	6.5

The estimated tax cash flows relating to the project are:

Figures in US$m

Year	Cash flow
0	8.0
1	(9.0)
2	(3.0)
3	(3.5)
4	(2.5)

A management fee of 20% on all project cash flows is payable by Hill Street Inc to Everage Ltd in return for managing the project. It is assumed that:

■ there are no exchange controls in the USA and Australia that may prevent the remittance of cash flows from the investment
■ foreign currency exchange rates are not expected to vary over the period of the project.

We will make the appropriate calculations, assuming that Hill Street Inc requires a 15% return on Australian investments, to determine whether or not the project should be accepted.

The following calculation of the NPV of the project uses cash flows that are net of tax.

Year	Cash outflows US$m	Cash inflows US$m	Discount factor at 15%	Present values US$m
0	−12.00		1.00	−12.00
1		4.00	0.87	3.48
2		6.00	0.76	4.56
3		7.00	0.66	4.62
4		4.00	0.57	2.28
				NPV +2.94

The NPV of the project is + US$2.94m, and being positive is therefore value-creating.
If we deduct the 20% management fee from the cash flows years one to four we can re-calculate the NPV as follows:

Year	Cash outflows US$m	Cash inflows US$m	Discount factor at 15%	Present values US$m
0	−12.00		1.00	−12.00
1		3.20	0.87	2.78
2		4.80	0.76	3.65
3		5.60	0.66	3.70
4		3.20	0.57	1.82
				NPV −0.05

The revised NPV of the project is now − US$0.05m, and being negative indicates that the project is not value-creating and suggests that it should not be undertaken. However, it should be noted that the opportunity of an otherwise good investment project that would increase shareholder wealth is being rejected because of the level of management fees paid between companies within the group. An alternative way of managing the project may therefore be considered.

Residual assets values

An investment in a new overseas subsidiary by a parent company must consider an estimate of the residual value of its assets, even though the company may be regarded as a going concern and may be assumed to exist in perpetuity. An estimate of the residual values of its assets at a point in time is required so that a realistic appraisal of the investment may be made, and also because the parent company may have plans to dispose of the subsidiary some time in the future.

Progress check 11.6

What are the additional factors that need to be considered in international investment appraisal compared with appraisal of domestic investment projects?

International investment cost of capital

Many of the issues relating to the evaluation of domestic investments apply equally to international investment appraisal. There are in addition some unique factors relating to the evaluation of international investment. As with the appraisal of domestic investment projects, assuming that the NPV method is employed, international investment projects pose the same difficult question about which is the most suitable discount rate to use. For international investment projects there are a number of discount rate options that may be considered to calculate NPV, for example:

- a weighted average cost of capital (WACC)
- the WACC of the parent company
- the WACC of the overseas subsidiary company
- the WACC of similar overseas companies
- a discount rate higher than a domestic discount rate to reflect the additional risk of an overseas investment
- the return required from overseas projects with similar risk
- a required return specific to the investment.

In practice, the use of a company's WACC as the discount rate to evaluate an investment is inherently inaccurate because of the difficulties in its calculation and the fact that WACC may change because of the change in gearing as a result of additional financing of a new investment from either debt or equity. On the other hand, the arbitrary use of a discount rate that reflects the additional risk of an overseas investment is also unsatisfactory, as is a return required from overseas projects with similar risk, because this type of risk (currency risk, interest rate risk, country or political risk) may be identified and managed.

The general consensus appears to be that the most appropriate discount rate for appraisal of an international investment should be a project-specific cost of capital that reflects the particular features and risk profile of the specific project. This discount rate may also allow for, for example, currency exchange rates, interest rates, and taxation specific to the individual overseas investment project. It may also take into account the type of financing, debt or equity, and its relevant risks.

The discount rate used will also depend on whether the investment is financed totally by equity or totally by debt or some combination of debt and equity. This then poses the additional questions about how the individual costs of financing should be determined. We have discussed the use of the CAPM to calculate cost of equity in Chapter 5. The CAPM does not require growth projections and while it is probably the best method of calculating a cost of equity its use in international investment appraisal is not without its problems. These include the determination of, for example: the time period; which market portfolio to consider; the market premium; the beta value of the project. Some of these issues are considered by Adrian Buckley (Buckley, A (2004) *Multinational Finance*: London, Financial Times Press) in the development of an international version of the capital asset pricing model.

A possible alternative to NPV to evaluate an overseas investment project may be to use an **adjusted present value (APV)** described by Stewart Myers (Myers, SC 'Interactions of corporate finance and investment decisions: implications for capital budgeting', *Journal of Finance* 29 (1), pages 1–25 (1974)). This is based on the Miller and Modigliani II model (see Chapter 5), which assumes that WACC is reduced because of the debt tax shield. The APV method first requires the 'base case' NPV to be calculated. The 'base case' NPV is the present value of the cash flows of the investment, regardless of tax and financing, discounted at the rate of return that shareholders would require if the project were totally equity-financed. This required rate of return is the parent company's ungeared beta (β). Then the cash flows relating to the 'adjustments' of tax and financing are discounted using a risk-adjusted cost of debt. The two present values are then added to give an APV, which is acceptable to the company if it is above zero. It can be seen that the APV method may be particularly useful in dealing with international investments, which have diverse sources of finance, but it still has the problem of being able to estimate accurate and appropriate discount rates.

Progress check 11.7

Explain the significance of the choice of discount rate in international investment appraisal.

In practice, international investment appraisal is a little more complex than the appraisal of a domestic investment. Some of the main issues are the volatility of foreign currency exchange rates, the estimated profitability and cash flows of the project, the risks involved in an overseas investment, and the management of such risks. Let's look at an example that includes some of these issues.

Worked example 11.6

Martin plc, a UK multinational company, has equity with a market value of £150m and debt capital with a market value of £100m. The company's current cost of equity is 12%, and its after-tax cost of debt is 7%.

Martin plc has secured a contract worth Aus$80m to supply and install plant and equipment for a company in Australia. The payment terms of the contract set by Martin plc, which are non-negotiable, are:

- Aus$20m payment to be made on completion of stage one of the contract at the end of year one
- Aus$24m payment to be made on completion of stage two of the contract at the end of year two
- Aus$36m payment to be made on completion of stage three of the contract at the end of year three

The estimated cost of the supply and installation of the plant and equipment is Aus$70m.

Project cash outflows in respect of the project are expected to involve three currencies – Aus$, £ sterling, and euro – and cash flows are estimated as follows:

Year	0	1	2	3
Inflows				
Aus$	0	20	24	36
Outflows				
Aus$	6	3	7	4
UK £	3	3	1	3
€	3	3	4	5

The current exchange rates at the start of the project are:

$$£ = Aus\$2.50$$
$$€ = Aus\$1.67$$

At the start of the contract, foreign currency forecasts for each of the next three years have been made as follows:

- Aus$ will appreciate by approximately 5% against the £
- Aus$ will appreciate by approximately 10% against the €.

We are required to evaluate the investment using the base currency of £ sterling and advise Martin plc on the financial acceptability of the project. We should also point out the factors that may impact on the profitability of the project, the risks involved in the project, and make some suggestions as to how to hedge against these risks.

We can summarise the expected exchange rates based on the forecasts provided for the subsequent three years:

Year	0	1	2	3
Aus$/£	2.500	2.375	2.256	2.143
Aus$/€	1.670	1.503	1.353	1.217
therefore €/£	1.497	1.580	1.667	1.761

The estimated cash flows for the project can now be translated into a single currency, £ sterling:

Figures in £m

Year	0	1	2	3
Inflows				
Aus$ in £	0.000	8.421	10.638	16.799
Outflows				
Aus$ in £	2.400	1.263	3.103	1.867
£	3.000	3.000	1.000	3.000
€ in £	2.004	1.899	2.399	2.839
Total outflows	7.404	6.162	6.502	7.706
Net cash flow	−7.404	2.259	4.136	9.093

We can determine the current WACC of Martin plc:

$$\text{WACC} = \frac{(£150\text{m} \times 12\%) + (£100\text{m} \times 7\%)}{(£150\text{m} + £100\text{m})} = 10\%$$

to use as an approximate discount rate to calculate the NPV of the project:

Year	Cash outflows £m	Cash inflows £m	Discount factor at 10%	Present values £m
0	−7.404		1.00	−7.404
1		2.259	0.91	2.056
2		4.136	0.83	3.433
3		9.093	0.75	6.820
				NPV +4.905

Using £ sterling as the base currency, and the company's current cost of capital, and assuming the three-year currency exchange rate forecasts are correct, the positive NPV is acceptable in financial terms because it adds £4,905,000 to the corporate value of the company. Therefore the project appears to be financially viable.

The company should also consider the potential risks of the project, for example:

- the reliability of the initial investment and cash flow forecasts, and therefore the profitability of the project
- the accuracy of the forecast future exchange rates
- the creditworthiness of the Australian customer.

To try and mitigate these risks Martin plc may, for example:

- obtain guarantees with regard to the cost estimates they have been given before agreeing to the project
- take out credit insurance with regard to the Australian customer
- use currency swaps, options, or forward contracts to try and cover the downside risk related to foreign exchange movements (see Chapter 12).

Financing international investment

Multinational companies with investments in overseas subsidiaries have the opportunity to access and exploit inefficiencies in the international capital markets, with regard to potentially lower costs of foreign equity and debt capital, and financial assistance from foreign governments. The lowest possible average cost of capital must be the objective but this has to be at an acceptable level of risk.

We discussed financing generally in Chapter 7, which was concerned mainly with sources of finance within a company's home country, and primarily the UK. As shown in Figure 11.3, international financing requires the consideration of additional factors, which include:

- currency risk
- interest rate risk
- home country and overseas taxation
- financial gearing
- country or political risk.

An overseas subsidiary may be financed using the currency of the parent company's home country or the foreign currency of the subsidiary's country (see Chapter 7 – Eurobonds). The method chosen will form part of the group's foreign currency risk exposure strategy (see Chapter 12). Borrowing may take place in local foreign currency, in which case foreign exchange translation exposure may be managed by matching foreign currency interest and capital repayments with foreign currency operational cash inflows.

There will inevitably be differences between the tax regimes in the parent company's home country and the countries of overseas subsidiaries. There may be differences in the ways in which profits and losses, and dividends and interest are treated for taxation. In general, because interest is tax deductible whereas dividends are not, then it may be advantageous for overseas subsidiaries to maximise their use of debt finance rather than equity, up to the maximum levels of gearing that may be allowed by governments within specific countries.

Gearing considerations relate to the levels of debt and equity in the parent company, the overseas subsidiary, and other similar companies in the foreign country. For the parent company, equity investment in an overseas subsidiary is of higher risk than debt capital, and although interest payments must be made they may be far more stable and predictable than dividend payments. An overseas subsidiary's use of local equity capital, while risky for investors, may

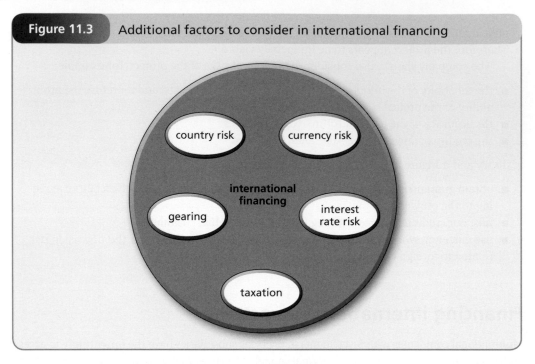

Figure 11.3 Additional factors to consider in international financing

also be risky for the company depending on the efficiency of that particular country's equity market. An overseas subsidiary may have difficulties with access to local debt finance, which may involve costly bank fees and higher interest rates if the parent company is not known and does not have high creditworthiness in the foreign country.

The parent company may guarantee the overseas subsidiary's borrowing if its own overall level of gearing is acceptable, and then the subsidiary's borrowing may be treated independently as a separate issue. The borrowing strategy of the overseas subsidiary may then exploit local tax and interest rate benefits, and the possibility of foreign government subsidies and grants. If an overseas subsidiary is financed locally using banks in that country and using local foreign government support, then political risk is mitigated since the likelihood of expatriation of the company's assets or interference in its affairs are less likely to happen. Overseas subsidiaries whose borrowings are not guaranteed by their parent company each need to independently consider optimisation of their own capital structures.

Progress check 11.8

What are the various types of financing that may be used to support international investment?

Risk and international investment

Buckley (Buckley, A (2004) *Multinational Finance*: London, Financial Times Press) defines political risk as the exposure to a change in the value of an investment or a cash position resultant upon government actions. Political risk, usually described as country risk, is the level of exposure a company faces as a consequence of a change in government action. This exposure to such country risk may be seen in the potential change in value of an investment, project, or cash receipts following changes in government policy.

The country risk or political risk associated with international investment can be considerable. It is important for a company to not only recognise the existence of such risk, and its potential impact on the company's international activities, but also to be aware of the possible strategies available to try and eliminate, or mitigate, the consequences of such risk. While such risks can develop in a number of different ways, they are generally related to overseas government actions and policies that seek to:

- expropriate company assets and profits
- impose foreign exchange currency controls
- impose price intervention policies that discriminate between the overseas country and home country
- impose tax laws that offer preferential treatment to overseas country companies
- impose social and work-related regulations that offer preferential treatment of overseas country companies
- impose regulations that restrict access to local finance
- restrict the movement of company assets and resources.

These overseas government policies may impact on an international company's ability to:

- undertake commercial activities
- generate profits
- repatriate or reinvest such profits for future growth,

and their effects can be substantial. Therefore the recognition, assessment, and management of such risk are important aspects of a company's international investment activities.

An international competitive advantage can only be gained by accepting some degree of country risk. Once a company has identified and recognised the existence of a potential country risk, it must then consider how this may impact on the company's activities. How can the company eliminate or mitigate the consequences of these risks? Companies may be willing to trade off higher levels of risk for higher overall returns. While the most extreme risk-averse strategy would be one of avoidance, that is the rejection of any investment projects in politically, socially, or economically uncertain countries, such an elimination strategy misses potential opportunities of investment projects that may yield high returns. In general, companies tend to adopt management strategies that seek to minimise country risk rather than eliminate it altogether. These management strategies may be either defensive, which protect or safeguard a company's overall position, or offensive, which aggressively consolidate a company's overall position, and include:

- obtaining insurance against the possibility of **expropriation of assets**
- negotiating overseas government concessions and guarantees to minimise the possibility of expropriation of company assets
- structuring the company's financial and operating policies to ensure they are acceptable to and consistent with regulatory requirements
- developing close social and political relationships with overseas country institutions
- internationally integrating operations to include overseas and home country companies to ensure that the overseas companies are dependent on home country companies
- locating research and development activities and any proprietary knowledge and technology in the home country to reduce the possibility of expropriation
- establishing global trademarks for company products and services to ensure such rights are legally protected domestically and internationally
- encouraging where possible the establishment of local participation in company activities
- encouraging local overseas shareholders to invest in the company's activities

- maintaining high levels of local overseas borrowing to protect against the adverse impact of exchange rate movements
- encouraging the movement of surplus assets from overseas country companies to the home country companies.

Progress check 11.9

Why is country risk so important to multinational companies?

Summary of key points

- Internationalisation, with regard to the increasing geographical dispersion of economic, cultural, social, educational, technological, and political activities across national borders, has an increasing impact on the role of the financial markets and the activities of international companies.

- The international financial marketplace is an interrelated network of buyers and sellers in which exchange activities occur in the pursuit of profit and reward, and has obvious significance for international companies.

- Companies may wish to undertake overseas operations for a variety of reasons, but particularly to gain access to overseas markets by enabling them to get closer to their customers.

- Companies may engage in various types of international operations, for example through exporting, use of agents, licensing, franchising, or the establishment of a branch, joint venture, or an overseas subsidiary.

- International companies may consider foreign direct investment (FDI) in terms of investments in new or expanded facilities overseas.

- There are additional, unique features associated with international investment appraisal in a multi-currency, overseas environment, compared with the appraisal of domestic investment projects, for example taxation, foreign currency cash flows, overseas interest rates, transfer prices, royalties, management fees, exchange controls, and country risk.

- The evaluation of international investment using NPV requires the choice of a suitable cost of capital as a discount rate, the most appropriate of which may be the required return specific to the individual investment.

- The choice of financing for international investments requires the consideration of currency risk, interest rate risk, taxation, gearing, and country risk.

- Country risk, which is also called political risk, is the exposure a company faces as a consequence of a change in government action, against which it may protect itself through, for example, insurance, negotiation, development of close relationships, establishment of a local presence, and the use of local financing.

Glossary of key terms

adjusted present value (APV) A method of investment appraisal where the basic investment, excluding the impacts of tax and financing, is discounted using an ungeared cost of equity, the result of which is then added to the result of discounting the tax and financing cash flows, using an appropriate cost of debt.

expropriation of assets Expropriation refers to the action of a government taking away a business or its assets from its owners, which may occur mainly in countries where property laws are not concrete and well defined.

foreign direct investment (FDI) FDI may be inward (domestic investment by overseas companies) or outward (overseas investment by domestic companies).

joint venture A business entity in which a company holds an interest on a long-term basis and is jointly controlled by that company and one or more other venturers under a contractual arrangement (FRS 9). A joint venture may also refer to a project undertaken by two or more persons or entities joining together with a view to profit, often in connection with a single operation.

transfer price The price at which goods or services are transferred between different units of the same company.

Assessment material

Questions

Q11.1   Explain the corporate financing implications of internationalisation.

Q11.2   Outline the roles of the key participants in the international financial marketplace.

Q11.3   Explain why companies may wish to engage in international markets.

Q11.4   Critically compare the different types of indirect international operations.

Q11.5   Critically compare the different types of direct international operations.

Q11.6   Describe the route by which a multinational company may ultimately establish a subsidiary company in a foreign country.

Q11.7   Outline the alternative methods of international investment appraisal.

Q11.8   Explain the advantages and disadvantages of the various discount rate options that may be used in the NPV evaluation of international investments.

Q11.9   Outline the risks associated with international investment.

Q11.10   Describe the strategies that may be adopted by multinational companies with regard to country risk.

Discussion points

D11.1   'Internationalisation is the only way that medium-sized and large companies can survive and prosper in the 21st century.' Discuss.

D11.2   'The cost of setting up an overseas subsidiary far outweighs any benefits.' Discuss.

D11.3   Chairman of a UK plc: 'The calculation of WACC is a straightforward matter and I don't see why it should be any more complicated if we are using it to evaluate an investment in an overseas subsidiary.' Discuss.

Exercises

Solutions are provided in Appendix 2 to all exercise numbers highlighted in colour.

Level I

E11.1   *Time allowed – 30 minutes*

Describe the main elements of the international financial marketplace.

E11.2   *Time allowed – 30 minutes*

Why do companies choose indirect methods like exporting rather than direct international operations like FDIs?

E11.3   *Time allowed – 30 minutes*

In what ways does international investment appraisal differ from domestic investment appraisal?

E11.4   *Time allowed – 45 minutes*

Explain the various ways in which an FDI may be evaluated, and compare the alternative choices of discount rate that may be used in such evaluations.

Level II

E11.5   *Time allowed – 45 minutes*

There is currently an economic recession throughout the continent of Indulosia, which has hit one of its countries, Zorbia, particularly hard. The UK Bank of Penderyn has made loans totalling £0.5bn to the government of Zorbia, for which it has received no repayments because of the widespread recession. Representatives of the Bank of Penderyn have had extensive discussions with officials of the Zorbian central bank and have now received a proposal. 'We acknowledge the Bank of Zorbia's debt with the Bank of Penderyn and, in order to satisfy its outstanding commitments to the Bank, the Zorbian government proposes that the outstanding debts of £0.5bn be exchanged for equity shares in a number of recently privatised Zorbian utility companies. The approximate current market value of these shares at today's exchange rate of £1 = 4.5 Zors is 1.35bn Zors.'

You are required to advise the Bank of Penderyn with regard to its overseas operation, and suggest how it may respond to the Zorbian government's proposal and recommend alternative courses of action that the bank may consider.

E11.6   *Time allowed – 45 minutes*

Explain and compare each of the alternative sources of financing an FDI, and their advantages and disadvantages to a multinational company.

E11.7   *Time allowed – 45 minutes*

Benjamin plc is a UK first-tier supplier of integrated automotive systems to a number of French car manufacturers. Benjamin plc has issued share capital of 666,667 fully paid up £1 ordinary shares with a current *ex dividend* market price of £3 per share, and 1,000,000 £1, 5% preference shares with a current market price of £1 per share. A dividend of 10p per share has recently been paid to ordinary shareholders. The company also has £800,000 7% debentures redeemable at par in three years' time. The debentures have a current *cum interest* market value of £104.

Benjamin has recently received a proposal for a contract for £20m to supply some of its systems to be used in French police vehicles.

The contract is expected to last four years and the estimated cash flows are:

Year	Cash flow
0	£(20.0m)
1	€11.0m
2	€13.5m
3	€10.0m
4	€3.5m

Benjamin plc is proposing the engagement of a UK-based management company to oversee the project. A management fee of £100,000 per annum is payable to the company in years one to four for their management of the French police contract. The UK corporation tax rate is assumed to be 35% on net profit payable in each year following the year in which the profit was earned. The £ sterling/euro exchange rates for the four years of the contract have been estimated at:

Year 1	£1 = €1.70
Year 2	£1 = €1.75
Year 3	£1 = €1.80
Year 4	£1 = €1.85

Required:

Benjamin plc uses its current weighted average cost of capital to evaluate overseas investments. On this basis, and ignoring French taxes, advise the company as to whether the contract should be accepted.

E11.8   *Time allowed – 45 minutes*

Provide a detailed explanation of country (political) risk, and its relevance with regard to a multinational company's decision to establish a new overseas subsidiary in a fast-growing, low-tax country. Outline the legitimate ways in which the multinational may minimise the risks you have described.

E11.9   *Time allowed – 45 minutes*

Lee Ltd is a UK company proposing to invest in a project in Singapore. The company expects the investment project to generate net profits of SGD2,000m per year.

You may assume that:

- Singapore corporation tax is 18%
- a withholding tax of 10% is payable on all foreign dividend remittances
- UK corporation tax is 30% with full tax credits available for taxes paid in Germany
- foreign exchange rates will not change over the life of the investment
- no exchange controls exist between the UK, Singapore, and Germany to prevent the remittance of investment cash flows.

Required:

Calculate the after-tax cash flows in the following situations:

(i)   **All the project profits are remitted to the UK.**
(ii) **All the project profits are reinvested in Singapore.**
(iii) **The investment is managed by a wholly owned German subsidiary with the dividends remitted to Germany for further investment outside the UK.**

E11.10 *Time allowed – 45 minutes*

Drex plc is a UK-based retail company with a market capitalisation of £800m. Because of increasing competition in the UK market, the company is considering two alternative mutually exclusive investment options:

- Option 1 is to invest £200m in the development of a range of new retail outlets in Norway.
- Option 2 is to invest £200m in a new subsidiary in Malaysia.

Because of financing constraints, the company can select only one of the options. The company is considering raising the required £200m from a combination of a rights issue and secured borrowing.

The risk and return profile of each option is as follows:

	Return	Standard deviation
New retail outlets in Norway	12%	0.04
New subsidiary in Malaysia	12%	0.05

The after-tax return on the capital invested in the existing UK business has been 10% per annum for the past few years with a standard deviation of 0.03. The correlation of project returns with the UK business is as follows:

- The correlation of the return on the Norway option with the average after-tax returns of the UK business is 0.8.
- The correlation of the return on the Malaysian project with the average after-tax returns of the UK business is 0.3.

Required:

Prepare a report for the board of Drex plc explaining and advising which of the above two projects the company should undertake.

12

Financial risk management

Chapter contents

Learning objectives

Completion of this chapter will enable you to:

- Explain what is meant by financial risk and consider its implications.
- Describe the various types of financial risk.
- Explain the use of the exchange rate equivalency model in the context of alternative financial strategies.
- Analyse the issues relating to interest rate risk.
- Analyse the issues relating to foreign currency exchange rate risk.
- Appreciate the importance of financial risk management.
- Consider the various methods used for the hedging of financial risks.
- Explain the use of some of the wide range of derivatives available for companies to hedge foreign currency exchange rate and interest rate risk.
- Evaluate the alternative financial risk management strategies.
- Describe how behavioural finance may explain irrational behaviour of investors.

Introduction

In Chapters 13 to 15 we will look at financial risk in general (as distinct from the business risk faced by a business) relating to the company's financial structure, or gearing, as it moves through its life cycle. Business risk relates to the variability of a company's operating profit or cash flow, dependent on levels of selling prices, demand volumes, cyclical trends, and the relationship between its level of fixed cost and total cost (operational gearing). The level of business risk varies from one industry to another. Financial risk with regard to a company's financial structure relates to the impact on profits of its commitment to and ability to pay interest, the level of interest rates, and the possibility of bankruptcy.

More specific types of financial risk are considered in this chapter relating to movements in foreign currency exchange rates and interest rates. These are financial risks that may be faced by companies arising from:

- trade (selling or buying) with overseas organisations
- transactions (trade or investment) denominated in currencies other than £ sterling (for UK companies)
- investment in assets or businesses located overseas
- financial investment overseas.

This chapter introduces what is broadly called the exchange rate equivalency model, which can be used to explain relationships between exchange rates, interest rates, and inflation rates. It forms a basis on which a number of techniques of international financial management are based.

A company may previously have had very little experience of doing business outside the UK. However, international interest and demand for its products will lead to its involvement in trade and possibly investment in countries in, for example, Europe, Africa, Asia, North America, and South America. The development of such business may not only contribute to securing the longer-term future of the company, but also restore market confidence generally in the company's performance.

Companies may seek to establish a foothold in an increasingly competitive and unpredictable global marketplace to enhance shareholder value, but find that it is rarely risk-free. The volatility of global markets is seen in the pressures of international supply and demand, continuing deregulation of international markets, and the unremitting expansion of international corporate trading activities. The minimisation of risk, particularly the risk of financial loss, has become an increasingly important role for 21st century corporate financial managers.

The existence of the risk of financial loss may result from a range of interrelated social, political, and economic factors. In an international context the risk of financial loss may result from:

- the imposition of excessive legal restrictions
- restrictive exchange controls
- loss of goods in transit
- customer payment default
- failure to meet payment deadlines
- contractual obligations not being satisfied.

This chapter discusses the types of financial risk that companies may face when trading or investing internationally, and the various techniques that they may use to minimise the risks associated with those activities.

Risk and uncertainty

It is useful to clarify what is meant by risk as distinct from uncertainty, although the two words are often used to mean the same thing. After a decision has been made the actual outcome may not be what was expected, but may be better or worse. The two approaches to analysing this are:

- uncertainty analysis, which is an unquantified approach that takes a view about how much the actual outcomes may be better or worse than rational estimates
- risk analysis, which is a quantified approach about how future outcomes may vary, expressed as probabilities.

The first approach, uncertainty analysis, in its simplest form considers the most likely outcome, and also the worst and best possible outcomes. A range of estimated outcomes may, for example, assist managers in assessing investment projects and rejecting those where the worst outcome might involve an unacceptable level of loss. This approach also enables a manager to compare alternative investment projects and choose the one offering attractive returns within acceptable levels of uncertainty.

The maximin, maximax, and minimax regret decision rules are forms of uncertainty analysis that may be applied where it is not possible to assign meaningful probabilities to alternative courses of action.

The maximin decision rule is used by a risk-averse decision-maker who wants to make a conservative decision. This type of decision-maker looks at the worst possible outcome of each decision alternative and chooses the one that has the least worse consequence. The decision is to select the option that offers the least unattractive worst outcome. This means choosing the option that maximises the minimum profit, or minimises the maximum loss (when it is then called the minimax rule).

The maximax decision rule is used by a risk-taking decision-maker who looks at the best possible outcome of each decision alternative and chooses the one that has the highest best consequence. The decision is to select the option that offers the most attractive best outcome. This means choosing the option that maximises the maximum profit.

The maximin and maximax decision rules are illustrated in Worked example 12.1.

Worked example 12.1

Right plc is considering three possible sales prices for a new product and has estimated the following sales volumes at each price over the life of the product:

Price per unit	£100	£105	£110
Expected sales volumes (units)			
Best	150,000	140,000	120,000
Likely	135,000	126,000	118,000
Worst	100,000	80,000	60,000

The costs over the life of the product are:

Fixed costs £5m
Variable costs £50 for each product

Which sales price should a company choose?

Price per unit	£100	£105	£110
Contribution per product	£50	£55	£60
Total profit/(loss)			
Best	£2.50m	£2.70m	£2.20m
Likely	£1.75m	£1.93m	£2.08m
Worst	£0.00m	£(0.60)m	£(1.40)m

Based on the *best sales volume*, the highest profit is at a price of £105 per product. Also, the likely profit at that price is slightly higher than at a price of £100, but the worst profit is a loss, which is lower than break-even at a price of £100.

Based on the *likely sales volume*, profit at a price of £100 is almost as good as at a price of £105, but it is not as good as at a price of £110. However, although a price of £110 gives the highest profit at the likely sales volume, the profit at the best volume is the worst of the three prices and at the worst sales volume there is a loss, which is a higher loss than at the price of £105.

Based on the *worst sales volume*, a price of £100 guarantees that the company does not make a loss.

Using the maximin, or in this case the minimax, decision rule, a risk-averse decision-maker will choose a price of £100 because it is the least unattractive position of the worst sales volumes, estimated at break-even, even though at likely and best sales volumes the profits are the lowest and next lowest.

Using the maximax decision rule, a risk-taking decision-maker will choose a price of £105 because it is the highest best position estimated at £2.70m profit, although at a worst sales volume a loss is estimated and at a likely sales volume the profit is next lowest.

Whenever a decision is made there is likely to be subsequent regret by the decision-maker that an alternative decision had not been made. The extent of this regret is effectively a loss of opportunity, and a regret for any combination of actions and circumstances is equal to the benefit gained from the best action in those circumstances less the actual benefit gained in those circumstances. The minimax regret decision rule is that the decision option selected should be the one that minimises the maximum potential regret, for any of the possible outcomes. This is illustrated in Worked example 12.2.

Worked example 12.2

An investor is considering two investments A and B which have different expected returns, dependent on whether the market is weak or strong, which are shown in the table below:

Investment	Return	
	Weak market	**Strong market**
A	£11,000	£15,000
B	£2,000	£21,000

We will consider which investment should be chosen, assuming it is not possible to assign probabilities to the likely market condition.

Using the maximin rule, the payoff selected is the least unattractive worst outcome.
Worst outcomes:
$$A = £11,000$$
$$B = £2,000$$
The decision is to choose A, which provides the least worse return

Using the maximax rule, the largest payoff is selected assuming that the best possible outcome will occur.
Best outcomes:
$$A = £15,000$$
$$B = £21,000$$

The decision is to choose B, which provides the best maximum return.

Using the minimax regret rule, the payoff selected aims to minimise the maximum possible regret, for any of the possible outcomes.

The regret table below shows the return that may be forgone for each project, depending on whether the outcome is a weak or strong market.

Choice	Regret table	
	Weak market occurs	**Strong market occurs**
A	£0 (i)	£6,000 (iii)
B	£9,000 (ii)	£0 (iv)

Regret   (i) 11–11   (ii) 11–2   (iii) 21–15   (iv) 21–21

$$\text{The maximum regret for investment A} = £6,000$$
$$\text{The maximum regret for investment B} = £9,000$$

The decision should be to choose project A, because it provides the minimum maximum likely regret.

The outcome of a decision may be uncertain, but for some decisions it is possible to use risk analysis by assigning probabilities to various outcomes. Estimates of probabilities may be assessed from previous experience or from comparisons with similar situations. The probabilities are used to measure the likelihood that an event or state of nature will occur. A probability distribution lists all possible outcomes for an event and the probability of each one occurring, a very simple example of which is illustrated in Worked example 12.3.

Worked example 12.3

Two students, Janet and John, have just sat the same examination. Whether they have passed or failed the examination is called the outcome of the event (the examination). The probability of each outcome has been estimated by their tutor and the results are shown in the probability distribution below.

Outcome	Janet probability	John probability
Pass examination	0.8	0.6
Fail examination	0.2	0.4
	1.0	1.0

Because the probabilities each add up to one it means that one or other outcome (pass or fail) will happen with certainty. The probability distribution provides more meaningful information than merely stating that the estimated outcomes are that both students are likely to pass.

In practice, probability distributions will include a great deal more data than illustrated in Worked example 12.3. Instead of presenting huge probability distributions for many alternatives, it is more convenient to use summary measures of these data to assess risk. We illustrated the use of three of these – expected values, standard deviation, coefficient of variation – in some of the worked examples in Chapter 4.

Risk is both complex and subjective. In general, the risk of financial loss arises where the outcome of particular events, processes, and transactions are deemed to be uncertain. For example, a low-risk event is an event where the outcome is fairly predictable, whereas a high-risk event is an event where the outcome is fairly unpredictable. The term risk normally encapsulates notions of chance, speculation, and uncertainty.

Types of financial risk

Within the global trading environment, sources of financial risk for a UK company are:

- country – economic and social infrasructures, government policy, legal restrictions, exchange controls, trade restrictions
- property – products, services, businesses, financial investments, land, and buildings
- credit – terms of trading, method of settlement, and likelihood of non-payment
- interest rates – UK and overseas interest rates
- foreign currency exchange rates – the relative values of worldwide currencies.

We have considered credit risk in Chapter 10. In this chapter we will look in some detail at financial risk arising from movements in interest rates and foreign currency exchange rates. Country risk is an area of risk which may have a significant impact on potential levels of property risk, credit risk, interest rate volatility, exchange rate volatility, and the alternative settlement strategies available to companies importing or exporting products or services overseas.

Many alternative international settlement strategies exist: open account; consignment payment; payment in advance; documentary collection; letter of credit; counter-trade. However, their selection and use, while partly dependent upon mutual negotiation, is based on:

- perceived risk associated with the specific country
- perceived risk associated with the nature of the transaction
- terms generally on offer within the country for similar products or services
- terms offered by competitors trading within the specific country
- requirements and trading history of the importing or exporting company
- financial implications in terms of cash flow requirements and levels of financial charges for the importing or exporting company.

The strategic management of financial risk is clearly important to companies that use debt financing. Financial risk relating to changing levels of foreign currency exchange rates, and possibly both UK and foreign interest rates, is extremely important to multinational businesses, and companies operating in global markets.

In 1934, the United States government fixed the rate at which the US$ was convertible into gold at US$35 per ounce. The Bretton Woods agreement of 1944 fixed £ sterling relative to the US$ at US $4.03 = £1. Therefore £ sterling also had a known 'gold parity'. All major world currencies were also fixed in value either to the US$ or the £, and therefore indirectly to gold. The UK Government devalued the £ in 1949 to US$2.80, and then in November 1967 to US$2.40. During this entire period up until 1971 foreign exchange remained relatively stable. From 1971 everything changed. In mid-1971, the United States suspended the convertibility of US$ into gold. During the following couple of years the Deutschmark and other European currencies were 'floated', and no longer fixed against the US$, and then subsequently re-fixed. The so-called 'Snake' agreement in April 1972 allowed several European currencies to fluctuate by a small percentage around some agreed exchange rates. In June 1972, the £ sterling left the 'Snake', floated and fell in value. In February 1973, the US$ was devalued. In March 1973, the European currencies broke their links with the US$ completely, maintaining links only between each other, and then the Deutschmark was revalued again in June 1973.

Things came to a head in October 1973 when the members of the OPEC (Organization of the Petroleum Exporting Countries) countries quadrupled the price of oil. The formal links that had previously held world currencies together, and had maintained their stability, had already been dismantled. Therefore, it was virtually impossible for the currency markets to absorb the first oil price crisis of 1973, and since that time the world has continued to experience repeated currency crises of increasing frequency and scale. Most currencies now float freely against each other, which means that their relative values are not fixed but vary from one minute to another for a variety of reasons.

Since 1971, exchange rates have moved much faster and more frequently than ever before. Even currencies that may be considered to be relatively stable can experience major movements on their exchange rates during the short term and over the longer term. It is not uncommon to see high levels of exchange rate volatility during a year, and exchange rates at the beginning and the end of a year may also be significantly different. During the period 1975 to 1993, for example, the year-on-year US$/£ exchange rate movements regularly ranged between 10 and 35%, although between 1993 and 2001 year-on-year movements tended to be less volatile.

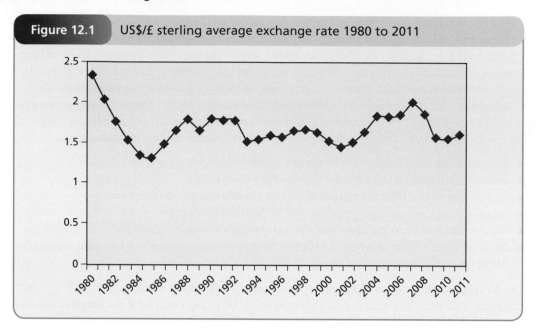

Figure 12.1   US$/£ sterling average exchange rate 1980 to 2011

However, from 2002 to date US$/£ exchange rate movements have again increased in volatility up to around 35% (see Figure 12.1). Timing is therefore the all-important factor in considering the appropriate actions required to eliminate or mitigate the impact of such foreign currency exchange rate movements on the profits of a business. It is because companies undertake transactions and hold assets and liabilities denominated in currencies other than their local currency that they face exposure to movements in exchange rates.

Progress check 12.1

Why is financial risk particularly important to international companies?

The level of financial risk is greater the higher a company is geared financially. A company with high debt faces the risk that interest rates may rise, which will have a directly adverse impact on profit. The company also faces the risk that it may earn insufficient levels of profit over the term of a loan to ensure that it is able to service the loan and ultimately repay the loan. At very high levels of debt, a company may face the further risk of bankruptcy, actioned by a lender's lack of confidence that future interest commitments and loan repayments may not be capable of being met. The level of interest risk faced by a company may be measured by its income gearing (the reciprocal of interest cover), which compares its interest payments as a percentage of profit before interest and tax. It may be argued that a low-geared company also faces the risk of lost opportunities of increased profits should future interest rates decrease. Interest rates were particularly volatile during the 1970s and 1980s, and as a consequence it became essential during that time for companies to closely manage their exposures to interest rate risk.

There is obviously a need for companies to identify the types of financial risk that they face and to take the appropriate actions to mitigate such risks. The level of such actions (which are called hedging), with regard to interest rates depends on:

■ the size and complexity of the company's borrowings
■ the proportion of floating and fixed interest debt

- the volatility of interest rates
- the currencies in which loans are denominated.

In terms of foreign currency exchange rate risk the level and type of hedging depend on the type of transaction (buying or selling), number and values of transactions, and level of investments denominated in foreign currency, and the specific countries with which business is conducted. The increasing uncertainty surrounding foreign currency exchange rates, increasing globalisation, and the massive increase in international trade, means that exchange risk management has become critically important to companies. Their failure to insure or hedge against exchange rate movements may significantly impact on profits and may even result in the ultimate demise of the business. It is useful to regard interest and exchange rate management as a form of insurance. As individuals we insure ourselves against loss or injury. In the same way, companies insure themselves by hedging against adverse movements in interest rates and foreign currency exchange rates.

Since 1971 there has necessarily been an increased awareness by companies of the benefits of managing and hedging both their interest and exchange rate risk exposures. The importance of hedging by companies is related to size of the potential losses that may result from adverse movements in interest and exchange rates. In the next few sections we will look at the different types of interest rate and foreign currency exchange risk faced by companies and the hedging techniques available to control and manage such risk. There are a growing number of complex financial instruments, called derivatives, which are available for the hedging of exposure to the risk of movements in both interest rates and foreign currency exchange rates. The accounting rules covering the reporting of derivatives are currently a hot topic. Much discussion and disagreement continues both within the UK and between various other countries with regard to the control and reporting of derivatives by companies, particularly in the light of the various examples of their misuse (note Enron and see the section later about the use of derivatives).

Exchange rate equivalency model

In an increasingly global economy, the international financial environment is a complex network of social, political, and economic interrelationships in which the supply of, and demand for capital, commodities, currencies, and assets are continually affected by, for example:

- government controls and restrictions with regard to the international trade of goods and services
- government controls and restrictions on capital flows and currency movements
- the relative power of market players
- the general level of market expectations.

Within this dynamic setting, theories and hypotheses have been developed to explain the relationships between:

- interest rate differentials
- inflation rate differentials
- movements in spot currency exchange rates
- movements in forward currency exchange rates.

The exchange rate equivalency model is a model that has been developed from a number of assumptions of market perfection, for example:

- the existence of no significant market imperfections
- the existence of no political or economic barriers to the mobility of capital and currencies
- the existence of no long-term sustainable arbitrage opportunities.

The exchange rate equivalency model may be defined as a hypothetical relationship in which:

- the nominal interest rate differential between two countries is assumed to be equal to
- the expected inflation rate differential between those two countries and equal to
- the differential between the forward rate and the spot rate of the currencies over a given period and equal to
- the rate of change of the expected spot exchange rate of those two countries.

The exchange rate equivalency model includes combinations of each of the above elements represented in the following theories and hypotheses:

- **Fisher Effect** (or Fisher's closed hypothesis)
- **Interest Rate Parity Theory**
- **Purchasing Power Parity Theory**
- **Expectations Theory** of exchange rates
- **International Fisher Effect** (or Fisher's open hypothesis),

which may be expressed in diagrammatic form (shown in Figure 12.2), and also algebraically (see Figure 12.3).

We may use the US$ and £ sterling to illustrate each of the elements of the exchange rate equivalency model, as follows:

$$i_\$ = \text{USA US\$ interest rate} \qquad f_0 = \text{US\$/£ forward exchange rate}$$
$$i_£ = \text{UK £ interest rate} \qquad s_0 = \text{US\$/£ spot rate}$$
$$p_\$ = \text{USA inflation rate} \qquad e_t = \text{US\$/£ expected spot rate}$$
$$p_£ = \text{UK inflation rate}$$

to illustrate the US$/£ sterling interrelationships and algebraic equations expressed in Figure 12.3.

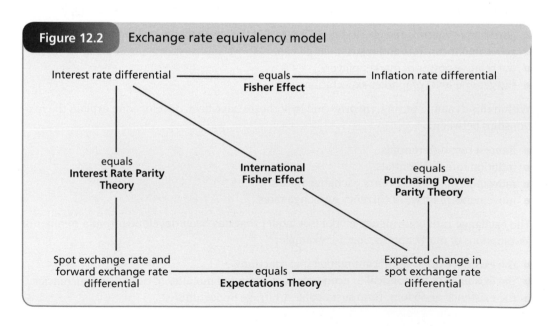

Figure 12.2 Exchange rate equivalency model

Interest rate differential ——— equals ——— Inflation rate differential
Fisher Effect

equals
Interest Rate Parity Theory

International Fisher Effect

equals
Purchasing Power Parity Theory

Spot exchange rate and forward exchange rate differential ——— equals ——— Expected change in spot exchange rate differential
Expectations Theory

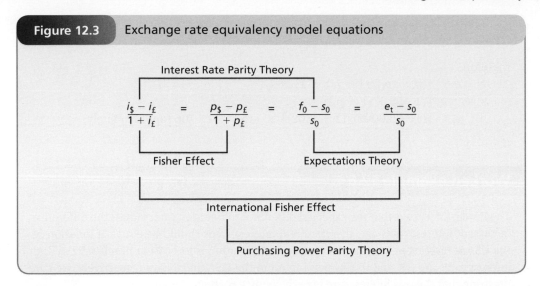

Figure 12.3 Exchange rate equivalency model equations

Worked example 12.4

The Interest Rate Parity Theory says that the ratio between the risk-free interest rates in two different countries is equal to the ratio between the forward and spot exchange rates.

There is an opportunity to invest US$500,000 for one year in a one-year US$ bond paying 3% per annum, or obtain a one-year Japanese yen bond paying 0.05% per annum. The spot rate is 115 ¥/US$, and the one-year forward rate is 111.706 ¥/US$.

We can determine if one bond is better than the other (ignoring transaction costs).

Value of the US$ bond after one year = US$500,000 × 1.03 = US$515,000
If US$ are exchanged for ¥ at the spot rate US$500,000 × 115 = ¥57,500,000
Value of the ¥ bond after one year = ¥57,500,000 × 1.0005 = ¥57,528,750
And then ¥ are exchanged for US$ ¥ 57,528,750 @ 111.706 = US$515,000

Both bonds have the same value in US$ (apart from rounding differences), which they should have by definition in the Interest Rate Parity Theory.

Worked example 12.5

The Purchasing Power Parity Theory of exchange rates says that the expected change in spot exchange rates equals the expected difference in inflation rates. If inflation in the USA is forecast at 2% (p_s) this year and Japan's inflation is forecast at a minus 0.92% (p_Y), we can calculate the expected spot rate one year ahead (e_t), given a current spot rate of 115 ¥/US$ (s_0).

$$\frac{p_Y - p_s}{1 + p_s} = \frac{e_t - s_0}{s_0}$$

therefore

$$e_t = [(p_Y - p_s)/(1 + p_s) + 1] \times s_0$$
$$= [(1 + p_Y)/(1 + p_s)] \times s_0$$
$$e_t = [(1 - 0.0092)/(1 + 0.02)] \times 115 = 111.706 \text{ (approximately)}$$

Worked example 12.6

The Fisher Effect says that the expected difference in inflation rates equals the difference in current interest rates and therefore real interest rates should be equal. If inflation in the USA is forecast at 2% this year and Japan's inflation is forecast at minus 0.92%, and interest rates are 3% and 0.05% per annum in the USA and Japan respectively, we can illustrate that the real interest rate in each country is about the same.

$$\text{USA real interest rate} \quad = \frac{1 + 3\%}{1 + 2\%} = \frac{1.03}{1.02} = 1.0098 = 0.98\%$$

$$\text{Japan real interest rate} = \frac{1 + 0.05\%}{1 - 0.92\%} = \frac{1.0005}{0.9908} = 1.0098 = 0.98\%$$

Worked example 12.7

Nishanota can manufacture one of its passenger car models in the UK for a total cost of £11,200, including its profit margin. At a current exchange rate of 0.56 £/US$ the car sells for US$20,000 in the USA. If the US$ is expected to rise in value against £ sterling to an exchange rate of 0.60 £/US$, we can calculate what price the car may be sold at by Nishanota in the USA while still protecting its profit margin.

$$\frac{£11,200}{0.60} = US\$18,667$$

If the US$ had been expected to fall in value against £ sterling to an exchange rate of say 0.55 £/US$, the price would have to have been increased to over US$20,000 at US$20,364.

The exchange rate equivalency model's theories and hypotheses' explanations of movements in interest rates, inflation rates, spot currency exchange rates, and forward currency exchange rates form a basis for many international financial management techniques. However, the validity of these interrelationships is not beyond question, and evidence from research undertaken over the last 25 years remains inconclusive as to the precise nature of the relationship between interest rates, inflation rates, and exchange rate movements. There are concerns regarding the lack of empirical support with regard to both the short-term and long-term validity of many of the model's underpinning theories and hypotheses.

- Fisher Effect – some researchers have found a positive relationship between interest rate movements and inflation rate movements while other researchers have found little evidence of such a relationship.
- Interest Rate Parity Theory – empirical testing has suggested that an actual relationship between interest rate differentials and forward exchange rate premiums and discounts may exist in the shorter term, although substantial deviations were found in the medium to longer term.
- Purchasing Power Parity Theory – some researchers have found that purchasing power parity does hold in the medium to longer term. Other researchers have found significant deviations, leading to suggestions that other influential factors beyond the inflation and exchange rate relationship may impact differently on inflation rates and exchange rates.
- International Fisher Effect – some researchers have found Fisher's open hypothesis to hold well in the medium to longer term, whereas other researchers have found significant deviations.
- Expectations Theory – researchers have found conflicting evidence. Some have found that the forward rate is a good unbiased predictor of the future exchange rate, while other researchers have found this not to be the case.

Such criticisms imply that the assumption that market forces, underpinned by an implicit interrelationship between interest rates, inflation rates, and exchange rates, freely determine the movements of currency exchange rates, which is clearly not the case. The reason for this is that often the largest player within the foreign exchange market, the national central bank, intervenes for reasons other than those of profit maximisation. The intervention of national central banks in the foreign exchange markets often occurs for other than primarily economic reasons.

Despite the criticisms, the exchange rate equivalency model is a useful model that has been deduced from the series of interrelationships between the relative levels of:

- interest rates
- inflation rates
- purchasing power,

which provides an approximation of how the interaction of inflation rates and interest rates may affect the movement of currency exchange rates.

In the absence of any significant market imperfections, arbitrage opportunities, speculation, political and economic barriers to the mobility of international capital, the exchange rate equivalency model provides an opportunity to estimate and predict the effects and impact of changes in:

- inflation rates, on interest rates
- interest rates, on currency exchange rates
- inflation rates, on currency exchange rates
- spot exchange rates of a particular currency, on forward exchange rates of that particular currency.

Interest rate risk

Interest rate risk is faced by businesses, whether they may be either or both lenders or borrowers of funds. If a company borrows money at a specific fixed rate of interest it faces a risk that market interest rates may subsequently fall and so it will have an opportunity cost of interest (and *vice versa* an opportunity gain should market interest rates increase). If a company lends by investing surplus funds at a specific fixed rate of interest it faces a risk that market interest rates may subsequently increase and so it will have an opportunity cost of lost interest (and *vice versa* an opportunity gain of interest should market interest rates fall).

The way in which interest rates affect lenders or borrowers of funds depends on whether the agreed rates are fixed or floating rates. Floating rates of interest are usually stated as the LIBOR (London Interbank Offer Rate) rate of interest + or − a number of percentage points (for example, LIBOR + 2%). Therefore, interest paid or received will vary as LIBOR varies.

The impacts on lenders or borrowers of funds at fixed or floating rates may be broadly summarised as follows:

- A borrower of funds at a fixed interest rate faces the risk of a fall in general interest rates. This is because competitors who have borrowed at floating rates will benefit from lower interest payments, higher profit, improved cash flow, and lower financial risk and therefore a lower cost of capital.
- A borrower of funds at a floating interest rate faces the risk of:
  - a rise in general interest rates, resulting in higher interest payments, reduced profit, worsened cash flow, and higher financial risk and therefore a higher cost of capital
  - inaccurate and unreliable forecasts of future interest cash outflows
  - the possibility of bankruptcy following large increases in interest rates, particularly if their level of gearing is high.
- A lender of funds at a fixed interest rate faces the risk of a rise in general interest rates. This is because competitors who have invested at floating rates will benefit from higher interest receipts, higher profit, and improved cash flow.
- A lender of funds at a floating interest rate faces the risk of:
  - a fall in general interest rates, resulting in lower interest receipts, reduced profit, and worsened cash flow
  - inaccurate and unreliable forecasts of future interest cash inflows.

In addition to the above situations, interest rate risk occurs when a business may be a lender and also a borrower of funds. It is unlikely that a company will have loans and investments of the same level at floating or fixed rates of interest, but if they do then the financial risk of borrowing may offset to some extent the risk of lending. It is probably more likely that a company will have loans and investments at differing floating rates or at floating rates that may or may not both be linked to LIBOR. A company which is both the lender and borrower faces the risk of:

- loans and investments which are not similar in size
- different floating rates
- floating rates that are inconsistently based (for example linked to LIBOR)
- interest rate revisions at different dates.

> **Progress check 12.2**
>
> What is interest rate risk?

Exchange rate risk

In increasingly global markets, businesses are even more likely to be engaged in transactions denominated in currencies other than that of their own country. A foreign currency exchange rate is broadly the rate at which one unit of a currency may be exchanged for one unit of another

Figure 12.4	Euro/£ sterling forward exchange rates at 14 June 2012	
	Bank buys euros	Bank sells euros
Spot rate	0.8066	0.8074
One month forward	0.8067	0.8078
Three months forward	0.8069	0.8083
One year forward	0.8084	0.8143

Figure 12.5	Example of euro/£ sterling forward exchange rates

14 June 2012

Spot	1 month	3 months	1 year
0.8066 – 0.8074	+1/4	+3/9	+18/69

currency. The rates at which currencies may be exchanged today are different from the rates at which currencies may be exchanged, for example, next week, next month, or next year.

The exchange rates at which currencies may be bought and sold today are determined by a number of factors but effectively reflect the demand and supply of the currencies. There is a spread between the rate at which a currency is bought and the rate at which it is sold. The spread of the rate for immediate buying or selling is called the **spot rate**. The spot rate actually means the exchange rate at which a currency is bought or sold today for value two working days later.

The exchange rate agreed today at which currency may be bought or sold at some time in the future is called a **forward rate**. Forward rates are determined by the current spot rate, the amount of time elapsing between now and the future transaction date, and the differential between the core interest rates applicable to each currency. The table in Figure 12.4 provides an illustration of the spreads of exchange rates at which a customer may buy or sell euros from or to a bank in exchange for £ sterling at the spot rates, and the rates in three months' time, and one year's time. For example, a customer could buy €1 from the bank (bank sells) for spot £0.8074, or sell €1 to the bank (bank buys) for £0.8066 spot on 14 June 2012.

The table in Figure 12.4 shows that each of the €/£ forward rates are higher than the spot rates. The forward rates are said to be at a **discount** to the spot rates. This is because at 14 June 2012 the € interest rate was higher than the UK £ sterling rate of interest. If forward exchange rates are lower than the spot rates they would be described as being at a **premium** to the spot rates.

The table in Figure 12.5 illustrates the way in which exchange rates are generally quoted in the financial media.

The plus sign means that the forward rate is at a discount to the spot rate and the three months bank selling forward rate is 0.8074 + 0.0009 = 0.8083€/£ (three months bank buying forward rate 0.8066 + 0.0003 = 0.8069€/£). If, for example, the ¥ interest rate had been lower than the UK £ sterling interest rate then the € forward rates would be at a premium to the £ and the appropriate premium (for example, −3/9) would be deducted from the spot rates. Very often the + and − signs are not quoted in the media and it is assumed that it is generally known by currency dealers whether or not a forward exchange rate is at a premium or a discount.

Progress check 12.3

What is meant by describing a forward exchange rate as being at a premium or at a discount to the spot rate?

Exchange rate risk arises because the values of foreign currencies are not now fixed against some standard like gold but 'float' so that their comparative values vary from day to day due to the influence of, for example, economic and political factors. **Economic risk**, for example, relates to the risk of the impact of long-term movements in exchange rates on the competitive position of companies engaged in international markets. Economic risk may be avoided by not trading in such markets, but that does not avoid the economic risk of the company's home country. The exposure of businesses to exchange rate risk is broadly defined within two classifications, which are called **transaction exposure** and **translation exposure**. Transaction exposures relate to relatively short-term revenue transactions and translation exposures relate to the balance sheet and generally for periods in excess of one year.

Businesses may be engaged in transactions with suppliers or customers in countries other than their own country. A UK business may sell overseas or buy from overseas but may not necessarily invoice the customer or be invoiced by the supplier in £ sterling. An overseas customer may not accept an invoice in £ sterling because they require to be invoiced in their own domestic currency. An overseas supplier may insist on invoicing in their own domestic currency. The cost of selling or buying a currency on the day that a transaction takes place is related to the exchange rate on that day which is known by both parties to the transaction. If the transaction is paid and settled on that day then no risk, or exposure, arises.

Most business transactions are credit transactions, where goods or services are not paid for until some time after the original transaction. Foreign exchange rate risk arises precisely because such credit terms are given. If goods and services are purchased in the currency of the vendor then the business has a payables foreign exchange transaction exposure. If the business contracts to sell in the currency of the customer then the business has a receivables foreign exchange transaction exposure. Transaction exposure is therefore the risk of a difference occurring on a foreign currency transaction between the value of the transaction in local currency at the transaction date and the value of the transaction in local currency at the settlement date. The transaction exposure is due to a risk of a movement in the exchange rate between those two dates.

Worked example 12.8

A customer in the USA insists on being invoiced for goods amounting to US$10,000 in US$ by Bruce plc, which is a UK company. At the time of delivery of the goods the value of the US$ sale in £ at the exchange rate on 13 May was £6,250 (£ = US$1.60). The US$10,000 sales invoice was issued a few days later and the exchange rate had changed to £ = US$1.62, which equals £6,173. The customer had agreed to pay two months later and the day they settled the invoice the exchange rate had moved again to £ = US$1.75, which equals £5,714. What is the value of the sale?

If a sales invoice is rendered in foreign currency, financial reporting standards require it to be valued at the exchange rate at the date of the transaction, or at an average rate for the period if exchange rates do not fluctuate significantly. In the above example the US$10,000 sale should be recorded at £1 = US$1.60 which equals £6,250. The US$10,000 was received two months later when £ sterling had appreciated to 1.75 against the US$ and so the US$10,000 was now worth only £5,714. Bruce plc therefore also made a loss on exchange of £536 (£6,250 − £5,714).

Transaction exposure relates to transactions and current assets and current liabilities denominated in foreign currencies, generally occurring within one year. Assets and liabilities appearing on a company's year-end balance sheet must be translated using the company's local currency at the exchange rate at each balance sheet date. The precise exchange rate used for valuation will be the market closing exchange rates on those dates (or it may be forward rates, which we shall discuss later). In addition, this issue arises particularly with regard to the translation of the assets and liabilities of overseas subsidiaries, which are denominated in the currencies of their country. For a holding company, at each year-end date the assets and liabilities of its overseas subsidiaries must be translated at the appropriate year-end exchange rates into its local currency for consolidation into its group accounts. Translation exposure relates to the risk that such translations may result in losses or gains as a result of movements in foreign currency exchange rates.

Worked example 12.9

A UK company has taken on a long-term loan of US$500m. In the first year at 31 December £1 = US$1.55 and in the second year at 31 December £1 = US$1.45. What is the translation loss to the company between years one and two?

	US$m	31 December exchange rate	£m
year 1	500	1.55	322.6
year 2	500	1.45	344.8
year 2 translation loss			22.2

Throughout the life of the loan the company will have translation exposures because of the movements in the £/US$ exchange rate over the period of the loan.

The assets and liabilities of a company that has transactions in foreign currencies are originally valued using the exchange rates at the time that the original transactions took place. The assets and liabilities that have not been realised in cash by the date that the next balance sheet is prepared must then be revalued at the exchange rates effective at the balance sheet date. These revaluations will result in a foreign exchange gain or loss and will therefore affect reported profit, but because they are unrealised such translation exposures are effectively only 'paper' transactions and therefore do not affect cash flows. Gains and losses on exchange will affect cash flow only when the assets and liabilities are realised and valued at the exchange rates on the dates they are paid. Nevertheless, for public companies, translation exposures may have a significant impact on their market perception because of their effect on profit.

Financial risk management

Businesses may manage the types of financial risk we have described above, relating to exchange rates and interest rates, by matching and offsetting assets and liabilities and cash flows, or choosing particular types of assets and liabilities. The following are examples of the management of such risk exposure, which are concerned with balance sheet structure:

■ An export company may invoice customers in its own currency only, thus avoiding any foreign currency exchange rate risk, but at the same time incurring a business risk of lost sales opportunities from customers who prefer to be invoiced in their own currencies.

■ Interest rate risk may be mitigated if companies hold a mix of loans with both fixed and floating interest rates – an increase in interest rates provides a benefit from holding fixed interest loans, whereas a reduction in interest rates provides a benefit from having floating interest loans.

■ Foreign currency exchange rate transaction risk may be reduced if accounts payable denominated in specific foreign currencies are matched and offset against accounts receivable denominated in the same currencies.

■ Foreign currency exchange rate transaction risk may be reduced if accounts payable denominated in specific foreign currencies are paid perhaps earlier than the agreed settlement dates if exchange rates are expected to move unfavourably over the subsequent period.

■ Foreign currency exchange rate translation risk may be reduced by a company increasing its liabilities through borrowing in the same currency as the currency in which a non-current asset is purchased, the term of the loan being the same as the anticipated life of the asset.

Management of its assets and liabilities is not the only technique that a company may use to reduce or mitigate financial risk. The past 40 years or so has seen an enormous increase in the various types of **hedging** techniques that are available to businesses in the management of their risk exposure. These began with **foreign exchange forward contracts**, and **money market hedging** (of interest rates) and **forward interest rate agreements (FRAs)** through lending and borrowing in the money market. Since the early days, hedging techniques have been developed into a huge range of what are called **derivatives** (see the later section on the use of derivatives). Derivatives are defined in the financial reporting standards as financial instruments that derive their value from the prices or rates of some underlying items, which include equities, bonds, commodities, interest rates, exchange rates, and stock market and other indices. Derivatives include **futures contracts**, **swaps**, **options**, and **swaptions**. Options (not to be confused with foreign exchange option forward contracts) may either be standard **traded options** or **over-the-counter (OTC) options**.

Mini case 12.1

Organisations need robust financial risk management procedures in place and the effect of failure to do so can be disastrous.

In March 2012 the Financial Services Authority (FSA) issued a Final Notice to the Royal Bank of Scotland (which was saved from financial collapse by the UK Government in 2008) that the Authority decided to publish a statement to the effect that the bank had contravened regulatory requirements.

Central to this decision was considerable criticism of RBS's risk management systems. The report identified the key aspects of this, which are listed below:

1. There were serious deficiencies in the control framework, which meant that it failed to provide robust oversight and challenge to the business.

2. There were serious deficiencies with the framework for the management of credit risk across the portfolio, which meant that there was a lack of focus on the need to manage risk across the portfolio as a whole.
3. There were serious deficiencies in the distribution framework, which meant that it did not operate effectively to reduce the risk in the portfolio.
4. There were serious deficiencies in the process for the identification and management of transactions that showed signs of stress, which meant that they were neither identified promptly nor managed effectively.

Hedging financial risks

Foreign exchange forward contracts

Foreign exchange forward contracts are used by businesses or individuals to buy or sell agreed amounts of currencies for delivery at specified future dates. Such contracts may be fixed foreign exchange forward contracts or option foreign exchange forward contracts. A fixed foreign exchange forward contract is a contract, for example, between a company and a bank, to exchange two currencies at an agreed exchange rate on a specific date (see Worked example 12.10). A foreign exchange forward option contract extends this idea to allow the bank or the company to call for settlement of the contract, at two days' notice, between any two dates that have been agreed between the bank and the company at the time of agreeing the contract (see Worked example 12.11).

Worked example 12.10

A UK company, Broadcal plc, expects to receive €100,000 from a customer at a specified date in three months' time. Today's spot rate against £ sterling is 1.2790 and the three-month fixed forward rate to sell € for £ is 1.2690. The company anticipates that £ sterling may strengthen against the € over the next few months in which case they would receive fewer pounds when they sell their €. They would prefer to 'fix' the amount now that they are going to realise in £ sterling in three months' time. How can they do this?

They can do this by selling €100,000 to their bank at 1.2690 by promising to deliver €100,000 on a specified date in three months' time, at which time they will receive £78,802 in return.

Alternatively, the company in Worked example 12.10 may consider a foreign exchange option forward contract instead of a fixed forward contract, an example of which is shown in Worked example 12.11.

Worked example 12.11

Broadcal plc expects to receive €100,000 from a customer at any time over the next three months up to a specific date. Today's spot rate against £ sterling is 1.2790 and the three-month option forward rate to sell € for £ is 1.2740. The company anticipates that £ sterling may strengthen against the € over the next few months in which case they would receive fewer pounds when they sell their €. They would prefer to 'fix' the amount now that they are going to realise in £ sterling over the next three months. How can they do this?

They can do this by selling €100,000 to their bank at 1.2740 by promising to deliver €100,000 at any time over the next three months (up to an agreed date), at which time they will receive £78,493 in return.

In using forward contracts, as we can see from Worked examples 12.10 and 12.11, the cash flows occur not when the forward contracts are agreed but at the settlement dates specified in the contracts. Forward contracts provide a hedge against downside risk through protection from adverse exchange rate (or interest rate) movements. However, such contracts, which are normally arranged through banks, are legally binding contracts and so any potential benefits from favourable movements in exchange rates (and interest rates) are lost.

If a transaction is to be settled at a contracted exchange rate using a forward foreign exchange contract then the exchange rate specified in the contract should be used to value that purchase or sale in the accounts of the business. Such a trading transaction is then said to be covered by a matching forward contract. At the end of each accounting period, all trade receivables denominated in a foreign currency should be translated, or revalued, using the rates of exchange ruling at the period-end date, or, where appropriate, the rates of exchange determined under the terms of any relevant forward contract currency agreements. Where there are related or matching forward contracts in respect of trading transactions, the rates of exchange specified in those contracts should be used.

A similar treatment applies to all monetary assets and liabilities denominated in a foreign currency, that is, cash and bank balances, loans, and amounts payable and receivable. An exchange gain or loss will result during an accounting period if a business transaction is settled at an exchange rate which differs from that used when the transaction was initially recorded, or, where appropriate, that used at the last balance sheet date. An exchange gain or loss will also arise on unsettled transactions if the rate of exchange used at the balance sheet date differs from that used previously. Such gains and losses are recognised during each accounting period and included in the profit or loss from ordinary activities.

Progress check 12.4

UK International Ltd invoiced a customer in the USA for goods to the value of US$50,000 on 31 December 2012. The US$ cheque sent to UK International by the customer was received on 31 January 2013 and was converted into £ sterling by the bank at US$1.55 to £1. Discuss the two transactions, the invoice and its settlement, and their impact on UK International's income statement and its balance sheet as at 31 December 2012.

Money market hedging

A money market hedge may be used by companies that, for example, want to borrow funds for a specific period for an investment at some time in the future, but are also expecting interest rates to have increased by that time. Exposure to this risk may be hedged by borrowing funds now for the whole term until the end of the required specific period. The funds are then placed on deposit at market rates until the loan is actually required. If interest rates fall or rise during the period up until when the loan is actually needed, the company will either pay more or less loan interest but also receive more or less deposit interest. Any loss would be considered a cost of hedging against the risk of paying a higher interest rate over the specific period of the loan.

Eurocurrency loans are another means of money market hedging. Eurocurrency is nothing to do with Europe or the euro. Eurocurrency refers to funds deposited in a bank when those funds are denominated in a currency differing from the bank's own domestic currency. A Eurocurrency loan may provide a hedge against an exposure to foreign exchange rate risk.

The company in Worked example 12.10 may consider a money market hedge as shown in Worked example 12.12, instead of a foreign exchange fixed forward contract.

Worked example 12.12

Broadcal plc expects to receive €100,000 from a customer at a specified date in three months' time and would like this settled at today's spot rate against £ sterling of 1.2790. The company anticipates that the £ sterling may strengthen against the € over the next few months in which case they would receive fewer pounds when they sell their €. Broadcal plc can negotiate an immediate € loan from its bank at 6.5% per annum, and it can immediately exchange the € for £ sterling at the spot rate of 1.2790. The proceeds may then be used to earn interest on deposit at say 5.0% per annum for three months. The €100,000 received in three months' time is then used to repay the € loan to the bank. We can look at the details of these transactions.

Assuming that the € loan interest rate is 6.5% per annum (1.625% for 3 months), and £ sterling deposit interest rate is 5.0% per annum (1.25% for 3 months):

The present value of the € to be borrowed is €100,000/1.01625 = €98,401
(€98,401 borrowed for 3 months is €98,401 × 1.01625 = €100,000)

£ sterling value of €98,401 = €98,401/1.2790 = £76,936
The value of £76,936 in 3 months' time = £76,936 × 1.0125 = £77,898

Broadcal plc should not therefore consider using this hedge since the amount of £ sterling received (£77,898) is less than that obtained from using the fixed foreign exchange forward contract (£78,802) that we saw in Worked example 12.10.

Progress check 12.5

What is hedging?

Forward interest rate agreement (FRA)

A company may enter into agreements with a bank concerning interest rates relating to its future borrowing or lending. Such forward interest rate agreements (FRAs) are normally used only for very large sums of money (millions rather than thousands of pounds) and for periods of more than one year. An FRA, for example, may fix the interest rate on a loan at a specific date in the future.

If interest rates rise and the actual rate on the specific future date is higher than the FRA rate then the bank will pay the difference to the company. If interest rates fall and the actual rate on the specific future date is lower than the FRA rate then the company will pay the difference to the bank.

An FRA may be used by a company to protect the downside interest rate risk on its borrowings. On the other hand, the company will not gain from any favourable interest rate movements.

The use of derivatives

International Financial Reporting Standard 9: Financial Instruments (IFRS 9) defines a derivative as a financial instrument or other contract whose value changes in response to the change in a specified interest rate, financial instrument price, commodity price, foreign exchange rate, index of prices or rates, credit rating or credit index, or other variable.

The use of derivatives has been a hot topic over the past few years and there are many *pros* and *cons* related to their use. Not least of these is the International Accounting Standards debate about their disclosure or not in the reports and accounts of public companies. Derivatives do represent financial commitments for a company, which may give rise to losses, and they may also present an opportunity for their misuse through unauthorised trading. Their proper use provides significant benefits for companies, but their misuse, as demonstrated by Nick Leeson's resultant downfall of Barings Bank, may be avoided through appropriate management controls, monitoring systems, and risk management. Management controls include:

- authorised limits on individual deals and positions
- limitations as to the types of derivatives used.

Monitoring systems include:

- regular valuation and monitoring of dealers' positions
- reporting on unauthorised dealing.

Risk management includes:

- setting the exposure policy for the treasury function: a profit centre or a cost centre
- a foreign exchange rate and interest rate exposure risk management strategy appropriate to the particular business
- identification and measurement of likely risk exposures
- selection of appropriate management techniques, hedging techniques, and derivatives.

The short-term aspect of the use of derivatives with regard to financing should be noted. They only have a relatively short life and are therefore only able to mitigate changes in the prices or rates of the underlying items, such as interest rates and exchange rates, for a limited period of time.

So, what are these derivatives that are available to companies and have generated so much excitement? We will look at the following, which are some of the main financial instruments available to companies:

- options
- futures
- swaps
- swaptions.

Progress check 12.6

What is a derivative?

Options

Options are not the same as forward contract options, but are more similar to share options. Options are available as currency options and as interest rate options. A currency option is an agreement that enables a company to buy or sell an amount of foreign currency at a specified exchange rate at some future date. The agreement gives the right to the company to buy or sell but it is under no obligation to do so and may simply abandon the option. Similarly, share options provide an agreement with the right to buy or sell shares at a specific share price, and interest rate options provide an agreement with the right to borrow or lend at a specific interest rate, and again the company is under no obligation to buy or sell. Each of these types of option is used to reduce or eliminate risk exposure, by providing the flexibility to take advantage of favourable foreign currency exchange rate, share price, and interest rate movements.

Options are useful for companies that need to issue price lists for their goods or services in foreign currencies, or who make tenders for overseas contracts in foreign currencies. In both situations, companies do not have a certainty of receiving specific amounts of foreign currency at specific dates and therefore foreign currency forward contracts would not be appropriate. They need a financial instrument that provides flexibility to deal with variable and uncertain foreign currency cash flows. The cost of this flexibility is an **option premium**, which has to be paid when the option is bought and is non-returnable.

The right to borrow or lend a specific amount of money by a particular date at a guaranteed interest rate, the **strike rate**, can be provided with an interest rate option. The right must be exercised or not by the time the agreed date is reached. An interest rate option, for example, may guarantee the interest rate on a loan up to a specific date in the future. If interest rates fall and the actual rate by the date that the option expires is lower than the option rate then the company will not want to exercise the option. If interest rates rise and the actual rate by the date that the option expires is higher than the option rate then the company will want to exercise the option.

Variations of interest rate options are available which are called **interest rate caps** and **interest rate collars**. Interest rate caps are options in which there is a 'ceiling' interest rate (as opposed to a 'floor' interest rate). An interest rate collar enables a borrower to buy an interest rate cap and simultaneously sell an interest rate 'floor' which therefore fixes the minimum cost for the company, which is lower than if an interest cap only had been used. The trade-off for this cost minimisation is that the company will not derive the benefit from a fall in interest rates below the 'floor' level.

Worked example 12.13

Jenkin plc currently borrows at 7% per annum. The finance director has advised that if interest rates were to rise above 8.5%, then this would represent a serious financial risk for the company at current gearing levels. Jenkin plc is therefore considering how it may benefit from a cap and collar agreement.

Jenkin plc may buy an interest rate cap at 8.5% from its bank, with a floor of 6.5%. The bank will have to reimburse Jenkin for the cost of any rise in interest rate above 8.5%. The bank pays Jenkin plc for agreeing to the floor of 6.5%, which Jenkin plc has effectively sold to the bank to partly offset the cost of the cap. If interest rates fall below the floor rate of 6.5% then the bank will benefit.

The premium for interest rate options is higher than FRA premiums. However, interest rate options may be standardised or tailor-made with regard to interest rates, amounts, currencies, and time periods.

Companies may obtain two different types of option:

■ a traded option is available, for example, only for specific currencies, and is a standardised option with regard to its specified amount and term, and is bought and sold on an options exchange

■ an over-the-counter (OTC) option is an option that is tailor-made by the bank to meet a company's specific requirements.

Traded options

Traded options are bought and sold on exchanges like LIFFE (the London International Financial Futures and Options Exchange). LIFFE is a London exchange for traded options (and futures contracts) and enables investors to hedge against the risk of movements in interest rates, gilt-edged securities prices, bonds prices, foreign currency exchange rates, and equity share prices. Similarly, for example, the New York Board of Trade (NYBOT) provides risk managers and investors with a marketplace for futures contracts and options in commodities such as sugar, cotton, coffee, and cocoa; and the Dubai Gold and Commodities Exchange (DGCX) is a marketplace for gold and silver, and also steel, cotton, and other commodities.

The standard sizes of options tend to be fairly large (for example, in units of the equivalent of millions of £ sterling), and they mature every quarter in March, June, September, and December. A traded option to buy currency or borrow funds is called a **call option** and an option to sell currency or lend funds is called a **put option**. A currency option may be agreed at the spot rate (termed **at the money**) or at a more or less favourable rate than the spot rate (termed **out of the money**). An **American option** is an option that can be exercised at any time within the specified option period. A **European option** must be exercised at the end of the specified option period.

Disadvantages of traded options are that they are not negotiable and are not available for every currency. Traded option premiums are typically about 5% of the total transaction, and must be paid for when they are purchased, but the determination of actual premiums is a complicated process (in much the same way as applies to traded options in securities), which is dependent on:

■ the movements and volatility of the foreign currency exchange rates and interest rates markets
■ the strike price
■ the time periods up to when the options expire.

An increase in interest rates, for example, will reduce the value of interest rate put options but increase the value of interest rate call options. Put options and call options, however, will both have a greater value in volatile currency and interest rate markets. The higher the volatility the more opportunity there is for the company having the option to gain; equally, the greater is the potential for a loss for the bank which is creating the option, and therefore the premium they charge is higher.

The higher the strike price of an interest rate option contract, the higher the price of a put option and the lower the price of a call option. An option becomes more valuable the longer the time there is until its expiry date, because it can continue to be used as a hedge by a company against adverse interest rate or currency exchange rates movements.

The value of an option can be divided into two parts: **time value** and **intrinsic value**. The time value of an option is a reflection of current interest rates. An option that is out of the money has no intrinsic value, but it can still have a time value. The time value of an option is at its maximum at the start of the option period and proportionately decreases throughout the option period down to zero at the option expiry date.

The intrinsic value of the option is the difference between the strike rate and the current rate. It represents the value of an option if it is exercised immediately and only has a value if it is **in the money**. If it is out of the money it does not have an intrinsic value. For example, if a euro/sterling currency option is agreed with a strike rate of €1.30/£ and the current exchange rate is €1.20/£, then it is in the money and will have intrinsic value. However, if the option had been agreed with a strike rate of €1.10/£ it would be out of the money and would not have an intrinsic value.

Over-the-counter (OTC) options

Companies can obtain OTCs from banks and other financial institutions and they are tailor-made to meet the specific requirements of the company. An OTC agreement includes the name of the foreign currency or the interest rate, the amount, and the period of the term of the option. OTC options, as well as traded options, may also include floors, caps, and collars.

A foreign currency exchange rate or an interest rate floor provides a guaranteed rate of exchange, or a rate of interest, for a company to deal in at a future date should the exchange rate or interest rate move below this rate. A foreign currency exchange rate, or an interest rate, cap provides a guaranteed ceiling rate of exchange, or a rate of interest, for a company to deal in at a future date should the exchange rate or interest rate move above this rate. A collar combines the use of a floor and a cap by providing a lower and upper limit to an interest rate or exchange rate at which to buy or sell currencies, or borrow or lend funds. Worked example 12.14 illustrates the use of a currency option.

Progress check 12.7

Describe put options and call options.

Worked example 12.14

Dewdrop plc is tendering for a contract in US$ with a USA company called Snowdrop Inc. Dewdrop's expected costs of the contract are £3.00m but Dewdrop plc is prepared to accept a low margin in order to get the contract and is proposing a tender price of £3.20m. The contract will be awarded in six months' time. The current six-month forward US$/£ exchange rate is US$1.75 and so Dewdrop plc is prepared to bid a price of US$5.6m. The board of Dewdrop plc is considering the use of using a currency option. Let's first consider two possible loss-making scenarios.

The first scenario is where Dewdrop plc may arrange a forward currency contract and wait six months to see if it has been awarded the contract.

The second scenario is where Dewdrop plc arranges no forward cover but waits to see if it obtains the contract and then sells the US$ income at the spot rate in six months' time.

If Dewdrop assumes that it will be awarded the contract in six months' time then it may consider taking a six-month forward contract to sell US$5.6m at the six months forward rate of US$1.75/£.

If after six months Dewdrop fails to get the contract then it will have to buy US$5.6m at the spot rate which we will assume has strengthened to US$1.45/£ to close out the forward contract.

Dewdrop plc sale of US$5.6m six months forward at US$1.75/£	= £3.20m
Dewdrop plc purchase of US$5.6m at spot in six months' time at US$1.45/£	= £3.86m
Loss	= £0.66m

If Dewdrop does not take a six-month forward contract, but does nothing and waits six months to see if it is awarded the contract, Dewdrop may then be awarded the contract in six months' time when we will assume the spot rate may have fallen to US$2.15/£.

Dewdrop plc sale of US$5.6m at spot in six months' time at US$2.15/£	= £2.60m
Dewdrop plc cost of contract	= £3.00m
Loss	= £0.40m

Let's consider the situation if Dewdrop plc does neither of the above but instead arranges a currency option to sell US$5.6m at US$1.75/£ in six months' time at a fixed premium of £100,000.

If Dewdrop does not win the contract it can abandon the contract and its cost will be just the option premium of £100,000. But if at that time the US$ has weakened to say US$2.05/£ Dewdrop can make a profit by exercising the option contract and buying US$ at the spot rate:

Dewdrop plc sale of US$5.6m at the option rate in six months' time at US$1.75/£	= £3.20m
Dewdrop plc purchase of US$5.6m at the spot rate in six months' time at US$2.05/£	= £2.73m
Profit	= £0.47m

If Dewdrop wins the contract and the exchange rate is unchanged then Dewdrop can exercise the option:

Dewdrop plc sale of US$5.6m at the option rate in six months' time at US$1.75/£	= £3.20m
Option premium	= £0.10m
Dewdrop plc cost of contract	= £3.00m
Profit	= £0.10m

If Dewdrop wins the contract and the US$ has strengthened against £ sterling to, say, US$1.45/£ Dewdrop can abandon the option and sell its US$ at the spot rate:

Dewdrop plc sale of US$5.6m at the spot rate in six months' time at US$1.45/£	= £3.86m
Option premium	= £0.10m
Dewdrop plc cost of contract	= £3.00m
Profit	= £0.76m

There are a number of *pros* and *cons* for companies using options to cover interest rate or currency exchange rate exposure risk. The disadvantages are that:

- the premiums are high and so options are not a cheap method
- there is a difficulty in traded options being able to perfectly match both the duration and size of a company's exposure, because of their standardisation.

The advantages are:

- the opportunity to gain from favourable movements in exchange and interest rates
- that OTC options may be used to hedge non-standard interest rate and currency exchange rate exposures.

Futures

A futures contract is a contract like a forward contract, but with a futures contract an intermediary creates a standardised contract so that the two parties to the contract do not have to negotiate the terms of the contract. A financial future is an agreement between two parties on the future price of a financial variable at an agreed price. Futures on loans or deposits are used as a hedge against movements in interest rates. Similarly foreign currency futures are used as a hedge against movements in exchange rates. A futures contract is not an actual sale or purchase relating to loans or foreign currency. With a futures contract there is always a winner and a loser, which is unlike, for example, the sales and purchases of stocks and shares.

Financial futures contracts can be traded because they are standardised contracts. Forward contracts cannot be traded because they are not standardised. However, this disadvantage of forward contracts is balanced by the fact that they are not standardised and can be tailor-made in line with company requirements, with regard to their values and time spans. Futures are somewhat similar to traded options, as they are both standardised contracts, but futures require the payment of a **margin** rather than a premium. The margin is the percentage of a futures ◀️||| contract value that must be placed on deposit with a broker. Because a futures contract is not an actual sale, only a fraction of the value, the margin, needs to be paid to open the contract.

If a company wants to protect itself against the risk of interest rates falling then it may buy interest rate futures contracts. If a company wants to protect itself against the risk of interest rates rising then it may sell interest rate futures contracts. Interest rate futures contracts generally have a standard size of US$1m and a period of three months. Interest rate futures contract prices are quoted by subtracting the interest rate from the nominal value of 100. For example, an interest rate futures contract nominal price of 91 means an interest rate of 9% (100 − 91). The minimum amount by which the price of an interest rate futures contract can move is called a **tick**. A tick is a movement of 0.01% of the contract price. Gains (or losses) on interest rate ◀️||| futures contracts are indicated by the changes in the nominal price.

The initial margin for a futures contract is usually around 1% to 3% of the contract value, payable to a futures exchange, for example the London International Futures and Options Exchange (LIFFE) in the UK. LIFFE no longer offers currency futures, but these may still be traded on Far East and North American exchanges.

As with any other financial instrument, there are advantages and disadvantages with using currency and interest rate futures contracts. The advantages of futures contracts are:

- favourable movements in exchange rates and interest rates are credited immediately to the company's margin account
- futures contracts can be bought and sold on the futures markets which determine their prices
- an advance payment premium is not applicable to futures contracts.

The disadvantages with futures contracts are:

- because of their standardised contracts, futures contracts may not be a perfect hedge in terms of amounts and timing
- an advance premium does not have to be paid for futures contracts, but a margin must be paid
- futures contracts only hedge against downside risk – there are no opportunities of gains for companies from favourable movements in exchange rates and interest rates
- because markets are not totally efficient, basis risk exists where exchange rates and interest rates are not aligned with futures contracts prices and therefore futures contracts may not be 100% efficient.

Progress check 12.8

What are the differences between currency futures and foreign exchange forward contracts?

The way in which foreign currency exchange rate futures may be used is shown in Worked example 12.15, and Worked example 12.16 illustrates the use of interest rate futures.

Worked example 12.15

Dewdrop plc is purchasing materials today, 28 February, in US$ from the USA company Snowdrop Inc. The cost is US$680,000 and payment has been agreed for 28 March. The spot rate to buy US$ is currently US$1.60/£ (which is also the 28 March futures price). The US$ can be bought forward at 28 March at US$1.45/£.

The board of Dewdrop plc is considering the use of currency futures, which may be bought and sold in blocks of £85,000 with a margin of 2%, compared with the use of a forward exchange contract.

Dewdrop plc can use currency futures to hedge against the risk of £ sterling falling against the US$. The cost to buy US$680,000 at 28 March is £425,000 (US$680,000/1.60). The futures must be bought and sold in blocks of £85,000. Dewdrop plc, therefore, sells five US$ sterling futures contracts (which means the company takes delivery of US$ in return for £ sterling) at the rate of US$1.60/£. Dewdrop plc must also immediately deposit £1,700 (2% of £85,000) per contract with the futures exchange, a total of £8,500.

On 28 March Dewdrop plc must pay US$680,000 for the materials, at which time let's assume £ sterling will have weakened to spot rate US$1.47/£ to buy US$ and US$1.48/£ to sell US$.

Dewdrop plc has to 'close out' its futures contracts at US$1.48/£:

Giving a profit
(US$680,000 @ US$1.48/£ less US$680,000 @ US$1.60/£)	=	£34,459
Dewdrop plc buys US$680,000 @ US$1.47/£ to pay Snowdrop Inc	=	£462,585
Net cost to Dewdrop plc	=	£428,126
Plus the margin	=	£8,500
Total cost of materials using currency futures	=	£436,626

We can compare this with the cost of a forward exchange contract US$1.45/£:

Dewdrop plc buys US$680,000 forward for delivery 28 March @ US$1.45/£ = £468,966

If the board of Dewdrop plc believe there is a risk that the £ sterling may weaken against the US to around US$1.47/£ by 28 March, then given the current spot and forward contract rates currency futures appear to be the cheapest option.

Worked example 12.16

On 30 April, Dewdrop plc is arranging a US$1m three-month loan from 31 July. The current 30 April interest rate is 7% but the finance director is expecting that interest rates may rise over the next few months. The 31 July futures price is 92, and the interest rate is 8%.

If the interest rate at 31 July rose to 10%, what would be the benefit to Dewdrop plc of using an interest rate futures contract?

If the market were assumed to be inefficient, what would be the hedge efficiency if the futures price was 91, and the interest rate was still 8%?

Dewdrop plc would need to sell a US$1m interest rate futures contract at 92 to hedge against interest on the three-month loan required at 31 July.

If the interest rate at 31 July rises to 10% then the contract price movement is 200 ticks [(10 − 8)/0.01].

One tick is 0.01% of the contract price per quarter so the value of one tick is

$$US\$1m \times 0.01\% \times 3/12 \qquad\qquad = US\$25$$

Dewdrop plc may close out its interest rate futures contract at 31 July by buying a contract at 90 (100 − 10), giving a profit of

$$200 \text{ ticks} \times US\$25 \qquad\qquad = \underline{US\$5,000}$$

which is the same as calculating

$$(US\$1m \times 10\% \times 3/12) - (US\$1m \times 8\% \times 3/12) \quad = US\$5,000$$

Dewdrop plc may then offset the profit of US$5,000 against the higher cost of borrowing the US$1m at 10% at 31 July.

The cost of borrowing US$1m × 10% × 3/12 = US$25,000
compared with the cost at 8% of US$1m × 8% × 3/12 = US$20,000
an increase in interest of US$5,000

The profit on closing out the futures contract is the same as the increase in cost of interest because the futures contract price is the same as the movement in interest rate and therefore it provides a perfect hedge with 100% efficiency.

If the interest rate was 8% but the futures price was 91, instead of the expected 92 in an efficient market, we now have an element of basis risk amounting to 92 − 91, or 1 percentage point. Basis risk gradually reduces over the period of the contract, which would be 0.33 percentage points over each of the three months. The level of basis risk indicates the level of efficiency of the hedge.

Dewdrop plc would need to sell a US$1m interest rate futures contract at 91 to hedge against interest on the three-month loan required at 31 July.

Now at 31 July Dewdrop plc gains only

$$[(10 - 9)/0.01] \text{ or } 100 \text{ ticks} \times US\$25 \qquad\qquad = \underline{US\$2,500}$$

The additional higher interest cost of Dewdrop plc borrowing the US$1m at 10% at 31 July is

The cost of borrowing US$1m × 10% × 3/12	= US$25,000
compared with the cost at 8% of US$1m × 8% × 3/12	= US$20,000
an increase in interest of	US$5,000

The hedge effectively reduces the new interest cost by only US$2,500. The efficiency of the hedge is therefore US$2,500/US$5,000 or 50%.

Swaps

The cash flows of some companies may vary as interest rates, exchange rates, commodity prices, etc. vary, resulting from particular risk profiles. Specific risk profiles may not be acceptable to companies. For example, a company may have a loan with a floating interest rate when in fact it would prefer a fixed interest rate. Or a company may have accounts receivable denominated in US$ when in fact it would prefer its receivables to be denominated in Japanese yen. In 1981 swaps were devised to allow businesses to change their risk profiles to acceptable risk profiles.

Swaps can be arranged by companies as a hedge against currency exchange rates and interest rates exposures for relatively long time periods, at a relatively low cost compared with, say, options. Swaps are flexible not only with regard to the time period but are also flexible in terms of the amount, unlike standardised derivatives.

Swaps protect against downside risk but they don't enable companies to take advantage of opportunities arising from favourable currency and interest rate movements. There may also be a risk of default on, for example, payment of interest by one of the parties involved in the swap, and so it is crucial that swap agreements are only entered into with other parties who have only the highest credit status.

An interest rate swap is an agreement between two companies in which each company agrees to exchange the 'interest rate characteristics' of two different financial instruments of an identical loan. The mechanics of swaps are to effectively exploit the comparative advantages of a company's loans and currency dealings with another company's loans and currency dealings to provide both companies with a hedge against their exchange rate and their interest rate exposure risks. The companies do not normally deal directly with each other but deal through an intermediary, normally a bank, which receives a fee from both companies. Swaps are generally much longer-term derivatives than options and futures for periods of, for example, two years, five years, and even ten years. The interest rate swaps market is now much bigger than the currency swaps market, although currency swaps were the first swaps to be developed.

In a currency swap, two parties formally agree to swap amounts of currency and interest payments over an agreed period of time. A currency swap therefore also includes an interest rate swap. A currency swap between two companies can enable a company to borrow money in the particular foreign currency it requires while eliminating any exposure to exchange rate risk on the interest payments as well as exposure to exchange rate risk on the loan itself. Currency swaps can also facilitate, for example, a multinational group company's borrowing of money in international money markets through one of its companies based in a country (and currency) where interest rates are low, but which does not actually require the loan. The group company may then swap the loan into the currency in which they actually want to borrow at a lower rate than they would have paid if they had borrowed in that currency at the outset.

A currency swap procedure involves a number of steps, which may be summarised as follows:

- agree the currencies and the capital amounts to be included in the swap
- agree the period of the swap
- agree the exchange rate to be used in the swap (usually the current spot rate)
- exchange the agreed amounts of currencies between the two companies, for example £ sterling and euros, at the agreed exchange rate
- exchange the interest payments between the two companies at agreed dates over the period of the swap
- at the maturity date of the swap, exchange back the swap amounts at the agreed exchange rate.

If they feel that it is to their advantage, companies may prefer to use variations of the currency swap described above. For example, companies may buy the required currencies at spot rates in the currency market and exchange interest payments only, and then at the maturity date of the swap exchange the capital amounts at an agreed exchange rate.

As with interest rate swaps, currency swaps may comprise any combination of floating and fixed interest rates payable on the currency amounts to be swapped. The following Worked examples 12.17, 12.18, and 12.19 are examples of various types of currency swaps.

Worked example 12.17

A German company has agreed to sell some large drilling equipment to a company in North America. It will be paid US$20m in three years' time in US$. The German company wants to arrange a currency swap to hedge its exchange rate risk exposure.

The German company may agree with another company to swap the US$ for euros in three years' time at an agreed US$/£ exchange rate. The German company will give the other company US$20m in three years' time and receive euros in return.

Worked example 12.18

An American corporation has a subsidiary engineering company in the UK. The USA group wants to purchase a small Scotch whisky distillery in Scotland, UK. The USA group company needs a £1.32m loan to finance the purchase of the distillery. The US$/£ sterling spot rate is US$1 = £0.55. The UK subsidiary of the US corporation also has a loan requirement. It wants to raise US$2.4m to purchase some state-of-the-art machine tools which it will import from the USA.

For both companies to eliminate their foreign exchange exposure risk they could borrow in their own countries on behalf of each other. The USA parent company could borrow the US$2.4m, and the UK subsidiary company could borrow the £1.32m.

Worked example 12.19

A French water company has placed a purchase order to buy some new water treatment equipment from a company in the UK, agreed to be paid for in £ sterling. On placing the order, to fund the £ sterling purchase of the equipment the water company agreed a fixed interest £ sterling loan from a UK bank, on which interest is payable monthly. The water company's income is all denominated in euros, and so its finance director has had discussions with a French bank about the possibility of a currency swap to eliminate its foreign currency exchange rate exposure risk.

The swap agreement will have an agreed euro/£ sterling exchange rate used by the French company to obtain a euro loan from a French bank at the same value as the £ sterling loan, and which will have a floating interest rate. The equivalent euro capital sum will be used to calculate the euro floating rate monthly interest payments which the water company will make to the French bank, in return for the French bank paying to the water company the fixed £ sterling monthly interest payments on its £ sterling loan, which the company will then pay on to the UK bank.

At the end of the period of the swap the water company will repay the euro capital sum to the French bank and in return will receive a £ sterling payment, converted at the agreed exchange rate, which it will use to repay its £ sterling loan to the UK bank. The currency swap will have enabled the French water company to make its £ sterling interest payments and repay its £ sterling loan in its own currency, euros, and so avoid any exposure to exchange rate risk.

An interest rate swap is an arrangement whereby two companies contractually agree to exchange payments on different terms, one at a fixed interest rate and the other at a floating interest rate. With an interest rate swap it is the comparative advantages of each company's floating or fixed interest rates that provide the opportunity for both companies to gain.

The **plain vanilla swap**, or generic swap, is the commonest form of interest rate swap. The floating interest payments on a specific loan amount for a specific period are swapped with the fixed interest payments based on the same loan amount for the same period. In a plain vanilla swap there is:

- a fixed interest rate paying company
- a floating interest rate paying company.

One company may have a better credit rating and an absolute advantage over another company because it can borrow at a lower fixed rate and a lower floating rate. However, the other company may have a comparative advantage over the first company. This is because, although both its floating and fixed borrowing rates are higher than the first company's, its floating rate as a percentage of its fixed rate is lower than the same percentage for the first company. The swap gain is the spread of fixed rates less the spread of floating rates.

Progress check 12.9

What is an interest rate swap agreement?

The plain vanilla swap is best illustrated with an example.

Worked example 12.20

Two companies, Lofix plx and Hifix plc, make their interest payments yearly.

	Lofix plc	**Hifix plc**
fixed rate	6.0%	7.0%
floating rate	LIBOR	LIBOR + 0.3%

Lofix borrows US$1m at its fixed interest rate of 6%, and Hifix borrows US$1m at its floating interest rate of LIBOR + 0.3%.

Lofix wants to change its risk profile by having a floating rate because it believes that interest rates may fall in the near future.

Hifix wants to change its risk profile by having a fixed rate because it believes that interest rates may rise in the near future.

The companies think that they can both gain by swapping interest payments. If LIBOR is 4.75%, and the bank's arrangement charge is 0.2%, what swap can be made and what is the gain for each company?

Lofix has an absolute advantage because it can borrow at a lower fixed rate and a lower floating rate than Hifix. But Hifix has a comparative advantage over Lofix because its floating rate is proportionately less expensive than Lofix at 72.1% (5.05/7) versus 79.2% (4.75/6).

If the two companies swap interest payments then:

- Hifix is better off by 1% because it is paying interest at 6% instead of 7%.
- Lofix is worse off by 0.3% because it is paying 5.05% (4.75 + 0.3) instead of 4.75%.
- If Hifix makes a payment of 0.3% to Lofix, then Lofix is neither better nor worse off.
- But, Hifix is still 0.7% better off.

The benefits of the swap need to be split evenly between Lofix and Hifix and so:

- Hifix will therefore have to make a 0.35% payment to Lofix so that Lofix will then have a floating rate of LIBOR − 0.35%, which is 4.4%.
- Hifix will then have a fixed rate of 7% − 0.35%, which is 6.65%.
- Both companies are better off by 0.35%.

In practice, Lofix plc and Hifix plc would not actually swap interest payments, but they would make balancing payments from one to the other for the difference between the fixed and floating rate. The balancing payments will vary as the floating rate varies. The swap would be arranged for the companies through their bank as an intermediary and the arrangement fee charged by the bank will reduce the benefit gained from the swap by both companies. The bank's arrangement fee of 0.2% is to be shared between Hifix plc and Lofix plc, at 0.1% each, as follows:

- Lofix would therefore have a final floating rate of LIBOR − 0.25%, which is 4.5%.
- Hifix would have a final fixed rate of 7% − 0.25%, which is 6.75%.
- Both companies gain by 0.25% (and the bank will be better off by 0.2%).

There are other types of interest rate swaps besides plain vanilla swaps, for example **basis swaps** which involve the swap of two floating rate interest payments that have been determined on different bases.

Swaptions

A further variation on the swap is the swaption, which is really a combination of a swap and an option. Swaptions are like options but, although they may have lower premiums than options, they are not as flexible because companies cannot benefit from favourable exchange rate and interest rate movements.

Financial risk management strategy

We have discussed ways in which businesses may manage to reduce or mitigate particular types of financial risk relating to exchange rates and interest rates through:

- matching and offsetting assets and liabilities and cash flows
- choosing particular types of assets and liabilities
- hedging.

The hedging strategy adopted differs from one company to another. A company may, for example, hedge none of its exposures, or all of its exposures, or 70% of its exposures. The strategy relating to the level of hedging must be determined with regard to an assessment of the expected benefits from hedging or the potential losses that may arise from not hedging. Despite the many disadvantages of hedging, like high costs and the complex nature of derivatives, our own first-hand experience of treasury management in multinational companies has identified many benefits from hedging:

- protection of downside risk – an insurance policy to provide a 'guaranteed' income level over the short term
- avoidance of bankrupty resulting from large interest rate rises, where the company is highly geared
- smoothing of cash flows for more accurate forecasting and planning
- competitive advantage gained from reducing the risk from high gearing and high levels of foreign currency exposures
- opportunities for changing the nature of existing debt or increasing further borrowing resulting from interest rate hedging.

Hedging is used to reduce or mitigate risk, but the use of hedging itself is not without its own risks. In the mid-1990s the Barings Bank debacle saw losses of almost £1bn in futures on the Far East exchanges, which resulted in the bank going under. This happened as a result of the bank's inadequate internal control systems relating to the activities of its dealers, and in particular trader

Nick Leeson. In the 2000s during the investigations into the fall of Enron, the company's imaginative activities in the unregulated sector of the over-the-counter derivatives market illustrated the problems of such unregulated trading in derivatives. More recently, in 2012, the problems with the complexity of these financial instruments were exposed at a number of major banks as the press extract below indicates.

Derivatives – beware!

Barclays has become the first bank to face claims in a British court that it manipulated the key inter-bank borrowing rate. The bank is accused of fixing Libor to provide borrowing rates it knew to be incorrect, according to papers filed with the High Court by a care home operator. Graiseley Properties and Graiseley Investments, which own and run the 30-strong chain of Guardian Care Homes across the country, have issued legal proceedings against Barclays, in a £36m claim against the bank.

Investigators across the world, including the UK Financial Services Authority, the SEC in the United States, as well as European, Canadian and Japanese regulators, are currently investigating claims that the world's largest banks, including Barclays, RBS and Lloyds Banking Group, suppressed Libor. Libor is used to price more than £200 trillion of financial products around the world, including everything from home loans to the most complex credit derivatives.

The Libor allegations are contained in a legal writ issued by Guardian Care Homes against Barclays over claims its investment banking arm mis-sold the business two interest rate hedging products. The care home operator, which last year settled a similar interest rate swap mis-selling claim against Lloyds Banking Group, alleges that Barclays sold it two multi-million pound hedges without explaining the potential downsides of the complex derivatives. The company is claiming about £12m in interest rate payments it says it should not have made, as well as a further £24m in break costs – the price of cancelling the derivative contracts – for the hedges.

The swap mis-selling claim is just the latest to hit Barclays. Last month, the bank settled a claim brought by a Newport-based landlord that it had mis-sold them an interest rate swap, while earlier this month an East London Turkish patisserie owner filed a legal claim alleging the bank mis-sold it a complex interest rate hedging product despite him and his wife not speaking any English. The claims against Barclays are part of allegations that all of Britain's big banks mis-sold interest rate hedges to small business customers.

Yesterday, a group of more than 40 MPs met in Westminster to discuss the growing outcry. But the inclusion of allegations that Barclays knowingly gave Libor rates that it knew to be untrue marks a potentially significant turning point in the cases, which have so far centred purely on the mis-selling claims. In the case of Guardian Care Homes, the claim is that a January 2009 decision by Barclays that the company was in breach of a loan-to-value covenant could have been incorrect if the Libor rate, off which the business's hedging products were valued, was being suppressed. The exit costs on the hedges taken out by the company increased as interest rates fell and were added to the business's total borrowings, meaning a lower Libor rate resulted in higher break costs. 'We were hugely sensitive to even small changes in Libor and it could have meant they [Barclays] put us in breach of our loan covenants when we were not,' said Gary Hartland, managing director of Guardian Care Homes.

The claim is the first in a UK court to specifically include Libor manipulation in a legal case against a bank. Barclays, as well as the UK's other major banks, has been named in several US investor lawsuits over the sale of derivative products linked to Libor. A spokesman for Barclays said: 'This action is completely without merit and we will contest it vigorously. Barclays is satisfied that it provides sufficient information to enable a client to make an informed, commercial decision about the products it offers.'

Source: **Barclays accused over Libor rate fix**, by Harry Wilson © *The Daily Telegraph*, 25 April 2012

The report and accounts disclosure requirements and tax treatment of derivatives are uncertain and complex. Currently, there is considerable debate regarding the accounting treatment of derivatives, their valuation and disclosure of information. From 2001, IAS 39 (Financial Instruments; Recognition and Measurement) was the standard for treatment of derivatives, but in November 2009, the International Accounting Standards Board (IASB) commenced the phased introduction of IFRS 9 (Financial Instruments), intended to clarify and simplify the treatment of complex financial instruments. However, IFRS 9's phased implementation leaves considerable grounds for uncertainty as IAS 39 is not yet entirely replaced and in October 2010 the IASB restructured IFRS 9 carrying forward elements of IAS 39 unchanged. In December 2011 the IASB deferred the effective date of the revised IFRS 9 to January 2015.

Progress check 12.10

What are the risks associated with hedging foreign currency risk and interest rate risk?

Behavioural finance

Any strategy that seeks to mitigate risk requires an understanding of the environment in which decisions are made, and the behaviour of investors is an important aspect. The last 20 years has seen considerable growth in the discipline of **behavioural finance**. The observation that markets and financial agents do not always seem to act entirely rationally has led to the development of research which seeks to explain and quantify the behaviours which deviate from what might be expected of the rational economic agent.

We would expect a rational economic agent to consistently adjust his perceptions whenever new information is made available to him and his actions would be consistently self-interested. However, as the press extract below illustrates, people do not always act in the way we might expect them to do, even though it may seem obvious to us. Indeed, we often think that if we were in the same situation we would obviously act differently, but the reality is that probably we would not.

Predicting human behaviour – a racing certainty?

An old horse-racing tipster scam takes the following elegant form: send predictions about the winner in a 10-horse race to 10,000 people, with 10 different predictions each sent to 1,000 people. After the race, focus on the 1,000 who received a successful prediction and send each of them a prediction of the winner in another 10-horse race; again, 10 different predictions, equally spread. After the second race, 100 people will have received two successive winning predictions and will be unaware of the 9,900 who have not. As a final flourish, forecast another 10-horse race and you will have 10 people, each of whom has received 3 successive correct forecasts against substantial odds. Then simply write to each of them and ask for a few thousand pounds in exchange for your next three tips.

Punters can be forgiven, I feel, for falling for such nonsense – because it is at least cleverly constructed nonsense. But a recent working paper, written by two behavioural economists, Nattavudh Powdthavee and Yohanes Riyanto, makes me wonder whether such classic scams are overkill. They conducted a laboratory experiment (actually, two: one in Thailand and one in Singapore, both with undergraduate students as subjects), which duplicated the old fraud. The twist was that the mechanics of the trick were entirely transparent. The tips were given in sealed, numbered envelopes – each set of envelopes unique to each student.

Instead of horse-racing, the students were shown coin-flips and given a number of good reasons to believe that the coin-flips were random: the coins came from the participants, not the experimenters; the coins were changed every couple of flips; participants, rather than the experimenters, would perform the actual flips. The students were told that each numbered envelope contained a forecast of the next coin flip. The students were given tokens to gamble with and invited to bet on each coin-flip, with the stake to double or to disappear. The students were also invited to pay a fixed price to look inside each envelope ahead of time. After each coin-flip, the students could open the prediction for free and see whether it was correct or not.

You can appreciate that the forecasts here are transparently useless. With almost 400 students, some were bound to witness a string of correct forecasts by chance. The question is, would the students who randomly received correct predictions through sheer fluke actually start to pay for future predictions? And how long would it take for them to start buying? The researchers answer these questions pithily: 'Yes, and not long.' After witnessing a single correct forecast, students were more likely to pay to see a second forecast; this effect becomes large and statistically very significant after a second correct forecast. After witnessing four correct coin-toss forecasts, more than 40 per cent of students were willing to pay to see the fifth, although the chance of four correct predictions is a not-exactly-stunning one in 16. In some senses this should be no surprise. Behavioural economists and psychologists have known for some time that people see patterns that just aren't there. Powdthavee and Riyanto also speculate that this is a particular feature of Thai culture.

But what gives pause for thought is the obvious uselessness of the tips. A horse-racing tipster will boast of insider knowledge and hint that racing results are pre-arranged for the convenience of the cognoscenti. Nobody believes that there is much 'insider knowledge' about the next toss of the coin. Of course, the cultivated readers of the FT would not make the same crass errors as the young students did. But, just in case, next time you see an investment manager touting impressive returns on a couple of funds, ask yourself how many other funds the company manages.

Research in behavioural finance has drawn upon many sources, but frequently upon cognitive psychology to try to investigate and understand what makes apparently rational people act in irrational ways. This work has strong practical implications in managing risk in companies and in financial planning, for example in deciding when to issue more shares. An example would be the January effect, where it is observed that share prices increase throughout the month of January. The effect is seen in small stocks or shares, which outperform the market in general. While several reasons have been put forward for the phenomenon, there have been several years where the effect has not materialised.

The research on behavioural finance covers a lot of ground. However, we can identify two groups of related theories that have frequently been used as a basis for seeking to explain seemingly unusual financial behaviour patterns.

The first set of theories is linked to the concept of cognitive bias, that is to say that new information is processed not in a way that revises or updates current mental paradigms, but in a way that reinforces the patterns we have already developed and by which we view the world. This set of biases includes the following:

- framing
- mental accounting
- regret avoidance
- prospect theory.

Framing

The important thing about information is the way in which it is given to individuals. Investors, for example, make decisions depending upon the way in which information is framed. An investor may have a portfolio making reasonable returns, but based on the current performance begins to buy riskier securities to extend the portfolio. They frame their new investments as winnings, seeing their initial portfolio as a baseline, rather than viewing the portfolio, and its performance, as a whole.

Mental accounting

Investors compartmentalise investments and the income stream from them and apply different rules to the different types of investment. For example, an investor may build a balanced portfolio of £400,000 shares and £400,000 of bonds (50%:50%), but mentally ignore a home equity loan of £200,000. In reality his portfolio has a value of £600,000 and is constructed 67%:33%.

The danger with mental accounting is that investors may concentrate overly on one aspect of their finances to the detriment of their overall financial situation.

Regret avoidance

Regret avoidance is the situation where we prefer to continue a course of action, irrespective of the potential outcomes, rather than admit we made a bad decision in the past. An investor may have bought shares which are declining in value but rather than sell them at a loss, and face up to the regret of the loss, the investor holds on to the shares as they continue to decline. His loss gets greater as he refuses to face the regret of the actual loss he will face when the decision to sell is realised.

This bias is relevant in many aspects of business. For example, a manager may continue to invest in a bad project rather than accept he was wrong in the first place, withdraw from the project and have to admit that to shareholders.

Prospect theory

Prospect theory was developed by psychologists Daniel Kahneman and Amos Tversky who argued that decision-making under risk can be viewed as a choice between prospects or gambles.

We have an irrational tendency to be less willing to gamble with profits than with losses and from an investor point of view this means selling quickly if he is earning profits but not selling if he is running losses. The investor is therefore focusing simply on outcomes rather than viewing the process holistically. That is to say, gains and losses are evaluated both separately and relatively, as opposed to simultaneously and in terms of absolute values or states of wealth.

The second set of theories deals with heuristic information processing. These are the ways in which people discover information for themselves and use this information to create a 'rule of thumb', which enables them to make short-cut decisions. While this saves time and helps decision-making, the rules are only as good as the information upon which they are based, and the situations in which they are applied. It may be that a rule is founded on a set of information that is not an adequate approximation of future occurrences or it is applied in the wrong circumstances. This would clearly lead to poorer decisions being made than if the new situation was assessed more conscientiously.

Heuristic information processing includes:

- herding
- overconfidence
- conservatism
- representativeness.

Herding

Herding is probably the most visible psychological aspect of investor behaviour because when it occurs its impacts are multiplied. It stems from a short-cut in the decision process in that investors think others have information they don't have and simply follow what others do. Since most of us are relatively lazy, it saves investors the effort of coming to their own conclusions. Several studies of the contagion caused by the Asian financial crisis of 1997 attribute it to the herding effect. Similarly, the dot.com bubble of the early 2000s can be seen as the impact of herding behaviour among investors.

Overconfidence

Overconfidence has recently become the subject of much study. Terrance Odean of the University of California, Berkeley has carried out a number of studies on overconfidence in investors and traders. His work suggests that investors overestimate the precision of their knowledge about a stock's value and also tend to believe more strongly in their own assessments than in those of others.

The clear danger in an overconfident investor is that he tends to trade more than a less confident investor. But on the basis of his (unsubstantiated) superior knowledge he usually realises a far worse performance than an investor who trades less.

Research also strongly suggests that men are more overconfident then women.

Conservatism

Conservatism is the hesitation of an investor to act on new information, where such information should dictate an action or a change in strategy. Once the investor has a strategy he may be unwilling to take notice of new information that suggests his strategy is wrong – once he has a system, it may be very hard to make him change.

We tend to assume that rational investors rapidly process new information once it is made public and act upon it, but in fact many do not.

Representativeness

People have short-term time horizons and place more emphasis on events in the recent past. A stock or share may have performed poorly over the past five years, but has recently begun to perform well. An investment in this security may appear to be an attractive proposition despite what the long-term evidence would suggest.

With representativeness there are two interrelated phenomena. When we have a large sample we tend to take the most recent events as representative and ignore the long term. But in cases where we have limited information, we are apt to assume that the few instances we have are representative of long-term performance. For example, a gambler who has backed the winners in the first three races of a meeting may be more inclined to wager more money on the fourth race than normal, simply because he judges the outcome of the fourth race in terms of the very limited information of the first three.

Mini case 12.2

The impact of behavioural finance is starting to move from the academic world to the investment world. In 2006, Barclays Wealth began incorporating behavioural finance as part of its portfolio construction in an attempt to ensure its clients' portfolios were matched to their attitudes to investment. In that time, Barclays stated that behavioural finance was an important part of their investment philosophy and in light of this in March 2012 they launched a new micro-site that provides research, blogs and videos on behavioural finance. The site indicates that as an exciting and relatively new field of research, behavioural finance uses psychology to understand why investors make the financial decisions they do, and how these individual decisions combine to drive markets.

Barclays, however, is not the only financial institution to embrace behavioural finance techniques. In July 2010, Allianz Global Investors announced the creation of the Allianz Global Investors Centre for Behavioural Finance. The Centre was created with the aim of applying the insights from behavioural finance to designing better financial solutions for investors.

Summary of key points

- An awareness of financial risk, as distinct from business risk, is crucially important to companies with regard to their levels of gearing and investment and trade in foreign currencies.

- There are various types of financial risk relating to a company's capital structure, its interest rate agreements, and foreign currency transactions.

- The exchange rate equivalency model explains relationships between interest rates, inflation rates, spot currency exchange rates, and forward currency exchange rates, and forms a basis of many international financial management techniques.

- An exposure to interest rate risk is faced by companies that lend or borrow money at either floating or fixed rates of interest.

- The economic risk element of exchange rate risk is faced by all companies; the other two elements, translation and transaction risk, are faced only by companies that trade, borrow, or invest overseas.

- The appropriate management of financial risk is important because of the volatility of both exchange rates and interest rates.

- Financial risk, relating to exchange rates and interest rates, may be managed by matching and offsetting assets and liabilities and cash flows; choosing particular types of assets and liabilities; or hedging.

- There are a number of methods that may be used for the hedging of financial risks:
  - foreign currency fixed or option forward contracts
  - money market hedging
  - forward interest rate agreements (FRAs)
  - derivatives.
- There is a wide range of derivatives available for companies to hedge foreign currency exchange rate and interest rate risk, including:
  - options–traded and over-the-counter (OTCs)
  - futures
  - swaps
  - swaptions.
- The financial risk management strategy adopted by a company must consider its attitude to risk; state its objectives; identify its exposures; value the exposures; assess the risk; assess the appropriate risk management techniques.
- There are many distinct benefits to be gained by companies that hedge financial risk, despite the complexity and cost.
- The problems with the use of derivatives relate to their accounting treatment and financial reporting, and also the lack of adequate internal controls to ensure their proper use.
- The action of investors may not be entirely rational; psychological traits are being explored in behavioural finance theory to try to understand and explain the sometimes seemingly irrational behaviour of investors.

Glossary of key terms

American option An option that can be exercised at any time within the specified option period.

at the money A currency option that is agreed at the spot rate.

basis swap A swap agreement which involves the exchange of two floating rate interest payments that have been determined on different bases.

behavioural finance The area of finance theory which studies and researches into why investors do not always behave as rationally as expected. The discipline seeks to understand the impacts other than pure financial gain, which affect financial decision-making in groups and individuals.

call option An option to buy a specified underlying asset at a specified exercise price on, or before, a specified exercise date.

derivative A financial instrument that derives its value from the price or rate of some underlying item. Underlying items include equities, bonds, commodities, interest rates, exchange rates, and stock market and other indices (and for companies like Enron, the weather!).

discount The difference between the specified forward rate and the spot rate ruling on the date of a foreign exchange forward contract, where the forward rate is higher than the spot rate.

economic risk Economic risk relates to the risk of the impact of long-term movements in exchange rates on the competitive position of companies engaged in international markets, which may be avoided by not trading in such markets. Economic risk in a company's home country cannot be avoided.

European option An option that must be exercised at the end of the specified option period.

Expectations Theory The Expectations Theory of exchange rates regards today's forward foreign currency exchange rate as a reasonable expectation of the future spot rate.

Fisher Effect Also known as Fisher's closed hypothesis, the Fisher Effect describes the long-run relationship between expectations about a country's future inflation and interest rates. Normally, a rise in a country's expected inflation rate should eventually cause an equal rise in the interest rate (and *vice versa*).

foreign exchange forward contract A fixed forward contract is an agreement to exchange different currencies at a specified future date and at a specified exchange rate. The difference between the specified rate and the spot rate ruling on the date the contract was entered into is the discount (see above) or premium (see below) on the forward contract (FRS 23). An option forward contract is an agreement to exchange different currencies on or before a specified future date and at a specified exchange rate.

forward interest rate agreement (FRA) An agreement which a company may enter into with a bank concerning interest rates relating to its future borrowing or lending of very large sums of money (millions rather than thousands of pounds) and normally for periods of more than one year.

forward rate The exchange rate at which a currency may be bought or sold some time in the future.

futures contract A contract relating to currencies, commodities, or shares that obliges the buyer (or issuer) to purchase (or sell) the specified quantity of the item represented in the contract at a predetermined price at the expiration of the contract. Unlike forward contracts, which are entered into privately, futures contracts are traded on organised exchanges, carry standard terms and conditions, have specific maturities, and are subject to rules concerning margin (see below) requirements.

hedging The use of transactions (hedges) to reduce or eliminate an exposure to risk.

interest rate cap A variation on an interest rate option in which there is a 'ceiling' interest rate, as distinct from a 'floor' interest rate.

interest rate collar An interest rate collar enables a borrower to buy an interest rate 'cap' and simultaneously sell an interest rate 'floor' which therefore fixes the minimum cost for the company, which is lower than if an interest 'cap' only had been used.

Interest Rate Parity Theory The theory that the lending and borrowing interest rates differential between two countries is equal to the differential between the forward foreign currency exchange rate of the two countries and the spot exchange rate.

International Fisher Effect Also known as Fisher's open hypothesis, the International Fisher Effect states that an expected change in a foreign currency spot exchange rate between two countries is approximately equivalent to the difference between the nominal interest rates of the two countries for that time.

in the money In the money refers to a situation when the strike price of an option is below the current market price for a call option or above the current market price for a put option. Such an option has an intrinsic value (see below).

intrinsic value The difference between the strike rate and the current rate of an option. It represents the value of an option if it is exercised immediately and only has a value if it is in the money. If it is out of the money it does not have an intrinsic value.

margin The percentage of a futures contract value that must be placed on deposit with a broker. Because a futures contract is not an actual sale, only a fraction of the value, the margin, needs to be paid to open the contract.

money market hedge A money market hedge is used by companies, for example, that want to borrow funds for an investment at some time in the future for a specific period, but are also expecting an increase in interest rates by that time.

option A right of an option holder to buy or sell a specific asset on predetermined terms on, or before, a future date.

option premium The cost of an option, which has to be paid when the option is bought and is non-returnable.

out of the money A currency option that is agreed at a more or less favourable rate than the spot rate.

over-the-counter (OTC) option An option that is tailor-made by the bank to meet a company's specific requirements. It is an option that is traded directly between licensed dealers, rather than through an organised options exchange.

plain vanilla swap (or generic swap) The commonest and simplest form of interest rate swap. The floating interest payments on a specific loan amount for a specific period are swapped with the fixed interest payments based on the same loan amount for the same period. In a plain vanilla swap there is a fixed interest rate paying company and a floating interest rate paying company.

premium The difference between the specified forward rate and the spot rate ruling on the date of a foreign exchange forward contract, where the spot rate is higher than the forward rate.

Purchasing Power Parity Theory The theory that foreign currency exchange rates are in equilibrium when their purchasing power is the same in each of the two countries at the prevailing exchange rates. This means that the exchange rate between two countries should equal the ratio of the two countries' price level of a fixed basket of goods and services. When a country experiences inflation, and its domestic price level is increasing, its exchange rate must depreciate in order to return to purchasing power parity.

put option An option to sell a specified underlying asset at a specified exercise price on, or before, a specified exercise date.

spot rate In general, a spot rate is the rate of interest to maturity currently offered on a particular type of security. With regard to foreign currency, the spot rate actually means the exchange rate at which a currency is bought or sold today for value two working days later.

strike rate In an interest rate option, the strike rate is the right to borrow or lend a specific amount of money by a particular date at a guaranteed interest rate, which must be exercised or not by the time the agreed date is reached.

swap An arrangement whereby two organisations contractually agree to exchange payments on different terms, for example in different currencies, or one at a fixed interest rate and the other at a floating interest rate.

swaption A combination of a swap and an option. It is like an option but, although having a lower premium than an option, it is not as flexible because companies cannot benefit from favourable exchange rate and interest rate movements.

tick The minimum amount by which the price of an interest rate futures contract can move, and which is a movement of 0.01% of the contract price.

time value The time value of an option is a reflection of current interest rates, which is at its maximum at the start of the option period and proportionately decreases throughout the option period down to zero at the option expiry date. An option that is out of the money has no intrinsic value, but it can still have time value.

traded option A traded option is available, for example, only for specific currencies, and is a standardised option with regard to its specified amount and term, and is bought and sold on an options exchange.

transaction exposure The susceptibility of an organisation to the effect of foreign exchange rate changes during the transaction cycle associated with the export or import of goods and services. Transaction exposure is present from the time a price is agreed until the payment has been made or received in the domestic currency.

translation exposure The susceptibility of the balance sheet and income statement (profit and loss account) to the effect of foreign exchange rate changes.

Assessment material

Questions

Q12.1 Identify the sources of financial risk faced by companies and outline the reasons why such exposure to risk has increased so much in recent years and continues to increase.

Q12.2 What has been the impact of the 1973 oil crisis with regard to the world currency markets and foreign currency exchange rates.

Q12.3 What are the financial risks related to the level of a company's gearing?

Q12.4 Explain the implications of the financial risk faced by companies having fixed interest loans compared with those having floating interest rate loans.

Q12.5 Outline what is meant by the 'spread' of foreign currency exchange spot rates.

Q12.6 Describe the relationship between foreign currency spot rates and future rate (one month, three months, six months, etc.) premiums and discounts.

Q12.7 Explain, with regard to the foreign currency exchange rate risks faced by companies, what is meant by economic exposure; transaction exposure; translation exposure.

Q12.8 What are the main types of hedging techniques available to companies in their management of foreign exchange and interest rate risk exposures.

Q12.9 Briefly describe how the use of derivatives: options; futures; swaps; and swaptions, may be used to hedge both foreign exchange and interest rate risk.

Discussion points

D12.1 'Continuing economic instability worldwide has been inevitable ever since the USA suspended the convertibility of US$ into gold in the early 1970s.' Discuss.

D12.2 'Derivatives are not a new invention, but an unnecessary evil that have been with us for a very long time.' Discuss.

D12.3 'An interest rate swap agreement cannot really be a win–win situation for the two companies involved and the bank arranging the swap – someone must lose.' Discuss.

Exercises

Solutions are provided in Appendix 2 to all exercise numbers highlighted in colour.

Level I

E12.1 *Time allowed – 15 minutes*

Build-It-Fast plc is a UK company that exports a range of DIY products to Switzerland. On 1 July 2012 the company had recently agreed a large supply contract with a building retailer in Geneva. The supply contract is for goods and services worth (Swiss francs) CHF75,000,000. The treasurer of Build-It-Fast plc is concerned about the future of the £ sterling/CHF exchange rate, and believes that over the next six months the value of the CHF may fall significantly. The Swiss supply contract is due to be paid on 31 December 2012. The following exchange rate information is available:

Exchange rates quoted for 1 July 2012:

Spot rate (dealers buying rate)	£1 = CHF1.4369
Spot rate (dealers selling rate)	£1 = CHF1.4107
Forward rate – 3 months forward	0.0050–0.0075 discount
Forward rate – 6 months forward	0.0100–0.0125 discount

You are required to calculate:

(i)   the cost to Build-It-Fast of buying and selling Swiss francs on the spot market on 1 July 2012

(ii) the spread on the 3-month forward rate, and the 6-month forward rate for the Swiss francs

(iii) the forward rate for 3-month and 6-month contracts to buy and sell Swiss francs

(iv) how much would be received in £ sterling if the treasurer of Build-It-Fast plc were able to sell the Swiss francs on 1 July 2012

(v)   how much the treasurer would receive in £ sterling were he to sell the Swiss francs 6 months forward on 31 December 2012.

E12.2 *Time allowed – 30 minutes*

Anthony plc is a UK company that exports high-quality electronic components worldwide, and has contracted a large order to sell components to Germany. The contract is worth €6,500,000. The electronic components were delivered on 1 September 2012, and the contract is due to be paid on 1 March 2013. The deal was organised by the company's marketing department, but the company's financial manager is very concerned because he believes the profit margin on the contract is very low. He suspects that the euro may fall substantially against the £ sterling over the next 6 months.

Spot rate on 1 September 2012	£1 = €1.12
Forward rate to sell euro 6 months forward	£1 = €1.14
UK – £ lending interest rate	10% p.a.
Germany – euro borrowing interest rate	8% p.a.

> **Required:**
>
> As the finance manager of Anthony plc, prepare a report to the board explaining what options are available to the company, and explain the implications regarding the relevant part of the exchange rate equivalency model.

E12.3   *Time allowed – 30 minutes*

The UK partnership, Ray & Co, is a worldwide importer and exporter of materials. On 30 September 2012 Ray & Co contracted to buy 2,000 tonnes of melinium from a vendor in Cambrasia at a price of Cam$7,000 per tonne, for immediate settlement on shipment. The 7,000 tonnes of melinium were to be shipped directly to a client in Pembolia, allowing one month's credit from shipment date, and Ray's selling price was PF300 per tonne. 1,000 tonnes of melinium were to be shipped during October 2012 and 1,000 tonnes were to be shipped during November 2012. Ray & Co agreed cover with their bank for these transactions in sterling on the forward exchange market.

The £ sterling exchange rates at 30 September 2012 were as follows:

	Cambrasian dollars (Cam$)/£	Pembolian francs (PF)/£
Spot	200–201	7–7.75
1 month forward	1–2 cents discount	5–3 centimes premium
2 months forward	2–3 cents discount	8–6 centimes premium
3 months forward	3–4 cents discount	13–11 centimes premium

Commission on all transactions is payable at 0.05% with a maximum of £20 per transaction.

> **Required:**
> **Calculate:**
>
> (i)   The profit that Ray & Co would have earned on the complete deal.
> (ii)   The impact on Ray & Co's profit if:
>   (a)   the November 2012 shipment had been cancelled
>   (b)   the November 2012 shipment had been delayed until January 2013.

E12.4   *Time allowed – 30 minutes*

Blud Ltd sells small boats to customers in Spain. A delivery has just been made to a customer in Barcelona. Blud Ltd has invoiced €40,000, payable in three months' time. Blud's finance director has obtained the following information about £/€ foreign exchange rates and UK £ sterling and € interest rates:

£/€ sterling exchange rates
Spot	1.1648–1.1652
3 months forward	100–100 premium

Interest rates

UK £ sterling		Spain euro	
Deposit	Borrowing	Deposit	Borrowing
2.5%	5.0%	3.0%	6.1%

Required:

(i)   How should Blud Ltd's finance director maximise Blud Ltd's sterling receipt from the sale of the boat?

(ii)   If, in addition to the above, Blud Ltd was required to make a payment of €20,000 to a Spanish supplier in three months' time, what may the finance director do to minimise the company's foreign currency exposure risk?

E12.5   *Time allowed – 30 minutes*

On 1 May 2012 Cookies plc needed to make a payment of US$730,000 in three months' time. The company considered three different ways in which it may hedge its transaction exposure – foreign exchange forward contract; money market; currency option – based on the following foreign currency exchange rate and interest rate data:

Exchange rates:

US$/£ sterling spot rate	1.6188–1.6199
Three month US$/£ forward rate	1.6109–1.6120

Interest rates:

	Borrowing %	Lending %
US$	3.15	1.85
£ sterling	5.00	1.50

Foreign currency option prices in cents per US$ for a contract size of £25,000:

Exercise price	Call option (July 2012)	Put option (July 2012)
US$/£1.70	2.5	7.5

Required:

Calculate the cost of the transaction using each of the three different methods considered by Cookies plc to determine which is the cheapest for the company.

Level II

E12.6   *Time allowed – 45 minutes*

On 30 April 2012 Gleeson plc had a short-term borrowing requirement for £10m on 1 August 2012 for a period of three months. The borrowing rate of interest at 30 April 2012 was 7% and the board of directors was concerned that interest rates may increase over the next six months. The finance director was asked to look at the use of interest rate futures with regard to the following two scenarios:

(a)   interest rates increase by 1% and the futures market price moves by 1%

(b)   interest rates fall by 2% and the futures market price moves by 1.5%.

They also suggested the possibility of buying an interest guarantee at 7%, for which the cost would be 0.3% of the value of the loan. At 30 April 2012 the price of July sterling three-month time deposit futures was 93.25. The standard contract size was £500,000, and the minimum price movement, one tick, was 0.01% of the loan per annum.

Required:

(i)   Assess the impact of the use of interest rate futures for each of the scenarios (a) and (b) above and calculate each of the hedge efficiencies.

(ii) Determine whether for each of the scenarios (a) and (b) above the total cost of the loan would have been cheaper if the interest guarantee had been acquired.

E12.7   *Time allowed – 45 minutes*

Houses plc has a very good credit rating and is able to borrow funds at a fixed rate of 5.2%. Houses plc may also borrow funds at a floating rate of LIBOR plus 3.0% (LIBOR is currently 1.10%).

Thinice plc has a less favourable credit rating, being seen as a company with a slightly higher risk profile and so is able to borrow funds at a less favourable fixed rate of 6%. Thinice plc can borrow funds at a floating rate of LIBOR plus 3.5%.

Houses plc currently has a large fixed interest loan, and Thinice has a loan of the same size on which it pays a floating rate of interest. Houses plc would prefer to be paying a floating rate of interest but Thinice would like its loan to be at a fixed interest rate.

Required:

Make the unrealistic assumption that a bank will not be involved in an interest rate swap arranged between the two companies in which they have an equal share of any gain. Make the appropriate calculations to illustrate how both companies may benefit from such an agreement. Your calculations should show: the total gain of the swap; the gain to each company; the borrowing rates of each company after the swap has taken place.

E12.8   *Time allowed – 45 minutes*

The finance director of Privet plc wants to arrange a £5m six-month loan in three months' time, but is worried that the current borrowing interest rate of 8% may move adversely over the next few months. The finance director is considering various hedging options: an interest rate futures contract; a forward rate agreement (FRA); an interest rate cap.

Explain how each of these financial instruments may be used to benefit Privet plc, and discuss the disadvantages of their use.

Millpot Ltd is a designer and manufacturer of fine pottery, aimed particularly at the mass market, via shops, large retail chains, and mail order companies. The company was founded many years ago by Martin Griffin, who was the managing director and was involved in the sales and marketing side of the business.

Towards the end of 2009 when Martin was due to retire, Emily Griffin, Martin's daughter, joined the company as managing director, along with Richard Higgins as marketing director. Emily had worked as a senior manager with Plato plc, a large UK designer and manufacturer of giftware, of which Richard had been a director. Emily and Richard capitalised on their experience with Plato to present some very innovative ideas for developing a new product range for Millpot. However, Emily and Richard's ideas for expanding the business required additional investment, the majority of which was spent during the financial year just ended on 31 March 2012.

The share capital of Millpot Ltd, 800,000 £1 ordinary shares, had all been owned by Martin himself. On retirement he decided to transfer 390,000 of his shares to his daughter Emily, and to sell 390,000 shares to Richard Higgins. Martin gifted his remaining 20,000 shares to Dennis Brown, who was the production director and had given the company many years of loyal service. Richard had used a large part of his personal savings and had taken out an additional mortgage on his house to help finance his investment in the business. This was, of course, paid to Martin Griffin and did not provide any additional capital for the business.

In order to raise additional share capital, Emily and Richard asked Martin's advice about friends, family, and business contacts who may be approached. Martin suggested approaching a venture capital company, Foxhole Ltd, which was run by a friend of his, Bill Fox. Foxhole already had a wide portfolio of investments in dot.com and service businesses, and Bill was interested in investing in this type of growing manufacturing business. He had known Martin and the Griffin family for many years, and was confident that Emily and Richard would make a success of the new ideas that they presented for the business. Additional capital was therefore provided from the issue of 800,000 new £1 shares at par to Foxhole Ltd, to become the largest shareholder of Millpot Ltd. Millpot Ltd also had a bank loan, which it increased during 2011/12, and had a bank overdraft facility.

The directors of the newly structured Millpot Ltd, and its shareholders were as follows:

Emily Griffin	Managing director	390,000 shares
Richard Higgins	Marketing director	390,000 shares
Dennis Brown	Production director	20,000 shares
Bill Fox	Non-executive director	
Foxhole Ltd		800,000 shares

As a non-executive director of Millpot Ltd, Bill Fox attended the annual general meetings and review meetings that were held every six months. He didn't have any involvement with the day-to-day management of the business.

The new range at Millpot did quite well and the company also began to export in a small way to North America. Emily and Richard were pleased by the way in which the sales of the business had grown and in the growth of their customer base. They had just received a large order from Potto, a German company, which was regarded as an important inroad into the European market. If Potto became a regular customer, the sales of the company were likely to increase rapidly over the next few years and would establish Millpot as a major player in the market.

In the first week of May 2012, the day that Millpot received the order from Potto, Emily also received a letter from the bank manager. The bank manager requested that Millpot Ltd immediately and considerably reduce their overdraft, which he felt was running at a level which exposed the bank and the company to a higher level of risk than he was prepared to accept. Emily Griffin was very angry and felt very frustrated. Emily, Richard, and Dennis agreed that since they had just had such a good year's trading and the current year looked even better, the reduction in the overdraft facility was going to seriously jeopardise their ability to meet the commitments they had to supply their customers.

When they joined the company, Emily and Richard decided that Millpot, which had always been production led, would become a design and marketing led business. Therefore, a great deal of the strategic planning was concerned with integrating the product design and development with the sales and marketing operations of the business. Over the past three years Emily and Richard had invested in employing and training a young design team to help continue to develop the Millpot brand. The marketing team led by Richard had ensured that the enthusiasm of their key customers was converted into new firm orders, and that new orders were received from customers like Potto. The order book grew until it had now reached the highest level ever for the company.

In addition to his role as production director, Dennis had always tended to look after the books and any financial matters. Dennis wasn't an accountant and he hadn't had any formal financial training. But, as he said, he had a small and experienced accounts team who dealt with the day-to-day transactions; if ever there had been a problem, they would ask Millpot's auditors for some advice. As soon as she received the letter from the bank, Emily called the bank manager to try and persuade him to continue to support the overdraft facility at the current level, but with no success. Emily also convened an urgent meeting of the directors, including Bill Fox, to talk about the letter and the draft accounts of the business for the year ended 31 March 2012. The letter from the bank was distributed to all the directors before the meeting.

Richard Higgins was very worried about his investment in the company. He admitted that his accounting knowledge was fairly limited. He thought that the company was doing very well, and said that the draft accounts for the year to 31 March 2012 seemed to confirm their success. Profit before tax was more than double the profit for 2011. He couldn't understand why the cash flow was so bad. He appreciated that they had spent a great deal of money on the additional plant and equipment, but they had already had a bank loan to help with that. He thought that the cash situation should really be even better than the profit because the expenses included £1.5m for depreciation, which doesn't involve any cash at all.

Emily Griffin, still appeared very angry at the lack of support being given by the bank. She outlined the impact that the overdraft reduction would have on their ability to meet their commitments over the next year. She said that the bank's demand to cut their overdraft by 50% over the next three months put them in an impossible position with regard to being able to meet customer orders. Millpot Ltd couldn't find an alternative source of such a large amount of money in such a short time.

Richard, Emily, and Dennis, had, before the meeting, hoped that Bill Fox would be prepared to help out by purchasing further additional new shares in the company or by making a loan to the company. However, it was soon made clear by Bill that further investment was not a possible option.

Foxhole Ltd had made a couple of new investments over the past few months and so did not have the money to invest further in Millpot. As a venture capitalist, Foxhole had actually been discussing the possible exit from Millpot by selling and trying to realise a profit on the shares. Finding a prospective buyer for their shares, or floating Millpot on the alternative investment market (AIM), did not currently appear to be a realistic option.

Bill Fox had been so much involved in running his own business, Foxhole Ltd, that he had neglected to monitor the financial position of Millpot Ltd as often and as closely as he should have done. At the directors' meeting he realised that he should have been much more atten-tive and there was now a possibility that Millpot would not provide the returns his company expected, unless things could be drastically improved.

The financial statements of Millpot Ltd for the past two years are shown below:

Income statement for the year ended 31 March

	2011 £000	2012 £000
Revenue	7,000	11,500
Cost of sales	3,700	5,800
Gross profit	3,300	5,700
Operating expenses	2,200	3,100
Operating profit	1,100	2,600
Interest paid	200	500
Profit before tax	900	2,100
Income tax expense	200	400
Profit for the year	700	1,700
Dividend	200	300
Retained earnings for the year	500	1,400
Retained earnings brought forward	1,100	1,600
Retained earnings carried forward	1,600	3,000

Balance sheet as at 31 March

	2011 £000	2012 £000
Non-current assets	4,300	7,200
Current assets		
Inventories	1,200	2,900
Trade receivables	800	1,900
Other receivables	100	200
Cash and cash equivalents	100	–
Total current assets	2,200	5,000
Total assets	6,500	12,200
Current liabilities		
Borrowings and finance leases	–	2,100
Trade payables	600	1,300
Other payables	100	200

(continued)

Income tax payable	200	400
Dividends payable	200	300
Total current liabilities	1,100	4,300
Non-current liabilities		
Loan	2,200	3,300
Total liabilities	3,300	7,600
Net assets	3,200	4,600
Equity		
Ordinary shares (£1)	1,600	1,600
Retained earnings	1,600	3,000
Total equity	3,200	4,600

Cash generated from operations for the year ended 31 March 2012

	£000
Profit before tax	2,100
Depreciation charges	1,500
Adjust finance costs	500
Increase in inventories	(1,700)
Increase in trade and other receivables	(1,200)
Increase in trade and other payables	800
Cash generated from operations	2,000
Interest paid	(500)
Income taxes paid	(200)
Net cash generated from operating activities	1,300

Statement of cash flows for the year ended 31 March 2012

	£000
Cash flows from operating activities	
Cash generated from operations	2,000
Interest paid	(500)
Income taxes paid	(200)
Net cash generated from operating activities	1,300
Cash flows from investing activities	
Purchases of tangible assets	(4,400)
Net cash outflow from investing activities	(4,400)
Cash flows from financing activities	
Proceeds from borrowings	1,100
Dividends paid to equity shareholders	(200)
Net cash inflow from financing activities	900
Decrease in cash and cash equivalents in the year	(2,200)
Cash and cash equivalents and bank overdrafts at beginning of year	100
Cash and cash equivalents and bank overdrafts at end of year	(2,100)

Analysis of cash and cash equivalents and bank overdrafts as at 31 March 2012

	At 1 April 2011	At 31 March 2012
	£000	£000
Cash and cash equivalents	100	–
Bank overdrafts	–	(2,100)
Cash and cash equivalents and	100	(2,100)
bank overdrafts		

The directors of Millpot Ltd were unable to agree on a way of dealing with the financial problem faced by the company. Emily thought it best that she continue to try and negotiate with the bank manager, and believed that she could change the bank manager's mind if she:

■ presented him with the accounts for 31 March 2012, which showed such good results

and

■ made him fully aware of the implications of the reduction in the overdraft facility on the future of Millpot.

However, Richard and Dennis said that they were aware that Millpot Ltd had exceeded its agreed overdraft limit a few times over the past two years and so they were not confident that Emily could persuade the bank to change its mind. They suggested that they should try and find another investor prepared to provide additional funds for the business, to keep the business going. They really believed that the year-end accounts showed how successful Millpot had been over the past two years and that their track record was sufficient to attract a potential new investor in the business. Bill didn't agree. He felt that this would not be a practical solution. More importantly, Foxhole didn't want to have another large shareholder in the company because it would dilute its shareholding, and also reduce its influence over the future direction of the business. However, Bill agreed that immediate and radical action was necessary to be taken by the company.

After hours of argument and discussion, it became apparent that the problem would not be resolved at the meeting. Therefore, it was agreed by all present that expertise from outside the company should be sought to help the company find an acceptable and viable solution to the problem. The directors decided to approach Lucis Consulting, which specialises in helping businesses with financial problems, and to ask them to produce a plan of action for their consideration.

Required:
As a member of the Lucis team, prepare a report for the board of directors of Millpot Ltd which analyses the problems faced by the company and which sets out a detailed plan of action for dealing with its problems. Your report should include consideration of the following questions:

(i)   What are the weaknesses in Millpot Ltd's current organisational structure?
(ii)   What are some of the financial procedures and controls that Millpot Ltd lacks?
(iii)   At which stage in its life cycle do you consider Millpot Ltd is currently at?
(iv)   How does Millpot Ltd appear in terms of profitability and cash flow?
(v)   What are the weaknesses in Millpot Ltd's investment and growth plans and their financing?

Your report should be supported by appropriate analyses for the years ended 31 March 2012 and 31 March 2011.

Part II

FINANCIAL STRATEGY

Introduction to Part II

Part I of this book is about corporate finance, which is concerned with the effective use of financial resources to create corporate value. Part II is concerned primarily with how the use of appropriate financial strategies not only creates corporate value but reflects it in increased shareholder value.

Chapter 13 sets the scene by looking at the product life cycle (PLC) and how this may be reflected in a theoretical business life cycle (BLC) model that describes the stages through which businesses may typically progress from their initial start-up through to their decline and possible demise. The financial parameters relating to each stage of this simplified business life cycle will be identified, and appropriate financial strategies will be discussed that may be used to exploit the specific circumstances in order to create shareholder value. It considers both financial risk and business risk and the relationship between them, and how these may change through each of the stages of the BLC. Each of the sources of external finance present different levels of financial risk and the choice of these is considered with regard to the BLC, together with their corresponding levels of interest and dividends.

Chapter 14 focuses specifically on start-up businesses and their transition to their growth phase. These stages of company development are considered with regard to their risk profiles and options about how they may best be financed. This chapter also looks at how companies may finance new investment, and how they may move from private to public ownership and become quoted on a stock exchange.

Chapter 15 takes the development of the business a step further by looking at how companies, after experiencing a period of turbulence and surviving a market shakeout, enjoy a period of maturity, but which may ultimately result in decline. These stages are considered with regard to their risk profiles and possible changes in their methods of financing. This chapter also looks at how mature companies may become takeover targets and some of the strategies that may be employed to delay or avoid decline.

Chapters 16 and 17 look at specific strategies used by companies with regard to mergers and acquisitions (M&As). It considers the reasons, justifications, and motives for M&As, and how target companies may be valued. The financing of acquisitions may involve the use of additional debt or equity and alternative financial strategies. A number of defences against a hostile takeover are examined, applicable both before and after a takeover bid has been made. The post-takeover position of the acquiring company and the acquired company are considered with regard to each of the major stakeholders.

Chapter 18 is concerned with the way in which companies may be restructured or reorganised and the influences and reasons for these strategies. This chapter considers the strategies and techniques used in demergers, privatisations, management buy-outs (MBOs), and management buy-ins (MBIs).

13

The business life cycle and financial strategy

Chapter contents

Learning objectives

Completion of this chapter will enable you to:

- Outline the product life cycle (PLC) model.
- Explain the BCG matrix and its strategic implications.
- Explain a simple business life cycle (BLC) model.
- Explain the inverse correlation between business risk and financial risk.
- Consider business risk and financial risk throughout the life cycle of a business.
- Recognise the changing levels of earnings per share (eps) and cash flow during the different stages of the business life cycle.
- Identify the various sources of business finance throughout the business life cycle.
- Consider how dividend levels, the P/E ratio, and the share price may change during the different stages of the business life cycle.

Introduction

As a product moves through the various stages of its development from its conception, start-up, or launch to its decline and possible eventual demise, levels of sales, profits, and cash flow may be expected to change significantly. The **product life cycle (PLC)** model tries to identify the separate stages in this development.

The PLC model may be criticised for its oversimplification, the reasons for which will be considered in this chapter. However, in order to provide a framework in which to consider financial strategy, we will extend the PLC model to describe theoretically how a company may also develop and progress through its stages of growth, maturity, and so on. Businesses in practice do not usually provide a single product or service; it is more likely that they may have a portfolio of many different products or services, each with a different life cycle. Businesses may also include a number of divisions or subsidiaries that also provide many different products or services, each with differing life cycles. Diversified companies may be involved in an even greater range of industrial sectors, businesses, and products. We are assuming that the PLC model describes distinctly separate phases in the development of a product, which may or may not be strictly accurate. If we extend this principle as applying to a company it is certainly true that in practice a phase like the mature phase of a company will also include elements of, for example, growth or decline.

Despite its oversimplification and inherent weaknesses we will use this form of product life cycle model and broaden it into the context of the entire business to examine appropriate financial strategies that may be adopted by companies to create shareholder value. This chapter will introduce this type of life cycle as applied to a business, the stages of which will each be considered separately and in more detail in Chapters 14 and 15.

Product life cycle (PLC)

Products (and services) developed and provided by businesses may be considered at three different levels, examples of which are shown in Figure 13.1. Generic products may be considered at the industry level, types of product at the sector of industry level, and branded versions of those products at the individual product level.

The life cycle of such products may apply in different ways at each of the different levels. At the industry level the mature stage tends to span a very long period. Whereas at the individual product level, which includes brands and makes of product, each stage in the life cycle may be of varying length with no common pattern. Each may be assumed to conform to the type of life cycle model illustrated by the curve in Figure 13.2.

The product life cycle (PLC) looks at the tracking of movements of sales, and therefore profits and cash flows, where market share is changing throughout the entire cycle. The PLC reflects what sales levels were over the life of the product, but the model may also be used to consider what future trends in sales, profits, and cash flows may be. At each stage of the cycle different levels of business risk will be faced at the industry level, sector of industry level, and individual product level with regard to political, economic, social, technological, environmental, and legal pressures, substitute and competing products, and competitors.

There are four separate stages in the product life cycle, separated by a period of instability or turbulence between the growth and maturity stages, and the effects of experience are seen throughout the entire cycle:

- start-up – which is the introductory phase of the launch of a product
- growth – in which new entrants are attracted into the marketplace
- turbulence – where increasing production capacity results in overcapacity, and then turmoil in the market resulting in a shakeout
- maturity – where demand and supply are in balance
- decline – where there is market saturation and therefore replacement or new product development is required.

During the pre-start-up and start-up phases there will be high costs of introducing a new product, during which time cash flows are likely to be highly negative, and this situation may also continue through to the growth phase. As the product becomes established during the growth phase, and into the mature phase, operating costs may be reduced as a result of economies of scale.

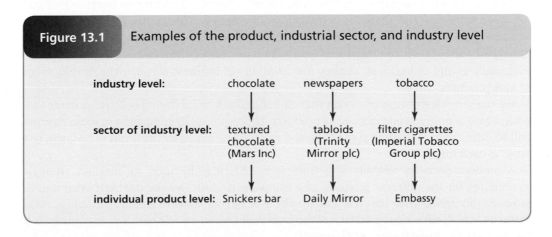

Figure 13.1   Examples of the product, industrial sector, and industry level

industry level:	chocolate	newspapers	tobacco
sector of industry level:	textured chocolate (Mars Inc)	tabloids (Trinity Mirror plc)	filter cigarettes (Imperial Tobacco Group plc)
individual product level:	Snickers bar	Daily Mirror	Embassy

Figure 13.2	The product life cycle (PLC)

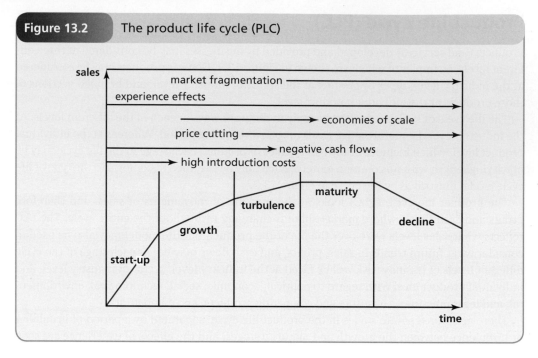

The parameters of the PLC are sales and time, and as the growth in sales of a product increases its prospects of future growth decline. During the high-growth phase of a product, competitors are attracted into the market with the aim of taking market share and earning profits. This will provide increased capacity to meet increasing demand as the market grows. As the growth in demand slows down this will eventually result in overcapacity, followed by a period of competition and price-cutting. Continued competition and price-cutting will result in a shakeout in which many companies will be forced out of the market.

The end of this period of turbulence marks the beginning of the mature phase of the life cycle, which sees a more stable demand and supply situation. The remaining companies that have survived the shakeout in that particular market may go on to enjoy high levels of sales and some stability in their levels of profits and cash flows.

The mature phase will not last forever. Market fragmentation will inevitably take place and demand for the majority of products will start to decline. This may be because demand has been saturated and there is no further requirement for these products. Or it may be because products have become obsolete, or they have been replaced by substitutes or enhanced versions. Once companies' products have reached the decline stage they may eventually go out of business, or they may continue in business through the development of new products.

We can see that a change in market share is a significant factor during each stage in the PLC with regard to products and competing products. The responses by companies to these changes will be different at each stage of the cycle and will be determined by the levels of business risk faced at each stage.

A product portfolio analysis is a framework that may be used to consider strategic alternatives for the different products of a company. It illustrates the different attributes of products throughout their life cycle, and may be used by companies to identify suitable growth, maturity, and decline strategies. One of the most well-known models of this type of analysis is the Boston Consulting Group (BCG) matrix.

Progress check 13.1

Explain what is meant by the product life cycle (PLC) and how this may be applied to consider the life cycle of a business.

Boston Consulting Group (BCG) matrix

The BCG matrix shows the changing positions of portfolios of products within a company by considering the two dimensions of market share and market growth. This model looks at the rate of growth of the market and relative market share compared to the next largest competitor up or down in the market. The relative market share of a company with a portfolio of products is illustrated in the BCG matrix in its comparison with the rate of market growth. These factors together with cash flows and profitability are important with regard to the successful development of any business. The relative market share rather than absolute market share is the significant factor. For example, a company achieving a market share of 40% may sound excellent. However, it would not be such a good position for the company if there was only one competitor, which had 60% of the market.

The BCG matrix can be used to determine how resource priorities may be allocated between products in the product portfolio of a company. To ensure sustainable long-term value creation, a company should have a portfolio of products that contains an appropriate balance of:

■ growth products that may require the further investment of company resources
■ low-growth products that may generate resources for investment by the company elsewhere.

The basic premise underpinning the matrix is that the greater the market share a product has, or the faster the market for a product grows, the better it is for the company.

The BCG matrix (see Figure 13.3) shows a company with a number of different products, which may be grouped into categories called:

Figure 13.3 The Boston Consulting Group (BCG) box

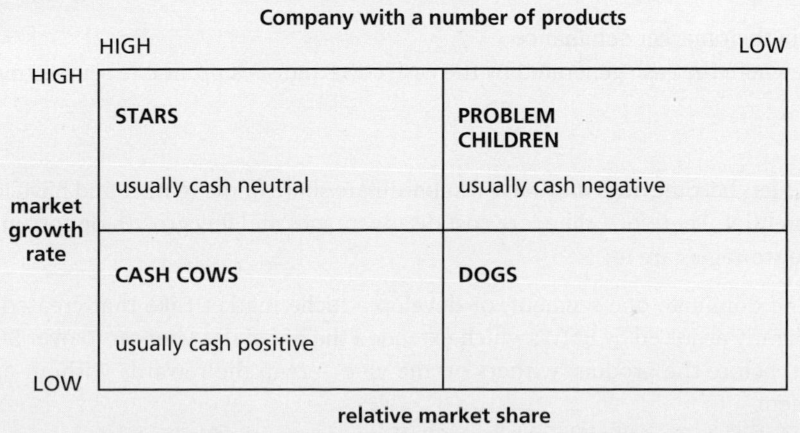

Company with a number of products

	HIGH		LOW
HIGH	**STARS** usually cash neutral	**PROBLEM CHILDREN** usually cash negative	
market growth rate			
	CASH COWS usually cash positive	**DOGS**	
LOW			

relative market share

- problem children
- stars
- cash cows
- dogs.

Problem children

The products within this category have high growth potential, but a low market share, and provide low profit margins, and so need cash. If no cash is provided to support their development then their growth potential may not be achieved and they become dogs.

Possible strategies are to:

- invest sufficiently in product development and promotion to try and obtain a high share of new business and ensure that the products become stars
- acquire competing businesses as a way of obtaining products that are either actual or potential stars.

Alternatively, if the company does not consider that either of these options is viable then it may get out of that market.

Stars

The products within this category are growing very fast, and so cash is needed to support this growth. The company aims to obtain high growth and a dominant market share with these products to make itself a market leader.

Possible strategies are to:

- protect market share through the creation of entry barriers to the market like the establishment of brand names and the benefits of economies of scale
- reinvest earnings for future growth
- actively seek to try and take a share of new business from competitors
- seek out new products and markets to protect the company's future.

Cash cows

Products described as cash cows have low market growth, although a dominant market share. These products are very profitable and strongly cash positive. Possible strategies are to:

- maintain their market dominance
- use elsewhere the cash generated by the cash cows and seek profitable reinvestment.

Dogs

When products become dogs they have a subordinate share of the market and have low market growth potential. Therefore, there are cost disadvantages and few growth opportunities.

Possible strategies are to:

- focus and dominate one segment, or develop a niche market (like that created by Rover, subsequently acquired by BMW, which extended the life of the Mini car to over 50 years)
- 'harvest' before the product 'withers on the vine' – reap the rewards without any further investment
- divest while there is still some value – sell off that part of the business
- abandon declining products and get out of the market.

A dog may possibly be revived through increased marketing. The life of products may also be continued by developing products like, for example, spare parts for products that are no longer in production in order to service customer requirements.

Generally, the BCG approach looks at cash rather than profit, but we may question whether the overall BCG rationale itself is sound. Although it may be difficult to define each of the variables, it may nevertheless be a little prescriptive. Does high growth result in high sales revenues and mean that there is little price competition? Does a high market share provide economies of scale and price-setting power, and result in the company achieving the role of market leader?

Companies are continually seeking ways to minimise risk, maximise revenue, and endeavour to increase market share. The basis of these strategies is the development of consistent and sustainable cash flows from sales of products and services. However, while the possession of cash cow products or services that command a large market share of an already mature market is important, future survival and success of a company cannot rest solely on such products and services. Future success is dependent upon having a balanced portfolio of products and services, represented by each of the boxes in the BCG matrix:

- problem children products or services occupying the introductory stage of the product life cycle
- star products or services occupying the growth stage of the product life cycle
- cash cow products or services occupying the maturity stage of the product life cycle
- dog products or services occupying the decline stage of the product life cycle.

Progress check 13.2

Describe the BCG matrix and its various components.

It is possible to use the BCG matrix to visualise the position of products, in order to assess appropriate strategies. It is the varying nature of a company's portfolio of products and services that directly affects the levels of risk faced by a company throughout its life cycle. Each of the boxes in the BCG matrix can be seen to be very similar to each of the phases in the PLC. The market growth rate in the BCG matrix relates to the sales volume growth of the PLC model, as products move from their start-up (problem children), to growth (stars), maturity (cash cows), and decline (dogs). Problem children effectively represent new start-up products requiring high levels of resources for market research, investment, research and development, operations, promotion, and advertising.

The business life cycle (BLC)

The concept of the **business life cycle (BLC)** has many different meanings. A business life cycle may fall into an annual pattern like the seasonal activities of, for example, a farming business. Alternatively, businesses that undertake projects such as the construction of a water desalination plant or a nuclear power plant, may have business life cycles that span many years. The business cycle may also be considered at a macroeconomic level relating to cyclical changes in the economic environment in terms of growth, inflation, and interest rates.

From the BCG matrix in Figure 13.3, which applies to a company having a portfolio of products, we can see how closely it imitates the PLC graph in Figure 13.2, particularly if we assume that negative growth may be possible (as in the decline stage) when the company has a large proportion of dogs. We will apply this model of the life cycle to businesses or divisions that may be active in particular industrial sectors. The four main phases of the PLC model: start-up or introduction phase; growth phase; mature phase; decline phase, will be used to describe the stages of corporate development and referred to the business life cycle (BLC).

We are using this business cycle approach because it is the time-tested way in which both industries and companies appear to have developed for hundreds of years right up to the present day. In the UK there are many good examples of this business life cycle pattern and the ways in which the risks to which they were exposed shaped the future of industries, products, and companies. Look at, for example, the coal mining, shipbuilding, and pottery industries illustrated in Mini cases 13.1, 13.2, 13.3, and 13.4.

Mini case 13.1

Coal had been used as a fuel for centuries but emerged as the main source of energy for the Industrial Revolution. Its use grew substantially in the early 19th century because of its abundance throughout the UK in Wales, Scotland, and the North of England. It was also able to be cheaply transported using canals and the railways. By the late 19th century there was enormous expansion of the coal industry and a great dependence on exports, and it became a mature industry throughout the 20th century.

The coal industry declined by the end of the 20th century as its use was replaced with oil and natural gas, and because of social costs and political pressures. Despite its decline it remains one of the cheapest sources of energy, although it may still be environmentally unfriendly.

Mini case 13.2

The UK as an island nation has a maritime history and so shipbuilding began a very long time ago but started seriously in the North of England in the 14th century and continued to grow up to the 18th century. During the 19th century, shipbuilding was transformed into a modern industry. Its boom years in the early 20th century were stimulated by the demand for warships and repair facilities. This was followed by a slump in the mid-1920s economic depression but was revived briefly in the 1940s because of Second World War demand. The industry again slumped in the 1960s because of reduced demand and an increase in foreign competition, and its decline continued throughout the late 20th century.

The business life cycles seen in industries have also been reflected in the life cycles of industrial sectors and in companies, the phases of each cycle tending to be shorter than those observed in industries. At both the sector of industry level and at the company level there is a wide range of good examples of the business life cycle, for example sporting newspapers (for example the *Sporting Life*), holiday camps (for example Butlin's), family cars (for example Rover), and vinyl music albums.

Mini case 13.3

Traditionally, there has been an abundance of both coal and clay in the UK and particularly in the Staffordshire area. The pottery industry had very early beginnings, and a medieval pottery industry appeared to be thriving in the 13th century in some parts of the UK. Growth of the industry took place between the mid-17th century and mid-18th century through industrialisation. By the mid-18th century a substantial industry had been established which then matured throughout the 19th century.

However, the pottery industry started to decline in the latter part of the 20th century because of changes in fashion, the availability of cheaper substitutes, and low-cost foreign competition, to its virtual demise in the 21st century. The majority of pottery and ceramics production now takes place elsewhere than in the UK, and in countries where production costs are considerably lower. Major companies like Wedgewood and Spode have now disappeared.

Mini case 13.4

Mass production of shellac gramophone records began in Germany at the end of the 19th century and 78 rpm records continued to be produced worldwide throughout the first half of the 20th century. Magnetic tape recording emerged in the early 1940s and vinyl records developed in the late 1940s. 78s were then superseded by tape and vinyl 45 rpm and 33 rpm records in the 1950s. Many companies started up during this period of the 1950s producing vinyl albums and enjoying rapid growth with the birth of rock music and then the Beatles phenomenon. These companies reached a period of maturity, which ran through the 1960s and 1970s.

Then in the early 1980s the first CDs were marketed which saw the merging of the consumer music industry with the computer revolution. This signalled the imminent death of the vinyl album (and tape cassettes), which disappeared by the 1990s (although there has been a recent revival of vinyl mainly as collector items). As the growth in demand for Internet digital downloads continues to increase throughout the early part of the 21st century, the CD is likely to become a relic of yet another bygone age.

We can see from the above examples that the types of risk and levels of risk faced by businesses are different during each phase of the business life cycle. Therefore different strategies should be adopted by companies at each stage of the cycle relating to, for example, marketing, human resources, operations, finance, and so on. In this book we are concerned with financial strategy. This chapter and the chapters that follow consider the financial strategies that may be most appropriate for companies at each stage of the business life cycle. In this context we will look at financial strategy with regard to:

- approaches to financial risk
- levels of earnings, or profitability, and cash flow
- types and levels of investment
- sources of finance – debt and equity
- gearing, or capital structure
- levels of dividends

- levels of earnings retention
- share price,

and with the aim of maximisation of shareholder wealth through creation of shareholder value consistent with levels of perceived risk and returns required by investors.

In our use of the business life cycle we will consider a specific view of the development of a company through each of the phases we have described. Throughout the business life cycle (BLC), companies face continual change and the effect of their experience continues to influence the ways in which they behave and make decisions throughout the whole cycle.

New products and new businesses take some time to gain acceptance by potential customers and so initial sales growth is usually very slow. In the start-up phase, and as companies develop and grow, they inevitably incur high start-up and introduction costs. There are likely to be only a few companies in any new market. Since output is initially quite low then unit costs will be high, as will be the cost of advertising and promotion and costs of rectification of initial teething problems. Therefore, the start-up phase of the BLC is likely to see negative net cash flows, which may continue right through into the growth phase. As a business develops through its growth phase and its output and sales increase, economies of scale may be achieved from which it may reap the rewards of increased profitability during its mature phase.

As output increases throughout the growth phase, unit costs will fall as a result of economies of scale. Strong demand will ensure some stability in sales prices. However, a strong market will also attract competitors, and so profitability will suffer from increased costs of product improvement, promotion, and distribution necessary for a business to try and maintain a dominant position in the market.

During the growth phase of a business turbulence in the market is normally seen in a great deal of price-cutting by competitors. The turbulence phase is the period of uncertainty and change in the market that occurs towards the end of the growth phase from which only the strongest players survive to go on and enter the mature phase.

During the mature phase the rate of sales growth normally reduces to a level that is usually the longest and most successful period of the life cycle. In general, most products on the market at any point in time are in their mature stage, where the company's sales and profits are both good. In the mature phase, new entrants may be tempted to enter such established and profitable markets, but to a lesser extent than during the growth phase. Whether during the growth phase or mature phase, increasing competition inevitably leads to production overcapacity. Sales of the products and services of some businesses may start to decline and some players will leave the market. Eventually, total market demand may decline either quickly or slowly depending on the level of introduction of substitutes or replacement products. The businesses that remain in the market usually either seek to 'harvest' the maximum possible return from a product before it eventually 'withers on the vine', or try to prolong the life of a product through modifications and development of niche markets. However, most businesses will leave the market during the decline phase because of falling profits. Those that remain in the market for too long in the decline phase before either getting out or seeking alternatives may simply become insolvent.

There are a number of drawbacks that should be considered in the use of a business life cycle (and product life cycle):

- each stage is not clearly defined
- the length of each stage is not certain

- the location of a product or a business at a point in time is not accurate
- the shape of the curve outlined in the life cycle model may not always occur in actuality
- extrapolation of the life cycle graph may not be accurate
- the life cycle is not inevitable – it depends on what strategic decisions are made and which actions are taken
- some products and businesses may never decline (note the extremely long lifespan of a product like Kellogg's Corn Flakes)
- the strategic implications of the life cycle will depend on the nature of the competition
- the life cycle model may not necessarily be the case in the real world.

Life cycle analysis is therefore not an exact science. Businesses are usually never exactly clear about which stage in the cycle they are at any point in time. The business life cycle model we are using is therefore not a prescriptive model used to forecast the lives of products or businesses.

We are using the business life cycle to describe generally how businesses and products may develop relative to the market, and to provide a framework that can be used to indicate which financial strategies may be most appropriate at each stage in the cycle.

Business risk and the life cycle

As we have seen in Chapter 4, businesses face both unsystematic risk and systematic risk. Unsystematic risk (or non-market risk) is risk unique to a company or a project that can be mitigated through diversification into other businesses or projects. Systematic risk (or market risk) is risk that cannot be diversified away. One element of systematic risk is business risk, and the other element is financial risk. Business risk is associated with systematic influences on a company's specific business sector. The level of business risk relates to the risk to a company's operating profits and varies from one industry to another. Different levels of business risk may be faced at different stages in its life cycle (see Figure 13.4), examples of which we saw in Mini cases 13.1, 13.2, 13.3, and 13.4.

Business risk relates to the variability of a company's operating profit or cash flow. During the start-up phase of the business life cycle sales are low and costs are very high. Profit and cash flow are dependent on the levels of sales made by a company, and on the levels and type of costs incurred by a company.

Sales are determined by selling price and sales volume, and the seasonal and cyclical trends of sales. It is possible to assess the risk to profits from changes in both selling price and demand volumes. The product may not succeed. Even if the product is very good, market demand may not be as high as expected when it reaches the mature stage of the life cycle, and may not be sufficient to warrant the initial investment. Competition and substitute or replacement products may curtail the length of the product's life. It may therefore be difficult to hold on to whatever market share is achieved, and demand for the product could fall off very quickly. For these reasons the risk to variability in the operating profit or cash flow can therefore be seen to be very high during the start-up phase of the life cycle.

If a product or a business survives the start-up phase of the cycle then the product is proven and has been accepted by the market. However, business risk is still faced by the company in terms of:

- being able to maintain sufficiently high market demand through to the mature stage of the cycle

| Figure 13.4 | Levels of business risk that may be faced by a company during its life cycle |

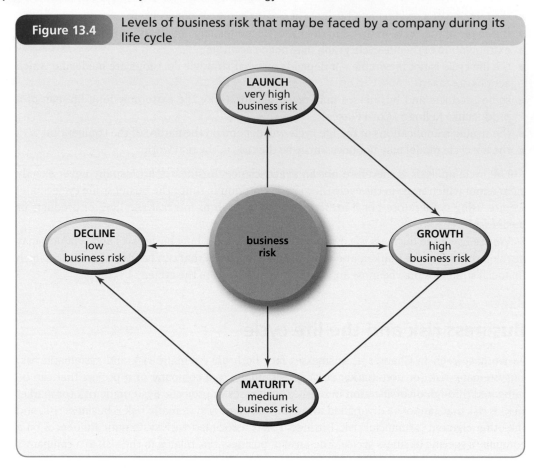

- competition and substitute or replacement products, which may curtail the length of the product's life
- holding on to market share
- the potential for a rapid decline in demand for the product.

Operational gearing

The risk to profits may be assessed by considering the company's level and structure of its costs, represented by its **operational gearing** (or operational leverage). Operational gearing may be considered simply as the relationship between fixed costs and total costs. A high proportion of fixed costs to total costs represents high operational gearing. The higher the operational gearing the greater is the advantage to the business of increasing sales volumes – the benefits of economies of scale. But, if sales are falling then a highly operationally geared business would find the high proportion of fixed costs a problem that may cause a swing from profit to loss. High operational gearing therefore indicates a high level of business risk.

Various operational gearing ratios may be used to assess the impact of fixed costs on a company. One example is the ratio that follows, which compares a company's contribution with its profit before interest and tax (PBIT):

$$\frac{\text{contribution}}{\text{PBIT}} = \frac{\text{revenue } - \text{ variable costs}}{\text{revenue } - \text{ variable costs } - \text{ fixed costs}}$$

This relationship shows the extent to which fixed costs may be increased before the company gets into a loss-making situation. It also shows the relationship between a given increase in sales revenue and the resultant impact on PBIT. Operational gearing increases as fixed costs rise and as variable costs fall. Unit contribution is the difference between the selling price and unit variable cost, measuring the incremental profit from one additional unit of a product or service. Since high fixed cost and low variable cost indicate a high contribution percentage, then high operational gearing indicates a high contribution percentage, and therefore high business risk. The degree of operational gearing may be seen from the following ratio:

$$\text{degree of operational gearing } = \frac{\text{change in PBIT}}{\text{PBIT}} \times \frac{\text{revenue}}{\text{change in revenue}}$$

This relationship measures the percentage change in PBIT for a given percentage change in sales and indicates a company's sensitivity to changes in its fixed costs. It may be used to measure the sensitivity of a business or a project to its fixed costs and the impact of the cyclicality of its revenues. From the above relationship we can expect that during the growth phase the business risk of variability in the operating profit (PBIT) is not as high as during the start-up phase, but it is still high. The growth in the market generally during the growth phase means that a business is also likely to achieve high sales growth. Because of its high costs during the growth phase the company is unlikely to earn high profits until it gets towards the end of this phase and the benefits of economies of scale start to be seen.

An illustration of the relationship between the degree of operational gearing (DG) and business performance is shown in Game Group Mini case 13.5.

Mini case 13.5

In March 2012 the UK video games retailer Game Group plc went into administration following several years of indifferent business performance.

The table shows the sales revenue and PBIT shown in the company's annual financial statements from 2003 to 2011.

	2011 £000	2010 £000	2009 £000	2008 £000	2007 £000	2006 £000	2005 £000	2004 £000	2003 £000
Revenue	1,625,034	1,772,358	1,971,905	1,491,914	801,306	645,118	576,586	606,660	560,065
PBIT	28,475	88,590	126,540	75,192	32,965	8,223	27,036	18,572	27,421

We can calculate the % change in PBIT % and change in revenue year on year. From these percentages the degree of operational gearing (DG) can be calculated from 2004 until 2011, the last full year of trading before the company went into administration.

	2011 £000	2010 £000	2009 £000	2008 £000	2007 £000	2006 £000	2005 £000	2004 £000
Year on year change in PBIT	−60,115	−37,950	51,348	42,227	24,742	−18,813	8,464	−8,849
PBIT change % of this year PBIT	−211%	−43%	41%	56%	75%	−229%	31%	−48%
Year on year change in revenue	−147,324	−199,547	479,991	690,608	156,188	68,532	−30,074	46,595
This year revenue % of change in revenue	−1,103%	−888%	411%	216%	513%	941%	−1,917%	1,302%
DG=% PBIT change × % revenue change	2,327%	382%	168%	121%	385%	−2,155%	−594%	−625%

The company was formed in 1991, and in the latter years prior to its demise we can see extreme swings in its degree of operational gearing.

Assuming that a business survives the shakeout that occurs from the turbulence phase of the life cycle it is then able to move into its mature phase, having established a relatively high market share. Because of this, the business faces a lower degree of business risk than in its growth phase. However, the business is still uncertain as to how long its mature phase will last and:

- how competition and substitute or replacement products may still curtail the length of the product's life
- how the business may hold on to its market share
- whether there may be a rapid decline in demand for the product, for whatever reason.

Business risk due to variability in the operating profit or cash flow during the mature phase is therefore at a medium or moderate level. The only element of business risk remaining as the business moves into the decline phase is the speed at which demand for the product may fall. The level of business risk during this phase, therefore, is relatively low. The problem frequently met when products reach this phase is deciding exactly when to drop them, unless new life can be breathed into them, or whether they can be rejuvenated to produce further sales at reduced costs.

Financial risk and its inverse correlation with business risk

Financial risk is the risk of impact of interest on earnings measured by a company's financial gearing. Financial risk increases as levels of debt are increased and the company is committed to high levels of interest payments. The level of financial gearing therefore impacts on both the company's profits and its ability to pay dividends. The total of systematic or market risk faced by the company comprises the two elements of business risk and financial risk. We have seen how business risk decreases as a company moves through its life cycle. Therefore, financial risk may be correspondingly increased throughout the life cycle without creating an unacceptable level of combined total systematic risk for the company. Financial risk is increased from increased gearing through taking on higher levels of debt. A comparison of Figures 13.4 and 13.5 illustrates this inverse correlation between business and financial risk.

Figure 13.5	Levels of financial risk that may be faced by a company during its life cycle

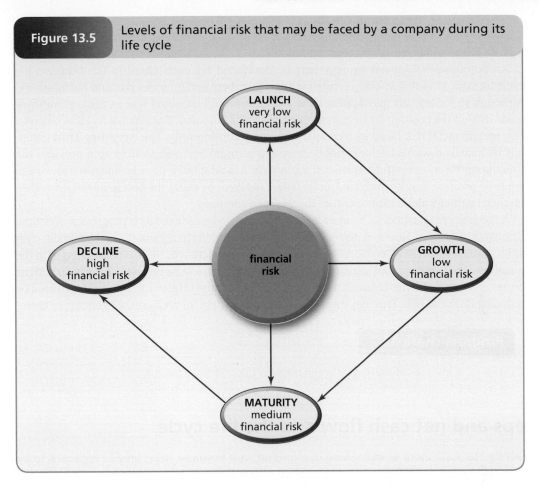

During its start-up phase, a company normally makes no operating profit and there is a high risk of business failure. Therefore business risk is very high. Consequently, financial risk should be low, which would normally mean that a start-up business is funded by equity rather than debt. However, this may not always be the case, and there are many instances of start-up companies being financed partly by debt, particularly by venture capitalists who may prefer this method of financing.

In the growth phase, operating profits should start to grow but will be volatile and there is likely to be some competition from new entrants to the market. Therefore, although lower than during the launch phase, business risk is nevertheless still likely to be high. If a small amount of debt is taken on in addition to equity then there will be some financial risk, although at a low level.

During the mature phase, a company's operating profits should be very high, with less volatility than during the growth phase, and therefore there is only a medium level of business risk. There is therefore scope for an increase in financial risk and so more debt may be taken on by the company without increasing total systematic risk. Financial risk is therefore likely to move to a medium level from the relatively low level seen in the growth phase.

In the decline phase, the business has no growth prospects and so business risk is low. Debt levels are likely to be fairly high and so financial risk is high, not only because of interest payments, but at extremely high levels of debt there is also a risk of insolvency. However, it should be noted that not all mature and declining companies are necessarily saddled with huge debts. Some companies may have been able to repay all or most of their debt incurred during their mature phase and before going into decline.

An appropriate financial strategy may be developed for each phase in the business life cycle by exploiting this inverse correlation that exists between financial risk and business risk. Although in theory this may appear quite logical it should be noted that in the real business environment the position is rarely so simple and straightforward. The relative levels of business risk and financial risk faced by a company will vary considerably. The weighting must generally be heavily towards business risk because it is a sound business strategy that provides the foundation for a successful business. If a company has adopted a poor business strategy then while its position may be mitigated, or its failure delayed, by using the best financial strategies, financial strategy alone cannot ensure success for a company.

A company may expect its business risk to continue to be reduced as it progresses over time through its life cycle. However, this may not happen if sudden changes occur in the market, such as increased competition, economic recession, or an introduction of substitute products. If in the meantime the company had increased its financial risk to exploit its inverse relationship with its business risk, a sudden increase in business risk would require total risk to be quickly reduced by reducing financial risk. This may involve a repayment of debt, or an increase in equity, or both.

> ### Progress check 13.3
>
> Explain the inverse correlation between business risk and financial risk.

eps and net cash flow and the life cycle

During the start-up or launch phase of a product or a business, sales may be expected to be very low or even non-existent, and therefore cash inflows will be zero or negligible. On the other hand, it is very likely that cash outflows will be very high because of high start-up costs. Because the inflow of cash from sales is low and cash outflows are high in respect of, for example, research and development costs, and marketing costs, net cash flow as well as eps may therefore be expected to be very highly negative (see Figure 13.6).

During its growth phase a business has an increasing inflow of cash from sales but cash outflows remain high because of working capital requirements, marketing costs, and continued investment in non-current assets for production, and possibly in improved quality initiatives and new product development. The level of net cash flow is dependent on the rate of growth the company is achieving, but is likely to be neither highly negative nor highly positive. As sales increase, eps will grow but may still be at relatively low levels because of high marketing costs, and because the benefits of economies of scale may not yet have been achieved.

The mature phase of a business usually sees cash inflows from sales at their highest levels and cash outflows are reduced because the company does not have to invest in new plant and machinery for further growth. In addition, since the product is now established then there is no need to continue to incur high levels of marketing costs. The net cash flow and eps at the mature phase of a business are therefore likely to be very highly positive.

During the decline phase of a business both cash inflows and cash outflows will be severely reduced. The eps of the business is likely to be low and reducing as sales levels fall. The net cash flow of the business is likely be low or negative, and its level is very much dependent on the rate of decline of the business.

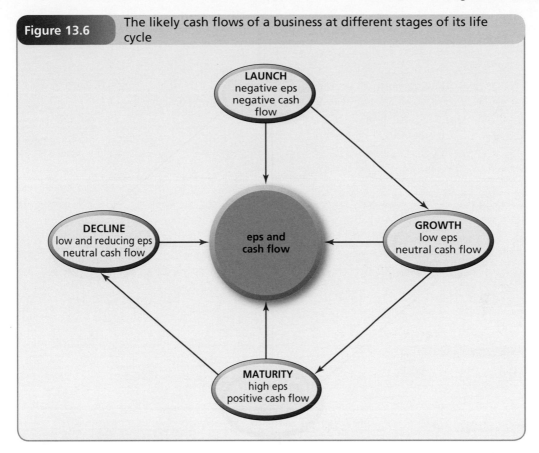

Figure 13.6 The likely cash flows of a business at different stages of its life cycle

---

How may a company's net cash flow vary during each stage of the BLC?

Sources of funding and the life cycle

When a company is in its start-up phase, business risk will be very high and financial risk very low. Equity, very often provided by venture capitalists, is usually the source of financing for start-up companies rather than debt (see Figure 13.7). This is because debt carries a fixed commitment for interest payments, which is difficult to meet during start-up when there are usually losses rather than profits, and negative cash flows. There is no such commitment with equity capital. During the start-up phase, the high returns required by equity shareholders will not be realised until funds are available for the company to pay dividends or unless shareholders dispose of their shares at a price higher than when they were acquired.

During the growth phase of the company business risk is high and financial risk is low. Equity continues to be the main source of funds. But if business risk is reduced then a small amount of debt may be taken on. During this phase the original providers of equity capital may recover their investment at an increased value from:

Figure 13.7 Sources of possible funding during a company's life cycle

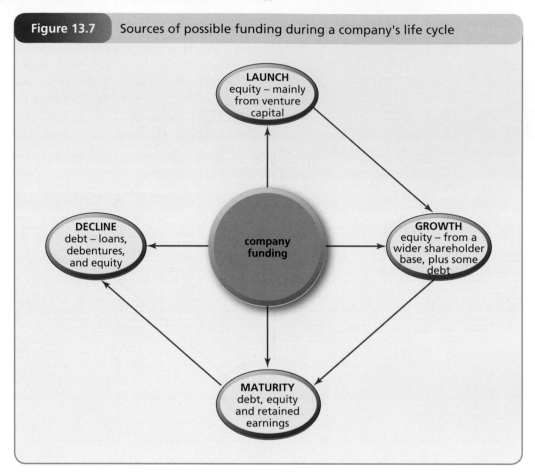

- sale of their shares to existing or new shareholders
- public flotation of the company, which therefore widens the share ownership
- buy-out of the company by its management, with or without the help of new external investors or lenders (see Chapter 18).

During the mature phase of the company business risk is at a medium level and financial risk is at a medium level. The company may continue to be funded largely by equity capital and also from its retained earnings, but financial risk may be increased to a medium level so the company's gearing may also be increased by taking on additional debt capital.

During the decline phase of the company business risk is low, therefore financial risk may be increased. The level of debt may be increased because this cheap source of funding may 'help' declining profits because of its relatively low cost compared with other financing. Such debt may be secured on the residual value of the assets which remain tied up in the business.

Progress check 13.5

Why may equity be preferable to debt financing during a company's start-up phase?

Dividends and the life cycle

In this section we will consider the levels of dividends that may be paid by considering a company's financial performance throughout each of its phases in the business life cycle (see Figure 13.8). The relationship between levels of dividends and each phase of the business life cycle is very much a generalisation and may not always be the case for all companies at all times and in every circumstance.

During its start-up phase the company has no distributable profits and negative cash flows and therefore the dividend payout ratio must be zero. During its growth phase as eps and cash flows start to increase there may be a nominal amount of dividend paid. The level of dividend payout will depend on the level of growth achieved by the company, with regard to the level of profit it has earned and conditional on its having sufficient cash flow.

During its mature phase the company would expect to maintain a high dividend payout ratio because there will be distributable profits even after debt interest, and there should be sufficient cash flow to pay high dividends. The company may now have few new investment opportunities. Therefore growth prospects are very limited, and so investors have less chance of capital gains and so will demand a high level of dividends. A possible agency problem may manifest itself here. Shareholders will generally require a high dividend payout during the company's mature phase but the directors or managers of the business may alternatively prefer to hold on to funds to give themselves increased operational flexibility.

In the decline phase, the company may decide to use all the free cash flow that it has generated to pay dividends. This total dividend payout ratio means that dividends are likely to exceed profit.

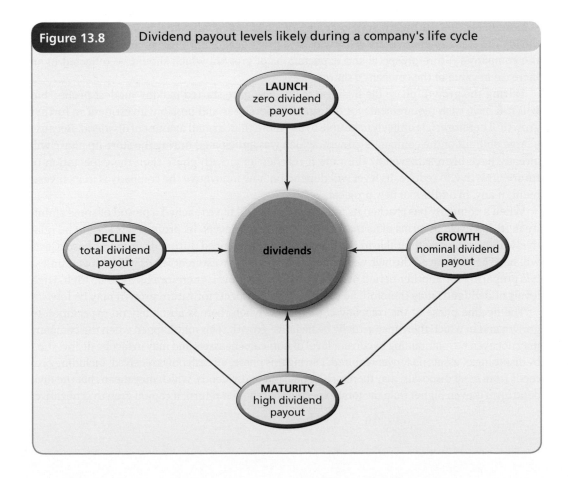

Figure 13.8 Dividend payout levels likely during a company's life cycle

In addition to consideration of the life cycle, there are a number of alternative theories relating to the dividend decision, which we will look at in Chapter 15, for example:

■ residual theory – the company pays dividends only when all other investment opportunities have been exhausted
■ Miller and Modigliani dividend irrelevancy theory – dividends are irrelevant to the market value of the shares
■ traditional view – the company pursues a growth strategy from profitable reinvestment to maximise the market value of the company's shares.

Shareholders' returns and the life cycle

One of the strategic financial decisions that companies have to make is 'Should we pay dividends now or retain earnings to reinvest in the company to provide future increased corporate value that will result in higher dividends in the future plus an increase in share price?'

Shareholders receive their returns in two ways: dividends; capital appreciation from an increase in share price. The levels of dividend payments and capital growth are usually very different throughout each stage in the life cycle of the business as illustrated in Figure 13.9.

During a company's start-up phase losses are likely to be made and cash flows will be highly negative. In addition, if the company is funded by debt as well as by equity then interest will also have to be paid. Therefore, dividends cannot be paid unless adequate cash is acquired by, for example, taking on more debt for that purpose. This is highly unlikely to happen, and so it is more likely that during the start-up phase of a business no dividend will be paid. However, during the start-up phase there is likely to be a great deal of enthusiasm and optimism about the company's future prospects and expectations of growth, which should be reflected in an increase in value of the company's shares.

During the growth phase the business is likely to have started making modest profits, but will still have cash requirements for funding its operations and possibly investment in further growth. Therefore, it is unlikely to be able to pay more than a small amount of dividend. Because a large amount of the company's growth, which was anticipated during the start-up phase will already have been achieved by the time it reaches its growth phase then the expectation of future growth will reduce. Its level will depend on how innovative the company is in its investment, if any, in additional new projects.

When a company has reached its mature phase it will have reached a period of some stability in its life cycle in terms of its market share and sales levels. Its profit levels should be relatively high and less vulnerable to the fluctuations experienced during its growth phase. Costs will have been reduced through economies of scale, and investment levels will be lower unless it is preparing for another period of high growth. Cash flow is therefore likely to be high. High levels of dividends may therefore be paid, but the prospects for future growth may be low.

The decline phase of the company is the period when there is absolutely no expectation of growth and in which there may actually be negative growth. This may happen when the company may not even be maintaining its current level of non-current assets and may in fact be disinvesting by disposing of assets no longer required. During this phase, all cash flows received, including proceeds from asset disposals, may therefore be paid out in dividends, which may mean that the dividend level is even higher than the total expected shareholder return, if capital growth is negative.

Figure 13.9 Shareholder returns likely during a company's life cycle

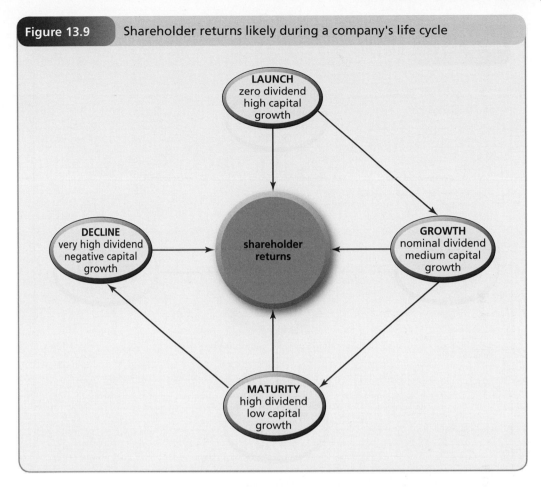

There is generally an offsetting relationship between the dividend payout ratio and the expected level of capital growth. This relationship should be considered in the context of a company decreasing its overall risk profile as it matures and then moves into decline. The decreasing risk profile means that over time the rate of return demanded by investors will get lower and lower. The way in which this may apply at each stage in the business life cycle is illustrated in Worked example 13.1.

Worked example 13.1

During Grovidend Ltd's start-up phase the annual total shareholder return (TSR) required by investors is represented wholly by expected capital growth in the value of its shares because expected future growth prospects of the company are high. We will assume that shareholders initially require a return of 30%, which at the start-up stage is all from capital growth, with no dividends being paid, as shown in Figure 13.10.

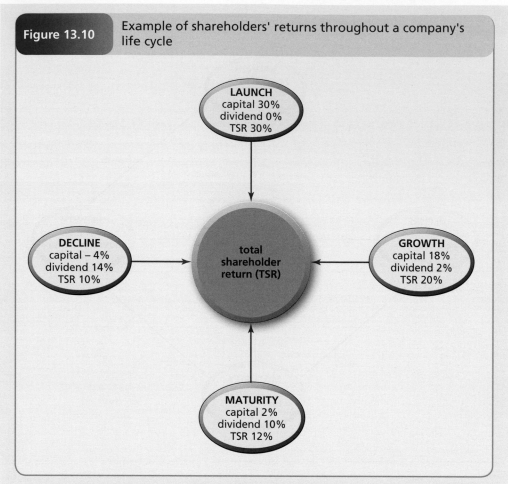

Figure 13.10 Example of shareholders' returns throughout a company's life cycle

During the growth phase of the company the TSR required by investors may have fallen to, say, 20%, as overall risk levels fall. Most of this will still be expected from capital growth (for example 18%), and if the company is making some profit and has sufficient cash flow it may pay out a small dividend (for example 2%). As the company progresses through its growth phase the prospects of future growth will gradually reduce unless the product is exceptionally highly successful.

During the mature phase the overall return required by investors will have again reduced to say 12%, as the overall risk level continues to reduce, but the majority of this will now be expected from the dividend yield (for example 10%). The growth element of TSR expected by investors will be much reduced (to 2% for example), because the company's growth prospects are still reducing. However, this lack of future growth is more than offset by the dividend yield.

The decline phase shows a total dividend payout ratio of, say, 14%, which may be higher than the total annual return expected by investors, which has again reduced to, say, 10%. Therefore, capital growth may be negative during the decline stage at, for example, −4%.

For the shareholder, income tax is payable on dividends, and capital gains tax is payable on the share price gains when the shares are disposed of. In theory, if the after-tax returns from both were similar then shareholders should be indifferent as to whether a dividend is paid or not (but in practice this would also depend on their individual tax positions). If a dividend is not paid, then the value of shares should increase to reflect the present value of future cash flows generated from reinvestment of funds, which were available to be paid out as dividends.

However, shareholders do actually like to receive dividends and achieve growth in the share price, which is not always achievable as illustrated in the press extract below. During the last 25 years, up until the 2008 global financial crisis, booming economic growth led to a preference among the growing number of institutional investors for capital growth. But in periods of economic slump cash returns in the form of dividends become more desirable. Also, the growth of institutional investors may limit fund raising activities since many value-oriented investment funds are not allowed to buy shares that do not pay dividends.

The choice between dividends and capital growth

There are more than 800 companies on the AIM, excluding investment vehicles, and only 187 of them pay a dividend. I have lost count of the number of chief executives who, when asked if their sights are set on paying a dividend, argue that investors in AIM companies would prefer capital growth. That might have been the case in the past, but times have changed.

Gervais Williams, the experienced small-cap fund manager who made the headlines when he left Gartmore last year, has resurfaced at MAM Funds, which is itself quoted on AIM. He is convinced that lifting income will come back into fashion in this age of austerity, and has had little trouble raising £50m for MAM's Diverse Income Trust.

As the name implies, he will be looking at every type of dividend-paying company.

The portfolio is expected to comprise 10 per cent FTSE 100, 25 per cent mid-cap and 65 per cent AIM and micro-cap companies.

By looking outside the FTSE 350, he will be able to widen the range of his investments considerably. In 2001 the biggest six income generators in the FTSE 100 paid a third of the index's total dividend, but this year they will pay almost half. Meanwhile, industrial goods and services companies paying a dividend account for just 3 per cent of the FTSE 100, but 24 per cent of the FTSE All-Share, excluding the FTSE 100.

Mr Williams also has a theory as to why small companies, which used to grow faster than the large corporations, have not done so for years, leading to large redemptions from small-cap funds. Data for UK pension funds shows that 25 years ago 70 per cent of their assets were allocated to a broad range of UK equities, including tiddlers. But increasing globalisation has seen pension funds almost halve their allocation to the UK while turning to large and mid-cap companies overseas in order to reduce risk.

Mr Williams argues that the credit boom made the past 25 years an extraordinary period for capital growth, but that the hangover from the crunch will persist. While the world economy is flat and there is little income growth from big corporations, smaller companies with cash flow and a rising dividend stream will become increasingly attractive. The example of BP and the Gulf of Mexico oil spill shows how a single event can lead to both a sharp reduction in income and capital value at a large corporation. 'For over 25 years we have trained small-caps to pay no dividend, but to reinvest and go for growth,' he says. As a result, even those that do pay a dividend are often under-distributing. His figures show that while the 54 dividend-paying companies in the FTSE Fledgling give a yield of 4.4 percent – well above the 3 per cent yield on the FTSE 350 – the AIM payers have a yield of just 0.6 per cent.

There are plenty of small-cap companies that are growing their income faster than other parts of the market. Those that have yet to start paying a dividend have no grounds for complaint if their share price drifts in an illiquid market. They should wake up to the fact that a dividend keeps a brake on the downside.

Winner pays all

Further evidence that dividends are increasing in importance can be found in the vote at last week's annual meeting of Burford Capital. The specialist in commercial dispute litigation in the US courts was one of only a handful of flotations on AIM in 2009, when it promised 'an intention to pay cash dividends from net realised gains in a manner that provides an ongoing level of dividend income to shareholders'. Out of a total of 180m shares in issue, almost 162m were voted in favour of the payment of a maiden dividend. Not only is the proportion of shares voted astonishing, but the vote was unanimous.

Meanwhile, it appears that providing investors with an income is essential for any company hoping to win an accolade. All five on the shortlist for this week's Growth Company Investor AIM Company of the Year award pay dividends. Majestic Wine, the winner, increased its interim dividend by 18 per cent for the six months to September 27. Quercus, publisher of The Girl With the Dragon Tattoo, was named Plus Company of the Year at the same event, following up its triumph as Company of the Year at the Plus Markets awards last week. The company last month announced a maiden dividend of 5p and a special dividend of 7p 'in recognition of the exceptional performance of The Millennium Trilogy', as Stieg Larsson's Dragon Tattoo and its sequels are known.

Source: Blackwell, D. (2011) Desire for dividends outweighs capital growth, *Financial Times*, 19 May.
© The Financial Times Limited 2012. All Rights Reserved.

Price/earnings (P/E) ratio, the share price, and the life cycle

A company's share price is dependent on the level of activity in the market for its shares. The higher the demand to buy the shares, the higher will be the share price because the supply in the short term, the number of shares in issue, is fixed. The demand to buy shares partly reflects performance that the company has already achieved and partly reflects an expectation of future performance. Future performance relates to the expected present value of future net cash flows, which the market feels that the company is able to achieve. Because an element of the share price includes an expectation of value to be created from future opportunities, the prospects of capital growth of a company are reflected in its published price/earnings (P/E) ratio.

As we have already discussed, very high growth prospects during a company's start-up phase are likely to be followed by high growth during the growth phase, then medium growth during the mature phase, and no growth or negative growth during the decline phase. Therefore, we can see that because the P/E ratio bears a direct relationship to expected future growth then it may be expected to fall over the company's life cycle (see Figure 13.11).

A company's share price equals its eps multiplied by its P/E ratio. During the start-up and growth phases nearly all shareholders' returns are generated from capital growth. As the rate of growth declines the share price may increase to a level that provides an acceptable level of shareholder return through a growth in eps, which takes account of the declining P/E ratio (applied to these earnings as they grow), and the changing dividend payout ratio which reduces expectations of future growth as the company matures.

Figure 13.11   P/E (price/earnings) ratio and share price likely during a company's life cycle

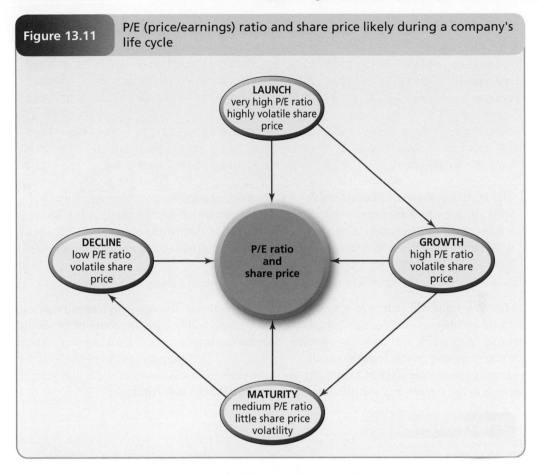

We may generalise about how the P/E ratio and share price may change during the life cycle of a business. In the start-up phase of a business the P/E ratio may be very high because of the expectation of high future levels of growth. The share price should increase but may be highly volatile because there is a high potential for failure of new businesses.

During the growth phase the P/E ratio may still be high, as growth expectations are still reasonably high. The share price may still be volatile because there will be continued uncertainty about whether the level of growth expected by investors will actually be achieved.

The level of JD Wetherspoon's P/E ratio during the past few years shows a company in a phase of growth heading towards maturity (see Mini case 13.6 below).

Mini case 13.6

Founded in 1979, JD Wetherspoon is a UK company that had a chain of 823 public houses as at the end of July 2011. The company was floated on the London Stock Exchange in October 1992 and at the end of its first year after flotation its annual report and accounts showed a P/E ratio of 23.2 (using a year-end share price of 341p and eps of 14.7p).

The company is now in a phase of growth towards maturity as it continues to increase its property portfolio. From the share price and eps extracted from its annual reports over the last eleven years we can calculate the P/E ratio and the variation between its high and low share price for each year, as shown in the table below.

	2001	2002	2003	2004	2005	2006	2007	2008	2009	2010	2011
Share price pence											
Highest price	418.5	440.5	327.5	324.0	287.0	446.0	772.5	608.0	486.0	556.0	473.0
Lowest price	298.5	262.5	159.0	225.5	222.5	275.5	428.0	167.75	205.75	378.7	389.1
% change (low to high)	40.20	67.81	105.97	43.68	28.99	61.89	80.49	262.44	136.21	46.82	21.56
Year-end price	339.5	283.5	233.5	254.5	276.0	445.0	576.5	231.25	450.0	428.4	434.5
eps	14.2	16.6	17.0	17.7	16.4	24.1	28.1	25.2	18.2	29.3	35.4
Year-end P/E ratio	23.9	17.1	13.7	14.4	16.8	18.5	20.5	9.2	24.7	14.6	12.3

The numbers show a relatively stable picture of a company approaching maturity. The wide variation in share prices during 2008 could be attributed to uncertainty in this sector following the smoking ban in public houses, which was implemented in July 2007. This uncertainty may also have impacted on levels of share trading causing the variations in the P/E ratio during 2007 and 2008.

The P/E ratio will reduce to a medium to low level during the company's mature phase, because earnings should be high but growth expectations will be low. The share price should become fairly stable and with less volatility, because the largest part of total investor returns are now provided mostly from dividends.

During the decline stage of a company the share price normally declines and is also volatile because of the uncertainty surrounding how long the business may continue.

Progress check 13.6

In what ways do equity shareholders receive returns from their investment in a company and how does this differ from returns received by debt holders?

In Chapters 14 and 15 we will link together each of the parameters we have considered in this chapter for each of the phases in the business life cycle. By looking at the complete picture of the company with regard to risk, gearing, dividends, and so on, during its start-up, growth, maturity, and decline phases we can consider the financial strategies that may be adopted to achieve an increase in shareholder value. Chapters 16, 17, and 18 take this a step further by considering additional financial strategies related to diversification and reorganisation, achieved through mergers and acquisitions (M&As) and business restructuring.

Summary of key points

- The product life cycle (PLC) model may be used to describe the separate phases in the development of a product.

- The Boston Consulting Group (BCG) matrix may be used in a similar way to the PLC to assess the strategic financial implications at each phase in the development of a business and its products or services.

- The business life cycle (BLC) may be used as a framework describing the separate phases in the development and growth of a company.

- Levels of business risk and financial risk faced by companies change throughout the different phases in their life cycles, and there is an inverse correlation between these types of risk, which together make up systematic or market risk.

- The levels of both earnings per share (eps) and cash flow vary during the different phases of the life cycle.

- One or more different sources of finance may be more appropriate throughout the separate phases of the business life cycle, with different combinations appropriate at each stage.

- The P/E ratio and total shareholder returns change as a business moves through each phase of its life cycle.

- Dividend policy may be determined with reference to the company's position in the life cycle.

Glossary of key terms

business life cycle (BLC) The business life cycle has many different meanings, including:

- an annual pattern, for example a business whose activities follow a seasonal cycle or a business that undertakes a project which spans many years
- changes in the economic environment, at a macroeconomic level, in terms of growth, inflation, and interest rates
- the development of a company through a number of clearly defined phases, in the same way as the PLC.

operational gearing The relationship of fixed costs to total costs. The greater the proportion of fixed costs, the higher the operational gearing, and the greater the advantage to the business of increasing sales volume. If sales revenues fall, a business with high operational gearing may face a problem from its high level of fixed costs.

product life cycle (PLC) The period which begins with the initial product specification and ends with the withdrawal from the market of both the product and its support. It is characterised by defined stages that include research, development, introduction, maturity, decline, and abandonment.

Assessment material

Questions

Q13.1 Outline the disadvantages associated with use of life cycle models.

Q13.2 Compare the Boston Consulting Group (BCG) matrix approach with that of the life cycle model.

Q13.3 Why should a company not expect the level of business risk it faces to remain constant during its entire life cycle?

Q13.4 For each of the major stages in the life cycle of a typical company describe the main cash inflows and outflows, their likely magnitudes, and the resultant net cash flows.

Q13.5 Describe the factors that influence the level of financial risk faced by a company.

Q13.6 Explain the significance of financial risk to a company.

Q13.7 Outline the relationship between business risk and financial risk during the life cycle of a company and explain why the distinction between these two forms of risk is important.

Q13.8 Analyse the ways in which a company's financing needs change over its life cycle.

Q13.9 Discuss the reasons why companies may consider adopting different capital structures as they progress from their initial start-up through to maturity.

Q13.10 Why do companies pay dividends?

Q13.11 What are the key factors that influence a company in deciding the level of dividends it will pay?

Discussion points

D13.1 'Every business should aim to maximise its number of BCG "cash cows".' Discuss.

D13.2 'Earnings per share (eps) tell shareholders everything they need to know about a company.' Discuss.

D13.3 'A shareholder is indifferent as to whether a dividend is paid or not.' Discuss.

Exercises

Solutions are provided in Appendix 2 to all exercise numbers highlighted in colour.

Level I

E13.1 *Time allowed – 30 minutes*

Outline a typical product life cycle (PLC) with reference to one specific industry.

E13.2 *Time allowed – 30 minutes*

Compare the BCG (Boston Consulting Group) matrix with the business life cycle approach. How do these two approaches assist in the development of appropriate financial strategies?

E13.3 *Time allowed – 30 minutes*

Outline the life cycle of a typical business, and explain the movements and net effects of its cash flows during each of the phases of its cycle.

E13.4 *Time allowed – 30 minutes*

In what ways does risk impact on a business as it moves through each phase of its life cycle? What strategies may a business adopt in response to such risks?

E13.5 *Time allowed – 30 minutes*

> Explain the inverse correlation between financial risk and business risk, and how a company may use this to develop an appropriate financial strategy, during each stage of its life cycle.

E13.6 *Time allowed – 30 minutes*

> Explain the circumstances necessary for a company to be able to pay dividends to shareholders.

Level II

E13.7 *Time allowed – 45 minutes*

> Clearly explain why you would agree or disagree with the statement that 'a company's shareholders would never want the company to invest in projects with negative NPVs'.

E13.8 *Time allowed – 45 minutes*

> Explain the ways in which a company may exploit the changing levels of business risk it faces to develop appropriate financial strategies in order to increase shareholder value.

E13.9 *Time allowed – 60 minutes*
The following is the capital structure of a company in the automotive industry:

	Number of units	Price per unit £	Market value
Ordinary shares	115,000,000	26.00	£2,990,000,000
Preference shares	10,000,000	32.50	£325,000,000
Warrants	14,400,000	13.50	£194,400,000
Bonds	2,000,000	650.00	£1,300,000,000

Due to large losses incurred during the past few years, the company had £2bn of tax losses carried forward. Therefore, the next £2bn of profit would be free from corporation tax. The consensus among financial analysts is that the company would not have cumulative profits in excess of £2bn over the next five years.

The majority of the preference shares are held by banks. The company had agreed to buy back the preference shares over the next few years, and needed to decide whether to issue new debt or equity shares to raise the funds needed to do this.

> Analyse the company's financial structure and outline the implications of its funding options. Explain what would be the best funding option for the company and why.

E13.10 *Time allowed – 60 minutes*

In one of the back issues of *Fortune* magazine (4 May 1981) an article entitled 'Fresh evidence that dividends don't matter' relating to the largest 500 corporations in the USA, stated that: 'All told, 115 companies of the 500 raised their payout every year during the period 1970–79. Investors in this ... group would have fared somewhat better than investors in the 500 as a whole: the median total annual compound return of the 115 companies was 10.7% during the decade versus 9.4% for the 500.'

Explain whether or not, in your opinion, the *Fortune* magazine article indicated evidence that investors prefer dividends to capital gains, and why this may be so.

14

Financial strategies from start-up to growth

Chapter contents

Learning objectives

Completion of this chapter will enable you to:

- Outline the key aspects in the profile of a start-up business.
- Identify the sources of financial and other support for start-up businesses.
- Explain the significant role that venture capitalists (VCs) may play in the support and development of new businesses.
- Describe the relationship between perceived risk and the return required by investors in a start-up business.
- Outline the key aspects in the profile of a growth business.
- Explain how the transition from the start-up phase of a business to its growth phase may take place.
- Describe the relationship between perceived risk and the return required by investors in a growth business.
- Identify the various types of capital market.
- Outline the process by which a company flotation takes place, its initial public offering (IPO).
- Consider the ways in which a company may finance new projects.
- Explain the way in which a rights issue is made and the implications for a company and its shareholders.

Introduction

We saw in Chapter 13 how the PLC model and also the BCG model identify the separate phases in the development of a business and its products. This chapter will focus on the start-up introduction phase and growth phase of products and the business life cycle. During its early stages of start-up and growth a business usually requires additional external financing. The individuals who launch new businesses are inevitably optimistic and enthusiastic about their new ventures. However, the risks of not succeeding are high and so the returns expected from investments in such ventures are also necessarily high. The investment required to support new businesses may be provided by **venture capitalists (VCs)** that specialise in providing funds for this type of investment.

We will consider the changes that take place when a company moves from its start-up phase to its growth phase, as it becomes much more market-orientated. During its growth phase a company may finance future growth by raising funds via financial institutions and private investors. A company may be floated on a stock exchange during its growth phase, through an initial public offering (IPO), before it reaches its mature stage when the opportunities for capital gains from increases in the share price may be limited.

Companies may finance new projects out of retained earnings or additional new project financing. Chapter 14 closes with a look at **secondary public offerings (SPOs)** such as rights issues, which are a source of new funding; existing shareholders are given rights to buy additional new shares at a discount to the market price in proportion to their existing shareholdings.

A profile of start-up businesses

Figure 14.1 provides a profile of a start-up business that summarises each of the variables that we considered in Chapter 13. Business risk is very high because of the uncertainty relating to both products (or services) and markets.

Start-up businesses are usually totally funded by equity, which is highly risky for the investors. Equity capital represents low financial risk for the business since it does not have to be repaid, and dividends do not have to be paid at all and may not be paid if the company is not making sufficient profits. Financial risk is also very low if there is no debt funding and therefore no commitments to interest payments.

External providers of equity funding for a start-up business include private equity companies and venture capitalists (VCs). Venture capitalists are ideal investors for start-ups, because they are professionals who are well aware of the high level of business risk associated with businesses in their launch or start-up phase.

In order to keep financial risk as low as possible, start-up businesses may therefore aim to avoid the use of debt capital. VCs usually provide equity capital, and they are prepared to take high risks for which they expect high returns. Their returns are in the form of capital gains achieved from an increase in share price. VCs are not restricted to providing equity and may also provide debt and other types of capital.

Although high business risk is faced by start-up companies it is not necessarily so for VCs. VCs invest in some businesses that are riskier than others. Sometimes VCs win and sometimes they lose, but they can mitigate the overall risks they face by developing a portfolio of investments. Once the growth phase is over, VCs may want to cease to be investors in a business and

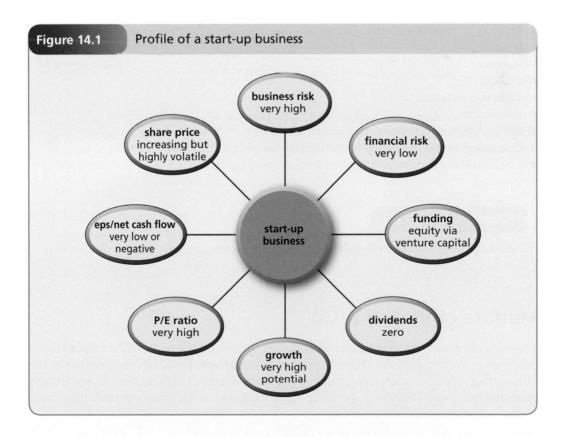

| Figure 14.1 | Profile of a start-up business |

business risk very high

share price increasing but highly volatile

financial risk very low

eps/net cash flow very low or negative

start-up business

funding equity via venture capital

P/E ratio very high

dividends zero

growth very high potential

realise their gains. This may then be the time for a public flotation on a stock exchange, or a
management buy-out (MBO) of the company (see Chapter 18).

Sources of support for a start-up business

Start-up, high-risk businesses are needed by the UK economy to replace declining industries.
During the pre-launch stages of a new business there may be high costs of research and development (R&D) and costs of the development of new product concepts, which are generally
sunk costs. Capital is necessary for these types of cost, which is termed **seed capital**. For products that still seem attractive for further development after the initial investment, further capital is required, which is called **start-up capital**, and is required to support operational requirements and marketing costs.

There is now an extremely wide range of support for new businesses in the UK. These
include:

- the Department of Business, Innovation and Skills (BIS)
- trade associations
- the former Regional Development Agencies (RDAs) such as the Welsh Development Agency
  in Wales
- Local Enterprise Partnerships (which replaced RDAs that finally disappeared in March 2012)
- national assemblies such as the Welsh Assembly
- knowledge networks such as Business Link (*www.businesslink.gov.uk*).

In the UK, the BIS provides a great deal of help and support in the areas of:

- regulations and environmental issues
- innovation
- training
- exports
- European business
- investment
- Intellectual Property Office, for patents, trademarks, copyrights, etc.
- Companies House, for details of professional bodies, business contacts, etc.
- Small Business Service, for details of local support schemes.

Progress check 14.1

Outline the range of support available for start-up businesses and the types of support that
they may provide.

Venture capitalists (VCs)

VCs are professional investors who provide funding for new businesses usually in return for an
equity stake in the companies. The failure of some investments by VCs should be offset by the
outstanding success of other investments, giving them an overall high return. VCs are actually
generally risk-averse. They may specialise in particular industrial sectors but still maintain a
portfolio of investments in other sectors.

VCs have a short investment horizon (three to five years) and an important consideration for them is their 'exit strategy' of how to leave companies after success, making room for new investors with lower return expectations. The future growth prospects and the P/E ratios of start-up companies are very high, with an expectation of high capital gains. VCs usually sell out for capital gain before a company is cash positive and paying dividends. The re-financing of such businesses after exit by VCs is something we have already introduced and will discuss again later in this book.

Examples of venture capitalists are:

- Investors in Industry (3i)
- Equity Capital for Industry
- Business Expansion Scheme funds
- specialist areas, usually subsidiaries, within the clearing banks.

Another source of funding for start-up businesses is that provided by large, established companies. The press extract below examines the growth of major corporations' provision of venture capital in Germany and in so doing throws light on the motivations of such venture capitalists and their role in encouragement of innovation and industrial development.

A growing breed of venture capitalist

A handful of Germany's leading companies are backing start-ups in the hunt for new ideas as well as financial returns, writes Chris Bryant.

When BMW last year launched its 'i' sub-brand to steer the German carmaker towards a greener, lightweight future, the sleek designs for its prototype i3 and i8 electric vehicles were hailed as a 'disruptive vision of the future'. But BMW's announcement that, alongside this, it was also establishing a $100m New York-based venture capital unit to invest in complementary start-ups, marked another radical break with the past. 'We want to attract young entrepreneurs and start-up companies to come to us with their ideas and innovations and ask us for support,' says Ulrich Kranz, head of Project i.

A handful of German companies – including Siemens, BASF, SAP and Deutsche Telekom – have operated venture capital units for years. But as the economy has recovered from the crisis, more and more proudly self-sufficient industrialists are turning to venture capital as a way of making better use of low interest-bearing cash resources.

In doing so, German companies are reflecting a global trend. A record 83 corporate venture funds were raised last year, primarily in the US and Asia, according to Global Corporate Venturing, a trade magazine. Recent high-profile examples include General Motors, which set up a $100m VC subsidiary in 2010, and Google, which founded a $100m VC arm in 2009. Yesterday a EUR300m fund was launched by France Télécom-Orange, Publicis Groupe and Iris Capital Management to invest in digital start-ups. In Germany, Evonik Industries, a speciality chemicals company, said in January it planned to invest up to EUR100m in start-ups and venture capital funds in the coming years. Boehringer Ingelheim, the pharmaceuticals company, in 2010 launched a EUR100m corporate VC fund and the same year RWE, the utility, consolidated existing VC activities into a new fund called Innogy Venture Capital, which invests in renewable energy companies. Merck set up a fund to invest in biotech start-ups in 2009.

While these corporate venture capital units are expected to make a profit over the long term, the primary motivation for companies founding them is rarely financial. 'The driving force is the desperate need for innovation,' says Hendrik Brandis, managing partner at Earlybird Venture Capital, a German VC firm. 'The corporate world has discovered that fundamental breakthrough innovations are more likely to be implemented first in dynamic start-ups.'

BASF, the world's largest chemical company by sales, is using the model to help it develop a new generation of photovoltaic material technology. In 2007, its subsidiary BASF Venture Capital invested in Heliatek, a Dresden-based start-up engaged in the design and development of organic solar cells. 'It's about accelerating the development of innovation within the company and that can happen faster via co-operation with start-ups,' says Dirk Nachtigal, head of the venture capital arm, which was established in 2001 and yesterday announced a $13.5m investment in a US speciality chemicals business.

Similarly, BMW was keen to offer customers new services beyond just zero-emissions vehicles. One of i Ventures' first investments was in Parkatmyhouse, which links people seeking to rent a parking space or garage with those who have one to spare. Anthony Eskinazi, who founded Parkatmyhouse five years ago, says that in comparison to working with a traditional VC, dealing with BMW offers 'more time to make sure the product is as good as it can be'. He adds: 'And if we want to do a big campaign and BMW sees the benefit of it, we don't have to think on a start-up level or a funded start-up … we're talking about a much bigger thing.'

Claus Schmidt, joint managing director of Robert Bosch Venture Capital, the VC arm of Bosch, Germany's largest private industrial conglomerate, says: 'Sometimes [start-ups] are looking for a strong brand name among their investors and sometimes they are looking to gain operational excellence. Many of these start-ups suffer from inability to transfer good ideas in prototypes into manufacturable products. So they come and talk to us.'

Corporate venture capital activity in Germany last peaked around the turn of the millennium when the digital revolution lured media companies such as Bertelsmann and Axel Springer into the market. When the dot.com bubble burst, some corporate VC units were closed and other companies reduced their activities.

Although corporate VC units are back in vogue, they still account for just 10–15 per cent of total global VC investments. Expected to make a profit over the long term, they typically invest alongside a VC as part of a consortium, taking a minority stake. The practice remains a luxury that only larger companies can afford. About $100m in investment firepower is typically required to start a fund, and even with careful management about 25–40 per cent of venture-backed investments fail.

New fields such as biotechnology, digital media, electromobility – electric vehicles – and renewable energy are also transforming the pace and nature of innovation. Markus Thill, the other joint managing director at Robert Bosch VC, says: 'If you look at the changes in technology that are happening at the moment you will see quite a lot of acceleration in the market. It's not only getting faster, it's also getting more complex and more diversified.'

The process of nurturing new initiatives outside the company will not bring a short-term profit. 'Teaming up with a start-up is something that complements our industrial research and development. It's an innovation tool out of a spectrum that includes R&D, acquisitions, joint ventures, licensing and university co-operations,' says Ralf Schnell, head of Siemens Venture Capital. '[But] if you got into this business, you have to understand it's a long-term investment. You can't go in and get out next year.'

The advantages of a venture capital unit extend far beyond compiling a portfolio of minority equity stakes in young companies. Some of the greatest benefits include the many contacts the unit makes when scouting for promising start-ups. This puts an early-stage start-up on a larger company's radar and can lead to customer–supplier relationships or joint initiatives. 'We can introduce companies that colleagues in our various business units perhaps haven't heard of yet,' says Mr Thill. 'That is very much part of our strategic purpose – as a matchmaker between start-ups and Bosch business units.'

A bid for bigger venture backing

In spite of a wealth of innovative, niche-focused, small and medium-sized businesses – collectively known as the Mittelstand – Germany has until recently lacked a fully fledged start-up scene. However, in recent years a lively cluster of digital start-ups has emerged in Berlin, drawing investment and entrepreneurs from overseas.

According to Earlybird Venture Capital, a German VC fund, there was at least $4.4bn in venture-backed trade sales and initial public offerings in Germany during the past 24 months – the highest in Europe. These included Groupon's acquisition of Citydeal, a Berlin-based provider of coupon deals, and Ebay's $200m acquisition of Brands for Friends, a German online shopping club.

The country has a long tradition of public support for research and development and universities, but compared with the US it still receives only a fraction of the venture capital investments needed to commercialise ideas. This is partly because Germany has only four independent domestic VC funds bigger than $100m. To help redress the balance, the German government in 2005 created the High-Tech Gründerfonds, a public–private partnership, to invest in start-ups. It received backing from companies including BASF, Siemens and Daimler, and – as of March 2011 – it had completed 228 investments.

Progress check 14.2

What is a venture capitalist?

Risk and return in start-up

Start-ups are investment intensive, but also risk intensive. There is risk attached to the provision of seed capital to support:

- R&D costs in identifying new products
- applied research costs
- product development costs,

and risk attached to the provision of start-up capital to support the introduction of the launch phase of the business, which includes costs of operating facilities and marketing.

Systematic risk is reflected in the impact on the returns on a company's shares as a result of external factors like government policy, interest rates, and economic cycles. In the initial period of a start-up business, this systematic risk does not exist. By definition, a start-up business has not been in existence long enough for such factors to have any significant impact on the returns on its shares. Systematic risk will start to increase as the start-up progresses. For example, a business selling fashion clothing is likely to suffer very quickly from an economic downturn.

However, such systematic risk is difficult to measure if there is no share price history. A start-up business does face the unique or unsystematic risk of the company performing badly or failing.

During the start-up phase, earnings per share (eps) are usually negative or at best very low because of the high start-up costs and very low sales levels. Usually, there can be no dividends paid by a start-up business because:

- funds are needed for investment
- dividends are not legally payable if the company does not have distributable reserves.

Therefore, for a start-up company it is not possible to apply a dividend growth model to estimate the expected returns of investors. Also, it may not be possible to use the Capital Asset Pricing Model (CAPM) in a start-up situation because although there will be unsystematic risk, it is likely that there will be no systematic risk. It should be remembered that CAPM brings together portfolio theory, share valuation theory, the cost of capital theory, and gearing theory, and is concerned with:

- how systematic risk can be measured
- how systematic risk affects required returns and share prices,

and so even if any systematic risk were present during the start-up phase it may not be possible to measure it because of the lack of a share price history.

A start-up company's share price may increase rapidly, but is likely to be very volatile because of the high potential for new business failures. How can the expected returns of a new business be estimated? Well, this may be estimated by using a probability-adjusted cash flow forecast, which allows for as wide a range of present value cash flows as possible, using a realistic discount rate, which is illustrated in Worked example 14.1. It may also be estimated by using a much higher discount rate, reflecting a high level of risk and unadjusted cash flows.

Worked example 14.1

Helen Hywater is considering a start-up business, which requires an initial investment of £100,000, the returns on which are dependent on the outcomes of one of three opportunities, which may be available, one of which is certain to go ahead. It is not yet known with certainty which opportunity will go ahead and each of them generates different yearly net cash flows over two years, with a different likelihood of occurrence. The estimated cost of capital for the business is 10% per annum.

The forecast probabilities and net cash flows for each year are:

Opportunity	Probability of occurrence	Per annum cash flow
A	0.5	£75,000
B	0.2	£25,000
C	0.3	£45,000
	1.0	

The total of the probabilities is one, which indicates that one of the options is certain to occur. Even though one opportunity will definitely go ahead Helen needs to consider if she should make the investment at all.

We first need to use the probabilities to calculate the expected annual cash flows – the weighted average of the expected outcomes for each year.

Opportunity	Cash flow £	Probability	Expected cash flow £
A	75,000	0.5	37,500
B	25,000	0.2	5,000
C	45,000	0.3	13,500
Expected per annum cash flows			56,000

To calculate the expected NPV over the two years we need to discount the expected annual cash flows using the discount rate of 10% per annum.

Year	Expected cash flow £	Discount factor at 10%	Expected present value £
1	56,000	0.91	50,960
2	56,000	0.83	46,480
Total	112,000		97,440
Initial investment			100,000
Expected NPV			−2,560

The negative expected NPV of £2,560 indicates that Helen should not go ahead with the start-up.

It should be noted that the above technique of expected net present value has used an average expected cash flow, which:

- in the example is not actually capable of occurrence
- may not represent the real situation if the underlying risk of outcomes worse than the average are ignored.

If the expected per annum cash flow from opportunity A had been £150,000 instead of £75,000, giving an expected £62,690 positive NPV, Helen may have been keen to proceed with the investment. However, she should also consider the impact on the business if, for example, opportunity B had been the one that subsequently became available.

Worked example 14.1 uses the technique of expected NPV in which financial estimates are very uncertain. In practice, it may be very difficult for a start-up venture, with unproven products and new markets, to use such an approach. In such cases, qualitative rather than quantitative information would be much more influential in guiding the decision to go ahead with the start-up. It should be noted that although the expected NPV approach is a useful method it may have more value when it is used for averaging repeated projects of a similar nature to make it a valid application.

With regard to Worked example 14.1 it may be useful to consider the possible impact of additional information on the decision on whether or not to go ahead with the start-up, for example:

- viability of the products relating to each opportunity
- reactions of potential customers

- customer orders already received
- previous experience of starting a business
- previous experience within the industry
- the role of due diligence
- the role of VCs:
  - are they needed?
  - are they good or bad?
  - exit strategies
  - impact on other shareholders
- the consequences should the business fail
- financing.

In a start-up there is a need for as low a financial risk as possible, or preferably no financial risk. Therefore it is recommended that there is no use of debt at all. There is no advantage in the use of debt by a start-up company because debt only increases default risk, which mitigates any value of the tax shield, the tax benefit of loan interest (unlikely to be required during the start-up phase). Default risk is the risk of not being able to pay interest and the ultimate repayment of the loan. In a start-up business there is a high likelihood of default because of the relatively high premium paid for debt financing – the high cost of debt.

Progress check 14.3

What are the major risks faced by a start-up business?

A profile of growth businesses

Figure 14.2 provides a profile of a business that has moved into its growth phase, and which summarises each of the variables that we considered in Chapter 13. Once a product has been successfully launched, sales revenues should start to increase rapidly. A high degree of business risk continues to be faced until required sales levels and market share have been achieved. However, there is a reduction in business risk from the level faced during the start-up phase. Because of this a modification of business strategy may be required that should include:

- an accent on marketing
- a focus on increasing sales
- an aim of increasing market share.

Most businesses during their growth phases that are seeking to finance investment, innovation, and growth are generally well served by a variety of private-sector sources of external finance. Equity finance, or debt finance secured on the assets of the business, may be neither suitable nor available to all companies. Companies that have become too large or are in a fast-growing stage of their growth phase may find it difficult to obtain additional funds from existing individual shareholders. On the other hand, they may be insufficiently developed to obtain a stock market listing, or they may have insufficient assets to secure adequate levels of debt finance. This difficulty in obtaining conventional financing results in what is often referred to as the funding gap or the financing gap.

To assist such companies, which are often SMEs (small and medium-sized enterprises) the UK Government instigated the following initiatives:

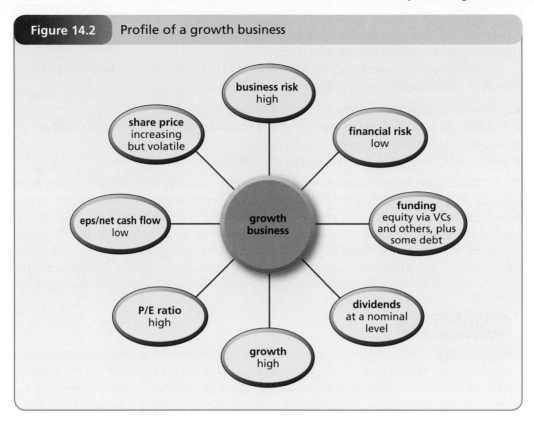

Figure 14.2   Profile of a growth business

- establishment of a number of local, regional, and national agencies to offer advice to SMEs
- development of the Enterprise Finance Guarantee (EFG) scheme which is operated by the Government in partnership with 42 leading financial institutions, and is designed to enable loans to be made to SMEs that are unable to offer any security (collateral)
- promotion of the use of Venture Capital Trusts (VCTs) and the Enterprise Investment Scheme (EIS) by offering a number of tax reliefs to encourage individuals to invest in small companies which are facing a funding gap, either indirectly through a mediated fund such as a VCT, or directly by investing in a company through the EIS.

Another source of funding for such companies is business angels (BAs). These are essentially wealthy individuals who invest, usually equity, in businesses with high growth potential. Some BAs invest their own capital, but there are also now many BAs who act on behalf of networks or investment syndicates.

In general BAs invest in businesses which:

- need an investment of between £10,000 and £250,000
- have a potential for a high rate of return
- are at an early stage of their development or expansion.

The main advantages of using a BA are that they often make quick investment decisions, and often without the need for complex business assessments. BAs are also able to bring valuable experience to a new business venture, because they often possess specialist local knowledge since most BAs tend to invest within 100 miles of their homes or offices.

A disadvantage in using BAs is that investments may be infrequent and irregular, and as a consequence, they may be difficult to locate, although the UK Business Angels Association (UKBAA) can be used to trace potential investors.

The UKBAA is the national trade association for the UK's business angel networks and their associates and affiliates. The association seeks to:

- promote the recognition of business angel networks (BANs)
- highlight the contribution that business angels can make to the entrepreneurial culture
- support member groups
- lobby the UK Government to encourage a fair and equitable marketplace.

The UK Business Angels Association (*www.ukbusinessangelsassociation.org.uk*), which until its re-branding on 2 July 2012 was called the British Business Angels Association, held its first AGM in June 2005, and is currently sponsored by Lloyds TSB (*www.lloydstsbbusiness.com*), Smith & Williamson LLP (*www.smith.williamson.co.uk*), and Nesta (*www.nesta.org.uk*). The UKBAA is also supported by the investment fund Business for Growth (*www.businessgrowthfund.co.uk*), by the Government's Capital for Enterprise (*www.capitalforenterprise.gov.uk*) funding initiative, and the BBA, the trade association for the UK banking and financial services sector (*www.bba.org.uk*).

Mini case 14.1

In May 2011, the Department for Business, Innovation and Skills (BIS) published its annual commissioned report on the business angel market in the UK 2009/10. The report looks at the visible angel market in the UK, defined as the activities of the business angel networks that are members of the British Business Angel Association (BBAA) and LINC Scotland.

The report makes it clear that angel activities via these associations have picked up since 2000, with investment tripling from £6.7m in 2000/01 to £18.2m in 2009/10. What also stands out from the report is the sectors in which angels tend to invest and the stage of the business growth cycle at which investment is most prevalent. The figures below extracted from the report highlight that the main areas of investment are high-tech businesses and that the level of business development which attracts angels is early stage, after the business has successfully negotiated start-up and is establishing itself. Angels are clearly twice as likely to invest in a business that has established a track record than they are to invest in the start-up stage.

Angel investment by industry

Industry	2008/2009		2009/2010	
	Number	%	Number	%
IT/Internet/software/telecoms	68	22.7%	69	22.9%
Medical/healthcare/biotech/pharmaceutical	52	17.4%	66	21.9%
Clean tech/environment/recycling/energy	21	7.0%	27	9.0%
Technology/hardware	31	10.4%	0	0.0%
Manufacturing/electronics/engineering	33	11.0%	43	14.3%

Industry	2008/2009		2009/2010	
	Number	%	Number	%
Business services	17	5.7%	25	8.3%
Retail	11	3.7%	10	3.3%
Property/property development	10	3.3%	0	0.0%
Media/creative industries	15	5.0%	32	10.6%
Food and drink	7	2.3%	0	0.0%
Automobile	4	1.3%	0	0.0%
Tourism/hospitality	6	2.0%	0	0.0%
Other	24	8.0%	29	9.6%
Total	299		301	

The transition from start-up to growth

The need to develop a sustainable competitive advantage is a good indicator of the level of business risk carried over from start-up to growth. In many companies we may see the construction of major entry barriers through factors such as learning curve cost reductions, economies of scale, and establishment of brand identities.

In the transition from start-up to growth there is a change of company focus from R&D and the development of technology to market-orientation. An example of this was seen in the pharmaceutical industry in the 1980s and 1990s where Glaxo, after their initial trials success and registration of patents, focused very heavily on marketing Zantac.

Consumers sometimes expect many new features in products, and sometimes companies may be guilty of 'over-engineering' products by providing too many unnecessary features. Despite the expectations of new features in products, commercial considerations may necessarily take precedence. A large number of new features and frequent design changes may result in delays in getting the product into the marketplace. Speed to the marketplace and the creation of appropriate barriers to entry are factors that are critical to the success of a growth business.

A change in the profile of investors

When a company moves from its start-up phase to its growth phase its financial risk remains low and the company is likely to continue to be financed by equity funding. Since VCs are unlikely to continue to fund businesses indefinitely, growth businesses are likely to seek a number of new investors. Additional new investors may also be required to finance further expansion of the business. Therefore, as a growth business develops and its prospects of future growth and its P/E ratio are still high, its VCs begin to implement their exit strategies. At this time current eps will be low but growth can be expected from an increasing market share. However, there is a lower expected return by investors since the product is now proven. There is lower business risk than during the start-up phase but it may still be high in periods of rapid sales growth.

There may be nominal dividends paid but cash is primarily required for further investment. The share price may be increasing but continues to be volatile because expected sales levels may still not actually have been achieved. New investors may need to be found to replace VCs and to fund additional investment for growth.

Because the VCs are seeking an exit, the company needs to consider the ways in which they may be replaced as investors. One option may be to remain as a limited (Ltd) company but to increase the number of private investors from, for example, friends and family. Alternatively, the company may become a public limited company (plc) by inviting the public to buy its shares through obtaining a flotation on the stock exchange or the Alternative Investment Market (AIM).

The first option of remaining a limited company is the cheapest one, but it has a big disadvantage in the lack of marketability of the shares. The shareholders of a Ltd company have no easy route for selling their shares.

The second option, which is called 'going public' (rather than remaining private) has a number of important implications:

- the business must take appropriate measures for the protection of investors
- the costs of flotation of the company are very high
- there is a requirement for the disclosure of a large amount of financial and non-financial information to maintain the confidence of investors and the financial markets in the company.

Risk and return in growth

As we have already discussed, high business risk continues in the growth phase of a business because there is still a risk of expected growth that may not materialise. Major entry barriers can be constructed during rapid growth periods to keep out competitors, once a product's potential has been identified. These include branding, the costs of which may be justified in the anticipation of growing future sales. They also include economies of scale, leading to low-cost production.

So, what returns will prospective investors require from IPOs of growth companies? Systematic risk is relevant for growth companies, which are sensitive to the changes in the external environment. Because a growth company faces systematic risk in addition to unsystematic risk, we can determine an estimate of the return required by investors using CAPM. Unsystematic risk is risk that can be diversified away. Systematic risk cannot be diversified away and, as we saw in Chapter 5, is reflected in CAPM in its basic form in the relationship:

$$R_s = R_f + \beta(R_m - R_f)$$

where:

R_s = the required return on a share
R_f = the risk-free rate of return
β = the beta factor of the share — the measure of volatility of the security in terms of its *systematic or market risk* (where beta for the market as a whole is 1.0)
R_m = market rate of return.

The estimated return required by shareholders is implied by the β (beta) value of the company, the relative measure of its systematic risk compared to the whole market. If the company is a growth business where there is little or no company history, the β value for the company may be estimated from similar companies that are already publicly quoted. In order to use the CAPM for this purpose we need to consider betas in a little more detail. The beta of a company comprises its equity beta and its debt beta. The beta that we have discussed so far is the equity beta, or geared beta, which reflects the total systematic risk faced by the company. Systematic risk comprises business risk and financial risk.

Business risk only is reflected in the company's ungeared beta, also called its asset beta. A company's ungeared beta reflects the weighted average of its equity beta and debt beta multiplied by the market values of its equity and debt, represented by the relationship:

$$\beta_u = \beta_e \times \frac{E}{E + D(1 - t)} + \beta_d \times \frac{D(1 - t)}{E + D(1 - t)}$$

where:

E = market value of the company's equity
D = market value of the company's debt
β_u = ungeared beta
β_e = equity beta
β_d = debt beta
t = corporation tax rate

From the above equation we can see that if the company is financed totally by equity its ungeared beta will equal its equity beta. If the company has a mix of debt and equity financing then its equity beta will always be higher than its ungeared beta.

It is a big assumption, but if we assume that the companies we are considering always meet their interest payments and so there is no risk of default then in the short term we may assume that their debt betas are zero. The ungeared beta equation can therefore be rewritten and represented as:

$$\beta_u = \beta_e \times \frac{E}{E + D(1 - t)}$$

or

$$\beta_e = \beta_u \times \frac{E + D(1 - t)}{E}$$

Companies may be involved in more than one business sector, or in different investment projects, each of which will have different levels of business risk and therefore different ungeared betas. If we are trying to determine an approximate return expected from a growth company we can identify quoted companies which are involved in the same type of business, and therefore with the same risk profiles, and use the equity betas of these companies to provide an estimated return using CAPM.

The equity betas of these companies must first be ungeared to eliminate the impact of their different levels of gearing. Their gearing and levels of risk are likely to be different from the company whose return we are trying to evaluate.

In addition, the ungeared betas we have calculated for these companies must be adjusted to eliminate the effects of any business sectors that they are involved in which are not relevant to the business we are trying to evaluate. The average of the ungeared betas of these companies may then be used to provide an estimated, surrogate ungeared beta for the company we are evaluating. This surrogate beta may then be geared up, using the respective proportions of debt and equity, to provide an estimated equity beta for the company. Finally, the surrogate equity beta, along with the risk-free rate and market rate of return, may then be used in the basic CAPM formula to calculate the expected return for the company. Let's look at an example of this.

Worked example 14.2

Packtical is a UK company in the packaging industry, which is currently financed with 90% equity and 10% debt. The company is in its growth phase and requires additional capital. A prospective investor wants to determine what the current level of return should be for Packtical. The prospective investor has identified four companies similar to Packtical, each with different beta values and levels of gearing. Three of the companies are involved wholly in the packaging industry. However, 40% of one of the companies, Pack & Carry plc, is also involved in the logistics and distribution business, which is considered to be 60% more risky than packaging.

The most recent financial data provided for each of the four companies is as follows:

	Equity beta	Debt %	Equity %	Tax rate %
Happy Packers plc	1.20	40	60	30
Flopack plc	1.25	30	70	30
Packmaster plc	1.30	25	75	30
Pack & Carry plc	1.35	50	50	30

The risk-free rate of return is 3%, represented by the yield on UK Government Treasury stock. The packaging market sector average return is 8%. Packtical's tax rate is 30%. Let's calculate Packtical's expected return

We will assume that the debt for each of the companies is risk-free and therefore their debt betas are zero. The ungeared betas for each company can therefore be calculated using:

$$\beta_u = \beta_e \times \frac{E}{E + D(1 - t)}$$

Happy Packers plc:

$$\beta_u = 1.20 \times \frac{60\%}{60\% + 40\% \times (1 - 30\%)}$$

$$\beta_u = 1.20 \times \frac{60\%}{60\% + (40\% \times 70\%)}$$

$$\beta_u = 1.20 \times 0.68$$

$$\beta_u = 0.82$$

Flopack plc:

$$\beta_u = 1.25 \times \frac{70\%}{70\% + 30\% \times (1 - 30\%)}$$

$$\beta_u = 0.96$$

Packmaster plc:

$$\beta_u = 1.30 \times \frac{75\%}{75\% + 25\% \times (1 - 30\%)}$$

$$\beta_u = 1.05$$

Pack & Carry plc:

$$\beta_u = 1.35 \times \frac{50\%}{50\% + 50\% \times (1 - 30\%)}$$

$$\beta_u = 0.79$$

Because logistics represents 40% of Pack & Carry plc's business and is considered 60% more risky than the packaging business then its ungeared beta must be adjusted accordingly to calculate its packaging ungeared beta as follows:

$$\beta_u = 0.4 \times \text{logistics } \beta_u + 0.6 \times \text{packaging } \beta_u$$

and

$$\text{logistics } \beta_u = 1.6 \times \text{packaging } \beta_u$$

therefore

$$\beta_u = 0.4 \times 1.6 \times \text{packaging } \beta_u + 0.6 \times \text{packaging } \beta_u$$
$$0.79 = 1.24 \times \text{packaging } \beta_u$$

therefore

Pack & Carry plc's packaging $\beta_u = 0.64$

The average of the Pack & Carry plc's adjusted ungeared beta and the other three ungeared betas is

$$\frac{0.82 + 0.96 + 1.05 + 0.64}{4} = 0.87$$

0.87 may be used as the surrogate ungeared beta for Packtical in order to calculate its surrogate equity beta by using the variation of the ungeared beta equation:

$$\beta_e = \beta_u \times \frac{E + D(1 - t)}{E}$$

$$\beta_e = 0.87 \times \frac{90\% + 10\% \times (1 - 30\%)}{90\%}$$

$$\beta_e = 0.94$$

We can now calculate Packtical's estimated return by using the basic CAPM formula:

$$R_s = R_f + \beta_e(R_m - R_f)$$
$$R_s = 3\% + 0.94 \times (8\% - 3\%)$$
$$R_s = 0.077$$

Packtical's expected return is therefore 7.7%.

Although the sort of data illustrated in Worked example 14.2 may be used for comparison, it nevertheless uses historical information. It should also be remembered that CAPM assumes that the capital markets are perfect, when in fact they are not. Nevertheless, the capital markets may in fact reflect a fairly high level of efficiency. Although the results of the type of analysis shown in Worked example 14.2 are therefore very much estimates and an indication of what actual returns may be, they may be reasonably accurate. Their accuracy will of course depend on the accuracy of the estimates of betas, risk-free and market returns, and the gearing of the companies being assessed.

Types of capital market

A market is a place of exchange, where the legal title and possession of an asset is exchanged for the legal title or possession of another asset, or the legal promise that such an exchange will take place in the future.

The assumed characteristics within such a market are that buyers and sellers:

- are rational
- are predominantly profit driven
- have access to relevant and useful information
- are well informed
- risk buying and selling in the market for a reward or a gain.

The capital markets are effectively no different from any other market and possess the characteristics common to many other types of market. The main difference is that buyers and sellers deal in particular types of securities and other financial assets, and in a variety of different currencies.

In addition, there are many types of capital or financial markets, for example markets where the buyers and sellers meet face to face. In commodity or asset markets activity is restricted to the buying and selling of particular commodities and assets. Private markets have access restricted to buying and selling by particular organisations.

The main characteristics of the capital markets are that there are many buyers and sellers, and there is generally freedom of access. There are many buyers and sellers in the market who will undertake activities of both buying and selling. The information regarding commodities and assets available in the markets is widely available to all (or at least many) of the buyers and sellers.

Capital markets are markets that exist for the trading of long-term financial instruments or securities. The capital markets exist for companies, for public sector securities, and include Eurobonds. Eurobonds are nothing to do with Europe! In Chapter 7, we looked at a diagrammatic representation of all the different types of securities and financial instruments. It included Eurobonds which were described in some detail. They are bonds that are denominated in currencies other than the currencies of the countries in which they are sold, for example a Japanese yen bond that is sold in the USA.

Capital markets enable companies to raise funds via financial institutions and private investors. The most important capital markets for companies are those dealing with ordinary shares, preference shares, and debt in general, which includes bonds, debentures, unsecured loan stock, and convertible loan stock. Capital markets comprise what are termed **primary markets** (see Figure 14.3) and **secondary markets** (see Figure 14.4).

The London Stock Exchange (LSE) is the place that deals in both equity (shares) and bonds (debt) in the UK. The LSE acts in both the primary and secondary markets, and includes two key sections:

- the Official List, comprising companies which are normally large and well established, and which have been trading for at least 3 years – the expected value of their shares after issue should exceed £700,000 and at least 25% of their share capital must be held by the public

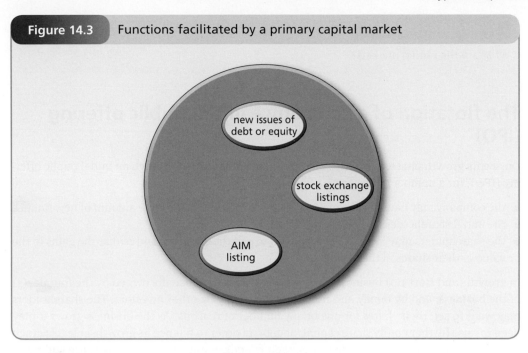

Figure 14.3 Functions facilitated by a primary capital market

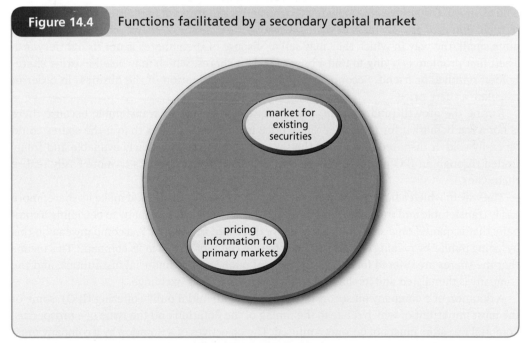

Figure 14.4 Functions facilitated by a secondary capital market

- the Alternative Investment Market (AIM), which opened in the UK in June 1995, is for smaller companies which do not meet the requirements of the Official List – its intention is to keep regulations to a minimum.

A secondary market is used for existing securities – the buying and selling of stocks and shares – which increases their liquidity and therefore their value. It also provides pricing information for primary markets, which increases the efficiency with which new funds may be allocated.

What are the capital markets?

The flotation of a company – initial public offering (IPO)

During its growth phase, a business may consider 'going public' through an initial public offering (IPO), for a number of reasons:

- the company may have big expansion plans for which it needs a large amount of new finance
- the initial shareholders may want to dispose of their shares
- the shareholders may include VCs who wish to exit the company and realise the gains in the value of their shares in the business.

In growth (and start-up) businesses the ordinary shares are usually owned by the founder(s) of the business, and by family and friends, and possibly by other investors. The shareholders may want to sell their shares for one of any number of reasons. As the business grows it may need to raise further equity share capital, or debt, in order to finance its growth, at levels much higher than the founders of the business, their friends, family, and maybe VCs, are willing or able to afford. Other investors include VCs who will certainly want to realise gains in the value of their shares as the business develops. Because the number of shareholders is likely to be quite small, the way in which they may sell or dispose of their shares is not straightforward. Their first problem is trying to find a buyer for their shares, which may be an existing shareholder, relative, or friend. Second, they must obtain a valuation of the business in order to calculate a share price.

During the growth (and start-up) phase, shares are not easily transferable because there is not a ready market for them. The share price is likely to be lower than if the shares could be easily sold or disposed of. Making the shares of the business publicly available and freely traded through an IPO makes it possible for the shareholders and VCs to more easily realise their gains.

The way in which a business may obtain additional new financing, and make its shares more easily transferable and tradeable, is to go from being an unquoted company to becoming a company that is quoted on a stock exchange. As we discussed in Chapter 7, a company can do this by 'going public' by making an initial public offering (IPO) of shares in its company. This means that the shares are offered for sale to the general public and to financial institutions, and the company is then listed and its shares may be traded on a stock exchange.

A flotation of a company must consider the rules of an initial public offering (IPO), some of the most important of which relate to the timing of the flotation and the issue of a prospectus. Potential investors must not become confused. The objectives of a flotation by a company must be clearly stated.

We can see from the following press extract about Abu Dhabi-based healthcare provider NMC that floating a company during its mature phase may be difficult. The company was founded nearly 40 years ago and was intending to float at the higher end of its share price range in order to raise £160m. However, the final share price at flotation was at the lower end, significantly reducing the funds raised from the flotation.

Mini case 14.2

The IPO market became buoyant in the last quarter of 2010 largely thanks to a number of high-profile Chinese offerings. The shares in Dangdang, China's largest online book retailer, closed at US$29.91, 87% above their offer price and Youku.com, the Chinese equivalent of YouTube, fetched US$33.44 which was 161% above its offer price. The shares were American Depositary Receipts (ADRs), instruments representing a foreign stock that is traded on a USA exchange, which allowed Dangdang to raise US$272m and Youku US$203m.

In the last quarter of 2010, of 49 IPOs on the New York Stock Exchange 18 were Chinese companies. However, the enthusiasm soon waned in the wake of concerns about fraud, poor business models, and weak financial controls. The result was that the number of Chinese IPOs were not successful, and in the middle of 2011 research company Renaissance Capital published a report which showed that anyone who had invested in all the 68 Chinese IPOs on the USA stock market from 2008 to the middle of 2011 would have made an average loss of 23.5% compared to a gain of 25% on a portfolio of the 254 non-Chinese IPOs.

The lack of interest in Chinese IPOs persisted until VIPSHOP, an online discount retailer, listed on the NYSE in March 2012 raising US$71.5m.

During a company's mature phase its share price may be high, even though it may be offering higher dividends. The opportunities for large capital gains from the flotation of a company in its mature stage are therefore usually quite limited.

Difficulties in setting the right price for an IPO

NMC Health, an Abu Dhabi-based healthcare provider, has raised £117m from a flotation on the London Stock Exchange amid signs that initial public offering activity is picking up in Europe. The company, which operates hospitals in the United Arab Emirates, sold 55.7m shares at 210p each, towards the lower end of the 200p to 280p price range initially indicated by bankers. The issue price values NMC at about £390m. 'We could have priced it higher, but we and the company wanted to see it trade well in the after-market,' said Christopher Laing, managing director of emerging equity capital markets at Deutsche Bank, the IPO's global co-ordinator and book-runner. NMC's shares rose to as high as 225p in initial trading, dropping to a low of 207p before closing at 210p.

Although NMC, founded by BR Shetty, an Indian businessman, operates in the defensive healthcare sector, the flotation of an emerging market company in London underlines the tentative recovery of Europe's IPO market, after a dismal second half of 2011. The amount raised in global IPOs slumped 43 per cent from the fourth quarter of last year to just US$15.5bn in the first three months of 2012, according to Thomson Reuters data.

But Europe saw two large deals in late March, nurturing hopes that more companies may seek to list after Easter and the release of first-quarter earnings figures. In March, Ziggo, a Dutch cable company, raised EUR804m and DKSH, a Swiss trading house, raised [CHF] SFr821m (US$124m) – the two largest global deals in the quarter. The London market, however, has remained relatively quiet for IPOs since Glencore listed last May. 'Six months ago NMC's IPO wouldn't have been possible, no matter how good the company is,' Mr Laing said.

The hospital group, the largest private healthcare provider in the oil-rich UAE, plans to use the flotation proceeds to buy Healthcare Suites in Dubai and build a maternity-dedicated hospital in Abu Dhabi. Longer term it will look to expand elsewhere in the Middle East, starting with Qatar, said Binay Shetty, chief operating officer of NMC's healthcare division.

Some emerging market companies, particularly in the Gulf, have occasionally been met by scepticism by London investors, given the region's sometimes poor corporate governance and transparency. Damas, a regional jewellery chain and gem retailer that listed on Dubai's flagship Nasdaq Dubai exchange in 2008, shocked investors in 2010 when it emerged that the company's founding family had conducted US$165m in 'unauthorised transactions', which forced the company into a debt restructuring. However, Mr Laing said Damas had not been a matter of concern to investors in NMC, and company executives said that they would adhere to the standards required by a premium London listing.

Source: Wigglesworth, R. (2012) NMC's flotation raises £117m, *Financial Times*, 2 April. © The Financial Times Limited 2012. All Rights Reserved.

Flotation is very costly. It is also extremely time-consuming, and burdensome with regard to the high volume of regulations and disclosure required from companies obtaining a listing.

Therefore, the company must be clear about the benefits of flotation. As well as providing an explanation of its reason for flotation the company should:

- indicate its target market
- state why the company is suitable for flotation
- outline the method of flotation.

Financing new projects

Growth companies may want to invest in new high-growth projects, which they may finance out of retained earnings. They may alternatively require additional new project financing.

But which new projects should be accepted by the company? Should new projects have the same risk profile or a different risk profile to the existing business? For new projects with similar risk profiles to the existing business the returns should be the same as the current investors' expected returns.

Should the returns from new projects be greater than the company's existing WACC? It really depends on the level of risk. Project risks must be considered against expected project returns.

Should WACC be used as a hurdle rate in the appraisal of investments in new projects? If it is, then many low-risk, financially attractive projects may be missed. On the other hand, many unattractive, high-risk investments may be accepted.

We have discussed capital investment appraisal and the use of WACC in Chapter 7. The ways in which the investments in new projects are financed also have an impact on the company's risk profile. The way in which the risk profile of the company changes is dependent on whether the additional funding is from debt or equity. The assessment of investment in new projects in terms of returns and risk must be considered along with the methods of financing. For most growth companies their WACC may actually be the same as their cost of equity.

Rights issues

High-growth companies may finance new project investments from their retained earnings or from IPOs. New equity may also be obtained from secondary public offerings (SPOs). SPOs of shares in a company may be made at current market prices, or more usually at a discount to current market prices, which are called rights issues. Rights issues are share issues offered to existing shareholders who are given rights to buy additional new discounted shares in proportion to their existing holdings. If they do not wish to take them up, current investors may sell these rights options to other potential investors.

Let's look at an example that illustrates the use of a rights issue.

Worked example 14.3

A company has share capital of 100,000 ordinary shares. The company needs to raise additional capital of £37,500 to fund an investment in a new project and decides to issue 25,000 new shares and offer them to existing shareholders at £1.50 each. The market price of a share in the company is £2, which includes the rights.

What will the share price be following the rights issue?

Pre rights number of shares	= 100,000
Number of new shares issued	= 25,000
Rights issue share price	= £1.50
The theoretical value of new total 125,000 shares	= (100,000 × £2) + (25,000 × £1.50)
	= £237,500
The theoretical *ex rights* share price	= £237,500/125,000
	= £1.90
The price of the right is therefore £1.90 − £1.50	= 40p per share

In theory, the share price will fall to £1.90 for the old and new shares. This may or may not be so in practice. The level at which the share price may finally settle will depend on the stock market's reaction to the company's new investment opportunity and its methods of financing it.

If a company requires additional capital to invest in new projects it needs to consider its current return on capital and the expected returns on the new projects. In a rights issue the number of new shares issued and the issue price will have an impact on the company's post-issue eps. Rights issues are normally underwritten by merchant banks, who guarantee to take any unsold shares, which insures against the share price falling below the rights issue price.

If we assume that a company wishes to raise a specific amount of additional funding, then:

- at a high issue price the number of shares is less but eps is increased
- at a low issue price the number of shares is more but eps is 'diluted'.

It may be noted that dilution of percentage ownership will occur to those shareholders who do not take up the rights offer. Dilution of market value of the shares may occur if the rights issue results in a larger than expected fall in share price. The issue price should really make no difference to its attractiveness to existing shareholders. The 'break-even' point is the rights price that results in an eps equal to the current pre-rights eps, which is illustrated in Worked example 14.4.

Worked example 14.4

A company that achieves a profit after tax of 20% on capital employed has the following capital structure:

400,000 ordinary shares of £1	£400,000
Retained earnings	£200,000

In order to invest in some new profitable projects the company wishes to raise £252,000 from a rights issue. The company's current ordinary share price is £1.80.

The company would like to know:

- the number of shares that must be issued if the rights price is £1.60; £1.50; £1.40; £1.20, the effect on eps

and

- the share price that causes no dilution of eps.

Capital employed is £600,000 [£400,000 + £200,000]
Current earnings are 20% of £600,000 = £120,000

$$\text{Therefore, earnings per share (eps)} = \frac{£120,000}{400,000} = 30p$$

After the rights issue, earnings should be 20% of £852,000 [£600,000 + £252,000], which equals £170,400.

Rights price £	Number of new shares £252,000/rights price	Total shares after rights issue	eps £170,400/total shares pence
1.60	157,500	557,500	30.6
1.50	168,000	568,000	30.0
1.40	180,000	580,000	29.4
1.20	210,000	610,000	27.9

We can see that at a high rights issue share price the eps are increased. At lower issue prices the eps are diluted. The 'break-even point', with no dilution, is where the rights price equals the original capital employed per share £600,000/400,000 = £1.50.

Progress check 14.5

What is a rights issue?

In Chapter 15 we will be discussing the mature phase of a business. While rights issues may be used by growth companies it should also be noted that they are also widely used by mature companies as a method of obtaining additional new finance.

Summary of key points

- The regular introduction of new start-up businesses provides an important contribution to a country's economy.
- There is a wide range of sources of financial and other support for start-up businesses.
- Venture capitalists (VCs) play a significant role in providing financing for start-up and growth businesses because they are prepared to accept the high risks of such ventures for which they expect correspondingly high returns.
- During the transition from the start-up phase of a business to its growth phase there is a change of company focus from R&D and technology to market-orientation.
- Alternative types of capital market enable companies to fund future growth by raising funds via financial institutions and private investors.
- A company may be floated on a stock exchange during its growth phase, through an initial public offering (IPO), before it reaches its mature stage when the opportunities for capital gains for its initial investors may be limited.
- Whether companies finance new high-growth projects out of retained earnings or additional new project financing, they need to consider whether the new projects have the same risk profile or a different risk profile to the existing business.
- New funding may also be obtained by a company from secondary public offerings (SPOs) such as rights issues in which existing shareholders are given rights to buy additional new discounted shares in proportion to their existing shareholdings.

Glossary of key terms

management buy-out (MBO) The purchase of a business from its existing owners by members of the management team, generally in association with a financing institution, for example a merchant bank or venture capitalist, who may buy part of the business, a division, or a subsidiary, or sometimes the whole group. Where a large proportion of the new finance required to purchase the business is raised by external borrowing, the buy-out is described as leveraged.

primary market A capital market in which securities are issued for the first time.

secondary market A capital market in which securities are traded once they have been issued.

secondary public offering (SPO) An issue of existing shares in a company at their market price, or possibly at a discount to current shareholders.

seed capital High-risk equity investment into a new business by venture capitalists or other investors in order to finance the period of pre-start-up before launch.

start-up capital High-risk capital that enables the new business to launch and become established, such that it can ultimately raise equity from other private investors or on an established stock exchange, at which time venture capitalists would expect to realise their holding of shares, and in so doing make a significant capital gain.

venture capitalist (VC) A provider of a specialised form of finance for new companies, buy-outs, and small growth companies which are perceived as carrying above-average risk.

Assessment material

Questions

Q14.1 What is the usual method of funding start-up companies, and how does this relate to their financial risk profiles?

Q14.2 Explain the main features of the investment behaviour of venture capitalists.

Q14.3 What are the features of unsystematic risk faced by a start-up business and how may the effects of these be mitigated?

Q14.4 Why is the profile of a company's investors likely to change as it moves from its start-up phase through into its growth phase?

Q14.5 Why are the capital markets important for growing companies, and how are primary markets different from secondary markets?

Q14.6 How can companies experiencing 'dynamic growth' react in terms of their financial strategy?

Q14.7 Outline the difficulties that may be faced by a company that is involved in an IPO.

Q14.8 In what ways may a growth company finance its investments in new projects and how are these linked to the way in which such investments may be evaluated?

Discussion points

D14.1 'The returns of 30% to 40% per annum expected by VCs are too high and restrict the growth potential of a business.' Discuss.

D14.2 'An IPO is inevitable if a company expects to grow indefinitely.' Discuss.

D14.3 'Shareholders always gain if they exercise their rights in a rights issue, and they always lose if they do not.' Discuss.

Exercises

Solutions are provided in Appendix 2 to all exercise numbers highlighted in colour.

Level I

E14.1 *Time allowed – 30 minutes*

> Outline the various types of capital required for new businesses and their sources.

E14.2 *Time allowed – 30 minutes*

> Explain the risk profile of a typical start-up business and the type of returns expected by investors.

E14.3 *Time allowed – 30 minutes*

> Explain the risk profile of a typical growth business and the type of returns expected by investors.

E14.4 *Time allowed – 45 minutes*

> Explain the role of venture capitalists and when and how they may become involved, and cease to become involved, in the development of a company.

Level II

E14.5 *Time allowed – 45 minutes*

> What alternative methods of funding may be considered by a growth company that requires additional capital to finance new projects?

E14.6 *Time allowed – 45 minutes*

> Outline why a company may consider an IPO, and explain the requirements for this. What are the advantages and disadvantages of an IPO to a company?

E14.7 *Time allowed – 60 minutes*

Gregor is a growing UK electrical component company financed by 20% debt and 80% equity. The provision of additional capital for expansion is currently being negotiated with an investor. The investor knows of three companies similar to Gregor, with the following financial data:

	Equity beta	Debt %	Equity %	Tax rate %
Pike plc	1.10	30	70	30
Rudd plc	1.15	25	75	30
Tench plc	1.25	20	80	30

Each of the companies is engaged in the electrical components industry. In addition, 50% of Pike plc's business is involved in computer repairs, which is considered to be 50% more risky than electrical components. The risk-free rate of return is 4%. The electrical components ➡

market sector average return is 10%. Gregor's tax rate is 30%. The debt for each of the companies is risk-free and therefore their debt betas are zero.

> **Required:**
> Calculate Gregor's current level of return.

E14.8 *Time allowed – 60 minutes*

Rightlyso plc has 4m ordinary £1 shares in issue, and the current share price is £8 per share. The company has announced a one-for-four rights issue by offering shares at £5.50 to all current shareholders. One shareholder, Mr Thomas, owns 1,200 shares and he is concerned that the value of his shareholding in Rightlyso plc will be diminished because the rights offer price is so much below the current market price of the shares.

> **Required:**
> Evaluate the impact of the following four options on the wealth of Mr Thomas as a shareholder of Rightlyso plc, assuming that the actual market value of the shares will be the same as the theoretical *ex rights* share price:
>
> (i)   Mr Thomas exercises 100% of his rights.
> (ii) Mr Thomas exercises 50% of his rights and sells 50%.
> (iii) Mr Thomas sells all his rights.
> (iv) Mr Thomas does not exercise his rights.

Case Study III: Derlex Ltd

Derlex Ltd is a new UK-based fashion start-up company created by two enthusiastic, confident, and ambitious undergraduate students, Alex Welch and Derek Kirby. Created in 2011, the company operates under the UK-registered Brown Circle brand name, and produces a range of high-quality sportswear products (polo shirts, bags, caps, etc.), which are sold over the Internet, and through a few selected retail outlets. With its products and services aimed at the proactive sports-orientated 20- to 50-year old, the company's aim is to:

- produce and deliver a quality product and service
- develop customer loyalty for the Brown Circle product portfolio
- create and maintain a financially viable and sustainable business.

The company's mission is to '… establish the Brown Circle brand as an inspirational symbol of style and class'.

The initial start-up costs of the company were fairly small and mainly administrative and management orientated, for example company registration costs, brand name registration costs, and product design costs.

The directors' financial projections indicated low cash inflows for 2012 but high and increasing cash inflows for 2013 and subsequent years. During early 2012, product manufacturing costs, distribution and marketing costs, and other retail development costs, for example website design fees, began to be incurred. Additional funding was now required over and above that initially invested by the two directors, Alex Welch and Derek Kirby. Some start-up grants were available from a range of both UK Government sponsored business agencies, and university-related agencies, but such funding was limited. The additional funding was required to finance:

- immediate short-term operational costs
- further product and service delivery plans.

The options available, in addition to the start-up business grants, were:

- short- to medium-term debt, including loans and overdraft facilities
- additional equity capital.

Required:

Draft a report for Alex Welch and Derek Kirby, which outlines the current position of the business and the appropriate financial strategies that it may adopt. Your report should explain the differences between a start-up company, growth company, and mature company, and the financial strategies that each may follow. The advantages and disadvantages of alternative strategies should be explained, with recommendations of the financial strategies that are most likely to increase shareholder value and how they will achieve this.

Bircom plc is a large UK-based machine component manufacturing company in its growth phase. The company has six production facilities located in Glasgow, Birmingham, Leeds, York, Swindon, and Bristol, and four wholesale outlets located in Manchester, Bradford, Sheffield, and Cambridge. The company's head office is in Birmingham.

In 2012 the sales of Bircom plc's products accounted for approximately 27% of the total market for machine components in the UK, which was an increase of 5% each year since 2007. The company is now the single largest machine component manufacturer in the UK. Such rapid growth in market share has been due to the development and establishment of a market brand name through extensive economies of scale, low cost and high-quality manufacturing.

Over the past few years Bircom plc's performance has consistently exceeded market expectations. Currently, the company's shares have a β of 0.80. The expected return in the market in which Bircom is operating is 9% and the risk-free rate of return is 4%.

The company is considering expanding its current production facilities during 2013 by investing in additional production facilities in Scotland and Wales. These additional production facilities would require a capital outlay of £40m. The company's directors have risk-assessed the revenues that may be generated from the new facilities associated with the expansion plan, and have estimated that cash flows could vary as follows:

Probability	Expected net cash flows £m
0.10	2
0.25	6
0.40	8
0.15	10
0.10	14

The directors of Bircom plc have also estimated that:

- annual total net revenues will commence in year one as soon as the new facilities are complete and online
- annual fixed operational costs of the new production facilities are expected to be £2m per year and will be incurred from the commencement of the project
- annual total net sales revenues will remain at the same level for the life of the production facilities, which is expected to be eight years
- the production facilities are anticipated to be sold at the beginning of year nine, when each is expected to realise £2m.

For project evaluation purposes, and to take into account the possible business risk associated with the expansion project, the directors of Bircom plc have decided to add a 2% risk premium to its current cost of capital. The company is currently totally financed by equity.

Required:

(i)   What are the advantages of using CAPM as the basis for calculating a company's cost of capital?

(ii)   Why should a DCF-based method of investment appraisal be preferable to the accounting rate of return or payback?

(iii)   Calculate the expected value of the NPV of Bircom plc's expansion programme, and the minimum level of net revenues required to justify the investment.

(iv)   Explain and evaluate the alternative methods of funding that may be used to finance Bircom's project.

(v)   Bircom plc is currently financed totally by equity, but we have not been told which of the various types of shareholders own the shares. Discuss the implications for the various possible types of investor in Bircom plc (which is in its growth phase), with regard to the alternative ways in which the investment in this project may be funded.

(vi)   What other factors may have an impact on Bircom's investment decision?

(vii)   Outline some of the actions that may be taken to assist in ensuring the viability of the project.

(viii) Recommend, giving reasons, which you feel may be the most appropriate financial strategies for Bircom plc in terms of creation of corporate value.

15

Financial strategies from growth to maturity to decline

Chapter contents

Learning objectives

Completion of this chapter will enable you to:

- Identify the features of the turbulence phase of the business life cycle.
- Outline the key aspects in the profile of a mature business.
- Describe the transition from growth to maturity.
- Describe the relationship between perceived risk and the return required by investors in a mature business.
- Explain the way in which mature companies may be most appropriately financed.
- Consider the factors which impact on a company's dividend policy.
- Describe the situations in which companies may become targets for takeover.
- Outline the key aspects in the profile of a declining business.
- Describe the transition from maturity to decline.
- Describe the relationship between perceived risk and the return required by investors in a declining business.
- Consider the ways in which a company may delay its decline.
- Explain the way in which a declining company may reduce its debt ratio.

Introduction

In Chapter 14 we looked in more detail at the start-up phase and growth phase of the BLC model. This chapter will look at the period of turbulence that occurs during the growth phase, during which time there is a great deal of activity with companies entering, and then leaving the marketplace as they become unable to compete. The period of relative stability which follows then sees the more successful businesses entering their mature phase, which they hope will continue for as long as possible, until they may move into the decline phase and perhaps likely demise of products (and possibly companies).

The turbulence phase of the business life cycle

As companies move out of their growth phase but before they reach their mature phase they face a period of turbulence. A period of fast growth in demand attracts many entrants into the market, despite the barriers that may have been constructed to deter their entry. The turbulence period generally occurs towards the end of the growth phase, when risk will have reduced but growth indicates the opportunities for returns, which are attractive to new entrants to the market. An increase in capacity and the battles for market share, created by the new entrants, then result in price competition.

The period of turbulence and turmoil as a result of overcapacity is followed by a shakeout of companies that are unable to compete successfully, which then leads to a period of stability. The companies that lack the funding or the ability to compete are forced out of the market, with only the most successful companies moving on into their mature phase. The mature phase of the business life cycle cannot start until this position is resolved. The mature market is then one which becomes relatively stable.

The turbulence period and subsequent shakeout for businesses may be illustrated by what happens in the popular music industry. A singer or band may identify a new sound or unique way of delivering songs and music. If they are successful then many more similar artists appear on the scene who may copy and possibly improve on the original theme or idea. The inevitable shakeout that eventually occurs results in only very few of these artists standing the test of time and going on to become established names for an extended period of time.

A profile of mature businesses

Companies that have successfully completed and moved out of the growth phase will have survived the turbulence period resulting from aggressive price competition and the excess capacity built up in the growth stage. After the shakeout has occurred and surplus capacity has been removed the successful growth companies then move into the mature phase where their business risk exposure is much reduced as expected sales levels and market share are achieved.

During its mature phase a company's goal should be to maintain its market share and improve efficiency. We can see from Figure 15.1 that earnings per share (eps) should be high during the mature stage, and may increase as a result of gains from efficiency improvements. There is reduced business risk during a company's mature phase and so financial risk may be increased through an increase in debt levels and benefits gained from additional tax shields. Overall financial risk may be maintained at a medium level through a mix of debt and equity financing.

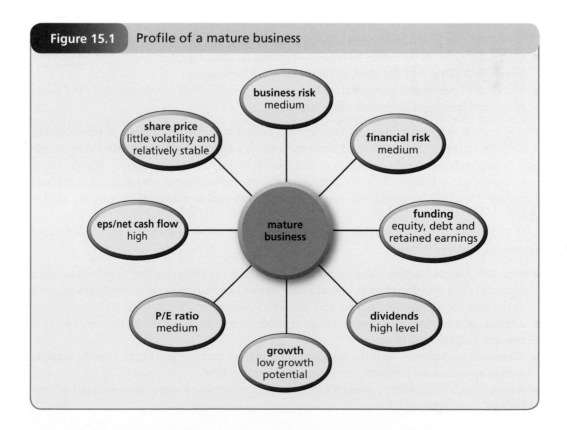

Figure 15.1   Profile of a mature business

A further source of funding now becomes available during the mature phase. This is retained earnings, which in addition to debt and equity may be used to fund investment in new projects. The amount of retained earnings available for investment is dependent on the company's dividend policy. Dividends are likely to be paid out at a high level in order to maintain a high level of total shareholder returns because share price increases, reflected in a lower P/E ratio, will be low as future growth prospects will now be lower. The company's share price is likely to be fairly stable with little volatility since the largest part of shareholder returns are now in the form of dividends.

> ### Progress check 15.1
>
> What are some of the key differences in the profile of a mature company compared with a growth company?

The transition from growth to maturity

When a company moves into its mature phase a change in managerial focus is required in order to profitably maintain the high level of sales it has achieved. Management must recognise that demand for their product may inevitably decline, and it may be a problem if they do not shift their managerial focus. There may be no justification to assume a prolonged high growth period. Consequently, management incentives based on growth should not be used during the mature stage of a business.

There are many examples of companies which, as a result of market pressure or lack of consumer demand, seek to reposition their product portfolios. Throughout the early 2000s we saw how:

- Coca-Cola continued to suffer from falling demand for soda-based drinks and as a result was forced to produce a raft of new products to reverse the slide
- McDonald's continued to suffer from bad press and was aiming to relocate its brand name with a new healthy-living marketing campaign.

Strong brands developed during a high growth period may not be capable of repositioning during the maturity stage, and to try and carry out such repositioning may prove very expensive. It may be better for the company to transfer the brand to another product, which is in or entering the growth stage. This is a practice that is widespread among large consumer goods companies. Marketing expenditure may need to be increased to maintain the existing market share.

In recent years, companies that have used their brand name to diversify their portfolio of successful products include:

- Procter & Gamble, which has made regular use of brand extension, and in particular with regard to the extension of its strongest brand names like Fairy Soap into new markets, such as the very successful Fairy Liquid, and then Fairy Automatic
- Armani, which extended its portfolio and expanded into everything from minimalist sofas to five-star holiday resorts
- Nike, which straddled both the casual fashion market and the hard-core athletic markets with innovative new products, marketing, and partnerships
- Kodak, which redefined its products and activities to become a major player in digital photography and printing.

Risk and return in maturity

As a company moves through its mature stage its unique, or unsystematic, risk level declines and cash flows become more predictable and stable. The demand for the product will have matured, and so profits are less volatile year-to-year, but they cannot be expected to grow dramatically.

During the mature phase, business risk relates primarily to how long this stage may last and whether levels of profit and cash flow may be maintained, rather than risk associated with issues of growth and market share. Therefore, this lower level of business risk means that investors may expect lower returns, which therefore results in a lower cost of equity to the company. The company should adopt the appropriate financial strategy to ensure that such reduced returns are acceptable.

We have seen from the CAPM that the beta (β) value for the market as a whole is one. If a company has a β less than one it means that its returns are less volatile than the market as a whole. If a company has a β greater than one it means that its returns are more volatile than the market as a whole.

A growing company is likely to have a β greater than one (higher systematic risk and higher volatility). Stability of earnings and cash flows in the company's mature stage means that its unsystematic risk has reduced, and this also means therefore that its level of systematic (market) risk has increased as a percentage of total risk. However, the β of the company (which was high during its growth phase) is likely to move downwards towards one as it moves through its mature stage (although it may never actually reach one). This is because the company's level of growth will have reduced and so it is now becoming less affected by the impact of external market changes. It therefore follows that the mature company's total returns will become much closer to that of the market as a whole. It should be noted that this may not always be the case; some utilities companies, which are generally companies in mature industries, often have very low beta values.

By delivering less volatile results year on year a mature company therefore communicates its lower overall risk profile, due to lower unsystematic risk. This is important to maintain stability in its share price and to avoid share price reductions.

Through the start-up and growth phases capital gains were high, but they decrease as maturity increases. Also, there is less need for the company to invest than there had been during the period of rapid growth.

Shareholders' reductions in capital gains may be mitigated by higher dividends. This is payable from the high level of profits and cash flows, which are helped by the value of the tax shield from increased debt. The inverse correlation may be noted as the reduction in business risk is offset by the higher financial risk as a result of increased debt funding.

> **Progress check 15.2**
>
> Outline the types of risk normally faced by a mature company.

Debt financing in maturity

There are, during a company's mature phase, high levels of earnings and cash flows accompanied by a high level of stability. The change in financial strategy from almost total equity to an increasing proportion of debt, can add considerable value for shareholders of a maturing company. The company is now a high taxpayer because of its high earnings, which leads to:

- a relevance of the tax shield – the reduction in tax payable due to the use of the tax-allowable deduction of debt interest against taxable income

- a decrease in the probability of financial distress, as the company is able to service debt (pay interest) and repay its debt
- business failure becoming less likely.

Therefore debt financing is justified during a company's mature stage and is recommended.

Dividends – why are they paid?

There are a number of reasons for paying dividends to shareholders, which are illustrated in Figure 15.2, and are discussed in the sections that follow.

Taxation

Dividend policies are greatly influenced by the tax systems under which businesses operate:

- corporate tax systems, because dividends are paid out of post-tax, distributable profits
- personal tax systems, because investors pay tax on the dividends they receive, with the amount of tax payable dependent on investors' individual tax positions.

Shareholders may, for example, prefer capital gains based on the share price, which may be taxed at a lower effective rate for them as individuals, rather than dividends which may be

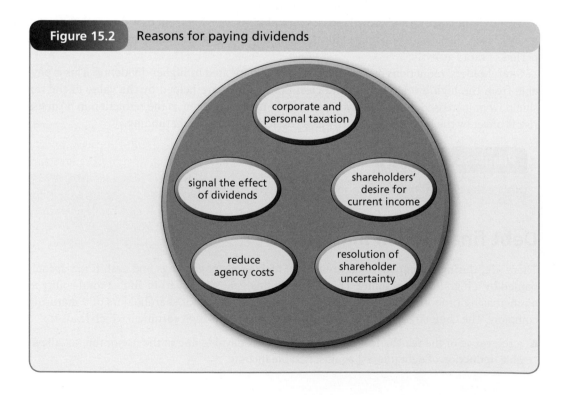

Figure 15.2　Reasons for paying dividends

taxed at a higher rate. Shareholders can choose when to realise a capital gain, because they may sell their shares whenever they want to. But shareholders do not have a choice about the timing of tax payable on dividends; UK companies pay dividends normally twice a year (and in practice, the timing of their payments is quite important for a company with regard to its cash flow planning).

Desire for current income

There is a huge demand for dividends from pension funds and other institutions, and from many trusts and endowments, which can only spend the dividend portion of their returns. These institutional investors, and many individual investors who have a current regular income requirement, want high dividend shares. Such investors cannot rely on gains from increases in share prices. Generally as salaries rise and the number of individual pensioners increases then pension funds, for example, require a regular income flow provided by dividends to ensure that funds are consistently available to provide pension payments. This is not only to those pension holders who are in retirement but also to the dependents of pension holders in accordance with their particular schemes.

The high level of increasing demand for high-dividend shares created by institutional and individual investors' requirements for current income from dividends will therefore push up the prices of such shares, particularly if dividends are rising. Equally, if a company's dividends are falling then its shares will be less in demand by these investors. The lack of demand for these shares following a fall in their dividends will effectively result in their share price falling.

In some circumstances, some types of institutional investors provide a demand for low-dividend shares that also have capital growth potential. These institutions provide investment packages at a low cost for individual investors. The institutional investors manage funds that are invested in low-dividend shares, from which they expect capital growth. These funds receive dividends, which together with their controlled sale of shares to realise gains, enable them to pay their investors specific levels of return.

Uncertainty resolution

£1 of dividend may be valued by investors more highly than £1 of retained earnings because investors regard future cash flows from new projects as being at a higher level of risk. Gordon (Gordon, MJ 'Optimal investment and financing policy', *Journal of Finance* 18, pages 264–72 (1963)) described this as an 'early resolution of uncertainty'. It may be argued that a company's current high-dividend policy benefits shareholders because it resolves uncertainty. Investors may evaluate the price of a share, or the value of the company, by forecasting and discounting future dividends. Forecasts of dividends to be received in the distant future have even greater uncertainty than forecasts of dividends in the shorter term; the greater the level of uncertainty then the lower is their present value. Therefore, it may be argued that if companies pay small dividends now in order to invest retained earnings in new projects to provide higher dividends at a later date, then the current share price will remain low.

Are short-term dividends less uncertain than dividends in the distant future? Well, the riskiness (uncertainty) of dividends depends on a company's business and financial risk. The bird-in-the-hand argument that dividends received now are worth more (just because they are received now) than dividends received in future years implies that the risk of the company may increase over time. However, this argument is fallacious as there is no reason to believe that risk increases over time for all companies.

Agency costs

There are agency theory implications that we may consider with regard to dividend payments. A company may have surplus cash but is unable to invest it in value-adding projects because its directors or managers may be reluctant to accept a higher level of risk attached to them. In such circumstances, the alternative of payment of dividends to shareholders is seen as a positive sign of good corporate governance. If new investment projects are available for consideration then payment of surplus cash to shareholders may be seen as an automatic vetting system for the appraisal of such investments. If managers reject these investment opportunities then it may be assumed that they have been appraised and considered unacceptable.

In Chapter 2 we saw the potential conflict between shareholders and directors, or managers, when ownership and control of a company is separated. The agency problem arises as a result of the directors not acting in the best interests of the shareholders. For example, a high retention of profits and cash by directors merely to provide a cushion for easier day-to-day management of operations means that a lower level of dividends may be paid out. Therefore the payment of dividends may be considered to be lowering the agency costs of equity. In this example, this results from reducing the amount of free cash flow available to managers, which therefore reduces the agency costs of holding on to cash that would otherwise have been paid out to shareholders in dividends (or invested in profitable new projects).

Companies that pay dividends may also periodically need to raise external funds rather than using retained earnings. The primary market to some extent therefore acts as a control against managers deviating from shareholders' best interests. The costs of issuing new equity shares may be offset by the lower agency costs of directors not acting in the best interests of shareholders.

We also saw in Chapter 2 that there may sometimes be an agency problem with regard to the relationship between debt-holders and shareholders. For example, shareholders may prefer the use of debt for investments by the company in new, high-risk projects. Shareholders may subsequently receive the benefit of the rewards gained from the success of such investments from the receipt of dividends and an increase in share price, but it is the debt-holders who bear the risk. A dividend may therefore be viewed as a transfer of wealth from debt-holders to shareholders. Another example is a company that, even if it is in financial distress, may be reluctant to cut dividends. This may impact on the ability of the company to repay debt. To protect themselves, debt holders can ensure that their loan agreements include provisions that dividends may only be paid if the company has positive earnings, cash flow, and working capital above pre-specified levels.

The dividend information content effect

There is an asymmetry of information between managers and shareholders, and so dividend decisions are seen by shareholders as providing information about the company and its performance. Also, when managers know more than individuals outside the business about a company's future prospects then they can signal this knowledge to investors through changes in dividend policy. Changes in dividends consequently have an information content and dividend policy is important in a semi-strong form efficient market. Increases in share price are generally observed to be associated with announcements of dividend increases. The rise in the share price following the dividend signal is called the information content effect.

Increases in dividends are not a credible signal about future performance if the higher level of dividends cannot be sustained at the company's current level of performance. If managers effectively lie about future performance by raising dividends, they may have to cut dividends in the future, which is something that very few managers are willing to do. Therefore, the information content effect implies that a share price may rise when dividends are raised if dividends simultaneously cause shareholders to upwardly adjust their expectations of future earnings.

We saw in Chapter 5 how, if a company's dividends grow at a regular rate, its share price and therefore its market value may be calculated using the dividend growth model equation:

$$S = v_1 / (K_e - G)$$

where

S = share price
K_e = cost of equity
v_1 = expected dividend
G = expected growth rate

This formula implies that the share price may be increased by a company through increasing its dividend. However, this assertion is not necessarily true. A company generates earnings, which may be retained for future investments or used to pay dividends, in any proportion it may choose. If we divide both sides of this equation by the company's eps we may re-write it as:

$$\frac{S}{eps} = \frac{v_1}{eps} \times \frac{1}{(K_e - G)}$$

S/eps is the company's P/E ratio and v_1/eps is the dividend payout ratio.
Therefore:

$$P/E \text{ ratio} = \text{dividend payout ratio} \times 1/(K_e - G)$$

We can see that if the company were to increase its dividend then its dividend payout ratio would also increase. The company's cost of equity, K_e, is also likely to increase because of its increased dividend. In addition, less earnings would be available for future investment and so the growth rate, G, would decrease (unless further external funding was available to finance new projects, which may also increase the cost of equity). Therefore, $1/(K_e - G)$ would increase. This means that changes in the two elements in the right-hand side of the equation are likely to balance out. The P/E ratio may therefore remain unchanged or it may decrease. A weakness of the dividend growth model lies in its implicit assumption that a company's future dividend growth cannot be greater than the rate of increase of its cost of equity, which in practice is not necessarily true.

Dividend policy and payment of dividends

The strongest argument about how companies pay dividends is that they are seen as a signalling device to the market. This may say to shareholders of a growth company that future growth prospects are not as exciting as in the past.

Mini case 15.1

Revisions to dividend policies by companies are always noticed by the markets, but when a company reverses its policy despite reassurances to the contrary, it is likely that there are problems within the company.

Telefónica, the Spanish telecommunications company, announced in December 2011 that it was reducing its dividend payout by 14% despite having continued to inform shareholders during previous months that their dividends were safe. The principal problems lay with the need for the industry to replace outdated technologies and the difficulty of squeezing more revenue out of highly saturated developed markets.

A policy of large acquisitions and necessary high capital expenditure had meant that Telefónica had one of the lowest ratios of dividends to total debt among its competitors. The dividend reduction was explained by the company as being necessary to improve financial flexibility.

The company announced a reduction of its dividend from €1.75 to €1.50 with 20 cents of the payout being made in share buy-backs. The company was also heavily indebted with a debt ratio of 2.49 times. Part of the problem was that the company had had to make many redundancies during 2011, generating a large one-off charge against profits.

For a mature company, paying out dividends may act as a signal that the company is doing well. An increase in levels of dividend indicates a stable level of post-tax profits. Reinvestment needs are covered by raising debt funding in reasonable proportions, in addition to the lower level of retained earnings. The P/E ratio decreases as the share price approaches a steady state value and the market will reassess the potential for future growth.

There are a number of different ways in which dividends may be paid. We will take a look at:

- **cash dividends**
- **share dividends**
- **share re-purchase** (or share buy-back).

Cash dividends

Companies, normally twice a year in the UK, declare so many pence payable as dividends per share held by each shareholder. The interim dividend is normally paid during the financial year, and the final dividend is paid after the financial year end and after it has been approved by the shareholders at the company's AGM. These so-called cash dividends are therefore made by payments to shareholders twice a year for the appropriate amounts.

There are a number of alternative cash dividend policies that a company may adopt:

- fixed % of earnings payout, which is simple to operate and gives a clear signal to the financial markets about performance, but provides a straitjacket regarding reinvestment of earnings
- zero payout, which is unacceptable unless it is supported by a high expectation of future growth levels
- constant payout, which is used to create stability, and to avoid cuts in dividends and to maintain the share price level
- steadily increasing payout, which increases investor expectations, but may lead to future cuts in the dividend.

Let's look at two examples of companies' dividend policies.

Worked example 15.1

Stanolly plc started as a two-man small business 10 years ago. The company continues to be managed and controlled by its original proprietors, Stanley and Oliver. The company had grown slowly in the early years since its initial launch, but had then achieved much greater growth more recently. In 2012 the company was floated on the AIM. Whereas previously Stanley and Oliver had owned virtually all the ordinary share capital, around 45% of the shares are now owned by the general public.

Stanolly's performance over the five years to 2011 is shown below:

Year	Number of ordinary shares in issue	Profit before tax £000	Dividend £000
2007	2,000,000	440	220
2008	2,000,000	450	230
2009	2,000,000	470	240
2010	2,000,000	630	310
2011	2,500,000	825	410

In 2012 the number of shares in issue was increased to 3 million. The profit before tax was £1,005,000, and the directors considered paying a dividend of £480,000 for 2012. The directors needed to determine whether their dividend policy was appropriate given their current status now that Stanolly was an AIM-quoted company.

The company's dividend policy in the past looks to have been based on paying dividends at a more or less fixed 50% of earnings, as illustrated in the table below:

Year	Earnings per share pence	Dividend per share pence	Dividend payout ratio %
2007	22.0	11.0	50.0
2008	22.5	11.5	51.1
2009	23.5	12.0	51.1
2010	31.5	15.5	49.2
2011	33.0	16.4	49.7
2012	33.5	16.0 (proposed)	47.8

A fixed percentage dividend policy may be appropriate when a company has moved from its growth phase to maturity when there is less volatility and some stability in the company's eps.

The 16p (£480,000/3m) dividend per share proposed for 2012 would mean a reduction from 2011, which would be unpopular with shareholders and may result in a drop in share price. The shareholders may be satisfied with the same level of dividend as 2011 at 16.4p per share which would give a higher payout ratio at 49%, which would still be slightly lower than 2011. This would create some stability and indicate the expectation of further capital growth. A higher dividend of say 20p per share may indicate that the company was approaching maturity with limited expectations of future growth.

Worked example 15.2

Hammans plc expects to achieve earnings next year of £2.8m. These earnings are expected to continue in perpetuity without any growth unless a proportion of earnings is retained, which means that paying 100% of earnings as dividends will restrict the company to no growth. If Hammans plc were to retain 30% of its earnings, an annual growth rate in earnings (and hence dividends) of 2% in perpetuity could be achieved. If the company were to retain 70% of its earnings an annual growth in earnings (and hence dividends) of 3% could be achieved.

The return currently required by Hammans plc's shareholders is 10%. If Hammans plc retains 30% of its earnings, the required rate of return would probably rise to 12%. If Hammans plc were to retain 70% of earnings, the required rate of return would probably rise to as much as 14%.

We will determine an optimum retention policy for Hammans plc.

(a) No retentions, 100% dividend payout

The formula $S = v_1/(K_e - G)$ relates to share price (S), expected divided per share (v_1), cost of equity (K_e), and expected growth rate (G). This may be re-stated in total terms as:

$$P_0 = D_1/(r - G)$$

using the current market value of the shares (P_0), total expected dividends (D_1), and shareholders' expected returns (r).

$$P_0 = \frac{£2.80m}{0.10 - 0.00}$$

$$P_0 = \underline{£28.0m}$$

(b) 30% retention, 70% dividend payout

$$P_0 = \frac{£1.96m \times 1.02}{0.12 - 0.02}$$

$$P_0 = \underline{£19.99m}$$

(c) 70% retention, 30% dividend payout

$$P_0 = \frac{£0.84m \times 1.03}{0.14 - 0.03}$$

$$P_0 = \underline{£7.87m}$$

The above calculations suggest an optimum dividend policy of 100% dividend payout ratio for Hammans Ltd, which would result in a market capitalisation of £28m.

Share dividends

Share dividends may be paid instead of cash dividends by capitalising the profits that would have been paid out in dividends and issuing shares instead. Dividends paid in shares are taxable in the same way as cash dividends. The company is effectively retaining its earnings and its cash for reinvestment. The difference for shareholders is that they may either hold on to the additional shares or sell them for cash.

Share re-purchase

It is the responsibility of the financial manager to use the resources of the company in the most efficient way in support of the objective of maximisation of shareholder wealth. During its mature phase, one of these resources, cash, is often surplus to the company's immediate requirements to maintain the business. Companies sometimes argue that their reason for holding on to surplus cash is just in case it may be required to finance acquisitions. However, there has often been increased pressure from institutional investors for companies to return their surplus cash rather than hold it for this purpose. The company may decide to return this cash to its investors either by paying special 'one-off' dividends or by buying back some of its shares. The choice between paying dividends or buying back shares depends on many factors, including taxation.

A company's purchase of its own shares may take place where all shareholders accept the purchase on a *pro rata* basis. The company may use its excess cash to buy its own shares in one of two ways. The first, and most common, is when a company buys shares on the open market, just as private investors do when they buy shares through a broker. The company has to get authority from its shareholders in order to buy back the shares. This is usually done at a general meeting of the company. There have been many examples of share buy-backs by companies, particularly over the past 20 years or so. For example, in 2005 Unilever plc and Unilever NV announced their commencement of an aggregate €500m share buy-back programme. The purchase of shares by the boards of directors on behalf of the companies was authorised in general meetings of shareholders of each company.

In the second and less common method a company may announce a tender offer. This involves all shareholders submitting a price they would be prepared to accept for their shares. In the UK, whichever of the two methods is used, the purchased shares are usually cancelled (although technically according to the Companies Act 2006 some shares may be held as treasury shares), and the company's share capital is reduced. The company cannot then sell back the shares in the market at a later date. The P/E ratio should remain unchanged. Earnings per share (eps) will increase because the number of shares in issue decreases, and so the share price should increase to compensate for the non-receipt of dividends.

From the shareholders' viewpoint share re-purchase or share buy-backs are generally good news. If there are fewer shares on the market then, unless demand for the shares changes for some other reason, the share price should rise. For the company, eps will be slightly reduced because of the reduction in interest received from the investment of its surplus cash, but this should be more than compensated by the increase in eps as a result of the reduction in number of shares.

We'll look at an illustration of the use of a share buy-back in Worked example 15.3.

Worked example 15.3

Thriller plc is a company in its mature phase and makes profits after tax of £15m each year, which includes after-tax interest received of £1.5m per annum. Thriller currently has cash of £25m. Its number of equity shares in issue is 100m. The current share price is £1. We will look at what may happen if the company uses all its cash resources of £25m to buy back some of its shares.

Thriller's current eps are £15m/100m = 15p
and its P/E ratio is £1.0/15p = 6.67 times

If Thriller uses all of its £25m cash it can buy 25m shares (£25m/£1).

Because it will not now be receiving interest on its cash balances its profits after tax will fall to £13.5m (£15 − £1.5m).

The number of shares remaining will be 75m (100m − 25m); therefore eps will increase to 18p (£13.5m/75m).

If shareholders believe that the P/E ratio of 6.67 times is still appropriate, then they may be willing to pay £1.20 (18p × 6.67) for the shares. Therefore, in theory the share price should increase after the share buy-back. In practice, the share price will depend on how the market perceives a company's disposal of its cash, and which stage it is at in its business life cycle.

If Thriller plc had any growth prospects shareholders may be willing to pay more than £1.20, because Thriller's potential profit growth would increase after returning the cash to shareholders, which was providing no more than average returns. However, in practice, investors are unlikely to see Thriller plc, a mature company, as having any growth prospects – it had not been able to invest its £25m surplus cash in new value-adding projects.

Therefore, it is likely that investors may not even be willing to pay £1.20 per share.

Worked example 15.4

Using the information from Worked example 15.3, let's consider what would happen if the original share price had been lower than £1 at, say, 50p, or higher than £1 at say, £2.50.

If the share price had been lower than £1 at say 50p then:

- £25m cash would have bought 50m shares (£25m/50p)
- eps would have been 27p (£13.5m/50m)
- the P/E ratio would have been 1.85 times (50p/27p)

If the original share price had been higher than £1 at say £2.50 then:

- £25m cash would have bought 10m shares (£25m/£2.50)
- eps would have remained at the original 15p (£13.5m/90m)
- the P/E ratio would have been 16.67 times (£2.50/15p)

The share price of £2.50 is the 'equilibrium' price, which equals the original earnings level of 15p multiplied by the £25m cash divided by the annual interest of £1.5m. At any share price above £2.50 eps will fall, and the P/E ratio will increase.

A company is therefore much more likely to buy back its shares when its P/E ratio is at a relatively low or medium level. Also, because the company needs a lot of surplus cash to make a buy-back worthwhile, it is much more likely to be mature businesses that buy back their shares.

Worked example 15.5 looks at a company that is considering the choice between:

- a residual dividend policy in which its total free cash flow (operating cash flow less net investment in non-current assets and working capital) is paid out in dividends
- paying dividends at a maintainable, regular growth rate each year, together with the possibility of share re-purchase.

Worked example 15.5

Baker plc has 24m equity shares in issue, and has estimated its net operating cash flows (after interest and taxation) for the next five years as follows:

Year	Net operating cash flow £m
2013	4
2014	12
2015	5
2016	6
2017	4

which have been calculated before the deduction of additional investments in fixed capital and working capital as follows:

Year	Investment cash flow £m
2013	3
2014	2
2015	3
2016	3
2017	2

We will consider some alternative dividend policies that may be adopted by Baker plc.

We can calculate the annual cash flows available and the dividend per share payable if a residual (or total) dividend policy is adopted, which are shown in the table below:

Year	Operating cash flow £m	Investment cash flow £m	Free cash flow £m	Dividend per share pence
2013	4	3	1	4.17 (£1m/24m)
2014	12	2	10	41.67 (£10m/24m)

(*continued*)

2015	5	3	2	8.33 (£2m/24m)
2016	6	3	3	12.50 (£3m/24m)
2017	4	2	2	8.33 (£2m/24m)

Alternatively, the company may adopt a dividend policy based on maintainable regular dividend payments. We can calculate an appropriate annual dividend growth rate, the annual dividend payments, and the amounts that may be available for the company to purchase its own shares.

We may assume that to ensure an affordable and maintainable dividend the company could pay £1m in dividends in 2013, and the amount could increase each year up to £2m by 2017. To achieve this, the annual dividend percentage growth rate, G, can be calculated as follows:

$$(1 + G)^4 = \text{£2m}/\text{£1m}$$
$$1 + G = \sqrt[4]{\text{£2m}/\text{£1m}}$$
$$1 + G = 1.189$$
$$G = 18.9\%$$

The maintainable dividends payable for the years 2013 to 2017 are shown in the table below, calculated using the annual growth rate of 18.9%. The table also shows free cash flows, and the net cash available after dividends available for the company to purchase its own shares.

Year	Free cash flow	Maintainable dividends payable	Maintainable dividends per share	Net cash flow available for share purchase
	£m	£m	pence	£m
2013	1	1.000	4.17 (£1m/24m)	0.000
2014	10	1.189	4.95 (£1.189m/24m)	8.811
2015	2	1.414	5.89 (£1.414m/24m)	0.586
2016	3	1.682	7.01 (£1.682m/24m)	1.318
2017	2	2.000	8.33 (£2m/24m)	0.000

It may be noted that if a share buy-back were not undertaken by the company then a special dividend may be paid in the years 2014, 2015, and 2016, calculated as follows:

2014 £8.811m/24m = 36.71p per share
2015 £0.586m/24m = 2.40p per share
2016 £1.318m/24m = 5.49p per share

Progress check 15.4

What are the key factors that a company may consider in determining its dividend policy?

Dividend policy – some practical issues

If a company pays a dividend then less funds will be available within the company for reinvestment, and therefore there is likely to be a reduction in future earnings and dividends. In theory the fall in the *ex dividend* market price will not equal the amount of dividend because:

- when the dividend is declared the shareholders' view of the riskiness of the company may change
- the actual dividend may differ from the dividend declared.

Porterfield (Porterfield, JTS (1965) *Investment Decisions and Capital Costs*, New Jersey: Prentice Hall) suggested that a dividend should only be paid if the market value of the share after the declaration of dividend (V_1) plus the declared dividend per share (D_0) is greater than or equal to the market value of the share before the declaration of dividend (V_0):

$$V_1 + D_0 \geq V_0$$

or

$$D_0 \geq V_0 - V_1$$

However, the situation is complicated by the fact that tax rate differentials may apply with regard to personal income tax and capital gains tax. If we assume that the dividend is D and the personal income tax rate is t, then when dividends are paid the net income to shareholders would be:

$$D \times (1 - t)$$

If c is the rate of capital gains tax and we assume that V_0 is the current market value of the share without a capital gain, and V_1 is the future market value of the share with a capital gain then when earnings are retained in order to achieve capital growth, income to shareholders would be:

$$(V_1 - V_0) \times (1 - c)$$

Shareholders would prefer reinvestment by the company if

$$(V_1 - V_0) \times (1 - c) > [D \times (1 - t)]$$

Dividend policy should attempt to maximise the sum of

$$(V_1 - V_0) \times (1 - c) + [D \times (1 - t)]$$

If the rate of capital gains tax is less than the rate of personal income tax ($c < t$) then there should be a preference in favour of retained earnings, although there is no certainty that retaining the dividends will necessarily generate an equivalent amount of capital gains. In the UK both c and t are often scaled depending on the shareholder's overall tax position.

The dividend argument – relevancy and irrelevancy

We may question whether dividend policy is relevant or irrelevant. There are two schools of thought regarding the dividend argument:

- dividend policy is irrelevant to maximisation of shareholder wealth
- dividend policy is relevant to maximisation of shareholder wealth.

The dividend irrelevancy argument

The most well-known supporters of the irrelevancy argument were Miller and Modigliani (Miller, MH and Modigliani, F 'Dividend policy, growth and the valuation of shares', *Journal of Business* 34, pages 411–33 (1961)), who suggested that in a tax-free world shareholders are indifferent between dividends and capital gains, and the value of a company is determined solely by the earnings power of its assets and investments. They argued that if a company with investment opportunities decides to pay a dividend resulting in retained earnings being insufficient to fund investment opportunities then the company would borrow funds. The loss in value in the existing shares as a result of borrowing instead of using internal funds would be exactly equal to the amount of dividend paid. They further suggested that the irrelevancy argument was valid whether the additional funds are raised by equity capital or by debt capital.

The dividend relevancy argument

Supporters of the relevancy argument suggest that different levels of taxes on dividends and capital gains can create a preference for either a high dividend payout or a high retention policy. They therefore reject the irrelevancy argument and suggest that the existence of:

- imperfect markets
- imperfect information
- the inherent uncertainty of future outcomes,

means that investors will prefer the early resolution of uncertainty and are willing to pay a higher price for the shares that offer the greater current dividends.

Gordon (Gordon, MJ 'The savings investment and valuation of a corporation', *Review of Economics and Statistics* 44, pages 37–51 (1962)) suggested that the higher the earnings retention rate, the greater was the required future return from investments to compensate for risk. He also suggested that the risk attitude of investors will ensure that shareholders' expected returns will rise for each successive year in the future to reflect growing uncertainty.

Takeover targets

Mature companies may run the risk of retaining profits for no 'profitable' use by investing in new projects with low returns. The result is a decline in the overall rate of return provided by the business. This may result from a disregard of the risk profile of new projects and possible agency problems.

If the transition from growth to maturity is not properly managed the share price may stay high for too long and then fall too sharply so then the company may become a takeover target (see Chapter 16). Business risk during the mature phase relates to how long the stable levels of profits and cash flow may be maintained. In August 2011, Immarsat, a UK satellite telecoms company founded in 1979, announced a revision of its meagre growth forecast for 2013 from 4% to 0%. The company, which provides telecommunications via 11 satellites in areas where communications are difficult, had developed a strong customer base and is in a strong financial position, but greater terrestrial coverage and the winding down of military deployments in Iraq and Afghanistan were hitting growth. The position of good cash flows and steady customer bases but no real growth prospects put Immarsat in the frame as a potential takeover target (see the press extract below).

Mature takeover target

Sadly, there is still plenty of action in Afghanistan. But for investors in Inmarsat – the UK satellite company that provides phones and internet services to ships, aircraft and soldiers in such remote places – some action in the boardroom would be welcome. Over the past year, the company's share price has fallen by two-fifths as a stalled shipping industry and cutbacks in military activity hurt business. Is this a perfect moment to make a bid?

Inmarsat's shares jumped 4 per cent yesterday on speculation that it may be a takeover target. EADS and General Electric have been aired as possible candidates. The Franco-German aerospace group bought Vizada, one of Inmarsat's main distributors, last year for €1bn and adding Inmarsat may open some prospect of synergies. Cost savings are less obvious for GE, though.

That said, Inmarsat's tepid medium-term outlook could be a turn-off for a publicly listed acquirer. Its earnings before interest, tax, depreciation and amortisation in 2012 are forecast to fall by 4 per cent and there is little prospect of growth in 2013. That perhaps opens the door for private equity. In a leveraged buy-out scenario, if a buyer paid, say, £2.5bn – or £5.54 per share, a 30 per cent premium to Inmarsat's undisturbed share price – funded half with debt, then even assuming no ebitda growth over five years, it could produce an internal rate of return of 12 per cent. Not bad.

Boosting Inmarsat's appeal is that its long-term future looks favourable. It has yet to materially tap into emerging markets and its new global broadband satellites could boost its military business revenues late next year. Current investors may be fed up with the lack of action but a private buyer with a longer-term perspective should be able to find value in the business. For Inmarsat's long-suffering shareholders, that would be a relief.

Source: Inmarsat, Lex column (2012), *Financial Times*, 9 February.
© The Financial Times Limited 2012. All Rights Reserved.

Diversification of a business may result in destroying overall value. A mature company has low risk and share price volatility. If it diversifies into launch and growth products, its investors' perception of risk increases. They will then demand a higher return to compensate for the higher perceived risk. The company may not then have any significant competitive advantage and so it may not be able to deliver the increased return. The consequence would be a reduction in shareholder value.

A profile of declining businesses

A summary of the financial parameters of a declining business is shown in Figure 15.3. The strong positive cash flow of a mature company cannot continue forever, as product demand eventually dies away. Business risk continues to decrease from the mature phase as a business

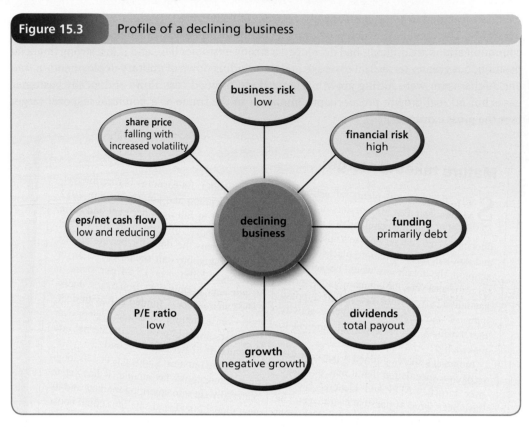

Figure 15.3 Profile of a declining business

moves into decline because reinvestment is low and growth prospects are negative, which is reflected in its low P/E ratio. Low business risk may be complemented by the high financial risk resulting from the high level of interest payments to service the use of debt financing, and from paying out a high level of dividends.

In its decline phase, a company's eps are likely to be low and their trend will be downwards, which will be reflected in a declining share price along with a high level of volatility. The company's dividend payout policy may allow its dividends to exceed its post-tax profits. This is due to inadequate financial justification to reinvest even at levels of its depreciation, which means that the company may fail to maintain its non-current asset levels. All excess cash may be paid out in dividends, and if dividends are higher than profits then this effectively means repayment of capital.

When the decline phase has been reached, the previously unknown length of the maturity phase is then known. The question that then arises is 'For how much longer can the business continue?'

Risk and return in decline

When a business reaches its decline phase the financial costs of the company require review. As sales reduce, the company should reduce its fixed costs and get into short-term variable contracts on as much expenditure as possible. The increasing use of debt financing means that the company may benefit from the lower cost of capital due to the general lower cost of debt compared with equity and the benefit of whatever debt interest tax shield it can use.

In its mature phase the company could accept the operating gearing risk connected with fixed cost, because of its relatively high and stable levels of profits and cash flow. But, in the decline phase there is a risk that arises because of the company's exposure to sudden changes in the external environment. This can lead to large losses if the company still has a big proportion of fixed costs compared with its total costs.

In the decline phase of a business the focus must be on short-term financial impacts. This may include, for example, the use of the payback method for decision-making to justify expenditure, as opposed to the use of discounted cash flow (DCF) techniques.

The use of return on investment (ROI) as a performance indicator, in which depreciation is charged as an expense, must assume that a business intends maintaining its asset base by reinvesting at its level of depreciation. This is not valid during the decline phase, at which time the business is very unlikely to be reinvesting at its current level of depreciation.

Worked example 15.6

Sleepers Ltd is an old established UK retail company. The shareholders of the company expect to receive a dividend of 30p per share each year into the foreseeable future. The current year's dividend is about to be declared.

The directors of the company are considering three options:

Option 1: retain the existing dividend policy
Option 2: increase the dividend to 35p this year – however, as a consequence of a potential reduction in retained earnings, it would be expected that future dividends would fall to 25p per share
Option 3: decrease the dividend to 25p this year – however, as a consequence of a potential increase in retained earnings, it would be expected that future dividends would increase to 35p per share.

The cost of shareholders' capital (and shareholders' expected return) is 12%.
Let's determine which dividend policy may be recommended.

We will assume that the *cum dividend* share price (S) is represented by the current dividend (v_0) plus a value calculated from using the simple dividend model, which is the future annual dividend (v_1) divided by the shareholders' cost of equity (K_e) in perpetuity (see the section on cost of equity in Chapter 5).

Option 1

Using

$$S = v_0 + v_1/K_e$$

if a dividend of 30p is declared and shareholders' expectations of future dividends remain at 30p then the estimated price of the shares *cum dividend* would be:

$$30p + (30p/0.12) = £2.80$$

Option 2

If a dividend of 35p is declared and shareholders' expectations of future dividends fall to 25p then the estimated price of the shares *cum dividend* would be:

$$35p + (25p/0.12) = £2.43$$

Option 2 would reduce the estimated share price by 37p to £2.43, and therefore an increase in dividend to 35p per share is not recommended.

Option 3

If a dividend of 25p is declared and shareholders' expectations of future dividends increase to 35p then the estimated price of the shares *cum dividend* would be:

$$25p + (35p/0.12) = £3.17$$

Option 3 would increase the estimated share price by 37p to £3.17, and therefore a decrease in dividend to 25p per share may be recommended.

Strategies to delay decline

As we have seen, during a company's decline phase business risk is low and so financial risk may be increased through increased debt financing (borrowing against assets) and a very high dividend payout ratio, which may even be higher than profit levels (which is effectively a repayment of equity capital). The benefit to a company in its decline phase from an increase in its level of debt is illustrated in Worked example 15.7.

Worked example 15.7

Sailaway Ltd is a company that has been in business for over 100 years but is now in its twilight years. One of Sailaway's assets is a machine that it expects to be able to be used productively over the next three years, after which time it believes it will be able to sell it for an estimated £200,000. The equity shareholders of the company currently expect a return of 12% per annum. Sailaway Ltd is able to obtain a loan at 7% per annum. Given that its cost of debt is lower than its cost of equity, we can determine how the company may increase its debt in order to increase shareholder value.

In three years' time we may expect the disposal proceeds of the asset of £200,000 to be distributed to the shareholders. The value of these proceeds to the shareholders, in real terms, is the present value of the expected disposal value of the asset, which is:

$$\frac{£200,000}{1.12^3} = £142,356$$

The company could immediately borrow £163,260 (£200,000/1.07^3) at 7% per annum, secured against the expected value of the machine after three years and these funds could be used now for distribution to shareholders. This sum is greater than the present value of the expected disposal value of the asset. Therefore, additional value will have been created for the shareholders as a result of Sailaway Ltd increasing its debt/equity ratio.

In practice, the actual amount that Sailaway may be allowed to borrow will depend on the lender's view of the accuracy of the estimate of the disposal value of the machinery after three years.

As a business moves into decline, there may be a conflict between shareholders and managers, who may want to avoid the final act of winding it up. This is one of the key issues in the agency problem. In the decline phase, diversification is difficult due to lack of financing if the core business is already in decline. It is also not recommended because of the lack of increase in shareholder value derived from diversification.

The decline phase does not necessarily mean the depressing death of a business. A re-focus may result in the growth of a niche market and provide domination of a market segment that may be extended for an indefinite period. See Mini case 15.2 about Rover's Mini car, which has remained in production for 50 years!

Mini case 15.2

The original Mini was designed for Rover by Alec Issigoni and developed for mass production in the 1960s but was still selling volumes of around 30,000 per year in the 1990s, although mostly to Japan by that time. It was the first British-manufactured car to sell a total of 5,000,000 units. By the 1980s, a niche market had been established and the Rover company at that time considered that the market for the Mini could be further developed and expanded by enhancing the product and building on the success of the increased interest in smaller cars as a result of increasing fuel costs. Enhancement of the product also gave the opportunity to reduce costs and improve profitability throughout the whole **value chain**, through the use of **value analysis** and *kaizen* to improve production efficiency. The success of the 'new' Mini in the late 1990s was so great that it became one of the few products that BMW chose to develop further into the BMW Mini following its takeover of that part of the Rover Group.

An examination of the reasons for the decline of a business may reveal opportunities that a company may consider. The following options may be looked at for adding value to a business in a decline stage that is expected to last for a while:

- split up the business
- acquire several small competitors
 - make a **deep discount rights issue** to fund such acquisitions.

A large group may use the strategy of splitting a large group and running it as separate businesses. The company may acquire several of its small competitors within the industry at low cost and regain market share, so that:

- rationalisation by removing spare capacity may give an opportunity to increase selling prices
- the relative bargaining position with suppliers and customers may be improved
- decline may actually be turned round so that, in BCG terms, many small dogs may become one large cash cow.

Acquisition of competitors may be financed by further debt or by a deep discount rights issue. A deep discount rights issue has a very low share issue price, and may be appropriate to finance such acquisitions. However, there is a risk that such a strategy might fail if investors have simply lost confidence in the company.

Progress check 15.5

How may the managers of a company try and extend the decline phase of its life cycle?

Reducing the debt ratio

We may consider a counter-argument to that which supports an increase in debt during the decline phase of a business. A company in its decline stage may benefit from a reduction in its level of debt.

When a company is in decline it starts to see its sales volumes and revenues reduce. Unless it is able to radically reduce its level of fixed costs then its profits will also quickly start to decline. One of the company's fixed costs is the interest it may be paying on long-term debt, which is also a drain on the cash flow much needed by the company at this time to pay out dividends. Additionally, if profits are reducing then the company normally has less need for the tax shield provided by debt.

A declining business may therefore try to increase shareholder value by reducing its debt/equity ratio. Reductions in debt, and therefore costs of debt, and reductions in shareholders' expected returns reduce risk perceptions and add value.

An increase of equity in a company's capital structure normally leads to an increase in WACC, because the cost of equity is generally greater than the cost of debt. A company in decline may currently be incurring higher costs of debt than its competitors by having to pay a substantial premium on its debt interest rate. If existing funding contains substantial risk premiums, then these can be removed by changing the financial strategy (by increasing equity), so that the inverse effect of a reduced WACC may be achieved. Therefore, an increase in shareholder value may be achieved due to the reduction in risk premium.

In Worked examples 15.8 and 15.9 we look at the consequences of a company increasing its equity through a rights issue in order to repay debt and reduce its gearing.

Worked example 15.8

Four Seasons plc had 25 million £1 ordinary shares in issue. It also had total debt capital of £50m. On 14 August 2012 the closing price of Four Seasons plc's shares was £2.39. The company had seen its market share decline slowly over the previous year or two. Due to further even more adverse market conditions the period between 15 August and 29 August 2012 saw a further decline in the company's share price. On 29 August the company's share price closed at £2. On 30 August, Four Seasons plc announced its intention to raise additional share capital through a £25m one-for-one rights issue at a deeply discounted price of £1 per share. The reason for raising this additional share capital was to drastically reduce its gearing ratio. We will calculate the *ex rights* share price, and the value of the company and its gearing ratio after the rights issue.

We can assume that no other external factors influence the share price of the company.

29 August original number of shares in issue, 25m shares at a market value of £2 = £50m
30 August one-for-one rights issue of 25m shares at £1 per share = £25m
Post-rights issue of 50m shares at £1.50 (theoretical *ex rights* share price) = £75m

	Equity £m	Debt £m	Equity plus debt £m	Gearing ratio
Pre rights value of Four Seasons plc (25m × £2)	50	50	100	0.5:1
Ex rights value of Four Seasons plc (50m × £1.50)	75	25	100	0.25:1

The deeply discounted rights issue means that to raise such a large amount of money a very large number of shares have to be issued but at the very low price. The low price is assumed to be in order to attract shareholders to invest more new funds.

Worked example 15.9

In addition to the information given in Worked example 15.8, we are told that Four Seasons plc's operating profit for the last financial year was £18m. The interest rate on its debt is 12% per annum before tax. Four Seasons' cost of equity is 15%. The corporation tax rate is 30%. Four Seasons plc has decided to distribute all profit after interest and tax in dividends and repay its debt. In this example we will consider the impact of the rights issue and repayment of debt on the company's cost of equity, share price, and the P/E ratio. We will also calculate the change in the company's WACC and how this may impact on the corporate value as a result of the reduction in Four Seasons' gearing.

Let's consider the income statement before the rights issue.

	£m		Number of shares in issue	eps
Operating profit	18			
Interest	6	12% × £50m		
	12			
Corporation tax	4	30% × £12m		
Profit after tax	8		25m	32p (£8m/25m)

The share price at 29 August 2012 was £2 and so the P/E ratio was 6.25 (£2/32p). If Four Seasons plc was in a steady state situation of zero growth then we may use the dividend growth model (with G being zero) to derive a cost of equity, which would be equal to the inverse of the P/E ratio = 1 × 100%/6.25 = 16%. We are informed that the company's cost of equity is in fact 15%. The reason for this is that the company is not yet in a steady state situation when its dividend growth rate would be zero and so its cost of equity is somewhat lower at 93.75% of the steady state level.

Let's consider the income statement after the rights issue.

	£m		Number of shares in issue	eps
Operating profit	18			
Interest	3	12% × £25m		
	15			
Corporation tax	5	30% × £15m		
Profit after tax	10		50m	20p (£10m/50m)

If Four Seasons plc were at the steady state level of total decline then the growth rate G would be zero. We have calculated the theoretical *ex rights* share price at £1.50; therefore the steady state P/E ratio = 7.5 (£1.50/20p).

Four Seasons plc may still be assumed to be in the same state of decline and so we can again assume the cost of equity to be lower in the same proportion of 93.75% of the steady state level as before the rights issue, therefore

cost of equity would equal 93.75% of 1 × 100%/7.5 = 12.5%
therefore the P/E ratio would be 10%/12.5% = 8

If the P/E ratio is 8 then with eps of 20p, this would imply a share price of £1.60, instead of the theoretical share price of £1.50. The increase in share price reflects the likely reaction of the market because of the reduction in total interest and the reduction in shareholders' returns, resulting in an increase in value for shareholders.

WACC before the rights issue

debt D = £50m   equity E = £50m   corporation tax rate t = 30%
cost of debt K_d = 12%   cost of equity K_e = 15%

$$\text{WACC} = K_e \times E/(E + D) + K_d(1 - t) \times D/(E + D)$$
$$\text{WACC} = 15\% \times 50/(50 + 50) + 12\% \times (1 - 30\%) \times 50/(50 + 50)$$
$$\text{WACC} = 7.5\% + 4.2\%$$
$$\text{WACC} = 11.7\%$$

WACC after the rights issue

debt D = £25m   equity E = £75m   corporation tax rate t = 30%
cost of debt K_d = 12%   cost of equity K_e = 12.5%

$$\text{WACC} = K_e \times E/(E + D) + K_d \times (1 - t) \times D/(E + D)$$
$$\text{WACC} = 12.5\% \times 75/(75 + 25) + 12\% \times (1 - 30\%) \times 25/(75 + 25)$$
$$\text{WACC} = 9.375\% + 2.1\%$$
$$\text{WACC} = 11.475\%$$

WACC has been reduced following the rights issue and therefore the net present value of Four Seasons plc's future cash flows will be increased.

Progress check 15.6

Is there just one appropriate financial strategy that a business may usually adopt with regard to its capital structure during its decline phase?

During their mature phase, companies may have run out of ideas for new investment projects. The payment of special dividends and share buy-backs may do something to maintain share price levels. However, mature companies are often targets for acquisition, particularly if their shares appear to be under-priced compared with the value of their net assets. Chapters 16 and 17 look at mergers and acquisitions (M&As) and how they may be financed.

Summary of key points

- A period of market turbulence usually occurs towards the end of the growth phase of the BLC, and the resultant shakeout sees only the most successful companies moving on into their mature phase.

- During the transition from growth to maturity a change in managerial focus is normally required to maintain a high level of sales with increased profitability.

- The level of unsystematic risk reduces as a company moves through its mature phase as profits and cash flows become more stable and predictable.

- The existence of the tax shield is a key factor that may lead mature companies to change their financing strategy from total equity to an increasingly high proportion of debt.

- A company's dividend policy varies considerably as it moves through each of the phases of its life cycle, and is also influenced by both corporate and personal taxation systems.

- Mature companies may become targets for takeover possibly because of agency problems, and if they run out of suitable new investment project ideas, and so are unable to maintain their overall shareholder returns.

- Product demand does not last for ever and so there is an inevitable move from the mature phase into the decline phase.

- As a company moves into a decline phase its managers must reassess the risk associated with its level of fixed costs, and identify ways in which they may be reduced.

- The decline phase does not necessarily mean the quick death of a business or product and there are many ways in which the decline phase may be extended.

- Shareholder value may be increased during the decline phase following a reduction in the company's debt ratio, or possibly as a result of an increase in its debt ratio.

Glossary of key terms

cash dividend A dividend paid to shareholders in cash six-monthly or yearly.

deep discount rights issue A rights issue in which the company's shares are offered to existing shareholders at a very large discount on the current market price.

share dividend A share dividend (also called a scrip dividend) is a partial or total alternative to a cash dividend, where shareholders accept more ordinary shares in the company instead of cash.

share re-purchase (or share buy-back) A mechanism whereby a company can re-purchase shares from its shareholders to reduce the number of shares in issue. This may be done because the company believes its share price is too low, or if the company has a surplus of cash for which it has no alternative value-adding uses. Share re-purchases may be an alternative to special cash dividend payments. The shares may be bought on the open market or by tender.

value analysis (and value engineering) Value analysis is the broad term usually used to include both value analysis and value engineering. Value engineering relates to design improvements resulting in cost savings and applies to products under development, while value analysis applies to products currently in production.

value chain The sequence of business activities by which, in the perspective of the end user, value is added to the products or services produced by an organisation.

Assesment material

Questions

Q15.1 Describe the period of turbulence that occurs between a company's growth phase and its mature phase.

Q15.2 How does a company's risk profile change after it has moved into its mature phase?

Q15.3 Outline the ways in which debt financing may benefit a mature company.

Q15.4 Explain the tax and cash flow planning implications with regard to a company's dividend policy.

Q15.5 Explain three of the reasons why companies pay dividends to shareholders.

Q15.6 Explain the dividend information content effect and the ways in which this impacts on shareholders.

Q15.7 Why do mature companies so often become the targets for hostile takeovers?

Q15.8 Explain how a conflict of interest between the shareholders and directors of a company may manifest itself during the decline stage of its life cycle.

Q15.9 Describe the financial strategies that a company may adopt in order to delay its decline.

Discussion points

D15.1 Company chairman: 'If we continue to pay no dividends for the foreseeable future and reinvest all of the earnings of the business then shareholders will be happy because of the value that will be added to the company.' Discuss.

D15.2 'The ways in which dividends are paid is irrelevant to the company and its shareholders.' Discuss.

D15.3 'Once a company has moved into its decline phase then its inevitable demise is certain to occur very quickly.' Discuss.

Exercises

Solutions are provided in Appendix 2 to all exercise numbers highlighted in colour.

Level I

E15.1   *Time allowed – 30 minutes*

> **Explain the risk profile of a typical mature business and the type of returns expected by investors.**

E15.2   *Time allowed – 30 minutes*

> **Explain the risk profile of a typical declining business and the type of returns expected by investors.**

E15.3   *Time allowed – 30 minutes*

> **Why is a company's dividend policy likely to change over its life cycle?**

E15.4   *Time allowed – 30 minutes*
Wane plc is an established retail company with retail outlets in South Wales and the North East of England.

The company is considering four alternative dividend policies:

- Option 1 – pay a dividend of 6.5p per share for each year in perpetuity.
- Option 2 – pay a dividend of 5.5p in 2012 with growth thereafter of 6% per year.
- Option 3 – pay a dividend of 5p in 2012 with growth of 9% for each of the next four years, and with 5% growth thereafter.
- Option 4 – pay a dividend of 5p in 2012 with growth of 10% for each of the next four years, and with 4% growth thereafter.

The company estimates that:

- if Option 1 is adopted the company's cost of equity will be 7%
- if Option 2 or Option 3 are adopted the company's cost of equity will rise to 10%
- if Option 4 is adopted the company's cost of equity will rise to 12%.

The company currently has an issued share capital of 785,000 ordinary shares.

> **Required:**
>
> **Using the above information advise the company as to which dividend option would maximise the value of the company.**

E15.5   *Time allowed – 30 minutes*

Wooden plc is an all equity financed company with the following history of annual dividend payments:

Year	Dividend per share
Current year	9.0p
1 year ago	8.5p
2 years ago	8.0p
3 years ago	7.8p
4 years ago	7.0p

The current year's dividend has recently been paid. Wooden plc has an opportunity to invest in a new retail facility, the cost of which would be funded from internal funds over the next three years. If the company invests in the new retail facility, dividends for the next three years will have to be reduced to 6.0p. Once the retail facility is complete, however, the company expects the dividend will increase to 10.0p and grow (as a result of the increased revenue benefits of the new retail outlet) by 8% per annum for the foreseeable future.

The company requires a rate of return of 12% for its shareholders, and has an issued share capital of 1,650,000 ordinary shares.

Required:

(i)   If the company does not develop the retail facility and dividends continue to grow at the historical rate, what would the value of the company be using the dividend valuation model?

(ii)   If the company develops the retail facility and dividends are reduced for the following three years, what would the value of the company be, using the dividend valuation model?

Level II

E15.6   *Time allowed – 30 minutes*

Solva plc is a company that is financed by £1 ordinary share capital and redeemable debentures. The debentures carry a nominal rate of 12% per annum, and have a current market value at par. The company has paid an annual dividend of 15p per share in the past and is expected to continue to do so in the future.

The market value per share is currently £2.50 *ex dividend*. The total market value of the equity is £5,000,000 and the market value of the debentures is £2,500,000. The company has a dividend policy of paying out all residual income as a dividend to shareholders.

The company has the option to redeem all the debentures in the next financial year. The finance director of the company has suggested that a rights issue of shares (at a price of £2.00 per share) could be used to raise the finance to repay all the outstanding debentures. If the debentures are redeemed, the finance director expects the cost of equity to fall by 1%.

Required:

Determine the market value of Solva plc after the debentures have been redeemed and compare this with the company's current market value. You may ignore any possible impact of taxation.

E15.7 *Time allowed – 45 minutes*

> Outline the alternative dividend policies for a company at each stage of its development. Explain the relationship between the dividend payout ratio and expected capital growth in share value.

E15.8 *Time allowed – 45 minutes*

Angle plc is a UK-based manufacturing company. The company is currently financed by a combination of ordinary share capital and debentures. The ordinary shares have a current market value of £3.00 *ex dividend*. The total market value of the equity is £9,000,000. The debentures are 7% irredeemable debentures and have a current market value at par. The total market value of the debentures is £4,000,000. The company has recently paid an annual dividend of 30p per share, and anticipates future dividends to remain at that level for the foreseeable future.

Angle plc is now considering a major new development that will cost the company £4,000,000. Annual net cash flows from the new development are expected to be £500,000 (before interest) in perpetuity. The company proposes to finance the new development using a new issue of 7% debentures at par.

The increase in debt is not expected to change either the market value or the cost of existing debentures. However, the increase in gearing will increase the financial risk for shareholders, and if the new development is undertaken and financed by debt, the company expects the company's cost of equity to increase by 2%.

Assume the business risk of the company will be unaffected by the new development, and that all net earnings (earnings after the deduction of interest) will be paid out as dividends in the year they are received. The impact of taxation may be ignored.

> **Required:**
>
> Advise Angle plc if they should undertake the project, and calculate the impact of the method of financing the development on the value of the company.

E15.9 *Time allowed – 45 minutes*

Cresswell plc is a mature company making post-tax profits of £30m a year. Its profit includes after-tax interest received of £2m a year. Cresswell currently has a cash surplus of £20m. Its number of equity shares in issue is 100m. The current share price is £2. Cresswell plc is considering using its £20m cash surplus to buy back some of its shares.

> **Required:**
>
> (i) Calculate Cresswell's eps and P/E ratio before and after the share buy-back.
>
> (ii) Explain whether or not the share buy-back should be undertaken by Creswell and why.

E15.10 *Time allowed – 45 minutes*

Using the information from Exercise 15.9, discuss the implications for Cresswell plc and its shareholders if the original share price had been higher than £2 at, say, £3, or if it had been even higher.

Kite Ltd is a first-tier supplier to major passenger car and commercial vehicle manufacturers. As a first-tier supplier Kite provides systems that fit directly into motor vehicles, which they have manufactured from materials and components acquired from second-, third-, fourth-tier, etc., suppliers. During the 2000s, through investment in R&D and technology, Kite had come to be regarded as one of the world's leaders in design, manufacture, and supply of innovative automotive systems.

In the late 2000s, Kite started business in one of the UK's many development areas. It was established through acquisition of the business of Mayfly from the Nuthatch Group. Mayfly was a traditional, mass production automotive component manufacturer, located on a brownfield site in Fordmead, once a fairly prosperous mining area. Mayfly had pursued short-term profit rather than longer-term development strategies, and had a poor image with both its customers and suppliers. This represented a challenge but also an opportunity for Kite to establish a world-class manufacturing facility.

A major part of Kite's strategic plan was the commitment to investing £30m to relocate from Fordmead to a new fully equipped 15,000 square metre purpose-built factory on a 20-acre Greenfield site in Dingfield, which was finally completed during the year 2012. At the same time, it introduced the changes required to transform its culture and implement the operating strategies required to achieve the highest level of industrial performance. By the year 2012 Kite Ltd had become an established high-quality supplier and was close to achieving its aim of being a world-class supplier of innovative automotive systems.

In December 2012 a seven-year bank loan was agreed with interest payable half-yearly at a fixed rate of 8% per annum. The loan was secured with a floating charge over the assets of Kite Ltd. The financial statements of Kite Ltd for the years ended 31 December 2011 and 2012 are shown below, prior to the payment of any proposed dividend.

Income statement for the year ended 31 December 2012

	2012 £000	2011 £000
Revenue	115,554	95,766
Cost of sales	(100,444)	(80,632)
Gross profit	15,110	15,134
Distribution costs	(724)	(324)
Administrative expenses	(12,348)	(10,894)
Operating profit	2,038	3,916
Finance costs	(1,182)	(1,048)
Finance income	314	76
Profit for the year from continuing operations	1,170	2,944
Income tax expense	–	–
Profit for the year	1,170	2,944

The company has no recognised gains and losses other than those included above.

Balance sheet as at 31 December 2012

	2012 £000	2011 £000
Non-current assets		
Tangible assets	42,200	29,522
Total non-current assets	42,200	29,522
Current assets		
Inventories	5,702	4,144
Trade and other receivables	18,202	16,634
Cash and cash equivalents	4	12
Total current assets	23,908	20,790
Total assets	66,108	50,312
Current liabilities	23,274	14,380
Non-current liabilities		
Borrowings and finance leases	6,000	–
Provisions	1,356	1,508
Accruals and deferred income	1,264	1,380
Total non-current liabilities	8,620	2,888
Total liabilities	31,894	17,268
Net assets	34,214	33,044
Equity		
Share capital	22,714	22,714
Retained earnings	11,500	10,330
Total equity	34,214	33,044

Statement of cash flows for the year ended 31 December 2012

	2012 £000	2011 £000
Cash flows from operating activities		
Net cash generated from operating activities	11,742	2,578
Cash flows from investing activities		
Purchases of non-current assets	(20,490)	(14,006)
Proceeds from sales of non-current assets	12	30
Interest received	314	76
Proceeds from Government grants	1,060	1,900
Net cash outflow from investing activities	(19,104)	(12,000)
Cash flows from financing activities		
Proceeds from issue of ordinary shares	–	8,000
Proceeds from borrowings	6,000	–
Net cash inflow from financing activities	6,000	8,000
Decrease in cash and cash equivalents in the year	(1,362)	(1,422)
Cash and cash equivalents and bank overdrafts at beginning of year	(1,974)	(552)
Cash and cash equivalents and bank overdrafts at end of year	(3,336)	(1,974)

Required:

(i) Prepare a SWOT analysis for Kite Ltd and identify what you consider may be the main risks faced by Kite Ltd, both internally and external to the business.

(ii) Prepare a report for shareholders that describes Kite's financial status.

(iii) The company has stated that it has achieved high levels of quality and customer satisfaction, but would you as a shareholder be satisfied with the financial performance and financial position of the business.

(iv) At what stage in its life cycle would you consider Kite Ltd to be and what are your reasons?

(v) What currently may be the appropriate financial strategies for Kite Ltd?

16

Mergers and acquisitions (M&As)

Learning objectives

Completion of this chapter will enable you to:

- Describe what is meant by mergers, acquisitions, amalgamations, and takeovers.
- Outline the principles underlying mergers and acquisitions (M&As).
- Identify the various types of M&A.
- Explain how market imperfections may be used to identify potential takeover targets.
- Appreciate the differences between 'good' and 'bad' reasons used to justify M&As.
- Consider the financial motives in M&As.
- Consider the managerial motives in M&As.
- Compare the various methods used for the valuation of M&A target companies.
- Explain some of the further reasons for share valuation and the use of share valuation models.

Introduction

Mergers and **acquisitions**, which are also called **amalgamations** and **takeovers**, are generally referred to as M&As. This chapter explains what is meant by M&As and considers why M&As take place between businesses. The obvious reason why M&As should take place in a competitive market environment is because it may be felt that shareholder wealth may be increased as a result. We shall see that this may not necessarily be the case, and also how it may not be the only reason why they take place at all. In order for M&As to take place the businesses involved need to be valued in a way that is acceptable and agreed by all the parties involved. We will look at a range of methods used to value businesses and consider the circumstances in which they may be most appropriate.

This chapter closes by considering some of the reasons, other than for M&As, why businesses may need to be valued. We will also look at some further methods that may be used to value the shares of both quoted and unquoted companies.

What are mergers, acquisitions, amalgamations, and takeovers?

Companies need to grow in order to generate increased dividend flows and capital gains for their shareholders. This growth may be achieved organically which is usually slow and costly, although smaller companies can achieve dynamic growth organically much more easily than larger companies.

Companies may try to reverse or accelerate the business life cycle. A company in its decline phase or mature phase may try to reverse its business cycle through investment in new product areas in order to try and create a new growth phase. Alternatively, a company may try and accelerate its business life cycle, for example, to justify growth values already priced into its shares. They may try to achieve this through dynamic changes in the structure of the business, and such changes may be achieved through mergers or acquisitions.

Underlying principles of M&As

A merger or an acquisition occurs when two businesses combine into one. Companies A and B may merge to become company C, which becomes a new entity. A merger is therefore a meeting of two equals to form a new venture.

However, mergers are rare, and what occurs more commonly is the acquisition, or takeover, which involves one company A acquiring the share capital of another company B, without a new entity being formed. Usually, in an acquisition, the larger company is the acquirer and a smaller company is the target, but this is not always the case.

In M&As, the combined expected present values of future cash flows of the combination of the two companies involved should be greater than the sum of the expected present values of future cash flows of the two individual companies, in order to create additional shareholder value. This may not be the case if a large premium is paid to shareholders of the target company. If the price paid by the acquiring company for the target company is higher than the added value that is gained from future expected cash flows then there will be no increase in shareholder value.

The costs of a takeover or a merger may be very high indeed. The cost of a proposed takeover that does not subsequently take place may also be considerable, such as the legal and advisory costs incurred in Sir Philip Green's abortive attempt to acquire Marks & Spencer in July 2004, which is described in Mini case 16.1. Such costs also include losses incurred by investors in share dealings in addition to the fees paid by the company to legal and financial advisers.

Mini case 16.1

In June 2004 Philip Green proposed an offer of between 290p and 310p a share in cash for M&S, along with a 25% stake in his newly formed business Revival Acquisitions. This valued M&S at around £9bn. Later in June 2004, Green upped his offer to 370p per share.

To win back shoppers and to try and fend off Green, the M&S board appointed Stuart Rose as CEO. Rose, who had started his career with the company, reorganised some of M&S's cluttered stores, cut unpopular lines, and sold non-core businesses such as financial services. The M&S board had to decide whether they had done enough to convince shareholders to give the business the time needed to restore flagging sales. M&S's board of directors did persuade the shareholders that they could add more value for them and they rejected both of Green's offers.

In early July 2004, Green came back with an increased offer of 400p per share. It was then reported in the press that to persuade shareholders to reject this latest bid, Stuart Rose would unveil his rescue plans for M&S by offering them a sweetener in the form of a special dividend or share buy-back, which would come from the sale and leaseback of dozens of M&S properties.

On 12 July 2004, M&S's pension trustees dropped a bombshell into the battle for control of the company by warning Philip Green that he may have to inject hundreds of millions of pounds into the pension fund if his bid for M&S succeeded. This could be as much as an extra £785m a year over three years. Analysts said the trustees' statement could be the beginning of a 'poison pill' that could torpedo Green's £9.1bn takeover proposal for the company. (See more about the 'poison pill' in the section about equity restructuring in Chapter 17.)

On 14 July 2004 Philip Green dramatically dropped his £9.1bn bid for Marks & Spencer, blaming the retailer's board for blocking a formal offer. Green walked away after nearly 3,000 small shareholders offered almost total support to the board at the M&S annual meeting in London. At the time Green said 'we will see who is the best retailer; there is only one vote that counts and that is the customer's'. Stuart Rose spelled out his plan to return £2.3bn to M&S shareholders, worth £1 per share, and announced the sale of the retailer's financial services offshoot to HSBC. He also planned to buy the Per Una range of women's fashion from its creator George Davies and make savings of up to £320m a year.

During 2005, M&S started to show some signs of recovery. In November 2006, M&S reported that sales revenues and profits before tax had increased significantly for the first half of 2006. The price of their shares soared to an all-time high of slightly over £7 per share at the news, which was £3 more than Sir Philip Green offered in 2004. Stuart Rose said that the company had gained market share in all areas in which it traded.

M&S's success continued in the second half of 2006 and in January 2007 Stuart Rose revealed that they had also had a good Christmas. Like-for-like sales for the third quarter ended 30 December 2006 rose 5.6%, and total sales gained 9.2%. Internet sales soared more than 70%, and international sales increased by 18.2%.

According to the City analysts, shareholders regarded the turnaround in M&S's fortunes as a testament to Rose's skills and leadership abilities. With hindsight, the group's performance indicated that M&S's shareholders had made the right decision in rejecting Green's takeover bids. Stuart Rose was rewarded with a knighthood in the 2008 New Year's Honours List.

Progress check 16.1

What is a merger (amalgamation) and what is an acquisition (takeover)?

Types of M&A

Mergers and acquisitions take place in a number of ways and there are various types of M&A. The most common of these are shown in Figure 16.1 and are discussed in the sections that follow.

Horizontal integration

One company A may take over or merge with another company B operating in the same industry at a similar level of production so that their operations may be combined. Horizontal integration relates to a merger or takeover involving a competing business and may be defined as:

■ the merging of two or more companies at the same level of production

or

■ the acquisition of a competitor or a number of competitors at the same level of production in pursuit of market power or economies of scale.

Figure 16.1   The ways in which mergers and acquisitions (M&As) may take place

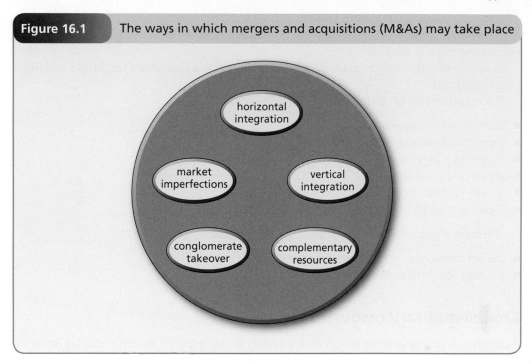

There are numerous examples of horizontal integration, which include Morrisons plc's acquisition of Safeway plc, Wal-Mart Inc's acquisition of Asda plc, and Granada plc's and Carlton plc's formation of ITV plc.

The main benefits of horizontal integration may be seen in:

- economies of scale – selling more of the same or a similar product
- economies of scope – sharing resources common to different products
- increased market power (over immediate suppliers and those further down the supply chain)
- reduced costs of marketing, selling, and distribution.

The main problems faced by companies involved in horizontal integration include:

- possible legal issues regarding the creation of market monopolies – horizontal integration by acquisition of a competitor may increase market share above a level that allows fair competition
- anticipated economic gains may not materialise (note Morrisons plc's poor results initially, following its takeover of Safeway).

Vertical integration

Vertical integration relates to a merger or takeover involving another business that may be a customer or a supplier. The merger or takeover involves two companies that are active in different stages of production within the same industry.

Vertical forward integration involves a move forward down the supply chain by company A acquiring company B to secure an outlet for company A's products; company A merges with or may take over one or more of its customers.

Vertical backward integration involves a move backward up the supply chain by company A acquiring company B to secure supply of raw materials; company A merges with or may take over one or more of its suppliers.

Examples of vertically integrated companies include Apple Computers Inc, BP plc, and Royal Dutch Shell plc.

The main benefits of vertical integration include:

- increased economies of scale
- greater economies of scope
- improved cost efficiency
- greater competitiveness
- reduced threats from suppliers or customers
- higher degree of control over the entire value chain.

The main disadvantages of vertical integration include:

- the limitation of a company's reaction to change
- the high cost to sustain such a company.

Complementary resources

A company A may acquire or merge with company B that uses, for example, similar materials or distribution channels. Company B may be a business that is using the same suppliers as the acquiring company A.

The combined operations of the companies can benefit from cost reductions from increased purchasing power and rationalisation of operations. There may be an increase in purchasing power derived from the larger size of the combined entity. There may also be rationalisation as a result of the pooling of knowledge and resources and elimination of the duplication of processes and effort.

Conglomerate takeover

A conglomerate takeover involves the acquisition of a company B engaged in a totally different line of business to that of the acquiring company A. To the acquiring company A this means moving into new, unknown areas involving high risk, but also potentially high returns. However, this strategy is questionable with regard to whether it is able to add shareholder value.

An example of a conglomerate takeover was Vivendi Universal's diversification into film and music production and telecommunications in the 1990s. Another high-profile conglomerate takeover was the food group Ranks Hovis McDougall's (RHM) acquisition by the multinational engineering conglomerate Tomkins plc in 1992, for which it has been suggested it paid much more than its fair value. Tomkins' massive growth had been achieved mainly through acquisition and prior to, and after the RHM acquisition, it continued to report continued year-on-year increases in earnings per share (eps). The problem with conglomerate takeovers, as Tomkins plc found, was that increases in eps were not necessarily reflected in a growth in share price. During the 1990s, as the Tomkins group ran out of ideas for investment in new growth projects, it returned cash to shareholders through buying back its shares and subsequently sold off RHM and other significant parts of the group.

Market imperfections

A target company may be one that is for some reason undervalued in the market, which is therefore by definition an inefficient or semi-efficient market. The share price may not reflect the earning potential of the company or the value of its assets.

The participants in a proposed takeover may not agree on the price of the target company's shares. Very often, acquiring companies may 'overpay' for acquisitions, as in the case of Tomkins and RHM. The benefits of the synergy effect (2 + 2 = 5) may be questioned. Is the whole new entity worth considerably more than the worth of the two separate entities, or considerably less?

Let's look at an example.

Worked example 16.1

Oliver plc and Ramsey plc are rival food retail companies both operating in the UK. The following information is available on each company:

	Oliver plc	Ramsey plc
Most recent dividends per share	£0.35	£0.15
Most recent earnings per share	£0.62	£0.25
Number of shares in issue	6m	3m
Current market price of shares	£8.80	£3.15
Current weighted average cost of capital	10%	10%

The management of Oliver plc is currently considering making a formal cash offer of £5.20 for each of Ramsey plc's shares.

The current management of Ramsey plc expect future dividends will grow by 5% each year in perpetuity. However, if the company is acquired by Oliver plc, the management of Oliver plc expect cost reductions and economies of scale will increase the growth rate to 7% each year in perpetuity. The transaction costs of the proposed acquisition are expected to be £1.2m.

We will use Gordon's dividend growth model (see Chapter 5) to calculate the value created by the acquisition. The market share price (S) is determined from the current dividend (v), the shareholders' required rate of return (K_e), and the expected dividend growth rate (G), as follows:

$$S = \frac{v \times (1 + G)}{(K_e - G)}$$

We will also calculate the value created for each group of shareholders if the cash offer of £5.20 is accepted by Ramsey plc's shareholders, and calculate the increase or decrease in value that would result if, due to integration problems, only 50% of the anticipated acquisition benefits were realised.

Value created by the acquisition

Ramsey plc – value before the acquisition

Using $S = \dfrac{v \times (1 + G)}{(K_e - G)}$

$S = £0.15 \times 1.05/(0.10 - 0.05)$ $= £3.15$ per share
value $= 3$ million $\times £3.15$ $= £9.45m$

Ramsey plc – value after the acquisition

$S = £0.15 \times 1.07/(0.10 - 0.07)$ $= £5.35$ per share

value $= 3$ million $\times £5.35$	$= £16.05m$
costs	$£1.20m$
	$£14.85m$
value prior to acquisition	$£9.45m$
total value created	$£5.40m$

Cash offer of £5.20 per share

Ramsey plc

$3m \times (£5.20 - £3.15)$ $= £6.15m$ value gained by Ramsey shareholders

Oliver plc

$3m \times (£5.35 - £5.20) - £1.20m$ $= (£0.75m)$ value lost by Oliver shareholders
total value created $£5.40m$

Value created if only 50% of the anticipated acquisition benefits are realised

loss of acquisition benefits $50\% \times £5.40m = £2.70m$

Ramsey plc

$3m \times (£5.20 - £3.15)$ $= £6.15m$ value gained by Ramsey shareholders

Oliver plc

$3m \times (£5.35 - £5.20) - (£1.20m + £2.70m) = (£3.45m)$ value lost by Oliver shareholders

total value created $£2.70m$

Reasons and justifications for M&As

The level of mergers and acquisitions increased worldwide in the 2000s peaking in 2007, both in value and volume of transactions. The years following 2007 saw an equally rapid decline in M&A activity until 2011 when global M&A activity climbed back to 2005 levels. The chart shown in Figure 16.2 illustrates that the pattern was replicated in Europe with clear peaks and troughs in M&A activity over the past 15 years. We can see a growth in values and volumes for the few years leading up to the 2008 global financial crisis but then a falling-back in the subsequent years to date.

Although M&A activity had levelled out in Europe at the end of 2011, a report in the *Daily Mail* in October 2011 noted that Britain was the second most active country in mergers and acquisitions in 2011, having secured 14 acquisition deals with a combined value of more than £52bn.

Back in 2005, CNN reported on the fact that 70% of the big M&A deals worldwide over the previous two years had failed to create value; 50% of M&A deals had actually destroyed shareholder value. More recent research suggests that, in spite of the general popularity of mergers and acquisitions, 60 to 80% of mergers worldwide fail to create value. An example of what initially appeared to be a huge success that ultimately turned sour, was the Royal Bank

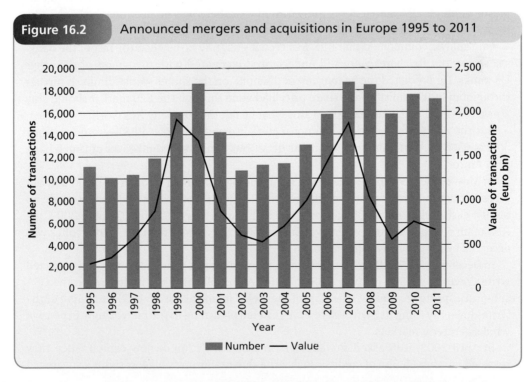

Figure 16.2 Announced mergers and acquisitions in Europe 1995 to 2011

Source: Thomson Financial, Institute of Mergers, Acquisitions and Alliances (IMAA) analysis.

of Scotland's acquisition in March 2000 of the much larger NatWest Bank, which is illustrated in Mini case 16.2.

Mini case 16.2

NatWest Bank plc was very much in need of a turnaround (see Nohria, N and Weber, J *The Royal Bank of Scotland: Masters of Integration*, Harvard Business School Case number 404026, 15 August, 2003). In March 2000, it was acquired by Royal Bank of Scotland (RBS), which was a much smaller outfit. 70% of RBS's revenue growth had been organic. However, this reverse takeover dramatically improved the company's revenues, profits, and market capitalisation. The additional gains following the takeover included:

- RBS's improved competitive position in all its businesses, giving them many market leader positions
- significantly improved cost/income ratio to make it one of the most efficient players in the banking industry
- the bringing of new customers to all segments of the bank
- an increase in the satisfaction of existing customers
- an increase in employee morale and pride they felt in being part of a winning organisation.

In January 2007, RBS's share price achieved its highest point ever at £20 per share. In 2006, Citigroup predicted that RBS was undervalued by £10bn because of a so-called 'management discount' based on the market's view of the bank's focus on acquisitions rather than generating shareholder value. However, RBS's chief executive, Sir Fred Goodwin, countered that by confirming that the bank was on track to exceed the market's expectation for profits of about £9.16bn in 2006, and stressed that there was no need for the bank to be looking at major acquisitions.

One analyst commented that RBS was growing slightly faster than the rest of the banking sector, but its shares were still under-priced compared with the shares of the other UK banks. He predicted the 'management discount' on the shares would diminish further throughout 2007 and since the share price had gone through the £20 mark it should stay above that level and continue up towards what he felt the company was worth.

But the analysts' predictions did not materialise and things at RBS were not as they appeared to be, particularly following its disastrous and ill-timed takeover of Dutch bank ABN Amro.

In May 2007, a consortium led by RBS, including Santander and Fortis Bank, laid out plans to outgun Barclays with an offer worth €71.1bn (£48.2bn) for ABN Amro, made up of 79% cash and in July 2007 increased the cash proportion to 93%. In October 2007, the RBS team clinched victory, after rival Barclays withdrew from the race, and its offer was accepted by 86% of ABN's shareholders.

In December 2007, RBS tried to ease investor fears when it revealed lower-than-expected write-downs of £1.5bn for both RBS and ABN Amro following the meltdown in the USA sub-prime mortgage market (the start of the global financial crisis). It offset £250m of the write-downs by using its own cash reserves instead of turning to the increasingly expensive wholesale credit markets.

In April 2008, RBS asked shareholders to pump in £12bn of new capital when they revealed another £5.9bn of credit crunch write-downs. Europe's biggest rights issue forced

CEO Sir Fred Goodwin on the defensive, although he dismissed talk of his resigning. In August 2008, Sir Fred again insisted he was the best man for the job despite unveiling the group's first loss in 40 years as a public company – pre-tax losses of £691m were the second biggest banking loss in UK corporate history.

In November 2008, former Abbey National boss Stephen Hester replaced Sir Fred as CEO of RBS, as the UK Government took a 58% stake in the bank for £15bn as part of a mammoth capital raising. In January 2009 the Government launched a second bank rescue plan, increasing its stake in RBS, as the bank announced that losses for 2008 could be up to £28bn, with the majority made up of write-downs on the ABN Amro acquisition.

In February 2009, history was made as RBS reported a loss of £24.1bn for 2008, the biggest in British corporate history. The Government asked Sir Fred, the former CEO, to give up his annual pension worth about £700,000. In March 2009, the bank's annual report said that Sir Fred was paid £1.3m in 2008. The Government took a stand on Sir Fred's pension and said it would vote against RBS's 2008 executive pay proposals.

In 2009, the Financial Services Authority launched a formal investigation into what exactly led to 2008's emergency Government rescue of RBS. By December 2010, although the FSA had criticised Sir Fred and other RBS executives a for a 'series of bad decisions' in 2007 and 2008 during the financial crisis, they escaped any sort of punishment.

However, Fred Goodwin had cost UK taxpayers £45bn as he steered RBS to disaster. There was great public pressure and a committee of senior civil servants and Government lawyers considered the case for Fred's knighthood to be rescinded. The loss of his title was immediate and he had to return the official medal and ribbon that went with his knighthood to Buckingham Palace. His wife Joyce, formerly Lady Goodwin, became plain Mrs Goodwin.

While the RBS/NatWest integration initially appeared to have been a success, we can see from the Mini case that management sometimes may forget the underlying principles for justifying M&As. Directors and managers of businesses are employed by companies to manage their assets in the most effective way to maximise shareholder wealth. The main justification of M&As therefore must be that target companies really should be worth more than they will cost the acquiring companies. This means that the expected future present value cash flows of the combined companies, minus the costs of acquisition, must amount to more than the expected future present value cash flows of the two individual companies.

However, we should not conclude that all M&As are failures and do not create value for shareholders. Some of the impacts of mergers and acqustions may be 'good' and some may be 'bad', and may affect the company and customers alike as the press extract below relating to M&A activity in Ireland between 2009 and 2011 illustrates.

How successful are M&As?

Recent years have seen increased consolidation within the agriculture and food, financial and media sectors in Ireland, according to Ibrahim Bah, manager, mergers division, the Competition Authority. 'Compared to the pre-crisis period, we have seen more mergers involving increased consolidation within the same industry or sector as opposed to mergers across different industries or mergers involving private equity firms,' he said. 'Mergers involving increased consolidation within the same industry may be more likely to raise competition concerns, in which case pre-notification discussions would be beneficial to the merging businesses and also the Competition Authority,' Bah said.

The number of mergers and acquisitions notified to the Competition Authority decreased in 2009 compared to previous years, and also relative to 2010 and 2011 to date. The dip in 2009, Bah said, reflected the initial impact of the financial and economic crisis on business and the availability of funding for mergers. 'Whether total mergers in 2012 will be near 2009 or 2011 levels will likely depend on general economic conditions and, in particular, on financial stability and the availability of funds to finance merger transactions,' he said.

A total of 46 mergers were notified to the Competition Authority in 2010, compared to 37 up to November of this year, with one currently active, Connacht Gold/Donegal Creameries in the dairy food and agri trade sector. The Competition Authority does not keep statistics on all mergers that occur in the state and does not exercise any discretion, for example, in terms of sector or size of transaction, on which mergers it regulates. Any observations on the number or size of transactions, or the sectors, within which mergers take place, reflect broader economic trends rather than any strategic decisions of choices on the part of the Competition Authority, Bah said.

Businesses may restructure by merging together or through one or more businesses acquiring another. 'A key element of a merger or acquisition is that there is a change in ownership and control of one or more of the businesses involved as a result of the restructuring. It is common to use the term merger to cover both mergers and acquisitions,' Bah said. 'A merger may result in greater success and profitability for the merged business than would otherwise have been the case for the separate businesses.'

Merger regulation, Bah said, focuses on how a change in market structure is likely to impact consumers, due to a likely alteration in the ability and incentives of the merged business and other competitors. 'The relevant test for assessing a notified merger is whether or not it will lead to a substantial lessening of competition in any market for goods or services in the state. This test is interpreted in terms of consumer welfare and, in most cases, whether the merger will lead to a sustainable price increase for consumers,' said Bah. 'Some mergers may be pro-competitive and may result in the merged business being able to compete more effectively to the benefit of consumers. Consumers may benefit from lower prices and/or better quality of goods or services.'

Some mergers may not, however, benefit consumers. 'For example, a merger may result in a reduction in choice for consumers and the merged business being able to sustain a significant increase in prices or a reduction in output. This outcome would be a substantial lessening of competition and not good for consumers, including business customers,' Bah said.

The Competition Authority is required by law to review any merger notified to it. It aims at all times to make sure that mergers are reviewed in an efficient and effective manner, said Bah. 'Mergers that are unlikely to result in harm to consumers are not held up any more than is necessary. At the same time, the Competition Authority actively protects the interests of consumers including through its power to remedy or block mergers that are likely to harm them,' he said. Businesses may contact the Competition Authority before notifying a merger. Pre-notification discussions can help parties to prepare their notification, according to Bah. 'They also offer the opportunity for the parties to provide an introductory explanation about the business activities of the notifying parties and also to discuss at an early stage potential competition concerns and possible remedial actions.'

The Competition Act 2002 obliges merging parties to notify mergers which satisfy specified turnover thresholds. This Act also sets out clear and specific assessment criteria and the review process which the Competition Authority is required to apply.

The general rule is that a merger transaction must be notified by the merging businesses to the Competition Authority if, in the most recent financial year: The world-wide turnover [revenue] of each of two or more of the parties is not less than €40,000,000; each of two or more of the parties carries on business in any part of the island of Ireland; and the turnover in the state of any one of the parties is not less than €40,000,000. Notwithstanding this rule, businesses may also voluntarily notify a transaction to the Competition Authority. This rule does not apply to a merger involving media businesses, or to one covered by the Credit Institutions (Financial Support) Act 2008.

Businesses are required to notify a merger transaction if they carry on a media business in the state. 'Currently, there are no notification turnover threshold criteria for media mergers,' said Bah. The Competition Act 2002 allows for the possibility that a media merger cleared by the Competition Authority on competition grounds after a full investigation may still be blocked by the Minister for Enterprise, Jobs and Innovation on public interest grounds.

Under Section 7 of the Credit Institutions (Financial Support) Act 2008, where the Minister for Finance has formed the opinion that a proposed merger or acquisition involving a credit institution is necessary to maintain the financial stability of the state, that merger or acquisition must be notified to the Minister for Finance rather than to the Competition Authority. In addition, the Credit Institutions (Stabilisation) Act 2010, allows the overriding of both the Competition Act, 2002 and the Credit Institutions (Financial Support) Act 2008 as they relate to banking sector mergers.

In the vast majority of cases, the Competition Authority's merger reviews are completed after an initial investigation or at 'phase one'. Where the Competition Authority is unable to clear the transaction at phase one, it proceeds into a full investigation or 'phase two'. These investigations, Bah said, involve reviewing and analysing information provided by the merging parties, submissions and consultations with third parties and other research. At phase one, the Competition Authority has one month after the 'appropriate' date to decide. At phase two, the Competition Authority's deadline for a decision is four months after the appropriate date. Within this deadline, the Competition Authority must decide to either clear the merger – with or without conditions – or prohibit the merger. The appropriate date is usually the date on which a notification is received by the Competition Authority, Bah said.

These deadlines may change where the Competition Authority formally required further information from the parties, he said. 'In such an instance, the appropriate date becomes the date at which the information is received by the Competition Authority and a revised deadline for a decision is one month from this new date,' he said. The merging parties may make proposals to the Competition Authority to alter the original transaction to address competition concerns. If proposals are made at phase one, then the deadline for an Authority decision is 45 days from the appropriate date rather than one month.

Source: **Corporate Transactions & Financing: Keeping an eye on M&A activity**, commercial reports section © *Sunday Business Post*, 4 December 2011

Very broadly, the good reasons a company may have for M&As are to:

■ support value-creating growth – note from the above article that 'a merger may result in greater success and profitability for the merged business than would otherwise have been the case for the separate businesses'
■ complement business strategies in terms of products, market, technologies, etc. – note from the above article, 'some mergers may be pro-competitive and may result in the merged business being able to compete more effectively to the benefit of consumers'
■ stop a competitor merging with or taking over a business.

Figure 16.3   Justifications supporting the reasons for M&As

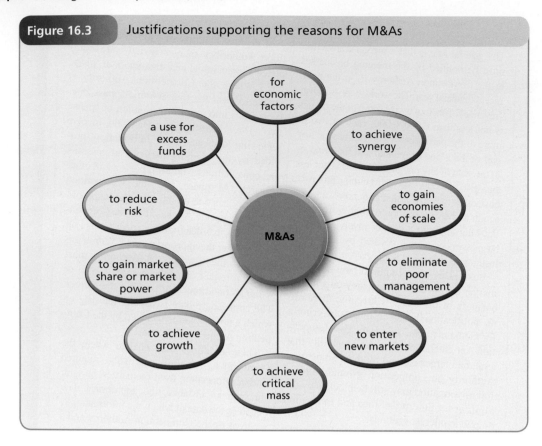

The bad reasons a company may have for M&As are to:

■ increase earnings per share (eps)
■ build empires by buying companies rather than running them successfully.

The main justifications supporting the reasons for M&As are shown in Figure 16.3, and are each considered in the sections that follow.

Economic factors

If company managers believe that shareholder wealth will be enhanced then that is a good reason for going ahead with an acquisition. The managers therefore believe that the two companies t (target) and p (predator) will be worth more in combination than as separate entities. In other words, the present values (PV) of the future cash flows of the combined entity will be greater than the present values of the future cash flows of the individual entities, which may be represented as:

$$PV_{t\&p} > PV_t + PV_p$$

Synergy

The assets of two companies, and the activities in which two companies are engaged, may complement each other. Synergy is the creation of wealth due to an increase in the output of the combined companies over the sum of outputs of the separate companies, using the same resources. The shorthand commonly used to denote synergy is:

$$2 + 2 = 5$$

It may be noted that Rappaport's seven drivers of value may be used to quantify synergies derived from an acquisition (see Chapter 2).

Economies of scale

Economies of scale are similar to the synergy effect, but economies of scale are due to the benefits that occur because of the larger scale of operations after the merger or acquisition. Economies of scale are most likely in horizontal mergers because of the higher level of sales revenues achieved with a lower cost base. However, economies of scale may also occur in vertical mergers.

Elimination of inefficient management

A company may be poorly run because managers are satisfying their own requirements, instead of seeking to maximise shareholders' wealth (see the agency problem in Chapter 2). The share price may therefore decline and attract prospective buyers who believe that they may manage the company's assets more efficiently.

The elimination of ineffective management following a merger or an acquisition may be a more attractive option than a vote by shareholders to remove them. A vote by shareholders to remove ineffective management may also take a long time and may not be totally effective.

Entry to new markets

The achievement of growth by a company organically or internally may be too slow or too costly. Companies may want to develop new areas by product, business type, or geographically. To achieve these aims, a merger or an acquisition may be a quicker option. It may also be a cheaper option because, for example, there will be no costs of acquiring new premises, and additional personnel and marketing costs.

This strategy is particularly popular in the retail trade where starting from scratch is particularly costly and time-consuming. An example was Iceland's acquisition of Bejam in 1987. Through that acquisition Iceland was able to break into the North of England geographical market instead of competing there with Bejam from a zero base.

Critical mass

Smaller businesses may merge to achieve critical mass. Small companies may lack credibility because of their:

- small size, which usually means they have a shortage of buying power, knowledge, etc.
- lack of resources for research and development, in terms of funding and specialist skills
- lack of investment in brands, with possibly no brands developed at all.

Merging companies can pool resources to provide a critical mass to finance the above requirements. Smaller companies involved in such mergers may then take advantage of an existing brand and an existing knowledge base.

Growth

When businesses have successfully moved through their start-up phase and are reaching the growth stage they may find it hard to grow further organically. A takeover provides a quick solution to provide further growth. Note British American Tobacco (BAT), which took over Allied Dunbar and Eagle Star, both financial institutions, as part of their growth strategy, using surplus cash.

An alternative for a cash rich mature company, as we have already discussed in Chapter 15, is to return funds to shareholders through a share re-purchase or by paying shareholders a special dividend.

Market share or market power

Companies may use horizontal mergers or takeovers to increase their market share. Swallowing up the competition therefore gives such businesses the ability to earn monopoly profits.

Companies may use vertical integration to increase their buying power in raw materials and distribution resources. They may do this either through merger or takeover of customer or supplier companies (vertical forward or vertical backward integration).

However, a legislative obstacle of referral to the Monopolies and Mergers Commission may cause financial damage and damage to the reputation of a company. Time may therefore be lost and any advantages eroded or eliminated because the price of the deal may increase, and very high legal fees may be incurred.

Risk reduction

A company may acquire another company in a different line of business. Such diversification may be justified in terms of reducing shareholder risk. Note the example of a business that sells both ice cream and umbrellas in order to reduce total overall business risk. When the weather is hot and sunny, people will buy ice cream, but they will not need to buy umbrellas; when the weather is cold and rainy, people will need to buy umbrellas, but they are less likely to buy ice cream.

If a company is involved in many different businesses then the volatility in its levels of profits and cash may also be smoothed. An example is a conglomerate takeover. The many examples of conglomerate takeovers in the 1980s and 1990s showed tremendous growth in eps and cash flow. However, as we have already discussed earlier in this chapter, although eps may be increased it is not necessarily true that the share price will also increase. Conglomerates have historically not added value for shareholders and it is often the case that cash surpluses are returned to shareholders for their investment elsewhere, rather than being invested in new projects within the conglomerates themselves.

Excess funds

Some companies may build up large amounts of cash that may not be earning sufficient returns to meet the expectations of shareholders. GEC/Marconi, for example (see Mini case 16.3), did just that through the 1980s and 1990 by building up cash excesses, which were surplus to their growth requirements.

Mini case 16.3

GEC (re-named Marconi in 1999) during the 1980s and 1990s was a cash rich, mature company that City analysts felt should be returning funds to the shareholders. But Marconi wanted to reverse its mature position back into the growth phase by investing in the high-tech, fast-growing dot.com and telecoms industry. It used its surplus cash to make acquisitions in this industrial sector, rather than return it to shareholders. However, it went further than this and took on high levels of debt to finance even further acquisitions. In the early 2000s, the dot.com and telecoms industry collapsed and this also resulted in Marconi's gradual collapse and decline. Effective from 1 January 2006, the Marconi name and most of the assets were acquired by the Swedish company Ericsson, with Marconi still used as a brand within Ericsson. The remainder of the Marconi company was renamed telent plc.

As a mature business, Marconi should not have been funded totally by equity, but then when it reversed its cycle into an industry with high business risk to become a growth company it should not have become highly geared by taking on such high levels of debt. It was perhaps an example of a company trying to do the right things, but doing them in the wrong way.

If companies are cash rich but sufficient numbers of appropriate value-adding new projects cannot be found in which to invest, then excess funds may be more usefully invested in the acquisition of other companies. Rather than following Marconi's example, acquisitions necessarily require consideration of the appropriate relationships between risk and return, and the matching of such investments with the appropriate types of funding.

Financial motives in M&As

There are some further motives for acquisitions, which may be divided into financial motives, and also managerial motives considered in the following section. We will first consider four financial motives, which relate to:

- target company undervaluation
- corporation tax
- unemployed tax shields
- earnings per share – 'bootstrapping'.

Target company undervaluation

One justification of a takeover may be that the target company is considered to be a bargain. The target company may be perceived as being undervalued in the market because its share price is low. The implication of this may be that the capital markets are not totally efficient, or are viewed as inefficient, if the share price does not reflect the value or the potential value of the business.

Even if capital markets are generally seen as efficient, some companies may be difficult to value with certainty so there is a further possibility of undervaluation.

Corporation tax

A company may have run out of carried forward tax losses to utilise against current and future years' profits. Therefore, this may result in it paying out a high proportion of its profits in tax.

The tax benefits from unused capital allowances in a target company may therefore be considered for utilisation by a takeover company. The target company may, for example, be making losses or low profits but may have high levels of unused tax allowances.

Unemployed tax shields

A low-geared company may have a high proportion of its capital in equity or it may be totally financed with equity. Such a company may therefore want to acquire a tax shield or increase its own tax shield to reduce its tax liability. It may achieve this by merging with, or taking over, a highly geared company. Such a highly geared target company will have a high level of debt and therefore be making high interest payments.

Bootstrapping

An acquiring company, which is seeking to take over another company, may have a higher P/E ratio compared with the company it is seeking to take over, the target company. The acquiring company may therefore increase its overall combined earnings by a greater proportion than its increase in share capital if the takeover is financed by a share-for-share issue (see Worked example 16.2). This type of activity, where a company tries to boost its eps through acquisition, is called 'bootstrapping'.

Worked example 16.2

The following data relates to the share capital of two companies A, the acquiring company, and B the target company:

Company	A	B
number of ordinary shares	200m	25m
earnings	£20m	£5m
eps	10p	20p

Company A has proposed a deal in which it may offer to company B shareholders 10m shares in company A for 25m shares in company B.

The data relating to the combined entity AB will then be:

Company	AB
number of ordinary shares	210m
earnings	£25m
eps	11.9p

The post-acquisition eps is therefore higher than the pre-acquisition eps of company A, although it is lower than the pre-acquisition eps of company B.

How would you generally distinguish between 'good' and 'bad' motives for M&As?

Managerial motives in M&As

There may be M&A situations in which the shareholders' wealth maximisation objective is secondary to managers' personal objectives in wishing to enhance their own positions. In such situations, the basis of such takeovers may therefore be a manifestation of the agency problem between shareholders and managers or directors. The motives behind such takeovers may be to increase managers':

- emoluments – salary, car, bonus, pension, club membership, etc.
- power – a seat on the main board of directors, and wider responsibility
- security – creating a situation in which they are unlikely to lose their jobs – managers may believe, rightly or wrongly, that they will be more secure in a larger organisation.

From a shareholder perspective, of course, these types of takeover cannot be justified. If a takeover does go ahead on this basis then the underlying agency problem may be overcome through the introduction of an executive share option scheme. If directors and managers become shareholders then in theory they should have the same objective as all other shareholders – the maximisation of shareholder wealth.

Target company valuation

When a company is considering a takeover of, or a merger with, another company, it must carry out an appraisal of the company in terms of what it may be worth, as well as what sort of fit and synergy effects the deal will provide. The takeover bid price offered may then be an estimated 'fair value' in excess of, for example, the current market share price. What the target company may be worth can be considered using one of many different approaches. There are a number of ways in which the estimated fair value may be determined.

The three broad approaches to company valuation are:

- stock market valuation of the company's shares
- valuation of the company's assets
- valuation of the company's future earnings or cash flows – a going concern valuation.

Stock market valuation

The valuation of a company's shares may be based on the stock market valuation at the current market price. This method is very simple to use. It involves the multiplication of the number of ordinary shares issued by the company by the current market share price. Whether or not the result is a 'fair price' depends on the efficiency of the stock market.

This method may be a useful starting point, but may not be a 'fair price' because:

- the share price may reflect only infrequent trading in the shares, and the volume of trading in shares may greatly affect the share price
- the company may be a private limited (Ltd) company and therefore not quoted on a stock exchange
- post-acquisition benefits are ignored, which are based on the intentions of the acquiring company.

Worked example 16.3 illustrates a stock market valuation of Flatco plc.

Worked example 16.3

The 2012 balance sheet, income statement, and additional information for Flatco plc are shown in Figures 8.3, 8.4, and 8.5 in Chapter 8.

Predco plc is negotiating its acquisition of Flatco plc and its directors are considering its valuation using a variety of methods. The financial data relating to Predco plc for the same period is as follows:

Profit after tax	£570,000
WACC	17%
P/E ratio	12.5

The directors of Predco plc believe that the company will continue to increase its profit after tax by 3% per annum for the foreseeable future as a result of economies of scale and synergies obtained from the takeover. Many of Flatco plc's processes use identical equipment to Predco and so the directors also believe that they may sell off a number of assets for £250,000 during 2013.

We will consider Flatco plc in terms of its stock market valuation.

$$\text{number of ordinary shares in issue} = \frac{\text{balance sheet value of ordinary shares}}{\text{nominal value of each ordinary share}}$$
$$= £1,200,000/£1$$
$$= 1.2\text{m shares}$$
$$\text{stock market valuation of Flatco plc} = \text{number of ordinary shares in issue}$$
$$\times \text{market price per share}$$
$$= 1.2\text{m} \times £2.75$$
$$= £3,300,000$$

The three main asset-based approaches to company valuation are shown in Figure 16.4.

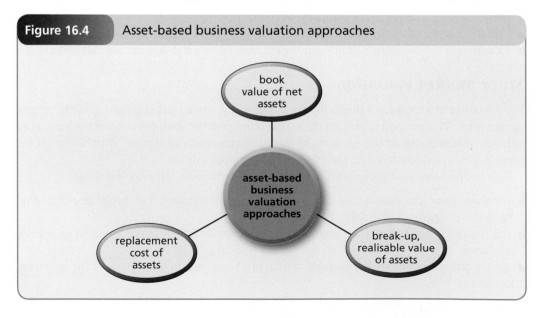

Figure 16.4 Asset-based business valuation approaches

Book value of net assets valuation

If we consider the net book value of a company's non-current assets in its balance sheet, together with its working capital, and then deduct the value of its loans, debentures, etc., the result is a balance sheet total of net assets. This may be represented as:

book value of net assets valuation
= non-current assets + net current assets − long-term debt

There are a number of obvious limitations to this method of valuation. First, asset valuations based on historical costs, which may be factual and available directly from the balance sheet, do not necessarily reflect the current valuation of assets. There may also be prior charges on assets, made by lenders to the company.

Second, the valuation of inventories may be unreliable or unrealistic because of type of valuation method that may have been used, and it may not always be possible to recover the full cost of inventories through sales.

Third, the valuation of trade receivables may be unreliable or unrealistic because of the particular doubtful debts policy adopted and the collectability of the accounts receivable at the values shown in the balance sheet.

Fourth, intangible non-current assets such as goodwill, human capital, and brand names, are ignored, unlike some other models like those based on earnings or dividend yield, or the super profits model (see later).

Fifth, costs such as development expenditure would also have a value related to future profits, which may be much higher than their value as assets, currently stated in the company's balance sheet.

Sixth, not all liabilities may have been quantified and there may be hidden liabilities.

Even if the book value of net assets were totally reliable it would really be only a lower limit valuation. The net assets model may be used as a measure of security in a share value. The value of shares in a particular class is equal to the net tangible assets attributable to that class of share.

Worked example 16.4

Using the data from Worked example 16.3 the directors of Predco plc may calculate a book value of net assets valuation of a share in Flatco plc.

	£000
total assets less current liabilities	3,543
less	
intangible non-current assets	(416)
	3,127
less	
long-term debt	(173)
	2,954
net asset value	£2,954,000
number of ordinary shares	1.2m
value per ordinary share	= £2,954,000/1,200,000
	= £2.46 per share

It can be seen from the above calculation that the valuation of the company based on the historical costs of its book assets is around 10% less than the stock market valuation in Worked example 16.3.

Break-up, realisable value of assets valuation

As an alternative to net assets valuation, assets may be valued according to their net realisable value. However, valuation is not necessarily a simple matter. The realisable value of the target company's assets is the residual amount that could be realised if they were sold separately on the open market, after deducting any liquidation costs and other liabilities. If the market value, that is the total value of the shares, is below the break-up value, which is the market value of the individual assets within the company, then the company is undervalued.

Replacement cost of assets valuation

The costs of acquiring the separate assets of a target company may be determined on an open market basis. These are the costs to replace the assets, rather than what they could be sold for. The advantage of this method is that replacement cost valuations are more relevant than historical cost book valuations or current realisable valuations.

Disadvantages are that this method ignores goodwill, and it is usually difficult to identify separate assets, like separate individual factories, machinery, etc., and determine their replacement cost. Assets may also be complementary and therefore their separate valuation may not be totally realistic; how much use is a left shoe to a two-legged person if they don't also have the right shoe to accompany it?

The six main earnings-based, or income-based, or going concern, approaches to company valuation are shown in Figure 16.5.

Capitalised earnings valuation

The capitalised earnings method calculates the value of a company by capitalising annual maintainable expected earnings, using its earnings yield (earnings per share divided by the current share price, which is the reciprocal of the P/E ratio) or return on investment (ROI).

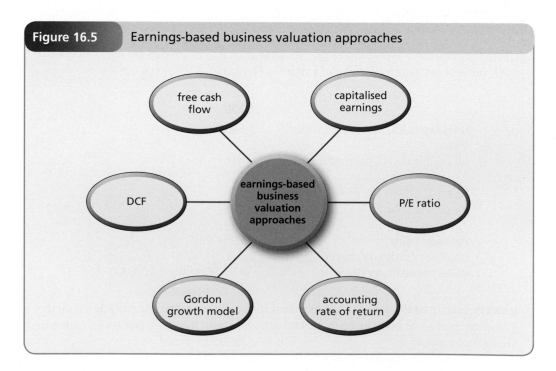

| Figure 16.5 | Earnings-based business valuation approaches |

Expected earnings may be estimated using average historical earnings and adding an uplift for synergy and economies of scale. This, of course, is very subjective.

The required earnings yield used to capitalise earnings should reflect the size of the business and the type of industry. The choice of required earnings yield may also be an estimate, rather than a precise calculation.

Worked example 16.5

Using the data from Worked example 16.3 the directors of Predco plc may calculate a capitalised earnings valuation of Flatco plc.

$$\text{capitalised earnings value} = \frac{\text{annual maintainable expected earnings}}{\text{required earnings yield}}$$

$$\text{required earnings yield} = \text{eps/share price}$$

$$\text{Flatco plc required earnings yield} = \frac{£0.45 \times 100}{£2.75} = 16.364\%$$

(which is also the reciprocal of its P/E ratio: $1 \times 100/6.11$)

$$\text{Flatco plc capitalised earnings value} = \frac{£540,000}{0.16364} \text{ (assuming that current earnings are}$$

$$\text{equal to its maintainable expected earnings)}$$

$$= £3,300,000 \text{ (rounded up)}$$

Price/earnings (P/E) valuation

The P/E method of valuation multiplies the target company's distributable earnings by an appropriate P/E ratio (the company market valuation divided by distributable earnings).

Possible P/E ratios which may be used for this type of valuation include:

■ the predator, or acquiring company, P/E ratio
■ the target company P/E ratio
■ a weighted average combination of the predator company P/E and the target company P/E ratio.

If the target company's P/E ratio is used, the resultant valuation will be the same as a capitalised earnings valuation of the target company. The P/E ratio used normally depends on who is making the valuation and for what purpose.

The P/E ratio model is a method of valuing a large controlling interest in a company or a whole company, where the owners can decide on the dividend and profit retention policy. It is an earnings-based valuation, as can be seen from the relationship:

$$\text{P/E ratio} = \frac{\textbf{market value of shares}}{\textbf{earnings per share (eps)}}$$

This relationship can be rewritten as:

$$\textbf{market value} = \textbf{eps} \times \textbf{P/E ratio}$$

where

$$eps = \frac{profit\ after\ tax\ (PAT)\ -\ preference\ share\ dividends}{number\ of\ ordinary\ shares\ in\ issue}$$

and therefore

$$market\ value = \frac{(PAT\ -\ preference\ share\ dividends)\ \times\ P/E\ ratio}{number\ of\ ordinary\ shares\ in\ issue}$$

The growth component reduces during the life cycle of a company as expansion of the business slows down. The P/E ratio reflects any expected future growth of a company, which is already incorporated in the share price. The share price moves only with respect to changes in expectations of future growth.

A growth of the P/E ratio is not a guarantee of a rise of the share price. A high P/E ratio is a signal to company managers that investors expect a future growth of eps. Low dividends and high reinvestments mean that managers expect growth. A lower P/E ratio is a signal that prospects of growth are decreasing. Growing dividends per share and low reinvestment is not the basis for growth.

Worked example 16.6

Using the data from Worked example 16.3 the directors of Predco plc may calculate a price/earnings ratio valuation of Flatco plc. Predco plc must decide on a suitable P/E ratio and then multiply this by Flatco plc's eps. Flatco plc's eps may be its historical eps or its expected future eps. Predco may also use one of a number of P/E ratios: Predco plc's P/E ratio; Flatco plc's P/E ratio; the weighted average of the P/E ratios of the two companies. We will consider valuations of Flatco plc using its historical (2012) eps and the three different P/E ratios.

Predco plc P/E ratio

Market value of Flatco plc = Flatco 2012 eps × Predco P/E × number of Flatco ordinary shares

= £0.45 × 12.5 × 1,200,000

= £6,750,000

Flatco plc P/E ratio

Market value of Flatco plc = Flatco 2012 eps × Flatco P/E × number of Flatco ordinary shares

= £0.45 × 6.11 × 1,200,000

= £3,300,000 (rounded up, and equal to the capitalised earnings valuation)

Weighted average P/E ratio

The combined earnings
(profit after tax) = £540,000 + £570,000

= £1,110,000

$$\text{Flatco plc P/E ratio weighted by combined earnings} = \frac{6.11 \times £540,000}{£1,110,000}$$

$$\text{Predco plc P/E ratio weighted by combined earnings} = \frac{12.5 \times £570,000}{£1,110,000}$$

$$\text{Weighted average P/E ratio} = \frac{6.11 \times £540,000}{£1,110,000} + \frac{12.5 \times £570,000}{£1,110,000}$$

$$= 2.97 + 6.42$$

$$= 9.39$$

$$\text{Market value of Flatco plc} = £0.45 \times 9.39 \times 1,200,000$$

$$= £5,070,600$$

Accounting rate of return model

The accounting rate of return (ARR) model may be used with regard to takeovers to assess the maximum an acquiring company can afford to pay, because it considers the post-acquisition profits.

The ARR model is different from the P/E ratio method, which is concerned with a market rate of return required by investors. The ARR model considers the accounting rate of return (or ROCE) required from the company whose shares are to be valued:

$$\text{market value} = \frac{\text{estimated future profits}}{\text{required ROCE}}$$

For a takeover bid, profits will usually be adjusted for changed circumstances following the takeover, such as:

- directors' pay
- interest payable
- the impacts of post-takeover rationalisation and the engagement of new management.

Gordon growth model valuation

The Gordon growth model, or dividend growth model, may be used to value a company by calculating the present value of future dividends accruing to its shares, which are expected to grow each year. The company valuation is calculated using the formula:

$$\frac{v \times (1 + G)}{(K_e - G)}$$

where

v is the current dividend payment

G is an annual dividend growth percentage, calculated using the historical values of the target company's dividends

K_e is the cost of equity or shareholders' return of the target company using the CAPM.

In practice, there may be a great deal of difficulty in estimating an annual dividend growth percentage for the target company.

Discounted cash flow (DCF) valuation

The DCF valuation model is an appropriate method to use when one company intends to acquire another company, and to then provide further investment in order to improve future profits. A DCF method of company valuation assumes that the maximum amount the predator company would pay for the target company is the difference between the present values of its pre- and post-acquisition cash flows. This may be represented as:

> **present values of the target (t) and predator (p) companies' post-acquisition cash flows**
> **less**
> **present values of the predator (p) company's pre-acquisition cash flows**

or

$$PV_{t\&p} - PV_p$$

The model normally uses after-tax cash flows and an after-tax cost of capital (WACC). Cash flows net of tax, and ignoring any purchase consideration (acquisition price), are discounted to calculate the NPV. The NPV is then the maximum purchase price that should be paid.

If estimates of future cash flows are not readily available, they may be determined using an approximation of cash flow like EVA (economic value added). We discussed EVA in Chapter 8, which is calculated by deducting the cost of using the company's assets from its profit after tax. The cost of using the company's assets is calculated by multiplying its WACC by an evaluation of its net assets.

In theory, the DCF method is the preferred business valuation method. It is based on cash flows rather than profits, or earnings. The earnings valuation approaches we have looked at are based on accounting profit, which is an extremely subjective measure. This is because the determination of profit is reliant on the many accounting conventions and standards, and the various alternative asset valuation method choices available to companies. The capital markets are not totally efficient and even if they were a stock market valuation may rarely provide a 'fair' value of a company. A company's share price is based on many factors, including the information available about the company, the reports of financial analysts, the demand for its shares, and the volume of trading.

When we looked at investment appraisal in Chapter 6 we saw that if a company invests in a project that generates a positive NPV then it will increase the wealth of the business by that amount. Elsewhere in this book we have discussed how this increase in corporate value may be reflected in shareholder value. The value of a company may be considered in terms of the total NPV of each of its investment projects. The acquisition of another business is the same as an investment in any other project. It should be appraised using DCF in the same way as any other long-term project to determine the value being added to the business.

The accuracy of any valuation method is dependent on the accuracy and reliability of the data, and who is making the valuation, and for what purpose. Although DCF may be the preferred method it is not without its difficulties, which relate mainly to:

- quantifying the synergy and economies of scale effects on estimated future cash flows
- deciding on future cash flow time horizons – five years, or multiples of five years are usually used
- deciding on an appropriate discount rate – the predator's WACC may be used, but not if the target company has significantly different risk characteristics, in which case the CAPM may be used to allow for the systematic risk of the target company.

Worked example 16.7

Using the data from Worked example 16.3 the directors of Predco plc may use the DCF method to compare the present value of the future cash flows of the combined entity with the present values of its future cash flows if the acquisition did not go ahead. Distributable earnings (profit after tax) may be taken as an approximation of cash flows:

Present value of future cash flows – no acquisition

Predco plc current distributable earnings   = £570,000

discount factor = Predco plc WACC   = 17%

$$\text{present value of future expected cash flows} = \frac{£570,000}{0.17}$$
$$= £3,352,941$$

Present value of future cash flows – with acquisition

Predco plc post-acquisition distributable earnings = £570,000 + £540,000

which it is assumed will increase in subsequent years by 3% per annum.

   The present values of future cash flows can then be calculated using Predco plc's WACC, adjusted for the inflation rate of 3% applied to distributable earnings.

 cash flow from the disposal of surplus assets during 2013 = £250,000

The present value of the disposal proceeds can be calculated by multiplying it by the discount factor for 2013 (year one) using Predco plc's WACC rate of 17%, which is 0.855.

$$\text{present value of post-acquisition cash flows} = \frac{£1,110,000 \times 1.03}{(0.17 - 0.03)} + (£250,000 \times 0.855)$$
$$= \frac{£1,143,300}{0.14} + £213,750$$
$$= £8,166,428 + £213,750$$
$$= £8,380,178$$

The difference between the present values of the future cash flows assuming acquisition and no acquisition are:

$$£8,380,178$$
$$\text{less } \underline{£3,352,941}$$

maximum price that should be paid by Predco plc for Flatco plc = $\underline{£5,027,237}$

Free cash flow model

Free cash flow is a widely used financial term that is used with many different meanings. In Chapter 1 we explored the differences between profit and cash flow. Operating profit differs from operating cash flow because:

- depreciation reduces profit but does not represent outflows of cash
- working capital is required because sales revenues and expenses (or costs or expenditure) are not necessarily accounted for when cash transfers occur, and inventories are not always used as soon as they are purchased,

and at the net profit level there are further differences between profit and cash flow. This is because revenues and expenses do not include all the events that impact on the financial position of the company, for example, investments in assets, interest, taxation, dividends, and the issue of new shares and loans.

Here we will use a standard definition of free cash flow that is very similar to the statement of cash flows example we saw in Figure 8.7 in Chapter 8. This is illustrated in Figure 16.6. The present value of a company's free cash flows, calculated as shown in Figure 16.6, may be used to provide a business valuation using an appropriate cost of capital, similar to the calculations we saw in Worked example 16.7.

In practice, an actual valuation of a company may be determined using shareholder value analysis (SVA) developed by Alfred Rappaport (Rappaport, A (1986) *Creating Shareholder Value: The New Standard for Business Performance*, London: Free Press). SVA is an extension of the use of free cash flows, and assumes that the value of a company may be determined from the NPV of its future free cash flows using an appropriate cost of capital. The SVA calculation usually involves the use of detailed estimates of a company's free cash flows for a planning period of say five or ten years and a 'terminal' value. The terminal value may be taken as the value of the company's net assets at the end of the planning period. Instead of using a terminal value, the company's free cash flow for each year after the planning period may be estimated in detail. Alternatively, the terminal value may be based on, for example, the fifth, eighth, or

| Figure 16.6 | The elements of free cash flow |

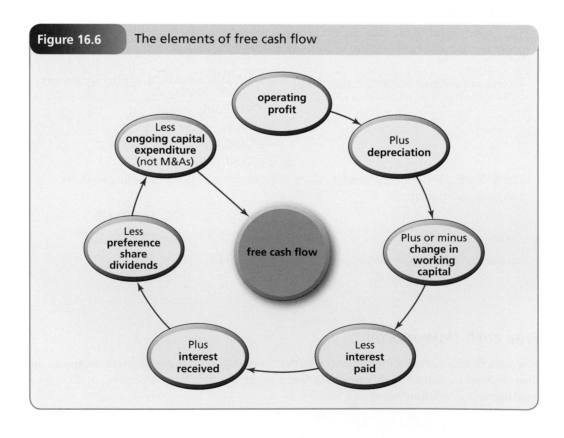

tenth year's free cash flow, and calculated using a similar formula to the Gordon growth model. The terminal value equals:

$$\frac{C_t \times (1 + G)}{(r - G)}$$

where

C_t is the free cash flow for the last year in the planning period (for example year 10)
r is the discount rate
G is the long-term sustainable growth rate after the last year in the planning period.

SVA may be used for company valuation, but it may also be used to calculate additional value created from alternative strategies. Used in this way, which is very similar to the use of EVA (see Chapter 8), there is no need to determine a terminal value. The use of SVA for the valuation of a business is illustrated in Worked example 16.8.

Worked example 16.8

Jalfreda plc has forecast its free cash flows for years 1 to 10 as follows:

Year	1	2	3	4	5	6	7	8	9	10
£m	−1.0	−1.2	−1.1	0.5	0.7	0.9	2.5	4.7	6.8	7.2

Jalfreda has estimated its long-term sustainable growth rate after year 10 at 4% per annum. Its cost of capital is 12%, which may be used as a discount rate.

Let's use free cash flow to provide a valuation of Jalfreda plc.

The terminal value based on Jalfreda's year 10 cash flow may be calculated as follows:

$$\frac{\text{free cash flow for year 10} \times (1 + \text{the long-term growth rate})}{\text{discount rate} - \text{long-term growth rate}}$$

$$= \frac{£7.2m \times (1 + 4\%)}{12\% - 4\%}$$

$$= \frac{£7.2m \times 1.04}{0.08}$$

$$= £93.6m$$

The present values of Jalfreda plc's free cash flows, including the year 10 terminal value of £93.6m, can be calculated as follows:

Year	Free cash flows £m	Discount factor at 12%	Present value of free cash flows £m
1	−1.0	0.893	−0.893
2	−1.2	0.797	−0.956
3	−1.1	0.712	−0.783

(continued)

4	0.5	0.636	0.318
5	0.7	0.567	0.397
6	0.9	0.507	0.456
7	2.5	0.452	1.130
8	4.7	0.404	1.899
9	6.8	0.361	2.455
10	100.8	0.322	32.458
	(7.2 + 93.6)	total present value	£36.481m

(Note that in this example we have used discount factors calculated to three decimal places instead of to two decimal places as shown in the tables in Appendix 1.)

The total present value of Jalfreda plc's free cash flows is £36,481,000, which may be used as a basis for the valuation of the company.

Other reasons for share valuation

We have seen how a takeover bid price offered may be an estimated 'fair value' in excess of the current stock market share price valuation. Similarly, a proposed merger of companies may require an assessment of the share value of each company. The share prices of publicly quoted companies (plcs) may be quoted on a stock exchange or the Alternative Investment Market (AIM), in which case a stock market valuation of such companies is readily available.

However, both quoted and unquoted companies may need to be valued for a number of other reasons in addition to takeover and merger valuations:

- shares may need to be used to supply collateral, or security, for loans
- a private limited (Ltd) company may want to 'go public', that is floated on a stock exchange or the AIM, and therefore needs to fix a share issue price for the initial public offering (IPO)
- since there is not a ready market for shares in a limited (Ltd) company, its shares may need to be valued to be sold
- individual holdings of shares may need to be valued for inheritance tax or capital gains tax purposes
- a subsidiary within a group of companies may need to be valued if it is to be sold off.

Some further share valuation models

One or other of the business valuation methods we have considered above may be used for reasons other than takeovers and mergers, as appropriate. There are also some further valuation methods, three of which are illustrated in Figure 16.7.

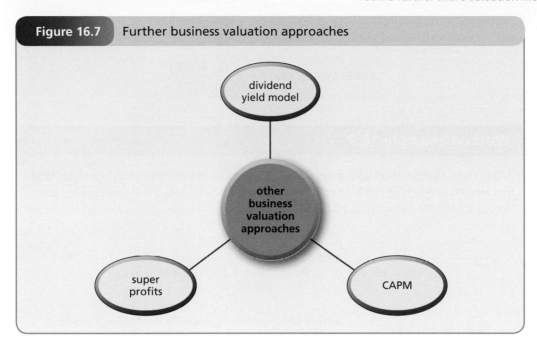

Figure 16.7   Further business valuation approaches

Dividend yield model

The dividend yield model is suitable for the valuation of small shareholdings in unquoted companies. It is based on the principle that small shareholders are mainly interested in dividends, rather than capital gains from the increase in value of their shares. The market valuation of a company's shares may be represented as:

$$\text{market value} = \frac{\text{dividend per share}}{\text{expected dividend yield \%}}$$

assuming a constant level of future dividends. The multiplication of this value by the number of ordinary shares in issue gives a market valuation of the company.

Alternatively, the Gordon dividend growth model, discussed earlier, may be used if future dividend growth may be predicted. If a dividend method is used for shareholders who wish to sell their shares, the valuation offer price compensates them for the increases in future dividends they would be giving up.

Capital Asset Pricing Model (CAPM)

The CAPM (see Chapter 5) may be used to value shares for a stock market listing by establishing a required equity yield. The market valuation of a company's shares may be determined by dividing its cost of equity into its dividend (which may be adjusted for any expected future dividend growth).

$$\text{cost of equity} = \text{risk-free rate of return} \\ + [\beta \times (\text{market rate} - \text{risk-free rate of return})]$$

or

$$K_e = R_f + \beta(R_m - R_f)$$

If we assume a current dividend of v and a future dividend growth rate of G% per annum then using the Gordon dividend growth model:

$$\text{market valuation} = \frac{v \times (1 + G\%)}{(K_e - G\%)}$$

Worked example 16.9

Using the data from Worked example 16.3 the directors of Predco plc may use the CAPM to value Flatco plc. The risk-free rate of return R_f is 1% per annum and the market rate of return R_m is 2.5% per annum. Flatco plc's beta factor $\beta = 1.13$.

$$\text{Using}\quad K_e = R_f + \beta \times (R_m - R_f)$$
$$\text{Flatco plc cost of equity} = 1\% + 1.13 \times (2.5\% - 1\%)$$
$$= 2.695\%$$

$$\text{Flatco plc market value} = \frac{\text{current 2012 dividend}}{\text{cost of equity}} \text{(assuming no dividend growth)}$$
$$= \frac{\pounds 70{,}000}{0.02695}$$
$$= \pounds 2{,}597{,}403$$

It should be noted that this valuation is lower than Flatco plc's book value of its net assets valuation of £2,954,000 at 31 December 2012, and lower than the valuation based on its share price 31 December 2012 of £2.75 × 1,200,000 = £3,300,000.

Super profits model

A rather out-of-fashion method, the super profits method applies a 'fair return' to the net tangible assets. But what is a fair return? This model then compares the 'fair return' with expected profits. Any excess of fair return over expected profits, the super profits, is used to calculate goodwill. Goodwill is therefore taken to be a fixed number of years of super profits. The market value is then calculated by adding goodwill to the company's tangible assets valuation. This method is now rarely used and has a number of disadvantages:

- difficulty and subjectivity of establishing a 'fair return'
- profit numbers are subjective and therefore not ideal
- the number of years of super profits used is arbitrary.

Progress check 16.4

Outline in general why there may be so many different methods used to provide a valuation of a business.

Mini case 16.4 compares the market share price at 25 February 2012 of a major UK plc, Tesco, and compares this with a number of alternative valuations, which we have discussed above.

Mini case 16.4

The financial statements and note 27 to the accounts of Tesco plc for the years to 25 February 2012 and 26 February 2011 are shown in Figures 16.8 and 16.9 below.
The market price of Tesco shares 25 February 2012 was 318.2p (26 February 2011: 406,5p).

Figure 16.8 — Tesco plc consolidated balance sheet as at 25 February 2012

Tesco plc
Consolidated balance sheet as at

	25 February 2012 £m	26 February 2011 £m
Non-current assets		
Goodwill and other intangible assets	4,618	4,338
Property, plant and equipment	25,710	24,398
Investment property	1,991	1,863
Investments in joint ventures and associates	423	316
Other investments	1,526	938
Loans and advances to customers	1,901	2,127
Derivative financial instruments	1,726	1,139
Deferred tax assets	23	48
	37,918	35,167
Current assets		
Inventories	3,598	3,162
Trade and other receivables	2,657	2,330
Loans and advances to customers	2,502	2,514
Derivative financial instruments	41	148
Current tax assets	7	4
Short-term investments	1,243	1,022
Cash and cash equivalents	2,305	2,428
	12,353	11,608
Assets of the disposal group and non-current assets classified as held for sale	510	431
	12,863	12,039
Current liabilities		
Trade and other payables	(11,234)	(10,484)
Financial liabilities:		
Borrowings	(1,838)	(1,386)
Derivative financial instruments and other liabilities	(128)	(255)
Customer deposits and deposits by banks	(5,465)	(5,110)
Current tax liabilities	(416)	(432)
Provisions	(99)	(64)
	(19,180)	(17,731)
Liabilities of the disposal group classified as held for sale	(69)	-
Net current liabilities	**(6,386)**	**(5,692)**
Non-current liabilities		
Financial liabilities:		
Borrowings	(9,911)	(9,689)
Derivative financial instruments and other liabilities	(688)	(600)
Post-employment benefit obligations	(1,872)	(1,356)
Deferred tax liabilities	(1,160)	(1,094)
Provisions	(100)	(113)
	(13,731)	(12,852)
Net assets	**17,801**	**16,623**
Equity		
Share capital	402	402
Share premium	4,964	4,896
Other reserves	40	40
Retained earnings	12,369	11,197
Equity attributable to owners of the parent	17,775	16,535
Non-controlling interests	26	88
Total equity	**17,801**	**16,623**

Figure 16.9	Tesco plc consolidated income statement for the year to 25 February 2012 and Note 27 to the accounts

Tesco plc
Consolidated income statement for the 52 weeks ending

	25 February 2012 £m	26 February 2011 £m
Continuing operations		
Revenue	64,539	60,455
Cost of sales	(59,278)	(55,330)
Gross profit	**5,261**	5,125
Administrative expenses	(1,652)	(1,640)
Profits arising on property-related items	376	432
Operating profit	**3,985**	3,917
Share of post-tax profits of joint ventures and associates	91	57
Finance income	176	150
Finance costs	(417)	(483)
Profit before tax	**3,835**	3,641
Taxation	(879)	(864)
Profit for the year from continuing operations	2,956	2,777
Discontinued operations		
Loss for the year from discontinued operations	(142)	(106)
Profit for the year	**2,814**	2,671
Earnings per share from continuing and discontinued operations		
Basic	34.98p	33.10p
Diluted	34.88p	32.94p

Tesco plc
Notes to the accounts

Note 27 Called up share capital

Ordinary shares of 5p each

	2012 Number	2012 £m	2011 Number	2011 £m
Allotted, called up and fully paid:				
At beginning of the year	8,046,468,092	402	7,985,044,057	399
Share options exercises	23,490,825	1	36,535,102	1
Share bonus awards issues	32,656,313	2	24,888,933	2
Shares purchased for cancellation	(70,802,785)	(3)	–	–
At end of the year	8,031,812,445	402	8,046,468,092	402

Tesco plc valuations as at 25 February 2012

Market capitalisation

25 February 2012 £25.54bn = 8,032m shares × 318.2p, or £3.18 per share
26 February 2011 £32.75bn = 8,046m shares × 406.5p, or £4.07 p per share

➡

Book value of net assets

	£m
Total net assets	
(non-current assets – net current liabilities)	
(£37,918 − £6,386)	31,532
Less intangible non-current assets	4,618
	26,914
Less long-term debt	9,911
	17,003

At 25 February 2012 Tesco had 8,032m shares in issue, therefore the value per share would be

£17,003m/8,032m = £2.12 per share (compared with the actual share price of £3.18)

Capitalised earnings valuation

$$\text{capitalised earnings value} = \text{annual maintainable expected earnings}/\text{required earnings yield}$$
$$\text{required earnings yield} = \text{eps/market share price}$$

At 25 February 2012 eps = 34.98p per share, and the quoted share price was 318.2p per share. Therefore the required earnings yield would be:

$$(34.98p \times 100)/318.2p = 10.99\%$$

Profits on ordinary activities after tax can be used as an approximation of the annual maintainable expected earnings, therefore the capitalised earnings valuation would be:

£2,956m/0.1099 = £26.90bn
£26,900m/8,032m = £3.35 per share (compared with the actual share price of £3.18)

Dividend growth model valuation

Growth may be estimated using past dividends (the total of interim and final dividends) obtained from prior years reports' and accounts:

2008	10.90p
2009	11.96p
2010	13.05p
2011	14.46p
2012	14.76p

The annual growth rate G may be calculated over the four years as follows:

$$(1 + G)^4 = 14.76p/10.90p$$
$$(1 + G) = \sqrt[4]{14.76p/10.90p}$$
$$1 + G = 1.08$$
$$G = 0.08 \text{ or } 8\%$$

Using G = 8%, the market price of the shares on 25 February 2012 mv = 318.2p, and the current dividend v = 14.76p, we can estimate the required shareholders' return K_e, as follows:

$$\text{market valuation mv} = \frac{v \times (1 + G)}{(K_e - G)}$$

$$K_e = \frac{v \times (1 + G)}{mv} + G$$

$$K_e = \frac{14.76p \times 1.08}{318.2p} + 0.08$$

$$\text{estimated shareholder return } K_e = 0.13 \text{ or } 13\%$$

Share valuation without growth using the dividend valuation model

14.76p/13% = £1.13 per share (compared with the actual share price of £3.18)

Share valuation with growth using the Gordon growth model

$$\frac{14.76p \times 1.08}{(13\% - 8\%)} = £3.19 \text{ per share (compared with the actual share price of £3.18)}$$

Summary of key points

■ Mergers, or amalgamations, are now quite rare and what occurs more commonly are acquisitions, or takeovers.

■ In mergers and acquisitions (M&As) the combined expected present values of future cash flows of the combined companies should be more than the sum of the expected present values of future cash flows of the two separate companies.

■ M&As may occur as a result of horizontal integration, vertical integration, complementary resources, conglomerate takeover, and from the exploitation of market imperfections that have resulted in the market undervaluation of companies.

■ There are a number of 'good' and 'bad' reasons used to justify M&As.

■ The financial motives for M&As include taxation benefits, gains from target company undervaluation, and enhancement of eps.

■ Managerial motives for M&As result from managers' desire to enhance their own position with regard to emoluments, power, and security.

■ There are a large number of methods that may be used to value an M&A target company based broadly on the valuation of its shares, assets, future earnings or cash flows, and P/E ratios.

■ Businesses may need to be valued for a number of reasons other than M&As, for example for security for loans, or if a company wishes to be floated on a stock exchange.

Glossary of key terms

acquisition See takeover.

amalgamation See merger.

merger (or **amalgamation**) A merger (or amalgamation) is a business combination that results in the creation of a new reporting entity formed from the combining parties, in which the shareholders of the combining entities come together in a combination for the mutual sharing of the risks and benefits of the combined entity, and in which no party to the combination in substance obtains control over any other, or is otherwise seen to be dominant, whether by virtue of the proportion of its shareholders' rights in the combined entity, the influence of its directors, or otherwise (FRS6). A demerger takes place when the merger process is reversed, and separate entities emerge from the merged body.

takeover (or **acquisition**) A takeover (or acquisition) is the acquisition by a company of a controlling interest in the voting share capital of another company, usually achieved by the purchase of a majority of the voting shares.

Assessment material

Questions

Q16.1   Outline the ways in which a merger differs from a takeover.

Q16.2   How and why do mergers and acquisitions take place?

Q16.3   Explain the fundamental principles underlying M&As.

Q16.4   In what ways may market imperfections be exploited by takeover activity?

Q16.5   Outline the business and financial reasons for company mergers.

Q16.6   Describe six justifications for M&As.

Q16.7   Differentiate between the financial motives and managerial motives for M&As, and illustrate both with some examples.

Q16.8   Which Acts of Parliament and financial institutions monitor and control merger and acquisition activities in the UK?

Q16.9   Consider why a growth in eps may not necessarily be reflected in a growth in share price, and support this with examples.

Q16.10 Describe the motivation for takeovers and analyse why target companies often employ defence strategies in response to a hostile takeover.

Q16.11 Outline the reasons why shareholders may require valuations of their businesses.

Q16.12 Critically compare the use of net asset valuations and earnings valuations of companies.

Discussion points

D16.1   Discuss the likely winners and losers following the possible acquisition of Marks & Spencer plc by someone like Philip Green.

D16.2 Discuss the possible benefits to the economy of any country resulting from a high level of M&A activity.

D16.3 Discuss the possible behaviour of share prices during a merger, the impact of a merger announcement on the share prices of the two companies involved, and how this may be measured.

Exercises

Solutions are provided in Appendix 2 to all exercise numbers highlighted in colour.

Level I

E16.1   *Time allowed – 15 minutes*

A large group called Pitch plc has shown interest in acquiring the shares of Perfecto plc, a smaller company in the same industry. Perfecto plc is quoted on the AIM and its balance sheet as at 30 September 2012 is shown below:

Perfecto plc

Balance sheet as at 30 September 2012

	£000
Non-current assets	
Tangible	902
Intangible	203
Total non-current assets	1,105
Inventories	161
Trade receivables	284
Prepayments	295
Cash and cash equivalents	157
Total current assets	897
Total assets	2,002
Borrowings and finance leases	–
Trade payables	277
Income tax payable	70
Dividends payable	20
Accruals	10
Total current liabilities	377
Debenture	85
Trade payables	77
Provisions	103
Total non-current liabilities	265
Total liabilities	642
Net assets	1,360
Share capital	600
Share premium account	105
Retained earnings	655
Total equity	1,360

The profits on ordinary activities after tax for the past five years have been:

	£000
2012	150
2011	140
2010	160
2009	150
2008	130

Perfecto plc has paid dividends of £40,000 for each of the past five years. The company has forecast that its dividends will increase by 4% over subsequent years.

The nominal value of Perfecto plc's ordinary shares is £1 each, and its share price at 30 September 2012 was £1.84, and its P/E ratio 7.36 times.

The directors of Perfecto had the tangible non-current assets of the company valued at £1.8m at 30 September 2012 (not reflected in the balance sheet at that date).

Pitch plc's profit after tax for 2012 was £800,000, and its WACC 6%. Its P/E ratio at 30 September 2012 was 9 times. An investigation into the proposed takeover has determined incremental net cash flows, over and above that expected from the separate companies, may be achieved by the group following its acquisition of Perfecto plc, as follows:

	£000
2013	130
2014	130
2015	150
2016	100
2017	130

You are required to provide a valuation of Perfecto plc using the book value of its net assets.

E16.2   *Time allowed – 15 minutes*

Using the data from E16.1 provide a valuation of Perfecto plc using the replacement cost of its net assets.

E16.3   *Time allowed – 15 minutes*

Using the data from E16.1 provide a capitalised earnings valuation of Perfecto plc.

E16.4   *Time allowed – 15 minutes*

Using the data from E16.1 provide a P/E ratio valuation of Perfecto plc.

Level II

E16.5   *Time allowed – 15 minutes*

Using the data from E16.1 provide a DCF valuation of Perfecto plc.

E16.6   *Time allowed – 15 minutes*

Using the data from E16.1 provide a CAPM valuation of Perfecto plc. You may assume that Perfecto plc has a β factor of 1.2, and the risk-free rate of return is 1% per annum and the market rate of return is 6.5% per annum.

E16.7   *Time allowed – 15 minutes*

Horse plc is considering the acquisition of Cart plc. Horse plc has a current market value of £100,000,000. Cart plc has a current market value of £50,000,000. If the acquisition occurs, expected economies of scale will result in savings of £2,500,000 per annum for the foreseeable future. The required rate of return on both companies and the proposed combination is 10%. The transaction costs will amount to £2,000,000.

Calculate:

(i)   The present value of the gain from the merger.
(ii)   The value that would be created for Horse plc's shareholders if a cash offer of £70,000,000 is accepted by Cart plc's shareholders.

E16.8   *Time allowed – 30 minutes*

The Burns Group plc is investigating the viability of acquiring Allen Ltd, which is currently earning profits after tax of around £1,000,000 per annum. Burns Ltd's financial advisers consider that Allen's post-tax profits may be increased to £1,200,000 per annum following the acquisition. Each company in the Burns group has a target of earning a post-tax return on capital employed of 8%.

Required:

(i)   Calculate a valuation of Allen Ltd based on the accounting rate of return.
(ii)   Indicate how the Burns Group may negotiate an acceptable takeover price.
(iii) What are the advantages to Burns of using an ARR valuation?

E16.9   *Time allowed – 30 minutes*

Morecambe plc is considering taking over Wise Ltd, which has net tangible assets of £850,000 and current earnings of £110,000 per annum. Morecambe's directors believe that 9% per annum is a fair return in their industry.

Required:

(i)   Calculate a valuation of Wise Ltd based on the super-profits method and assuming goodwill is equal to four years' super-profits.
(ii)   What are the disadvantages to Morecambe plc's use of this method of valuation?

E16.10 *Time allowed – 30 minutes*

Porgy plc is a large electronics company. The company is currently undertaking a large expansion programme, and is considering the acquisition of Bess plc, a smaller retail company. Porgy plc currently has a stock market value of £90,000,000 while Bess plc has a stock market value of £40,000,000. The management of Porgy plc expects the acquisition of Bess plc to generate significant economies of scale and cost savings. They expect the market value of the combined company to be £158,000,000.

To secure the required share capital in Bess plc, the management of Porgy plc have decided to pay a premium of £20,000,000. Additional transaction costs are expected to be £5,000,000. The required rate of return on both companies and the proposed combination is 10%. Porgy plc has 45,000,000 shares in issue and Bess plc has 20,000,000 shares in issue.

Required:

(i) Calculate the present value that would be created by the acquisition.
(You can assume the management of both Porgy plc and Bess plc are shareholder wealth maximisers, and that the initial savings will continue in perpetuity.)

(ii) If Porgy plc decides to purchase the shares of Bess plc with a cash offer, calculate the price Porgy plc would offer for each of Bess plc's shares.

(iii) If shares are offered in such a way that Bess plc's shareholders would possess 1/3 of the merged company, what value would be created for Porgy plc's shareholders?

(iv) If a cash offer of £60,000,000 was accepted by ALL Bess plc's shareholders what value would be created for Porgy plc's shareholders?

(v) Explain the reasons which the management of Bess plc may suggest as to why the offer made by Porgy plc should be rejected.

(vi) Outline the tactics the managers of Bess plc could employ to effectively contest the bid.

E16.11 *Time allowed – 45 minutes*

Black Ltd is a profitable company and the owners are also the directors. The directors have decided to sell their business, and have identified organisations interested in its purchase: White plc; Scarlet plc; Brown plc. Black Ltd's latest balance sheet and additional financial information are shown below:

Black Ltd financial position at the most recent balance sheet date

	£
Non-current assets	
Land and buildings	800,000
Plant and equipment	450,000
Motor vehicles	55,000
Total non-current assets	1,305,000
Current assets	
Inventories	250,000
Trade and other receivables	127,000
Cash and cash equivalents	8,000
Total current assets	385,000
Total assets	1,690,000

(continued)

Current liabilities		
Trade and other payables		180,000
Income tax payable		50,000
Total current liabilities		230,000
Total assets less current liabilities		1,460,000
Non-current liabilities		
Secured loan		400,000
Net assets		1,060,000
Equity		
300,000 ordinary shares @ £1		300,000
Retained earnings		760,000
Total equity		1,060,000

Black Ltd's profit after tax and interest over the previous five years has been:

	£
Year 1	90,000
Year 2	80,000
Year 3	105,000
Year 4	90,000
Year 5	100,000

Black Ltd's annual divided has been £45,000 for the past six years. The company's five-year plan forecasts an after-tax profit of £100,000 for the next 12 months, with an increase of 4% per annum over each of the next four years. As part of their preparations to sell the company, the directors of Black Ltd have had the non-current assets revalued by an independent expert, which is not reflected in the most recent balance sheet:

	£
Land and buildings	1,075,000
Plant and equipment	480,000
Motor vehicles	45,000

The average dividend yield and P/E ratio of the three interested public companies in the same industry as Black Ltd over the past three years have been:

	White plc		Scarlet plc		Brown plc	
	Dividend yield (%)	**P/E**	**Dividend yield (%)**	**P/E**	**Dividend yield (%)**	**P/E**
Most recent year	12.0	8.5	11.0	9.0	13.0	10.0
Previous year	12.0	8.0	10.6	8.5	12.6	9.5
Three years ago	12.0	8.5	9.3	8.0	12.4	9.0
Average	12.0	8.33	10.3	8.5	12.7	9.5

Large companies in the industry apply an after-tax cost of capital of about 18% to acquisition proposals when the investment is not backed by tangible assets, as opposed to a rate of only 14% on the net tangible assets. The following is an estimate of the net cash flows which would ➡

accrue to a purchasing company, allowing for taxation and the capital expenditure required after the acquisition to achieve the company's target five-year profit plan:

	£
Year 1	120,000
Year 2	120,000
Year 3	140,000
Year 4	70,000
Year 5	120,000

Required:

The directors of Black Ltd have asked you for your assessment of the ordinary share price a potential purchaser may be willing to pay.

Using the above information prepare six alternative valuations which a prospective purchaser may consider.

E16.12 *Time allowed – 45 minutes*
Explain why companies may consider making mergers and acquisitions, and critically examine some of the 'good' reasons and the 'bad' reasons for these strategies.

E16.13 *Time allowed – 45 minutes*
Critically comment on six ways in which a company may justify the acquisition of another company.

Financial strategies in M&As

Learning objectives

Completion of this chapter will enable you to:

■ Describe how cash, equity shares, and debt may be used to finance mergers and acquisitions (M&As).

■ Recognise the differences between the use of debt and the use of equity in the financing of M&As.

■ Explain the financial strategies relating to M&As and the ways in which suitable target companies may be identified.

■ Outline the range of takeover defences that may be made by a company to avoid being taken over before a formal takeover bid has been made.

■ Consider the range of takeover defences that may be made by a company to repel a takeover once a formal takeover bid has been made.

■ Explain the impact of M&As on shareholders, directors, managers, employees, and financial institutions.

Introduction

This chapter looks at the ways in which M&As may be financed, involving the use of cash, debt, or equity in one way or another. We will consider the advantages and disadvantages of each method of financing and particularly the differences between the use of debt or equity.

Suitable target companies must be identified for acquisition or merger and appropriate financial strategies developed to derive the optimum benefits from such activity. The benefits from the synergies expected to result from M&As then need to be evaluated, before deals are completed.

There is a wide range of defences that may be used by companies to avoid being merged or taken over. Some of these defences may be used before a formal offer has been made, and, if these are unsuccessful, some other defences may be employed after a formal bid has been received. This chapter closes by considering the impact of M&As on the major stake-holders in both target companies and acquiring companies. These include shareholders, directors, managers, employees, and financial institutions.

Financing acquisitions

Because of the sheer size of most mergers and acquisitions, the financing implications are extremely significant. The choice of the most appropriate financing method for M&As is therefore a very important decision for a board of directors.

The main methods used to finance M&As are shown in Figure 17.1. We will discuss each of these methods, which include a **vendor placing**, in the sections that follow. We will also discuss what is termed a **mixed bid**, and consider the use of debt compared with equity in the financing of M&As.

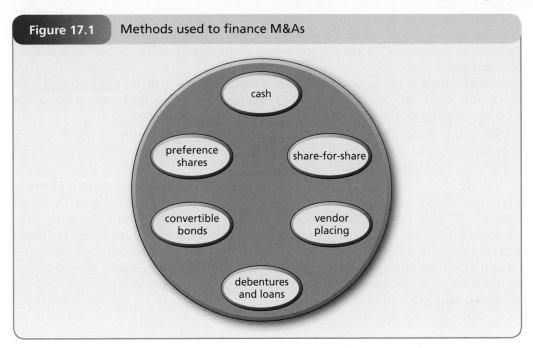

Figure 17.1 Methods used to finance M&As

Cash

The purchase of a target company's shares for cash is attractive to its shareholders because the value is certain. There is an advantage to the target company in that no share selling costs will be incurred. However, there is also a disadvantage in that there may be a capital gains tax liability for the shareholders of the target company. An advantage to the takeover bidding company is that the offer for the target company makes it clear that the number of shares will not be changed, as that would lead to a dilution of earnings per share (eps).

The cash to fund a takeover may be provided from:

- cash provided internally from a company's retained earnings
- external use of mezzanine finance – debt that has risk and return characteristics somewhere between equity and debt
- external leverage, from high amounts of debt finance.

However, if a company making a takeover bid does not have sufficient cash to pay for the shares in the target company, it will be at a disadvantage if it has to borrow to fund the takeover.

A cash purchase of a business is classed as a takeover and so the rules of merger accounting may not be applied. Merger accounting is explained in more detail in the later section on vendor placings.

Share-for-share

A bidding company, or predator company, may offer a deal whereby the target company's shareholders receive a fixed number of shares in the predator company in exchange for the shares they hold in their own company.

The advantages to the target company are that its shareholders still retain an equity interest in the new combined business, and they do not incur brokerage costs or capital gains tax liabilities on their shares. So, the target company shareholders still remain part owners of the new business.

A disadvantage to the acquiring company is the cost of the share-for-share method compared with a cash offer. The brokerage costs incurred by the acquiring company are usually very high and may be a significant factor in appraisal of a potential takeover.

The value of shares offered by the acquiring company will vary over time so the offer needs to be generous enough to prevent it becoming unattractive if the predator's share price drops any time after the takeover bid has been made.

At a later date the takeover company may subsequently increase the number of shares in issue, resulting in a dilution of the shares held by the target company shareholders. Therefore, although the target company shareholders may initially feel that they have a reasonable number of shares, this may subsequently be reduced as a proportion of the total number of issued shares. A decrease in gearing, because of an increase in the number of ordinary shares, may move the predator from its optimal capital structure in theory and therefore increase its cost of capital. The AOL acquisition of Time Warner was a very large share-for-share deal, which is outlined in Mini case 17.1.

Mini case 17.1

The largest ever acquisition up to that time took place in the year 2000. It was AOL's takeover of Time Warner. The US$163bn deal announced on 10 January 2000 involved the issue of shares in a combined new entity, which would be valued at around US$350bn. For every share held in their respective companies, each AOL shareholder would receive 1 new share and each Time Warner shareholder would receive 1.5 new shares. The AOL shareholders would have 55% of the new entity and the Time Warner shareholders would end up with 45%.

We will consider the implications of this share-for-share deal for the shareholders of each company.

The announcement of the deal immediately pushed up the share prices of both companies. However, AOL was an Internet, new economy, dot.com business and very much larger than Time Warner, which was a traditional media group valued at around US$80bn. Before the announcement of the acquisition, Time Warner's share price and P/E ratio were relatively low, reflecting its position as a traditional media company. AOL's share price and P/E ratio were relatively high, reflecting the dot.com boom, which perhaps valued AOL higher than its real worth. It is likely that the high premium being paid to the Time Warner shareholders (1.5 shares for each share held, compared with 1 share to AOL shareholders) reflected this apparent over-valuation.

On 12 January 2000, the value of the takeover dropped as AOL's share price fell 8% after analysts downgraded its future performance prospects; Time Warner's share price fell by 5.5%. By 15 January, the value of the acquisition had fallen to US$145bn. Some analysts warned that the value of the deal may fall to as low as US$128bn; they felt that the acquisition was less than a perfect match, which may hamper AOL's growth, and was more to do with 'huge corporate egos, bloated investment banking fees and awesome executive bonuses' (see *Daily Telegraph* various media and business sections articles, 11 to 15 January 2000).

Vendor placing

A vendor placing is a variation on a cash offer, which allows the acquiring company to apply **merger accounting** rules rather than **takeover accounting** rules to the post-merger company. A cash offer is classified as a takeover and the accounting rules relating to mergers cannot be applied.

UK takeover, or acquisition, accounting rules require the following:

- a restatement of net assets to fair value at the acquisition date
- profits of the target company to be included from the acquisition date
- the difference between the purchase price paid for the target company and its net assets fair value to be accounted for as goodwill.

UK merger accounting rules require the following:

- no restatement of net assets to fair value
- profits of the target company to be included for the whole of the accounting period
- the difference between the purchase price paid for the target company and its net assets fair value to be added to or deducted from reserves.

Merger accounting is allowed if the two groups of shareholders continue their shareholdings as before the companies combine, but on a combined basis. The companies combine on an equal footing. A vendor placing involves the acquiring company offering shares to the target company with the option to continue their shareholding, and at the same time arranging for the new shares to be placed with institutional investors and for cash to be paid to the target company's shareholders. The institutional investors, for example insurance companies and pension funds, are approached by the company's sponsor (a merchant bank or stockbroker), before the issue takes place and offer the shares at a fixed price. The company's sponsor underwrites the issue and therefore takes up any unplaced shares. Other potential investors (both institutional and the general public) cannot buy shares that have been placed until after the listing and official dealing takes place. Compared with other share issue methods, placings have lower costs, but since companies use them because they want to issue their shares to institutions the spread of shareholding is relatively narrow (see the section about new issues in Chapter 7).

Another variation on the cash offer is a vendor rights issue. A vendor rights issue is the same as a vendor placing, but instead the shares are offered to the acquiring company's shareholders.

Debentures and loans

A debenture, which is a type of bond, is a written acknowledgement of a debt that includes the terms regarding payment of interest and the principal. A debenture is normally secured on a specific asset, or the assets in general, of a company.

The use of securities other than the shares of the acquiring company as a means of paying the target company is now rare in the UK. It is not entirely clear why this should be so, but in the UK the use of debentures, preference shares, and loans in M&As fell from around 25% in the 1970s, to 15% in the 1980s, to 1% in the 1990s.

Debt is largely unacceptable to target company shareholders, who have previously shown their preference for higher risks and returns associated with their being equity shareholders.

However, the issue of debt by an acquiring company as a means of payment for a target company does not lead to dilution of eps. In addition, the interest payments on debt are tax efficient. These are potentially very big plusses for a predator company.

Bonds

A bond is a debt that offers a fixed rate of interest over a fixed period of time, and has a fixed redemption value.

The use of bonds leads to an increase in the predator company's gearing. A big disadvantage of bonds is that they require the build-up of cash reserves by the company with which to pay off the loans on maturity.

Convertible bonds

To overcome some of the problems of using straight bonds, a company may issue convertible bonds. Convertible bonds, which are an example of hybrid securities, offer bond-holders a means of benefiting from future corporate growth.

Convertible bonds are 'two stage' financial instruments, which:

- start their life as a convertible debenture or a convertible preference share
- include an option to convert them into ordinary shares at a later date.

The predator company receives a number of advantages from the use of convertible bonds:

- dilution of eps will not occur until much later when the bonds are converted into ordinary shares – therefore, earnings increase without increasing the number of shares until a much later date
- convertibles tend to pay a lower coupon rate (or interest rate), which greatly benefits the cash flow of the company
- convertibles reduce the short-term carrying cost of company financing, that is interest rather than dividends.

There are a number of commonly used terms associated with convertibles, or convertible bonds, which are listed below:

- **coupon yield** is the interest paid on the nominal value of a bond (or a loan, or debenture)
- **straight bond value** is the market value dependent on the coupon rate relative to market interest rates
- convertible bonds issued at par (the nominal price of the bond used for setting the interest rate) normally have a lower coupon rate than straight bonds because the investor has to pay for the conversion rights – the bonds will become ordinary shares at a later date
- **conversion ratio** is the number of ordinary shares that will be obtained from the conversion of one unit of the convertible bond
- **conversion value** is the market value of the ordinary shares into which a unit of the convertible bond may be converted
- convertible bond value is the market value dependent on the straight bond value, current conversion value, time up to conversion, and the ordinary shares risk and return expectation.

Preference shares

Preference shares are shares rather than loans but do not constitute part of the ownership of the company. Preference shares carry a fixed rate of dividend, which is a prior claim on profits, and they may have a prior claim on capital. The use of preference shares as a means of payment in a takeover is even more rare than the use of debt.

In a takeover, preference shares are less attractive to the predator company than ordinary shares because they lack flexibility, and also because their dividends are distributed from post-tax profit and so are not allowable for tax.

In a takeover, preference shares do not offer ownership to the target company's shareholders, and neither do they provide the security of a cash offer.

Mixed bids

Mixed bids of share-for-share offers supported by a cash alternative have become increasingly popular in the UK. There are two main reasons for this:

- mixed bids are acceptable to target company shareholders because they can choose the method that best suits their individual liquidity preferences and tax positions
- rule 9 of the City Code on Takeovers and Mergers 1988 (City Code) applies.

Rule 9 of the City Code requires companies, which are acquiring 30% or more of a target company's shares, to make a cash offer (or cash alternative if a share-for-share offer is being made) at the highest price paid by the predator company for the target company's shares over the previous 12 months.

The City Code is a set of rules and principles that governs the way in which takeovers and mergers of public companies are carried out in the UK. The code applies to all UK resident companies.

The City Code does not specifically concern itself with the commercial aspects of a takeover or merger, or with the way a company conducts its business, but is designed to ensure the protection and equal treatment of shareholders in certain takeover and merger situations, and where there are changes in the individuals and groups that control that company. The City Code also sets out a detailed timetable under which all such takeovers and mergers are conducted, and covers issues such as:

- the conditions of an offer
- information availability regarding target and predator company shareholders
- target company restrictions with regard to its directors
- how the approach to a target company should be made
- the announcement of the takeover bid
- obligations of the target company board of directors
- conduct of companies during the offer.

International Financial Reporting Standard IFRS 3: Business Combinations, and the Statement of Financial Accounting Standards SFAS 141: Business Combinations, published by the Financial Accounting Standards Board (FASB), provide further information on the requirements of mergers and acquisitions. The extra detail contained in these standards relates largely to the recognition of events and the identification of non-controlling interests (previously called minority interests), identification of the acquirer, rules on disclosure, and determination of an acquisition date.

Progress check 17.1

Which method of financing an M&A may be preferred by the shareholders of a target company, and why?

Debt versus equity in financing acquisitions

The cost of debt to a company is generally lower than its cost of equity at low levels of gearing, because of the low risk and high risk respectively to investors, associated with debt and equity.

Financial leverage (gearing) is the use of debt finance to increase the return on equity by deploying borrowed funds in such a way that the return generated is greater than the cost of servicing the debt. The return must be greater than the debt interest rate.

If the return on deployed funds is less than the cost of servicing the debt, the effect of the leverage is to reduce the return on equity. That is, the return rate is less than the debt interest rate.

As we saw in Chapter 7 there are many different sources of finance available to businesses comprising various forms of debt and equity and combinations of the two. Debt and equity may be looked at in terms of their perceived risk and the return required from them. The range of types of financing and their attributes is shown in Figure 17.2. Government debt (low risk, low return) and equity, or ordinary share capital (high risk, high return) represent the extremities of a continuum of financial instruments, which includes secured and unsecured, long- and short-term debt, and preference shares. Financial instruments are available with a range of combinations of risk and potential return. Sometimes in trying to distinguish between debt and equity the boundaries become blurred. There are literally hundreds of hybrid financial instruments on the market. They represent additional possibilities for further sophistication in company financing.

A rights issue (see Chapters 7 and 14) is one way in which equity financing may be used to fund an acquisition. Mini case 17.2 shows how Balfour Beatty plc used this technique in 2009 and considers the impact on the company's share ownership and gearing.

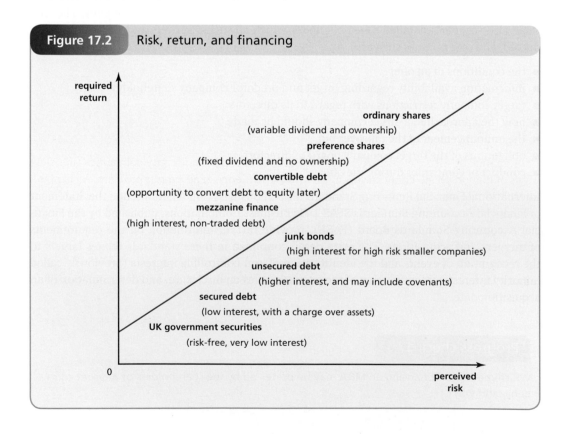

Figure 17.2 Risk, return, and financing

Mini case 17.2

One of the benefits of using a rights issue to fund an acquisition lies in the opportunity to maintain the same profile of shareholders after the funds have been raised without increasing the gearing of the company outside normal levels.

In September 2009 Balfour Beatty plc, a UK engineering and construction company, announced the acquisition of the US professional services business Parsons Brinckerhoff in a $626m (£380m) takeover.

Balfour Beatty plc offered a 3 for 7 rights issue at 180 pence per ordinary share (a discount of 48%) to raise approximately £353m, net of issue expenses. The outcome was that existing shareholders bought 97% of 199.5m new shares, with the remaining 6m shares bought by other investors.

After the acquisition, the overall spread of shareholders therefore altered only marginally, and the gearing ratio remained at a level acceptable to the company.

Balfour Beatty plc gearing 2006 to 2010

2010	2009	2008	2007	2006
115%	140%	104%	158%	160%

Financial strategy in acquisitions

There are a number of important strategic factors that relate to the financial aspects of acquisitions. There is a financial role in evaluating the value of potential synergies, the evaluation of $2 + 2 = 5$, rather than involvement in the achievement of the synergies themselves. Another financial role is to identify a potential target company that is not adopting an optimum financial strategy to maximise shareholders' wealth. Various alternative options may be considered for the valuation of potential target companies, in order to consider the maximum purchase prices that may be offered. It should be noted that the financial structure of the target company may also need to be changed, for example through leverage.

A financially astute corporate raider (a takeover expert) can identify companies that show signs of inappropriate financial strategies or some evidence of an agency problem. An example of a clear sign of an inappropriate financial strategy is a mature group that has very large net cash surpluses. This may indicate the group's reluctance to invest in new projects. A predator company may acquire such a group, and strip off the cash, then leverage the company, by taking on debt, on the basis of the cash generation capability of its core business.

We will consider a number of aspects related to the identification of suitable target companies for acquisition, including **greenmailing** and the **earn-out method**, which are summarised in Figure 17.3.

Diversified companies

A group that has diversified into growth areas with competitive advantages offers even greater opportunities for a predator to increase post-acquisition value. This is because parts of the business may still be in the growth phase, not yet having reached maturity.

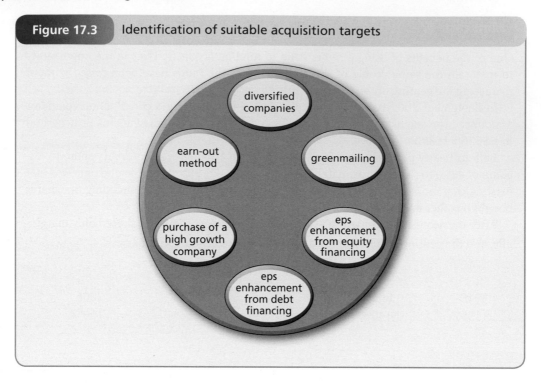

Figure 17.3 Identification of suitable acquisition targets

A diversified group should ideally be valued at a minimum of the weighted average P/E applicable to its component businesses. However, in practice this may be difficult to ascertain. If some of the newly acquired parts of the group company do not perform well after acquisition they may be sold for appropriately high P/E multiples.

Greenmailing

A corporate raid is a particular type of hostile takeover in which the target company is acquired and then broken up. Predator companies who are corporate raiders may have a significant impact on the strategies of targeted companies without taking complete control of them. This may be achieved by acquiring just a small part of target companies.

A corporate raider may buy a stake in a company that is considered to be significantly under-valued, and in this way 'greenmail' the management, which is effectively accusing them of running the company to the detriment of the shareholders by not aiming to maximise share-holder wealth. The greenmail threat is to acquire the entire company, sack the management, and implement a new strategy.

In the USA, where companies have acquired shares in such target companies, this tactic has been used and has resulted in management offers to buy out the corporate raiders' stakes, with inevitable large capital gains to the raider.

eps enhancement using equity financing

Most plcs see eps as their most important financial measure. However, it should be noted, as we have previously discussed, that enhancement of eps is not one of the 'good' reasons for an acquisition. Rightly or wrongly, even though cash measures are probably better, eps is a key element in maintaining share price levels, because:

$$\text{share price} = \text{eps} \times \text{P/E}$$

If equity rather than cash is used to finance a takeover deal then there will be an impact on the eps of the combined entity. The level of impact on eps will depend on the target company's P/E ratio, as follows:

- if the P/E ratio of the bidding company is greater than the P/E ratio of the target company – then eps will be increased
- if the P/E ratio of the bidding company is less than the P/E ratio of the target company – then eps will be diluted
- if the P/E ratio of the bidding company is the same as the P/E ratio of the target company – then eps will be unchanged.

Worked examples 17.1 and 17.2 illustrate the impact on eps of an equity-financed acquisition at different levels of the target company's P/E ratio.

Worked example 17.1

Presley plc wants to acquire Richard plc by offering shares to Richard's shareholders. The price that Presley plc will pay is the market capitalisation of Richard plc. To keep the calculations simple we will assume that they each have 1,000,000 ordinary shares in issue and their current share prices are both £4.

We will consider the impact of the takeover on Presley's combined company eps at different levels of P/E for Richard plc.

Presley plc's P/E ratio greater than Richard plc's P/E ratio

	Presley plc	Richard plc
issued shares	1,000,000	1,000,000
net profit after tax	£0.16m	£0.20m
eps	16p	20p
share price	£4	£4
P/E ratio	25	20

number of Presley plc shares in issue after the takeover	2,000,000
total net profit	£0.36m
eps	18p

The combined company's eps have increased to 18p from Presley's 16p.

Presley plc's P/E ratio the same as Richard plc's P/E ratio

	Presley plc	Richard plc
issued shares	1,000,000	1,000,000
net profit after tax	£0.20m	£0.20m
eps	20p	20p
share price	£4	£4
P/E ratio	20	20

number of Presley plc shares in issue after the takeover	2,000,000
total net profit	£0.40m
eps	20p

The combined company's eps are unchanged at 20p.

Presley plc's P/E ratio less than Richard plc's P/E ratio

	Presley plc	Richard plc
issued shares	1,000,000	1,000,0 00
net profit after tax	£0.20m	£0.16m
eps	20p	16p
share price	£4	£4
P/E ratio	20	25

number of Presley plc shares in issue after the takeover	2,000,000
total net profit	£0.36m
eps	18p

The combined company's eps have decreased to 18p from Presley's 20p.

In Worked example 17.1 if the numbers of issued shares and share prices of the two companies had been different then the solution would just require a recalculation of the price paid for the acquisition. Worked example 17.2 illustrates the impact on eps and net assets of an equity-financed acquisition where the numbers of issued shares and share prices of the two companies are different.

Worked example 17.2

Python plc is a UK manufacturing company, which has an issued share capital of 2m £1 ordinary shares. The company's net assets (excluding goodwill) are £2.5m and the company's average annual earnings are £2m. Python plc currently has a P/E ratio of 10. Pig

Ltd is a UK manufacturing company, which has an issued share capital of 1m £1 ordinary shares. The company's net assets (excluding goodwill) are £3.5m and the company's average annual earnings are £500,000. The shareholders of Pig Ltd have recently accepted an all-equity offer from Python plc, and the offer values Pig Ltd's shares at £6 each.

We will calculate Python plc's earnings and net assets per share before and after the acquisition of Pig Ltd.

Python plc – before the acquisition:

eps	= £2m/2m shares	= £1.00
net assets per share	= £2.5m/2m shares	= £1.25

Python has a P/E ratio of 10, and therefore the current market value of Python's shares is £10 (10 × £1).

Pig Ltd – before the acquisition:

eps	= £0.5m/1m shares	= £0.50
net assets per share	= £3.5m/1m shares	= £3.50

Python plc's offer of £6 per share for Pig Ltd gives Pig a P/E ratio of 12 (£6/£0.50). Because Python's P/E ratio is lower than Pig's P/E ratio, Python's earnings will therefore be diluted as follows:

The market value of Pig Ltd is £6 million (1 million × £6), therefore Python plc would have to issue 600,000 shares to finance the deal (£6 million/(£1 × 10).

Python plc – after the acquisition:

eps	= (£2m + £0.5m)/(2m + 0.6m shares)	= £0.96
net assets per share	= (£2.5m + £3.5m)/2.6m shares	= £2.31

Python plc's eps have been diluted to 96p from £1, but the company's net assets per share have increased to £2.31 from £1.25.

Pig plc – after the acquisition:

For Pig Ltd the opposite is the case. In total, Pig Ltd's shareholders would receive 600,000 shares in Python plc for the 1,000,000 shares they used to hold in Pig Ltd – 6 shares for every 10 shares they had each held.

Pig Ltd eps:
10 old Pig shares would earn 10 × £0.50 eps = £5.00
6 new Python shares would earn 6 × £0.96 eps = £5.76,

which is an increase of 76p/6, or 12.7p per share.

Pig Ltd net assets per share:
10 old Pig shares would be worth 10 × £3.50 = £35.00
6 new Python shares would be worth 6 × £2.31 = £13.86,

which is a decrease of £21.14/6, or £3.52 per share.

eps enhancement using debt financing

If debt instead of equity is used to finance a takeover deal then the interest rate paid on the debt will have an impact on the eps of the combined entity. The extent of the impact on eps will depend on the P/E ratio of the target company, as follows:

- if the post-tax interest rate is less than the inverse of the P/E ratio of the target company – then eps will be increased
- if the post-tax interest rate is greater than the inverse of the P/E ratio of the target company – then eps will be diluted.

This is similar to eps enhancement using equity financing, but in this situation the increased growth prospects are offset by increased financial risk due to increased debt and higher interest.

The impact of the use of debt financing for a takeover at different levels of interest rate is illustrated in Worked example 17.3.

Worked example 17.3

Presley plc (see Worked example 17.1) wants to acquire Richard plc and finance the takeover totally by debt. The price that Presley plc will pay is the market capitalisation of Richard plc. The companies each have 1,000,000 ordinary shares in issue and the current share prices are both £4.

We will consider the impact of the takeover on Presley's combined company eps if it is able to finance the acquisition through borrowing £4m at 4%, 5%, or 6% per annum. The corporation tax rate is 20%.

Presley plc's cost of debt is 4%

	Presley plc	**Richard plc**
issued shares	1,000,000	1,000,000
net profit after tax	£0.20m	£0.16m
eps	20p	16p
share price	£4	£4
P/E ratio	20	25
cost of additional debt @ 4%	£0.128m	
£4m × 4% × (1 − 20%)		
number of shares in Presley plc		
after the takeover	1,000,000	
total net profit £0.36 − £0.128m	£0.232m	
eps	23.2p	

The combined company's eps have increased to 23.2p from Presley's 20p. The after-tax cost of debt is 4% × (1 − 20%) = 3.2%, which is less than the reciprocal of Richard plc's P/E ratio 1 × 100%/25 = 4%.

Presley plc's cost of debt is 5%

	Presley plc	Richard plc
issued shares	1,000,000	1,000,000
net profit after tax	£0.20m	£0.16m
eps	20p	16p
share price	£4	£4
P/E ratio	20	25
cost of additional debt @ 5%	£0.16m	
£4m $\times$ 5% $\times$ (1 − 20%)		
number of shares in Presley plc		
after the takeover	1,000,000	
total net profit £0.36 − £0.16m	£0.20m	
eps	20p	

The combined company's eps remain at 20p. The after-tax cost of debt is 5% $\times$ (1 − 20%) = 4%, which equals the reciprocal of Richard plc's P/E ratio 1 $\times$ 100%/25 = 4%.

Presley plc's cost of debt is 6%

	Presley plc	Richard plc
issued shares	1,000,000	1,000,000
net profit after tax	£0.20m	£0.16m
eps	20p	16p
share price	£4	£4
P/E ratio	20	25
cost of additional debt @ 6%	£0.192m	
£4m $\times$ 6% $\times$ (1 − 20%)		
number of shares in Presley plc		
after the takeover	1,000,000	
total net profit £0.36 − £0.192m	£0.168m	
eps	16.8p	

The combined company's eps have been diluted to 16.8p from Presley's 20p. The after-tax cost of debt is 6% $\times$ (1 − 20%) = 4.8%, which is greater than the reciprocal of Richard plc's P/E ratio 1 $\times$ 100%/25 = 4%.

As in Worked example 17.1, if in Worked example 17.3 the numbers of issued shares and share prices of the two companies had been different then the solution would just require a recalculation of the price paid for the acquisition.

Purchasing a high-growth company

The usual takeover or merger scenario is where a large company may bid for and acquire, for example, a smaller people-based, owner-managed company. The acquisition price will reflect the high expectation of synergy benefits and economies of scale achieved from the takeover of the target company. However, post-acquisition, its managers, the key asset of the business, may leave or may not be motivated to achieve the expected benefits that have been paid for. In addition to this, the acquisition purchase price may have been too high, and the expected benefits may not be achieved.

Earn-out method

Very often, what is called an earn-out method is used to acquire small companies that are expected to have very good future prospects. An earn-out method may also be used to resolve differences of opinion on the value and the potential of a target company.

The eventual price paid for an acquisition may be tied to the subsequent growth rate in the early years following transfer of ownership. The earn-out deal may be that the target company shareholders receive part payment on acquisition, with the balance deferred a couple of years until a specific agreed level of profits has been achieved.

Because the risk of future performance is transferred to the existing owners, the acquisition price will be higher than normally expected. For an earn-out to be effective the vendor shareholders should also be the key managers in the company, to guarantee their commitment.

Compensation, in terms of the acquisition price, must be adequate reward to the vendors for 'waiting' for payment.

Progress check 17.2

What are the key financial strategies that may be adopted in the identification of M&A target companies?

Takeover pre-bid defences

We may question why a proposed takeover bid may be opposed at all. The directors of a target company may oppose a takeover bid because:

- they want to retain their jobs and they think that avoiding a takeover will achieve this (the most usual reason)
- they believe that they can create more value than would be created following a takeover.

Companies may try and avoid being taken over before a formal takeover bid has been made and the purpose of this is:

- to make a company difficult and expensive to take over
- early detection of a bid is an advantage to get a defence in place quickly
- to maintain consistency with the shareholder wealth maximisation objective.

Companies may use one or more of a number of pre-bid defences, which are shown in Figure 17.4.

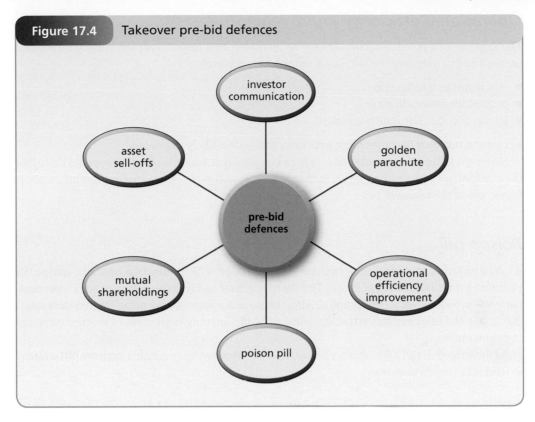

Figure 17.4   Takeover pre-bid defences

Investor communication

Maintaining good relations with investors and analysts may make a potential takeover difficult and expensive. It may prove very costly for a potential acquiring company to persuade shareholders about the benefits of the takeover. It may also require an unacceptably high offer price to induce them to accept.

Managers need to keep investors well informed about policies, strategies, and performance, and about their aim to satisfy their risk and return preferences. Target companies may also make commitments to shareholders that potential predator companies feel unable to support.

Golden parachute

Golden parachutes are extremely generous termination packages that may be contracted with senior managers, which effectively increase the cost of a takeover. These may be introduced into directors' contracts if there is a threat of a takeover.

For the predator company the removal of managers surplus to requirements after the takeover may then be very costly, because of the high cost of termination packages. This may be sufficient to make a takeover unattractive and therefore deter a potential predator company.

Operational efficiency improvement

The expense of a potential takeover may be increased by a target company raising its eps and share price (so reducing the likelihood of takeover) through:

- overheads cost reduction
- production rationalisation
- labour productivity improvement,

so that the takeover becomes more expensive and so less likely to proceed.

However, shareholders and others may be concerned at why it took a takeover bid threat for these initiatives to be put in place. Perhaps these should have been initiated by the directors regardless of the takeover bid.

Poison pill

A takeover target company may purchase its own shares, which reduces a predator company's ability to gain a controlling position. The share purchase reduces the equity of the target company as a proportion of its total capital. Also, the resultant increased gearing (higher debt ratio) may make the takeover less attractive because of the ongoing high costs of interest payment commitments.

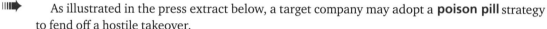 As illustrated in the press extract below, a target company may adopt a **poison pill** strategy to fend off a hostile takeover.

Illumina poison pill

US diagnostics company Illumina has moved to fend off Roche's $5.7bn hostile takeover bid by announcing that it will adopt a 'poison pill' to protect its shareholders. Through the rights agreement, Illumina shareholders can buy new common stock if a bidder acquires 15 per cent of the company's shares. The move is intended to deter Roche, the Swiss drug-maker, or other potential acquirers by making Illumina more expensive to acquire. 'The Illumina board has taken this action to ensure that our stockholders receive fair treatment and protection in connection with any proposal or offer to acquire the company, including the proposal announced by Roche,' said Jay Flatley, Illumina's chief executive.

The bid for Illumina comes as deal-making in the healthcare sector has proved resilient amid the economic slump. Large pharmaceutical and biotechnology companies are doing deals as they try to replace revenues lost from drugs coming off patent and to establish their position in emerging treatment and diagnostic areas.

In a second high-profile healthcare deal this week, Amgen of the US yesterday unveiled a $1.16bn agreed takeover of Micromet, a biotech business founded in Germany with a leading experimental cancer compound and a broader technology with scope for a wider range of treatments. The $11 per share cash offer gives Amgen control of Micromet's experimental drug Blinatumomab, currently in mid-stage clinical trials for acute lymphoblastic leukaemia and non-Hodgkin's lymphoma, with scope for a range of other diseases.

Separately yesterday, Celgene, another US biotech group that specialises in cancer therapies, said that it was acquiring Avila Therapeutics for $350m in cash plus another $575m pending the development of some of its drug candidates.

This week's activity follows an up-tick in deal-making in the sector that started late last year. Illumina's decision to put in place a poison pill suggests the company's board is intent on forcing Roche to pay a higher price for the company. Illumina's shares are already trading substantially above Roche's $44.50 cash offer, although they slipped 4.5 per cent to close at $52.65 yesterday.

Industry advisers were this week doubtful that a counter-bidder would emerge for Illumina, given Roche's reputation and previous success in launching hostile bids and its financial firepower.

Another example of the type of poison pill a target company may adopt is to plant into its capital structure, for example, rights of shareholders to buy future loan stock or preference shares, thus increasing the cost of possible acquisition. The potential future ongoing cost of interest payments makes the takeover look more expensive, and therefore less attractive, and therefore less likely to take place. This strategy has the same impact as the target company buying back its own shares.

There are a number of other types of poison pill that may be effected by potential takeover target companies:

- staggering the retirement of directors, which may hinder rather than prevent a takeover
- issuing of new shares to 'friendly' shareholders to dilute the holding of a potential acquiring company
- changing the rules of the company so that a super-majority of, say, 75% is required, rather than the normal 50%, for a takeover to proceed.

Let's look at an example of another type of poison pill in Mini case 17.3.

Mini case 17.3

In September 2001, Royal Caribbean Cruises Ltd and P&O Princess Cruises plc announced their proposed 'merger of equals'. In December 2001, the Carnival Corporation launched a hostile takeover of P&O Princess.

At first, Princess spurned the offer, then did an about-face, announcing that it would auction itself off to the highest bidder. In January 2002, the Carnival Corporation raised its offer in a final attempt to break up the UK cruise group's pre-arranged merger with Royal Caribbean. The value of the Carnival offer was now substantially greater than Royal Caribbean's. The management of P&O Princess continued to favour the pairing with Royal Caribbean, and advised investors of this through its website.

Various governmental regulators in the USA, the UK, and Europe needed to consider their approval of any merger. The Carnival Corporation wanted the legitimacy of P&O's merger with Royal Caribbean to be tested in the UK courts because it would be a poison pill and against the shareholders' interests according to the City Code. (See more about the City Code in the earlier section about mixed bids.) Carnival said it would avoid paying the poison pill by delaying the completion of its takeover of Princess until January 2003.

Approval for both deals was given by the European Commission, and by the UK and USA regulators. By early 2003 P&O Princess Cruises plc had agreed to its takeover by Carnival with a US$5.5bn agreement.

Worked example 17.4 below shows the effect of a poison pill strategy on the percentage of shares of a target company held by a predator company, and the likely impact on the viability of the possible takeover.

Worked example 17.4

Fly plc has 10m shares in issue and additional authorised share capital of 10m shares. Spider plc also has share capital of 10m and has offered Fly plc shareholders one share in Spider for every one share they hold in Fly.

Spider may then acquire and cancel the shares in Fly.

Let's consider the outcome, and the use of a poison pill defence by Fly plc.

The outcome of Spider's acquisition of Fly would be:

shares in Fly	10m
existing shares in Spider	10m
new issue to acquire Fly	10m
total	20m
ownership of new entity	
Fly shareholders	50%
Spider shareholders	50%

In defence of the acquisition Fly plc may consider a poison pill strategy of issuing 10m shares to existing shareholders at their nominal value. If Fly plc activates the poison pill then:

shares in Fly	20m
existing shares in Spider	10m
new issue to acquire Fly	20m
total	30m
ownership of new entity	
Fly shareholders	67%
Spider shareholders	33%

The loss of control by Spider shareholders may make the takeover unattractive and prevent Spider plc taking any further action.

Mutual shareholdings

Some companies may have sufficient trust in each other to collude to prevent a takeover. Such collusion is a device that may ensure that a significant proportion of equity is kept within 'friendly hands'.

Target companies may arrange for other companies to take mutual shareholdings in each other to block potential takeover bids through such strategic alliances.

Asset sell-offs

The use of divestment as a pre-bid defence involves the disposal of some key assets, which would be particularly attractive to a predator company. Non-core, low-growth businesses may be sold off by a potential takeover target company.

The divestment may then enable a concentration by the target company on markets in which the company is strong. This may then give the company some focus, in addition to helping to repel a hostile bid. The result of such a strategic divestment by a target company should be an increase in profits, eps, and share price. This then achieves the objective of increasing the cost of a potential takeover, which as a result becomes less likely to go ahead.

Progress check 17.3

Outline the pre-bid defences that may be used by a takeover target company.

Takeover post-bid defences

If none of the pre-bid defences have been successful then there are also a number of post-bid defences that may be used by target companies to repel a bid once one has been made. These are shown in Figure 17.5.

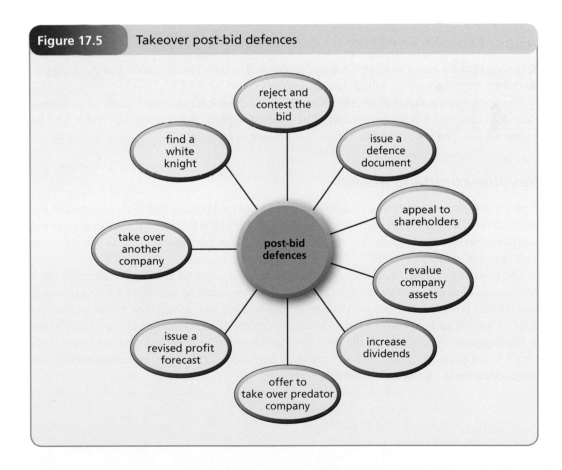

Figure 17.5   Takeover post-bid defences

Reject and contest the bid

The initial takeover bid may be attacked to signal to the predator that the target company will contest the takeover. This device is to let the predator know that the takeover bid is not welcome and will be defended.

This rejection may be enough to scare off the predator. But, why should the directors do this? It may be that the directors believe that the bid undervalues the company, or that synergies will not be achieved, or maybe they feel that the takeover is a threat to their own positions.

Issue a defence document

The board of directors of the target company may prepare a formal document, which is circulated to its shareholders praising its own performance and criticising the bidding company and its offer.

This document may criticise the bid by saying that:

- promised synergies are unlikely to be realised
- shareholder value will not be increased
- the takeover may represent a risk to shareholders,

and to be credible, such a document must be very carefully prepared, and it is important that its assertions are borne out by subsequent events.

Appeal to shareholders

Target companies may also make a pre-emptive appeal to their shareholders. The directors can do this by immediately circulating the shareholders.

The appeal to the shareholders should explain how the bid is not in the shareholders' favour from a logical and a price perspective. They should explain that shareholder value will be higher without the takeover than if the takeover were to go ahead.

Revalue company assets

A target company may revalue its assets, before or after a takeover bid. This can involve the revaluation of land and buildings (see an example of this in the following press extract), or the capitalisation of brand names that the company may have purchased, to make the company look stronger or more valuable.

The predator company may then need to make an increased offer, to up its bid following a revaluation of assets. However, if the capital markets are efficient, and since no new information is being provided, the existing share price may be a fair one. In that case, financial analysts will be aware of such assets even if they have not been revalued, so this will already be reflected in the company's share price. If the asset revaluation tactic is successful, and the target company's share price increases, then the predator may consider that the price required for the target company is too high and therefore withdraw.

The real value of a company's assets

Minerva took the extraordinary step of reinstating its chairman in spite of his re-election to the board being voted down by investors led by major shareholder and hostile bidder Nathan Kirsh's KiFin. At the property company's annual meeting yesterday, Mr Kirsh's KiFin investment vehicle and its associates voted against a resolution to re-elect Oliver Whitehead. This left the company briefly without a chairman, but the board met immediately after the AGM to reappoint Mr Whitehead. He will act as chairman during the course of the unsolicited offer from KiFin. The company said: 'During KiFin Limited's unsolicited offer, the board believes that the interests of all shareholders should be protected and the role of a strong, independent chairman is the most important aspect of this.'

KiFin, which controls 29.9 per cent of the company's shares, called a poll on the resolution. The poll received 29m votes in favour of the re-election of Mr Whitehead and 48m votes against. Minerva said more than 99.3 per cent of independent shareholders – excluding KiFin and its associates – voted in favour.

Two weeks ago, KiFin launched a 50p-a-share takeover bid for Minerva, valuing the company at £85m. Minerva this week wrote to shareholders rejecting KiFin's offer as it significantly undervalued the company. It also released an updated net asset value for the company at 95p per share, after a revaluation of its properties. Mr Whitehead later said: 'Minerva has high-quality developments in excellent locations. KiFin's offer of only 50p per share significantly undervalues the company, and your board has no hesitation in rejecting this highly opportunistic bid.'

John Matthews, senior independent director of Minerva, said: 'The board is very disappointed by this deliberately disruptive behaviour by a shareholder that has made a bid for the company. We have decided to reappoint Oliver as chairman during the course of the unsolicited offer as it is critical that all shareholders' interests are protected.'

Mr Whitehead was chief executive and then chairman of Alfred McAlpine until June 2007, and formerly group chief executive of Babcock International Group.

Minerva also announced the sale of its headquarters on Wigmore Street in London to Standard Life Investment for £40.75m, a premium of 20 per cent to the property's book value as reported at June 30 2009. Salmaan Hasan, chief executive of Minerva, said: 'This disposal of a non-core asset is another key milestone achieved by Minerva as the market recovers and as we continue to make progress.'

Source: **Minerva overrides shareholders by reinstating chairman**, by Daniel Thomas © *Financial Times*, 5 December 2009

Increase dividends

A target company may announce an increase in dividend and its intention to pay future increased dividends. Again, there is the problem of a potential lack of credibility. It is reasonable for shareholders to question why current and future dividends should have suddenly been improved.

A dividend increase may persuade target company shareholders to reject a takeover offer. Or it may not, particularly if the shareholders remain unconvinced as to why increased dividends were not paid prior to a takeover offer. If promises of increased dividends are not kept, then the share price may fall. The company may then become an even easier target for takeover.

Offer to take over the predator company – Pac-Man defence

⟶ The **Pac-Man defence** was named after the computer game in which the monster you are pursuing all of a sudden turns around and eats your monster instead. The idea is to counter an unwanted takeover bid by turning the tables and bidding yourself. A flaw in the strategy is that the moment the Pac-Man defence is deployed, the industrial logic of the deal has essentially been recognised. The only remaining question is who ends up eating whom.

⟶ Using the Pac-Man defence a target company may make a counter-bid for the shares of the predator company. This is also sometimes referred to as a **reverse takeover**. This usually involves a smaller more dynamic company attempting to acquire a larger company, but it is not always the case. This option is difficult and expensive but has occasionally been used successfully in the USA. The Pac-Man defence was used in the UK by Warner Music against EMI in June 2006 (see Mini case 17.4).

Mini case 17.4

EMI had been trying, on and off for more than six years, to acquire Warner Music, but one way or another they seemed incapable of pulling it off.

EMI's first attempt was thwarted by the competition regulators. Subsequently, the merger of BMG and Sony, and the way in which the industry had been structurally transformed by music downloads, encouraged Eric Nicoli, the EMI chairman, to believe that the regulators might prove more amenable. However, there had been a change of ownership at Warner Music, which was also headed by a new chairman. He recognised the synergies and cost cuts that could be derived by combining with EMI, but he was not amenable to being taken over by EMI or anyone else. He therefore countered EMI's US$31 per share bid for Warner Music with a £3.20 per share cash offer for EMI.

Both offers were dependent on board recommendation and due diligence, which neither party was willing to give, and so there was an impasse. In the majority of takeovers, it is shareholders in the company being taken over that gain most out of the transaction. Usually, the gains achieved by any synergies are less than the premium paid for the company being taken over and so the investors in the acquiring company are usually no better or worse off. On that basis, EMI shareholders should have been keen to accept Warner Music's cash.

Mr Nicoli, the EMI chairman, had difficulty in getting the City's support through a rights issue to fund his purchase of Warner Music. However, Mr Bronfman, the Warner Music chairman, appeared to have persuaded his backers that the whole deal could be financed with debt. His financing was therefore more secure, even if it was much higher risk.

Warner Music's Pac-Man defence was successful because its offer was rejected by EMI and EMI didn't make a further counter offer for Warner Music.

Issue a revised profit forecast

A report may be prepared by the target company indicating a forecast profit improvement at better than market expectations. Again, this must be prepared very carefully by the directors of the target company to maintain credibility. It may be quite reasonable for shareholders to question why profit forecasts have now suddenly been improved. If the market accepts the revised profit forecast, the share price may rise and make the proposed takeover more expensive.

If the market does not accept the revised forecast then obviously this tactic will not work. If, subsequent to the revised forecasts, the profit levels are not achieved then the share price will drop, bringing an increased risk of takeover and a loss of credibility in the repeat use of such a defence. This may also possibly make a takeover even cheaper and easier, which therefore defeats the initial aim of the profit announcement.

Take over another company

The target company may buy new assets or companies that are incompatible with the predator company's business. Alternatively, the target company may sell off the 'crown jewels', the assets in which the predator company is particularly interested. This is similar to the pre-bid takeover defence divestment strategy.

Both of these strategies are employed to make the potential takeover less attractive to the predator company, and to encourage it to withdraw. However, the City Code on M&As restricts such selling off of assets once a takeover bid has been made.

Find a white knight

A device that is sometimes seen as a last resort is for the target company to seek out a more acceptable company, a **white knight**, to take it over. An example of this is shown in the press extract below. The argument is that it is better for a company to be taken over by a company of its choice rather than some other hostile bidder. The City Code on M&As allows this tactic only if any information passed to the white knight is also passed to the initial predator.

Alternatively, the target company, with shareholders' prior approval, may issue new shares to a white knight to dilute the predator company's holdings. This again includes the involvement of a 'friendly pair of hands'.

It should be noted that the use of either of these options to defend against a takeover bid requires the approval of shareholders.

Jousting match for white knight

The jousting match for Canadian uranium producer, Hathor Exploration, intensified yesterday as the white knight Rio Tinto trumped an unsolicited offer from its rival suitor Cameco for a second time. Rio Tinto increased its offer for the northern Saskatchewan-focused aluminium giant to C$654m (£404m), topping a revised offer by Canada's Cameco on Monday. Rio's latest bid is 4.5 per cent higher than Cameco's offer and 13 per cent more than its previous C$578m approach last month.

Rio made its first white knight bid after Hathor's board rejected an unsolicited approach from Cameco in September on the basis that it undervalued the company. Hathor's board, which said on Monday that it would review Cameco's latest offer before deciding whether to recommend it to its shareholders, unanimously backed Rio Tinto's latest offer yesterday. Cameco, the world's largest aluminium producer, declined to say if it would raise its offer further.

Acquiring the Vancouver-based Hathor would give Rio Tinto control of the Roughrider deposit in northern Saskatchewan's Athabasca Basin, which is estimated to contain about 35.4 million kilograms of nuclear reactor fuel. These will add to its interest in uranium mines in Australia and Namibia.

The uranium industry has seen its fortunes slump since the Fukushima disaster in March, which has prompted countries such as Japan and Germany to end their reliance on nuclear power. This has forced down the price of uranium by about a fifth to about $55 a pound. At the same time, the costs of extracting the metal are rising, further squeezing producers' profitability and investment plans. Nonetheless, Rio Tinto believes that the acquisition of Hathor would give the group a considerable boost.

Announcing its first offer, last month, its chief executive, Doug Ritchie, said: 'The medium- and long-term outlook for the uranium market is positive, with uranium assuming a significant role in the world's primary energy needs.' He added: 'This acquisition will allow us to build on the plat-

form successfully laid out by Hathor and we will continue to draw on their expertise and commitment. Canada is a country crucial to our business and growth plans.'

Although Rio is bullish about the longer-term prospects for uranium mining, it is less so about aluminium. On Wednesday, it announced the closure of its aluminium smelter in Lynemouth, a sign that the industry is feeling the pinch from lower metals prices and high costs.

Source: **Rio Tinto ups bid for Hathor to trump offer from Cameco**, by Tom Bawden © *The Independent*, 19 November 2011

The position of shareholders, managers, employees, and financial institutions in M&As

M&As obviously impact on shareholders, and directors and managers of both the target and acquiring companies. They also impact on other stakeholders like employees, and on financial institutions like insurance companies, pension funds, and merchant banks.

In theory, the economy should gain if assets are transferred from inefficient to efficient management. However, empirical research by Cowling *et al.* (Cowling, K, Stoneman, P, and Cubbin, J (1986) *Mergers and Economic Performance*, Cambridge: Cambridge University Press) in the 1980s suggested that in fact M&As at best had a neutral impact on the economy as a whole, and provided no great efficiency gains.

Shareholders

Target company shareholders generally appear to enjoy significant returns while predator company shareholders experience insignificant or negative returns.

A quantified look at both post-acquisition financial performance and share price movement by the financial press leads them to conclude more often than not that merger and takeover activity is not wealth-creating but instead involves the transfer of wealth from predator to target company shareholders.

Managers and employees

The directors and managers in predator companies generally benefit from successful takeovers. This is because their power and security is further strengthened. Post-takeover, managers have increased power and status from running a larger company, often reflected in increased rewards. However, this may not necessarily be totally to the benefit of the shareholders. Directors' jobs become more secure since it is more difficult for a larger company to be subsequently taken over. This may be beneficial for the shareholders if the new larger company is value-adding.

The directors and managers of target companies generally lose out after a takeover, because they may be deemed inefficient or surplus to requirements. There may be a duplication of departments, and particularly a duplication of senior management roles. Employees of target companies usually suffer in the same way, from the results of economies of scale, resulting in:

- redundancies from duplicated functions
- the closing down of unwanted parts of the acquired business.

After all, synergies and economies of scale are usually the very reasons and justifications of M&As, and so therefore there is usually a high chance of these outcomes.

Financial institutions

Financial institutions usually earn large fees from their advisory roles to target companies and acquiring companies in M&As. The financial institutions in M&As, such as merchant banks, investment banks, and M&A lawyers and accountants, are usually some of the really big winners, as well as the shareholders of the target companies.

Financial institutions are always one of the parties benefiting most from M&As because they are indispensable in a wide range of roles from advice on bid values, to organising pre- and post-bid defences, to arrangement of financing.

Progress check 17.4

What are the main impacts on the directors and managers of companies involved in M&As?

Summary of key points

- There are a number of ways in which mergers and acquisitions (M&As) may be financed which include the use of cash, equity shares, and debt.

- Cash may be the preferred option of the shareholders of a company being taken over, but both debt and equity are widely used in financing M&As.

- There are many advantages and disadvantages to shareholders that result from the use of cash, debt, or equity in the financing of M&As.

- The accounting treatment of an M&A is dependent on the type of deal and how it is financed.

- There are a number of financial strategies relating to acquisitions and the ways in which suitable target companies may be identified and potential synergies evaluated.

- Many different types of takeover defences may be used by a company before a formal takeover bid has been made to try and avoid being taken over.

- Many different types of takeover defences may be used by a company to repel a takeover once a formal takeover bid has been made.

- M&A deals may have significant impacts on shareholders, directors, managers, employees, and financial institutions.

Glossary of key terms

conversion ratio The number of ordinary shares that will be obtained from the conversion of one unit of a convertible bond.

conversion value The market value of the ordinary shares into which a unit of a convertible bond may be converted.

coupon yield The interest paid on the nominal value of a bond (or a loan, or debenture).

earn-out method Target company shareholders receive part payment on acquisition, with the balance deferred a couple of years until a specific agreed level of profits has been achieved so that the eventual price paid for the acquisition may be tied to the subsequent growth rate in the early years following transfer of ownership. This arrangement gives a measure of security to the new owners, who pass some of the financial risk associated with the purchase of a new enterprise to the target company.

golden parachute An extremely generous termination package that may be introduced into a target company's directors' contracts if there is a threat of a takeover, which effectively increases the cost of a takeover.

greenmailing A corporate raider may buy a stake in a company that is considered to be significantly undervalued, and in this way greenmail the management, accusing them of running the company to the detriment of the shareholders by not aiming to maximise shareholder wealth. The greenmail threat is to acquire the entire company, sack the management, and implement a new strategy.

merger accounting A method of accounting which treats two or more parties as combining on an equal footing. It is normally applied without any restatement of net assets to fair value, and includes the results of each for the whole of the accounting period. Correspondingly, it does not reflect the issue of shares as an application of resources at fair value. The difference that arises on consolidation does not represent goodwill but is deducted from, or added to, reserves (FRS 6).

mixed bid A share-for-share offer for a target company supported by a cash alternative, which means that its shareholders can choose the method that best suits their individual liquidity preferences and tax positions.

Pac-Man defence A reverse takeover, where a target company may make a counter-bid for the shares of the predator company.

poison pill A contractual obligation or a feature of the target company's capital structure that has the effect of increasing the cost of possible acquisition to make it less attractive to the predator company, and therefore less likely to take place.

reverse takeover See Pac-Man defence.

straight bond value The market value of a bond, which is dependent on the coupon rate relative to market interest rates.

takeover accounting A method of accounting which regards the business combination as the acquisition of one company by another: the identifiable assets and liabilities of the company acquired are included in the consolidated balance sheet at their fair value at the date of acquisition. The difference between the fair value of the consideration given and the fair values of the net assets of the entity acquired is accounted for as goodwill (FRS 6).

vendor placing A vendor placing involves the acquiring company offering shares to the target company with the option to continue their shareholding, and at the same time arranging for the new shares to be placed with institutional investors at a pre-determined price and for cash to be paid to the target company's shareholders.

white knight A more acceptable company which the target company may seek out to take it over with the rationale that it is better to be taken over by a company of its choice rather than some other hostile bidder.

Assessment material

Questions

Q17.1 Why is the method of financing important in M&As?

Q17.2 In what ways does a cash purchase of a business differ from a vendor placing?

Q17.3 How may eps be enhanced from a takeover?

Q17.4 Describe the various forms of equity restructuring that may be used by a target company to avoid its being taken over.

Q17.5 How may profit announcements, and changes in dividend policy, be used by target companies to provide defences after a takeover bid has been made?

Q17.6 Describe and explain the range of defence strategies used by companies facing a hostile takeover bid.

Q17.7 Outline the types of problem faced by employees and managers after their company has been taken over.

Discussion points

D17.1 'Takeovers merely satisfy the inflated egos of power-hungry company bosses.' Discuss.

D17.2 'The ways in which M&As are financed do not have any influence on their subsequent success.' Discuss.

D17.3 'There is no real defence against a takeover bid from a determined predator company.' Discuss.

D17.4 'The position of shareholders, managers, and employees in M&As is largely disregarded by both predator and target companies.' Discuss.

Exercises

Solutions are provided in Appendix 2 to all exercise numbers highlighted in colour.

Level I

E17.1 *Time allowed – 30 minutes*

Explain the advantages and disadvantages of using debt or equity in financing acquisitions.

E17.2   *Time allowed – 30 minutes*

Explain what is meant by a convertible bond and discuss the advantages from its use in financing a takeover.

E17.3   *Time allowed – 45 minutes*

Outline the alternative methods that may be used to finance an acquisition and the circumstances in which each method may be appropriate.

Level II

E17.4   *Time allowed – 45 minutes*

Explain some of the financial strategies that may be used in acquisitions and consider the possible impacts of these on both predator and target companies.

E17.5   *Time allowed – 45 minutes*

Discuss the reasons why a hostile takeover bid may be opposed by a target company. Outline three pre-bid and four post-bid defences and how they may be effectively employed to avoid a takeover.

E17.6   *Time allowed – 45 minutes*

Outline the differences between merger accounting rules and takeover accounting rules. What types of merger allow merger accounting rules to be used?

E17.7   *Time allowed – 45 minutes*

Explain the possible impact of M&As on shareholders, managers, and employees of both predator and target companies.

E17.8   *Time allowed – 45 minutes*
Blue Sky plc is a UK-based retail company. The company is considering expanding its retail operations and is considering the acquisition of rival company White Cloud plc. Blue Sky plc has a current market value of £80m, and White Cloud plc has a current market value of £50m. Blue Sky plc expects the acquisition of White Cloud plc to result in substantial economies of scale, which will result in savings of £2.75m per year in perpetuity.

Blue Sky plc requires a rate of return on all investments of 10% per annum and has estimated that, as a result of the acquisition, transaction costs of £5m will be incurred.

Required:

(i) Briefly explain the main reasons why a company would seek to acquire another company.

(ii) Calculate the present value of the gain to Blue Sky plc from the acquisition of White Cloud plc.

(iii) If a cash offer of £65m is accepted by White Cloud plc's shareholders what value would be created for Blue Sky plc's shareholders?

(iv) If a share offer is made providing White Cloud plc's shareholders with a 30% holding in Blue Sky plc after the acquisition, what value would be created for Blue Sky plc's shareholders?

(v) If White Cloud plc were to contest the offer, what possible defences could the company use to defend itself against the takeover bid?

E17.9 *Time allowed – 45 minutes*

Arkwright plc is a UK-based manufacturing company. The company has a weighted average cost of capital of 10%, and is financed partly by equity (cost 12%) and partly by debt capital (cost 8%).

The company is considering acquiring Granville Ltd, a design company. The acquisition of Granville Ltd would cost £10m. However, the acquisition is expected to yield additional annual profits of £2m before interest charges.

The company expects to finance the investment with a further loan at a cost of 8% per annum. As a result of this additional borrowing, the company expects its cost of equity to rise to 15%. The company pays out all profits in dividends, which are currently £3.6m a year.

You may assume the traditional view of WACC and gearing.

Required:

(i) Calculate the effect of acquiring Granville Ltd on the value of Arkwright plc's equity.

(ii) Calculate the extent to which the change in the value of Arkwright plc's equity is caused by:
   (a) the NPV of the project at the current WACC
   (b) the method of financing.

(iii) Briefly explain why the company's cost of equity would increase as the company increases its total borrowing.

18

Reorganisations and restructuring

Chapter contents

Learning objectives

Completion of this chapter will enable you to:

- Explain the reasons why company reorganisations and restructuring may take place.
- Outline the ways in which company reorganisations and restructuring may be made.
- Identify the financial strategies that may be adopted in response to issues internal to a company that may necessitate its reorganisation.
- Identify the financial strategies that may be adopted in response to issues external to a company that may necessitate its reorganisation.
- Appreciate the differences between the two forms of 'privatisation': sale by government; return to private ownership.
- Consider the use of management buy-outs (MBOs) and management buy-ins (MBIs) as methods of restructuring and refinancing companies.
- Outline the problems that may be faced by MBOs and MBIs.

Introduction

As businesses grow and develop they inevitably face many challenges as well as opportunities resulting from changes in their internal operations and structures, and factors in their external environment. The development of a business may result in internal changes to its financial structure resulting in its gearing being too high or too low. Alternatively, there may be external factors that impact on the company such as its shares trading at a price well below their fair value. This chapter will consider the reorganisations of companies that involve the adoption of appropriate financial strategies in response to both internal and external issues.

In the past, many UK businesses and some entire industrial sectors became Government-owned as a result of political decisions or because they may have suffered financial problems and therefore needed rescuing. Subsequently, during the latter part of the last century, many businesses were restructured by being sold back by the UK Government to the private sector, through public flotation. Such sales by government are examples of **privatisation**. The other type of privatisation dealt with in this chapter is a return to private ownership, moving from plc to Ltd company status. We will consider the reasons and the timings of these returns to private ownership, which are called **re-privatisations**.

Two other forms of company restructuring are management buy-outs (MBOs) and **management buy-ins (MBIs)**. This chapter will look at how a company may be purchased from its shareholders and managed by its existing managers (MBO) or managed by a new team of managers brought in from outside the company (MBI). We will also look at some of the problems encountered and to be overcome by MBOs and MBIs in order to ensure their success.

Reasons for reorganisations and restructuring

In the following sections we will look at how company restructuring takes place when:

- a company is in trouble due to internal issues, such as inappropriate financial strategies
- a company experiences a market under-pricing of its shares, which is an example of an external issue.

The financial strategy of any business should generally change over time as it progresses through its business life cycle and in accordance with the development of its business strategy.

The financial strategy of a company may be wrong because:

- it has too little debt
- it may have too much debt,

which are gearing problems and are issues that are internal to the company.

A company's shares may be trading at a market value considerably below a fair value. This is the perception of the company's share price by the market, which may not be an efficient market. Major changes in business strategy may be stimulated by the threat of a takeover. These are issues that are external to the company.

There are a number of ways in which a company may respond to these internal and external issues. We will consider financial strategies in response to both.

Reorganisation – financial strategies in response to internal issues

A mature company may, for example, have too little debt because it has continued to be financed by equity for some time. This may have been deliberate company policy, even if it may have been misguided. Such a company can re-balance its levels of debt and equity in three ways, which are shown in Figure 18.1.

If a company has a high level of equity compared to its level of debt, and assuming it has the cash available, it may pay out a special dividend far in excess of normal levels, which enables shareholders

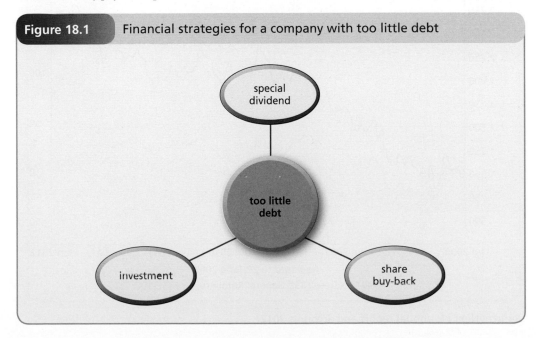

| Figure 18.1 | Financial strategies for a company with too little debt |

to reinvest their funds. Alternatively, it may undertake a share buy-back (see Chapter 15). In a share buy-back, as we have seen, a company buys back its shares on the open market, and cancels them in its balance sheet (in the UK) and therefore reduces its equity and increases its gearing (assuming it is financed by both debt and equity). An example of this is shown in Mini case 18.1 below.

Mini case 18.1

Next plc, the UK clothing retailer, has been undertaking an annual share buy-back programme since 2000. The impact has been to maintain a high share price, and outperform competitors. The downside has been consistently high levels of gearing. The chart below shows the number of shares re-purchased and the amount of cash returned to shareholders by Next since 2008. It also shows the impact on the company's share price and gearing over that period.

	2012	2011	2010	2009	2008
Cash returned to shareholders £m	291.1	221.6	120.1	53.6	412.9
Shares re-purchased m	12.5	10.0	5.9	3.9	26.1
Gearing %	74.85	66.98	79.59	78.37	117.20

The graphs in Figure 18.2 below show how Next plc's share price outperformed both the FTSE General Retailers and the FTSE 100 indices between July 2008 and January 2012.

Such strategies of share re-purchase and returns of cash to shareholders are only sustainable if a company is generating high levels of free cash flow, which as a major high street retailer Next plc has been able to do.

Figure 18.2   Next share price performance July 2008 to January 2012

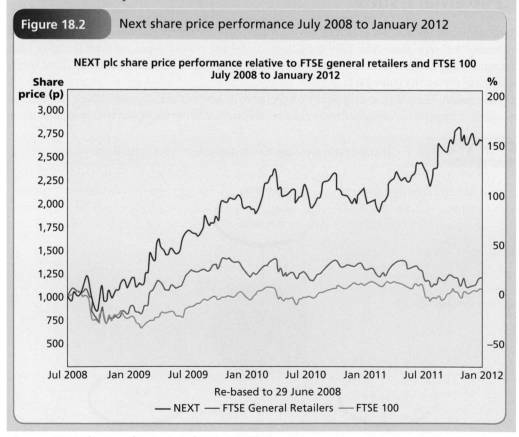

NEXT plc share price performance relative to FTSE general retailers and FTSE 100 July 2008 to January 2012

Re-based to 29 June 2008
—— NEXT —— FTSE General Retailers —— FTSE 100

Source: Next plc annual report and accounts 2012.

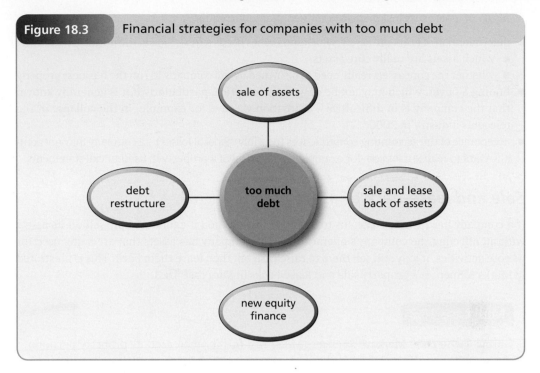

Figure 18.3 Financial strategies for companies with too much debt

If a company has a comparatively low level of debt and therefore a high level of equity then it can use that equity to invest in value-enhancing new projects. Alternatively, a company may have too much debt due to a misguided financial strategy, or because of a failure to adapt to changing circumstances, for example falling operating profits. Such a company may adopt one or more of the financial strategies shown in Figure 18.3.

Sale of assets

Companies may sell surplus assets to raise cash, and if the assets are non-core assets then this may be a simple method to action. A company may dispose of some of its assets for a number of reasons and in a number of ways. For example, core assets may be sold to a financing company and then leased back, to provide an immediate increase in cash flow. This is illustrated in Tesco's proposed split of its property portfolio in Mini case 18.2.

Mini case 18.2

In March 2006, the *Daily Telegraph* reported that the UK's biggest retailer, Tesco plc, was planning to place its £12bn (US$21bn) freehold property into a real estate investment trust (REIT) to enable it to use the money raised from selling shares in the REIT to buy back its own shares. After the report appeared saying that the company planned to unlock more value from its property assets, shares in the supermarket giant rose to a record high. Tesco denied that it had immediate plans to do this, but its finance director, Andrew Higginson, said: 'We're obviously interested [in REITs] in the sense that we're a big property company. We've got people looking at whether it's a good idea.'

A sale of assets surplus to operational requirements requires:

- determination of non-core assets, which sometimes needs a fresh look at the business regarding:
  - which assets are really core assets
  - whether the core assets really need to be owned by the company to run the business properly
- finding a buyer, which may not be easy at a good price, particularly if it is generally known that the company is in difficulties – a situation we saw, for example, in the collapse of the telecoms industry in 2000
- acceptance of the accounting consequences (possibly disposal losses) – a company may not actually want to realise a loss on, for example, the disposal of a property in its financial statements.

Sale and lease-back of assets

If a company has no assets surplus to its requirements then it cannot simply sell off its assets without affecting the company's operations. If the company has assets that are being used for its core activities, it may still sell them to raise cash but then lease them back. This is illustrated in Marks & Spencer's property sale and lease-backs in Mini case 18.3.

Mini case 18.3

During 1999/2000 Marks & Spencer (M&S) had further increased its property portfolio through the acquisition of 19 Littlewoods stores. By 2001 M&S continued to suffer from the sales shortfalls that had affected the company over the previous three years. M&S needed to improve its cash flow and had already announced that it would be closing six of the Littlewoods stores. M&S also signed a number of sale and lease-back agreements relating to a significant proportion of its UK properties. In this way it could benefit from the immediate cash flow of selling the properties, in return for renting back the properties on an annual basis over subsequent years.

New equity finance

Cash may be raised from new investors through an issue of new equity, or from existing equity shareholders. A deep discount rights issue may be most appropriate for raising equity from existing shareholders (see Chapter 15). In this way, by offering shares to existing shareholders at such a huge discount on the current market price of its shares a company may be assured of raising the level of new finance it requires. The press extract below describes China Citic Bank's rights issue in June 2011, which raised cash to improve its capital ratio. The effectiveness of rights issues depends on timing and a depressed market can damage the impact of the share offering.

A successful deep discount rights issue

China Citic Bank Corp launched a Rmb26bn ($4.01bn) dual rights issue on June 24 becoming the latest Chinese bank to boost its capital ratio. Citic will sell 2.48bn 'H' shares at HK$4 ($0.51) each and 5.32bn 'A' shares for Rmb3.33 each, offering two new shares for every 10 existing shares. But the company's stock has plummeted 9.3% since the beginning of June. 'The 'H' share price is much cheaper than we thought it would be,' said a China bank analyst at Macquarie. 'This has been bad timing for the bank as its stock price was already very suppressed.'

The rights price is just 0.9 times the book value. The 'H' share rights price represents a 20.14% discount to the bank's trading average for the 10 days before stock closed on Thursday at HK$5.02. Bank of China, China Construction Bank and ICBC offered discounts of around 40% on their rights issues last year, but their stocks had not slumped before launch.

Bankers expect the deal to do well because it is cheap, and because the bank's two big shareholders – Citic Group and BBVA – have both agreed to take up their full entitlements: around 75% of the deal. 'The bank needs very little to get it out in the market with these stakes secured,' said the analyst.

Several smaller banks are likely to follow Citic's example over the next few months. China Minsheng Bank is planning a Rmb29bn dual rights issue, and China Merchants Bank also intends to raise around Rmb140bn of capital – although it is unclear how much, if any, of this will come through a rights issue. China's five biggest banks – Agricultural Bank of China, Bank of China, Bank of Communications, China Construction Bank and ICBC – must have a 9.5% tier one capital ratio by 2013 to comply with local regulations, said an analyst. But China's other banks have until the end of 2016 to raise their capital ratios to 8.5%.

Citic's tier one capital is now 8.5%, but it needs to raise capital to maintain this ratio, said an analyst. China Merchants Bank meanwhile has a tier one ratio of 8%, as does Minsheng.

CICC and Citic Securities are joint global coordinators and underwriters of the deal, which will be marketed throughout July. The bank will announce the results of the rights issue – which represents around 16.7% of the enlarged share capital of the bank – on July 29.

Source: **Citic Bank surprises with cheaply priced rights issue** (uncredited article) © *Euroweek*, 30 June 2011

Citic Bank managed to raise funds by offering a 20% discount on its shares, but even deep discounted rights issues can fail if the timing of the issue is not right, as illustrated in the Pendragon press extract below.

A badly timed deep discount rights issue

Car dealer Pendragon's shares fell almost 7pc as it emerged that almost a third of the company's £75.2m rights issue was left on the books of the investment banks advising on the capital-raising. Pendragon carried out a nine-for-eight issue of new shares at 10p in July, when its shares were trading at around 21p.

Yesterday, the company said its brokers, RBS Hoare Govett, Barclays Capital and Arden Partners had failed to find investors willing to buy the rump of the heavily discounted rights issue. As a result, Pendragon's joint underwriters and sub-underwriters have been forced to take on the remaining 242.7m shares, 32pc of the rights issue.

This means the brokers are vulnerable to major changes in Pendragon's share price. Nick Bubb, an analyst at Arden Partners, which advised the company on the fundraising, said: 'Pendragon was unfortunate that the period of the rights issue announced on July 14 coincided with a major slump on global stockmarkets, but the 68pc take-up is creditable in the circumstances.'

Pendragon carried out the capital-raising to help it reduce its huge debt pile, much of which was accrued in 2006 when the company bought rival car dealer Reg Vardy for £500m. As part of the balance sheet restructuring, the company's lending banks have agreed new three-year loan terms and will cut its £300m debt burden to around £220m by December. This will allow the company to pay a dividend next year. Pendragon has also agreed to give pension trustees £36m of security in 17 of its properties in exchange for wiping out the £40m pension deficit.

The car dealer is expected to unveil interim results next week, according to Arden Partners. Mr Bubb said: 'We remain happy with our forecasts. Last week's riots in England don't seem to have impacted on September pre-orders for new cars. We

expect Pendragon to say ... that 2011 is going according to plan.

'The new car market is soft and so top-line sales are under some pressure, but operating costs are also falling and, with a steady gross margin, the earnings before interest and tax line is broadly flat in the UK, with the strong US business adding a bit of growth overall.'

Pendragon shares fell 0.7 to 10.5p.

Source: **Banks mop up Pendragon rights issue**, by Ben Harrington © *Daily Telegraph*, 18 August 2011

An alternative to straight equity is a convertible debt, providing advantages with regard to the company's eps and its cost of financing. Earnings per share are not immediately affected if such additional finance is provided, as there is no initial increase in the number of ordinary shares in issue. Since the cost of debt is generally lower than the cost of equity and has the benefit of the tax shield, then the cost of financing may also not be significantly increased, if at all. There is also the advantage of some downside risk protection for shareholders (if the share price should fall) and also an upside opportunity to make the risk worthwhile (if the share price should rise). In 2004 the hotel chain Accor restructured its business through an extension of its range of leisure products and casino interests, and its acquisition of 30% of the shares in the holiday village business Club Med Accor issued a €280m convertible bond to pay for its 30% stake.

Debt restructure

A company's short-term survival may be aided if lenders can be convinced of the advantages of waiving interest payments or extending the term of a loan. Arrangements with creditors, for example the banks and other debt-holders, may be negotiated to restructure debt. This usually works only if the banks are owed significant sums by the company. It is often said that: 'if you owe the bank £1 million then you have a problem; if you owe the bank £1 billion then the bank has a problem'.

If a company is in financial difficulties, then to avoid the possible liquidation of the company, a debt-for-equity swap may be effected to release existing loans in exchange for an equity stake. If the debt-holders become shareholders then they may share in its recovery. If, on the other hand, the company's creditors force it to repay debt then the company may go bust. Therefore the creditors will lose out.

Debt renegotiation is always difficult because of the different interests of various stakeholders. Another disadvantage of a debt-for-equity swap is the dilution of existing shareholdings, which may result in a conflict between debt-holders and shareholders. In the Endemol press extract below, creditors of the company wanted a debt–equity swap which would give them controlling interests in the heavily indebted media company but at the same time potential takeovers, particularly from Time Warner, were being mooted. The extract highlights the complexities surrounding the process of a debt–equity swap. Ultimately, the Time Warner bid came to nothing and in January 2012, Endemol's three owners agreed a restructuring which handed control to several major creditors.

The difficulties in debt restructuring

Time Warner has made an approach worth about € 1bn (US$1.4bn) for Endemol, the European television production group behind Big Brother and Deal Or No Deal, setting up a debate among creditors about whether to sell the group or continue with plans for a debt-for-equity swap. Time Warner declined to comment, but Endemol confirmed that it had received an approach from the US media group.

Four people familiar with the talks said that the group, which owns the Warner Brothers film and TV studios, had made a non-binding offer. Two of the people said that it faced competition from Silvio Berlusconi's Mediaset empire, which has joined forces with Clessidra, an Italian private equity group, and made its interest known. Mediaset, Goldman Sachs Capital Partners and Cyrte (an investment vehicle run by Endemol co-founder Jon de Mol) bought Endemol for €3.4bn in 2007, but were caught out by the crisis that followed the collapse of Lehman Brothers, which had handled the sale.

Creditors have spent months haggling over its €2.8bn debt load. Earnings before interest, tax, depreciation and amortisation are estimated to be between €135m and €150m this year. The two approaches – putting an enterprise value of €1bn on Endemol – had come in the past two weeks and were not far off the creditors' valuation, two people close to the situation said, but one of them said that creditors saw the offers as opportunistic and unlikely to succeed.

Creditors would consider in the next week whether to push ahead with a debt-for-equity swap that would cut debt to about €500m or pursue an auction to flush out other bidders, he added. Endemol's largest creditors include the private equity funds Apollo, Centerbridge and Providence Equity, and banks such as Barclays, Goldman Sachs, Royal Bank of Scotland and the Lehman estate. The funds have agreed a restructuring with Goldman and Cyrte but were still in talks with Lehman and RBS, one of the people said. Creditors have extended a waiver on the debt until mid-November and could do so again. Endemol said: 'Endemol is an attractive asset but this doesn't change anything. Talks with lenders are ongoing and we are confident discussions will end in an agreement which will put the company on a firm footing for the future.'

For Time Warner, an Endemol deal would confirm its focus on international expansion, following its acquisition of 31 per cent of CME, the eastern European channel owner and televison producer, its backing of a buy-out of Shed Media, a British television production company, and its acquisition of Chilevision, the Chilean broadcaster.

Progress check 18.1

What are the main financial strategies that may be adopted in response to internal restructuring issues?

Reorganisation – financial strategies in response to external issues

A company may be at a market value much lower than a fair value of its shares and therefore vulnerable to a possible takeover bid. To forestall an opportunistic takeover bid the company has a number of options:

- increase public relations activity to change market perception – the company may use public relations to explain its true value to shareholders and analysts
- a **demerger**, or a **spin-off** of some of the business units or divisions of the business, to demonstrate value
- go private – de-list the company from a public plc to a private Ltd company.

There are two meanings to the term 'going private':

- a sale by government
- a re-privatisation.

Demergers

A company may have, in the past, diversified into areas where it had no real prospects of developing and so a successful core business may have developed into a larger group without providing any additional value. Both shareholders and analysts may find diversified groups very difficult to understand, which may lead to market under-pricing of the shares of such a group.

The splitting up of diversified groups, or conglomerates, may clarify individual investments. In general, the post-split sum of the market values of the separated companies is usually greater than the value of the whole group before the split.

Companies may be split in the following ways:

- demerger
- spin-off
- sale of a subsidiary.

A demerger is where one listed company becomes two or more listed companies, generally of equal size and initially with the same shareholders, although this is not always necessarily the case (see the press extract below which reported on Punch Taverns' tenanted and managed public houses demerger).

Punch without spirit

Punch Taverns is sounding out equity analysts as to whether they will cover the highly indebted tenanted pub company following its demerger from the more promising managed pubs business this summer.

Brunswick, the company's public relations firm, rang round the sector's 20 or so equity analysts in April. A slight majority of those contacted by the FT said they would carry out equity research coverage on both Spirit plc – which will run the managed pubs and which has been valued at between 45p and 100p a share – and Punch plc, which will hold more than 5,000 tenanted pubs and is expected to trade as a penny stock. Ian Dyson, Punch Taverns' chief, will become chief executive of Spirit – but intends to sit on the board of Punch plc during the transition.

The PR team put no pressure on analysts who have yet to decide, but they did try to persuade at least one person who does not plan to cover the tenanted group. 'They said: 'You have to',' he recalled. 'And I said: 'No, I don't'.' Three analysts asked by the FT were undecided. Five said they would cover both businesses. One City analyst who plans to cover both Spirit and Punch said: 'I suspect that a load of people will dump Punch as soon as they can.' But Paul Hickman at Peel Hunt argued that because there would probably be substantial trading in the shares after the demerger, it would be unusual for many analysts to discontinue their coverage. Other analysts said the decision would be made during conversations with bosses. For those who do not cover Young & Co or Shepherd Neame – small UK pub groups – it might be strange to make an exception for the new Punch plc, which is expected to have a very small market capitalisation.

John Beaumont, analyst with Matrix, did a sum-of-the-parts analysis of the new Punch – including £2.5bn in debt, £120m of cash and a stake in drinks distributor Matthew Clarke. 'Until negotiations with bondholders have been successfully completed – which could take many months after demerger – we find it difficult to see why the market would give it a value of much more than a few pennies,' Mr Beaumont said.

Mr Dyson has said the internal split at Punch should be nearly complete by June. Decisions about external advisers, including PR teams, bankers and solicitors, will not be announced until after the demerger. If JPMorgan and Citigroup, the joint brokers for Punch Taverns, were to stay on as brokers for both Sprit and Punch, they would continue equity research coverage. Punch needs approval for the demerger by the UK pensions regulator and Ambac, an insurance company backing bonds issued by Punch and Spirit.

Source: Jacobs, R. (2011) Punch Taverns tries to gauge extent of coverage after group is split, *Financial Times*, 2 May.
© The Financial Times Limited 2012. All Rights Reserved.

A demerger may be contrasted with a spin-off, which is, for example, where a company divests itself of a division by distributing shares to its own shareholders usually in the form of a dividend. In a spin-off a subsidiary or division of a company may be actioned without any money changing hands, or it may be sold off in an IPO (initial public offering) as illustrated in the Pfizer press extract below.

Pfizer spins off

Pfizer is considering plans to raise US$3bn this year through a part-flotation of its animal health division, as it examines ways to spin off a business valued at as much as US$18bn. The pharmaceuticals group, the world's second largest by market capitalisation, has been talking to bankers about arranging an initial public offering that would place up to 19.9 per cent of the unit's shares in the autumn, in what is known as an equity carve-out or partial spin-off, according to people familiar with the talks.

Floating a stake in a business ahead of a spin-off is a common tactic to establish a shareholder following, improving its ability to trade as a stand-alone company. The value of spin-offs globally is set to double this year. Pfizer, whose animal health business is the largest in the world, said it was still evaluating all options for the division. It is set to announce a decision in the coming months.

Last year Pfizer revealed plans to shed the animal health division and its infant nutrition unit as part of efforts to streamline activities after investor criticism over poor returns. It appointed JPMorgan to explore alternatives for Animal Health, which has attracted the attention of Germany's Bayer and other companies. But a full-blown sale of the business was unlikely because of the tax hit that would be incurred by Pfizer, some of those familiar with the process said.

Analysts at Credit Suisse last year estimated the value of the unit at US$14.7bn to US$18.4bn. They described it as a market leader with a 19 per cent share of a market estimated at US$20bn. Morgan Stanley and Centerview are running an auction for the infant nutrition business, with Danone and Nestlé seen by people familiar with the pro-cess as frontrunners. That auction was in the second round of bidding, with offers valuing the business at about US$10bn, the people said.

The spin-offs highlight an increasing trend for companies to refocus their businesses by disposing of non-core assets, often after pressure from shareholders.

The global value of corporate spin-offs – whereby a division of a company is spun off as an independent listed business or is sold – is set to rise to £250bn in 2012, up 92 per cent from last year, according to analysis from Deloitte and The Spinoff Report, a specialist corporate break-up adviser.

The added value from the break-up of a company may be derived from:

- identification of the clearly defined segments of the business
- identification of the separate financial strategies of each business
- improved corporate governance
- better use of management incentives
- removal of the 'conglomerate discount', the reduced share price.

The size of a business is not necessarily a protection against takeover and the increasing power of corporate raiders. The current tendency is to reverse the trend of conglomeration. In this way, diversification strategies are reversed to concentrate on fewer core businesses.

As we have seen, demergers may be undertaken to improve the value attributed to the business by the financial markets. This was clearly illustrated by the break-up, or demerger, of British Telecom in 2001 into two separate businesses BT Group plc and mmO2 (subsequently re-branded as O2). BT Group plc retained the telecoms business and O2 took up the wireless business. O2 in particular has performed extremely successfully over the past few years.

Worked example 18.1

A demerger relates to the division of a corporate entity into a number of independent corporate entities. Why would a company choose to demerge and what are the potential problems that may arise out of such a strategy?

The possible reasons for a company considering a demerger are that:

- specific parts of the business may represent a poor strategic fit
- one or more subsidiaries may no longer complement the business's core activities
- there may be unprofitable activities
- parts of the business may have high-risk cash flows.

The potential problems that may arise from a demerger strategy are:

- economies of scale may be lost
- subsequent costs may be increased
- the company's asset backing may be reduced
- there may be a loss of operational synergies.

Privatisation – sale by government

A public sector organisation (a nationalised industry) may be 'publicly' floated (in the private sector!). This is a sale by government. We need to look at the reasons for such a privatisation and consider why and how the organisation came to be owned by a government in the first place.

Some businesses may have been acquired initially by a government by historical accident or because they were in financial distress and then ended up being rescued and owned by government. Subsequently, these businesses may then be returned to the private sector without subsequent controls, which it is argued that existing competition should provide. This argument says that controls may be exercised through the market. In the UK we have seen many examples like the rail network, the communications industry, and the motor industry, which may prompt us to question the effectiveness of market-driven controls.

Some businesses are effectively 'owned' by the UK Government, because of social policies or because of their strategic importance. Examples were the utilities and defence industries in the UK. A subsequent return to private ownership may require external regulation. An example of the type of control that may be put in place is a restriction to prevent foreign ownership of shares in the business of a defence contractor.

Privatisation through sale by government may run the risk of abuse of monopoly power by new owners. Privatisation of a major utility creates a natural monopoly, the abuse of which may be a great economic threat.

The removal or control of monopoly power may be achieved through:

- competition, which is difficult to achieve and may prove very expensive
- the subsequent introduction of regulatory controls.

We may question whether the introduction of competition post-privatisation really does provide the removal of, or adequate control over, the abuse of monopoly power.

Privatisation – return to private ownership

A publicly quoted company (plc) may be returned to private ownership, and this is called re-privatisation. A company may feel that its plc status may no longer be appropriate and may wish to revert to a more restricted and closely held ownership. We have already discussed an example of this in Richard Branson's Virgin Group. Subsequently, however, Branson appeared to change his strategy by offering parts of his business back to the public as separate entities.

The reasons for re-privatisation are usually linked to the company's original reasons for 'going public' and its position in its life cycle when this occurred. The original flotation may have been a cash-in or a cash-out flotation. A cash-in flotation is used to raise funds for the continued expansion of the company. A cash-out flotation is used to obtain an exit route for existing shareholders rather than to raise any new money. An example is the exit of venture capitalists from a growth company.

A company that floated in its mature, cash-positive phase should not want to re-privatise. If a mature company does want to re-privatise, it may be relatively easy to re-finance due to its strong cash position, the most common method being a management buy-out (MBO).

A reversal is more likely if the company was floated in its growth phase, when most of the initial financing was injected into the company. Then, as the company matured, cash flow would have become increasingly positive and so it would not have needed to raise additional funds. The main advantage that the shareholders of such a company would have from being public is the marketability of their shares. However, if shareholders still have high growth expectations, which the company may not be able to deliver, then the company may consider a reversal to private status.

Investors in a company that floated in its growth phase may no longer anticipate significant capital growth and the main advantage of plc status, the marketability of their shares, may not still apply. If only a small proportion of shares are publicly owned, a leveraged buy-out may be used. This means that the existing equity shareholders, who own a very large majority of the shares may obtain a relatively small loan to finance the purchase of the small number of shares that are in public hands. There is not a huge number of examples of this strategy; a company called Caparo Engineering employed this technique in 1991.

A company which floated on very high growth expectations (perhaps resulting from a breakdown of communications between the company and its investors) that it failed to deliver, may reverse its plc status as a part of a strategic repositioning. An example of this was where Andrew Lloyd Webber bought back his public Really Useful Group because of the pressure from other shareholders who required him to continually produce hit musicals.

A low share price and possibly insignificant dividends may lead to acceptance of any reasonable re-privatisation offer. Shareholders may be anxious to realise a realistic return on their investment. A change of management team and development of new strategies may also be necessary to avoid selling out at a heavily discounted share price. This strategy is called a management buy-in (MBI). An MBI is the same as an MBO except that the management team is a group of managers that is brought in from outside rather than managers who are already within the business.

Progress check 18.2

What are the main financial strategies that may be adopted in response to external restructuring issues?

Management buy-outs (MBOs)

A management buy-out (MBO) is the purchase of a business from its existing owners by members of the current management team, generally in association with a financial institution, for example a merchant bank or a venture capitalist. The management team may buy a part of a group, a division, or a subsidiary, or sometimes the whole group.

If a large proportion of the new finance, required to buy the business, is raised by external borrowing then the buy-out is described as a **leveraged MBO**. If the debt financing is greater than the equity then the MBO is said to be highly leveraged (or highly geared).

The impetus for an MBO

Where does the impetus for an MBO come from? Well, this may be seen from looking at the reasons why:

- a holding company may favour a buy-out
- management may favour a buy-out.

A holding company may favour an MBO for a number of reasons:

- to regain focus through disposal of a non-core business, because part of the business may have become non-core (for example the Chrysalis Group – see Mini case 18.4)
- to release funds to support the rest of the group – the release of capital may be for potentially more profitable investments
- to pass on a family business following retirement of the owners.

Mini case 18.4

LBC and Heart 106.2FM were London radio stations owned by the Chrysalis Group. In 2005 the group was in talks to sell off its books division in a £12.5m management buy-out. Chrysalis said that the business had reported 'extremely disappointing' full-year results and its write-downs related to the sale of the company to its management would create a significant exceptional loss. The chief executive of Chrysalis, Richard Huntingford, said the MBO deal would allow the group to start its new financial year in 'the right strategic shape', and referring to the books division he said 'it closes a chapter and one that has not been a happy experience for us'.

Management may favour a buy-out for a number of different reasons:

- to run the business autonomously without head office interference – ambitious management may see the potential for high growth
- fear that their division will be closed or outsourced, and so they will want to protect their jobs which may, for example, be threatened by outsourcing
- to run their own business rather than work for a new owner, therefore seeking independence and possibly greater job security.

Whether the MBO is driven by the management or the owners of the business will influence the early stages of development of an MBO. The particular reason will be an important influence on the attitudes of potential financiers and other stakeholders.

If the owners of a business have indicated their approval for an MBO then the management team will be able to pursue this in their own way, without interference, and approach alternative providers of finance and funding. This is the simplest situation since there is no conflict if the shareholders have accepted in principle.

If it is the directors or senior managers of the company that show initial interest in an MBO then their fiduciary duty may initially be questioned. Management should, by definition, be acting in the best interests of the shareholders. Management's interest in an MBO brings into question whose interests they are pursuing and is a further example of the agency problem.

Although the frequency of MBOs has reduced in recent years they still remain an attractive option for companies even though an MBO may or may not be in the best interests of the shareholders. In the CPA Global press extract below we can see that shareholders received a cash payment but were left with a minority stake in the company.

A Jersey-based MBO

CPA Global, the patent and legal services group, is set to complete on Thursday a management buy-out financed by Intermediate Capital Group, the private equity investor. The £440m deal will be structured as a scheme of arrangement in a Jersey court. It is the latest sign that the UK buy-out market, which fell to a 25-year low by deal volume last year, is picking up as banks start lending to private equity again.

ICG is best known as a provider of mezzanine finance, a hybrid between debt and equity, for private equity deals. But since 2007 the group's minority partners team has also been investing equity directly in management buy-outs. CPA, which was founded 40 years ago by UK law firms to manage patent renewals, is owned by more than 300 shareholders. Many of these are partners at the founding law firms who are reaching retirement age.

The sale of the Jersey-based company has been structured as a scheme of arrangement to help secure the green light from its diverse shareholder base. More than 90 per cent of shareholders approved the scheme last week. The deal is being financed with £175m of bank and mezzanine loans and a £50m revolving credit facility, provided by Lloyds Banking Group, HSBC, Bank of Ireland, Calyon, Bank of Scotland, Ares Capital Europe and ICG itself.

If the Royal Court of Jersey approves the scheme of arrangement on Thursday, CPA's 300 shareholders will receive a cash payment of about £260m and be left with 31 per cent of the company's equity. ICG is expected to take a stake of about 47 per cent, and the remaining 22 per cent will be held by management, led by chief executive Peter Sewell.

The deal includes an option for a co-investor to buy a further 9 per cent from the 300 selling shareholders. CPA employs 1,600 people. It generated £150m of revenues last year, with £45m of earnings before interest, tax, depreciation and amortisation. It has two businesses. The first is a patent renewals operation, which has a 35 per cent share of the renewals market. The second is a more recent move into the fast-expanding market for providing legal services to multinational companies, such as Rio Tinto.

ICG recently agreed the £975m sale of Marken, which provides distribution services to the pharmaceutical industry, to Apax Partners. Marken was one of the biggest and most profitable investments by the group's minority partners team.

Management may need to consider the feasibility of an MBO, before they approach the owners. This is a good approach because if the MBO is not feasible then the management team can drop the idea, and no-one is any the wiser. If the management team approach the owners and then fail to obtain the necessary financing they will find themselves in a very weak position. If the MBO is feasible they may then seek to obtain the necessary funding and then approach the owners of the business in a much stronger position. It is a good idea to first see how the company feels about an MBO, but there may possibly be legal problems regarding disclosure of information.

Alternatively, the management team may approach the owners before considering the MBO deal at all. This is the 'above the board' approach. The management team continue to respect their fiduciary duties by talking to owners before determining whether a deal can be done or not. However, if the owners of the business baulk at the idea then the management team could lose their jobs since they have no fall-back position.

Regardless of where the impetus for the buy-out originates, the management team need to approach the providers of finance, which may be venture capitalists (VCs), and consider the choice of debt or equity financing. The range of alternative providers of finance may only get involved with deals up to a particular level, or only within particular industries. The management team also need to approach and engage professional advisers, such as lawyers, accountants, and bankers. Since the management team is likely to lack experience in all these areas, particularly in managing the MBO project itself, and the various options with regard to financing, they should also appoint an MBO project manager.

Worked example 18.2

Management buy-outs have become increasingly popular over recent years. Which factors dictate whether the management buy-out will be successful?

Management buy-outs often occur as part of a corporate dis-investment strategy. The reasons for the dis-investment, together with the nature of the assets and liabilities of the business being divested, must be fully explored and understood by the buy-out team. The success of an MBO depends primarily on the skills of the management team and the price being paid for the MBO.

The stages of an MBO deal

Support for the deal must be secured before the MBO takes place, and the tax and legal implications must be fully considered. A fair price must be negotiated and agreed for the MBO, and a potential problem may be inadequate financing and asset backing. Following the MBO there may possibly be a loss of some employees if the business plans to relocate to another area. The maintenance of employee rights must be ensured for those employees that are retained.

Venture capitalists are the usual source of MBO funding, and normally provide a standard list of the stages of such a deal. The stages of a typical MBO deal are illustrated in Figure 18.4.

Due diligence is undertaken by the venture capitalists on both the company and the management team through trade references and references obtained from individuals, banks, professional bodies, and other sources. It is necessary to determine whether the management team is capable of seeing the MBO deal through and running the business. An assessment must be made to ascertain whether the management team has any serious flaws, and normally appraisals are carried out to determine whether there is one or more of the management team that may need to be replaced.

The management team may also carry out due diligence on the venture capitalists (or any other providers of capital) to confirm that they are good, reliable, supportive, and trustworthy investors. It is important that VCs are hands-on and likeable, and able to get on well with the management team.

The structuring of an MBO requires a balancing of the needs of each of the parties by resolving the issues of:

- the requirements of each of the parties
- the amount that the business can afford to pay for the buy-out
- funding requirements.

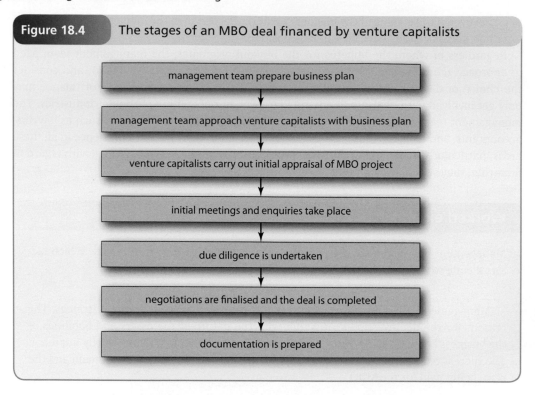

Figure 18.4 The stages of an MBO deal financed by venture capitalists

> management team prepare business plan
>
> ↓
>
> management team approach venture capitalists with business plan
>
> ↓
>
> venture capitalists carry out initial appraisal of MBO project
>
> ↓
>
> initial meetings and enquiries take place
>
> ↓
>
> due diligence is undertaken
>
> ↓
>
> negotiations are finalised and the deal is completed
>
> ↓
>
> documentation is prepared

Each of the parties involved in an MBO will have different requirements. Lenders are generally looking for low-risk investments, and require downside risk protection provided by, for example, covenants and security (leverage). Each of the members of the management team are usually motivated by wanting to be their own boss and the expectation of job security. They want to get a share in the equity of the business, and to get rich. Venture capitalists want a high return on equity, and a planned exit route out of the company, usually within a few years.

An MBO will have an impact on the cash flow of the business with regard to its being able to provide a return to both lenders and investors. Therefore, the amount that the management team can afford to pay for the business needs to be considered in terms of forecast profit levels, and its proposed levels of funding through debt and equity, and levels of interest cover and cash flow cover required (see Worked example 18.3).

Worked example 18.3

Jetrac Ltd is a well-established private company. The owners of the company are considering disposing of all their business interests, and have asked the senior management group of the company if they would be interested in buying the company. The owners of the company have suggested a valuation of the company at £75m. The earnings of Jetrac Ltd for the year ending 31 March 2012 were £4m after interest and tax, and dividends were £2.5m. Earnings and dividends are expected to grow at 4% per annum for the foreseeable future. We may assume that investments in similar companies to Jetrac Ltd currently achieve a return of 8% per annum.

We are required to calculate what may be considered to be a fair value of the share capital of the company.

A fair value of the company may be calculated as follows:

$$\frac{\text{retained earnings} \times \text{annual growth rate}}{\text{expected return} - \text{annual growth rate}} = \frac{£2.5\text{m} \times 1.04}{(0.08 - 0.04)}$$

$$= £65\text{m}$$

The owners of the company appear to be over-stating its value by £10m.

Funding requirements must be considered to cover the purchase price of the business that has been negotiated, the costs of further development of the business, and of course the professional fees, which are not insignificant. Professional fees usually amount to about 5% of the total deal. The three issues considered above are really the constraints in considering determination of:

- the total funding needed
- how much funding should be debt
- how much funding should be provided by the management team.

Funding needs to be determined with regard to how much is needed for the deal itself plus the professional fees, and also for working capital requirements. While debt is generally at a lower cost than equity, the level of gearing will affect the return on equity. Also, debt usually requires security and so debt levels are dependent on the asset backing that the business is able to provide and the quality and levels of cash flows the business can generate.

In addition to external funding for an MBO, the level of finance provided by the management team is also important. How much funding should the management team provide? In an MBO, each manager generally puts in the equivalent of one year's salary and maybe more. The MBO team needs to decide upon how much the relative ownership proportions should be. They also need to specify the level of returns they require and determine a dividend policy for the business.

Documentation for the MBO deal necessarily includes all sale and purchase agreements, loan agreements, covenants, new articles and memorandum of association for the new company, employment contracts, key employee insurance, etc.

Worked example 18.4

The management of a plc are interested in making an offer to its shareholders for an MBO. Assuming that the shareholders' approval to pursue the MBO in principle has been provided, we will consider some of the factors that the management team may need to consider.

Typically, the management team will agree as to who will become the managing director. The team will appoint a firm of financial consultants and together they will assess the viability and suitability of the buy-out.

The consultants assist in the formulation of a business plan and an evaluation of the seller's asking price, and negotiation of the purchase of the business. The management team also needs to appoint legal consultants and select a firm of auditors, and ensure that due diligence tests are implemented.

If equity is required to fund the MBO then equity advisers must be selected and written offers obtained, followed by the selection of a lead investor and negotiation of the best equity deal.

After all necessary debt, equity, and other finance has been secured then all necessary legal documents are prepared and legal ownership is passed to the management team.

Worked examples 18.5, 18.6, and 18.7 illustrate how an MBO may be funded and the type of returns that may be expected by each of the parties involved in the deal.

Worked example 18.5

During 2011 a large UK plc, the Nikos Group, agreed an MBO by the directors of one of its subsidiaries, Chance Ltd. To finance the MBO deal, the directors of Chance have established a relationship with the ITCD bank and engaged venture capitalists Siluc. Chance's directors have agreed to buy the company for £18m and require a further £4m for working capital requirements and to cover the costs of the MBO. Between them the directors were able to invest a maximum of £500,000 in the MBO. They expected that the company's performance would immediately be greatly improved during the first year following the buy-out and they forecast an operating profit of £2.6m for the year ended 31 December 2012.

The ITCD bank agreed to provide loan capital at 6.5% per annum, but with two important covenants:

- interest cover during the first year must be maintained at a minimum of four times
- gearing must not be greater than 45% of total funding.

To assist during the planning and roll-out of the MBO, Siluc and the directors of Chance employed a financial adviser specialising in MBOs, whose first task was to recommend an appropriate financial structure.

The limit of the funding by the ITCD bank first needed to be established:

expected operating profit for 2012	= £2.6m
interest cover	= 4 times
therefore the maximum interest at 6.5% per annum	= £650,000
which meant a potential maximum loan of	£10m

However, the total funding requirement was £22m, to cover the purchase of the company including costs and working capital requirement. ITCD imposed the condition that the loan may not exceed 45% of the total funding.

45% of the total funding of £22m = £9.9m

Therefore, the maximum bank loan must be restricted to £9.9m even though £10m appeared possible based on the interest cover restriction.

Since the maximum bank loan was £9.9m, then the balance of funding required of £12.1m must be provided by the directors of Chance Ltd and Siluc, the venture capitalists, as follows:

Chance Ltd directors	=	£500,000	(4.1%)
Siluc	=	£11,600,000	(95.9%)
total		£12,100,000	(100.0%)

When the total funding requirements have been agreed, together with the level of debt and the contribution of the management team, then the balance required from venture capitalists can be assessed. The VC contribution may be in the form of ordinary shares, preference shares, or debt.

Worked example 18.6

Using the information from Worked example 18.5, we will consider the next issue that the financial adviser needed to address with Siluc and the directors, which was the terms of their investment in the MBO.

The directors indicated that they would feel disadvantaged and demotivated if they received only 4.1% of the ordinary share capital of the new business, compared to Siluc's 95.9%. They were expecting over 20% of the business.

The financial adviser suggested that this problem may be overcome by using preference gearing, where Siluc's investment would be partly in ordinary shares and partly in preference shares. He suggested £10m preference shares with a fixed dividend of 5% per annum.

The investments by Siluc and the directors of Chance would therefore be:

	Ordinary £1 shares	Preference £1 shares	Total
Chance Ltd directors	£0.5m (23.8%)	–	£0.5m
Siluc	£1.6m (76.2%)	£10.0m	£11.6m
	£2.1m (100.0%)	£10.0m	£12.1m

The decision about how much capital goes into ordinary shares and how much into preference shares is crucial in structuring the financing of an MBO. Preferential gearing is a method devised to give the management team proportionately more of the equity than their monetary contribution alone would deserve.

Preferential gearing is used to motivate management with the option to enlarge its participation if the MBO is successful through greater equity participation.

A convertible redeemable preference share is also a particularly suitable financial instrument for MBOs. These are preference shares that are convertible into ordinary shares at a later date. The terms of conversion into ordinary shares may be established so that preference shares can possibly start converting in three to five years, after it has been confirmed that a degree of success of the MBO has been achieved. This gives time for the MBO to establish itself.

Worked example 18.7

Using the information from Worked examples 18.5 and 18.6, we will consider the subsequent growth and future of the MBO. During the three years since the MBO, the business was transformed and improved so that profit forecasts were exceeded and £7.1m of the original loan had been repaid. If we assume that three years after a successful MBO, the Chance Ltd directors and Siluc, the venture capitalists, decide that they wish to sell the business, we may consider what sort of returns each may expect. The company still had growth potential and a prospective buyer had offered £27.5m for the business including taking over its remaining debt of £2.8m.

	MBO	Sale of business
total funding of MBO	£22.0m	
sale of business		£27.5m
less: bank loan	£(9.9)m	£(2.8)m
	£12.1m	£24.7m
less: preference share capital	£(10.0)m	£(10.0)m
equity capital	£2.1m	£14.7m
split of equity capital:		
Chance directors (23.8%)	£0.5m	£3.5m
Siluc (76.2%)	£1.6m	£11.2m
total equity capital	£2.1m	£14.7m

The directors of Chance Ltd can be seen to have increased their initial investment of £0.5m seven times to £3.5m over three years.

The venture capitalists made an initial investment of £11.6m (£1.6m being ordinary shares) and received dividends on their preference shares for three years at 5% on £10m, which at £0.5m per year is a total of £1.5m. Siluc's cash flows over three years may be summarised as follows:

Year	Cash flow £m	
0	(11.6)	initial capital investment
1	0.5	preference dividend
2	0.5	preference dividend
3	0.5	preference dividend
3	22.2	repayment of capital [£10.0m preference shares + £11.2m equity]

which in discounted cash flow terms represents a pre-tax internal rate of return of 61%.

Progress check 18.3

What is a management buy-out (MBO)?

Management buy-ins (MBIs)

A management buy-in (MBI) occurs when a group of experienced managers from outside the company, with a good track record, are brought into the company to run it. A buy-in may occur when a business runs into trouble and a group of outside managers sees an opportunity to take over the business and restore its profitability. We have over the past few years seen many examples of buy-ins, such as Gary Lineker's association with Leicester City football club in 2002, and Adrian Wright's £30m bid for Moss Brothers in 2005. A further, more recent example of a buy-in was the intervention of a consortium led by a former player, Ken Moss, to take over Wasps rugby union club in April 2012 (see the press extract below).

MBI Moss injection to make Wasps buzz

Wasps will be saved from going into administration if they avoid relegation from the Premiership next weekend, with former player Ken Moss understood to be heading up a consortium to buy the London club from owner Steve Hayes. The deal is expected to be finalised next week but remains dependent on the club, who are four points ahead of bottom-placed Newcastle, avoiding the drop. 'We just have to win. It's in our hands,' said Dai Young, the Wasps director of rugby. Wasps will go down if the Falcons win the match by 24 points or more and deny the hosts a losing bonus point.

Moss, who played for Wasps from 1985–90, has put together a deal that will inject the required £2million to keep the club afloat for another season. The consortium is also seeking investment to secure the club's long-term future. Wasps have enough funding to see out this season, but without fresh investment would be forced into administration. Rugby Football Union regulations state that any club who remain in administration beyond six weeks will be docked 22 points, which would see Wasps relegated to the Championship.

Hayes, who bought the club in 2008, is prepared to write off shareholder debts of about £10million, effectively reducing the asking price to £1.5million, the club's expected loss for the next 12 months. Moss's consortium would also have to take on a secured loan of £1.5million, but this would be offset by some of the club's shares in Premiership Rugby, which are thought to be worth almost £4million.

The deal would ensure that England internationals James Haskell and Tom Palmer and Wales fly-half Stephen Jones join Wasps next season to bolster the injury-hit squad. Moss has a record of success in the business world, making millions from the sale of IT company Bytech and later founding a successful online video platform.

The news comes as European Rugby Cup has confirmed that Wasps will play in next season's Heineken Cup if they stay in the Premiership and either Edinburgh or Clermont Auvergne win the tournament. Hayes, whom it recently emerged had been arrested and bailed as part of a Scotland Yard investigation into computer hacking, put Wasps up for sale last October, when Wycombe District Council withdrew its support for the construction of a new stadium. Hayes, who has funded the losses since buying Wasps in 2008, had hoped to recoup some of his investment by selling the club.

Source: **Wasps will be saved by former player Ken Moss – provided they avoid relegation from Premiership,** by Gavin Mairs © *Daily Telegraph*, 27 April 2012

Progress check 18.4

What is a management buy-in (MBI)?

Problems with MBOs and MBIs

MBO and MBI financing is normally by debt and equity with high risk and an expectation of high returns. We have already seen the importance of assessing the correct proportion of debt and equity, and the proportions held by management and outside investors. The deal may be structured using, for example, founder shares so that managers take the risks but can gain effective control and become fully committed to the project.

Managers may not willingly accept the board representation requirement that external financiers will insist upon. Alternatively, board representation by venture capitalists may demonstrate their commitment and a hands-on approach.

When an MBO takes place, there may be inadequate financing for new investment. This may be due to a lack of good advice leading to the lack of a realistic plan at the outset, which then results in a lack of funding. There may be difficulties in achieving a fair buy-out price. We saw this from looking generally at the variety of methods used in valuation of businesses in Chapter 16.

It should be noted that both MBOs and MBIs may result in tax and legal complications for the company and the management team. Managers who are involved in an MBO or MBI may have little accounting or financial management experience. Therefore, there may be a need to recruit a qualified accountant, which could significantly increase the costs of the MBO or MBI. The maintenance of the pension rights of previous employees may also result in high costs following the establishment of the MBO or MBI.

Following an MBO or MBI, employees may be unwilling to move geographically, or accept changes to work practices, remuneration, or other conditions. This, together with most of the other difficulties and problems, are really to do with the successful management of a large project and obtaining good advice regarding appropriate financing.

Summary of key points

- There are a number of reasons why companies may require reorganisation and restructuring, which may relate in particular to their levels of gearing and the market's perception of their share price.

- Company reorganisations may take place supported by a range of financial strategies.

- Changes to financial strategies may be introduced in response to issues both internal and external to a company that may necessitate its restructuring.

- Privatisation as a means of company restructuring may relate to a sale by government to the public, for example UK utility businesses, or it may relate to the return of a company to private ownership (to Ltd from plc status).

- Management buy-outs (MBOs) and management buy-ins (MBIs) are two further methods that may be used to restructure and refinance companies.

- There are many advantages to be gained but also many problems that may result from the establishment of MBOs and MBIs.

Glossary of key terms

demerger A demerger is the separation of a company into several separate parts, particularly where the company may have grown by acquisition.

leveraged MBO A management buy-out (MBO) in which a large proportion of the new finance required is raised by external borrowing, and if the debt financing is greater than the equity financing then the MBO is said to be highly leveraged (or highly geared).

management buy-in (MBI) If there are insufficient skills and expertise within the management team, the business may be purchased from its existing owners by the members of an external management team, generally in association with a financing institution. As with an MBO, where a large proportion of the new finance required to purchase the business is raised by external borrowing, the buy-out is described as leveraged.

privatisation In the UK privatisation is the process of selling a nationalised industry to private owners (e.g. the general public).

re-privatisation The process of selling a publicly quoted company (plc) to private owners. The company may feel that plc status may no longer be appropriate and may wish to return to a more restricted and closely held ownership.

spin-off A company reorganisation in which a division or a subsidiary of the company becomes a separate and independent legal entity.

Assessment material

Questions

Q18.1 Outline the reasons why a company may consider reorganisation or restructuring.

Q18.2 How may debt restructuring be used as a financial strategy in response to an internal issue faced by a company?

Q18.3 Explain the differences between a spin-off and a demerger, and why a large group of companies may prefer one strategy to the other.

Q18.4 Outline the process followed in the privatisation of utilities in the UK.

Q18.5 Explain the goals of a typical management buy-out (MBO), and describe the business and financial strategies that may be used to achieve these goals.

Q18.6 Explain why a plc may wish to return to private ownership and become a Ltd company.

Q18.7 What are the advantages and disadvantages of the various ways in which an MBO may be financed?

Q18.8 Why may an MBO be popular with the managers of a business?

Discussion points

D18.1 'The financial restructuring of a company is really only a means of delaying the inevitable death of the business.' Discuss.

D18.2 Discuss and critically examine the procedure followed in the privatisation of a public company with which you are familiar.

D18.3 'MBOs generally meet the selfish aspirations of a handful of ambitious managers, whereas MBIs may provide a more professional and experienced approach to taking a business forward.' Discuss.

Exercises

Solutions are provided in Appendix 2 to all exercise numbers highlighted in colour.

Level I

E18.1 *Time allowed – 45 minutes*

> Outline the internal issues relating to why companies may need to be restructured, and explain how such reorganisations may be undertaken.

E18.2 *Time allowed – 45 minutes*

> Explain the external strategic financial issues that may be faced by a business, and outline the reorganisation strategies that may be used in response to these.

E18.3 *Time allowed – 45 minutes*

> One of the meanings of 'privatisation' is the return of a public limited company (plc) to private ownership (Ltd). Explain why MBOs and MBIs are often used for such a 'reprivatisation' and outline some of the problems that may be encountered.

E18.4 *Time allowed – 45 minutes*

> Explain what is meant by a demerger and why a business may consider this strategy. How may value be added to a business as a result of a demerger?

Level II

E18.5 *Time allowed – 45 minutes*

> What is a leveraged MBO and how is it implemented? What are the advantages to a venture capitalist and to the management team from using debt or preference shares to finance an MBO.

E18.6 *Time allowed – 45 minutes*

> Explain some of the problems that might arise in an MBO or an MBI deal and provide some recommended courses of action that may eliminate or minimise the impact of such problems.

E18.7 *Time allowed – 60 minutes*

Pomfrit Ltd is a family-owned business and has an issued share capital of 1,500,000 ordinary shares. The shareholders have recently expressed their wish to sell all their shares in the company. As a result at a recent management meeting the company's managers decided to propose a management buy-out.

The earnings of the company over the next financial year are expected to be about £10m, and dividends are expected to be limited to £4m.

➡

During the next financial year the company was intending to invest £12m in new capital projects. These were planned to be funded as follows:

- retained earnings £6m
- new share issue £6m.

Over the next three years the management of the company were expecting to limit dividends to 25% of earnings. No further new issues of capital were planned and it was expected that all investments after the next year would be financed from retained earnings.

While the expected rate of return from shares with similar risk is about 10%, the management of Pomfrit Ltd anticipate that an average rate of return of 15% on the planned new investments can be achieved in the first three years, although from year four onwards the return is expected to be 10% per annum. In addition, from year four onwards the management of the company expect to be able to establish and maintain a dividend payout ratio of 50%.

> **Required:**
>
> **Calculate what you would consider to be an appropriate market price for Pomfrit Ltd's shares. You may ignore any impact of taxation.**

E18.8   *Time allowed – 60 minutes*

Gillie plc is a UK-based manufacturing company. The company is currently financed by £1 ordinary share capital and irredeemable debentures. The debentures carry a nominal rate of 10%, and have a current market value at par. The company has paid an annual dividend of 40p per share in the past and is expected to continue to do so in the foreseeable future. The market value per share is £2 *ex dividend*.

The total market value of the company's equity is £6,000,000 and the market value of the debentures is £2,000,000.

The company is considering a major reorganisation of the company's operations infrastructure. The proposed reorganisation will cost the company £2,000,000, and is expected to return annual net cash flows of £525,000 (before interest) in perpetuity.

The company proposes to finance the reorganisation project with a new issue of 10% debentures at par. The rights of the existing debenture holders will be protected, so it is expected that the cost of existing debt will be unchanged and its market value will remain the same.

The higher gearing is expected to increase the financial risk for the shareholders. Assuming that the reorganisation proceeds and is financed by debt, the cost of equity is expected to increase by 5%.

> **Required:**
>
> **Advise Gillie plc on whether they should undertake the reorganisation, and calculate by how much the choice in the method of financing affects the decision. You may ignore taxation and assume that all earnings before interest will be paid out as dividends in the year they are received.**

Chamberlain plc is an electrical goods manufacturing company, and its shares are quoted on the London Stock Exchange. Its balance sheet as at 30 September 2012 is shown below.

Balance sheet as at 30 September 2012

	£m
Non-current assets	350
Current assets	
Inventories	75
Trade and other receivables	225
Cash and cash equivalents	200
	500
Current liabilities	
Trade and other payables	225
Net current assets	275
Total assets less current liabilities	625
Non-current liabilities	
8% loan	125
Net assets	500
Equity	
Ordinary shares (£1)	50
Retained earnings	450
Total equity	500

The company is currently examining its future strategy by carrying out a strategic review of the business and considering diversification through acquisition. The board of directors of Chamberlain is looking at three possible takeover target companies:

- C-Price plc owns a number of electrical retail outlets throughout the UK and sells cut-price TVs and other multi-media products to the general public. Chamberlain plc have sought the company's view regarding an offer and the indication is that they will sell at the right price. Chamberlain believes it may gain through re-branding C-Price's products with its own brands.
- Packitin plc is a packaging company. If Chamberlain plc were to make a takeover bid, such a bid may be regarded as hostile by Packitin.

APPENDICES

Contents

Appendix 1

Present value tables

Present value of £1

The table shows the value of £1 to be received or paid, using a range of interest rates (r) after a given number of years (n). The values are based on the formula $V_n r = (1 + r)^{-n}$

Rate r % After n years	1	2	3	4	5	6	7	8	9	10	11	12
1	0.99	0.98	0.97	0.96	0.95	0.94	0.93	0.93	0.92	0.91	0.90	0.89
2	0.98	0.96	0.94	0.92	0.91	0.89	0.87	0.86	0.84	0.83	0.81	0.80
3	0.97	0.94	0.92	0.89	0.86	0.84	0.82	0.79	0.77	0.75	0.73	0.71
4	0.96	0.92	0.89	0.85	0.82	0.79	0.76	0.74	0.71	0.68	0.66	0.64
5	0.95	0.91	0.86	0.82	0.78	0.75	0.71	0.68	0.65	0.62	0.59	0.57
6	0.94	0.89	0.84	0.79	0.75	0.70	0.67	0.63	0.60	0.56	0.53	0.51
7	0.93	0.87	0.81	0.76	0.71	0.67	0.62	0.58	0.55	0.51	0.48	0.45
8	0.92	0.85	0.79	0.73	0.68	0.63	0.58	0.54	0.50	0.47	0.43	0.40
9	0.91	0.84	0.77	0.70	0.64	0.59	0.54	0.50	0.46	0.42	0.39	0.36
10	0.91	0.82	0.74	0.68	0.61	0.56	0.51	0.46	0.42	0.39	0.35	0.32
11	0.90	0.80	0.72	0.65	0.58	0.53	0.48	0.43	0.39	0.35	0.32	0.29
12	0.89	0.79	0.70	0.62	0.56	0.50	0.44	0.40	0.36	0.32	0.29	0.26
13	0.88	0.77	0.68	0.60	0.53	0.47	0.41	0.37	0.33	0.29	0.26	0.23
14	0.87	0.76	0.66	0.58	0.51	0.44	0.39	0.34	0.30	0.26	0.23	0.20
15	0.86	0.74	0.64	0.56	0.48	0.42	0.36	0.32	0.27	0.24	0.21	0.18

Rate r % After n years	13	14	15	16	17	18	19	20	30	40	50
1	0.88	0.88	0.87	0.86	0.85	0.85	0.84	0.83	0.77	0.71	0.67
2	0.78	0.77	0.76	0.74	0.73	0.72	0.71	0.69	0.59	0.51	0.44
3	0.69	0.67	0.66	0.64	0.62	0.61	0.59	0.58	0.46	0.36	0.30
4	0.61	0.59	0.57	0.55	0.53	0.52	0.50	0.48	0.35	0.26	0.20
5	0.54	0.52	0.50	0.48	0.46	0.44	0.42	0.40	0.27	0.19	0.13
6	0.48	0.46	0.43	0.41	0.39	0.37	0.35	0.33	0.21	0.13	0.09
7	0.43	0.40	0.38	0.35	0.33	0.31	0.30	0.28	0.16	0.09	0.06
8	0.38	0.35	0.33	0.31	0.28	0.27	0.25	0.23	0.12	0.07	0.04
9	0.33	0.31	0.28	0.26	0.24	0.23	0.21	0.19	0.09	0.05	0.03
10	0.29	0.27	0.25	0.23	0.21	0.19	0.18	0.16	0.07	0.03	0.02
11	0.26	0.24	0.21	0.20	0.18	0.16	0.15	0.13	0.06	0.02	0.01
12	0.23	0.21	0.19	0.17	0.15	0.14	0.12	0.11	0.04	0.02	0.008
13	0.20	0.18	0.16	0.15	0.13	0.12	0.10	0.09	0.03	0.013	0.005
14	0.18	0.16	0.14	0.13	0.11	0.10	0.09	0.08	0.03	0.009	0.003
15	0.16	0.14	0.12	0.11	0.09	0.08	0.07	0.06	0.02	0.006	0.002

Cumulative present value of £1

The table shows the present value of £1 per annum, using a range of interest rates (r), receivable or payable at the end of each year for n years.

Rate r % After n years	1	2	3	4	5	6	7	8	9	10	11	12
1	0.99	0.98	0.97	0.96	0.95	0.94	0.94	0.93	0.92	0.91	0.90	0.89
2	1.97	1.94	1.91	1.89	1.86	1.83	1.81	1.78	1.76	1.74	1.71	1.69
3	2.94	2.88	2.83	2.78	2.72	2.67	2.62	2.58	2.53	2.49	2.44	2.40
4	3.90	3.81	3.72	3.63	3.55	3.47	3.39	3.31	3.24	3.17	3.10	3.04
5	4.85	4.71	4.58	4.45	4.33	4.21	4.10	3.99	3.89	3.79	3.70	3.61
6	5.80	5.60	5.42	5.24	5.08	4.92	4.77	4.62	4.49	4.36	4.23	4.11
7	6.73	6.47	6.23	6.00	5.79	5.58	5.39	5.21	5.03	4.87	4.71	4.56
8	7.65	7.33	7.02	6.73	6.46	6.21	5.97	5.75	5.54	5.34	5.15	4.97
9	8.57	8.16	7.79	7.44	7.11	6.80	6.52	6.25	6.00	5.76	5.54	5.33
10	9.47	8.98	8.53	8.11	7.72	7.36	7.02	6.71	6.42	6.15	5.89	5.65
11	10.37	9.79	9.25	8.76	8.31	7.89	7.50	7.14	6.81	6.50	6.21	5.94
12	11.26	10.58	9.95	9.39	8.86	8.38	7.94	7.54	7.16	6.81	6.49	6.19
13	12.13	11.35	10.64	9.99	9.39	8.85	8.36	7.90	7.49	7.10	6.80	6.42
14	13.00	12.11	11.30	10.56	9.90	9.30	8.75	8.24	7.79	7.37	6.98	6.63
15	13.87	12.85	11.94	11.12	10.38	9.71	9.11	8.56	8.06	7.61	7.19	6.81

Rate r % After n years	13	14	15	16	17	18	19	20	30	40	50
1	0.89	0.88	0.87	0.86	0.85	0.85	0.84	0.83	0.77	0.71	0.67
2	1.67	1.65	1.63	1.61	1.59	1.57	1.55	1.53	1.36	1.22	1.11
3	2.36	2.32	2.28	2.25	2.21	2.17	2.14	2.11	1.81	1.59	1.41
4	2.97	2.91	2.86	2.80	2.74	2.69	2.64	2.59	2.17	1.85	1.61
5	3.52	3.43	3.35	3.27	3.20	3.13	3.06	2.99	2.44	2.04	1.74
6	4.00	3.89	3.78	3.69	3.59	3.50	3.41	3.33	2.64	2.17	1.82
7	4.42	4.29	4.16	4.04	3.92	3.81	3.71	3.61	2.80	2.26	1.88
8	4.80	4.64	4.49	4.34	4.21	4.08	3.95	3.84	2.93	2.33	1.92
9	5.13	4.95	4.77	4.61	4.45	4.30	4.16	4.03	3.02	2.38	1.95
10	5.43	5.22	5.02	4.83	4.66	4.49	4.34	4.19	3.09	2.41	1.97
11	5.69	5.45	5.23	5.03	4.83	4.66	4.49	4.33	3.15	2.44	1.98
12	5.92	5.66	5.42	5.20	4.99	4.79	4.61	4.44	3.19	2.46	1.99
13	6.12	5.84	5.58	5.34	5.12	4.91	4.71	4.53	3.22	2.47	1.99
14	6.30	6.00	5.72	5.47	5.23	5.01	4.80	4.61	3.25	2.48	1.99
15	6.46	6.14	5.85	5.58	5.32	5.09	4.88	4.68	3.27	2.48	2.00

Appendix 2

Solutions to selected chapter-end exercises

E2.2 Shareholder value

The term shareholder value was introduced by Alfred Rappaport (1986). Although there is no uniform definition of the term, as it is used in a variety of contexts, shareholder value is often interpreted as the maximising of shareholder benefit and implies a primary focus on raising company earnings and the share price. The most common methods of measuring shareholder value are:

- customer satisfaction and customer value-added (CVA)
- total cost analysis
- profitability analysis
- strategic profit model (SPM)
- economic value-added (EVA).

E2.5 Chancer Ltd – agency problem

The agency problem can be defined as a conflict of interest that may exist between the shareholders of a company (the principals) and the management of a company (the agents). For Chancer Ltd the additional borrowing of £30m secured against the company's existing assets would have a dramatic impact on the company's gearing ratio. The additional debt would increase interest payments, and unless substantial savings can be generated by the new head office development, this could have a negative effect on the value of the company's shares. As a result while the development would undoubtedly raise the profile of the company in the short term it could mean a loss of value for shareholders. To eliminate such a problem is difficult and good investor relations are a useful starting point.

E2.7 Efficient market hypothesis (EMH)

Market efficiency is really a myth due to the complex and unpredictable interrelationships that are now features of the financial marketplace. Modern sophisticated capital markets often exhibit clear inefficiencies, usually at the strong form level.

However, overall in terms of pricing, such markets are generally regarded as being partially efficient. But why are efficient markets important? Efficient markets are seen as promoting:

- increased volumes of transactions
- greater mobility of funds
- the involvement of a greater number of participants
- a more efficient allocation and reallocation of resources.

The implications of such efficiency is that while in the short term market outsiders may profit at margins greater than the market average because of chance or luck, it is unlikely that over the longer term market outsiders could consistently outperform the market and earn profits over and above the market average.

Abnormal gains are generally not available to rational market participants. The relevance of such an argument to a wholly economically driven market (a market functioning primarily on the mechanics of supply and demand) is beyond doubt. Where there are a number of powerful participants driven by other than wholly economic motives, for example electoral pledges founded on politically based ideologies, the appropriateness of such an argument can have a substantial impact on:

- the overall market mechanisms – the availability of market assets, commodities, or currencies
- the activities of other market participants as part of the supply and demand mechanism.

E2.8 Crosby plc

Key issues are volatility and market confidence. Although profits are similar, trends differ. Crosby has steady growth whereas Nash has growth but with a pattern that appears erratic and uncertain. Such growth patterns could indicate a lack of managerial competence and control.

These problems could clearly reduce market confidence in the company and hence affect the value of the company. It is, however, worth noting that other external conditions may well apply. These are conditions that may impact on either of the companies, for example potential growth opportunities, inherent goodwill within the companies, and the overall market conditions.

E2.9 Efficiency

In terms of stock markets and capital markets, pricing efficiency refers to the notion that prices rapidly reflect in an unbiased way all available information. Investment in financial assets should not on average produce abnormal returns.

Other types of efficiency include operational efficiency, which refers to the level of costs of carrying out transactions in capital markets. Allocational efficiency refers to the extent to which capital is allocated to the most profitable enterprise. This should be a product of pricing efficiency. Pricing efficiency emerges because the prices of assets are adjusted to reflect expected future cash flows. Market efficiency is important because it:

- promotes investor trust in the market and thus encourages capital investment
- promotes allocational efficiency
- improves market information and therefore choice of investments.

E2.10 Implications of EMH

This is essentially a discussion on the context of the efficient markets hypothesis and the alternative forms of tested pricing efficiency: weak; semi-strong; strong. There is no definitive answer but key issues that could be discussed may be:

- importance of information in market pricing
- relevance of past trends in market pricing
- levels of disclosure – public and private information.

E3.1 Accounting information and corporate governance

The role of accounting in corporate governance is wide and varied. The reports and financial statements of companies should ensure:

- openness
- integrity
- accountability.

Accounting standards should be precise and strictly adhered to. External auditors should check and confirm that the company has complied with corporate governance requirements. Internal auditors may be responsible for the detection, minimisation and elimination of fraud.

E3.2 Effective corporate governance

Major participants in the corporate financial environment include:

- shareholders
- creditors
- employees
- directors
- trades unions
- banks and other financial institutions
- Government agencies
- auditors.

All the above participants have a role to play in corporate governance either directly (for example auditors and directors) or indirectly (for example employees). With regard to corporate governance, directors' responsibilities are to ensure goal congruence between the objectives of the shareholders and those of the managers of the company. The agency problem arises when directors (agents) do not act in the best interest of their shareholders (principals).

Relevant reports include:

Cadbury Report (1992)

- Clarified key issues of corporate governance
- Defined corporate governance
- Provided a code of best practice
- Established roles of executive directors and non-executive directors
- Set standards of best practice in relation to financial reporting and accountability
- Establishment of audit committees for listed companies

Greenbury Code (1995)

- Made recommendations on directors' pay

Hampel Report (1996)

- Reviewed Cadbury and Greenbury reports

Combined Code of Practice

- Aim is to promote openness, integrity, and accountability
- Considers issues related to:
  - audit and the role of auditors
  - directors' obligations and responsibilities regarding:
    - duty of care
    - corporate manslaughter
    - insolvency
    - wrongful and fraudulent trading.

UK Corporate Governance Code (2010)

- The Code is backed by a 'comply or explain' approach
- Provides guidance on five tenets of good corporate governance:
  - leadership
  - effectiveness
  - accountability
  - remuneration
  - relations with shareholders.

E3.3 Share options

Past UK Governments have made managers' share option schemes tax efficient and therefore schemes are now very common among plcs.

Many plcs have found that their share prices react to specific management policies and decisions, for example takeovers and disposals of businesses. Users of financial information can assess these decisions, knowing of the options awarded to the directors.

Many plcs have found that they can only keep or attract high calibre managers by including share options in their remuneration packages. Investing institutions demand more and more information regarding directors' remuneration. This can influence their basic hold or buy or sell decisions. The financial press frequently includes criticism of specific companies.

E3.4 Perks

Directors do not necessarily own the company they work for; the shareholders do. Any monies (expenses) that a director takes from the company will affect the annual profit. Annual dividends are paid from the annual profits. The shareholders approve the accounts at the AGM, which includes remuneration of the directors. If the directors hide information regarding their remuneration and benefits from the shareholders, then that part of the accounts may not show a true and fair view of the company.

E3.5 Contracts

Before corporate governance codes of practice were introduced, shareholders found that their directors had powers that were increasing, especially regarding length of contract and compensation for loss of office. The financial press regularly commented on the compensation paid to a director, where company performance has been acknowledged to be poor, and the length of directors' contracts.

The Cadbury and Greenbury Committees recommended that directors' contracts should be no longer than three years (Cadbury) and then one year (Greenbury). These committees had looked at the evidence presented to them. Hampel (1998) provided that the contracts should be one year or less.

UK financial institutions also became proactive regarding the length of directors' contracts issue. They noted that in the past too many highly paid directors were awarding themselves contracts in which compensation for loss of office was very high.

E3.9 Tomkins plc

Equity shareholders are the owners of the company, and the level of their dividends usually varies with levels of profits earned by the company. Directors are appointed by the shareholders, and remunerated for their efforts. Major multinational companies are difficult to manage successfully over a long period of time. The remuneration of directors should reflect that difficulty.

The information that has been given about Tomkins plc shows that there is an executive director who earns a basic salary of just below £1m a year, an amount which most shareholders would like to see disclosed in the accounts and discussed at the AGM.

The bonus of £443,000 would also generate some interest among the institutions and individual shareholders. Institutions (and the UK Government) increasingly put pressure on directors if they feel that pay awards are excessive. The consultancy agreement for a non-executive director may also be of interest to the various users of the notes to the accounts.

E4.1 CML

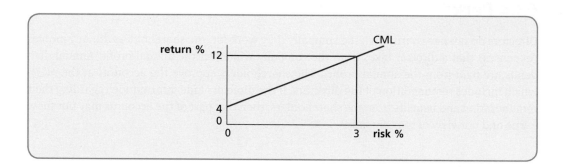

E4.2 Caldey plc and Tenby plc

(i) Perfect positive correlation

Probability	Caldey: 30% forecast return	Tenby: 70% forecast return	Combined portfolio return x			
p	%	%	%	$(x \times p)$	$(x - EV_x)$	$p(x - EV_x)^2$
0.20	3.0	8.4	11.4	2.28	(4.80)	4.61
0.60	3.6	12.6	16.2	9.72	–	–
0.20	4.2	16.8	21.0	4.20	4.80	4.61
			$EV_x = 16.20$		Variance =	9.22
					Standard deviation =	3.04

(ii) Perfect negative correlation

Probability	Caldey: 30% forecast return	Tenby: 70% forecast return	Combined portfolio return x			
p	**%**	**%**	**%**	**(x × p)**	**(x − EV_x)**	**p(x − EV_x)²**
0.20	3.0	16.8	19.8	3.96	3.60	2.59
0.60	3.6	12.6	16.2	9.72	–	–
0.20	4.2	8.4	12.6	2.52	(3.60)	2.59

$$EV_x = 16.20 \qquad \text{Variance} = \underline{5.18}$$

$$\text{Standard deviation} = \underline{2.28}$$

With perfect positive correlation the forecast returns from the shares of both companies are moving in the same direction, and this gives an expected return of 16.2% and a standard deviation or risk for the portfolio of 3.04%. With perfect negative correlation the forecast returns from the shares of both companies are varying inversely, and this gives the same expected return of 16.2% and a standard deviation or risk for the portfolio of 2.28% which is lower than with perfect positive correlation.

If there is no correlation, the level of risk would lie between 2.28% and 3.04%.

E4.3 Efficient portfolios

(i) An efficient portfolio is one which lies on the securities market line, or capital market line. Its rate of return is as high as can be expected for the level of risk involved.

(ii)

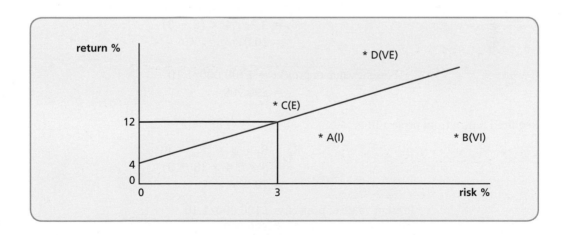

Portfolio A is quite inefficient as it lies below the capital market line (CML).
Portfolio B is very inefficient. It lies well below the CML.
Portfolio C is quite efficient, lying above the CML and yielding 3% above the market portfolio for the same level of risk.
Portfolio D is very efficient, yielding around 7.5% more than the expected rate of return for the level of risk faced.

(iii) We may calculate the beta value from a portfolio yielding a return of 11% from

$$R_p = R_f + \beta \times (R_m - R_f)$$
$$11 = 4 + \beta \times (12 - 4)$$
$$\beta = 7/8 = 0.875$$

(iv) We may calculate the return on a portfolio with a beta of 1.3 from:

$$R_p = R_f + \beta \times (R_m - R_f)$$
$$R_p = 4 + 1.3 \times (12 - 4)$$
$$R_p = 14.4\%$$

E4.4 French plc and Saunders plc

(i)   French plc

Required return from project I

$$R_p = R_f + \beta \times (R_m - R_f)$$
$$= 3 + 1.3 \times (8 - 3)$$
$$= 9.5\%$$

Present value of project $= £300,000/1.095$
$$= £273,973$$

Saunders plc

Required return from project II

$$R_p = R_f + \beta \times (R_m - R_f)$$
$$= 3 + 1.4 \times (8 - 3)$$
$$= 10.0\%$$

Present value of project $= £100,000/1.10$
$$= £90,909$$

Required return from project III

$$R_p = R_f + \beta \times (R_m - R_f)$$
$$= 3 + 1.4 \times (8 - 3)$$
$$= 10.0\%$$

Present value of project $= £100,000/1.10$
$$= £90,909$$

Required return from project IV

$$R_p = R_f + \beta \times (R_m - R_f)$$
$$= 3 + 0.8 \times (8 - 3)$$
$$= 7.0\%$$

Present value of project $= £200,000/1.07$
$$= £186,916$$

(ii) Total present value of Saunders plc's projects II, III, and IV

$$= £90,909 + £90,909 + £186,916$$
$$= £368,734$$

If Saunders plc goes ahead with its three proposed projects then its total beta factor will be

$$= \frac{(£90,909 \times 1.4) + (£90,909 \times 1.4) + (£186,916 \times 0.8)}{£368,734} = 1.1$$

(iii) Saunders plc has a higher present value and lower total systematic risk than French plc. Therefore in an efficient capital market Saunders plc would have a higher market value. Saunders plc will be a diversified company and if investors were not themselves able to hold well-diversified portfolios and therefore reduce their unsystematic risk as much as possible, then this company may be more likely to be highly valued by investors. In a large and developed capital market such diversification by individual investors is feasible and so the apparent benefit derived by Saunders plc through its own diversification may not give it an advantage over French plc.

E4.5 Investor risk

The risk relating to an investment in a equity share comprises two elements:

- Systematic risk, or market risk, is the element of total risk that is generally common to all stocks and shares. It is market risk which is dependent on general economic and market conditions. Systematic risk cannot be avoided and cannot be diversified away.
- Unsystematic risk is that element of risk which is specific to type of industry or business in which the company is engaged. For example, ice cream sales are adversely affected by a cold and rainy summer. However, this unsystematic risk could be offset by diversifying into securities which are either negatively correlated (or to unrelated economic sectors of the market). A portfolio of shares in an ice cream company, for example, may be diversified to include a company which sells umbrellas, the sales of which are likely to move in the opposite direction to those of a company selling ice cream.

Unsystematic risk may be reduced by diversification, and research has shown that unsystematic risk accounts for around 70% of the risk of a security. In an efficiently diversified portfolio, different types of security are chosen with regard to markets, technology, geographical areas, product and service types, etc.

E4.6 Abdul and Said

(i)

Abdul's total returns	$T = 12\%$
Risk-free rate of return	$R_f = 7\%$

Abdul's return on his market portfolio of equities $= R_e$
One quarter (25%) of Abdul's funds are in risk-free investment and so three-quarters (75%) of his funds are invested in equities.

Therefore

$$T = (0.25 \times R_f) + (0.75 \times R_e)$$
$$12 = (0.25 \times 7) + (0.75 \times R_e)$$
$$12 = 1.75 + (0.75 \times R_e)$$
$$R_e = 10.25/0.75$$
$$R_e = 13.67$$

The return on Abdul's equity investments is therefore 13.67%. Said's market portfolio of equities is similar to Abdul's market portfolio of equities and so we can assume also gives a return of 13.67%. Said is achieving a total return which is higher than this and so he also must be borrowing in funds at the risk-free rate.

Said's total returns	$T = 18\%$
Risk-free rate of return	$R_f = 7\%$
Said's return on his market portfolio of equities	$R_e = 13.67\%$
Said's proportion of additional borrowed funds	$= B$

$$T = (1 + B) \times R_e - (B \times R_f)$$
$$18 = (1 + B) \times 13.67 - (B \times 7)$$
$$18 = 13.67 + 13.67B - 7B$$
$$4.33 = 6.67B$$
$$B = 4.33/6.67$$
$$B = 0.65$$

Said has borrowed at the risk-free rate of 7% to increase his funds by 65% which are all invested in equities, which may be illustrated as follows:

100 equities @ 13.67 % gives a return of	13.67
65 (addition of 65% to his own funds borrowed and invested by Said)	
@ 13.67% gives a return of	8.88
Cost of 65 borrowed at the risk-free rate of 7%	(4.55)
Total return	18.00

(ii)

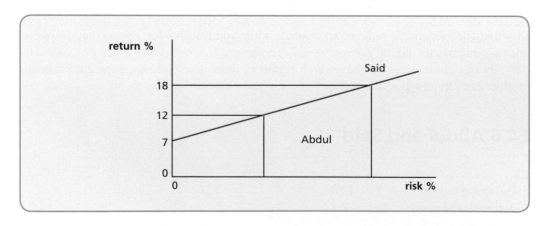

(iii) The capital market line is represented by

$$y = R_f + bx$$

where

Abdul's expected total return	$y = 12\%$	
risk-free rate of return	$R_f = 7\%$	
standard deviation or risk of Abdul's portfolio	$x = 8\%$	
slope of the capital market line (CML)	$= b$	

therefore

$$12 = 7 + 8b$$
$$b = 5/8$$
$$b = 0.625$$

The slope of the CML is 0.625 and this can be used to calculate the new risk (standard deviation) of the portfolio if Abdul increases his required return to 13%.

$$y = R_f + bx$$
$$13 = 7 + 0.625x$$
$$x = 9.6$$

Therefore for Abdul to increase his required return from 12% to 13% the risk will increase from 8% to 9.6%.

We can calculate Abdul's new portfolio as follows:

Abdul's total returns	$T = 13\%$	
Risk-free rate of return	$R_f = 7\%$	
Abdul's return on his market portfolio of equities	$R_e = 13.67\%$	
Abdul's proportion of funds invested in risk-free investments	$= R$	

$$T = (1 - R) \times R_e + (R \times R_f)$$
$$13 = (1 - R) \times 13.67 + (R \times 7)$$
$$13 = 13.67 - 13.67R + 7R$$
$$-0.67 = -6.67R$$
$$R = 0.67/6.67$$
$$R = 0.10$$

The proportion of funds invested in risk-free investments is therefore 10%. So in order to achieve an overall rate of return of 13%, Abdul would have to increase the proportion of his fund invested in equities from 75% to 90%, with a corresponding rise in the risk (standard deviation) of the portfolio to 9.6%.

E4.7 Bill Brownbridge

(i)

Probability		Company X					Company Y		
	Return					Return			
	%					%			
p	x	EV_X	$x - EV_X$	$p(x - EV_X)^2$		y	EV_Y	$y - EV_Y$	$p(y - EV_Y)^2$
0.3	30	9	5	7.5					
0.4	25	10	0	0.0					
0.3	20	6	(5)	7.5					

(*continued*)

		50	10	20	80.0
0.2		30	18	0	0.0
0.6		10	2	(20)	80.0
0.2					
EV$_X$ __25__ Variance	__15.0__	EV$_Y$ __30__		Variance	__160.0__

Expected return Company X = 25% $\sigma_X = \sqrt{15} = 3.87\%$
Expected return Company Y = 30% $\sigma_Y = \sqrt{160} = 12.65\%$
Portfolio return = (60% × 25%) + (40% × 30%) = 27%

(ii) $\sigma_p = \sqrt{[(a_X{}^2 \times \sigma_X{}^2) + (a_Y{}^2 \times \sigma_Y{}^2) + (2 \times a_X \times a_Y \times r \times \sigma_X \times \sigma_Y)]}$

where

σ = standard deviation
a = proportion of investment in portfolio
r = correlation coefficient of investment return, which for X and Y is zero

$$\sigma_p = \sqrt{[(0.6^2 \times 3.87^2) + (0.4^2 \times 12.65^2)]}$$
$$= \sqrt{[(0.36 \times 15) + (0.16 \times 160)]}$$
$$= \sqrt{(5.4 + 25.6)}$$
$$= \sqrt{31}$$
$$= 5.57\%$$

Risk company X = 3.87%
Risk company Y = 12.65%
Risk portfolio XY = 5.6%

(iii)

Portfolio and expected returns

A portfolio is a collection of different securities that make up an investor's total holding.

The expected return of a portfolio will be the weighted average of the expected returns of each of the securities in the portfolio. The risk in a security or portfolio of securities is that the actual return will not be the same as the expected return. The risk of a security or portfolio of securities can be measured as the standard deviation of the expected returns.

Risk and diversification

Portfolio theory suggests that the relationship of securities held in a portfolio is as important as the securities themselves.

Why does portfolio diversification appear to work?

The prices of different securities (equity or debt) do not move exactly together. Diversification works best when investment returns are negatively correlated. If investment returns show negative correlation then by combining them in a portfolio overall risk will be reduced. In general investors choose a portfolio that balances expected return and risk. This is represented in the investor's individual indifference curve.

Traditional investment theory suggests that if two portfolios have the same return but different risks then the least risk option should be chosen, and if two portfolios have the same risk but different returns the greatest return option should be chosen. This is the risk-averse assumption.

Does diversification affect all risk?

It depends on two key issues:

- size of the portfolio
- types of risk.

Size of portfolio: The risk-reducing impact of diversification is not linear but exponential. It works well with up to 20 or 30 investments, after which the impact becomes statistically minimal. **Types of risk** include systematic and unsystematic risk. Systematic risk (sometimes called market risk) includes economy-wide (macroeconomic) sources of risk that affect the overall market and differ between types of investments with some industries riskier than others. Diversification can only assist in reducing unsystematic risk. Systematic risk must be accepted by the investor, the return being higher returns than the risk-free rate of return. Unsystematic risk (sometimes called unique risk) includes risk factors that only affect one company or investment (that is inherent risk).

Implications of systematic and unsystematic risk

To avoid risk altogether the investor must invest in risk-free investments. A small portfolio of investments will have both systematic and unsystematic risk. In a balanced portfolio the portfolio systematic risk will in theory be equal to the average systematic risk in the market as a whole.

E5.3 Adam plc

(i) Dividend yield $= 5\%$, on share price of £25

Dividend per share therefore $= £25 \times 0.05 = £1.25$
P/E ratio $= 10$, therefore earnings per share $= £25/10 = £2.50$
Dividend payout ratio $= £1.25/£2.50 = 50\%$

(ii) Dividend growth model

$$K_e = \frac{v(1 + G)}{S} + G = \frac{£1.25 \times 1.03}{£25} + 0.03 = 0.0815 \text{ or } 8.15\%$$

(iii) CAPM

$$K_e = R_f + \{\beta_e \times (R_m - R_f)\} = 4\% + \{1.25 \times (10\% - 4\%)\} = 11.5\%$$

From the dividend model:

$$S = \frac{v(1 + G)}{(K_e - G)} = \frac{£1.25 \times 1.03}{(0.115 - 0.03)} = £15.15$$

The share price appears to be over-valued by £9.85 (£25 − £15.15).

(iv) Please refer to the relevant sections in Chapter 5 to check your solution.

(v) Assumptions for derivation of the CAPM:

- investors are risk averse
- everyone in the market has the same forecast
- investment opportunities are the same for all investors
- a perfect market and no transaction costs or taxation
- investors can borrow and lend freely at a risk-free rate of return
- all investors have a single-period planning horizon.

Theoretical implications:

- investors and companies require a return in excess of the risk-free rate to compensate for systematic risk
- investors and companies should not require a premium for unsystematic risk since it can be diversified away
- systematic risk varies between companies and projects and therefore rates of return required by investors and companies will vary
- a linear relationship is assumed between the return on an individual investment or security (R_s) and the average return from all securities in the market (R_m), which will tend to be positively correlated
- differential returns between R_s and R_m may be due to systematic risk
- the relationship between R_m and R_s can be used to derive a beta factor (β) for individual securities
- unsystematic risk can be mitigated through diversification.

E5.4 Lucky Jim plc

If shareholders' equity is E and the net financial debt D then the relative proportions of equity and debt in the total financing are:

$$\frac{E}{E + D} \text{ and } \frac{D}{E + D}$$

$$\frac{E}{E + D} = 2/3$$

$$\frac{D}{E + D} = 1/3$$

Cost of equity $K_e = 18\%$

Return on financial debt $K_d = 12\%$

$$\begin{aligned} \text{WACC} &= (2/3 \times 18\%) + \{1/3 \times 12\%(1 - 40\%)\} \\ &= 12\% + 2.4\% \\ &= 14.4\% \end{aligned}$$

$$\text{The present value of future cash flows in perpetuity} = \frac{\text{annual cash flows}}{\text{annual discount rate \%}}$$

$$= \frac{£35,000}{0.144}$$

$$= £243,056$$

Net present value, NPV $= £243,056 - £200,000 = +£43,056$

Using WACC to discount the cash flows of the project, the result is a positive NPV of £43,056 and therefore the project should be undertaken.

E5.5 Abey plc

(i)

	£
Current profits	2,250,000
Increase (£850,000 − extra interest 10% × £5,000,000)	350,000
New profits after project	2,600,000
New cost of equity	20%
New market value	13,000,000
Old market value	12,500,000 (earnings £2.25m/ cost of equity 18%)
Increase in shareholders' wealth	500,000

(ii)

NPV of the project using WACC 16%

$$(£850,000/0.16) - £5,000,000 = £312,500$$

The increase in the value of the equity is £500,000 (see above).
The +NPV of the project is £312,500 (see above).

Therefore the impact of financing the project is:

$$£500,000 - £312,500 = £187,500$$

E5.6 Homeslore plc

(i)   Growth in dividends 2006 to 2012

$$= \sqrt[6]{(£900/£570)}$$
$$= \sqrt[6]{1.5789}$$
$$= 1.079, \text{ a growth rate G of } 7.9\%$$

$$\text{current dividend } v = £900/4,500 = £0.20 \text{ per share}$$
$$\text{current share price } S = £4.60 - £0.20 = £4.40 \ ex \ dividend$$

using the dividend growth model

$$K_e = \frac{v(1 + G)}{S} + G = \frac{£0.20 \times 1.079}{£4.40} + 0.079 = 0.128$$

cost of equity = 12.8%

(ii) Cost of redeemable debt

Year	Cash flow £	Discount factor at 5%	Present value £
0	(90)	1.0000	(90.00)
1 – 5	5 – (5 × 0.30)	4.3295	15.15
5	100	0.7835	78.35
			3.50

Year	Cash flow £	Discount factor at 5%	Present value £
0	(90)	1.0000	(90.00)
1– 5	5 – (5 × 0.30)	4.2124	14.74
5	100	0.7473	74.73
			(0.53)

using interpolation 5% + {£3.50/(£3.50 + £0.53)} = 5.87% after tax
cost of debt = 5.87%

(iii) Weighted average cost of capital

Ordinary shares	£4.40 × 4.5m	£19,800,000	12.80%	£2,534,400
Debentures	£0.90 × 4.0m	£3,600,000	5.87%	£211,320
		£23,400,000		£2,745,720

WACC = £2,745,720/£23,400,000 = 11.73%

E5.7 Homeslore plc

(i) Using WACC 11.73%, discount factor Year 1 = 0.895, Year 2 = 0.801

Year 1{(£440,000 × 0.5) + (£200,000 × 0.4) + (£460,000 × 0.1)} × 0.895 = £309,670
Year 2{(£600,000 × 0.6) + (£580,000 × 0.2) + (£350,000 × 0.2)} × 0.801 = £437,346

PV of benefits	£747,016
Cost – Year 0	£700,000
NPV	£47,016

(ii) Justification for using WACC is that by using WACC only those investments which offer a return in excess of WACC are accepted, thereby contributing to the overall funds of the company. It is assumed that WACC reflects the long-term future capital structure of the company. Problems are that:
- floating rate debt is difficult to incorporate into a WACC calculation
- the risk profile of prospective projects may differ from the risk profile of the company
- WACC does not consider the risk of individual projects.

E5.8 Yor plc

(i)   Yor plc

Income statement for the year ended 30 September 2013

Figures in £m	Debentures	Shares
PBIT	15.6	15.6
Interest payable	(1.6)	(1.2)
Profit before tax	14.0	14.4
Tax on profit on ordinary activities	(3.5)	(3.6)
Profit on ordinary activities after tax	10.5	10.8
Retained profit at 1 October 2012	10.6	10.6
	21.1	21.4
Dividends	(3.3)	(4.6)
Retained profit at 30 September 2013	17.8	16.8

(ii)   Yor plc

Capital and reserves as at 30 September 2013

Figures in £m	Debentures	Shares
Share capital (£1 ord. shares)	10.0	14.0
Share premium (4m × £1.50)		6.0
Retained earnings	17.8	16.8
	27.8	36.8
Loans	30.0	20.0

(iii)

$$\text{earnings per share 2012} = \frac{\text{profit available for ordinary shareholders}}{\text{number of ordinary shares in issue}}$$

$$= \frac{\text{£7.8m}}{\text{10m}}$$
$$= 78\text{p}$$

(iv)   using debentures

$$\text{earnings per share 2013} = \frac{\text{£10.5m}}{\text{10m}} = \text{£1.05}$$

using shares

$$\text{earnings per share 2013} = \frac{\text{£10.8m}}{\text{14m}} = 77\text{p}$$

(v)

$$\text{dividend per share 2012} = \frac{\text{total dividends paid to ordinary shareholders}}{\text{number of ordinary shares in issue}}$$

$$= \frac{\text{£3.0m}}{\text{10m}} = 30\text{p}$$

(vi) using debentures

$$\text{dividend per share 2013} = \frac{£3.3m}{10m} = 33p$$

using shares

$$\text{dividend per share 2013} = \frac{£4.6m}{14m} = 33p$$

(vii)

$$\text{gearing} = \frac{\text{long-term debt}}{\text{equity} + \text{long-term debt}}$$

	Using debentures	Using shares
2012	**2013**	**2013**
$\dfrac{£20.0m}{£20.6m + £20.0m} = 49.3\%$	$\dfrac{£30.0m}{£27.8m + £30.0m} = 51.9\%$	$\dfrac{£20.0m}{£36.8m + £20.0m} = 35.2\%$

(viii)   Summary of results

Figures in £m		**Using debentures**	**Using shares**
	2012	**2013**	**2013**
Profit after tax	7.8	10.5	10.8
Dividends	(3.0)	(3.3)	(4.6)
Retained profit for year	4.8	7.2	6.2

The use of debentures to finance the new project will increase the 2012/2013 profit after tax, and available for dividends, by £2.7m or 34.6%, whereas if shares were used the increase would be £3.0m or 38.5%. Earnings per share will be increased to £1.05 (+27p) and decreased to 77p (−1p) respectively. However, retained profit would be increased by £2.4m (50%) and £1.4m (29.2%) respectively. The difference is because the gain from the lower interest cost in using shares is more than offset by the increase in dividends.

Dividend per share will be increased from 30p to 33p per share regardless of which method of financing is used.

Gearing at 30 September 2012 was 49.3%. If debentures are used to finance the new project then gearing will increase to 51.9%, but if shares are used to finance the new project then gearing will decrease to 35.2%. This represents a higher financial risk for the company with regard to its commitments to making a high level of interest payments. The company is therefore vulnerable to a downturn in business and also the possibility of its loans being called in and possible liquidation of the company.

E6.3 Rainbow plc

(i)   From a divisional point of view
Divisional managers are rewarded via a remuneration package which is linked to an ROI performance measure. Therefore they are likely to take a short-term view in appraising the investment proposals because they will be anxious to maintain their earnings. They would be interested in the short-term effect on ROI and perhaps on residual income (RI).

Project A

	Year			
	1	**2**	**3**	**4**
	£000	**£000**	**£000**	**£000**
NBV of asset at beginning of year	60	45	30	15
Net cash inflow	21	21	21	21
Depreciation	(15)	(15)	(15)	(15)
Operating profit	6	6	6	6
Imputed interest at 15%	(9)	(7)	(5)	(2)
Residual income	(3)	(1)	1	4
ROI %	(6/60)	(6/45)	(6/30)	(6/15)
	10.0	13.3	20.0	40.0

Project B

	Year			
	1	**2**	**3**	**4**
	£000	**£000**	**£000**	**£000**
NBV of asset at beginning of year	60	45	30	15
Net cash inflow	25	20	20	15
Depreciation	(15)	(15)	(15)	(15)
Operating profit	10	5	5	–
Imputed interest at 15%	(9)	(7)	(5)	(2)
Residual income	1	(2)	–	(2)
ROI %	16.7	11.1	16.7	–

Project C

	Year			
	1	**2**	**3**	**4**
	£000	**£000**	**£000**	**£000**
NBV of asset at beginning of year	60	45	30	15
Net cash inflow	10	20	30	40
Depreciation	(15)	(15)	(15)	(15)
Operating profit	(5)	5	15	25
Imputed interest at 15%	(9)	(7)	(5)	(2)
Residual income	(14)	(2)	10	23
ROI %	(8.3)	11.1	50.0	166.7

Red Division is likely to reject project A because of the potential adverse effect on the manager's remuneration in year 1.

Similarly, project C is also likely to be rejected due to adverse results in the early years, despite the long-term profitability of the project.

Project B is the most likely to be accepted if the manager takes a short-term view to protect his or her remuneration in the coming year, although the decision will be affected by the division's current level of ROI.

(ii)   From a company point of view

The company is likely to appraise the projects using discounted cash flow techniques.

Year	Discount factor at 15%	Project A Cash flow £000	Present value £000	Project B Cash flow £000	Present value £000	Project C Cash flow £000	Present value £000
1	0.87	21	18.27	25	21.75	10	8.70
2	0.76	21	15.96	20	15.20	20	15.20
3	0.66	21	13.86	20	13.20	30	19.80
4	0.57	21	11.97	15	8.55	40	22.80
			60.06		58.70		66.50
Initial investment			60.00		60.00		60.00
Net present value			+0.06		−1.30		+6.50

From the company point of view project A may be acceptable although the NPV is very small and there is no room for possible error in the estimates and the risk of a negative return would be very great. The final decision will depend among other things on the risk premium built into the cost of capital.

Project B would be unacceptable whereas project C would be acceptable from a company point of view.

(iii) Probable decision

Project	Division	Company
A	Reject	Accept
B	Accept	Reject
C	Reject	Accept

The table shows that there is unlikely to be goal congruence between the company and the manager of Red Division.

The divergence between the two points of view has occurred because they are each using different assessment crriteria. The views of the division and the company can be brought into line if they both use the same criteria in future. This would mean abandoning the practice of linking a manager's remuneration directly to short-term ROI because this is likely to encourage short-term thinking since ROI tends to be low in the early stages of an investment.

On the other hand it would be difficult to link remuneration to the net present value of individual projects because of the length of time before all the costs and benefits arise.

The specific problem with project A could be overcome through the use of annuity depreciation instead of the straight line method. The constant cash flows will then result in a smoother ROI profile over the life of the project. The manager would then be more likely to make the same decision as the company, although it depends to an extent on the division's current level of ROI.

The company may consider introducing the use of economic value added (EVA) as a measure of performance, which may be suitable for both divisional and economic performance.

E6.8 AAK

(i)

Year	Equipment cost £000	Running costs £000	Lighting, heating, etc. £000	Total outflow £000	Discount factor at 10%	Present value £000
0	120			120	1.00	120.000
1		40	15	55	0.91	50.050
2		44	15	59	0.83	48.970
3		48	15	63	0.75	47.250
4		52	15	67	0.68	45.560
5		56	15	71	0.62	44.020
Present value						355.850

We can assume that the annual sales revenue at the full level is S. We first need to calculate the present value of each year's expected sales.

Year	Revenue	Discount factor at 10%	Present value
1	0.4S	0.91	0.364S
2	0.7S	0.83	0.581S
3	1.0S	0.75	0.750S
4	1.0S	0.68	0.680S
5	1.0S	0.62	0.620S
Present value			2.995S

$$\text{contribution} = \text{revenue} - \text{variable costs}$$

Because the prices of drinks are to be set at double their direct (variable) costs then half of the total present value of sales 2.995S must represent direct costs and the other half must represent contribution.

$$\text{therefore contribution} = \frac{2.995S}{2} = 1.4975S$$

which is the present value of the contribution from the drinks.

To break even at an annual capital cost of 10% the present value of the contribution from drinks must equal the present value of the total outgoings, which is £355,850.

$$1.4975S = £355,850$$
$$S = £237,629$$

Therefore the required sales of drinks in each year are:

Year		£
1	£237,629 × 40%	95,052
2	£237,629 × 70%	166,340
3		237,629
4		237,629
5		237,629

(ii)   Aspects of the proposals that require further investigation:

- Can the facilities be used outside normal licensed opening hours for alternative uses in order to increase the contribution?
- Has market research been carried out to support the belief that there will be additional future benefits?
- Will the proposed cost plus drinks pricing method result in competitive prices?
- Perhaps there is a better way for this project to utilise the space and the capital, and perhaps food may be an option.

E6.9 Lew Rolls

(i)

Year	Super						Superlux			Exec			Excel		
	10% DF	20% DF	CF	10% DCF	20% DCF	CF	10% DCF	20% DCF	CF	10% DCF	20% DCF	CF	10% DCF	20% DCF
			£m	£m	£m	£m	£m	£m	£m	£m	£m	£m	£m	£m
0	1.00	1.00	−3	−3	−3	−7	−7	−7	−12	−12	−12	−15	−15	−15
1	0.91	0.83	1	0.91	0.83	2	1.82	1.66	0	0	0	10	9.10	8.30
2	0.83	0.69	1	0.83	0.69	2	1.66	1.38	0	0	0	10	8.30	6.90
3	0.75	0.58	1	0.75	0.58	2	1.50	1.16	7	5.25	4.06	0	0	0
4	0.68	0.48	1	0.68	0.48	2	1.36	0.96	7	4.76	3.36	0	0	0
5	0.62	0.40	1	0.62	0.40	2	1.24	0.80	7	4.34	2.80	0	0	0
Total			2	0.79	−0.02	3	0.58	−1.04	9	2.35	−1.78	5	2.40	0.20

(ii)   **Calculation of IRR**

From the table above calculate the IRR for each of the projects using interpolation/extrapolation as shown in Figures 6.3 and 6.4 in Chapter 6 to obtain:

	Super	Superlux	Exec	Excel
IRR	19.8%	13.6%	15.7%	20.9%
Ranking of projects (highest IRR ranked 1)	2	4	3	1

Net present value

	Super	Superlux	Exec	Excel
NPV of each project	£0.79m	£0.58m	£2.35m	£2.40m
NPV/£ invested	£0.263	£0.083	£0.196	£0.160
Ranking	1	4	2	3

NPV per £ invested is the more reliable evaluation method for appraisal of these alternatives. Therefore, given the £24m total constraint, the investment decision may be determined as follows:

	£m	NPV per £ invested	NPV £m
Super	3	£0.263	0.79
Exec	12	£0.196	2.35
Excel	9 (part)	£0.160	1.44
Superlux	0	0.083	0.00
Optimum total NPV	24		4.58

If IRR rankings were used to make the investment decision:

Excel	15	£0.160	2.40
Super	3	£0.263	0.79
Exec	6 (part)	£0.196	1.18
Superlux	0	£0.083	0.00
Total NPV	24		4.37

which is not optimal

(iv) and (v) Please refer to the relevant sections in Chapter 6 to check your solutions.

E7.1 Vine plc

The reduction in the company's cash flow for 2012 is explained as follows:

	£
PBIT	2,700
Depreciation	300
Inventories increase	(1,000)
Trade and other receivables increase	(1,900)
Trade and other payables increase	1,000
Operating cash flow increase	1,100
Non-current assets purchased	(2,700)
Dividends paid	(600)
Income tax paid	(1,000)
Share capital increase	600
Debentures increase	1,200
Cash flow decrease	(1,400)

Cash and cash equivalents have been reduced by £1.4m in the year (£1.5m − £0.1m). The company is generating profits but much of the sales revenue appears to be reflected in a high level of trade receivables, with the company investing heavily in increased inventory levels.

E7.2 Lamarr plc

Current market value of Lamarr plc is

	£
Current ordinary share capital	400,000 × £2.20 = 880,000
Rights issue	200,000
	1,080,000

Expected earnings of Lamarr plc = £1,080,000 × 16.5% = £178,200
Current eps (before rights issue) = ((£880,000 × 0.16)/400,000) = £0.352 or 35.2p

Rights issue @ £2.00

Shares issued = £200,000/£2.00 = 100,000
Total shares in issue = 400,000 + 100,000 = 500,000
Theoretical *ex rights* price £1,080,000/500,000 = £2.16
New eps £178,200/500,000 = 35.6p

Rights issue @ £1.80

Shares issued = £200,000/£1.80 = 111,111
Total shares in issue = 400,000 + 111,111 = 511,111
Theoretical *ex rights* price £1,080,000/511,111 = £2.11
New eps £178,200/511,111 = 34.9p

Rights issue @ £1.60

Shares issued = £200,000/£1.60 = 125,000
Total shares in issue = 400,000 + 125,000 = 525,000
Theoretical *ex rights* price £1,080,000/525,000 = £2.06
New eps £178,200/525,000 = 33.9p

E7.3 Emlyn plc

The company made a profit before tax of £9.4m in 2012, which was a return per share of 94p (£9.4m/10m shares). The share price is £2.50, and so the ratio of profit before tax to market value is 94p/£2.50, or 37.6%. This is the minimum return on new capital that should be expected, and so the assumption is that Emlyn plc will earn profit before additional interest and tax of 38% on the £5.5m that it raises.

(a) 6% bonds

(i) It may be difficult for the company to issue £5.5m bonds without having to provide security.

(ii) Earnings per share

Profit before additional interest is assumed to increase by 38% on new funds raised.

	£m
Profit before extra interest (£9.4m + 38% × £5.5m)	11.490
Less extra interest (6% of £5.5m)	(0.330)
Profit before tax	11.160
Tax @ 35%	(3.906)
Profit after tax	7.254
Number of ordinary shares	10m
eps	72.5p

which is a big increase over the 2012 level of 61p (£6.1m/10m).
(iii) Debt/equity ratio

$$\text{dividend payout ratio} = £3.8\text{m}/6.1\text{m} = 62.3\%$$

$$\text{retained earnings} = \text{PAT } £7.3\text{m} - \text{dividends } £4.5\text{m } (62.3\%) = £2.8\text{m}$$

$$\frac{\text{total debt}}{\text{total equity}} = \frac{£13.5\text{m} + £5.5\text{m}}{£23.6\text{m} + £2.8\text{m}} = 72.0\%$$

Assuming dividends are paid at the same level as 2012 at 62.3% of PAT, the financial gearing, represented by the debt/equity ratio would rise to 72.0%, compared to the already high level of 57.2% (£13.5m/£23.6m) for 2012. This could have an adverse effect on the willingness of the bank, suppliers and other investors to grant further credit.

(b) Ordinary shares

(i)   The ordinary shares one-for-four rights issue is at a discount to the current market price at a price of £2.20 per share. This would result in the issue of 10m × 0.25 = 2.5m new shares, which at an issue price of £2.20 per share would raise £5.5m.

(ii)   Earnings per share

Profit before additional interest is assumed to increase by 38% on new funds raised.

	£m
Profit before extra interest	11.490
(£9.4m + 38% × £5.5m)	
Tax @ 35%	(4.022)
Profit after tax	7.468
Number of ordinary shares	12.5m
eps	59.7p

which is a fall from the 2012 level of 61p.

(iii) P/E ratio

The P/E ratio on the basis of 2012 earnings is £2.50/61p = 4.1 times.

If this P/E ratio is applied to an eps of 59.7p, we would expect the share price to fall to about £2.44 (4.1 × 59.7p).

This compares with a theoretical *ex rights* price of

	£
4 shares, market value £2.50	10.00
1 new shares issued at £2.20	2.20
5 shares theoretical value	12.20
Theoretical *ex rights* price £12.20/5	2.44

The share price after the rights issue may fall, but only to around its theoretical *ex rights* price of £2.44 per share.

(iv) Debt/equity ratio

$$\text{retained earnings} = \text{PAT } £7.5\text{m} - \text{dividends } £4.7\text{m } (62.3\%) = £2.8\text{m}$$

$$\frac{\text{total debt}}{\text{total equity}} = \frac{£13.5\text{m}}{£23.6\text{m} + £2.8\text{m}} = 51.1\%$$

Assuming dividends are paid at the same level as 2012 at 62.3% of PAT, the financial gearing, represented by the debt/equity ratio would fall to 51.1%, compared to 57.2% for 2012 and this would put the company in a slightly better position to raise further finance in the future, if required, by raising new debt capital.

(c) 7% preference shares

   (i)   Earnings per share

Profit before additional preference share dividends is assumed to increase by 38% on new funds raised.

	£m
Profit before extra interest	11.490
(£9.4m + 38% × £5.5m)	
Tax @ 35%	(4.022)
	7.468
Preference dividend 7% × £5.5m	(0.385)
Profit after tax	7.083
Number of ordinary shares	10m
eps	70.8p

which is a big increase over the 2012 level of 61p.

   (ii)   Debt/equity ratio

$$\text{retained earnings} = \text{PAT £7.1m} - \text{dividends £4.4m (62.3\%)} = \text{£2.7m}$$

Preference shares are usually included with prior charge capital for gearing calculations, and so debt/equity would increase to

$$\frac{\text{£13.5m} + \text{£5.5m}}{\text{£23.6m} + \text{£2.7m}} = 72.2\%$$

Assuming dividends are paid at the same level as 2012 at 62.3% of PAT, the financial gearing, represented by the debt/equity ratio would rise to 72.2%, compared to 57.2% for 2012 and this is a level of gearing about which other creditors might have reservations about granting credit to the company.

Recommendations

The company should make either a rights issue of new equity or an issue of bonds. An issue of preference shares would improve eps, but not as much as an issue of bonds and so would not be as beneficial.

An issue of bonds would substantially increase eps, due to the low after-tax cost of the bonds, which an issue of new equity would not. However, because of the high level of gearing, the perceived risk of the company would rise, and the share price would probably fall to a lower P/E level.

In conclusion, a rights issue would probably be the most suitable method of financing since this would provide an extra injection of equity capital that would put the company in a good position for further growth in the future, without any harmful effects on eps or on the share price (allowing for the dilution with the issue).

E7.4 Globe plc

   (i)   We need to examine whether the company's requirements regarding the rights issue are viable.

(a) Total earnings after the redemption of the loan stock would be £263,000.

	£	£
Current earnings are 500,000 × 50p		250,000
Additional earnings after redeeming the bond		
Interest saved £400,000 × 5%	20,000	
Less tax on interest @ 35%	(7,000)	
		13,000
Earnings after redeeming the bond		263,000

If eps should be diluted by no more than 12%, they will be no less than 44p.
Therefore, the number of shares in issue will be:

$$\frac{\text{total earnings}}{\text{eps}} = \frac{£263,000}{£0.44} = 597,727 \text{ shares}$$

Therefore, the additional number of shares issued should not be more than 97,727.
The rights issue price will then be:

$$\frac{£400,000}{97,727} = £4.09$$

This is not viable because it is above the current market share price of £3.80.

(b) A rights issue price at 10% below the current share price would be £3.80 × 90% = £3.42.
116,959 shares would have to be issued to raise £400,000, and so the eps would be:

$$\frac{£263,000}{500,000 + 116,959} = 42.6\text{p, which is 14.8\% below the current eps 50p}$$

(c) If Globe plc makes a one-for-four issue, the number of shares issued would be 125,000
(500,000/4), and to raise £400,000 the issue price per share would be:

$$\frac{£400,000}{125,000} = £3.20$$

which is 15.8% below the current market value, and not 10% as required.

(ii) The theoretical *ex rights* price of the shares would be:

	£
Market value *cum rights* of four shares (4 × £3.80)	15.20
Rights issue price of one share @ £3.20	3.20
Theoretical value of five shares	18.40

The theoretical *ex rights* price would be £3.68 per share (£18.40/5).
The eps would be:

$$\frac{£263,000}{500,000 + 125,000} = 42\text{p}$$

The P/E ratio would be $\dfrac{£3.68}{42\text{p}}$ = 8.8 times

(iii) A rights issue of ordinary shares can be made to raise a substantial amount of new long-
term capital.

If an issue of shares to new shareholders is chosen as an alternative to a rights issue, it is a Stock Exchange requirement that prior approval must have been obtained within the past 12 months, from the shareholders in a general meeting, for the issue of shares for cash other than as a rights issue. A rights issue is more likely to be successful than a public issue, because:

- the offer is to existing investors who are familiar with the company
- existing shareholders may wish to take up the rights offer in order to preserve their relative shareholdings in the company
- the offer price, below the current market price, would be set in such a way as to attract shareholders into acceptance. The cost of a rights issue would also be less than that of an offer for sale.

The main drawback to a rights issue is its cost. Placings are cheaper, and would probably be preferred for smaller issues

A rights issue would be preferable to raising long-term loan capital:

- where the interest rate on the loan capital which must be offered to attract investors is unacceptably high
- where the company's level of gearing would become unacceptably high, possibly causing a reduction in the market value of the ordinary shares as a result of the extra financial risk to shareholders
- where the company wishes to reduce its level of gearing.

A dilution in net earnings per share would generally be expected as a result of a rights issue, at least in the short term. This should be acceptable to shareholders provided that the return obtained on their total investment is at least as high as it was before the rights issue.

Consider a company that has in issue 1m ordinary shares with a market value of £2m and current annual earnings of £250,000 or 25p eps. It decides to make a one-for-four rights issue to finance a new investment. The offer price is £1.50 per share.

The current P/E ratio is 8 (share price £2 and eps 25p).

The theoretical market value of the 1,250,000 shares in issue after the rights issue is

4 × £2	£8.00	
1 @ £1.50	£1.50	
5	£9.50 = £1.90 per share × 1,250,000 = £2,375,000	

If the P/E ratio is to be maintained at 8, then the market value of the 1,250,000 shares must be sustained by annual earnings of:

$$£2,375,000/8 = £296,875$$
$$\text{eps would be } £296,875/1,250,000 = 23.75\text{p}$$

Provided that the company pursues a consistent dividend policy by maintaining a constant dividend cover ratio then the shareholders would be happy with their return despite eps dropping from 25p to 23.75p.

E7.5 Wiltel plc

Redemption value of debt V_n = £3.50 × 4 = £14 per £10 debt or £140 per £100 debt

Debt interest i = £8 pre-tax and £8 × (1 − 25%) = £6 after tax

Current market value of debt V_0 = £106

We want to find the market rate of return on bonds expected by investors (R_d), using:

$$V_0 = i/(1 + R_d) + i/(1 + R_d)^2 + i/(1 + R_d)^3 + \cdots + (i + V_n)/(1 + R_d)^n$$

Therefore £106 = £6/(1 + R_d) + £6/(1 + R_d)^2 + (£6 + £140)/(1 + R_d)^3

This may be solved using the interpolation technique we saw in Chapter 6, and we will calculate NPV using estimated rates of 12% and 15%.

	Cash flows		£ present values at 12%	£ present values at 15%
Year 0		£106.00	−106.00	−106.00
Year 1 – 3	£8 × (1 − 0.25) =	£6.00	14.41	13.70
Year 3	40 × £3.50	= £140.00	99.65	92.05
			+8.06	−0.25

Using interpolation we can calculate the cost of convertible debt
Therefore the company's cost of the convertible debt is 14.9%.

$$\frac{£0.25}{x} = \frac{£8.06}{(15\% - 12\% - x\%)}$$

$$0.25 \times (3 - x) = 8.06 \times x$$

$$0.75 - 0.25x = 8.06x$$

$$0.75 = 8.06x + 0.25x$$

$$0.75 = 8.31x$$

$$\frac{0.75}{8.31} = x$$

$$0.09 = x$$

Cost of the convertible debt = 15% − 0.09% = 14.91%

An alternative calculation may be used to give the same result:

$$= 12\% + \left\{ \frac{£8.06}{£8.06 + £0.25} \times (15\% - 12\%) \right\}$$

Cost of the convertible debt = 14.91%

E7.7 Nimrod plc

The advantages of a market listing include:

- easier access to capital
- the company will enjoy a higher profile and enhanced status with its customers and suppliers
- it may be a possible first step towards a full Stock Exchange listing
- it presents an opportunity for the company to create a market for its shares and widen its shareholder base
- it provides increased opportunities to make acquisitions.

The disadvantages of a market listing include:

- increased scrutiny by investors, analysts, and the press
- specific requirements for the company to keep investors informed
- the company may be subject to irrational market share price movements
- the company may be subject to short-termist pressure from shareholders.

The main differences between a listing on the London Stock Exchange and a listing on the AIM include:

London Stock Exchange

- there is a requirement for a minimum 25% shares to be in public hands
- normally a three-year trading record is required for the company
- shareholder prior approval is required for substantial acquisitions and disposals
- there is a minimum market capitalisation.

AIM

- there is no minimum number of shares required to be in public hands
- there is no minimum trading record requirement
- there is no prior shareholder approval required for acquisitions and disposals
- a nominated adviser is required at all times
- there is no minimum market capitalisation requirement.

E7.8 Curtis E Carr & Co

(i)

$$\text{PV of purchase} = £150,000 - (£5,000/(1.10)^7)$$
$$= £150,000 - (£5,000 \times 0.5132)$$
$$= (£150,000 - £2,566)$$
$$= £147,434$$

The equivalent annual cost of the purchase would be:

$$£147,434/7 \text{ year annuity factor @10\%}$$
$$£147,434/4.8684 = £30,284$$

The annual lease payment is less than the equivalent annual purchase cost therefore the company should lease.

(ii) Please refer to the relevant section in Chapter 7 to check your solution.

E8.1 Priory Products plc

(i) Net debt to equity

Net debt	100	250	800
Equity	300	500	800
Debt/equity (%)	33%	50%	100%

(ii) Long-term loans to equity and long-term loans

Long-term loans	200	200	600
Equity plus LTL	500	700	1,400
Gearing (%)	40%	29%	43%

Capital turnover

$$\text{Capital turnover 2012} = \frac{\text{revenue}}{\text{average capital employed in year}} = \frac{£456}{£288} = 1.6 \text{ times}$$

$$\text{Capital turnover 2011} = \frac{£491}{£260.5} = 1.9 \text{ times}$$

Capital turnover 2010 is not available because we do not have the capital employed figure for 31 March 2009.

Report on the profitability of Hardy plc

Sales revenue for the year 2012 was 7.1% lower than sales revenue in 2011, which was 16.9% above 2010. It is not clear whether these sales revenue reductions were from lower volumes, fewer products, or changes in selling prices.

Gross profit improved from 34.0% in 2010 to 34.2% in 2011 to 35.3% in 2012, possibly from increased selling prices and/or from lower costs of production.

Operating profit to sales revenue increased from 11.9% in 2010 to 12.4% in 2011 but then fell to 11.4% in 2012, despite the improvement in gross profit, because of higher levels of distribution costs and administrative expenses.

ROCE dropped from 23.4% to 18.1%, reflecting the lower level of operating profit. Return on equity increased from 12.6% in 2010 to 13.0% in 2011 but then fell sharply in 2012 to 9.0%. This was because of the large fall in profit after tax in 2012.

Capital turnover was reduced from 1.9 times in 2011 to 1.6 in 2012, reflecting the fall in sales levels in 2012 over 2011.

Efficiency ratios for Hardy plc for 2012 and the comparative ratios for 2011 and 2010
Collection days

$$\text{Collection days 2012} = \frac{\text{trade receivables} \times 365}{\text{revenue}} = \frac{£80 \times 365}{£456} = 64 \text{ days}$$

$$\text{Collection days 2011} = \frac{£70 \times 365}{£491} = 52 \text{ days}$$

$$\text{Collection days 2010} = \frac{£53 \times 365}{£420} = 46 \text{ days}$$

Payables days

$$\text{Payables days 2012} = \frac{\text{trade payables} \times 365}{\text{cost of sales}} = \frac{£38 \times 365}{£295} = 47 \text{ days}$$

$$\text{Payables days 2011} = \frac{£38 \times 365}{£323} = 43 \text{ days}$$

$$\text{Payables days 2010} = \frac{£26 \times 365}{£277} = 34 \text{ days}$$

Inventories days (inventory turnover)

$$\text{Inventories days 2012} = \frac{\text{inventories}}{\text{average daily cost of sales in period}} = \frac{£147}{£295/365} = 182 \text{ days (26.0 weeks)}$$

$$\text{Inventories days 2011} = \frac{£152}{£323/365} = 172 \text{ days (24.6 weeks)}$$

$$\text{Inventories days 2010} = \frac{£118}{£277/365} = 156 \text{ days (22.3 weeks)}$$

Operating cycle days

$$\text{Operating cycle 2012} = \text{inventories days} + \text{collection days} - \text{payables days} = 182 + 64 - 47$$

$$= 199 \text{ days}$$
$$\text{Operating cycle 2011} = 172 + 52 - 43$$

$$= 181 \text{ days}$$

$$\text{Operating cycle 2010} = 156 + 46 - 34$$
$$= 168 \text{ days}$$

Operating cycle %

$$\text{Operating cycle \% 2012} = \frac{\text{working capital requirement}}{\text{revenue}}$$

$$= \frac{(£147 + £80 - £38) \times 100\%}{£456} = 41.4\%$$

$$\text{Operating cycle \% 2011} = \frac{(£152 + £70 - £38) \times 100\%}{£491} = 37.5\%$$

$$\text{Operating cycle \% 2010} = \frac{(£118 + £53 - £26)}{£420} = 34.5\%$$

Asset turnover

$$\text{Asset turnover 2012} = \frac{\text{revenue}}{\text{total assets}} = \frac{£456}{£385} = 1.18 \text{ times}$$

$$\text{Asset turnover 2011} = \frac{£491}{£374} = 1.31 \text{ times}$$

$$\text{Asset turnover 2010} = \frac{£420}{£303} = 1.39 \text{ times}$$

Report on the efficiency performance of Hardy plc

Average customer settlement days worsened successively over the years 2010, 2011 and 2012 from 46 to 52 to 64 days. This was partly mitigated by some improvement in the average payables days which increased from 34 to 43 to 47 days over the same period. The average inventories days worsened from 156 to 172 to 182 days over 2010, 2011, and 2012. Therefore, mainly because of the poor receivables collection performance and increasingly high inventories levels, the operating cycle worsened from 168 days in 2010 to 181 days in 2011 and to 199 days in 2012 (operating cycle 34.5% to 37.5% to 41.4%). Asset turnover reduced from 1.39 to 1.31 times from 2010 to 2011 and then to 1.18 in 2012, reflecting the degree to which sales revenue had dropped despite increasing levels of total assets.

Liquidity ratios for Hardy plc for 2012 and the comparative ratios for 2011 and 2010

Current ratio

$$\text{Current ratio 2012} = \frac{\text{current assets}}{\text{current liabilities}} = \frac{£253}{£93} = 2.7 \text{ times}$$

$$\text{Current ratio 2011} = \frac{£251}{£90} = 2.8 \text{ times}$$

$$\text{Current ratio 2010} = \frac{£197}{£66} = 3.0 \text{ times}$$

Quick ratio (acid test)

$$\text{Quick ratio 2012} = \frac{\text{current assets} - \text{inventories}}{\text{current liabilities}} = \frac{£253 - £147}{£93} = 1.1 \text{ times}$$

$$\text{Quick ratio 2011} = \frac{£251 - £152}{£90} = 1.1 \text{ times}$$

$$\text{Quick ratio 2010} = \frac{£197 - £118}{£66} = 1.2 \text{ times}$$

Defensive interval

$$\text{Defensive interval 2012} = \frac{\text{quick assets}}{\text{average daily cash from operations}}$$

$$= \frac{£253 - £147}{(£70 + £456 - £80)/365} = 87 \text{ days}$$

$$\text{Defensive interval 2011} = \frac{£251 - £152}{(£53 + £491 - £70)/365} = 76 \text{ days}$$

The defensive interval 2010 is not available because we do not have the trade receivables number for 31 March 2009.

Report on the liquidity of Hardy plc
The current ratio and the quick ratio have both dropped over the three years from 3.0 to 2.7 times, and 1.2 times to 1.1 times respectively. The defensive interval has increased from 76 days to 87 days at which level the company could potentially survive if there were no further cash inflows.

(ii) There are a number of areas that require further investigation. The following five ratios may be particularly useful to assist this investigation:
- return on capital employed, ROCE
- receivables collection days
- payables days
- inventories days
- current ratio.

(iii) The relevant information has not been provided to enable the following investment ratios to be calculated for Hardy plc, which would have improved the analysis of Hardy plc's performance:

Earnings per share, eps

Cannot be calculated because we do not have details of the number of ordinary shares in issue.

Dividend per share

Cannot be calculated because we do not have details of the number of ordinary shares in issue.

Dividend cover

Cannot be calculated because we have not been able to calculate earnings per share, eps, and dividend per share.

Dividend yield %

Cannot be calculated because we have not been able to calculate dividend per share, and we do not have the market prices of the company's shares.

Price/earnings ratio, P/E

Cannot be calculated because we have not been able to calculate earnings per share, and we do not have the market prices of the company's shares.

Capital expenditure to sales revenue %

Cannot be calculated because we do not have details of capital expenditure.

Capital expenditure to gross non-current assets %

Cannot be calculated because we do not have details of capital expenditure.

E8.10 Dandy plc

As discussed in Chapter 8, there are many alternative ways in which ratios may be presented. This exercise illustrates some variations on the ratios shown in Chapter 8.

(i)

Return on net assets (return on capital employed)

$$\frac{\text{profit before interest and tax}}{\text{total assets less current liabilities and long-term liabilities}} \times 100$$

2010	2011	2012
(£1,600/£3,400) × 100	(£2,400/£4,700) × 100	(£1,200/£5,350) × 100
47.1%	**51.1%**	**22.4%**

Return on equity

$$\frac{\text{profit after tax}}{\text{equity}} \times 100$$

2010	2011	2012
(£1,000/£3,400) × 100	(£1,300/£4,700) × 100	(£650/£5,350) × 100
29.4%	**27.7%**	**12.1%**

Gross profit to sales revenue

$$\frac{\text{gross profit}}{\text{sales revenue}} \times 100$$

2010	2011	2012
(£5,600/£11,200) × 100	(£5,000/£8,000) × 100	(£3,200/£6,000) × 100
50.0%	**62.5%**	**53.3%**

PBIT to sales revenue

$$\frac{\text{profit before interest and tax}}{\text{sales revenue}} \times 100$$

2010	2011	2012
(£1,600/£11,200) × 100	(£2,400/£8,000) × 100	(£1,200/£6,000) × 100
14.3%	**30.0%**	**20.0%**

Asset turnover

$$\frac{\text{sales revenue}}{\text{total assets}}$$

2010	2011	2012
(£11,200/£7,900)	(£8,000/£11,200)	(£6,000/£13,200)
1.42 times	**0.71 times**	**0.45 times**

Inventories days

$$\frac{\text{inventories}}{\text{cost of sales}} \times 365$$

2010	2011	2012
(£1,700/£5,600) × 365	(£1,800/£3,000) × 365	(£2,200/£2,800) × 365
111 days	**219 days**	**287 days**

Collection days

$$\frac{\text{trade receivables}}{\text{sales revenue}} \times 365$$

2010	2011	2012
(£2,900/£11,200) × 365	(£5,550/£8,000) × 365	(£5,000/£6,000) × 365
95 days	**253 days**	**304 days**

Payables days

$$\frac{\text{trade payables}}{\text{cost of sales}} \times 365$$

2010	2011	2012
(£1,300/£5,600) × 365	(£1,200/£3,000) × 365	(£1,000/£2,800) × 365
85 days	**146 days**	**130 days**

Operating cycle

$$\text{inventories days} + \text{collection days} - \text{payables days}$$

2010	2011	2012
$111 + 95 - 85$	$219 + 253 - 146$	$287 + 304 - 130$
121 days	**326 days**	**461 days**

Current ratio

$$\frac{\text{current assets}}{\text{current liabilities}}$$

2010	2011	2012
(£5,300/£3,500)	(£9,200/£3,500)	(£8,100/£3,350)
1.51:1	**2.63:1**	**2.42:1**

Quick ratio (acid test)

$$\frac{\text{current assets} - \text{inventories}}{\text{current liabilities}}$$

2010	2011	2012
(£5,300 − £1,700)/£3,500	(£9,200 − £1,800)/£3,500	(£8,100 − £2,200)/£3,350
1.03:1	**2.11:1**	**1.76:1**

Debt/equity ratio

$$\frac{\text{total debt}}{\text{total equity}}$$

2010	2011	2012
(£1,000/£3,400) × 100	(£3,000/£4,700) × 100	(£4,500/£5,350) × 100
29.4%	**63.8%**	**84.1%**

Earnings per share

$$\frac{\text{profit after tax}}{\text{number of ordinary shares}}$$

2010	2011	2012
£1,000/2,000	£1,300/2,200	£650/2,500
50p	**59p**	**26p**

Price/earnings ratio

$$\frac{\text{current market price per share}}{\text{earnings per share}}$$

2010	2011	2012
£0.80/£0.50	£0.90/£0.59	£0.45/£0.26
1.60	**1.53**	**1.73**

Dividend yield

$$\frac{\text{dividend per share}}{\text{current market price per share}}$$

2010	2011	2012
(£600/2,000)/£0.80	(£200/2,200)/£0.90	(£300/2,500)/£0.45
37.50%	10.10%	26.67%

Dividend cover

$$\frac{\text{profit after tax}}{\text{total dividend}}$$

2010	2011	2012
£1,000/£600	£1,300/£200	£650/£300
1.67	6.50	2.17

Multivariate analysis – Altman Z score

$$Z = 1.2R_1 + 1.4R_2 + 3.3R_3 + 0.6R_4 + 0.999R_5 \text{ for a public company}$$

(note that the private company formula is slightly different)
where

$R_1 = $ working capital/total assets
$R_2 = $ retained earnings/total assets
$R_3 = $ earnings before interest and tax (PBIT)/total assets
$R_4 = $ market value of equity/total liabilities
$R_5 = $ sales revenue/total assets

For a public company

Z score above 2.99 indicates that a company is likely to be successful
Z score below 1.81 indicates that a company is likely to fail
Between 1.81 and 2.99 indicates that a company's future is indeterminate.

	2010	**2011**	**2012**
Figures in £000			
working capital	1,800	5,700	4,750
total assets	7,900	11,200	13,200
retained earnings	1,400	2,500	2,850
PBIT	1,600	2,400	1,200
total liabilities	4,500	6,500	7,850
MV of equity	1,600	1,980	1,125
sales revenue	11,200	8,000	6,000
R_1	0.228	0.509	0.360
R_2	0.177	0.223	0.216
R_3	0.203	0.214	0.091
R_4	0.356	0.305	0.143
R_5	1.418	0.714	0.455

2010

$$Z = 1.2(0.228) + 1.4(0.177) + 3.3(0.203) + 0.6(0.356) + 0.999(1.418)$$
$$Z = 2.82 \text{ (indeterminate)}$$

2011

$$Z = 1.2(0.509) + 1.4(0.223) + 3.3(0.214) + 0.6(0.305) + 0.999(0.714)$$
$$Z = 2.53 \text{ (indeterminate)}$$

2012

$$Z = 1.2(0.360) + 1.4(0.216) + 3.3(0.091) + 0.6(0.143) + 0.999(0.455)$$
$$Z = \textbf{1.58 (failure likely based on financial statement factors)}$$

(ii) Please refer to the relevant sections in Chapter 8 to check your solution.

E9.1 Hearbuy plc

Hearbuy plc sales plan – formulae

	A	B	C	D	E	F	G	H	I	J
1	Model			Sales		Year 1	Year 2	Year 3	Year 4	Total
2	assumptions									
3	Growth		0.2	Units 000		=2684/5.368	=+F3+$C$3*F3	=+G3+$C$3*G3	=+H3+$C$3*H3	=SUM(F3:I3)
4										
5	Price/unit		50	Units £m		=(F3*$C$5)/1000	=(G3*$C$5)/1000	=(H3*$C$5)/1000	=(I3*$C$5)/1000	=SUM(F5:I5)

Hearbuy plc sales plan – numbers

	A	B	C	D	E	F	G	H	I	J
1	Model			Sales		Year 1	Year 2	Year 3	Year 4	Total
2	assumptions									
3	Growth		20.0%	Units 000		500.0	600.0	720.0	864.0	2,684.0
4										
5	Price/unit		£50	Units £m		25.0	30.0	36.0	43.2	134.2

E9.2 Hearbuy plc

Hearbuy plc income statement for Year 1

Model assumptions	C	Income statement Figures in £m	F Year 1	Column F formulae
		Total sales revenue	25.00	
% sales revenue	70.0%	Cost of sales	(17.50)	+ F6*$C$7
% sales revenue	30.0%	PBIT	7.50	+ F6 + F7
% of debt	10.0%	Interest	(0.45)	+ 4.5*$C$9
		PBT	7.05	+ F8 + F9
% of PBT	35.0%	Tax	(2.47)	+ F10*$C$11
		Net profit	4.58	+ F10 + F11
% of net profit	60.0%	Dividends	(2.75)	+ F12*$C$13
% of net profit	40.0%	Retained earnings	1.83	+ F12 + F13

E9.3 Hearbuy plc

Hearbuy plc four-year plan

Model assumptions	C	Income statement	F	G	H	I	Column I
		Figures in £m	Year 1	Year 2	Year 3	Year 4	formulae
Growth	20.0%	Total sales revenue	25.00	30.00	36.00	43.20	+H6+$C6*H6
% sales revenue	70.0%	Cost of sales	(17.50)	(21.00)	(25.20)	(30.24)	+I6*$C$7
% sales revenue	30.0%	PBIT	7.50	9.00	10.80	12.96	+I6+I7
% of debt	10.0%	Interest	(0.45)	(0.45)	(0.80)	(1.22)	+H21*$C$9
		PBT	7.05	8.55	10.00	11.74	+I8+I9
% of PBT	35.0%	Tax	(2.47)	(2.99)	(3.50)	(4.11)	+I10*$C$11
		Net profit	4.58	5.56	6.50	7.63	+I10+I11
% of net profit	60.0%	Dividends	(2.75)	(3.34)	(3.90)	(4.58)	+I12*$C$13
% of net profit	40.0%	Retained earnings	1.83	2.22	2.60	3.05	+I12+I13

Model assumptions	C	Balance sheet	F	G	H	I	Column I
		Figures in £m	Year 1	Year 2	Year 3	Year 4	formulae
Growth	20.0%	Non-current assets	13.50	16.20	19.44	23.33	+H18+$C6*H18
% of sales revenue	60.0%	Working capital	15.00	18.00	21.60	25.92	+I6*SCS19
		Total assets	26.67	28.50	34.20	41.04	49.25	+I18+I19
		Debt	(4.50)	(4.50)	(7.98)	(12.22)	(17.38)	+H24–I27
			22.17	24.00	26.22	28.82	31.87	+I20+I21
		Equity	22.17	24.00	26.22	28.82	31.87	+H23+I14
		Additional funding required		3.48	4.24	5.16		+I20-H20–I14

E9.5 Hearbuy plc

No additional debt

Model assumptions	C	Income statement	F	G	H	I	Column I
		Figures in £m	Year 1	Year 2	Year 3	Year 4	formulae
Growth	6.87%	Total sales revenue	25.00	26.72	28.56	30.51	+H6+$C6*H6
% sales revenue	70.00%	Cost of sales	(17.50)	(18.70)	(19.99)	(21.36)	+I6*$C$7
% sales revenue	30.00%	PBIT	7.50	8.02	8.57	9.15	+I6+I7
% of debt	10.00%	Interest	(0.45)	(0.45)	(0.45)	(0.45)	+H21*$C$9
		PBT	7.05	7.57	8.12	8.70	+I8+I9
% of PBT	35.00%	Tax	(2.47)	(2.65)	(2.84)	(3.05)	+I10*$C$11
		Net profit	4.58	4.92	5.28	5.65	+I10+I11
% of net profit	60.00%	Dividends	(2.75)	(2.95)	(3.17)	(3.40)	+I12*$C$13
% of net profit	40.00%	Retained earnings	1.83	1.97	2.11	2.25	+I12+I13

Model assumptions	C	Balance sheet		F	G	H	I	Column I
		Figures in £m		Year 1	Year 2	Year 3	Year 4	formulae
Growth	6.87%	Total assets	26.67	28.50	30.46	32.55	34.79	+H18+$C6*H18
		Debt	(4.50)	(4.50)	(4.49)	(4.47)	(4.46)	+H19–I22
			22.17	24.00	25.97	28.08	30.33	+I18+I19
		Equity	22.17	24.00	25.97	28.08	30.33	+H21+I14
		Additional funding required			−0.01	−0.02	−0.01	+I18–H18–I14
		effectively zero						
		Retention ratio	0.4	1.83/4.58				
		Return on capital employed	0.2066	4.58/22.17				
		Equity/ assets ratio	0.8313					

$(0.4 \times 0.2066 \times 0.8313)$
$= 0.0687 = 6.87\%$ **Growth rate**

E9.6 Hearbuy plc

Constant gearing ratio

Model assumptions	C	Income statement	F	G	H	I	Column I
		Figures in £m	Year 1	Year 2	Year 3	Year 4	formulae
Growth	8.26%	Total sales revenue	25.00	27.07	29.30	31.72	+ H6 + $C6*H6
% sales revenue	70.00%	Cost of sales	(17.50)	(18.95)	(20.51)	(22.20)	+ I6*$C$7
% sales revenue	30.00%	PBIT	7.50	8.12	8.79	9.52	+ I6 + I7
% of debt	10.00%	Interest	(0.45)	(0.45)	(0.49)	(0.52)	+ H21*$C$9
		PBT	7.05	7.67	8.30	9.00	+ I8 + I9
% of PBT	35.00%	Tax	(2.47)	(2.68)	(2.90)	(3.15)	+ I10*$C$11
		Net profit	4.58	4.99	5.40	5.85	+ I10 + I11
% of net profit	60.00%	Dividends	(2.75)	(3.00)	(3.24)	(3.51)	+ I12*$C$13
% of net profit	40.00%	Retained earnings	1.83	1.99	2.16	2.34	+ I12 + I13

Model assumptions	C	Balance sheet Figures in £m	F Year 1	G Year 2	H Year 3	I Year 4	Column I formulae
Growth	8.26%	Total assets	26.67	28.50	30.85	33.40	36.16	+H18+$C6*H18
		Debt	(4.50)	(4.50)	(4.86)	(5.25)	(5.67)	+H19–I22
			22.17	24.00	25.99	28.15	30.49	+I18+I19
		Equity	22.17	24.00	25.99	28.15	30.49	+H21+I14
		Additional funding required			0.36	0.39	0.42	+I18–H18–I14
		Retention ratio	0.4	1.83/4.58				
		Return on capital employed	0.2066	4.58/22.17				

(0.4 × 0.2066)
= 0.0826 = 8.26% **Growth rate**

E9.7 Marx

(i)

	Chico	Groucho	Harpo
Average net operating assets	£7.5m	£17.5m	£12.5m
Operating profit	£1.5m	£1.4m	£2.0m
ROCE%	20%	8%	16%
Ranking of ROCE%	1	3	2

(ii)

	Chico	Groucho	Harpo
Average net operating assets	£7.5m	£17.5m	£12.5m
Divisional WACC	7%	5%	10%
Operating profit	£1.5m	£1.4m	£2.0m
Administrative expenses	£0.80m	£0.30m	£0.65m
Net income	£0.70m	£1.10m	£1.35m
Net assets × WACC	£0.525m	£0.875m	£1.250m
EVA = Net income − (NA × WACC)	£0.175m	£0.225m	£0.100m
Ranking of EVA	2	1	3

(iii) Please refer to the relevant section in Chapter 9 to check your solution.

(iv), (v) and (vi)

The ROCE% of each division is currently above its WACC with Chico being by far the best performer, followed by Harpo and then Groucho. Chico and Harpo would be reluctant to pursue an investment opportunity that is expected to yield a return of 9% because they currently earn 20% and 16% respectively. In the case of Chico this represents a lost opportunity for Marx plc because taking on the investment would add value since Chico's WACC is 2% lower than the project's 9%. Harpo's decision not to take on the investment is in the best interest of Marx plc since Harpo's WACC is 1% above the project's 9%. Groucho would be keen to pursue an investment opportunity that is expected to yield a return of 9% because it currently earns only 8%. Groucho's decision to take on the investment is also in the best interest of Marx plc since Groucho's WACC is 4% below the project's 9%.

The current EVA of Groucho is the highest, followed by Chico and then Harpo. If performance is measured using RI, then Chico and Groucho would take on an investment opportunity that yields 9% because even after capital charges on net operating assets at 7% and 5% respectively it would add to their residual incomes. If performance is measured using EVA, Harpo would not take on an investment opportunity that yields 9% because after the capital charge on net operating assets at 10% there would be a reduction to residual income.

E9.8 Arby Ltd

(i)

Figures in £	Oct	Nov	Dec	Jan	Feb	Mar
Sales revenue	200,000	205,000	180,000	200,000	205,000	200,000
Bad debts	7,000	7,175	6,300	7,000	7,175	7,000
Opening cash balance	25,000	−40,000	−15,500	−55,175	−62,975	−100,975
Cash sales 30%	60,000	61,500	54,000	60,000	61,500	60,000
Credit sales		133,000	136,325	119,700	133,000	136,325
Cash receipts	60,000	194,500	190,325	179,700	194,500	196,325
Wages	90,000	105,000	90,000	85,000	90,000	100,000
Materials	0	30,000	65,000	67,500	67,500	62,500
Overheads	35,000	35,000	35,000	35,000	35,000	35,000
Non-current assets			40,000		40,000	
Cash payments	125,000	170,000	230,000	187,500	232,500	197,500
Closing cash balance	−40,000	−15,500	−55,175	−62,975	−100,975	−102,150
Materials	60,000	70,000	65,000	70,000	55,000	70,000
50%		30,000	30,000	35,000	32,500	35,000
50%			35,000	32,500	35,000	27,500
	0	30,000	65,000	67,500	67,500	62,500

(ii) Please refer to the relevant sections in Chapter 9 to check your solution.

E10.1 Oliver Ltd

Production costs

		£	
Raw materials	[40% × £5,300,000]	2,120,000	held in inventory on average 4 days
Direct labour	[25% × £5,300,000]	1,325,000	
Overheads	[10% × £5,300,000]	530,000	
		3,975,000	finished goods held in inventory on average 7 days

The production cycle is 14 days

Working capital requirement

			£	£
Raw materials	[£2,120,000 × 4/365]	=		23,233
Work in progress				
Raw materials	[£2,120,000 × 14/365]	=	81,315	
Direct labour	[£1,325,000 × 14/365 × 25%]	=	12,705	
Overheads	[£530,000 × 14/365 × 25%]	=	5,082	
				99,102
Finished goods	[£3,975,000 × 7/365]	=		76,233
Trade receivables	[£5,300,000 × 60/365]	=		871,233
Trade payables	[£2,120,000 × 30/365]	=		(174,247)
Total working capital requirement				895,554

E10.5 Worrall plc

Cost of sales is 80% of sales			
Variable cost of sales	80% × 90%		= 72% of sales
Therefore			
Contribution			= 28% of sales
Proposed trade receivables			
Sales revenue, increased by 20% is	120% × £8m = £9.6m		
Credit allowed increased to 90 days	£9.6m × 90/365		= £2,367,123
Current trade receivables	£8m × 60/365		= £1,315,068
Increase in trade receivables			= £1,052,055
Gains			
Increase in contribution	(£9.6m − £8.0m) × 28%		= £448,000
Losses			
Increase in bad debts	(3% × £2,367,123) − (2% × £1,315,068)	=	£44,713
Increase in financing costs	£1,052,055 × 10%	=	£105,206
Total losses			£149,919
Net gain per annum	(£448,000 − £149,919)		£298,081

The net gain to Worrall Ltd is £298,081 per annum and so an increase to 90 days' credit may be recommended.

E11.5 Bank of Penderyn

This is about the minimisation of loss and the Bank of Penderyn has a responsibility not only to its shareholders but also to its account holders. However, it is also about how to deal with payment default arising from excessive country risk.

In terms of courses of action available to the Bank of Penderyn, there are perhaps three courses of action open:

1 reject the offer
2 seek to renegotiate the offer
3 accept the offer.

If the Bank were to reject the offer, it would need to decide on what action to take. It could, for example, pursue international legal action against the central bank of Zorbia for immediate recovery of the outstanding loans. This course of action, while undoubtedly legitimate and ethically correct, is likely to be costly and ultimately fruitless given the problems associated with third world debt. In addition, even if the course of action were to be successful, it would be unlikely given the current political and economic instability in many Indulosian countries, that the Bank would ever be able to sequestrate sufficient Zorbian assets to cover the outstanding loans.

Alternatively, the Bank could seek to sell the outstanding debt on the open market. It would be likely that this course of action would not produce a sum sufficient to cover the outstanding debt. It would be likely that the market value of the debt would be substantially less than the current book value of the outstanding debt.

The Bank's second course of action would be to seek a renegotiation of the settlement terms. However, given that the Bank of Penderyn may not be the only bank involved in the debt default and the offer has emerged after considerable discussion it seems unlikely that this would produce any improvement.

The Bank's final course of action, and perhaps the only feasible course of action, would be to accept the offer and seek to minimise overall losses.

Compared to the outstanding value of the loans this represents a potential loss of £0.2 billion at current exchange rates. However this loss may be exacerbated by the existence of Zorbian exchange control restrictions which may prevent the disposal of the shares and repatriation of the funds to the UK and the lack of any double taxation agreement between Zorbia and the UK, which may mean that any allowable repatriation of funds could be subject to excessively high withholding taxes. This could substantially increase the potential loss.

In addition, the excessive market disposal of shares in previously publicly owned Zorbian Utilities may result in a considerable downturn in the market value per share resulting in an even greater potential loss accruing.

There are a number of ways in which the Bank could seek to minimise this potential loss. First, the Bank of Penderyn may seek to undertake an equity swap to avoid exchange limits and restrictions imposed on programme trading in equities. Second, the Bank of Penderyn may consider the use of equity options to protect against a potential downturn in share prices. Third, the Bank may simply seek to hold on to the shares in the anticipation that the share prices may rise.

E11.7 Benjamin plc

Calculate the company's weighted average cost of capital, based on:

■ cost of ordinary share capital
■ cost of preference share capital
■ cost of debentures.

Using the dividend model (without growth) calculate the cost of ordinary share capital and cost of preference shares as follows:

Cost of ordinary shares $=$ £0.10/£3.00 $=$ 0.0333 or 3.33%
Cost of preference share capital $=$ £0.05/£1.00 $=$ 0.05 or 5.00%

Because the debentures are redeemable, to calculate the cost of debentures we need to calculate the internal rate of return (IRR):

The debentures are 7% and the *cum interest* price is £104
Therefore the *ex interest* price is $=$ £104 $-$ £7 $=$ £97

Calculate net present value (NPV) using a 7% and 5% discount rate:

Year	Cost	Interest	Tax	Net
	£	£	£	£
0	(97.00)			(97.00)
1		7.00	(2.45)	4.55
2		7.00	(2.45)	4.55
3	100.00	7.00	(2.45)	104.55

Discounting at 7%:

Year	Cash flow	Discount	Present value
	£	factor	£
0	(97.00)	1.00	(97.00)
1	4.55	0.93	4.23
2	4.55	0.87	3.96
3	104.55	0.82	85.7
			NPV (3.11)

Discounting at 5%:

Year	Cash flow	Discount	Present value
	£	factor	£
0	(97.00)	1.00	(97.00)
1	4.55	0.95	4.32
2	4.55	0.91	4.14
3	104.55	0.86	89.91
			NPV 1.37

Using the interpolation method discussed in Chapter 6 the IRR may be calculated as:

$$\frac{3.11}{x} = \frac{1.37}{(2-x)}$$
$$3.11(2-x) = 1.37x$$
$$6.24 - 3.11x = 1.37x$$
$$6.24 = 1.37x + 3.11x$$
$$6.24 = 4.48x$$
$$x = \frac{6.24}{4.48}$$
$$x = 1.39$$
$$\text{Cost of debentures} = 7 - 1.39 = 5.61\%$$

Alternatively the IRR may be calculated as follows:

$$5\% + \frac{£1.37 \times (7\% - 5\%)}{(£1.37 + £3.11)} = 5.61\%$$

Using each of the above costs of capital we can calculate the weighted average cost of capital:

	Market Value £	Cost of capital	Weighting £
Ordinary shares	2,000,000	0.0333	66,600
Preference shares	1,000,000	0.0500	50,000
Debentures (£97 × 800,000)	776,000	0.0561	43,534
	3,776,000		160,134

$$\text{Weighted average cost of capital} = \frac{£160,134}{£3,776,000} = 0.0424 = 4.24\%$$

Convert all cash flows into £ sterling:

Year	Cash flows	Exchange rate	Cash flows £m
0	£(20.0m)	1.00	(20.00)
1	€11.0m	1.70	6.47
2	€13.5m	1.75	7.71
3	€10.0m	1.80	5.56
4	€3.5m	1.85	1.89

Make adjustments for management fees and corporation tax:

Year	Cash flows £m	Management fee £m	Corporation tax 35% cash flows less management fee £m	Net cash flows £m
0	(20.00)	0.00	0.00	(20.00)
1	6.47	0.10	0.00	6.37
2	7.71	0.10	2.23	5.38
3	5.56	0.10	2.66	2.80
4	1.89	0.10	1.91	(0.12)
5	0.00	0.00	0.63	(0.63)

Evaluate the £ sterling net cash flows of the project using the company's weighted average cost of capital, a discount rate of 4.24%:

Year	Cash flows £m	Discount factor at 4.24%	Present value £m
0	(20.00)	1.000	(20.00)
1	6.37	0.959	6.11
2	5.38	0.920	4.95
3	2.80	0.883	2.47
4	(0.12)	0.847	(0.10)
5	(0.63)	0.813	(0.51)
			NPV (7.08)

Using the company's weighted average cost of capital the project gives a negative NPV of £7.08m and so will reduce shareholder value. Therefore on a financial evaluation basis Benjamin plc should reject the project.

E11.9 Lee Ltd

(i) All the project profits are remitted to the UK

		Singapore $000
Profit		2,000,000
Singapore corporation tax		(360,000)
(18% × 2,000,000)		
Dividend before tax		1,640,000
Withholding tax (10%)		(164,000)
Net dividend received		1,476,000
UK corporation tax	600,000	
(30% × 2,000,000)		
Foreign tax credit	(524,000)	
		(76,000)
Net annual cash flow after tax		1,400,000

(ii) All the project profits are reinvested in Singapore

	Singapore $000
Profit	2,000,000
Singapore corporation tax (18% × 2,000,000)	(360,000)
Net annual cash flow after tax	1,640,000

(iii) The investment is managed by a wholly owned German subsidiary with the dividends remitted to Germany for further investment outside the UK

	Singapore $000
Profit	2,000,000
Singapore corporation tax (18% × 2,000,000)	(360,000)
Dividend before tax	1,640,000
Withholding tax (10%)	(164,000)
Net annual cash flow after tax	1,476,000

In summary:

If all the project profits are reinvested in Singapore the net annual cash flow would be $1,640,000,000.

If the cash flows remain in Singapore, then the withholding tax of 10% is not imposed.

If all the project profits are remitted to the UK the net annual cash flow would be $1,400,000,000. However, if the investment in Singapore is held via a German holding company with the dividends remitted to Germany for further investment outside the UK, the net annual cash flow would be $1,476,000,000.

This difference of $76,000,000 is due to the differential tax rates between Singapore and the UK – that is, the effective overall tax in the UK is greater than the effective overall tax in

Singapore. The tax credit in the UK for overseas tax is limited to the tax imposed in the UK. However, if there is greater convergence between the tax rates between Singapore and the UK, the differential benefit becomes less.

Assume, for example, if the Singapore withholding tax was not 10%, but 14%.

If all the project profits were remitted to the UK, the net annual cash flow would be:

		Singapore $000
Profit		2,000,000
Singapore corporation tax		(360,000)
(18% × 2,000,000)		
Dividend before tax		1,640,000
Withholding tax (14%)		(229,600)
Net dividend received		1,410,400
UK corporation tax (30% × 2,000,000)	600,000	
Foreign tax credit	(589,600)	
		(10,400)
Net annual cash flow after tax		1,400,000

If the investment was managed by a wholly owned German subsidiary with the dividends remitted to Germany for further investment outside the UK, the net annual cash flows would be:

	Singapore $000
Profit	2,000,000
Singapore corporation tax (18% × 2,000,000)	(360,000)
Dividend before tax	1,640,000
Withholding tax (14%)	(229,600)
Net annual cash flow after tax	1,410,400

E11.10 Drex plc

The overall expected after tax return of the UK company on existing projects is (£800m × 10%) plus either of the new projects (£200m × 12%).

With the Norwegian project the return would be:

$$(0.80 \times 0.10) + (0.20 \times 0.12) = 10.4\%$$

With the Malaysian project the return would be:

$$(0.80 \times 0.10) + (0.20 \times 0.12) = 10.4\%$$

Both are the same. However, the risk (standard deviation) on each project and the expected correlation between the new project returns and the existing business are not the same.

We can calculate the variance of a two-investment (x and y) portfolio p as follows:

$$\sigma_p^2 = (\alpha_x^2 \times \sigma_x^2) + (\alpha_y^2 \times \sigma_y^2) + (2 \times \alpha_x \times \alpha_y \times r \times \sigma_x \times \sigma_y)$$

where

σ^2 = variance

α = proportion of investment in portfolio

r = correlation coefficient of returns of the two investments and the risk (standard deviation) is $\sqrt{\sigma_p}$

For the Norwegian project portfolio variance would be:

$(0.80)^2 \times (0.03)^2 + (0.20)^2 \times (0.04)^2 + 2(0.80) \times (0.20) \times (0.80) \times (0.03) \times (0.04) = 0.0009472$

For the Norwegian project the standard deviation is $\sqrt{0.0009472} = 0.3078$ or 3.1%

For the Malaysian project the portfolio variance would be:

$(0.80)^2 \times (0.03)^2 + (0.20)^2 \times (0.05)^2 + 2(0.80) \times (0.20) \times (0.30) \times (0.03) \times (0.05) = 0.00082$

For the Malaysian project the standard deviation is $\sqrt{0.00082} = 0.02863$ or 2.9%

The Malaysian project should be chosen because it has the lower risk. By doing this, the company's overall variability of income would be reduced by approximately 13.4%.

That is:

$$1 - (0.00082/0.0009472) = 1 - 0.866 = 13.4\%$$

E12.3 Ray & Co

(i)   The foreign exchange operations may have occurred as follows:

On 30 September 2012, Ray & Co would have arranged four foreign exchange transactions:

1   to obtain sufficient Cam\$ to purchase 1,000 tonnes in October 2012, at the spot rate
2   to obtain sufficient Cam\$ to purchase 1,000 tonnes in November 2012, at the one-month forward rate, that is, at the beginning of November 2012
3   to sell PF to be received from the customer (for the first 1,000 tonnes) in November 2012, at the end of November 2012 (two months forward)
4   to sell PF to be received by the end of December 2012 on the final 1,000 tonnes at the end of December 2012 rate (three months forward).

The bank selling rate (customer buying rate) is the left-hand column of figures quoted, and the bank buying rate (customer selling rate) for foreign currency is the right-hand column of figures.

Purchases of melinium

		Cam\$	£
(1) October 2012:	7,000 Cam\$ × 1,000 tonnes @ 200 Cam\$/£	7,000,000	35,000
(2) November 2012:	7,000 Cam\$ × 1,000 tonnes @ 201 Cam\$/£ (200 + 1 discount)	7,000,000	34,826
Total purchases			69,826

Sales of melinium

		PF	£
(3) October 2012:	300PF × 1,000 tonnes @ 7.44 PF/£ (7.5 − 0.06 premium)	300,000	40,323
(4) November 2012:	300 Cam\$ × 1,000 tonnes @ 7.39 PF/£ (7.5 − 0.11 premuim)	300,000	40,595
Total sales			80,918

The commission of 0.05% (maximum £20) is as follows:

(1) $0.05 \times £35,000/100 =$ £17.50
(2) $0.05 \times £34,826/100 =$ £17.41
(3) $0.05 \times £40,323/100 = £20.16$, therefore £20.00
(4) $0.05 \times £40,595/100 = £20.30$, therefore <u>£20.00</u>

Total commission   <u>£74.91</u> or £75

	£
Sales revenue	80,918
Less cost of sales	(69,826)
Gross profit	11,092
Less commission	(75)
Profit	11,017

(ii)   If the November 2012 shipment had been cancelled after Ray & Co had entered into the forward exchange contracts, the contracts would still have to be honoured. They would still have to buy Cam$7,000,000 at a rate of 201, and would have to sell PF300,000 at a rate of 7.39. Without the November 2012 shipment, Ray & Co would be obliged to 'close out' the contracts. They would have to:

- sell the Cam$ they must buy, at the spot rate available at the time
- buy PF at the available spot rate (or at a suitable forward rate) on the foreign exchange market, for resale.

In both of the above transactions there would probably have been a loss because the resale of the foreign currencies would probably earn less in £ sterling than it would cost Ray & Co to buy them (depending on how exchange rates have moved since the original forward exchange contracts were entered into) and incur commission costs.

If the November 2012 shipment had been delayed for two months until January 2013, the contracts entered into at the end of September 2012 would still have to be honoured.

The Cam$7,000,000 would have been obtained too early and it is unlikely that Ray & Co would have had enough funds in the business to hold them for two months. Ray & Co may have sold the Cam$ they needed to buy in November 2012, and would have made a loss on this transaction, and then entered into another forward exchange contract to obtain Cam$7,000,000 in November 2012.

The merchant would have had to sell PF300,000 in December 2012, in which case he would have had to buy this amount at the spot rate in order to re-sell it. There would have been a loss on this transaction, just as if the November 2012 shipment had been cancelled.

The merchant would then probably have decided to enter into another forward exchange contract to sell PF300,000 two months later than originally expected, that is, in February 2013.

The effect of a delay in shipment would then have been similar to the effect of a cancellation, with the exception that Ray & Co would have arranged two further foreign exchange contracts, one to buy more Cam$ and the other to sell forward more PF. Ray & Co would really have been trying to extend each of their forward exchange contracts by a further two months. Ray & Co's bank may have offered them slightly better exchange rates to extend the contracts than they would have had to use to close out the contracts and make new contracts.

E12.4 Blud Ltd

(i)

The finance director of Blud Ltd could take a chance on the future changes in the €/£ sterling exchange rate, and do nothing for three months. When the €40,000 are received, they can then be exchanged at the spot rate, whatever that happens to be.

However, this is not recommended. The company should have a policy of hedging against foreign exchange risk, in view of its regular export sales. There are two principal methods to consider:

- a forward exchange contract
- the currency market.

Forward exchange contract

The forward exchange rate for Blud Ltd to sell €40,000 in three months' time is as follows.

Spot rate	1.1652
Less premium	(0.0100)
Forward rate	1.1552

The sterling value of the receipts will be:

$$\frac{€40,000}{1.1552} = £34,626$$

The currency market

The euros will be received in three months, so Blud Ltd should borrow euros now. At a borrowing rate of 6.1% per annum or 1.525% per three months, the amount to be borrowed to become €40,000 payable in three months' time is:

$$\frac{€40,000}{1.01525} = €39,399$$

The borrowed euros will be converted into £ sterling at the spot rate of 1.1652 to yield:

$$\frac{€39,399}{1.1652} = £33,813$$

Assuming that these funds could be invested to earn the deposit rate for £ sterling (2.5% per annum or 0.625% for three months) this would have a value in three months' time of:

$$£33,813 \times 1.00625 = £34,024$$

A forward exchange contract appears to be the more profitable, and is therefore recommended.

(ii)

The payment of €20,000 could be partially matched with the receipt of €40,000, so that the foreign exchange risk exposure is eliminated by using euro receipts to make euro payments. A forward exchange contract should be taken out for the remaining €20,000, and the net receipts will be:

$$\frac{€20,000}{1.1552} = £17,313$$

E12.5 Cookies plc

Foreign exchange forward contract

Forward contract fixed at 1 August 2012

$$\frac{US\$730{,}000}{1.6109} = £453{,}163$$

Total cost of the payment of US$730,000 = £453,163

Money market

Assuming it has sufficient £ sterling Cookies plc could buy US$ and lend it in the money market

Three-months US$ lending rate = 1.85%/4 = 0.4625%

The amount today required to become US$730,000 in three months' time:

$$\frac{US\$730{,}000}{1.004625} = US\$726{,}639$$

Cost of buying US$726,639 at the current spot rate is:

$$\frac{US\$726{,}639}{1.6188} = £448{,}875$$

The three-month £ sterling lending rate = 1.5%/4 = 0.375%
Three months' interest lost on £448,875 = £448,875 × 0.00375 = £1,683
Total cost of the payment of US$730,000 = £448,875 + £1,683 = £450,558

Currency option

Put options may be used and each contract would deliver 1.7 × £25,000 = US$42,500

The number of contracts required is:

$$\frac{US\$730{,}000}{US\$42{,}500} = 17.18, \text{ or } 17 \text{ contracts}$$

Cost of the put option contracts:

$$0.075 \times US\$42{,}500 \times 17 = US\$54{,}188$$

£ sterling cost of the options:

$$\frac{US\$54{,}188}{1.6188} = £33{,}474$$

£ sterling required to deliver 17 × US$42,500 or US$722,500 = 17 × £25,000 = £425,000

$$\text{Shortfall} = US\$730{,}000 - US\$722{,}500 = US\$7{,}500$$

Cost of shortfall in £ sterling using the US$/£ three-month forward rate

$$\frac{US\$7{,}500}{1.6109} = £4{,}656$$

Total cost of using options = £33,474 + £425,000 + £4,656 = £463,130

The money market is the cheapest method in this example for Cookies plc to use to hedge its US$730,000 transaction exposure, at a cost of £450,558.

E12.6 Gleeson plc

(i)

One tick has a value of 0.0001 × £500,000 × 3/12 = £12.50

$$1\% = 100 \text{ ticks}$$

(a) Gleeson would sell £10m of interest rate futures contracts − 20 at 93.25, or 6.75% − to hedge against an interest rate rise on the three-month loan required on 1 August. If the futures rate increased by 1% then at 1 August Gleeson would close out its contracts by buying contracts at 92.25, or 7.75%

giving a profit of £10m × 1% × 3/12 = £25,000

or 20 × 100 ticks @ £12.50 = £25,000

If the interest rate increased by 1% then Gleeson would offset the futures contracts profit of £25,000 against the increased cost of borrowing £10m at 8% at 1 August

cost of borrowing £10m × 8% × 3/12 = £200,000

cost of borrowing £10m × 7% × 3/12 = £175,000

increased interest cost = £25,000

The hedge efficiency is

$$\frac{£25,000}{£25,000} = 100\%$$

which is a perfect hedge.

(b) Gleeson would sell £10m of interest rate futures contracts − 20 at 93.25, or 6.75% − to hedge against an interest rate fall on the three-month loan required on 1 August. If the futures rate fell by 1.5% then at 1 August Gleeson would close out its contracts by buying contracts at 94.75, or 5.25%

giving a loss of £10m × 1.5% × 3/12 = £37,500

or 20 × 150 ticks @ £12.50 = £37,500

Gleeson would offset the futures contracts loss of £37,500 against the lower cost of borrowing £10m at 5% at 1 August

cost of borrowing £10m × 5% × 3/12 = £125,000

cost of borrowing £10m × 7% × 3/12 = £175,000

reduced interest cost = £50,000

The hedge efficiency is $\dfrac{£50,000}{£37,500} = 133\%$.

(ii)

Futures hedging costs

(a) Interest £10m × 8% × 3/12	= £200,000
less gain from futures contracts £25,000	= £175,000
(b) Interest £10m × 5% × 3/12	= £125,000
plus loss from futures contracts £37,500	= £162,500

The premium for the guarantee is £10m × 0.3% = £30,000.
If the interest rate increases then the cost of servicing the loan is:

$$£10m × 7% × 3/12 = £175,000$$
$$\text{plus premium } £30,000 = £205,000$$

This costs more than the futures contracts hedge in (a) above and so would not be beneficial.
If the interest rate falls then the cost of servicing the loan is:

$$£10m × 5% × 3/12 = £125,000$$
$$\text{plus premium } £30,000 = £155,000$$

This costs less than the futures hedge in (b) above and so would be beneficial.

E12.7 Houses plc

Houses plc has an absolute comparative advantage over Thinice plc with regard to its fixed interest rate:

5.2% compared with 6%

Houses plc's fixed interest rate loan is 0.8% cheaper than Thinice plc may obtain.

Houses plc also has an absolute comparative advantage over Thinice plc with regard to its floating interest rate:

4.10% (1.10 + 3.00) compared with 4.60% (1.10 + 3.50)

Thinice plc floating interest rate loan is 0.5% more expensive than Houses plc may obtain.

However, Thinice plc has a relative comparative advantage with regard to its lower cost of floating interest compared with its cost of fixed interest.

Thinice plc's floating interest rate compared with its fixed interest rate is:

$$\frac{4.60\%}{6.0\%} = 76.7\%$$

Houses plc's floating interest rate compared with its fixed interest rate is:

$$\frac{4.10\%}{5.2\%} = 78.8\%$$

Therefore, since both companies have loans of the same value, they may both gain from a swap arrangement.

If the two companies arranged an interest rate swap, Thinice plc would effectively pay Houses plc's fixed rate of interest on its loan at 5.2%, while Houses plc would effectively pay Thinice plc's floating rate of interest on its loan at 4.60%.

Thinice plc is saving on the fixed rate, and is better off by 0.8% (6% − 5.2%).

Houses plc is worse off by 0.5% because of paying more on its floating rate (4.10% − 4.60%).
The net benefit is therefore 0.3% (0.8% − 0.5%).

If the gain of 0.3% is shared equally between the two companies, then both companies should be better off by 0.15%.

Therefore, Thinice plc should pay Houses plc 0.65%, and will then be better off by 0.15% (0.8% − 0.65%).

Houses plc will then be better off by 0.15% (−0.5% + 0.65%).

The result of the swap is that:

Houses plc will pay a floating interest rate of LIBOR + 2.85% (3.95%) compared with LIBOR + 3.0% (4.10%) instead of the fixed interest rate of 5.2%.

Thinice plc will pay a fixed interest rate of 5.85% compared with 6% instead of the floating rate of 4.60% (LIBOR + 3.50%).

E12.8 Privet plc

Forward rate agreements (FRAs) are agreements to fix the interest rate applying to a loan (borrowing or lending) for some period in advance. For example, a company can enter into an FRA with a bank that fixes the rate of interest for borrowing at a certain time in the future. If the actual interest rate proves to be higher than the rate agreed, the bank pays the company the difference. If the actual interest rate is lower than the rate agreed, the company pays the bank the difference. FRAs do not involve actual lending or borrowing of the principal sum. FRAs are usually for amounts of at least the currency equivalent of US$1,000,000.

In Privet's case, an FRA could be combined with taking out a loan for £5m, which would be separately arranged. This would enable Privet effectively to fix its borrowing costs in three months' time.

Interest rate futures are similar to FRAs, except that the terms, the amounts, and the periods involved are standardised. An interest rate future is a binding contract between a buyer and a seller to deliver or take delivery of (respectively) a specified interest rate commitment on an agreed specified date at an agreed price.

Futures contracts can be sold now in the expectation that, if interest rates increase, the contract value will fall: they can then be purchased at a lower price thus generating profits on the deal which can compensate for the increase in interest rate. If interest rates move in the opposite direction, there will be a loss on the contract, but this should be offset by the saving on the interest costs on the loan taken out as a result of the fall in rates. Interest rate futures can thus be used as a hedge against interest rate changes, and are available for a maximum period of one to two years.

The standard rates futures contracts are traded on futures exchanges. The London International Financial Futures provides a market for a limited number of interest rate contracts, including three-month sterling time deposits, three-month Eurodollar, 20-year gilts, and 20-year US Treasury bonds. The cost of the contract being provided is reflected in a margin or initial deposit.

Interest rate futures provide Privet with another method of hedging against interest rate risk. Because of the standardised nature of the contracts, however, it will probably not be possible to hedge the risk perfectly.

Interest rate guarantees (IRGs) are more expensive for a company to obtain than FRAs. They are agreements with a bank on the maximum borrowing rate that will apply at a certain time in the future. For example, a company might obtain an IRG from its bank that the interest rate will not exceed 14%. If it does, the bank must pay the company the difference. If market interest rates turn out to be lower, the company is not bound to accept 14%. Instead, it can abandon the guarantee and borrow at the lower existing market rate. IRGs are sometimes referred to as interest rate options or interest rate caps, and have a maximum maturity of one year. Longer-term interest rates options (such as caps, floors, and collars) are also available.

Similar hedging against interest rate risk is possible with IRGs as with FRAs. The main difference is that, unlike with an FRA, with IRGs the seller has to be paid a premium, whether or not the option involved in the guarantee is exercised. Against this relative disadvantage of IRGs, they do offer the advantage that the option holder, while being protected against adverse interest rate movements, can take full advantage of favourable interest rate movements. If interest rates fall, the guarantee need not be used; the company can borrow the money at the lower interest rates, having paid the premium for the IRG. FRA and interest rate futures do not offer the same possibility of gaining from favourable interest rate movements.

Privet could make use of IRGs to avoid exposure to the risk of interest rate rises while benefiting from falls in rates. However, to pay for these advantages, a premium must be paid for an IRG, which makes them relatively expensive.

Please refer to the relevant sections of Chapter 12 for a full discussion on hedging.

E14.7 Gregor

The ungeared betas for each company can be calculated using:

$$\beta_u = \beta_e \times \frac{E}{E + D(1 - t)}$$

Tench plc

$$\beta_u = 1.25 \times \frac{80\%}{80\% + 20\% \times (1 - 30\%)}$$

$$\beta_u = 1.25 \times \frac{80\%}{80\% + (20\% \times 70\%)}$$

$$\beta_u = 1.25 \times 0.85$$

$$\beta_u = 1.06$$

Rudd plc

$$\beta_u = 1.15 \times \frac{75\%}{75\% + 25\% \times (1 - 30\%)}$$

$$\beta_u = 1.15 \times 0.81$$

$$\beta_u = 0.93$$

Pike plc

$$\beta_u = 1.10 \times \frac{70\%}{70\% + 30\% \times (1 - 30\%)}$$

$$\beta_u = 1.10 \times 0.77$$

$$\beta_u = 0.85$$

Because computer repairs represents 40% of Pike plc's business and is considered 50% more risky than the electrical components business then its ungeared beta must be adjusted accordingly to calculate its electrical components ungeared beta as follows:

$$\beta_u = 0.5 \times \text{computer repairs } \beta_u + 0.5 \times \text{electrical components } \beta_u$$

and

$$\text{computer repairs } \beta_u = 1.5 \times \text{electrical components } \beta_u$$

therefore

$\beta_u = (0.5 \times 1.5 \times \text{electrical components } \beta_u) + (0.5 \times \text{electrical components } \beta_u)$
$0.85 = 1.25 \times \text{electrical components } \beta_u$

therefore

$$\text{Pike plc's electrical components } \beta_u = 0.68$$

The average of Pike plc's adjusted ungeared beta and the other two ungeared betas is

$$\frac{1.06 + 0.93 + 0.68}{3} = 0.89$$

0.89 may be used as the surrogate ungeared beta for Gregor in order to calculate its surrogate equity beta by using the variation of the ungeared beta equation:

$$\beta_e = \beta_u \times \frac{E + D(1 - t)}{E}$$

$$\beta_e = 0.89 \times \frac{80\% + 20\% \times (1 - 30\%)}{80\%}$$

$$\beta_u = 1.18 \times 0.89$$
$$\beta_e = 1.05$$

We can now calculate Gregor's estimated return (R_s) by using the basic CAPM formula:

$$R_s = R_f + \beta_e(R_m - R_f)$$
$$R_s = 4\% + 1.05 \times (10\% - 4\%)$$
$$R_s = 0.1030$$

Gregor's expected return is therefore 10.3%.

E15.4 Wane plc

Option 1

$$6.5p/0.07 = 92.86p$$

Therefore the value of the company would be £0.93 × 785,000 = £730,050
Option 2

$$5.5p/(0.10 - 0.06) = 137.5p$$

Therefore the value of the company would be £1.375 × 785,000 = £1,079,375
Option 3

	Dividend		**Discount factor**	**PV**
	pence		**at 10%**	**pence**
2012	5.00	×	0.909	4.55
2013	5.45	×	0.826	4.50
2014	5.94	×	0.751	4.46
2015	6.47	×	0.683	4.42

(*continued*)

2016	7.05	×	0.621	4.38
2016	148.05*	×	0.621	91.94
				114.25

*$7.05 \times 1.05/(0.10 - 0.05) = 148.05$p

Therefore the value of the company would be £1.14 × 785,000 = £894,900

Option 4

	Dividend pence		Discount factor at 12%	PV pence
2012	5.00	×	0.893	4.46
2013	5.50	×	0.797	4.38
2014	6.05	×	0.712	4.31
2015	6.66	×	0.636	4.24
2016	7.32	×	0.567	4.15
2016	95.16*	×	0.567	53.96
*$7.32 \times 1.04/(0.12 - 0.04) = 95.16$				75.50

Therefore the value of the company would be £0.755 × 785,000 = £592,675
Option 2 gives the maximum valuation of the company.

E15.5 Wooden plc

(i)
$$(1 + G)^4 = (9/7)$$
$$(1 + G)^4 = 1.286$$
$$(1 + G) = \sqrt[4]{1.286}$$
$$G = 1.065 - 1$$
$$G = 6.5\%$$

Using the dividend growth model

$$S = \frac{v(1 + G)}{(K_e - G)}$$

$$S = £0.09 \times 1.065/(0.12 - 0.065) = £1.74$$

Therefore the value of the company would be £1.74 × 1,650,000 = £2,871,000

(ii)

	Dividend pence		Discount factor at 12%	PV pence
Year 1	6	×	0.893	5.36
Year 2	6	×	0.797	4.78
Year 3	6	×	0.712	4.27
Year 4	10	×	0.636	6.36
Year 4	270*	×	0.636	171.72
				192.49

*$10.0 \times 1.08/(0.12 - 0.08) = 270.00$

Therefore the value of the company would be £1.92 × 1,650,000 = £3,168,000
It would therefore appear that the sacrifice of short-term dividends is worthwhile.

E15.6 Solva plc

	Current market value		**Current returns**
	£		**£**
Equity	5,000,000	2m shares $\times$ 15p	300,000
Debt	2,500,000	£2.5m debt $\times$ 12%	300,000
	7,500,000		600,000

Cost of equity using the dividend growth model and assuming zero dividend growth:

$$K_e = \frac{v}{S} = \frac{15p}{£2.50} = 6\%$$

Current market value £7,500,000
Rights issue at £2 per share to redeem debt of £2.5m

$$£2,500,000/£2 = 1,250,000 \text{ shares}$$

Total shares

$$\text{Original shares } £5,000,000/£2.50 = 2,000,000$$
$$\text{Rights issue } £2,500,000/£2.00 = 1,250,000$$
$$\text{Total shares} \quad 3,250,000$$

Estimated new cost of equity after debt redemption $= 6\% - 1\% = 5\%$
Share price using the dividend growth model and assuming zero dividend growth:

$$S = \frac{v}{K_c} = \frac{15p}{5\%} = £3$$

Total new market value 3,250,000 shares $\times$ £3	$= £9,750,000$
Original market value	$= £7,500,000$
Increase in market value	$= £2,250,000$

E15.8 Angle plc

	Current market value		**Current returns**
	£		**£**
Debt	4,000,000	£4m debt $\times$ 7%	280,000
Equity	9,000,000	3m shares $\times$ 30p	900,000
	13,000,000		1,180,000

Cost of equity using the dividend growth model and assuming zero dividend growth:

$$K_e = \frac{v}{S} = \frac{30p}{£3.00} = 10\%$$

$$WACC = \frac{£1,180,000}{£13,000,000} \times 100 = 9.076923\%$$

New development evaluation

$$NPV = \frac{£500,000}{0.09076923} - £4,000,000 = +£1,508,475$$

Therefore the new development is worthwhile.

	£	
Current dividend	900,000	
Current interest	280,000	
	1,180,000	
New development earnings	500,000	
	1,680,000	
New total interest	(560,000)	(£4m + £4m) debt × 7%
	1,120,000	

New cost of equity 10% + 2% = 12%

Therefore, new value of equity = £1,120,000/0.12	=	£9,333,333
Current value of equity	=	£9,000,000
Increase in value of equity	=	£333,333
New value of company at WACC = £1,680,000/0.09076923	=	£18,508,475
Current value of company = £8,000,000 + £9,333,333	=	£17,333,333
Increase in value		£1,175,142
NPV of project		£1,508,475
Increase in value of equity		£333,333

E15.9 Cresswell plc

(i)
Cresswell's current eps are £30m/100m = 30p and its P/E ratio is £2.0/30p = 6.67 times
  If Cresswell uses all its £20m cash it can buy 10m shares (£20m/£2).
  Because it will not now be receiving interest on its cash balances its profits after tax will fall to £28m (£30 − £2m).
  The number of shares remaining will be 90m (100m − 10m); therefore eps will increase to 31.1p (£28m/90m), and if its share price remained unchanged its P/E ratio would fall to £2.0/31.1p = 6.43 times.

(ii)

If shareholders believe that the P/E ratio of 6.67 times is still appropriate, then they may be willing to pay £2.07 (31.1p × 6.67) for the shares. Therefore, in theory the share price should increase after the share buy-back. In practice, the share price will depend on how the market perceives a company's disposal of its cash, and its stage in its business life cycle.

discussion of the law in this area. Note that the definition of 'employee' for statutory adoption pay (SAP) purposes is different. The implications of this are discussed later in this chapter under 'Statutory adoption pay – eligible persons'.

Share fishermen and women and the police are excluded from the right to SAL – Ss.199(2) and 200 ERA. However, seafarers employed on ships registered under S.8 of the Merchant Shipping Act 1995 are covered provided that the ship is registered as belonging to a port in Great Britain, that under his or her contract of employment the worker does not work wholly outside Great Britain, and that he or she is ordinarily resident in Great Britain – S.199(7) and (8). Crown employees and parliamentary staff are also covered – Ss.191, 194 and 195, but members of the armed forces are not – S.192 (read with para 16, Sch 2). (Note, however, that similar arrangements to the statutory scheme exist for armed service personnel.)

6.46 *Employee shareholders.* Section 31 of the Growth and Infrastructure Act 2013, which came into force on 1 September 2013, added a new S.205A to the ERA that introduced a new type of employment contract: an 'employee shareholder' contract. Under this type of contract, an individual agrees to waive certain employment rights, including the right to claim ordinary unfair dismissal, in return for at least £2,000 worth of free shares in the employer's company. These shares are subject to a number of favourable tax concessions. The right to take SAL is not one of the rights that an individual must waive in order to become an employee shareholder and such an employee is therefore entitled to take SAL in the normal way. However, an employee shareholder is required to give 16 weeks' notice of his or her intention to return to work during a period of adoption leave (as opposed to the eight weeks' notice that would usually be required) – S.205A(3)(b) (see the section 'Returning to work after adoption leave' below, under 'Notice of return during adoption leave – employee shareholders'). For more information about employee shareholder status, see IDS Employment Law Handbook, 'Atypical and Flexible Working' (2014), Chapter 7, 'Employee shareholders'.

6.47 **Foster parents.** Local authority foster parents who are approved prospective adopters are entitled to claim OAL where a child is placed with them with a view to adoption under S.22C of the Children Act 1989. These placements are commonly known as 'fostering for adoption' placements. Under S.22C of the Children Act 1989, a local authority in England is under a duty to consider a 'fostering for adoption' placement where it is considering adoption as an option for the child's long-term care (whether as the only option, or as one of several) but it does not yet have authorisation to place the child for adoption. The right to adoption leave applies to foster parents who are notified of having been matched with a child on or after 5 April 2015.

The necessary amendments to the PAL Regulations were made by the Paternity and Adoption Leave (Amendment) (No.2) Regulations 2014 SI 2014/3206. As

as is 'just and equitable having regard to the extent of each respondent's responsibility for the infringement' – S.57ZQ(10).

Unlawful detriment. Section 47C(1) ERA stipulates that an employee 'has the **6.36** right not to be subjected to any detriment by any act, or any deliberate failure to act, by his employer done for a prescribed reason'. Subsection (2) goes on to state that 'a prescribed reason' must be one that is prescribed by regulations and which relates, among other things, to the right to paid or unpaid time off to attend adoption appointments under S.57ZJ or S.57ZL. The prescribed reasons are set out in Reg 28 of the Paternity and Adoption Leave Regulations 2002 SI 2002/2788 ('the PAL Regulations') and provide that an employee has the right not to be subjected to any detriment by any act, or any deliberate failure to act, by the employer because:

- the employee took or sought to take paid or unpaid time off to attend an adoption appointment, or
- the employer believed that the employee was likely to take such time off.

An employee is therefore protected from suffering any detrimental treatment related to the fact that he or she took or requested time off in connection with an expected adoption placement. This is the case regardless of whether the employee is the primary or the secondary adopter; in other words, the legislation protects both those who request paid leave in order to attend an adoption meeting and those who request unpaid leave for the same reason.

Agency workers benefit from more explicit protection in relation to time off in **6.37** order to attend adoption appointments. S.47C(5)(c) and (d) ERA, which was inserted by the Children and Families Act 2014 on 1 October 2014, gives agency workers a right not to be subjected to a detriment by the temporary work agency or the hirer on certain grounds. The grounds are that the agency worker:

- took or sought to take time off for an adoption appointment under S.57ZN or S.57ZP ERA, or
- (in the case of the primary or sole adopter) received or sought to receive remuneration under S.57ZO for time off to attend an adoption appointment.

The enforcement of claims under S.47C(1) and (5) for a refusal to allow time off for adoption meetings is discussed in Chapter 12, 'Detriment and unfair dismissal', under 'Right not to suffer detriment – remedies'.

Automatically unfair dismissal. Section 99 ERA and Reg 29 PAL Regulations **6.38** provide that an employee is regarded as automatically unfairly dismissed if the reason or principal reason for the dismissal (or his or her selection for redundancy) is connected to the fact that the employee took or sought to take paid or unpaid time off under S.57ZJ or S.57ZL ERA, or the employer believed that the employee was likely to take such time off. There is no minimum service requirement for the right to claim automatically unfair dismissal under S.99.

Section 99 and Reg 29 apply to employees. As a result, agency workers are only covered if they are employees employed under a contract of employment, which is generally not the case. The employment status of agency workers is discussed in detail in IDS Employment Law Handbook, 'Atypical and Flexible Working' (2014), Chapter 1, 'Agency workers', under 'Employment status'.

6.39 **Asserting a statutory right.** If an employee is dismissed because he or she has tried to exercise the right to take time off for adoption appointments, the employee may also be able to claim that he or she has been dismissed for asserting a statutory right. Under S.104(1) ERA an employee's dismissal will be automatically unfair if the reason or principal reason for the dismissal was that:

- the employee brought proceedings against the employer to enforce a relevant statutory right, or

- the employee alleged that the employer had infringed a relevant statutory right.

It is immaterial whether the employee actually has the statutory right in question or whether it has been infringed, but the employee's claim to the right must be made in good faith – S.104(1) ERA. Furthermore, it is sufficient that the employee made it reasonably clear to the employer what the right claimed to have been infringed was; it is not necessary actually to specify the right – S.104(3).

6.40 Dismissals for asserting a statutory right are dealt with in detail in IDS Employment Law Handbook, 'Unfair Dismissal' (2010), Chapter 12, 'Dismissal for asserting a statutory right'.

6.41 **Discrimination.** The ERA provisions against unlawful detriment and dismissal protect employees (or agency workers, in the case of unlawful detriment) wanting to take time off work for pre-adoption meetings. Such claims could potentially be accompanied by a claim for unlawful discrimination under the Equality Act 2010 (EqA), which would allow the claimant to seek an award of compensation for injury to feelings (a head of damages not available in a straightforward claim under the ERA). The EqA outlaws discrimination on a number of grounds, including sex, pregnancy and maternity, marriage and civil partnership, and sexual orientation. Several different types of claim could arise in the context of the right to time off to attend adoption appointments. For example, it would amount to direct sex discrimination contrary to S.13 EqA to refuse to allow a man to exercise his statutory right to paid time off for adoption appointments where a woman would not be refused a similar request. A claim would also be likely to succeed where the employer has granted all requests for time off but has subsequently made it clear to a man (but not a woman) taking

time off for this reason that his adoption appointments are harming his career prospects. It would similarly amount to direct discrimination, albeit on the ground of sexual orientation, to refuse the right to time off for adoption appointments to a lesbian or gay employee intending to adopt a child but not to a heterosexual employee.

An indirect sex discrimination claim, based on the premise that more women than men are likely to take paid time off for adoption appointments (as they will have the main responsibility for the child), is also a possibility. Indirect discrimination occurs under S.19 EqA where an employer applies to a woman a provision, criterion or practice which it applies or would apply equally to a man but which puts, or would put, women at a particular disadvantage when compared with men, which puts her at that disadvantage, and which the employer cannot show to be a proportionate means of achieving a legitimate aim.

For further discussion of discrimination law in this area, see Chapter 13, **6.42** 'Discrimination and equal pay'. For a more in-depth analysis, see IDS Employment Law Handbook, 'Discrimination at Work' (2012).

Ordinary adoption leave **6.43**

Section 75A ERA provides that an employee who satisfies certain conditions is entitled to take ordinary adoption leave (OAL). (As we will see under 'Additional adoption leave' below, these conditions are also pertinent to additional adoption leave (AAL) because the main condition for entitlement to AAL is that the employee has taken OAL.)

Who has the right? **6.44**
SAL is available to employees – regardless of their length of service – who:

- are matched with a child for adoption (see 'Conditions of entitlement – adopter' below)

- foster a child with a view to adoption (see 'Foster parents' below), or

- are intended parents in a surrogacy arrangement who have, or have applied or intend to apply for, a parental order (see 'Intended parents in surrogacy arrangement' below).

Employees only. OAL can only be taken by employees and not other types of **6.** 'worker' or the self-employed. 'Employee' means an individual who has entered into or works under a contract of employment, which is defined as a contract of service or apprenticeship, whether express or implied, and (if express) whether oral or in writing – Reg 2(1) PAL Regulations. These definitions are identical to those that apply for the purposes of unfair dismissal and redundancy under the ERA and reference should be made to IDS Employment Law Handbook, 'Contracts of Employment' (2014), Chapter 2, 'Employment status', for a full explained under 'Conditions of entitlement' below, an employee qualifies for OAL under Reg 15(1) PAL Regulations if he or she is matched with a child for adoption. Reg 2(4)(c) provides that a person is 'matched with a child for adoption' when a decision has been made under S.22C of the Children Act 1989 that the child is to be placed with a local authority foster parent who is also an approved prospective adopter. A 'prospective adopter' is defined as someone who has been approved as suitable to adopt a child and has been notified of that decision – Reg 2(1).

Regulation 15(1A) prevents a local authority foster parent taking two periods **6.48** of OAL in respect of the same child – i.e. when the child is placed with him or her under the 'fostering for adoption' scheme and then again when the child is placed with him or her for adoption. Once the foster parent has taken OAL at the time of the child's 'fostering for adoption' placement, his or her entitlement to OAL under the PAL Regulations is extinguished.

Note that the spouse, civil partner or partner of the foster parent may be entitled to statutory paternity leave – see Chapter 7, 'Paternity leave and pay'. The shared parental leave scheme is also open to foster parents – see Chapter 8, 'Shared parental leave and pay', under 'Who has the right?'.

Intended parents in surrogacy arrangement. Where a child is born via a **6.49** surrogacy arrangement, the surrogate mother (i.e. the woman who is carrying or has carried the child) is regarded as the child's mother – S.33 Human Fertilisation and Embryology Act 2008. This means that surrogate mothers are entitled to take full statutory maternity leave and pay, regardless of whether or not they continue to have contact with the child following the birth. Various attempts to argue that it should be the intended mother in a surrogacy arrangement who should be entitled to maternity leave and pay have failed before the courts – see, for example, CD v ST 2014 ICR D26, ECJ. However, in November 2012 the Government announced that it would legislate to extend statutory adoption leave and pay to intended parents in a surrogacy arrangement ('Modern Workplaces – Government Response on Flexible Parental Leave', November 2012).

The Paternity, Adoption and Shared Parental Leave (Parental Order Cases) Regulations 2014 SI 2014/3096 ('the Leave (Parental Order Cases) Regulations'), which came into force on 1 December 2014 and apply where the expected week of birth began on or after 5 April 2015, extend the right to take adoption leave to intended parents in a surrogacy arrangement who have:

- gained a parental order under S.54(1) of the Human Fertilisation and Embryology Act 2008 in respect of a child, or

- applied or intend to apply for such an order within six months of the child's birth, which they expect the court to make.

235

6.50 Such parents are referred to as 'parental order parents' in the legislation. The intended parent who is entitled to take adoption leave is the one who has elected to be 'Parent A' in accordance with Reg 2(4) PAL Regulations (as modified by Reg 6(c) Leave (Parental Order Cases) Regulations). A person elects to be Parent A in relation to a child if he or she agrees this with the other parental order parent. The other parental order parent may be eligible for statutory paternity leave provided he or she is the spouse, civil partner or partner of Parent A when the child is born – see Chapter 7, 'Paternity leave and pay'. The shared parental leave scheme is also available to parental order parents – see Chapter 8, 'Shared parental leave and pay', under 'Who has the right?'.

The specific rules that apply to parental order parents are discussed under 'Intended parents in a surrogacy arrangement' below and in the appropriate places throughout this chapter.

6.51 ## Conditions of entitlement

Regulation 15(1) PAL Regulations provides that an employee is entitled to OAL in respect of a child (i.e. a person who is, or when placed with an adopter for adoption was, under the age of 18 – Reg 2(1)) if the employee:

- satisfies the conditions specified in Reg 15(2) (see 'Regulation 15(2) conditions' below), and

- has complied with the notice and (where applicable) evidential requirements in Reg 17 (see 'Notice and evidential requirements for OAL' below).

6.52 **Regulation 15(2) conditions.** The conditions specified in Reg 15(2) PAL Regulations are that the employee:

- is the 'child's adopter'; and

- has 'notified the [adoption] agency that he agrees that the child should be placed with him and agrees as to the date of placement'. An 'adoption agency' has the meaning given to it by S.2(1) of the Adoption and Children Act 2002 in relation to England and Wales and by S.119(1) of the Adoption and Children (Scotland) Act 2007 in Scotland – Reg 2(1).

For these purposes, 'placed for adoption' means:

- placed for adoption under the Adoption and Children Act 2002 or the Adoption of Children (Scotland) Act 2007, or

- placed in accordance with S.22C of the Children Act 1989 with a local authority foster parent who is also an approved adopter (see 'Who has the right? – foster parents' above) – Reg 2(1).

6.53 The placement begins on the date on which the child goes to live with the employee with a view to being formally adopted by court order. In Coventry City Council v O and ors 2011 EWCA Civ 729, CA, the Court of Appeal held that for the purposes of the Adoption and Children Act 2002, a child is 'placed' for adoption when he or she begins to live with the proposed adopters or, if the child is already living with them in their capacity as foster carers, when the adoption agency formally allows him or her to continue to live with them in their fresh capacity as prospective adopters.

Removal of qualifying service condition. The right to OAL was originally **6.54** only available to employees who had been 'continuously employed for at least 26 weeks' with the employer ending with the week in which he or she was 'notified of having been matched with the child' – Reg 15(2)(b) PAL Regulations. However, this provision was repealed on 5 April 2015 by the Paternity and Adoption Leave (Amendment) Regulations 2014 SI 2014/2112. Accordingly, employees who are matched with a child for adoption on or after 5 April 2015 are entitled to OAL irrespective of how long they have been working for their employer. (However, there is still a qualifying service requirement in order to qualify for SAP – see under 'Statutory adoption pay – conditions of entitlement' below.)

Adopter. An 'adopter' is defined as 'a person who has been matched with [a] **6.55** child for adoption' – Reg 2(1) PAL Regulations. An employee is 'matched with a child for adoption' when an adoption agency decides that that employee would be a suitable adoptive parent for the child, either individually or jointly with another person – Reg 2(4)(a). Where two people have been matched jointly, the 'adopter' is 'whichever of them has elected to be the child's adopter for the purposes of [the] Regulations' – Reg 2(1). An employee elects to be a child's adopter if he or she and the other person agree, at the time at which they are matched with the child, that the employee and not the other person will be the adopter – Reg 2(4A).

An adopter may therefore be an individual who adopts or one member of a couple where the couple adopt jointly. This means that where a couple adopt jointly only one member of that couple can claim OAL. However, the other member of the couple, or the partner of an individual who adopts, may be entitled to paternity leave and pay – see Chapter 7, 'Paternity leave and pay'. The fact that adoption leave is only available to those who have been matched with a child through an agency means that, for example, stepfathers and stepmothers who wish to adopt their stepchildren are not eligible for adoption leave.

Overseas adoptions. By virtue of Reg 4(2) of the Paternity and Adoption Leave **6.56** (Adoption from Overseas) Regulations 2003 SI 2003/921 the definition of 'adopter' is modified slightly to refer to 'a person by whom [a] child has been or is to be adopted' (as opposed to a person who has been matched with a child for adoption). For further discussion of overseas adoptions, see 'Overseas adoptions' below.

6.57 **Adopting more than one child.** An employee's entitlement to OAL is not affected by the placement for adoption of more than one child as part of the same arrangement – Reg 15(4). This means that an employee is only entitled to one period of OAL in respect of each placement, even if more than one child is adopted as part of the same arrangement.

6.58 **Overseas adoptions**

Taken by themselves, the PAL Regulations only cover adoptions where a child is matched and placed for adoption under UK law. However, by virtue of the Paternity and Adoption Leave (Adoption from Overseas) Regulations 2003 SI 2003/921, the PAL Regulations also apply, with the necessary modifications, to the adoption of children from overseas. Note, though, that OAL is not available in respect of overseas adoptions where the employee has taken shared parental leave in respect of the child – Reg 15(1A) PAL Regulations (as substituted by Reg 9 of the 2003 Regulations).

The requirement of 26 weeks' continuous employment was removed in respect of adoptions from overseas with effect from 5 April 2015 by Reg 25(d) of the Shared Parental Leave and Paternity and Adoption Leave (Adoptions from Overseas) Regulations 2014 SI 2014/3092.

Any significant differences between the rules governing domestic and overseas adoptions will be highlighted throughout this chapter where relevant.

6.59 **Intended parents in a surrogacy arrangement**

As mentioned above, a parental order parent – i.e. the intended parent of a child born via a surrogacy arrangement who has applied, or intends to apply, for a parental order in respect of the child, or whose application has already been granted – is entitled to take OAL in respect of a child whose expected week of birth began on or after 5 April 2015. This is made possible by the Leave (Parental Order Cases) Regulations, which provide that the PAL Regulations also apply, with the necessary modifications, where a child is adopted by a parental order parent.

6.60 **Modifications.** For the purposes of adoption by a parental order parent, Reg 6(a) Leave (Parental Order Cases) Regulations provides that Reg 2(1) PAL Regulations is modified to omit the definitions of 'adopter' and 'child'. Furthermore, the conditions for entitlement in Reg 15(2) PAL Regulations are modified to provide that an employee is entitled to OAL if he or she is:

- one of the child's parental order parents, and

- has elected to be Parent A – Reg 13(a) Leave (Parental Order Cases) Regulations.

A 'parental order parent' is a person who applies, or intends to apply, with another person for a parental order in respect of the child within six months of the child's birth and expects the court to make such an order, or whose application to the court has already been granted – Reg 6(a) Leave (Parental Order Cases) Regulations. The parental order application is made under S.54(1) of the Human Fertilisation and Embryology Act 2008 and, if granted, provides that the child is to be treated in law as the child of the two applicants. A person elects to be Parent A in relation to a child if he or she agrees this with the other parental order parent – Reg 6(c) Leave (Parental Order Cases) Regulations.

Regulation 15(4) PAL Regulations is also slightly modified to state that Parent **6.61** A will be entitled to adoption leave under Reg 15 regardless of whether more than one child is born, or expected to be born, as a result of the same pregnancy – Reg 13(b) Leave (Parental Order Cases) Regulations.

Notice and evidential requirements for OAL
6.62

Regulation 17 PAL Regulations sets out various notice and evidential requirements with which the employee must comply. Special rules apply to adoptions from overseas and in respect of parental order parents, which are mentioned in the appropriate sections below.

Notice. Under Reg 17(1) the employee must give the employer notice of his or **6.63** her intention to take OAL, specifying:

- the date on which the child is expected to be placed with him or her for adoption ('the expected placement date'). This will be the date the adoption agency has informed the employee that it expects to place the child with him or her. This is not the same as the date on which the child is actually placed, which may well be different. Furthermore, the expected date may change. It is not clear whether the employee is obliged to give notice of such change but to be on the safe side he or she should probably do so, and

- the date on which the employee has chosen his or her leave period to begin in accordance with Reg 16 – see 'Commencement and duration of OAL' below.

The notice must be in writing if the employer so requests and must be given to the employer no more than seven days after the date on which the employee is notified of having been matched with the child for adoption or, where that is not reasonably practicable, as soon as is reasonably practicable – Reg 17(2) and (6).

'Notified of having been matched'. An employee is notified of having been **6.64** matched with a child on the date on which he or she receives notification of the agency's decision – Reg 2(4)(b) PAL Regulations. Where the employee is a foster parent (see 'Who has the right? – foster parents' above), he or she is notified of having been matched with a child on the date on which he or she receives notification from the adoption agency of the decision to place the child with him or her for adoption – Reg 2(4)(d) PAL Regulations.

239

6.65 *Adoption from overseas.* In the case of adoption from overseas, the employee must give his or her employer notice of each of the following matters:

- the date on which the employee received an official notification and the date on which the child is expected to enter Great Britain (notice of which must be given no more than 28 days after the date he or she received the official notification or the date on which he or she completes 26 weeks' continuous employment with the employer, whichever is later. (Note that the reference to 26 weeks' continuous employment has not been removed despite the fact that the 26 weeks' qualifying period for claiming OAL no longer applies)

- the date on which the employee has chosen to begin his or her period of adoption leave (notice of which must be given to the employer at least 28 days prior to that date), and

- the date on which the child enters Great Britain (notice of which must be given no more than 28 days after that) – Reg 9 Paternity and Adoption Leave (Adoption from Overseas) Regulations 2003.

Note that the notice deadlines are more rigid in the case of overseas adoption (unless the employer agrees to relax or waive them), as there is no room for flexibility on the basis that it is not reasonably practicable for the employee to meet them.

6.66 *Parental order parents.* Where a parental order parent is adopting a child through a surrogacy arrangement, the employee must give the employer notice of the following matters:

- the expected week of the child's birth (notice of which must be given in or before the 15th week before the expected week of the child's birth)

- the date on which the child was born (notice of which must given as soon as reasonably practicable after the child's birth) – Reg 14 Leave (Parental Order Cases) Regulations.

6.67 **Evidence.** Where the employer requests it, the employee must also provide evidence of his or her entitlement to adoption leave. Reg 17(3) states that the evidence must be in the form of one or more documents issued by the adoption agency that matched the employee with the child and must contain the following:

- the name and address of the agency

- the date on which the employee was notified that he or she had been matched with the child, and

- the date on which the agency expects to place the child with the employee.

Note that the name and date of birth of the child is no longer required.

For the purpose of complying with the above requirements, a 'Matching Certificate: Statutory Adoption Leave and Pay' is available online. This form confirms that the named person has been matched with a child for adoption and must be completed by the adoption agency. It gives all the information required by Reg 17(3).

Adoption from overseas. In the case of adoption from overseas, the employee **6.68** must provide (again, where the employer requests it) a copy of the official notification together with evidence of the date of the entry of the child into Great Britain – Reg 9 Paternity and Adoption Leave (Adoption from Overseas) Regulations 2003.

Parental order parents. Where the employer requests it, a parental order **6.69** parent must also provide a parental statutory declaration, which is a statutory declaration stating that the employee has applied, or intends to apply, under S.54 of the Human Fertilisation and Embryology Act 2008 with another person for a parental order in respect of the child within the applicable time limit, and expects the order to be granted – Reg 14 Leave (Parental Order Cases) Regulations.

Varying the commencement date. An employee who has given notice under **6.70** Reg 17(1) PAL Regulations may vary the date he or she has chosen as the date on which OAL will begin provided that he or she gives the employer notice of the variation. The deadlines for giving the notice of variation are:

* where the employee wishes to begin the period of leave on the date on which the child is placed with him or her for adoption, 28 days before the date specified in the employee's earlier notice as the expected placement date

* where the employee wishes to begin the period of leave on a predetermined date, 28 days before the predetermined date

* or if it is not reasonably practicable to give 28 days' notice in either of the above situations, as soon as is reasonably practicable – Reg 17(4).

Again, the notice only needs to be given in writing if the employer so requests – Reg 17(6).

Adoption from overseas. In the case of adoption from overseas, an employee **6.71** wishing to vary the start date of his or her OAL to begin on the date on which the child enters Great Britain must give notice of this 28 days before the date specified in the employee's earlier notice as the expected placement date – Reg 9 Paternity and Adoption Leave (Adoption from Overseas) Regulations 2003.

Parental order parents. In the case of parental order parents, there is no option **6.72** to choose the date on which OAL begins and hence no power to vary the date on which OAL starts.

241

6.73 **Employer's response to notice.** An employer must, within 28 days of receipt of the employee's notice of intention to take OAL, notify the employee of the date on which the employee's full entitlement to leave ends, taking into account the additional adoption leave to which the employee will be entitled (see 'Additional adoption leave' below) – Reg 17(7) PAL Regulations. This will inform the employee of when he or she has to return to work. This notice does not have to be in writing (and the employee has no statutory right to insist that it is).

The notice must be given to the employee:

● within 28 days of the date on which the employer received the employee's notice – Reg 17(8)(a), or

● in the case of an employee's notice to vary the OAL start date, within 28 days of 'the date on which the employee's [OAL] period began' – Reg 17(8)(b).

6.74 *Less than 28 days' notice.* If the employer '[does] not notify the employee in accordance with Reg 17(7) and (8)' (which in essence means failing to give at least 28 days' notice), it will lose the right to postpone the employee's return if the employee gives less than the prescribed eight weeks' notice in the event of his or her wishing to return to work early – Reg 25(5) (see 'Returning to work after adoption leave – notice of return during adoption leave' below). Furthermore, if the employer '[gives] less than 28 days' notice of the date on which [adoption leave ends]' and it is not reasonably practicable for the employee to return on this date, any detriment suffered by the employee as a result of coming back too late will be unlawful under Reg 28 and any dismissal will be automatically unfair under Reg 29 – Regs 28(1)(c)(ii) and 29(3)(c)(ii). For these purposes, it is not necessary for the employer's notice of the end date to be given within the more restrictive 28-day time limit prescribed by Reg 17(8), provided it is given 28 days or more before the end of the adoption leave period.

6.75 *No notice.* If the employer '[does] not notify [the employee] in accordance with Reg 17(7) and (8) *or otherwise*' (our stress), any detriment as a result of coming back too late will be unlawful and any dismissal will be automatically unfair if the employee reasonably believed that adoption leave had not ended – Regs 28(1)(c)(i) and 29(3)(c)(i). The meaning of the words 'or otherwise' in this context is somewhat unclear and confusing. We would suggest that a reasonable interpretation would be that the consequences described in Regs 28(1)(c)(i) and 29(3)(c)(i) apply either where:

● no notice at all is given, or

● some purported notice is given that fails to comply with the strict requirements of the above regulations.

242

Commencement and duration of OAL

6.76

OAL begins on the date chosen by the employee and lasts for 26 weeks – Reg 18(1) and (2) PAL Regulations. An employee is entitled to choose to begin OAL on:

- the day on which the child is placed with him or her for adoption – Reg 16(1)(a) (or in the case of adoption from overseas, the date on which the child enters Great Britain – Reg 9 Paternity and Adoption Leave (Adoption from Overseas) Regulations 2003), or

- a predetermined date, specified in a notice under Reg 17 (see 'Notice and evidential requirements for OAL' above), which is no more than 14 days before the expected placement date and no later than that date – Reg 16(1)(b) (or in the case of adoption from overseas, which is no later than 28 days after the date on which the child enters Great Britain).

Where an employee has chosen to start the leave on the date on which the child is placed (or enters Great Britain) and the employee is at work that day, the leave period will start on the following day – Reg 18(3) PAL Regulations.

If the employee has varied the start date under Reg 17(4) (see 'Notice and evidential requirements for OAL' above), leave will commence on the new date (or the last date specified if there has been more than one variation) – Reg 18(2).

6.77

There are three situations in which OAL (or indeed, additional adoption leave) may end early. These are where:

- the placement has been 'disrupted', in which case the adoption leave will end eight weeks after the week during which the disrupting event took place – Reg 22 (see 'Disrupted placement during adoption leave' below)

- the employee is dismissed while he or she is absent on OAL (or additional adoption leave), in which case the dismissal brings the leave period to an end – Reg 24, and

- the employee gives the employer notice that he or she intends to end it early. Notice may be given under either Reg 25 (where the employee wants to return to work early) or the special leave curtailment procedure (where the employee wants to take shared parental leave) – see 'Returning to work after adoption leave – notice of return during adoption leave' below.

Parental order parents. In the case of parental order parents, the employee cannot choose the date on which his or her OAL will begin. OAL always begins on the day on which the child is born and lasts for 26 weeks. If the employee is at work on that date, the employee's leave begins on the day after that date. However, the employee's OAL (or AAL) may end early under Reg 22 (see 'Disrupted placement during adoption leave' below) or Reg 24 (the employee

6.78

is dismissed) – Reg 15 Leave (Parental Order Cases) Regulations. OAL may also end early where the employee curtails his or her OAL under the shared parental leave provisions.

6.79 Additional adoption leave

Section 75B ERA provides that an employee who satisfies certain prescribed conditions is entitled to take additional adoption leave (AAL). AAL is a period of 26 weeks beginning on the day after the last day of the employee's OAL period – Reg 20(2) PAL Regulations.

6.80 Entitlement to AAL

An employee will be entitled to AAL in respect of a child provided the following conditions are satisfied:

- the child was placed with the employee for adoption (or in the case of adoption from overseas, the child has entered Great Britain; or in the case of parental order parents, the employee is Parent A)

- the employee took OAL in respect of the child, and

- the OAL period did not end prematurely either by dismissal or by disrupted placement (see 'Ordinary adoption leave – commencement and duration of OAL' above) – Reg 20(1) PAL Regulations.

Like OAL, AAL may come to an end prematurely by virtue of dismissal or disrupted placement. It may also end early where the employee gives the employer notice that he or she wants to return to work early, or gives the employer a leave curtailment notice under Reg 9(1) of the Maternity and Adoption Leave (Curtailment of Statutory Rights to Leave) Regulations 2014 SI 2014/3052 in order to take shared parental leave – see Chapter 8, 'Shared parental leave and pay', under 'Curtailing maternity or adoption leave'.

6.81 OAL v AAL

Following amendments made by the Maternity and Parental Leave etc and the Paternity and Adoption Leave (Amendment) Regulations 2008 SI 2008/1966, many (but not all) of the differences in respect of the terms and conditions that continue to apply during periods of OAL and AAL have been eliminated – see 'Terms and conditions during adoption leave' below. Furthermore, there is a great deal of similarity between OAL and AAL in respect of terms and conditions that apply following the employee's return from adoption leave – see 'Terms and conditions following return' below. The main distinction between the two is in respect of the right to return to work – see 'Returning to work after adoption leave' below.

Terms and conditions during adoption leave 6.82

Sections 75A(3) and 75B(4) ERA and Reg 19(1) PAL Regulations provide that an employee who takes OAL or AAL is:

- entitled to the benefit of all the terms and conditions of employment that would have applied if he or she had not been absent, and

- bound by any obligations arising under those terms and conditions (except in so far as they are inconsistent with the employee's right to take OAL or AAL).

'Terms and conditions of employment' for these purposes includes 'matters connected with an employee's employment whether or not they arise under his or her contract of employment, but... does not include terms and conditions about remuneration' – Ss.75A(4) and 75B(5) ERA and Reg 19(2). 'Remuneration' is sums payable to an employee by way of wages or salary – Reg 19(3).

In other words, an employee's contract of employment continues during OAL 6.83 or AAL (unless either party brings it to an end) and he or she must be treated in all respects as if he or she was not absent, both in terms of the benefits to which he or she is entitled and the obligations he or she owes the employer. This is subject to two exceptions. The first is that the employee is not entitled to receive remuneration (unless, of course, he or she is contractually entitled to continue to be paid during OAL and/or AAL – see 'Contractual and composite adoption rights' below). However, most employees will be entitled to SAP (which is made 'in a like manner to payments of remuneration') – see 'Statutory adoption pay' below. The second exception is that the employee is not bound by any obligations that are inconsistent with the fact that he or she is taking SAL (e.g. the obligation actually to turn up and work).

The current position is in marked contrast to the one that prevailed prior to amendments in 2008. Previously, the terms and conditions that applied during AAL were far more limited than those that applied during OAL. However, following amendments by the Maternity and Parental Leave etc and the Paternity and Adoption Leave (Amendment) Regulations 2008 SI 2008/1966, the distinction between OAL and AAL was eliminated to ensure that the employee's terms and conditions are preserved throughout the whole 52-week period of SAL.

The terms and conditions that apply during adoption leave are very similar to 6.84 those that apply during maternity leave. Maternity leave is dealt with in detail in Chapter 3, 'Maternity leave', and reference should be made to that chapter for a detailed discussion of the meaning of 'remuneration' and a consideration of how a period of maternity leave impacts on matters such as annual leave, notice

245

rights and pension rights – see Chapter 3, 'Maternity leave', under 'Terms and conditions during maternity leave'. Below, we provide a brief analysis of these issues in the context of adoption leave.

6.85 Remuneration

As stated above, an employee is not entitled to receive remuneration during adoption leave (unless contractually entitled to do so). Unfortunately, deciding what amounts to remuneration is not always straightforward. Reg 19(3) PAL Regulations provides that 'only sums payable to an employee by way of wages or salary are to be treated as remuneration'. As noted in Chapter 3, 'Maternity leave', under 'Terms and conditions during maternity leave – remuneration', this definition seems to cover only the actual monetary payments that an employee receives from his or her employer for his or her work (i.e. the monetary elements of an employee's contract that are replaced by SAP or contractual adoption pay) and not other benefits which the employee receives through his or her employment. However, HMRC takes the view that benefits which have a transferable cash value (e.g. housing allowance, luncheon vouchers, etc) should also be treated as remuneration (in contrast to non-cash benefits in kind) – see its guidance note, 'Statutory maternity leave – salary sacrifice and non-cash benefits' (July 2014), which applies to both maternity and adoption leave. (Note that the guide is now only available on the Government's national archive site.)

In addition, benefits that are provided for business use only (such as a mobile phone or company car), while they do not amount to remuneration, may be withdrawn during SAL, even if they do not have a transferable cash value. This is because they are provided for the sole purpose of enabling the employee to carry out his or her duties – duties from which he or she is exempt while on SAL.

6.86 Non-cash benefits. In contrast, an employee should continue to receive any non-cash benefits during SAL that he or she would have received had he or she not been absent because these do not count as remuneration within the meaning of Reg 19(3). This is the case even if these benefits were provided as part of a salary sacrifice arrangement. Such non-cash benefits might include the following:

- gym membership
- participation in share schemes
- reimbursement of professional subscriptions, and
- the private use of a company car or mobile phone.

6.87 Pay rises. Although not entitled to receive remuneration during SAL, employees must not be denied the benefit of any pay rises awarded during their absence.

246

Profit-related pay, bonuses and commission. The purpose for which and the 6.88 terms under which profit-related pay, bonuses and commission are paid and the period over which they are calculated will determine whether they fall within the scope of 'wages or salary'. If, for instance, the payment relates to work the employee did before he or she commenced SAL, he or she should be entitled to it regardless of the fact that he or she is absent from work when it is actually paid. If, however, the payment relates to work that would have been done during the SAL period if the employee had not been absent, it amounts to 'wages or salary' for that period and need not be paid.

An employer can make a pro rata reduction to reflect the fact that the payment covers a period during part of which the employee was on leave – see Hoyland v Asda Stores Ltd 2005 ICR 1235, EAT (discussed in Chapter 3, 'Maternity leave', in the section 'Terms and conditions during maternity pay', under 'Remuneration – profit-related pay, bonuses and commission').

Note that, depending upon the rules of a bonus scheme, days spent 'keeping in touch' during adoption leave under Reg 21A PAL Regulations may need to be counted as days worked for the purposes of calculating any *pro rata* reduction in an annual bonus to reflect absence – see 'Keeping in touch during adoption leave – work during adoption leave' below. Where payment of a bonus is dependent solely on a condition that the employee is in active employment on the date on which it is awarded, an employee on adoption leave might be well advised to arrange a 'keeping-in-touch' day for the date in question to avoid losing out on the bonus altogether. This would be subject to the employer's agreement (see 'Keeping in touch during adoption leave – work during adoption leave' below) but the withholding of agreement in these circumstances could possibly amount to a detriment under Reg 28 (given the adverse consequences) – see 'Detriment and unfair dismissal rights' below.

Bonuses dependent on qualifying service. Where a payment is dependent upon 6.89 a period of qualifying service, both OAL and AAL must count towards that period of service. Note, however, the position in respect of pensions and other employment-related benefits during unpaid AAL – see 'Pensions and other service-related benefits' below.

Discretionary and ex gratia benefits. As noted under 'Terms and conditions 6.90 during adoption leave' above, Ss.75A(4) and 75B(5) ERA state that 'terms and conditions of employment' include 'matters connected with an employee's employment *whether or not* they arise under the contract of employment' (our stress). In other words, employees absent on adoption leave may be entitled to one-off non-contractual discretionary bonuses, so long as they do not amount to 'remuneration'.

6.91 **Sick pay**
Employees are not entitled to claim statutory sick pay during the adoption pay period and/or during adoption leave.

6.92 **Adoption pay period.** Employees may not claim statutory sick pay during the adoption pay period – S.171ZP(1) SSCBA. See 'Statutory adoption pay – period of payment of SAP' below for further details.

6.93 **Adoption leave.** Similarly, an employee cannot claim contractual (or statutory) sick pay during adoption leave (whether paid or unpaid), as this amounts to remuneration. The EAT reiterated this point in Department of Work and Pensions v Sutcliffe EAT 0319/07 (in the context of maternity leave) – for further details see Chapter 3, 'Maternity leave', under 'Terms and conditions during maternity leave – sick pay'.

6.94 Annual leave
Annual leave gives rise to special considerations in the context of SAL. Although annual leave continues to accrue during SAL, case law suggests that it cannot be taken concurrently with adoption leave.

6.95 **Accrual of leave.** Paid annual leave (both contractual and statutory) that would normally accrue while the employee was at work should continue to accrue during SAL (as should any other benefits which accrue over a period of time, such as seniority rights and pensionable service – for further details, see 'Pensions and other service-related benefits' below). Statutory annual leave entitlement is governed by Reg 13 of the Working Time Regulations 1998 SI 1998/1833 ('the Working Time Regulations') – see IDS Employment Law Handbook, 'Working Time' (2013), Chapter 4, 'Annual leave', in the section, 'Right to paid annual leave', under 'Basic annual leave' and 'Additional annual leave'.

6.96 *'Holiday credits' systems.* In Adcock and ors v H Flude and Co (Hinckley) Ltd EAT 521/97, a case concerning maternity leave, the EAT held that holiday credits paid under a system for calculating the holiday entitlement of pieceworkers constituted 'remuneration'. However, this case may no longer be good law and should be treated with considerable caution – see Chapter 3, 'Maternity leave', in the section 'Terms and conditions during maternity leave', under 'Annual leave – "holiday credits" systems'.

6.97 **Can an employee take paid holiday during adoption leave?** The current legal position appears to be that the two rights cannot be exercised at the same time. In other words, an employee has to bring his or her adoption leave to an end if he or she wants to take paid annual leave, or take his or her annual leave before he or she starts adoption leave. This position is based, at least in part, on the ECJ's decision in Merino Gómez v Continental Industrias del Caucho SA 2005 ICR 1040, ECJ (a maternity leave case) – for further details, see Chapter 3, 'Maternity leave', in the section 'Terms and conditions during maternity leave', under 'Annual leave – can an employee take paid holiday during maternity leave?'.

'Lost' holiday. Given that employees may not take annual leave concurrently **6.98** with adoption leave, the question arises as to when they may take their annual leave entitlement. The difficulty is that Reg 13(9)(a) of the Working Time Regulations states that the basic four-week statutory leave entitlement is to be taken in the same year to which it relates. SAL (like statutory maternity leave) may last for up to 52 weeks. Unless an employee's adoption leave starts and ends in the same leave year, and ends with enough time left to allow the leave to be taken, he or she will be unable to take his or her basic statutory annual leave entitlement after his or her adoption leave finishes (although a relevant agreement may allow him or her to carry over the 1.6 weeks of additional statutory leave, or enhanced contractual leave, into the following leave year – see Reg 13A(7)). The joined cases of Stringer and ors v Revenue and Customs Commissioners; Schultz-Hoff v Deutsche Rentenversicherung Bund 2009 ICR 932, ECJ, raise questions as to whether the UK's approach is compatible with the EU Working Time Directive (No.2003/88) (which the Working Time Regulations implement). A detailed discussion of this in the context of maternity leave – where identical considerations apply – can be found in Chapter 3, 'Maternity leave', in the section 'Terms and conditions during maternity leave', under 'Annual leave – "lost" holiday'.

In May 2011, the Government launched a 'Consultation on Modern Workplaces' proposing, among other things, that in the light of Merino Gómez v Continental Industrias del Caucho SA (above), the Working Time Regulations should be amended to allow carry-over of both *basic* and *additional* annual leave that is untaken due to absence on family-related leave, including adoption leave. Although the Modern Workplaces consultation closed on 8 August 2011, the Government's response to the annual leave proposals is still awaited.

Notice rights
6.99

If an employee gives or receives notice of termination during SAL, the question arises as to how much statutory and/or contractual notice pay is due.

Statutory notice pay. The amount payable during the statutory notice period **6.100** to an employee who gives notice or is given notice while on adoption leave depends on the length of contractual notice owed by the employer. Ss.87–89 ERA provide for full salary to be paid to employees where they are given notice, or give notice, in certain situations. One of these situations is where the notice is given to, or by, an employee during his or her adoption leave (Ss.87(1)–(3), 88(1)(c) and 89(3)(b)). These provisions only apply, however, where the notice to be given by the employer does not exceed the statutory minimum (set out in S.86(1)) by one week or more – S.87(4). If the notice to be given by the employer

249

does exceed the statutory minimum by one week or more, then an employee who is given notice (or who gives notice) during his or her adoption leave period will be entitled to no more during the notice period than the normal statutory or contractual adoption pay that would otherwise have applied. For further details and for an explanation of how the amount of pay due under Ss.88 and 89 is calculated, see Chapter 3, 'Maternity leave', in the section 'Terms and conditions during maternity leave', under 'Notice rights – statutory notice pay'.

6.101 **Contractual notice.** Given that an employee is entitled to the benefit of all his or her terms and conditions of employment during his or her adoption leave period other than those relating to remuneration, he or she must be entitled to his or her period of contractual notice in the same way as any other employee. However, since notice pay is in effect the wages or salary payable for the weeks of notice, it would fall within the definition of 'remuneration' (under Ss.75A(4) and 75B(5) ERA and Reg 19(2) of the PAL Regulations). As a result, an employee on SAL would not be entitled to full salary during a contractual notice period. He or she would, however, still be entitled to any statutory or contractual adoption pay during that period. Furthermore, depending on how much contractual notice he or she is owed by the employer, the employee may be entitled to full salary for as much of his or her contractual notice period as is equivalent to the statutory minimum – see 'Statutory notice pay' above.

6.102 ## Continuity of employment

Since an employee's contract of employment continues during SAL, the period of leave will count towards his or her period of continuous employment for the purposes of statutory employment rights (see S.212(1) ERA). SAL will also count for the purposes of any contractual rights dependent on a period of qualifying service (for example, pay increments and rights dependent on seniority – but see 'Pensions and other service-related benefits' below in respect of pensions and other employment-related benefit schemes during periods of unpaid AAL). Reg 27(1)(a) PAL Regulations makes it clear that an employee has the right to return from SAL 'with his [or her] seniority, pension rights and similar rights as they would have been if he or she had not been absent' – see 'Returning to work after adoption leave' below for further details.

Note that the ECJ has held that where a woman was appointed to a post as a civil servant while on maternity leave, the date of her appointment, not the date on which she actually took up her post at the end of that leave, should be used for the purpose of calculating her seniority under the EU Equal Treatment Directive (No.76/207) (now the recast EU Equal Treatment Directive (No.2006/54)) – Herrero v Instituto Madrileño de la Salud 2006 IRLR 296, ECJ. The same principle would apply where the employee's appointment occurs during a period of adoption leave.

Pensions and other service-related benefits

6.103

The employer's obligations in respect of pensions and other similar benefits during adoption leave depend on whether the employee is on a paid or unpaid period of adoption leave. 'Paid adoption leave' in this sense covers any period during which SAP is paid, and/or any period during which the employee is entitled to be paid under a contractual adoption scheme.

Pension rights, etc during paid adoption leave. Under para 5B of Schedule 5 **6.104** to the Social Security Act 1989 any employment-related benefit scheme, including any occupational pension scheme, is subject to the 'normal employment requirement', by virtue of which an employee's *paid* adoption leave must be treated as if it were a period during which he or she was working normally for his or her usual remuneration. This applies to both final salary schemes and money purchase schemes – in the case of the latter, this could be a personal pension plan or a stakeholder scheme – and regardless of whether or not the employee returns to work after adoption leave. (Similar, but not identical, provisions apply with respect to paid maternity leave, paid paternity leave, paid shared parental leave and paid parental leave – see Chapter 3, 'Maternity leave', under 'Terms and conditions during maternity leave – pensions'; Chapter 7, 'Paternity leave and pay', in the section 'Employment protection during and after paternity leave', under 'Terms and conditions during paternity leave – pension and other service-related benefits during paid leave'; Chapter 8, 'Shared parental leave and pay', in the section 'Employment protection during and after SPL', under 'Terms and conditions during SPL – pension and other service-related benefits during paid leave'; and Chapter 10, 'Unpaid parental leave', in the section, 'Key elements', under 'Terms and conditions during unpaid parental leave – pension benefits'.)

The general effect of para 5B is to ensure that employment-related benefit schemes do not contain any 'unfair adoption leave provision', which is defined as a provision that offends the 'normal employment requirement' by discriminating between an employee who is on paid adoption absence and an employee who is working normally.

Employer's contributions. The employer's contributions to a pension or other **6.105** employment-related benefit scheme during adoption leave must be based on the employee's notional pay (i.e. the pay he or she would have received had he or she been working normally) as opposed to the actual pay he or she receives during adoption leave.

In final salary schemes an employee is guaranteed a pension based on final salary and it is the actuary who decides from time to time what level of contributions are needed from employers to fund the liabilities of the pension scheme as a whole. In such schemes an employer's contributions are not specifically designated to any one employee. Accordingly (depending upon the actuary's advice), an employer may or may not have to pay greater contributions

251

to take account of men or women in the scheme taking family-related leave, such as adoption leave.

6.106 *Employee's contributions.* In a contributory scheme, whether money purchase or based on final salary, the employee only has to make contributions based on the amount of pay he or she actually receives during paid adoption leave (whether that is statutory or contractual adoption pay), not his or her normal salary – para 5B(3), Sch 5. This may lead to funding problems for money purchase schemes – see Chapter 3, 'Maternity leave', in the section 'Terms and conditions during maternity leave', under 'Pensions – pension rights during paid maternity leave', for a consideration of these problems (in the context of maternity leave).

6.107 **Pension rights, etc during unpaid adoption leave.** The rights to protected membership and accrual of benefits under para 5B of Schedule 5 to the Social Security Act 1989 apply only in respect of periods of paid adoption leave. The question thus arises as to whether employees are entitled to have pension rights or other employment-related benefit rights maintained during any periods of unpaid adoption leave. The Government takes the approach that the answer depends upon whether the employee is on unpaid OAL (because he or she does not qualify for statutory or contractual adoption pay) or on unpaid AAL (either because he or she does not qualify for statutory or contractual adoption pay or because the 39-week adoption pay period has expired).

6.108 *Unpaid OAL.* The Government's position is that during OAL the employer should continue to make contributions to any occupational pension scheme as if the employee were working normally and on the basis of his or her normal remuneration. This is confirmed in the HMRC guidance note, 'Statutory maternity leave – salary sacrifice and non-cash benefits' (July 2014), which states that 'the law... requires that employers continue pension contributions during [ordinary maternity leave], regardless of whether the employee is in receipt of maternity pay'. As is made clear in its introduction, the guide also applies to adoption leave so the same will be true where the employee is on OAL but not in receipt of adoption pay. (Note that the guide is now only available on the Government's national archive site.)

This view is, presumably, drawn from the fact that S.75A(3) ERA and Reg 19 PAL Regulations, taken with S.75A(4), require that all normal contractual terms and conditions – save for remuneration – be maintained during OAL. The Government's view, historically, has been that pension rights and other similar benefits do not fall within the exclusion of 'remuneration'. After all, pension contributions are not 'sums payable to an employee' within the meaning of Reg 19(3). The Government's approach (in the context of maternity leave at least) accords with the ECJ's decision in Boyle and ors v Equal Opportunities Commission 1999 ICR 360, ECJ. In that case, which concerned, among other things, the proper interpretation of the EU Pregnant Workers

Directive (No.92/85), the ECJ ruled that the accrual of pension rights under an occupational scheme is one of the rights connected with the employment contracts of workers within the meaning of Article 11(2)(a) of the Directive. See Chapter 3, 'Maternity leave', in the section 'Terms and conditions during maternity leave', under 'Pensions – pension rights during unpaid OML', for further discussion of the Government's position, the Boyle decision and their general implications.

Unpaid AAL. The Government takes a different approach to unpaid AAL, **6.109** however. In the Government's guidance notes, 'Employee rights when on leave', it states that 'pension contributions usually stop if a period of leave is unpaid, unless your contract says otherwise'. However, this is misleading as it suggests that an employer need not continue to make pension contributions during any period of unpaid OAL, which – as we saw above – is incorrect. It nevertheless confirms the Government's view that the employer is not required to make contributions to the employee's occupational pension scheme during unpaid periods of AAL (unless of course the contract provides otherwise). The employee's contributions will also stop during any such period of unpaid adoption leave, unless the occupational pension scheme rules allow him or her to make voluntary contributions.

In fact, the position would appear to be slightly more complicated than this in that what is required is a comparison with the equivalent maternity leave provisions. As discussed above, Reg 19(1)(a) PAL Regulations provides that an employee who takes OAL or AAL is entitled to the benefit of all the terms and conditions of employment that would have applied if he or she had not been absent (except for those relating to remuneration). This mirrors the wording of Reg 9(1)(a) of the Maternity and Parental Leave etc Regulations 1999 SI 1999/3312 ('the MPL Regulations'). However, the PAL Regulations contain no equivalent of Reg 9(4) MPL Regulations, which, in essence, stipulates that, with regard to the accrual of rights under an employment-related benefit scheme during additional maternity leave (AML), nothing in Reg 9(1)(a) MPL Regulations should be taken to impose a requirement which exceeds the requirements of para 5 of Schedule 5 to the Social Security Act 1989 (now replaced by S.75 of the Equality Act 2010 (EqA)). As stated in Chapter 3, 'Maternity leave', in the section 'Terms and conditions during maternity leave', under 'Pensions – pension rights during unpaid AML', the effect of this provision is that an employee on unpaid AML is not entitled to the benefit of the accrual of rights under an occupational pension scheme (unless the contract or scheme provides otherwise), since unpaid maternity leave is not covered by Schedule 5 (see now S.75(9) EqA).

However, since the PAL Regulations contain no equivalent of this provision, **6.110** and if, as appeared to be accepted by the Government, pension rights do not fall within the exclusion of 'remuneration', there appears, at first sight, no

253

logical reason to distinguish between OAL and AAL for these purposes. It therefore appears arguable that for placements occurring on or after 5 October 2008, pension accruals should continue throughout unpaid AAL, as well as unpaid OAL.

Nevertheless, this is inconsistent with the Government's stated approach (see above). In fact, it may well be that the omission of an equivalent to Reg 9(4) of the MPL Regulations (regarding terms and conditions during leave) is an oversight and, indeed, may be immaterial in view of the fact that the PAL Regulations contain a very similar provision to Reg 9(4). The provision in question – Reg 27(2) – concerns the right to return from leave (thus mirroring Reg 18A MPL Regulations). As discussed under 'Returning to work after adoption leave' below, the effect of Reg 27(2) appears to be that an employee is not entitled to return with his or her seniority, pensions and similar rights as if he or she had not been absent in so far as these constitute rights under an employment-related benefits scheme during unpaid AAL. If this is the effect of Reg 27(2), then arguably pension accruals do not need to be paid throughout unpaid AAL, despite there being no provision in Reg 19 to that effect.

6.111 (Note that any days on which the employee is paid for carrying out work during a period of unpaid AAL under the 'keeping-in-touch' scheme will come within the provisions of Schedule 5B and therefore employers must make contributions to any applicable employment-related benefit scheme in respect of such days – see 'Keeping in touch during adoption leave – working during adoption leave' below.)

6.112 **Continuity for 'pensionable service' purposes.** Again, a distinction must be made between paid and unpaid leave (and then between unpaid OAL and unpaid AAL).

6.113 *Paid adoption leave.* Paragraph 5B of Schedule 5 to the Social Security Act 1989 provides that an employee's paid adoption leave should be treated as if it were a period during which he or she was working normally for the purposes of pension, sickness and other employment-related benefit schemes. In addition, as pointed out above, Reg 27(1)(a) PAL Regulations makes specific provision for an employee's 'seniority, pension rights and similar rights' to be preserved during his or her OAL and AAL. Thus, in respect of the period of absence covered by statutory and/or contractual adoption pay, an employee is entitled to add the length of that period to the periods on either side of his or her adoption leave when computing his or her pensionable service.

6.114 *Unpaid adoption leave.* Regulation 27(2) PAL Regulations provides that in the case of accrual of rights under an employment-related benefit scheme, Reg 27(1)(a) in so far as it applies to AAL should not be taken to impose a requirement which exceeds the requirements of paras 5, 5B and 6 of Schedule 5 to the Social Security Act 1989. In other words, a period of unpaid OAL does count as pensionable service, but a period of unpaid AAL need not (unless, of course, the rules of the particular pension or employment-related benefit scheme expressly provide that the entire period of adoption absence will count in this regard).

However, as adoption leave does not break the employee's continuity of service (see 'Continuity of employment' above), the employee's pensionable service before and after any unpaid AAL must be treated as continuous – i.e. he or she must not be treated as having left and then rejoined the scheme.

Remedies   6.115

An employee who is denied the non-remuneration benefits of his or her contract during SAL may bring a claim for breach of contract in the county court. He or she may also be able to bring a breach of contract claim in an employment tribunal where the claim arises or is outstanding on the termination of the employee's employment. Furthermore, if the breach amounts to an unauthorised deduction from wages he or she will be able to bring a claim under the protection of wages provisions contained in Part II of the ERA. 'Wages' in this context could include bonuses, commissions and adoption pay but not benefits in kind such as medical insurance or use of a company car – S.27 ERA. Breach of contract claims are dealt with in IDS Employment Law Handbook, 'Contracts of Employment' (2014), Chapter 10, 'Breach of contract', while deduction from wages claims are dealt with in IDS Employment Law Handbook, 'Wages' (2011), Chapter 3, 'Protection of wages – 1', and Chapter 4, 'Protection of wages – 2'.

An employee on SAL denied the terms and conditions to which he or she is entitled will also be able to rely on Reg 28 PAL Regulations, which provides that an employee must not to be subjected to any detriment by any act, or deliberate failure to act, by his or her employer because the employee took or sought to take OAL or AAL. He or she may also be entitled to resign and claim unfair constructive dismissal under Reg 29. Regs 28 and 29 are discussed under 'Detriment and unfair dismissal rights' below.

Discrimination claims. Any unfavourable treatment of an employee on SAL   6.116 may give rise to a claim under the discrimination provisions of the EqA. For a woman on adoption leave who suffers less favourable treatment, the claim could be for direct or (perhaps more likely) indirect sex discrimination. She could also bring a claim for harassment. For a man, on the other hand, the claims would most likely only be for direct sex discrimination and/or harassment, rather than indirect sex discrimination, since it is difficult to imagine that he would be able to show a specific 'provision, criterion or practice' relating to adoption leave that puts men at a particular disadvantage when compared with women. Note also that as same-sex couples are eligible to adopt, claims for sexual orientation discrimination could also be relevant. In addition, the EqA makes it unlawful to discriminate, either directly or indirectly, against married persons and civil partners on the ground of their marital or civil partnership status. For further consideration of discrimination law in the context of family leave, see Chapter 13, 'Discrimination and equal pay'. A detailed discussion of discrimination law generally is contained in IDS Employment Law Handbook, 'Discrimination at Work' (2012).

6.117 Employee's obligations

Sections 75A(3)(b) and 75B(4)(b) ERA and Reg 19(1)(b) PAL Regulations provide that an employee taking SAL is bound by any obligations arising under his or her terms and conditions of employment, except in so far as they are inconsistent with his or her right to take SAL. In other words, the employee is not bound by, for example, his or her usual obligation to turn up and work, but is still bound by all the other terms and conditions of his or her contract, including any implied terms such as the implied term of mutual trust and confidence or the implied obligation of good faith. (A full discussion of these and other implied terms can be found in IDS Employment Law Handbook, 'Contracts of Employment' (2014), Chapter 3, 'Contractual terms', under 'Principal implied terms'.)

If an employee breaches any of the terms or conditions of his or her contract during SAL the employer may treat him or her in the same way as he would treat any other employee in these circumstances. The employer should, however, be careful not to treat the employee less favourably because of the fact that he or she is on SAL, since the employer could end up being liable for unlawful detriment or possibly some form of unlawful discrimination – see Chapter 12, 'Detriment and unfair dismissal', and Chapter 13, 'Discrimination and equal pay'. The employer should be particularly wary of penalising an employee for unauthorised absence in circumstances where it neglected or delayed informing the employee of the date on which he or she was due to return to work and the employee failed to do so in time – Reg 28(1)(c) (see 'Ordinary adoption leave – notice and evidential requirements for OAL' above and 'Detriment and unfair dismissal rights' below).

6.118 Keeping in touch during adoption leave

The Work and Pensions Act 2006 introduced statutory provisions to promote contact between employer and employee during periods of adoption leave as well as to enable the employee to carry out a limited amount of paid work during such leave without this having a detrimental impact on his or her SAP entitlement. These provisions – implemented by way of the Maternity and Parental Leave etc and the Paternity and Adoption Leave (Amendment) Regulations 2006 SI 2006/2014 – are discussed below.

'Reasonable contact' during adoption leave

6.119

As part of the Government's move to encourage better communication during family-related leave, it amended the PAL Regulations in 2006 to clarify that 'reasonable contact' from time to time during the SAL period, which either the employer or the employee is entitled to make, will not bring that period to an end – Reg 21A(4). An example given in Reg 21A(4) is contact 'to discuss an employee's return to work'. It will normally be the employer who initiates contact during the employee's adoption leave period, for example, in order to inform the employee of changes in the workplace. In its guidance notes, 'Adoption leave and pay', Acas recommends that the employer and employee should agree when and how the employer will keep in contact during the employee's absence from work. Excessive contact, or non-urgent contact in the early stages of the adoption, may not be reasonable.

The wording of Reg 21A(4) mirrors that of Reg 12A MPL Regulations (relating to work during maternity leave). The analysis in Chapter 3, 'Maternity leave', under '"Reasonable contact" during maternity leave' is therefore relevant.

Work during adoption leave

6.120

The PAL Regulations were also amended to introduce 'keeping-in-touch' (KIT) days, whereby an employee can work for his or her employer on up to ten days during SAL without bringing the leave to an end, and without extending the total duration of the SAL period – Reg 21A(1) and (6). Moreover, Reg 27A of the Statutory Paternity Pay and Statutory Adoption Pay (General) Regulations 2002 SI 2002/2822 provides that work an employee carries out under the KIT provisions will not involve him or her losing any SAP – see the section 'Statutory adoption pay' below, under 'Disentitlement to SAP – working for the employer during the adoption pay period'. Previously, if an employee did even as little as one day's work, he or she would be barred from receiving statutory adoption pay for that entire week. These provisions are mirrored in the maternity leave and pay schemes – see Chapter 3, 'Maternity leave', under 'Work during maternity leave', and Chapter 5, 'Statutory maternity pay', under 'Disentitlement to statutory maternity pay – working during the maternity pay period'.

As with the 'reasonable contact' provision in Reg 21A(4) (see '"Reasonable contact" during adoption leave' above), the purpose of the KIT scheme is to facilitate communication between employer and employee during the statutory leave period and to prepare the employee for his or her return to work.

Regulation 21A(3) PAL Regulations provides that 'work' means any work done under the contract of employment, and may include training or any activity undertaken for the purpose of the employee keeping in touch with the workplace. Such work for only part of a day will still constitute 'a day's work' for the purposes of the KIT provisions – Reg 21A(2). Note also that such work can be carried out at any time during the statutory leave period. Since the

6.121

257

Regulations do not specify whether KIT days should be taken as a single block or separately, this issue is left to be agreed between the parties.

The Regulations make it clear, however, that any such work must be by agreement between the parties. The employee has no right to work during SAL, and the employer has no right to require an employee to work during SAL – Reg 21A(5). In fact, pressuring an employee to work during SAL could expose the employer to liability for discrimination. In Chigboh-Anyadi v Wickramapathirana t/a Edmunds Solicitors ET Case No.3200926/05, a maternity leave case, C-A worked as an assistant solicitor for a small firm that was highly dependent on publicly funded legal work. While C-A was on maternity leave, her employer needed to prepare to face an audit conducted by the Legal Services Commission. He put pressure on C-A to continue to work during her maternity leave, on the basis that if she did not, the business would suffer and her job would be 'on the line'. She felt a sense of obligation to help and carried out paid work on 30 days during her leave. A tribunal found that she was denied 'the full benefit of maternity leave', and that her perception of having suffered a real loss was genuine and 'exacerbated by the discovery that her sacrifice had been in vain when, without due process, she was dismissed as redundant'. It upheld her claim of unlawful discrimination on the ground of her pregnancy in being pressured into working while on maternity leave. Although this case was brought under the special pregnancy and maternity discrimination provisions in S18 EqA, similar facts in an adoption leave scenario might well amount to either direct or indirect sex discrimination under S.13 or S.19 EqA.

6.122 The Government's commitment to employees on adoption leave being genuinely free to choose whether or not to make use of KIT days is further underlined by the fact that the PAL Regulations provide that an employee who undertook, considered undertaking, or refused to undertake KIT days is entitled to the protection against detriment offered by S.47C ERA – Reg 28(1)(bb). Furthermore, Reg 29(3)(b) provides that the dismissal of an employee because he or she undertook, considered undertaking, or refused to undertake KIT days will be automatically unfair under S.99 ERA. Regs 28 and 29 are discussed under 'Detriment and unfair dismissal rights' below and in Chapter 12, 'Detriment and unfair dismissal'.

Note that an employee who shares his or her leave with a partner under the shared parental leave (SPL) scheme is entitled to take up to 20 'shared parental leave in touch' days (SPLIT days) while absent on SPL without bringing his or her entitlement to SPL or shared parental pay to an end. SPLIT days can be taken in addition to KIT days, so the employee may be able to work for the employer for up to a total of 30 days if he or she takes both SAL and SPL. See further Chapter 8, 'Shared parental leave and pay', under 'Planning and booking periods of leave – staying in touch days'.

Payment for KIT days. There is no provision for KIT days to be paid, so **6.123** payment will be a matter for agreement between the employer and the employee. However, the employer must ensure that the employee receives at least the national minimum wage. SAP may be offset against any contractual pay agreed. Note, however, that payment for KIT days during a period of otherwise unpaid AAL may have consequences with regard to pension contributions. HMRC advises in its guidance note, 'Statutory maternity leave – salary sacrifice and non-cash benefits' (which applies to both maternity and adoption leave), that if an employee receives pay for any KIT days during a period that would otherwise be unpaid statutory leave, the employer must make pension contributions in respect of those remunerated KIT days – see further Chapter 3, 'Maternity leave', under 'Terms and conditions during maternity leave – pensions'. (Note that the guide is now only available on the Government's national archive site.)

'Without bringing... statutory adoption leave to an end'. The express **6.124** statement in Reg 21A that an employee may take up to ten KIT days 'without bringing his [or her] statutory adoption period to an end' could be taken to imply that the employee's adoption leave will end if he or she works for more than ten days. This is the assumption made in HMRC's guide, 'Statutory Adoption Pay: employee circumstances that affect payment', which states: 'If your employee does more than [ten days'] work for you in their SAP pay period you cannot pay SAP to them for any week in which they do such work and their adoption leave will come to an end.' However, nothing in the legislation expressly states this. Adoption leave may only be ended early by the employee:

- giving the employer eight weeks' notice of his or her return to work under the provisions of Reg 25 (see 'Returning to work after adoption leave – notice of return during adoption leave' below), or

- if he or she intends to take SPL, by following the procedure set out in Reg 9(1) of the Maternity and Adoption Leave (Curtailment of Statutory Rights to Leave) Regulations 2014 SI 2014/3052 to curtail the amount of adoption leave he or she intends to take, which again requires at least eight weeks' notice – Reg 10(2)(a) (see Chapter 8, 'Shared parental leave and pay', under 'Curtailing maternity or adoption leave').

That said, under Reg 25(2) PAL Regulations the employer may accept less or no notice of an employee's return to work at its discretion. This provision states that if an employee attempts to return without giving eight weeks' notice, or by giving shorter notice, the employer 'is entitled' to postpone his or her return – the implication being that it need not exercise that entitlement. This raises a danger that where an employee carries out work during the adoption leave period, this could be perceived as an attempt to return from adoption leave, and, where the employer does not exercise its Reg 25(2) entitlement to postpone that return, the adoption leave comes to an end. Thus, Reg 21A was drafted to

259

make it clear that taking up to ten KIT days will not inadvertently end the employee's adoption leave.

6.125 The position where an employee works in excess of the statutory ten KIT days remains ambiguous, however. Arguably, working for more than ten days during adoption leave will, in the circumstances described above, bring the adoption leave period to an end. But we suggest that this outcome may be prevented. The simplest route, if the adoption leave has eight weeks or less to run, would be for the employer formally to exercise its entitlement under Reg 25(2) to postpone the employee's return to the end of the adoption leave period, while in practice allowing him or her to work occasional days. Alternatively, the employee may provide a written statement that in working additional days he or she is not attempting to return from adoption leave early. The difficulty with the latter approach is that adoption leave, being a statutory right, is governed by legislation and not by the parties' agreement, except to the extent that the legislation provides for such agreement. Thus, a tribunal might interpret the adoption leave legislation to the effect that working during adoption leave, over and above KIT days, constitutes an attempt to return to work, regardless of the parties' intentions. In practice, however, we envisage that tribunals will rarely be called upon to decide the question as the parties are likely to simply assume that adoption leave continues in the absence of any clear authority to the contrary. Disagreement is most likely to arise where, for example, an employee considers that he or she has agreed to work extra 'KIT' days, but the employer is under the impression that it has negotiated an early return.

The position regarding payment of SAP must be considered separately – see the section 'Statutory adoption pay' below, under 'Disentitlement to SAP – working for the employer during the adoption pay period'.

6.126 Overseas adoptions. The Explanatory Notes to the 2006 Amendment Regulations specifically refer to adoption from overseas (where the child enters Great Britain on or after 1 April 2007). Oddly, however, the Amendment Regulations relating to adoption pay do not similarly refer to adoption from overseas. Therefore the extent of their application to adoption from overseas is unclear.

6.127 Disrupted placement during adoption leave

Regulation 22(1) PAL Regulations deals with various situations in which a child's placement is terminated during ordinary or additional adoption leave. It applies where:

- an employee has begun a period of adoption leave before the placement of the child and the adoption agency notifies the employee that the child will not be placed with him or her (note that this does not apply to adoption from overseas)

- the child dies during adoption leave

- the child is returned after being placed for adoption (i.e. either under Ss.31–35 of the Adoption and Children Act 2002 or S.25(6) of the Adoption and Children (Scotland) Act 2007, or following termination of a placement under S.22C of the Children Act 1989), or

- (in the case of adoption from overseas only) the child ceases to live with the adopter.

Regulation 22(2)(a), read with Reg 22(3), provides that in these situations, the employee's adoption leave period will end eight weeks after the end of:

- the week during which the employee is notified that the placement will not take place

- the week during which the child dies

- the week during which the child is returned, or

- (in the case of adoption from overseas only) the week during which the child ceases to live with the adopter.

A 'week' for these purposes means seven days beginning with Sunday – Reg 22(4).

6.128 This eight-week period provided for in Reg 22 allows an adoptive, or prospective adoptive, parent time to come to terms with the ending of the placement or the child's death before returning to work. It also allows time for him or her to give the employer the eight weeks' notice required by Reg 25 if he or she wishes to return to work before the end of his or her adoption leave – see 'Returning to work after adoption leave – notice of return during adoption leave' below.

Special provision is made if the 26 weeks' OAL (or, as the case may be, AAL) period would have ended within eight weeks of the week in which the event occurs. If the disrupting event occurs during OAL, the employee's OAL continues until the expiry of the 26 weeks and he or she is then entitled to AAL, which will end eight weeks after the week in which the event occurred – Reg 22(2)(b). If the disrupting event occurs during AAL, the employee's AAL continues until the expiry of the 26 weeks – Reg 22(2)(c).

6.129 **Parental order parents.** In surrogacy cases, Reg 22(1) PAL Regulations is modified to provide that a child's placement is terminated during ordinary or additional adoption leave where:

- the employee does not apply for a parental order within the time limit set in S.54(3) of the Human Fertilisation and Embryology Act 2008

261

- the employee's application for a parental order for the child is refused, withdrawn or otherwise terminated without the order being granted and any time limit for an appeal or new application has expired, or

- the child dies during adoption leave – Reg 17(a) Leave (Parental Order Cases) Regulations.

Regulation 22(2)(a), read with a modified Reg 22(3), provides that in these situations, the employee's adoption leave period will end eight weeks after the end of:

- the week during which the time limit in S.54(3) of the Human Fertilisation and Embryology Act 2008 for an application for a parental order for the child expires

- the week in which the employee's application for a parental order is refused, withdrawn or otherwise terminated without the order being granted, or

- the week during which the child dies – Reg 17(b) Leave (Parental Order Cases) Regulations.

6.130 Returning to work after adoption leave

An employee has the right to return to work after adoption leave, normally to the same job he or she had before he or she left. A failure to allow an employee to return will amount to dismissal.

6.131 Notice of return during adoption leave

An employee returning to work at the end of his or her AAL is not required to give the employer notice of return. (The employer should have informed the employee of the return date in response to the employee's notice of his or her intention to take adoption leave – see 'Ordinary adoption leave – notice and evidential requirements for OAL' above.) The employee can simply turn up to work on the first working day after his or her AAL ends. However, if the employee wishes to return to work before the end of the AAL period (and this includes an employee who wishes to return before or at the end of his or her OAL period), he or she must give the employer at least eight weeks' notice of the date on which he or she intends to return – Reg 25(1) PAL Regulations (or 16 weeks if he or she is an 'employee shareholder' – see 'Employee shareholders' below). There is no requirement that this notice be in writing (nor is there provision for the employer to request that it be in writing).

If an employee attempts to return to work early without having given at least eight weeks' notice, the employer is entitled to postpone the employee's return to a date that will secure the full period of notice – Reg 25(2) PAL Regulations. The employer may not, however, delay the employee's return beyond the end of the AAL period – Reg 25(3). If the employer has exercised the right to defer an employee's return date on account of inadequate notice having been given by the employee, but the employee nevertheless returns to work before the date specified by the employer, the employee has no contractual right to be paid until the deferred return date – Reg 25(4).

Importantly, the employee's obligation to give notice of an earlier return to **6.132** work, the employer's right to postpone that return where inadequate notice has been given, and the employer's right not to pay an employee who returns early without having given sufficient notice, do not apply where the employer failed to notify the employee of the date on which the employee's AAL period would end in accordance with Reg 17(7) and (8) (see 'Ordinary adoption leave – notice and evidential requirements for OAL' above) – Reg 25(5).

Note that where the employee wishes to cut short his or her adoption leave in order to make use of the new system for shared parental leave, he or she must follow the procedure set out in the Maternity and Adoption Leave (Curtailment of Statutory Leave) Regulations 2014 SI 2014/3052, including the notice requirements. The procedure is discussed in detail in Chapter 8, 'Shared parental leave and pay', under 'Curtailing maternity or adoption leave', and 'Notice and evidential requirements for SPL'.

More than one change of return date. The Maternity and Parental Leave etc **6.133** and the Paternity and Adoption Leave (Amendment) Regulations 2006 SI 2006/2014 inserted Reg 25(2A) and (2B) into the PAL Regulations, allowing an employee to change his or her mind once he or she has given notice to return to work early or had his or her return postponed after returning to work without giving sufficient notice. In essence, Reg 25(2A) provides that an employee who decides to return to work earlier than the 'original return date' must give the employer not less than eight weeks' notice of the new date on which he or she now intends to return to work. Alternatively, if the employee wishes to return to work later than the 'original return date' he or she must give the employer not less than eight weeks' notice ending with the 'original return date'.

The 'original return date' is defined as:

- the date which the employee initially notified the employer as being the date of his or her return to work under Reg 25(1), or

- the date to which his or her return was postponed by the employer under Reg 25(2) – Reg 25(2B).

Employee shareholders. The notification requirements applicable to employees **6.134** who are 'employee shareholders' within the meaning of S.205A(1) ERA are slightly different to those that apply to normal employees. S.205A(3) provides that in the case of employee shareholders, all references in Reg 25 to 'eight weeks' notice' are to be read as if there were substituted '16 weeks' notice'.

In other words, employee shareholders who wish to return early from AAL must give 16 weeks' notice of the date on which they wish to return under Reg 25(1), and, if they change their mind in the circumstances described in Reg 25(2A) or (2B), they must give 16 weeks' notice of the revised date.

Employee shareholder status is explained in IDS Employment Law Handbook, 'Atypical and Flexible Working' (2014), Chapter 7, 'Employee shareholders'.

6.135 **Disrupted placement.** If the employee's adoption leave is curtailed (whether during OAL or AAL) because of a disrupted placement under Reg 22 PAL Regulations (see 'Disrupted placement during adoption leave' above), the end of the employee's AAL is treated, for the purposes of Reg 25, as the date on which AAL would have ended if the adoption leave had not been curtailed – Reg 25(6). This means that, for the purposes of the provisions on early return and the employer's right to postpone it for inadequate notice, the employee's adoption leave period is treated as if it had not been curtailed. Therefore, the employee must still give at least eight weeks' notice of an intention to return early and, if he or she fails to do so, the employer may postpone the date of return (even though under Reg 22 adoption leave ends eight weeks after a disrupted placement). The employee must thus notify the employer on the day the placement ends that he or she will be returning to work in eight weeks' time (assuming he or she wants to be sure that the employer will not postpone his or her return).

6.136 *Example.* Employee Y expects a child to be placed with her for adoption on 9 September 2014. Y decides to start her adoption leave on 3 September 2014 (having notified her employer in accordance with Reg 17). However, on 6 September Y is informed by the adoption agency that the placement will not take place. Y's leave will, therefore, end on 1 November (eight weeks later). For the purposes of Reg 25, however, her adoption leave period is treated as continuing until 9 September 2015. Therefore, Y needs to give her employer notice under Reg 25 that she wishes to return to work, starting back on 2 November 2014. This notice should be given at least eight weeks in advance, i.e. on or before 6 September 2014.

6.137 **Right to return after adoption leave**

As we discussed under 'Terms and conditions during adoption leave' above, many of the differences between OAL and AAL were eliminated – in respect of the terms and conditions that apply *during* the leave period – by amendments made by the Maternity and Parental Leave etc and the Paternity and Adoption Leave (Amendment) Regulations 2008 SI 2008/1966. There is also a great deal of similarity between OAL and AAL in respect of terms and conditions that apply following the employee's return from adoption leave – see below. However, there is still a distinction between OAL and AAL in respect of the right to return to work itself.

Different rules apply depending on whether the employee is returning from an isolated period of OAL, from a period of OAL that is the last of two or more consecutive periods of statutory leave, or from a period of AAL. These rules, which are outlined briefly below, have significant similarities with those that apply where an employee is returning from a period of maternity leave and reference should be made to Chapter 4, 'Returning to work after maternity leave', for a more detailed analysis of their application.

Ordinary adoption leave. An employee who returns to work after OAL **6.138** which was:

- an isolated period of leave, or

- the last of two or more consecutive periods of statutory leave, which did not include any period of unpaid parental leave of more than four weeks, or any period of statutory leave which, when added to other periods of statutory leave (excluding unpaid parental leave) taken in relation to the *same* child, exceeded 26 weeks in relation to that child

is entitled to return to the job in which he or she was employed before the absence – Reg 26(1) PAL Regulations (as amended by Reg 9 of the Paternity and Adoption Leave (Amendment) Regulations 2014 SI 2014/2112 with effect from 1 December 2014).

Note that where, during an employee's SAL, it is not reasonably practicable by reason of *redundancy* for the employer to continue to employ the employee under his or her existing contract, the employee is entitled to be offered any suitable alternative vacancy on terms and conditions that are 'not substantially less favourable to her' – Reg 23. In other words, the provisions of Reg 26 (above) do not apply where the redundancy exception in Reg 23 applies – Reg 26(4). Reg 23 is considered in greater detail under 'Redundancy and adoption leave' below.

Where the employee is returning from a period of OAL that does not fall within **6.139** Reg 26(1), he or she is entitled to return to the job in which he or she was employed before the absence unless it is not reasonably practicable for the employer to allow the employee to return to that job, in which case the employee is entitled to return to another job which is both suitable for the employee and appropriate for him or her to do in the circumstances – Reg 26(2)(b). See Chapter 4, 'Returning to work after maternity leave', under 'Returning after additional maternity leave – reinstatement not reasonably practicable', for a further analysis of this exception in the context of maternity leave.

To summarise: an employee returning to work after taking OAL is entitled to return to exactly the same job he or she left except when:

- the OAL follows consecutively on from periods of statutory leave (excluding unpaid parental leave) adding up to more than 26 weeks taken in relation

265

to the same child, or a period of unpaid parental leave lasting more than four weeks, and

- it is not reasonably practicable for a reason other than redundancy for the employee to return to the same job.

6.140 *Employee's 'job'.* The job in which the employee was employed before the absence for the above purposes is the job in which he or she was employed:

- immediately before the period of leave began (where he or she is returning from an isolated period of leave), or

- immediately before the first period of leave (where he or she is returning from consecutive periods of statutory leave) – Reg 26(3) PAL Regulations.

'Job' is defined in the ERA as 'the nature of the work which [the employee] is employed to do in accordance with his [or her] contract and the capacity and place in which he [or she] is so employed' – S.235(1). This is identical to the definition of 'job' in the MPL Regulations and reference should therefore be had to Chapter 4, 'Returning to work after maternity leave', under 'Returning after ordinary maternity leave – employee's "job"', for a more detailed consideration of its meaning.

6.141 **Additional adoption leave.** An employee who returns after a period of AAL (whether or not preceded by another period of statutory leave) is entitled to return to the job in which he or she was employed before the absence except when it is not reasonably practicable (for a reason other than redundancy) for the employer to allow the employee to return to that job. Should the exception apply, the employee is entitled to return to another job that is both suitable and appropriate for him or her to do in the circumstances – Reg 26(2)(a) PAL Regulations.

See Chapter 4, 'Returning to work after maternity leave', under 'Returning after additional maternity leave – reinstatement not reasonably practicable', for a further analysis of this exception in the context of maternity leave (where very similar provisions apply).

6.142 **Failure to allow return.** A refusal to allow an employee to return after adoption leave in accordance with Regs 26 and 27 (see 'Terms and conditions following return' below) of the PAL Regulations may amount to a detriment or dismissal, which, in the case of the latter and depending on the reasons for it, may be unfair – see 'Detriment and unfair dismissal rights' below. (Note, however, that the right to return after adoption leave does not apply where the employee has been made redundant during his or her leave period under Reg 23 – Reg 26(4). Reg 23 is discussed under 'Redundancy and adoption leave' below.)

Terms and conditions following return   6.143

As we saw above, generally speaking, an employee is entitled to return from adoption leave to the job in which he or she was employed before the absence. This means that the employee is entitled to return to exactly the same job he or she had before taking leave. Where the exceptions in Reg 26(2) PAL Regulations apply (see 'Right to return after adoption leave' above), the employee is entitled to return to another job that is both suitable and appropriate. In all cases, however, the employee is entitled to return on terms and conditions not less favourable than those that would have applied had the employee not been absent – Reg 27(1)(b). This is not the same as saying that the employee is entitled to the terms and conditions that applied before he or she went on adoption leave. What it means is that the employee is entitled on his or her return to the benefit (or indeed possibly detriment) of any changes in terms and conditions at work that have taken place during his or her absence and which would have applied to the employee if he or she had been at work during that time. See further Chapter 4, 'Returning to work after maternity leave', under 'Returning after ordinary maternity leave – terms and conditions "not less favourable"', for a detailed analysis in the context of maternity leave (where very similar provisions apply).

The requirement that an employee be treated as if he or she had not been absent refers to the absence since the beginning of an isolated period of ordinary adoption leave or the beginning of the first consecutive period of statutory leave, as the case may be – Reg 27(3).

Seniority, pensions and similar rights. Prior to the Maternity and Parental   6.144
Leave etc and the Paternity and Adoption Leave (Amendment) Regulations 2008 SI 2008/1966, Reg 27 of the PAL Regulations made special provision for seniority, pension rights and similar rights when returning from AAL. However, Reg 27 was amended to provide that an employee is entitled to return from adoption leave (whether OAL or AAL) with his or her seniority, pension rights and similar rights as they would have been if he or she had not been absent – Reg 27(1)(a). This amendment has effect where the expected placement date (or actual date a child from overseas enters Great Britain) is on or after 5 October 2008. For placements that occurred before 5 October 2008, therefore, the old law will continue to apply in respect of seniority, pension and similar rights – more specifically, old Reg 27(1)(a). Basically, this provided that the period of AAL did not count towards seniority or pension rights, or towards any other similar rights which depended on a period of qualifying service. However, the period of leave did not break the employee's continuity of service and the employee was entitled to the pension and seniority rights, etc that would have applied had the two periods either side of the leave (including the period of OAL) been continuous.

For placements occurring on or after 5 October 2008, a period of AAL, like OAL, counts towards seniority or pension rights, and towards any other similar

267

rights that depend upon a period of qualifying service. However, Reg 27(2) provides that nothing in Reg 27(1)(a) concerning the treatment of AAL is to be 'taken to impose a requirement which exceeds the requirements of paras 5, 5B and 6 of [Schedule 5 to the Social Security Act 1989]'. Para 5B provides for the preservation, during paid adoption leave, of the accrual of rights under an employment-related benefit scheme. (Paras 5 (now replaced by S.75 EqA) and 6 apply similar provisions during periods of paid maternity and 'family' leave.) The effect of Reg 27(2), therefore, appears to be that an employee is not entitled to return with his or her seniority, pensions and similar rights as if he or she had not been absent in so far as these constitute rights under an employment-related benefits scheme during unpaid AAL. However, the employee is entitled to the employment-related benefit rights that would have applied had the two periods either side of the unpaid AAL been continuous. In other words, the employee's rights are preserved exactly as they were at the beginning of the unpaid AAL period. See 'Terms and conditions during adoption leave – pensions and other service-related benefits' above, and Chapter 3, 'Maternity leave', under 'Terms and conditions during maternity leave – pensions', for a full discussion of the effect of unpaid leave on such benefits.

6.145 Contractual and composite adoption rights

Employers are entitled to offer contractual rights to adoption leave and pay that are more favourable than those available under the statutory scheme. For example, a contract may allow the employee to receive normal contractual remuneration during at least part of the total leave period. An employee who is entitled to statutory adoption leave and who also has a contractual right to adoption leave may not exercise the two rights separately, but may take advantage of whichever is the more favourable in any particular respect – Reg 30(1) and (2)(a) PAL Regulations.

If the employee does combine elements of a contractual right and the statutory right, the various statutory provisions that apply to the statutory right are modified to give effect to the more favourable contractual terms – Reg 30(2)(b). Where an employee combines elements of a contractual right and a statutory right, the result is referred to as a composite right. For further details of composite rights, see Chapter 3, 'Maternity leave', under 'Contractual and composite maternity rights'.

6.146 Detriment and unfair dismissal rights

The Employment Act 2002 inserted provisions into the ERA protecting employees taking adoption leave from being subjected to a detriment or being unfairly dismissed. These rights are outlined below and are discussed further in Chapter 12, 'Detriment and unfair dismissal'. Note that an employee who is dismissed during his or her SAL will still be entitled to receive SAP for the full 39-week pay period once he or she has qualified for it – see 'Statutory adoption pay' below.

Protection from detriment

6.147

Under S.47C ERA, employees have the right not to be subjected to any detriment by any act, or any deliberate failure to act, of their employer for a reason which relates to (among other things) adoption leave. Reg 28(1) PAL Regulations sets out the details of the right, providing that an employee has the right not to be subjected to any detriment by his or her employer because:

- the employee took or sought to take time off for adoption appointments (from 5 April 2015) (see 'Time off for adoption appointments' above)

- the employer believed that the employee was likely to take time off to attend adoption appointments (from 5 April 2015)

- the employee took or sought to take OAL or AAL

- the employer believed that the employee was likely to take OAL or AAL

- the employee undertook, considered undertaking or refused to undertake 'KIT work' (see 'Work during adoption leave' above)

- the employee failed to return after a period of AAL and the employer had failed to notify the employee in accordance with Reg 17(7) and (8) or otherwise of the date on which the AAL period would end (see 'Ordinary adoption leave – notice and evidential requirements for OAL' above) and the employee reasonably believed that the period had not ended, or

- the employer had given the employee less than 28 days' notice of the date on which the AAL period would end and it was not reasonably practicable for the employee to return on that date.

Any detriment that amounts to a dismissal is specifically excluded by Reg 28(2) as dismissals are dealt with by Reg 29 – see 'Protection from unfair dismissal' below.

Protection from unfair dismissal

6.148

Section 99 ERA renders dismissals for reasons relating to, among other things, adoption leave automatically unfair if:

- the reason or principal reason for the dismissal is 'of a prescribed kind'; or

- the reason or principal reason for the dismissal takes place 'in prescribed circumstances'.

This means that once it is established that dismissal was for one of the prescribed reasons, there is no consideration of whether the employer's actions were

269

reasonable – the prescribed reason automatically renders the dismissal unfair. Furthermore, there is no minimum service requirement for the right to claim under S.99. 'Prescribed' means prescribed by regulations made by the Secretary of State – in this case, the PAL Regulations.

6.149 Regulation 29(1) and (3) provides that an employee who is dismissed will be taken to be unfairly dismissed under S.99 if the reason or principal reason for the dismissal is:

- that the employee is redundant and Reg 23 has not been complied with (see 'Redundancy and adoption leave' below) – Reg 29(1)(b), or

- connected with the fact that:

  – the employee took or sought to take time off to attend adoption appointments (where the effective date of termination falls on or after 5 April 2015) – Reg 29(3)(zc) (see 'Time off for adoption appointments' above)

  – the employer believed that the employee was likely to take time off to attend adoption appointments (where the effective date of termination falls on or after 5 April 2015) – Reg 29(3)(zd)

  – the employee took or sought to take adoption leave – Reg 29(3)(a)

  – the employer believed that the employee was likely to take OAL or AAL – Reg 29(3)(b)

  – the employee undertook, considered undertaking or refused to undertake 'KIT work' (see 'Work during adoption leave' above) – Reg 29(3)(bb), or

  – the employee failed to return after a period of AAL and the employer

    (i) had failed to notify the employee in accordance with Reg 17(7) and (8) or otherwise of the date on which the AAL period would end (see 'Ordinary adoption leave – notice and evidential requirements for OAL' above) and the employee reasonably believed that the period had not ended, or

    (ii) had given the employee less than 28 days' notice of the date on which the AAL period would end and it was not reasonably practicable for the employee to return on that date – Reg 29(3)(c).

6.150 Cases on adoption leave (and pay) are relatively rare. However, a claim of automatic dismissal under S.99 ERA/Reg 29 was upheld by the employment tribunal in Coulombeau v Enterprise Rent-A-Car (UK) Ltd ET Case No.2600296/06. There, C decided to embark on the training necessary to become an adopter after discovering that she could not have children. She underwent a considerable amount of training and took several days' leave to have supervision meetings with social workers. C was subsequently suspended by her employer pending the investigation of three charges of dishonesty and misconduct that had been made against her. The investigation took several weeks and culminated in a disciplinary hearing which led to her being dismissed. The tribunal found that the employer thought that C was likely to need time off and for that reason orchestrated her dismissal. The dismissal therefore fell within Reg 29(3)(b) and was automatically unfair. Interestingly, the tribunal also upheld a claim for direct sex discrimination, as it was satisfied that the employer would not have dismissed a man for the same offence and that there was clear evidence of a discriminatory climate when it came to dealing with complaints made by women against men. C was awarded a substantial amount for injury to feelings – £12,000. In making this award, the tribunal took into account not only the way the employer's treatment of her had made her feel but also the fact that she would need to defer the adoption process (because she would need to find another job and stay long enough to gain the support of her new employer before embarking on the process again).

'Connected with' adoption leave. The meaning of the words 'connected with' **6.151** in Reg 29(3) was considered by the EAT in Atkins v Coyle Personnel plc 2008 IRLR 420, EAT – a case concerning paternity leave. There it was suggested that some causal connection (as opposed to mere association) is necessary between dismissal and leave. This case is fully discussed in Chapter 7, 'Paternity leave and pay', in the section 'Employment protection during and after paternity leave', under 'Protection from unfair dismissal – "connected with"', and Chapter 12, 'Detriment and unfair dismissal', under 'Automatically unfair dismissal – paternity leave'.

Termination of employment contract. For an employee to claim unfair **6.152** dismissal, he or she must first show that there has been a termination of the employment contract. Note that if the employer refuses to take the employee back after his or her adoption leave, this will amount to a dismissal – see further Chapter 4, 'Returning to work after maternity leave', under 'Failure to allow employee to return – automatically unfair dismissal'. (Although Chapter 4 relates to maternity leave, similar considerations will apply in the context of adoption leave.)

Exception. It used to be the case that, by virtue of Reg 29(4) PAL Regulations, **6.153** Reg 29(1) did not apply where the employer had five employees or fewer when certain conditions were met. However, this exception no longer applies, as Reg 29(4) was revoked by the Maternity and Parental Leave etc and the Paternity and Adoption Leave (Amendment) Regulations 2006 SI 2006/2014 (which came into force on 1 October 2006).

There is now only one situation in which the automatically unfair dismissal provisions of Reg 29(1) do not apply – where the employee is offered a suitable job by an associated employer.

271

6.154 *Offer from associated employer.* By virtue of Reg 29(5), Reg 29(1) does not apply to render a dismissal automatically unfair in relation to an employee if:

- it is not reasonably practicable for a reason other than redundancy for the employer (who may be the same employer or a successor) to permit the employee to return to a job which is both suitable for the employee and appropriate for him or her to do in the circumstances

- an associated employer offers the employee a job of that kind, and

- the employee accepts or unreasonably refuses that offer.

This might happen where, for example, there is a business reorganisation within a group of companies that does not involve redundancies. Two employers are associated if one is a company of which the other (directly or indirectly) has control, or both are companies of which a third person (directly or indirectly) has control – Reg 2(6).

6.155 Where Reg 29(5) applies, although the dismissal will not be automatically unfair, the employee will still be able to bring a claim of unfair dismissal under the 'ordinary' unfair dismissal provisions contained in Ss.95–98 ERA. He or she may also be able to claim, for example, sex discrimination (see Chapter 13, 'Discrimination and equal pay'). In an ordinary unfair dismissal claim, various matters must be established, such as whether the complainant has the requisite qualifying service, whether he or she was indeed dismissed, the reason for the dismissal, and whether or not the employer acted reasonably in dismissing for that reason – see further Chapter 12, 'Detriment and unfair dismissal', under '"Ordinary" unfair dismissal'. Where there is a dispute as to whether the exception applies, it is for the employer to show that the provisions of Reg 29(5) were satisfied – Reg 29(6).

6.156 Redundancy and adoption leave

An employee who becomes redundant during adoption leave has a right to be offered a suitable alternative vacancy, and a failure to offer such a vacancy (where one exists) will result in an automatically unfair dismissal. Furthermore, an employee will be automatically unfairly dismissed if he or she is selected for redundancy on grounds relating to his or her adoption leave in preference to other comparable employees.

6.157 Suitable available vacancy

Special provisions apply where, during an employee's SAL period, it is not practicable by reason of redundancy for the employer to continue to employ the employee under his or her existing contract of employment – Reg 23 PAL Regulations. In these circumstances, where there is a suitable available vacancy, the employee is entitled to be offered alternative employment with his or her employer, the employer's successor or an associated employer before the end of the employee's employment under the existing contract – Reg 23(2). Two employers are associated if one is a company of which the other (directly or indirectly) has control or both are companies of which a third person (directly or indirectly) has control – Reg 2(6).

The suitability of a job is judged from the perspective of an objective employer, not from the employee's perspective – Simpson v Endsleigh Insurance Services Ltd 2011 ICR 75, EAT.

The new contract must take effect immediately on the ending of the previous contract and must be such that: **6.158**

- the work to be done is of a kind which is both suitable in relation to the employee and appropriate for him or her to do in the circumstances, and

- its provisions as to the capacity and place in which the employee is to be employed, and as to the other terms and conditions of employment, are not substantially less favourable to the employee than if he or she had continued to be employed under the previous contract – Reg 23(2) and (3).

If a suitable available vacancy exists and the employer fails to offer it to the employee (either at all or before the termination of the employee's existing contract), the dismissal will be automatically unfair under S.99 ERA if the reason or principal reason for the dismissal is redundancy – Reg 29(1)(b) (see 'Automatically unfair dismissal' below). If, however, such a vacancy genuinely does not exist or the employer does offer the vacancy but the employee unreasonably refuses it, the dismissal will almost certainly be fair and he or she will lose the right to a redundancy payment – see S.141 ERA.

If there is no suitable available vacancy, the employee's employment (and his or her adoption leave period) will come to an end by reason of redundancy. The employee will, however, be entitled to his or her notice period (see 'Terms and conditions during adoption leave – notice rights' above) and to a written statement of the reasons for dismissal (without having to request it) – see S.92(4A) ERA. The employee will also be entitled to a redundancy payment (statutory or contractual), provided he or she has sufficient qualifying service. An employee who is dismissed during his or her paid adoption leave will still be entitled to receive statutory adoption pay for the full 39-week period once he or she has qualified for it. **6.159**

Automatically unfair dismissal **6.160**
There are two situations where an employee's dismissal by reason of redundancy will be automatically unfair. In both, redundancy must be 'the reason or principal reason for the dismissal'.

273

The first situation is when the employer has failed to comply with its obligations under Reg 23 PAL Regulations with regard to offering suitable alternative employment (see 'Suitable available vacancy' above) – Reg 29(1)(b). Note that this situation is limited to redundancy during adoption leave by virtue of Reg 23.

The second situation in which a redundancy dismissal will be automatically unfair is where:

- the circumstances constituting the redundancy applied equally to one or more employees in the same undertaking who held positions similar to that held by the employee and who have not been dismissed by the employer, and

- the reason (or, if more than one, the principal reason) for which the employee was selected for dismissal was one of the reasons listed in Reg 29(3) (see 'Detriment and unfair dismissal rights – protection from unfair dismissal' above) – Reg 29(2).

6.161 In this situation, the employee essentially has to show that he or she was selected for redundancy on grounds relating to his or her adoption leave in preference to other comparable employees. In such a case, dismissal would be automatically unfair even if the employer has complied with its obligations under Reg 23. Note that Reg 29(2) (unlike Reg 29(1)(b)) is not limited to redundancy during adoption leave. It can also apply to redundancy before or after adoption leave so long as the reason the employee was selected for redundancy relates to adoption leave.

Where the reason for dismissal is not related to the employee's adoption leave and, where applicable, the employer has complied with Reg 23, dismissal will not be automatically unfair. However, the employee may still be able to bring a claim for 'ordinary' unfair dismissal and/or unlawful discrimination. Furthermore, if an employer fails to follow a fair procedure when selecting an employee on adoption leave for redundancy, the employee will be able to claim unfair dismissal in the ordinary way (provided he or she has sufficient qualifying service).

6.162 **Comparison with maternity leave**
Similar provisions apply during maternity leave and reference should be made to Chapter 4, 'Returning to work after maternity leave', under 'Redundancy during maternity leave', for further details. Note that Regs 7(5), 10 and 20 MPL Regulations are equivalent to Regs 24, 23 and 29 PAL Regulations. See also IDS Employment Law Handbook, 'Redundancy' (2011), Chapter 3, 'Alternative job offers', and in particular the section on 'Offers during maternity, adoption or paternity leave', for further information about alternative job offers.

Statutory adoption pay   6.163

The Employment Act 2002 established a right to statutory adoption pay (SAP) for adoptive parents. S.4 inserted Part 12ZB into the Social Security Contributions and Benefits Act 1992 (SSCBA), entitled 'Statutory Adoption Pay', and references to section numbers below are to provisions of the SSCBA. The main regulations dealing with SAP are the Statutory Paternity Pay and Statutory Adoption Pay (General) Regulations 2002 SI 2002/2822 ('the General Regulations') and references to regulations in this section are to these Regulations unless otherwise stated. (For Northern Ireland the equivalent provisions are contained in the Statutory Paternity Pay and Statutory Adoption Pay (General) Regulations (Northern Ireland) 2002 SR 2002/378.)

The remainder of this chapter considers the individual qualifying conditions for SAP (which are independent of the qualifying conditions for SAL) and the circumstances in which an employee may become disentitled to SAP. We also deal with the payment of SAP. In particular, we outline the current rates of adoption pay, the manner in which SAP is paid, the period during which these payments are payable and the circumstances in which employees in receipt of SAP are disentitled to statutory sick pay (SSP).

Adoption from overseas   6.164
Note that the SSCBA and the General Regulations only cover adoptions within the UK. However, special regulations have been made providing for these provisions to have effect, with the necessary modifications, in relation to overseas adoptions – see the Social Security Contributions and Benefits Act 1992 (Application of Parts 12ZA and 12ZB to Adoptions from Overseas) Regulations 2003 SI 2003/499 and the Statutory Paternity Pay (Adoption) and Statutory Adoption Pay (Adoption from Overseas) (No.2) Regulations 2003 SI 2003/1194. The adoption pay provisions for overseas adoptions effectively mirror those that apply in relation to the leave entitlement. Note that for the purpose of claiming SAP where a child is adopted from overseas, model self-certificate form SC6, 'Statutory adoption pay and adoption leave when adopting from abroad', should be used. The form can be obtained from the HMRC website.

Eligible persons   6.165
Eligibility for SAP extends beyond employees in the strict sense; it also covers office holders and 'employed earners', although certain conditions apply.

'Employee'. Section 171ZL SSCBA makes it clear that SAP is payable only to 6.166 employees who satisfy conditions of eligibility based on length of service and average earnings. The usual definition of employee for most statutory employment law rights is someone who works under a contract of service or is

275

an apprentice. Indeed, this is the definition of 'employee' for the purposes of entitlement to adoption leave – see 'Ordinary adoption leave – who has the right?' above. The definition for SAP purposes, however, is slightly wider. It mirrors the definition of 'employee' for statutory maternity pay (SMP) purposes and reference should be made to Chapter 5, 'Statutory maternity pay', for a more in-depth analysis.

Section 171ZS(2) provides that 'employee' means a person:

- who is gainfully employed in Great Britain either under a contract of service or in an office (including elective office), and

- with earnings, within the meaning of Parts 1 to 5 of the Act. 'Earnings' are defined in S.3 SSCBA as 'any remuneration or profit derived from an employment'. Earnings will therefore typically include any salary or wages and other forms of reward such as bonuses, commission and tips.

6.167 **Office holders.** As can be seen, S.171ZS applies to office holders, not just those employed under a contract of service. A company director, for example, is an office holder but is not always employed under a contract of service, in which case he or she would not be entitled to SAL. He or she is likely nonetheless to qualify for SAP, given the wide definition of 'earnings' (see above). However, another condition of entitlement to SAP is being on adoption leave – see 'Conditions of entitlement' below. Therefore, if the office holder in question is not entitled to SAL (because he or she is not an employee in the common legal sense) the right to SAP will only apply where the office holder in question has a contractual right to adoption leave.

6.168 **'Employed earners'.** A person who falls under the category of 'employed earners' (under the Social Security (Categorisation of Earners) Regulations 1978 SI 1978/1689) is 'treated as an employee' for SAP (but not SAL) purposes – Reg 32(1). In other words, he or she has to be working for someone who is liable to pay the employer's share of Class 1 national insurance contributions. Note that an employee does not have to pay national insurance to qualify for SAP. Therefore, SAP may be available in some cases where SAL is not available on account of the fact that the person in question is not an 'employee' for the purposes of the statutory adoption scheme. A person who notionally qualifies for SAP but does not have a statutory right to adoption leave would have to rely upon a contractual right to such leave in order to take advantage of his or her SAP rights.

There is no Class 1 national insurance contribution liability if an employee's earnings in a pay period are less than the lower earnings limit for national insurance (£112 per week for the tax year 2015/16). Therefore, employees earning less than the national insurance lower earnings limit, while they may be entitled to SAL, are not entitled to SAP. However, while low-paid parents on adoption leave may not be entitled to SAP, they may be entitled to income support. The Social Security (Paternity and Adoption) Amendment Regulations

2002 SI 2002/2689 amended the Income Support (General) Regulations 1987 SI 1987/1967 and the Jobseeker's Allowance Regulations 1996 SI 1996/207 to clarify that:

- a person on adoption leave is not to be treated as engaged in remunerative work for the purposes of entitlement to income support under the SSCBA, and

- remuneration received while on adoption leave is not to be counted as earnings when calculating entitlement to jobseeker's allowance under the Jobseekers Act 1995.

Foster parents. Following recent changes, local authority foster parents who **6.169** are prospective adopters and who have been notified that a child is, or is expected, to be placed with them by a local authority in England under S.22C of the Children Act 1989 are now entitled to SAP. S.171ZL(9) SSCBA makes it clear that 'fostering for adoption' placements should be treated in the same way as adoption placements in terms of entitlement to SAP. However, once the parent is entitled to SAP in respect of a child who is, or is expected to be, placed with him or her in a 'fostering for adoption' placement, that person does not again become entitled to SAP when the child is placed with him or her for adoption – S.171ZL(10). Further amendments are contained in the Statutory Paternity Pay and Statutory Adoption Pay (Parental Orders and Prospective Adopters) Regulations 2014 SI 2014/2934. The changes apply in relation to children matched with a person who is notified of having been matched on or after 5 April 2015. For more information on local authority foster parents, see the section 'Ordinary adoption leave' above, under 'Who has the right? – foster parents'.

Intended parents in a surrogacy arrangement. The Statutory Paternity Pay **6.170** and Statutory Adoption Pay (Parental Orders and Prospective Adopters) Regulations 2014 SI 2014/2934 ('the Pay (Parental Orders) Regulations') extend SAP to intended parental order parents in a surrogacy arrangement. A 'parental order parent' is a person who applies, or intends to apply, with another person for a parental order in respect of the child within six months of the child's birth and expects the court to make such an order, or whose application to the court has already been granted.

The Pay (Parental Orders) Regulations provide that the General Regulations apply, with the necessary modifications, to parental order parents. The modifications apply in respect of children whose expected week of birth begins on or after 5 April 2015. Further amendments are made by the Social Security Contributions and Benefits Act 1992 (Application of Parts 12ZA, 12ZB and 12ZC to Parental Order Cases) Regulations 2014 SI 2014/2866. For more information on parental order parents, see the section 'Ordinary adoption leave' above, under 'Who has the right? – intended parents in a surrogacy arrangement'.

277

6.171 **Agency workers.** Agency workers are not usually classed as employees in the traditional sense (though some may be) and therefore most will not qualify for SAL. However, agency workers can be treated as employed earners (under the 1978 Regulations) and may thus be more likely to qualify for SAP – see Chapter 5, 'Statutory maternity pay', in the section 'Qualifying for statutory maternity pay', under 'Definition of "employee" – agency workers', for further details.

6.172 **Crown servants.** Crown servants are treated as employees for SAP purposes under S.171ZQ.

6.173 **Employees working abroad.** Certain employees working abroad are eligible for SAP by virtue of the Statutory Paternity Pay and Statutory Adoption Pay (Persons Abroad and Mariners) Regulations 2002 SI 2002/2821. These employees are:

- those gainfully employed in another Member State of the European Economic Area (EEA) who would be employees for the purposes of the SSCBA if they were working in Great Britain (the EEA comprises the 28 Member States of the EU together with Iceland, Norway and Liechtenstein) and who are subject to UK legislation under EU Council Regulation No.1408/71 on the application of social security schemes to employed persons and their families moving within the Community

- those who are employees or are treated as such under the category above and who are working in Great Britain in the week in which they are notified of having been matched with a child for adoption but who have worked for the same employer in another EEA Member State in any week during the 26 weeks prior to that week

- those who are absent from Great Britain but in respect of whom an employer has secondary Class 1 national insurance liability

- mariners employed on a 'home-trade ship' (even though they may not be employed in Great Britain) so long as their employer has a place of business within the UK. However, mariners engaged in employment on a 'foreign-going ship' or on a 'home-trade ship with an employer who does not have a place of business within the United Kingdom' are not covered even if they may have been employed in Great Britain. 'Home-trade ship' has the same, rather technical, meaning as in Reg 115 of the Social Security (Contributions) Regulations 2001 SI 2001/1004 and includes every ship or vessel employed in trading or going within the UK, the Channel Islands, the Isle of Man, and Europe. 'Foreign-going ship' is any ship that is not a 'home-trade ship'

- persons working on the continental shelf.

The corresponding Regulations in Northern Ireland are the Statutory Paternity Pay and Statutory Adoption Pay (Persons Abroad and Mariners) Regulations (Northern Ireland) 2002 SR 2002/382.

Exclusions. A person who is in employed earner's employment is not treated as **6.174** an employee for the purposes of SAP if either:

- his or her employer is not resident or present in Great Britain in accordance with Reg 145(1) of the Social Security (Contributions) Regulations 2001 SI 2001/1004, or

- an international treaty or convention (which is binding on the UK) exempts his or her employer from the provisions of the SSCBA or renders the SSCBA unenforceable against the employer – Reg 32(3) General Regulations.

Conditions of entitlement
6.175
Under S.171ZL(1) SSCBA an employee who satisfies various conditions is entitled to be paid SAP following the placement of a child for adoption. These conditions, set out in S.171ZL(2) and read with S.171ZL(3), require that the employee:

- is a person with whom a child is, or is expected to be, placed for adoption under the law of the UK (which includes a child being placed under S.22C of the Children Act 1989 – S.171ZL(9)(a))

- has been 'in employed earner's employment' for a continuous period of at least 26 weeks ending with the week in which he or she is notified of having been matched with a child for adoption

- has ceased to work for the employer (i.e. he or she has taken adoption leave)

- has normal weekly earnings for eight weeks ending with the week in which the adopter is notified of being matched with the child for adoption that are not less than the lower earnings limit for the payment of national insurance contributions, and

- has elected to receive SAP. The employee must give the employer a declaration that he or she has elected to receive SAP and not statutory paternity pay – see 'Evidence of entitlement to SAP' below.

(Note that the Welfare Reform Act 2012 introduced a new condition that, at the end of the week in which the adopter is notified of being matched with the child, the employee must legally be 'entitled to be in employment' under UK immigration law. This provision is not yet in force.)

Under S.171ZL(4) and (4A) an employee may not elect to receive SAP if he or **6.176** she has elected to receive statutory paternity pay (see Chapter 7, 'Paternity leave and pay'), or:

279

- the child is, or is expected to be, placed for adoption with him or her as a member of a couple (meaning a married couple or, in the case of adoption under the law of England, Wales and Scotland only, civil partners, or two people – whether of different sexes or the same sex – living as partners in an enduring family relationship – S.171ZL(4B))

- the other member of the couple also satisfies the conditions in S.171ZL(2) (i.e. is entitled to SAP, see above), and

- the other member of the couple has elected to receive SAP.

6.177 **Continuous employment.** To qualify for SAP, an employee must have been employed for a continuous period of at least 26 weeks ending with the 'relevant week', which means the week in which the child's adopter is notified of being matched with the child – S.171ZL(2)(b) and (3) SSCBA. An employee will be taken to be in 'employment' for these purposes so long as his or her contract of employment continues in existence: the employee does not need to attend his or her workplace and do any work in order to have a contract of employment in existence.

Continuous employment for the purposes of claiming SAP is based on employment by the same employer without a break. However, the General Regulations also provide for continuity to be preserved in some cases where there have been breaks in an employee's employment and where there is a change of employer – see 'Breaks in employment' below.

6.178 The general rules for computing continuity of employment contained in Ss.210–219 ERA (see IDS Employment Law Handbook, 'Continuity of Employment' (2012), Chapter 1, 'The general framework') are incorporated with some variations into the SAP scheme by Regs 33–37 of the General Regulations. These rules have similarities with the rules regarding continuous employment for SMP purposes – see Chapter 5, 'Statutory maternity pay', under 'Continuous employment', for further details. (Note that for SAL purposes, continuous employment is calculated in accordance with the continuity provisions in the ERA – see 'Ordinary adoption leave – conditions of entitlement' above.)

6.179 *Breaks in employment.* Regulation 33 sets out the circumstances in which weeks when there is no contract of employment in existence nevertheless count as a period of continuous employment. These parallel the circumstances set out in S.212 ERA and are weeks during the whole or part of which the employee is:

- incapable of work because of sickness or injury – Reg 33(1)(a). Not more than 26 consecutive weeks may count under this provision – Reg 33(2), so if the employee is incapable of work for longer than 26 weeks, continuity will be broken

- absent from work on account of a temporary cessation of work – Reg 33(1)(b), or

- absent from work in circumstances such that, by arrangement or custom, he or she is regarded as continuing in employment for any purpose – Reg 33(1)(c).

An employee must return to work following his or her absence to preserve continuity under one of the grounds above – Reg 33(1). (In the case of absence through sickness or injury, he or she must return before the 26-week cut-off date.) This means that if, just before the relevant week, an employee's contract is terminated for one of the reasons set out above, and the reason for the absence continues beyond the relevant week, then the break in employment will only be bridged for the purposes of showing continuity if he or she is re-employed by the employer before commencing adoption leave.

Spasmodic employment. As noted above, a period of absence during which a **6.180** contract of employment does not subsist will only be counted as continuous employment under Reg 33 of the General Regulations once the employee returns to work after that absence and only if the absence was for one of the three specified reasons set out in Reg 33(1). There is an exception to this general rule, however, in the case of spasmodic employment. The exception applies where it is the custom of the employer to offer work for a fixed period of not more than 26 consecutive weeks:

- on two or more occasions in a year for periods that do not overlap

- to those persons who had worked for it during the last or a recent such period.

If both these conditions apply and the employee is absent from work because of incapacity arising from some specific disease or bodily or mental impairment, then continuous employment will be preserved for SAP purposes (and the period of absence will count towards continuity) even though he or she does not in fact return to work before starting adoption leave – Reg 33(3).

Re-employment after complaint of unfair dismissal. Where an employee is **6.181** dismissed and then re-employed in consequence of:

- the employee presenting an unfair dismissal complaint – Reg 34(1)(a)

- the employee claiming in accordance with a dismissals procedure agreement under S.110 ERA – Reg 34(1)(b)

- action taken by an Acas conciliator under Ss.18A–18C of the Employment Tribunals Act 1996 – Reg 34(1)(c), or

- a decision arising out of the required use of a (now repealed) statutory dispute resolution procedure contained in Schedule 2 to the Employment Act 2002 – Reg 34(1)(d),

281

the interval between dismissal and re-employment counts as a period of continuous employment – Reg 34(2). The re-employment must be by the employee's employer, a successor or associated employer to fall within this provision. A 'successor' is a person who, in consequence of a change occurring in the ownership of the undertaking, or part of the undertaking, for the purposes of which the employee was employed, has become the owner of the undertaking or part – Reg 34(3) and S.235 ERA. Two employers are associated if one is a company directly or indirectly controlled by the other or both are companies over which a third person has direct or indirect control – Reg 34(3) and S.231 ERA.

6.182 *Stoppage because of a trade dispute.* If there is a week or part of a week when an employee does not work because there is a stoppage of work due to a trade dispute within the meaning of S.35(1) of the Jobseekers Act 1995 at his or her place of employment, there is no break in continuity of employment – Reg 35(1). But any such week will not count in computing the total period of continuous employment unless the employee can prove that at no time did he or she have a direct interest in the trade dispute – Reg 35(3).

Dismissal of an employee during a stoppage of work breaks continuity of employment and, in contrast to the rules on continuity in the ERA, continuity is not restored for the purposes of qualifying for SAP if re-employment takes place unless the employee can prove that he or she never had a direct interest in the trade dispute – Reg 35(3). Unless the employee can prove this, continuity will be treated as ending on the first day on which he or she stopped work – Reg 35(2). A trade dispute is defined in the Jobseekers Act as 'any dispute between employers and employees, or between employees and employees, which is connected with the employment or non-employment or the terms of employment or the conditions of employment of any persons, whether employees in the employment of the employer with whom the dispute arises, or not'. This appears to be wider than the definition in S.244 of the Trade Union and Labour Relations (Consolidation) Act 1992 governing industrial action.

6.183 *Change of employer.* Regulation 36 sets out the circumstances in which employment is treated as continuous even though the identity of the employer changes. These are where:

- the employer's trade or business or undertaking (which may be established under an Act of Parliament) is transferred to another person – Reg 36(a)

- one employer is substituted by another under an Act of Parliament – Reg 36(b)

- the employee is re-employed following the death of the employer by the employer's personal representatives or trustees – Reg 36(c)

- there is a change in the employing partners, personal representatives or trustees – Reg 36(d)

- employment is transferred to an associated employer – Reg 36(e). 'Associated employer' has the meaning given in S.231 ERA – i.e. two or more employers are associated if one is a company directly or indirectly controlled by the other or both are companies over which a third person has direct or indirect control

- the employee is transferred between two employers, one being a local authority and the other being the governors of a school maintained by the same local authority – Reg 36(f).

The circumstances correspond with those set out in S.218 ERA – see IDS Employment Law Handbook, 'Continuity of Employment' (2012), Chapter 4, 'Change of employer', for full details.

Reinstatement after service with the armed forces. Section 1 of the Reserve **6.184** Forces (Safeguard of Employment) Act 1985 provides a right for a reservist to be taken back into employment after demobilisation, no matter how long the military service has lasted. Within six months of the end of military service, an employer is obliged to re-employ any reservist who was employed by it in the four-week period prior to being called up, on the terms and conditions that would have applied if there had been no call-up. Reg 37 General Regulations provides that, where a person enters the employment of the employer within that six-month period, his or her previous employment with that employer and the period of employment beginning in that six-month period will be treated as continuous.

Dismissal to avoid adoption pay. Where an employer has terminated an **6.185** employee's contract of employment solely or mainly for the purpose of avoiding SAP liabilities, the employee will still be entitled to SAP from the former employer if he or she has been employed continuously for at least eight weeks at the time of the dismissal – Reg 30. Regardless of the dismissal, the employee is deemed to have been employed up to the end of the relevant week, and his or her normal weekly earnings are calculated on the basis of the last eight weeks in respect of which he or she has been paid. Note that the dismissal would also be automatically unfair and could constitute an act of unlawful discrimination – see Chapter 12, 'Detriment and unfair dismissal', and Chapter 13, 'Discrimination and equal pay'.

Normal weekly earnings. As noted above, one of the conditions for entitlement **6.186** to SAP is that the employee's weekly earnings are at least the lower earnings limit for paying primary Class 1 national insurance contributions (£112 for the tax year 2015/16). Regs 39 and 40 General Regulations deal with the calculation of normal weekly earnings. These regulations mirror the provisions relating to the calculation of normal weekly earnings for SMP – see Chapter 5,

283

'Statutory maternity pay', under 'Normal weekly earnings'. Basically, the normal weekly earnings for SAP are the average weekly earnings over a period of at least eight weeks:

- starting on a 'normal pay day' (i.e. a day on which he or she is contractually due to be paid), and

- finishing on the last normal pay day to fall before the first day of the week after the week in which the adopter is notified of being matched with the child for adoption.

For example, assume X is a full-time employee whose pay day falls on the last Friday of every month. She was notified of being matched with a child for adoption on Wednesday, 15 August 2014. The first day of the week after notification is Monday, 20 August. Therefore, X's average weekly earnings are calculated over a period ending on Friday, 27 July (the last normal pay day to fall before 15 August) and starting from Friday, 25 May 2014 (the last pay day to fall at least eight weeks before 27 July).

6.187 Notice requirements for SAP

As noted under 'Period of payment of SAP' below, SAP will only be payable if the adopter gives the employer at least 28 days' notice of the date from which he or she expects liability to pay SAP to begin or, if that is not reasonably practicable, as soon as is reasonably practicable – S.171ZL(6) SSCBA. The notice must be in writing if the employer so requests – S.171ZL(7).

At the same time as giving notice under S.171ZL(6), the adopter must also inform the employer of the date on which the child is expected to be placed for adoption – Reg 23(1) General Regulations. Where the employee has chosen (in accordance with Reg 21(1)(a)) to begin the adoption pay period on the date that the child is placed for adoption (and has notified the employer of the date from which he or she expects the liability to pay SAP to begin in accordance with S.171ZL(6)), the employee must give the employer further notice as soon as is reasonably practicable of the date the child is actually placed for adoption – Reg 23(2).

6.188 Parental order parents.

Note that in the case of parental order parents, Reg 23 is modified so as to provide that the employee must give the employer notice of the following matters:

- the expected week of the child's birth, and

- the date on which the child is born (notice of which must given as soon as reasonably practicable) – Reg 19 Pay (Parental Orders) Regulations.

Evidence of entitlement to SAP

6.189

Under Reg 24 General Regulations, employees need to provide evidence to prove eligibility for SAP (whether the employer asks for it or not). Note that an employee only needs to provide evidence of entitlement to SAL if the employer requests it (see 'Ordinary adoption leave – notice and evidential requirements for OAL' above). An employee must give the employer evidence of his or her entitlement to SAP by providing the employer with a document (known as a 'matching certificate') or documents issued by an approved adoption agency stating:

- the name and address of the approved adoption agency

- the name and address of the person claiming entitlement to SAP

- the expected placement date or, where the child has already been placed for adoption, the placement date, and

- the date on which the person claiming payment of SAP was informed by the adoption agency that the child would be placed with him or her – Reg 24(1)(a) and (2).

The employee must also give the employer a declaration that he or she has elected to receive SAP and not statutory paternity pay – Reg 24(1)(b).

Both the evidence of entitlement and the declaration must be provided at least 28 days before the date chosen as the beginning of the adoption pay period or, if that is not reasonably practicable, as soon as is reasonably practicable thereafter – Reg 24(3).

6.190

Parental order parents. In surrogacy cases, the employee must give the employer a declaration that he or she has elected to receive SAP and not statutory paternity pay. Where the employer requests it, a parental order parent must also provide a statutory declaration, which is a declaration stating that the employee has applied, or intends to apply, under S.54 of the Human Fertilisation and Embryology Act 2008 with another person for a parental order in respect of the child within the applicable time limit, and expects the order to be granted – Reg 20 Pay (Parental Orders) Regulations.

6.191

Rate of SAP

6.192

Following amendments introduced by S.124 of the Children and Families Act 2014, the rate of SAP payable has been brought into line with the rate payable for SMP (see Chapter 5, 'Statutory maternity pay', under 'Rates of statutory maternity pay'). SAP is paid for:

- the first six weeks at the 'earnings-related rate', which is 90 per cent of the employee's 'normal weekly earnings' – S.171ZN(2E)(a) and (2F) SSCBA (For the meaning of 'normal weekly earnings', see 'Conditions of entitlement – normal weekly earnings' above.)

285

- the remaining 33 weeks at the 'prescribed rate', which is currently £139.58 (for the tax year 2015/16), or at the earnings-related rate if that is lower – S.171ZN(2E)(b) and (2F) SSCBA. (The 'prescribed rate' is subject to revision every April.)

The new rate of SAP applies in relation to any adoption pay period which begins on or after 5 April 2015 – Reg 13 Children and Families Act 2014 (Commencement No.3, Transitional Provisions and Savings) Order 2014 SI 2014/1640. Prior to that date, SAP was paid at the rate set out in Reg 3 of the Statutory Paternity Pay and Statutory Adoption Pay (Weekly Rates) Regulations 2002 SI 2002/2818, which provided that the weekly rate of SAP was the lesser of the 'prescribed rate' or 90 per cent of the employee's normal weekly earnings.

The level of SAP is not affected by how many children are placed for adoption as part of the same arrangement – S.171ZL(5) SSCBA.

6.193 Period of payment of SAP

Provided the adoption is not disrupted (see 'Disruption of adoption' below) or the employee has not ended his or her adoption leave early (see 'Returning to work after adoption leave – notice of return during adopton leave' above) SAP is paid for a continuous period of 39 weeks – Reg 21(5) General Regulations. This 39-week period is termed the 'adoption pay period'.

Note that prior to amendment (by the Statutory Paternity Pay and Statutory Adoption Pay (General) and the Statutory Paternity Pay and Statutory Adoption Pay (Weekly Rates) (Amendment) Regulations 2006 SI 2006/2236) the adoption pay period was 26 weeks. The 2006 Regulations make no mention of overseas adoption and the extent of their application to such adoption is therefore unclear.

6.194

An employee can choose to begin the adoption pay period on:

- the date on which the child is placed with him or her or, where he or she is at work on that day, on the following day – Reg 21(1)(a)

- a predetermined date, specified by the adopter, which is no more than 14 days before the expected placement date and no later than that date – Reg 21(1)(b).

Where the employee has chosen a predetermined date under Reg 21(1)(b), the adoption pay period cannot begin earlier than 28 days after notice has been given in accordance with S.171ZL(6) SSCBA (see 'Notice requirements for SAP' above) unless the employer agrees to the adoption pay period beginning earlier – Reg 21(3). There is an exception where the beginning of the adoption pay period would be later than the date of placement, in which case the adoption pay period will begin on the date of placement – Reg 21(4).

An employee can change his or her mind about the starting date of the adoption **6.195** pay period provided that he or she gives the employer notice complying with S.171ZL(6) – Reg 21(6). This means that the employee must give the employer notice of the change at least 28 days before the date on which he or she expects SAP to begin, or if that is not reasonably practicable, as soon as is reasonably practicable thereafter.

Parental order parents. In the case of parental order parents, there is no option **6.196** to choose the date on which the adoption pay period begins. Instead, the adoption pay period always begins on the day on which the child is born or, where the person is at work on that day, the following day – Reg 17 Pay (Parental Orders) Regulations.

Future extension of adoption pay period. As noted at the beginning of this **6.197** chapter, the Work and Families Act 2006 introduced a framework for various amendments to maternity, adoption and other parental rights. S.2 of the 2006 Act amended S.171ZN(2) SSCBA to provide that the adoption pay period shall be 'of a duration not exceeding 52 weeks'. This paves the way for Reg 21(5) (which, as noted above, sets out the actual duration of the adoption pay period – currently 39 weeks) to be amended accordingly. This, in effect, would mean that the adoption pay period would cover the whole of the employee's AAL, as well as OAL. However, the introduction of the extended pay period has been postponed indefinitely.

Reduction of the adoption pay period. Conversely, S.171ZN(2A) SSCBA, **6.198** which was inserted by the Children and Families Act 2014 on 30 June 2014, provides that regulations may provide for the duration of the adoption pay period to be reduced. This is to take account of the new provisions on shared parental pay. Accordingly, Reg 9 of the Statutory Maternity Pay and Statutory Adoption Pay (Curtailment) Regulations 2014 SI 2014/3054 allows eligible adopters to curtail their adoption pay period in order to enable them, or their partner, to take shared parental leave – and receive statutory shared parental pay. The shared parental leave scheme is discussed in detail in Chapter 8, 'Shared parental leave and pay'.

Disruption of adoption
6.199

Regulation 22(1)–(3) and (5) General Regulations provides that the adoption pay period will terminate:

- (where the child dies after being placed for adoption) eight weeks after the end of the week during which the child dies

- (where the child is returned after being placed, i.e. under Ss.31–35 of the Adoption and Children Act 2002 or S.25(6) of the Adoption and Children (Scotland) Act 2007, or following termination of a placement under S.22C

287

of the Children Act 1989) eight weeks after the end of the week during which the child is returned, or

- (where the adoption pay period has begun before the child has been placed for adoption but the placement does not take place) eight weeks after the end of the week during which the prospective adopter is notified that the placement will not be made.

For these purposes, a 'week' means seven days beginning with Sunday – Reg 22(4).

These are very similar to the provisions of Reg 22 PAL Regulations governing disrupted placement in the course of the adoption leave period (see 'Disrupted placement during adoption leave' above).

6.200 **Parental order parents.** In surrogacy cases, Reg 22(1) General Regulations is modified to provide that the adoption pay period will terminate where:

- the child dies during adoption leave
- the employee does not apply for a parental order within the time limit set in S.54(3) of the Human Fertilisation and Embryology Act 2008, or
- the employee's application for a parental order for the child is refused, withdrawn or otherwise terminated without the order being granted and any time limit for an appeal or new application has expired – Reg 18(a) Pay (Parental Orders) Regulations.

Regulation 22(2), read with a modified Reg 22(3), provides that in these situations, the adoption pay period will end eight weeks after the end of:

- the week during which the child dies
- the week during which the time limit in S.54(3) of the Human Fertilisation and Embryology Act 2008 for an application for a parental order for the child expires, or
- the week in which the employee's application for a parental order is refused, withdrawn or otherwise terminated without the order being granted – Reg 18(b) Pay (Parental Orders) Regulations.

6.201 **Payment of statutory adoption pay**

Payments of SAP may be made 'in a like manner to payments of remuneration' but must not include payment in kind or by way of the provision of board or lodgings or of services or other facilities – Reg 41 General Regulations. Therefore deductions such as PAYE tax and national insurance contributions need to be made.

According to HMRC's 'Employer's Helpbook for statutory adoption pay' (E16 (2012)), this also means that, although SAP is a weekly payment, it can nevertheless be aligned to the employee's usual pay period. Therefore, if an employee is normally paid monthly, SAP can be paid on her normal pay day in any one month, in which case she will be entitled to receive the total sum of SAP payments that have fallen due since her last pay day.

Liability for SAP

6.202

Generally, the liability to pay SAP is on the employer who employs the employee claiming SAP – S.171ZM(1) SSCBA. However, a former employer will be liable to make payments of SAP to a former employee where the employee had been employed for a continuous period of at least eight weeks and his or her contract of service was brought to an end by the former employer solely, or mainly, for the purpose of avoiding liability for SAP – Reg 30(1) General Regulations.

In such a case, regardless of the date of dismissal, for the purposes of SAP the employee is treated as if he or she had been employed for a continuous period ending with the week in which he or she was notified of having been matched with the child for adoption – Reg 30(2)(a). (A parental order parent is treated as if he or she had been employed for a continuous period ending with the week immediately preceding the 14th week before the expected week of the child's birth – Reg 23 Pay (Parental Orders) Regulations.) The employee's normal weekly earnings will be calculated on the basis of his or her last eight weeks' earnings (under the former contract of service) – Reg 30(2)(b). Note that the dismissal would also be automatically unfair and could constitute an act of unlawful discrimination – see Chapter 12, 'Detriment and unfair dismissal', and Chapter 13, 'Discrimination and equal pay'.

Aggregation of earnings under different contracts/employers. If an employee 6.203 works under more than one contract for the *same* employer, then the employer must treat the different contracts as one for the purposes of SAP – Reg 38(3) General Regulations. However, an employer is not required to aggregate earnings under different contracts if such aggregation is not reasonably practicable because the earnings under the respective contracts are separately calculated – Reg 14 Social Security (Contributions) Regulations 2001 SI 2001/1004 ('the 2001 Regulations'). Similar provisions apply where an employee is employed under separate contracts with two associated employers – Reg 15(1) 2001 Regulations.

Where an employee works under more than one contract for *different* employers who are not associated, he or she is not usually entitled to aggregate his or her earnings since liability for paying national insurance contributions lies separately with each individual employer (he or she may be entitled to SAP from each one, however). In a few rare cases (other than those concerning associated employers) the earnings paid to an employee under two contracts can be aggregated and treated as a single payment of earnings for national insurance purposes – see Reg 15(1) 2001 Regulations. In these situations,

289

liability for SAP is apportioned between the employers, either in the proportions which they agree or, if they cannot agree, in the proportion which the employee's earnings bear to the amount of the aggregated earnings – Reg 38(1) and (2) General Regulations.

6.204 *NHS employees.* The Statutory Paternity Pay and Statutory Adoption Pay (National Health Service Employees) Regulations 2002 SI 2002/2819 make provision for certain NHS employees whose contracts of employment have been divided into two or more contracts with different bodies to elect to have those contracts treated as one contract, and for one of the employee's employers to be regarded as his or her employer for the purposes of entitlement to SAP (as well as statutory paternity pay – see Chapter 7, 'Paternity leave and pay').

6.205 **HM Revenue and Customs.** Regulation 43 General Regulations makes HMRC liable to pay SAP that is due where the employer has failed to do so.

The basic position is that HMRC becomes liable where:

- it has decided that an employer is liable to pay SAP

- the time for appealing against its decision has expired, and

- no appeal against the decision has been lodged (or leave to appeal against the decision is required and has been refused).

Where HMRC becomes liable for the payment of SAP, the first payment will be made as soon as reasonably practicable after it becomes liable, and payments thereafter will be made at weekly intervals – Reg 45.

6.206 *Insolvency.* Where the employer is insolvent, HMRC will be liable as from the week in which the employer first becomes insolvent until the end of the adoption pay period – Reg 43(2).

6.207 *Legal custody or imprisonment.* HMRC will be liable to pay SAP instead of the employer where SAP is due:

- in respect of a period directly after a week during any part of which the employee was detained in legal custody or sentenced to a term of imprisonment (not suspended), or

- during a period of detention in legal custody where the employee is released without charge, subsequently found not guilty and released, or is convicted but does not receive a custodial sentence – Regs 44 and 27 (see 'Disentitlement to SAP' below).

6.208 **Persons/employees unable to act**
Where SAP is payable to a person who is unable for the time being to act and no receiver has been appointed by the Court of Protection with power to receive SAP on his or her behalf (or, in Scotland, the person's estate is not being

administered by any tutor, curator or other guardian acting or appointed in terms of law), HMRC may, upon written application by a person over 18, appoint that person to exercise any right to payment on behalf of the person unable to act – Reg 46(1) General Regulations. SAP is then payable to that person and he or she will take on the employee's rights and obligations in respect of SAP.

Disentitlement to SAP

6.209

There are several circumstances in which an employer will not be liable to pay SAP because the employee becomes disentitled. Note that an employee does not become disentitled simply because he or she does not return to work after adoption leave.

Working for employer during adoption pay period. Under S.171ZN(3) SSCBA an employer is not liable to pay SAP to an employee in respect of any week during any part of which the employee works under a contract of service for the employer. It is immaterial whether the contract of service under which the work is carried out existed immediately before the adoption pay period or not – S.171ZN(4). 'Week' means a period of seven days beginning with the day of the week on which the adoption pay period began – S.171ZN(8).

6.210

There is one important proviso to this. As noted under 'Keeping in touch during adoption leave' above, if the employer and the employee agree, an employee can work for up to ten keeping-in-touch ('KIT') days without losing his or her SAP entitlement for the weeks in which that work is done. The amount of pay the employee receives for work done is subject to agreement but the minimum the employer must pay is the SAP rate the employee is entitled to.

Therefore, if a week in the SAP pay period contains only KIT days, SAP should be paid as normal. However, if a week in the SAP pay period contains the last of the KIT days plus an additional day or days of work, or only additional days where the employee has used up all his or her KIT days, the employer must stop SAP for that week and for any additional week in which work is done.

6.211

Working for another employer during adoption pay period. The general rule is that an employee loses entitlement to SAP from an employer (Employer A) in respect of any week of the adoption pay period during which he or she works for another employer (Employer B) who is not liable to pay SAP – S.171ZN(5) SSCBA. Furthermore, in such a situation, Employer A is not liable to pay SAP for the remainder of the adoption pay period, starting from the week the employee started to work for Employer B – Reg 26(1) General Regulations. Even if the employee stopped working with the other employer before the end of the adoption pay period, he or she would seemingly not be entitled to receive SAP for the remainder of the period.

6.212

'Week' for these purposes means a period of seven days beginning with the day of the week on which the adoption pay period began – S.171ZN(8).

6.213 However, there is an exception under Reg 25 General Regulations, which preserves an employee's entitlement to SAP from Employer A when he or she works for Employer B during the SAP period if:

- Employer B is not liable to pay him or her SAP, and

- he or she worked for Employer B in the week in which he or she was notified of being matched with the child (or, in the case of a parental order parent, in the week immediately preceding the 14th week before the expected week of the child's birth – Reg 21 Pay (Parental Orders) Regulations).

The effect of this provision is that an employee who has a second, low-paid job at the time the adoption agency tells him or her that he or she has been matched with a child is not obliged to give up that job during adoption leave in order to preserve entitlement to SAP from the main employer. However, the requirement that the employee must have worked for Employer B during the notification week prevents the employee from taking up a new job while claiming SAP from Employer A.

6.214 It appears that the employee only has to show that he or she worked for Employer B at some point during the notification week, so one day of work would suffice. However, the wording of Reg 25 suggests that the employee does actually have to be working for Employer B during the notification week. So if, for example, the employee works for Employer B in alternate weeks and does not happen to be working for Employer B during the notification week (even if he or she is still employed by him), the employee would lose entitlement to SAP from Employer A if he or she worked for Employer B during the SAP period. It is the duty of the employee to inform Employer A that he or she has started work for another employer if this affects Employer A's liability to pay SAP – Reg 26(2). This notification must be in writing if Employer A so requests – Reg 26(3).

6.215 **Illness and death.** There is no liability to pay SAP in respect of any week:

- during any part of which the adopter is entitled to statutory sick pay, or

- following the week in which the person claiming it has died – Reg 27(1)(a) and (b) General Regulations.

(Where the child dies during the SAP pay period, the pay period will end eight weeks after the end of the week in which the child dies, if it was not due to end earlier – Reg 22.)

6.216 **Legal custody or imprisonment.** Similarly, there is no liability on the employer to pay SAP in respect of any week during any part of which the person entitled to it is detained in legal custody or sentenced to a term of imprisonment (except where the sentence is suspended) – Reg 27(1)(c). However, HMRC is liable to pay SAP in respect of any week during which the employee is detained in legal custody if the employee is:

* subsequently released without charge

* subsequently found not guilty of any offence and released, or

* convicted of an offence but does not receive a custodial sentence – Reg 27(2) (see 'Liability for SAP – HM Revenue and Customs' above).

SAP and contractual remuneration   6.217

Under S.171ZP(4) SSCBA, any entitlement to SAP does not affect any right to remuneration under the contract of employment. However, certain contractual payments to an employee can be offset against SAP and *vice versa* – S.171ZP(5). If any contractual remuneration is payable for any week during which SAP is due, it can be treated as reducing or extinguishing the liability to SAP for that week. Similarly, if SAP is paid for any week, it can go towards discharging any liability to pay contractual remuneration in respect of that period.

Payments that are to be treated as contractual remuneration for these purposes are sums payable under a contract of service:

* by way of remuneration ('remuneration' is not defined in the General Regulations but the definition of remuneration for adoption leave purposes may provide some guidance – see 'Terms and conditions during adoption leave – remuneration' above)

* for incapacity for work due to sickness or injury

* by reason of the adoption of a child – Reg 28 General Regulations.

If any of the above payments is payable for any week during which SAP is due, **6.218** it can be treated as reducing or extinguishing the liability to SAP for that week.

Alternatively, the employer can pay SAP in the normal way and withhold a corresponding sum from any contractual payment falling within Reg 28. In effect, this means that an employee can never claim SAP in addition to his or her contractual pay.

Termination of employment before start of SAP   6.219

Where an employee who is entitled to SAP is dismissed or leaves employment before the adoption pay period has begun, his or her right to SAP is retained – Reg 29 General Regulations. The adoption pay period will then begin:

* 14 days before the expected placement date, or

- on the day immediately following the employee's last day of employment where the termination occurs on or within 14 days before the expected placement date – Reg 29(1).

In these circumstances the notice requirements set out in S.171ZL(6) SSCBA and Reg 23 General Regulations (see 'Notice requirements for SAP' above) do not apply – Reg 29(2).

6.220 *An example.* Employee Z is dismissed on 6 March and the expected placement date is 25 April. Therefore the adoption pay period will begin on 11 April. However, if the expected placement date was instead 15 March, the adoption pay period would begin on 7 March (the day after dismissal).

6.221 **Parental order parents.** In surrogacy cases, Reg 29 is modified so as to provide that the adoption pay period will begin on the day the child is born – Reg 22 Pay (Parental Orders) Regulations.

6.222 **Contracting out**

Any agreement will be void to the extent that it purports to:

- exclude, limit or modify any provision of the SAP scheme, or
- require an employee to contribute to any costs incurred by the employer under such schemes – S.171ZO(1) SSCBA.

However, some agreements to make deductions from SAP are acceptable. Under S.171ZO(2) an agreement between employer and employee authorising deductions from SAP is not void if the employer is contractually authorised to make the same deductions from the equivalent contractual remuneration. So, an employer may be able to continue making deductions in respect of, for example, pension contributions or trade union subscriptions.

Similarly, SAP is treated as earnings, so an employer should make any statutory deductions (such as income tax and national insurance contributions) that are due.

7 Paternity leave and pay

Who has the right?

Entitlement to paternity leave (birth)

Entitlement to paternity leave (adoption)

Entitlement to paternity leave (surrogacy)

Commencement and duration of paternity leave

Notice and evidential requirements for paternity leave

Employment protection during and after paternity leave

Statutory paternity pay

Since April 2003, fathers (and other eligible employees) have been entitled to **7.1** take up to two weeks' paid paternity leave on the birth or placement for adoption of a child. This right was introduced with the dual aim of supporting the child's mother or adopter and helping to care for the child in the initial period following the birth or placement for adoption. The right is now also available to foster parents and intended parents in a surrogacy arrangement.

The right to take paternity leave is governed by Ss.80A–80E of the Employment Rights Act 1996 (ERA) and Part 2 of the Paternity and Adoption Leave Regulations 2002 SI 2002/2788 ('the PAL Regulations'). (The equivalent provisions in Northern Ireland are the Paternity and Adoption Leave Regulations (Northern Ireland) 2002 SR 2002/377.) The right to statutory paternity pay (SPP) is governed by the Social Security Contributions and Benefits Act 1992 (SSCBA) and the Statutory Paternity Pay and Statutory Adoption Pay (General) Regulations 2002 SI 2002/2822 (or, in Northern Ireland, the Statutory Paternity Pay and Statutory Adoption Pay (General) Regulations (Northern Ireland) 2002 SR 2002/378). Many of the qualifying conditions for each right are the same and so there is a considerable amount of duplication. In this chapter we set out the details of all the Regulations that apply to each particular right for the sake of precision and ease of location. Further information on the rights of new fathers and adoptive parents can be found on the Government's public service information website www.gov.uk, as well as the Acas website www.acas.org.uk.

Abolition of additional paternity leave. Until very recently, fathers (and other **7.2** eligible employees) also had the right to take additional paternity leave (APL) of up to 26 weeks following the birth or adoption of a child if the mother or adopter returned to work early (see the Additional Paternity Leave Regulations

295

2010 SI 2010/1055). They also had a right to additional statutory paternity pay (ASPP) if the mother or adopter had not used up his or her entitlement to statutory maternity pay, maternity allowance or statutory adoption pay at the time of his or her return to work (see the Additional Statutory Paternity Pay (General) Regulations 2010 SI 2010/1056). However, the additional paternity leave and pay scheme was abolished on 5 April 2015 by S.125 of the Children and Families Act 2014. In its place the Government has introduced the right for parents whose baby is expected on or after 5 April 2015 to take shared parental leave and pay.

This new scheme allows a woman who is eligible for statutory maternity leave and statutory maternity pay to choose to curtail her entitlement to maternity leave and pay and to share the balance with the father of her child (or her spouse, civil partner or partner). Unlike APL, where the mother 'transferred' her unused leave to the father, the shared parental leave and pay scheme allows parents to share the remaining pot of leave. Similar rights apply to employees who adopt (for children who are placed for adoption on or after 5 April 2015) and to parents of a child born through a surrogacy arrangement if they have a parental order (or have applied or intend to apply for such an order) and are eligible for adoption leave. For full details of this new shared parental leave and pay scheme, see Chapter 8, 'Shared parental leave and pay'.

7.3 Note that the right to APL and ASPP still applies in respect of children born (or placed for adoption) before 5 April. Details of the scheme can be found in the previous edition of this Handbook, 'Maternity and Parental Rights' (2012), Chapter 7, 'Paternity leave and pay', under 'Additional paternity leave' and 'Additional statutory paternity pay'.

7.4 Unpaid parental leave and time off rights. The right to statutory paternity leave is in addition to the right to take up to 18 weeks' unpaid parental leave and the right to unpaid time off to care for dependants for urgent family reasons – see further Chapter 10, 'Unpaid parental leave', and Chapter 11, 'Time off for dependants'.

7.5 European law. Unlike the right to maternity leave, the right to paternity leave in domestic law does not derive from an EU Directive. Attempts to legislate for paternity leave at EU level have not proved successful. In October 2008, for example, the European Commission published proposals to amend the EU Pregnant Workers Directive (No.92/85) to give men at least two weeks' non-transferable paternity leave, on the same terms and conditions as maternity leave (except for duration). Had this proposal been adopted, UK law would have had to allow for two weeks' statutory paternity leave paid at 90 per cent of actual wages (as is the case with the start of maternity leave), as opposed to being capped at (currently) £139.58. However, the revised Directive as approved by the European Parliament was rejected by the Council of Ministers in December 2010.

Who has the right?

Inevitably, when one refers to 'paternity' leave and pay, one thinks predominantly of fathers. While fathers certainly can – and do – take paternity leave, they are not the only ones eligible. Notably, women may also be entitled, depending upon the circumstances. The following individuals are entitled to paternity leave and pay, provided they satisfy the relevant qualifying conditions:

- fathers of newborn children (whether or not they are biological fathers)
- adoptive parents (specifically, the person in the couple not taking adoption leave/pay)
- foster parents (who are not taking adoption leave/pay)
- intended parents in a surrogacy arrangement (who are not taking adoption leave/pay).

We consider each category in turn below. First, however, we look at the definition of 'employee', as only those workers who are 'employees' can benefit from the right to paternity leave and pay.

Employees only

Only employees can benefit from the right to paternity leave and pay. The definition of 'employee' for paternity leave purposes is different from the definition of employee for SPP purposes. This means that some workers who are excluded from the right to take paternity leave may nonetheless be entitled to SPP, and vice versa.

Definition of 'employee' – paternity leave. Paternity leave can only be taken 7.8 by employees and not by other types of 'worker' or the self-employed – see Ss.80A–80BB of the Employment Rights Act 1996 (ERA). 'Employee' for these purposes means an individual who has entered into or works under (or, where the employment has ceased, worked under) a contract of employment, which is defined as a contract of service or apprenticeship, whether express or implied, and (if express) whether oral or in writing – S.230(1) ERA and Reg 2(1) PAL Regulations. These definitions are identical to those that apply for the purposes of unfair dismissal and redundancy and reference should be made to IDS Employment Law Handbook, 'Contracts of Employment' (2014), Chapter 2, 'Employment status', for discussion of the law in this area.

Members of the armed forces, share fishermen and the police are specifically excluded from the statutory right to take paternity leave – Ss.192 (read with para 16, Sch 2), 199(2) and 200 ERA. However, seafarers employed on ships registered under S.8 of the Merchant Shipping Act 1995 are covered provided that the ship is registered as belonging to a port in Great Britain; that under the contract of employment the employee does not work wholly outside Great

297

Britain; and that he or she is ordinarily resident in Great Britain – S.199(7) and (8). Crown employees are also covered, as are parliamentary staff – Ss.191, 194 and 195.

7.9 **Definition of 'employee' – SPP.** The definition of 'employee' for SPP purposes differs from the definition that applies for paternity leave purposes. S.171ZJ SSCBA, which governs SPP, provides that 'employee' means a person:

- who is gainfully employed either under a contract of service or as an office holder (including an elective office), and

- with general earnings, as defined by S.7 of the Income Tax (Earnings and Pensions) Act 2003 (i.e. any salary, wages or fee; any gratuity or other profit or incidental benefit of any kind if it is money or money's worth; or anything else that constitutes an emolument of the employment).

In addition, there are special cases where a worker will be considered an employee for SPP purposes, despite not falling within the definition set out in S.171ZJ.

7.10 As a result of this wider definition, some workers who are excluded from the right to take paternity leave may nonetheless be entitled to SPP, which they could presumably take if they have a contractual right to paternity leave. In addition, there may be rare cases where a worker satisfies the conditions for paternity leave – but not for SPL.

For further discussion of eligibility for SPL, see 'Statutory paternity pay – employed earners' below.

7.11 **Birth fathers, spouses and partners**
The child's father is eligible for paternity leave and pay by virtue of Reg 4(2)(b)(i) PAL Regulations and Reg 4 General Regulations. The mother's spouse, civil partner or partner can also claim paternity leave and pay, i.e. even if not the child's biological father – Reg 4(2)(b)(ii) PAL Regulations and Reg 4 General Regulations.

A 'civil partner' is a person who has entered into a civil partnership with a person of the same sex under the Civil Partnership Act 2004. A 'partner' is a person, whether of a different sex or of the same sex, who lives with the mother and the child in 'an enduring family relationship' but is not a relative of the mother – Reg 2(1) PAL Regulations (this definition also applies to SPP by virtue of Reg 4 General Regulations). Thus in certain circumstances a woman will be able to take 'paternity' leave upon the birth of a child. The relatives of the mother who are expressly prohibited from being a partner for these purposes are the mother's parents, grandparents, sisters, brothers, aunts and uncles, whether they are full blood or half blood or, in the case of an adopted person, such of those relationships as would exist but for the adoption (i.e. her birth family) – Reg 2(2) and (3)(a) PAL Regulations. The mother's adoptive, or former adoptive, parents are also prohibited from being a partner but not other adoptive relationships – Reg 2(3)(b) PAL Regulations. Thus, if the mother is adopted, her adoptive parents would be excluded but not, it seems, her adoptive brother. The Regulations offer no indication of what is meant by 'an enduring family relationship', but we assume that the enduring nature will be measured by reference to the time the relationship with the mother has already lasted rather than on any forecast of how long the relationship with the mother (and baby) will last in the future. Presumably the degree of commitment to the relationship will also be a relevant factor.

Where an employee is the biological father of the child, he must have (or expect **7.12** to have) responsibility for the upbringing of that child in order to qualify for SPP – Reg 4(2)(c)(i) PAL Regulations and Reg 4 General Regulations. Where an employee is the spouse or partner of the mother, he (or she) must have (or expect to have) the main responsibility for the child (apart from any responsibility of the mother) – Reg 4 General Regulations and Reg 4(2)(c)(ii) PAL Regulations.

Adoptive parents   **7.13**
Paternity leave and pay is available to an adopter's spouse, civil partner or partner where a child is placed for adoption – Reg 8(2)(b) PAL Regulations and Reg 11(1) General Regulations. The right applies only in relation to children who are under 18, or under 18 when placed with an adopter for adoption – Reg 2(1) PAL Regulations. The meanings of 'civil partner' and 'partner' are discussed under 'Birth fathers, spouses and partners' above. An 'adopter' is a person who has been matched with the child for adoption or, where two people have been matched jointly, whichever of them has elected to be the child's adopter for these purposes – Reg 2(1) PAL Regulations; Reg 2(1) General Regulations. A person elects to be a child's adopter if he or she and the other person agree at the time they are matched that he or she (and not the other person) will be the adopter – Reg 2(4)(c) PAL Regulations. The adopter will, of course, be entitled to claim adoption leave – see Chapter 6, 'Adoption leave and pay'.

The spouse or partner must have or expect to have the main responsibility (apart from the responsibility of the adopter) for the upbringing of the child – Reg 8(1)(c) PAL Regulations and Reg 11(1)(b) General Regulations.

It is possible for a woman to take paternity leave where a couple adopts a child **7.14** and the adoptive father takes adoption leave, or where two women in a relationship adopt a child. Following the introduction of the Civil Partnership Act 2004 and changes made to the Adoption and Children Act 2002, the same rights and entitlements are available to two people of the same sex who are living together as partners or as civil partners and who are adopting a child together. Again, one person can take adoption leave and the other paternity leave.

299

7.15 Adoption from overseas. Employees who adopt from overseas are also entitled to paternity leave and pay by virtue of the following Regulations:

- the Employment Rights Act 1996 (Application of Section 80B to Adoptions from Overseas) Regulations 2003 SI 2003/920

- the Paternity and Adoption Leave (Adoption from Overseas) Regulations 2003 SI 2003/921

- the Social Security Contributions and Benefits Act 1992 (Application of Parts 12ZA, 12ZB and 12ZC to Adoptions from Overseas) Regulations 2003 SI 2003/499, and

- the Statutory Paternity Pay (Adoption) and Statutory Adoption Pay (Adoptions from Overseas) (No.2) Regulations 2003 SI 2003/1194.

7.16 Foster parents

As a result of changes introduced by the Paternity and Adoption Leave (Amendment) (No.2) Regulations 2014 SI 2014/3206 ('the PAL (Amendment) (No.2) Regulations'), local authority foster parents who are approved prospective adopters are entitled to claim adoption leave where a child is placed with them with a view to adoption under S.22C of the Children Act 1989 – see Chapter 6, 'Adoption leave and pay', under 'Ordinary adoption leave – who has the right?'. Reg 2(4) PAL Regulations (as amended) makes it clear that a child is 'placed for adoption' if he or she is 'placed… with a local authority foster parent who is also a prospective adopter'. The spouses, civil partners and partners of such foster parents are entitled to paternity leave. The conditions of eligibility are the same as apply to the spouses and partners of adoptive parents – see 'Entitlement to paternity leave (adoption)' below. The new rights apply to foster parents who are notified of having been matched with a child on or after 5 April 2015. (A foster parent is notified of having been matched with a child on the date on which he or she receives notification from the adoption agency of the decision to place the child with him or her for adoption – Reg 2(4)(d) PAL Regulations.)

Regulation 15(1A) prevents a spouse/partner taking two periods of paternity leave in respect of the same child – i.e. when the child is placed with him or her under the 'fostering for adoption' scheme and then again when the child is placed with him or her for adoption. Once the spouse/partner has taken paternity leave at the time of the child's 'fostering for adoption' placement, his or her entitlement to paternity leave under the PAL Regulations is extinguished. The same applies in respect of a foster parent's entitlement to statutory adoption leave (SAL) – Reg 8(1A)(c).

7.17 Foster parents have correlative rights to statutory adoption pay (SAP) and SPP by virtue of the Statutory Paternity Pay and Statutory Adoption Pay (Parental Orders and Prospective Adopters) Regulations 2014 SI 2014/2934.

Surrogacy 7.18

Under the Paternity, Adoption and Shared Parental Leave (Parental Order Cases) Regulations 2014 SI 2014/3096 ('the Leave (Parental Order Cases) Regulations') the right to take adoption leave and paternity leave has been extended to parents in a surrogacy arrangement who:

- have acquired a parental order under S.54(1) of the Human Fertilisation and Embryology Act 2008 in respect of a child, or

- have applied, or intend to apply within six months of the child's birth, for a parental order, which it is expected will be granted by the court.

Such parents are referred to as 'parental order parents' by the legislation. The parent who is entitled to take adoption leave is the one who has elected to be 'Parent A' in accordance with Reg 2(4) PAL Regulations (as modified by Reg 6 Leave (Parental Order Cases) Regulations). Simply put, a person elects to be Parent A in relation to a child if this is agreed by the couple. The other parent is eligible for statutory paternity leave provided he or she is the spouse, civil partner or partner of Parent A when the child is born. The new rights apply where the expected week of birth began on or after 5 April 2015.

Parental order parents have correlative rights to SAP and SPP by virtue of the **7.19** following Regulations:

- the Social Security Contributions and Benefits Act 1992 (Application of Parts 12ZA, 12ZB and 12ZC to Parental Order Cases) Regulations 2014 SI 2014/2866, and

- the Statutory Paternity Pay and Statutory Adoption Pay (Parental Orders and Prospective Adopters) Regulations 2014 SI 2014/2934 ('the Pay (Parental Orders) Regulations').

Entitlement to paternity leave (birth) 7.20

Under Reg 4(1) PAL Regulations an employee is entitled to paternity leave following the birth of a child where the purpose of the absence is:

- to care for the child, or

- to support the child's mother

provided that he or she satisfies the conditions contained in Reg 4(2) (see below) and has complied with the notice and evidential requirements set out in Reg 6 (see 'Notice and evidential requirements for paternity leave – notice requirements (birth)' below). An employee is not entitled to paternity leave for purposes other than those specified in Reg 4(1). Although S.80A(5)(a) ERA states that regulations may specify things which are, or are not, to be taken as done for the purpose of caring for a newborn child or supporting the child's mother, the PAL

Regulations contain no such provision. Note that in the case of multiple births, only one period of paternity leave can be taken – Reg 4(6).

7.21 The conditions of entitlement to paternity leave set out in Reg 4(2) are that the employee:

- has been continuously employed for at least 26 weeks ending with the 15th week before the expected week of birth – Reg 4(2)(a). Continuous employment is calculated in accordance with the continuity provisions in the ERA – Reg 2(5) (see IDS Employment Law Handbook, 'Continuity of Employment' (2012), Chapter 1, 'The general framework'). The 'expected week' of birth means the week beginning with midnight between Saturday and Sunday in which it is expected that the child will be born – Reg 2(1)

- is the father of the child; or is the mother's spouse, civil partner or partner but is not the child's father – Reg 4(2)(b) (see 'Who has the right? – birth fathers, spouses and partners' above)

- has, or expects to have, if the child's father, responsibility for the upbringing of the child. If the employee is the mother's spouse, civil partner or partner, but not the child's father, he or she must have, or expect to have, the main responsibility (apart from any responsibility of the mother) for the upbringing of the child – Reg 4(2)(c) (see 'Who has the right? – birth fathers, spouses and partners' above).

7.22 Note that in order to claim statutory paternity pay, the employee must stay in the same employment, or in employment with an associated employer, until the day on which the child is born – see 'Statutory paternity pay – qualifying for SPP' below. There is no equivalent condition expressly attached to paternity leave.

It is important to note that an employee is not eligible for paternity leave if he or she has taken any shared parental leave (SPL) in respect of the child – Reg 4(1A) PAL Regulations. Fathers (or spouses/partners) should therefore make sure they take their paternity leave entitlement before taking any SPL. Commonly, they will do so while the mother is on compulsory maternity leave. Full details of the SPL scheme can be found in Chapter 8, 'Shared parental leave and pay'. Compulsory maternity leave is dealt with in Chapter 3, 'Maternity leave', under 'Compulsory maternity leave'.

7.23 Special cases
The PAL Regulations provide that a person who would satisfy the above conditions but for the fact that certain specified events – listed below – have occurred will not lose his or her right to paternity leave.

7.24 Premature birth. Regulation 4(3) states that an employee will be treated as having satisfied the continuous employment condition in Reg 4(2)(a) if he or she would have satisfied it but for the fact that the child was born earlier than expected. In other words, where the child is born prematurely, the fact that this results in the employee having less than 26 weeks' continuous employment by the date of the birth will be disregarded for the purpose of qualifying for paternity leave.

Death of mother. Regulation 4(4) provides that an employee will be treated as **7.25** satisfying the condition relating to the employee's relationship with the child's mother in Reg 4(2)(b) if he or she would have satisfied it but for the fact that the child's mother has died.

Stillbirth or death of child. Lastly, Reg 4(5) states that an employee will be **7.26** treated as satisfying the condition relating to the upbringing of the child in Reg 4(2)(c) if he or she would have satisfied it but for the fact that the child was stillborn after 24 weeks of pregnancy or has died. Where a pregnancy ends before 24 weeks and the child does not survive – in other words, the mother has a miscarriage – the father (or mother's spouse/partner) will not be able to take paternity leave. However, he or she may be able to take some unpaid time off – see Chapter 10, 'Unpaid parental leave'.

Entitlement to paternity leave (adoption) 7.27

Under Reg 8(1) PAL Regulations an employee is entitled to be absent from work on paternity leave where the purpose of the absence is:

- to care for a child, or

- to support the child's adopter

provided he or she also satisfies the conditions specified in Reg 8(2) (see below) and has complied with the notice and evidential requirements in Reg 10 (see 'Notice and evidential requirements for paternity leave – notice requirements (adoption)' below). Although S.80B(5)(a) ERA states that regulations may specify things which are, or are not, to be taken as done for the purpose of caring for a child or supporting the child's adopter, no such provision is contained in the PAL Regulations.

The conditions of entitlement to paternity leave in Reg 8(2) are that **7.28** the employee:

- has been continuously employed for at least 26 weeks ending with the week in which the child's adopter is notified of having been matched with the child – Reg 8(2)(a). A 'week' is defined as the period of seven days beginning with Sunday – Reg 8(3). Continuous employment is calculated in accordance with the continuity provisions in the ERA – Reg 2(5) (see IDS Employment Law Handbook, 'Continuity of Employment' (2012), Chapter 1, 'The general framework')

303

- is either married to, or the civil partner or the partner of, the adopter – Reg 8(2)(b) (see 'Who has the right? – adoptive parents' above)

- has, or expects to have, the main responsibility (apart from the responsibility of the adopter) for the upbringing of the child – Reg 8(2)(c) (see 'Who has the right? – adoptive parents' above).

Note that in order to claim SPP, the employee must stay in the same employment, or employment with an associated employer, until the day on which the child is placed for adoption – see 'Statutory paternity pay – qualifying for SPP' below. There is no equivalent condition expressly attached to paternity leave.

7.29 An employee is still entitled to take paternity leave if the child's adopter dies during the child's placement or if the child's placement with the adopter has ended – Reg 8(4) and (5). Where more than one child is being adopted as part of the same arrangement only one period of paternity leave can be taken – Reg 8(6).

An employee is not, however, eligible for paternity leave if he or she has taken any shared parental leave in respect of the child – Reg 8(1A) PAL Regulations. Similarly, where the employee has exercised the right to paid time off under S.57ZJ ERA to attend adoption appointments, he or she is then no longer entitled to take paternity leave in respect of the same child when the child is placed for adoption – Reg 8(1A)(b). The right for employees to take time off work to attend appointments in advance of a child being placed with them for adoption is fully discussed in Chapter 6, 'Adoption leave and pay', under 'Time off for adoption appointments'.

7.30 Adopting children from outside UK
The PAL Regulations by themselves only cover domestic adoptions. However, two sets of regulations – the Employment Rights Act 1996 (Application of Section 80B to Adoptions from Overseas) Regulations 2003 SI 2003/920 and the Paternity and Adoption Leave (Adoption from Overseas) Regulations 2003 SI 2003/921 ('the Adoption from Overseas Regulations') deal with the entitlement to paternity leave in respect of adoptions from overseas. The first set of Regulations mentioned above modifies S.80B ERA to extend the powers under which the Secretary of State may make regulations in order to deal with this scenario. Pursuant to that power, the second set of Regulations – by virtue of Reg 3 – modifies the relevant provisions of the PAL Regulations in relation to their application to overseas adoptions.

The right to paternity leave is available to an employee if the child's adopter has received an official notification of his or her suitability to adopt – Reg 8(2)(a) PAL Regulations, as modified by Reg 7 Adoption from Overseas Regulations. Official notification means written notification issued by or on behalf of the relevant domestic authority that it is prepared to issue a certificate to the overseas authority concerned with the adoption of the child, or has issued a certificate and sent it to that authority, confirming, in either case, that the adopter is eligible to adopt and has been assessed and approved as being a suitable adoptive parent – Reg 4(2)(b) Adoption from Overseas Regulations. The relevant domestic authority in England will normally be the Department for Education; in Wales, the National Assembly for Wales; and in Scotland, the Scottish Ministers.

The paternity leave provisions in the case of overseas adoptions are by and **7.31** large the same as those applying to UK adoptions, except that the employee must have 26 weeks' continuous employment by the end of the week in which the adopter receives official notification or by the time he or she wants the leave to begin, whichever is later – Reg 8(2)(b) PAL Regulations, as modified by Reg 7 Adoption from Overseas Regulations. Paternity leave cannot be taken until the child enters Great Britain – Reg 9(2) PAL Regulations, as modified by Reg 7 Adoption from Overseas Regulations.

The main differences relate to the notice requirements. These are discussed under 'Notice and evidential requirements for paternity leave – notice requirements (adoption)' below.

Entitlement to paternity leave (surrogacy) 7.32

The right to statutory adoption leave and paternity leave applies to parents of a child born through a surrogacy arrangement if they have a parental order under S.54(1) of the Human Fertilisation and Embryology Act 2008 (or have applied or intend to apply for such an order). They are referred to as 'parental order parents' by the Paternity, Adoption and Shared Parental Leave (Parental Order Cases) Regulations 2014 SI 2014/3096 ('the Leave (Parental Order Cases) Regulations'). The person who is entitled to take adoption leave is the one who has agreed to be 'Parent A'. Parent A's spouse, civil partner or partner is entitled to paternity leave, provided he or she satisfies the relevant qualifying conditions – see 'Who has the right? – surrogacy' above.

The conditions for paternity leave are set out in Reg 8, i.e. the same as for adoptive parents. Importantly, however, these provisions are modified by Part 2 of the Leave (Parental Order Cases) Regulations.

Under Reg 8(1) PAL Regulations (as modified) an employee is entitled to be **7.33** absent from work on paternity leave where the purpose of the absence is:

- to care for a child, or

- to support Parent A.

He or she must also satisfy the conditions specified in Reg 8(2) (as modified) (see below), and comply with the notice and the evidential requirements in Reg 10 (as modified) (see 'Notice and evidential requirements for paternity

305

leave – notice requirements (surrogacy)' below). Reg 8(2) (as modified) provides that the employee must:

- have been continuously employed for at least 26 weeks ending with the 15th week before the expected week of birth – Reg 8(2)(a)

- be either married to, or the civil partner or the partner of, Parent A – Reg 8(2)(b) (see 'Who has the right? – surrogacy' above)

- have, or expect to have, the main responsibility (apart from the responsibility of Parent A) for the upbringing of the child – Reg 8(2)(c), or

- be a parental order parent of the child – Reg 8(2)(d).

7.34 An employee will be treated as satisfying the condition relating to the employee's relationship with the child's mother in Reg 8(2)(b) if he or she would have satisfied it but for the fact that Parent A has died – Reg 8(4) (as modified). In addition, an employee will be treated as having satisfied the continuous employment condition in Reg 8(2)(a) if he or she would have satisfied it but for the fact that the child was born earlier than expected – Reg 8(7) (inserted by Reg 9 Leave (Parental Order Cases) Regulations). Lastly, an employee will be treated as satisfying the condition relating to the upbringing of the child in Reg 8(2)(c) if he or she would have satisfied it but for the fact that the child was stillborn after 24 weeks of pregnancy or has died – para 8(5) (as modified).

7.35 Commencement and duration of paternity leave

An employee entitled to paternity leave may choose to take either one week's leave or two consecutive weeks' leave – Reg 5(1) (birth); Reg 9(1) (adoption). He or she cannot take odd days or two weeks that are not consecutive. A 'week' is not defined in Reg 5/Reg 9, but under S.80A(7) ERA it is defined as any period of seven days. S.171ZE(11) SSCBA, which governs the payment of SPP, similarly defines a 'week' as any period of seven days. It therefore seems that the week may commence on any day. This is reinforced by Reg 5(2)(a)/ Reg 9(3)(a), which provide that the employee may begin his or her leave on the day on which the child is born/placed for adoption (see below).

There is a 56-day period within which paternity leave must be taken. This is dealt with by Reg 5(2) for birth parents, Reg 9(2) for adoptive parents, and Reg 9(2) (as modified by Reg 10 Leave (Parental Order Cases) Regulations) for parental order parents.

7.36 When can paternity leave be taken? (birth/surrogacy)

For birth and parental order parents, paternity leave cannot begin before the day of the child's birth and must be completed within 56 days of the birth – Reg 5(2)(a)/Reg 9(2) (as modified). Where more than one child is born as a result of the same pregnancy, S.80A(6) ERA stipulates that time starts to run for the purpose of the 56-day period from the date of the birth of the first child.

Where the child is born before the first day of the expected week of birth, Reg 5(2)(b) provides that the time starts to run on that day (the first day of the expected week of birth). So if, for example, the child is born two weeks prematurely, the 56-day period is effectively extended by 14 days. Surprisingly, Reg 9 (as modified) makes no such provision for parental order parents.

7.37 The requirement that leave cannot begin before the day of the child's birth or the expected week of birth means that prospective fathers cannot take paternity leave for any kind of ante-natal care or emergency. In Miller v Larchford Ltd ET Case No.2100727/08 there was a period of 13 days between the date the claimant's partner went into labour and the date she eventually gave birth. Shortly after the birth, the claimant was dismissed, since he had not returned to work after his partner had initially gone into hospital. He claimed that the reason for his dismissal was connected with the fact that he took paternity leave and therefore automatically unfair under S.99 ERA and Reg 29 (see 'Employment protection during and after paternity leave – protection from unfair dismissal' below). The tribunal dismissed his claim, finding that the paternity leave period could not begin before the child was born. As a consequence, he could not rely on the provisions affording special protection during paternity leave.

Where the employee wants to be present during labour and the birth itself he or she should make use of the right to unpaid time off for domestic emergencies – see further Chapter 11, 'Time off for dependants'. He or she may also be eligible to take unpaid parental leave – see Chapter 10, 'Unpaid parental leave'.

7.38 **Choosing the start date.** Provided the leave is taken within the relevant 56-day period, the employee may choose to begin his or her leave on:

- the date on which the child is born

- the date falling such number of days after the birth as specified in the employee's notice of intention to take paternity leave under Reg 6/Reg 10 (as modified) (see 'Notice and evidential requirements for paternity leave' below), or

- a predetermined date specified in the notice which is later than the first day of the expected week of birth – Reg 5(3)/Reg 9(2) (as modified).

Paternity leave begins on the date specified in the employee's notice of intention, or where he or she has varied that date under Reg 6(4) or (6)/Reg 10(4) or (5) (as modified), on the varied date (or the last such date if he or she has varied the date more than once) – Reg 7(1)/Reg 11(1) (as modified). The only exception is where the employee has chosen to begin his or her leave on the date on which the child is actually born and he or she is at work on that day, in which case his or her leave begins on the following day – Reg 7(2)/Reg 11(2) (as modified).

7.39 When can paternity leave be taken? (adoption)
Paternity leave consequent upon adoption must be taken during the period of 56 days beginning with the date on which the child is placed with the adopter – Reg 9(2). Where more than one child is placed for adoption as part of the same arrangement, S.80B(6) ERA stipulates that the date of the child's placement in Reg 9(2) should be read as referring to the date of placement of the first child for the purpose of the 56-day period.

7.40 Choosing the start date. The employee can choose to begin a period of leave on:

- the date on which the child is placed with the adopter
- the date falling such number of days after the date on which the child is placed with the adopter as the employee may specify in a notice under Reg 10 (see 'Notice and evidential requirements for paternity leave – notice requirements (adoption)' below), or
- a predetermined date, specified in a notice under Reg 10, which is later than the date on which the child is expected to be placed with the adopter – Reg 9(3).

Paternity leave begins on the date specified in the employee's notice under Reg 10(1) (see below) or, where he or she has varied the date under Reg 10(4) or (6), on the varied date (or the last such date if he or she has varied the date more than once) – Reg 11(1). If the employee has chosen to start his or her leave on the date on which the child is placed for adoption and he or she is at work on that day, the leave will begin on the following day – Reg 11(2).

7.41 Notice and evidential requirements for paternity leave

An employee who intends to take paternity leave must give his or her employer a notice of his or her intention to do so. Furthermore, the employee must provide the employer with a signed declaration upon request. For birth fathers (or spouses/partners of birth mothers) the notice and declaration must comply with Reg 6, for adoptive parents it must comply with Reg 10, and for parental order parents it must comply with Reg 10, as modified by Reg 11 Leave (Parental Order Cases) Regulations.

Notice requirements (birth)   **7.42**

Under Reg 6 an employee must give his employer notice of his intention to take paternity leave, specifying:

- the expected week of the child's birth

- the length of the absence (either one week or two consecutive weeks – see 'Commencement and duration of paternity leave' above)

- the date on which the employee has chosen to begin his leave – Reg 6(1).

The notice must be given to the employer in or before the 15th week before the expected week of birth or, where that is not reasonably practicable, as soon as is reasonably practicable – Reg 6(2). The notice must be in writing if the employer so requests – Reg 6(8). There is no requirement to provide the employer with any medical evidence of the pregnancy.

Once the notice is received by the employer, it is advisable to discuss the date **7.43** the employee is expected to return to work from paternity leave. However, the employer is not under any legal obligation to give the employee confirmation of the end date of the paternity leave period.

Where an employer requests it, the employee must – within 14 days of receipt of the request – also give the employer a signed declaration that the purpose of his or her absence from work is to take care of a child or support the child's mother; that he or she is the father of the child or the mother's spouse, partner or civil partner; and that he or she has or expects to have responsibility for the upbringing of the child – Reg 6(3). A model self-certificate of entitlement to paternity leave and pay (form SC3, 'Becoming a parent') is available from HMRC (at www.hmrc.gov.uk). The form tells employees about their entitlement to SPP and includes a tear-off statement on which the employee fills in the expected or actual date of the child's birth and the date on which he or she has chosen his or her paternity leave to begin. There is also a declaration for the employee to sign. (Note that, while the employee need only complete this form for paternity leave if the employer requests it, he or she must complete it to be eligible for SPP – see 'Statutory paternity pay – notice requirements for SPP' below. However, the employee only has to complete the form once to be entitled to both leave and pay.)

An employee who has given notice under Reg 6(1) may vary the date he or she **7.44** has chosen to begin leave by giving his or her employer notice of the variation:

- where the variation is to provide for the leave to begin on the date of the child's birth, at least 28 days before the first day of the expected week of birth

- where the variation is to provide for the leave to begin on a date that is a specified number of days (or a different specified number of days) after the birth date, at least 28 days before the date falling that number of days after

309

the first day of the expected week of birth. For example, if the employee wants the leave period to start 14 days after the child's birth and the expected week of birth begins on 17 August, he or she must notify the employer of the new date by 3 August (i.e. 28 days before 31 August (which is 14 days after 17 August))

- where the variation is to provide for the leave to begin on a predetermined date (or on a different predetermined date), at least 28 days before that date

or, if it is not reasonably practicable to give 28 days' notice, as soon as is reasonably practicable – Reg 6(4). The notice of variation must be in writing if the employer so requests – Reg 6(8).

7.45 Where an employee has chosen to begin his or her period of leave on a particular predetermined date and the child is not yet born by that date, the employee must vary his or her choice of date by substituting a later predetermined date or exercising an alternative option under Reg 5(3) (see 'Commencement and duration of paternity leave – when can paternity leave be taken? (birth/surrogacy)' above), and give his or her employer notice of the variation as soon as possible – Reg 6(6). To recap, Reg 5(3) provides that the employee may also choose to begin his or her leave on:

- the date on which the child is born, or

- the date falling such number of days after the birth (as specified in the employee's notice).

The variation notice must be in writing if the employer so requests – Reg 6(8). Where the employee varies the start date of the leave period, it would be advisable to complete another self-certificate form SC3.

7.46 In all cases, the employee must give his or her employer a further notice of the date on which the child was born, as soon as is reasonably practicable after the child's birth – Reg 6(7). The notice must be in writing if the employer so requests – Reg 6(8).

Paternity leave begins on the date specified in the employee's notice or the date in the varied notice or, if more than one variation has been made, the date in the last notice – Reg 7(1) (see further 'Commencement and duration of paternity leave – when can paternity leave be taken? (birth/surrogacy)' above).

7.47 Notice requirements (adoption)
An employee who wishes to take paternity leave upon the adoption of a child must give his or her employer a notice of intention, specifying:

- the date on which the adopter was notified that he or she had been matched with the child

- the date on which the child is expected to be placed with the adopter

- the length of the period of paternity leave that the employee has chosen to take (either one week or two consecutive weeks), and

- the date on which he or she has chosen to begin that leave (see 'Commencement and duration of paternity leave – when can paternity leave be taken? (adoption)' above) – Reg 10(1).

Notice must be given to the employer no more than seven days after the date on which the adopter is notified of having been matched with the child or, where that is not reasonably practicable, as soon as is reasonably practicable – Reg 10(2). The notice must be in writing if the employer so requests – Reg 10(8).

Once the notice is received by the employer, it is advisable to discuss the date **7.48** the employee is expected to return to work from paternity leave. However, the employer is not under any legal obligation to give the employee confirmation of the end date of the leave period.

Where the employer requests it, an employee must – within 14 days of receipt of the request – also give his or her employer a signed declaration that the purpose of the absence is to care for a child or support the child's adopter, and that he or she satisfies the conditions of entitlement in Reg 8(2)(b) and (c) – i.e. that he or she is married to, or the civil partner or the partner of, the adopter and that he or she has the main responsibility (apart from the adopter) for the child's upbringing – Reg 10(3).

A model self-certificate of entitlement to paternity leave and pay in respect of a **7.49** child placed for adoption (form SC4, 'Becoming an adoptive parent') is available from HMRC (at www.hmrc.gov.uk). Note that, for the purpose of taking paternity leave, the employee only has to give the employer a signed declaration if the employer requests one. However, the employee must give the employer a signed declaration in order to be entitled to SPP – see 'Statutory paternity pay' below – although only one declaration needs to be given to entitle the employee to both leave and pay.

An employee who has given notice under Reg 10(1) may vary the date he or she has chosen to begin his or her leave by giving the employer a notice of variation:

- where the variation is to provide for the employee's period of leave to begin on the date on which the child is placed with the adopter, at least 28 days before the date specified in the employee's notice as the date on which the child is expected to be placed with the adopter

- where the variation is to provide for the employee's period of leave to begin on a date that is a specified number of days (or a different specified number of days) after the date on which the child is placed with the adopter, at least 28 days before the date falling that number of days after the date specified in the employee's original notice as the date on which the child is expected to be placed. For example, if the employee wants the leave period to start

311

14 days after the date on which the child is placed with the adopter, and the date specified in the employee's original notice as the date on which the child is expected to be placed is 17 August, he or she must notify the employer of the new date by 3 August (i.e. 28 days before 31 August (which is 14 days after 17 August))

- where the variation is to provide for leave to begin on a predetermined date specified in the notice, at least 28 days before that date

or, if it is not reasonably practicable for the employee to give 28 days' notice of a variation, as soon as is reasonably practicable – Reg 10(4). The notice of variation must be in writing if the employer so requests – Reg 10(8).

7.50 Where an employee has chosen to begin his or her period of leave on a particular predetermined date and the child is not placed with the adopter by that date, the employee must vary his or her choice of date by substituting a later predetermined date or exercising an alternative option under Reg 9(3) (see 'Commencement and duration of ordinary paternity leave – when can paternity leave be taken? (adoption)' above). To recap, Reg 9(3) provides that the employee can also choose to begin a period of leave on:

- the date on which the child is placed with the adopter, or

- the date falling such number of days after the date on which the child is placed with the adopter (as specified in the employee's notice).

The notice of variation must be given as soon as is reasonably practicable, in writing if the employer so requests – Reg 10(6) and (8).

In all cases the employee must give his or her employer a further notice, as soon as is reasonably practicable after the child's placement, of the date on which the child was placed – Reg 10(7). The notice must be in writing if the employer so requests – Reg 10(8).

7.51 **Adoption from overseas.** If the child is being adopted from outside the UK, then different notice requirements apply. These fall into three stages.

At the first stage, the employee must inform the employer of:

- the date on which the adopter received official notification – Reg 10(1)(a) PAL Regulations, as modified by Reg 7 Adoption from Overseas Regulations, and

- the date the child is expected to enter Great Britain – Reg 10(1)(b) PAL Regulations, as modified by Reg 7 Adoption from Overseas Regulations.

Where the employee has the necessary 26 weeks' qualifying service with the employer by the time the adopter receives official notification, he or she must provide the employer with this information within 28 days of the adopter receiving official notification. Where the employee does not yet satisfy the service requirement (but will by the time he or she wants the leave to begin), he or she must provide the employer with the information within 28 days of completing the service requirement – Reg 10(2)(a) PAL Regulations, as modified by Reg 7 Adoption from Overseas Regulations.

At the second stage, the employee must give the employer at least 28 days' **7.52** notice of the intended start date for paternity leave – Reg 10(1)(c) and (2)(b) PAL Regulations, as modified by Reg 7 Adoption from Overseas Regulations. This information can also be given at the first stage. If the employee subsequently decides to change the start date, he or she must give at least 28 days' notice before the new start date – Reg 10(4) PAL Regulations, as modified by Reg 7 Adoption from Overseas Regulations.

At the third stage, which is after the child has entered Great Britain, the employee must notify the employer of the actual date the child entered the country, no later than 28 days after that date – Reg 10(1)(d) and (2)(c) PAL Regulations, as modified by Reg 7 Adoption from Overseas Regulations.

If the employer so requests, notification must be given in writing – Reg 10(5) **7.53** PAL Regulations, as modified by Reg 7 Adoption from Overseas Regulations. HMRC form SC5, 'Statutory Paternity Pay and paternity leave when adopting from abroad', can be used for this purpose.

Notice requirements (surrogacy)   7.54

A parental order parent who wishes to take paternity leave must give his or her employer a notice of intention specifying:

- the expected week of the child's birth

- the length of the absence (either one week or two consecutive weeks)

- the date on which the employee has chosen to begin his leave – Reg 10(1) (as modified by Reg 11 Leave (Parental Order Cases) Regulations).

The notice must be given to the employer in or before the 15th week before the expected week of birth – Reg 10(2) (as modified). Interestingly, unlike the equivalent provision for birth and adoptive parents (see above), there is no scope for the notice period to be shortened in cases where it was not reasonably practicable to submit the notice in time. The notice must be in writing if the employer so requests – Reg 10(8) (as modified).

Where an employer requests it, the employee must – within 14 days of receipt **7.55** of the request – also give the employer a signed declaration that the purpose of his or her absence from work is to take care of a child or support Parent A; that he or she is married to, or the civil partner or the partner of, Parent A; that he or she has the main responsibility (apart from Parent A) for the child's upbringing; and that he or she is a parental order parent of the child – Reg 10(3) (as modified).

An employee who has given notice under Reg 10(1) may vary the date he or she has chosen to begin the leave by giving his or her employer notice of the variation:

- where the variation is to provide for the leave to begin on the date of the child's birth, at least 28 days before the first day of the expected week of birth

- where the variation is to provide for the leave to begin on a date that is a specified number of days (or a different specified number of days) after the birth date, at least 28 days before the date falling that number of days after the first day of the expected week of birth

- where the variation is to provide for the leave to begin on a predetermined date (or on a different predetermined date), at least 28 days before that date – Reg 10(4) (as modified).

7.56 Again, unlike the equivalent provisions for birth and adoptive parents (see above), there is no scope for the notice period to be shortened in cases where it was not reasonably practicable to submit the notice within the prescribed time limit. The notice of variation must be in writing if the employer so requests – Reg 10(8).

Where an employee has chosen to begin his or her period of leave on a particular predetermined date and the child is not yet born by that date, the employee must vary his or her choice of date by substituting a later predetermined date or exercising an alternative option under Reg 9(3) (see 'Commencement and duration of paternity leave – when can paternity leave be taken? (birth/surrogacy)' above), and give the employer notice of the variation as soon as possible – Reg 6(6). To recap, Reg 9(3) (as modified for parental order parents) provides that the employee may also choose to begin his or her leave on:

- the date on which the child is born, or

- the date falling such number of days after the birth (as specified in the employee's notice).

7.57 The notice must be in writing if the employer so requests – Reg 6(8).

In all cases, the employee must give his or her employer a further notice of the date on which the child was born, as soon as is reasonably practicable after the child's birth – Reg 10(6) (as modified). The notice must be in writing if the employer so requests – Reg 10(8) (as modified).

7.58 Employment protection during and after paternity leave

Section 80C ERA gives employees important rights during and after paternity leave. These are detailed in Regs 12–14 PAL Regulations and discussed below.

Terms and conditions during paternity leave
7.59

Reg 12(1) PAL Regulations provides that an employee who is absent on paternity leave (whether as the result of the birth or adoption of a child):

- is entitled to the benefit of all of the terms and conditions of employment that would have applied if he or she had not been absent, and

- is bound by any obligations arising under those terms and conditions except in so far as they are inconsistent with the employee's right to take paternity leave.

Identical provision is made with regard to overseas adoptions by Reg 27 Adoption from Overseas Regulations.

'Terms and conditions of employment' has the meaning given to it by S.80C(5) ERA and includes matters connected with an employee's employment whether or not they arise under his or her contract of employment, but excludes terms and conditions about remuneration – Reg 12(2). For these purposes, only sums payable to an employee by way of wages or salary are to be treated as remuneration – Reg 12(3).

The effect of these provisions is that an employee's contract of employment **7.60** continues during paternity leave (unless either party brings it to an end) and the employee must be treated in all respects as if he or she were not absent, in terms of both the benefits to which he or she is entitled and the obligations he or she owes the employer. The only exceptions to this are that the employee is not entitled to receive his or her normal remuneration (unless, of course, his or her contract expressly states that he or she will continue to be paid during paternity leave – see 'Contractual and composite paternity rights' below) and he or she is not bound by any obligations that are inconsistent with the fact that he or she is taking paternity leave (e.g. the obligation actually to turn up and work). However, he or she will be entitled to statutory paternity pay – see 'Statutory paternity pay' below.

These provisions are similar to those that apply to employees taking maternity leave and reference should be had to Chapter 3, 'Maternity leave', under 'Terms and conditions during maternity leave', for a detailed discussion of the meaning of remuneration and the status of various benefits during the leave period, including non-cash benefits (e.g. private medical insurance or gym membership), bonus payments, annual leave and notice pay. Similar provisions also apply to adoption leave – see Chapter 6, 'Adoption leave and pay', under 'Terms and conditions during adoption leave'.

Sick pay. It is important to note that, unlike SMP, there is no prohibition on **7.61** employees claiming statutory sick pay during the paternity pay period (see Chapter 3, 'Maternity leave', under 'Terms and conditions during maternity leave – sick pay'). However, Reg 18 of the Statutory Paternity Pay and Statutory

315

Adoption Pay (General) Regulations 2002 SI 2002/2822 provides that there is no liability to pay SPP to an employee in respect of any week during any part of which he or she is entitled to statutory sick pay. This is discussed further under 'Statutory shared parental pay – payment of SPP' below.

7.62 **Pension and other service-related benefits during paid leave.** Pension and other service-related benefits are discussed at length in Chapter 3, 'Maternity leave', under 'Terms and conditions during maternity leave', and Chapter 6, 'Adoption leave and pay', under 'Terms and conditions during adoption leave', but it is worth setting out here the specific provisions – contained in para 5A of Schedule 5 to the Social Security Act 1989 – that govern an employer's obligations in respect of these benefits in the context of paid paternity leave. 'Paid paternity leave' in this sense covers any period during which SPP is paid or any period during which the employee is entitled to be paid under a contractual paternity scheme – para 5A(4).

Under para 5A any employment-related benefit scheme, including any occupational pension scheme, is subject to the 'normal employment requirement', by virtue of which an employee's *paid* paternity leave must be treated as if it were a period during which he or she was working normally for his or her usual remuneration. This applies to both final salary schemes and money purchase schemes – in the case of the latter, this could be a personal pension plan or a stakeholder scheme.

7.63 The general effect of para 5A is to ensure that employment-related benefit schemes do not contain any 'unfair paternity leave provisions', which are defined as any provision that offends the 'normal employment requirement' by discriminating between an employee who is on paid paternity leave and an employee who is working normally – para 5A(4).

7.64 *Employer's contributions.* The employer's contributions to a pension or other employment-related benefit scheme during paid paternity leave must be based on the employee's notional pay (i.e. the pay he or she would have received had he or she been working normally) as opposed to the actual pay he or she receives during paternity leave – para 5A(3).

In final salary schemes an employee is guaranteed a pension based on final salary and it is the actuary who decides from time to time what level of contributions are needed from employers to fund the liabilities of the pension scheme as a whole. In such schemes an employer's contributions are not specifically designated to any one employee. Accordingly (depending upon the actuary's advice), an employer may or may not have to pay more contributions to take account of men in the scheme taking paternity leave.

7.65 *Employee's contributions.* In a contributory scheme, whether money purchase or based on final salary, the employee only has to make contributions based on the amount of pay he or she actually receives during paid paternity leave, not his or her normal salary – para 5B(3). This could lead to funding problems for money purchase schemes and employers may need to make up the shortfall.

Right to return after paternity leave

7.66

Section 80C(1)(c) ERA establishes a right to return to work from paternity leave to a job 'of a kind prescribed by regulations'. This is dealt with by Reg 13 PAL Regulations. Under Reg 13(1) an employee who returns to work after an isolated period of paternity leave is entitled to return to the job in which he or she was employed before the absence. Less straightforwardly, Reg 13(1) also entitles an employee to return to the same job if he or she returns to work after a period of paternity leave which was the last of two or more consecutive periods of statutory leave which did not include:

- any period of unpaid parental leave of more than four weeks

- any period of statutory leave which when added to any other period of statutory leave (excluding unpaid parental leave) taken in relation to the same child means that the total amount of statutory leave taken in relation to that child totals more than 26 weeks.

An employee who returns to work after a period of paternity leave not falling within Reg 13(1) is entitled to return from leave to the job in which he or she was employed before his or her absence, or, if it is not reasonably practicable for the employer to permit this, to another job which is both suitable for the employee and appropriate for him or her to do in the circumstances – Reg 13(2).

The job in which an employee was employed before his or her absence is the **7.67** job in which he or she was employed either immediately before the isolated period of paternity leave or, in the case of consecutive periods of statutory leave, immediately before the first such period – Reg 13(3).

Note that unlike other types of statutory leave (see, for example, Chapter 4, 'Returning to work after maternity leave', under 'Redundancy during maternity leave'), there is no exception to Reg 13 in cases of redundancy.

Terms and conditions. An employee who has the right to return under Reg 13 **7.68** PAL Regulations is entitled to return on terms and conditions not less favourable than those that would have applied, and with his or her seniority, pension rights and similar rights as they would have been, if he or she had not been absent – Reg 14 PAL Regulations. If his or her return is from consecutive periods of statutory leave, he or she should be treated as if he or she had not been absent since the beginning of the first such period – Reg 14(3).

Regulation 14(1)(a) PAL Regulations sets down special rules with respect to an employee's seniority, pension rights and similar rights where the employee is returning from consecutive periods of statutory leave that included a period of additional adoption leave or (as the case may be) additional maternity leave. In these circumstances, the employee's right to return is a right to return with seniority, pension rights and similar rights as they would have been if the period or periods of employment prior to the additional adoption leave or additional maternity leave were continuous with the period of employment following it. In other words, the period of additional adoption leave or additional maternity leave does not count towards seniority or pension rights, or towards any other similar rights which depend upon a period of qualifying service; for example, a service-related pay increment. However, the employee is entitled to the pension and seniority rights, etc, that would have applied had the two periods either side of the leave been continuous.

7.69 This position may alter if the employee received pay during any part of the additional adoption leave period or the additional maternity leave period. Reg 14 PAL Regulations is subject to the provisions governing equal treatment in pension schemes found in paras 5B and 6 of Schedule 5 to the Social Security Act 1989 and S.75 of the Equality Act 2010 – Reg 14(2). The provisions of S.75 and para 5B are considered at length in Chapter 3, 'Maternity leave', under 'Terms and conditions during maternity leave – pensions', and Chapter 6, 'Adoption leave and pay', under 'Terms and conditions during adoption leave – pensions and other service-related benefits'. Para 6 deals with paid leave for 'family reasons' and provides that any member of a pension scheme taking paid leave should, for the purposes of his or her occupational pension benefits, be treated as if he or she is working normally but only receives the remuneration in fact paid to him or her for that period. In effect, for money purchase schemes this means that the employee and the employer need only pay pension contributions on the amount of remuneration actually paid. For final salary schemes, the employee likewise pays any contributions on the amount of remuneration actually paid. The employer's contributions to a final salary scheme depend on actuarial advice and are not specifically designated to any one employee.

Schedule 5 to the 1989 Act applies to all service-related benefits, not just occupational pension schemes. As a result, what has been written above in relation to pensions applies equally to other benefits such as sickness or invalidity benefits and death benefits during any paid family leave.

7.70 **Refusal to allow return.** A refusal to allow an employee to return to his or her old job after paternity leave in accordance with these provisions may amount to a detriment or a dismissal, which, depending on the reasons for it, may be unfair – see 'Protection from detriment' and 'Protection from unfair dismissal' below.

7.71 ## Contractual and composite paternity rights
Employers may offer contractual rights to paternity leave and pay that are more favourable than those available under the statutory scheme. For example, a contract may allow for a longer period of leave than that provided by the

PAL Regulations, or for the employee to receive normal contractual remuneration during the leave period. An employee who is entitled to SPL and who also has a contractual right to paternity leave may not exercise the two rights separately, but may take advantage of whichever is the more favourable in any particular respect – Reg 30(1) and (2)(a) PAL Regulations. Where an employee combines elements of a contractual right and a statutory right, the result is referred to as a composite right. In these circumstances, the various statutory provisions that apply to the statutory right are modified to give effect to the more favourable contractual terms – Reg 30(2)(b). For further details of composite rights see Chapter 3, 'Maternity leave', under 'Contractual and composite maternity rights'.

Protection from detriment
7.72

An employee has the right not to be subjected to any detriment by his or her employer because the employee took or sought to take paternity leave – S.47C ERA and Reg 28(1)(a) PAL Regulations. For example, denying an employee the opportunity of participating in a training programme because he or she is on paternity leave at the time constitutes detrimental treatment. However, any detriment that amounts to a dismissal is specifically excluded by Reg 28(2), as dismissals are dealt with by Reg 29 PAL Regulations – see 'Protection from unfair dismissal' immediately below.

The right not to suffer detriment in respect of the various types of family leave discussed in this Handbook is considered at length in Chapter 12, 'Detriment and unfair dismissal', under 'Right not to suffer detriment'.

Protection from unfair dismissal
7.73

Employees who are dismissed for reasons connected with paternity leave are given special protection by virtue of Reg 29(1)(a) and (3)(a) PAL Regulations. These provisions stipulate that an employee who is dismissed will be regarded as unfairly dismissed under S.99 ERA if the reason or principal reason for the dismissal is connected with the fact that the employee took or sought to take paternity leave. S.99 renders dismissals for reasons relating to, among other things, paternity leave *automatically* unfair – i.e. without any consideration of whether the decision to dismiss was reasonable, and there is no minimum service requirement for the right to claim. Automatically unfair dismissals under S.99 are discussed in detail in Chapter 12, 'Detriment and unfair dismissal', under 'Automatically unfair dismissal'.

'Connected with'. The meaning of the phrase 'connected with' for the purpose 7.74 of Reg 29 PAL Regulations was considered by the EAT in Atkins v Coyle Personnel plc 2008 IRLR 420, EAT. In that case, A was on paternity leave but remained contactable at home. Following an angry e-mail and telephone exchange with his employer about a work matter, the employer told him on the phone that he was sacked. Considering his claim for automatically unfair

319

dismissal – A lacked the requisite qualifying period for ordinary unfair dismissal – an employment tribunal found that the reason for the dismissal was not connected with the fact that A had taken paternity leave, but was rather a result of frustration and annoyance at A's attitude, which culminated in the telephone argument. On appeal, the EAT upheld this finding. It further made obiter (i.e. non-binding) comments on the meaning of 'connected with' in Reg 29. According to the EAT, the fact that the words 'connected with' might on the dictionary definition be taken to mean 'associated with' does not mean that a causal connection between the dismissal and the paternity leave is unnecessary. It is not sufficient that the dismissal was associated with the paternity leave, since that is a very vague concept and so wide that it would be enough for the employee merely to establish that he was on paternity leave when he was dismissed. Such an interpretation cannot have been intended, and for the same reasons nor can it have been intended merely to apply a test of asking whether the dismissal would have occurred 'but for' the fact that the employee was on paternity leave. 'Connected with' in Reg 29 means causally connected with rather than some vaguer, less stringent connection.

The Atkins case is also considered in Chapter 12, 'Detriment and unfair dismissal', under 'Automatically unfair dismissal – paternity leave', in the context of case law on dismissals for reasons 'connected with' an employee's maternity leave, which advocates a less narrow interpretation of the phrase. However, as the EAT put it in Atkins, the exact interpretation of the phrase 'connected with' is 'both sterile and semantic', as it is ultimately a task for the tribunal to determine as a matter of fact whether there is a connection between the taking of leave and the dismissal. Once that determination is made, it will be a rare case where it will be interfered with on appeal.

7.75 No ambiguity existed over the reason for the employee's (constructive) dismissal in Jackson v Instant Installations Ltd ET Case No.2801865/07. In that case, J asked for two weeks' paternity leave. The employer refused the request by shouting at him, 'You're not fucking having an extra fortnight off. No fucker else gets it. I don't give a fuck.' Hearing his claim under S.99 ERA, the tribunal found that the treatment meted out to J amounted to a breach of the implied term of trust and confidence, entitling him to treat himself as constructively dismissed. The dismissal was automatically unfair because the reason for it was that J sought to take paternity leave.

7.76 **Job offer by associated employer.** There is one situation in which the automatically unfair dismissal provisions do not apply. By virtue of Reg 29(5) PAL Regulations, Reg 29(1) does not apply to render a dismissal automatically unfair if:

- it is not reasonably practicable for a reason other than redundancy for the employer (who may be the same employer or a successor of his) to permit the employee to return to a job which is both suitable for the employee and appropriate for him to do in the circumstances

- an associated employer offers the employee a job of that kind, and

- the employee accepts or unreasonably refuses that offer.

In this situation the fairness or otherwise of the dismissal will be for an employment tribunal to decide in the normal way, applying the test of reasonableness set out in S.98(4) ERA. Where there is a dispute as to whether this exception applies, it is for the employer to show that the provisions of Reg 29(5) were satisfied – Reg 29(6).

For the purposes of these Regulations, any two employers shall be treated as **7.77** associated if (a) one is a company of which the other (directly or indirectly) has control, or (b) both are companies of which a third person (directly or indirectly) has control – Reg 2(6).

Redundancy. An employee will also be regarded as unfairly dismissed if the **7.78** reason or principal reason for the dismissal is that the employee was redundant and it is shown that:

- the circumstances constituting the redundancy applied equally to one or more employees in the same undertaking who held positions similar to that held by the employee and who have not been dismissed by the employer, and

- the reason (or, if more than one, the principal reason) for which the employee was selected for dismissal was connected with the fact that the employee took, or sought to take, paternity leave – Reg 29(2) PAL Regulations.

It is important to note that where, during paternity leave, it is not reasonably practicable by reason of redundancy to continue to employ the employee, but the employer has a suitable available vacancy within the company, the employer is not obliged to offer it to him or her. In this respect, paternity leave differs from maternity and adoption leave where the employer must give preferential treatment to employees absent on such leave where there is a redundancy situation – see Chapter 4, 'Returning to work after maternity leave', under 'Redundancy during maternity leave', and Chapter 6, 'Adoption leave and pay', under 'Redundancy and adoption leave'. However, employees absent on paternity leave in these circumstances may still be able to argue that the selection for redundancy made the dismissal automatically unfair under Reg 29(2) or that it was unfair under the 'ordinary' unfair dismissal provisions. Alternatively, the dismissal may amount to unlawful sex discrimination – see 'Protection from discrimination' below.

Asserting a statutory right. If the employee is dismissed because he or she **7.79** sought to exercise the right to paternity leave, he or she may be able to claim that he or she was dismissed for asserting a statutory right. Under S.104(1)

321

ERA an employee's dismissal will be automatically unfair if the reason or principal reason for the dismissal was that:

● the employee brought proceedings against the employer to enforce a relevant statutory right, or

● the employee alleged that the employer had infringed such a right.

There is no minimum period of qualifying service for a claim under S.104. Dismissals for asserting a statutory right are discussed in Chapter 12, 'Detriment and unfair dismissal', under 'Automatically unfair dismissal – asserting a statutory right'.

7.80 ## Protection from discrimination

Denying an employee a period of paternity leave or subjecting him or her to any detriment in relation to taking such leave may also give rise to a claim of unlawful discrimination. Potential claims for sex discrimination under the EqA in the context of paternity leave include claims for direct discrimination (e.g. the employer allows female employees taking paternity leave more time off than male employees taking such leave) or harassment (e.g. a woman taking paternity leave is subjected to derogatory remarks related to her sex). However, the most common complaint in relation to paternity leave is likely to be a claim for indirect discrimination.

Indirect sex discrimination occurs where an employer operates a seemingly gender-neutral practice which in reality has a disproportionate effect on one sex. Where a man has been refused paternity leave, has suffered a detriment or been dismissed because he took, or sought to take, paternity leave, he may be able to bring a claim for indirect discrimination, on the basis that men are more likely than women to take paternity leave and will therefore be disproportionately affected by a refusal or other detriment. In Jackson v Instant Installations Ltd ET Case No.2801865/07, for example, J asked for two weeks' paternity leave, which was refused by the employer. The tribunal found that the employer would have reacted the same way if a woman had requested paternity leave, and J was therefore unable to show that he had suffered direct discrimination. However, his indirect discrimination claim succeeded before the tribunal, as the employer's refusal would have a greater impact on men. As the employer failed to justify its actions, the claim was upheld.

7.81 Other potential claims include discrimination on grounds of marital or civil partnership status or sexual orientation. Given that same-sex partners are entitled to take paternity leave, claims of sexual orientation discrimination could be brought where an employer refuses to grant paternity leave to same-sex couples but allows such leave in relation to heterosexual couples. A detailed discussion of discrimination law is contained in Chapter 13, 'Discrimination and equal pay'.

Statutory paternity pay 7.82

Like paternity leave, the right to statutory paternity pay (SPP) is enjoyed by fathers (biological or otherwise), spouses, partners and civil partners of new mothers, adoptive parents, foster parents and parental order parents in a surrogacy arrangement. Full details can be found under 'Who has the right?' above. The conditions of entitlement to SPP are contained in the Social Security Contributions and Benefits Act 1992 (SSCBA), as amended by S.2 of the Employment Act 2002, and the Statutory Paternity Pay and Statutory Adoption Pay (General) Regulations 2002 SI 2002/2822 ('the General Regulations'). In this section we consider the individual qualifying conditions for SPP and the payment of SPP. For details on the administration and enforcement of the SPP scheme, see Chapter 9, 'Administering statutory payments'.

Employed earners 7.83

Only employees who are in 'employed earner's employment' can benefit from SPP. However, the definition of 'employee' for SPP purposes differs from the definition that applies for paternity leave purposes. S.171ZJ(2) SSCBA, which governs SPP, provides that 'employee' means a person:

* who is gainfully employed either under a contract of service or as an office holder (including an elective office)

* with general earnings, as defined by S.7 of the Income Tax (Earnings and Pensions) Act 2003 (i.e. any salary, wages or fee; any gratuity or other profit or incidental benefit of any kind if it is money or money's worth; or anything else that constitutes an emolument of the employment).

In addition, there are special cases where a worker will be considered an employee for SPP purposes, despite not falling within the definition set out in S.171ZJ(2). Reg 32(1) General Regulations provides that a person is taken to be an employee for the purposes of SPP if he or she is treated as an employed earner by virtue of the Social Security (Categorisation of Earners) Regulations 1978 SI 1978/1689. This applies regardless of the age of the person provided that the person, if he or she is under the age of 16, would have been treated as an employed earner by virtue of the 1978 Regulations had he or she been over that age – Reg 32(1A). A person who is in employed earner's employment under a contract of apprenticeship is treated as an employee for the purposes of SPP – Reg 32(2).

To be an 'employed earner' the employee must work for someone who is 7.84 liable to pay the employer's share of his or her Class 1 national insurance (NI) contributions. This means that the person must earn at least as much as the lower earnings limit for national insurance of £112 a week for the tax year 2015/16.

323

However, a person who is in employed earner's employment is not treated as an employee for the purposes of SPP if either:

- his or her employer is not resident or present in Great Britain in accordance with Reg 145(1) of the Social Security (Contributions) Regulations 2001 SI 2001/1004, or

- his or her employer is a person who is exempt from the provisions of the SSCBA or against whom the provisions of the Act are not enforceable – Reg 32(3).

Crown servants are treated as employees for SPP purposes under S.171ZH SSCBA.

7.85 In the majority of cases workers who qualify for statutory paternity leave will also be entitled to SPP and vice versa, but there are a few exceptions. First, those who are not 'employees' under S.230(1) ERA (and who therefore do not qualify for paternity leave) may nevertheless qualify for SPP because they are employed earners. This exception may apply to agency workers or office holders, such as members of the police, judiciary and armed forces, MPs and some company directors. Presumably, the right to SPP will apply where they have a contractual right to paternity leave. Secondly, employees earning less than the NI lower earnings limit are not entitled to SPP but may be entitled to statutory paternity leave and income support. This is discussed further under 'Low-paid parents' immediately below.

7.86 **Low-paid parents.** As noted above, to qualify for SPP a person must be an 'employed earner' – that is, working for someone who is liable to pay the employer's share of his or her Class 1 NI contributions. There is no Class 1 NI contribution liability if an employee's average weekly earnings are less than the lower earnings limit for national insurance of £112 a week for the tax year 2015/16. Therefore, employees earning less than the NI lower earnings limit are not entitled to SPP. They may, however, be entitled to statutory paternity leave and income support.

The Social Security (Paternity and Adoption) Amendment Regulations 2002 SI 2002/2689 amended the Income Support (General) Regulations 1987 SI 1987/1967 to enable low-paid parents taking paternity leave to receive income support. Para 14B of Schedule 1B to the 1987 Regulations extends entitlement to income support to a person who is entitled to and taking paternity leave under S.80A or S.80B ERA and who satisfies either or both of the following conditions:

- he or she is not entitled to statutory paternity pay under Part 12ZA of the SSCBA, or to any remuneration (which means payment of any kind) from his employer in respect of that leave

- he or she is entitled to working tax credit, child tax credit, housing benefit or council tax benefit on the day before that leave begins.

Employees working abroad. Certain employees working abroad are entitled **7.87** to SPP by virtue of the Statutory Paternity Pay and Statutory Adoption Pay (Persons Abroad and Mariners) Regulations 2002 SI 2002/2821. These employees are:

- those gainfully employed in another Member State of the European Economic Area (EEA) who would be employees for the purposes of the SSCBA if they were working in Great Britain (the EEA comprises the 27 Member States of the EU together with Iceland, Norway and Liechtenstein) and who are subject to UK legislation under EC Council Regulation No.1408/71 on the application of social security schemes to employed persons and their families moving within the Community

- those who are employees or are treated as such under the category above and who are working in Great Britain in the week immediately preceding the 14th week before the expected week of birth (birth) or in the week in which the adopter is notified of having been matched with a child for adoption (adoption) but who had worked for the same employer in another EEA Member State during the 26 weeks prior to that week

- those who are absent from Great Britain but in respect of whom an employer has secondary Class 1 NI liability

- mariners engaged in employment on board a home-trade ship with an employer who has a place of business within the UK, even though they may not be employed in Great Britain. However, mariners engaged in employment on a foreign-going ship or on a home-trade ship with an employer who does not have a place of business within the UK are not covered even if they may have been employed in Great Britain

- persons working on the continental shelf.

The corresponding Regulations in Northern Ireland are the Statutory Paternity Pay and Statutory Adoption Pay (Persons Abroad and Mariners) Regulations (Northern Ireland) 2002 SR 2002/382.

Qualifying for SPP   7.88
An employee who satisfies various conditions set out in Ss.171ZA(2) and 171E(4) SSCBA and Reg 4(2)(b) and (c) PAL Regulations is entitled to be paid SPP following the birth of a child. While the PAL Regulations apply to paternity *leave*, Reg 4 General Regulations provides that the conditions set out in Reg 4(2)(b) and (c) PAL Regulations also apply to SPP. Similarly, an employee who satisfies the conditions set out in Ss.171ZB(2) and 171E(4) SSCBA and Reg 11 General Regulations is entitled to SPP following the placement of a

325

child for adoption. (By virtue of the following Regulations, these provisions apply, with the necessary modifications, to overseas adoptions: the Social Security Contributions and Benefits Act 1992 (Application of Parts 12ZA, 12ZB and 12ZC to Parental Order Cases) Regulations 2014 SI 2014/2866; and the Statutory Paternity Pay and Statutory Adoption Pay (Parental Orders and Prospective Adopters) Regulations 2014 SI 2014/2934).

7.89 The conditions for each type of parent are alike and can be discussed together. They are as follows:

- the employee has, or expects to have, responsibility for the child (if he is the biological father) or the *main* responsibility for the child (in all other cases) – Reg 4(2)(c) PAL Regulations (birth); Reg 11(1) General Regulations (adoption); and Reg 9 Pay (Parental Orders and Prospective Adopters) Regulations

- the employee has been in employed earner's employment for a continuous period of 26 weeks ending with the 'relevant week' (see 'Relevant week' below) and remains continuously employed by that employer until the day on which the child is born/placed for adoption – S.171ZA(2)(b) and (d) (birth); S.171ZB(2)(b) and (d) (adoption). Note that a parental order parent must remain in continuous employment until the day on which the child is *born* – Schedule 1 SSCBA (Parental Order Cases) Regulations. This requirement is further discussed under 'Continuous employment' below

- the employee's normal weekly earnings for the eight weeks ending with the 15th week before the relevant week (see '"Relevant week"' below) are not less than the lower earnings limit for the payment of NI contributions in force at the end of that week (£112 per week for the tax year 2015/16) – S.171ZA(2)(c) (birth); S.171ZB(2)(c) (adoption). This requirement is further discussed under 'Normal weekly earnings' below

- it is the employee's purpose at the beginning of the statutory pay week to care for the child or support the child's mother/adopter/Parent A – S.171ZE(4) (see 'Caring for child or supporting the other parent' below)

- in the case of adoptive parents or parental order parents, the employee in question has elected to receive SPP – S.171ZB(2)(e). A person may not elect to receive SPP if he or she has elected to receive statutory adoption pay (see Chapter 6, 'Adoption leave and pay') – S.171ZB(4).

(Note that the Welfare Reform Act 2012 has introduced an additional condition that, at the end of the relevant week (see '"Relevant week"' below), the employee must have been 'entitled to be in that employment' under UK immigration law. This provision is not yet in force.)

7.90 **'Relevant week'.** For fathers (biological or otherwise) and parental order parents, the relevant week is the 15th week before the expected week of birth – S.171ZA(3) and Schedule 1 to the SSCBA (Parental Order Cases) Regulations. For adoptive parents, the relevant week is the week in which the adopter is notified of being matched with the child – S.171ZB(3).

Continuous employment. To qualify for SPP, an employee must have been **7.91** employed for a continuous period of at least 26 weeks ending with either:

- the 15th week before the expected week of the child's birth (this applies to parental order parents, as well as fathers), or

- the week in which the child's adopter is notified of being matched with the child

and remain in continuous employment until the day on which the child is born/ placed for adoption – Ss.171ZA(2) and 171ZB(2), and Schedule 1 SSCBA (Parental Order Cases) Regulations.

Where a father or parental order parent would have satisfied the continuous employment requirement if the baby had not been born prematurely, the requirement is treated as having been satisfied, provided the employee's normal weekly earnings in the eight weeks ending with the week immediately preceding the week in which the child is born are not less than the lower earnings limit (see further 'Normal weekly earnings' below) – Reg 5 General Regulations and Schedule 1 SSCBA (Parental Order Cases) Regulations.

Continuous employment for the purposes of claiming SPP is based on **7.92** employment by the same employer without a break. However, the General Regulations also provide for continuity to be preserved in some cases where there have been breaks in an employee's employment or where there is a change of employer – see 'Breaks in employment' and 'Change of employer' below. The general rules for computing continuity of employment contained in Ss.210– 219 ERA (see IDS Employment Law Handbook, 'Continuity of Employment' (2012), Chapter 1, 'The general framework') are incorporated with some variations into the SPP scheme – Regs 33–37 General Regulations.

Breaks in employment. Regulation 33 sets out the circumstances in which **7.93** weeks when there is no contract of employment in existence nevertheless count as a period of continuous employment. These replicate the circumstances set out in S.212 ERA and are:

- weeks during the whole or part of which the employee is incapable of work because of sickness or injury – Reg 33(1)(a). Not more than 26 consecutive weeks may count under this regulation – Reg 33(2)

- weeks during the whole or part of which the employee is absent from work on account of a temporary cessation of work – Reg 33(1)(b)

327

- weeks during the whole or part of which the employee is absent from work in circumstances such that, by arrangement or custom, he or she is regarded as continuing in employment for any purpose – Reg 33(1)(c).

An employee must return to work for his or her employer after the incapacity for or absence from work to preserve continuity – Reg 33(1).

7.94 *Spasmodic employment.* Where it is the custom of the employer:

- to offer work for a fixed period of not more than 26 consecutive weeks

- to offer work for up to 26 weeks on two or more occasions in a year for periods that do not overlap, and

- to offer the work available to those persons who had worked for it during the last or a recent such period

but the employee is absent from work because of incapacity arising from some specific disease or bodily or mental impairment, then that period will be counted as continuous employment and the condition in Reg 33(1) that the employee 'returns to work for his or her employer after the incapacity for or absence from work' does not apply – Reg 33(3).

7.95 *Re-employment after complaint of unfair dismissal.* Regulation 34 covers the situation where an employee is dismissed and then re-employed in consequence of:

- the employee presenting an unfair dismissal complaint – Reg 34(1)(a)

- the employee claiming in accordance with a dismissals procedure agreement under S.110 ERA – Reg 34(1)(b)

- action taken by an Acas conciliator under Ss.18A–18C of the Employment Tribunals Act 1996 – Reg 34(1)(c).

(Note that Reg 34 also expressly applies in respect of a decision arising out of the use of a statutory dispute resolution procedure contained in Schedule 2 to the Employment Act 2002 – Reg 34(1)(d). However, these procedures were repealed as from 6 April 2009.)

7.96 If any of the above applies, the interval between dismissal and re-employment counts as a period of continuous employment. The re-employment may be by the employee's employer, a successor or associated employer to fall within this provision – Reg 34(2). A 'successor' is a person who in consequence of a change occurring in the ownership of the undertaking, or part of the undertaking for the purposes of which the employee was employed, has become the owner of the undertaking or part thereof – Reg 34(3) and S.235 ERA. Two employers are associated if one is a company directly or indirectly controlled by the other or both are companies over which a third person has direct or indirect control – Reg 34(3) and S.231 ERA.

328

Stoppage because of a trade dispute. If there is a week or part of a week when **7.97** an employee does not work because there is a stoppage of work due to a trade dispute within the meaning of S.35(1) of the Jobseekers Act 1995 at his or her place of employment, there is no break in continuity of employment. But any such week does not count in computing the total period of continuous employment – Reg 35(1). In contrast to the rules on continuity in the ERA, dismissal of an employee during a stoppage of work breaks continuity of employment and continuity is not restored if re-employment takes place. In these circumstances, continuity will not be treated as extending beyond the commencement of the day he stopped work – Reg 35(2). However, the provision in Reg 35(1) that the period of work stoppage does not count towards continuous employment and the provision in Reg 35(2) relating to those dismissed during the stoppage do not apply to an employee who proves that at no time did he have a direct interest in the trade dispute in question – Reg 35(3).

A trade dispute is defined in the Jobseekers Act as 'any dispute between employers and employees, or between employees and employees, which is connected with the employment or non-employment or the terms of employment or the conditions of employment of any persons, whether employees in the employment of the employer with whom the dispute arises, or not'. This appears to be wider than the definition in S.244 of the Trade Union and Labour Relations (Consolidation) Act 1992 governing industrial action.

Change of employer. Regulation 36 sets out the circumstances in which **7.98** employment is treated as continuous even though the identity of the employer changes. The circumstances correspond with those set out in S.218 ERA (except that Reg 36 does not cover transfers of employment between certain health service employers) – see IDS Employment Law Handbook, 'Continuity of Employment' (2012), Chapter 4, 'Changes of employer', for full details. The circumstances in which continuity is preserved are where:

- the employer's trade or business or an undertaking (which may be established under an Act of Parliament) is transferred to another person – Reg 36(a)

- one employer is substituted by another under an Act of Parliament – Reg 36(b)

- the employee is re-employed following the death of the employer by the employer's personal representatives or trustees – Reg 36(c)

- there is a change in the employing partners, personal representatives or trustees – Reg 36(d)

- employment is transferred to an associated employer – Reg 36(e). 'Associated employer' has the meaning given in S.231 ERA – i.e. two or more employers are associated if one is a company directly or indirectly controlled by the other or both are companies over which a third person has direct or indirect control

329

- the employee is transferred between two employments where both employers are either the governors of a school maintained by the same local authority or are that authority – Reg 36(f).

7.99 *Reinstatement after service with the armed forces.* Section 1 of the Reserve Forces (Safeguard of Employment) Act 1985 provides a right for a reservist to be taken back into employment after demobilisation, no matter how long the military service has lasted. Within six months of the end of military service, an employer is obliged to re-employ any reservist who was employed by it in the four-week period prior to being called up on the terms and conditions which would have applied if there had been no call-up. Reg 37 General Regulations provides that, where a person enters the employment of the employer within that six-month period, his or her previous employment with that employer and the period of employment beginning in that six-month period will be treated as continuous.

7.100 **Normal weekly earnings.** To qualify for SPP, an employee's normal weekly earnings for the eight weeks ending with the 'relevant week' must be no less than the lower earnings limit for the payment of NI contributions in force at the end of that week (£112 per week for the tax year 2014/15, rising from £111 per week in 2014/15) – Ss.171ZA(2)(c) and 171ZB(2)(c). For the meaning of 'relevant week', see '"Relevant week"' above.

Regulations 39 and 40 General Regulations deal with the calculation of normal weekly earnings. These regulations mirror the provisions relating to the calculation of normal weekly earnings in the statutory maternity pay legislation – see Chapter 5, 'Statutory maternity pay', under 'Normal weekly earnings'. Basically, 'normal weekly earnings' are the average weekly earnings over a period of at least eight weeks up to and including the last normal pay day to fall on or before:

- the first day of the 15th week before the baby is due (for fathers and parental order parents), or

- the first day of the week after the week in which the adopter is notified of being matched with the child for adoption (for adoptive parents).

All the pay that the employee received in that period must be taken into account, and pay means earnings which are liable for Class 1 NI contributions, or earnings which would be liable if they were high enough.

7.101 **Aggregation of earnings under different contracts/employers.** If an employee works under more than one contract for the *same* employer, then the employer must treat the different contracts as one for the purposes of SPP – Reg 38(3) General Regulations. However, an employer is not required to aggregate earnings under different contracts if such aggregation is not reasonably practicable because the earnings under the respective contracts are separately calculated – Reg 14 Social Security (Contributions) Regulations 2001 SI 2001/1004 ('the 2001 Regulations'). Similar provisions apply where an employee is employed under separate contracts with two associated employers – Reg 15(1) 2001 Regulations.

Where an employee works under more than one contract but for *different* employers who are not associated, he or she is not usually entitled to aggregate his or her earnings since liability for paying national insurance contributions lies separately with each individual employer (the employee may be entitled to SPP from each one, however). In a few rare cases (other than those concerning associated employers) the earnings paid to an employee under two contracts can be aggregated and treated as a single payment of earnings for NI purposes – see Reg 15(1) 2001 Regulations. In this situation, liability for SPP is apportioned between the employers, either in the proportions which they agree or, if they cannot agree, in the proportions which the employee's earnings bear to the amount of the aggregated earnings – Reg 38(1) and (2) General Regulations.

7.102 *NHS employees.* The Statutory Paternity Pay and Statutory Adoption Pay (National Health Service Employees) Regulations 2002 SI 2002/2819 make provision for certain NHS employees whose contract of employment has been divided into two or more contracts with different bodies to elect to have those contracts treated as one contract, and for one of the employee's employers to be regarded as his or her employer for the purposes of entitlement to SPP.

7.103 **Caring for child or supporting the other parent.** Under S.171ZE(4) SPP is only payable to an employee if it is his or her purpose at the beginning of the statutory pay week to:

- care for the child, or
- support the child's mother/adopter/Parent A.

'Statutory pay week' is the week chosen by the employee as the week in which SPP will be payable – S.171ZE(11).

Rates of SPP
7.104

SPP is paid at the weekly rate set out in Reg 2 of the Statutory Paternity Pay and Statutory Adoption Pay (Weekly Rates) Regulations 2002 SI 2002/2818 ('the Weekly Rates Regulations'). This is the lesser of:

- £139.58 (the rate was £138.18 for pay weeks commencing prior to 5 April 2015), or
- 90 per cent of the employee's normal weekly earnings. For the meaning of 'normal weekly earnings' see 'Qualifying for SPP – normal weekly earnings' above.

These rates are subject to change every April.

331

Note that no extra SPP is payable for multiple births in respect of the same pregnancy or for the placement for adoption of more than one child as part of the same arrangement – Ss.171ZA(4) and 171ZB(6).

7.105 **Period of payment of SPP**
SPP is payable in respect of a period of two consecutive weeks over a 56-week qualifying period – S.171ZE(2)(a) and (3). The employee may elect for SPP to be paid in respect of a period of a week instead – Reg 6(3)/Reg 12(3). This corresponds with the employee's right under the PAL Regulations to choose whether to take one or two weeks' paternity leave – see 'Commencement and duration of paternity leave' above.

7.106 **Qualifying period for SPP.** For fathers and parental order parents, the 56-week qualifying period within which SPP is payable begins with:

- the date of birth of the child, or

- the first day of the expected week of birth, whichever is the later – Reg 8/ Reg 14 (as modified by Reg 13 Pay (Parental Orders and Prospective Adopters) Regulations.

In cases of multiple births the relevant date is the date on which the first child is born – S.171ZE(9), Schedule 1 SSCBA (Parental Order Cases) Regulations.

7.107 For adoptive parents, the 56-week qualifying period begins with the date of the child's placement for adoption – Reg 14. Where more than one child is placed for adoption as part of the same arrangement, the relevant date is the date of placement of the first child – S.171ZE(10).

Regulation 8/Regulation 14 General Regulations and Reg 5/Reg 9 PAL Regulations (discussed under 'Commencement and duration of paternity leave' above) taken together mean that paternity leave and the paternity pay period must be completed within eight weeks of the child's birth/placement.

7.108 **Choosing when the SPP period will begin.** A father or parental order parent may choose the SPP period to begin on:

- the date on which the child is born or, where the employee is at work on that day, the following day

- the date falling such number of days after the date on which the child is born as the employee may specify; or

- a predetermined date, specified by the employee, which is later than the first day of the expected week of birth (for fathers), or which is later than the expected week of birth (for parental order parents) – Reg 6(1)/ Reg 12(1) (as modified by Reg 11 Pay (Parental Orders and Prospective Adopters) Regulations).

332

It is worth noting that, in what is likely to be an oversight, Reg 12(1) (as modified) does not stipulate that the predetermined date must be later than *the first day* of the expected week of birth.

Similar provisions apply for adoptive parents claiming paternity pay, who may **7.109** choose the SPP period to begin on:

- the date on which the child is placed for adoption or, where the employee is at work on that day, the following day

- the date falling such number of days after the date on which the child is placed for adoption as the employee may specify; or

- a predetermined date, specified by the employee, which is later than the day on which the child is to be placed with the adopter – Reg 12(1).

These dates correspond to those on which an employee may start his or her paternity leave – see 'Commencement and duration of paternity leave' above – thereby ensuring that the date on which leave starts coincides with the day on which the pay period starts.

An employee can vary the start date of the SPP period provided that he or she **7.110** gives the employer notice. Reg 6(4)/Reg 12(4) provide that the employee must give the employer notice of the change at least 28 days before the date from which the employee expects the liability to pay SPP to begin or, if that is not reasonably practicable, as soon as is reasonably practicable.

Notice requirements for SPP   7.111

An employee is only entitled to SPP if he or she gives his or her employer notice of the date he or she expects the SPP period to begin, in writing if the employer so requests – S.171ZC(1) and (2). A birth father's notice must be given in or before the 15th week before the expected week of birth or, if that is not reasonably practicable, as soon as is reasonably practicable – Reg 5A. An adoptive parent's notice must be given no more than seven days after the date on which the adopter is notified of having been matched with the child for adoption or, if that is not reasonably practicable, as soon as is reasonably practicable – Reg 11A.

Where an employee has chosen the SPP period to begin on the date on which the child is born/placed for adoption under Reg 6(1)(a)/Reg 12(1)(a) or the date falling such number of days after that date as the employee has specified in his or her notice under Reg 6(1)(b)/Reg 12(1)(b) (see 'Period of payment of SPP' above), he or she must also give the employer further notice of the date on which the child was born/placed for adoption as soon as is reasonably practicable after the child's birth/placement – Reg 7(1) (birth)/Reg 13(1) (adoption).

Where an employee has chosen a predetermined date under Reg 6(1)(c)/ **7.112** Reg 12(1)(c) and notified that date to the employer, and the date of the child's

333

birth/placement is later than the date specified, the employee must give the employer notice as soon as is reasonably practicable that the SPP period will begin on a date different to that originally chosen – Reg 7(2)/Reg 13(2). That date may be any date chosen in accordance with Reg 6(1)/Reg 12(1) – Reg 7(3)/Reg 13(3).

Note that the notice requirements for parental order parents seeking SPP are the same as for birth fathers, i.e. based upon the date of birth – Regs 11A and 13 (as modified by Regs 10 and 12 Pay (Parental Orders and Prospective Adopters) Regulations).

7.113 Evidence of entitlement to SPP

In order to be able to claim SPP an employee must give the employer evidence in writing of his or her entitlement, together with a written declaration. The nature of the evidence and written declaration required differs depending upon whether the situation is one of birth, adoption or surrogacy – see 'Evidence of entitlement (birth)', 'Evidence of entitlement (adoption)' and 'Evidence of entitlement (surrogacy)' below.

In the case of birth fathers (or spouses, civil partners or partners of birth mothers) and parental order parents seeking SPP, the information and declaration must be given to the employer in or before the 15th week before the expected week of birth or, where that is not reasonably practicable, as soon as is reasonably practicable thereafter – Reg 9(3)/Reg 15(3) (as modified by Reg 14 Pay (Parental Orders and Prospective Adopters) Regulations). An adoptive parent seeking SPP must give the information and declaration to his or her employer no more than seven days after the adopter is notified of having been matched with the child or, where that is not reasonably practicable, as soon as is reasonably practicable – Reg 15(3).

7.114 **Evidence of entitlement (birth).** Where a father (or mother's spouse/partner) is claiming SPP upon the birth of a child, he or she must provide the following information:

- his or her name

- the expected week of the child's birth and, where the birth has already occurred, the date of birth

- the date from which it is expected that the liability to pay SPP will begin

- whether the period chosen in respect of which SPP is to be payable is a week – Reg 9(1)(a) and (2).

The employee must also provide a written declaration that he or she is the father of the child or the civil partner, partner or spouse of the child's mother; that he or she is taking leave either to care for a child or support the mother;

and that he or she has or expects to have responsibility for bringing up the child – Reg 9(1)(b).

A model self-certificate of entitlement to paternity leave and pay (form SC3, **7.115** 'Becoming a birth parent') is available from HMRC. The form tells employees about their entitlement to SPP and includes a tear-off statement on which the employee can fill in the expected week of birth or, if the child has already been born, the date of birth and the date on which the employee has chosen his or her leave to begin. There is also a declaration for the employee to sign. Employers can also request a completed self-certificate as evidence of entitlement to paternity *leave* (see 'Notice and evidential requirements for paternity leave – notice requirements (birth)' above). Where employees provide a completed SC3, they should therefore be able to satisfy the notice and evidence conditions for both paternity leave and pay.

Where the employer so requests, the employee must inform it of the date of the child's birth within 28 days, or as soon as is practicable thereafter – Reg 9(4). Note that there is no requirement for the father to give his or employer any medical evidence of the pregnancy or birth.

Evidence of entitlement (adoption). An adoptive parent wishing to claim SPP **7.116** must provide his or her employer with the following information:

- his or her name
- the date on which the child is expected to be placed for adoption or, where the child has already been placed for adoption, the date of the placement of the child
- the date from which it is expected that liability to pay SPP will begin
- whether the period chosen in respect of which SPP is to be payable is a week
- the date the adopter was notified that he or she had been matched with the child for the purposes of adoption – Reg 15(1)(a) and (2).

The employee must also provide: **7.117**

- a declaration that he or she has or expects to have responsibility for the upbringing of the child and is either married to, or the civil partner or partner of, the child's adopter
- a declaration that the purpose of the leave is to care for an adopted child or support the child's adopter
- where the employee is entitled to both SPP and SAP, a declaration that he or she has elected to receive SPP and not SAP – Reg 15(1)(b) and (c).

335

Where the employer so requests, the employee must also inform it of the date of the child's placement within 28 days, or as soon as is reasonably practicable thereafter – Reg 15(4).

7.118 A model self-certificate of entitlement to paternity leave and pay in respect of a child placed for adoption (form SC4, 'Becoming an adoptive parent') is available from HMRC. For the purpose of claiming SPP where a child is adopted from overseas, the model self-certificate form SC5, 'Statutory Paternity Pay and paternity leave when adopting from abroad', can be used (available from HMRC). Employers can also request a completed self-certificate as evidence of entitlement to paternity leave (see 'Notice and evidential requirements for paternity leave – notice requirements (adoption)' above). Where employees provide a completed SC4/SC5, they should therefore be able to satisfy the notice and evidence conditions for both paternity leave and pay.

7.119 **Evidence of entitlement (surrogacy).** A parental order parent wishing to claim SPP must provide his or her employer with the following information:

- his or her name
- the expected week of birth
- the date from which it is expected that liability to pay SPP will begin
- whether the period chosen in respect of which SPP is to be payable is a week
- the date on which the child was born – Reg 15(1)(a) and (2) (as modified by Reg 14 Pay (Parental Orders and Prospective Adopters) Regulations).

7.120 The employee must also provide:

- a declaration that he or she has or expects to have responsibility for the upbringing of the child and is either married to, or the civil partner or partner of, Parent A
- a declaration that the purpose of the leave is to care for the child or support Parent A
- where the employee is entitled to both SPP and SAP, a declaration that he or she has elected to receive SPP and not SAP – Reg 15(1)(b) and (c).

Where the employer so requests, the employee must also inform it of the date of the child's birth within 28 days, or as soon as is reasonably practicable thereafter – Reg 15(4) (as modified by Reg 14 Pay (Parental Orders and Prospective Adopters) Regulations).

7.121 **Payment of SPP**

Payments of SPP may be made in a like manner to payments of remuneration but must not include payment in kind or by way of the provision of board or lodgings or of services or other facilities – Reg 41 General Regulations.

SPP should be paid on the day that has been agreed for the payment, the day when payments by way of remuneration are normally made, or, in the absence of agreement or normal practice, the last day of the calendar month – Reg 42(1).

Section 171ZE(10A) SSCBA allows SPP to be calculated at a daily rate, which is one seventh of the weekly rate. Although SSP is payable in blocks of one or two weeks, employers may find it easier to use a daily rate for SPP where, for example, the pay period straddles two monthly pay periods. If the SPP calculation – on the basis of either the daily or the weekly rate – produces a figure that includes a fraction of a penny, the payment must be rounded up to the nearest whole penny – Reg 4 Weekly Rates Regulations.

Liability for SPP. Generally, the liability to pay SPP is on the employer who **7.122** employs the employee claiming SPP – S.171ZD(1). However, a former employer will be liable to make payments of SPP to a former employee in any case where the employee had been employed for a continuous period of at least eight weeks and his or her contract of service was brought to an end by the former employer solely, or mainly, for the purpose of avoiding liability for SPP – Reg 20(1).

In such a case the employee shall be treated as if he or she had been employed for a continuous period ending with the child's birth or, as the case may be, the placement of the child for adoption, and his or her normal weekly earnings will be calculated by reference to his or her normal weekly earnings for the period of eight weeks ending with the last day in respect of which he or she was paid under his former contract of service – Reg 20(2).

Liability of HMRC. Regulation 43 General Regulations makes HMRC liable **7.123** to pay SPP that is due where the employer has failed to do so. Where the employer is insolvent, HMRC will be liable as from the week in which the employer first becomes insolvent until the end of the paternity pay period – Reg 43(2). Where HMRC becomes liable for the payment of SPP, the first payment will be made as soon as reasonably practicable after it becomes liable, and payments thereafter will be made at weekly intervals – Reg 45.

Persons unable to act. Where SPP is payable to a person who is unable for the **7.124** time being to act and no receiver has been appointed by the Court of Protection with power to receive SPP on his or her behalf (or, in Scotland, where his or her estate is not being administered by any tutor, curator or other guardian acting or appointed in terms of law) HMRC may, upon written application by a person over 18, appoint that person to exercise any right to payment on behalf of the person unable to act – Reg 46.

Disentitlement to SPP. There are several circumstances in which an employer **7.125** will not be liable to pay SPP to an employee.

337

7.126 *Working for the employer paying SPP during the paternity pay period.* Under S.171ZE(5) an employer is not liable to pay SPP to an employee in respect of a statutory pay week during any part of which the employee works under a contract of service for the employer. It is immaterial whether the contract of service under which the work is carried out existed immediately before the statutory pay week or not – S.171ZE(6).

7.127 *Working for another employer during the paternity pay period.* The general rule is that SPP is not payable to an employee in respect of a statutory pay week during any part of which he or she works for an employer who is not liable to pay him or her SPP – S.171ZE(7). Reg 17(1) provides that where SPP is being paid to a person who works during the SPP period for an employer who is not liable to pay him or her SPP there is no liability to pay SPP in respect of any remaining part of the SPP period. However, this is subject to Reg 10(b)/Reg 16(b), which provide that SPP is still payable to an employee who works for another employer who is not liable to pay SPP during any part of a statutory pay week provided that the employee worked for that employer in the 15th week before the expected week of the child's birth or, in the case of adoption, in the week in which the adopter was notified of being matched with the child.

'Statutory pay week' is defined in S.171ZE(11) as a week chosen by the employee as a week in respect of which SPP will be payable. 'Week' means any period of seven days – S.171ZE(11).

7.128 Where Reg 17(1) applies, it is the duty of the employee to inform the original employer that he or she has started work for another employer within seven days of the first day during which he or she works during the SPP period – Reg 17(2). This notification must be in writing if the original employer so requests – Reg 17(3).

7.129 *Illness and death.* There is no liability to pay SPP in respect of any week during any part of which the employee is entitled to statutory sick pay or in respect of any week following that in which the employee has died – Reg 18(a) and (b).

7.130 *Legal custody.* Regulation 18(c) provides that there is no liability to pay SPP in respect of any week during part of which the employee is in legal custody or sentenced to a term of imprisonment (except where the sentence is suspended), or which is a subsequent week within the same SPP period.

7.131 **SPP and contractual remuneration.** Under S.171ZG(1), any entitlement to SPP does not affect any right to remuneration under any contract of employment. However, certain contractual payments to an employee can be offset against SPP – S.171ZG(2)(a). Similarly, any SPP paid to an employee for any week will go towards discharging any liability to pay contractual remuneration in respect of that period – S.171ZG(2)(b).

The payments which are to be treated as contractual remuneration are sums payable under a contract of service:

- by way of remuneration
- for incapacity for work due to sickness or injury
- by reason of the birth or adoption of a child – Reg 19.

Contracting out. Any agreement will be void if it purports to exclude, limit or **7.132** modify any provision of the SPP scheme or if it purports to require an employee to contribute to any costs incurred by the employer under such a scheme – S.171ZF(1). However, some agreements to make deductions from SPP are acceptable. Under S.171ZF(2) an agreement between employer and employee authorising deductions from SPP is not void if the employer is authorised to make the same deductions from contractual remuneration. So an employer may be able to continue making deductions in respect of, for example, pension contributions, trade union subscriptions or a season ticket loan. Similarly, SPP is treated as earnings, so an employer should make any statutory deductions (such as income tax and NI contributions) that are due.

8 Shared parental leave and pay

A new statutory system of shared parental leave and pay was introduced on **8.1** 1 December 2014 by the Children and Families Act 2014. The scheme allows a woman who is eligible for statutory maternity leave (SML) and statutory maternity pay (SMP) to choose to bring both to an early end and share the balance with the father of her child (or her spouse, civil partner or partner). While the statutory scheme came into force on 1 December 2014, it only applies to children due on or after 5 April 2015. Employees who adopt enjoy similar rights to shared parental leave and pay (for children who are placed for adoption on or after 5 April 2015), as do intended parents of a child born through a surrogacy arrangement (if they apply for a parental order and are eligible for adoption leave). While these rights are to all intents and purposes identical to the rights afforded to birth parents, there are obviously some necessary differences to cater for the particular circumstances.

Unpaid parental leave. Shared parental leave should not be confused with the **8.2** right to parental leave contained in Part III of the Maternity and Parental Leave etc Regulations 1999 SI 1999/3312 ('the MPL Regulations'), which entitles qualifying parents to take up to 18 weeks' unpaid leave to care for a child. Unpaid parental leave is discussed in Chapter 10, 'Unpaid parental leave'.

341

8.3 Background and overview

Prior to the 2010 general election, the Conservative and Liberal Democrat parties were both committed to introducing a more flexible system of leave for parents wishing to share caring responsibility for their children. This was reflected in the subsequent coalition agreement and the May 2011 'Consultation on modern workplaces'. In its response to that consultation, the Government announced that it would implement a package of measures to encourage fathers to take a greater role in caring for their babies and to enable working families to share the leave and pay that up till then had only been available to the mother.

The enabling provisions for these measures – which derive from the Children and Families Act 2014 – came into force on 30 June 2014: new Ss.75E–75K of the Employment Rights Act 1996 (ERA) govern shared parental leave (SPL) and new Ss.171ZU–171ZZ5 of the Social Security Contributions and Benefits Act 1992 (SSCBA) govern statutory shared parental pay (SSPP). The details of the scheme are set out in the following Regulations:

- the Shared Parental Leave Regulations 2014 SI 2014/3050 ('the SPL Regulations')

- the Statutory Shared Parental Pay (General) Regulations 2014 SI 2014/3051 ('the SSPP Regulations')

- the Maternity and Adoption Leave (Curtailment of Statutory Rights to Leave) Regulations 2014 SI 2014/3052 ('the Leave (Curtailment) Regulations')

- the Statutory Maternity Pay and Statutory Adoption Pay (Curtailment) Regulations 2014 SI 2014/3054 ('the Pay (Curtailment) Regulations')

- the Maternity Allowance (Curtailment) Regulations 2014 SI 2014/3053 ('the MA (Curtailment) Regulations').

8.4 To assist employers and employees in understanding the new rules, the Department for Business, Innovation and Skills (BIS) has published an 'Employer's Technical Guide to Shared Parental Leave and Pay' ('the Technical Guide') and Acas has published 'Shared Parental Leave: a good practice guide for employers and employees' ('the Acas Guide'). BIS has also developed an online calculator to help prospective parents calculate their eligibility for shared parental leave and their pay entitlements.

8.5 Who has the right?

The following persons are eligible for SPL and SSPP, provided they satisfy the relevant qualifying conditions:

- birth parents
- adoptive parents
- foster parents, and
- intended parents in a surrogacy arrangement ('parental order parents').

We consider each category in turn below. First, however, we look at the definition of 'employee', as only those workers who are employees can benefit from the right to shared parental leave and pay.

Employees only
8.6

Only employees can benefit from the right to shared parental leave and pay. The definition of 'employee' for SSPP purposes is wider than the definition of employee for SPL purposes.

Definition of 'employee' for SPL purposes. Only employees, as defined by 8.7 S.230(1) ERA, can benefit from the right to SPL, and not other types of worker or the self-employed – Ss.75E–75K ERA. In other words, the right to SPL is afforded only to those who have entered into or work under (or where employment has ceased, worked under) a contract of employment – which is defined as a contract of service or apprenticeship, whether express or implied, and (if express) whether oral or in writing. These definitions of 'employee' and 'contract of employment' are common to many statutory employment rights, including statutory maternity leave, adoption leave and paternity leave – see Chapter 3, 'Maternity leave', under 'Entitlement to maternity leave – employees only'; Chapter 6, 'Adoption leave and pay', under 'Ordinary adoption leave – who has the right?'; and Chapter 7, 'Paternity leave and pay', under 'Who has the right?'. Reference should be made to IDS Employment Law Handbook, 'Contracts of Employment (2014), Chapter 2, 'Employment status', under 'Statutory definitions of "employee"', for a full discussion of the law in this area.

Definition of 'employee' for SSPP purposes. The definition of 'employee' for 8.8 SSPP purposes is slightly wider than that which applies for SPL purposes. It mirrors the definition that applies in respect of SMP, and indeed statutory adoption pay and paternity pay – see Ss.171(1) (maternity), 171ZS (adoption) and 171ZJ (paternity) SSCBA. S.171ZZ4 SSCBA, which governs SSPP, states that 'employee' means a person:

- who is gainfully employed either under a contract of service or as an office holder (including an elective office), and

- with general earnings, as defined by S.7 of the Income Tax (Earnings and Pensions) Act 2003 (i.e. any salary, wages or fee; any gratuity or other profit or incidental benefit of any kind if it is money or money's worth; or anything else that constitutes an emolument of the employment).

343

In addition, there are special cases where a worker will be considered an employee for SSPP purposes, despite not falling within the definition set out in S.171ZZ4. This means that SSPP may be available in some cases where SPL is not available (on account of the fact that the individual in question is not an 'employee' for the purposes of the SPL scheme) – see further 'Statutory shared parental pay – qualifying for SSPP' below.

8.9 Birth parents

Birth parents are eligible for shared parental leave and pay by virtue of Part 2 SPL Regulations and Part 2 SSPP Regulations. The child's mother or expectant mother can share leave with:

- the child's father, or

- her spouse, civil partner or partner at the date of birth – Regs 3(1), 4 and 5 SPL Regulations/Regs 2(1), 4 and 5 SSPP Regulations.

The father of the child will, of course, not necessarily be the mother's husband or partner (and vice versa), in which case the mother will have to decide with whom she wishes to share the leave. She cannot, however, share the leave with more than one person.

8.10 A 'partner' means a person (whether of a different sex or the same sex) who lives with the mother and child in an 'enduring family relationship' but is not a blood relative of the mother. The relatives of the mother who are expressly prohibited from being a partner for these purposes are her parents, grandparents, sisters, brothers, aunts and uncles, whether they are full blood or half blood or, in the case of an adopted person, such of those relationships as would exist but for the adoption (i.e. her birth family) – Reg 3(1) and (2) SPL Regulations/ Reg 2(1)–(3) SSPP Regulations. The mother's adoptive, or former adoptive, parents are also prohibited from being a partner but not other adoptive relationships. Thus, if the mother is adopted, her adoptive parents would be excluded but not, it seems, her adoptive brother.

The Regulations offer no indication of what is meant by 'an enduring family relationship', but one assumes that the enduring nature will be measured primarily by reference to the time an individual's relationship with the mother has lasted rather than on any forecast of how long the relationship with the mother (and baby) will last in the future. Presumably the degree of commitment to the relationship will also be a relevant factor.

8.11 Not all birth parents are entitled to SPL, as they must also satisfy the conditions set out in Part 2 SPL Regulations – see further 'Shared parental leave (birth)' below. The conditions for SSPP are discussed under 'Statutory shared parental pay – qualifying for SSPP' below.

Adoptive parents
8.12

Adoptive parents are eligible for shared parental leave and pay by virtue of Part 3 SPL Regulations and Part 3 SSPP Regulations. The adopter can share leave with his or her spouse, civil partner or partner – Regs 20 and 21 SPL Regulations/Regs 17 and 18 SSPP Regulations. The adopter for these purposes is the person with whom the child is, or is expected to be, placed for adoption – Reg 3(1) SPL Regulations/Reg 2(1) SSPP Regulations. Where two people have been matched jointly, Reg 3(1) SPL Regulations provides that the primary adopter is whoever has elected to be the child's adopter for the purposes of the Paternity and Adoption Leave Regulations 2002 SI 2002/2788 ('the PAL Regulations'). A person elects to be a child's adopter if he or she and the other person agree at the time they are matched that he or she will be the adopter – Reg 2(4)(c) PAL Regulations. The definition of adopter is the same as that which applies for the purposes of adoption leave and paternity leave – see Chapter 6, 'Adoption leave and pay', under 'Ordinary adoption leave – conditions of entitlement', and Chapter 7, 'Paternity leave and pay', under 'Entitlement to paternity leave (adoption)'. The meanings of 'partner' are discussed under 'Birth parents' above.

Not all adoptive parents are eligible for SPL. They must also satisfy the conditions set out in Part 3 SPL Regulations – see 'Shared parental leave (adoption)' below. These conditions replicate those that apply for birth parents, differing only to reflect the circumstances. The conditions for SSPP are discussed under 'Statutory shared parental pay – qualifying for SSPP' below.

Adoption from overseas. Employees who adopt from overseas are also entitled 8.13 to shared parental leave and pay by virtue of the following Regulations:

- the Employment Rights Act 1996 (Application of Sections 75G and 75H to Adoptions from Overseas) Regulations 2014 SI 2014/2091

- the Shared Parental Leave and Paternity and Adoption Leave (Adoptions from Overseas) Regulations 2014 SI 2014/3092, and

- the Statutory Shared Parental Pay (Adoption from Overseas) Regulations 2014 SI 2014/3093.

The right arises in relation to children who enter Great Britain on or after 5th April 2015.

Foster parents
8.14

The Paternity and Adoption Leave (Amendment) (No.2) Regulations 2014 SI 2014/3206 ('the PAL (Amendment) (No.2) Regulations') provide new rights to adoption leave for local authority foster parents who are approved prospective adopters where a child is placed with them with a view to adoption under S.22C of the Children Act 1989 – see Chapter 6, 'Adoption leave and pay', under 'Ordinary adoption leave – who has the right?'. The Regulations also provide

345

new statutory paternity leave rights to the spouses, civil partners and partners of those foster parents – see Chapter 7, 'Paternity leave and pay', under 'Who has the right? – foster parents'. Foster couples (comprising the foster parent and his or her spouse, civil partner or partner) have the right to SPL (under Part 3 SPL Regulations) and SSPP (under Part 2 SSPP Regulations). Reg 3(1) SPL Regulations and Reg 2(1) SSPP Regulations make it clear that a child is 'placed for adoption' for the purposes of SPL and SSPP if he or she is 'placed... with a local authority foster parent who is also a prospective adopter'. The conditions of eligibility are the same as for adoptive parents – see 'Shared parental leave (adoption)' and 'Statutory shared parental pay – qualifying for SSPP' below.

8.15 Surrogacy

Where a child is born via a surrogacy arrangement, the surrogate mother (i.e. the woman who is carrying or has carried the child) is regarded as the child's mother – S.33 Human Fertilisation and Embryology Act 2008. This means that surrogate mothers are entitled to take full statutory maternity leave and pay, regardless of whether or not they continue to have contact with the child following the birth. The same applies to mothers who give their child up for adoption following the birth. In order to be eligible for shared parental leave and pay, however, the mother must have shared responsibility for caring for the child – Reg 4(2)(b) and (3)(b) SPL Regulations/Reg 4(2)(b) and (3)(a) SSPP Regulations. This requirement will preclude surrogate mothers from being entitled to SPL and SSPP.

The intended mother in a surrogacy arrangement is not entitled to take SML even if, as anticipated, she ends up caring for the child following the birth (since the MPL Regulations only apply to birth mothers). The ECJ has confirmed that a woman who becomes a mother through a surrogacy arrangement is not entitled to maternity leave under EU law – CD v ST 2014 ICR D26, ECJ, and Mayr v Bäckerei und Konditorei Gerhard Flöckner OHG 2008 IRLR 387, ECJ. These cases are discussed in Chapter 3, 'Maternity leave', under 'Entitlement to maternity leave – surrogacy'.

8.16 However, under the Paternity, Adoption and Shared Parental Leave (Parental Order Cases) Regulations 2014 SI 2014/3096 ('the Leave (Parental Order Cases) Regulations') the right to take adoption leave and paternity leave has been extended to parents in a surrogacy arrangement who have:

- acquired a parental order under S.54(1) of the Human Fertilisation and Embryology Act 2008 in respect of a child, or

- applied or intend to apply for such an order, which they expect to be made, within six months of the child's birth.

Such parents are referred to as 'parental order parents' by the legislation. The parent who is entitled to take adoption leave is the one who has elected to be

'Parent A' in accordance with Reg 2(4) PAL Regulations (as modified by Reg 6 Leave (Parental Order Cases) Regulations). Simply put, a person elects to be Parent A in relation to a child if this is agreed by the couple. The other parent is eligible for statutory paternity leave provided he or she is the spouse, civil partner or partner of Parent A when the child is born. For full details, see Chapter 6, 'Adoption leave and pay', under 'Ordinary adoption leave – who has the right?', and Chapter 7, 'Paternity leave and pay', under 'Who has the right? – surrogacy'.

Parental order parents are eligible for SPL if Parent A is eligible for adoption **8.17** leave – Part 3 SPL Regulations, as modified by Part 4 Leave (Parental Order Cases) Regulations. Parent A can share leave with the other parental order parent, provided they are married, in a civil partnership or in an enduring family relationship when the child is born – Reg 21 Leave (Parental Order Cases) Regulations. The conditions of eligibility for parental order parents are discussed under 'Shared parental leave (surrogacy)' below.

Shared parental leave (birth) 8.18

Birth parents are eligible for SPL by virtue of Part 2 SPL Regulations – see 'Who has the right? – birth parents' above. The child's mother or expectant mother can share leave with:

* the child's father, or

* her spouse, civil partner or partner at the date of birth – Regs 4 and 5 SPL Regulations.

For simplicity's sake, throughout this chapter we use the term 'father' (as shorthand for 'father/spouse/partner') to describe the person who is eligible to share leave with the birth mother (unless the context otherwise requires). However, it should always be borne in mind that the mother can choose to share leave with someone who is not the child's biological father.

The conditions for SPL consequent upon the birth of a child are set out in **8.19** Part 2 SPL Regulations. The mother must satisfy the conditions in Reg 4, and the father must satisfy those in Reg 5. There is a great deal of similarity between the two sets of requirements. They can be summarised as follows:

* the employee must have been working with the same employer for 26 weeks by the end of the 'relevant week' and remain in continuous employment until the week before he or she starts any period of SPL – see 'Continuous employment' below

* the employee must share the main caring responsibility for the child with the other parent – see 'Main caring responsibility' below

347

- the other parent must satisfy the 'employment and earnings test' set out in Reg 36 – see 'Employment and earnings test' below

- the mother must be entitled to SML and have ended that entitlement. Note that if the mother is not entitled to SML, the father (but not the mother) can still claim SPL if she is entitled to SMP or Maternity Allowance and has ended that entitlement – see 'Mother must be eligible for SML' and 'Mother must curtail SML' below.

8.20 There are also a number of notification and evidential requirements that need to be satisfied, discussed in detail under 'Notification and evidential requirements' below. In brief, they are as follows:

- the employee must give a notice of entitlement to his or her employer in accordance with Reg 8 (if the mother) or Reg 9 (if the father) – Regs 4(2)(e) and 5(2)(c)

- the employee must, if requested, give his or her employer the child's birth certificate and/or the name and address of the other parent's employer – Regs 4(2)(f) and 5(2)(d), and

- the employee must give a 'period of leave notice' in accordance with Reg 12 in order to book the period (or periods) of SPL he or she wishes to take – Regs 4(2)(g) and 5(2)(e).

Note that the conditions for adoptive parents – set out in Reg 20 and Reg 21 – are very similar and are discussed under 'Shared parental leave – adoption' below.

8.21 Continuous employment

To be eligible for SPL, the employee must have been continuously employed for 26 weeks up to and including the 'relevant week' – Regs 4(2)(a), 5(2)(a) and 35(1)(a) SPL Regulations. In addition, the employee must remain in continuous employment until the week before he or she starts any period of SPL – Reg 35(1)(b). Note that this contrasts with SML, where there is no minimum qualifying service – see Chapter 3, 'Maternity leave', under 'Entitlement to maternity leave'. The 'relevant week' for these purposes is the week immediately preceding the 14th week before the expected week of childbirth (EWC) – Reg 35(3)(a). Put more simply, it is the 15th week before the EWC. The 'expected week' of childbirth means the week, beginning with midnight between Saturday and Sunday, in which it is expected that the child will be born – Reg 3(1).

8.22 Premature births. Reg 35(2) states that an employee will be treated as having satisfied the continuous employment condition in Reg 35(1)(a) if he or she would have satisfied it but for the fact that the child was born earlier than expected.

Main caring responsibility   8.23

The employee must – at the date of birth – share the main caring responsibility for the child with the other parent – Regs 4(2)(b) and (3)(b); and 5(2)(b) and (3)(b). The Regulations offer no indication of what is meant by 'main caring responsibility'. It is unclear whether the fact that the parents are living together as husband and wife or as partners is in itself sufficient to establish that they share the main caring responsibility for the child, or whether evidence of how they have agreed to share the childcare will also be required. If the mother and father are separated, this will not necessarily preclude them from sharing the main caring responsibility for the child. All will depend upon the particular circumstances of the case and, crucially, what has been agreed between them.

Employment and earnings test   8.24

While there is no minimum earnings threshold for employees claiming SPL, the other parent must satisfy the 'employment and earnings test' set out in Reg 36 – Regs 4(3)(a) and 5(3)(a) SPL Regulations. The test requires the other parent to have:

• been an employed or self-employed earner in Great Britain for a total of 26 weeks (which do not have to be continuous) in the period of 66 weeks leading up to the EWC ('the calculation week'), and

• earned an average of £30 a week in 13 of those weeks (whether or not continuous).

'Employed earner' is defined by S.2(1)(a) SSCBA as 'a person who is gainfully employed in Great Britain either under a contract of service, or in an office (including elective office) with earnings'. Earnings includes 'any remuneration or profit derived from an employment' – S.3. 'Self-employed earner' means 'a person who is gainfully employed in Great Britain otherwise than in employed earner's employment' – S.2(1)(b). Under the Social Security (Categorisation of Earners) Regulations 1978 SI 1978/1689, certain categories of persons who do not have a contract of service or hold an office with earnings are nonetheless treated as 'employed earners' for national insurance (NI) purposes. Conversely, certain categories of persons are treated as 'self-employed earners' notwithstanding that they are employed under a contract of service or are in an office with general earnings. The same categories apply for the purposes of the 'employment and earnings test'. Those falling into the category of 'employed earners' under the 1978 Regulations include office cleaners, ministers of religion, persons employed by their spouse or civil partner, certain entertainers and certain agency workers. The category of 'self-employed earners' is smaller, comprising examiners, moderators and invigilators.

As noted in the Technical Guide, self-employed parents will not be eligible for   8.25
SPL and SSPP but if they satisfy the employment and earnings test this may

enable their employed partner to access them – an example of 'shared' parental leave not actually being shared at all.

8.26 Mother must be eligible for SML

The mother can only qualify for SPL if she is entitled to SML in respect of the child in question – Reg 4(2)(c) SPL Regulations. As explained in Chapter 3, 'Maternity leave', SML is divided into 26 weeks' ordinary maternity leave (OML) and a further 26 weeks' additional maternity leave (AML). The conditions for eligibility – which are discussed in Chapter 3 under 'Entitlement to maternity leave' – are much less stringent than those for SPL, meaning that this particular hurdle will be easily passed if the mother satisfies the conditions for SPL.

The father's right to SPL, on the other hand, is dependent upon the mother being entitled to SML *or* SMP (or Maternity Allowance) – Reg 5(3)(c) SPL Regulations. In other words, where the mother is entitled to SML, both she and the father will be entitled to SPL (provided the other qualifying conditions are met). However, if the mother only qualifies for SMP or Maternity Allowance, she cannot claim SPL but the father can. In these circumstances, the term 'shared parental leave' is something of a misnomer since the father will not be sharing the statutory leave with anyone.

8.27 Normally a mother who is entitled to SML will also be entitled to SMP (or Maternity Allowance), and vice versa, so this scenario will rarely arise. However, in certain circumstances, the mother may be eligible for one and not the other. For example, the definition of 'employee' for the purpose of claiming SMP (and Maternity Allowance) is wider than the definition for SML purposes, meaning that women who only fall within the wider definition may only be able to claim SMP (see Chapter 3, 'Maternity leave', under 'Entitlement to maternity leave – employees only', and Chapter 5, 'Statutory maternity pay', under 'Qualifying for statutory maternity pay – definition of "employee"'). Conversely, in order to qualify for SMP, a woman must have completed 26 weeks' continuous service by the 15th week before the EWC (or 26 non-continuous weeks in the 66 weeks preceding the EWC for Maternity Allowance) (see Chapter 5, 'Statutory maternity pay', under 'Continuous employment'). No such requirement exists for SML, meaning that a woman who has not completed 26 weeks' service could claim SML but not SMP.

8.28 Mother must curtail SML

Where the mother is entitled to SML, she must cut short that entitlement in order to take advantage of SPL – Regs 4(2)(d) and 5(3)(d)(i). This she can do by either:

● returning to work early, or

- giving a leave curtailment notice to her employer, in accordance with Part 2 of the Maternity and Adoption Leave (Curtailment of Statutory Rights to Leave) Regulations 2014 SI 2014/3052 ('the Leave (Curtailment) Regulations').

Both options are considered under 'Curtailing maternity or adoption leave' below.

Note that the mother *must* take SML in the two weeks after birth by virtue of S.72(1) ERA and Reg 8 MPL Regulations. This is known as the 'compulsory maternity leave period'. For factory workers the compulsory maternity leave period is four weeks after giving birth – S.205 Public Health Act 1936. In other words, mothers cannot waive their compulsory maternity leave period for the purposes of SPL. This is made clear by Reg 6(2)(a) Leave (Curtailment) Regulations, which provides that the leave curtailment date must be at least one day after the end of the compulsory maternity leave period under the MPL Regulations (or the four-week period under the Public Health Act 1936 if applicable).

As explained under 'Mother must be eligible for SML' above, there will be a **8.29** limited number of cases where the mother is not entitled to SPL but the father is (because the mother is entitled to SMP or Maternity Allowance but not SML). In such cases, in order for the father to take advantage of SPL the mother must cut short her 'maternity pay period' (i.e. the 39 weeks that SMP is payable) or her 'Maternity Allowance period' (i.e. the 39 weeks that Maternity Allowance is payable). (The mother must similarly curtail her maternity pay period or Maternity Allowance period if she and/or the father wish to claim SSPP – see 'Statutory shared parental pay – curtailing maternity pay or allowance' below.)

What if parent or child dies?   8.30

Where the mother, father or child dies before the end of the period during which SPL may be taken, special provisions contained in Part 1 of the Schedule to the Regulations apply – Reg 19 SPL Regulations. If the mother dies, the father does not lose his entitlement to SPL and the requirement for the mother to have curtailed her SML and SMP (or Maternity Allowance) does not apply, although if she has already done so the curtailment still has effect – see paras 1 and 2 of the Schedule.

If the father dies, the mother does not lose her entitlement to SPL, provided she has given her employer a notice of entitlement in accordance with Reg 8 SPL Regulations – see 'Notice and evidential requirements for SPL – notice of entitlement (birth)' below. Again, the relevant statutory provisions are modified to factor in this 'special circumstance' – see paras 4 and 5 of the Schedule.

If the child dies, the parents are entitled to take any period of SPL already booked (see 'Planning and booking periods of leave' below) but cannot book any further periods of leave – para 5 of the Schedule.

8.31 Shared parental leave (adoption)

Adoptive parents are eligible for SPL by virtue of Part 3 SPL Regulations – see 'Who has the right? – adoptive parents' above. The 'adopter' for these purposes (i.e. the one who is entitled to take statutory adoption leave (SAL) and who must cut short that leave in order to opt in to SPL) is the person with whom the child is, or is expected to be, placed for adoption. Where two people have been matched jointly, the adopter is whoever has elected to be the child's adopter – Reg 3(1) SPL Regulations. The right to SPL extends to local authority foster parents who are approved prospective adopters where a child is placed with them with a view to adoption under S.22C of the Children Act 1989, as well as employees who adopt from overseas – see the section 'Who has the right?', under 'Adoptive parents – foster parents' above.

The conditions for SPL consequent upon the adoption of a child are set out in Part 3 SPL Regulations. The adopter must satisfy the conditions in Reg 20 and the adopter's spouse or partner must satisfy those in Reg 21. There is a great deal of similarity between the two sets of requirements. They can be summarised as follows:

- the employee must have been working with the same employer for 26 weeks by the end of the 'relevant week' and remain in continuous employment until the week before he or she starts any period of SPL – see 'Continuous employment' below

- the employee must share the main caring responsibility for the child with his or her spouse/partner – see 'Main caring responsibility' below

- the employee's spouse or partner must satisfy the 'employment and earnings test' set out in Reg 36 – see 'Employment and earnings test' below

- the adopter must be entitled to SAL and have ended that entitlement. Note that if the adopter is not entitled to SAL but is entitled to statutory adoption pay (SAP), the adopter's spouse (or partner) can still claim SPL, provided the adopter ends that entitlement – see 'Adopter must be entitled to SAL' and 'Adopter must curtail SAL' below.

8.32 There are also a number of notification and evidential requirements that need to be satisfied, discussed in detail under 'Notification and evidential requirements' below. In brief, they are as follows:

- the employee must give a notice of entitlement to his or her employer in accordance with Reg 24 (if the adopter) or Reg 25 (if the adopter's spouse or partner) – Regs 20(2)(e) and 21(2)(c)

- the employee must, if requested, give his or her employer certain information about the child's adoption and/or the name and address of the other parent's employer – Regs 20(2)(f) and 21(2)(d), and

- the employee must give a 'period of leave notice' in accordance with Reg 28 in order to book the period (or periods) of SPL he or she wishes to take – Regs 20(2)(g) and 21(2)(e).

These provisions governing SPL for adoptive parents are almost identical to those governing SPL for birth parents (see 'Shared parental leave (birth)' above).

Continuous employment   8.33

To be eligible for SPL, the employee must have been continuously employed for 26 weeks up to and including the 'relevant week' – Regs 20(2)(a), 21(2)(a) and 35 SPL Regulations. A similar requirement applies to birth parents (see 'Shared parental leave (birth) – continuous employment' above), except that 'relevant week' is defined as the week in which the principal adopter was notified of having been matched for adoption with the child – Reg 35(3)(b).

Main caring responsibility   8.34

The employee must share the main caring responsibility for the child with his or her spouse/partner at the date of the child's placement for adoption – Regs 20(2)(b) and (3)(b), and 21(2)(b) and (3)(b). This is the same as the requirement for birth parents (see 'Shared parental leave (birth) – main caring responsibility' above), except the responsibility must be shared at the date of the child's placement for adoption (as opposed to his or her birth). The Regulations offer no indication of what is meant by 'main caring responsibility'. If a couple have been matched with a child jointly by an adoption agency, that may go some way to establishing that they share the main caring responsibility for the child. Other relevant considerations might include how they have agreed to share the childcare and what domestic arrangements are in place to implement this.

Employment and earnings test   8.35

While there is no minimum earnings threshold for employees claiming SPL, their spouse or partner must satisfy the 'employment and earnings test' set out in Reg 36 – Regs 20(3)(a) and 21(3)(a) SPL Regulations. The test requires the spouse or partner to have:

- been an employed or self-employed earner in Great Britain for a total of 26 weeks (which do not have to be continuous) in the period of 66 weeks leading up to the week in which the adopter was notified of having been matched for adoption with the child ('the calculation week'), and

- earned an average of £30 a week in 13 of those weeks (whether or not continuous).

353

This test is identical to that which applies to birth parents, except that the calculation week for birth parents is the expected week of birth – see 'Shared parental leave (birth) – employment and earnings test' above.

8.36 Adopter must be eligible for SAL

The adopter can only qualify for SPL if he or she is entitled to SAL in respect of the child in question – Reg 20(2)(c) SPL Regulations. As detailed in Chapter 6, 'Adoption leave and pay', SAL is divided into 26 weeks' ordinary adoption leave (OAL) and a further 26 weeks' additional adoption leave (AAL). The conditions for eligibility are set out in that chapter under 'Ordinary adoption leave' and 'Additional adoption leave'. The spouse or partner's right to SPL, on the other hand, is dependent upon the adopter being entitled to SAL *or* statutory adoption pay (SAP) – Reg 21(3)(c) SPL Regulations. In other words, where the adopter is entitled to SAL, both the adopter and his or her spouse/partner will be entitled to SPL (provided the other qualifying conditions are met). However, if the adopter only qualifies for SAP, the adopter cannot claim SPL but his or her spouse/partner can.

8.37 Adopter must curtail SAL

Where the adopter is entitled to SAL, he or she must cut short that entitlement in order to take advantage of SPL – Regs 20(2)(d) and 21(3)(d)(i) SPL Regulations. This can be done by either:

- returning to work early, or

- giving a leave curtailment notice to the employer, in accordance with Part 3 Leave (Curtailment) Regulations.

Both options are considered under 'Curtailing maternity or adoption leave' below. Note that Reg 10(2)(a) of the Leave (Curtailment) Regulations provides that the adopter cannot curtail the first two weeks of SAL. This is despite the fact that there is no compulsory adoption leave period under the PAL Regulations.

8.38 As explained under 'Adopter must be eligible for SAL' above, there will be limited circumstances where the adopter will not be entitled to SPL, but his or her partner will (because the adopter is entitled to SAP but not to SAL). In such a case, the adopter must cut short his or her 'adoption pay period', i.e. the 39 weeks that SAP is payable – see Chapter 6, 'Adoption leave and pay', under 'Statutory adoption pay – period of payment of SAP'. (The adoption pay period must similarly be curtailed in order to claim SSPP – see 'Statutory shared parental pay – curtailing adoption pay' below.)

8.39 What if parent/child dies or placement disrupted?

Where the adopter, his or her partner or the child dies, or the child is returned after being placed for adoption, before the end of the period during which SPL may be taken, special provisions contained in Part 2 of the Schedule to the Regulations apply – Reg 34 SPL Regulations. If the adopter dies, the spouse/ partner does not lose his or her entitlement to SPL and the requirement for the adopter to have curtailed his or her SAL or SAP does not apply, although if he or she has already done so the curtailment still takes effect – paras 6 and 7 of the Schedule.

If the adopter's spouse or partner dies, the adopter does not lose his or her entitlement to SPL, provided the adopter has given a notice of entitlement to the employer – see 'Notice and evidential requirements for SPL – notice of entitlement (adoption)' below.

If the child dies or is returned to the adoption agency after being placed, the **8.40** parents are entitled to take any period of SPL already booked (see 'Planning and booking periods of leave' below) but cannot book any further periods of leave – see para 10 of the Schedule to the SPL Regulations.

Shared parental leave (surrogacy)   8.41

The right to SPL applies to parents of a child born through a surrogacy arrangement if they have a parental order (or have applied or intend to apply for such an order) and are eligible for adoption leave. They are referred to as 'parental order parents' by the Paternity, Adoption and Shared Parental Leave (Parental Order Cases) Regulations 2014 SI 2014/3096 ('the Leave (Parental Order Cases) Regulations'). The person who is entitled to take adoption leave – and hence who must cut short that leave in order to opt in to SPL – is the one who has agreed to be 'Parent A' – see further 'Who has the right? – surrogacy' above.

The conditions for SPL for such parents are set out in Part 3 SPL Regulations, i.e. the same as for adoptive parents. Importantly, however, these provisions are modified by Part 4 Leave (Parental Order Cases) Regulations. Parent A must satisfy the conditions set out in Reg 20 SPL Regulations (as modified) and Parent A's spouse or partner the conditions in Reg 21 (as modified). There is a great deal of similarity between the two sets of requirements. They can be summarised as follows:

- the employee must have been working with the same employer for 26 weeks by the end of the 'relevant week' and remain in continuous employment until the week before he or she starts any period of SPL – see 'Continuous employment' below

- the employee must share the main caring responsibility for the child with his or her spouse/partner – see 'Main caring responsibility' below

- the employee's spouse or partner must satisfy the 'employment and earnings test' set out in Reg 36 – see 'Employment and earnings test' below

- Parent A must be entitled to statutory adoption leave (SAL) and have ended that entitlement. Note that if the adopter is not entitled to SAL but is entitled to statutory adoption pay (SAP), the adopter's spouse (or partner) can still claim SPL, provided the adopter ends that entitlement – see 'Adopter must be entitled to SAL' and 'Adopter must curtail SAL' below.

8.42 There are also a number of notification and evidential requirements that need to be satisfied. In brief, they are as follows:

- the employee must give a notice of entitlement to his or her employer in accordance with Reg 24 (if Parent A) or Reg 25 (if Parent A's spouse or partner) – Regs 20(2)(e) and 21(2)(c)

- the employee must, if requested, give his or her employer evidence in the form of a parental order (if available) and/or the name and address of the other parent's employer – Regs 20(2)(f) and 21(2)(d), and

- the employee must give a 'period of leave notice' in accordance with Reg 28 in order to book the period (or periods) of SPL he or she wishes to take – Regs 20(2)(g) and Reg 21(2)(e).

8.43 Continuous employment

To be eligible for SPL, the employee must have been continuously employed for 26 weeks up to and including the 'relevant week' – Regs 20(2)(a), 21(2)(a) and 35 SPL Regulations. The 'relevant week' for these purposes is the 15th week before the week in which the baby is due to be born – Reg 31 Leave (Parental Order Cases) Regulations. This is the same as the continuity of employment requirement for birth parents – see 'Shared parental leave (birth) – continuous employment' above. As with birth parents, an employee will be treated as having satisfied the continuous employment condition in Reg 35(1)(a) if he or she would have satisfied it but for the fact that the child was born earlier than expected.

8.44 Main caring responsibility

The employee must share the main caring responsibility for the child with his or her spouse/partner at the date of the child's birth – Regs 22 and 23 Leave (Parental Order Cases) Regulations. This mirrors the requirement for birth parents, but differs from the requirement for adoptive parents (where the responsibility must be shared at the date of the child's placement for adoption) – see 'Shared parental leave (birth) – main caring responsibility' and 'Shared parental leave (adoption) – main caring responsibility' above.

8.45 Employment and earnings test

While there is no minimum earnings threshold for employees claiming SPL, their spouse or partner must satisfy the 'employment and earnings test' set out in Reg 36 – Regs 20(3)(a) and 21(3)(a) SPL Regulation. The test requires the spouse or partner to have:

- been an employed or self-employed earner in Great Britain for a total of 26 weeks (which do not have to be continuous) in the period of 66 weeks leading up to the expected week of birth ('the calculation week'), and

- earned an average of £30 a week in 13 of those weeks (whether or not continuous).

Note that, in contrast to the test for adoptive parents, the calculation week is the expected week of birth, and not the date on which the child is matched for adoption – Reg 32 Leave (Parental Order Cases) Regulations.

Parent A must be eligible for SAL   8.46
Parent A can only qualify for SPL if he or she is entitled to SAL in respect of the child in question – Reg 20(2)(c) SPL Regulations. The spouse or partner's right to SPL is dependent upon Parent A being entitled to SAL *or* SAP – Reg 21(3)(c) SPL Regulations.

Parent A must curtail SAL   8.47
Where Parent A is entitled to SAL, he or she must cut short that entitlement in order to take advantage of SPL – Regs 20(2)(d) and 21(3)(d)(i) SPL Regulations. This can be done either by:

- returning to work early, or

- giving an adoption leave curtailment notice to the employer, in accordance with Part 3 Leave (Curtailment) Regulations (i.e. the same procedure as applies for adoption).

Both options are considered under 'Curtailing maternity or adoption leave' below.

There will be limited circumstances where Parent A will not be entitled to SPL but his or her partner will (because Parent A is entitled to SAP but not to SAL). In such a case Parent A must cut short his or her adoption pay period. (The adoption pay period must similarly be curtailed in order to claim SSPP – see 'Statutory shared parental pay – curtailing adoption pay' below.

What if parent/child dies or parental order not granted?   8.48
The provisions that apply to adoption cases where a parent or child dies, or the placement is disrupted, apply equally to surrogacy situations but with modifications. Reg 30 Leave (Parental Order Cases) Regulations modifies Reg 34 SPL Regulations to provide that Part 2 of the Schedule to the SPL Regulations applies where Parent A, his or her spouse or partner or the child dies; the intended parents do not apply for a parental order within the time

limit set down in S.54(3) of the Human Fertilisation and Embryology Act 2008; or their application is refused, withdrawn or otherwise terminated. Reg 33 Leave (Parental Order Cases) Regulations makes the necessary knock-on modifications to para 10 of the Schedule to deal with these situations. See 'Shared parental leave (adoption) – what if parent/child dies or placement disrupted?' above.

8.49 Curtailing maternity or adoption leave

An employee who is entitled to SML or SAL must cut short that entitlement in order to take advantage of SPL – Regs 4(2)(d) and 5(3)(d)(i) SPL Regulations. This can be done by either:

*   returning to work early – see 'Returning to work early' below, or
*   giving a leave curtailment notice to the employer in accordance with the Maternity and Adoption Leave (Curtailment of Statutory Rights to Leave) Regulations 2014 SI 2014/3052 ('the Leave (Curtailment) Regulations') – see 'Giving a leave curtailment notice' below.

The curtailment provisions for parental order parents in a surrogacy arrangement are identical to those that apply for adoptive parents.

8.50   Note that under Reg 8 MPL Regulations, the mother *must* take SML in the two weeks after birth (four weeks under the Public Health Act 1936 if she is a factory worker) and she cannot waive this compulsory maternity leave period for the purposes of SPL. This is made clear by Reg 6(2)(a) Leave (Curtailment) Regulations, which provides that the leave curtailment date must be at least one day after the end of the compulsory maternity leave period under the MPL Regulations (or the four-week period under the Public Health Act 1936 if applicable). There is no equivalent compulsory adoption leave period for adopters under the PAL Regulations. Nevertheless, Reg 10(2)(a) Leave (Curtailment) Regulations provides that the adopter cannot curtail the first two weeks of SAL. In addition, even if the adopter returns to work straightaway, Reg 22(1)(b) SPL Regulations makes it clear that the first two weeks back do not count for the purposes of calculating the amount of SPL in adoption cases. Therefore the maximum amount of SPL that can be made available for both birth and adoptive parents is 50 weeks (since both SML and SAL comprise 52 weeks).

8.51   **Returning to work early**
The first method by which maternity/adoption leave can be curtailed is by the mother/adopter returning to work early. The procedure for doing this is set out in Reg 11 MPL Regulations for SML, and Reg 25 PAL Regulations for SAL (full details can be found in Chapter 4, 'Returning to work after maternity leave', under 'Date of return to work – notice of intention to return early', and

Chapter 6, 'Adoption leave and pay', under 'Returning to work after adoption leave – notice of return during adoption leave'). Whether returning early from SML or SAL, the employee must give the employer at least eight weeks' notice of the date on which he or she intends to come back to work – Reg 11(1)/Reg 25(1). There is no requirement that this notice be in writing. The employer may accept less or no notice at its discretion. If an employee attempts to return to work early without having given eight weeks' notice, the employer is entitled to postpone the return to a date that will secure the full eight-week notice period – Reg 11(2)/Reg 25(2). The employer may not, however, delay the employee's return beyond the end of the full 52-week maternity/adoption leave period – Reg 11(3)/Reg 25(3).

An employee must also give eight weeks' notice if he or she decides to change the return date having previously given notice of early return, or where he or she decides to return later than any date to which the employer has postponed the return under Reg 11(2)/Reg 25(2). If the employee wishes to return to work earlier, he or she must give the employer not less than eight weeks' notice of the new intended return date; if he or she wishes to return later, he or she must give the employer at least eight weeks' notice ending with the original return date (or the postponed return date) – Reg 11(2A)(a) and (b)/Reg 25(2A)(a) and (b). There is no limit on the number of times an employee may change his or her mind as to the return date, provided Reg 11/Reg 25 is complied with.

8.52 Where a mother or adopter returns to work early, the amount of SPL available is 52 weeks less the number of weeks' SML/SAL taken – Regs 6(1)(b) and 22(1)(b)(i) SPL Regulations. As noted above, the mother must take compulsory maternity leave, which will be deducted from the 52-week period. While there is no compulsory adoption leave under the PAL Regulations, the first two weeks of SAL will always be deducted, whether or not this is taken by the adopter – Reg 22(1)(b)(ii).

Giving a leave curtailment notice

8.53 The second way in which maternity or adoption leave can be curtailed is by the mother/adopter giving a leave curtailment notice to the employer in accordance with the procedure set out in the Leave (Curtailment) Regulations. The procedure for curtailing SML is set out in Part 2 of those Regulations (Regs 5–8), while the procedure for curtailing SAL is set out in Part 3 (Regs 9–12). The requirements are, however, very similar and can be discussed together. For convenience, we use the term 'other parent' to describe the person for whom the employee is curtailing his or her leave. Of course, in the case of an adopter, it will strictly speaking be his or her spouse/partner – see 'Who has the right? – adoptive parents' above. In the case of the mother it could be the father, spouse or partner – see 'Who has the right? – birth parents' above.

An employee can curtail SML or SAL by giving his or her employer a leave curtailment notice, together with either of the following:

- his or her notice of entitlement to SPL. As discussed under 'Notice and evidential requirements for SPL' below, an employee who is eligible for and intends to take SPL must provide his or her employer with a written notice of entitlement, or

- a 'declaration of consent and entitlement' signed by him or her in support of the other parent's notice of entitlement – Regs 5(1) and 9(1). This is a written declaration signed by the mother/adopter, stating that the other parent has given a notice of entitlement to his or her employer and that the mother/adopter has consented to the amount of leave which the other parent intends to take – Reg 3(1)(a) and (b).

8.54 A leave curtailment notice must be in writing and must state the date on which the mother's OML or AML, or the adopter's OAL or AAL, is to end – Regs 6(1) and 9(1). This is known as the 'leave curtailment date' – Reg 3(1). The leave curtailment date must be:

- at least eight weeks after the date on which the employee gave the curtailment notice to his or her employer – Regs 6(2)(b) and 10(2)(a). This means that the employee must give the notice at least eight weeks before the date he or she wishes SML/SAL to end

- (if curtailing SML) at least one day after the end of the compulsory maternity leave period under the MPL Regulations (or the four-week period under the Public Health Act 1936 if applicable) – Reg 6(2)(a)

- (if curtailing SAL) at least two weeks after the first day of OAL – Reg 10(2)(b), and

- where the employee is curtailing a period of AML/AAL, at least one week before the last day of that period – Regs 6(2)(c) and 10(2)(c).

If the employee is entitled to SML/SAL with more than one employer, he or she must give curtailment notices to each of them 'at the same time' (presumably the same date will suffice, although this is not entirely clear) – Regs 5(3) and 9(3). However, this does not apply in respect of an employer for whom he or she has already returned to work on or before the date the notices are given – Regs 5(4) and 9(4).

8.55 Effect of a leave curtailment notice
Once the leave curtailment notice has been given to the employer (along with a notice of entitlement or declaration of consent), the employee's SML/SAL will end on the leave curtailment date – Regs 7(1) and 11(1). This does not mean that SPL cannot be taken before that date. The effect of the leave curtailment notice is simply to shorten the amount of maternity/adoption leave available and

allow the balance to be taken as SPL instead – Regs 6(1)(a) and 22(1)(a) SPL Regulations. The shared leave itself can be taken at any time from the date of birth (or the date the child is placed for adoption) – Regs 7(1) and 23(1) SPL Regulations. For example, there is nothing to stop the father from taking SPL while the mother is still on SML, provided the date upon which her SML will end has already been fixed (i.e. she has given her employer a curtailment notice at least eight weeks in advance of the leave curtailment date). Of course, in addition to any entitlement to SPL, the father (or adopter's partner) has the right to take two weeks' paternity leave within 56 days of the birth (or placement for adoption) (provided he or she has not already taken a period of SPL). The logistics of taking SPL is discussed under 'Planning and booking periods of leave' below.

Can a leave curtailment notice be revoked?   8.56

As noted under 'Returning to work early' above, it is possible for an employee who has given notice of an early return to work to change the return date, provided he or she complies with the procedure set out in Reg 11 MPL Regulations (if on maternity leave) or Reg 25 PAL Regulations (if on adoption leave). The potential for changing one's mind once a leave curtailment notice has been served is more restricted, particularly so far as adoption leave is concerned.

Revoking a maternity leave curtailment notice. A maternity leave curtailment 8.57
notice can only be revoked prior to the leave curtailment date, and then only in the following prescribed circumstances:

- if it transpires that neither parent is entitled to SPL or SSPP, the notice may be withdrawn up to eight weeks after it was given – Reg 8(1)(a) and (2)(a) Leave (Curtailment) Regulations. However, if the parents discover this after the eight-week period is up, the Technical Guide makes it clear that the mother's SML has to end on the date specified in the curtailment notice, as it cannot now be withdrawn (although this does not affect her SMP or Maternity Allowance period). The Guide does not expect this scenario to arise, describing it as merely a 'theoretical possibility'

- provided the notice was served before the child's birth, the mother may withdraw it without a reason up to six weeks following the birth – Reg 8(1)(b) and (2)(b)

- if the father dies, the notice may be withdrawn within a reasonably practicable time of his death – Reg 8(1)(c) and (2)(c).

The procedure for withdrawal is straightforward and involves the mother sending a 'revocation notice' in writing to her employer simply stating that she is revoking her leave curtailment notice and (where applicable) the date of death – Reg 8(3). If the mother has given a leave curtailment notice to more than one employer, she must give a revocation notice to each of those employers – Reg 8(4).

8.58 Where the mother sends a revocation notice under Reg 8(1)(b) (i.e. within six weeks of birth), she is entitled to send her employer another leave curtailment notice, setting out a new leave curtailment date – Reg 8(6). In other words, she and the father can subsequently opt in to SPL at a later date. However, as the Technical Guide makes clear, if revocation occurs under Reg 8(1)(a) or Reg 8(1)(c) (i.e. due to an absence of entitlement or following the death of the father), there is no further opportunity to opt in to SPL. The Guide also confirms that any SPL and SSPP taken by the father in the period between birth and when a mother revokes her notice to end her maternity leave must be deducted from any entitlement to SPL and SSPP, should the couple subsequently opt in at a later stage.

8.59 **Revoking an adoption leave curtailment notice.** Like maternity leave, once an adoption leave curtailment notice has been served, it can only be revoked prior to the leave curtailment date, and then only if:

- it transpires that neither parent is entitled to SPL or SSPP, in which case the notice may be withdrawn up to eight weeks after it was given – Reg 12(1)(a) and (2)(a) Leave (Curtailment) Regulations

- the spouse or partner dies, in which case the notice may be withdrawn within a reasonably practicable time thereafter – Reg 12(1)(b) and (2)(b).

Unlike maternity leave (where the curtailment notice may be withdrawn without a reason up to six weeks following the birth) there is no provision for an adoption leave curtailment notice to be withdrawn without a reason following the child's placement for adoption. In addition, there is no further possibility of opting in to SPL once an adoption leave revocation notice has been given to the employer – Reg 12(6).

8.60 The procedure for withdrawal involves the adopter sending a 'revocation notice' in writing to the employer stating that he or she is revoking the leave curtailment notice and (where applicable) the date of the spouse or partner's death – Reg 12(3). If the adopter has given a leave curtailment notice to more than one employer, he or she must give a revocation notice to each of those employers – Reg 12(4).

8.61 ## Notice and evidential requirements for SPL

To be eligible for SPL, it is not enough simply to curtail maternity/adoption leave (discussed under 'Curtailment of maternity or adoption leave' above). There are also a number of detailed notice requirements that need to be complied with. First, an employee who intends to take SPL must provide his or her employer with a written notice of entitlement, accompanied by signed declarations in support. For birth parents, the notice and declarations must comply with the conditions set out in Regs 8 and 9 SPL Regulations. For adoptive parents, the notice and declarations must comply with the conditions set out in Regs 24 and 25 SPL Regulations. Furthermore, the employee must provide the employer with certain additional information upon request. The prescribed information is set out in Reg 10 for birth parents and Reg 26 for adoptive parents. Finally, the employee must send the employer a 'period of leave notice' in order to actually book the period (or periods) of leave he or she wishes to take – Regs 12 (birth) and 28 (adoption). We examine each of these requirements in turn for both birth and adoptive parents. Similar notice and evidential requirements apply for parental order parents in a surrogacy arrangement – Regs 24 and 25 SPL Regulations, as modified by Regs 25 and 26 Leave (Parental Order Cases) Regulations. We highlight the main differences where relevant under 'Notice of entitlement (surrogacy)' below.

Notice of entitlement (birth)
8.62

As noted above, an employee who is eligible for and intends to take SPL must provide his or her employer with a written notice of entitlement, accompanied by signed declarations in support. So far as birth parents are concerned, the mother's notice of entitlement must comply with Reg 8 SPL Regulations – Reg 4(2)(e). A notice sent by the father must comply with the almost identical requirements in Reg 9 – Reg 5(2)(c). In either case, the notice must be submitted at least eight weeks before the employee intends to take SPL. It must also be accompanied by a signed declaration from both the employee and the other parent (see 'Declarations to support mother's notice of entitlement' and 'Declarations to support father's notice of entitlement' below) – Regs 8(1) and 9(1). Note that a mother's maternity leave curtailment notice must be accompanied by either her notice of entitlement to SPL or her signed declaration in support of the father's notice of entitlement – Reg 5(1) Leave (Curtailment) Regulations (see 'Curtailment of maternity or adoption leave – giving a leave curtailment notice' above).

The notice of entitlement itself (whether sent by the mother or the father) must provide the following information:

- the names of the mother and father

- the start and end dates of any period of SML taken or to be taken by the mother, if she is eligible for SML. If the mother is not eligible for SML, she cannot claim SPL. However, the father will still be eligible for SPL if the mother is entitled to SMP or Maternity Allowance (see 'Shared parental leave (birth) – mother must be eligible for SML' above). In that case, his notice of entitlement must instead state the period in respect of which SMP or Maternity Allowance is payable

- the total amount of SPL available (see 'Amount of shared parental leave – amount of SPL (birth)' below)

- the expected week of birth

- the date of birth. Note that where the child is not yet born, this information must be provided as soon as reasonably practicable after the birth and, in any event, before the first period of SPL to be taken by the employee

- how much SPL the mother and father each intend to take

- an 'indication' as to when the employee giving the notice intends to take SPL, including the start and end dates for each period of leave – Regs 8(2) and 9(2).

8.63 A notice of entitlement should not be confused with a period of leave notice that fixes the precise period (or periods) during which leave is to be taken (colloquially known as a 'booking notice') – see 'Period of leave notice' below. Regs 8(6) and 9(5) expressly state that the 'indication' as to intended leave periods contained in a notice of entitlement is non-binding and must not be treated as a period of leave notice, unless otherwise indicated. The Acas Guide confirms that the employee does not have to take the leave on the dates specified in the notice of entitlement. The intention at this stage is to give the employer some idea of what is being considered. Nevertheless, Regs 8(6) and 9(5) also suggest that if the notice of entitlement expressly states that it is to be treated as a period of leave notice, it must be treated as such.

It appears that the information provided in the notice of entitlement as to how much SPL each parent intends to take *is* binding, unless the employee gives his or her employer a written notice to vary this. Reg 11 SPL Regulations enables an employee to vary the notice of entitlement by giving his or her employer a written notice of variation – see 'Varying notice of entitlement' below.

8.64 Declarations to support mother's notice of entitlement. Where the mother is applying for SPL, she must sign a declaration that:

- she satisfies or will satisfy the conditions for SPL in Reg 4(2) SPL Regulations (discussed under 'Shared parental leave (birth)' above)

- the information given in her notice of entitlement is accurate

- she will immediately inform her employer if she ceases to care for the child – Reg 8(3)(a) SPL Regulations.

8.65 In addition, the father must sign a declaration stating:

- his name, address and NI number (or that he does not have an NI number)

- that he satisfies or will satisfy the conditions in Reg 4(3) enabling the mother to take SPL (discussed under 'Shared parental leave (birth)' above)

- that he is the child's father. If the person signing the declaration is not the father, he (or she) must instead confirm that he (or she) is the mother's spouse, civil partner or partner

- that he consents to the amount of leave the mother intends to take

- that he consents to the mother's employer processing the information in his declaration – Reg 8(3)(b).

Both declarations must be given to the mother's employer with her notice of entitlement – Reg 8(1).

Declarations to support father's notice of entitlement. Where the father is **8.66** applying for SPL, he must sign a declaration that:

- he satisfies or will satisfy the conditions for SPL in Reg 5(2) SPL Regulations (discussed under 'Shared parental leave (birth)' above)

- the information given in his notice of entitlement is accurate

- he is the child's father. If the person applying for SPL is not the father, he (or she) must instead confirm that he (or she) is the mother's spouse, civil partner or partner

- he will immediately inform his employer if the mother tells him that she has revoked her maternity leave curtailment notice or her maternity pay/Maternity Allowance period curtailment notice, as the case may be (see 'Curtailing maternity or adoption leave – can a leave curtailment notice be revoked?' above, and 'Statutory shared parental pay – curtailing maternity pay or allowance' below)

- he will immediately inform his employer if he ceases to care for the child – Reg 9(3)(a).

In addition, the mother must sign a declaration stating: **8.67**

- her name, address and NI number (or that she does not have an NI number)

- that she satisfies or will satisfy the conditions in Reg 5(3) SPL Regulations enabling the father to take SPL (discussed under 'Shared parental leave (birth)' above)

- that she consents to the amount of leave the father intends to take

- that she will immediately inform the father if she revokes her curtailment notice

- that she consents to the father's employer processing the information in her declaration – Reg 9(3)(b).

Both declarations must be given to the father's employer with his notice of entitlement – Reg 9(1).

365

8.68 Notice of entitlement (adoption)

So far as adoptive parents are concerned, the adopter's notice of entitlement must comply with Reg 24 SPL Regulations – Reg 20(2)(e). A notice sent by the adopter's spouse or partner must comply with the almost identical requirements in Reg 25 – Reg 21(2)(c). In either case, the notice must be submitted at least eight weeks before the employee intends to take SPL. It must also be accompanied by a declaration from both the employee and his or her spouse/partner (see 'Declarations to support adopter's notice of entitlement' and 'Declarations to support spouse/partner's notice of entitlement' below) – Regs 24(1) and 25(1). Note that the adopter's adoption leave curtailment notice must be accompanied either by his or her entitlement to SPL or by his or her signed declaration in support of the spouse/partner's notice of entitlement – Reg 9(1) Leave Curtailment Regulations (see 'Curtailing maternity or adoption leave – effect of a leave curtailment notice' above).

The notice of entitlement itself (whether sent by the adopter or his or her spouse/partner) must provide the following information:

- the names of the adopter and his or her spouse/partner

- the date that the adopter was notified of having been matched for adoption with the child

- the date that the child is expected to be placed for adoption and the date of the placement. Note that where the child has yet to be placed for adoption, this information must be provided as soon as reasonably practicable after the placement and, in any event, before the first period of SPL to be taken by the employee

- the start and end dates of any period of SAL taken or to be taken by the adopter (if eligible for SAL). If the adopter is not eligible for SAL, he or she cannot claim SPL. However, the adopter's spouse or partner will still be eligible for SPL if the adopter is entitled to SAP (see 'Shared parental leave (adoption) – adopter must be eligible for SAL' above). In that case, the spouse/partner's notice of entitlement must instead state the period in respect of which SAP is payable

- the total amount of SPL available (see 'Amount of shared parental leave – amount of SPL (adoption)' below)

- how much SPL the employee and his or her spouse/partner each intend to take

- an indication as to when the employee giving the notice intends to take SPL, including the start and end dates for each period of leave – Regs 24(2) and 25(2).

Regs 24(6) and 25(5) expressly state that the 'indication' as to intended leave **8.69** periods contained in the notice of entitlement is non-binding and must not be treated as a period of leave notice (colloquially known as a 'booking notice'), unless otherwise indicated – see further 'Period of leave notice' below. However, it appears that the information provided in the notice of entitlement as to how much SPL each parent intends to take *is* binding, unless the employee gives his or her employer a written notice to vary this. Reg 27 SPL Regulations enables an employee to vary the notice of entitlement by giving his or her employer a written notice of variation – see 'Varying notice of entitlement' below.

Declarations to support adopter's notice of entitlement. Where it is the **8.70** adopter applying for SPL, he or she must sign a declaration that:

- he or she satisfies or will satisfy the conditions for SPL in Reg 21(2) SPL Regulations (see 'Shared parental leave (adoption)' above)

- the information given in his or her notice of entitlement is accurate

- he or she will immediately inform the employer if he or she ceases to care for the child – Reg 24(3)(a) SPL Regulations.

In addition, the adopter's spouse/partner must sign a declaration stating: **8.71**

- his or her name, address and NI number (or that he or she does not have an NI number)

- that he or she satisfies or will satisfy the conditions in Reg 20(3) enabling the adopter to take SPL (see 'Shared parental leave (adoption)' above)

- that he or she is the adopter's spouse, civil partner or partner

- that he or she consents to the amount of leave the adopter intends to take

- that he or she consents to the adopter's employer processing the information in the declaration – Reg 24(3)(b).

Both declarations must be given to the adopter's employer with his or her notice of entitlement – Reg 24(1).

Declarations to support spouse/partner's notice of entitlement. Where the **8.72** spouse/partner is applying for SPL, he or she must sign a declaration that:

- he or she satisfies or will satisfy the conditions for SPL in Reg 21(2) SPL Regulations (see 'Shared parental leave (adoption)' above)

- the information given in his or her notice of entitlement is accurate

- he or she is the adopter's spouse, civil partner or partner

- he or she will immediately inform the employer if the adopter tells him or her that the adoption leave curtailment notice or the adoption pay period curtailment notice, as the case may be, has been revoked (see 'Curtailing

367

maternity or adoption pay – can a leave curtailment notice be revoked?' above, and 'Statutory shared parental pay – curtailing adoption pay' below)

- he or she will immediately inform the employer if he or she ceases to care for the child – Reg 25(3)(a).

8.73 In addition, the adopter must sign a declaration stating:

- his or her name, address and NI number (or that he or she does not have an NI number)

- that he or she satisfies or will satisfy the conditions in Reg 21(3) SPL Regulations enabling his or her spouse/partner to take SPL

- that he or she consents to the amount of leave the spouse/partner intends to take

- that he or she will immediately inform the spouse/partner if the SAL curtailment notice (or SAP curtailment notice, as the case may be) is revoked

- that he or she consents to his or her spouse/partner's employer processing the information in the declaration – Reg 25(3)(b).

Both declarations must be given to the spouse/partner's employer with his or notice of entitlement – Reg 25(1).

8.74 Notice of entitlement (surrogacy)
Regs 24 and 25 SPL Regulations (see 'Notice of entitlement (adoption)' also apply to parental order parents in a surrogacy arrangement, but as modified by Regs 25 and 26 Leave (Parental Order Cases) Regulations. The main differences are that instead of setting out details about the child's adoption, the notice of entitlement must contain:

- the expected week of birth

- the date of birth (where the notice is given before birth, this information must be given as soon as reasonably practicable after birth), and

- if the parental order has been granted, the date on which it was granted.

The requirements relating to the declarations in support are, however, identical.

8.75 Varying notice of entitlement
As noted above, the information provided in a notice of entitlement regarding the amount of SPL each parent intends to take is binding, unless the employee gives his or her employer a written notice to vary this. Regs 11 (birth) and 27 (adoption) SPL Regulations enable an employee to vary the notice of entitlement by giving his or her employer a written notice of variation. The notice of variation must contain:

368

- an 'indication' as to when the employee intends to take SPL, including the start and end dates for each period of leave. This 'indication' is non-binding and must not be treated as a period of leave notice (colloquially known as a 'booking notice' – see 'Period of leave notice' below) unless otherwise indicated

- a description of the periods of SPL to be taken by the employee and the other parent, as set out in their respective booking notices or any variation to a booking notice (variation of booking notices is discussed under 'Planning and booking periods of leave – varying periods of leave' below)

- a description of the periods of SSPP to be taken by the employee and the other parent, as set out in their notices to claim SSPP (see 'Statutory shared parental pay – notification and evidential requirements' below), and

- a declaration signed by the employee and the other parent that they agree the variation – Regs 11(3) and (4), and 27(3) and (4).

There is no limit to the number of notices of variation that may be given – Regs 11(6) and 27(6). In addition, there is no time limit within which a notice of variation must be given.

Information that may be requested by employer   8.76
Within 14 days of being given a notice of entitlement, the employer may request certain additional information. The prescribed information is set out in Regs 10 and 26 SPL Regulations (for birth and adoptive parents respectively) and Reg 27 Leave (Parental Order Cases) Regulations (for parental order parents).

Birth parents. Within 14 days of being given the notice of entitlement by the 8.77 employee, the employer may request a copy of the child's birth certificate and/ or the name and address of the other parent's employer – Reg 10(1) and (2) SPL Regulations. The employee must provide that information within a further 14 days – Reg 10(3)(a) and (5)(a). If the birth certificate has yet to be issued, the employee must instead provide a signed declaration which states the date and location of the child's birth and that a birth certificate has not yet been issued – Reg 10(3)(b). If the child has not yet been born at the time of the employer's request, the birth certificate (or signed declaration) must be provided within 14 days of the birth – Reg 10(4). Finally, if the other parent has no employer, the employee must send a declaration to confirm this – Reg 10(5)(b).

Adoptive parents. Within 14 days of being given the notice of entitlement by 8.78 the employee, the employer may request the name and address of his or her spouse/partner's employer, and evidence of the following (in the form of one or more documents issued by the adoption agency):

- the name and address of the adoption agency

369

- the date that the adopter was notified of having been matched for adoption with the child

- the date on which the adoption agency expects to place the child with the adopter – Reg 26(1) and (2) SPL Regulations.

The employee must provide that information within a further 14 days – Reg 26(3) and (4)(a). If the employee's spouse or partner has no employer, the employee must send a declaration to confirm this – Reg 26(4)(b).

8.79 **Parental order parents (surrogacy).** Within 14 days of being given the notice of entitlement by the employee, the employer may request the name and address of his or her spouse/partner's employer, and evidence in the form of a parental order (if available) – Reg 26(1) and (2) SPL Regulations (as modified by Reg 27 Leave (Parental Order Cases) Regulations).

The employee must provide that information within a further 14 days – Reg 26(3) and (4)(a). If the employee's spouse or partner has no employer, the employee must send a declaration to confirm this – Reg 26(4)(b).

8.80 **Period of leave notice**

In order to fix the precise period during which leave is to be taken, the employee must give at least one 'period of leave notice' in accordance with Reg 12 (birth) or Reg 28 (adoption). This notice is referred to as a 'booking notice' in the Technical Guide. A booking notice can request either one continuous period or two or more 'discontinuous' periods of SPL. It must be in writing, contain the start and end dates of each period of leave requested and be given to the employer at least eight weeks before the start date of the first period requested in the notice – Regs 12(1)–(3) and 28(1)–(3).

If the notice is given before the child is born, the start date can be expressed either as the day on which the child is born or as a number of days following that date. The end date can also be expressed as a number of days following the birth. This applies to parental order parents as well as birth parents – Reg 12(4)(c) SPL Regulations/Reg 28 Leave (Parental Order Cases) Regulations. So far as adoptive parents are concerned, if the notice is given before the child is placed for adoption, the start date can be expressed either as the day on which the child is placed for adoption or as a number of days following that date – Reg 28(4)(c) SPL Regulations.

8.81 A booking notice may not be given before a notice of entitlement – Regs 12(5)(a) and 28(5)(a). It may, however, be given to the employer at the same time as a notice of entitlement (or a variation of a notice of entitlement) – Regs 12(4)(a) and 28(4)(a). Note that a notice of entitlement (or indeed a variation of a notice of entitlement) may be treated as a period of leave notice if this is expressly stated in the notice – Regs 8(6), 9(5) and 11(6) (birth), and 24(6), 25(5) and 27(6) (adoption).

An employee can request a variation of the period(s) of leave contained in the booking notice by giving a written notice – Regs 15 (birth) and 31 (adoption). However, he or she is limited to a maximum of three booking/variation notices (unless the employer agrees otherwise or one of the limited exceptions applies), whether for continuous or discontinuous periods of leave – Regs 16(1) (birth) and 32(1) (adoption). An employer cannot refuse a request for a continuous block of leave (provided it satisfies the notice requirements set out above). However, it is not bound to accept the pattern of leave proposed in a notice requesting discontinuous periods of leave.

Booking and varying periods of leave is discussed under 'Planning and booking periods of leave' below.

Amount of shared parental leave

8.82

Put simply, the total amount of SPL available to parents who wish to share leave under the SPL Regulations depends upon the amount of SML (or SAL) that the mother (or adopter) has taken and/or proposes to take. The relevant provisions are, however, slightly more complex and are discussed under 'Amount of SPL (birth)' and 'Amount of SPL (adoption)' below. The provisions for parental order parents in a surrogacy arrangement are identical to those that apply for adoption. The period within which SPL can be taken – which is obviously relevant to the amount that can be taken – is discussed under 'When SPL can be taken' below.

Amount of SPL (birth)

8.83

The total amount of SPL available to birth parents who wish to share leave depends upon the amount of SML that the mother has taken and/or proposes to take. As previously explained, in order to create a right to SPL, the mother must cut short her 52-week SML entitlement – comprising 26 weeks' ordinary maternity leave (OML) and 26 weeks' additional maternity leave (AML). This she can do by either:

- returning to work early, or

- giving a curtailment notice to her employer to end her maternity leave on a specific date (see 'Curtailing maternity or adoption leave' above).

Regulation 6 SPL Regulations explains how to calculate SPL in any particular case. This differs depending upon which of the above two methods the mother has chosen to curtail her SML. If she returns to work before the end of her maternity leave period, the amount of SPL available is 52 weeks less the number of weeks of SML taken – Reg 6(1)(b). If she gives her employer a leave curtailment notice, the amount of SPL available is 52 weeks less the number of weeks of SML:

8.84

371

- beginning with the first day of SML taken by the mother, and

- ending with the leave curtailment date (i.e. the date specified in the notice), irrespective of whether or not the mother returns to work before that date – Reg 6(1)(a).

Under the Maternity and Parental Leave etc Regulations 1999 SI 1999/3312 ('the MPL Regulations'), a mother is required to take a minimum of two weeks' maternity leave immediately following birth (or four weeks under the Public Health Act 1936 if she works in a factory or workshop). This means that the maximum amount of SPL available can never be more than 50 weeks. The minimum amount is one week – see Reg 6(2)(c) Leave (Curtailment) Regulations.

8.85 **Total amount if mother not entitled to SML.** In a limited number of cases a mother will be entitled to SMP (or Maternity Allowance), but not SML. In these circumstances she will not be able to take SPL but, provided he meets the requisite qualifying conditions, the father will. In such a case, the mother must give a 'maternity pay period curtailment notice' to her employer (or a 'Maternity Allowance period curtailment notification' to the Secretary of State) – Reg 5(3)(d)(ii) and (iii) SPL Regulations/Reg 6 Statutory Maternity Pay and Statutory Adoption Pay (Curtailment) Regulations 2014 SI 2014/3054 ('the Pay (Curtailment) Regulations')/Reg 4 Maternity Allowance (Curtailment) Regulations 2014 SI 2014/3053 ('the MA (Curtailment) Regulations'). This is discussed further under 'Statutory shared parental pay – curtailing maternity pay or allowance' below.

Where the mother gives such a notice *before* returning to work, the amount of leave available is 52 weeks less the number of weeks of SMP/Maternity Allowance payable to the mother up to the curtailment date (i.e. the date upon which the mother wishes her maternity pay/allowance to end, as specified in her notice) – Reg 6(2)(b) and (3)(b) SPL Regulations. Where she gives such a notice *after* returning to work, the amount of SML available is 52 weeks less the number of weeks of SMP/Maternity Allowance payable to her before she came back – Reg 6(2)(a) and Reg (3)(a) SPL Regulations. Note that in such a case the curtailment date is the last day of the week in which that notice is given, irrespective of the date specified in the notice – Reg 7(5) Pay (Curtailment) Regulations/Reg 5(5) MA (Curtailment) Regulations.

8.86 The maximum number of weeks of SPL that can be made available is 50. This is because Reg 7(2)(b) Pay (Curtailment) Regulations and Reg 5(2)(b) MA (Curtailment) Regulations specifically provide that if the mother does not have the right to OML (and hence does not have the right to compulsory maternity leave), the curtailment date must be at least two weeks after the end of the pregnancy. (Note that this two-week minimum period also applies to factory workers who are not eligible for OML, despite the fact that factory workers who *are* eligible for OML are entitled to a four-week compulsory maternity leave period under the Public Health Act 1936.)

Regulation 7(2)(d) Pay (Curtailment) Regulations provides that the curtailment date must be at least one week before the last day of the maternity pay period. Since the maternity pay period is 39 weeks (see Chapter 5, 'Statutory maternity pay', under 'The maternity pay period'), this means that the minimum amount of SPL that will be available is 14 weeks (i.e. 52 weeks minus 38 weeks), although, of course, the father is not obliged to take the whole period as SPL.

Amount available for each birth parent. The amount of SPL available to the 8.87 mother on the one hand and the father on the other will, of course, depend upon what has been agreed between them (as set out in their notices of entitlement and accompanying declarations of consent – see 'Notice and evidential requirements for SPL – notice of entitlement (birth)' above). The formula for the calculation is found in Reg 6(4) (for the mother) and Reg 6(5) (for the father). These provide that an employee's entitlement is the total amount of SPL available (calculated according to the above-mentioned rules), less:

- any SPL which the other parent has booked in a period of leave notice (or in a variation to that notice) – see 'Planning and booking periods of leave' below

- any period of leave which an employee is required to take by the employer under Reg 18. (An employer may require an employee to take leave under this provision where the employee informs it that he or she has ceased to care for the child less than eight weeks before he or she is due to take a period of leave – see 'Planning and booking leave – change of circumstances' below), and

- any weeks of SSPP to which the other parent is entitled and during which the other parent is not absent on SPL. As noted under 'Who has the right – employees only' above, office holders and employed earners may be entitled to SSPP, even if they are not employees within the strict meaning of S.230(1) ERA and are not therefore entitled to SPL. The individual must still be absent from work in order to claim SSPP – for example, in reliance on a contractual entitlement to parental leave. Any such weeks of absence taken by the other parent will be deducted under Reg 6(4)(c) and (5)(c).

Amount of SPL (adoption)   8.88
The total amount of SPL available to adoptive parents depends on the amount of SAL that the adopter has taken and/or proposes to take. If the adopter returns to work before the end of his or her adoption leave, the amount of SPL available is 52 weeks less the number of weeks' SAL taken – Reg 22(1)(b) SPL

Regulations. If he or she gives the employer a leave curtailment notice, the amount of SPL available is 52 weeks less the number of weeks of SAL:

- beginning with the first day of SAL taken by the adopter, and

- ending with the leave curtailment date, irrespective of whether or not the adopter returns to work before that date – Reg 22(1)(a).

While there is no compulsory adoption leave period under the Paternity and Adoption Leave Regulations 2002 SI 2002/2788, it is not possible for the adopter to curtail the first two weeks of OAL. Reg 10(2)(b) Leave (Curtailment) Regulations states that the leave curtailment date must be at least two weeks after the first day of OAL, meaning that the maximum amount of SPL available is 50 weeks. In addition, Reg 22(1)(b) makes it clear that if the adopter returns to work during the first two weeks of adoption leave, the total amount of SPL available is still only 50 weeks. The minimum amount is one week – see Reg 10(2)(c) Leave (Curtailment) Regulations.

8.89 Total amount if adopter not entitled to SAL. As previously explained, where the adopter is not entitled to SAL, but is entitled to SAP, he or she cannot take SPL but his or her spouse/partner can, provided the spouse/partner meets the requisite qualifying conditions and the adopter gives an 'adoption pay period curtailment notice' to the adopter's employer – Reg 21(3)(d)(ii) SPL Regulations/ Reg 11 Pay (Curtailment) Regulations. The procedure is considered further under 'Statutory shared parental pay – curtailing adoption pay' below. Where the adopter gives such a notice *before* returning to work, the amount of SPL available to the spouse or partner is 52 weeks less the number of weeks of SAP payable to the adopter up to the curtailment date (i.e. the date upon which the adopter wishes the adoption pay period to end, as specified in the notice) – Reg 22(2)(b) SPL Regulations. Where the adopter gives such a notice *after* returning to work, the amount of SML available is 52 weeks less the number of weeks of SAP payable to the adopter before he or she came back – Reg 22(2)(a). Note that in such a case the curtailment date is the last day of the week in which that notice is given, irrespective of the date specified in the notice – Reg 12(4) Pay (Curtailment) Regulations.

The maximum number of weeks' SPL that can be made available is 50. This is because Reg 12(2)(c) Pay (Curtailment) Regulations provides that the curtailment date must be at least two weeks after the first day of the adoption pay period. Reg 12(2)(d) states that the curtailment date must be at least one week before the last day of the adoption pay period. Since the adoption pay period is 39 weeks, this means that the minimum amount of SPL that can be made available is 14 weeks (i.e. 52 minus 38), although of course the adopter's spouse/partner is not obliged to take the whole period as SPL.

8.90 Amount available for each adoptive parent. The amount available to the adopter on the one hand and the adopter's spouse/partner on the other will, of course, depend on what has been agreed between them (as set out in their notices of entitlement and accompanying declarations of consent) – see 'Notice and evidential requirements for SPL– notice of entitlement (adoption)' above. The formula for the calculation is found in Reg 22(3) SPL Regulations for the adopter and Reg 22(4) for the adopter's spouse/partner. These provide that an employee's entitlement is the total amount of SPL available (calculated according to the above-mentioned rules), less:

- any SPL which his or her spouse/partner has booked in a period of leave notice (or in a variation to that notice) – see 'Planning and booking periods of leave' below

- any period of leave which is required to be taken in accordance with Reg 33. (An employer may require an employee to take leave under this provision where the employee informs it that he or she has ceased to care for the child less than eight weeks before he or she is due to take a period of leave – see 'Planning and booking periods of leave – change of circumstances' below) and

- any weeks of SSPP to which the spouse/partner is entitled and during which he or she is not absent on SPL. As noted under 'Who has the right – employees only' above, office holders and employed earners may be entitled to SSPP, even if they are not employees within the strict meaning of S.230(1) ERA and are therefore not entitled to SPL. The individual must still be absent from work in order to claim SSPP – for example, in reliance on a contractual entitlement to parental leave. Any such weeks of absence taken by the spouse/partner will be deducted under Reg 22(3)(c) and 22(4)(c).

When SPL can be taken   8.91
SPL can be taken as one continuous period or in discontinuous periods – see further 'Planning and booking periods of leave' below. The period within which such leave can be taken is set out in Regs 7(1) and 23(1) SPL Regulations (for birth parents and adoptive parents respectively) and Reg 24 Leave (Parental Order Cases) Regulations for parental order parents in a surrogacy arrangement. For birth and parental order parents, the period begins on the date the child is born (or, if more than one child is born from the same pregnancy, the date the first child is born) and ends the day before that child's first birthday. For adoptive parents, it begins on the date the child is placed for adoption (or if more than one child is placed for adoption through a single placement, the date of the placement of the first child) and ends the day before the first anniversary of that placement.

The 52-week period during which SPL can be taken is fixed and cannot be extended. Any entitlement to SPL that is not taken within that period will be lost. This is most likely to occur in situations where only one parent qualifies for SPL and he or she chooses to utilise the flexibility of the scheme to take discontinuous periods of leave, returning to work between each period of absence. That parent will almost certainly be unable to take his or her full SPL entitlement within the fixed 52-week period. However, that parent will not necessarily suffer financially. In fact, he or she may be better off, as well as having the benefit of remaining involved at work. The parent could arrange to take up to 37 weeks of SPL in discontinuous blocks (the number of weeks for which he or she could claim SSPP) and will also be paid (in accordance with his or her contract of employment) when at work in the periods between those blocks of leave.

8.92 Planning and booking periods of leave

The statutory scheme offers parents a considerable amount of flexibility when it comes to how they wish to take SPL, provided it is taken within the relevant 52-week period (see 'Amount of shared parental leave – when SPL can be taken' above). For example, it is possible for them to take leave at the same time (see 'Concurrent periods of leave' below) or separately. In addition, they can take SPL in one continuous block or in two or more 'discontinuous' blocks – see 'Continuous periods of leave' and 'Discontinuous periods of leave' below. There is also scope for them to vary planned periods of SPL that have already been agreed with their employer – see 'Varying periods of leave' below. Finally, an employee may also work for up to 20 days while taking SPL without bringing his or her entitlement to an end – see 'Keeping in touch days' below. However, the system for booking leave is somewhat less flexible and may have an impact on how parents plan their leave. In particular, an employee is restricted to submitting three 'period of leave' (or booking) notices, unless the employer agrees to more. This is discussed under 'Booking leave' immediately below.

8.93 Booking leave

In order to be able to take any leave at all, an employee must submit a 'period of leave notice' – referred to as a 'booking notice' in the Technical Guide. A booking notice can either request one continuous period of leave or two or more 'discontinuous' periods of leave. Crucially, an employee can only submit a maximum of three booking notices, whether for continuous or discontinuous periods of leave (unless the employer agrees to more) – Regs 16(1) (birth) and 32(1) (adoption). This maximum number includes variation notices (see 'Varying periods of leave'). The following types of notice are disregarded for these purposes:

- a notice requesting discontinuous periods of SPL that was withdrawn by the employee on or before the 15th day after the notice was given and before it has been agreed by the employer – Regs 16(2)(a) and 32(2)(a)

- a notice given in response to a request from the employer to vary the period of leave – Regs 16(2)(c) and 32(2)(c)

- a notice given as a result of the child being born earlier or later than the EWC (in the case of a birth parent) – Reg 16(2)(b), or

- a notice given as a result of the child being placed for adoption earlier or later than the date expected (in the case of an adoptive parent) – Reg 32(b).

Note that where an employee has more than one employer, the limit applies in respect of each employer – Regs 16(3) (birth) and 32(3) (adoption).

The general requirements of a booking notice are discussed under 'Notice **8.94** and evidential requirements for SPL – period of leave notice' above. They are the same whether or not the notice is requesting continuous or discontinuous periods of leave. In brief, the notice must be in writing, contain the start and end dates of each period of leave requested and be given to the employer at least eight weeks before the start date of the first period requested in the notice – Regs 12(1)–(3) (birth) and 28(1)–(3) (adoption). There is, however, a critical distinction between a 'continuous leave' notice and a 'discontinuous leave' notice: an employer cannot refuse a request for a continuous block of leave, provided it satisfies the relevant notice requirements (see 'Notice and evidential requirements for SPL – period of leave notice' above), whereas it is not bound to accept the pattern of leave proposed in a notice requesting discontinuous periods of leave.

Continuous periods of leave   **8.95**

Employees have an absolute right to book and take a period of SPL in one continuous block. Regs 13 (birth) and 29 (adoption) state simply that 'where an employee gives a notice… which requests one continuous period of SPL, the employee is entitled to take that period of leave'. In other words, the employer cannot refuse a request for a continuous block of leave, provided that request satisfies the relevant notice requirements (see 'Notice and evidential requirements for SPL – period of leave notice' above).

Therefore, if an employee wishes to take a single block of leave, he or she simply needs to send a booking notice in accordance with Reg 12 (if the birth provisions apply) or Reg 28 (if the adoption provisions apply), and the employer will have to agree. As noted above, an employee can give a combined total of three booking notices, unless his or her employer agrees to accept more. Therefore, an employee who wishes to take three separate periods of SPL over the 52-week period could submit three notices for each period of leave, thus guaranteeing that he or she will be able to take the leave as desired. Since each notice is requesting a continuous period of leave, the employer will have to accept the pattern of leave requested. However, the employee would not then be able to vary the leave, as variation notices count towards the three permissible notices (unless the employer otherwise agrees).

377

8.96 Discontinuous periods of leave

Employees have the right to request two or more periods of discontinuous leave in a single booking notice; for example, a period of five weeks' leave, then two weeks back at work, followed by another period of leave. However, where he or she does so, the employer is not bound to accept the pattern of leave proposed. Upon receipt of such a request, the employer has two weeks in which to:

- consent to the discontinuous periods of leave requested

- propose alternative dates for the periods of leave, or

- refuse the periods of leave without proposing alternative dates – Regs 14(2) (birth) and 30(2) (adoption).

If the employer agrees to the employee's proposed dates, or the employee agrees with the alternative dates proposed by the employer, the employee is entitled to take that leave as agreed – Regs 14(3) and 30(3). If agreement cannot be reached within the two-week window, the employee is entitled to take the total amount of leave requested as a continuous block – Regs 14(4) and 30(4). This is essentially the default position. In these circumstances, the employee must choose a start date that falls at least eight weeks after the date on which the booking notice was given and notify his or her employer of that start date within five days of the end of the two-week negotiation period. If the employee fails to choose a start date, his or her leave will commence on the start date of the first period of leave that was initially requested – Regs 14(5) and 30(5). Finally, the employee has the right to withdraw a notice requesting discontinuous periods of SPL on or before the 15th day after the notice was originally given, unless agreement has been reached over periods of leave – Regs 14(6) and 30(6). In these circumstances, the withdrawn notice will not count towards the limit of three booking notices an employee can submit (and neither will the request to withdraw the notice) – Regs 16(2)(a) and 32(2)(a). The employee can then submit an entirely new request for either continuous or discontinuous leave. Note that the Regulations do not prescribe how a 'discontinuous leave' notice may be withdrawn. There appears to be nothing to prevent the employee from doing so verbally, for example.

8.97 Concurrent periods of leave

An employee may be absent on SPL at the same time as the other parent is absent on SPL, SML, SAL, statutory paternity leave or unpaid parental leave in relation to the same child; or in receipt of Maternity Allowance, SMP, SAP, statutory paternity pay or SSPP in relation to the same child – Regs 7(5) and 23(5). In other words, as long as the relevant notice requirements have been complied with, both parents can take periods of leave, and not just SPL, concurrently, within the relevant 52-week period. The necessary notice

378

requirements are discussed under 'Curtailing maternity or adoption leave' and Notice and evidential requirements for SPL' above.

Staying in touch days
8.98

As we have seen, the relative flexibility of the SPL scheme means that an employee can return to work between periods of leave. In addition, an employee may work for up to 20 days *while taking SPL* without bringing his or her entitlement to an end – Reg 37(1) and (2) SPL Regulations. These are referred to as 'shared parental leave in touch' days (SPLIT days) in both the Technical Guide and the Acas Guide. Reg 37(2) provides that an employee can take up to 20 SPLIT days 'for each employer' during the period within which SPL can be taken. The Technical Guide explains that this means that an employee on SPL can work for up to 20 days per employer if he or she has more than one employer. Under this provision, any work carried out under the contract of employment (including any training or activity undertaken for the purposes of keeping in touch with the workplace) on any day constitutes a day's work – Reg 37(3) and (4). Days can be worked continuously or as odd days. An employee does not have to take a SPLIT day at the request of his or her employer. Similarly, an employee has no right to take SPLIT days – Reg 37(6). However, both parties may agree that it would be beneficial for the employee to attend work in order to, for example, attend a training session or a team meeting. A SPLIT day does not have the effect of extending the total duration of a period of SPL – Reg 37(7).

As SPLIT days allow for an employee to work under the terms of his or her contract of employment, he or she is entitled to be paid for that work. The rate of pay may be dictated by the terms of the employment contract or agreed on a case-by-case basis, but must comply with the employer's statutory obligations, such as ensuring that the employee is paid the national minimum wage. The employee would also be entitled to receive SSPP for any week that he or she works, although this could be offset against any contractual pay agreed.

Reg 37(5) makes it clear that any day on which contact is made between employer and employee to discuss the employee's return to work, or any other reasonable contact, does not count as a SPLIT day.
8.99

Varying periods of leave
8.100

An employee who wishes to vary a period of booked leave must submit a variation notice in writing to his or her employer. Regs 15 and 31 deal with variation notices for birth and adoptive parents respectively. They provide that a variation notice must state the periods of leave the employee is currently entitled to take, namely:

- any continuous period of leave requested in a single notice – see 'Continuous periods of leave' above

379

- any discontinuous periods of leave requested in a single notice that have been agreed to by the employer – see 'Discontinuous periods of leave' above

- any continuous leave to be taken as a result of the employer's rejection of a discontinuous leave notice – see 'Discontinuous periods of leave' above.

The notice can vary the start or end date of any period of SPL, in which case it must be given no less than eight weeks before both the date to be varied and the new date. It may also change a single period of leave into discontinuous periods of leave or vice versa. Finally, it can cancel the amount of leave requested, in which case it must be given not less than eight weeks before the date on which the cancelled leave is due to commence.

8.101 If the employee's variation notice relates to one continuous period of leave, Regs 13 (birth) and 29 (adoption) apply – see 'Continuous periods of leave' above. In other words, the employer cannot refuse the employee's variation request and the employee will be entitled to take the period of leave as varied (or treat the leave as cancelled), provided the notice complies with the requirements of Reg 15/Reg 31. If the employee's variation notice relates to discontinuous periods of leave, Regs 14 (birth) and 30 (adoption) apply – see 'Discontinuous periods of leave' above. In other words, the employer is not bound to accept the varied pattern of leave proposed and has two weeks in which to:

- consent to the varied periods of leave requested

- propose alternative dates for the periods of leave, or

- refuse the varied periods of leave without proposing alternative dates (in which case the total amount of leave must be taken as a continuous block).

8.102 A variation notice counts towards the maximum of three notices that an employee can submit in order to book leave, unless it is given:

- in response to a request from the employer to vary the period of leave – Regs 16(2)(c) and 32(2)(c)

- as a result of the child being born earlier or later than the EWC (in the case of a birth parent) – Reg 16(2)(b), or

- as a result of the child being placed for adoption earlier or later than the date expected (in the case of an adoptive parent) – Reg 32(2)(b).

Note that the employee has the entirely separate right to withdraw a notice requesting discontinuous periods of SPL on or before the 15th day after the notice was originally given, where that notice has not been agreed by the employer – Regs 14(6) and 30(6). In these circumstances, the withdrawn notice will not count towards the limit of three booking notices an employee can submit, and neither will the request to withdraw the notice – see further 'Discontinuous periods of leave' above.

Change of circumstances

It is possible that, once SPL has been agreed, the employee's circumstances change such that he or she is no longer responsible for caring for the child, and therefore no longer needs to take leave under the SPL regime. If the employee informs the employer of this more than eight weeks before he or she is due to take a period of SPL, he or she will not have to take the leave. However, if he or she does so less than eight weeks before a period of SPL (or during such a period), the position is different. The provisions for birth parents are set out in Reg 18. Parallel provisions apply to adoptive parents – Reg 33. Regs 18(1) and 33(1) provide that where the mother/adopter informs the employer that he or she has ceased to care for the child less than eight weeks before he or she is due to take a period of SPL, the employer can require him or her to take a period of leave if it is not reasonably practicable to accommodate the change. The Technical Guide explains that this is to enable the employer to have eight weeks to stand down any cover arrangements that might have been put in place in anticipation of the employee's absence on shared parental leave. Of course, if it is reasonably practicable to allow the mother/adopter to return to work, the employer must allow this.

Regulations 18(2) and 33(2) make similar provision in respect of a father or spouse/partner whose circumstances have changed, either because he or she has ceased to care for the child or because the mother/adopter has informed him or her that she or he no longer satisfies the condition in Reg 5(3)(d)/ Reg 21(3)(d) (which sets out the requirements for the mother/adopter to curtail his or her entitlement to SML, SMP or Maternity Allowance, or SAL or SAP, so that the father or spouse/partner can take SPL). This is intended to cover the situation where the mother/adopter has revoked his or her maternity leave/adoption leave curtailment notice (or maternity pay (or Maternity Allowance)/adoption pay curtailment notice, as the case may be). The Technical Guide makes the point that entitlement to SSPP ceases immediately on revocation of the mother's notice to end her maternity pay/Maternity Allowance as the pay or allowance period is reinstated. Consequently, if the father is required by his employer to be absent in the period following revocation of a pay curtailment notice, then he would not be entitled to SSPP in that period. The same would also be true in the case of adoption.

Any leave an employer requires an employee to take under Reg 18/Reg 33 must be treated as SPL for the purposes of the Regulations – Regs 18(4) and 33(4). This means that it will be deducted from the overall amount of SPL available – see 'Amount of shared parental leave' above.

Where an employer requires an employee to take leave under Reg 18/Reg 33, it must start on the date on which the next period of SPL was due to start – Regs 18(5)(a) and 33(5)(a). If the employee is on a period of SPL at the time, the leave that is required to be taken starts on the date the employer is informed of the change in circumstances – Regs 18(6)(a) and 33(6)(a).

8.103

8.104

381

8.105 Any SPL that an employer requires an employee to take under Reg 18/Reg 33 must be brought to an end as soon as it is reasonably practicable for the employer to accommodate the employee's change in circumstances and to allow the employee to work – Regs 18(5)(b) and (6)(b), and 33(5)(b) and (6)(b). In any event, it must end no later than the date on which the next period of SPL was due to end (or, if the employee is on SPL at the time, the date that that period of SPL is due to end), or eight weeks after the employer is informed of the change in circumstances, whichever is earlier – Regs 18(5) and (6)(b), and 33(5)(b) and (6)(b).

Note that Reg 18 does not apply where the change of circumstances is the death of the mother, father or child – Reg 18(3). In these circumstances, the special provisions contained in Part 1 of the Schedule to the SPL Regulations apply – see 'Shared parental leave (birth) – what if parent or child dies?' above. Similarly, Reg 33 does not apply where the change of circumstances is the death of the adopter, his or her spouse/partner or child, or where the placement has been disrupted – Reg 33(3). In these circumstances, the special provisions contained in Part 2 of the Schedule to the SPL Regulations apply – see 'Shared parental leave (adoption) – what if parent/child dies or placement disrupted?' above.

8.106 Employment protection during and after SPL

The employment protection afforded to employees under the SPL Regulations mirrors that which exists for employees who take maternity, paternity or adoption leave. The protection derives from Ss.75I and 75J ERA and the detail is set out in Regs 37–44 SPL Regulations.

8.107 Terms and conditions during SPL

Regulation 38 SPL Regulations provides that an employee who is absent on SPL (whether as the result of the birth or the adoption of a child) is entitled to the benefit of all the terms and conditions of his or her employment which would have applied if he or she were not absent – Reg 38(1)(a). By the same token, the employee remains bound by any obligations arising under his or her contract, except where those obligations are inconsistent with the SPL regime – Reg 38(1)(b). 'Terms and conditions of employment' has the meaning given to it by S.75I(2) ERA and includes matters connected with an employee's employment whether or not they arise under his or her contract of employment, but excludes terms and conditions about remuneration – Reg 38(2). For these purposes, only sums payable to an employee by way of wages or salary are to be treated as remuneration – Reg 38(3).

These provisions are the same as those that apply to employees taking maternity leave and reference should be had to Chapter 3, 'Maternity leave', under 'Terms and conditions during maternity leave', for a detailed discussion of the meaning of remuneration and the status of various benefits during the leave period, including non-cash benefits (e.g. private medical insurance or gym membership), bonus payments, annual leave, notice pay and pension and other service-related benefits. Similar provisions also apply to adoption leave and paternity leave – see Chapter 6, 'Adoption leave and pay', under 'Terms and conditions during adoption leave'; and Chapter 7, 'Paternity leave and pay', under 'Employment protection during and after paternity leave – terms and conditions during paternity leave'.

Sick pay. It is important to note that, unlike SMP, there is no prohibition on **8.108** employees claiming statutory sick pay during the SSPP period (see Chapter 3, 'Maternity leave', under 'Terms and conditions during maternity leave – sick pay'). However, Regs 14 and 26 of the Statutory Shared Parental Pay (General) Regulations 2014 SI 2014/3051 provide that there is no liability to pay statutory shared parental pay to an employee in respect of any week during any part of which he or she is entitled to statutory sick pay. This is discussed further under 'Statutory shared parental pay – payment of SSPP' below.

Pension and other service-related benefits during paid leave. Pension and **8.109** other service-related benefits are discussed at length in Chapter 3, 'Maternity leave', under 'Terms and conditions during maternity leave', and Chapter 6, 'Adoption leave and pay', under 'Terms and conditions during adoption leave', but it is worth setting out here the specific provisions – contained in para 5C of Schedule 5 to the Social Security Act 1989 (SSA) – that govern an employer's obligations in respect of these benefits in the context of paid SPL.

Under para 5C any employment-related benefit scheme, including any occupational pension scheme, is subject to the 'normal employment requirement', by virtue of which an employee's *paid* shared parental leave must be treated as if it were a period during which the employee was working normally for his or her usual remuneration. This applies to both final salary schemes and money purchase schemes – in the case of the latter, this could be a personal pension plan or a stakeholder scheme. 'Paid shared parental leave' in this sense covers any period during which SSPP is paid or any period during which the employee is entitled to be paid under a contractual shared parental leave scheme – para 5C(4).

The general effect of para 5C is to ensure that employment-related benefit **8.110** schemes do not contain any 'unfair shared parental leave provisions', which are defined as any provision that offends the 'normal employment requirement' by discriminating between an employee who is on paid shared parental leave and an employee who is working normally – para 5C(4).

Employer's contributions. The employer's contributions to a pension or other **8.111** employment-related benefit scheme during paid SPL must be based on the employee's notional pay (i.e. the pay the employee would have received had he

383

or she been working normally) as opposed to the actual pay he or she receives during shared parental leave – para 5C(2).

In final salary schemes an employee is guaranteed a pension based on final salary and it is the actuary who decides from time to time what level of contributions are needed from employers to fund the liabilities of the pension scheme as a whole. In such schemes an employer's contributions are not specifically designated to any one employee. Accordingly (depending upon the actuary's advice), an employer may or may not have to pay more contributions to take account of employees taking SPL.

8.112 *Employee's contributions.* In a contributory scheme, whether money purchase or based on final salary, the employee only has to make contributions based on the amount of pay he or she actually receives during paid leave, not his or her normal salary – para 5C(3). This could lead to funding problems for money purchase schemes and employers may need to make up the shortfall.

8.113 Staying in touch days

An employee may work for up to 20 days while absent on SPL without bringing his or her entitlement to an end – Reg 37(1) and (2) SPL Regulations. These are referred to as 'shared parental leave in touch' days (SPLIT days) in both the Technical Guide and the Acas Guide and are discussed under 'Planning and booking periods of leave – staying in touch days' above.

8.114 Contractual and composite rights to SPL

Employers may offer contractual rights to SPL that are more favourable than those available under the statutory scheme. For example, a contract may allow the employee to receive normal contractual remuneration during at least part of the total leave period. An employee who is entitled to SPL under the SPL Regulations and who also has a contractual right to SPL may not exercise the two rights separately, but may take advantage of whichever is the more favourable in any particular respect – Reg 45(a) SPL Regulations. Where an employee combines elements of a contractual right and a statutory right, the result is referred to as a 'composite right'. In these circumstances, the various statutory provisions that apply to the statutory right are modified to give effect to the more favourable contractual terms – Reg 45(b). For further details of composite rights, see Chapter 3, 'Maternity leave', under 'Contractual and composite maternity rights'.

8.115 Returning to work after SPL

Regulation 40(1) SPL Regulations provides that an employee is entitled to return to the same job after a period of SPL where the total amount of 'relevant statutory leave' taken in relation to the child does not exceed 26 weeks. 'Relevant statutory leave' for these purposes comprises SML, SAL, SPL and paternity leave (but not unpaid parental leave). If, for example, a mother takes a total of 13 weeks' OML and 13 weeks' SPL, she will be entitled to return to the same job when returning from her final period of SPL. If the total amount of 'relevant statutory leave' exceeds 26 weeks, an employee is only entitled to return to the same job where it is reasonably practicable for the employer to allow this. Otherwise, the employee must be offered another job which is both suitable and appropriate for him or her – Reg 40(2). This would apply, for example, if an adopter returns from SPL, having taken a total of 14 weeks' SAL and 13 weeks' SPL.

Reg 40(2) also applies where the employee is returning from two or more consecutive periods of statutory leave (the last of which was SPL) which included a period of unpaid parental leave of more than four weeks, a period of AML or a period of AAL. For these purposes the 26-week threshold does not apply. If, for example, an employee took a period of five weeks' unpaid parental leave, immediately followed by a period of ten weeks' SPL, he or she loses the automatic right to return to the same job.

In other words, an employee has the automatic right to return to the same job **8.116** from a period of SPL if:

- he or she has taken less than 26 weeks' relevant statutory leave, *and*

- where the period of SPL was the last of two or more consecutive periods of statutory leave, this did not include a period of AML or AAL, or a period of unpaid parental leave of more than four weeks – i.e. it *can* include a period of OML, OAL, statutory paternity leave or less than four weeks' unpaid parental leave.

Where these two conditions are not satisfied – i.e. where more than 26 weeks' relevant statutory leave has been taken, or where the period of SPL before the employee returned to work was the last of two or more consecutive periods of relevant statutory leave, which included a period of unpaid parental leave of more than four weeks, a period of AML, or a period of AAL – the employee only has the right to return to the job in which he or she was employed before the absence where it is reasonably practicable for the employer to allow this – Reg 40(2).

Note that Reg 40 does not apply at all where it is not practicable, by reason of **8.117** redundancy, for the employer to continue to employ the employee under his or her existing contract – Reg 40(4). In these circumstances, Reg 39 applies – see 'Redundancy during SPL' below.

The right under Reg 40(1) is to return to the job in which the employee was employed before the absence. This means the job in which the employee was employed immediately before any isolated period of SPL, or, if the return is from consecutive periods of leave provided for in Part 8 ERA (i.e. SML, SAL, SPL, unpaid parental leave and parental leave), immediately before the first

385

such period – Reg 41(2). 'Job' means the nature of the work which the employee is employed to do under the contract and the capacity and place in which the employee was employed before the absence – Reg 41(1). It is important to establish just what the employee's contract states he or she is employed to do as this may be wider than what he or she actually does. If so, the employer may be entitled to require the employee to do different work on his or her return, or even work different shifts or at a different place of work, provided this is within the scope of the contract.

8.118 **Terms and conditions.** The employee's right to return under Reg 40 is the right to return 'on terms and conditions not less favourable than those which would have applied if there had been no absence' – Reg 41(3). This applies whether the employee is returning to the same job or to a suitable and appropriate alternative job. This is not the same as saying that the terms and conditions must be not less favourable than they were when the employee went on leave, since changes to which the employee would have been subjected had he or she not been on leave might have occurred during the leave period. Any such changes to terms and conditions, whether to the benefit – such as a pay rise – or detriment of the employee, will apply to the employee on his or her return. For further discussion on this topic, see Chapter 4, 'Returning to work after maternity leave', under 'Returning after ordinary maternity leave – terms and conditions "not less favourable"'.

Under Reg 41(3)(a), an employee returning from a period of SPL must be treated as though he or she had not been absent for the purposes of seniority, pension rights and similar contractual rights which depend on length of service. The period of leave will therefore be included in the service calculation. In the case of accrual of rights under an employment-related benefit scheme, Reg 41(3)(a) does not impose a requirement which exceeds those set out in para 5C of Schedule 5 to the Social Security Act 1989 (see 'Terms and conditions during SPL – pension and other service-related benefits during paid leave' above) – Reg 41(4).

8.119 **Refusal to allow return.** A refusal to allow an employee to return after SPL in accordance with Regs 40 and 41 SPL Regulations may amount to a detriment or dismissal, which, in the case of the latter and depending on the reasons for it, may be unfair – see 'Protection from detriment' and 'Protection from dismissal' below.

8.120 **Redundancy during SPL**
Special provisions apply where, during a period of SPL, it is not practicable by reason of redundancy for the employer to continue to employ the employee under his or her existing contract of employment – Reg 39. In these circumstances, the employee is entitled to be offered any suitable alternative vacancy that exists with the employer, the employer's successor or an associated

employer, before his or her existing contract ends – Reg 39(2). It is essentially an obligation on the employer to give preferential treatment to employees on SPL above those who are not on SPL. The new contract must take effect immediately on the ending of the previous contract. Furthermore, the work offered must be both 'suitable in relation to the employee and appropriate for the employee to do in the circumstances'. The new contract's provisions as to the capacity and place in which the employee is to be employed, and its other terms and conditions, must also not be substantially less favourable to the employee than if he or she had continued to be employed under the previous contract – Reg 39(3). A failure to offer such a vacancy will result in a finding of automatic unfair dismissal – Reg 43(1)(b) (see 'Protection from dismissal' below). If, however, such a vacancy genuinely does not exist or the employer offers such a vacancy but the employee unreasonably refuses it, the dismissal will almost certainly be fair and the employee will lose the right to a redundancy payment – see S.141 ERA.

If there is no suitable available vacancy, the employee's employment (and his or her SPL) will come to an end by reason of redundancy. The employee will, however, be entitled to his or her notice period and to a written statement of the reasons for dismissal (without having to request it) – see S.92(4A) ERA. The employee will also be entitled to a redundancy payment (statutory or contractual), provided he or she has sufficient qualifying service.

Protection from detriment   8.121
Under S.47C ERA, employees are entitled not to be subjected to any detriment by any act, or any deliberate failure to act, by their employer for any reason specified in Reg 42 SPL Regulations. The reasons are that:

- the employee took, sought to take, or made use of the benefits of SPL – Reg 42(1)(a)

- the employer believed that the employee was likely to take SPL – Reg 42(1)(b), or

- the employee undertook, considered undertaking, or refused to undertake work during the SPL period in accordance with Reg 37 (see 'Staying in touch days' above) – Reg 42(1)(c).

An employee 'makes use of the benefits of [SPL] if, during a period of [SPL], the employee benefits from any of the terms and conditions of employment preserved by Regulation 38 during that period' – Reg 42(3). (For more information about the effects of Reg 38, see 'Terms and conditions during SPL' above). Reg 42 does not apply where the detriment in question amounts to dismissal – Reg 42(3). Instead, Reg 43 applies – see 'Protection from dismissal' below.

387

8.122 The right not to suffer detriment in respect of the various types of family leave discussed in this Handbook is considered at length in Chapter 12, 'Detriment and unfair dismissal', under 'Right not to suffer detriment'.

8.123 ### Protection from dismissal

Section 99(1) ERA provides that an employee will be regarded as having been unfairly dismissed if the reason or principal reason for the dismissal is of a prescribed kind, or the dismissal takes place in prescribed circumstances. 'Prescribed' in this context means prescribed by regulations. S.99(3) sets out the prescribed reasons or circumstances caught by these provisions, which expressly include reasons related to 'shared parental leave' – S.99(3)(bb).

The relevant prescribing regulations in this context are the SPL Regulations, Reg 43(1) of which provides that an employee who is dismissed will be regarded as unfairly dismissed under S.99 ERA if the reason or principal reason for the dismissal is:

- of a kind specified in Reg 43(3), or

- that the employee is redundant and Reg 39 has not been complied with. (Reg 39 applies to redundancies during shared parental leave and is dealt with under 'Redundancy during SPL' above.)

8.124 The reasons for dismissal specified in Reg 43(3) SPL Regulations are reasons connected with the fact that:

- the employee took, sought to take, or made use of the benefits of, SPL – Reg 43(3)(a)

- the employer believed that the employee was likely to take SPL – Reg 43(3)(b), or

- the employee undertook, considered undertaking, or refused to undertake work in accordance with Reg 37 (see 'Staying in touch days' above) – Reg 43(3)(c).

An employee will also be regarded as unfairly dismissed if he or she is selected for redundancy for one of the above reasons and the circumstances constituting the redundancy applied equally to one or more employees in the same undertaking who held positions similar to that held by the employee and who have not been dismissed by the employer – Reg 43(2).

8.125 Note that unlike the equivalent provisions in the Maternity and Parental Leave etc Regulations 1999 SI 1999/3312 and Paternity and Adoption Leave Regulations 2002 SI 2002/2788, there is no exception to the automatically unfair dismissal provisions that apply to SPL where an associated employer makes a suitable and appropriate job offer to the employee – see further Chapter 12, 'Detriment and unfair dismissal' under 'Automatically unfair dismissal – exception for job offers from associated employers'.

Protection from discrimination

8.126

Potential claims for sex discrimination under the Equality Act 2010 (EqA) in the context of SPL include claims for direct discrimination (e.g. where the employer allows female employees taking family leave more time off than male employees taking such leave) or harassment (e.g. where a woman taking parental leave is subjected to derogatory remarks related to her sex). However, the most common complaint is likely to be a claim for indirect discrimination.

Indirect sex discrimination occurs where an employer operates a seemingly gender-neutral practice which in reality has a disproportionate effect on one sex. Where a man has been refused SPL, has suffered a detriment or been dismissed because he took, or sought to take, SPL, he may be able to bring a claim for indirect discrimination if it can be established that men are more likely than women to take parental leave and will therefore be disproportionately affected by a refusal or other detriment.

Other potential claims include discrimination on grounds of marital or civil partnership status or sexual orientation. Given that same-sex partners are entitled to take SPL, claims of sexual orientation discrimination could be brought where an employer refuses to grant SPL to employees in a same-sex relationship but allows such leave in relation to employees in a heterosexual relationship. A detailed discussion of discrimination law is contained in Chapter 13, 'Discrimination and equal pay'.

8.127

Statutory shared parental pay

8.128

Like SPL, the right to SSPP is enjoyed by:

- birth parents
- adoptive parents
- foster parents, and
- parental order parents in a surrogacy arrangement.

Full details can be found under 'Who has the right?' above.

Qualifying for SSPP

8.129

The conditions for SSPP are set out in the Statutory Shared Parental Pay (General) Regulations 2014 SI 2014/3051 ('the SSPP Regulations'). Part 2 covers birth parents and Part 3 covers adoptive parents. More specifically, Reg 4 deals with the entitlement of the mother; Reg 5, the father (who may be

389

the birth father and/or the spouse or partner of the mother); Reg 17, the adopter; and Reg 18, the adopter's spouse or partner. Parental order parents must also satisfy the conditions in Part 3, but as modified by the Statutory Shared Parental Pay (Parental Order Cases) Regulations 2014 SI 2014/3097 ('the Pay (Parental Order Cases) Regulations'). Statutory references in this section are to the SSPP Regulations, unless otherwise indicated.

In essence, the conditions for SSPP are the same as (or similar to) those for SPL but with additional requirements relating to the employee's weekly earnings and the period (or periods) in respect of which SSPP is paid. There is also a wider definition of 'employee' for SSPP purposes – see 'Wider definition of employee' below.

8.130 The requirements that are similar or the same as for SPL are as follows:

- the employee must have been working with the same employer for 26 weeks by the end of the 'relevant week' and remain in continuous employment until the week before the pay period is due to start – Regs 4(2)(a), 5(2)(a) and 30 (birth), and 17(2)(a), 18(2)(a) and 31 (adoption). For birth parents and parental order parents, the 'relevant week' is the 15th week before the expected week of birth – Reg 30(3) SSPP Regulations/Reg 14 Pay (Parental Order Cases) Regulations. For adoptive parents it is the week in which the adopter was notified of having been matched with the child – Reg 31(2) SSPP Regulations. (Note that special rules apply where the employee is absent from work without a contract of employment during the 26-week period in certain defined circumstances, including as a consequence of sickness or injury or a temporary cessation of work, or as a result of industrial action or a change of employer – Regs 34–38 SSPP Regulations. These are very similar to the exceptions that apply to SAP – see Chapter 6, 'Statutory adoption leave and pay', in the section 'Statutory adoption pay', under 'Conditions of entitlement – continuous employment')

- the employee must share the main caring responsibility for the baby with the other parent – as at the date of birth (in the case of birth parents and parental order parents) or the date of the child's placement for adoption (in the case of adoptive parents) – Regs 4(2)(b), 4(3)(a), 5(2)(b) and 5(3)(a) (birth), and 17(2)(b), 17(3)(a), 18(2)(b) and 18(3)(a) (adoption); and Reg 6 Pay (Parental Order Cases) Regulations

- the mother/adopter must be entitled to SMP/SAP and have ended that entitlement – Regs 4(2)(d), 4(2)(e), 5(3)(c) and 5(3)(d) (birth), and 17(2)(d), 17(2)(e), 18(3)(c) and 18(3)(d) (adoption). If the mother is not entitled to SMP but is entitled to Maternity Allowance, the father can claim SSPP, provided she ends that entitlement – Reg 5(3)(c) and (d)

- the other parent must satisfy the 'employment earnings test' set out in Reg 29 – Regs 4(3)(b) and 5(3)(b) (birth), and 17(3)(b) and 18(3)(b) (adoption); and Reg 13 SSPP (Parental Order Cases) Regulations. The test is identical to that which must be satisfied by the other parent so far as SPL is concerned – see further 'Shared parental leave (birth) – other parent must satisfy "employment and earnings test"', 'Shared parental leave (adoption) – spouse/partner must satisfy "employment and earnings test"', and 'Shared parental leave (surrogacy) – spouse/partner must satisfy "employment and earnings test"' above

- the employee must provide a notice to claim SSPP at least eight weeks before he or she wishes the payment period to start – Regs 4(2)(c) and 5(2)(c) (birth), and 17(2)(c) and 18(2)(c) (adoption); and Regs 6 and 7 SSPP (Parental Order Cases) Regulations.

The conditions listed above are essentially the same as for SPL, except that **8.131** instead of being entitled to SML/SAL (and ending that entitlement), the mother/adopter must be entitled – and end entitlement to – SMP/SAP. This is discussed further under 'Curtailing maternity pay or allowance' and 'Curtailing adoption pay' below. In addition, there are separate notice requirements for SSPP – see further 'Notice and evidential requirements for SSPP' below. Full details of the conditions for SPL can be found under 'Shared parental leave (birth)', 'Shared parental leave (adoption)' and 'Shared parental leave (surrogacy)' above.

The additional conditions that need to be satisfied for SSPP are as follows:

- the employee's normal weekly earnings for the eight weeks ending with the 'relevant week' must be not less than the lower earnings limit for paying Class 1 NI contributions (£112 per week for the tax year 2015/16) – Regs 4(2)(a) and 5(2)(a) and 30 (birth), and 17(2)(a), 18(2)(a) and 31 (adoption)

- during each period in respect of which SSPP is paid, the employee must intend to care for the child, be absent from work and (where he or she is an employee within the meaning of S.230(1) ERA) be absent on SPL – Regs 4(2)(f)–(h) and 5(2)(d)–(f) (birth), and 17(2)(f)–(h) and 18(2)(d)–(f) (adoption).

Before looking at these additional requirements in more detail, it is worth highlighting another distinction between SPL and SSPP regarding the definition of 'employee'.

Wider definition of 'employee'. Only employees who are in 'employed earner's **8.132** employment' are entitled to SSPP – S.171ZU Social Security Contributions and Benefits Act 1992 (SSCAB). The definition of 'employee' for these purposes is slightly wider than the definition that applies for SPL purposes (which is restricted to individuals who have entered into or work under a contract of service or apprenticeship – S.230(1) ERA). S.171ZZ4 SSCBA – which governs SSPP – provides that 'employee' means a person:

391

- who is gainfully employed either under a contract of service or as an office holder (including an elective office), and

- with general earnings, as defined by S.7 of the Income Tax (Earnings and Pensions) Act 2003 (i.e. any salary, wages or fee; any gratuity or other profit or incidental benefit of any kind if it is money or money's worth; or anything else that constitutes an emolument of the employment).

8.133 This definition covers office holders as well as those employed under a contract of service. A company director, for example, is an office holder but is not always employed under a contract of service, in which case he or she would not be entitled to SPL. However, he or she is likely nonetheless to be able to qualify for SSPP, given the wide definition of 'general earnings'.

In addition (as with statutory maternity, paternity and adoption pay), there are special cases where someone will still be considered an employee for SSPP purposes, despite not falling within the definition set out in S.171ZZ4. Reg 33 SSPP Regulations provides that a person is taken to be an employee for the purposes of SSPP if he or she is treated as an employed earner by virtue of the Social Security (Categorisation of Earners) Regulations 1978 SI 1978/1689. This applies regardless of the age of the person provided that the person, if he or she is under the age of 16, would have been treated as an employed earner by virtue of the 1978 Regulations had he or she been over that age – Reg 33(3). A person who is in employed earner's employment under a contract of apprenticeship is treated as an employee for the purposes of SSPP – Reg 33(4).

To be an 'employed earner' the employee must work for someone who is liable to pay the employer's share of his or her Class 1 NI contributions. This means that the person must earn at least as much as the lower earnings limit for national insurance of £112 a week for the tax year 2015/16.

8.134 However, a person who is in employed earner's employment is *not* treated as an employee for the purposes of SSPP if either:

- his or her employer is not resident or present in Great Britain in accordance with Reg 145(1) of the Social Security (Contributions) Regulations 2001 SI 2001/1004, or

- his or her employer is a person who is exempt from the provisions of the SSCBA or against whom the provisions of the Act are not enforceable – Reg 33(5).

Crown servants are treated as employees for SSPP purposes under S.171ZZ2 SSCBA.

Broadly speaking, the effect of these provisions is that the vast majority of those whose earnings attract Class 1 NI contributions qualify for SSPP, whether or not they are employed under a contract of service (and whether or not they are office holders). This means that SSPP may be available in some cases where

SPL is not available (on account of the fact that the individual in question is not an 'employee' for the purposes of the SPL scheme). Presumably, the right to SSPP will apply where they have a contractual right to shared parental leave. Conversely, employees earning less than the NI lower earnings limit are not entitled to SSPP but may be entitled to SPL and income support.

Normal weekly earnings. Regulations 30(1)(b) and 31(1)(b) SSPP Regulations **8.135** stipulate that to qualify for SSPP, the employee's normal weekly earnings for the eight weeks ending with the 'relevant week' must be no less than the lower earnings limit for paying Class 1 NI contributions (£112 for the tax year 2015/16). As noted in the Technical Guide, the same requirement applies for statutory maternity, paternity and adoption pay. For birth parents and parental order parents, the 'relevant week' is the 15th week before the expected week of birth – Reg 30(3) SSPP Regulations and Reg 14 SSPP (Parental Order) Regulations. For adoptive parents, it is the week in which the adopter was notified of having been matched with the child – Reg 31(2) SSPP Regulations.

The calculation of normal weekly earnings is governed by Reg 32 (for both birth and adoptive parents). In essence, it is based on the employee's average weekly earnings over a period of at least eight weeks:

• starting on the last 'normal pay day' to fall before the 'appropriate date', and

• finishing on the last 'normal pay day' to fall at least eight weeks earlier than this – Reg 32(2).

A 'normal pay day' is a day on which the employee is contractually due to be **8.136** paid – Reg 32(9)(c). The 'appropriate date' for birth parents and parental order parents is the first day of the 14th week before the expected week of birth or the first day in the week in which the child is born, whichever is earlier – Reg 32(9)(a)(i) SSPP Regulations/Reg 15 Pay (Parental Order Cases) Regulations. For adoptive parents, it is the first day of the week after the adopter was notified of being matched with the child – Reg 32(9)(a)(ii) SSPP Regulations.

'Earnings' for the purposes of the 'normal weekly earnings' test means gross earnings and includes any remuneration or profit derived from a person's employment – Reg 32(7). 'Earnings' also includes certain additional payments or benefits that an employee may receive, such as statutory sick pay and statutory maternity, paternity, adoption and shared parental pay – Reg 32(8). As with SMP etc, certain payments are expressly excluded from earnings for SSPP purposes, including payments in kind, employer's pensions contributions and redundancy payments – Reg 32(7). (These mirror the payments that are excluded from earnings for NI purposes.)

8.137 It is worth emphasising that this lower earnings limit requirement does not apply to SPL. This means that employees who are earning less than the NI lower earnings limit may be entitled to SPL but not SSPP.

8.138 **Conditions during the payment period.** During the payment period (or periods), the parent in question must:

- intend to care for the child – Regs 4(2)(f) and 5(2)(d) (birth), and 17(2)(f) and 18(2)(d) (adoption)

- be absent from work – Regs 4(2)(g) and 5(2)(e) (birth), and 17(2)(g) and 18(2)(e) (adoption)

- where the parent is an employee within the meaning of S.230(1) ERA, be absent on SPL – Regs 4(2)(h) and 5(2)(f) (birth), and 17(2)(h) and 18(2)(f) (adoption).

As discussed under 'Wider definition of "employee"' above, office holders and employed earners may be entitled to SSPP, even if they are not employees within the strict meaning of S.230(1) ERA and are therefore not entitled to SPL. The effect of Regs 4(2)(h), 5(2)(f), 17(2)(h) and 18(2)(f) is that where the parent is not a 'S.230(1) employee', he or she does not need to be absent on SPL in order to claim SSPP. However, as Regs 4(2)(g), 5(2)(e), 17(2)(g) and 18(2)(e) make clear, he or she must still be absent from work – for example, in reliance upon some contractual entitlement to leave.

8.139 There are three qualifications to the 'absent from work' requirement. First, the parent is not prevented from working 'other than for an employer' – Regs 15(1)(a) (birth) and 27(1)(a) (adoption). This means the parent could do freelance or voluntary work, for example, without losing his or her SSPP entitlement. Secondly, the requirement does not prevent the parent from working for an employer:

- that is not liable to pay SSPP, and

- for which he or she worked in the relevant week – Regs 15(1)(b) (together with Reg 12(1)(a)) (birth), and 27(1)(b) (together with Reg 24(1)(b)) (adoption). For birth parents and parental order parents, the relevant week is the 15th week before the expected week of birth – Reg 12(1)(a)(ii) SSPP Regulations/Reg 12 SSPP (Parental Orders) Regulations. For adoptive parents, it is the week immediately preceding the 14th week before the expected week of placement – Reg 24(a)(ii) SSPP Regulations.

8.140 Finally, the parent is entitled to work for up to 20 'shared parental leave in touch' (SPLIT) days for his or her employer without losing entitlement to SSPP – Regs 15(1)(c) (together with Reg 12(1)(b)) (birth), and 27(1)(c) (together with Reg 24(1)(b)) (adoption). SPLIT days are discussed under 'Planning and booking periods of leave – staying in touch days' above.

394

Curtailing maternity pay or allowance

8.141

The mother must curtail her maternity pay period (MPP) (i.e. the 39-week period during which SMP is payable) if she and/or the father wish to claim SSPP – Regs 4(2)(e) and 5(3)(d) SSPP Regulations. Where the mother is entitled to Maternity Allowance but not SMP, she can enable the father to take SSPP by curtailing her 39-week Maternity Allowance period (MAP) – Reg 5(3)(d). As the Technical Guide explains, when a mother returns to work before the end of her MPP and without curtailing it, that period does not end but continues to 'run in the background'. This means that if a woman is absent from work for whatever reason in the 39-week period in which her MPP continues to run, her employer must pay her SMP. Similarly, if the mother is entitled to Maternity Allowance, this will be payable through Jobcentre Plus if she is absent from work for whatever reason while the 39-week period continues to run. Full details of these pay periods can be found in Chapter 5, 'Statutory maternity pay', under 'The maternity pay period' and 'Maternity Allowance'.

Thus, in order to create an entitlement to SSPP (for herself and/or the father), the mother *must* end her maternity pay or allowance period. The procedure for curtailing the MPP is set out in Part 2 of the Statutory Maternity Pay and Statutory Adoption Pay (Curtailment) Regulations 2014 SI 2014/3054 ('the Pay (Curtailment) Regulations'). Reg 7 provides that the mother must submit a 'maternity pay period curtailment notice' in writing to the person who is liable to pay her SMP, specifying the date on which she wants her maternity pay period to end. This will usually be her current employer, although there may be cases where liability rests elsewhere. For example, if the employer becomes insolvent, liability for SMP passes to HMRC.

Alternatively, if a woman wishes to curtail her MAP, she must notify the Secretary of State of the date it will come to an end, in accordance with Reg 5(1) Maternity Allowance (Curtailment) Regulations 2014 SI 2014/3053 ('the MA (Curtailment) Regulations'). Interestingly, there is no express requirement for this notice to be in writing. Therefore, it may be that this requirement is satisfied by, for example, the mother simply telephoning her local job centre.

8.142

It is worth noting that, unlike a leave curtailment notice (see 'Shared parental leave (birth) – curtailing maternity or adoption pay' above), there is no need for the curtailment notice for maternity pay or allowance to be accompanied by another document, such as a notice of entitlement.

Date on which MPP/MAP can end. As with a leave curtailment notice, there are a number of restrictions as to the date a woman can choose to end her maternity pay or Maternity Allowance period – Reg 7(2) Pay (Curtailment) Regulations/Reg 5(2) MA (Curtailment) Regulations. It must be:

8.143

• the last day of a week

___

395

- if the mother has the right to OML, at least one day after the end of the compulsory maternity leave period under the Maternity and Parental Leave etc Regulations 1999 SI 1999/3312 (or the four-week period under the Public Health Act 1936 if applicable). If not, it must be at least two weeks after the end of the pregnancy

- at least eight weeks after the date on which the mother gave the curtailment notice – Reg 7(2)(c)/Reg 5(2)(c). Note that in the case of Maternity Allowance, the Secretary of State may reduce this eight-week period in any particular case if he or she considers it appropriate to do so – Reg 5(3) MA (Curtailment) Regulations

- at least one week before the last day of the maternity pay or Maternity Allowance period.

The term 'week' in this context bears the same meaning as that which applies in respect of the MPP under S.165(8) SSCBA (i.e. a period of seven days beginning with the day of the week in which the pay period begins) – Reg 7(6)/Reg 5(6).

8.144 **Effect of curtailment notice.** If the notice is properly served, the mother's MPP/MAP (and thus her entitlement to SMP/Maternity Allowance) will end on the specified date, provided that:

- the mother was actually entitled to SMP/Maternity Allowance in the first place, and

- the conditions as to continuity of employment, normal weekly earnings and partner's employment and earnings are satisfied (see 'Qualifying for SSPP' above) – Regs 4–6 Pay (Curtailment) Regulations/Regs 3 and 4 MA (Curtailment) Regulations.

The effect of the curtailment notice is simply to reduce the amount of maternity pay/allowance available to the mother and allow the remaining balance to be claimed as SSPP – Reg 10(1)(a)(ii) SSPP Regulations. (Although note that there will be cases where an SMP or Maternity Allowance curtailment notice also enables the father to take shared parental *leave*. This is discussed under 'Shared parental leave (birth) – mother must curtail SML' above.)

8.145 **Revoking a curtailment notice.** A curtailment notice for maternity pay/ allowance may be revoked within six weeks of the birth, provided the notice itself was given before the birth – Reg 8(1)(a) and (2)(a) Pay (Curtailment) Regulations/Reg 6(1)(a) and (2)(a) MA (Curtailment) Regulations. A notice given after birth cannot be revoked unless the father dies, in which case it can be revoked within a reasonable period of his death – Reg 8(1)(b) and (2)(b)/ Reg 6(1)(b) and (2)(b). Note that, unlike leave curtailment, there is no provision stating that a revocation notice must be given before the date specified in the curtailment notice in order for the revocation to be effective.

Under the revocation procedure the mother must give notice stating that she is revoking her earlier curtailment notice and (where the notice is being revoked because the father has died) the date of the father's death. A notice revoking curtailment of the MPP must be given in writing to the person liable to pay the mother's SMP (usually her employer) – Reg 8(2) and (3) Pay (Curtailment) Regulations. A notice revoking curtailment of the MAP must be given to the Secretary of State and does not have to be in writing – Reg 6(2) and (3) MA (Curtailment) Regulations. This requirement is likely to be satisfied by the mother contacting her local Jobcentre Plus.

Where the mother sends a revocation notice under Reg 8(1)(a) Pay **8.146** (Curtailment) Regulations (i.e. within six weeks of birth), she is entitled to send her employer another pay curtailment notice setting out a new curtailment date – Reg 8(5). The same applies in respect of Maternity Allowance – Reg 6(4) MA (Curtailment) Regulations. In other words, she and the father can subsequently opt in to SSPP (and/or SPL) at a later date. However if revocation occurs following the death of the father, there is no further opportunity to opt in to SSPP/SPL.

Curtailing adoption pay
8.147

The adopter must similarly curtail his or her 39 week adoption pay period (APP) to enable him or her, and his or her spouse/partner, to claim SSPP – Regs 17(2)(e) and 5(3)(d) SSPP Regulations. If he or she is not eligible for adoption pay, there is no opportunity for the adopter or the adopter's spouse/partner to claim SSPP. The APP curtailment procedure is set out in Part 3 of the Pay (Curtailment) Regulations. It is similar to the procedure for MPP curtailment set out in Part 2. Reg 12 requires the adopter to submit an 'adoption pay period curtailment notice' in writing to the person who is liable to pay his or her SAP (usually the employer), specifying the date on which he or she wants the APP to end. Unlike a leave curtailment notice (see 'Curtailing maternity or adoption pay' above), there is no need for an APP curtailment notice to be accompanied by another document, such as a notice of entitlement.

Date on which APP can end. As with an MPP curtailment notice, there are a **8.148** number of restrictions as to the date an adopter can choose to end his or her APP – Reg 12(2) Pay (Curtailment) Regulations. It must be:

- the last day of a week

- at least eight weeks after the date on which the adopter gave the curtailment notice

- at least two weeks after the first day of the APP

- at least one week before the last day of the APP.

397

The term 'week' in this context bears the same meaning as that which applies in respect of the APP under S.171ZN(8) SSCBA (i.e. a period of seven days beginning with the day of the week in which the pay period begins) – Reg 12(5).

8.149 **Effect of curtailment notice.** If the notice is properly served, the adopter's APP (and thus his or her entitlement to SAP) will end on the specified date, provided:

- the adopter was actually entitled to SAP in the first place

- the conditions as to continuity of employment, normal weekly earnings and partner's employment and earnings are satisfied (see 'Qualifying for SSPP' above) – Regs 9–11 Pay (Curtailment) Regulations.

The effect of the curtailment notice is simply to reduce the amount of SAP available to the adopter and allow the remaining balance to be claimed as SSPP – Reg 22 SSPP Regulations. (Although note that there will be cases where an SAP curtailment notice also enables the adopter's spouse or partner to take shared parental *leave*. This is discussed under 'Shared parental leave (adoption) – adopter must curtail SAL' above.)

8.150 **Revoking an APP curtailment notice.** The potential for revoking an APP curtailment notice is very limited indeed. It may only be revoked if the adopter's spouse or partner dies, in which case the adopter must send a revocation notice in writing to the person liable to pay SAP stating that he or she is revoking the APP curtailment notice and the date of death. The notice must be given within a reasonable period from the date of death – Reg 13 Pay (Curtailment) Regulations. Once the revocation notice has been given, there is no further opportunity to opt in to SSPP – Reg 13(5).

8.151 **Notice and evidential requirements for SSPP**

An employee who intends to claim SSPP must provide notice to his or her employer in accordance with the SSPP Regulations. The Acas Guide confirms that this notice – which must be given at least eight weeks before the employee wishes to start claiming SSPP – can be included in the notice of entitlement to take SPL (see 'Notification and evidential requirements for SPL' above). A notice from birth parents must comply with the conditions set out in Reg 6 (if sent by the mother) and Reg 7 (if sent by the father). A notice from adoptive parents must comply with Reg 19 (if sent by the adopter) and Reg 20 (if sent by the adopter's spouse or partner). Similar notice and evidential requirements apply for parental order parents in a surrogacy arrangement – Regs 19 and 20, as modified by Regs 8 and 9 Pay (Parental Order Cases) Regulations. We highlight the main differences where relevant under 'Notice to claim SSPP (surrogacy)' below.

8.152 **Notice to claim SSPP (birth).** The notification requirements for birth parents are set out in Part 2 SSPP Regulations. While the mother must comply with Reg 6 and the father with Reg 7, the provisions are very similar. At least eight weeks before the employee wishes to start claiming SSPP, he or she must give the employer the following information:

- his or her name
- the expected week of birth
- the actual date of birth. (Note that where the child is not yet born, this information must be provided as soon as reasonably practicable after the birth but, in any event, before the employee wishes to start claiming SSPP)
- the total number of weeks in respect of which he or she would be entitled to claim SSPP (disregarding any intention of the other parent to claim SSPP)
- the number of weeks in respect of which he or she intends to claim SSPP
- the number of weeks in respect of which the other parent intends to claim SSPP
- the period or periods during which the employee intends to claim SSPP.

Within the same time frame, the employer must be provided with written **8.153** declarations from both the employee and the other parent. The employee's signed declaration must affirm that:

- the information he or she has given is correct
- he or she meets (or will meet) the qualifying conditions for SSPP – see 'Qualifying for SSPP' above
- he or she will immediately inform the person liable to pay SSPP if SMP or Maternity Allowance is no longer being curtailed.

Furthermore, where the mother is applying for SSPP, her written declaration must also specify the date on which her MPP or MAP began, and the number of weeks by which it is, or will be, reduced.

In support of the employee's claim for SSPP, the other parent must sign a written **8.154** declaration stating:

- that he or she consents to the employee's intended claim
- that he or she meets (or will meet) the required conditions to enable the employee to qualify for SSPP – see 'Qualifying for SSPP' above
- his or her name, address and NI number (or that he or she has no such number), and
- that he or she consents to the processing of the information in the written declaration.

Notice to claim SSPP (adoption). So far as adoptive parents are concerned, **8.155** the adopter's notice must comply with Reg 19 and the spouse/partner's notice

---

399

must comply with Reg 20. Again, the notification requirements are very similar. At least eight weeks before the employee wishes to start claiming SSPP, he or she must give the employer the following information:

- his or her name

- the date on which the adopter was notified that he or she had been matched with the child

- the date of the child's placement for adoption. (Note that where the child is not yet placed for adoption, this information must be provided as soon as reasonably practicable after placement but, in any event, before the employee wishes to start claiming SSPP)

- the total number of weeks in respect of which the employee would be entitled to claim SSPP (disregarding any intention of his or her spouse/partner to claim SSPP)

- the number of weeks in respect of which he or she intends to claim SSPP

- the number of weeks in respect of which the employee's spouse or partner intends to claim SSPP

- the period or periods during which the employee intends to claim SSPP.

8.156 Within the same time frame, the employer must be provided with signed written declarations from both the employee and the employee's spouse or partner. The employee's signed declaration must affirm that:

- the information he or she has given is correct

- he or she meets (or will meet) the qualifying conditions for SSPP – see 'Qualifying for SSPP' above

- he or she will immediately inform the person liable to pay SSPP if SAP is no longer being curtailed.

Furthermore, where the adopter is applying for SSPP, his or her written declaration must also specify the date on which his or her APP began and the number of weeks by which it is, or will be, reduced.

8.157 In support of an employee's claim for SSPP, the spouse/partner must sign a written declaration stating:

- that he or she consents to the employee's intended claim

- that he or she meets (or will meet) the required conditions to enable the employee to qualify for SSPP – see 'Qualifying for SSPP' above

- his or her name, address and NI number (or that he or she has no such number), and

- that he or she consents to the processing of the information in the written declaration.

Notice to claim SSPP (surrogacy). Regulations 19 and 20 SSPP Regulations **8.158** also apply to parental order parents in a surrogacy arrangement, but as modified by Regs 8 and 9 Pay (Parental Order Cases) Regulations. The main differences are that instead of setting out details about the child's adoption, the notice must state the expected week of birth and the date of birth. (Where the notice is given before birth, the latter information must be given as soon as reasonably practicable after birth.)

In addition, where the person who has elected to be Parent A is applying for SSPP, he or she must give the employer:

- a statutory declaration in accordance with Reg 24 of the Statutory Paternity Pay and Statutory Adoption Pay (General) Regulations 2002 SI 2002/2822 ('the Pay (General) Regulations') as evidence of his or her entitlement to SAP in respect of the child, i.e. a declaration that he or she has elected to receive SAP and not statutory paternity pay

- a copy of the parental order (if this has been granted), or

- a 'parental order statutory declaration', which is a declaration stating that the employee has applied, or intends to apply, under S.54 of the Human Fertilisation and Embryology Act 2008 with another person for a parental order in respect of the child within the applicable time limit, and expects the order to be granted.

Request for further information by employer. Within 14 days of receiving a **8.159** notice to claim SSPP (together with declarations in support), an employer may request certain additional information, which the employee must then provide (also within 14 days) – Regs 6(1)(c) and 7(1)(c) (birth), and 19(1)(c) and 20(1)(c) (adoption). Where the employee is a birth parent or a parental order parent, the employer may request:

- a copy of the child's birth certificate or, if one has not been issued, a declaration signed by the employee that it has not been issued and/or

- the name and address of the other parent's employer or a declaration signed by the employee that the other parent has no employer – Regs 6(4) and 7(4) SSPP Regulations/Regs 8 and 9 Pay (Parental Order Cases) Regulations.

In addition, for parental order parents the employer may request a parental order statutory declaration, if this has not already been provided with the notice to claim SSPP (see 'Notice to claim SSPP (surrogacy)' above).

Where the employee is an adoptive parent, the employer may request evidence, **8.160** in the form of one or more documents issued by the adoption agency that matched the adopter with the child of:

401

- the name and address of the adoption agency

- the date on which the adopter was notified that he or she had been matched with the child

- the date on which the adoption agency was expecting to place the child with the adopter, and

- the name and address of his or her spouse/partner's employer or a declaration signed by the employee that his or her spouse/partner has no employer – Regs 19(4) and 20(4).

8.161 **Varying a notice to claim SSPP.** Employees may vary the period or periods during which they both wish to claim SSPP by giving a notice in writing to their employer at least eight weeks before the beginning of the first period they wish to vary – Reg 8(1) (birth) and Reg 21(1) (adoption). In addition, an employee may vary the number of weeks in respect of which he or she intends to claim SSPP by giving a notice in writing to the employer which specifies the number of weeks during which the employee and the other parent have exercised, or intend to exercise, an entitlement to SSPP – Regs 8(2) and (3) (birth), and 21(2) and (3) (adoption). There is no time limit within which this notice must be given. However, it must be accompanied by a signed declaration from the other parent consenting to the variation.

8.162 **Amount of SSPP**

The weekly rate of pay of SSPP is the smaller of the following two amounts:

- £139.58 (from 5 April 2015)

- 90 per cent of the normal weekly earnings of the individual claiming SSPP – Reg 40(1) SSPP Regulations.

The total amount of SSPP available to birth parents in any particular case depends, in essence, on the amount of SMP that the mother has taken and/or proposes to take – or to put it another way, the amount by which she wishes to cut short her SMP entitlement – see 'Amount of SSPP if SMP cut short' below. Of course, the mother must be entitled to SMP in the first place – if not, there is no possibility of her creating a shared entitlement to SSPP. She can, however, create a right to SSPP for the father if she is entitled to Maternity Allowance – see 'Amount of SSPP if Maternity Allowance cut short' below.

8.163 The total amount of SSPP available to adoptive parents depends upon the amount of SAP that the adopter has taken and/or proposes to take – see 'Amount of SSPP if SAP cut short' below. If he or she is not eligible for adoption pay, neither the adopter nor his or her spouse/partner can claim SSPP.

8.164 **Amount of SSPP if SMP cut short.** It is impossible to discuss the amount of SSPP without first considering the amount of SMP available to the mother.

Entitlement to SMP arises during the mother's 'maternity pay period' (MPP), which lasts 39 weeks. The earliest that the MPP can start is the beginning of the 11th week before the expected week of birth (unless the child is born earlier, in which case the MPP starts on the day after the birth) – S.165(2) SSCBA and Reg 2(3) Statutory Maternity Pay (General) Regulations 1986 SI 1986/1960. The latest the MPP can start is the day after the woman gives birth. The woman can choose to start her MPP on any day of the week – S.165(8).

As discussed under 'Curtailing maternity pay or allowance' above, in order to create a right to SSPP, the mother must cut short her MPP by giving her employer an MPP curtailment notice in accordance with Part 2 of the Pay (Curtailment) Regulations. The date she chooses to curtail her MPP – which will, of course, determine the amount of SSPP available – is subject to the following restrictions:

- it must be the last day of a week – Reg 7(2)(a) Pay (Curtailment) Regulations

- if the mother has the right to OML, it must be at least one day after the end of the compulsory maternity leave period under the Maternity and Parental Leave etc Regulations 1999 SI 1999/3312 (or the four-week period under the Public Health Act 1936 if applicable). If not, it must be at least two weeks after the end of the pregnancy – Reg 7(2)(b)

- it must be at least eight weeks after the date on which the mother gave the curtailment notice – Reg 7(2)(c).

8.165 The effect of Reg 7(2)(b) is that the mother cannot curtail her MPP until at least two weeks after she has given birth. This means that the maximum amount of SSPP that can be made available is 37 weeks (since, as noted above, the MPP must begin the day after the birth). The minimum amount that can be made available is one week – Reg 7(2)(d).

Where the mother gives an MPP curtailment notice (which satisfies the requirements of the Pay (Curtailment) Regulations) before she returns to work, the total amount of SSPP available is 39 weeks less the number of weeks to which the MPP has been reduced – Reg 10(1)(a)(ii) SSPP Regulations. For example, a mother whose MPP begins on Tuesday 21 April 2015 wishes to terminate it on Monday 7 September 2015 (instead of Monday 18 January 2016) and to return to work on 23 September. She gives her employer a curtailment notice in February 2015 (i.e. well in advance of the eight weeks' notice of curtailment required by the Pay (Curtailment) Regulations). This has the effect of reducing her MPP to 20 weeks. Therefore, the total amount of SSPP available is 19 weeks.

8.166 Note that the mother *must* serve an MPP curtailment notice in order to reduce her entitlement to SMP. Unlike SML, it will not be cut short simply by her returning to work (see 'Curtailing maternity or adoption leave – returning to work early' above). As BIS explains in its Technical Guide, when a mother

403

returns to work before the end of her MPP and without curtailing it, that period does not end but continues to 'run in the background'.

It is possible for the mother to serve the curtailment notice after returning to work. However, if she does so the curtailment date will be the last day of the week in which that notice is given, irrespective of the date specified in the notice – Reg 7(5) Pay (Curtailment) Regulations. In such circumstances, the amount of SSPP available is 39 weeks less the number of weeks' SMP payable to the mother before she came back to work – Reg 10(1)(a)(i) SSPP Regulations. For example, the mother in the example above returns to work on Wednesday 23 September 2015 (her MPP having begun on Tuesday 21 April). The following day, she gives her employer a curtailment notice, specifying Monday 30 November as the curtailment date. Notwithstanding this, the curtailment date will be Monday 28 September. Since there were 22 weeks' SMP payable to the mother before she came back, the total amount of SSPP available is 17 weeks.

8.167 **Amount of SSPP if Maternity Allowance cut short.** As noted previously, if the mother is not entitled to SMP there is no possibility of her creating a *shared* entitlement to SSPP for the father. However, if she is eligible for Maternity Allowance (a social security benefit payable to women whose service with their current employer does not qualify them for SMP), she can create a right to SSPP solely for the father by curtailing the 39-week period over which her Maternity Allowance is payable. The procedure for doing so is set out in the MA (Curtailment) Regulations and is discussed in detail under 'Curtailing maternity pay or allowance' above. In brief, a woman who wishes to curtail her Maternity Allowance period must give the Secretary of State eight weeks' notice of the date it will come to an end. If she gives the notice before returning to work, the total amount of SSPP available is 39 weeks less the number of weeks to which the Maternity Allowance period has been reduced – Reg 10(1)(a)(ii). Where she gives such a notice after returning to work, the amount of SSPP available is 39 weeks less the number of weeks' Maternity Allowance payable to her before she came back – Reg 10(1)(a)(i) SSPP Regulations.

8.168 **Amount of SSPP if SAP cut short.** As noted under 'Curtailing adoption pay' above, in order to create a right to SSPP, the adopter must cut short his or her APP by giving his or her employer an APP curtailment notice in accordance with Part 3 of the Pay (Curtailment) Regulations. The date she chooses to curtail her APP – which will determine the amount of SSPP available – is subject to the following restrictions:

- it must be the last day of a week – Reg 12(2)(a)

- it must be at least eight weeks after the date on which the adopter gave the curtailment notice – Reg 12(2)(b)

- it must be at least two weeks after the first day of the APP – Reg 12(2)(c).

404

The effect of Reg 12(2)(c) is that the adopter cannot curtail his or her APP until at least two weeks after the first day of the APP. This means that the maximum amount of SSPP that can be made available is 37 weeks, since the APP must at the latest begin the day after the child is placed with the adopter – see Chapter 6, 'Adoption leave and pay', under 'Statutory adoption pay – period of payment of SAP'. The minimum amount that can be made available is one week – Reg 12(2)(d) Pay (Curtailment) Regulations.

Where the adopter gives an APP curtailment notice (which satisfies the **8.169** requirements of the Pay (Curtailment) Regulations) before he or she returns to work, the total amount of SSPP available is 39 weeks less the number of weeks to which the APP has been reduced – Reg 22(1)(a)(ii) SSPP Regulations. Note that the adopter *must* serve an APP curtailment notice in order to reduce his or her entitlement to SAP. Unlike SAL, it will not be cut short simply by his or her returning to work (see 'Curtailing maternity or adoption leave – returning to work early' above). It is possible for the adopter to serve the APP curtailment notice after returning to work. However, if he or she does so the curtailment date will be the last day of the week in which that notice is given, irrespective of the date specified in the notice – Reg 12(4) Pay (Curtailment) Regulations. In such circumstances, the amount of SSPP available is 39 weeks less the number of weeks' SAP payable to the adopter before he or she came back to work – Reg 22(1)(a)(i) SSPP Regulations.

Period over which SSPP is payable   8.170

The period over which SSPP is payable is determined by Regs 11 and 23 SSPP Regulations (for birth parents and adoptive parents respectively). Reg 11 provides that SSPP is not payable on or after the child's first birthday. The same applies to parental order parents by virtue of Reg 11 Pay (Parental Order Cases) Regulations. Furthermore, it is not payable to the *mother* before the end of her MPP. An example: a mother's MPP begins on Tuesday 21 April 2015 and she gives birth the following Thursday (30 April 2015). She has already curtailed her MPP so that it will end on Monday 7 September 2015, having given her employer a curtailment notice back in February (well in advance of the eight weeks' notice of curtailment required by the Pay (Curtailment) Regulations). This means that her MPP is reduced to 20 weeks and the total amount of SSPP available is 19 weeks. The effect of Reg 11 is that the mother can (if she chooses to take SPL) claim SSPP any time between 8 September and 29 April 2016. The father would be able to claim SSPP any time from the birth of the child on 30 April 2015 until 29 April 2016.

As for adoption, Reg 23 provides that SSPP is not payable on or after the first anniversary of the date on which the child was placed for adoption. Furthermore, it is not payable to the *adopter* before the end of his or her APP.

405

8.171 Death or disrupted placement

If the mother or adopter dies, the other parent does not lose his or her entitlement to SSPP, although the provisions of the SSPP Regulations are modified by its Schedule to factor in this 'special circumstance' – see paras 1, 4 and 5 of the Schedule (for birth parents), and 7, 10 and 11 (for adoptive parents). Crucially, the requirement for the mother/adopter to have curtailed SMP/SAP does not apply, although if curtailment happened prior to death this will still have effect. If the other parent dies, the mother/adopter does not lose her (or his) entitlement to SSPP, provided she (or he) satisfies the relevant notice requirements, discussed under 'Notice and evidential requirements for SSPP' above. Again, the relevant statutory provisions are modified to factor in this 'special circumstance' – see paras 2 and 3 (for birth parents), and 8 and 9 (for adoptive parents). If the child dies or – in the case of adoptive parents only – is returned to the adoption agency, the parents are entitled to take any period of SSPP already notified to their respective employers (see 'Notice and evidential requirements for SSPP' above) but cannot book any further periods – see paras 6 (for birth parents) and 12 (for adoptive parents).

8.172 Payment of SSPP

Payments of SSPP may be made in like manner to payments of remuneration but must not include payment in kind or by way of the provision of board or lodgings or of services – Reg 43 SSPP Regulations. It should be paid on the day that has been agreed for the payment, the day when payments by way of remuneration are normally made, or, in the absence of agreement or normal practice, the last day of the calendar month – Reg 44(5).

The weekly rate of pay of SSPP is the lesser of:

- £139.58 (from 5 April 2015), or

- 90% of the normal weekly earnings of the individual claiming SSPP – Reg 40(1) SSPP Regulations.

Section 171ZY(6) SSCBA allows SSPP to be calculated at a daily rate, which is one seventh of the weekly rate. If the SSPP calculation – on the basis of either the daily or the weekly rate – produces a figure that includes a fraction of a penny, the payment must be rounded up to the nearest whole penny – Reg 40(2) SSPP Regulations.

8.173 Liability for SSPP. Generally, the liability to pay SSPP is on the employer that employs the employee claiming SSPP — S.171ZX(1). However, a former employer will be liable to make payments of SSPP to a former employee in any case where the employee had been employed for a continuous period of at least eight weeks and his or her contract of service was brought to an end by the former employer solely, or mainly, for the purpose of avoiding liability for SSPP – Reg 42(1).

406

In such a case the employee will be treated as if he or she had been employed for a continuous period ending with the Saturday before the 'relevant period' – Reg 42(2)(a). The 'relevant period' is the period

- ending on the last pay day under the former contract of employment, and

- beginning with the day after a contractual pay day that falls at least eight weeks earlier – Reg 42(2)(b).

Aggregation of earnings under different contracts/employers. If an employee **8.174** works under more than one contract for the same employer, then the employer must treat the different contracts as one for the purposes of SPL – Reg 39(3) SSPP Regulations. However, an employer is not required to aggregate earnings under different contracts if such aggregation is not reasonably practicable because the earnings under the respective contracts are separately calculated – Reg 14 Social Security (Contributions) Regulations 2001 SI 2001/1004 ('the 2001 Regulations'). Similar provisions apply where an employee is employed under separate contracts with two associated employers – Reg 15(1) 2001 Regulations.

Where an employee works under more than one contract for different employers who are not associated, he or she is not usually entitled to aggregate his or her earnings since liability for paying national insurance contributions lies separately with each individual employer (he or she may be entitled to SSPP from each one, however). In a few rare cases (other than those concerning associated employers) the earnings paid to an employee under two contracts can be aggregated and treated as a single payment of earnings for national insurance purposes – see Reg 15(1) 2001 Regulations. In these situations, liability for SSPP is apportioned between the employers, either in the proportions which they agree or, if they cannot agree, in the proportion which the employee's earnings bear to the amount of the aggregated earnings – Reg 39(1) and (2) SSPP Regulations.

Liability of HM Revenue and Customs. Regulation 45 SSPP Regulations **8.175** makes HMRC liable to pay SSPP that is due where the employer has failed to do so. Where the employer is insolvent, HMRC will be liable as from the week in which the employer first becomes insolvent until the last week that the employee is entitled to SSPP – Reg 45(3). Where HMRC becomes liable for the payment of SSPP, the first payment will be made as soon as reasonably practicable after it becomes liable, and payments thereafter will be made at weekly intervals — Reg 47.

Persons unable to act. Where SSPP is payable to a person who is unable for the **8.176** time being to act and no receiver has been appointed by the Court of Protection with power to receive SSPP on his or her behalf (or, in Scotland, where his or her estate is not being administered by a guardian acting or appointed under the Adults with Incapacity (Scotland) Act 2000) HMRC may, upon written

407

application by a person over 18, appoint that person to exercise any right to payment on behalf of the person unable to act — Reg 48.

8.177 **Disentitlement to SSPP.** There are several circumstances in which an employer will not be liable to pay SSPP to an employee.

8.178 *Working for any employer during a 'statutory pay week'.* The general rule is that SSPP is not payable in respect of a 'statutory pay week', during any part of which the employee is working for any employer – S.171ZE(4). Where the employee has multiple employers, this includes not only the employer that is liable to pay SSPP, but also those that are not liable to pay. 'Statutory pay week' means a week in respect of which an employee has chosen to exercise an entitlement to SSPP – Regs 12(4) SSPP Regulations (birth) and 24(4) (adoption).

There are exceptions to this general rule. An employee is entitled to work for up to 20 'shared parental leave in touch' (SPLIT) days for his or her employer without losing entitlement to SSPP – Regs 15(1)(c) and 12(1)(b) (birth), and 27(1)(c) and 24(1)(b) (adoption). SPLIT days are discussed under 'Planning and booking periods of leave – staying in touch days' above.

8.179 In addition, an employee is not prevented from working for an employer:

- that is not liable to pay SSPP, and

- for which he or she worked in the relevant week – Regs 15(1)(b) and 12(1)(a) (birth) and Regs 27(1)(b) and 24(1)(b) (adoption). For birth parents and parental order parents, the relevant week is the week immediately preceding the 14th week before the expected week of birth – Reg 12(1)(a)(ii) SSPP Regulations/Reg 12 Pay (Parental Order Cases) Regulations. For adoptive parents, it is the week immediately preceding the 14th week before the expected week of placement – Reg 24(a)(ii) SSPP Regulations.

The employee must notify the employer liable to pay SSPP if he or she receives SSPP in respect of any week specified in a notice to claim SSPP (see 'Notice and evidential requirements for SSPP' above) during which he or she was working for any employer that does not fall within the above exception. This must be done within seven days of the first day during which he or she does such work, in writing if the employer so requests – Regs 12(2) and (3) (birth), and 24(2) and (3) (adoption).

8.180 *Illness and death.* There is no liability to pay SSPP in respect of any week during any part of which the employee is entitled to statutory sick pay or in respect of any week following that in which the employee has died – Regs 14(1)(a) and (b) (birth), and 26(1)(a) and (b) (adoption).

8.181 *Legal custody.* There is no liability to pay SSPP in respect of any week during part of which the employee is in legal custody or sentenced to a term of imprisonment (except where the sentence is suspended) – Regs 14(1)(c) (birth) and 26(1)(c) (adoption). Note that there is liability to pay SSPP in respect of any subsequent period not falling within Reg 14(1)(c)/Reg 26(1)(c). However, liability for payment rests with HMRC, rather than the employer – Reg 46(a).

Regs 14(2) and 26(2) make it clear that there is liability to pay SSPP in respect of any week during any part of which the employee who is entitled to SSPP is detained in legal custody where he or she is:

• subsequently released without charge

• subsequently found not guilty of any offence and is released

• is convicted of an offence but does not receive a custodial sentence.

Again, however, HMRC is liable for payment – Reg 46(b).

SSPP and contractual remuneration. Under S.171ZZ(1), any entitlement to 8.182 SSPP does not affect any right to remuneration under any contract of employment. However, certain contractual payments to an employee can be offset against SSPP — S.171ZZ(2)(a). Similarly, any SSPP paid to an employee for any week will go towards discharging any liability to pay contractual remuneration in respect of that period — S.171ZZ(2)(b).

The payments that are to be treated as contractual remuneration arc sums payable under a contract of service:

• by way of remuneration

• for incapacity for work due to sickness or injury

• by reason of the birth or adoption of a child — Reg 41.

Contracting out. Any agreement will be void if it purports to exclude, limit or 8.183 modify any provision of the SSPP scheme or if it purports to require an employee to contribute to any costs incurred by the employer under such a scheme — S.171ZZ(1). However, some agreements to make deductions from SSPP are acceptable. Under S.171ZZ(2) an agreement between employer and employee authorising deductions from SSPP is not void if the employer is authorised to make the same deductions from contractual remuneration. So an employer may be able to continue making deductions in respect of, for example, pension contributions, trade union subscriptions or a season ticket loan. Similarly, SSPP is treated as earnings, so an employer should make any statutory deductions (such as income tax and NI contributions) that are due.

9 Administering statutory payments

> **Statutory maternity pay**
>
> **Statutory adoption pay and statutory paternity pay**
>
> **Statutory shared parental pay**

In this chapter we consider how statutory maternity pay (SMP), statutory **9.1** adoption pay (SAP), statutory paternity pay (SPP) and statutory shared parental pay (SSPP) are administered. We outline the means by which employers fund their liabilities to make the statutory payments to their employees, the records they must keep, what happens if an employee's claim for a statutory payment is rejected, and how disputes over entitlement are dealt with.

All of the statutory payments are administered in essentially the same way. However, while the rules are similar, they are not identical. A body of rules and regulations governing the administration of SMP has built up over a number of years. SAP and SPP, on the other hand, are comparatively recent schemes, and although exactly the same rules apply in relation to each, they differ in some respects from the rules that apply to SMP. Finally, a number of new administrative provisions have been introduced as a result of the recent implementation of the SSPP scheme. For these reasons, this chapter is divided into three sections – one focusing on the administration of SMP, one on administering SAP and SPP, and another on administering SSPP.

Note that HM Revenue and Customs (HMRC) has produced various guides to **9.2** help employers comply with their obligations with regard to the administration of statutory payments. These guides are referred to in this chapter where relevant and can be found on the government website (www.gov.uk).

Statutory maternity pay $\qquad$ **9.3**

Since 18 April 2005, overall responsibility for the administration of SMP has been with HMRC – S.7 Commissioners for Revenue and Customs Act 2005 and Art 2(2)(c) Commissioners for Revenue and Customs Act 2005 (Commencement) Order 2005 SI 2005/1126. By virtue of S.163(1)(d) of the Social Security Administration Act 1992, SMP can be paid out of the National Insurance (NI) Fund.

Any references to the 'maternity pay period' (MPP) in this chapter are to the 39 weeks of SMP available to women who satisfy the qualifying conditions for claiming SMP (see Chapter 5, 'Statutory maternity pay', under 'Qualifying for statutory maternity pay').

9.4 Recovery of payments

Every employer is under an obligation to pay SMP but, depending on the size of the organisation, may be able to recover most or all of the monies paid out. Employers who do not qualify for small employers' relief (see 'Small employers' above) can recover 92 per cent of the amount they pay out by way of SMP – Reg 4(a) Statutory Maternity Pay (Compensation of Employers) and Miscellaneous Amendment Regulations 1994 SI 1994/1882 ('the 1994 Regulations'). Small employers can recover 100 per cent – Reg 4(b)(i).

There are two ways in which employers may seek recovery:

- by applying for advance funding (see 'Advance funding' below), or

- by making deductions from payments they are liable to make to HMRC (see 'Deductions from employer's HMRC liability' below).

9.5 The principles governing the recovery of SMP payments from HMRC are set out in S.167 SSCBA and the 1994 Regulations. The equivalent rules that deal with recovery of SMP payments in Northern Ireland are the Social Security Contributions and Benefits (Northern Ireland) Act 1992 and the Statutory Maternity Pay (Compensation of Employers) and Miscellaneous Amendment Regulations (Northern Ireland) 1994 SR 1994/271.

Basic information about recovering SMP, including relevant HMRC contact details, is set out in HMRC's guide, 'Get financial help with Statutory Maternity and Paternity Pay'.

9.6 'Small employers'. 'Small employers' are entitled to recover 100 per cent of the SMP they have paid to employees – Reg 4(b)(i) 1994 Regulations. They are also entitled to an additional payment – known as the 'compensation rate' – to compensate for the employers' NI contributions paid on SMP – Reg 4(b)(ii). The rate of payment is currently 3 per cent of the SMP which a small employer has paid – Reg 3. Qualifying employers can recover the payments either by applying for advance funding under Reg 5 (see 'Advance funding' below), or by deducting the payments from such amounts as would otherwise be due to HMRC under Reg 6 (see 'Deductions from employer's HMRC liability' below).

A 'small employer' is defined as an employer whose gross Class 1 NI contributions payments, including employer's and employees' shares, do not exceed £45,000 for the qualifying tax year – Reg 2(1) and (2) 1994 Regulations. The limit of £45,000 was set in April 2004 and, to date, remains unchanged – see the Statutory Maternity Pay (Compensation of Employers) Amendment Regulations 2004 SI 2004/698.

The qualifying tax year is the tax year preceding that in which the qualifying **9.7** day in question falls – Reg 1(4) 1994 Regulations. For example, if the employee's qualifying day (being the first day in the 15th week before the expected week of childbirth – see Chapter 5, 'Statutory maternity pay', under 'Qualifying for statutory maternity pay – qualifying conditions') is 26 April 2015, the qualifying tax year is 2014/15. If the employer's gross (i.e. employer's plus employee's) Class 1 NI contributions for the tax year 2014/15 were £45,000 or less, it will be able to recover 103 per cent of the employee's SMP. The total of the employer's and employee's NI contributions for the tax year will be recorded by the employer on the Employer Annual Return (form P35, available from HMRC).

Special rules apply where the employer has made contributions payments in one or more, but not all, of the income tax months in the qualifying tax year. In these circumstances, the amount of its contributions payments in the tax year must be estimated by adding together all the payments it has made, dividing the total amount by the number of months in which it has made those payments, and multiplying the resulting figure by 12 – Reg 2(3) 1994 Regulations. An 'income tax month' begins on the sixth day of any calendar month and ends on the fifth day of the following calendar month – Reg 1(4).

Where the employer has not made any contributions payments at all in the **9.8** qualifying tax year, but has made such payments in one or more income tax months that fall both:

- in the tax year in which the qualifying day falls, and

- before the qualifying day or, where there is more than one such day in that tax year, before the first of those days

then the amount of its contributions payments for the qualifying year must be estimated in accordance with Reg 2(3) (see above) but as if the amount of the contributions payments falling in those months had fallen instead in the corresponding tax months in the qualifying tax year – Reg 2(4) 1994 Regulations.

Advance funding   9.9
Where in any income tax month or quarter the amount of SMP that an employer is entitled to recover under Reg 4 1994 Regulations exceeds the aggregate of what it is required to pay:

- to HMRC by way of
  - PAYE
  - student loan deductions
  - NI contributions
  - Construction Industry Scheme deductions

- to its employees by way of SAP, SPP and SMP

the employer can apply to HMRC for an advance of funds to pay that excess (or so much of it as remains outstanding) to the employee(s) concerned – Reg 5(1) 1994 Regulations.

An 'income tax month' begins on the sixth day of any calendar month and ends on the fifth day of the following calendar month – Reg 1(4). An 'income tax quarter' is the period beginning on 6 April and ending on 5 July; the period beginning on 6 July and ending on 5 October; the period beginning on 6 October and ending on 5 January; or the period beginning on 6 January and ending on 5 April – Reg 1(4).

9.10 The amount requested by way of advance funding must not exceed the total amount the employer is entitled to recover under Reg 4, which will be either 92 per cent or 103 per cent of the SMP paid (see 'Recovery of payments' above) – Reg 5(3). The employer can apply for advance funding where it experiences a shortfall in funds in any income tax month or quarter or where it considers that it will experience such a shortfall on the date of the next SMP payment – Reg 5(2). The request can be faxed or posted to the HMRC Accounts Office, or submitted online.

Regulation 5 covers the situation where the money the employer saves by not making its usual payments to HMRC in respect of PAYE, NI contributions, etc (see 'Deductions from employer's HMRC liability' below) does not give it enough money to pay out all the statutory payments it is liable to make in any particular month or quarter. (Note that the employer will also take into account any payments it will have to make in respect of its employees' statutory sick pay, tax rebates or tax credits when deciding whether it has sufficient funds.) In these circumstances, the employer can ask the Accounts Office for the balance of the amount it is entitled to recover. The provision is particularly aimed at helping small employers – i.e. those entitled to recover 103 per cent in respect of any statutory payments they have to make.

9.11 Even if an employer qualifies for advance funding, it is always open to it not to make use of the facility but, instead, to carry over any balance owed to it to the next month or quarter and recover it from its tax liability to HMRC at that point – see 'Deductions from employer's HMRC liability' below.

9.12 **Overpayments.** Regulation 7A 1994 Regulations allows HMRC to recover any overpayments generated by advance funding. An HMRC officer will decide, to the best of his or her judgement, the amount of the overpayment – that is, the part of the advance funding that was not used by the employer to pay SMP – and give written notice of the decision to the employer – Reg 7A(1) and (2). The officer's decision may cover advance funds provided for one or more income tax months or quarters in a tax year and in respect of a class or classes of employees specified in the decision (without naming the individual employees), or in respect of one or more specifically named employees – Reg 7A(3).

The officer's decision will be treated as an assessment and as if the amount of funds determined were income tax charged on the employer, and Part 6 of the Taxes Management Act 1970 on the collection and recovery of unpaid taxes will apply accordingly – Reg 7A(4). Where the decision relates to more than one employee, the funds can be recovered by HMRC in one set of proceedings or in separate proceedings – Reg 7A(5)–(7).

Deductions from employer's HMRC liability   9.13

Regulation 6 1994 Regulations allows employers to recover payments of SMP by making one or more deductions from the types of payment set out in Reg 5(1) – namely, income tax, NI contributions, student loan deductions and Construction Industry Scheme deductions. Prior to changes made by the Statutory Maternity Pay (Compensation of Employers) Amendment Regulations 2003 SI 2003/672, deductions were only possible from the employer's NI contributions.

Deductions may not be made from payments for any income tax month or quarter earlier than the one in which SMP was paid, or from payments made later than six years after the tax year in which SMP was paid – Reg 6(a) and (b). An employer cannot make a deduction where it has either received an advance payment under Reg 5 (see 'Advance payment' above) or made a request in writing for an advance payment and has not received notification from HMRC that its request has been refused – Reg 6(c) and (d).

Timing of deductions made from NI contributions. Where an employer has **9.14** made a deduction from an NI contributions payment under Reg 6, the date on which it is to be treated as having been paid for the purposes of S.167(6) SSCBA (which stipulates the date on which any deduction from an employer's contributions payment is deemed to have been paid and received by HMRC towards discharging the employer's liability in respect of Class 1 contributions) will be:

- where the deduction did not extinguish the contributions payment, the date on which the remainder of the contributions payment, or the first date on which any part of the remainder of the contributions payment, was paid – Reg 7(a)

- where the deduction extinguished the contributions payment, the 14th day after the end of the income tax month during which the employer paid the earnings in respect of which the contributions payment was due – Reg 7(b).

Payments to employers by HMRC. If the employer has been unable to deduct, **9.15** in accordance with Reg 6, the total amount it is entitled to recover under Reg 4

415

(see 'Recovery of payments' above), it may make a written request to HMRC for the outstanding sum – Reg 6A 1994 Regulations.

9.16 Pay rises during maternity leave

In Chapter 5, 'Statutory maternity pay', we discuss the SMP implications of a pay rise awarded to the employee before the end of the maternity leave period. In short, a woman must benefit from any pay rise that is awarded between the beginning of the period used to calculate SMP and the end of maternity leave, irrespective of whether the increase has been backdated to a date within the calculation period (i.e. in the case of SMP, the eight-week period ending with the 15th week before the expected week of childbirth). This was established by the European Court of Justice in Alabaster v Woolwich plc 2005 ICR 695, ECJ, and the Statutory Maternity Pay (General) (Amendment) Regulations 2005 SI 2005/729, which were brought into force on 6 April 2005, made amendments to that effect. For further details of this important case, see Chapter 5, Statutory maternity pay', under 'Normal weekly earnings – pay rises', and Chapter 13, 'Discrimination and equal pay', under 'Equal pay – pay rises during maternity leave'.

Where an employer has paid an employee arrears of SMP as a result of a pay rise, it will be able to recover the relevant percentage of the additional SMP paid (i.e. 92 per cent or 103 per cent for small employers) from its payments to HMRC as normal.

9.17 Record keeping

It is obligatory for employers to keep certain records for three years after the end of the tax year in which an employee ends her maternity pay period. For each employee concerned these records must show:

- the date of the first day of absence from work wholly or partly because of pregnancy or confinement. This date will be the first notified day of absence or (if different) the actual first day of absence

- the weeks in the tax year for which SMP was paid and the amount paid in each week, and

- any week in that tax year which was within an employee's maternity pay period but for which no payment of SMP was made, together with the reasons why no payment was made – Reg 26(1) Statutory Maternity Pay (General) Regulations 1986 SI 1986/1960 ('the SMP Regulations').

Employers must also retain for the same period maternity certificates or other evidence relating to the expected week of confinement (EWC) or, where appropriate, evidence of the actual date of confinement – Reg 26(2) SMP Regulations. In the majority of cases, employers will retain form MAT B1 given to them by the employee as evidence of her EWC – see Chapter 3, 'Maternity leave', under 'Entitlement to maternity leave', and Chapter 5, 'Statutory maternity pay', under 'Medical evidence'. If an employer has returned a maternity certificate to an employee so that she can pursue a separate claim for maternity allowance, it is sufficient for it to retain a copy – Reg 26(3). Employers should not retain birth certificates as evidence of confinement but should simply keep a record of the date of birth – Reg 26(4).

9.18 HMRC publishes a convenient record sheet – form SMP2, 'Statutory maternity pay (SMP) record sheet' – which provides a means by which employers can record the details mentioned above. However, use of this form is voluntary.

In addition to the records required under Reg 26, Reg 26A(1) and (2) provides that HMRC officers may, by written notice, require employers to produce any of the records listed in Reg 26A(4) that are in the employer's possession or power and that (in the officer's reasonable opinion) may contain information relevant to satisfy the officer that SMP has been paid and is being paid to employees who are entitled to it. The records are:

- any wage sheet
- any deductions working sheet, or
- any other document that relates to the calculation or payment of SMP to its employees or former employees

whether kept in written form, electronically or otherwise – Reg 26A(4).

9.19 Documents and records must be produced to the officer 'at the place of keeping' within 30 days of the date of the notice – Reg 26A(1) and (2). The 'place of keeping' means:

- such place in Great Britain that the employer and the authorised officer may agree upon, or
- in the absence of such agreement, any place in Great Britain where the records are normally kept, or
- in the absence of such agreement and if there is no such place where the records are normally kept, the employer's principal place of business in Great Britain – Reg 26A(5).

The production of records under Reg 26A is without prejudice to any lien that a third party may have in respect of the records – Reg 26A(3).

9.20 Regulation 26A does not stipulate for how many years the employer must keep the documents and records listed in Reg 26A(4), but HMRC's guide, 'Statutory Maternity Pay and Leave: employer guide', advises that an employer 'must keep records for three years from the end of the tax year they relate to', which presumably includes the records kept in order to comply with Reg 26A.

417

Employers must also keep proper accounting records for the purposes of reclaiming SMP and NI compensation rate from HMRC. In this regard, the following forms should be maintained:

- the employees' deductions working sheets (form P11) (or substitute)
- the employees' end-of-year summaries (form P14)
- the employer's annual returns (form P35).

Employers should not forget to record any additional payment of SMP made as a result of a pay rise and any advance funding they may have received in respect of their SMP liability.

9.21 **Penalties.** If the employer fails to maintain the required records, it will be liable to a penalty of up to £3,000 – S.113A(3) Social Security Administration Act 1992 (SSAA). If the employer fails to produce any document or record, or provide any information as required by Reg 26A, that is punishable by a fine of up to £300 (and it remains a punishable offence even if the failure is later remedied) – S.113A(1)(a), (b), (2)(a) and (5). Continued failure after a penalty is imposed is punishable by a further fine of up to £60 for each day on which the failure continues – S.113A(2)(b).

An employer will be treated as having complied with the requirements under Regs 26 and 26A if it complied with them within such further time as allowed by the officer, had a reasonable excuse for not complying, or, where such an excuse no longer applied, complied without unreasonable delay thereafter – S.113A(7) SSAA.

9.22 The mechanics of the penalty regime set out in Schedule 1 to the Employment Act 2002 apply, with the necessary modifications, to penalties imposed under S.113A – S.113A(8) and (9) SSAA. In brief, paras 1 and 2 deal with determining and notifying penalties, para 3 sets out the procedure for appealing against a penalty determination, and paras 4 and 5 deal with penalty proceedings before the First-tier Tribunal and the Upper Tribunal respectively. The remaining paragraphs of the Schedule cover mitigation of penalties, time limits, interest and interpretation.

For a quick reference guide to the penalties that can be imposed, see HMRC's guide, 'Statutory pay: employer penalties'.

9.23 **Rejecting claims for SMP**

It is for the employer to decide whether or not to pay SMP to a particular employee. An employer who decides that an employee is not entitled – for example, because the employee has given insufficient notice of her impending absence – should explain to her the reasons for non-payment. If the employee does not agree with the employer's decision, she has a right to ask the employer for a written statement specifying, as applicable:

- which weeks (if any) of the maternity absence the employer regards as weeks for which SMP is payable

- the amount of SMP to which the employer considers the employee is entitled for each of those weeks

- the reasons the employer does not consider itself liable to pay SMP for the other weeks (which may mean all the weeks) in the period – S.15(2) SSAA.

If the employee's request is reasonable, the employer must supply the information within a reasonable time.

Where an employer decides that it has no liability to pay SMP to an employee 9.24 who has given appropriate notice, it must give her details of the reasons for its decision within seven days of the decision being made or, if earlier, within 28 days of the day the woman gave notice of her intended absence (or confinement if that had occurred) – Reg 25A(1)(a), (2) and (4)(b)(i) SMP Regulations. The employee's maternity certificate (MAT B1) should be returned to her – Reg 25A(4)(a).

The employer must also give to the employee who is not entitled to SMP a completed form SMP1, 'Employee not entitled to Statutory Maternity Pay: form for employers'.

Legal custody/imprisonment during SMP period. SMP ceases to be payable 9.25 if an employee is taken into legal custody. If the employer has made one or more payments and decides, before the end of the maternity pay period, that no more are due because the employee has been detained in legal custody or sentenced to a term of imprisonment which was not suspended, the employer must provide her with the following information:

- details of its decision and the reasons for it

- details of the last week in which liability to pay SMP arose

- the total number of weeks in the maternity pay period in which there was a liability to pay SMP – Reg 25A(1)(b) and (3) SMP Regulations.

These details have to be provided within seven days of the employer being notified of the woman's detention or sentence – Reg 25A(4)(b)(ii). The woman's maternity certificate (MAT B1) should also be returned to her – Reg 25A(4)(a).

Disputes over entitlement to SMP
9.26

If the employee is dissatisfied with her employer's decision as to her entitlement to SMP, she may refer the matter to an HMRC officer for a formal decision – Reg 2(1)(b) Statutory Sick Pay and Statutory Maternity Pay (Decisions) Regulations 1999 SI 1999/776 ('the 1999 Regulations'). An officer can only decide the matter on the basis of an application by the employee concerned or on his or her own initiative – Reg 2(2). This means that the employer

419

cannot apply for a determination, although HMRC will give general guidance to employers.

Applications for a formal decision must:

- be made in writing in a form approved by HMRC (or in such other manner, being in writing, as the officer may accept as sufficient in the circumstances)

- be delivered and sent to an HMRC office within six months of the earliest day in respect of which entitlement to SMP is in issue

- state the period in respect of which entitlement is in issue

- state the grounds (if any) on which the employer has refused to pay – Reg 3 1999 Regulations.

9.27 **Provision of information to HMRC.** Under Reg 25 SMP Regulations, any woman claiming to be entitled to SMP (or any other person who is a party to proceedings relating to SMP) must, if he or she receives notification from an HMRC officer that any information is required from him or her for the determination of any question arising in connection with the woman's entitlement to SMP, furnish that information to HMRC within ten days.

Failure to provide the information or document requested is punishable with a fine not exceeding £300 – S.113A(1)(b) and (2)(a) SSAA. Continued failure after a penalty is imposed is punishable by a further fine of up to £60 for each day on which the failure continues – S.113A(2)(b). No penalty can be imposed after the failure has been remedied – S.113A(4).

9.28 A person will be treated as having complied with the requirement under Reg 25 if he or she complied with it within such further time as allowed by the officer, had a reasonable excuse for not complying with it, or, where such an excuse no longer applied, complied without unreasonable delay thereafter – S.113A(7).

Appeals against a penalty determination are governed by Schedule 1 to the Employment Act 2002, with the necessary modifications – S.113A(8) and (9) SSAA (see 'Record keeping – penalties' above).

9.29 **Appeals**
Either the employer or the employee can appeal to the First-tier Tribunal, and thereafter to the Upper Tribunal, against a decision made by an HMRC officer relating to entitlement to SMP – S.11(2)(a) Social Security Contributions (Transfer of Functions, etc) Act 1999. Notice of appeal must be submitted in writing within 30 days after the date on which notice of the decision was issued – S.12(1). It must be given to the HMRC officer who gave notice of the decision, and must specify the grounds of appeal – S.12(2) and (3).

420

Fraud

9.30

Where a person fraudulently or negligently:

- makes any incorrect statement or declaration in connection with claiming SMP, or

- provides any incorrect document or record or provides any incorrect information required to be produced to an HMRC officer in respect of SMP under Regs 26A or 25 SMP Regulations (see 'Record keeping' and 'Disputes over entitlement to SMP – provision of information to HMRC' above)

he or she is liable to a fine not exceeding £3,000 – S.113B(1) SSAA.

Similarly, where an employer fraudulently or negligently:

- makes an incorrect payment of SMP, or

- receives an overpayment as a result of an advance payment made to it under Reg 5 1994 Regulations (see 'Advance funding' above)

it is liable to a fine not exceeding £3,000 – S.113B(2) and (3) SSAA.

Appeals against a penalty determination are governed by Schedule 1 to the Employment Act 2002, with the necessary modifications – S.113B(4) and (5) (see 'Record keeping – penalties' above).

Enforcement

9.31

Once an employer has been notified of a formal decision that it is liable to pay SMP and the time limit for bringing an appeal has expired, SMP must be paid on the date specified in Reg 29 SMP Regulations. This provides that where either no appeal has been brought or the appeal has been finally disposed of, the employer (or former employer) must pay the SMP no later than the first pay day after:

- the day on which the employer receives notification that the appeal has been disposed of

- the day on which the employer receives notification that leave to appeal has been refused, or

- in all other cases where no appeal has been brought, the day on which the time for bringing an appeal expires – Reg 29(2) and (3).

If the employer's accounting methods are such that it is not practicable for it to make the payment on the first pay day, the employer must make the payment no later than the following pay day – Reg 29(4).

Where the employer would not have remunerated the employee for her work in **9.32** the week in question as early as the pay day specified in Reg 29(3) or (4), the employer must pay the employee on the first day on which she would have been remunerated – Reg 29(5).

421

'Pay day' in this context means the contractual or customary pay day. If there is no contractual or customary pay day, e.g. because the woman is paid at irregular intervals, it means the last day of a calendar month – Reg 29(1).

9.33 **Insolvent employers.** Where an employer is insolvent, the Secretary of State takes over the employer's liability to pay SMP (which is paid out of the NI Fund). Reg 7(3) SMP Regulations stipulates that such liability runs from the week in which the employer first becomes insolvent until the end of the maternity pay period. Reg 7(4)(a) defines 'insolvency' for this purpose in England and Wales, and Reg 7(4)(b) sets out the applicable definition in Scotland.

9.34 **Penalties.** Where an employer refuses or repeatedly fails to make a payment of SMP after a formal decision holding that it is liable to do so, it is liable to a penalty of up to £3,000 – S.113A(6) SSAA.

An employer will be treated as having complied with the requirement to pay SMP if it complied with it within such further time as allowed by the officer, had a reasonable excuse for not complying or, where such an excuse no longer applied, complied without unreasonable delay thereafter – S.113A(7) SSAA.

Appeals against a penalty determination are governed by Schedule 1 to the Employment Act 2002, with the necessary modifications – S.113A(8) and (9) SSAA (see 'Record keeping – penalties' above).

9.35 **Acas**

Acas conciliation officers have no powers or duties in connection with disputes over SMP brought under the statutory procedures outlined above. They can become involved in disputes over time off for ante-natal care, the right to return to work after maternity leave, and suspension or dismissal from work on maternity grounds, but these are matters arising under employment protection legislation. It should be noted, however, that an employee may be able to claim for unauthorised deductions from wages under the Employment Rights Act 1996 if SMP is withheld by an employer. If such a claim is brought, Acas can become involved with a view to conciliating the claim. Deductions from wages claims are dealt with in IDS Employment Law Handbook, 'Wages' (2011), Chapter 3, 'Protection of wages – 1', and Chapter 4, 'Protection of wages – 2'.

9.36 ## Statutory adoption pay and statutory paternity pay

As with SMP, overall responsibility for the administration of SAP and SPP rests with HMRC – S.7 Commissioners for Revenue and Customs Act 2005 and Art 2(2)(c) Commissioners for Revenue and Customs Act 2005 (Commencement) Order 2005 SI 2005/1126. By virtue of S.163(1)(d) SSAA, SAP and SPP can be paid out of the NI Fund provided that regulations specifically authorise this. Reg 3 of the Statutory Paternity Pay and Statutory Adoption Pay (Administration) Regulations 2002 SI 2002/2820 ('the SPP and SAP (Administration) Regulations') provides that authorisation.

The rules governing the way in which SAP and SPP are administered are contained in Ss.6–16 of the Employment Act 2002 and in the SPP and SAP (Administration) Regulations. These rules mirror those dealing with SMP discussed under 'Statutory maternity pay' above.

The equivalent rules covering the administration of SAP and SPP in Northern Ireland are the Statutory Paternity Pay and Statutory Adoption Pay (Administration) Regulations (Northern Ireland) 2002 SR 2002/379. **9.37**

Abolition of additional statutory paternity leave and pay. Until recently, eligible employees had the right to take additional paternity leave (APL) of up to 26 weeks following the birth or adoption of a child if the mother (or adopter) returned to work early. They also had a right to additional statutory paternity pay (ASPP) if the mother or adopter had not used up his or her entitlement to statutory maternity pay, maternity allowance or statutory adoption pay at the time of his or her return to work. **9.38**

However, S.125 of the Children and Families Act 2014 abolished the additional paternity leave and pay scheme (birth and adoption) as of 5 April 2015 and in its place the Government introduced the right, for parents whose baby is expected on or after 5 April 2015, to take shared parental leave and pay. This new scheme allows a woman who is eligible for statutory maternity leave and SMP to choose to curtail her entitlement to leave and pay and to share the balance with the father of her child (or her spouse, civil partner or partner). Similar rights apply to employees who adopt and to parents of a child born through a surrogacy arrangement if they have a parental order (or have applied or intend to apply for such an order) and are eligible for adoption leave. For full details of this new shared parental leave and pay scheme, see Chapter 8, 'Shared parental leave and pay'. For information about the administration of statutory shared parental pay, see 'Statutory shared parental pay' below.

Numerous legislative amendments have been made so that, from 5 April 2015, 'statutory paternity pay' refers only to what was previously known as 'ordinary statutory paternity pay' (OSPP). However, the right to APL and ASPP still applies in respect of: **9.39**

- children whose expected week of birth ends on or before 4 April 2015
- children placed for adoption on or before 4th April 2015 – articles 14–16 Children and Families Act 2014 (Commencement No. 3, Transitional Provisions and Savings) Order 2014 SI 2014/1640.

423

Thus, the legislation dealing with the administration of SPP as it applied to OSPP and ASPP continues to be relevant in respect of parents whose baby was due/placed for adoption before 5 April 2015. Further details of the additional paternity leave and pay scheme can be found in the previous edition of this Handbook, 'Maternity and Parental Rights' (2012), Chapter 7, 'Paternity leave and pay', and Chapter 8, 'Administering statutory payments'. Details of the paternity leave and pay scheme as it applies from 5 April 2015 can be found in this Handbook in Chapter 7, 'Paternity leave and pay'.

9.40 In this chapter we set out the law as it applies to the administration of statutory paternity pay (SPP) in relation to babies due (or placed for adoption) on or after 5 April 2015.

9.41 Recovery of payments

As is the case for SMP, employers who are not entitled to small employers' relief (see immediately below) are entitled to recover 92 per cent of the total SAP or SPP that they have paid – Reg 3(1)(a) SPP and SAP (Administration) Regulations. Basic information about recovering SPP, including relevant HMRC contact details, is set out in the HMRC guide, 'Get financial help with Statutory Maternity and Paternity Pay'. This guide also applies to the recovery of SAP.

There are two ways in which employers may seek recovery of payments:

- by applying for advance funding (see 'Advance funding' below), or

- by deducting the payments from such amounts as would otherwise be due to HMRC (see 'Deductions from employer's HMRC liability' below) – Reg 3(2).

9.42 **'Small employers'.** 'Small employers' are entitled to recover 100 per cent of the gross SAP and SPP paid to employees, and are also entitled to an additional payment equal to the amount to which the employer would have been entitled under S.167(2)(b) SSCBA had the payment been a payment of SMP – Reg 3(1)(b) SPP and SAP (Administration) Regulations. This additional payment – known in relation to SMP as the 'compensation rate' – is to compensate for the employer's NI contributions paid on the SAP and SPP. The compensation rate for SMP since April 2011 is 3 per cent of the gross SMP paid – Reg 3 Statutory Maternity Pay (Compensation of Employers) and Miscellaneous Amendment Regulations 1994 SI 1994/1882 as amended by the Statutory Maternity Pay (Compensation of Employers) Amendment Regulations 2011 SI 2011/725. The same rate applies to SAP and SPP.

The definition of a 'small employer' is the same as that in relation to SMP – S.7(3) Employment Act 2002 – that is, an employer who paid or was liable to pay NI contributions payments of £45,000 or less in the qualifying tax year.

Advance funding   9.43

Where in any income tax month or quarter the amount of SAP or SPP that an employer is entitled to recover under Reg 3 SPP and SAP (Administration) Regulations exceeds the aggregate of the total amount that it is due to pay to the HMRC by way of:

- PAYE

- student loan deductions

- NI contributions

- Construction Industry Scheme deductions

the employer can apply to HMRC for an advance of funds to pay the SAP or SPP (or so much of it as remains outstanding) to the employee – Reg 4(1). An 'income tax month' begins on the sixth day of any calendar month and ends on the fifth day of the following calendar month – Reg 2(1). An 'income tax quarter' is the period beginning on 6 April and ending on 5 July; the period beginning on 6 July and ending on 5 October; the period beginning on 6 October and ending on 5 January; or the period beginning on 6 January and ending on 5 April – Reg 2(1).

In other words, Reg 4 caters for the situation where the payments the employer   9.44
would usually make to HMRC do not, if held back, give it enough money to pay its employees the amount of SAP or SPP to which they are entitled in any income tax month or quarter. In these circumstances, the employer can apply to the HMRC Accounts Office for an advance. The maximum it can claim is the amount it is entitled to recover, which will be either 92 per cent or 103 per cent (see 'Recovery of payments' above) – Reg 4(3). The employer can apply for advance funding where it experiences a shortfall in funds in any income tax month or quarter or where it considers that it will experience such a shortfall on the date of the next SAP or SPP payment – Reg 4(2). The request can be faxed or posted to the HMRC Accounts Office, or submitted online.

Although the statutory provisions mentioned above refer to advance funding in circumstances where the employer has insufficient funds to pay SAP or SPP to its employees, in practice, it will factor in all the statutory payments it has to make in any income tax month or quarter – including any SMP payable – when considering whether to apply for advance funds under that provision (see 'Statutory maternity pay – advance funding' above).

Overpayments. If an HMRC officer decides that, to the best of his or her   9.45
judgement, any amount of the funds provided to the employer by way of advance funding under Reg 4 SPP and SAP (Administration) Regulations was not used to pay SAP or SPP, he or she will notify the employer of the decision in writing – Reg 8(1) and (2). The officer's decision will be treated as an assessment and as if the amount of funds determined were income tax charged

425

on the employer, and Part 6 of the Taxes Management Act 1970 on the collection and recovery of unpaid taxes will apply accordingly – Reg 8(4). The officer's decision may cover advance funds provided for any one or more income tax months or quarters in a tax year and in respect of a class or classes of employees specified in the decision (without naming the individual employees), or in respect of one or more specifically named employees – Reg 8(3). Where the decision relates to more than one employee, the funds can be recovered by HMRC in one set of proceedings or in separate proceedings – Reg 8(5) and (6).

9.46 Deductions from employer's HMRC liability

Regulation 5 SPP and SAP (Administration) Regulations allows an employer to recover payments of SAP and SPP by making deductions from the four types of payment set out in Reg 4(1)(a)–(d) – namely, PAYE, NI contributions, student loan and Construction Industry Scheme deductions. Deductions may not be made from payments for any income tax month or quarter earlier than the one in which SAP or SPP was paid, or from payments made later than six years after the tax year in which SAP or SPP was paid – Reg 5(a) and (b).

An employer cannot make a deduction where it has either received an advance payment for the amount it is permitted to recover (see under 'Advance funding' above) or has made a request in writing for an advance payment and has not received notification from HMRC that its request has been refused – Reg 5(c) and (d).

9.47 Timing of deductions made from NI contributions. Where an employer has made a deduction from an NI contributions payment under Reg 5, the date on which it is to be treated as having been paid for the purposes of S.7(5) of the Employment Act 2002 (which stipulates the date on which any deduction from an employer's contributions payment is deemed to have been paid and received by HMRC) will be:

- where the deduction did not extinguish the contributions payment, the date on which the remainder of the contributions payment, or the first date on which any part of the remainder of the contributions payment, was paid – Reg 7(a); and

- where the deduction extinguished the contributions payment, the 14th day after the end of the income tax month or quarter during which the employer paid the earnings in respect of which the contributions payment was due – Reg 7(b).

9.48 Payments to employers by HMRC. If the total amount that an employer is or would otherwise be entitled to deduct under Reg 5 SPP and SAP (Administration) Regulations is less than the payment to which it is entitled under Reg 3 (see 'Recovery of payments' above) in an income tax month or quarter, it may make a written request to HMRC for payment of the outstanding sum – Reg 6.

Record keeping   9.49

It is obligatory for employers to keep certain records for three years after the end of the tax year in which they made payments of SAP or SPP – Reg 9 SPP and SAP (Administration) Regulations. For each employee concerned the records must show:

- if the employee's adoption pay period or paternity pay period began in that year, the date on which the pay period began and the evidence of entitlement to SAP or SPP provided by the employee. (The evidence of entitlement the employee must provide to the employer is explained in Chapter 6, 'Adoption leave and pay', under 'Statutory adoption pay – evidence of entitlement to SAP'; and in Chapter 7, 'Paternity leave and pay', under 'Statutory paternity pay – evidence of entitlement to SPP')

- the weeks in that tax year in which SAP or SPP was paid and the amount paid in each week; and

- any week in that tax year which was within the employee's adoption or paternity pay period but for which no payment of SAP or SPP was made and the reason no payment was made.

HMRC publishes forms that employers may use to keep a record of SAP and SPP payments, which are available online.

Inspection of employer's records. Regulation 10 SPP and SAP (Administration)   9.50
Regulations provides that HMRC officers can require employers to produce the following documents and records listed in Reg 10(2) for inspection:

- wages sheets

- deductions working sheets

- records kept in accordance with Reg 9 (above), and

- other documents and records relating to the calculation or payment of SAP or SPP.

An officer may require the employer to produce all documents in one or more of the above categories for a particular year or may request production of specified documents from the relevant categories.

Regulation 10 does not stipulate for how many years the employer must keep   9.51
the documents and records listed in Reg 10(2), but it requires them to be produced 'in respect of the years specified by [the] officer'. The HMRC guide, 'Statutory Adoption Pay and Leave: employer guide', advises employers to

427

keep the records for at least three years after the end of the tax year to which they relate.

The HMRC officer has the power to take copies of, or make extracts from, any document or record produced and may remove any document or record at a reasonable time and for a reasonable period – Reg 10(4). Where the officer removes a document or record, he or she must provide the employer with a receipt, and, if the document or record is reasonably required for the proper conduct of a business, the officer must provide a copy of it (free of charge) within seven days – Reg 10(5). The removal of any document under Reg 10(4) will not break any lien that is claimed on the document or record – Reg 10(6).

9.52 If the employer keeps its documents and records on computer, it must provide the HMRC officer with the facilities to obtain the information from the computer files if required to do so – Reg 10(7).

Documents and records must be produced at such time as the officer may reasonably require 'at the prescribed place' – Reg 10(1). The 'prescribed place' means:

- such place in Great Britain as the employer and the authorised officer may agree upon, or

- in default of such agreement, the place in Great Britain at which the documents and records are normally kept, or

- in default of such agreement and if there is no such place at which the documents and records are normally kept, the employer's principal place of business in Great Britain – Reg 10(3).

9.53 (Note that the definition of 'prescribed place' is exactly the same as the definition of 'place of keeping' used in the equivalent provision relating to SMP – see 'Statutory maternity pay – record keeping' above.)

Employers must also keep proper accounting records for the purposes of reclaiming SAP or SPP and NI compensation rate from HMRC. In this regard, employers should maintain the following forms:

- the employees' deductions working sheets (form P11) (or alternative)

- the employees' end-of-year summaries (form P14)

- the employer's annual returns (form P35).

Where the employer has received advance funding this should also be recorded.

9.54 Penalties. If an employer fails to keep the required records it will be liable to a fine of up to £3,000 – S.11(3) Employment Act 2002. No penalty can be imposed after the failure has been remedied – S.11(4). If the employer fails to produce any document or record, provide any information or make any return in order that an HMRC officer can establish that SAP or SPP (as appropriate) has been paid (or is being paid) in accordance with the Regulations, that is punishable by a fine of up to £300 (and remains a punishable offence even if the failure is later remedied) – S.11(1)(a), (2)(a) and (5). Continued failure to produce the document or record after a penalty is imposed is punishable by a further fine of up to £60 for each day on which the failure continues – S.11(2)(b).

The employer will be treated as having complied with the requirements under Regs 9 and 10 SPP and SAP (Administration) Regulations if it complied with them within such further time as allowed by the officer, had a reasonable excuse for not complying or, where such an excuse no longer applied, complied without unreasonable delay thereafter – S.11(7) Employment Act 2002.

The mechanics of the penalty regime, including appeals against a penalty **9.55** determination, are set out in Schedule 1 to the Employment Act 2002 – S.11(8). In brief, paras 1 and 2 of the Schedule deal with determining and notifying penalties, para 3 sets out the procedure for appealing against a penalty determination and paras 4 and 5 deal with penalty proceedings before the First-tier Tribunal and the Upper Tribunal respectively. The remaining paragraphs of the Schedule cover mitigation of penalties, time limits, interest and interpretation.

Rejecting claims for SAP or SPP
9.56

It is for the employer to decide in the first instance whether or not it is liable to pay SAP or SPP to a particular employee. Should an employer decide that it has no liability to make such payment to an employee who has given evidence of entitlement, it must give the employee details of the decision and its reasons for that decision – Reg 11(1) SPP and SAP (Administration) Regulations. In terms of timing, those reasons must be given to the employee:

- in the case of SPP (adoption) or SAP, within 28 days of the end of the seven-day period starting on the date on which the adopter is notified of having been matched with the child – Reg 11(3)(b)(ii). An adopter is notified of having been matched with a child on the date on which he or she receives notification that an adoption agency has decided that he or she would be a suitable adoptive parent for the child – Reg 11(4)

- in the case of SPP (birth), within 28 days of the day the employee gave notice of his intended absence or the end of the 15th week before the expected week of birth, whichever is the later – Reg 11(3)(b)(i).

In addition, the employer must return any evidence of entitlement to the employee who provided it – Reg 11(3)(a) SPP and SAP (Administration) Regulations.

HMRC has published forms that employers may use to inform employees that **9.57** they are not entitled to SAP or SPP. These are available online.

429

9.58 **Legal custody/imprisonment during periods of SAP or SPP.** SAP ceases to be payable in respect of any week during any part of which the person entitled to it is detained in legal custody or sentenced to a term of imprisonment (except where the sentence is suspended) – Reg 27(1)(c) Statutory Paternity Pay and Statutory Adoption Pay (General) Regulations 2002 SI 2002/2822 ('the SPP and SAP (General) Regulations'). If, during the adoption pay period, the employer decides that it has no further liability to pay SAP because the employee has been detained in legal custody or sentenced to a term of imprisonment which was not suspended, it must give the employee:

- details of its decision and the reasons for it

- details of the last week in respect of which liability to pay SAP arose

- the total number of weeks within the adoption pay period in which such a liability arose – Reg 11(2) SPP and SAP (Administration) Regulations.

These details must be provided within seven days of being notified of the employee's detention or sentence – Reg 11(3)(c). The employer must also return any evidence of entitlement to SAP (although no specific time limit is attached to this requirement) – Reg 11(3)(a).

9.59 Note that if an employee who has been detained in legal custody is released without charge, is subsequently found not guilty and is released, or is convicted but does not receive a custodial sentence, his or her right to SAP is revived and so he or she will be entitled to any part of the entitlement not paid by the employer – Reg 27(2) SPP and SAP (General) Regulations. However, special provision is made in these circumstances for the employer's liability to be met by the Commissioners of HMRC – see Reg 44 2002 Regulations.

SPP ceases to be payable by an employer in respect of any week during any part of which the employee is detained in legal custody or sentenced to a term of imprisonment (except where the sentence is suspended), or which is a subsequent week within the same SPP period – Reg 18(c) SPP and SAP (General) Regulations. Unlike SAP, it would appear that an employee loses his or her entitlement to SPP entirely in these circumstances, as Reg 18(c) applies not just to the week of imprisonment, but to any subsequent weeks. And unlike custody/imprisonment during the SAP period, there is no provision for HMRC to pick up the tab in circumstances where an employee is released without charge, is subsequently found not guilty and is released, or is convicted but does not receive a custodial sentence.

9.60 **Disputes over entitlement to SAP or SPP**

If an employee is dissatisfied with the employer's decision regarding his or her entitlement to SAP or SPP, he or she may refer the matter to HMRC for a decision – Reg 12(1) SPP and SAP (Administration) Regulations. An HMRC officer can only decide the matter on the basis of an application by the employee

430

concerned or on his or her own initiative – Reg 12(2). This means that the employer cannot apply for a determination, although HMRC will give general guidance to employers.

Applications by an employee for a decision must:

- be made in a form approved by HMRC

- be made to an officer within six months of the earliest day in respect of which entitlement to SAP or SPP is in issue

- state the period in respect of which entitlement is in issue

- state the grounds (if any) on which the employer has refused to pay – Reg 13.

Provision of information to HMRC. Under Reg 14(1) SPP and SAP **9.61** (Administration) Regulations, an HMRC officer can ask any of the persons listed below to furnish any information or document that is reasonably required from him or her to ascertain whether SAP or SPP is or was payable, and such information must be provided within 30 days of being notified of the request. The persons so specified are:

- the employee claiming entitlement to SAP or SPP

- the employee's current or former spouse, civil partner or partner

- the employee's current or former employer

- employment agencies

- any servant or agent of any of the above – Reg 14(2).

Penalties. Failure to provide the information or document requested is **9.62** punishable by a fine not exceeding £300 – S.11(1)(b) and (2)(a) Employment Act 2002. Continued failure after a penalty is imposed is punishable by a further fine of up to £60 for each day on which the failure continues – S.11(2)(b). However, no penalty can be imposed after the failure has been remedied – S.11(4).

A person will be treated as having complied with the requirement to provide the information if he or she complied with it within such further time as allowed by the officer, had a reasonable excuse for not complying or, where such an excuse no longer applied, complied without unreasonable delay thereafter – S.11(7).

Appeals against a penalty determination are governed by Schedule 1 to the **9.63** Employment Act 2002 – S.11(8) (see 'Record keeping – penalties' above).

Appeals
9.64

Either the employer or the employee can appeal to the First-tier Tribunal, and thereafter to the Upper Tribunal, against a decision made by an HMRC officer

431

relating to entitlement to SAP or SPP – S.11(2)(a) Social Security Contributions (Transfer of Functions, etc) Act 1999. Notice of appeal must be submitted in writing within 30 days after the date on which notice of the decision was issued – S.12(1). It must be given to the HMRC officer who gave notice of the decision, and must specify the grounds of appeal – S.12(2) and (3).

9.65 Fraud

Where a person fraudulently or negligently:

- makes any incorrect statement or declaration in connection with claiming SAP or SPP, or

- provides any incorrect information or document required to be produced to an HMRC officer in respect of SAP or SPP (see 'Provision of information to HMRC' above)

he or she is liable to a fine – S.12(1) and (2) Employment Act 2002. For SAP, the maximum fine is £3,000. For SPP, the maximum fine is £300.

9.66 Similarly, where an employer fraudulently or negligently:

- makes an incorrect payment of SAP or SPP

- produces any incorrect document or record, provides any incorrect information or makes any incorrect return (see 'Record keeping' above), or

- receives incorrect payments in connection with the recovery of SAP or SPP

it is liable to a fine – S.12(3)–(5). If the employer's offence relates to SAP it is liable to a fine of up to £3,000. If it relates to SPP, the maximum fine is £300.

Appeals against a penalty determination are governed by Schedule 1 to the Employment Act 2002 – S.12(6) (see 'Record keeping – penalties' above).

9.67 Supply and use of information

Under S.13 of the Employment Act 2002, certain information relating to SAP and SPP held by HMRC, or by people providing services to HMRC, may be supplied to other specified parties – S.13(1). These parties are the Secretary of State, the Department for Social Development (in Northern Ireland), the Department for Employment and Learning (in Northern Ireland) or a person providing services to any of these people or organisations – S.13(2). The information may be supplied 'for use for the purposes of functions relating to social security, child support or war pensions'.

Conversely, S.14 allows information held by the various people and organisations mentioned in S.13(2) to be supplied to HMRC (or to a person providing services to HMRC) for the purposes of functions relating to SAP or SPP.

Section 15 authorises HMRC to use information held by it in relation to one **9.68** function for the purpose of any of its other functions specified in S.15(2). These include functions in relation to SAP, SPP, statutory shared parental pay, tax, NI contributions, statutory sick pay and SMP.

Enforcement   **9.69**
The rules relating to enforcement of SAP and SPP are set out in Reg 42 SPP and SAP (General) Regulations, which specifies the dates by which an employer must pay SAP or SPP once it has been notified of a decision by HMRC that it is liable to pay and the time for bringing an appeal has expired. Where either no appeal has been brought or the appeal has been finally disposed of, the employer (or former employer) must pay the relevant payment no later than the first normal pay day after:

- the day on which the employer receives notification that the appeal has been disposed of

- the day on which the employer receives notification that leave to appeal has been refused, or

- in all other cases where no appeal has been brought, the day on which the time for lodging an appeal expires – Reg 42(2) and (3).

If the employer's accounting methods are such that it is not practicable for it to make the payment on the first normal pay day, the employer must make the payment no later than the following pay day – Reg 42(4).

Where the employer would not have remunerated the employee for his or her **9.70** work in the week in question as early as the pay day specified above, the employer must pay the employee on the first day on which the employee would have been remunerated – Reg 42(5).

'Pay day' in this context means the contractual or customary pay day. If there is no contractual or customary pay day, e.g. because the employee is paid at irregular intervals, it means the last day of a calendar month – Reg 42(1).

Insolvent employers. Where an employer is insolvent, the Commissioners of **9.71** HMRC take over the employer's liability to pay SAP or SPP (which is paid out of the NI Fund). Reg 43(2) SPP and SAP (General) Regulations provides that such liability runs from the week in which the employer first becomes insolvent until the end of the adoption pay period or, as the case may be, the end of the SPP period. Reg 43(3)(a) defines 'insolvency' for this purpose in England and Wales, and Reg 43(3)(b) sets out the applicable definition in Scotland.

Penalties. Where an employer is liable to make payments of SAP or SPP and **9.72** refuses or repeatedly fails to do so, it is liable to a penalty of up to £3,000 – S.11(6) Employment Act 2002.

433

The employer will be treated as having complied with the requirement to pay SAP or SPP if it complied with that requirement within such further time as allowed by the officer, had a reasonable excuse for not complying or, where such an excuse no longer applied, complied without unreasonable delay thereafter – S.11(7) Employment Act 2002.

9.73 Appeals against a penalty determination are governed by Schedule 1 to the Employment Act 2002 – S.11(8) (see 'Record keeping – penalties' above).

9.74 Statutory shared parental pay

A new statutory system of shared parental leave and pay was introduced on 1 December 2014 under powers granted by the Children and Families Act 2014. The scheme allows a woman whose baby is due to be born on or after 5 April 2015 to bring her SML or SMP to an early end and share the balance with the father of her child (or her spouse, civil partner or partner) as shared parental leave (SPL) and statutory shared parental pay (SSPP). Qualifying adoptive parents enjoy similar rights to shared parental leave and pay (for children who are placed for adoption on or after 5 April 2015), as do qualifying parents whose baby is born through a surrogacy arrangement. For more information about the shared parental leave and pay scheme, see Chapter 8, 'Shared parental leave and pay'.

Responsibility for the administration of SSPP rests with HMRC – para 26B of Schedule 1 to the Commissioners for Revenue and Customs Act 2005.

9.75 Recovery of payments

The principles governing the recovery of SSPP payments from HMRC are set out in S.7 of the Employment Act 2002 (as amended) and the Statutory Shared Parental Pay (Administration) Regulations 2014 SI 2014/2929 ('the SSPP (Administration) Regulations'). (Regulations to introduce shared parental leave and pay in Northern Ireland have not yet been enacted. However, the power to enact such regulations is being brought into force under the Work and Families Act (Northern Ireland) 2015 on a date which has yet to be appointed.)

An employer who does not qualify for small employers' relief is able to recover 92 per cent of the SSPP it pays out – Reg 3(1)(a). An employer who qualifies for small employers' relief will be able to recover 100 per cent of the amount of SSPP paid out plus an additional payment to compensate for the employers' NI contributions paid on SSPP – Reg 3(1)(b)(i)–(ii) SSPP (Administration) Regulations. In other words, a total of 103 per cent. The rate of the additional payment is that which applies in relation to the recovery of SMP under S.167(2)(b) SSCBA (currently 3 per cent) – Reg 3(1)(b)(ii). The definition of 'small employer' is exactly the same as that which applies for the purposes of SMP – S.7(3) Employment Act 2002 – that is, an employer who paid or was liable to pay NI contributions payments of £45,000 or less in the qualifying tax year.

As with the other benefits discussed in this chapter, there are two ways in which **9.76** employers can seek recovery of SSPP:

- by applying for advance funding under Reg 4 SSPP (Administration) Regulations (see 'Advance funding' below), or

- by deducting the payments from such amounts as would otherwise be due to HMRC under Reg 5 (see 'Deductions from employer's HMRC liability' below) – Reg 3(2).

Advance funding   **9.77**
Where in any income tax month or quarter the amount of SSPP that an employer is entitled to recover under Reg 3 exceeds, or is expected to exceed, the aggregate of what it is required to pay to HMRC by way of:

- PAYE

- student loan deductions

- NI contributions

- Construction Industry Scheme deductions

the employer can apply to HMRC for funds to pay the SSPP (or so much of it as remains outstanding) to the employee(s) concerned – Reg 4(1) and (2) SSPP (Administration) Regulations.

An 'income tax month' begins on the sixth day of any calendar month and ends on the fifth day of the following calendar month – Reg 2(1). An 'income tax quarter' is the period beginning on 6 April and ending on 5 July; the period beginning on 6 July and ending on 5 October; the period beginning on 6 October and ending on 5 January; or the period beginning on 6 January and ending on 5 April – Reg 2(1).

The amount requested must not exceed the total amount the employer is **9.78** entitled to recover under Reg 3 (either 92 per cent or 103 per cent of the SSPP paid, depending on the size of the employer – see 'Recovery of payments' above) – Reg 4(3).

Overpayments. Regulation 8 SSPP (Administration) Regulations allows **9.79** HMRC to recover any overpayments generated by advance funding. An HMRC officer will decide, to the best of his or her judgement, the amount overpaid and give written notice of his or her decision to the employer – Reg 8(1) and (2). The decision may cover advance funds provided for one or more income tax months or quarters in a tax year and in respect of a class or classes of employees

435

specified in the decision (without naming the individual employees), or in respect of one or more specifically named employees – Reg 8(3).

The officer's decision will be treated as an assessment and as if the amount of funds determined were income tax charged on the employer, and Part 6 of the Taxes Management Act 1970 on the collection and recovery of unpaid taxes will apply accordingly – Reg 8(4). Where the decision relates to more than one employee, the funds can be recovered by HMRC in one set of proceedings or in separate proceedings – Reg 8(5)–(6).

9.80 Deductions from payments to HMRC

Under Reg 5 SSPP (Administration) Regulations, an employer can recover the amount that it is entitled to recover under Reg 3 by making one or more deductions from the aggregate of the payments set out in Reg 4(2)(b)(i)–(iv) – namely, income tax, NI contributions, student loan deductions and Construction Industry Scheme deductions.

An employer cannot make deductions from payments for any income tax month or quarter earlier than the one in which the SSPP was paid, or from payments made later than six years after the tax year in which the SSPP was paid – Reg 5(a) and (b). An employer cannot make a deduction where it has either received an advance payment under Reg 4 (see 'Advance funding' above) or has made a request in writing for an advance payment and has not received notification from HMRC that its request has been refused – Reg 5(c) and (d).

9.81 **Timing of deductions made from NI contributions.** Where an employer has made a deduction from an NI contributions payment under Reg 5, the date on which it is to be treated as having been paid for the purposes of S.7(5) of the Employment Act 2002 (which stipulates the date on which any deduction from an employer's contributions payment is deemed to have been paid and received by HMRC towards discharging the employer's liability in respect of Class 1 contributions) will be:

- where the deduction did not extinguish the contributions payment, the date on which the remainder of the contributions payment, or the first date on which any part of the remainder of the contributions payment, was paid – Reg 7(a)

- where the deduction extinguished the contributions payment, the 14th day after the end of the income tax month during which the employer paid the earnings in respect of which the contributions payment was due – Reg 7(b).

9.82 **Payments to employers by HMRC.** If the employer has been unable to deduct, in accordance with Reg 5, the total amount it is entitled to recover under Reg 3 (see 'Recovery of payments' above), it may make a written request to HMRC for the outstanding sum – Reg 6 SSPP (Administration) Regulations.

Record keeping

9.83

The following records must be maintained by an employer for three years after the end of the tax year in which it makes SSPP payments to an employee:

- if the employee's SSPP period began in that tax year, the date when that period began and the evidence that the employee provided to the employer of his or her entitlement to SSPP. (The evidence of entitlement that the employee must give the employer is dealt with in Chapter 8, 'Shared parental leave and pay', under 'Notice and evidential requirements for SPL'

- details of the weeks in that tax year in which SSPP was paid to the employee and the amount paid in each week

- details of any week in that tax year which fell within the employee's payment period for SSPP but for which no payment of SSPP was made, and the reason no payment was made – Reg 9 SSPP (Administration) Regulations.

Penalties. If an employer fails to keep the required records it will be liable to a fine of up to £3,000 – S.11(3) Employment Act 2002. No penalty can be imposed after the failure has been remedied – S.11(4).

9.84

The employer will be treated as having complied with the requirements of Reg 9 if it complied with them within such further time as allowed by an HMRC officer, had a reasonable excuse for not complying or, where such an excuse no longer applied, complied without unreasonable delay thereafter – S.11(7) Employment Act 2002.

The mechanics of the penalty regime, including appeals against a penalty determination, are set out in Schedule 1 to the Employment Act 2002 – S.11(8). In brief, paras 1 and 2 of the Schedule deal with determining and notifying penalties, para 3 sets out the procedure for appealing against a penalty determination and paras 4 and 5 deal with penalty proceedings before the First-tier Tribunal and the Upper Tribunal respectively. The remaining paragraphs of the Schedule cover mitigation of penalties, time limits, interest and interpretation.

9.85

For a quick reference guide to the penalties that can be imposed see HMRC's guidance, 'Statutory pay: employer penalties'.

Inspection of employers' records

9.86

An employer is required, whenever called upon to do so by any authorised officer of HMRC, to provide the following documents and records to that officer for inspection:

- all wages sheets, deductions working sheets, records kept in accordance with Reg 9 (see 'Records to be maintained by employers' above) and any other

437

documents relating to the calculation or payment of SSPP to employees in respect of the years as may be specified by the HMRC officer, or

- such of those wages sheets, deductions working sheets or other documents and records as may be specified by the officer – Reg 10(2) SSPP (Administration) Regulations.

The documents and records must be provided at such time as the HMRC officer reasonably requires, and they must be made available at the 'prescribed place' – Reg 10(1). The 'prescribed place' means:

- any such place in Great Britain as agreed between the employer and the HMRC officer

- in the absence of agreement between the employer and HMRC, the place in Great Britain where the documents and records are normally kept, or

- if there is no place where the documents and records are normally kept, the employer's principal place of business in Great Britain – Reg 10(3).

9.87 (Note that the equivalent provision relating to SMP refers to the 'place of keeping'. However, the definitions of 'place of keeping' and 'prescribed place' are exactly the same.)

Where the records are maintained by computer, the employer is required to provide the HMRC officer with all the facilities necessary to access the information – Reg 10(7).

9.88 The HMRC officer is permitted to take copies of, or make extracts from, the documents or records produced and, if necessary to do so, at a reasonable time and for a reasonable period, to remove any of the documents or records – Reg 10(4). If a document or record is removed, the HMRC officer will provide a receipt as evidence of its removal – Reg 10(5)(a). If the document or record is reasonably required for the proper conduct of the employer's business, the HMRC officer is required to provide a copy of it to the employer, free of charge, within seven days – Reg 10(5)(b).

Where a lien is claimed on a document produced in accordance with Reg 10(1), the removal of the document under Reg 10(4)(b) will not be regarded as breaking that lien – Reg 10(6).

9.89 **Penalties.** If an employer fails to provide the above documentation to the HMRC officer so that he or she can establish whether SSPP has been paid (and is being paid), in accordance with the relevant regulations, the employer will be liable to a fine of up to £300 – S.11(1)(a) and (2)(a) Employment Act 2002. A penalty can be imposed even after the failure has been remedied – S.11(5). Continued failure after a penalty is imposed is punishable by a further fine of up to £60 for each day on which the failure continues – S.11(2)(b).

Rejecting claims for SSPP 9.90

Where an employer who has been given evidence of an employee's entitlement to SSPP pursuant to the Statutory Shared Parental Pay (General) Regulations 2014 SI 2014/3051 believes that it has no liability to make payments of SSPP to that employee, it is to give the employee details of its decision and the reasons for it – Reg 11(1) SSPP (Administration) Regulations. It must provide this information within 28 days of the day the employee gave evidence of his or her entitlement to SSPP – Reg 11(4)(b). Similar provisions apply where an employer has made one or more payments to the employee but decides, before the end of the SSPP period, that it has no further liability to make payments because the employee has been detained in legal custody (see below). In either case, the employer must return to the employee any evidence the employee provided of his or her entitlement to SSPP – Reg 11(4)(a).

Legal custody/imprisonment during SSPP period. SSPP ceases to be payable 9.91 if the employee is taken into legal custody. If the employer has made one or more payments and decides, before the end of the maternity pay period, that no more are due because the employee has been detained in legal custody or sentenced to a term of imprisonment which was not suspended, the employer must provide the employee with the following information:

• details of its decision and the reasons for it

• details of the last week in which liability to pay SSPP arose, and

• the total number of weeks in the SSPP period in which there was a liability to pay SSPP – Reg 11(2) and (3) SSPP (Administration) Regulations.

These details must be provided within seven days of the employer being notified of the employee's detention or sentence – Reg 11(4)(c).

While SSPP is no longer payable by the employer in these circumstances, 9.92 HMRC will become responsible for making SSPP payments in any period of entitlement that falls after the employee is released – see 'Liability of HMRC to pay SSPP – employee taken into legal custody or imprisoned' below.

Disputes over entitlement to SSPP 9.93

If an employee disputes a decision that he or she is not entitled to SSPP, he or she can refer the matter to an HMRC officer for a formal decision – Reg 12(1) SSPP (Administration) Regulations. An officer can only decide the matter on the basis of an application by the employee concerned or on his or her own initiative – Reg 2(2). In other words, an employer cannot apply for a determination of the matter.

The employee's application must:

• be made in writing in a form approved by HMRC

439

- be delivered and sent to an HMRC office within six months of the earliest day in respect of which entitlement to SSPP is in issue

- state the period in respect of which entitlement is in issue, and

- state the grounds (if any) on which the employer has refused to pay – Reg 13.

9.94 **Provision of information to HMRC.** Under Reg 14(1) SSPP (Administration) Regulations, an HMRC officer can ask any of the persons listed below to furnish any information or document that is reasonably required from him or her to ascertain whether SSPP is or was payable, and such information must be provided within 30 days of being notified of the request. The persons so specified are:

- any person claiming to be entitled to SSPP

- any person who is, or has been, the spouse, civil partner or partner of a person claiming to be entitled to SSPP

- the employer, or former employer, of the person claiming to be entitled to SSPP

- employment agencies

- any person who is a servant or agent of any of the persons listed above.

9.95 **Penalties.** Failure to provide the information or document requested is punishable by a fine not exceeding £300 – S.11(2)(a) Employment Act 2002. No penalty can be imposed after the failure has been remedied – S.11(4). Continued failure after a penalty has been imposed is punishable by a further fine of up to £60 for each day on which the failure continues – S.11(2)(b).

Appeals against a penalty determination are governed by Schedule 1 to the Employment Act 2002 – S.11(8) (see 'Record keeping – penalties' above).

9.96 **Appeals**

Either the employer or the employee can appeal to the First-tier Tribunal, and thereafter to the Upper Tribunal, against a decision made by an HMRC officer relating to entitlement to SSPP – S.11(2)(a) Social Security Contributions (Transfer of Functions, etc) Act 1999. Notice of appeal must be submitted in writing within 30 days after the date on which notice of the decision was issued – S.12(1). It must be given to the HMRC officer who gave notice of the decision, and must specify the grounds of appeal – S.12(2) and (3).

9.97 **Fraud**

Where a person fraudulently or negligently:

- makes any incorrect statement or declaration in connection with claiming SSPP, or

- provides any incorrect information or document required to be produced to an HMRC officer in respect of SSPP (see under 'Provision of information to HMRC' above)

he or she is liable to a fine of up to £3,000 – S.12(1) and (2) Employment Act 2002.

Similarly, where an employer fraudulently or negligently:

- makes an incorrect payment of SSPP

- produces any incorrect document or record, provides any incorrect information or makes any incorrect return (see 'Record keeping' above), or

- receives incorrect payments in connection with the recovery of SSPP

it is liable to a fine of up to £3,000 – S.12(3)–(5).

Appeals against a penalty determination are governed by Schedule 1 to the Employment Act 2002 – S.12(6) (see 'Record keeping – penalties' above).

Supply and use of information 9.98

Under S.13 of the Employment Act 2002, certain information relating to SSPP held by HMRC, or by people providing services to HMRC, may be supplied to other specified parties – S.13(1). These parties are the Secretary of State, the Department for Social Development (in Northern Ireland), the Department for Employment and Learning (in Northern Ireland) or a person providing services to any of these people or organisations – S.13(2). The information may be supplied 'for use for the purposes of functions relating to social security, child support or war pensions'.

Conversely, S.14 allows information held by the various people and organisations mentioned in S.13(2) to be supplied to HMRC (or to a person providing services to HMRC) for the purposes of functions relating to SSPP.

Section 15 authorises HMRC to use information held by it in relation to one 9.99 function for the purpose of any of its other functions specified in S.15(2). These include functions in relation to SAP, SPP, SSPP, tax, NI contributions, statutory sick pay and SMP.

Enforcement 9.100

Regulation 44 of the Statutory Shared Parental Pay (General) Regulations 2014 SI 2014/3051 ('the SSPP (General) Regulations') sets out the time limits within which SSPP must be paid where an HMRC officer has made a decision that an employer (or former employer) is liable to make a payment of SSPP and the time limit for bringing an appeal against that decision has expired. Where either no appeal has been brought or any appeal brought has been finally

441

disposed of, the employer (or former employer) must pay the SSPP no later than the first pay day after:

- the day on which the employer receives notification that the appeal has been disposed of

- the day on which the employer receives notification that its appeal has been refused, or

- in all other cases where no appeal has been brought, the day on which the time limit for bringing an appeal expires – Reg 44(1) and (2).

9.101 Where it is impracticable, in light of the employer's accounting methods, for the employer to make the payment on the date specified in Reg 44(2), it must make the payment no later than the next following pay day – Reg 44(3). However, where the employer would not have remunerated the employee for his or her work in the week in question as early as the pay day specified in Reg 44(2) or (3), the employer must pay the employee on the first day on which the employee would have been remunerated – Reg 44(4).

'Pay day' in this context means the contractual or customary pay day, or, if there is no contractual or customary day, the last day of a calendar month – Reg 44(5).

9.102 Liability of HMRC to pay SSPP

Where an HMRC officer has decided that an employer is liable to make payments of SSPP, the time for appealing that decision has expired and no appeal has been lodged or leave to appeal against the decision has been refused, HMRC will be liable to pay the SSPP:

- for any week in respect of which the employer was liable to pay SSPP but did not do so, and

- for any subsequent weeks that the employee is entitled to SSPP – Reg 45(1) and (2) SSPP (General) Regulations.

9.103 Insolvent employer. HMRC will be liable to make payments of SSPP if an employer becomes insolvent. It will be liable as from the week that the employer first becomes insolvent until the last week that the employee is entitled to SSPP – Reg 45(3). Reg 45(4) defines 'insolvency' for this purpose in England and Wales, and Reg 45(5) sets out the applicable definition in Scotland.

9.104 Employee taken into legal custody or imprisoned. Where an employer ceases to be liable to pay SSPP because the employee is in legal custody or has been sentenced to a term of imprisonment that is not suspended, HMRC will take responsibility for making payments in any period thereafter in which SSPP becomes payable (i.e. after the employee is released) – Reg 46(a) SSPP (General) Regulations. HMRC will also be liable in respect of any period during which the employee was detained in legal custody but was subsequently released without charge, found not guilty of any offence and released, or convicted, but not given a custodial sentence – Reg 46(b). For more information about when SSPP is payable to an employee who is legally detained or imprisoned, see Chapter 8, 'Shared parental leave and pay', in the section 'Statutory shared parental pay', under 'Payment of SSPP – disentitlement to SSPP'.

Timing of payments by HMRC. Regulation 47 SSPP (General) Regulations 9.105 provides that where HMRC is liable to make payments of SSPP under Reg 45 or Reg 46, the first payment will be made as soon as reasonably practicable after it becomes so liable, and any subsequent payments will be made at weekly intervals. Payment will be made by means of an instrument of payment or by any such other means as appears to HMRC to be appropriate in the circumstances of the particular case.

10 Unpaid parental leave

Statutory framework and guidance

Unpaid parental leave schemes

Key elements

Default scheme

Remedies

In the previous chapters, we examined in detail the main entitlements available **10.1** to employees upon the birth or adoption of a child: maternity, paternity and adoption leave and pay. We also looked at the possibility of both parents sharing any unused portion of maternity or adoption leave and pay under the shared parental leave scheme. All of these entitlements are associated with the first year following the birth or adoption of the child. In this chapter, we turn our attention to the right to take unpaid parental leave in order to care for a child. This right is available to an eligible employee from the child's birth or adoption until the child reaches the age of 18. However, in contrast to the other rights mentioned above, there is no statutory obligation to pay the employee during this period of leave.

Parental Leave Directives. The right to unpaid parental leave has its origins **10.2** in the EU Parental Leave Directive (No.96/34), which was adopted in June 1996. This put into effect a framework agreement on parental leave concluded by the cross-industry organisations BUSINESSEUROPE (formerly known as UNICE), CEEP and ETUC. The Framework Agreement formed an annex to the Directive. The relevant provisions of this Directive were implemented into UK law by the Maternity and Parental Leave etc Regulations 1999 SI 1999/3312 ('the MPL Regulations') and the Maternity and Parental Leave etc (Northern Ireland) Regulations 1999 SR 1999/471, both of which came into force on 15 December 1999. The statutory right to unpaid parental leave, as originally introduced, allowed eligible employees time off work to care for a child up to the age of five.

With effect from 8 March 2012, the original Parental Leave Directive was repealed and superseded by a revised Parental Leave Directive (No.2010/18), referred to throughout this chapter as the 'revised Directive' (as opposed to the 'original Directive'). The revised Directive was issued following a renegotiated and revised Framework Agreement between the parties to the original framework agreement. This forms an annex to the revised Directive. The provisions of the revised Directive were transposed by the Parental Leave (EU Directive) Regulations 2013 SI 2013/283 on 8 March 2013. These amended the MPL Regulations so that the total amount of unpaid parental leave that a qualifying employee is entitled to take in respect of an individual child increased from 13 to 18 weeks. The same change was made in Northern Ireland by the Parental Leave (EU Directive) (Maternity and Parental Leave) Regulations (Northern Ireland) 2013 SR 2013/25.

10.3 **'Unpaid parental leave' and 'shared parental leave'.** In May 2011 the Government launched a public consultation – as part of its 'Modern Workplaces' consultation – on proposals for a fundamental redesign of the right to parental leave. The key objective was to offer parents greater choice and flexibility in their parental leave arrangements, with the hoped effect that this would lead to a cultural shift towards more shared parenting. A plan for a flexible parental leave system was drawn up, which was built around giving parents the opportunity of sharing their statutory leave and pay entitlements in the first year of the child's life but which also incorporated the existing right to take unpaid parental leave in subsequent years. In the end, however, the Government opted for two separate systems of parental leave: a new system of *shared* parental leave and pay and the existing system of *unpaid* parental leave. In addition, the Government decided that it would be consistent with its commitment to encouraging shared parenting to increase the age limit for entitlement to unpaid parental leave to 18. The change was implemented on 5 April 2015.

In this chapter, we examine how the statutory right to unpaid parental leave operates in practice. We also highlight the recent changes that were made to the scope of the right. It is worth reiterating in this context that, despite the similar terminology, the new right to shared parental leave and pay (discussed in full in Chapter 8, 'Shared parental leave and pay') has no impact on the right to unpaid parental leave; the two are entirely separate. In order to avoid any confusion, we refer to the statutory right to unpaid parental leave as 'unpaid parental leave' throughout this chapter. This is to emphasise that the right under the statute is only to unpaid parental leave. That is not, of course, to say that the right can never be paid. An employer may offer more generous benefits to individual employees under the terms of their contracts of employment. However, in the majority of cases, employees will not have a contractual right (or indeed a right under a workforce or collective agreement) to be paid while absent from work on this type of family leave.

10.4 Statutory framework and guidance

The rules on unpaid parental leave are contained in the MPL Regulations, made under Ss.76–80 of the Employment Rights Act 1996 (ERA), as substituted by Schedule 4 to the Employment Relations Act 1999. Similar rules apply in Northern Ireland – see the Maternity and Parental Leave etc (Northern Ireland) Regulations 1999.

The right has been amended on numerous occasions. Early changes included the extension of the total amount of leave from 13 weeks to 18 weeks where the child is disabled; the removal of the requirement that the child must be born on or after 15 December 1999 for the parent to qualify; and changes to the treatment of pensions during unpaid parental leave. Despite this, it appears that the take-up rate for unpaid parental leave has been low. The 'Fourth Work-Life Balance Employee Survey', published by the Department for Business, Innovation and Skills in July 2012, revealed that only 11 per cent of parents questioned had taken unpaid parental leave in 2011. Earlier surveys also revealed that unpaid parental leave was generally taken for fairly short periods.

Since the 2012 survey, the right has been extended twice – see 'Recent changes **10.5** to the statutory right' immediately below – and more employees have subsequently become entitled to it. Nevertheless, it is unlikely that this will result in a significant rise in the take-up rate. The Government's own estimate of the impact of extending the right to parents with children between the ages of five and 18 is that annual take-up of unpaid parental leave will be in the range of 6 to 12 per cent of eligible parents with a child aged between five and seven, but that this take-up decreases with the age of the child, as the need for unpaid parental leave reduces over time ('Modern Workplaces – Government Response on Flexible Parental Leave, Impact Assessment', November 2012). The main reason for the generally low take-up rate is thought to be that parental leave is unpaid unless there is a contractually enhanced right to payment. As long as the statutory right remains unpaid, the take-up rate is likely to remain low.

Recent changes to the statutory right **10.6**

As mentioned above, a number of important changes were recently made to the unpaid parental leave system. The impetus for these came from the obligation to implement the provisions of the revised Parental Leave Directive into UK law and the Government's commitment to introducing family-friendly reforms as part of its 'Modern Workplaces' consultation.

Member States were required to bring in legislation to give effect to the revised Directive by 8 March 2012, although under Article 3(2) they were given a maximum additional period of one year if this proved necessary to take account of 'particular difficulties'. The UK Government relied on this provision in order to delay implementation of the Directive until March 2013 pending its review of parental leave undertaken as part of its 'Modern Workplaces' consultation.

Following the conclusion of that consultation, the Parental Leave (EU **10.7** Directive) Regulations 2013 SI 2013/283 were introduced on 8 March 2013. These increased the total amount of unpaid parental leave that a qualifying employee is entitled to take in respect of an individual child from 13 to 18 weeks, so as to comply with clause 2(2) of the revised Framework Agreement. The Regulations also introduced a provision – new Reg 16A MPL

447

Regulations – which requires the Secretary of State to review the operation and effect of those provisions which implement the Directive and to publish a report within five years (i.e. by March 2018) and every five years after that. Following a review, it will fall to the Secretary of State to consider whether the relevant provisions should remain as they are, or be revoked or amended, although this could only be done through further secondary legislation. The amount of leave available to eligible employees was also increased in Northern Ireland – see the Parental Leave (EU Directive) (Maternity and Parental Leave) Regulations (Northern Ireland).

Another outcome of the 'Modern Workplaces' consultation was the Government's decision to increase the age limit of children covered by the unpaid parental leave scheme. It acknowledged that there was a gap in the provisions in respect of parents of older children who might need to deal with non-emergency caring responsibilities, such as planned medical appointments. In order to meet this need, the Government decided to increase the upper age limit of children in respect of whom unpaid parental leave could be taken from five to 18 years. The Maternity and Parental Leave etc (Amendment) Regulations 2014 SI 2014/3221 implemented the new age limit with effect from 5 April 2015. Accordingly, each parent in England, Wales and Scotland is now entitled to take up to 18 weeks' unpaid parental leave for each child under the age of 18.

10.8 At the time of writing, the Maternity and Parental Leave etc (Northern Ireland) Regulations 1999 SR 1999/471 had not yet been amended to extend the right to unpaid parental leave to all parents of children aged under 18. However, this change is anticipated: the Northern Ireland Department for Education and Learning, which has responsibility for the Regulations, indicated in its response to the 2013 consultation, 'Sharing parental rights – extending flexibility at work', that it would 'extend unpaid parental leave to cover all employees who are parents of children aged up to 18'.

10.9 Outline of the statutory right

As we have seen above, the current right to unpaid parental leave entitles parents of both sexes (who fulfil the qualifying conditions) to take up to 18 weeks' unpaid leave to care for a child. The MPL Regulations contain a number of 'key elements', which apply to all qualifying employees and cannot be contracted out of, together with a 'default or fallback' scheme, which can be varied by agreement but applies automatically in the absence of any other agreement between the employer and his employees. The means by which agreements as to unpaid parental leave can take effect are explored under 'Unpaid parental leave schemes' below. After that, we consider the key elements that make up the minimum framework of parental leave rights (see 'Key elements' below) and the nature of the default scheme that automatically applies in the absence of any other agreement (see 'Default scheme' below).

448

Guidance on the operation of the right 10.10

The Government has provided guidance on the right to unpaid parental leave for employers and employees, which can be found on the 'Parental leave' page of its website – www.gov.uk ('the Government guidance'). This guidance is in five parts: overview, entitlement, eligibility, notice period and delaying leave. Prior to publication of the Government guidance, a number of different explanatory documents on the statutory right to unpaid parental leave were available:

- 'Parental leave', which was aimed at employees.

- 'Parental leave and time off for dependants', which was aimed at employers. This replicated some, but not all, of the information set out in its predecessor, the more detailed 'Parental leave – a guide for employers and employees' (PL 509), which was produced by what was then known as the DTI but which is no longer available.

These can now be found on the National Archives website but they are no longer updated (as from 17 October 2012). However, we refer to passages of the old guidance below where relevant.

Unpaid parental leave schemes 10.11

Before examining in detail the substance of the statutory right to unpaid parental leave and the means by which employees can enforce their right to take such leave, it is first necessary to understand the way in which agreements on parental leave can take effect and consider what flexibility there is for deviating from the statutory provisions.

There is a major conceptual difference between unpaid parental leave and maternity leave. With maternity leave there is a comprehensive statutory scheme that applies as a minimum. Any agreement made between a woman and her employer can only improve upon the woman's statutory maternity rights. Where there is a conflict between the woman's contractual rights and the statutory rights, the woman may rely on whichever is the more favourable. This is known as a 'composite right' – see Chapter 3, 'Maternity leave', under 'Contractual and composite maternity rights'. This means that a woman always has the statutory maternity scheme as a fallback.

The situation is different in relation to unpaid parental leave. The Government 10.12 has specifically drafted the legislation to allow for flexibility. As noted under 'Statutory framework and guidance – outline of the statutory right' above, there are certain key elements that apply as a legal minimum. These cannot be changed by agreement unless it is to improve upon them. However, employers and employees then have, in effect, a blank sheet on which to work out the details of their parental leave scheme in a workforce or collective agreement.

449

In the absence of either, the default scheme contained in the MPL Regulations will apply as a legal minimum. There are four ways in which agreements as to unpaid parental leave can take effect:

- automatic application of the default scheme

- individual agreement

- collective agreement

- workforce agreement.

10.13 In each case the key elements discussed below apply as a minimum. But it is possible to be flexible about other matters relating to parental leave. The extent to which each of the four options allows deviation from the statutory default scheme is governed by the combined effect of Regs 16 and 21.

Regulation 21 MPL Regulations applies where an employee is entitled to statutory unpaid parental leave and also has a corresponding right to parental leave under his or her contract of employment. In this situation Reg 21(2) provides that the employee may not exercise the statutory right and the contractual right separately but he or she may take advantage of whichever right is the more favourable. It is therefore necessary to know which of the statutory rights apply to the employee in question. This is where we must consider the effect of Reg 16.

10.14 Regulation 16 MPL Regulations states that where an employee's contract does not include a provision which:

- confers a right to parental leave, and

- incorporates or operates by reference to a collective or workforce agreement

the default scheme will apply.

The effect of Regs 16 and 21, therefore, is that where a collective or workforce agreement that satisfies Reg 16 is used, an employee or employer cannot fall back on the statutory default scheme under Reg 21. The collective or workforce agreement completely displaces the statutory default scheme, even if this results in less favourable terms for the employees. So, for example, in a collective or workforce agreement the parties could agree that the circumstances in which the employer could postpone leave would be wider than allowed under the default scheme. Where a collective or workforce agreement is not used, or where the terms of the collective or workforce agreement do not satisfy Reg 16, then the default scheme applies as a minimum.

10.15 There are two important points to note about Reg 16. First, the contract must confer a specific entitlement to parental leave. This could be contained in either an individual employee's contract or in the collective or workforce agreement or other document which is itself incorporated into the employee's contract.

Secondly, the employee's contract must 'incorporate or operate by reference to' a collective or workforce agreement. This means that the collective or workforce agreement must be incorporated into, or referred to in, the employee's contract of employment. Existing employees will have to consent to any new agreement unless their contracts provide that the terms of collective or workforce agreements are incorporated automatically (which is more likely to be the case with collective agreements than workforce agreements). If these two requirements are not complied with, then the default scheme will apply as a minimum (subject to any more favourable contractual rights). Incorporation of contractual terms is considered in detail in IDS Employment Law Handbook, 'Contracts of Employment' (2014), Chapter 5, 'Incorporated terms', and Chapter 9, 'Variation of contract', under 'Collective agreements – incorporation'.

We now look in more detail at each of the four possible ways listed above by which terms relating to unpaid parental leave can take effect.

Automatic application of the default scheme

10.16

If no unpaid parental leave agreement (whether via an individual agreement or via a collective or workforce agreement) has been reached between employer and employee, then the default scheme set out in Schedule 2 to the Regulations will automatically apply. This is considered in detail under 'Default scheme' below.

Individual agreement

10.17

Employers and employees can agree to amend the default scheme in an individual agreement (e.g. in a contract of employment or other contractual document which does not qualify as a workforce or collective agreement), but because of the combined effect of Regs 16 and 21 discussed above, any individual agreement can only improve upon the default scheme. If a provision of an individual agreement is less favourable to the employee than the corresponding provision in the default scheme, then the employee may choose to rely on the more favourable statutory right – Reg 21(2)(a) MPL Regulations.

Collective agreement

10.18

A 'collective agreement' is defined by Reg 2(1) as an agreement within the meaning of S.178 of the Trade Union and Labour Relations (Consolidation) Act 1992 (TULR(C)A). That is, 'any agreement or arrangement made by or on behalf of one or more trade unions and one or more employers or employers' associations' and relating to, among other things, terms and conditions of employment. A collective agreement may therefore cover a number of other matters in addition to parental leave.

The trade union(s) in question must be independent within the meaning of S.5 TULR(C)A. This means that the union(s) must not be under the domination or control of any employer, and must not be liable to interference by any employer (arising out of the provision of financial or material support or by any other means) tending towards such control. Under S.8 TULR(C)A the Certification Officer has exclusive jurisdiction to decide whether a trade union is independent and may issue a certificate of independence, which will be conclusive proof of independent status. For further information, see IDS Employment Law Handbook, 'Trade Unions' (2013), Chapter 1, 'Trade unions', under 'Independence – certificate of independence'.

10.19 Workforce agreement

The mechanism of a workforce agreement was first introduced in the working time legislation and follows a similar format in relation to unpaid parental leave. The rules governing such agreements are contained in Schedule 1 to the MPL Regulations. Essentially, a workforce agreement provides a non-union means of reaching an agreement relating to parental leave. Employees whose terms and conditions are covered to any extent in a collective agreement cannot be covered by a workforce agreement. This is because the provisions concerning workforce agreements apply only in respect of 'relevant members of the workforce', and such members are defined in para 2 of Schedule 1 as 'all of the employees employed by a particular employer, excluding any employee whose terms and conditions of employment are provided for, wholly or in part, in a collective agreement'.

Under Schedule 1 to the MPL Regulations a number of criteria must be satisfied for a workforce agreement to be valid. The agreement must:

- be in writing – para 1(a)

- have effect for a specified period that does not exceed five years – para 1(b)

- apply either to all of the relevant members of the workforce or to all relevant members of the workforce who belong to a particular group – para 1(c)

- be signed by:
  - the representatives of the workforce or of the particular group of workers (excluding, in either case, any representative who is not a relevant member of the workforce on the date on which the agreement is first made available for signature), or
  - in the case of an employer who employs 20 or fewer employees on the date when the agreement is first made available for signature, either the appropriate representatives as defined above or a majority of the employees employed by the employer – para 1(d).

10.20 Before the agreement is made available for signature, the employer must provide all the employees to whom it is intended to apply on the date on which it comes into effect with copies of the text of the agreement and such guidance as those employees might reasonably require in order to understand the agreement fully – para 1(e).

As stated above, 'relevant members of the workforce' are 'all of the employees employed by a particular employer, excluding any employees whose terms and conditions of employment are provided for, wholly or in part, in a collective agreement'. Where an agreement relates to a 'particular group', this is defined as meaning 'relevant members of a workforce who undertake a particular function, work at a particular workplace or belong to a particular department or unit within their employer's business' – para 2.

Election of representatives. As noted above, a workforce agreement must be **10.21** signed by elected representatives, except where the employer employs 20 or fewer employees, in which case the agreement may be signed instead by a majority of those employees. The requirements relating to the election of representatives are set out in para 3 of Schedule 1. They are as follows:

- the number of representatives to be elected must be determined by the employer

- the candidates for election must be relevant members of the workforce, and the candidates for election as representatives of a group must be members of that group

- no employee who is eligible to be a candidate may be unreasonably excluded from standing

- all the relevant members of the workforce or group must be entitled to vote

- the employees entitled to vote must be able to vote for as many candidates as there are representatives to be elected

- the election must be conducted so as to secure that, so far as is reasonably practicable, those voting do so in secret, and the votes given at the election are fairly and accurately counted.

These election requirements are in the same form as the requirements for **10.22** electing representatives for the purpose of signing a workforce agreement under the Working Time Regulations 1998 SI 1998/1833 – see IDS Employment Law Handbook, 'Working Time' (2013), Chapter 1, 'Scope and key concepts', in the section 'Agreements', under 'Workforce agreements – election of representatives'. However, it is unclear whether a representative elected under those Regulations could act as a representative in respect of a workforce agreement under the MPL Regulations without being specifically re-elected for that purpose. There is nothing in Schedule 1 which stipulates that the representatives must be elected for that specific purpose; merely, as mentioned in para 2, that they must be 'duly elected to represent the members of a particular group' in accordance with the requirements set out above. To avoid having to conduct multiple

453

elections, an employer may wish to make it clear, before holding any elections for workforce representatives, that the representatives are to have authority in respect of all future workforce agreements.

Commentators have criticised the provisions for the election of representatives on a number of grounds, including the lack of any express requirement that the representatives be genuinely independent of the employer. There is also concern over the fact that there is no specific means of redress for workers who believe that the election process has not been properly conducted, although in such circumstances an employee could argue that the workforce agreement was invalid and seek to rely on the fallback provisions of the default scheme. Furthermore, there is no explicit requirement that representatives should consult with the workers whom they represent during the course of the negotiations with the employer. Finally, workforce representatives have no right to time off for training, in contrast to the position of employee representatives in relation to collective redundancies and transfers.

10.23 **Protection from detriment or dismissal.** Workers who are elected as representatives under the MPL Regulations, or who stand for election, have the right not to be dismissed or to be subjected to a detriment as a result of their activities or functions. Employees who refuse to sign a workforce agreement have similar protection – Regs 19 and 20. For further details, see Chapter 12, 'Detriment and unfair dismissal'.

10.24 Key elements

The MPL Regulations lay down a minimum framework of unpaid parental leave rights. These key elements apply in every case, even where a workforce or collective agreement is in place, and may be improved upon (from the employee's perspective) but never reduced. They are not listed separately in the Regulations but are contained for the most part in Regs 13–15 and 17–18A.

The key elements that always apply can be summarised as follows:

- the right to take unpaid parental leave is available to employees with one year's service who have responsibility for a child
- up to 18 weeks' unpaid leave may be taken for each child
- leave is to be taken for the purpose of caring for a child
- the right to take unpaid leave applies until the child reaches the age of 18 (note that until the Maternity and Parental Leave etc (Amendment) Regulations came into force on 5 April 2015, the right to take leave was restricted to the child's first five years, subject to some exceptions – see 'Age of child' below)

- the employee remains employed while on leave and certain minimum terms and conditions continue to apply

- the employee is entitled to return after leave either to the same job or to another suitable job depending on the circumstances.

The stated policy behind the unpaid parental leave statutory provisions is to **10.25** encourage employers and employees to reach their own agreements on parental leave. However, any such agreement can only improve upon the key elements. The old guidance, 'Parental leave and time off for dependants', suggested the following ways in which a parental leave scheme could be enhanced:

- paying employees full or half pay while they are on leave

- allowing employees to take more than their maximum statutory parental leave entitlement (see 'Length of leave' below)

- specifying a notice period that is less than 21 days (see 'Default scheme – notice' below).

Employees with one year's service
10.26

In order to qualify for unpaid parental leave the parent must be an employee and have been continuously employed for a period of not less than a year – Reg 13(1).

Employee. An employee is an individual who has entered into or works under **10.27** a contract of employment, which is defined as a contract of service or apprenticeship, whether express or implied, and (if express) whether oral or in writing – Reg 2(1). These definitions are identical to those that apply for the purposes of unfair dismissal and redundancy under the Employment Rights Act 1996 (ERA) – see IDS Employment Law Handbook, 'Contracts of Employment' (2014), Chapter 2, 'Employment status'.

Members of the armed forces, share fishermen and women and the police are excluded from the right to take unpaid parental leave – Ss.192 (read with para 16, Sch 2), 199(2) and 200 ERA. However, seafarers employed on ships registered under S.8 of the Merchant Shipping Act 1995 are covered provided that the ship is registered as belonging to a port in Great Britain, that under his or her contract of employment the worker does not work wholly outside Great Britain, and that he or she is ordinarily resident in Great Britain – S.199(7) and (8) ERA. Crown employees and parliamentary staff are also covered – Ss.191, 194 and 195.

One year's continuous service. In its 'Modern Workplaces' consultation, the **10.28** Government briefly entertained the idea of removing the one-year qualifying period for unpaid parental leave. However, in the consultation response it made it clear that it wanted to retain this requirement. Accordingly, an

455

employee must have been with the employer for at least a year to take unpaid parental leave.

The Regulations do not specify the date on which continuous service should be calculated, although it can be inferred from Reg 13(1) MPL Regulations that it should be measured at the date on which the leave is to start. If an employee changes employer, he or she will have to work for a further year before taking unpaid parental leave. Continuous service should be calculated in accordance with the provisions of Chapter 1 of Part XIV ERA – see IDS Employment Law Handbook, 'Continuity of Employment' (2012), Chapter 1, 'The general framework'.

10.29 Responsibility for a child

To take unpaid parental leave, an employee must have, or expect to have, responsibility for a child – Reg 13(1)(b) MPL Regulations. Reg 13(2), when read with Reg 2(1), states that an employee has responsibility for a child if:

- he or she has 'parental responsibility' for the child under the Children Act 1989 (or 'parental responsibilities' under the Children (Scotland) Act 1995) or has acquired such responsibility (or responsibilities) in accordance with the provisions of the Children Act 1989 (or the Children (Scotland) Act 1995) – Reg 13(2)(a); or

- he has been registered as the child's father under S.10(1) or S.10A(1) of the Births and Deaths Registration Act 1953 or S.18(1) or (2) of the Registration of Births, Deaths and Marriages (Scotland) Act 1965 – Reg 13(2)(b).

Regulation 13(2)(b) was added to ensure that unmarried fathers were entitled to unpaid parental leave by providing that an employee has responsibility for a child for the purposes of the Regulations if he is registered as the father of the child on the birth certificate. This provision was necessary at the time as, before 1 December 2003, unmarried fathers (unlike unmarried mothers) did not automatically acquire parental responsibility, even if they were named as the father on the child's birth certificate (although they could acquire parental responsibility as a result of a court order or by entering into a formal agreement with the child's mother – Ss.2(2) and 4 Children Act 1989). However, the legal position of unmarried fathers was subsequently changed. S.111 of the Adoption and Children Act 2002 amended S.4 of the Children Act 1989 to provide that, in the case of children born on or after 1 December 2003, unmarried fathers have parental responsibility if they appear on the birth certificate, having registered the birth jointly with the mother.

10.30 The Children Act 1989 also includes provisions – i.e. Ss.2(1A), (2A) and 4ZA – for the mother's female partner to automatically have, or to acquire, parental responsibility in relation to a child. Furthermore, intended parents in a surrogacy arrangement who have been granted, or are intending to apply for, a

456

parental order under S.54(1) of the Human Fertilisation and Embryology Act 2008 are entitled to take unpaid parental leave.

Adoptive parents. Employees who adopt a child are entitled to take unpaid **10.31** parental leave. Previously, they were given parental responsibility on the making of an adoption order but as a result of S.25(3) of the Adoption and Children Act 2002, which came into force on 30 December 2005, parental responsibility is now given from the date of placement. However, this change has had little, if any, effect on the right to take unpaid parental leave, since Reg 13(1) provides that parental leave can be taken by anyone who 'has, or *expects to have*' (our stress) parental responsibility, even if they have not yet acquired it, and so would normally be available from the date of placement in any event, since at that point the potential adopters will expect to acquire parental responsibility.

According to the Government guidance, foster parents are not entitled to unpaid parental leave unless they have secured parental responsibility through the courts. However, this is no longer entirely accurate. Local authority foster parents who are approved adopters and who have children placed with them under the 'fostering for adoption' scheme – i.e. with a view to adoption – from 5 April 2015 are now entitled to unpaid parental leave. For more information on the 'fostering for adoption' scheme, see Chapter 6, 'Adoption leave and pay', in the section 'Ordinary adoption leave', under 'Who has the right? – foster parents'.

Step-parents. It is unclear in what circumstances – other than those involving **10.32** a straightforward adoption as described above – an employment tribunal would define someone who is not a child's natural parent as having an expectation of acquiring parental responsibility. For example, what if a stepfather, who has not adopted his stepchild but intends to do so, wishes to take unpaid parental leave? Is it possible to say that he expects to acquire parental responsibility merely because he intends to apply for adoption?

Normally, if the child's natural father is alive and has parental responsibility, his consent would be required before the child could be adopted, unless the court was to override his wishes in the interests of the child. This could provide a barrier to step-parents who wish to take unpaid parental leave, unless the employer is willing to take a more lenient view. S.112 of the Adoption and Children Act 2002, which came into force on 30 December 2005, amended the Children Act 1989 (by inserting a new S.4A) to make it possible for step-parents to acquire parental responsibility without adopting the child (and therefore without severing the parental responsibility of the natural parents) but this must be done either by an agreement between the step-parent and both natural parents, or by an application to the court if there is disagreement. 'Step-parent' is defined in the Act as a person who is married to, or is the civil partner of, the child's parent who has parental responsibility for the child.

457

10.33   Note that the qualifications for paternity leave in respect of employees who are not the child's natural parent are less stringent than for unpaid parental leave. An employee can qualify for paid paternity leave if he or she is married to the mother or lives with her in an enduring family relationship and expects to have responsibility for the upbringing of the child, without necessarily acquiring formal parental responsibility – see Chapter 7, 'Paternity leave and pay', under 'Who has the right?'

10.34   **Guardians, etc.** It is also possible for someone other than a natural or adoptive parent, such as a guardian (which may include another relative), to acquire parental responsibility for a child. If an individual has acquired parental responsibility for the child, he or she will be entitled to unpaid parental leave if the qualifying conditions are met.

To summarise, there are two main points to note when considering the question of responsibility for a child. First, parents do not have to live with their children to qualify for the right to take unpaid parental leave. Secondly, step-parents and (most) foster parents do not automatically have the right to unpaid parental leave unless they have or expect to have formal parental responsibility.

10.35   **Length of leave**
Each parent may currently take up to a total of 18 weeks' unpaid leave for each individual child – Reg 14(1) MPL Regulations (although under the default scheme an employee can take no more than four weeks in respect of each individual child in any one year – see 'Default scheme – how leave may be taken' below). Until the Parental Leave (EU Directive) Regulations came into force on 8 March 2013, the right was to 13 weeks' unpaid leave for each child and 18 weeks' unpaid leave in respect of a child entitled to disability living allowance.

As with maternity leave, there is no limit on the number of children in respect of whom leave can be taken – four children means four lots of 18 weeks. But unlike maternity leave, in the case of multiple births or the adoption of more than one child at the same time, a parent may take the full amount of leave for each child. The right is non-transferable, so the father cannot transfer his leave entitlement to the mother or vice versa. However, provided they give the appropriate notices and meet the other qualifying conditions, employees may, if they wish, take unpaid parental leave immediately after a period of maternity, paternity or adoption leave. They may similarly decide to take it after a period of shared parental leave.

10.36   The right is to take 18 weeks' unpaid parental leave in total with all employers, so someone who takes four weeks and then moves to a different employer will only qualify for 14 weeks from the second employer (once he or she has served any qualifying period with that employer). This raises questions over record keeping, which are discussed under 'Default scheme – how leave may be taken' below.

Regulation 14(2) defines the meaning of a 'week's leave' where the period for which an employee is normally required to work under his or her contract of employment in the course of a week does not vary. In these circumstances, a week's leave is 'a period of absence from work which is equal in duration to the period for which he [or she] is normally required to work'. This means that a week's leave for an employee who usually works from Monday to Friday is five days. For an employee who works Mondays and Tuesdays, a week's leave is two days.

10.37 Regulation 14(3) deals with the situation where the period for which the employee is normally required to work varies from week to week, or where he or she is normally required under the contract to work in some weeks but not in others. In these circumstances, a week's leave is calculated by dividing the total amount of time the employee is normally required to work in a year by 52. The old guidance, 'Parental leave and time off for dependants', set out the example of an employee who is contracted to work three days a week for 30 weeks, four days a week for 18 weeks, and two days a week for four weeks. Such an employee would calculate the number of days' leave in his or her average week by dividing the total number of days worked in these periods by 52. Reg 14(4) goes on to deal with the situation where an employee takes leave in periods shorter than the period that constitutes for him or her a week's leave under Reg 14(2) or (3). In such a case the employee completes a week's leave when the aggregate of the periods of leave he or she has taken equals the period constituting a week's leave for him or her under whichever of Reg 14(2) or (3) is applicable. This in itself is relatively straightforward. However, if the default scheme applies to an employee then, unless he or she is the parent of a disabled child (or a child entitled to armed forces independence payment), he or she is unable to take leave in periods shorter than a week and so the provisions in Reg 14(4) do not apply – see New Southern Railway Ltd (formerly South Central Trains Ltd) v Rodway 2005 ICR 1162, CA, discussed under 'Default scheme – how leave may be taken' below.

Leave is unpaid

10.38 One of the most controversial aspects of the right to parental leave is the fact that it is unpaid. In November 1999 the Social Security Select Committee of the House of Lords recommended in its report, 'Social Security Implications of Parental Leave', that the state should fund a flat-rate payment of up to £100 a week. It recommended that this should be available to all employees taking statutory parental leave, regardless of income. The Government did not implement the recommendation, but instead introduced specific provisions for two weeks' paid paternity leave (see Chapter 7, 'Paternity leave and pay'), and extended the statutory maternity and adoption pay period to 39 weeks

459

(see Chapter 5, 'Statutory maternity pay', under 'The maternity pay period', and Chapter 6, 'Adoption leave and pay', under 'Statutory adoption pay – period of payment of SAP').

We have already noted that the revised EU Parental Leave Directive provided for the period of unpaid parental leave to be extended from 13 to 18 weeks, and this was implemented into UK national law from 8 March 2013 by the Parental Leave (EU Directive) Regulations and the Parental Leave (EU Directive) (Maternity and Parental Leave) Regulations (Northern Ireland). While noting in para 20 of its Preamble that 'experiences in Member States have shown that the level of income during parental leave is one factor that influences the take up by parents, especially fathers', the revised Directive leaves it to Member States to determine the level of income during parental leave. There seems little prospect in the immediate future that the current Government will decide to introduce paid parental leave. In fact, we would argue that this is even less likely now that the Government has introduced the shared parental leave scheme, which enables fathers to take paid time off from work after the birth of a child where the mother has curtailed her entitlement to maternity leave and pay – see Chapter 8, 'Shared parental leave and pay', for details.

10.39 Note that some lower-paid employees may qualify for income support during unpaid parental leave. There may also be other benefits available, such as housing benefit and council tax reduction. There is also the possibility of tax credit awards – for instance, working tax credit and child tax credit.

10.40 Caring for the child

An employee is entitled to be absent from work on unpaid parental leave for the purpose of caring for a child – Reg 13(1) MPL Regulations. Under S.76(5)(a) ERA, regulations made by the Secretary of State may specify things which are, or are not, to be taken as done for the purpose of caring for a child. However, the MPL Regulations are silent on this matter, although the old guidance, 'Parental leave and time off for dependants', did provide some assistance. It stated that caring for a child means looking after the welfare of a child and can include making arrangements for the good of a child. It does not necessarily mean being with the child 24 hours a day. The old Guidance gave the following examples of ways in which leave might be used:

- to spend more time with the child

- to accompany a child during a stay in hospital

- to check out new schools

- to help settle a child into new childcare arrangements

- to enable the family to spend more time together – for example, taking the child to stay with grandparents.

The old Guidance suggested that if an employee uses unpaid parental leave for some other purpose – for example, to do other work – then the employer could deal with this situation according to the usual disciplinary procedures. However, employers have no specific right to seek evidence from an employee as to the reason for taking leave.

Note that, under the default scheme, an employee can only take unpaid parental **10.41** leave in blocks of a week or more – see 'Default scheme – how leave may be taken' below. Therefore, unless there is an agreement in place whereby the employee can take shorter periods of parental leave, it may not be the most appropriate type of leave for activities such as hospital appointments or visiting new schools. A day's paid annual leave may be a better option or, in the case of a sudden illness or emergency, the employee may be able to take time off to care for the child under S.57A ERA (see Chapter 11, 'Time off for dependants', under 'Circumstances in which time off may be taken – reasons for time off').

Age of child   **10.42**

An employee may not exercise any entitlement to unpaid parental leave in respect of a child after the date of the child's 18th birthday – Reg 15 MPL Regulations. This is a simplified version of the provision that was in force until 5 April 2015, which had restricted the right to unpaid parental leave to the first five years of the child's life, subject to some notable exceptions (see 'Position before April 2015' below). The change was effected by Reg 4 of the Maternity and Parental Leave etc (Amendment) Regulations.

As was previously the case, where the default scheme applies and the employer exercises the right to postpone an employee's leave, then the employee can still take the leave up to the end of the period to which it is postponed. However, a period of unpaid parental leave cannot be postponed until after the date of the child's 18th birthday. See 'Default scheme – postponement of leave by the employer' below for further details concerning the provisions on postponement.

The Maternity and Parental Leave etc (Northern Ireland) Regulations have not, **10.43** as yet, been similarly amended to provide employees with a right to take unpaid parental leave in respect of a child up to and including the date of the child's 18th birthday. As a result, the current position in Northern Ireland is the same as it was in Great Britain prior to 5 April 2015.

Position before April 2015. As a general rule, unpaid parental leave could **10.44** not be taken after a child's fifth birthday – old Reg 15(1). This meant that, unless there was a contractual scheme that extended the age limit, the right to parental leave would not normally assist parents for whom childcare during the school holidays was a problem. However, there were three exceptions to the five-year rule:

- where a child was entitled to disability living allowance (under the Social Security Contributions and Benefits Act 1992), leave could be taken up to (but not including) the child's 18th birthday. This exception also applied (but only from 8 April 2013) where a child was entitled to personal independence payment (under the Welfare Reform Act 2012) or armed forces independence payment (under the Armed Forces and Reserve Forces (Compensation Scheme) Order 2011 SI 2011/517) – old Reg 15(3) MPL Regulations. These two additions were necessary as both benefits were newly introduced on 8 April 2013: personal independence payment replaced disability living allowance for those aged 16 and over and armed forces independence payment was introduced to support service personnel seriously injured as a result of their service

- in the case of an adopted child (who was not entitled to disability living allowance, personal independence payment or armed forces independence payment) leave could be taken up to (but not including) the fifth anniversary of the date of placement or the date of the child's 18th birthday, whichever was the earlier – old Reg 15(1). The five-year limit ran from the day the child was placed with the prospective adopters, not the date a formal adoption order was made

- in a case where the default scheme applied and the employer exercised the right to postpone an employee's leave, then the employee could still take the leave up to the end of the period to which it was postponed, even if the normal cut-off date would have been exceeded – old Reg 15(4).

10.45 Terms and conditions during unpaid parental leave

The contract of employment continues during unpaid parental leave, but only to the extent set out in the MPL Regulations. Reg 17 sets out the terms and conditions of employment that continue to apply during unpaid parental leave.

10.46 **Employer's obligations.** An employee on unpaid parental leave is entitled to the benefit of his or her employer's implied obligation of trust and confidence and also to any terms and conditions of employment relating to:

- notice of termination by the employer

- compensation in the event of redundancy

- disciplinary or grievance procedures – Reg 17(a) MPL Regulations.

10.47 **Employee's obligations.** An employee on unpaid parental leave is bound by his or her implied obligation of good faith and also any terms and conditions of employment relating to:

- notice of termination by the employee

- disclosure of confidential information

- acceptance of gifts or other benefits

- the employee's participation in any other business – Reg 17(b) MPL Regulations.

All other terms and conditions of employment are in effect suspended during the parental leave period unless the contract provides otherwise. For example, the continuation of terms and conditions relating to matters such as access to a company car or mobile phone, and perks such as health club membership, remain a contractual matter between employer and employee. Special provisions apply in respect of pensions and other service-related benefits, however (see below).

The expression 'terms and conditions of employment' includes matters **10.48** connected with an employee's employment whether or not they arise under his or her contract of employment (and therefore may include discretionary benefits or a non-contractual redundancy procedure, for example) – S.77(2)(a) ERA. Furthermore, the expression is not confined to express terms and conditions but includes any implied terms (such as the implied duty of confidentiality).

A detailed consideration of the specific terms and conditions listed in Reg 17 falls outside the scope of this Handbook. Further information can be found in IDS Employment Law Handbook, 'Contracts of Employment' (2014). Below we discuss some specific issues that arise in the context of unpaid parental leave.

Remuneration. As noted above, there is no statutory obligation to pay the **10.49** employee during a period of parental leave. S.77(2)(b) ERA specifically states that remuneration is excluded from the terms and conditions of employment that continue during parental leave. Whether any payment is made is a matter for agreement between employer and employee. For more details on what is meant by 'remuneration', see Chapter 3, 'Maternity leave', under 'Terms and conditions during maternity leave – remuneration'.

Notice rights. Treatment of an employee's notice rights during a period of **10.50** unpaid parental leave will depend on whether the notice period is statutory or governed by contract.

Statutory notice pay. An employee who is given notice (or who gives notice) **10.51** during a period of parental leave is entitled to be paid his or her wages during the statutory notice period set out in S.86(1) ERA despite the fact that he or she is absent from work on parental leave – Ss.88(1)(c) and 89(3)(b). This right to payment does not apply, however, to notice given by the employer or employee where the period of notice to be given by the employer in the contract is at least one week more than the statutory notice period – S.87(4). The same rules apply during maternity leave, and the topic is discussed further in Chapter 3, 'Maternity leave', under 'Terms and conditions during maternity leave – notice rights'.

However, the effect of S.87(4) ERA appears to run counter to the ECJ's decision in Meerts v Proost NV 2010 All ER (EC) 1085, ECJ, and undermine the notice rights employees had before taking parental leave. In that case, the European Court held that the Framework Agreement on Parental Leave, annexed to the original EU Parental Leave Directive, entitles a worker dismissed without the statutory period of notice while on part-time parental leave to be paid compensation based on his or her full-time salary rather than on the reduced salary received while on parental leave. Clause 2(6) of the Framework Agreement (now clause 5(2) of the Framework Agreement of the revised Directive) is intended to prevent the loss or reduction of rights, such as notice rights, 'acquired or in the process of being acquired' at the start of parental leave, and to ensure that at the end of that leave the worker's rights are maintained. In the Court's view, national legislation reducing employment rights for those availing themselves of parental leave could discourage workers from taking such leave and encourage employers to dismiss workers on parental leave rather than others.

Statutory notice rights are considered in greater detail in IDS Employment Law Supplement, 'Notice Rights' (2006).

10.52 *Contractual notice.* Since contractual notice rights are specifically preserved by Reg 17 MPL Regulations, an employee on parental leave will be entitled to his or her period of contractual notice in the same way as any other employee. However, since contractual notice pay is in effect the remuneration payable for weeks of notice, and 'remuneration' is specifically excluded from the scope of Reg 17 by S.77(2)(b) ERA (see above), the employee is not entitled to be paid his or her salary during any part of the contractual notice period that falls within the parental leave period. The employee would, however, be entitled to any contractual parental leave pay payable during that period. Again, the argument could be made that a failure to pay an employee his or her full salary in respect of a contractual notice period that falls within a parental leave period is contrary to EU law. Although Meerts v Proost NV (above) involved a dismissal without statutory notice, the ECJ's reasoning would appear to apply equally to failure to give contractual notice.

10.53 **Holiday entitlement.** Entitlement to 28 days' paid annual holiday (pro rata for part-time staff) under the Working Time Regulations 1998 SI 1998/1833, as amended, continues to accrue during a period of unpaid parental leave. There is no requirement for the employee to be actually working for annual leave to accrue under those Regulations, provided the worker's contract subsists (which it does, under the MPL Regulations). The accrual of additional holiday under an employee's contract of employment during parental leave is a matter for agreement between employer and employee.

10.54 **Pension benefits.** Any period of unpaid parental leave that started before 6 April 2003 can be disregarded when calculating seniority and pensionable service (unless the rules of the particular scheme state otherwise). In these circumstances, the period of employment prior to the leave period will be treated as continuous with that following the employee's return to work – Reg 18(5)(b) MPL Regulations. However, since 6 April 2003 the old Reg 18 has been replaced by new Regs 18 and 18A, which provide that periods of leave starting on or after that date must be counted for the purposes of seniority, pension rights and similar rights, as if the employee had not been absent.

Since parental leave is generally unpaid, contributions to a money purchase scheme by employer and employee will usually be nil, unless the rules of the scheme provide otherwise. However, for final salary schemes, the level of employers' contributions depends on actuarial advice and not directly on the amount of an employee's earnings. Since parental leave counts as pensionable service, the employer may have to continue making contributions in order to keep the fund at an appropriate level.

10.55 The position is more complicated if the employer has agreed to provide any element of paid parental leave. In these circumstances, Schedule 5 to the Social Security Act 1989 applies. Para 6 of Schedule 5 deals with paid leave for 'family' reasons and provides that any member of a pension scheme taking such leave should, for the purposes of his or her occupational pension benefits, be treated as if he or she is working normally but only receives the remuneration in fact paid to him or her for that period. This provision applies to money purchase and final salary schemes. For money purchase schemes this in effect means that the employee and the employer need only pay pension contributions on the amount of remuneration actually paid. (This differs from the rules on maternity leave, which provide that the employer must continue to pay pension contributions as if the employee were working and earning her full salary.) For final salary schemes, the employee likewise pays contributions on the amount of remuneration actually paid. However, the employer's contributions to a final salary scheme depend on actuarial advice and are not specifically designated to any one employee. So if the employee is receiving less than full salary while on parental leave, the employer may in the long run end up having to make up the shortfall in order to maintain the level of benefits.

For further consideration of pension rights during paid leave, see Chapter 6, 'Adoption leave and pay', under 'Terms and conditions during adoption leave – pension and other service-related benefits'.

10.56 **Other service-related benefits.** Schedule 5 to the 1989 Act applies to all service-related benefits, not just occupational pension schemes. As a result, what has been written above in relation to pensions applies equally to other benefits such as sickness or invalidity benefits and death benefits during any paid family leave. Similarly, Reg 18A MPL Regulations applies (regardless of whether the leave is paid or not) to 'seniority, pension rights and similar rights' and therefore seniority and length of service for all contractual purposes is preserved.

10.57 Social security benefits. Rights relating to social security benefits are not protected under the Parental Leave Directive (under either the original or the revised versions) and so rights will not be maintained during parental leave. Under Clause 2(8) of the Framework Agreement on Parental Leave (annexed to the original Directive), matters relating to social security in connection with the right to take parental leave are left to Member States and national law and exactly the same stipulation is made in Clause 5(5) of the revised Framework Agreement annexed to the revised Directive.

In Gómez-Limón Sanchez-Camacho v Instituto Nacional de la Seguridad Social (INSS) and ors 2009 3 CMLR 41, ECJ, G-L reduced her working hours to two thirds of her previous full-time hours in accordance with her rights under Spanish law, and her salary and social security contributions were reduced accordingly. She subsequently developed a condition that left her permanently unable to work and became entitled to a state invalidity pension calculated according to her employer's contributions on her reduced hours. G-L argued that her pension should have been calculated according to what she would have received had she remained full time. The ECJ held that the Framework Agreement on Parental Leave does not apply to social security benefits, since provision had been made for these to be determined separately, and it did not amount to a breach of European law to calculate such benefits on the basis of reduced hours of work even if the reduction was because of parental responsibilities.

10.58 Continuity of employment. Since an employee's contract continues during unpaid parental leave, a period of leave will count as continuous service for the purposes of statutory employment protection rights, such as the right to a redundancy payment. A period of parental leave where the remuneration payable to an employee is less than the amount that would have been payable had he or she been working is disregarded when calculating a 'week's pay' for the purposes of Ss.220–229 ERA – see Reg 22 MPL Regulations. Instead, account is taken of remuneration in earlier weeks.

10.59 Bonuses. Generally, whether or not a bonus is paid to an employee who is on unpaid parental leave is a matter for the contract of employment. However, there may be sex discrimination arguments to consider. In Lewen v Denda 2000 ICR 648, ECJ, the German employer refused to pay a Christmas bonus to a woman who was taking parental leave. The woman claimed that this was discriminatory and contrary to Article 141 of the EC Treaty (now Article 157 of the Treaty on the Functioning of the European Union) guaranteeing the right to equal pay for equal work. The European Court held that it was not discriminatory for an employer to refuse to pay a Christmas bonus to a female worker on parental leave where the sole condition of the bonus was that the employee be in active employment at the time the bonus was awarded. However, where the bonus was awarded retroactively as pay for work performed during the year, the employer must pay a part of the bonus proportionate to the period that the employee actually worked during the year.

The nature and purpose of a bonus payment will therefore be of crucial importance. Generally, an employee will be entitled to the bonus if it relates to performance or work done before the leave began. However, it is clear from the above case that a performance-related bonus does not have to be paid for a period of parental leave and it is not discriminatory for an employer to make a pro rata reduction to a bonus paid for work performed over the year to reflect a period of parental leave. So, for example, if the employee has taken four weeks' parental leave during the year, the amount of the bonus could be reduced by 4/52 or one thirteenth.

Remedies. An employee who is denied the terms and conditions of employment to which he or she is entitled during unpaid parental leave may bring a claim for breach of contract in the county court. However, given the nature of the rights preserved by Reg 17 MPL Regulations, an employment tribunal claim under Regs 19 or 20 may be more appropriate. Reg 19 provides that an employee is entitled not to be subjected to any detriment by any act, or deliberate failure to act, by the employer done because he or she has taken or sought to take unpaid parental leave. Reg 20 covers the right to claim automatically unfair dismissal where the employee has been dismissed for a reason connected with the fact that he or she took or sought to take unpaid parental leave. These provisions are discussed further under 'Remedies' below, and in Chapter 12, 'Detriment and unfair dismissal'. **10.60**

Sex discrimination. Any unfavourable treatment of an employee on unpaid parental leave may also give rise to a claim of indirect sex discrimination, in view of the fact that more women than men take unpaid parental leave. Sex discrimination law is discussed under 'Remedies' below, and in Chapter 13, 'Discrimination and equal pay'. **10.61**

Returning to work after unpaid parental leave **10.62**
Regulations 18 and 18A MPL Regulations deal with employees' rights on returning to work after a period of unpaid parental leave. Two different rules apply depending on the circumstances.

An employee returning after a period of unpaid parental leave of four weeks or less, which was:

- an isolated period of unpaid parental leave; or
- a period of unpaid parental leave that was the last of two or more consecutive periods of statutory leave which did not include (i) a period of unpaid parental leave of more than four weeks or (ii) any period of statutory leave which, when added to any other period of statutory leave (excluding unpaid

467

parental leave) taken in relation to the same child, means that the total amount of leave taken in relation to that child totals more than 26 weeks

has the right to return to the same job in which he or she was employed before the absence – Reg 18(1).

10.63 'Statutory leave' means leave provided for in Part 8 of the Employment Rights Act 1996 – Reg 2(1). This includes maternity leave, adoption leave, shared parental leave, unpaid parental leave and paternity leave. 'Job' means the nature of the work that the employee is employed to do in accordance with the contract and the capacity and place in which the employee is so employed – Reg 2(1). It is important to establish just what the employee's contract states he or she is employed to do as this may be wider than what he or she actually does. If so, the employer may be entitled to require the employee to do different work on his or her return, or even work different shifts or at a different place of work, provided this is within the scope of the contract.

The right to return under this head is identical to the right to return from ordinary maternity leave – for further details see Chapter 4, 'Returning to work after maternity leave', under 'Returning after ordinary maternity leave'.

10.64 An employee returning after:

- a period of unpaid parental leave of more than four weeks whether or not preceded by another period of statutory leave; or

- a period of unpaid parental leave of four weeks or less that was the last of two or more consecutive periods of statutory leave which included (i) a period of unpaid parental leave of more than four weeks or (ii) any period of statutory leave which, when added to any other period of statutory leave (excluding unpaid parental leave) taken in relation to the same child, exceeded a total of 26 weeks taken in relation to that child

has the right to return to the same job in which he or she was employed before the absence *unless* it is not reasonably practicable for the employer to permit the employee to return to that job. In these circumstances the employer must permit the employee to return to another job that is both suitable for him or her and appropriate for him or her to do in the circumstances – Reg 18(2) MPL Regulations. The right to return under this head is identical to the right to return from additional maternity leave – for further details see Chapter 4, 'Returning to work after maternity leave', under 'Returning after additional maternity leave'.

10.65 In Blundell v Governing Body of St Andrew's Catholic Primary School and anor 2007 ICR 1451, EAT, the Appeal Tribunal gave guidance on the meaning of the 'same job' provisions in Reg 18. While the case concerned an employee returning to work in the context of maternity leave, it would apply equally to a situation where an employee returns to work following a period of unpaid parental leave. The claimant taught at a primary school where teachers usually teach pupils of a particular age for two years and then move on to another class. Shortly before her return from maternity leave, the claimant was offered either a floating role or a 'year two' class. She complained that that was not the 'same job' she had performed before she went on leave, when she had taught a reception class. The tribunal disagreed and the claimant appealed to the EAT.

On appeal, the EAT noted that Reg 2(1) provides that 'job' must be defined by reference to 'the nature of the work which the employee is employed to do in accordance with her contract and the capacity and place in which she is so employed'. The phrase 'in accordance with her contract' qualifies only the 'nature' of the work, not 'capacity' and 'place'. 'Capacity' is more than 'status', though may encompass it, and is a factual label, descriptive of the function which the employee serves in doing work of the nature she does. Similarly, the word 'place' is not purely contractual. Thus, if a contract had a mobility clause by virtue of which the returnee could be assigned to a different workplace, the employer could not make her transfer because she would suffer both the dislocation and the unsettling need to familiarise herself with that workplace at a time when she was vulnerable, and still learning to accommodate the needs of her newborn alongside those of work. The Regulations' aim is to provide that a returnee comes back to a work situation as near as possible to the one she left. The level of specificity with which the three matters 'nature', 'capacity' and 'place' are to be addressed is likely to be critical, and is essentially a matter of factual determination for the tribunal.

Applying this to the instant case, the EAT concluded that the claimant had been **10.66** offered the 'same job' on her return from maternity leave. The nature of her work, according to her contract, was that of a teacher. But her role was viewed more realistically as a class teacher than as a reception teacher, since she would in any event have been asked to move after each two-year period. Finally, the place of work could not be said to be the reception classroom, but the school.

Note that Clause 6(1) of the revised Framework Agreement annexed to the revised EU Parental Leave Directive states that 'in order to promote better reconciliation, Member States and/or social partners shall take the necessary measures to ensure that workers, when returning from parental leave, may request changes to their working hours and/or patterns for a set period of time. Employers shall consider and respond to such requests, taking into account both employers' and workers' needs.' However, this did not necessitate any major change in UK law, as employees returning from unpaid parental leave were already entitled to request flexible working – see IDS Employment Law Handbook, 'Atypical and Flexible Working' (2014), Chapter 4, 'Flexible working', under 'Right to request flexible working'. Note, though, that S.80F(8)(a)(ii) of the Employment Rights Act 1996 was amended by Reg 2 of the Parental Leave (EU Directive) Regulations, so as to provide that employees

469

who are agency workers are entitled to request flexible working upon return from unpaid parental leave (agency workers are otherwise excluded from the right to request flexible working).

10.67 Nature of rights on return

Under Reg 18A(1)(b) MPL Regulations the employee's right to return under Reg 18 is the right to return 'on terms and conditions not less favourable than those which would have applied if [he or] she had not been absent'. This applies whether the employee is returning to the same job or to a suitable and appropriate alternative job in the circumstances set out above. This is not the same as saying that the terms and conditions must be not less favourable than they were when the employee went on leave, since changes to which the employee would have been subjected had he or she not been on unpaid parental leave might occur during the leave period. Any such changes to terms and conditions, such as a pay rise, will apply to the employee on his or her return. For further information, see Chapter 4, 'Returning to work after maternity leave', under 'Returning after ordinary maternity leave – terms and conditions "not less favourable"'.

10.68 Pensions and seniority.
Under Reg 18A(1)(a), an employee returning from a period of unpaid parental leave – however long – must be treated as though he or she had not been absent for the purposes of seniority, pension rights and similar contractual rights which depend on length of service. The period of leave will therefore be included in the service calculation. This is a change from the position prior to 6 April 2003, when unpaid parental leave did not count for seniority, pensions or similar rights. See 'Terms and conditions during unpaid parental leave – pension benefits' above.

Again, an employee who is denied the terms and conditions of employment to which he or she is entitled on return to work from a period of unpaid parental leave may be able to bring a claim under Regs 19 or 20 (see Chapter 12, 'Detriment and unfair dismissal') or a claim for sex discrimination or equal pay under the Equality Act 2010 (see Chapter 13, 'Sex discrimination and equal pay').

10.69 Failing to return after unpaid parental leave

If an employee wishes to resign rather than return to work after unpaid parental leave, notice must be given in the normal way in accordance with the terms of his or her contract of employment. If no contractual notice period is specified, the employee must give the minimum statutory notice of one week stipulated in S.86(2) ERA.

A late return from unpaid parental leave should be dealt with under the disciplinary procedure in the same way as any other unauthorised absence. However, if the employee is unable to return due to illness, he or she should be treated in the same way as any other employee who is off sick.

Redundancy during unpaid parental leave

10.70

If a redundancy situation arises while an employee is on unpaid parental leave, he or she should be treated in exactly the same way as any other employee would be. This would include consulting with the employee individually, including the employee in any collective consultation, and considering him or her for alternative employment. However, it is unlawful for the employer to select an employee for redundancy solely or partly on the basis that he or she is taking, proposing to take or has taken unpaid parental leave. The dismissal would be automatically unfair – see Chapter 12, 'Detriment and unfair dismissal', under 'Automatically unfair dismissal'.

In Riežniece v Zemkopības ministrija and anor 2013 ICR 1096, ECJ, the European Court confirmed that the original EU Parental Leave Directive and the original Framework Agreement on Parental Leave did not prohibit an employer from including a worker who has taken parental leave in a recession-led redundancy selection exercise. The ECJ noted that, in accordance with clause 2(4) of the Framework Agreement, an employer was not prevented from dismissing a worker who had taken parental leave, provided the dismissal was not on the grounds of the application for, or the taking of, parental leave. Furthermore, clause 2(5) of the Framework Agreement meant that an employer was not precluded from assessing that worker with a view to transferring him or her to an equivalent or similar post consistent with that worker's employment contract. In short, an employer was allowed to reorganise his business in order to ensure the efficient management of his organisation, subject to compliance with the applicable rules of EU law. However, the employer must ensure that the criteria used in the redundancy selection exercise do not infringe the principle of non-discrimination in the EU Equal Treatment Directive (No.76/207) (now the recast EU Equal Treatment Directive (No.2006/54)) – see 'Remedies – sex discrimination' below. Furthermore, the employer will not comply with his obligation to offer the employee a similar job on his or her return from parental leave where he offers the employee an alternative position that he knows will soon be abolished.

Default scheme

10.71

The default scheme set out in Schedule 2 to the MPL Regulations automatically applies in the absence of any other agreement. Remember that an employer can provide a scheme that is less favourable to employees than the default scheme only by means of a workforce or collective agreement – see 'Unpaid parental leave schemes' above. So, for example, it could be agreed in a qualifying workforce or collective agreement that employees may take all 18 weeks' leave at once – an improvement on the default scheme – but that an employee wishing to do so must give 18 weeks' notice – a longer period of notice than would otherwise be required under the default scheme. If an employer simply wants

471

to improve on the default scheme, a collective or workforce agreement can be used but an individual agreement will suffice.

Paragraph 1 of Schedule 2 sets out three conditions that must be complied with before an employee is entitled to take unpaid parental leave under the default scheme. These are that:

- the employee has complied with any request made by his or her employer to produce for the employer's inspection evidence of entitlement of the kind specified in para 2

- the employee has given the appropriate notice under paras 3–5

- the employer has not postponed leave in accordance with para 6.

Each of these requirements is examined separately below.

10.72 **Evidence**
Under para 1(a) of Schedule 2 to the MPL Regulations an employer may require the employee to produce evidence of entitlement to unpaid parental leave. The evidence to be produced for these purposes is such evidence as may reasonably be required of:

- the employee's responsibility or expected responsibility for the child in respect of whom the employee proposes to take unpaid parental leave – para 2(a)

- the child's date of birth, or, in the case of adoption, the date on which the placement began – para 2(b).

Prior to 5 April 2015, the employer could also require the employee to produce evidence of the child's entitlement to disability living allowance, personal independence payment or armed forces independence payment where the employee's entitlement to take leave under Reg 15 or to take a particular period of leave under para 7 – see 'How leave may be taken' below – depended upon whether the child was entitled to that allowance or payment – para 2(c). This provision was repealed by Reg 6 of the Maternity and Parental Leave etc (Amendment) Regulations with effect from 5 April 2015.

10.73 The Regulations do not provide any further detail as to the nature of the evidence that could be required. However, the evidence should be such evidence as may 'reasonably be required'. Thus it is likely to include documents such as a birth certificate, a parental responsibility order or papers confirming a child's adoption. The consultation document on parental and maternity leave (URN 99/1043) indicated that it would not be reasonable to ask for documents other than the normal ones, like a birth certificate, that the employee can easily get hold of. The Government guidance states: 'Employers can ask for proof (like a birth certificate) as long as it's reasonable to do so – e.g. they can't ask for proof each time an employee requests leave.'

The employee's obligation is to produce the evidence for the employer's inspection. As this is a condition of entitlement to leave under the default scheme, the employee must comply with any request before he or she can take the leave in question. An employee who tries to claim leave dishonestly can be dealt with under an employer's normal disciplinary procedures.

Notice   10.74

An employee wishing to take a period of unpaid parental leave must give his or her employer notice under para 1(b) of Schedule 2 to the MPL Regulations. The notice must specify the dates on which the period of leave is to begin and end and must be given to the employer at least 21 days before the date on which that period is to begin – para 3, Sch 2. There is no provision requiring that the notice be in writing, and so oral notice would suffice. However, there must be evidence of a formal application for leave. In Yohanna-Washington v South London and Maudsley NHS Trust ET Case No.2302238/04 the employment tribunal held that it was not sufficient for the claimant to mention to her employer that she needed time off to look after her children. Since there was no evidence of a formal application for leave having been made, her claim that the employer had unlawfully refused her parental leave could not proceed.

The requirement to give 21 days' notice means that in most cases it will not be possible to take unpaid parental leave to deal with a sick child. However, the employee may be able to take a short amount of unpaid time off under the right to dependant care leave under S.57A ERA – see further Chapter 11, 'Time off for dependants'. In the consultation paper, 'Work and Parents: Competitiveness and Choice' (December 2002), the Government considered extending the notice period to 28 days so as to harmonise it with the notice periods for starting maternity, paternity and adoption leave. In the end, however, this option was not taken up and the notice period remains at 21 days.

Leave starting with child's birth or adoption. There are special provisions   **10.75** allowing a certain amount of flexibility for new fathers and new adoptive parents who wish to take time off when the child is born or placed for adoption, since the exact date of birth or placement cannot always be predicted accurately.

New fathers. Paragraph 4 of Schedule 2 to the MPL Regulations sets out the   **10.76** notice requirements for an employee who is the father of the child in respect of whom the leave is to be taken where the leave is to begin on the date on which the child is born. The notice must specify the expected week of childbirth and the duration of the period of leave and must be given to the employer at least 21 days before the beginning of the expected week of childbirth. Provided that the father has given 21 days' notice of the expected week of childbirth, he may start his leave as soon as the baby is actually born, even if this is earlier or later than was expected.

10.77 *New adoptive parents.* Paragraph 5 of Schedule 2 deals with new adoptive parents who wish to take leave beginning on the date of placement for adoption. In these circumstances, the notice must specify the duration of the period of leave and the week in which placement is expected to occur and must be given to the employer at least 21 days before the beginning of that week. The Regulations recognise that it may not always be possible to give 21 days' notice. One reason for this may be that the adoptive parents themselves may not get 21 days' notice of the date on which the placement will start. Para 5(b) therefore states that if it is not reasonably practicable to give 21 days' notice, notice must be given as soon as is reasonably practicable. Having given the appropriate notice, adoptive parents should be able to start leave as soon as the child is placed with them for adoption, even if this occurs earlier or later than the week specified in the notice.

Of course, if the employee is entitled to statutory adoption leave (see Chapter 6, 'Adoption leave and pay') then he or she will normally wish to take advantage of that right instead of taking unpaid parental leave from the date of placement. Unpaid parental leave can be taken immediately after a period of adoption leave, but in that situation para 5 of the default scheme does not apply. The employee will in any case have plenty of time during the adoption leave to give 21 days' notice of the actual dates for the unpaid parental leave in the normal way.

10.78 **Paternity leave.** If the employee is entitled to paid paternity leave (see Chapter 7, 'Paternity leave and pay') then he will normally wish to take this instead of, or as well as, unpaid parental leave. Where the father wants to take a period of paternity leave followed by a period of unpaid parental leave, the notice requirements in the default scheme are somewhat unsatisfactory. There is no provision allowing an employee to specify that he wishes unpaid parental leave to start immediately after paternity leave, without having to give 21 days' notice of specific start and end dates. The flexibility under paras 4 and 5 only applies where unpaid parental leave is due to start on the date of birth or placement. However, where paternity leave is due to start on the date of birth or placement then the exact date on which paternity leave will end (and unpaid parental leave will start) may not be known until birth or placement actually takes place. Since paternity leave currently only lasts two weeks, for any employee not entitled to or opting not to take shared parental leave there will not be enough time for the employee to give 21 days' notice of the exact date he wishes to start unpaid parental leave. In order to make the scheme more workable, employers may wish to consider allowing fathers to specify that they want to take unpaid parental leave straight after paternity leave without fulfilling the notice requirements of the default scheme to the letter. Where an employee seeks to take unpaid parental leave from the date of birth or placement in accordance with paras 4 and 5, the employer has no power to postpone the leave – see 'Postponement of leave by the employer' below. The employer can, however, postpone a period of unpaid parental leave which the employee wishes to take straight after adoption or paternity leave.

Failure to give notice. If an employee gives no notice or inadequate notice, he or she will lose the right to take unpaid parental leave on that occasion. However, he or she may still be able to take a short period of unpaid leave under the right to time off for dependant care leave – see Chapter 11, 'Time off for dependants'. **10.79**

Altering dates of leave. The MPL Regulations do not specifically address the situation in which an employee, having given notice that he or she wishes to take unpaid parental leave, asks to rearrange the dates. However, in Kiiski v Tampereen Kaupunki 2008 1 CMLR 5, ECJ, the European Court of Justice held that a Finnish collective agreement that failed to recognise a new pregnancy as a valid reason for altering the dates and duration of prearranged parental leave, with the result that the claimant was unable to take up paid maternity leave, gave rise to discrimination contrary to the EC Equal Treatment Directive (No.76/207) (which has now been consolidated into the recast EU Equal Treatment Directive (No.2006/54)) and the EU Pregnant Workers Directive (No.92/85). Although similar circumstances will rarely arise in the United Kingdom – as the law provides for only 18 weeks' unpaid parental leave per child – if they do, the employer will be obliged, as a result of the ECJ's decision, to allow the employee to cancel or rearrange her parental leave dates in order to take maternity leave. **10.80**

Postponement of leave by the employer

10.81

Paragraph 6 of the default scheme contained in Schedule 2 to the MPL Regulations deals with the circumstances in which an employer can postpone an employee's requested period of unpaid parental leave. Subject to the exceptions relating to new fathers and adoptive parents mentioned above (and discussed in more detail under 'exceptions' below), an employer may postpone leave where he considers that 'the operation of his business would be *unduly disrupted* if the employee took leave during the period identified in his [or her] notice' – para 6(b) (our stress). Reg 2(1) defines a business as including a trade or profession and any activity carried on by a body of persons (whether corporate or unincorporated).

However, the employer cannot postpone leave indefinitely. Under para 6(c) the employer must agree to permit the employee to take a period of leave of the same duration as the period requested by the employee, to be commenced on a specific date no later than six months after the commencement date originally requested by the employee. Furthermore, the period of leave must in any case end before the 18th birthday. Under para 6(d) the employer must give the employee notice in writing of the postponement, stating the reason for the postponement and specifying the start and end dates for the period of unpaid

475

parental leave to which the employer would agree. Presumably most employers would try to agree these dates in discussion with the employee rather than imposing them, but there does not seem to be any explicit requirement to do so. The employer must give the written notice to the employee not more than seven days after the employee gave his or her notice to the employer – para 6(e).

10.82 While para 6 allows the employer to postpone the period of leave requested by the employee, the employer cannot reduce the amount of leave requested or break it up into shorter periods. Furthermore, once leave has been postponed, the employer must let the employee take leave in accordance with the postponement. There is no provision in the default scheme for the employer to postpone a second time if he finds that further business disruption would ensue. An employer wishing to do this would have to have put in place a scheme under a workforce or collective agreement (but not an individual's contract) that allowed further postponements.

Examples of when an employer may be justified in postponing leave:

- when work is at a seasonal peak

- where a significant proportion of the workforce applies for unpaid parental leave at the same time

- where the employee's role is such that his or her absence at a particular time would unduly harm the business

- where a replacement cannot be found within the notice period

- in the education sector where postponement is necessary to ensure the continuation of education.

10.83 Clause 2(3)(e) of the Framework Agreement annexed to the original Parental Leave Directive covered the first four of these examples. However, the equivalent clause in the revised Framework Agreement (as annexed to the revised Directive (No.2010/18)) stops short of giving specific examples of grounds for postponement of leave, contenting itself with asserting that: 'Member States and/or social partners may... define the circumstances in which an employer, following consultation in accordance with national law, collective agreements and/or practice, is allowed to postpone the granting of parental leave for justifiable reasons related to the operation of the organisation. Any problem arising from the application of this provision should be dealt with in accordance with national law, collective agreements and/or practice' – Clause 3(1)(c). In this way, the 'modalities of application' – being the term used for the heading to Clause 3 – are less specific and prescriptive than the antecedent provision in the original Framework Agreement.

The government guidance simply states that employers must have a 'significant reason' for postponing unpaid parental leave. It adds that this may be the case where the employee's requested leave period would 'cause serious disruption to the business'. However, the legislation talks of undue disruption and the first three of the five potentially valid reasons for an employer postponing leave listed above would arguably fall within that description. In and of themselves, the fourth and fifth grounds also seem to be eminently justifiable reasons for requiring a postponement of leave in specific difficult situations. In any case, the Explanatory Notes to the Employment Relations Act 1999 (which originally introduced the right to unpaid parental leave) stated that difficulty in finding a short-term replacement or otherwise covering the employee's absence on parental leave may be relevant in establishing undue disruption, and thus gave backing to the fourth example listed. As for the fifth – namely, where the postponement is necessary to ensure the continuation of education – this was an example that was specifically suggested in the Government consultation document that preceded the MPL Regulations (URN 99/1043).

10.84 As S.80 ERA allows employees to complain when their employer has unreasonably postponed leave (see 'Remedies – preventing or unreasonably postponing leave' below), employment tribunals considering complaints relating to postponement will be concerned with issues of reasonableness. This may include balancing the needs of the employer against the competing desire of the employee. During the committee stage of the Employment Relations Bill, Ian McCartney, then Minister of State at the Department of Trade and Industry, said: 'A parent who wants to be with a child recovering from an operation cannot postpone that need, but one who simply wants some time with a child might be asked not to take it during a rush period in the workplace' – Hansard Standing Committee E, 23 February 1999, col 112.

Note that the employer may not in any case postpone the leave so that it would end on or after the child's 18th birthday – para 6(c), Sch 2.

10.85 **Exceptions.** As noted above, under the default scheme an employer cannot postpone leave where a new father has given notice under para 4 to take unpaid parental leave starting from the date of birth or a new adoptive parent has given notice under para 5 to take leave starting with the date of placement. This is because para 6(1)(a) – which deals with postponement of leave – specifically states: 'An employer may postpone a period of parental leave where neither paragraph 4 nor paragraph 5 applies.' Again, this is an obstacle that could be removed by a workforce or collective agreement. However, with the availability of paternity and adoption leave, the right to take unpaid parental leave in these circumstances is likely to fall into disuse for all but a minority of employees, so the restriction is likely to be of limited practical significance.

How leave may be taken

10.86 Two provisions in the default scheme limit the way in which an employee can take unpaid parental leave.

477

10.87 **Minimum periods of leave.** Under para 7 of Schedule 2 to the MPL Regulations, unpaid parental leave may only be taken in periods constituting a week's leave for the purposes of Reg 14 or multiples of a week. This means that an employee cannot take anything less than a week's unpaid parental leave at any one time. This was confirmed by the Court of Appeal in New Southern Railway Ltd (formerly South Central Trains Ltd) v Rodway 2005 ICR 1162, CA. In that case R had informed his employer that he wished to take a day's parental leave on 26 July to look after his two-year-old son. The employer responded on 24 July, telling R that he would not be able to take the time off because his job could not be covered. R nevertheless spent the day with his son, staying away from work. SCT Ltd charged R with the disciplinary offence of being absent from work without permission. At the disciplinary hearing that followed, the employer withdrew this charge and instead issued R with a written warning about his absence.

R subsequently brought an employment tribunal claim alleging that he had been subjected to a detriment, contrary to S.47C ERA, by reason of his taking unpaid parental leave. The key issue was whether R had a statutory right to take one day's parental leave, since para 7 of Schedule 2 to the Regulations stated that parental leave can only be taken in blocks of a week or multiples thereof. The tribunal held that para 7 should be interpreted as meaning that an absence of less than a week exhausts one week's entitlement to unpaid parental leave, rather than that an employee is excluded altogether from taking unpaid parental leave for a period of less than a week. It went on to conclude that R had been entitled to take a day's parental leave, and that in being charged with a disciplinary offence, required to attend a disciplinary hearing and being given a written warning, he had been subjected to a detriment for a prescribed reason within the meaning of S.47C ERA.

10.88 On appeal, the EAT and, subsequently, the Court of Appeal held that the tribunal's interpretation of para 7 was flawed. In the Court of Appeal's view, the heading to para 7 – 'Minimum periods of leave' – was significant. Furthermore, the Court held that the language of that paragraph was unambiguous and any other interpretation would be artificial. In Lord Justice Keene's view, 'employers might well prefer to be able to make arrangements for temporary employees to cover for a week during an employee's absence, rather than to face the problems arising from an employee being absent for a single day or two odd days'. This, felt the Court, is 'not so unbalanced a situation in the relationship between employer and employee in this default case as to cast doubt on the natural meaning of the words in the Schedule'. Since R worked more than one day a week, he had been unable to take a single day's parental leave under the statutory scheme. It followed that the detriment he suffered as a result of his non-attendance at work did not fall within S.47C ERA, meaning that his claim must fail.

478

The decision in Rodway shows that parents who know in advance that they will need a day off to look after a child will, under the statutory default parental leave scheme, need to take a whole week off. This is likely to prove difficult for many parents as such leave is generally unpaid. By way of an alternative, they may be able to fall back on their statutory right to dependant care leave, as set out in Ss.57A and 57B ERA. However, although there is no minimum period of dependant care leave, the right to take such leave only applies in the context of childcare specifically where the need to take time off arises 'because of the unexpected disruption or termination of arrangements for the care of a dependant' – S.57A(1)(d). For further details, see Chapter 11, 'Time off for dependants', under 'Circumstances in which time off may be taken – reasons for time off'.

Exception. An exception is made in para 7 where the child in respect of whom **10.89** leave is being taken is entitled to disability living allowance, personal independence payment or armed forces independence payment. In this case the employee may take the leave in periods shorter than one week. The Government initially created this exception in recognition of the extra demands that the parents of disabled children face. The old 'Parental leave and time off for dependants' Guidance stated that such parents enjoy the flexibility to take leave a day at a time. This may enable an employee who works a five-day week to take, for example, one day's unpaid parental leave a week for, say, 20 weeks in a year (which would total four weeks' leave in that year – see below). On 8 April 2013, the exception was extended to cover children entitled to personal independence payment (which replaced disability living allowance for those aged 16 and over) and armed forces independence payment (which was introduced to support service personnel seriously injured as a result of their service).

Note that the employee is no longer required to produce evidence of entitlement to the allowance or payment in order to take a particular period of leave under para 7 – see 'Evidence' above. This requirement was repealed on 5 April 2015 by Reg 6 of the Maternity and Parental Leave etc (Amendment) Regulations.

Maximum annual leave allowance. Under para 8 of Schedule 2 to the MPL **10.90** Regulations an employee cannot take more than four weeks' leave in respect of any individual child during a particular year. The Government imposed this limit in response to pressure from employers' representatives. The four-week limit applies to all employees taking unpaid parental leave and there is no exception for the parents of children who are entitled to disability living allowance, personal independence payment or armed forces independence payment. The Government did consider lifting the restriction to a limited extent at some time in the future to enable parents to take their full entitlement in one block straight after maternity, paternity or adoption leave – see 'Balancing work and family life: enhancing choice and support for parents', published

479

jointly by what was then the DTI and the Treasury in January 2003. In the end, however, this option was not taken up. Nor did the Government revisit this topic when it consulted on introducing a new system of shared parental leave in 2011.

The definition of a year for these purposes is set out in para 9. This defines a year as the period of 12 months beginning either:

- on the date on which the employee in question first became entitled to take unpaid parental leave in respect of the child in question, or

- in a case where the employee's entitlement has been interrupted at the end of a period of continuous employment, on the date on which the employee most recently became entitled to take unpaid parental leave in respect of that child.

10.91 Each successive period of 12 months begins on the anniversary of the relevant date. The way in which a year is calculated means that each employee will have a different definition of a year for the purposes of working out his or her entitlement to four weeks' leave per year. The employee's unpaid parental leave year is likely to be different from his or her holiday year. This could cause some administrative headaches for employers unless they align the two by means of a workplace or collective agreement.

The combined effect of paras 7–9 is to limit considerably the opportunity for parents to use unpaid parental leave as a means of returning to work part time following maternity, paternity, adoption or shared parental leave. A mother (or father) wishing to change her (or his) working hours to cope with the demands of family life would be better advised to make a request for flexible working – see IDS Employment Law Handbook, 'Atypical and Flexible Working' (2014), Chapter 4, 'Flexible working'.

10.92 **Record keeping.** Although S.79(1)(b) ERA enables the Secretary of State to make regulations requiring employers or employees to keep records of unpaid parental leave taken, no such regulations have in fact been made and so there is no specific requirement on employers to keep such records. However, the Government accepted in the consultation document that preceded the MPL Regulations that employers will probably want to record unpaid parental leave as part of ordinary management procedures. As employees are entitled to 18 weeks' unpaid parental leave in total with all employers, it is likely that when an employee changes job the new employer will want to know how much of his or her entitlement has been used up. Employers could make enquiries of a previous employer or seek this information from the employee. Any dishonesty by an employee in declaring previous periods of leave should be dealt with under disciplinary procedures. Employers must be careful, however, when asking about previous periods of unpaid parental leave at interview or on an application form as discrimination could be inferred from such questions.

Remedies

10.93

There are a number of remedies available to an employee in relation to the right to unpaid parental leave. We discuss an employee's various options below, but it is worth remembering that all the potential claims discussed constitute 'relevant proceedings' for the purpose of S.18 of the Employment Tribunals Act 1996. This means that they are subject to the mandatory rules on early conciliation, which apply since 6 May 2014 and which require the employee to first notify Acas and be offered early conciliation of the dispute before a claim can be presented to an employment tribunal. The rules on early conciliation are discussed in detail in IDS Employment Law Handbook, 'Employment Tribunal Practice and Procedure' (2014), Chapter 3, 'Conciliation, settlements and ADR', under 'Early conciliation'.

Preventing or unreasonably postponing leave

10.94

An employee can complain to an employment tribunal under S.80(1) ERA that the employer:

- has unreasonably postponed a period of unpaid parental leave requested by the employee, or

- has prevented or attempted to prevent the employee from taking unpaid parental leave.

A complaint must be presented to the tribunal within three months of the date of the matters complained of, although the tribunal may allow an extension for such time as it considers reasonable where it is satisfied that it was not reasonably practicable for the employee to submit the claim in time – S.80(2)(b). Note that the three-month time limit may be extended where the parties are engaged in mediation to resolve a cross-border dispute or where the rules on early conciliation apply – S.80(2A). The law on time limits is explained in IDS Employment Law Handbook, 'Employment Tribunal Practice and Procedure' (2014), Chapter 5, 'Time limits'.

If the tribunal finds the employee's complaint to be well founded, it must make 10.95 a declaration to that effect and it may make an award of compensation to the employee – S.80(3). The amount of compensation shall be such amount as the tribunal considers to be just and equitable having regard to the employer's behaviour and any loss sustained by the employee that is attributable to the matters complained of – S.80(4). The reference to the employer's 'behaviour' in determining the level of compensation is unusual. Although tribunals do take into account an employer's behaviour when making awards of compensation – for example, in making awards for injury to feelings in discrimination cases – this is the first time to our knowledge that an employment statute has specifically directed the tribunal to take account of an employer's behaviour.

481

As yet there are no reported cases on what sort of behaviour tribunals ought to take into account. It may be that a totally unreasonable refusal of unpaid parental leave, where the employer has dismissed the employee's request out of hand, giving no reasons, is the sort of case where increased compensation will be awarded without the need for the employee to show actual loss. The following gives an indication of how tribunals may approach the issue of compensation in cases relating to unreasonable postponement of leave:

- **McDonald v Royal Mail Group plc** ET Case No.2602058/03: McD had applied for and had been granted three weeks' parental leave to follow the four weeks' annual leave and one week's paternity leave he planned to take after the birth of his child. Two months after the initial authorisation his manager wrote to him informing him that due to staffing arrangements the company was no longer able to permit him to take the full three weeks' parental leave and he was expected back in the office after two weeks' leave. On his return to work, McD registered a formal internal complaint and brought a S.80 claim before a tribunal. Some two months after his formal complaint, the employer accepted that the manager had acted incorrectly in postponing a week's parental leave and accordingly offered McD one week's annual leave with pay which he could take at a mutually convenient date, conditional on his withdrawing his tribunal complaint. He rejected this and proceeded with his tribunal claim. The employment tribunal noted that the employer only made an apology and a formal admission that it had 'unreasonably postponed the claimant's parental leave' some four or five months after leave was postponed. Even after that admission, it had continued to contend that McD was not entitled to any compensation. With this in mind, the tribunal awarded the claimant compensation of £850.

10.96 **Unlawful detriment**

Employees are also protected against detrimental treatment by their employer for reasons related to the right to take unpaid parental leave. By virtue of S.47C ERA and Reg 19 MPL Regulations, an employee is entitled not to be subjected to any detriment by any act, or any deliberate failure to act, by the employer done because he or she:

- took or sought to take unpaid parental leave, or

- declined to sign a workforce agreement for the purpose of the Regulations, or

- performed, or proposed to perform, any functions or activities as either a representative of members of the workforce or as a candidate in an election to become such a representative.

Detriment potentially covers a wide range of unfavourable treatment, including failure to promote, refusal of training or other opportunities, unjustified disciplinary action and reductions in pay. See Chapter 12, 'Detriment and unfair dismissal', under 'Right not to suffer detriment – meaning of "detriment"' for further details.

The following case highlights the fact that in order to be able to claim to have **10.97** suffered a detriment as a result of taking, or seeking to take, unpaid parental leave, the employee must have made it clear that he or she was relying on the right to take unpaid parental leave. In Tavernor v Associated Co-operative Creameries Ltd ET Case No.1902341/00 T had two children who were in receipt of disability living allowance and needed operations. At T's request, the employer agreed that he could use holidays and unpaid leave to take time off during their recuperative period. It was envisaged that he would wish to take two days off a week over a six-week period. However, problems ensued, mainly because T did not give proper notice or liaise with his superiors when he wanted to take leave. The Chief Engineer, L, spoke to T about his concerns and T subsequently raised a grievance. He took two days off work with the agreement of an Assistant Engineer but without seeking L's permission. On his return, L told him that further time off would lead to instant dismissal but T was later told at his grievance hearing that this threat should not have been made and did not stand. There was a full discussion about arrangements for future absences. Several months later there was a problem at home requiring T's urgent attention and he left without completing a time sheet and without giving the employer information on which jobs he had completed. On his return T was given a verbal warning for failing to complete the time sheet and he resigned in consequence. The employment tribunal dismissed his complaint of unlawful detriment. The agreed arrangement had been that T would be able to use holidays (including holidays brought forward from the following year), days in lieu or unpaid leave to cover his absences. At no time was parental leave mentioned and at the time of his initial request T had been unaware of his parental leave rights, although he subsequently became aware of them. The tribunal held that T had not sought to take parental leave and could not therefore seek redress under Reg 19. Overall, the employer had been sympathetic to T's situation and the warning was a justifiable sanction.

Similarly, an employee can only claim to have suffered a detriment contrary to S.47C ERA if he or she is actually entitled to take unpaid parental leave in the first place. In New Southern Railway Ltd (formerly South Central Trains Ltd) v Rodway 2005 ICR 1162, CA (see 'Default scheme – how leave can be taken' above), the Court of Appeal upheld the EAT's decision that, since the claimant could not lawfully take a single day off for unpaid parental leave, the detriment he suffered as a result of his non-attendance at work did not fall within S.47C ERA.

Automatically unfair dismissal
10.98

In addition, an employee will be regarded as automatically unfairly dismissed if the reason or principal reason for the dismissal (or selection for redundancy) is connected with the fact that the employee:

483

- took or sought to take unpaid parental leave, or

- declined to sign a workforce agreement for the purposes of the Regulations, or

- performed, or proposed to perform, any functions or activities as either a representative of members of the workforce or as a candidate in an election to become such a representative – S.99 ERA and Reg 20 MPL Regulations.

10.99 In Slaney v Universal Care Ltd ET Case No.2700900/02 S's wife was due to give birth and, as a result, he had arranged to take annual leave at the relevant time and was told that he would also be entitled to two to three days' compassionate leave. His wife gave birth on Tuesday 5 February and he took the rest of the week off. The following week, he returned to work to sort out some bookings and thereafter planned to take annual leave. UC Ltd contended that when S left, there were a number of work arrangements that had not been completed, and it contacted him to ask him to return to work. S refused, and reminded his employer that it was leave arranged in advance in order to be with his wife and baby. He was told that if he did not come back to the office, there would be a disciplinary hearing the following week. When S returned to work on 18 February, he was dismissed with immediate effect. The employment tribunal found that the reason for his dismissal was that he had failed to return to the office to deal with outstanding work at a time when he was asserting his statutory right to take parental leave. In its view, the employer's request had been unreasonable. S had informed his employer in advance of his intention to take leave. Furthermore, the fact that he had taken annual leave instead of unpaid leave did not mean that the time that he had spent at home immediately following the birth of his child and the few days thereafter could not be seen as parental leave. Moreover, the failure to comply with one lawful instruction in these circumstances did not justify a termination of employment. Accordingly, the tribunal found that S had been unfairly and wrongly dismissed.

Unfair dismissal is covered in detail in Chapter 12, 'Detriment and unfair dismissal'.

10.100 Asserting a statutory right

If an employee is dismissed because he or she has tried to exercise the right to take unpaid parental leave, he or she may also be able to claim to have been dismissed for asserting a statutory right. Under S.104 ERA an employee's dismissal will be automatically unfair if the reason or principal reason for the dismissal was that:

- the employee brought proceedings against the employer to enforce a relevant statutory right, or

- the employee alleged that the employer had infringed a relevant statutory right.

It is immaterial whether the employee actually has the statutory right in question or whether it has been infringed, but the employee's claim to the right must be made in good faith – S.104(2). Furthermore, it is sufficient that the employee made it reasonably clear to the employer what the right claimed to have been infringed was; it is not necessary actually to specify the right – S.104(3).

Dismissals for asserting a statutory right are dealt with in IDS Employment **10.101** Law Handbook, 'Unfair Dismissal' (2010), Chapter 12, 'Dismissal for asserting a statutory right'.

Sex discrimination
10.102

An employee who has a complaint in relation to the right to unpaid parental leave may be able to bring a sex discrimination claim. Since there is no limit on compensation for sex discrimination, an employee bringing such a case would not be bound by the cap which limits the amount of unfair dismissal compensation (£78,335 (from 6 April 2015) – or, if lower, 52 weeks' gross pay).

Direct sex discrimination. A claim of direct discrimination under S.13 of the **10.103** Equality Act 2010 (EqA) may be available to either a woman or a man who, because of his or her sex, has been treated less favourably than someone of the opposite sex. Take as an example the case of an employer who decides to modify the default scheme to allow women to take all 18 weeks of unpaid parental leave in one block directly after maternity leave. If the employer refuses to allow male employees 18 weeks' unpaid parental leave on the birth of a child and enforces the four-week annual maximum contained in the default scheme, then a claim of direct sex discrimination might be possible.

Indirect sex discrimination. A woman who has been refused unpaid parental **10.104** leave or has suffered a detriment or been dismissed because she took or sought to take unpaid parental leave may also be able to pursue a claim of indirect sex discrimination, on the basis that women are more likely than men to take unpaid parental leave and will therefore be disproportionately affected by a refusal or other detriment.

Indirect discrimination consists of four elements, all of which must be made out – see S.19 EqA 2010. These are that:

- the employer has applied a 'provision, criterion or practice' that applies (or would apply) equally to men and women but which

- puts or would put women at a particular disadvantage when compared to men

- puts the women in question at that disadvantage, and

- he cannot show to be a proportionate means of achieving a legitimate aim.

485

10.105 Prior to introducing the right to unpaid parental leave in 1999, the Government estimated that 35 per cent of women and only 2 per cent of men would take advantage of it. The 'Fourth Work-Life Balance Employee Survey', published by BIS in July 2012, suggests that in fact the take-up rates for women and men are similar. Contrary to the assumptions made by the Government, the survey revealed that in 2011 10 per cent of mothers took unpaid parental leave compared with 12 per cent of fathers. Based on these figures, a woman would struggle to show particular disadvantage. However, this conclusion should be treated with some caution as the figure for women may well be higher in practice. It is interesting to note in this regard that in Lewen v Denda 2000 ICR 648, ECJ, the European Court emphasised the finding of the court of first instance in Denmark that women in Denmark took parental leave 'far more often than men', although no statistics were cited. In that case, a failure to pay a Christmas bonus to a woman because she was on parental leave was found to be indirect sex discrimination – see Chapter 13, 'Discrimination and equal pay', under 'Equal pay – bonuses', for further details.

The finding in Lewen was referred to in Riežniece v Zemkopības ministrija and anor 2013 ICR 1096, ECJ, where the European Court held that it was for the national court to determine whether a similar finding was applicable to Latvia. If so, then in order to avoid indirect sex discrimination, the method for assessing workers in the context of the abolition of a post must not place those who had taken parental leave in a less favourable position than those who had remained in active service. The case concerned R, a principal adviser in the legal affairs division of the Latvian Government's Administrative Department, who took parental leave from 14 November 2007 to 6 May 2009. In 2009 the Department decided to abolish one of its principal adviser posts and all those who were potentially affected (including R) were assessed against criteria from the 2009 performance appraisal. Since R was not at work in 2009, the results of her last appraisal before going on leave were used to measure her against the 2009 criteria, notwithstanding that the 2006 and 2009 appraisals adopted different benchmarks.

10.106 As a result of this assessment, R's post was abolished. She brought a claim arguing that her dismissal was unlawful and her case reached the Senate of the Latvian Supreme Court, which referred a number of questions to the ECJ. The ECJ noted that the two sets of appraisals did not have the same objectives: the 2006 appraisal was aimed at assessing the quality of work, while the 2009 appraisal was carried out in the context of the abolition of a post. However, while the assessment of workers over two different periods was not a perfect solution, the ECJ considered that it was appropriate, given R's absence in 2009, provided the criteria used did not place workers who had taken parental leave at a disadvantage. The national court would need to satisfy itself that the assessment encompassed all workers liable to be affected by the abolition of the post; that it was based on criteria which did not differentiate between those who were, and those who were not, in active service; and that it did not involve the physical presence of workers, as this was a condition that those on parental leave were unable to fulfil.

Examples. We consider below two different situations in which a woman may **10.107** be able to argue indirect sex discrimination. The first involves a straightforward refusal to allow unpaid parental leave. The second involves a situation where unpaid parental leave has been allowed but later used as the basis of a decision affecting the employee:

- an employer has a policy of refusing all requests for unpaid parental leave. A woman who is refused unpaid parental leave could claim that this policy indirectly discriminates against her. The employer's policy is a 'provision, criterion or practice' – which applies to both men and women – that employees do not take any unpaid parental leave. However, if, in practice, this affects more women than men, and cannot be justified by the employer, then it would amount to indirect sex discrimination. It would also be a breach of the MPL Regulations and would enable the employee to bring a claim under S.80(1) ERA for unreasonable refusal (see 'Preventing or unreasonably postponing leave' above)

- an employer considering candidates for promotion decides to exclude any candidate who has taken more than one week of unpaid parental leave in the last year. A woman who is refused promotion because she has taken four weeks' unpaid parental leave over the last year could claim that this policy indirectly discriminated against her, if it is shown that women are more likely than men to take unpaid parental leave of more than one week. The employer would have to explain why this should be a relevant criterion in the selection process in order to show justification. The employee may also be able to bring a claim of unlawful detriment under S.47C ERA (see 'Unlawful detriment' above).

11 Time off for dependants

Right is unpaid

Who has the right?

Circumstances in which time off may be taken

Notice requirements

When is a refusal reasonable?

Remedies

Discrimination by association – disability and age

The EU Parental Leave Directive (No.2010/18) requires Member States and/or **11.1** management and labour to take the necessary measures to enable workers to take time off work 'on grounds of force majeure for urgent family reasons in cases of sickness or accident making the immediate presence of the worker indispensable' – Clause 7 of the framework agreement on parental leave annexed to the Directive. This provision is implemented in the United Kingdom by Ss.57A and 57B of the Employment Rights Act 1996 (ERA), which set out the right to time off for dependants.

The Department for Business, Enterprise and Regulatory Reform (BERR) (as it then was) produced a guide aimed at helping employers and employees understand the right to time off for dependants. This guide, 'Time Off for Dependants – A guide for employers and employees' (URN 07/1495), published in October 2007, includes answers to six frequently asked questions on practical issues relating to the legislation. Although not legally binding, this publication remains a significant source of guidance for tribunals and has been referred to in a number of cases.

A pared-down version of the guide is available on the Government website **11.2** (www.gov.uk) ('the online guidance'). This has replaced the separate guidance for employers and employees which used to be housed on the DirectGov and BusinessLink websites respectively.

Domestic emergencies not involving dependants. When the Government first **11.3** proposed legislation in this area, urgent domestic problems were covered so that, for example, disruption caused by flooding, fire or burglary would entitle the employee to take time off. However, this proposal was not enacted in S.57A ERA.

Filial leave. In November 2008, the European Commission announced its **11.4** intention to introduce a new right to 'filial leave', aimed primarily at employees

489

who look after an elderly or otherwise dependent relative. However, the proposal appears to have fallen by the wayside: when the European Social Partners agreed a new Parental Leave Directive in 2010, they chose not to deal with 'filial' or carers' leave; and a Commission research project in the area has not resulted in any concrete proposals for legislation.

11.5 Right is unpaid

It is important to be clear from the outset that the statutory right to time off to care for dependants does not include a right to be paid for that time, even though the period of absence occurs during working hours. An employee can only receive payment if his or her contract of employment specifically provides for this, and then only in the circumstances set out in the contract.

11.6 Who has the right?

The right to time off to care for dependants is available to all employees (male and female). An 'employee' is an individual who works under a contract of service, as opposed to a contract for services – S.230 ERA (see IDS Employment Law Handbook, 'Contracts of Employment' (2014), Chapter 2, 'Employment status').

No minimum period of qualifying service is necessary and the right applies regardless of whether the employee is full time or part time, permanent or temporary.

11.7 However, a number of classes of employee are excluded from the right to time off. These are:

- those employed in the armed forces – S.192 (read with para 16, Sch 2) ERA
- those employed in share fishing – S.199(2)
- those employed in the police service – S.200.

Under S.126 of the Criminal Justice and Public Order Act 1994, prison officers are covered by the employment protection legislation and so will qualify for the right to dependant care leave.

11.8 Circumstances in which time off may be taken

The circumstances in which an employee may take time off are set out in S.57A ERA. S.57A(1) states that an employee is entitled to be permitted to take a reasonable amount of time off during the employee's working hours in order to take action which is necessary:

490

- to provide assistance on an occasion when a dependant falls ill, gives birth or is injured or assaulted

- to make arrangements for the provision of care for a dependant who is ill or injured

- in consequence of the death of a dependant

- because of the unexpected disruption or termination of arrangements for the care of a dependant, or

- to deal with an incident involving a child of the employee which occurs unexpectedly in a period during which an educational establishment is responsible for the child.

These circumstances are dealt with in more detail under 'Reasons for time off' below.

According to the EAT in Qua v John Ford Morrison 2003 ICR 482, EAT, the **11.9** right is for employees to take a reasonable amount of time off work to take necessary action in respect of 'a variety of unexpected or sudden events affecting their dependants' and to make 'any necessary longer-term arrangements for their care'. This interpretation was approved in Cortest Ltd v O'Toole EAT 0470/07. The online guidance on the right to time off for dependants makes it clear that the right is intended to cover *unforeseen* matters and would not cover, for example, a parent taking a child to a hospital appointment. It suggests that if employees know in advance that they are going to need time off, they may be able to arrange with their employer to take annual leave. Alternatively, if the circumstances behind the need to take time off relate to the employee's child, the employee may qualify to take unpaid parental leave. This guidance does, however, need to be viewed in light of the decision in Royal Bank of Scotland plc v Harrison 2009 ICR 116, EAT, where the Appeal Tribunal took a more generous view of the circumstances in which the right is available – see 'Time off that is "necessary" – is an emergency required?' below.

'Reasonable' amount of time off

11.10

Under S.57A ERA an employee is entitled to take a 'reasonable' amount of time off. The concept of reasonableness is central to all statutory rights to time off and employment tribunals use their common sense and industrial experience to make judgements as to what is reasonable in any given set of circumstances. In Qua v John Ford Morrison (above) the Appeal Tribunal held that when determining what constitutes a reasonable amount of time off, a tribunal should always take into account the circumstances of the individual and should ignore any disruption or inconvenience to the employer.

The online guidance states: 'If your child falls ill you could take time off to go to the doctor and make care arrangements. Your employer may then ask you to

491

take annual leave or parental leave if you want to look after your child for longer.' This accords with the intention of Parliament as expressed by Lord Sainsbury of Turville: 'In all cases, the right will be limited to the amount of time which is reasonable in the circumstances of a particular case. For example, if a child falls ill with chicken pox the leave must be sufficient to enable the employee to cope with the crisis, to deal with the immediate care of the child and to make alternative longer-term care arrangements. The right will not enable a mother to take a fortnight off while her child is in quarantine. In most cases, whatever the problem, one or two days will be the most that are needed to deal with the immediate issues and sort out longer-term arrangements if necessary' (Hansard (HL Debates) 8 July 1999, cols 1084–85).

11.11 The Qua guidance on the question of reasonableness was approved by the EAT in Cortest Ltd v O'Toole (above). In that case C, who lived with his partner and their three young children, worked as a street lighting engineer. In December 2006, his relationship came under immense strain and, unable to cope, his partner left the family home to get some rest. Having been left alone with his children, C asked his employer for between one and two months off work to allow his family situation to return to normal (a request under S.57A(1)(d) ERA). The employer responded that C would be permitted the time off, provided that he resign on the understanding that he would be automatically reinstated when he was ready to return to work. The employer then alleged that C agreed to resign, although the tribunal held that he had in fact been dismissed. Moreover, because the dismissal was due to the employer's unreasonable refusal of a request for time off under S.57A, it was automatically unfair under S.99 ERA and Reg 20(3)(e)(iii) of the Maternity and Parental Leave etc Regulations 1999 SI 1999/3312 ('the MPL Regulations') (see 'Remedies' below). On appeal, the EAT had to consider among other things whether C's request for between one and two months off work was reasonable for the purposes of S.57A. The employer argued that the length of time involved was contrary to the intent of the legislation, which was designed to deal with emergencies. The EAT agreed, holding that 'a period as long as one month or even longer for care by a parent would rarely, almost never, fall within S.57A and cannot on the facts before the tribunal have done so here'. Accordingly, C's request for time off did not come within S.57A and the tribunal's finding of automatic unfair dismissal was reversed.

Another case which applied the Qua guidance was Uzowuru v London Borough of Tower Hamlets EAT 0869/04. U's employer granted him time off from the beginning of September 2002 until 23 September 2002 to go to Nigeria to visit his mother, whose health was deteriorating. By agreement, that absence was extended to 7 October, by which time U had requested more time off. Eventually, the employer summoned U to a disciplinary meeting for unauthorised absence on 28 July 2003 – which he did not attend because he was still in Nigeria – and he was dismissed as a result. An employment tribunal found that the requested time off was not reasonable for the particular situation, and therefore dismissed U's complaint that he had been dismissed as a result of taking time off under S.57A. That decision was upheld by the EAT.

However, 12 days' leave was found to be reasonable in Mura v Fancy That of **11.12** London Ltd ET Case No.2304256/04. In that case M was granted five days off to visit her seriously ill mother in Italy in June 2004. The following month M was again contacted by her family in Italy, this time to say that her mother was dying. On this occasion she requested five days off from 10 to 14 July and, again, the employer agreed. While M was in Italy, her mother's condition deteriorated and she told her employer that she had to extend her return date to 17 July. On 15 July, M's mother died. M then contacted her employer to say that she had to extend her stay further in order to deal with her mother's funeral arrangements. When she eventually returned to work on 22 July M was dismissed. The employment tribunal held that she had been automatically unfairly dismissed for taking time off under S.57A, in relation to both the time off that she had taken to provide assistance to her seriously ill mother (S.57A(1)(a)), and as a result of her mother's death (S.57A(1)(c)).

An even longer period of time off – 21 days – was found to be reasonable in Williams v Impact Business Group Ltd ET Case No.2702249/12, due to the severity of the condition and the lack of alternative arrangements. W's young son fell ill at school on Friday 1 June, and she left work to collect him and take him to hospital. After a number of tests and a transfer to a larger hospital, it was discovered that he had a ruptured appendix. He was discharged on 10 June, and needed to remain at home for a further week. W had no relatives who could care for her son, and he was too ill for a childminder to care for him. By contrast, however, the tribunal in Clifton v Enticott ET Case No.3104944/09 found that it was not reasonable for C to have four to six weeks off work to care for her daughter after a severe traffic accident. Although it accepted that there was a need for a woman, rather than C's husband, to provide personal care to her daughter (see immediately below), the tribunal did not consider that such a long period off work was reasonable when C had not taken any action to seek alternative arrangements.

Time off that is 'necessary'   11.13

The employer is required to permit the employee to take time off in order to take action which is 'necessary' to carry out one of the five activities listed in S.57A(1) ERA above.

In Qua v John Ford Morrison 2003 ICR 482, EAT, the Appeal Tribunal considered how employment tribunals should approach the question of whether it was necessary for an employee to take time off in any given situation. The EAT held that factors to be taken into account include the nature of the incident which has occurred, the relationship between the employee and the

493

dependant in question, and the extent to which anybody else can provide assistance. Two examples:

- **Clifton v Enticott** (above): C's 16-year-old daughter was hospitalised after a road traffic accident. Upon her discharge from hospital a week later, C sought to take between four and six weeks off under S.57A. An employment tribunal found that it was necessary for C to take time off to care for her daughter, even though C's husband was available: the nature of the daughter's injuries meant she needed help going to the toilet, and this was not appropriate for a male to provide to a 16-year-old girl. However, the tribunal went on to find that the amount of time off sought was unreasonable, given the lack of an investigation into alternative care arrangements

- **Morancie v PVC Vendo plc** ET Case No.3300938/01: M began working for her employer on 22 March 2001. On Sunday 25 March her one-year-old daughter was taken ill. M took her to hospital and remained there with her overnight. She telephoned her employer at 9 am on Monday and left a message explaining the situation, saying that she hoped to be able to return to work on Wednesday or Thursday. She was subsequently dismissed. She gave her employer a letter from the hospital explaining that she had stayed overnight because of her daughter's illness, but was told that her employer 'did not have time for people who had to look after children'. The employment tribunal held that, in the circumstances, M's presence at the hospital was necessary to provide 'assistance' within the meaning of S.57A(1)(a) ERA, in the form of assisting in the making of any decision, should a decision have been necessary regarding her daughter's medical care.

11.14 **Is an emergency required?** In the Qua case, the EAT described the circumstances that trigger the right to time off under S.57A as being 'unexpected or sudden', involving someone who depends on the claimant's help or care. This clearly suggests that nothing short of a genuine and unforeseen emergency will suffice – a view also expressed in the online guidance. However, the EAT took a broader view in Royal Bank of Scotland plc v Harrison 2009 ICR 116, EAT – a case concerned primarily with the meaning of the word 'unexpected' in S.57A(1)(d) (see 'Reasons for time off' below) but also relevant to the wider question of what amounts to a necessity for the purposes of S.57A as a whole. The EAT emphasised that it is for the employment tribunal in each case to find on the facts whether necessity has been established and that many factors will come into play, including considerations of urgency and time, but 'there are no hard and fast rules'. However, the Appeal Tribunal continued, 'the obvious principle that the greater the time to make alternative arrangements, the less likely it will be that necessity will be established, hardly needs to be stated'. In its view, if an employee failed to take appropriate steps to make alternative arrangements but had sufficient time in which to do so, a tribunal is unlikely to find as a fact that it was necessary for him or her to take the time off.

If, however, the time period between learning of the risk and the risk becoming fact was very short, then it will be easier for the employee to establish that it was necessary for him or her to take the time off.

An unlimited right to time off?   11.15
There is no formal statutory limit on the number of occasions on which an employee can exercise the right to take time off – a point clearly expressed in the online guidance. Does this mean that an employee is entitled to take any number of periods of time off, provided that he or she complies with the notice requirements in S.57A(2) ERA (see 'Notice requirements' below) and takes a 'reasonable' amount of 'necessary' time off on each occasion? Apparently not. In Qua v John Ford Morrison (above), Q had taken 17 days off work over a period of nine months under S.57A(1)(a) to care for her son, who suffered from a medical condition that caused him to suffer regular relapses. The EAT held that, in the context of a dependant with such a condition, where an employee has exercised the right to time off on one or more previous occasions and has been permitted time off, an employer can take into account the number and length of those previous absences, as well as the dates on which they occurred, when determining whether the time taken off or sought to be taken off on a subsequent occasion is reasonable and necessary. The EAT pointed out that the legislation was not intended to provide an employee with the right to take a day or more off each week on a regular basis whenever an existing medical condition caused a dependant to become unwell. (This aspect of the Qua decision is also considered under 'When is a refusal reasonable?' below.)

Although the EAT in Qua indicated that time off under S.57A is not in fact 'unlimited' in the true sense of the word, employers should proceed with caution before instigating absence management procedures simply because an employee has exercised the right on numerous occasions. For example, in Naisbett v Npower Ltd ET Case No.2502795/12 the employer called N to a meeting and issued her with a 'first written notification of concern' because she had taken a total of seven days of dependant care leave over the previous nine months. It warned that she could face dismissal if she had 'further unsatisfactory attendance due to time off for dependants'. An employment tribunal found that this time off was reasonable and necessary, and upheld N's claim that she had been subjected to an unlawful detriment for having taken it (see 'Remedies – unlawful detriment' below).

Reasons for time off   11.16
Section 57A(1) ERA stipulates five different types of circumstance in which an employee may take a reasonable amount of time off during working hours to take 'necessary' action. Each of these is discussed below.

To provide assistance on an occasion when a dependant falls ill, gives birth 11.17
or is injured or assaulted – S.57A(1)(a). The online guidance gives examples

_____

495

of how the time-off provisions might apply in practice. It states that the illness or injury under S.57A(1)(a) need not necessarily be serious or life-threatening and may be the result of a deterioration of an existing condition; for example, a nervous breakdown. The dependant may not require full-time care but there may be occasions when his or her condition deteriorates and the employee will need to take time off work. Any references to illness or injury include mental illness or injury – S.57A(6). The guidance states that S.57A(1)(a) would include a situation where a victim of an accident or assault was distressed rather than physically injured. It gives as an example the mugging of a dependant where the victim is not physically hurt. In this case the employee should be able to take time off work 'to comfort or help the victim'.

11.18 *'Occasion when a dependant falls ill'.* Section 57A(1)(a) provides that an employee is entitled to time off to assist on an occasion when a dependant falls ill. A line needs to be drawn here between the occasion when a dependant falls ill and the point at which a dependant is ill, which is dealt with under S.57A(1)(b). Ultimately, this is a question of fact to be determined by the tribunal on the circumstances of each case, although the EAT has made it clear that when a dependant is in hospital, a tribunal must carefully consider whether it was 'necessary for [the employee] to provide any further assistance' or make further arrangements for the provision of care within the meaning of S.57A(1)(a) or (b) – MacCulloch and Wallis Ltd v Moore EAT 51/02.

In Morancie v PVC Vendo plc ET Case No.3300938/01 (see 'Time off that is "necessary"' above) the employment tribunal gave a broad interpretation to the meaning of the phrase 'occasion when a dependant falls ill'. M was dismissed after she was absent from work to be with her hospitalised daughter. It is arguable on the facts of that case that the occasion when M's daughter fell ill should have been limited to the time needed to get to hospital and that M was not entitled to time off under S.57A(1)(a) to remain at hospital with her daughter. However, in the tribunal's view, the 'occasion' on which M's daughter 'fell ill' could be regarded as not merely the time the daughter was taken to hospital but the whole of the time when she was in hospital. Therefore M had been unfairly dismissed for taking time off under S.57A(1)(a).

11.19 In Rookley v Piper and Hannam ET Case No.3101822/03 an employment tribunal took a similar approach. There, R worked as an assistant in a shoe shop and had been scheduled to work on a Sunday in February. However, during the early hours of that day she had to take her son to hospital because he was suffering from gastroenteritis and she told her employer that she would be unable to work for that reason. The employer insisted that R attend work the following day, but she discovered that her son's nursery would not take him on the Monday because he was too unwell. Eventually, she was able to arrange for her father to look after the child and arrived at work on Monday morning. At the end of the working day R was dismissed by the employer, who stated that, due to her 'circumstances', she was unreliable. The employment tribunal found that R was automatically unfairly dismissed for taking time off under S.57A(1)(a).

However, in McDonald v NDI Momentum Ltd ET Case No.2409325/03 the employment tribunal adopted a more restrictive test. M was employed as an assistant accountant. In August 2003, her father suffered a heart attack and was admitted to hospital. M told her employer that this was the reason she required time off, whereas the real reason for her absence – which she did not mention – was that she needed to look after her chronically ill mother (who was dependent on her father). When she eventually returned to work M was dismissed because, according to the employer, 'things were not working out'. M claimed that she had been automatically unfairly dismissed for taking time off under S.57A(1)(a). The tribunal disagreed, holding that her father's hospitalisation was not a S.57A(1)(a) reason; he was in hospital, therefore she was not 'providing assistance' to him within the meaning of S.57A(1)(a).

The online guidance states that the illness suffered by a dependant can include **11.20** a deterioration of an existing condition. One of the questions raised in Qua v John Ford Morrison 2003 ICR 482, EAT (discussed extensively in previous sections of this chapter) was whether a dependant suffering from an existing medical condition that caused him or her to suffer regular relapses 'fell ill' each time there was a relapse. The EAT pointed out that whether an employee has 'fallen ill' within the scope of S.57A(1)(a) is a question of foreseeability, since the aim of S.57A(1)(a) is to allow an employee time off to deal with unforeseen or unexpected emergencies. If a dependant suffers from a medical condition that is likely to cause regular relapses, it cannot be said that the dependant's illness is unexpected or unforeseen and therefore the dependant will not have 'fallen ill' within the meaning of S.57A(1)(a). Accordingly, an employee who takes time off work to care for a dependant who suffers regular relapses as a result of an existing medical condition is not protected by the section if he or she is dismissed on account of those absences. However, the employee would be allowed reasonable time off in order to make longer-term care arrangements for the dependant under S.57A(1)(b) (see below). Whether a relapse or the deterioration of an existing condition is expected or foreseeable is a question of fact and degree to be decided by a tribunal on the facts of the case.

This aspect of the EAT's decision in Qua could have unfortunate consequences for employees who need to take time off under S.57A(1)(a) in anticipation of a dependant's death. Following Qua it is arguable that the impending death of a dependant would not amount to 'falling ill' if death was an expected or foreseeable consequence of the dependant's medical condition. Such an interpretation could, however, render S.57A incompatible with the Parental Leave Directive, which requires Member States to take 'the necessary measures to entitle workers to time off from work... on grounds of force majeure for

497

urgent family reasons in cases of sickness… making the immediate presence of the worker indispensable'. There can surely be no more urgent situation making the immediate presence of the worker indispensable than the impending death of a dependant. (Note that once the dependant has died the employee will be entitled to time off in order to take action that is necessary in consequence of the dependant's death under S.57A(1)(c) – see below.)

11.21 In Mura v Fancy That of London Ltd ET Case Nos.2304256/04 M worked as a sales assistant in a shop that sold items for the tourist trade. In June 2004, she was informed that her mother in Italy – who had a terminal illness – was seriously unwell. M requested five days off to visit her mother and the employer agreed. The following month M was again contacted by her family in Italy, this time to say that her mother was dying. On this occasion she requested five days off from 10 to 14 July and again the employer agreed. While M was in Italy her mother's condition deteriorated and she told her employer that she had to extend her return date to 17 July. On 15 July, M's mother died. M then contacted her employer again to say that she had to extend her stay further in order to deal with her mother's funeral arrangements. When she eventually returned to work on 22 July M was dismissed. An employment tribunal held that M had been automatically unfairly dismissed for taking time off under S.57A, in relation to both the time off that she had taken to provide assistance to her seriously ill mother (S.57A(1)(a)), and as a result of her mother's death (S.57A(1)(c)). It is interesting to note that, in this case, the tribunal had no hesitation in finding that the time M had taken off to tend to her dying mother – who was terminally ill – fell within the parameters of S.57A(1)(a).

11.22 **To make arrangements for the provision of care for a dependant who is ill or injured – S.57A(1)(b).** The online guidance suggests that this subsection is concerned with the making of 'longer-term' care arrangements for a dependant who is ill or injured, such as making arrangements to employ a temporary carer or taking a sick child to stay with relatives. As mentioned above, the EAT has made it clear that when a dependant is in hospital, an employment tribunal must carefully consider whether any further arrangements for the provision of care are expected or needed – MacCulloch and Wallis Ltd v Moore EAT 51/02.

11.23 **In consequence of the death of a dependant – S.57A(1)(c).** The current online guidance omits to mention time off in consequence of the death of a dependant. However, it seems clear that time off for making funeral arrangements or attending the funeral of a dependant would be covered by this provision. If the funeral is overseas, then employer and employee would need to agree a length of absence that is reasonable in the circumstances. For example, in Gomes v Top Class Investments Ltd ET Case No.2204585/03 the tribunal considered that it was reasonable for G to take three days off to attend her father's funeral in Portugal (see below under 'When is a refusal reasonable? – taking annual leave').

498

Section 57A(1)(c) is not restricted to arranging and attending the funeral: it also covers other matters such as registering the death and applying for probate if the deceased person had made a will – Forster v Cartwright Black 2004 ICR 1728, EAT. However, it does not include time off to deal with the emotional effects of bereavement. In the Forster case, F worked for a law firm from August 2002 until her dismissal just over ten months later. In October 2002, she took three days' sick leave, which was followed by a further 12 days off following the death of her father in January 2003. In May she had two days' sick leave due to an infection, and later that month her mother died. This necessitated F taking another five days off to deal with the consequences of that death. Before she was due to return to work, F became sick with an illness that her doctor certified as 'bereavement reaction'. On 10 June, her doctor issued her with a two-week sick note for the same reason, and on 12 June she was dismissed, the employer citing her general absence record as the reason. In subsequent tribunal proceedings, F alleged that her dismissal was automatically unfair as a result of her having taken time off under S.57A(1)(c). The employment tribunal rejected her claim, holding that the extended time that F had taken off in respect of her mother's death did not fall within the scope of that provision. The EAT agreed: although the death of a dependant may produce sadness, bereavement and unhappiness, the right contained in S.57A(1)(c) was not intended to introduce a right to compassionate leave following such a death.

Because of the unexpected disruption or termination of arrangements for the care of a dependant – S.57A(1)(d). The online guidance suggests that this subsection would cover matters such as a childminder failing to turn up, or a nursing home or nursery unexpectedly closing. An example: **11.24**

- **Nim v Union Grove Community Day Nursery** ET Case No.2305431/06: N, who had a seven-year-old son, worked as a nursery assistant. Early on the morning of 23 June 2006, N learned that her childminder was unable to collect the son from nursery and take him to a doctor's appointment which had been arranged for later that day. At around 10 am, N informed her employer of this and said that, as a result, she needed to leave work an hour and a half early at 3 pm. On her return to work N was summoned to a disciplinary meeting by her employer for failing to follow guidelines by not arranging to make up the time that she requested off. During the meeting, N said that she needed to 'refresh and take a long break', and explained that she wanted to take a week's unpaid leave to deal with 'family affairs'. The employer interpreted this as a resignation but an employment tribunal disagreed, holding that N had been automatically unfairly dismissed for taking time off to care for her son under S.57A(1)(d).

Although in Nim the tribunal held that the claimant's need to take one-and-a-half hours off work to look after her son was reasonable, the EAT has made it clear that it would not be permissible for the employee to become the primary carer under S.57A(1)(d) for a lengthy period of time. In Cortest Ltd v O'Toole EAT 0470/07 the EAT stated that the section was intended to give a parent 'the breathing space to enable a replacement carer to be found'.

11.25 *'Unexpected' disruption or termination.* As previously mentioned, the EAT in the Qua case described the circumstances that trigger the right to time off under S.57A as being 'unexpected or sudden', which suggests that nothing short of a genuine and unforeseen emergency will suffice. Indeed, the EAT in Cortest Ltd v O'Toole (above) – a case dealing with S.57A(1)(d) – held that the 'purpose of the legislation is to cover emergencies and enable other care arrangements to be put in place'.

However, in Royal Bank of Scotland plc v Harrison 2009 ICR 116, EAT, the Appeal Tribunal took a much broader approach. H worked part time as a home insurance claims adviser. She had two young children, who were looked after by a childminder when she was at work. On 8 December 2006 the childminder informed H that she would be unable to work on 22 December. On 13 December, having failed to secure alternative arrangements, H asked RBS if she could be absent on 22 December. RBS refused and informed her that she would be disciplined for unauthorised absence if she failed to attend work on that day. Left with no option, H remained at home with her children on 22 December and received a verbal warning as a result. An employment tribunal concluded that H's circumstances were sufficiently unexpected for the purposes of S.57A(1)(d) and thus upheld H's claim that she had been subjected to a detriment for exercising her right to time off. RBS appealed, arguing that the tribunal had applied too broad an interpretation to S.57A(1)(d) and had thus erred by viewing the disruption to H's childcare arrangements as unexpected.

11.26 The EAT upheld the tribunal's decision. It rejected the argument that Parliament, in enacting S.57A, was confined to providing for time off only on the ground of 'force majeure' (meaning irresistible compulsion or coercion) that is identified in the Parental Leave Directive. It was clear that Parliament was free to legislate for better protection than provided by the Directive. The decisions in the Qua and Cortest cases (see above) did not specifically address the meaning of 'unexpected' or 'necessary' in S.57A(1)(d), but the EAT considered that these words should be given their ordinary natural meaning: there was no justification for reading into the statutory wording a requirement that the disruption in the employee's childcare arrangements must be 'sudden' as well as unexpected. Although a tribunal may take into account 'the time which passes between the employee becoming aware of the risk of the relevant disruption and the risk becoming fact', that issue is 'primarily relevant to and will be considered by the tribunal as part of the question whether it was *necessary for the employee to take that time off*' (our stress). The question of whether time off is necessary is considered above under 'Time off that is "necessary"'.

To deal with an incident involving a child of the employee which occurs 11.27
unexpectedly in a period during which an educational establishment is
responsible for the child – S.57A(1)(e). According to the online guidance, this
category covers the situation where an employee needs to take time off to deal
with a serious incident involving his or her child during school hours. The
examples it gives are where the child has been involved in a fight, is distressed,
has been injured on a school trip or is being suspended from school.

Definition of 'dependant'
11.28

A 'dependant' is defined in S.57A(3) ERA as the employee's spouse or civil
partner, child, parent or person who lives in the same household as the employee
but who is not his or her employee, tenant, lodger or boarder. This clearly
covers non-married partners, including same-sex partners, and children, such
as stepchildren, who are not the employee's children but who live in the same
house. The definition also potentially covers other family members or friends
who live together. So, for example, an elderly aunt or grandparent who lives in
the employee's household would probably be a qualifying dependant. However,
the definition would not include, for example, a live-in housekeeper.

Section 57A(4) and (5) extends the definition of dependant contained in
S.57A(3) in certain circumstances. S.57A(4) states that for the purposes of
S.57A(1)(a) and (b) (see 'Reasons for time off' above) a dependant also includes
any person who reasonably relies on the employee (a) for assistance on an
occasion when the person falls ill or is injured or assaulted, or (b) to make
arrangements for the provision of care in the event of illness or injury. S.57A(5)
states that for the purposes of S.57A(1)(d) (see above), the definition of
dependant also includes any person who reasonably relies on the employee to
make arrangements for the provision of care where the arrangements for care
have been unexpectedly disrupted or terminated.

These extended definitions of dependant apply where the person 'reasonably 11.29
relies' on the employee. This means that the person need not necessarily be
related to the employee. The current online guidance does not deal with this
point, but the old Directgov guidance stated that these extended definitions
may apply where the employee is the primary carer or is the only person who
can help in an emergency. For example, a dependant may be an aunt who lives
nearby whom the employee looks after outside work and who falls ill
unexpectedly, or an elderly neighbour living alone who falls and breaks a leg,
where the employee is closest to hand at the time of the fall.

Abusing right to dependant care leave
11.30

An employer may be faced with an employee whom it suspects is not being
honest about his or her time off. Can the employer ask the employee for
evidence to support the time off taken in this situation? There is nothing in the
statute that requires the employee to produce evidence, either of the actual

501

incident or the employee's relationship to the dependant. However, employers who think that an employee is abusing the right to time off should deal with the situation according to their normal disciplinary procedures and it seems probable that as part of any investigation under such a procedure the issue of evidence to support the employee's explanation of his or her absences would arise. Further guidance on this issue is likely to come from the tribunals as more cases under S.57A ERA are heard. In the meantime, it may be advisable for employers to consider amending their disciplinary procedures to deal with matters related to dependant care leave.

Generally, employers will have to tread carefully when dealing with employees whom they suspect of abusing the right to time off. If a request is refused, the employee may complain to an employment tribunal that the employer unreasonably refused to allow time off. If, after time off has been taken, the employer takes disciplinary action against the employee, he or she may be able to claim that he or she has suffered a detriment. If the employer ultimately dismisses the employee, then the employee may be able to claim either that he or she has been automatically unfairly dismissed or that he or she has been dismissed for asserting a statutory right – see further 'Remedies' below.

11.31 In MacCulloch and Wallis Ltd v Moore EAT 51/02 M was employed as a sales assistant. In January 2001 she was informed that her father – who was in hospital following a car crash – had taken a turn for the worse. M told her employer that her father was dying and she was immediately granted time off to be with him in Ireland. However, after a while the employer began to suspect that M was not telling the truth about the reason for her absence and insisted that she get in touch. On Friday 19 January M contacted the employer to say that she intended to remain off work for another week, but was warned that she faced dismissal if she did not return to work after the weekend. Later that Friday the employer contacted the hospital where M's father was purportedly staying, and the staff there said that his condition was not life-threatening, although he would remain in hospital for some time. That weekend, unbeknown to the employer, M's father suffered a heart attack. On 26 January M discovered that she had been dismissed on the Monday when she had not turned up for work. Her father died the following day. The employment tribunal held that M had been automatically dismissed for taking time off under S.57A. However, the EAT overturned that decision, holding that the tribunal had failed to consider whether on the 'relevant date' (i.e. Friday 19 January – the date when M's request to extend her time off was refused), it had been reasonable for the employer to refuse that request. This involved consideration of a number of other questions, such as whether, on the relevant date, M had reasonably believed that her father was dying, or whether his already being in hospital on that date meant it had been reasonable and necessary for her to take time off to provide him with assistance or make arrangements for his care. The answers to these questions were essential for the tribunal to determine if M's request on

19 January fell within one or other of S.57A(1)(a) and 57A(1)(b), or both. The tribunal had mistakenly considered the above issues not on 19 January – the date when M had requested additional time off – but on 22 January – the date when M was required to return to work.

Notice requirements 11.32

The right to time off under S.57A(1) ERA is dependent on the employee telling the employer:

- the reason for his or her absence as soon as reasonably practicable, and

- how long he or she expects to be absent – S.57A(2).

The online guidance states that notice under S.57A(2) does not have to be in writing. In practice, many employees give such notice via telephone or other electronic means.

A question of fact. Whether or not the employee has complied with these 11.33 notice requirements is a matter for the employment tribunal to decide on the facts of each case. Three examples:

- **Giles v Tyco Healthcare UK Ltd** ET Case No.1701470/01: G worked as a sewing machinist for 12.5 hours a week while her two-year-old son attended playgroup. During the last weekend of July, her son became ill and her normal childminding arrangements could not cover the situation. She had already booked Monday and Tuesday of the following week as leave, and on the Monday she took her son to the doctor, who diagnosed him as suffering from chicken pox. On the Tuesday morning G visited her employer to explain that her son was ill and that, with no cover, she needed to take the remainder of the week off. An employment tribunal held that, by visiting her employer on the Tuesday morning, G had communicated the reason for her absence as soon as reasonably practicable. In the tribunal's view, it would have been unduly harsh to require G to have contacted her employer on the previous day

- **McDonald v NDI Momentum Ltd** ET Case No.2409325/03: M requested time off under S.57A(1)(a) to care for her father, who had been admitted to hospital following a heart attack. However, the real reason for her absence was to look after her chronically ill mother, who was dependent on her father. An employment tribunal rejected M's claim that she was 'providing assistance' to her hospitalised father within the meaning of S.57A(1)(a), although caring for her mother did fall within S.57A(1). However, as M had not informed her employer of the true reason behind her absence, she failed to comply with the notice requirements of S.57A(2) in that she did not give

503

her employer the reason for her absence under S.57A(1); namely, the need to care for her mother

- **Welsh v WA Riddell Transport** ET Case No.2502955/12: W was employed as a heavy goods vehicle (HGV) driver. His wife was nine months pregnant, and phoned him in a worried state to say that she was bleeding. W phoned the owner of WART, who told him to continue 30 miles further north where he could swap loads with another driver so that he could get home earlier. By the time W had reached the meeting point, his wife was hysterical and panicking. She refused to call an ambulance, saying she wanted W to take her to the hospital. W phoned the owner's son, who gave him permission to take the empty trailer back to the depot where he had left his car, so he could return home to take his wife to hospital. Shortly thereafter, the owner dismissed W over the phone, insisting that he had not done as he had been told. When W attempted to explain that he had been given permission by the owner's son, he was told 'you don't speak to him, you speak to me'. An employment tribunal found that W had a reasonable belief that his wife was entering labour, he had notified his employer of the need to take time off, and the action he took was necessary in the circumstances. It followed that he had been automatically unfairly dismissed for exercising his right to time off under S.57A.

11.34 **Notice need not use exact wording of statute.** The EAT has emphasised that employees are not required to use the exact wording of the statute when giving notice under S.57A(2), provided sufficient information is forthcoming. In Truelove v Safeway Stores plc 2005 ICR 589, EAT, T frequently had to work on Saturdays. But when it transpired that both he and his partner were required to work on Saturday 26 July, their babysitter made it clear that she could not look after their daughter that day. Initially, T tried to book the day off as leave but his request was refused. He then arranged for his sister to provide cover but that arrangement fell through at the last minute. With no other options available, T approached his manager on Friday 25 July and broached the possibility that he might be absent the following day because no one else was available to look after his daughter, although he failed to mention that the arrangement with his sister had fallen through. He then made a formal request for time off later that afternoon, which was refused by the employer. Left with no choice, T took the Saturday off without permission and was disciplined and suffered a deduction in bonus as a result.

The employment tribunal rejected T's claim under S.57B(1) that his employer had unreasonably refused him time off under S.57A, holding that he had failed to comply with S.57A(2) by not telling the employer how his right (under S.57A(1)(d) on this occasion) had arisen. This would have involved telling the employer that there had been an 'unexpected disruption' to his childcare arrangements. The EAT overturned the decision, stating that the tribunal's construction of S.57A(2) was too restrictive: the legislation was designed for parents facing a sudden and difficult situation, and they could not be expected to communicate in the language of the statute. Applying the guidance in Qua v John Ford Morrison 2003 ICR 482, EAT, the Appeal Tribunal said that – in the context of S.57A(1)(d) – there must be a communication which imparts an understanding into the mind of the employer 'that something has happened to disrupt what would otherwise be a stable arrangement affecting, in this case, a child and making it necessarily urgent for the employee to leave work'.

Not reasonably practicable to provide notice. The statute recognises that it **11.35** may not always be reasonably practicable to tell the employer the reason for the absence (or how long that absence might be) until the employee has returned to work. Where this is the case, the employee must tell the employer the reason for the absence on his or her return and the obligation to tell his or her employer how long he or she expects to be absent does not apply – S.57A(2)(b). This means that an employer may be notified of an employee's absence and the reason for it after the event. Neither the statute nor the online guidance gives any further assistance with identifying the circumstances in which it would not be reasonably practicable to inform the employer of the reason for the absence until after the employee's return to work. Where the employee is at work and has to leave to deal with an emergency, it is likely to be reasonably practicable to inform the employer of the reason for the absence before leaving. Even in cases where the employee is unable to attend work, it is suggested that in most cases it would still be reasonably practicable for the employee to telephone the employer to let him know the situation.

This point was illustrated by Ellis v Ratcliff Palfinger Ltd EAT 0438/13. In that case E failed to turn up for work for a week while he was at hospital with his partner before and during the birth of her baby. E's father telephoned E's employer on the first afternoon and E telephoned personally on the third day, but did not indicate how long he would be away. E argued that it had not been reasonably practicable for him to contact his employer any earlier because the battery on his mobile phone had run out. However, the employment judge did not accept that argument, noting that E could have recharged the battery, used a payphone at the hospital or borrowed someone else's phone. That conclusion was upheld by the EAT.

Updating the employer. In the Qua case (above), the EAT held that an **11.36** employee is not under a duty to report to the employer on a daily basis while time off is being taken. However, the later decision of the EAT in Ellis (also above) suggests that, if the likely duration of the absence changes, the employee should notify the employer. In the Ellis case, E left an answer-phone message with his employer on the third day of his absence, indicating that he would not be working the following day. However, he had failed to contact the employer again to give notice that he would be taking a fifth day's absence. This meant he had not satisfied the notice requirements.

11.37 **Effect of failure to give notice.** If an employee fails to comply with the requirements of S.57A(2), he or she will lose the right to time off under S.57A(1). In these circumstances, the employer should treat any leave taken in the same way as it would treat any other unauthorised leave.

In the event that the employee is dismissed for taking unauthorised leave, and he or she has sufficient qualifying service to claim unfair dismissal, the fairness of the dismissal will be determined according to S.98 ERA (see IDS Employment Law Handbook, 'Unfair Dismissal' (2010), Chapter 6, 'Conduct', under 'Absenteeism and lateness', in the section 'Absenteeism – unauthorised absences'). For example, in the Ellis case (above), after concluding that E had not been automatically unfairly dismissed for exercising his rights under S.57A, the employment tribunal went on to find that the decision to dismiss fell within the range of responses of a reasonable employer and was therefore fair.

11.38 It should be borne in mind that, since it is primarily women who need to take time off to look after dependants, any detrimental treatment of an employee in these circumstances – whether or not the time off meets the requirements of S.57A – may amount to sex discrimination. Sex discrimination in respect of an unreasonable refusal of leave is considered under 'Remedies' below.

11.39 When is a refusal reasonable?

An employee may bring a complaint under S.57B ERA that an employer has unreasonably refused to permit him or her to take time off – see 'Remedies' below. This suggests that there may be circumstances in which an employer's refusal to allow time off would be reasonable. Clearly, the employer will not always be in a position to refuse time off as he may only be notified after the event. But a refusal may be an option where an employee is actually at work when he or she is called away. There are two main grounds upon which dependant care leave can reasonably be refused:

- *where it is not necessary for the employee to take the time off.* As explored under 'Circumstances in which time off may be taken' in the sections 'Time off which is "necessary"' and 'Reasons for time off' above, the statutory right only applies to time off that is necessary for one of the five reasons outlined in S.57A(1). It is unlikely to be necessary for both parents take time off work to care for a sick child (although consideration would need to be given to the severity of the illness and the type of care required). Furthermore, the EAT in Royal Bank of Scotland plc v Harrison 2009 ICR 116, EAT, suggested that time off might not be necessary if the employee has not adequately explored alternative arrangements and there is time left to do so

- *where the amount of time off that is requested is unreasonable.* The online guidance indicates that right to time off under S.57A is directed at emergencies. The guidance gives the example of the employee's child falling ill. In such a situation the leave should be enough to help the employee cope with the crisis – to deal with the immediate care of the child, to visit the doctor and to make longer-term care arrangements. The guidance states that in most cases one or two days should be sufficient to deal with the immediate crisis, but that this will depend on individual circumstances. Clearly, then, this is not a right that would ordinarily lead to an employee taking a month or longer off work and employers may be inclined to reject requests for more than a few days off. There is, however, a risk of an employment tribunal subsequently concluding that a longer period off work was justified in the circumstances of the case – see, in particular, Mura v Fancy That of London Ltd ET Case Nos.2304256/04 and Williams v Impact Business Group Ltd ET Case No.2702249/12, the facts of which were considered under 'Circumstances in which time off may be taken – "reasonable" amount of time off' above.

It may also be reasonable for an employer to refuse time off where the employee **11.40** has had periods of time off in the past. This appears to be the conclusion of the EAT in Qua v John Ford Morrison 2003 ICR 482, EAT, where Mrs Recorder Cox QC (as she then was) stated: 'Where an employee has exercised the right on one or more previous occasions and has been permitted to take time off, for example, to deal with a dependant child's recurring illness, an employer can in our view take into account the number and length of previous absences, as well as the dates when they occurred, in order to determine whether the time taken off or sought to be taken off on a subsequent occasion is reasonable and necessary.' The Appeal Tribunal in that case was concerned with time off when a dependant falls ill under S.57A(1)(a) (see 'Reasons for time off' above), and was dealing with the issue of recurring illnesses in particular, so it is arguable that Mrs Recorder Cox's comments are limited to that scenario. However, the use of the words 'for example' implies a wider application.

According to the EAT in Qua, the disruption or inconvenience caused to the employer's business by the employee's absence are irrelevant factors that should not be taken into account in determining whether it will be reasonable to refuse to allow the employee time off.

Rearranging working hours **11.41**

The right is to time off during the employee's working hours. It will not be reasonable for an employer to require the employee to rearrange his or her working hours or to make up for lost time later. In Nim v Union Grove Community Day Nursery ET Case No.2305431/06 N was disciplined for taking time off to escort her son to a doctor's appointment in breach of the employer's policy that such time needed to be made up at a later date. The

507

employment tribunal said that this policy ignored the fact that N was not aware until the morning of the day in question that she would need time off in lieu, and 'it begs the question of how her taking time off in lieu at such short notice would have alleviated any difficulties the [employer] was anticipating it would have in covering for her during her absence'.

11.42 Taking annual leave

It will not be reasonable for an employer to insist that the employee take annual leave to cover a situation that falls within the ambit of S.57A ERA. In Gomes v Top Class Investments Ltd ET Case No.2204585/03 G worked as a chambermaid in the employer's hotel. In August 2003 she sought three days off to attend her father's funeral – a request under S.57A(1)(c) – in Portugal. The employer refused, but agreed that G could bring forward annual leave that she had booked for later that month in order to cover the period. A heated exchange followed, with G insisting that she should not have to use her annual leave in these circumstances, and she stormed off the premises. The following day, while preparing to fly to Portugal, G received a hand-delivered letter from her employer informing her that she had been dismissed for taking time off without permission, as G had made it clear that she would attend the funeral but would not use her annual leave for that purpose. The employment tribunal held that G had been automatically unfairly dismissed because she had taken time off under S.57A. It concluded that 'the time she sought was reasonable and necessary, due to the distance of the funeral'.

11.43 Remedies

There are a number of remedies that may be available to an employee who has been unreasonably refused time off under S.57A ERA or who has been disciplined as a result of taking time off.

11.44 Unreasonable refusal of time off

An employee may complain to an employment tribunal under S.57B(1) ERA that the employer has unreasonably refused to permit him or her to take time off as required by S.57A. A complaint must be presented to the tribunal within three months of the date when the alleged refusal occurred – S.57B(2)(a). However, if it was not reasonably practicable for the employee to present the complaint within the three-month time limit, the tribunal may extend the time limit by such further period as it considers reasonable – S.57B(2)(b). The time limit may also be extended to facilitate cross-border mediation or early conciliation. The law on time limits is fully explained in IDS Employment Law Handbook, 'Employment Tribunal Practice and Procedure' (2014), Chapter 5, 'Time limits'.

If the tribunal finds the employee's complaint to be well founded, it must make a declaration to that effect and may make an award of compensation to the employee. The amount of compensation must be such as the tribunal considers just and equitable having regard to the employer's default and any loss sustained by the employee that is attributable to the matters complained of – S.57B(4). Compensation could, therefore, include an amount representing the cost of providing substitute care for a dependant.

11.45 The date on which a tribunal should assess whether the employer's refusal was unreasonable or not (which is referred to as the 'relevant date') is the date on which the request for time off was made, not the date on which the employee was required to return to work – see MacCulloch and Wallis Ltd v Moore EAT 51/02.

Unlawful detriment
11.46

An employee is entitled not to be subjected to any detriment by any act, or any deliberate failure to act, by his or her employer because he or she took or sought to take time off under S.57A – S.47C ERA and Reg 19 MPL Regulations. 'Detriment' potentially covers a wide range of unfavourable treatment, including failure to promote, denial of training or other opportunities, unjustified disciplinary action and reduction in pay. In Royal Bank of Scotland plc v Harrison 2009 ICR 116, EAT, a verbal warning was held to amount to a detriment, and the three-month time limit was found to run from the date of the warning, not the date the employee was refused time off.

If an employment tribunal upholds a complaint of detriment relating to time off under S.57A, it will generally make an award for injury to feelings. An example:

• **Naisbett v Npower Ltd** ET Case No.2502795/12: In the period between March 2011 and February 2012, N had to take a total of seven days' absence to care for her infant son when he was too ill to attend nursery. On each occasion, she followed the employer's procedure on time off for dependants, and the leave was authorised by a manager. After the final absence, the employer invited N to a capability meeting where she was issued with a 'first written notification of concern' and warned that she could face dismissal if she had further unsatisfactory attendance due to time off for dependants. N complained to an employment tribunal that she had been subjected to a detriment for exercising her rights under S.57A. The tribunal upheld the claim, finding that the time off that N sought was both reasonable and necessary – there was nobody else available to look after her son in these circumstances. It recognised that N had not suffered any financial loss, but nonetheless considered that the written warning was a detriment because it could be taken into account in future disciplinary proceedings or when N applied for promotion. She was awarded £1,000 compensation for injury to feelings.

Unlawful detriment is dealt with in Chapter 12, 'Detriment and unfair dismissal'.

11.47 **Automatically unfair dismissal**

An employee will be regarded as automatically unfairly dismissed if the reason or principal reason for the dismissal (or selection for redundancy) is connected with the fact that the employee took or sought to take time off under S.57A – S.99(3)(d) ERA and Reg 20(3)(e)(iii) MPL Regulations.

In Qua v John Ford Morrison 2003 ICR 482, EAT, the Appeal Tribunal held that an employment tribunal should ask itself four questions in order to determine whether an employee has been automatically unfairly dismissed for taking time off for dependants.

11.48 **Question 1.** Did the employee take time off or seek to take time off from work during his or her working hours? If so, on how many occasions and when?

11.49 **Question 2.** If so, on each of those occasions did the employee:

● as soon as reasonably practicable inform the employer of the reason for the absence, and

● tell the employer how long he or she expected to be absent?

If not, were the circumstances such that the employee could not inform the employer of the reason until after he or she had returned to work?

If on the facts the tribunal finds that the employee did not comply with these requirements of S.57A(2) (see 'Notice requirements' above), then the right to take time off work under subsection (1) does not apply. The absences would then be unauthorised and the dismissal would not be automatically unfair. However, ordinary unfair dismissal might arise for consideration if the employee has the requisite length of service (see IDS Employment Law Handbook, 'Unfair Dismissal' (2010), Chapter 9, 'Conduct', under 'Absenteeism and lateness – absenteeism').

11.50 **Question 3.** If the employee did comply with the above requirements then the following questions arise:

● did the employee take or seek to take time off work in order to take action which was necessary to deal with one or more of the five situations listed at paras (a) to (e) of S.57A(1) (see 'Circumstances in which time off may be taken', under 'Time off that is "necessary"' and 'Reasons for time off' above), and

- if so, was the amount of time off taken or sought to be taken reasonable in the circumstances (see 'Circumstances in which time off may be taken – "reasonable" amount of time off' above)?

Question 4. If the employee satisfies questions 3(a) and (b), was the reason or principal reason for his or her dismissal that he or she had taken or sought to take that time off work? **11.51**

If the answer to the final question is in the affirmative, then the employee is entitled to a finding of automatic unfair dismissal and the tribunal should consider whether to order that the employer reinstate or re-engage the employee, or whether to make an award of compensation to the employee.

For further detail on unfair dismissal, see Chapter 12, 'Detriment and unfair dismissal'.

Asserting a statutory right **11.52**
If an employee is dismissed because he or she has tried to exercise the right to take time off to care for a dependant, he or she may also be able to claim that he or she has been dismissed for asserting a statutory right. Under S.104 ERA an employee's dismissal will be automatically unfair if the reason or principal reason for the dismissal was that:

- the employee brought proceedings against the employer to enforce a relevant statutory right, or

- the employee alleged that the employer had infringed a relevant statutory right.

It is immaterial whether the employee actually has the statutory right in question or whether it has been infringed, but the employee's claim to the right must be made in good faith – S.104(2). Furthermore, it is sufficient that the employee made it reasonably clear to the employer what the right claimed to have been infringed was; it is not necessary actually to specify the right – S.104(3).

Dismissals for asserting a statutory right are dealt with in detail in IDS Employment Law Handbook, 'Unfair Dismissal' (2010), Chapter 12, 'Dismissal for asserting a statutory right'.

Sex discrimination **11.53**
A woman who has been refused dependant care leave or has suffered a detriment or been dismissed because she took or sought to take time off under S.57A ERA may also be able to pursue a claim of indirect sex discrimination. This is because in reality women are more likely to bear the brunt of caring responsibilities than men and are therefore more likely to take or seek to take dependant care leave. By pursuing a claim of indirect sex discrimination, a

511

successful claimant would be able to seek an award of compensation for injury to feelings.

Indirect sex discrimination occurs when an employer applies to a woman 'a provision, criterion or practice' (PCP) which it applies or would apply equally to a man but which:

- puts or would put women at a particular disadvantage when compared with men

- puts her at that disadvantage, and which

- the employer cannot show to be a proportionate means of achieving a legitimate aim – S.19 Equality Act 2010.

11.54 The precise formulation of a claim would depend on the circumstances of the case. We consider below two different circumstances in which a woman may be able to argue indirect sex discrimination. The first involves a straightforward refusal to allow time off. The second involves a situation where time off has been allowed but is later used as the basis of a decision affecting the employee.

11.55 **Example 1:** An employer has a policy of refusing all requests for time off for dependant care leave. A woman who is refused time off could claim that this policy indirectly discriminates against her. She could argue that the employer has imposed a PCP, which applies to both men and women, that employees do not take any dependant care leave.

11.56 **Example 2:** An employer's policy is to not promote any candidate who has recorded four or more separate instances of dependant care leave in a year. A woman who is refused promotion because she has taken dependant care leave on four separate occasions over a year could claim that this policy indirectly discriminated against her. In this case the PCP is that to qualify for promotion the employee (whether male or female) must not have had more than three instances of dependant care leave per year.

Having formulated the PCP that the employer has applied, it would then have to be shown that that PCP put women at a particular disadvantage when compared with men. One of the most important factors here will be identifying the 'pool' that is chosen to effect the comparison. Once the pool has been established, the degree of adverse disparate impact must be ascertained. This is likely to involve arguments as to the extent to which women are more likely to be responsible for childcare and the care of the elderly than men and are thus more likely to take or seek to take dependant care leave. A tribunal may be persuaded to take judicial notice of this fact without the need for the woman to adduce detailed statistical evidence. It would then remain to be shown that the woman suffered a particular disadvantage. Once this had been done, the tribunal would consider whether the PCP could be justified. Any further detailed consideration of this subject is outside the scope of this chapter but reference should be made to Chapter 13, 'Discrimination and equal pay', and to IDS Employment Law Handbook, 'Discrimination at Work' (2012), Chapter 16, 'Indirect discrimination: proving disadvantage', and Chapter 17, 'Indirect discrimination: objective justification'.

Discrimination by association – disability and age

11.57

If an employee requests time off to care for a disabled or elderly dependant, or a child, any unreasonable refusal and/or subsequent dismissal or detriment by the employer may amount to unlawful direct discrimination under the Equality Act 2010. S.13(1) of that Act provides that 'a person (A) discriminates against another (B) if, because of a protected characteristic, A treats B less favourably than A treats or would treat others'. This is intended to cover, inter alia, the situation where an employer treats an employee less favourably than others because they have caring responsibilities for a child, an elderly person, or a person with a disability. For a detailed discussion of this subject, see IDS Employment Law Handbook, 'Discrimination at Work' (2012), Chapter 15, 'Direct discrimination', under 'Discrimination by association'.

Paragraph 3.19 of the Code of Practice on Employment published by the Equality and Human Rights Commission gives the following example of such discrimination: 'A lone father caring for a disabled son has to take time off work whenever his son is sick or has medical appointments. The employer appears to resent the fact that the worker needs to care for his son and eventually dismisses him. The dismissal may amount to direct disability discrimination against the worker by association with his son.'

However, it is important to recognise that S.13 EqA does not, by itself, make it **11.58** unlawful to discriminate against someone with caring responsibilities. The employee will have to show that he or she was treated less favourably than a similarly situated employee would have been treated in circumstances where the comparator is not associated with a person with the characteristic in question. Where an employer treats all employees requesting time off to care for dependants in the same way, regardless of age or disability or any other protected characteristic of the dependant, then there will be no unlawful discrimination.

12 Detriment and unfair dismissal

Right not to suffer detriment
Unfair dismissal
Automatically unfair dismissal
'Ordinary' unfair dismissal

The framework of family-friendly rights described in the preceding chapters of **12.1** this Handbook would be of little value to employees if an employer could avoid its obligations by dismissing them or penalising them for seeking to exercise those rights. Accordingly, the law provides a remedy for employees whose employer takes such action, and in this chapter we discuss the right not to be unfairly dismissed and the right not to suffer a detriment for exercising or seeking to exercise any of the rights described in Chapters 1–8 and 10–11.

The relevant law is contained in the Employment Rights Act 1996 (ERA) and in three sets of regulations. In respect of maternity and unpaid parental leave and the right to time off for dependants, the relevant regulations are the Maternity and Parental Leave etc Regulations 1999 SI 1999/3312 ('the MPL Regulations'). In respect of paternity leave and adoption leave, the relevant regulations are the Paternity and Adoption Leave Regulations 2002 SI 2002/2788 ('the PAL Regulations'). In respect of shared parental leave, the relevant regulations are the Shared Parental Leave Regulations 2014 SI 2014/3050 ('the SPL Regulations').

Note that, given the considerable scope for overlap with discrimination claims **12.2** based on the protected characteristics of sex (gender) and pregnancy and maternity under the Equality Act 2010 (EqA), it would be useful to read this chapter in conjunction with Chapter 13, 'Discrimination and equal pay'. Indeed, it would be unwise and impractical to consider the rights outlined in this chapter in isolation.

Right not to suffer detriment
12.3

The right not to suffer a detriment in respect of the various types of family leave discussed in this Handbook is contained in S.47C(1) ERA. It applies regardless of an employee's length of service or hours of work.

Section 47C(1) provides that an employee has the right 'not to be subjected to any detriment by any act, or any deliberate failure to act, by his employer' done

515

for a prescribed reason. A prescribed reason is one which is prescribed in regulations and must relate to one of the matters listed in S.47C(2), namely:

- pregnancy, childbirth or maternity – S.47C(2)(a)

- time off under S.57ZE to accompany a pregnant woman at an ante-natal appointment – S.47C(2)(aa)

- time off under S.57ZJ or S.57ZL to attend adoption appointments – S.47C(2)(ab)

- ordinary, compulsory or additional maternity leave – S.47C(2)(b)

- ordinary or additional adoption leave – S.47C(2)(ba)

- shared parental leave – S.47C(2)(bb)

- unpaid parental leave – S.47C(2)(c)

- paternity leave – S.47C(2)(ca)

- time off for dependants under S.57A – S.47C(2)(d).

12.4 The MPL Regulations, the PAL Regulations and the SPL Regulations set out the prescribed reasons under each of these heads and are dealt with below under the relevant subject headings. As outlined under 'Pregnancy, childbirth and maternity' below, the detriment provision in S.47C(2)(a) runs parallel to the provisions of the EqA. Arguably, therefore, S.47C is of greatest significance as a stand-alone provision in relation to the other parental rights listed above, since any sex discrimination claim based on a detriment suffered in relation to those rights would – unlike in the case of pregnancy or maternity discrimination – need to overcome the hurdle of establishing that the treatment was less favourable than that which would be accorded a comparator – see Chapter 13, 'Discrimination and equal pay', under 'Direct discrimination'.

Note that two of the matters listed in S.47C(2) have yet to be addressed in regulations: the right to time off under S.57ZE to accompany a pregnant woman at an ante-natal appointment (S.47C(2)(aa)) and the right to time off under S.57ZJ or S.57ZL to attend adoption appointments (S.47C(2)(ab)). These provisions came into effect on 5 April 2015, so it is anticipated that regulations will soon follow.

12.5 **Agency workers.** Section 129 of the Children and Families Act 2014 inserted new subsections (5)–(7) into S.47C ERA. These give agency workers the right not to be subjected to a detriment for exercising rights under Ss.57ZA–57ZP to time off for a pregnancy or adoption-related reason. They fall to be considered separately to the rights under S.47C(1) because they are explicitly stated not to apply to employees – S.47C(6) – and do not depend on the reason for detriment being 'prescribed in Regulations'.

516

Section 47C(5) stipulates that an agency worker has the right not to be subjected to any detriment by any act, or any deliberate failure to act, by the temporary work agency or the hirer done on the ground that:

- being a person entitled to time off to attend ante-natal appointments under S.57ZA, and entitled to remuneration under S.57ZB in respect of that time off, the agency worker exercised (or proposed to exercise) that right or received (or sought to receive) that remuneration – S.47C(5)(a)

- being a person entitled to time off to accompany a pregnant woman to ante-natal appointments under S.57ZG, the agency worker exercised (or proposed to exercise) that right – S.47C(5)(b)

- being a person entitled to time off to attend adoption appointments under S.57ZN, and entitled to remuneration under S.57ZO in respect of that time off, the agency worker exercised (or proposed to exercise) that right or received (or sought to receive) that remuneration – S.47C(5)(c)

- being a person entitled to unpaid time off to attend adoption appointments under S.57ZP, the agency worker exercised (or proposed to exercise) that right.

For the purposes of the above provisions, the terms 'agency worker', 'hirer' and **12.6** 'temporary work agency' have the same meaning as in the Agency Workers Regulations 2010 SI 2010/93 – see IDS Employment Law Handbook, 'Atypical and Flexible Working' (2014), Chapter 1, 'Agency workers', for full details.

There are no provisions protecting agency workers from being subjected to a detriment on grounds related to maternity, adoption, paternity and shared parental leave, for the simple reason that agency workers are not entitled to such leave – these rights are available to employees only.

Meaning of 'detriment'   **12.7**
There is no definition of 'detriment' in S.47C or in the MPL, PAL or SPL Regulations, but the concept appears to be very wide as the right is a right not to suffer *any* detriment. The term is also used in other employment and equality legislation, where it has similarly been given a wide meaning. For example, in Ministry of Defence v Jeremiah 1980 ICR 13, CA (a sex discrimination case), Lord Justice Brandon said that it meant simply 'putting under a disadvantage', while Lord Justice Brightman stated that a detriment 'exists if a reasonable worker would or might take the view that [the action of the employer] was in all the circumstances to his detriment'. This view was approved by the House of Lords in Shamoon v Chief Constable of the Royal Ulster Constabulary 2003 ICR 337, HL (also a sex discrimination case), where their Lordships emphasised that a sense of grievance which is not justified will not be sufficient to constitute a detriment. (For further consideration of the meaning of detriment under the Equality Act 2010, see IDS Employment Law Handbook, 'Discrimination at

517

Work' (2012), Chapter 25, 'Discrimination during employment', under 'Any other detriment – meaning of detriment'.)

It would seem, therefore, that the term 'detriment' is meant to be all-embracing in the sense that it would be unlawful for an employer to subject an employee to any adverse treatment for a prohibited reason. So, while a detriment would include the obvious examples of unjustified disciplinary action or a reduction in pay, it would also incorporate more subtle forms of treatment such as a failure to promote, a refusal of training or other opportunities, or a reduction in job status or content. Two examples:

- **Dixon v GB Eye Ltd** ET Case No.2803642/10: D worked as an export administrator. After her return from maternity leave, she discovered that she was working entirely on spreadsheets and, although this had formed part of her job prior to her maternity leave, she was no longer getting what she regarded as more interesting work as well. An employment tribunal considered that it was reasonable for D to regard the change in the character and frequency of her work as being to her detriment

- **Springer v Open Heavens Media Ltd and anor** ET Case No.2200573/12: the tribunal considered that S had been subjected to a detriment when her employer stated that she had lost her edge and was not hungry enough and that this might be due to her pregnancy. It considered that linking poor performance to pregnancy, in the absence of any evidence that there was a connection, would make a reasonable employee feel disadvantaged.

12.8 Even seemingly good-intentioned actions can amount to a detriment. For example, in Dean v Sodexho Ltd ET Case No.2901518/04 an employer was held to be in breach of S.47C after D was asked to keep the fact of her pregnancy to herself. The motivation for this instruction was that one of D's colleagues had been experiencing difficulty in conceiving and might be upset at the news. However, the employment tribunal held that the instruction subjected D to a detriment 'because she was denied the chance to share her good news with whomsoever she chose'.

12.9 **Exclusion of dismissal.** In the case of employees, if the detriment amounts to a dismissal it is specifically excluded from the provisions relating to detriment by Reg 19(4) MPL Regulations, Reg 28(2) PAL Regulations, and Reg 42(3) SPL Regulations, as such dismissals are dealt with separately under S.99 ERA – see 'Automatically unfair dismissal' below. In the case of agency workers, however, termination of a working assignment would amount to a detriment for the purposes of S.47C(5).

12.10 **Causation.** The wording of the three sets of Regulations makes it clear that employees have the right not to be *subjected to* any detriment for having exercised or sought to exercise one of the rights to family leave. Thus, the mere fact that a detriment arises is insufficient – there must be a link between the employer's act (or deliberate failure to act) and the exercise of the right. However, an employee does not have to show that the detriment was deliberately inflicted or that the employer acted with any malice. An administrative error that resulted in an employee not receiving her maternity pay for April until 22 May amounted to a detriment related to pregnancy in Gorge v Burns (Jewellers) Ltd ET Case No.2303442/98, particularly as the employee was unpaid at a time when it was known that she was unwell and near giving birth.

No appellate case law on causation has arisen under S.47C or the MPL, PAL or SPL Regulations. However, in the context of the right not to be subjected to a detriment because of having made a protected disclosure (S.47B ERA), the EAT observed that it would be difficult to talk of a failure to act as having 'caused' an ongoing detriment, since the detriment would have been caused by the ongoing course of events, and not by a failure to stop it. The EAT reasoned that the term 'subjected to' was therefore chosen by Parliament as a suitable linguistic alternative for conveying a sense of causation capable of operating in respect of both a positive act and a failure to act – Abertawe Bro Morgannwg University Health Board v Ferguson 2013 ICR 1108, EAT.

Post-employment detriment. There has not, as yet, been a ruling on whether **12.11** a former employee can bring a claim under S.47C arguing that he or she was subjected to a detriment *after* the employment had ended. Such a claim would typically arise where an employee believes that he or she has received a less favourable reference (or no reference at all) because he or she took advantage of one of the family leave rights during employment. However, rulings in respect of other 'detriment' provisions suggest that a tribunal would have jurisdiction to hear such a claim. In Rhys-Harper v Relaxion Group plc and other cases 2003 ICR 867, HL, the House of Lords held that an employee can bring a complaint under discrimination legislation in respect of conduct following termination of employment, provided the discrimination arises out of the employment relationship. In this regard, S.108 EqA now provides that a person (A) must not discriminate against another (B) if 'the discrimination arises out of and is closely connected to a relationship which used to exist between them'. Furthermore, in Woodward v Abbey National plc (No.1) 2006 ICR 1436, CA, the Court of Appeal took the view that it was appropriate to take the same approach in respect of S.47B ERA, which protects workers who have made a protected disclosure from suffering a detriment in the workplace. Part of the reasoning applied by the Court in Woodward was that the categories of worker to whom the whistleblowing provisions apply include those who '*worked* under a contract of employment' (our stress) – see S.230(3) ERA.

The reasoning applied in Woodward would seem to apply equally to other forms of detriment under the ERA, including detriment under S.47C. S.47C and the MPL, PAL and SPL Regulations apply to 'employees' only, but the definition of 'employees' includes individuals who, 'where the employment has

519

ceased, worked under a contract of employment' – S.230(1) ERA, Reg 2(1) MPL Regulations and Reg 2(1) PAL Regulations. The SPL Regulations do not define 'employees' but it would seem likely that tribunals would adopt the same definition as in the other Regulations.

12.12 There is therefore considerable scope to argue that employees are protected from detriment after their employment has terminated for having taken advantage of one of the family leave rights while they were employed. (Note, however, that a complaint under S.47C must normally be presented within three months of the act, or failure to act, complained of – see 'Remedies' below).

12.13 ## Pregnancy, childbirth and maternity
A woman who is subjected to detrimental treatment because of pregnancy or maternity leave can claim pregnancy and maternity discrimination under S.18 EqA (see Chapter 13, 'Discrimination and equal pay', under 'Direct discrimination – pregnancy and maternity discrimination'). However, there is also a free-standing statutory right not to be subjected to any detriment connected with pregnancy, childbirth or maternity – see S.47C ERA and Reg 19 MPL Regulations.

Under S.47C ERA employees are entitled not to be subjected to any detriment by any act, or any deliberate failure to act, by their employer for any reason specified in Reg 19(2) MPL Regulations. The reasons that are relevant here are that the employee:

- is pregnant – Reg 19(2)(a)

- has given birth to a child and the act or failure to act takes place during her ordinary or additional maternity leave period – Reg 19(2)(b) and (5) (see Chapter 3, 'Maternity leave', under ' General considerations – maternity leave periods', for an explanation of the two different types of maternity leave)

- is the subject of a maternity suspension on health and safety grounds within the meaning of S.66(2) ERA – Reg 19(2)(c) (see Chapter 2, 'Health and safety protection', under 'Suspension on maternity grounds')

- took, sought to take or availed herself of the benefits of any of the terms and conditions of her employment preserved by S.71 ERA and Reg 9 during her ordinary maternity leave period, or the terms and conditions preserved by S.73 ERA and Reg 9 during her additional maternity leave period – Reg 19(2)(d) (see Chapter 3, 'Maternity leave', under 'Terms and conditions during maternity leave')

- failed to return after a period of ordinary or additional leave in a case where the employer did not notify her (in accordance with Reg 7(6) and (7) or otherwise) of the date on which the period in question would end, and she reasonably believed that that period had not ended – Reg 19(2)(ee)(i)

(see Chapter 3, 'Maternity leave', under 'Entitlement to maternity leave – employer's notice of end date')

● failed to return after a period of ordinary or additional leave in a case where the employer gave her less than 28 days' notice of the date on which the period in question would end, and it was not reasonably practicable for her to return on that date – Reg 19(2)(ee)(ii) (see Chapter 3, 'Maternity leave', under 'Entitlement to maternity leave – employer's notice of end date')

● undertook, considered undertaking or refused to undertake work during her maternity leave period ('keeping-in-touch' days) in accordance with Reg 12A – Reg 19(2)(eee) (see Chapter 3, 'Maternity leave', under 'Work during maternity leave').

12.14 Note that the protection under Reg 19(2)(b) against suffering a detriment for having given birth to a child is restricted by Reg 19(5) to an act or failure to act that takes place during the employee's ordinary or additional maternity leave period. This reflects the position under European law, which gives special protection to women from the beginning of their pregnancy to the end of their maternity leave, and the right not to be discriminated against because of pregnancy and maternity, which lasts for 'the protected period' – see Chapter 13, 'Discrimination and equal pay', in the section 'Direct discrimination', under 'Pregnancy and maternity discrimination – protected period'.

Regulation 19(6) and (7) make provision for determining when a continuing act or a failure to act is done for the purposes of Reg 19(5) – i.e. during an employee's ordinary or additional leave period. Where a detrimental act extends over a period, the last day of that period is the date on which the act is taken to be done – Reg 19(6)(a). Where the detriment is a failure on the employer's part to act, the act is treated as done when the employer made the decision not to act – Reg 19(6)(b). Unless there is evidence to the contrary, an employer will be taken to have decided not to act either when it does something which is inconsistent with doing the failed act or, failing that, at the end of the period within which it might reasonably have been expected to have done it – Reg 19(7).

12.15 **Ante-natal appointments.** As we saw in Chapter 1, 'Time off for ante-natal care', a pregnant employee has the right to paid time off to attend ante-natal appointments – Ss.55–57 ERA. Reg 19(2) MPL Regulations makes no specific mention of a reason relating to time off work for the purpose of attending ante-natal appointments. However, there is a strong argument that the need for ante-natal care is so inextricably bound up with the fact that an employee is pregnant – which *is* one of the specific reasons set out in Reg 19(2) (see Reg 19(2)(a)) and therefore a reason that has been 'prescribed by regulations' for the purposes of S.47C(2) ERA – that the refusal of paid time off for ante-natal care, or any other detrimental treatment related to the fact that the

521

employee took or requested paid time off for ante-natal care, would appear to be caught by these provisions.

The same logic would not, however, apply to detriment on the ground that an employee exercised the right in S.57ZE to accompany a pregnant woman to an ante-natal appointment. Since the employee in such a scenario is not pregnant, there is no prospect of the detriment claim falling within Reg 19(2) MPL Regulations.

12.16 **IVF treatment.** There is no statutory right to time off for IVF (in vitro fertilization) treatment (unless it can be brought within the definition of ante-natal care – see further Chapter 1, 'Time off for ante-natal care', under 'Right to time off for ante-natal care – conditions') and no express provision under S.47C protecting women who suffer a detriment for a reason relating to IVF treatment. Moreover, none of the reasons specified in Reg 19(2) would seem capable of covering IVF treatment, particularly as the European Court of Justice (ECJ) has held that a woman undergoing IVF is not pregnant, and therefore not covered by the EU Pregnant Workers Directive (No.92/85) ('the Pregnant Workers Directive'), until the fertilized ova has been implanted in the uterus – Mayr v Bäckerei und Konditorei Gerhard Flöckner OHG 2008 IRLR 387, ECJ. Note, however, that a woman undergoing IVF treatment may be protected from dismissal for that reason under S.99 ERA – see 'Automatically unfair dismissal – pregnancy, childbirth and maternity' below. Furthermore, the less favourable treatment of a woman undergoing IVF treatment may amount to discrimination – see Chapter 13, 'Discrimination and equal pay', in the section 'Direct discrimination', under 'Pregnancy and maternity discrimination – protected period'.

12.17 **Surrogacy.** A woman who gives birth to a child as part of a surrogacy arrangement will be entitled to maternity leave in the usual way and protected from being subjected to a detriment for any of the reasons listed in Reg 19(2) MPL Regulations. However, the commissioning mother in such an arrangement does not enjoy an equivalent right to maternity leave. In C-D v S-T ET Case No.2505033/11 the claimant, whose partner had provided the sperm in a surrogacy arrangement, contended that she was entitled to maternity leave and benefits during the period of the surrogate mother's pregnancy and post-birth. After being denied such benefits by her employer on the ground that she herself was not pregnant, the claimant alleged before an employment tribunal that, in being denied the benefits she sought, she had suffered a detriment contrary to S.47C ERA and Regs 19 and 28 MPL Regulations. The tribunal considered that, while it was obvious that the claimant had not herself become pregnant or given birth, she had breastfed the child, which potentially engaged the Pregnant Workers Directive because Article 2(c) of that Directive specifically refers to breastfeeding. In order to clarify the position under EU law, the tribunal therefore decided to refer the matter to the ECJ for a preliminary ruling.

In CD v ST 2014 ICR D26, ECJ, the ECJ noted that the objective of the Pregnant Workers Directive is to encourage improvements in the health and safety at work of pregnant workers and workers who have recently given birth or who are breastfeeding. The Directive and European case law acknowledged that such workers are especially vulnerable, which makes it necessary to grant them maternity leave, and that their situation cannot be compared to that of a man or a woman on sick leave. The maternity leave is intended, first, to protect the worker's biological condition during and after pregnancy and, secondly, to protect the special relationship between a woman and her child following pregnancy and childbirth. That second objective only refers to the period after 'pregnancy and childbirth'. Thus, the granting of maternity leave pursuant to Article 8 of the Pregnant Workers Directive presupposes that the worker has been pregnant and has given birth to a child. This was confirmed by the ECJ's earlier decision in Mayr v Bäckerei und Konditorei Gerhard Flöckner OHG 2008 IRLR 387, ECJ, where the Court stated that it was apparent, both from the wording of Article 10 of the Directive, which protects against dismissal, and from the Directive's primary objective, that to benefit from the protection in Article 10 the pregnancy in question must have started. It followed that a commissioning mother who has had a baby through a surrogacy arrangement does not fall within the scope of Article 8 of the Directive, even though she may or does breastfeed the baby following the birth, because she has not been pregnant. Consequently, Member States are not required to grant such a worker a right to maternity leave under Article 8.

The ECJ's decision in CD v ST (above) has established that extending maternity **12.18** leave and benefits to commissioning mothers is not required under the minimum standards set down in the Pregnant Workers Directive. However, the Directive does not preclude Member States from introducing provisions more favourable to commissioning mothers who have babies through surrogacy and that is exactly what the UK has done. S.122 of the Children and Families Act 2014 and the Paternity, Adoption and Shared Parental Leave (Parental Order Cases) Regulations 2014 SI 2014/3096 together extend the right to adoption leave to commissioning mothers in surrogacy arrangements, on the condition that they have or intend to make an application for, a 'parental order' under S.54 of the Human Fertilisation and Embryology Act 2008. Any claim of detriment in connection with the exercise of these rights will therefore lie under the PAL or SPL Regulations – see 'Adoption leave' and 'Shared parental leave' below.

Unpaid parental leave
12.19

Under S.47C ERA, employees are entitled not to be subjected to any detriment by any act, or any deliberate failure to act, by their employer for any reason specified in Reg 19(2) MPL Regulations. The reasons that are relevant here are that the employee:

- took or sought to take unpaid parental leave – Reg 19(2)(e)(ii)

523

- declined to sign a workforce agreement on unpaid parental leave – Reg 19(2)(f), or

- being a representative of members of the workforce for the purposes of a workforce agreement on unpaid parental leave, or a candidate in an election in which any person elected will, on being elected, become such a representative, performed (or proposed to perform) any functions or activities as such a representative or candidate – Reg 19(2)(g).

An important factor to note in relation to claims brought under S.47C(2)(c) is that, under the MPL Regulations, unpaid parental leave can only be taken for a minimum of one week or in blocks of one or more weeks. Accordingly, in New Southern Railway Ltd (formerly South Central Trains Ltd) v Rodway 2005 ICR 1162, CA, an employee was not subjected to an unlawful detriment when his employer disciplined him for taking an unauthorised day's leave to look after his son – he did not have the right to take any less than a week's leave, with the result that the employer's action was not in breach of Reg 19(2)(e)(ii).

12.20 The following case highlights the fact that in order to be able to claim to have suffered a detriment as a result of taking, or seeking to take, unpaid parental leave, the employee must have made it clear that he or she was relying on the right to take unpaid parental leave:

- **Tavernor v Associated Co-operative Creameries Ltd** ET Case No.1902341/00: T had two children who were in receipt of disability living allowance and needed operations. At T's request, the employer agreed that he could use holidays and unpaid leave to take time off during their recuperative period. It was envisaged that he would wish to take two days off a week over a six-week period. However, problems ensued, mainly because T did not give proper notice or liaise with his superiors when he wanted to take leave. The Chief Engineer (L) spoke to T about his concerns and T subsequently raised a grievance. He took two days off work with the agreement of an Assistant Engineer but without seeking L's permission. On his return, L told him that further time off would lead to instant dismissal but T was later told at his grievance hearing that this threat should not have been made and did not stand. Several months later there was a problem at home requiring T's urgent attention and he left without completing a time sheet or giving the employer information on which jobs he had completed. On his return T was given a verbal warning for failing to complete the time sheet and he resigned in consequence. The employment tribunal dismissed his complaint of unlawful detriment. The agreed arrangement had been that T would be able to use holidays (including holidays brought forward from the following year), days in lieu or unpaid leave to cover his absences. At no time was parental leave mentioned and at the time of his initial request T had been unaware of his parental leave rights, although he subsequently became aware of them. The tribunal held that T had not sought to take parental leave and could not therefore seek redress under Reg 19. Overall, the employer had been sympathetic to T's situation and the warning was a justifiable sanction.

For full details of the right to unpaid parental leave, see Chapter 10, 'Unpaid parental leave'. It must be stressed that the right to unpaid parental leave under the MPL Regulations is entirely separate to the new system of shared parental leave under the SPL Regulations – see Chapter 8, 'Shared parental leave and pay', and, for discussion of the detriment provisions in the SPL Regulations, 'Shared parental leave' below.

Time off for dependants

12.21

Under S.47C, employees are entitled not to be subjected to any detriment by any act, or any deliberate failure to act, by their employer for any reason specified in Reg 19(2) MPL Regulations. The reason that is relevant under this head is that the employee took or sought to take time off under S.57A ERA (time off for dependants).

In Royal Bank of Scotland plc v Harrison 2009 ICR 116, EAT, a mother who had to take a day off work when she was unable to make alternative childcare arrangements was subjected to an unlawful detriment when her employer issued her with a warning. The EAT held that, for an employee to enjoy the right to time off because of a change in arrangements for the care of a dependant under S.57A, the change need not be sudden and unexpected, merely unexpected. The word 'unexpected' did not imply any temporal element.

For details of the right to take time off for dependants, see Chapter 11, 'Time off for dependants'.

Paternity leave

12.22

Under S.47C ERA, employees are entitled not to be subjected to any detriment by any act, or any deliberate failure to act, by their employer for any reason specified in Reg 28 PAL Regulations. The reason that is relevant under this head is that the employee took or sought to take paternity leave – Reg 28(1)(a). For details of the right to take paternity leave on the birth or adoption of a child, see Chapter 7, 'Paternity leave and pay'.

Note that there is no longer a distinction between 'ordinary' and 'additional' paternity leave – the latter, arising under the Additional Paternity Leave Regulations 2010 SI 2010/1055, was replaced by the system of shared parental leave with effect from 5 April 2015 – see Chapter 8, 'Shared parental leave and pay'.

Adoption leave

12.23

Under S.47C ERA, employees are entitled not to be subjected to any detriment by any act, or any deliberate failure to act, by their employer for any

525

reason specified in Reg 28 PAL Regulations. The reasons relevant under this head are that:

- the employee took or sought to take ordinary or additional adoption leave – Reg 28(1)(a)

- the employer believed that the employee was likely to take ordinary or additional adoption leave – Reg 28(1)(b)

- the employee undertook, considered undertaking or refused to undertake work during the adoption leave period ('keeping-in-touch' days) in accordance with Reg 21A – Reg 28(1)(bb), or

- the employee failed to return after a period of additional adoption leave in a case where the employer did not notify the employee (in accordance with Reg 17(7) and (8) or otherwise) of the date on which that period ended, and he or she reasonably believed that the period had not ended; or the employer gave the employee less than 28 days' notice of the date on which the period would end, and it was not reasonably practicable for him or her to return on that date – Reg 28(c).

For details of the right to adoption leave, see Chapter 6, 'Adoption leave and pay'.

12.24 Shared parental leave

Under S.47C ERA, employees are entitled not to be subjected to any detriment by any act, or any deliberate failure to act, by their employer for any reason specified in Reg 42 SPL Regulations. The reasons are that:

- the employee took, sought to take, or made use of the benefits of, shared parental leave – Reg 42(1)(a)

- the employer believed that the employee was likely to take shared parental leave – Reg 42(1)(b), or

- the employee undertook, considered undertaking, or refused to undertake work during the shared parental leave period ('shared parental leave in touch' days) in accordance with Reg 37 – Reg 42(1)(c).

For details of the right to shared parental leave, see Chapter 8, 'Shared parental leave and pay'.

12.25 Remedies

An employee who has suffered a detriment in contravention of S.47C ERA may make a complaint to an employment tribunal – S.48(1). On such a complaint it is for the employer to show the ground on which any act or deliberate failure to act was done – S.48(2). Presumably, the employee has the burden of showing that he or she has suffered a detriment, but this is not actually specified in the section.

A complaint must be presented to an employment tribunal before the end of three months beginning with the date of the act or the failure to act or, where there is a series of acts or failures, the last of them. Tribunals may, however, hear cases presented out of time if they consider that it was not reasonably practicable for the complaint to have been submitted within the three-month time limit – S.48(3) ERA. The time limit may also be extended to allow for early conciliation or cross-border mediation – Ss.207A and 207B ERA. Where a detrimental act extends over a period, the 'date of the act' means the last day of that period and a deliberate failure to act will be treated as done when the employer made the decision not to act. Unless there is evidence to the contrary, an employer will be taken to have decided not to act either when it does something which is inconsistent with doing the failed act or, failing that, at the end of the period within which it might reasonably have been expected to have done it – S.48(4).

12.26 Where a tribunal finds a complaint well founded it must make a declaration to that effect and may make an award of compensation – S.49(1) ERA. The compensation will be an amount that the tribunal thinks is 'just and equitable' in all the circumstances having regard to the infringement to which the complaint relates and any loss attributable to the employer's act or failure to act – S.49(2). When assessing the complainant's losses, the tribunal is directed to take account of any expenses reasonably incurred by the employee as a result of the employer's conduct and any benefits the employee might otherwise have had – S.49(3). The employee is, however, under a duty to mitigate his or her losses and the amount awarded may be reduced by any contributory conduct on the part of the employee concerned – S.49(4) and (5). There is no specified upper limit to the compensation that may be awarded in respect of any detriment suffered under the above provisions.

12.27 **Injury to feelings.** Unlike claims under the EqA in respect of detriments that amount to unlawful discrimination, there is no express provision for compensation to be awarded for injury to feelings under the ERA. However, the statutory language does not expressly rule out such an award either. Moreover, in Virgo Fidelis Senior School v Boyle 2004 ICR 1210, EAT (a whistleblowing detriment claim under S.47B ERA), the EAT reasoned that detriment claims are another species of discrimination claim, and that the guidelines on compensation set out in Vento v Chief Constable of West Yorkshire Police 2003 ICR 318, CA, should therefore be applied to the assessment of compensation under S.49 ERA (see IDS Employment Law Handbook, 'Whistleblowing at Work' (2013), Chapter 7, 'Enforcement and remedies', under 'Remedies in detriment claims – injury to feelings').

527

12.28 Unfair dismissal

Where maternity and parental rights are concerned, it is helpful to consider the law relating to unfair dismissal in two parts:

- automatically unfair dismissal under S.99 ERA, Reg 20 MPL Regulations, Reg 29 PAL Regulations and Reg 43 SPL Regulations

- 'ordinary' unfair dismissal under S.98 ERA.

Automatically unfair dismissals are discussed under 'Automatically unfair dismissal' below. The term 'automatically unfair' means that, once it is established that the reason for dismissal was one of a small band of 'inadmissible' reasons, there is no consideration of whether the employer's actions were reasonable – the inadmissible reason automatically renders the dismissal unfair. The final section of this chapter – '"Ordinary" unfair dismissal' – considers unfair dismissal in its normal guise, i.e. where the reason for dismissal does not lead to an automatic finding of unfairness. In these circumstances the tribunal has to determine the reasonableness of the employer's decision to dismiss in the normal way.

12.29 Definition of dismissal

Section 95 ERA contains a definition of dismissal that covers claims of both automatically unfair and ordinary unfair dismissal. A similar but not identical definition of dismissal for redundancy purposes is contained in S.136. Under S.95, an employee is dismissed by his or her employer if:

- his or her contract of employment is terminated by the employer, with or without notice – S.95(1)(a)

- he or she is employed under a limited-term contract (which includes a fixed-term contract) and the contract expires by virtue of the limiting event without being renewed under the same terms – S.95(1)(b)

- the employee terminates the contract under which he or she is employed (with or without notice) in circumstances in which he or she is entitled to terminate it without notice by reason of the employer's conduct (i.e. constructive dismissal) – S.95(1)(c).

The MPL, PAL and SPL Regulations make it clear that an employee's contract of employment subsists during all periods of statutory family leave. If an employee's contract is terminated by the employer during a period of family leave, he or she may therefore present a claim of unfair dismissal to an employment tribunal. If the reason for the dismissal was one of the inadmissible reasons connected with the statutory leave, then the dismissal is likely to be automatically unfair. If the reason was unconnected with the leave, the tribunal must decide upon the fairness of the dismissal in the usual way under S.98 ERA.

Note also that an employee who is not allowed to return to work at the end of **12.30** a period of statutory leave will have been dismissed because the contract will have been terminated. Depending on the reasons for the dismissal, the employee will be entitled to bring a claim for automatically unfair dismissal or ordinary unfair dismissal (or for a redundancy payment).

Where an employee simply fails to turn up for work at the end of his or her statutory leave period, the employer cannot simply assume that the employee has resigned. In Rashid v Asian Community Care Services Ltd EAT 480/99 a woman failed to return to work at the end of her maternity leave period. The EAT stated that it was impossible to infer repudiation just from a failure to turn up for work. There had to be a positive repudiation on the woman's part if it were to have the effect of terminating the contract. Although this case was decided under the old maternity leave provisions it is thought that the same principle would apply in respect of any of the family leave periods provided for under the MPL, PAL or SPL Regulations.

Constructive dismissal. As we have seen in the relevant chapters of this **12.31** Handbook, employees on ordinary or additional maternity leave, ordinary or additional adoption leave, paternity leave or shared parental leave, or who take time off to care for dependants, are entitled to the benefit of all their terms and conditions of employment, except remuneration, during their leave, while employees taking unpaid parental leave have the benefit of reduced terms and conditions during their leave. An employer's failure to provide the employee with the benefits of employment to which he or she is entitled during the leave period will amount to a breach of contract and may give the employee grounds to resign and claim constructive dismissal. In order for such a claim to succeed, the employer's breach must constitute a fundamental breach of contract.

For a detailed discussion on the meaning of dismissal, including constructive dismissal, see IDS Employment Law Handbook, 'Unfair Dismissal' (2010), Chapter 1, 'Dismissal'.

Automatically unfair dismissal   12.32

Employees who are dismissed for reasons connected with pregnancy, childbirth or any of the statutory rights to family leave (maternity, paternity, adoption or parental leave or time off for dependants) are given special protection by the ERA. The relevant provisions are contained in S.99 ERA and in the MPL, PAL and SPL Regulations. There is no minimum service requirement (qualifying period) for the right to claim automatically unfair dismissal under S.99.

Section 99 provides that an employee will be regarded as unfairly dismissed if the reason or principal reason for the dismissal is of a kind prescribed in regulations, or the dismissal takes place in prescribed circumstances – S.99(1)

529

and (2). A reason or set of circumstances prescribed under S.99(1) must relate to:

- pregnancy, childbirth or maternity – S.99(3)(a)

- time off under S.57ZE to accompany a pregnant woman to an ante-natal appointment – S.99(3)(aa)

- time off under S.57ZJ or S.57ZL to attend adoption appointments – S.99(3)(ab)

- ordinary, compulsory or additional maternity leave – S.99(3)(b)

- ordinary or additional adoption leave – S.99(3)(ba)

- shared parental leave – S.99(3)(bb)

- unpaid parental leave – S.99(3)(c)

- paternity leave – S.99(3)(ca) or

- time off for dependants – S.99(3)(d).

12.33 The reason or set of circumstances may also relate to redundancy or other factors – S.99(3).

There have not, as yet, been any regulations prescribing reasons for dismissal in relation to the rights to time off under Ss.57ZE, 57ZJ and 57ZL (although an employee dismissed for exercising these rights would be able to bring a claim of automatically unfair dismissal under S.104 ERA – see 'Asserting a statutory right' below). The MPL, PAL and SPL Regulations set out the detailed reasons under each of the other heads listed above (the 'inadmissible reasons'), which are discussed in the relevant sections below.

12.34 Burden of proof
The general rule is that an employee is not required to prove his or her case. He or she only has to produce some evidence to the tribunal to create a presumption in law that the dismissal was for an inadmissible reason under S.99. Where an employer argues that the dismissal was for a different reason and was fair, it must show the real reason for dismissal and that it was one of the acceptable reasons under S.98(1) or (2). Failure to do so will result in a finding of unfair dismissal. For a detailed discussion of S.98 dismissals, see IDS Employment Law Handbook, 'Unfair Dismissal' (2010), Chapter 3, 'Unfairness', under 'Reason for dismissal'.

The situation is somewhat different, however, where the claimant lacks the two years' continuous service required to claim ordinary unfair dismissal. There is no qualifying period to claim automatically unfair dismissal under S.99, but the effect of an employee having less than two years' continuous service is that the employee bears the burden of proof in showing that the reason for dismissal was a prescribed reason within the meaning of S.99 and the applicable regulations – Smith v Hayle Town Council 1978 ICR 996, CA.

As mentioned above, once it is found that the reason for dismissal was an **12.35** inadmissible reason, there is no room for the employer to argue that the dismissal was nonetheless reasonable in all the circumstances and therefore fair – see, for example, George v Beecham Group 1977 IRLR 43, ET.

Pregnancy, childbirth and maternity

12.36

Section 99(1) ERA provides that an employee shall be regarded as having been unfairly dismissed if the reason or principal reason for the dismissal is of a prescribed kind, or the dismissal takes place in prescribed circumstances. ('Prescribed' in this context means prescribed by regulations.) S.99(3) sets out the prescribed reasons or set of circumstances caught by these provisions, which expressly include reasons related to 'pregnancy, childbirth or maternity' (S.99(3)(a)) and 'ordinary, compulsory or additional maternity leave' (S.99(3)(b)).

The relevant prescribing regulations in this context are the MPL Regulations, Reg 20(1) of which provides that an employee who is dismissed will be regarded as unfairly dismissed under S.99 ERA if the reason or principal reason for the dismissal is:

- of a kind specified in Reg 20(3) – Reg 20(1)(a) (see below), or

- where the dismissal ends the employee's ordinary or additional maternity leave, that the employee is redundant and Reg 10 has not been complied with – Reg 20(1)(b) and Reg 20(4) (redundancy during maternity leave – and the provisions of Reg 10 – are dealt with in Chapter 4, 'Returning to work after maternity leave', under 'Redundancy during maternity leave').

The reasons for dismissal specified in Reg 20(3) are reasons connected with: **12.37**

- the pregnancy of the employee – Reg 20(3)(a) (which would encompass taking, or seeking to take, time off for ante-natal care)

- the fact that the employee has given birth to a child – Reg 20(3)(b). This only applies where the dismissal ends the employee's ordinary or additional maternity leave – Reg 20(4) (see Chapter 3, 'Maternity leave')

- maternity suspension on health and safety grounds within the meaning of S.66(2) ERA – Reg 20(3)(c) (see Chapter 2, 'Health and safety protection', under 'Suspension on maternity grounds')

- the fact that the employee took, sought to take or availed herself of the benefits of any of the terms and conditions of her employment preserved by S.71 ERA and Reg 9 during her ordinary maternity leave period, or the terms and conditions preserved by S.73 ERA and Reg 9 during her

531

additional maternity leave period – Reg 20(3)(d) and (5) (see Chapter 3, 'Maternity leave', under 'Terms and conditions during maternity leave')

- the fact that the employee failed to return after a period of ordinary or additional maternity leave in a case where: the employer did not notify her (in accordance with Reg 7(6) and (7) or otherwise) of the date on which the leave in question would end and she reasonably believed that the leave period had not ended; or the employer gave her less than 28 days' notice of the date on which the leave would end and it was not reasonably practicable for her to return on that date – Reg 20(3)(ee). (The notification provisions in Reg 7(6) and (7) are discussed in Chapter 4, 'Returning to work after maternity leave', under 'Date of return to work – postponing return')

- the fact that she undertook, considered undertaking or refused to undertake work ('keeping-in-touch' days) in accordance with Reg 12A – Reg 20(3)(eee) (see Chapter 3, 'Maternity leave', under 'Work during maternity leave').

An employee will also be regarded as unfairly dismissed if she is selected for redundancy for one of the above reasons – Reg 20(2) MPL Regulations. Automatically unfair redundancies are considered under 'Automatically unfair redundancy' below.

12.38 In much the same way as outlined under 'Right not to suffer detriment' above, the automatically unfair dismissal provisions relating to pregnancy, childbirth and maternity overlap with the pregnancy and maternity discrimination provisions of the EqA. Any dismissal found to be automatically unfair for any of the inadmissible reasons listed above will almost certainly also amount to pregnancy and maternity discrimination, or sex discrimination. There is nothing to prevent a claim being brought under both heads, and in practice it is wise to include a claim of discrimination since compensation for discrimination is not subject to the statutory ceiling that applies to unfair dismissal claims and the tribunal has the power to make an award for injury to feelings – see Chapter 13, 'Discrimination and equal pay', under 'Preliminary matters – overview of relevant UK and European law'.

12.39 **Pregnancy-related dismissals.** As we have seen above, Reg 20(1) and (3)(a) provides that a woman's dismissal is unfair where the principal reason for it is connected with her pregnancy. Protection under this provision is very wide and the phrase 'connected with her pregnancy' would certainly cover ante-natal care, miscarriages and pregnancy-related illnesses. It may also cover IVF treatment – see 'IVF treatment' below.

There is no appellate case law directly considering the test for causation in claims under Reg 20. However, in the sex discrimination case of O'Neill v Governors of St Thomas More Roman Catholic Voluntarily Aided Upper School and anor 1997 ICR 33, EAT, the Appeal Tribunal provided some guidance as to when a dismissal can be regarded as pregnancy-related. The case concerned an unmarried teacher at a Roman Catholic school, who had been unfairly constructively dismissed after she had become pregnant. An employment tribunal dismissed her sex discrimination complaint, finding that she had not been dismissed because she was pregnant but because the father was a Roman Catholic priest, a fact that had become public knowledge, making her position as a teacher of religious education untenable. On appeal, the EAT held that the issue of the paternity of the child, the ensuing scandal and the consequent untenability of the employee's position at the school were all causally related to the employee's pregnancy. It followed that she had been dismissed on pregnancy-related grounds.

Three examples of cases in which the dismissal was held to be pregnancy related: **12.40**

- **Pottinger v Eastbourne County Community Transport** ET Case No.3102143/04: P was employed to drive minibuses and cars, providing transport for the elderly and infirm. After becoming pregnant, and at a time when her employer was aware of her pregnancy, she took some elderly women shopping. One of the women complained that P was unwilling to carry her shopping for her, after which there was a heated discussion between the employer and P. She pointed out that she had previously had two miscarriages and was concerned about the effect that carrying heavy bags could have on her pregnancy. As a result of the discussion, P was dismissed. The employment tribunal found that the argument and subsequent dismissal were both as a result of her pregnancy and therefore the dismissal was automatically unfair

- **Shaw v Sunplee Ltd ET Case No.**1304585/12: S was dismissed from her role as a manager of a care home at a time when she was pregnant and was shortly to begin her maternity leave. An employment tribunal accepted that the employer had legitimate concerns over S's abilities as a manager and that, sooner or later, she would have been dismissed. However, the employer had not followed a proper procedure before dismissing her and had given no consideration to allowing her to return to her previous role of senior care assistant. Its decision to dismiss her at that time was related to her pregnancy

- **Bonnar v Swindells** ET Case No.2400514/99: B was off work sick from 20 November 1998 because of complications arising from her pregnancy. She telephoned her employer on 5 December to say that she had been given a further sick note for two weeks by her GP but had been advised that she would feel better after the first three months of pregnancy had passed. Her employment was terminated. The employment tribunal held that B had been unfairly dismissed on the ground of pregnancy. She was dismissed because it would be some time before she could return to work.

12.41 In Clayton v Vigers 1989 ICR 713, EAT, the Appeal Tribunal held that the dismissal of a woman on maternity leave was automatically unfair where the reason for that dismissal was that the employer was unable to obtain a temporary replacement for her. The EAT held that Reg 20(3)(a) had to be read widely and it was sufficient that the dismissal was associated with the 'after effects' of pregnancy. Note, however, that this decision would appear to conflict with the EAT's decision in the paternity leave case of Atkins v Coyle Personnel plc 2008 IRLR 420, EAT, where the Appeal Tribunal held – obiter – that 'connected with' means more than simply associated with – see 'Paternity leave' below.

12.42 *Illness at end of maternity leave.* Particular difficulties have arisen where employees have been dismissed after the date on which they were due to return to work at the end of their maternity leave period where they were suffering from an illness which was caused by, or had its basis in, pregnancy. The question then arises as to whether the protection from dismissal offered to pregnant employees under Reg 20(3)(a) extends beyond the end of a woman's maternity leave period – i.e. whether the dismissal is automatically unfair or whether it is an 'ordinary' dismissal subject to the reasonableness test in S.98(4) ERA. The EAT took the view in Caledonia Bureau Investment and Property v Caffrey 1998 ICR 603, EAT, that the protection contained in what was then S.99(1)(a) (and is now Reg 20(1) and (3)) can apply after the end of a period of statutory maternity leave. In that case a woman failed to return to work at the end of her ordinary maternity leave because of post-natal depression. Her employer dismissed her a few months later. The EAT held that the dismissal constituted a pregnancy-related dismissal and was automatically unfair.

It is strongly arguable, however, that Reg 20(3)(b) MPL Regulations was intended to overrule the Caffrey decision. Reg 20(3)(b) confers a right not to be dismissed for a reason connected with the fact that the employee has given birth to a child, but it is expressly restricted by Reg 20(4) to situations in which the dismissal ends the employee's ordinary or additional maternity leave. In other words, an employee is not protected under Reg 20(3)(b) from a childbirth-related dismissal that occurs *after* the end of her maternity leave period. This provision reflects the position under European law, which gives special protection to women during the period running from the beginning of their pregnancy to the end of their maternity leave – see Chapter 13, 'Discrimination and equal pay', under 'Direct discrimination – pregnancy and maternity discrimination'. The effect of Reg 20(4) is that any dismissal after the end of an employee's maternity leave for an illness that relates to childbirth will not be automatically unfair but the fairness or otherwise of the dismissal will be considered under the ordinary unfair dismissal principles.

12.43 At the time when Caledonia Bureau Investment and Property v Caffrey (above) was decided, S.99 did not outlaw dismissals connected to the fact that the employee had given birth to a child – it only referred to dismissals connected with pregnancy. The EAT was therefore only able to find in the employee's favour by treating her post-natal depression as a reason connected with pregnancy under Reg 20(3)(a), which has no express limitation in time. However, since the introduction of Reg 20(3)(b), it seems unlikely that post-natal depression would be treated as 'pregnancy-related' when it so obviously falls fairly and squarely within the scope of that provision, i.e. is connected with the fact that the employee has given birth to a child – after all, 'post-natal' means after-birth. Clarification from a higher court would be welcome. This is particularly so since the European Court of Justice has made it clear that special protection against dismissal under European law does not extend beyond the end of maternity leave – see Handels-og Kontorfunktionærernes Forbund (acting for Larsson) v Dansk Handel and Service (acting for Føtex Supermarked A/S) 1997 IRLR 643, ECJ. Note that the EAT declined to follow Caffrey in Lyons v DWP Jobcentre Plus 2014 ICR 668, EAT, when concluding that an employee dismissed after the end of her maternity leave period for absences due to post-natal depression had not suffered pregnancy and maternity discrimination contrary to S.18 EqA. However, that case did not involve a claim under S.99 ERA or the MPL Regulations, so the question of whether dismissal for post-natal depression falls within Reg 20(3)(a) or (b) has yet to be fully resolved.

Employer's knowledge of pregnancy. For a claim of automatically unfair **12.44** dismissal for a reason connected with pregnancy under Reg 20(3)(a) to succeed it is essential that the employer knew or believed that the woman was pregnant – see Del Monte Foods Ltd v Mundon 1980 ICR 694, EAT. In that case, M was warned repeatedly about her absences due to gastroenteritis and similar complaints. Eventually the decision was taken to dismiss her. One day later she phoned to say that she was pregnant but the employer went ahead with the dismissal anyway. The EAT said that, in order for S.99 and Reg 20 to apply, it was essential to show that the employer knew of M's pregnancy when the decision to dismiss her was taken. The mere fact that, after deciding to dismiss her, the employer learned of the pregnancy did not make the dismissal automatically unfair. The EAT did add, however, that the employer's decision not to retain the employee after being informed that she was pregnant might be relevant to determining whether the dismissal was fair in accordance with the general provisions dealing with unfair dismissal under S.98(4).

Doubts were cast over the correctness of the Del Monte Foods decision following the observations of Mr Justice Lindsay in HJ Heinz Co Ltd v Kenrick EAT 2000 ICR 491, EAT, that a connection between a pregnancy and a dismissal can be established whether or not the pregnancy featured in the employer's mind. However, the EAT in Ramdoolar v Bycity Ltd 2005 ICR 368, EAT, confirmed that an employer *must know or believe in the existence of an employee's pregnancy* in order to be liable for automatically unfair dismissal. The EAT went on to qualify its statement of the law by saying that it is

535

conceivable that, in limited circumstances, a dismissal will be automatically unfair under Reg 20 even though the employer neither knows nor believes that the employee is pregnant. Those circumstances are where an employer, suspecting that an employee might be pregnant, dismisses the employee before having those suspicions confirmed.

12.45 In Del Monte Foods Ltd v Mundon (above) the EAT said that it must be shown that the employer knew or *believed* that the employee was pregnant. In Gauci v Amphenol Ltd ET Case No.11684/83 G thought (erroneously) that she was pregnant and the employer took her at her word. She was subsequently dismissed when she refused to work with a substance that she thought would be dangerous to her. An employment tribunal found this to be an automatically unfair dismissal but went on to say that it would have been unfair under S.98(4) anyway.

12.46 *Absenteeism and pregnancy.* Employers need to tread carefully when dismissing for persistent absenteeism occasioned by pregnancy. Employment tribunals tend to treat such dismissals as pregnancy dismissals – and thus automatically unfair. Three examples:

- **Davis v Hampton Coaches (Westminster) Ltd** ET Case No.2300181/98: D was off sick on five occasions during her first four months of employment and away for medical appointments on three further occasions. On 20 October 1997 D told her employer that she was pregnant. On 30 October she was certified unfit for work for two weeks owing to a pregnancy-related condition. The employer wrote D a letter dated 3 November dismissing her for being absent and failing to make contact. According to the employer, the medical certificate was not received until 4 November. The employment tribunal held that D was unfairly dismissed on the ground of pregnancy. The employer took no action on D's absences until after being informed of her pregnancy and the letter dated 3 November was actually postmarked 8.15 pm on 4 November

- **Hill v The Old Rectory Nursing Home Ltd** ET Case No.2100018/07: H began working as a care assistant on 1 May 2005. On 20 February 2006, after eight episodes of sickness absence, she was given a final written warning that if her attendance did not improve she would be dismissed. In early June she informed her employer that she was pregnant. During June and July, H was off work on four occasions with pregnancy-related sickness. She was dismissed on 14 August because of her level of sickness absence. The employment tribunal found her dismissal automatically unfair

- **Louis v INP Ltd t/a Initial City Link** ET Case No.1501415/03: L had a number of pregnancy-related absences that led to INP Ltd dismissing her, the reason given being that she had failed to keep the company properly informed of her absences, which in turn had severely affected INP Ltd's delivery business. The employment tribunal held that the impact on the business, no matter how harsh, did not affect the fact that L had been dismissed due to her pregnancy-related absences. The dismissal was thus automatically unfair and also amounted to sex discrimination.

While employers should be cautious, all cases must be considered on their own **12.47** particular facts. In Wright v DHSS ET Case No.1448/77, for example, W was dismissed while absent due to being both sick and pregnant, but a tribunal found that it was the sickness and not the pregnancy that was the real reason for dismissal. W had a long record of absences caused by anxiety neurosis and depression. There was nothing to connect them with her pregnancy, although they might have been aggravated by it. The employment tribunal said that W's symptoms were 'a long-standing and underlying matter' and that the reason for dismissal was her mental condition and not her pregnancy. (This meant only that the dismissal was not automatically unfair: the tribunal went on to hold that it was unfair under the ordinary unfair dismissal provisions in S.98 ERA.)

IVF Treatment. As mentioned above, a woman is not protected under S.47 **12.48** ERA and Reg 19(2) MPL Regulations from being subjected to a detriment for undergoing or having undergone IVF treatment. However, the protection from dismissal under S.99 ERA and Reg 20 MPL Regulations is drafted in wider terms than the protection from detriment – for the dismissal to be automatically unfair it need only be 'connected with' the employee's pregnancy. And IVF treatment has been considered by employment tribunals to be a reason connected with pregnancy. Two examples:

- **Kaveri v Bermingham Power Ltd** ET Case No.08037/95: when K began working for BP Ltd, an employment agency, in January 1994 she told the company that she would need to take time off for IVF treatment. The employer said this would not be a problem. When K commenced the treatment she was off work from 28 October to 8 November. She came back to work at 8 am and at 8.30 was told she was being dismissed immediately because 'things were not working out'. There had been relatively minor criticisms made of her during the year. A tribunal held that K was dismissed because she was absent for IVF treatment and that IVF treatment was something which related to pregnancy. The dismissal was held to be unlawful sex discrimination

- **Dunne v Cardshops Ltd** ET Case No.09736/95: D was dismissed from her job after more than 20 years when, in response to being asked to deliver a box of cards, she said she could only do this if she could take a taxi there and back because she had just undergone IVF treatment. She was given a letter of dismissal the next day which said, in part: 'This is the first time that the company has had any idea that there is anything wrong with you, and if you are incapable of doing what is required then we can no longer employ you.' The employment tribunal held that D's dismissal was for a

537

reason connected with her pregnancy and therefore automatically unfair. It also constituted unlawful sex discrimination, as a result of which D was awarded £1,500 for injury to feelings.

12.49 These decisions pre-date the ECJ's ruling in Mayr v Bäckerei und Konditorei Gerhard Flöckner OHG 2008 IRLR 387, ECJ, that a woman is not pregnant, and therefore not covered by the EU Pregnant Workers Directive (No.92/85), until the fertilized ova has been implanted in the uterus. However, the wording to the Directive is narrower than S.99 and Reg 20 in that it requires Member States to prohibit dismissal during the period from 'the beginning of... pregnancy' to the end of maternity leave. It does not use the term 'connected with'. It is therefore highly arguable that undergoing IVF treatment continues to be covered by S.99 and Reg 20.

Note that in the Mayr case the Court observed that dismissing an employee who is undergoing IVF treatment is likely to amount to unlawful sex discrimination. This aspect of the case is discussed in Chapter 13, 'Discrimination and equal pay', in the section 'Direct discrimination', under 'Pregnancy and maternity discrimination – protected period'.

12.50 *Contributory conduct.* Contributory conduct on the part of the employee may be taken into account when assessing compensation for unfair dismissal. In Moon v Highland Electronics Ltd ET Case No.34342/83, for example, M was dismissed for persistent absenteeism when the employer knew that she was pregnant. The tribunal found that pregnancy was the principal reason for the dismissal, which was therefore automatically unfair. But they found that a number of M's absences were wilful and without due cause and that she had contributed 100 per cent to her dismissal by her conduct. No compensation was awarded. (Note that, unlike unfair dismissal compensation, there is no scope for a tribunal to reduce compensation for sex or pregnancy discrimination due to the claimant's contributory conduct.)

12.51 **Dismissals connected with childbirth or maternity leave.** If a woman is dismissed during her ordinary or additional maternity leave period, the maternity leave period ends at the time of the dismissal – Reg 7(5) MPL Regulations. Where this occurs, the employee is entitled to claim automatically unfair dismissal under Reg 20(3)(b) if the reason or principal reason for the dismissal is connected with the fact that she has given birth to a child. In Wakeman v Longworth and Jackson t/a Dotty Price Fashions ET Case No.20768/95, for example, W was not allowed to return to her job after taking maternity leave. Her employer maintained that the principal reason was that the lease of the shop she managed was precarious and the company did not want her to return to a precarious job. The tribunal held that the dismissal was automatically unfair. The lease had always been precarious. Had W not taken maternity leave she would not have been dismissed simply because, at some future date, the lease might no longer exist. The principal reason for the dismissal was related to the fact that she had been on maternity leave and therefore to the fact that she had given birth to a child.

The application of Reg 20(3)(b) MPL Regulations is limited by Reg 20(4) to dismissals that end the employee's ordinary or additional maternity leave. The reasoning behind this limitation is considered under 'Pregnancy-related dismissals' above.

12.52 In addition to the protection afforded by Reg 20(3)(b), a woman is entitled to claim automatically unfair dismissal if the reason or principal reason for her dismissal is that she took, sought to take, or availed herself of the benefits of ordinary or additional maternity leave – Reg 20(3)(d). As we saw in Chapter 3, 'Maternity leave', under 'Terms and conditions during maternity leave', during both ordinary and additional maternity leave a woman is entitled to the benefit of the terms and conditions of employment which would have applied if she had not been absent, except the right to receive remuneration – Ss.71(4) and (5) and 73(4) and (5) ERA.

In Moss v Cyprus t/a Valley Yarns ET Case No.2402081/98 (which was decided under the old legislation, which entitled all pregnant women to 14 weeks' maternity leave) a tribunal decided that a woman who was dismissed for having failed to return from her maternity leave on the due date had been automatically unfairly dismissed under the equivalent of Reg 20(3)(d). M began her maternity leave on 6 October. On 8 February she informed her employer that she would not be able to return to work on 11 February owing to sickness. Her maternity leave was actually due to end on 12 January. On 12 February the employer wrote to M saying that she was entitled to 14 weeks' maternity leave. As she had now been absent for 20 weeks she had lost the right to return. The tribunal held that M had been automatically unfairly dismissed. She had been dismissed because she took more maternity leave than she was entitled to take. That, in the tribunal's view, amounted to dismissal for a reason connected with the fact that the employee availed herself of the benefits of maternity leave.

12.53 However, it is arguable that the same construction given to the earlier legislation, even if it was right at the time (which is questionable), could not be given to the current Reg 20(3)(d). Regs 19(3), 19(3A) and 20(5) together provide that a woman avails herself of the benefits of ordinary or additional maternity leave if, during her leave period, she avails herself of the benefit of any of the terms and conditions of her employment preserved by Ss.71 or 73 ERA during that period. Those regulations clearly restrict the operation of Reg 20(3)(d) to events that occur *during* the ordinary or additional maternity leave period and do not extend to unauthorised absences that occur after the ordinary or additional maternity leave period has ended.

There are no provisions in the MPL Regulations stipulating quite what the effect of an employee's failure to return on time is. The preferred view is that if

539

the employer dismisses the employee for taking unauthorised absence, the fairness of the dismissal should be judged in the normal way under S.98(4) ERA. In deciding whether it was reasonable for the employer to have dismissed for that reason, the tribunal would then take account of whether the employee knew that such behaviour would be treated by her employer as a disciplinary matter and that dismissal was a possible sanction.

12.54 What is certain, however, is that employees cannot 'lose the right to return' after maternity leave. Their contract remains in force throughout their period of leave and no longer needs to be 'revived' on their return. Furthermore, the EAT made it clear in Rashid v Asian Community Care Services Ltd EAT 480/99 that it is not possible to infer that a woman has repudiated her contract from the mere fact that she has failed to return to work at the end of her maternity leave. There has to be a positive repudiation on the woman's part if it is to have the effect of terminating the contract.

12.55 Unpaid parental leave
Section 99(1) ERA provides that an employee shall be regarded as having been unfairly dismissed if the reason or principal reason for the dismissal is of a prescribed kind, or the dismissal takes place in prescribed circumstances. 'Prescribed' in this context means prescribed by regulations. S.99(3) sets out the prescribed reasons or set of circumstances caught by these provisions, which expressly include reasons related to 'parental leave' in so far as the reason or set of circumstances relates to 'action which an employee takes, agrees to take, or refuses to take, under or in respect of a collective or workforce agreement which deals with parental leave' (S.99(3)(c) and (4)). The term 'parental leave' in this context refers to the right to unpaid parental leave to care for a child under the MPL Regulations, rather than the right to shared parental leave under the SPL Regulations.

The relevant prescribing regulations in this context are the MPL Regulations. Under those Regulations, an employee who is dismissed will be regarded as unfairly dismissed under S.99 ERA if the reason or principal reason for the dismissal is connected with the fact that he or she:

- took or sought to take parental leave – Reg 20(3)(e)(ii) MPL Regulations

- declined to sign a workforce agreement for the purposes of the Regulations – Reg 20(3)(f), or

- being a representative of members of the workforce for the purposes of a workforce agreement on parental leave or a candidate in an election in which the person elected will become such a representative, performed (or proposed to perform) any functions or activities as such a representative or candidate – Reg 20(3)(g).

An employee will also be regarded as unfairly dismissed if he or she is selected **12.56** for redundancy for one of the above reasons – Reg 20(3). Automatically unfair redundancies are considered under 'Automatically unfair redundancies' below.

The right to take unpaid parental leave is discussed in detail in Chapter 10, 'Unpaid parental leave'. This right is entirely separate to the right to shared parental leave (see Chapter 8, 'Shared parental leave and pay'). Dismissal for a reason connected to shared parental leave is considered under 'Shared parental leave' below.

Time off for dependants
12.57

Section 99(1) ERA provides that an employee shall be regarded as having been unfairly dismissed if the reason or principal reason for the dismissal is of a prescribed kind, or the dismissal takes place in prescribed circumstances. 'Prescribed' in this context means prescribed by regulations. Included among the reasons caught by these provisions are those related to the right to time off for dependant care leave under S.57A in so far as the reason or set of circumstances relates to 'action which an employee takes, agrees to take, or refuses to take, under or in respect of a collective or workforce agreement which deals with parental leave' (S.99(3)(d) and (4)).

The relevant prescribing regulations in this context are the MPL Regulations. Under those Regulations, an employee who is dismissed will be regarded as unfairly dismissed under S.99 ERA if the reason or principal reason for the dismissal is connected with the fact that he or she took or sought to take time off to care for dependants under S.57A ERA – Reg 20(3)(e)(iii). An employee will also be regarded as unfairly dismissed if he or she is selected for redundancy for taking, or seeking to take, time off under S.57A – Reg 20(2). Automatically unfair redundancies are considered under 'Automatically unfair redundancy' below.

In Qua v John Ford Morrison 2003 ICR 482, EAT, the Appeal Tribunal held **12.58** that an employment tribunal should ask itself four questions in order to determine whether an employee has been automatically unfairly dismissed for taking time off for dependants.

Question 1. Did the employee take time off or seek to take time off from work **12.59** during his or her working hours? If so, on how many occasions and when?

Question 2. If so, on each of those occasions did the employee: **12.60**

- as soon as reasonably practicable inform the employer of the reason for the absence, and

- inform the employer of how long he or she expected to be absent?

- If not, were the circumstances such that the employee could not inform the employer of the reason until after he or she had returned to work?

541

If on the facts the tribunal finds that the employee did not comply with these requirements in S.57A(2) (see Chapter 11, 'Time off for dependants', under 'Notice requirements'), then the right to take time off work under subsection (1) does not apply. The absences would be unauthorised and the dismissal would not be automatically unfair. However, ordinary unfair dismissal might arise for consideration if the employee has the requisite length of service. In Ellis v Ratcliff Palfinger Ltd EAT 0438/13 E had been absent from work to take his heavily pregnant partner to hospital to give birth. He had not contacted his employer to inform it of his absence until the evening of the second day, and nor had he indicated the expected duration of his absence. He was subsequently dismissed for misconduct relating to his absence and failure to make contact. The EAT upheld a tribunal's decision that E had not been automatically unfairly dismissed under S.99 ERA, as he had not complied with the requirement in S.57A(2) to notify the employer 'as soon as reasonably practicable'. E had sufficient length of service to claim 'ordinary' unfair dismissal under S.98 ERA, but the EAT agreed with the tribunal that he had been fairly dismissed for misconduct – he had already been given a final written warning for conduct issues.

12.61 **Question 3.** If the employee did comply with the above notice requirements then the following questions arise:

- did the employee take or seek to take time off work in order to take action which was necessary to deal with one or more of the five situations listed at paras (a) to (e) of S.57A(1) (see Chapter 11, 'Time off for dependants', under 'Circumstances in which time off may be taken')?

- If so, was the amount of time off taken or sought to be taken reasonable in the circumstances?

12.62 **Question 4.** If the employee satisfies both parts of question 3, was the reason or principal reason for his or her dismissal that he or she had taken or sought to take that time off work?

If the answer to the final question is in the affirmative, then the employee is entitled to a finding of automatic unfair dismissal.

12.63 The majority of cases involving S.57A concern time off in relation to employees' children, but dependants can also include parents, spouses and civil partners. The right to time off encompasses action that is necessary on the death of a dependant, but this is limited to funeral arrangements, registering the death and other administrative matters; employees do not have a right to 'compassionate leave' upon the death of a dependant and do not enjoy protection from dismissal for having taken such leave – Forster v Cartwright Black 2004 ICR 1728, EAT.

Paternity leave

12.64

Section 99(1) ERA provides that an employee shall be regarded as having been unfairly dismissed if the reason or principal reason for the dismissal is of a prescribed kind, or the dismissal takes place in prescribed circumstances. 'Prescribed' in this context means prescribed by regulations. S.99(3) sets out the prescribed reasons or set of circumstances caught by these provisions, which expressly include reasons related to 'paternity leave' – S.99(3)(ca). The relevant prescribing regulations in this context are the PAL Regulations.

An employee who is dismissed will be regarded as unfairly dismissed under S.99 ERA if the reason or principal reason for the dismissal is connected with the fact that the employee took or sought to take paternity leave – Reg 29(1)(a) and (3)(a) PAL Regulations.

The meaning of 'connected with' in this context was considered by the EAT in 12.65 Atkins v Coyle Personnel plc 2008 IRLR 420, EAT. During a period of paternity leave, A engaged in angry e-mail and telephone correspondence with his employer, the end result of which was that his manager shouted to him down the phone that he was sacked. Considering his claim for automatically unfair dismissal – A lacked the requisite qualifying period for ordinary unfair dismissal – an employment tribunal found that the reason for the dismissal was not connected with the fact that A had taken paternity leave, but was rather a result of frustration and annoyance at his attitude, which culminated in the telephone argument. On appeal, the EAT upheld this finding, and further offered obiter views on the meaning of 'connected with' in Reg 29. According to the EAT, the fact that the words 'connected with' might on the dictionary definition be taken to mean 'associated with' does not mean that a causal connection between the dismissal and the paternity leave is unnecessary. It is not sufficient that the dismissal was associated with the paternity leave, since that is a very vague concept and so wide that it would be enough for the employee merely to establish that he was on paternity leave when he was dismissed. Such an interpretation cannot have been intended, and for the same reasons nor can a 'but for' test. 'Connected with' in Reg 29 means causally connected with rather than some vaguer, less stringent connection.

These obiter comments of the EAT in the Atkins case would seem to be at odds with the earlier decision in Clayton v Vigers 1989 ICR 713, EAT. There, another division of the EAT, in deciding that the dismissal of a woman on maternity leave because the employer had been unable to find a temporary replacement was automatically unfair, held that the words 'reasons connected with the pregnancy of the employee' did not require a direct causal connection. Rather, the reason for a woman's dismissal need only be 'associated with' her pregnancy. The Clayton decision was before the EAT in Atkins and Mr Justice Nelson rather surprisingly took the view that it supported a causal requirement. If this view is adopted by tribunals, it would not only act to limit the protection for

543

those who take paternity leave, but would also impact on the protection enjoyed by pregnant women and those on maternity leave.

12.66 In practice, the distinction between these two interpretations of the term 'connected with' may be of minimal importance – it is for tribunals to determine as a matter of fact whether there is a connection between the taking of leave and the dismissal, and it will be a rare case where such a determination will be interfered with on appeal.

An employee will also be regarded as unfairly dismissed if he is selected for redundancy for taking, or seeking to take, paternity leave – Reg 29(2) PAL Regulations. Automatically unfair redundancies are considered under 'Automatically unfair redundancy' below.

12.67 Note that there is no longer a distinction between 'ordinary' and 'additional' paternity leave – the latter, arising under the Additional Paternity Leave Regulations 2010 SI 2010/1055, was replaced by the system of shared parental leave with effect from 5 April 2015 – see 'Shared parental leave' below.

For details of the right to paternity leave, see Chapter 7, 'Paternity leave and pay'.

12.68 **Adoption leave**
Section 99(1) ERA provides that an employee shall be regarded as having been unfairly dismissed if the reason or principal reason for the dismissal is of a prescribed kind, or the dismissal takes place in prescribed circumstances. 'Prescribed' in this context means prescribed by regulations. S.99(3) sets out the prescribed reasons or set of circumstances caught by these provisions, which expressly include reasons related to 'ordinary or additional adoption leave' (S.99(3)(ba)).

The relevant prescribing regulations in this context are the PAL Regulations, under Reg 29(1) of which an employee who is dismissed will be regarded as unfairly dismissed under S.99 ERA if the reason or principal reason for the dismissal is:

- of a kind specified in Reg 29(3) – Reg 29(1)(a), or
- that the employee is redundant and Reg 23 has not been complied with – Reg 29(1)(b). (Reg 23 applies to redundancies during ordinary or additional adoption leave and is dealt with in Chapter 6, 'Adoption leave and pay', under 'Redundancy and adoption leave'.)

12.69 The reasons for dismissal specified in Reg 29(3) PAL Regulations are reasons connected with the fact that:

- the employee took or sought to take adoption leave – Reg 29(3)(a)

- the employer believed that the employee was likely to take ordinary or additional adoption leave – Reg 29(3)(b)

- the employee undertook, considered undertaking or refused to undertake work ('keeping-in-touch' days) in accordance with Reg 21A – Reg 29(3)(bb)

- the employee failed to return after a period of additional adoption leave in circumstances in which the employer did not notify him or her (in accordance with Reg 17(7) and (8) or otherwise) of the date on which that period would end, and the employee reasonably believed that the period had not ended; or the employer gave him or her less than 28 days' notice of the date on which the period would end and it was not reasonably practicable for him or her to return on that date – Reg 29(3)(c). (The notification provisions in Reg 17(7) and (8) are discussed in Chapter 6, 'Adoption leave and pay', under 'Ordinary adoption leave – notice and evidential requirements for OAL'.)

An employee will also be regarded as unfairly dismissed if he or she is selected for redundancy for one of the above reasons – Reg 29(2). Automatically unfair redundancies are dealt with under 'Automatically unfair redundancy' below.

While rights during adoption leave are, in many respects, analogous to those **12.70** enjoyed by women on maternity leave, there are no discrimination provisions in the EqA that directly refer to adoption leave. As a result, the protection granted by Reg 29 assumes a greater importance for employees who have been dismissed for a reason specified in that regulation. That is not to say, however, that employees cannot also bring a claim of sex discrimination. In Coulombeau v Enterprise Rent-A-Car (UK) Ltd ET Case No.2600296/06, for example, C embarked on the training necessary to become an adopter after discovering that she could not have children. This entailed a number of days' leave in order to meet with social workers. A senior manager, H, had visited the branch where C worked and, on hearing that she was training to become an adopter, commented that 'she'll be no bloody use to me then'. Thereafter, C was charged with misconduct and dishonesty, with further charges being included in the disciplinary process at H's behest. She was dismissed and that decision was upheld on appeal. The employment tribunal found that the reason for C's dismissal was that H believed she was likely to take adoption leave, with the result that the dismissal was automatically unfair by virtue of Reg 29(3)(b). It went on to find that, on the facts of the case, a man would not have been dismissed for the offences with which C was charged and that her dismissal also amounted to sex discrimination.

The right to take adoption leave is discussed in detail in Chapter 6, 'Adoption leave and pay'.

545

12.71 Shared parental leave

Section 99(1) ERA provides that an employee shall be regarded as having been unfairly dismissed if the reason or principal reason for the dismissal is of a prescribed kind, or the dismissal takes place in prescribed circumstances. 'Prescribed' in this context means prescribed by regulations. S.99(3) sets out the prescribed reasons or set of circumstances caught by these provisions, which expressly include reasons related to 'shared parental leave' – S.99(3)(bb).

The relevant prescribing regulations in this context are the SPL Regulations, under Reg 43(1) of which an employee who is dismissed will be regarded as unfairly dismissed under S.99 ERA if the reason or principal reason for the dismissal is:

- of a kind specified in Reg 43(3) – Reg 43(1)(a), or

- that the employee is redundant and Reg 39 has not been complied with. (Reg 39 applies to redundancies during shared parental leave and is dealt with in Chapter 8, 'Shared parental leave and pay', under 'Employment protection during and after SPL – redundancy during SPL'.)

12.72 The reasons for dismissal specified in Reg 43(3) SPL Regulations are reasons connected with the fact that:

- the employee took, sought to take, or made use of the benefits of, shared parental leave – Reg 43(3)(a)

- the employer believed that the employee was likely to take shared parental leave – Reg 43(3)(b), or

- the employee undertook, considered undertaking, or refused to undertake work ('shared parental leave in touch' days) in accordance with Reg 37 – Reg 43(3)(c).

An employee will also be regarded as unfairly dismissed if he or she is selected for redundancy for one of the above reasons – Reg 43(2). Automatically unfair redundancies are dealt with under 'Automatically unfair redundancy' below.

12.73 Exception for job offers from associated employers

The MPL and PAL Regulations contain an important exception to the automatically unfair dismissal provisions considered above under 'Pregnancy, childbirth and maternity', 'Unpaid parental leave', 'Time off for dependants' and 'Adoption leave'. However, it is no longer accurate to describe this as a 'general exception' to all of the forms of automatically unfair dismissal arising under S.99 ERA, since an equivalent provision has not been included in the SPL Regulations.

Regulation 20(1) MPL Regulations and Reg 29(1) PAL Regulations do not apply to render a dismissal automatically unfair in relation to an employee if:

546

- it is not reasonably practicable *for a reason other than redundancy* for the employer (who may be the same employer or a successor) to permit the employee to return to a job which is both suitable for the employee and appropriate for him or her to do in the circumstances

- an associated employer offers the employee a job of that kind, and

- the employee accepts or unreasonably refuses that offer – Reg 20(7)/ Reg 29(5).

Where there is a dispute as to whether this exception applies, it is for the employer **12.74** to show that the provisions in Reg 20(7)/Reg 29(5) were satisfied – Reg 20(8)/ Reg 29(6). (Note that, as emphasised above, this exception does not apply where the reason for dismissal is redundancy – for discussion of automatically unfair redundancies, see 'Automatically unfair redundancy' below.)

Two employers are associated if one is a company of which the other (directly or indirectly) has control, or both are companies of which a third person (directly or indirectly) has control – Reg 2(3) MPL Regulations and Reg 2(6) PAL Regulations.

If a tribunal finds that this exception applies, it must decide the fairness or **12.75** otherwise of the dismissal in the normal way, i.e. by applying the test of reasonableness set out in S.98(4) ERA (see 'Ordinary unfair dismissal' below and IDS Employment Handbook, 'Unfair Dismissal' (2010), Chapter 3, 'Unfairness', under 'Reasonableness of dismissal'). The dismissal may also give rise to a sex discrimination claim – see Chapter 13, 'Discrimination and equal pay'.

Automatically unfair redundancy
12.76
There are two circumstances in which redundancy will be automatically unfair:

- redundancy during maternity, adoption, or shared parental leave, where the employee was not offered a suitable available vacancy

- redundancy selection for an inadmissible reason.

Redundancy during maternity, adoption or shared parental leave. Regulation **12.77** 10 MPL Regulations, Reg 23 PAL Regulations and Reg 39 SPL Regulations deal with the situation in which an employee's existing job becomes redundant while he or she is absent on maternity leave, adoption leave or shared parental leave. Where there is a suitable available vacancy, the employee is entitled to be offered alternative employment before the existing contract ends, in preference to employees who are not absent on such leave. The new employment may be with the existing employer or his successor, or an associated employer, under a new contract of employment which complies with requirements specified in Reg 10(3), Reg 23(3) or Reg 39(3) (outlined below). The new employment

547

must take effect immediately on the ending of the employee's employment under the previous contract – Reg 10(2)/Reg 23(2)/Reg 39(3).

In order to comply with Reg 10/Reg 23/Reg 39, the new contract of employment must be such that:

- the work to be done under it is of a kind which is both suitable in relation to the employee and appropriate for him or her to do in the circumstances, and

- its provisions as to the capacity and place in which the employee is to be employed, and as to the other terms and conditions of employment, are not substantially less favourable to the employee than if he or she had continued to be employed under the previous contract – Reg 10(3)/Reg 23(3)/Reg 39(3).

12.78 Where the reason or principal reason for an employee's dismissal is redundancy and the provisions as to suitable alternative employment in Reg 10, Reg 23 or Reg 39 have not been complied with, the employee will be regarded as unfairly dismissed under S.99 ERA – Reg 20(1)(b)/Reg 29(1)(b)/Reg 43(1)(b). In Chagger v Mullis and Peake LLP ET Case No.3201677/09, for example, C worked as a solicitor in the employer's property team. She went on maternity leave in December 2007 and in her absence the firm decided to restructure the department in which she worked. C was not included in the new structure: internal memos referred to her being 'retrained out of the department'. In May 2008, C indicated that she would like to return on a three-day week. However, before C returned, the firm began a redundancy consultation, which resulted in C being dismissed for redundancy. An employment tribunal held that the selection criteria and scoring process used were ostensibly reasonable, but found that the firm had been influenced by the fact that C had taken maternity leave and by her future childcare requirements. Her dismissal was therefore pregnancy and maternity discrimination. In addition, the dismissal was automatically unfair under S.99 ERA because Reg 10 MPL Regulations gave her preference over employees who were not on maternity leave and there was a suitable alternative vacancy that could have been offered to her.

If there is no suitable alternative vacancy available, the ordinary rules on dismissal for redundancy apply (see '"Ordinary" unfair dismissal' below) unless the employee was selected for redundancy for a reason related to taking maternity, adoption leave, or shared parental leave – see 'Redundancy for an inadmissible reason – redundancy' below.

12.79 Regulations 10 and 20(1)(b) MPL Regulations, Regs 23 and 29(1)(b) PAL Regulations, and Regs 39 and 43(1)(b) SPL Regulations will render a redundancy dismissal unfair regardless of the fact that the employer acted reasonably in dismissing. The EAT made it clear in Community Task Force v Rimmer 1986 ICR 491, EAT, that the normal 'reasonableness' test contained in S.98(4) ERA does not apply. In that case the employer was a job creation agency funded largely by the Manpower Services Commission (MSC). When R's job became redundant during her maternity leave, the employer wanted to redeploy her to a new job in another division. However, the MSC refused to allow this: its policy was not to allow inter-divisional transfers but to recruit unemployed persons for new jobs. The MSC would have cut funding if the employer had gone ahead with moving R to the new job. The EAT upheld an employment tribunal finding that R had been automatically unfairly dismissed when the employer felt unable to offer her the job in the face of the MSC embargo. The EAT said that Reg 10 is not qualified by any consideration of what is economic or reasonable. The job in question was available and it could not become unavailable because of an eligibility rule imposed by a third party, or even because of the withdrawal of funding by a third party.

Note that these provisions for redundancy during maternity, adoption leave or shared parental leave do not apply to employees on unpaid parental leave, paternity leave or taking time off for dependants. However, employees in these circumstances may be able to claim that the selection for redundancy made the dismissal automatically unfair under Reg 20(2) MPL Regulations or Reg 29(2) PAL Regulations (see 'Redundancy for an inadmissible reason' below), or that the dismissal was unfair under the ordinary unfair dismissal provisions (see '"Ordinary" unfair dismissal' below), or that the dismissal amounted to unlawful discrimination because of sex or maternity/pregnancy (see Chapter 13, 'Discrimination and equal pay').

12.80 Redundancy during maternity leave is discussed further in Chapter 4, 'Returning to work after maternity leave', under 'Redundancy during maternity leave'; redundancy during adoption leave is considered in Chapter 6, 'Adoption leave and pay', under 'Redundancy and adoption leave'; and redundancy during shared parental leave is addressed in Chapter 8, 'Shared parental leave and pay', under 'Employment protection during and after SPL – redundancy during SPL'.

12.81 **Redundancy for an inadmissible reason.** An employee will be regarded as unfairly dismissed under S.99 ERA if the reason or the principal reason for the dismissal is redundancy and it is shown that:

- the circumstances constituting the redundancy applied equally to one or more employees in the same undertaking who held positions similar to that held by the employee and who have not been dismissed by the employer, and

- the reason (or, if more than one, the principal reason) for which the employee was selected for dismissal was a reason of a kind specified in Reg 20(3) MPL Regulations, Reg 29(3) PAL Regulations or Reg 43(3) SPL Regulations (i.e. one of the prescribed – or 'inadmissible' – reasons set out above under 'Automatically unfair dismissal' which relate to pregnancy; childbirth; maternity, unpaid parental, paternity, adoption or shared parental leave; and time off for dependants) – Reg 20(2)/Reg 29(2)/Reg 43(2).

549

In relation to maternity rights, these provisions give statutory effect to the view of the House of Lords in Brown v Stockton-on-Tees Borough Council 1988 ICR 410, HL, that the practical effect of what is now Reg 20(2) is that 'an employer faced with deciding which of several employees to make redundant must disregard the inconvenience that inevitably will result from the fact that one of them is pregnant and will require maternity leave. If the employer does not do so and makes that absence the factor that determines the pregnant woman's dismissal then the dismissal is to be deemed unfair.'

12.82 However, not all employees dismissed as redundant will be able to claim automatically unfair dismissal under S.99. Provided the employee is selected for redundancy for a reason unconnected with the statutory right, the fairness of the dismissal will be judged under S.98(4) in the usual way (see '"Ordinary" unfair dismissal – redundancy' below). For example, it would not be automatically unfair to dismiss where the employee's job ceased to exist and there was no suitable vacancy for him or her. An example:

- **Peppard v Martyn Jessop** ET Case No.1700350/98: the employer's hairdressing business was in financial difficulties. The only employees were P, who was a stylist, and a trainee. P told her employer that she was pregnant and soon afterwards her doctor signed her off work with high blood pressure. The employer realised that it could not keep the business open without staff, so the business was closed down and P was dismissed. An employment tribunal held that P was genuinely redundant. Although her absence was for a pregnancy-related reason, it was merely the trigger for the inevitable closure of the business.

Note, however, that in Flora v George Nares and Co ET Case No.32753/86 the tribunal took the view that when selecting a pregnant woman for redundancy for a reason unconnected with her pregnancy, the employer must take greater care than usual to consult and warn the employee of her impending redundancy because she will be losing her maternity rights.

12.83 Tribunals will pay close attention to any redundancy involving an employee who is exercising, or is about to exercise, any right to a period of statutory leave to ensure that redundancy is the real reason for the dismissal and not a cover for an inadmissible reason. For example, in Intelligent Applications Ltd v Wilson EAT 412/92 W was made redundant following the reallocation of her duties during her absence on maternity leave. An employment tribunal found that there had been a potential redundancy situation in W's department for some time. However, the reallocation of duties had taken place because W had gone on maternity leave – there had been no suggestion that the reorganisation would have taken place at that time for any other reason. The reason for W's dismissal, which was redundancy, had its origins in and was therefore connected with her pregnancy. The EAT upheld this decision on appeal. The stimulus to dealing with the overstaffing situation had been W's decision to take maternity leave and the reorganisation had taken the form which it did because of W's temporary absence from the company. Had the employer decided to deal with the overcapacity without considering the element of W's maternity leave, it was not inevitable that W would have been selected. The tribunal had therefore been entitled to hold that W's pregnancy had led to the decision to make her redundant and to infer a direct connection between the pregnancy and the dismissal.

Asserting a statutory right

12.84

An employee's dismissal may be automatically unfair under S.104 ERA where the reason or the principal reason for the dismissal is that the employee brought proceedings against the employer to enforce a 'relevant statutory right' – S.104(1)(a), or alleged that the employer had infringed such a right – S.104(1)(b). There is no minimum period of qualifying service for a claim under S.104. In the context of the rights covered by this Handbook, the following are included in the definition of a 'relevant statutory right':

- protection from detriment rights in relation to maternity, unpaid parental, paternity, adoption and shared parental leave and time off for dependants – S.47C ERA
- the right to paid time off for ante-natal care – Ss.55 and 56
- the right to accompany a pregnant woman to ante-natal appointments – S.57ZE
- the right to time off to attend adoption appointments – Ss.57ZJ and 57ZL
- the right to time off for dependants – S.57A
- the right to paid maternity suspension and alternative work – Ss.67 and 68
- the right to unpaid parental leave – S.76
- the right to receive a written statement of reasons for dismissal – S.92
- the right not to be unfairly dismissed – S.94
- the right to a redundancy payment – S.135.

Although not covered in this Handbook, a further statutory right that may be asserted in the context of maternity and parental rights is the right to request flexible working, which is also covered by S.104. For details of this right, see IDS Employment Law Handbook, 'Atypical and Flexible Working' (2014), Chapter 4, 'Flexible working'.

Whether or not the employee actually has the right asserted, and whether or **12.85** not the right has actually been infringed, is immaterial provided the employee is acting in good faith – S.104(2). It follows that an employee's genuine but mistaken belief that he or she has the statutory right in question will be enough

551

to found a claim. Thus, an employee who is dismissed because she has tried to take time off for ante-natal care may also be able to claim that she has been dismissed for asserting a statutory right (in addition to any other claim she may have for automatically unfair dismissal for an inadmissible reason). This possibility was raised by a tribunal in Sanders v Hesketh and anor t/a The Phoenix Club ET Case No.2401441/98, although the case was decided on other grounds – see Chapter 1, 'Time off for ante-natal care', under 'Remedies – discrimination', for further details.

For a detailed consideration of the right not to be dismissed for asserting a statutory right, see IDS Employment Law Handbook, 'Unfair Dismissal' (2010), Chapter 12, 'Dismissal for asserting a statutory right'.

12.86 Remedies

An employee who has been unfairly dismissed may seek reinstatement or re-engagement (with no financial loss) or, failing that, an award of compensation. These remedies are discussed in detail in IDS Employment Law Handbook, 'Unfair Dismissal' (2010). An employee who has been made redundant will be entitled to a redundancy payment provided he or she has at least two years' continuous service – see IDS Employment Law Handbook, 'Redundancy' (2008), Chapter 5, 'Qualifications and exclusions', under 'Qualifying service'. Both the basic award of compensation for unfair dismissal and a statutory redundancy payment are assessed according to a well-known statutory formula that is based on the number of completed years of service the claimant has acquired with the employer (up to a maximum of 20) and a multiplicand that varies according to the age of the claimant. The resulting figure is then used to determine how many weeks' pay the claimant is entitled to – for full details, see IDS Employment Law Handbook, 'Redundancy', Chapter 6, 'Redundancy payments', under 'Statutory redundancy pay scheme – formula for calculating statutory redundancy pay'.

Note that for the purposes of calculating a 'week's pay' under Ss.220–229 ERA, where the amount of a week's pay is calculated by reference to the average amount of remuneration paid over a 12-week period, any week during which the employee was absent from work on maternity, parental, paternity or adoption leave, with the result that the remuneration due for that week was less than the amount that would have been payable if he or she had been working, must be disregarded. Instead, account must be taken of remuneration in earlier weeks – Reg 22 MPL Regulations and Reg 31 PAL Regulations. The calculation of a week's pay is explained in IDS Employment Law Handbook, 'Wages' (2011), Chapter 10, 'A week's pay'.

12.87 **Injury to feelings.** Compensation for non-financial losses, including injury to feelings, cannot be awarded in unfair dismissal claims – Dunnachie v Kingston upon Hull City Council 2004 ICR 1052, HL. However, injury to feelings awards may well be available in detriment claims (see 'Right not to suffer detriment – remedies' above) and are certainly available in discrimination claims. Thus, it is rare for a claimant to bring a complaint solely under S.99 ERA.

Written reasons for dismissal

12.88

Article 10(2) of the EU Pregnant Workers Directive (No.92/85) provides that, if a worker is dismissed while she is pregnant or during her maternity leave, the employer 'must cite duly substantiated grounds for her dismissal in writing'. This is enacted in the UK by S.92(4) ERA, which provides that an employee is entitled to a written statement of the reasons for her dismissal if she is dismissed at any time while she is pregnant, or if she is dismissed after childbirth and her maternity leave period ends by reason of her dismissal. This entitlement applies irrespective of the employee's length of service and without her having to request it. A similar provision exists in relation to adoption leave – see S.92(4A) ERA.

If an employer unreasonably fails to provide an employee with written reasons under the above provisions, or if it supplies the employee with inadequate or untrue reasons, the employee may make a complaint to an employment tribunal within three months of the dismissal (although the time limit may be extended if the tribunal finds that it was not reasonably practicable to present the complaint in time or to allow for early conciliation or cross-border mediation). Where the tribunal finds the complaint well founded, it may make a declaration stating what the tribunal has found to be the proper reasons for dismissal and must order the employer to make a payment to the employee of two weeks' pay – S.93 (and S.111). Where an employee has not requested written reasons for dismissal and the employer had no knowledge of the fact that the employee was pregnant at the time of dismissal, it is unlikely that a tribunal would find that an employer had acted unreasonably in failing to supply them.

Employees who are not pregnant or on maternity or adoption leave when they are dismissed are entitled to a written statement of the reasons for their dismissal if they have two years' service and request one. Thus an employee with at least two years' service who is dismissed while on parental or paternity leave is entitled to request a written statement and the employer must provide the statement within 14 days – S.92(1)–(3).

12.89

For full details of the rights under S.92, see IDS Employment Law Handbook, 'Unfair Dismissal' (2010), Chapter 21, 'Written reasons for dismissal'.

'Ordinary' unfair dismissal

12.90

As we have seen under 'Automatically unfair dismissal' above, where an employee is dismissed or made redundant for an inadmissible reason connected with any of the statutory rights outlined in the preceding chapters, the dismissal will be automatically unfair under S.99 ERA and the relevant regulations. There

553

is no minimum service requirement for bringing a claim under S.99, and since such dismissals are automatically unfair, the 'reasonableness' test does not apply.

Where, on the other hand, an employee is dismissed during a period of statutory leave (or during pregnancy, or after returning to work from a period of leave) for reasons unconnected with the statutory right in question, the dismissal is not automatically unfair under S.99. However, the dismissal may still be unfair under the 'ordinary' unfair dismissal provisions contained in S.98 ERA. In an ordinary unfair dismissal claim, various matters have to be established, such as whether or not the complainant has the requisite qualifying service, the reason for the dismissal, and whether or not the employer acted reasonably in dismissing for that reason. These issues are dealt with fully in IDS Employment Law Handbook, 'Unfair Dismissal' (2010), Chapter 3, 'Unfairness'. However, given the peculiar circumstances of an employee on statutory leave, special considerations apply and these are discussed below.

12.91 Qualifying service for unfair dismissal

In order to bring a claim of 'ordinary' unfair dismissal under the ERA (as opposed to automatically unfair dismissal) an employee must have two years' continuous service – S.108(1) ERA.

The ERA applies to England, Wales and Scotland, but not to Northern Ireland, where the equivalent rights are to be found in the Employment Rights (Northern Ireland) Order 1996 SI 1996/1919. The qualifying period for the right to claim unfair dismissal under the Order is one year's continuous service.

12.92 Reason for dismissal and reasonableness

In proceedings for ordinary unfair dismissal, once the employee has established that he or she has the requisite period of continuous service, the employment tribunal must go on to consider the reason for the dismissal and the reasonableness of dismissing for that reason. Certain reasons for dismissal which are connected with pregnancy, childbirth or statutory leave will automatically render the dismissal unfair – see 'Automatically unfair dismissal' above. Here we briefly consider reasons for dismissal that are *potentially* fair.

An employer seeking to defend a claim of unfair dismissal must show that the reason for dismissal was one of the potentially fair reasons contained in S.98(1) and (2) – i.e. that it related to capability, conduct, retirement, redundancy or statutory restriction, or was for 'some other substantial reason of a kind such as to justify the dismissal of an employee holding the position which the employee held' (SOSR). A tribunal does not have to accept an employer's stated reason for dismissal if the evidence points to a different reason. For example, in James v Hillyards Removals ET Case No.1200887/98 J, who was pregnant, took three days off work because of sickness. On her return she was dismissed for redundancy. Someone had moved into her office after she left and the tribunal was satisfied that the only reason for the dismissal was J's pregnancy and resulting sickness absence.

Common reasons put forward by employers for dismissing an employee while **12.93** he or she is on a period of family leave are conduct, SOSR and redundancy. These are dealt with briefly below. For a more detailed discussion, see IDS Employment Law Handbook, 'Unfair Dismissal' (2010), Chapter 6, 'Conduct', and Chapter 8, 'Some other substantial reason'; and IDS Employment Law Handbook, 'Redundancy' (2011).

Note in this context that Reg 17(a)(iii) MPL Regulations provides that employees are entitled to the benefit of any terms relating to disciplinary procedures during unpaid parental leave. (Employees taking ordinary or additional maternity leave, ordinary or additional adoption leave, paternity leave, shared parental leave and time off for dependants need no special protection, since terms relating to disciplinary procedures will continue to apply in the normal way during the period of leave.) This means that employers are expected to carry out their normal disciplinary procedures in respect of employees who are on unpaid parental leave. However, the Regulations do not specify whether employees are required to give up leave time in order to attend disciplinary hearings. Presumably, whether or not an employer is acting reasonably in insisting that an employee return from leave in order to attend a disciplinary hearing will depend on the facts of each particular case.

Conduct during leave. Employees remain bound by certain contractual **12.94** obligations during periods of statutory leave. (The full extent of an employee's obligations is discussed in the relevant chapter relating to the particular type of leave question – see Chapter 3, 'Maternity leave'; Chapter 6, 'Adoption leave and pay'; Chapter 7, 'Paternity leave and pay'; Chapter 8, 'Shared parental leave and pay'; and Chapter 10, 'Unpaid parental leave'.) If an employee fails to honour his or her obligations during the leave period, the employee will be in breach of contract and the employer may have grounds to dismiss. If the reason for the dismissal is the employee's conduct, then the fairness of the dismissal will fall to be considered under the ordinary unfair dismissal provisions.

Conduct on return to work. Employers need to tread carefully when dismissing **12.95** an employee shortly after his or her return from a period of statutory leave because the employee concerned will almost certainly argue that the fact that he or she took leave was the real reason for the dismissal. For example, in Indans v Merit Ice Cream Ltd ET Case No.2305027/98 – a sex discrimination case – I was dismissed two days after she returned from maternity leave. Her employer maintained that she was dismissed because of poor work performance but I argued that she was dismissed because she had taken maternity leave. An employment tribunal found that I had indeed been dismissed for poor performance but, if she had not taken maternity leave, her employer would have addressed the problem at the time it arose. The tribunal held that I had suffered sex discrimination in that she was not given a proper opportunity to improve. It is almost certain that the dismissal would also have been unfair if I had brought her claim under that head.

12.96 **Some other substantial reason.** Employers occasionally dismiss staff who are on leave simply because they find the employee's replacement more suitable, and then argue that the dismissal is for SOSR. However, tribunals are unlikely to accept such arguments since the dismissal is nevertheless connected with the employee's reason for being absent – pregnancy or maternity, unpaid parental, shared parental, paternity or adoption leave, as the case may be – and is therefore automatically unfair. Furthermore, tribunals are reluctant to deny employees their statutory right to return even though the enforcement of that right means the dismissal of the replacement employee. In Rees v Apollo Watch Repairs plc 1996 ICR 466, EAT, a woman was refused the right to return after her maternity leave as the employer found her replacement more efficient. The EAT held that the refusal amounted to unlawful sex discrimination. (It would also have been an unfair dismissal.) The effective reason for the employee's dismissal was pregnancy since, but for her absence through pregnancy, the unfavourable comparison with her replacement would not have arisen.

(Note that the dismissal of replacement employees is discussed in Chapter 14, 'Replacement employees'.)

12.97 ## Redundancy
As we have seen under 'Automatically unfair dismissal – automatically unfair redundancy' above, special provision is made where an employee's job becomes redundant while he or she is absent on maternity, adoption or shared parental leave: the employee is entitled to be offered suitable alternative employment if such employment exists – Reg 10 MPL Regulations, Reg 23 PAL Regulations and Reg 39 SPL Regulations. If the employer fails to comply with this obligation the dismissal will be automatically unfair. Similarly, if an employee is dismissed for redundancy and the reason for his or her selection was one of the inadmissible reasons connected with pregnancy, childbirth or any of the statutory periods of leave, the dismissal will be automatically unfair – Reg 20(2) MPL Regulations, Reg 29(2) PAL Regulations, Reg 43(2) SPL Regulations. However, where an employer cannot comply with Reg 10, Reg 23 or Reg 39 because he has no suitable alternative employment, or if the dismissal is not for one of the inadmissible reasons, the ordinary rules on dismissal for redundancy apply.

In order to successfully defend a claim of unfair dismissal for redundancy, the employer must show that the employee was genuinely redundant within the statutory definition contained in S.139(1) ERA – i.e. that the employer has closed the business or ceased operations at the employee's workplace or that the requirement for employees to do work of a particular kind has diminished. If the employer fails to show this, the dismissal will be unfair because no reason for it has been established.

Two examples: **12.98**

- **Wilkinson v Addleshaw Booth and Co** ET Case No.2402991/98: while W, a part-time librarian, was on maternity leave her employer decided to appoint an information services manager and incorporate W's duties into this post. W was due to return to work on 29 June and was dismissed as redundant with effect from 2 July. The employment tribunal accepted that there was no other suitable job that could have been offered to W but held that the dismissal was unfair because, at the time she was dismissed, she was not genuinely redundant. The new post had not been filled and her old job was still available

- **Cochrane v Shaw Group UK Ltd** ET Case No.1305403/98: in May C informed her employer that she was pregnant and that her baby was expected in November. In July there was a significant downturn in business and the employer announced that operations in Wolverhampton, where C worked, were to close and that any remaining work would be transferred to the Derby premises. It was intended that C would continue in employment until the end of October, when the move was to take place, or the beginning of her maternity leave, whichever was the sooner. She would then be considered for alternative employment in Derby. C became ill with a pregnancy-related condition at the beginning of August. The employer decided to bring forward her redundancy to 31 August because it was thought she would be unable to return to work. C's dismissal was held to be unfair because her redundancy was brought forward only because she was pregnant. She was not genuinely redundant at the time of the dismissal.

Once an employer has established redundancy as the reason for dismissal under **12.99** S.98(1) and (2) ERA, a tribunal must go on to determine whether it acted reasonably in treating that reason as a sufficient reason for dismissal within the terms of S.98(4). Two examples:

- **Tanner v Amlin Corporate Services** ET Case No.1102370/06: during her maternity leave, T asked to return to work on a phased basis, building up to full-time working after four months. ACS decided it could not agree to her request as customers strongly preferred continuity in the customer services function. ACS had carried out a review of the customer services function during T's absence and concluded that there was no longer a requirement for a dedicated customer services team and T was made redundant as a result. An employment tribunal held that T's post was genuinely redundant, there was no suitable alternative vacancy, and the dismissal was not unfair

557

- **Linkinson-Cole v Glenfield Hospital NHS Trust** ET Case No.1901861/97: a cost-cutting exercise was carried out while L-C, a grade H nurse, was on maternity leave. 12 posts, including L-C's, were identified as probably no longer justified. There were two nurses working in L-C's field, L-C herself and a nurse on a lower grade, and it was decided that only one should be retained. L-C was made redundant. An employment tribunal accepted that there was a redundancy situation but held that L-C's dismissal was unfair because the employer had assumed that the remaining post had to be offered to the nurse on the lower grade and had not sought L-C's views on the matter.

12.100 Selection for redundancy must be carried out fairly and consultation is an integral part of a fair procedure. The fact that an employee is absent from work is no excuse for a failure to consult him or her. Two examples:

- **Waite v Thomassen UK Ltd** ET Case No.1900285/98: W's duties as office administrator were redistributed after a restructuring and her job disappeared as a result. She was not consulted until the day before she went on maternity leave and consultation took the form of a ten-minute meeting. A post arose while she was on maternity leave and an external candidate was appointed. W would have been appointed had she not been absent on maternity leave. When she returned, it was clear that her employer had not really expected her to come back and she found herself in a subordinate position. She resigned and successfully claimed unfair constructive dismissal. The fact that she was absent when the new post arose was no excuse for not consulting her

- **Blatt v North and anor** ET Case No.2301667/96: B and her employer were involved in negotiations over the terms of the renewal of B's fixed-term contract while she was on maternity leave. The employer had wanted to include a waiver of unfair dismissal and redundancy rights, but B would not agree and the clause was eventually removed. When B returned to work she was increasingly sidelined in favour of her assistant, H. A few months later there was a restructuring exercise and B and H applied for the same post. H was successful and B was made redundant. A tribunal found that B was dismissed because of the restructuring, not because of her pregnancy, but held that the dismissal was unfair because there had been no consultation with her.

12.101 Although an employer must not treat an employee who is pregnant or absent on maternity leave (or any other form of statutory leave) any less favourably than other employees, it does not have to give the employee preferential treatment. All an employer has to do is show that its selection of the employee for redundancy would have been fair if he or she had not been pregnant/absent from work. In Cunningham v Hillingdon Shirt Co Ltd ET Case No.9922/79, for example, C was told during her maternity leave that she was redundant and could not return. She argued that she should not have been selected because more junior staff had been retained. However, prior to starting her maternity leave, C had been given a final warning for being a disruptive influence in her department. The tribunal held that C was fairly dismissed. She would have been selected even if she had not been on maternity leave.

The consideration of alternative employment will also be relevant to the reasonableness of a redundancy dismissal. So for example, in Cochrane v Shaw Group UK Ltd (above), if the employer had followed the original plan and allowed C to continue in employment until the date of the closure of her workplace and had then considered alternative employment in Derby, her dismissal might not have been unfair even if there had been no suitable work for her to do there. (As mentioned above, special provisions apply where the employee is dismissed during maternity leave and there is a suitable alternative vacancy – see Reg 10 MPL Regulations.)

If a redundant employee unreasonably refuses an offer of suitable alternative **12.102** employment, the dismissal will almost certainly be fair and he or she will lose his or her right to a redundancy payment – S.141(2) ERA. If there is no suitable vacancy and if the employee is genuinely redundant, then the employee will normally be entitled to a redundancy payment, provided he or she has the requisite two years' qualifying service. Redundancy pay claims must be brought within six months of the dismissal – S.164 ERA.

For a full discussion of the law on redundancy, see IDS Employment Law Handbook, 'Redundancy' (2011).

13 Discrimination and equal pay

As we have seen in the preceding chapters, there is now an extensive body of **13.1** maternity and parental rights in the UK, and the Employment Rights Act 1996 (ERA) provides protection from detriment and dismissal for those who exercise such rights. However, as demonstrated in this chapter, the protection afforded by discrimination law is equally – arguably more – important.

Preliminary matters
13.2

For a long time, the two principal sources of anti-discrimination law that had a bearing on maternity and parental rights were the Equal Pay Act 1970 (EqPA) and the Sex Discrimination Act 1975 (SDA). Although both were introduced with the intention of narrowing the gender pay gap and eliminating widespread discrimination against women, for many years neither contained any provisions that directly referred to pregnancy or maternity leave. Instead, the majority of measures specifically aimed at protecting pregnant women and new mothers were, and to a large extent still are, to be found in the ERA.

The fact that the SDA and the EqPA made no special provision for pregnant women did not, however, prevent a copious body of case law being developed dealing with the protection of such women against discrimination on the ground of their sex. As a result, by the start of the 21st century, pregnancy and maternity could be regarded as a distinct branch of anti-discrimination law, or as a separate ground of direct discrimination. These case law developments were, in effect, codified in 2005 when the SDA was amended to include a specific provision dealing with discrimination on the grounds of pregnancy and maternity leave.

13.3 The Equality Act 2010 (EqA) repealed the SDA and the EqPA on 1 October 2010, replacing both statutes with equivalent provisions designed to protect against sex discrimination, pregnancy and maternity discrimination, and gender pay inequality. The EqA was introduced with the purpose of harmonising discrimination law, removing inconsistencies between the different strands and strengthening the law in certain respects. However, the basic structure of discrimination law remains, so that cases decided under the former statutes will continue to be relevant and are referred to throughout this chapter.

The main focus of this chapter is the impact of the specific provision protecting women from discrimination because of pregnancy and maternity, and how this overlaps with the general concepts of direct and indirect sex discrimination. But the application of discrimination law in this area is not restricted to pregnant women and those on maternity leave. Since many parents request, and are granted, part-time working or other flexible working arrangements in order to cope with the demands of family life, we also consider the ways in which women and men who seek family-friendly forms of working are protected by anti-discrimination laws. In addition, we consider how the law relating to equal pay can underpin an employee's contractual rights while on maternity leave. But first, by way of background, we provide a short introduction to the relevant legislation, both domestic and European.

13.4 Note that in this chapter, for ease of reference, we talk about discrimination against employees by employers. However, protection from discrimination extends to a wider class of worker than just employees, including contract workers, barristers, partners and crown employees. For a full analysis of the extent of the protection offered by discrimination law, see IDS Employment Law Handbook, 'Discrimination at Work' (2012), Chapter 28, 'Liability of employers, employees and agents', and Chapter 29, 'Liability of other bodies'.

13.5 Overview of relevant UK and European law

This section describes in outline the key legislative measures and case law – domestic and European – that govern discrimination in the context of the exercise of family-friendly rights.

13.6 **Equality Act 2010 – discrimination, harassment and victimisation.** The EqA – which, as noted above, has replaced the specific provisions of the SDA and EqPA – provides protection against discrimination in employment in relation to recruitment, promotion, transfer, training, the provision of facilities and access to benefits, or in relation to dismissal or any other detriment – S.39. Discrimination is prohibited in relation to certain 'protected characteristics', listed at S.4, which include sex, pregnancy and maternity, and marriage and civil partnership.

562

The two main forms of discrimination outlawed are:

- *direct discrimination* – where an employer treats a person less favourably because of a 'protected characteristic' than it treats or would treat others – S.13 EqA. The employer's motives are irrelevant if the treatment is based on a protected characteristic and any underlying good intentions will not make the treatment lawful. The issue of justifiability does not arise where there is direct discrimination. Direct discrimination covers treatment on the grounds of, among other things, sex and pregnancy and maternity. There is also specific protection from pregnancy and maternity discrimination under S.18. All these forms of discrimination are discussed under 'Direct discrimination' below

- *indirect discrimination* – where an employer applies to a person a 'provision, criterion or practice' (PCP) that it applies or would apply equally to others, but which puts or would put those with a particular protected characteristic at a particular disadvantage when compared with those who do not share that protected characteristic, and which puts the person at that disadvantage. Such treatment is unlawful if the employer cannot show the PCP to be a proportionate means of achieving a legitimate aim – S.19 EqA. Note that pregnancy and maternity are not 'protected characteristics' for the purpose of indirect discrimination (although sex is) – S.19(3). Indirect sex discrimination is discussed under 'Indirect sex discrimination' below.

Although the concepts of discrimination outlined above refer to employers, the **13.7** rights under the EqA are of broader application than those under the ERA. S.83(2) EqA provides that employment is defined as 'employment under a contract of service, a contract of apprenticeship or a contract personally to do work'. As a result of this wide definition, most 'workers' (i.e. those employed under a contract of personal service as well as those employed under a contract of employment) will be covered by the EqA. In addition, various non-employment but employment-like relationships are covered by the EqA, including the holding of an office, partnership in a law firm and membership of a barristers' chambers. However, the right to ordinary and additional maternity leave is confined to 'employees' only – S.230(1) ERA – with the result that non-employees (i.e. those who are *not* employed under a contract of employment) are only entitled to special protection under S.18 during their pregnancy and for the two weeks immediately following the end of their pregnancy. A similar restriction applies to the rights to paternity leave and pay, adoption leave and pay, shared parental leave and pay, unpaid parental leave, time off for dependants, time off for ante-natal care and the right to request flexible working.

Note that S.17 EqA prohibits discrimination on the grounds of pregnancy or maternity in the provision of goods and services as well as in the exercise of public functions, education and associations. The issues that this raises are beyond the scope of this Handbook.

563

13.8 *Harassment.* Section 26 EqA contains a specific provision outlawing harassment in respect of all the protected characteristics except pregnancy and maternity and marriage and civil partnership. S.26(1) provides that an employer harasses a person if it engages in unwanted conduct 'related to a relevant protected characteristic' – such as sex – *and* the conduct has the purpose or effect of:

- violating that person's dignity, or

- creating an intimidating, hostile, degrading, humiliating or offensive environment for that person.

Unwanted conduct 'of a sexual nature' is expressly covered in S.26(2) if it has the purpose or effect referred to above. In addition, an employer will also subject a person to harassment if, on the ground of that person's rejection of or submission to unwanted conduct of a sexual nature or unwanted conduct related to sex, it treats that person less favourably than it would treat him or her had he or she not rejected, or submitted to, the conduct – S.26(3). Harassment is discussed in greater detail under 'Harassment' below.

13.9 *Victimisation.* Section 27(1) EqA makes it unlawful for an employer to subject a person to a detriment because that person does (or the employer believes that person has done or may do) a protected act. The following are 'protected acts' for the purpose of S.27(1):

- bringing proceedings under the EqA

- giving evidence or information in connection with proceedings under the EqA

- doing any other thing for the purposes of or in connection with the EqA, and

- making an allegation (whether or not express) that the employer or another person has contravened the EqA – S.27(2).

This provision is intended to protect an individual from suffering adverse consequences as a result of making complaints of discrimination or harassment, whether during employment or after it has ended. For further details, see IDS Employment Law Handbook, 'Discrimination at Work' (2012), Chapter 19, 'Victimisation'.

13.10 *Compensation.* In Chapter 12, 'Detriment and unfair dismissal', we outline the provisions in the ERA that are designed to protect employees from dismissal and detriment on account of their having exercised maternity or parental rights. However, as pointed out frequently in that chapter, it is commonplace for a claim under the ERA to be brought alongside a discrimination claim. The primary reason for this concerns the remedies that are available to a successful claimant. Unlike in cases of 'ordinary' unfair dismissal, there is no statutory cap on the amount of compensation that can be awarded upon a finding of discrimination – a claimant can recover the full extent of his or her economic losses. In addition, a claimant who has been discriminated against can recover damages for 'injury to feelings'. Under the guidelines established in Vento v Chief Constable of West Yorkshire Police 2003 ICR 318, CA, and since updated by the EAT in Da'Bell v NSPCC 2010 IRLR 19, EAT, such awards should range from £600 in the least serious cases to £30,000 in the most serious.

The size of the award for injury to feelings depends on the facts of each case and the degree of hurt, distress and humiliation caused to the complainant by the discrimination. In Touati v Root Success Ltd ET Case No.2318259/10, for example, a tribunal awarded £10,000 for injury to feelings to an employee who was warned about a potential restructuring only hours after informing the employer of her pregnancy and who was made redundant without any consultation shortly thereafter. The tribunal found that the employer contrived the need for an urgent restructuring of the business as a pretext for dismissing her swiftly once it knew that she was pregnant. Similarly, in Stone v Ramsay Health Care UK Operations Ltd ET Case No.1400762/11 a tribunal decided that pregnancy and maternity discrimination suffered by an employee over a nine-month period merited an award for injury to feelings of £18,000. The tribunal's many criticisms of the employer's treatment of the employee during her maternity leave included its failure to inform her of the nature of a colleague's grievance against her (the colleague had taken umbrage at her failure to respond to work queries while she was on compulsory maternity leave), to agree 'keeping-in-touch' (KIT) days as requested by her or to include her in the annual pay review.

13.11 *Time limits.* Another aspect of discrimination law that differs from that under the ERA is the basis on which an extension to the time limit for bringing a claim may be granted. While, for example, a claim of detriment under S.47C ERA and a claim under the EqA both have a time limit of three months (subject to the early conciliation and cross-border mediation rules), the employment tribunal's discretion to extend time beyond that limit is more restricted under the ERA – a tribunal can only do so where it was 'not reasonably practicable' for the claimant to have brought the claim in time. In contrast, under the EqA a tribunal may extend the time limit to 'such other period as the employment tribunal thinks just and equitable' – S.123(1)(b). For an extensive discussion of the circumstances in which tribunals can and have exercised this discretion, see IDS Employment Law Handbook, 'Discrimination at Work' (2012), Chapter 34, 'Enforcing individual rights', under 'Time limits – extension of time limits', and IDS Employment Law Handbook, 'Employment Tribunal Practice and Procedure' (2014), Chapter 5, 'Time limits', under '"Just and equitable" extension – extension of time in discrimination cases'.

13.12 **Equality Act 2010 – equal pay.** The right to gender equality in contractual terms was introduced by the EqPA in 1975 and is now found in Chapter 3 of

Part 5 of the EqA, headed 'Equality of terms'. Briefly, these provisions are designed to ensure that the terms in a woman's contract of employment are not less favourable than those enjoyed by a comparable man unless the difference is due to a material factor, reliance on which does not involve direct or unjustified indirect discrimination. A comparable man in these circumstances is a man employed 'in the same employment' in:

- like work
- work rated as equivalent, or
- work of equal value – S.1 EqPA.

If the woman succeeds in her equal pay claim, her contract is deemed to be modified by means of a 'sex equality clause' so that it ceases to be less favourable than her comparator's contract.

13.13   The EqA also includes a 'maternity equality clause' (Ss.72–74) that enshrines, among other things, a woman's right to benefit from pay rises in the calculation of her contractual maternity pay, subject to certain conditions. There is no need to show equal work with a comparator.

As a general rule, the EqPA covered discriminatory contractual terms, while the SDA covered discrimination in the formation, operation, variation and termination of the contract – e.g. recruitment, non-contractual benefits, promotion and dismissal. It was not possible for a woman to use the SDA to complain about discriminatory contractual terms. This distinction is maintained by the EqA, so that a woman who wishes to complain of discriminatory contractual terms in relation to pregnancy and maternity must complain under the 'equal pay' provisions, namely Ss.64–80. We discuss these provisions in greater detail under 'Equal pay' below.

13.14   **Part-time Workers Regulations.** In July 2000 the provisions of the Part-time Workers (Prevention of Less Favourable Treatment) Regulations 2000 SI 2000/1551 came into force, giving part-time workers the right not to be treated less favourably than full-time workers unless that treatment is justified. These Regulations are of benefit to both women and men who have reduced their hours to accommodate childcare responsibilities – see 'Discrimination against part-time workers' below.

13.15   **Other family-friendly measures.** A number of legislative measures are aimed at making it easier for parents to combine work and childcare commitments, two of which will be referred to at various times throughout this chapter. They are the statutory right to request flexible working and the new scheme on shared parental leave. In IDS Employment Law Handbook, 'Atypical and Flexible Working' (2012), Chapter 4, 'Flexible working', we discuss the right to request flexible working which, since 30 June 2014, is available to all employees who have at least 26 weeks' continuous employment with the employer. However, it remains particularly useful for parents who wish to apply for flexible working patterns to help them balance their work and family life.

Parents of children born on or after 5 April 2015 also have the option of taking shared parental leave, provided the child's mother ends her maternity leave early. Under the scheme, parents can share up to 50 weeks of leave between them (except for the two weeks of compulsory maternity leave which must be taken by the mother) and they can decide whether they wish to take leave at separate times or together. Shared parental leave replaced additional paternity leave, which allowed eligible employees (usually fathers) the right to take up to six months' leave to care for a child if the child's mother returned to work without exercising her full entitlement to maternity leave. The shared parental leave scheme, which is also available to adoptive parents who end adoption leave early, is discussed in detail in Chapter 8, 'Shared parental leave and pay'.

European anti-discrimination legislation. The impact of European law in **13.16** this area has been significant, and it is therefore useful to be aware of the main anti-discrimination provisions emanating from Brussels. The most important of these is Article 157 of the Treaty on the Functioning of the European Union (TFEU) (formerly Article 141, and before that Article 119, of the EC Treaty), which embodies the principle of 'equal pay for equal work'. In addition, there is the recast EU Equal Treatment Directive (No.2006/54) ('the recast Equal Treatment Directive'), which relates to 'the implementation of the principle of equal opportunities and equal treatment of men and women in matters of employment and occupation'. This Directive consolidated seven different Directives dealing with gender equality, including the EU Equal Treatment Directive (No.76/207) and the EU Equal Pay Directive (No.75/117), although this is more often seen as a footnote to Article 157 than as a distinct measure in its own right. The seven consolidated Directives were repealed with effect from 15 August 2009 and references to those Directives elsewhere in EU legislation are now to be read as referring to the relevant part of the recast Directive.

The supremacy of EU law over national law means that Article 157 will always take precedence over national discrimination legislation (now contained in the EqA) and any employee can rely on that Article directly even if this means disapplying a provision of the national legislation. This is the doctrine of 'direct effect'. Where the employer is a 'public body' such as a government department or an NHS Trust, the terms of the EU Directives will also have direct effect and overrule inconsistent provisions of national law. Where the employer is not a public body, the national legislation must be interpreted by courts and tribunals whenever possible so as to comply with the Directives – see further IDS Employment Law Handbook, 'Discrimination at Work' (2012), Chapter 2, 'European discrimination law', under 'Indirect effect'.

13.17 In this context, it is important also to bear in mind the terms of the EU Pregnant Workers Directive (No.92/85) ('the Pregnant Workers Directive'). Although this Directive is, strictly speaking, separate from the main corpus of European anti-discrimination legislation, as it was introduced as a health and safety measure, this has not stopped the courts from referring to it when determining how the anti-discrimination legislation should be applied to women who are pregnant or on maternity leave. This is particularly true of equal pay claims brought before the European Court of Justice (ECJ) under Article 157, where the effect of the Pregnant Workers Directive has generally been to reduce the scope for women on maternity leave to claim equality of entitlement with male and female colleagues not on maternity leave – see, in particular, Gillespie and ors v Northern Health and Social Services Board and ors 1996 ICR 498, ECJ (discussed under 'Equal pay' below).

13.18 **European Convention on Human Rights.** Since the Human Rights Act 1998 came into force on 2 October 2000, claimants have been able to assert their rights under the European Convention on Human Rights (ECHR) in UK courts and employment tribunals. Article 8(1) of the Convention guarantees the right to respect for private and family life, and Article 14 provides that the enjoyment of the rights and freedoms under the Convention 'shall be secured without discrimination on any ground'. As a result, case law emanating from the European Court of Human Rights (ECtHR) on the scope of the Convention is pertinent when considering discrimination in the context of maternity and parental rights.

In Topcic-Rosenberg v Croatia 2013 ECHR 1131, ECtHR, T-R, a businesswoman, adopted a three-year-old-child in October 2006. Thereafter, she submitted a request to the Zagreb office of the Croatian Health Insurance Fund to establish her right to paid maternity leave. At that point in time, Croatian law (namely the 'Maternity Leave Act' and the 'Labour Act') provided that a woman could take maternity leave 45 days before the expected date of childbirth and could remain on such leave until the child's first birthday. However, although it went on to state that 'all rights guaranteed under this Act are applicable under equal conditions to an adoptive parent', the Maternity Leave Act did not specify how those rights should be applied in the event that a child was adopted *after* its first birthday. In these circumstances, the Fund construed the legislation to mean that, as her child was over one when adopted, T-R had no right to paid maternity leave. After appealing unsuccessfully to the Administrative Court and the Constitutional Court, T-R took her case to the ECtHR, arguing, among other things, that as an adoptive mother she had been discriminated against in respect of her right to maternity leave contrary to Article 14 read in conjunction with Article 8.

13.19 The Court noted that Article 14 complements the other substantive provisions of the ECHR and its Protocols. Although it has no independent existence, since it has effect solely in relation to 'the enjoyment of rights and freedoms' safeguarded by the Convention, it applies to those additional rights falling within the general scope of any Convention Article which a state had voluntarily decided to provide. The Court added that a difference in treatment was discriminatory if it had no objective and reasonable justification; in other words, if it did not pursue a legitimate aim or if there was no reasonable relationship of proportionality between the means employed and the aim sought to be realised. Applying those principles, the ECtHR held that a relationship arising from lawful and genuine adoption may be deemed sufficient to attract respect for family life under Article 8; that Article 14, taken with Article 8, applied to the issue concerning maternity leave and related allowances; and that, accordingly, if a state decided to create a parental or maternity leave scheme, it had to do so in a manner that was compatible with Article 14. In the instant case, the ECtHR reasoned that the Croatian authorities had interpreted the Maternity Leave Act in an 'excessively formal and inflexible' manner, and had ignored the general principle recognised under the Labour Act that the position of a biological mother at the time of birth corresponded to an adoptive mother's position immediately after adoption. Accordingly, as the Court could discern no objective and reasonable justification for the difference in treatment between T-R and a biological mother, it considered that that difference amounted to discrimination.

The right to respect for private and family life enshrined in Article 8 has also been successfully relied on to establish that men have the same entitlement as women to participate in a parental leave scheme provided by a Member State. In Markin v Russia 56 EHRR 8, ECtHR, M, a radio intelligence operator in the Russian military, was the sole carer for his three children. Under the Russian Labour Code, women and men were entitled to three years' parental leave. However, under the Russian Military Service Act, only female military personnel were entitled to parental leave in accordance with the Labour Code. M asked the head of his military unit for three years' parental leave to look after his children but his request was refused.

Having exhausted domestic legal avenues, M applied to the ECtHR, alleging **13.20** that the refusal to grant him parental leave breached his rights under Articles 8 and 14 of the Convention. A majority of the Court upheld his application. According to the Court, parental leave and parental allowances promote family life and Article 8 was therefore engaged. Although that Article did not include a right to parental leave or impose any positive obligation on states to provide parental leave allowances, if a state decided to create a parental leave scheme, it must to do so in a manner compatible with the prohibition on discrimination laid down in Article 14. The Court accepted that states have a wide margin of discretion when it comes to justifying discriminatory treatment. However, no such justification was provided in M's case. The Court stressed that parental leave was intended to enable the parent concerned to stay at home to look after

569

the child, and that men and women were similarly placed to take on that role. In contrast with maternity leave, which was intended to enable the woman to recover from childbirth and to breastfeed her baby, men and women were in an analogous situation in so far as parental leave was concerned. The difference in treatment could not therefore be justified by reference to the special role of women in raising children. Nor did the Court accept that, as many more men than women were in the military, denying men this right was necessary for the operational effectiveness of the army. Accordingly, the exclusion of male military personnel from the entitlement to parental leave on the ground of their sex was not objectively justified.

13.21 Direct discrimination

The EqA contains a number of prohibitions on various forms of sex and pregnancy-related discrimination which are intended to have much the same cumulative effect as those previously contained in the SDA. S.13 EqA sets out a 'general' prohibition on direct discrimination, which occurs where A treats B less favourably than it treats or would treat others 'because of a protected characteristic'. The protected characteristics are listed in S.4 and include 'sex' and 'pregnancy and maternity'. It follows that a claim of direct sex discrimination should be brought under S.13 as a claim of discrimination 'because of sex'. It is generally accepted that this is not significantly different to the right to bring a claim of sex discrimination under the SDA, which used slightly different terminology. For detailed analysis of the protection from direct discrimination under the EqA, see IDS Employment Law Handbook, 'Discrimination at Work' (2012), Chapter 15, 'Direct discrimination'.

The combined wording of Ss.4 and 13 EqA suggests that direct discrimination 'because of' pregnancy and maternity is also caught. However, this must be considered in the light of S.18, which creates a specific form of direct pregnancy and maternity discrimination (and is effectively the successor to S.3A SDA). S.18 provides that an employer (A) discriminates against a woman if, in the 'protected period' in relation to a pregnancy of hers, A treats her unfavourably:

- because of the pregnancy – S.18(2)(a), or

- because of illness suffered by her as a result of it – S.18(2)(b).

13.22 The 'protected period', in relation to a woman's pregnancy, starts when the pregnancy begins and, if she has the right to ordinary and additional maternity leave, ends either at the end of additional maternity leave or when she returns to work, if earlier – S.18(6)(a). If the woman does not have the right to ordinary and additional maternity leave, then the protected period lasts until the end of the period of two weeks beginning with the end of the pregnancy – S.18(6)(b). (Note that it now appears to be technically possible for a woman to choose to end her maternity leave early – and with it her protected period – without immediately returning to work. This seems to be the effect of the shared parental leave scheme, which applies to children born on or after 5 April 2015 and is discussed further under 'Pregnancy and maternity discrimination – protected period' below.)

Section 18 goes on to provide that it is also pregnancy and maternity discrimination against a woman if A treats her unfavourably:

- because she is on compulsory maternity leave – S.18(3), or

- because she is exercising or seeking to exercise, or has exercised or sought to exercise, the right to ordinary or additional maternity leave – S.18(4).

Note that, in these instances, there is no limitation to treatment occurring during a protected period.

The key difference between the special protection from pregnancy and maternity **13.23** discrimination in S.18 and the general protection from direct discrimination under S.13 is that S.18 does not require that a complainant compare the way she has been treated with the way a comparator has been or would have been treated. This comparator, who may be real or hypothetical, must be in circumstances that are not materially different to those of the complainant for the purpose of a S.13 claim – S.23(1). In contrast, S.18 requires simply that the complainant show she has been treated 'unfavourably' – no question of comparison arises. This recognises the fact – as confirmed by ECJ case law – that pregnancy is a condition unique to women, such that it makes no sense for a claimant to be required to compare her treatment with the treatment that would have been afforded to a man in similar circumstances.

Relationship between Ss.13 and 18 EqA. The question that then arises is, **13.24** how do the specific provisions on pregnancy and maternity discrimination interact with the general prohibition on direct discrimination laid down by S.13? The first thing to note is that there is a clear intention that, if a claim can be brought under S.18, it should be. S.18(7) stipulates that no claim of direct sex discrimination may be made under S.13 based on treatment of a woman that falls within S.18. The effect of this provision is that discrimination during the protected period of a woman's pregnancy and discrimination based on maternity leave should be addressed under S.18 and should not be framed instead as a direct sex discrimination claim under S.13. This interpretation also chimes with S.25(5), which states that 'pregnancy and maternity discrimination is discrimination within... S.18'. However, a claim for direct sex discrimination under S.13 will be available for pregnancy and maternity cases that fall outside the scope of the special protection in S.18 – for example, because the alleged discrimination takes place outside the protected period, or stems from an incorrect perception that a woman is pregnant, or from the claimant's association with a pregnant woman. In such cases the comparator approach will, on the face of it, apply. However, it is questionable whether this accords

571

with EU law, at least in a case where the treatment complained of is based on pregnancy (or perceived pregnancy) as distinct from the consequences of pregnancy (such as a pregnancy-related illness extending beyond the protected period of the woman's maternity leave).

It is notable that, as well as prohibiting direct sex discrimination, S.13 appears to cover direct discrimination because of the protected characteristic of pregnancy and maternity. This follows from the fact that S.13(1) refers to less favourable treatment 'because of a protected characteristic', and pregnancy and maternity appear in the list of protected characteristics in S.4. It is curious that, in a case falling within S.18, S.18(7) disapplies S.13 only 'so far as relating to *sex* discrimination' (our stress); it does not also expressly preclude a S.13 claim based on the protected characteristic of pregnancy and maternity. On the face of it, therefore, there is nothing to prevent a S.18 claimant from also bringing a S.13 claim of direct discrimination because of pregnancy or maternity, as distinct from sex – although, given that S.13 requires a comparator whereas S.18 does not, it is unclear what she would gain from doing so. This is a surprising conclusion and it is far from clear that this was the Government's intention. For a fuller discussion of the point, see IDS Employment Law Handbook, 'Discrimination at Work', Chapter 15, 'Direct discrimination', under 'Protected characteristics covered by S.13'.

13.25 **Case law decided under the SDA.** As noted in the introduction to this chapter, the preponderance of case law governing pregnancy and maternity discrimination was decided before the EqA came into force and generally pre-dates the introduction of specific prohibitions against pregnancy and maternity discrimination in 2005. However, as the introduction of S.3A SDA in 2005 was intended, for the most part, to consolidate the developments in case law in this area, these cases remain relevant, as do the general principles set down by European case law.

13.26 Pregnancy and maternity discrimination

As noted above, the most striking difference between the concept of direct discrimination under S.13 and pregnancy and maternity discrimination under S.18 is that the latter does not require a comparator – a woman who alleges she has been discriminated against on the ground of pregnancy or maternity need not compare her treatment with a man in similar circumstances (e.g. one whose attendance is erratic or who requires a lengthy period of absence for an operation) or with a woman who is not pregnant. The lack of a need for a comparator reflects the jurisprudence of the ECJ, which had for many years resulted in employment tribunals interpreting S.1(2)(a) SDA (the original provision outlawing direct sex discrimination) as not requiring a comparator in pregnancy and maternity discrimination cases, despite the statutory language suggesting that it did. Given the continuing importance of European law in this area, we begin by outlining some of the key ECJ decisions.

572

The common understanding that pregnancy discrimination amounts to sex discrimination derives from the cases of Dekker v Stichting Vormingscentrum voor Jong Volwassenen (VJV-Centrum) Plus 1992 ICR 325, ECJ; Handels-og Kontorfunktionærernes Forbund i Danmark (acting for Hertz) v Dansk Arbejdsgiverforening (acting for Aldi Marked K/S) 1992 ICR 332, ECJ; and Habermann-Beltermann v Arbeiterwohlfahrt, Bezirksverband Ndb/Opf eV 1994 IRLR 364, ECJ. These cases (usually abbreviated to Dekker, Hertz and Habermann-Beltermann) established that a refusal to recruit a woman, the dismissal of a woman or subjecting a woman to a detriment on the ground of pregnancy constitute direct discrimination on the ground of sex contrary to the principle of equal treatment.

A thornier issue for the ECJ arose in Webb v EMO Air Cargo (UK) Ltd 1994 **13.27** ICR 770, ECJ. In that case the claimant was engaged by the employer primarily in order to cover for another employee taking maternity leave, but she then became pregnant herself. The House of Lords was in no doubt that to dismiss a woman simply because she is pregnant or to refuse to employ a woman of childbearing age because she may become pregnant amounted to automatic direct sex discrimination on the basis that childbearing and the capacity for childbearing are unique characteristics of the female sex. However, the employer argued that it was not the fact that she was pregnant that was the problem, but the fact that she had been hired to cover someone else's maternity – a condition which, as a result of her own maternity leave, she would not be able to fulfil. Their Lordships asked the ECJ to indicate whether a court should regard the principal reason for dismissing or refusing to engage a woman in these circumstances as being her unavailability for work, as opposed to her pregnancy. In making this reference to the ECJ, their Lordships accepted that if the comparison approach was contrary to European law, they had a duty to attempt to construe the SDA (which at the time required comparators for all forms of direct discrimination) in accordance with European law.

In giving its judgment, the ECJ ruled that the protection afforded by European law to a woman during pregnancy and after childbirth cannot be dependent upon whether her presence during maternity leave is essential to the proper functioning of the undertaking that employs her. In the ECJ's view, any contrary interpretation would render the provisions of the Equal Treatment Directive ineffective.

The ECJ's ruling in Webb made it clear that, under European equality law, less **13.28** favourable treatment of a woman on the ground of her pregnancy or the consequences of that pregnancy amounts to direct sex discrimination without the need for a comparison with a man in similar circumstances. To compare a woman who is unavailable for work due to pregnancy with a man who is absent from work because of medical or other reasons – either of which might otherwise

573

justify the dismissal of a woman – was contrary to the Equal Treatment Directive (and continues to be contrary to the recast Equal Treatment Directive).

Note that while Webb establishes that a woman need not compare her treatment with a man to establish pregnancy discrimination, and that an employer cannot rely on such a comparison as a defence, there are circumstances where a comparison may be drawn in order to support a woman's claim of pregnancy discrimination. For example, a woman absent from work by reason of pregnancy may compare her treatment with the more favourable treatment afforded to a sick man in order to demonstrate that a different rule is being applied in a comparable situation – see Fletcher and ors v NHS Pensions Agency and anor 2005 ICR 1458, EAT.

13.29 **Maternity leave.** The issue of maternity (as opposed to pregnancy) was not specifically addressed in Webb v EMO Air Cargo (UK) Ltd (above), but did fall for consideration in Thibault v Caisse Nationale d'Assurance Vieillesse des Travailleurs Salariés (CNAVTS) 1999 ICR 160, ECJ. There the Court held that depriving a woman of her right to an assessment of her performance, and therefore of the possibility of qualifying for promotion, on the ground that she was absent on maternity leave for some of the assessment period, was contrary to EU law. A similar conclusion was reached by the ECJ in Napoli v Ministero della Giustizia, Dipartimento dell'Amministrazione Penitenziaria 2014 ICR 486, ECJ. There it was held that automatic exclusion of a female worker from a vocational training course because she had taken compulsory maternity leave constituted unfavourable treatment contrary to EU law, because it delayed her opportunity to be promoted to a higher grade.

Another pivotal case concerning the treatment afforded to women on maternity leave was Land Brandenburg v Sass 2005 IRLR 147, ECJ. There, S had been employed in the former East Germany, and had taken 20 weeks of maternity leave. Upon German reunification, her employment transferred to another body and became subject to a collective agreement. Under the terms of that agreement, S had to have 15 years' service to qualify for a higher salary grade. Her employer determined that only eight weeks of the maternity leave could be counted towards that service, since this was the period provided for under German law at the time of reunification and was the period referred to in the collective agreement. On a reference from the Bundesarbeitsgericht (Federal Labour Court), the ECJ ruled that the fact that a legislative measure grants women maternity leave of more than the minimum 14 weeks provided for in the Pregnant Workers Directive does not preclude that leave from being considered to be maternity leave as referred to in Article 8 of the Directive. The leave therefore comprised a period during which the rights connected with the employment contract must, under Article 11, be ensured.

13.30 The effect of the Sass decision on UK law was substantial, since it called into question the approach of according women different contractual rights on the basis of whether they were taking ordinary or additional maternity leave. As explained in Chapter 3, 'Maternity leave', under 'Terms and conditions during maternity leave', this distinction was abolished in October 2008 by the Work and Families Act 2006 and the Maternity and Parental Leave etc and the Paternity and Adoption Leave (Amendment) Regulations 2008 SI 2008/1966. In addition, S.3A SDA was introduced in 2005 and provided that any less favourable treatment of a woman on the grounds that she exercised or sought to exercise her right to ordinary, additional or compulsory maternity leave would amount to direct discrimination. This provision is now found in S.18(4) EqA.

The scope of S.18(4) EqA was considered in Holden and Co LLP v Russell EAT 0537/13, where the EAT upheld an employment tribunal's decision that R had been discriminated against when the employer failed to accept her properly notified return date at the end of her maternity leave. The EAT held that the unfavourable treatment fell within S.18(4) because the reason for R's treatment was that she had 'exercised or sought to exercise' the right to maternity leave. The EAT noted that neither party had put forward any authority on S.18(4) but held that that provision not only protects a woman at any point in time when she exercises, or seeks to exercise, her right to maternity leave but also in respect of the necessary consequences of that right. It took the view that the return date is a necessary or essential ingredient of the right to maternity leave and, accordingly, any unfavourable treatment in relation to it falls within S.18(4).

Impact on employer. The consequences of pregnancy for the employer, **13.31** financial or otherwise, are irrelevant in considering whether there has been pregnancy or maternity discrimination. In Webb v EMO Air Cargo (UK) Ltd (above) the ECJ said that the protection afforded by European law could not depend on whether the woman's presence at work during her maternity leave period was essential to the proper functioning of the business. This has been confirmed in later cases dealing with a variety of situations. In Tele Danmark A/S v Handels-og Kontorfunktionærernes Forbund i Danmark (HK) (acting on behalf of Brandt-Nielsen) 2004 ICR 610, ECJ, for example, the employee was unable to complete a substantial part of the six-month contract on which she had been engaged. The ECJ ruled that the dismissal of a worker on account of pregnancy constitutes direct sex discrimination whatever the nature and extent of the economic loss incurred by the employer as a result of her absence. In Mahlburg v Land Mecklenburg-Vorpommern 2001 ICR 1032, ECJ, the employee applied for a permanent job but was refused because national laws relating to pregnant women meant that she would not be able to take up the post until after the birth of her child. The ECJ held that this refusal amounted to sex discrimination. And in Busch v Klinikum Neustadt GmbH und Co Betriebs KG 2003 IRLR 625, ECJ, the fact that a pregnant nurse would have been unable to perform certain aspects of her duties did not permit the employer to prevent her returning early from a career break.

575

There are two main reasons why the law refuses to take account of the effect of a pregnancy on an employer's business: sexual equality and health and safety. The former is exemplified in Lord Griffiths' comment in Brown v Stockton-on-Tees Borough Council 1988 ICR 410, HL, that the 'considerable inconvenience' of keeping a woman's job open while she has a baby 'is a price that has to be paid as a part of the social and legal recognition of the equal status of women in the workplace'. The latter reason was raised by the ECJ in Tele Danmark A/S v Handels-og Kontorfunktionærernes Forbund i Danmark (HK) (acting on behalf of Brandt-Nielsen) (above) when the Court referred to 'the risk that a possible dismissal may pose for the physical and mental state' of workers who are pregnant or breastfeeding, including 'the particularly serious risk that they may be encouraged to have abortions'.

13.32 **Concealment of pregnancy.** Since pregnancy, or its consequences, cannot justify a dismissal, a failure to recruit or other detrimental treatment, it follows that a woman is not obliged to disclose the fact that she is pregnant before accepting a job or other opportunity offered to her. In Tele Danmark A/S v Handels-og Kontorfunktionærernes Forbund i Danmark (HK) (acting on behalf of Brandt-Nielsen) (above) the applicant knew at the time she was applying for the job that she was pregnant and that she expected to give birth in the fourth month of the six-month contract. When she finally told her employer of her pregnancy, she was dismissed on the basis that she had breached the duty of good faith in concealing the fact that she would be unavailable for work for a substantial part of the contract. The ECJ held that this was irrelevant and that her dismissal was an act of sex discrimination. Similarly, in Busch v Klinikum Neustadt GmbH und Co Betriebs KG (above) B, a nurse, was entitled under German Law to take a three-year career break (referred to in the case as 'parental leave') following the birth of her first child. However, following her discovery that she was pregnant again, she asked her employer if she could terminate her parental leave early and return to work. The employer consented to her returning early, but B did not disclose the fact that she was pregnant until after she started work. The employer then tried to rescind the consent on the grounds of 'fraudulent misrepresentation and mistake as to an essential characteristic', because B had known all along that she would be unable to perform all her duties when she returned and had, the employer argued, breached her duty of loyalty in failing to disclose the pregnancy. The German Government also contended before the Court that B's conduct was an abuse of process in that she was seeking to take advantage of the extra maternity pay she would get by returning to work before giving birth to the second child. The ECJ rejected these arguments and found that B had not been obliged to tell her employer of her pregnancy, since the employer would not have been permitted to take it into account in deciding whether to allow her to return early from her career break.

13.33 **Comparators.** As mentioned above, the jurisprudence of the ECJ has long recognised the unique position of women who are pregnant or on maternity leave. As far back as the early 1990s, Webb v EMO Air Cargo (UK) Ltd (above) and Dekker v Stichting Vormingscentrum voor Jong Volwassenen (VJV-Centrum) Plus (above) established that the law requires not just that women in these situations must be treated not less favourably than a comparable man, but that, in a number of respects, they should be treated *more* favourably. Despite this, the SDA's wording seemed to stubbornly allude to a comparative approach. When the Government first introduced a specific provision – new S.3A – relating to maternity and pregnancy discrimination in 2005 (in order to reflect the ECJ case law developments discussed in the sections above), the wording still required a form of comparison. The comparison was not with a man – rather, it was with how the woman would have been treated if she had not become pregnant or taken maternity leave. The now-disbanded Equal Opportunities Commission argued that this wording did not comply with EU law and successfully mounted a legal challenge. In R (Equal Opportunities Commission) v Secretary of State for Trade and Industry 2007 ICR 1234, QBD, the High Court asked the Government to recast the provision. However, when the Government finally complied with the Court's order in 2008, it opted simply to omit all the words appearing after 'less favourably'. For instance, S.3A(1)(a) was amended to read that the woman would be regarded as having been discriminated against if, on the ground of her pregnancy, the discriminator treated her 'less favourably'. This, of course, prompted the question: less favourably than what or whom? The somewhat clumsy wording of S.3A seemed to stem from a struggle to accept that, so far as the task of legislative drafting was concerned, it was inappropriate to treat pregnancy and maternity discrimination in the same way as direct sex discrimination.

Section 18 EqA has finally got rid of any notion of a comparison with others when it comes to establishing pregnancy and maternity discrimination. S.18(2) provides that a pregnant woman suffers discrimination if she is treated 'unfavourably' and that treatment is because of her pregnancy or an illness arising as a result of it. S.18(3) and (4) makes similar provision in relation to a woman's maternity leave.

Unfavourable treatment. The EqA does not define what it means by **13.34** 'unfavourable' treatment for the purpose of S.18. The Equality and Human Rights Commission (EHRC) has produced guidance on the Act in the form of the 'Code of Practice on Employment' (2010) and, although this does not tackle the concept of 'unfavourable' treatment directly as it relates to S.18, it does examine what the term means with regard to disability in S.15, which makes it unlawful for an employer to treat a disabled person 'unfavourably' because of something arising in consequence of a disability. The Code notes at para 5.7 that this means that the disabled person 'must have been put at a disadvantage'. Often the disadvantage will be obvious and it will be clear that the treatment has been unfavourable; for example, a person may have been refused a job, denied a work opportunity or dismissed from their employment. But sometimes unfavourable treatment may be less obvious. Even if an employer thinks that they are acting in the best interests of a disabled person, they may still treat that person unfavourably.

When it comes to the issue of pregnancy discrimination under S.18, although the Code does not elaborate on the definition of 'unfavourably' in isolation, it does give examples of treatment that will be covered by this section. Para 8.22 notes that the following would all be unlawful under S.18:

- failure to consult a woman on maternity leave about changes to her work or about possible redundancy

- disciplining a woman for refusing to carry out tasks due to pregnancy-related risks

- assuming that a woman's work will become less important to her after childbirth and giving her less responsible or less interesting work as a result

- depriving a woman of her right to an annual assessment of her performance because she was on maternity leave

- excluding a pregnant woman from business trips.

13.35 A failure to consult a woman on maternity leave about changes to her job was at issue in Smith-Twigger v Abbey Protection Group Ltd EAT 0391/13. S-T had agreed time-limited flexible working arrangements under which she worked Mondays to Thursdays. Another employee, A, worked only on Fridays and was on a fixed-term contract that expired at the same time as S-T's flexible working agreement. Thus, in practice, S-T and A operated in tandem but there was no formal 'job share' arrangement nor any reference in S-T's contract to A. S-T was on maternity leave when her flexible working agreement ran out and when A's contract expired. S-T complained that it amounted to unfavourable treatment contrary to S.18(4) EqA for APG Ltd not to have contacted her to discuss the end of her flexible working or to inform her that A had left. A tribunal rejected this claim and the EAT endorsed the tribunal's decision on appeal. In relation to A's departure, the EAT noted that there was no formal job share and that there is, in general, no obligation on an employer to discuss with one employee the termination of the contract of another. As for the flexible working arrangements, while there may be good practical reasons why employers consult with employees about the ending of such arrangements, if the employee knows that the agreement will expire on a particular date then there is no legal obligation on the employer to do so. S-T had a right to request further flexible working but the impetus for that would come from her, not her employer. Accordingly, S-T's claim fell at the first hurdle.

By contrast, in Stone v Ramsay Health Care UK Operations Ltd ET Case No.1400762/11 the employment tribunal had no difficulty in identifying acts of unfavourable treatment on which to base a claim of pregnancy and maternity discrimination. S, a general manager at the employer's hospital, went on maternity leave in February 2010. Two days after she gave birth, T, the interim manager, began contacting her about work matters. S initially responded to them but, when her baby developed colic, she stopped answering T's e-mails in order to care for her baby. In May T raised a grievance about S, complaining that S had been aggressive towards her on a recent visit to the hospital with her baby and that negative comments had been made by senior managers about S not doing her usual hospital walks and GP visits and on occasion leaving work early prior to going on maternity leave. T did not know that S had agreed these arrangements with W, her line manager, because she had been suffering from a pregnancy-related illness. Six weeks after receiving the grievance, W informed S that a grievance had been made against her, but refused to disclose either the identity of the complainant or the nature of the grievance. When asked when she wanted the grievance to be investigated, S opted to delay the investigation until after her return from maternity leave. In August S raised her own grievance, complaining about W's handling of the grievance against her, and lamenting W's failure to organise keeping-in-touch (KIT) days and include her in the annual pay review. S did not receive a formal response to her grievance. S returned to work in January 2011 and was eventually told that T had raised the grievance, what it was about, and that it would not be taken any further. In response, S made a formal complaint under the employer's Dignity at Work policy, raising serious allegations of discrimination. When the complaint was rejected, S resigned and brought a complaint under S.18.

13.36 The employment tribunal found that S had been subjected to 'a continuing series of unfavourable treatment/conduct', which included W's failure to make proper arrangements for staying in touch with S during her maternity leave in accordance with the employer's own policy; to include S in the annual pay review; to give S proper details of the grievance against her and to deal with it in a timely manner; to respond properly to S's own grievance of August 2010; to arrange the KIT days while she was on additional maternity leave; and to allow her the right to appeal against the rejection of her complaint under the Dignity at Work policy. In the absence of a non-discriminatory explanation for these failures, the tribunal found that S's claim was made out – the treatment was explained by her being on maternity leave. It noted in particular that there was a worrying lack of understanding at senior management level of the employer's procedures on pregnancy and maternity and the legal protections available to women in these situations, and a failure to take S's complaints of discrimination seriously. The tribunal also accepted that T's unjustified grievance against S was tainted by discrimination: it was prompted by T's unhappiness at S not responding to her wholly improper requests for support and assistance while S was on maternity leave and by dissatisfaction among the senior management team caused by S's pregnancy-related illness and the arrangements made with W for S to work at home because of her pregnancy.

579

Depriving a woman of an opportunity for promotion (together with the corresponding higher earning potential) because she is pregnant or on maternity leave will also amount to unfavourable treatment for the purpose of S.18. Furthermore, as the case of Commissioner of Police of the Metropolis v Keohane 2014 ICR 1073, EAT, shows, the employee does not have to wait and see if such a risk materialises before she is able to bring a complaint. In that case, K was a police constable in the Metropolitan Police Service (MPS), where she worked as a dog handler with two narcotics dogs. Her status as a dual narcotics dog handler enhanced her career prospects and gave her an opportunity to earn overtime. The MPS operated a policy relating to the 'retention, reallocation or withdrawal of police dogs' when handlers were either sick; performing recuperative or restricted duties; pregnant or on maternity leave; or suspended from operational duties. On 19 October 2010, K told the force that she was pregnant. While pregnant, she could not be deployed on operational duties for safety reasons. On 29 October she attended a meeting to discuss the reallocation of her police dogs. The Chief Inspector decided to reallocate Nunki Pippin, K's passive search dog, leaving her with one proactive search dog. K complained to an employment tribunal that this decision was unfavourable treatment because of her pregnancy, contrary to S.18(2). K brought a second claim under S.18(2) when the MPS refused her request to have the dog returned to her before the end of her maternity leave.

13.37 An employment tribunal found that both the decision to take away Nunki Pippin and the subsequent decision not to reallocate the dog to K amounted to unfavourable treatment because of her pregnancy. K had suffered a detriment as a result of the first decision in that she knew that there was a serious risk that on her return to work her working conditions would be different from those which she had enjoyed before she ceased operational duties. The subsequent loss of opportunity for overtime and damage to her career prospects that resulted from the refusal to reallocate Nunki Pippin were also detriments about which K was entitled to complain, despite their limited duration of eight months. On appeal, the EAT refused to interfere with the tribunal's decision.

13.38 **'Because of'.** In order for a discrimination claim to succeed under S.18 EqA, the unfavourable treatment must be 'because of' the employee's pregnancy or maternity leave. The meaning of this expression was considered by the EAT in Indigo Design Build and Management Ltd and anor v Martinez EAT 0020/14. There, His Honour Judge Richardson, sitting alone, noted that the term 'because of' is a change from the term used in the antecedent discrimination legislation, but he confirmed that, nonetheless, no change in legal approach was necessary and that the law required a consideration of the 'grounds' for the treatment. In so holding, HHJ Richardson referred to Onu v Akwiwu and anor; Taiwo v Olaigbe and anor 2014 ICR 571, CA, in which Lord Justice Underhill said: 'What constitutes the "grounds" for a directly discriminatory act will vary according to the type of case. The paradigm is perhaps the case where the discriminator applies a rule or criterion which is inherently based on the protected characteristic. In such a case the criterion itself, or its application, plainly constitutes the grounds of the act complained of, and there is no need to look further. But there are other cases which do not involve the application of any inherently discriminatory criterion and where the discriminatory grounds consist in the fact that the protected characteristic has operated on the discriminator's mind… so as to lead him to act in the way complained of. It does not have to be the only such factor: it is enough if it has had "a significant influence". Nor need it be conscious: a subconscious motivation, if proved, will suffice.' Turning to the instant case, HHJ Richardson concluded that the tribunal had failed to apply the correct legal test. This was not a case where the employer applied an inherently discriminatory criterion or rule but one where it was necessary to consider its mental processes in order to determine the employee's S.18 claim. Accordingly, the matter was remitted to the tribunal to be considered afresh.

The question of causation was also in issue in Commissioner of Police of the Metropolis v Keohane (above), where a police dog handler complained of unlawful discrimination under S.18(2) – i.e. unfavourable treatment because of her pregnancy – when the police decided to remove one of her narcotics dogs when she became pregnant and not to return the dog to her at the end of her maternity leave: she feared that the decision would damage her earnings capacity and career prospects upon her return to work. The police resisted the claim by contending that the decision was based on the need for the dog to remain operational. The tribunal was not convinced. Although it recognised that the police's decision was based partly upon its need to keep the dog operational, it went on to find that factors connected with the employee's pregnancy were operating on the Chief Inspector's mind in his decision-making process: he had referred to this being her second pregnancy within 17 months. The EAT could detect no error of law in the tribunal's decision. Since the tribunal had found as a fact that the employee's pregnancy was operative in the decision-making process, the unfavourable treatment was 'because of' the pregnancy within the meaning of S.18(2) and the claim was made out. The appeal was accordingly dismissed.

The EAT underlined the importance of the 'because of' enquiry in Sefton **13.39** Borough Council v Wainwright 2015 IRLR 90, EAT. In that case, W was employed by the Council as Head of Overview and Scrutiny. As part of a reorganisation, the Council proposed to abolish W's role and that of P, a man, and replace them with the combined role of Democratic Service Manager (DSM). W and P were both notified that they were at risk in July 2012. At that time, W had just begun maternity leave. The Council interviewed both P and W for the role in December 2012 and decided that P was better qualified. It therefore offered him the position and dismissed W as redundant in April 2013. W claimed that the dismissal was automatically unfair because the DSM role was a suitable available vacancy, which the Council was obliged to offer her under Reg 10 of the Maternity and Parental Leave etc Regulations 1999 SI 1999/3312 ('the MPL Regulations'), and that the dismissal was also discriminatory under S.18 EqA. An employment tribunal upheld both claims: it accepted that W's dismissal was automatically unfair by reason of the employer's breach of Reg 10 MPL Regulations and, apparently assuming that such a breach must automatically be discriminatory, it also upheld her claim of discrimination under S.18 EqA.

Overturning the tribunal's decision on discrimination, the EAT held that it had not followed the correct approach applicable to a S.18 claim. Although W was treated unfavourably while on maternity leave, in that she was selected for redundancy and not offered an alternative role, the treatment was not necessarily 'because of' pregnancy or maternity leave, as S.18 requires. The tribunal had failed to enquire as to the reason why W had been treated as she was. It was not entitled simply to assume that, because there had been a breach of Reg 10, there must also automatically have been a breach of S.18. The two forms of protection are different and it would go beyond the language of the statute to assume that a breach of Reg 10 is inherently discriminatory. While W's being on maternity leave was certainly the context for her unfavourable treatment, this did not inevitably mean that the latter was 'because of' the former. This part of the claim was therefore remitted to the tribunal.

13.40 Two further cases where the reason for the less favourable treatment was considered, albeit with different outcomes:

- **Tantum v Travers Smith Braithwaite Services** ET Case No.2203585/12: an employment tribunal found that T was discriminated against when her employer failed to offer her a permanent position as an associate solicitor in its real estate department at the end of her two-year training contract. The tribunal rejected the employer's submission that it had reduced the number of available posts from two to one due to business requirements. In its view, the proper inference to be drawn from the evidence before it was that the abolition of the second post – which meant that T missed out on a permanent position – was contrived in order to avoid the department having a newly qualified solicitor absent from work on maternity leave. T's claim under S.18 therefore succeeded

- **Maksymiuk v Bar Roma** EATS 0017/12: M was the only one of a number of bar staff at an Italian restaurant made redundant. She complained that the redundancy dismissal, coming shortly after her announcement that she was pregnant, was discriminatory under S.18, but the tribunal dismissed her complaint. It found that there was a genuine redundancy situation, which had arisen prior to the employer knowing of her pregnancy, and that she had scored lowest by reference to objective selection criteria: her pregnancy had played no role in selecting her for redundancy. On appeal, the EAT held that the tribunal was entitled to come to this conclusion and dismissed M's appeal.

Practical importance of S.18 pregnancy discrimination claims. Under S.99 **13.41** ERA and Reg 20 MPL Regulations it is automatically unfair to dismiss a woman on pregnancy- or maternity-related grounds, regardless of her hours of work or length of service. In addition, it is unlawful under S.47C ERA and Reg 19 MPL Regulations for an employer to subject a woman to any detriment short of dismissal on pregnancy or maternity-related grounds. Inevitably, these measures (discussed in more detail in Chapter 12, 'Detriment and unfair dismissal') diminish the need for women to rely on discrimination law to establish a cause of action. Nevertheless, a claim of discrimination under S.18 EqA (or, where appropriate, other provisions of the EqA) should always be considered in addition to any claim of unlawful dismissal or detriment since discrimination awards commonly include a sum for injury to feelings and, unlike unfair dismissal awards, are not subject to any upper limit on compensation. Furthermore, a pregnant employee refused a job at the recruitment stage would only be able to rely on a discrimination claim since she would not be an 'employee' for the purposes of claiming detriment or unfair dismissal.

Fixed-term and indefinite contracts. A situation left unresolved by the ECJ in **13.42** Webb v EMO Air Cargo (UK) Ltd 1994 ICR 770, ECJ, was whether a finding of sex discrimination is inevitable if a woman is denied employment for a fixed term in the future during the whole of which her pregnancy would make her unavailable for work. When the Webb case returned to the House of Lords as Webb v EMO Air Cargo (UK) Ltd (No.2) 1995 ICR 1021, HL, Lord Keith suggested (obiter) that he thought it was not. The issue was examined again in Caruana v Manchester Airport plc 1996 IRLR 378, EAT, in which an independent contractor, C, had worked on a series of fixed-term contracts, the last of which had been a one-year contract ending on 31 December 1992. When she gave notice that she would be commencing maternity leave on 11 December, the airport declined to renew her contract. The EAT noted that the circumstances of the case did not fall within the scope of Lord Keith's suggested exception, which his Lordship had expressed only in very tentative terms. Furthermore, in the EAT's view, the ECJ's judgment in Webb provided no basis for any wider exception than that suggested by Lord Keith. In the circumstances, the non-renewal of C's contract was an act of direct sex discrimination. The question still remained, however, as to whether (and to what extent) fixed-term contracts provided any exception to the general principle that unfavourable treatment on the ground of pregnancy automatically amounts to direct sex discrimination.

The ECJ finally laid the matter to rest in Tele Danmark A/S v Handels-og Kontorfunktionærernes Forbund i Danmark (HK) (acting on behalf of Brandt-Nielsen) 2004 ICR 610, ECJ, and Jiménez Melgar v Ayuntamiento de Los Barrios 2004 ICR 610, ECJ. In the Jiménez Melgar case the Court held that Article 10 of the Pregnant Workers Directive, which prohibits the dismissal of workers during the period from the beginning of pregnancy to the end of maternity leave, applies to women employed on fixed-term contracts. The ECJ

583

also held that the non-renewal of a fixed-term contract, when it ends as stipulated, is not a dismissal prohibited by Article 10, but would, if motivated by the fact that the worker is pregnant, constitute sex discrimination under the Equal Treatment Directive (and, by extension, now under the recast Equal Treatment Directive).

13.43 In the Tele-Danmark case a woman had been recruited to perform a six-month contract from 1 July to 31 December, and would undergo training during the first two months. At the time she was recruited she knew she was pregnant but kept this information from the employer until she was in post. She expected to give birth in early November and would have been entitled to take maternity leave from 11 September. When she told her employer about her pregnancy she was dismissed with effect from 30 September. The employer argued that, in withholding information about her pregnancy, she had not obtained the job in good faith because she knew she would not be able to perform a substantial part of the contract. The ECJ considered its earlier decision in Webb v EMO Air Cargo (UK) Ltd (above) and held that 'since the dismissal of a worker on account of pregnancy constitutes direct discrimination on grounds of sex, whatever the nature and extent of the economic loss incurred by the employer as a result of her absence because of pregnancy, whether the contract of employment was concluded for a fixed or an indefinite period has no bearing on the discriminatory character of the dismissal'. The Court noted that the duration of an employment relationship is uncertain, even if a worker is recruited on a fixed term, since the contract could be renewed or extended. Finally, the Court noted that the Equal Treatment Directive and the Pregnant Workers Directive did not make any distinction, as regards their scope, in respect of the duration of the employment relationship in question. Had the legislature wished to exclude fixed-term contracts it would have done so expressly.

Since the UK courts must interpret UK law in the light of these two cases, it is clear that any dismissal or other less favourable treatment of a woman on the ground of her pregnancy will automatically constitute direct sex discrimination, whatever the duration of the contract, whatever the impact on the employer, and whether or not she concealed her pregnancy at the time of recruitment. It should also be noted that the non-renewal of a fixed-term or limited-term contract amounts to a dismissal for the purposes of unfair dismissal law, and thus can be caught by the automatically unfair dismissal provisions outlined in Chapter 12, 'Detriment and unfair dismissal'.

13.44 **Protected period.** In Handels-og Kontorfunktionærernes Forbund i Danmark (acting for Hertz) v Dansk Arbejdsgiverforening (acting for Aldi Marked K/S) 1992 ICR 332, ECJ ('the Hertz case') the European Court established the concept of the 'protected period', which runs from *the inception of pregnancy to the end of a woman's statutory maternity leave*. This concept, which was first codified by S.3A(3)(a) SDA, is now found in S.18(6) EqA. In the majority of cases, the protected period will start when the pregnancy begins and end (in usual circumstances) when the woman returns from additional maternity leave (unless she decides to return to work earlier) – S.18(6)(a). The special protection against unfavourable treatment afforded by S.18 to pregnant workers and women exercising maternity rights applies throughout this period.

If the pregnant woman is not entitled to statutory maternity leave, the protected period ends two weeks after the end of the pregnancy (i.e. at the end of compulsory maternity leave) – S.18(6)(b). The two-week protected period applies, for example, to pregnant women who are job applicants, who are not 'employees', who have not complied with the notice requirements in relation to their pregnancy, or who miscarry before the 24th week of their pregnancy.

In addition, it now appears possible for a woman to choose to end her maternity **13.45** leave early – and with it her protected period – without returning to work. This is the effect of the shared parental leave scheme, which applies to children born on or after 5 April 2015. Under the scheme, a woman may elect to bring her maternity leave to an end early by giving a 'curtailment' notice to the employer, thus enabling the remaining portion of leave to be taken as shared parental leave. After cutting short her maternity leave, she may therefore decide not to return to work immediately but to take a period of shared parental leave instead, perhaps together with the child's father (or partner). In these circumstances, even though the protected period has not been brought to an end by virtue of either of the scenarios envisaged in S.18(6)(a) – the employee's return to work or the expiry of her additional maternity leave period – it would seem that it has nonetheless ended on the date specified in the curtailment notice. This is the effect of Reg 7 of the Maternity and Adoption Leave (Curtailment of Statutory Rights to Leave) Regulations 2014 SI 2014/3052, which provides that where the mother has brought forward the date on which her ordinary or additional maternity leave period ends by giving a valid curtailment notice, her statutory maternity leave period ends on the leave curtailment date given in the notice. Once the woman's maternity leave has been brought to an end in accordance with Reg 7, the special protection under S.18 no longer applies to her. The shared parental leave scheme is discussed in detail in Chapter 8, 'Shared parental leave and pay'.

Although the special protection afforded to a woman while pregnant or on maternity leave does not extend beyond the protected period, she may nevertheless be able to bring a claim under S.18(4) where she is treated less favourably *after* her maternity leave period *because* she has taken or sought to take maternity leave. For example, where she returns to work and her job has changed to her detriment while she was away, she will be able to bring a claim for unlawful discrimination on the ground that she took maternity leave. Similarly, if she is refused promotion following her return to work because she did not attend the required training courses, she will have a claim under S.18 if the training took place while she was on maternity leave.

13.46 Furthermore, S.18(5) provides that where unfavourable treatment because of pregnancy or a related illness is in implementation of a decision taken during the protected period, then the treatment is to be regarded as occurring during the protected period, even if the implementation occurs after the end of that period, i.e. after the woman has returned to work.

If the protected period has expired, it is still open to a woman to argue that the treatment meted out to her because of her pregnancy amounted to less favourable treatment because of *sex* contrary to S.13 EqA (direct discrimination) or S.19 EqA (indirect discrimination). It may also amount to pregnancy or maternity discrimination under S.13 – see 'Direct discrimination' above.

13.47 *Trying to conceive.* Section 18(6) clearly links the start of the protected period to the start of the pregnancy. Women who are trying to get pregnant and who suffer discrimination as a result cannot therefore bring a claim of discrimination under S.18. However, a woman who is discriminated against because she is trying to get pregnant – or may possibly get pregnant at some point in the future – may be able to claim direct discrimination because of sex under S.13. An example:

- **Cosson v Phoenix plc** ET Case No.2306029/04: C worked for a marketing company as an account director. She got married in May 2004 and in June suffered a miscarriage and was off work for a short time. She had a second miscarriage in September and was off work for two weeks as a result. On the last day of her absence, P plc telephoned her to tell her that she was to be made redundant, on the basis of 'last in, first out' (LIFO), as she had the shortest service in her pool. C claimed direct discrimination under S.1(2)(a) SDA. The employment tribunal considered that LIFO is not of itself an unfair selection method, but P plc had to discharge the burden of proving that LIFO was not adopted as a method of selecting C because she was trying to become pregnant. P plc did not produce credible and cogent evidence of the process by which it adopted LIFO as its selection criterion. In the absence of evidence that it made any meaningful attempt to consult with C or to consider her for alternative work, and in the light of the manner in which she was informed of her dismissal without warning while recovering from a miscarriage and remarks made by the owner of the company that enough women were becoming pregnant, the tribunal declared that C's selection for redundancy was an act of direct sex discrimination.

13.48 *IVF treatment.* While women who are trying to become pregnant fall outside the protected period, the issue is more complicated where the woman is undergoing in vitro fertilization (IVF) treatment. In these circumstances, the point at which the woman may enter the protected period – and become entitled to protection under S.18 – depends on the stage the treatment had reached when the alleged unfavourable treatment occurred.

The first case of note on this particular issue was Mayr v Bäckerei und Konditorei Gerhard Flöckner OHG 2008 IRLR 387, ECJ, where the ECJ held that women undergoing IVF treatment, who have had their ova fertilized but not yet implanted, are not 'pregnant' and have therefore not yet entered the protected period. Fertilized ova might be kept for an indeterminate period, and so to extend protection to women before the transfer to the uterus would result in female workers having protection even where the transfer was postponed for several years, or even abandoned. However, the ECJ went on to hold that the recast Equal Treatment Directive did preclude the dismissal of a woman at such an advanced stage of IVF treatment – that is, between follicular puncture and the immediate transfer of the fertilized ova into the uterus – where the reason for the dismissal was that the woman was undergoing such treatment.

The EAT took matters one step further in Sahota v Home Office 2010 ICR 772, **13.49** EAT. In that case S brought a number of complaints of sex discrimination that related to a period when she was undergoing IVF treatment. An employment tribunal dismissed her claim, partly because the acts she complained of were not done on the ground that she was undergoing IVF treatment. In upholding that decision the EAT noted that it was common ground between the parties – and indeed the tribunal had proceeded on this assumption – that implantation of fertilized eggs in the claimant's uterus marked the start of pregnancy. This was so even though the claimant had undergone two implantations and neither had been successful. The EAT was prepared to accept that the claimant could have been regarded as pregnant between the date of implantation and the date those attempts at IVF were discovered to have failed; in both cases periods of less than a month. On this analysis, the claimant would have been protected under S.18 for those periods.

The Appeal Tribunal also considered the argument that the result of Mayr was that any less favourable treatment of a woman because she was undergoing IVF treatment amounted to sex discrimination. The EAT rejected this argument, on the ground that if that were to be accepted, then any detrimental treatment related to gender-specific medical treatment would amount to sex discrimination, which would be contrary to the ECJ's decision in Handels og Kontorfunktionærernes Forbund i Danmark (acting for Hertz) v Dansk Arbejdsgiverforening 1992 ICR 332, ECJ. Instead, the EAT took the view that the decision in Mayr created 'a limited, and closely defined, exception only for the "important" stage between the follicular puncture and the *immediate* transfer of the in vitro fertilized ova' (our stress).

The combined effect of the Mayr and Sahota cases appears to be that between **13.50** the follicular puncture and implantation – if that follows 'immediately' – less favourable treatment of a woman because she is undergoing IVF treatment

587

would amount to sex discrimination. From implantation onwards, the woman is in the 'protected period' and so entitled to protection from pregnancy discrimination. In accordance with S.18(6) EqA, that protected period lasts until the end of maternity leave, in the usual way, or until two weeks after the implantation is ascertained to be a failure.

13.51 *Surrogacy arrangements.* Note that the situation of women who have a baby through a surrogacy arrangement is discussed under 'Surrogacy arrangements' below.

13.52 **'Pregnancy of hers'.** As discussed above, a claim for direct pregnancy and maternity discrimination under S.18 is available for as long as the claimant is in the protected period, which spans the time from the onset of her pregnancy until she returns to work at the end of her maternity leave. If further proof was needed that only a woman who is pregnant (or on maternity leave) can avail herself of protection under S.18, it is provided by the requirement in S.18(2) that the unfavourable treatment suffered by the claimant must relate to a 'pregnancy of hers'. On the face of it, S.18 does not therefore protect a woman who suffers unfavourable treatment because she is perceived to be pregnant but who is not actually pregnant. Similarly, it does not cover those who suffer discrimination because they are closely associated with a pregnant woman. However, this does not mean that the EqA provides no form of redress in these situations. Anyone suffering less favourable treatment either because of a perception that they are pregnant or because of their association with someone who is pregnant (or on maternity leave) may be able to complain of direct discrimination because of sex. We discuss the scope for claiming discrimination in these circumstances under 'Discrimination by association' and 'Discrimination by perception' below.

13.53 Pregnancy-related illness

A woman dismissed for a pregnancy-related illness *during* the protected period will be able to claim, without more, that her dismissal is automatically discriminatory under the special protection afforded by S.18 EqA (as to which, see under 'Pregnancy and maternity discrimination' above). However, if a woman is dismissed *after* the protected period for an illness arising out of pregnancy or childbirth, the dismissal falls to be compared to the analogous circumstances of a sick man, since the claim will be for direct sex discrimination (and/or direct pregnancy/maternity discrimination) under S.13 EqA. The issue then is whether a man would have been dismissed in the same or similar circumstances as the woman. If the answer to this question is 'yes', then the woman will not be able to claim that she has been discriminated against because of her sex – see 'Dismissal after protected period' below.

13.54 **Length of protected period.** In Brown v Rentokil Ltd 1998 ICR 790, ECJ, the European Court ruled that EU law prohibits the dismissal of a woman at any time during her pregnancy where the dismissal is based on her absence due to incapacity for work that is caused by an illness arising from her pregnancy. The dismissal of a woman during pregnancy cannot be based on her inability, as a result of her condition, to perform the duties that she is contractually employed to do. Although pregnancy is not comparable to a general illness, there may be complications that arise that require a woman to undergo strict medical supervision or rest absolutely for all or part of her pregnancy. Such disorders, which can lead to the inability to work, form part of the risks that are inherent in pregnancy and thus form a specific feature of pregnancy. The ECJ went on to confirm that the protected period first recognised in Handels-og Kontorfunktionærernes Forbund i Danmark (acting for Hertz) v Dansk Arbejdsgiverforening (acting for Aldi Marked K/S) 1992 ICR 332, ECJ covers a woman *throughout the entire period of her pregnancy and the period of maternity leave set out in national law.*

As noted above, the concept of 'protected period' is defined by S.18(6) EqA as beginning when pregnancy begins and ending (in usual circumstances) when the woman returns from additional maternity leave (unless she decides to return to work earlier). If the pregnant woman is not entitled to statutory maternity leave, the protected period ends two weeks after the end of the pregnancy (i.e. at the end of compulsory maternity leave) – S.18(6)(b). This fully accords with and reflects the ECJ's ruling in the Brown case.

Dismissal after protected period. The ECJ in Brown v Rentokil Ltd (above) **13.55** confirmed the decision in Handels-og Kontorfunktionærernes Forbund i Danmark (acting for Hertz) v Dansk Arbejdsgiverforening (acting for Aldi Marked K/S) (above) that, where an illness or other pathological condition arose after the end of maternity leave, then the issue is whether or not the woman is treated in the same way as a comparable man. If they are treated the same, there is no discrimination on the ground of sex.

However, the Court in Brown did go on to express doubts about another of its previous decisions – namely, Handels-og Kontorfunktionærernes Forbund (acting for Larsson) v Dansk Handel and Service (acting for Føtex Supermarked A/S) 1997 IRLR 643, ECJ. Contrary to what was suggested in that case, the ECJ in Brown was of the view that, when considering whether dismissal is justified, it is not possible to take account of pregnancy-related illness absences that occurred between the onset of pregnancy and the commencement of maternity leave. This clearly implies that, when dealing with the dismissal of a woman for continued absence after the period of her maternity leave has ended, an employer must ignore any absences on account of pregnancy that occurred between the beginning of her pregnancy and the end of her maternity leave. If during this protected period she had, say, 30 weeks' absence, and was dismissed after a further four weeks' absence following the end of her maternity leave, the question of whether she had been discriminated against would be judged by

589

comparison with how a man who had four weeks' sickness absence would have been treated. The relevant comparator would not be a man who had 34 weeks' sickness absence. This principle has since been applied by the EAT in Healy v William B Morrison and Son Ltd EAT 172/99.

13.56 It is a logical deduction from the ECJ's reasoning in Brown v Rentokil Ltd (above) that, once outside the protected period, any absence – including pregnancy-related absence – can be taken into account by an employer. It is true that the facts of Handels-og Kontorfunktionærernes Forbund i Danmark (acting for Hertz) v Dansk Arbejdsgiverforening (acting for Aldi Marked K/S) (above) upon which the reasoning in Brown is based concerned a woman whose illness, although connected with pregnancy, only manifested itself after the end of her maternity leave. But the logic of the Brown case suggests that even if a pregnancy-related illness manifests itself during the protected period, a woman loses the special protection against dismissal on account of such an illness once that period comes to an end. Thus, any period of absence on account of pregnancy illness that takes place after the period of maternity leave has expired can form the basis for dismissal. Whether or not such a dismissal is discriminatory is then a matter of how a man with the same amount of absence would have been treated. As a result, it seems likely that the EAT's decision in Caledonia Bureau Investment and Property v Caffrey 1998 ICR 603, EAT (a case decided before the ECJ's ruling in Brown and discussed in more detail in Chapter 12, 'Detriment and unfair dismissal', under 'Automatically unfair dismissal – pregnancy, childbirth and maternity'), can no longer be considered good law. In that case, the EAT held that any dismissal of a woman for a pregnancy-related illness constitutes discrimination, even when the dismissal takes place after the end of maternity leave.

The impact of the ECJ's ruling in Brown v Rentokil Ltd (above) is illustrated by the EAT's decision in Lyons v DWP Jobcentre Plus 2014 ICR 668, EAT. After the birth of her child in February 2010, L suffered from post-natal depression. She was due to return to work in September 2010 after six months' ordinary maternity leave and a period of annual leave but was signed off sick by her GP because of her depression. In March 2011, DWP dismissed L because she had been absent for approximately six months and was unlikely to return to satisfactory attendance within a reasonable time. An employment tribunal upheld L's claim of unfair dismissal (with a Polkey reduction of 50 per cent) but dismissed her claims of pregnancy and maternity discrimination under S.18 EqA and direct sex discrimination under S.13 EqA. On appeal, the EAT agreed with the tribunal that, while L had been treated unfavourably for a pregnancy-related illness, that treatment occurred after the end of the protected period (i.e. after her return from maternity leave) and was therefore not caught by S.18 EqA. Turning to the direct sex discrimination claim under S.13, the EAT felt that Caledonia Bureau Investment and Property v Caffrey (above), which was heavily relied on by L, would have been decided differently if the Appeal

Tribunal in that case had had the benefit of the ECJ's ruling in the Brown case. Applying the ECJ's reasoning in Brown, the EAT held that if a pregnancy-related illness arises during pregnancy or maternity leave but persists after the maternity leave period has ended and results in periods of sickness absence, the employer can take into account those absences when deciding whether to dismiss. Once the protected period has ended, S.13 EqA requires that these absences be treated in the same way as a man's absences for illness. The tribunal had therefore been entitled to conclude that L had not been subjected to direct sex discrimination.

Sickness dismissal clauses. The final point the European Court in Brown v **13.57** Rentokil Ltd (above) had to consider was whether its decision that the Equal Treatment Directive ruled out the dismissal of a woman during her pregnancy for incapacity for work caused by a pregnancy-related illness was affected by the fact that the complainant's contract of employment contained a term allowing the employer to dismiss workers of either sex after a stipulated number of weeks of continuous absence. In the ECJ's view, such a term made no difference. In short, the situation of a woman absent during the protected period for a pregnancy-related illness could not be compared to that of a man off sick and so the fact that they were both treated in the same way makes no difference. The application of the contractual term in circumstances such as B's constituted direct sex discrimination.

Unfavourable treatment short of dismissal. It goes without saying that the **13.58** above principles are not restricted simply to dismissal cases. Any unfavourable treatment of a woman because of a pregnancy-related illness is on the ground of pregnancy and thus on the ground of her sex. For example, in Stephenson v FA Wellworth and Co Ltd, unreported 21.3.97, NICA, the Northern Ireland Court of Appeal confirmed that it was unlawful for an employer to stop a pregnant woman from attending work when a pregnancy-related illness prevented her from fulfilling any duties involving lifting and carrying. Although employers have a right to suspend a new or expectant mother with pay on health grounds in certain circumstances (see Chapter 2, 'Health and safety protection', under 'Suspension on maternity grounds'), the employee may still be able to pursue a claim of unlawful discrimination if, in consequence, she has been unfavourably treated. For further discussion, see 'Statutory prohibition and pregnancy' below.

In Handels-og Kontorfunktionærernes Forbund i Danmark, acting on behalf of Pedersen and ors v Fællesforeningen for Danmarks Brugsforeningen, acting on behalf of Kvickly Skive and ors 1999 IRLR 55, ECJ, the ECJ held that it was contrary to European discrimination law for the employment legislation of a Member State (in this case Denmark) to provide that workers who are absent from work on account of sickness are entitled to receive full pay from their

591

employers, but pregnant workers who are off sick before the start of their maternity leave are only entitled to full pay if the illness is not pregnancy-related.

13.59 **Detriment and unfair dismissal.** An employee dismissed or subjected to a detriment because of a pregnancy- or childbirth-related illness will also have a cause of action under the MPL Regulations. Reg 20 provides that a dismissal will be unfair if it is for a reason connected with the pregnancy of the employee or the fact that she has given birth to a child, while Reg 19 provides that she is entitled not to be subjected to any detriment for the same reasons. This protection extends to the end of the maternity leave period – Regs 19(5) and 20(4), mirroring the 'protected period' under sex discrimination law. Note, though, that a dismissal after maternity leave ends could still be unfair under the general provisions of S.98 ERA. For more information on unfair dismissal and detriment, see Chapter 12, 'Detriment and unfair dismissal'.

13.60 Health and safety obligations

As discussed in Chapter 2, 'Health and safety protection', under 'Risk assessments', Reg 3 of the Management of Health and Safety at Work Regulations 1999 SI 1999/3242 ('the 1999 Regulations') provides that every employer must make a suitable and sufficient assessment of the risks to the health and safety of its employees to which they are exposed while they are at work, for the purpose of identifying the measures it needs to take to comply with its statutory health and safety duties. Reg 16 of the 1999 Regulations further states that where women of childbearing age work in an undertaking and the work is of a kind which could, by reason of her condition, involve risk to the health and safety of a new or expectant mother or to that of her baby, the risk assessment must include an assessment of that risk.

In Day v T Pickles Farms Ltd 1999 IRLR 217, EAT, the Appeal Tribunal held that an employment tribunal had wrongly decided that the duty to carry out a risk assessment under Reg 16 did not arise until the employer knew the employee was pregnant. As a consequence, the tribunal had failed to consider whether the employee had suffered a detriment capable of founding a sex discrimination claim. The EAT held that the duty arises whenever the employer employs women of childbearing age. Furthermore, it held that an employer's failure to fulfil any of the obligations imposed by the above statutory provisions may amount to a detriment giving rise to liability for direct sex discrimination under the SDA. It remitted the case to the tribunal to consider whether there had been any discrimination. What the EAT did not do in that case was examine whether the other elements of a discrimination claim were made out.

13.61 The EAT took matters one stage further in Hardman v Mallon t/a Orchard Lodge Nursing Home 2002 IRLR 516, EAT. The employment tribunal had found that the employee, H, had suffered no detriment when the employer failed to carry out a risk assessment. It then went on to find that in any case the fact that no risk assessment had been carried out in respect of any employees, male or female, meant that H had not been treated less favourably than a male comparator. The EAT disagreed and held, following the Day v Pickles case, that a failure to carry out a risk assessment amounted, *per se*, to a detriment. It also criticised the tribunal's use of the 'hypothetical male' comparator. The EAT held that, following the Webb v EMO Air Cargo (UK) Ltd line of ECJ cases (see 'Pregnancy and maternity discrimination' above), it was not necessary for the treatment of a pregnant woman to be compared with that accorded to a comparable male or non-pregnant female. In the EAT's view, the employer's failure *automatically* amounted to direct sex discrimination because it had a greater impact on pregnant employees. To hold otherwise would be to fail to interpret the SDA in such a way as to provide the protection required by the Pregnant Workers Directive.

The Hardman case, which can be seen as something of a high water mark in the application of the doctrine of direct discrimination to the protection of pregnant women, was decided before the SDA was amended to insert specific provisions relating to pregnancy discrimination. However, despite questions being raised about its reasoning, it was confirmed as still being of effect following the introduction of S.3A SDA in Stevenson v JM Skinner and Co EAT 0584/07.

13.62 With respect, there are difficulties with the EAT's analysis in both Hardman and Stevenson. If a risk assessment has not been carried out in respect of any employee, then all employees are in a comparable position – their health and safety is potentially jeopardised due to their employer's failure to assess the risks they face in the workplace. In these circumstances, the failure on the part of the employer has nothing to do with pregnancy, but is instead attributable to the employer's disregard for its obligations under the 1999 Regulations. As a result, the logical means by which to enforce the employee's right is a civil action for breach of those Regulations. By treating what is, in reality, a technical breach of health and safety regulations as an act of discrimination, the EAT has essentially made the requirement to carry out a risk assessment a 'strict liability' tort – an employee affected by a failure to assess risk need not prove damage and will invariably receive an award for injury to feelings.

Early indications suggest that a discrimination claim based on a failure to carry out a risk assessment will not be so easily made out under S.18 EqA. In Indigo Design Build and Management Ltd and anor v Martinez EAT 0020/14 M presented complaints to the employment tribunal alleging, among other things, that her employer's failure to conduct a health and safety risk assessment following notification of her pregnancy amounted to direct pregnancy discrimination in contravention of S.18(2) EqA. This provides that an employer discriminates against a woman if, in the 'protected period' in relation to a pregnancy of hers, it treats her unfavourably because of her pregnancy or because of illness suffered by her as a result of it. The tribunal upheld the claim

593

on the basis that, since a risk assessment is required under the 1999 Regulations, failure to provide it must be direct discrimination. The EAT overturned this decision. His Honour Judge Richardson, sitting alone, remarked that 'this is not the law'. Failure to carry out a risk assessment relating to pregnancy or maternity may be, but is not necessarily, 'because of' pregnancy or maternity leave. It may, for example, be a simple administrative error. Where, as in this case, the mental processes of the alleged discriminator are in issue, the tribunal should apply the same process of reasoning as is required in any other discrimination case.

13.63 Moral repercussions of pregnancy

There is little room, if any, for employers to argue that an employee can be lawfully dismissed because of the moral consequences arising out of her pregnancy. This follows the EAT's decision in O'Neill v Governors of St Thomas More Roman Catholic Voluntarily Aided Upper School and anor 1997 ICR 33, EAT, a case concerning a religious studies teacher at a Roman Catholic school who was not permitted to return to work after giving birth to a child she had conceived with a priest. The tribunal accepted that there were two distinct causes operating when the governors of the school decided not to allow the teacher to return. One was the pregnancy itself, but the circumstances surrounding the pregnancy were, it believed, the 'dominant' cause – namely, the identity of the child's father; the publicity the story had attracted; and the untenability of the teacher's position at the school. For this reason the tribunal concluded that her dismissal had not been 'on grounds of sex'. The EAT overturned this decision. The critical question, it said, was whether, on an objective consideration of all the surrounding circumstances, the teacher's dismissal had been on the ground of pregnancy (and hence her sex). It need not have been only on that ground. It need not even have been mainly on that ground. All that was required was that the teacher's pregnancy was 'an effective cause' of her dismissal. There were always 'surrounding circumstances' to a pregnancy, and the circumstances relied upon by the tribunal as the 'dominant' cause were all causally related to the fact that the teacher was pregnant. Her pregnancy precipitated and permeated the decision to dismiss her. She had, consequently, been discriminated against on the ground of her sex.

The EAT's approach in the O'Neill case gives a strong indication that Berrisford v Woodard Schools (Midland Division) Ltd 1991 ICR 564, EAT – a case pre-dating the ECJ's ruling in Webb v EMO Air Cargo (UK) Ltd 1994 ICR 770, ECJ (see under 'Pregnancy and maternity discrimination' above) – would be decided differently today. In the Berrisford case the EAT ruled that the complainant had not been dismissed for pregnancy but because, as an unmarried expectant mother, she was setting a poor moral example to the children in the school where she worked.

594

Statutory prohibition and pregnancy

13.64

The recast EU Equal Treatment Directive and the EqA provide for certain derogations from the principle of equal treatment on public policy grounds. Para 2 of Schedule 22 to the EqA provides protection for an employer in respect of any discriminatory act in relation to employment or vocational training if it is necessary to comply with:

- a requirement of an existing statutory provision concerning the protection of women

- a relevant statutory provision under Part I of the Health and Safety at Work etc Act 1974 and it is done for the purpose of the protection of women, or

- a requirement of a provision specified in Schedule 1 to the Employment Act 1989 (provisions concerned with protection of women at work).

However, the ECJ's ruling in Habermann-Beltermann v Arbeiterwohlfahrt, Bezirksverband Ndb/Opf eV 1994 IRLR 364, ECJ, suggests that this statutory defence may not apply if the result is that a woman is not appointed to a job or loses the job she already has on health and safety grounds. In that case the ECJ ruled that an employer could not rely on German laws preventing pregnant women from performing night work in order to dismiss a woman from her job. The prohibition on night work did not fall within Article 2(6) of the Equal Treatment Directive, as then in force, which permitted national legislation to derogate from the principle of non-discrimination where the legislation concerns the protection of women, because the effect of the legislation was to exclude women from the labour market.

Similarly, in Mahlburg v Land Mecklenburg-Vorpommern 2001 ICR 1032, **13.65** ECJ, the ECJ ruled that another German health and safety law (this time, prohibiting pregnant women from being employed in work where they might be exposed to dangerous substances) was incompatible with the Equal Treatment Directive. According to the Court, the previous case law made it clear that the application of provisions concerning the protection of pregnant women must not result in unfavourable treatment regarding their access to employment. Accordingly, it was not permissible for an employer to refuse to take on a pregnant woman on the ground that a prohibition on employment would prevent her being employed from the outset and for the duration of the pregnancy in a post of unlimited duration. As for the possible financial consequences of an obligation to take on pregnant women, in particular for small and medium-sized undertakings, Dekker v Stichting Vormingscentrum voor Jong Volwassenen (VJV-Centrum) Plus 1992 ICR 325, ECJ, had already established that a refusal to employ a woman on account of her pregnancy could not be justified on grounds relating to the financial loss that the employer would suffer for the duration of her maternity leave. The same principle, the ECJ believed, should also be applied to the financial loss caused by the fact that

595

the woman appointed could not be employed in the post concerned for the duration of her pregnancy.

In Busch v Klinikum Neustadt GmbH und Co Betriebs-KG 2003 IRLR 625, ECJ, the fact that a pregnant nurse would have been unable to perform certain aspects of her duties did not permit the employer to prevent her returning early from a career break. According to the ECJ, to accept that a pregnant employee might be refused the right to return to work before the end of parental leave due to temporary prohibitions on performing certain work duties for which she was hired would be contrary to the objective contained in the Equal Treatment Directive and the Pregnant Workers Directive and would rob those Directives of any practical effect. The Court pointed out that the latter Directive provides that, where there is a risk to the safety or health of a worker or a negative effect on her pregnancy or breastfeeding, the employer should temporarily adjust the worker's working conditions or hours or, if that is not possible, move the worker to another job or, as a last resort, grant the worker leave.

13.66 Employers should always carefully consider what alternative work is available for women who can no longer perform their normal duties because of pregnancy. In Iske v P and O European Ferries (Dover) Ltd 1997 IRLR 401, EAT, the employer was held liable for direct sex discrimination for refusing to offer a pregnant woman working on a ferry a transfer to available suitable shore-based work in circumstances where merchant shipping regulations precluded pregnant women from working at sea after their 28th week of pregnancy.

For further details of the statutory provisions which govern the suspension of pregnant women from work on health and safety grounds, see Chapter 2, 'Health and safety protection', under 'Suspension on maternity grounds'.

13.67 **Breastfeeding**
In addition to the health and safety obligations an employer may have with regard to mothers who are breastfeeding (discussed in Chapter 2, 'Health and safety protection', under 'Risk assessments – duties of employers'), an employer may be liable for sex discrimination if it refuses to permit a woman to breastfeed at work. There is no statutory right to take time off for breastfeeding or expressing milk and although S.13(6)(a) EqA provides that less favourable treatment of a woman because she is breastfeeding is less favourable treatment because of sex, S.13(7) states that this does not apply to work-related discrimination. Nonetheless, an employer's refusal to accommodate requests for changes to working hours or conditions to enable breastfeeding may give rise to a claim of indirect sex discrimination under S.19 EqA. The EHRC Code of Practice on Employment gives the following example:

'An employer refused a request from a woman to return from maternity leave part time to enable her to continue breastfeeding her child who suffered from eczema. The woman told her employer that her GP had advised that continued breastfeeding would benefit the child's medical condition. The employer refused the request without explanation. Unless the employer's refusal can be objectively justified, this is likely to be indirect sex discrimination' – para 8.45.

The situation of women who wish to continue breastfeeding or expressing milk after returning to work from maternity leave is discussed further in Chapter 4, 'Returning to work after maternity leave', under 'Returning after ordinary maternity leave – breastfeeding on returning to work'.

Surrogacy arrangements   13.68

Where a child is born through a surrogacy arrangement, it is the birth mother who is entitled to maternity leave, even if it is the commissioning mother who looks after the child from birth. For some time there was a question mark over whether denying the commissioning mother a period of maternity leave – and with it the resulting special protection – was in breach of EU law. However, this issue was resolved by the ECJ in CD v ST 2014 ICR D26, ECJ, where D had entered into a surrogacy arrangement to have a baby, but her request for leave and pay under the employer's 'special leave policy' was rejected. She complained to an employment tribunal of discrimination contrary to the EqA but the tribunal decided to stay the proceedings and make a reference to the ECJ, which rejected her complaint. According to the Court, a commissioning mother who has had a baby through a surrogacy arrangement is not entitled to the maternity leave provided for in Article 8 of the Pregnant Workers Directive. The Court noted that pregnant workers and workers who have recently given birth or who are breastfeeding are in an especially vulnerable situation that makes it necessary for them to be granted the right to maternity leave. While the Court had previously held that maternity leave is also intended to ensure that the special relationship between a woman and her child is protected, that objective concerns only the period after 'pregnancy and childbirth'.

Thus, the granting of maternity leave pursuant to Article 8 presupposes that the worker has been pregnant and has given birth to a child. This was confirmed by the ECJ's decision in Mayr v Bäckerei und Konditorei Gerhard Flöckner OHG 2008 IRLR 387, ECJ. There, the Court stated that it is apparent, both from the wording of Article 10 of the Directive (which protects against dismissal) and from the Directive's primary objective, that to benefit from the protection in Article 10 the pregnancy in question must have started. Consequently, Member States are not required to grant a commissioning mother such as D, who has had a baby through a surrogacy arrangement, a right to maternity leave under Article 8, even if she may or does breastfeed the baby following the birth (as D had in fact done). However, the Directive does not preclude Member States from introducing provisions more favourable to commissioning mothers who have babies through surrogacy.

597

13.69 The ECJ also went on to hold that the employer's refusal to provide maternity leave was not direct sex discrimination contrary to the recast Equal Treatment Directive. To constitute direct discrimination on the ground of sex within the meaning of Article 2(1)(a) of that Directive, the reason for the refusal to provide maternity leave must apply exclusively to workers of one sex. Under UK law a commissioning father who has a baby through a surrogacy arrangement is treated in the same way as a commissioning mother in a comparable situation, in that he is also not entitled to paid leave equivalent to maternity leave. It followed from this that the refusal of D's request was not based on a reason that applies exclusively to workers of one sex.

Nor was there indirect sex discrimination within the meaning of Article 2(1)(b) because nothing in the instant case established that the refusal of maternity leave put female workers at a particular disadvantage compared with male workers. Finally, D was not treated less favourably for reasons related to pregnancy or maternity leave contrary to Article 2(2)(c), because a commissioning mother who has had a baby through a surrogacy arrangement cannot, by definition, be subjected to less favourable treatment related to her pregnancy given that she has not been pregnant. Also, as held above, D was not entitled to maternity leave under the Pregnant Workers Directive. Accordingly, there was no breach of the Equal Treatment Directive.

13.70 In a similar Irish case, decided on the same day – Z v A Government Department 2014 IRLR 563, ECJ – the ECJ also held that it is not discriminatory to refuse maternity leave to a woman who has a baby by a surrogate because she has no uterus. Z had argued, among other things, that the refusal to provide her with leave equivalent to maternity leave amounted to disability discrimination contrary to the EU Equal Treatment Framework Directive (No.2000/78). Applying its decision in HK Danmark (on behalf of Ring) v Dansk almennyttigt Boligselskab and another case 2013 ICR 851, ECJ, the Court held that the concept of 'disability' within the meaning of the Directive must be understood as referring to 'a limitation which results in particular from long-term physical, mental or psychological impairments which… may hinder the full and effective participation of the person concerned in professional life on an equal basis with other workers'. In particular, the Directive was aimed at enabling a disabled person's access to or participation in employment. While Z's condition constituted a limitation resulting from physical, mental or psychological impairments and was of a long-term nature, it did not make it impossible for her to carry out her work or constitute a hindrance to the exercise of her professional activity. Furthermore, the Court did not dispute that the inability to have a child by conventional means might be a source of great suffering. However, this did not in itself, in principle, prevent a commissioning mother from having access to, participating in, or advancing in employment. Z's condition did not therefore constitute a 'disability' within the meaning of the Directive.

598

Note that while commissioning mothers in a surrogacy arrangement are not entitled to maternity leave, recent changes introduced by the Children and Families Act 2014 made paid adoption leave available to them for the first time. They are also entitled to convert the adoption leave into shared parental leave. The details are contained in the Paternity, Adoption and Shared Parental Leave (Parental Order Cases) Regulations 2014 SI 2014/3096, which came into force on 1 December 2014, and are dealt with in Chapter 6, 'Adoption leave and pay', and Chapter 8, 'Shared parental leave and pay', respectively.

Motherhood discrimination

13.71

Unfavourable treatment of a female employee because she has young children will be direct sex discrimination if it is shown that a man with young children would not have been treated in the same way. This type of motherhood discrimination – where a comparison with a man is called for – differs from situations where an employer has made an employment decision based on a discriminatory assumption about a woman's capacity for childbearing. As noted above, discrimination based simply on the fact of a woman's pregnancy or capacity for childbearing amounts to automatic sex discrimination without the need for a comparison with a man in similar circumstances.

Three cases that illustrate the sort of conduct founded on sex-based assumptions about the role of women that will ground a complaint of direct discrimination:

- **Hurley v Mustoe** 1981 ICR 490, EAT: H started a job as an evening waitress in a wine bar but was immediately dismissed when the employer discovered that she had young children. He argued that his policy was not to have employees with young children because they were unreliable. The employment tribunal held that there was no evidence at all that the employer would refuse to employ a man with young children, so this was unlawful direct sex discrimination

- **Khan v Kent Country Nurseries Ltd** ET Case No.11996/82: K applied for a job and her application showed that she had three young children. She received the reply: 'Regrettably I must decline your application since a young mum with three kiddies would be failing in her domestic duties to take up the opportunity that I offer.' The employment tribunal held that this was 'clear and unequivocal' direct discrimination. It was immaterial that the employer, although misguided, had good intentions

- **Wickramaratne v Wellingtons Estate Agents (Battersea) Ltd** ET Case No.2304283/00: W applied for a secretarial post. During her second interview the employer asked her if she would work on Saturdays. She said she was unhappy about Saturday working because she wanted to spend time with her family and her parents, who were preparing to leave the country. However, she agreed to work one Saturday in four. The employer offered her the post at a final interview but withdrew it on discovering that

599

she had a young baby. The employer claimed the offer was withdrawn because W had been dishonest in the information she had given at interview about her responsibilities. However, the employment tribunal found that the employer had not asked W about her responsibilities and that she had not been dishonest. Instead, the employer had made an assumption that, given that W had a baby, she had major responsibilities that would 'clearly interfere' with her work – an assumption it would not necessarily have made about a male in similar circumstances – and had therefore treated her less favourably than a hypothetical male comparator.

13.72 However, most sex discrimination claims stemming from motherhood are of *indirect* discrimination – the imposition of an unjustifiable and detrimental provision, criterion or practice that puts a woman at a particular disadvantage compared to a man. Cases arise most often when a woman wishes to return after maternity leave on different terms that would make it easier for her to cope with her new baby (see 'Indirect sex discrimination' below).

In British Telecommunications plc v Roberts and anor 1996 ICR 625, EAT, the Appeal Tribunal emphasised the limited scope for making a claim for direct discrimination in motherhood cases. That case concerned two women whose employer rejected their requests to return to work from maternity leave on a job-share basis. The employment tribunal upheld their claims of direct sex discrimination on the basis that the employer's failure to give proper or reasonable consideration to their requests followed directly from the fact of their pregnancies and subsequent maternity leave, and therefore constituted discrimination on the ground of sex.

13.73 However, the EAT held that this was the wrong approach. Women, it said, are not entitled to rely permanently on the fact that they have children to establish discrimination whenever they suffer any detriment in their employment: the ECJ's decision Handels-og Kontorfunktionærernes Forbund i Danmark (acting for Hertz) v Dansk Arbejdsgiverforening (acting for Aldi Marked K/S) 1992 ICR 332, ECJ (see under 'Pregnancy and maternity discrimination – protected period' above), was authority for the proposition that once a woman returns from maternity leave, the special 'protected period' is at an end and her treatment falls to be considered by comparison with a man in the same circumstances in the normal way. In the EAT's view, no other grounds existed for a claim of 'automatic' direct sex discrimination because having childcare responsibilities – unlike childbearing or the capacity to bear children – was not a circumstance unique to women. Accordingly, since there was no evidence in the case before it that a man in the same circumstances would have been allowed to job-share, or would have had his request considered more seriously, the employees' claims of direct discrimination were bound to fail. That, however, left open the possibility of there being indirect discrimination arising from the employer's refusal to allow a job share. The employment tribunal had made no findings in this respect and the EAT concluded that the only proper course was to remit the case so that the tribunal could consider that possibility.

Inappropriate questions to job applicants. It is unlawful for an employer to **13.74** discriminate against a job applicant in the arrangements it makes for determining who should be offered employment – S.39(1) EqA. Employers must therefore be careful not to make sex-based assumptions about childcare during interviews or in the design of job application forms/questionnaires. Questions about domestic and family arrangements are not barred entirely but should be restricted to where they are relevant to the requirements of the job. In particular, if the work involves long and anti-social hours it may well be legitimate for an employer to assess whether an individual's circumstances will affect the performance of the job – Woodhead v Chief Constable of West Yorkshire Police EAT 285/89. However, it will amount to unlawful sex discrimination if a man with young children is not, or would not be, asked the same questions – Smith v North Western Regional Health Authority ET Case No.29270/86.

While, for the sake of caution, questions about existing family arrangements or future plans for a family should be restricted to circumstances where they are directly relevant to the job, it should also be remembered that such questions do not automatically found a claim of sex discrimination – they are merely potential evidence of such discrimination. An example:

- **Rigg v Renold Chain Ltd** ET Case No.1902753/03: R applied for a post with RC Ltd. During the interview, she was asked whether she intended to start a family. Prior to this, R had suffered a number of miscarriages and thus found the question distressing. She was successful in interview and was offered the post, but at a lower salary than she had hoped for. After accepting the offer, she withdrew and claimed that she had been discriminated against by reason of her sex. An employment tribunal recognised that questions about domestic circumstances are potentially discriminatory, but noted that such a question, by itself, is not discriminatory. In the circumstances of the case there was no evidence of R having been treated less favourably than a man would have been – there was evidence that male applicants were asked the same question, and a man was eventually appointed to the role on a lower salary than R had been offered. Accordingly, R's claim failed.

Discrimination by persons other than employers **13.75**

In addition to the extensive provisions relating to discrimination in employment, the EqA covers discrimination by a number of other bodies in a work-related context. These include discrimination against contract workers (S.41); discrimination by partnerships (Ss.44 and 45), barristers' chambers (S.47) and advocates' stables (S.48); and discrimination in respect of public and personal offices (Ss.49–52). For a full analysis of these provisions and the other provisions

601

mentioned in this section, see IDS Employment Law Handbook, 'Discrimination at Work' (2012), Chapter 28, 'Liability of employers, employees and agents'.

13.76 *Secondary liability.* The discriminatory acts of an employee, if done in the course of his or her employment, will be treated as having been done by the employer – S.109(1) EqA. There is, however, a defence to a claim against the employer: that the employer took all reasonable steps to prevent the employee from doing that act, or from doing in the course of his or her employment anything of that description – S.109(4).

13.77 *Personal liability of employees and agents.* Where an employer is liable for the discriminatory acts of its employee under S.109 EqA, the employee may also be personally liable under S.110 EqA. S.110 incorporates some of the provisions of the SDA relating to aiding unlawful acts. It also makes it explicit that the employee who commits an act of sex or pregnancy discrimination is personally liable: previously, the same result was achieved by the circuitous route of making the employee liable for knowingly aiding the employer to do an unlawful act. One key difference is that under the EqA provisions it is no longer necessary to show that the employee knew that the act was unlawful. However, it is still necessary that the employer be secondarily liable under S.109 EqA, or that the employer would be so liable if it had not satisfied the 'all reasonable steps' defence.

13.78 *Instructing, causing and inducing discrimination.* Section 111 EqA makes it unlawful for a person to instruct, cause or induce someone to discriminate, harass or victimise another person on the ground of sex (or any other protected characteristic). The EHRC can enforce this section, but S.111(5) provides that both the recipient of the instruction and the intended victim can bring proceedings, so long as they have suffered some detriment. So, if an employer instructs an employee not to appoint a woman who was pregnant to a particular post, and the employee refuses to follow the instruction, the employee can bring a claim under S.111 if the employer then subjects that person to a detriment, such as refusing them a pay rise. S.111 also prohibits a person from causing or inducing another person to commit an act of discrimination, harassment or victimisation.

13.79 **Aiding discrimination.** A person may also be liable for aiding an act of discrimination. S.112 states that a person (A) must not knowingly help another (B) to carry out an act that he or she knows is unlawful under the EqA. The EHRC Code of Practice on Employment states that 'help' should be given its ordinary meaning, and that help given to someone to discriminate, harass or victimise will be unlawful 'even if it is not substantial or productive, so long as it is not negligible'. The example given is of a manager who wants to ensure that a female candidate is appointed and asks a junior employee in the HR department to find out the sex of candidates, where this information has been removed from application forms. In these circumstances, the junior employee is likely to be liable under S.112, even though the manager is unsuccessful at excluding male candidates (para 9.27).

The helper has to 'know' that discrimination, harassment or victimisation is a likely outcome, but this does not have to be the intention of the helper. Furthermore, S.112(2) provides that where the helper is relying on a statement by B that the act for which help is given is not unlawful, and it is reasonable for him or her to rely on that statement, then the helper will escape liability. The Code of Practice states that, in the example given above, if the manager told the junior employee that he was under a duty to balance the sexes in the workplace, and it is reasonable for the junior employee to rely on this, then he would escape liability. The Code states that '[w]hether it is reasonable to believe depends on all the relevant circumstances, including the nature of the action and the relationship of the helper to the person getting the help' (paras 9.29–30).

Furthermore, S.112(3) makes it a criminal offence for B to knowingly or **13.80** recklessly make such a statement to the helper. So, in the example from the Code, if the manager either knows the statement is not true, or 'simply does not care whether it is true or not', then the manager will be liable at civil law and will also have committed a criminal act. This is punishable by a fine not exceeding level 5 on the standard scale (currently £5,000) – S.112(4).

An example of aiding sex discrimination under the equivalent provisions of the SDA:

- **Miles v Gilbank and anor** 2006 ICR 1297, CA: G was employed by a hairdressing salon as a senior hair designer and trainee manager. There was a friendly atmosphere in the salon until February 2004 when G informed M, the salon manager and a major shareholder in the company, that she was pregnant. Thereafter, the atmosphere changed. Owing to the events that followed, G brought a sex discrimination claim before the employment tribunal against both the company and M personally. The tribunal concluded that there had been an 'inhumane and sustained campaign of bullying and discrimination' against G by M and her other managers. It found the salon liable for the acts of M and the other managers, and went on to find that M was personally liable for her own discriminatory acts and also for the other managers' discriminatory acts because she had aided them to commit an unlawful act. On appeal, the Court of Appeal held that, in order to 'aid' an act of discrimination, a person must do more than merely create an environment in which discrimination can occur. In this case, the tribunal had found that M had consciously fostered and encouraged within the salon a discriminatory culture that targeted G. She had made it clear to the other managers, both in the manner in which she dealt with G's complaints about them and through her own discriminatory conduct, that their treatment of G was acceptable. She had been in a position to put an end to the

603

discrimination but instead had encouraged it. In these circumstances, the tribunal had been entitled to hold that M had knowingly aided the other managers' unlawful acts.

13.81 Indirect sex discrimination

At the end of maternity leave, a woman has the statutory right to return to the job in which she was employed before her absence (unless, in the case of additional maternity leave, that is not reasonably practicable, in which case she is entitled to return to a suitable and appropriate alternative job – see Chapter 4, 'Returning to work after maternity leave', under 'Returning after additional maternity leave') – S.71(4)(c) ERA and Reg 18(2) MPL Regulations. Similar rights apply where the woman is returning to work after having taken a period of shared parental leave in addition to maternity leave – see Chapter 8, 'Shared parental leave and pay'. However, women are frequently unable, or unwilling, to return to their original job because of family responsibilities. For this reason many women prefer to return to work on a more flexible basis, or on reduced hours, or to vary their job content, or to join up with another employee in a job-share arrangement.

An employee whose request to vary her job in this way is refused may be able to claim unlawful indirect sex discrimination. A complaint of direct discrimination is likely to fail because the employer may be just as likely to have refused a man's request in similar circumstances. An indirect discrimination complaint, however, may be a different matter. Such discrimination occurs where an employer operates a seemingly gender-neutral practice which, in reality, has a disproportionate effect – often referred to as disparate adverse impact – on one sex.

13.82 Note that, while the EqA was intended to harmonise the protection from various forms of discrimination across all protected characteristics, not all protected characteristics are covered by every form of discrimination. One notable instance of this is that while 'pregnancy and maternity' is a protected characteristic under S.4, it is not a 'relevant' protected characteristic under S.19, which prohibits indirect discrimination – S.19(3). Thus, while a refusal of flexible working may give rise to an indirect *sex* discrimination claim, there is no prospect of an indirect pregnancy/maternity discrimination claim.

13.83 **Relationship with flexible working provisions.** The statutory right to request flexible working – dealt with in IDS Employment Law Handbook, 'Atypical and Flexible Working' (2014), Chapter 4, 'Flexible working' – provides a statutory framework within which qualifying employees may request, and employers are obliged to consider, changes to their terms and conditions of employment, such as working hours or place of work – Part 8A ERA. The right to request flexible working allows employees to apply for flexible work patterns to help them balance their work and family life (although it is worth noting that, since 30 June 2014, the statutory right is available to all employees with at least six months' qualifying service with the employer). The employer to whom a flexible working request is made must be careful to consider not only the flexible working provisions but also the implications of discrimination law, since in many cases it will be the latter that provides employees with the greater substantive rights.

Furthermore, where an employer concludes that an employee is not entitled to make a request under the flexible working provisions – for example, if the employee does not have sufficient continuity of service, or has already made a request within the last 12 months – the employer should be careful not to dismiss the request out of hand. To do so would be to risk a discrimination claim, since there are no similar qualifying conditions for such claims – see further IDS Employment Law Handbook, 'Atypical and Flexible Working' (2014), Chapter 4, 'Flexible working', under 'Discrimination claims'.

Proving indirect discrimination 13.84

There are four elements of the test for indirect discrimination that must be established if a woman is to succeed in her claim. These are:

- that the employer applies to a woman a provision, criterion or practice which it applies or would apply equally to a man – S.19(1) and (2)(a) EqA, but

- which puts or would put women at a particular disadvantage when compared with men – S.19(2)(b), and

- which puts her at that disadvantage – S.19(2)(c), and

- which the employer cannot show to be a proportionate means of achieving a legitimate aim – S.19(2)(d).

The above definition of indirect discrimination was introduced – in respect of sex – in October 2005 when it was inserted into the SDA by the Employment Equality (Sex Discrimination) Regulations 2005 SI 2005/2467. It mirrors that found in previous discrimination legislation pertaining to race, religion, sexual orientation and age and, as a result, case law decided under those other (now repealed) discrimination provisions is relevant to indirect sex discrimination cases under what is now S.19 EqA. For a detailed explanation and analysis of the former indirect sex discrimination provisions, see IDS Employment Law Handbook, 'Discrimination at Work' (2012), Chapter 16, 'Indirect discrimination: proving disadvantage', under 'Legislative history'.

As with allegations of direct discrimination, the intention of the discriminator 13.85 is irrelevant to consideration of indirect discrimination complaints. As will be seen, the example of full-time working is used to illustrate many of the relevant principles in this section. However, it should be noted that the practice of

605

requiring employees to work full time is not the only potentially discriminatory practice that arises in this context. Particular shift patterns, for example, or a long-hours culture, may well prevent women from competing equally in the job market and amount to discrimination if not objectively justified.

13.86 Provision, criterion or practice

The words 'provision, criterion or practice' are not defined in the EqA. As a result, cases that were decided under either of the previous definitions of indirect discrimination in the SDA continue to be relevant under the current statutory wording, although it is generally accepted that 'provision, criterion or practice' is wider than the original 'requirement or condition' formula. The meaning of a 'provision', a 'criterion' or a 'practice' was considered in British Airways plc v Starmer 2005 IRLR 863, EAT. There the employer refused to allow a female pilot to work 50 per cent of her full-time hours following her return from maternity leave. BA plc did, however, offer to reduce her hours to 75 per cent of full time. It argued that this decision could not amount to a PCP because it was a one-off discretionary management decision. As such, it could not be said to be a 'provision' or a 'criterion' or a 'practice'. The EAT held that, although the decision might not amount to a criterion or a practice, an employment tribunal had been entitled to find that it was a provision.

13.87 Examples of PCPs. All of the following have been held to constitute a PCP:

- a requirement to work full time – **Mitchell v David Evans Agricultural Ltd** EAT 0083/06

- a requirement to work full time in order to be eligible for management positions – O'Donnell and anor v Legal and General Resources Ltd ET Case Nos.3102905–6/03

- a requirement to work full time during core hours, which included 2.30 pm – 5 pm – Glass v Newsquest (North East) Ltd ET Case No.2508468/04

- a requirement to work three full days a week – Henery v Quoteline Insurance Services Ltd t/a Sureplan Insurance ET Case No.2502542/13

- a requirement that a police officer provide on-call cover one weekend in eight – Sweeney v Chief Commissioner of Sussex Police ET Case No.3103129/04

- a requirement to work full time in the office or at least 25 hours a week in the office – Giles v Cornelia Care Homes ET Case No.3100720/05

- a requirement to perform out-of-hours on-call duties – Oxford Health NHS Foundation Trust v Laakkonen and ors EAT 0536/12

- a practice of counting childcare absences when assessing attendance records for dismissal purposes – Ceesay v Deepdene Hostel Ltd and ors ET Case No.2302853/02.

606

In addition, examples of requirements or conditions under the original test that would amount to PCPs today include:

- a rule that part-time workers be selected for redundancy before full-time workers – Clarke and anor v Eley (IMI) Kynoch Ltd 1983 ICR 165, EAT

- a refusal to employ someone with young children (discrimination on the ground of marital status) – Hurley v Mustoe 1981 ICR 490, EAT

- a demand that teaching staff in a school take on extra-curricular activities – Briggs v North Eastern Education and Library Board 1990 IRLR 181, NICA

- a requirement that the employee work in any place within the UK to which she is directed pursuant to a contractual mobility clause – Meade-Hill and anor v British Council 1995 ICR 847, CA

- an informal policy indicating that requests to work part time or on a job-sharing basis would be refused – Cast v Croydon College 1998 ICR 500, CA.

13.88 The potential of indirect sex discrimination arising in the application of redundancy selection criteria was examined by the ECJ in Riežniece v Zemkopības ministrija and anor 2013 ICR 1096, ECJ. Although this case concerned an employee absent on parental leave, the same principles would apply where a redundancy situation arises when the employee is absent from work on maternity leave. R, a principal adviser in the legal affairs division of the Latvian Government's Administrative Department, took parental leave from November 2007 to May 2009. In 2009 the Department decided to abolish one of its principal adviser posts and all those who were potentially affected (including R) were assessed against criteria from the 2009 performance appraisal. Since R was not at work in 2009, the results of her last appraisal before going on leave were used to measure her against the 2009 criteria, notwithstanding that the 2006 and 2009 appraisals adopted different benchmarks.

As a result of this assessment, R's post was abolished. She brought a claim arguing that her dismissal was unlawful and her case reached the Senate of the Latvian Supreme Court, which referred a number of questions to the ECJ. The ECJ noted that the two sets of appraisals did not have the same objectives: the 2006 appraisal was aimed at assessing the quality of work, while the 2009 appraisal was carried out in the context of the abolition of a post. However, while the assessment of workers over two different periods was not a perfect solution, the ECJ considered that it was appropriate, given R's absence in 2009, provided the criteria used did not place workers who had taken parental leave at a disadvantage. The national court would need to satisfy itself that the assessment encompassed all workers liable to be affected by the abolition of the post; that it was based on criteria which did not differentiate between those who were, and those who were not, in active service; and that it did not involve

607

the physical presence of workers, as this was a condition that those on parental leave were unable to fulfil.

13.89 Importantly, the Court did not say that employers could not include employees away from work on family-related leave – be it parental or maternity leave – as part of a redundancy selection exercise. However, they must make sure that the criteria used to decide who is going to be made redundant are applied equally to everyone and do not put those employees on leave in a less favourable position than employees who remained at work. Conversely, the employer must not apply the criteria in such a way that unduly favours a female employee away on maternity leave. In Eversheds Legal Services Ltd v De Belin 2011 ICR 1137, EAT, for example, the employer was held to have discriminated against B, a male employee, when he was made redundant in preference to a female employee who was on maternity leave. In calculating their respective scores, the female employee was given the maximum notional score for a criterion measuring the period between work being done for clients and receipt of payment. As a result, B scored lowest and was dismissed. The EAT held that the employer unfairly favoured the female employee over B and upheld his direct sex discrimination claim. (This case is discussed further under 'Discrimination against men – direct discrimination' below.)

13.90 **'Particular disadvantage'**
The next stage in proving indirect discrimination is for the claimant to show that the PCP applied by the employer:

- puts or would put women at a particular disadvantage when compared with men – S.19(2)(b), and

- puts her at that disadvantage – S.19(2)(c).

In other words, the claimant must establish that women as a group suffer or would suffer a particular disadvantage as a result of the application of the relevant PCP (the so-called 'group disadvantage') and that the claimant herself suffers or would suffer that same disadvantage. The concept of 'particular disadvantage' is not new: it applied in the vast majority of employment cases before S.19 came into force.

13.91 **Defining 'disadvantage'.** What amounts to a 'disadvantage' for the purpose of S.19 is not defined in the EqA. However, the EHRC Code of Practice on employment states at para 4.9 that 'disadvantage' is to be construed as 'something that a reasonable person would complain about – so an unjustified sense of grievance would not qualify. A disadvantage does not have to be quantifiable and the worker does not have to experience actual loss (economic or otherwise). It is enough that the worker can reasonably say that they would have preferred to be treated differently.' This, in effect, summarises the House of Lords' decision in Shamoon v Chief Constable of the Royal Ulster

608

Constabulary 2003 ICR 337, HL, which considered discriminatory detriment under the Northern Irish equivalent of what was then S.6(2)(b) SDA. The equivalent provision is now S.39(2)(d) EqA, which provides that an employer (A) must not discriminate against an employee (B) 'by subjecting B to any other detriment'. It would therefore seem that the concept and scope of 'disadvantage' is similar to that of 'detriment' found in the original definitions of indirect discrimination in the SDA. In fact, tribunals frequently use the terms 'detriment' and 'disadvantage' interchangeably.

In Commissioner of Police of the Metropolis v Keohane 2014 ICR 1073, EAT, the EAT held that a 'risk' to the employee's career prospects was capable of being a 'disadvantage' within the meaning of S.19(2) EqA. There, the police force had a policy of removing a dog from its handler where the handler was likely to be non-operational for some time. A police officer employed as a dog handler claimed that she had suffered direct discrimination because of her pregnancy under S.18, and indirect sex discrimination under S.19, when the police force removed one of her two police dogs from her when she informed them of her pregnancy. An employment tribunal upheld the first claim, but rejected the second.

On appeal, the EAT overturned the employment tribunal's conclusion that **13.92** there was no indirect discrimination because there was only a 'potential disadvantage arising out of risk'. The EAT considered that the tribunal had been correct to recognise, in relation to the direct discrimination claim, that subjecting the claimant to 'a risk of adverse consequences' – in this case, that she might have no second dog upon her return to work, that she would lose the opportunity of overtime, and that her career prospects would be damaged – itself constituted a detriment, regardless of whether those consequences actually materialised on her return to work. In the EAT's view, there was no obvious reason why the same should not apply in the case of the indirect discrimination claim, stating: 'If one were to ask in respect of two persons whether one was disadvantaged by comparison with the other because one suffered a real risk of adverse events materialising, while the other did not, only one answer could be given: that one was indeed disadvantaged by comparison with the other.' Given that the claimant was disadvantaged by the removal of her dog, her claim of indirect discrimination was remitted to the tribunal to consider whether the police force could establish objective justification. (Note that the EAT's decision on the direct discrimination claim is discussed in the section 'Direct discrimination' above, under 'Pregnancy and maternity discrimination – unfavourable treatment', and 'Pregnancy and maternity discrimination – "because of"'.)

Group disadvantage. As noted above, under S.19(2)(b) EqA the claimant **13.93** must show that the PCP puts or would put women at a particular disadvantage when compared with men. This is a departure from the original approach to

609

indirect discrimination, which in effect required the claimant to show that the application of the requirement or condition or PCP had a disproportionate adverse impact on members of her sex compared with members of the opposite sex. This entailed a statistically driven comparative exercise and generated a huge amount of case law addressing the tricky issue of how to establish disproportionate impact – i.e. what amounts to a considerably larger or a considerably smaller proportion (depending on which test was in force) of women? While tribunals were prepared to apply their 'industrial knowledge' to the question of whether there had been adverse disparate impact, detailed statistical evidence was usually required. Given that it has now been some time since this test was abolished, the extensive body of case law that developed under it, much of which focused on the use of statistics to prove a claimant's case, is primarily of historical interest only and is not referred to in this chapter. However, discussion of the old test can be found in IDS Employment Law Handbook, 'Discrimination at Work' (2012), Chapter 16, 'Indirect discrimination: proving disadvantage', under 'Particular disadvantage – the statistical approach: relative proportions'.

The current test of particular disadvantage entails a comparative exercise, requiring a tribunal to assess whether the application of the PCP causes or would cause 'particular disadvantage' to members of the claimant's sex. The question now is how it should go about this process in view of the fact that the legislation no longer makes mention of the claimant having to demonstrate that a considerably larger or a considerably smaller proportion of her sex has been put to a particular disadvantage. Are statistics still relevant, and, if so, what is the statistical methodology that should be applied? Is the threshold lower for establishing disadvantage than it was for establishing a considerably larger or smaller proportion? The initial view of the Government when it consulted over the new test was that the move away from statistical comparison would make it easier to establish indirect sex discrimination. However, tribunals have continued to address the question of the correct 'pool' for the purpose of making a comparison.

13.94 The guiding principle for constructing the pool is that it should be defined by reference to the nature of the PCP in issue, and should accordingly be limited to those affected by that PCP. For example, in Pike v Somerset County Council and anor 2010 ICR 46, CA, the Court of Appeal held that the discriminatory effect of an employer's policy of not making pension contributions in respect of employees who had retired and returned to work part time should be tested only by reference to that policy's impact on those who had actually retired and re-entered employment, not the whole workforce. In the Court's view, the leading case – the House of Lords' decision in Secretary of State for Trade and Industry v Rutherford and anor (No.2) 2006 ICR 785, HL – made it clear that those who had no interest in the policy at issue – in this case, employees who had yet to retire – should not be brought into the pool.

In Hacking and Paterson and anor v Wilson EATS 0054/09 the Scottish EAT considered the appropriate pool for testing indirect sex discrimination with regard to family-friendly working, with surprising results. In that case, the Appeal Tribunal had to decide whether an employer's practice of refusing all flexible working requests from its property managers had an indirectly discriminatory impact. The EAT decided that the appropriate pool for comparison was restricted to property managers who wanted to work flexibly. But it rejected the employer's argument that this automatically meant that there would be no indirect discrimination, since everyone in the pool would have received a negative response. The EAT thought that the tribunal should consider whether the refusal of the claimant's request gave rise to a particular disadvantage, something that would depend on the consequences – for the claimant – of a refusal. If such disadvantage is established, the tribunal would then have to consider whether it is a disadvantage more likely to be experienced by women than men.

This might appear to throw a spanner in the works of indirect sex discrimination **13.95** claims brought on the basis of employers' flexible working policies. It had previously become commonplace for tribunals to assume disparate impact of rigid working practices on women, in view of their greater propensity to have childcare responsibilities, and so move straight to the question of objective justification (see 'Justification' below). The EAT's decision in Hacking suggests that this might not be assumed so readily in future – or at least, not conceded so readily by the employer. The EAT's comments that disadvantage to the claimant herself is not obvious in every case may create a further obstacle. The EAT observed that it is not only women with childcare responsibilities who potentially lose out from a refusal of flexible working – male as well as female employees seek flexible working for various reasons, such as combining jobs or pursuing other interests or educational courses. Furthermore, when it comes to disadvantage suffered as a result of a conflict between work and childcare commitments, while some women cannot sustain full-time work around their childcare commitments, others can but prefer to work part time. The EAT considered that it would be difficult to regard a woman who chose to work part time as disadvantaged when her request for flexible working was refused.

If specific proof of disparate impact is indeed required, it is worth noting that the choice of relevant pool can have a significant impact on the outcome. For example, it is generally a good deal easier to establish that a requirement to work full time places women at a particular disadvantage if the pool consists of all potential applicants for a job rather than merely a cross-section of a particular workforce. In the latter case, the proportion of women who are put at a disadvantage by the PCP may be so small in number that it becomes impossible to say that the application of the requirement has any discriminatory effect in practice. Where the selected pool happens to include a relatively small number of women, it may be that none of these, apart from the claimant, has childcare responsibilities or faces other impediments to full-time working.

13.96 That said, we would suggest that, even within the narrower pool suggested by the EAT in Hacking and Paterson and anor v Wilson (above), disparate impact should still be fairly easy to show. Although the EAT was correct to note that people may seek flexible working arrangements for a variety of reasons – even more so now that the statutory right to request flexible working is available to all – it is still overwhelmingly the case that the reason most women seek flexible working patterns is that they have primary responsibility for the care of a child, something far fewer men are likely to have. Tribunals will not lightly accept the suggestion that a woman who seeks flexible working arrangements in order to spend more time bringing up a child is not disadvantaged when such a request is refused. And tribunals will presumably still be entitled to apply either common knowledge or their industrial experience to the consideration of whether that disadvantage is one that tends to afflict women more than men.

Recent decisions lend support to the view that the suggestion in Hacking – that it is not inevitable that women are disproportionately adversely affected by a refusal to grant flexible working – is indeed premature. In Shackletons Garden Centre Ltd v Lowe EAT 0161/10, for example, the employer required all employees to work rotational shifts that included some weekends. The employee, who wanted to return from maternity leave working three fixed weekdays, complained to an employment tribunal of indirect sex discrimination. On the question of whether the PCP put women at a particular disadvantage, the tribunal came to the following conclusion: 'It is well recognised that significantly more women than men are primarily responsible for the care of their children. Accordingly the ability of women to work particular hours is substantially restricted because of those childcare commitments in contrast to that of men.' Although the EAT overturned the tribunal's finding of indirect discrimination on appeal, it did so on the basis that the tribunal had erred in finding that the employee had personally been disadvantaged by the employer's PCP (see under 'Individual disadvantage' below). It did not criticise the tribunal's finding that the PCP disadvantaged women as a group. On this point, it found itself in agreement with the tribunal, stating that the tribunal had been entitled to find that women are primarily responsible for childcare 'based on what is now well recognised in industrial and employment circles'.

13.97 These sentiments were echoed by the employment tribunal in Cooper v House of Fraser (Stores) Ltd ET Case No.2204356/11. There, the employer required all buyers in the women's wear department to work full time. The tribunal found that the PCP disadvantaged women because they were likely to be the main carers for children and particularly young children. It continued: 'It may be, as identified in [Hacking and Paterson and anor v Wilson (above)], that as time moves on the position is not as straightforward as that, with the development of different roles in society by men and women, more childcare responsibilities on men etc. However, we conclude, both from the statistics and from our own observations of how society operates, that it is still women who in the main have the burden of the care of very young children, and therefore a rule that states that they would not be permitted to work part time for an employer is going to be disadvantageous to women.' The statistics shown to the tribunal came from a document entitled, 'Working Time and Work Life Balance in European Countries' (2006), which showed that the part-time workforce mainly or exclusively consists of women, particularly mothers with young children. The tribunal concluded that the PCP disadvantaged women buyers as a group and the claimant in particular and, as the employer was unable to show justification, the claimant's claim under S.19 succeeded.

Individual disadvantage. The final step when making out a case of indirect 13.98 discrimination (prior to consideration of objective justification) requires the claimant to show that the PCP puts or would put her at the particular disadvantage – S.19(2)(c) EqA. For example, in Shackletons Garden Centre Ltd v Lowe (above) a complaint of indirect sex discrimination failed because the claimant was unable to show that she herself was adversely affected by a requirement to work on weekends. L worked as a sales assistant at a garden centre. Following her return from maternity leave, she objected to the employer's requirement that all employees must work rotational shifts involving some weekends. An employment tribunal agreed that she suffered indirect sex discrimination contrary to S.19. On appeal, the EAT upheld the tribunal's finding that the PCP relating to weekend working put women at a particular disadvantage. However, it overturned the tribunal's decision on the basis that it had failed to identify the specific disadvantage caused to L. There was insufficient evidence that childcare arrangements would be unavailable if she worked the rota system required by her employer. In those circumstances, it was unclear that she had suffered an individual disadvantage, as distinct from a 'self-inflicted detriment', and the case was remitted to a differently constituted tribunal.

The disadvantage suffered by the claimant under S.19(2)(c) must be the *same* disadvantage as the group disadvantage made out under S.19(2)(b). In Boon v Chief Constable of Leicestershire ET Case No.1900473/13 B worked as a police constable in the Leicestershire police force. During the course of her employment, she gave birth to two children but, as they were born 11 months apart, she took only one period of maternity leave. B and her husband, who also worked on the force but was a higher-ranking officer, decided that she would be the children's primary carer. In March 2008, B returned to work on reduced hours to enable her to look after the children. When her shift pattern later changed, B again reduced her hours to avoid working late shifts. In May 2011, the police force announced that it would introduce a new shift system to enable it to operate 24/7. Under the new system, everyone would be required to work some anti-social hours. Knowing that some groups, such as flexible workers, would be adversely affected, a panel was set up to address any issues caused by the new shift system on an individual basis. In addition, S, who had overall responsibility for flexible working, devised shift patterns for officers who had children and whose partners also worked in the force. In B's case, S dovetailed her shift pattern with that of her husband's to ensure that either one of them would be available to provide childcare. However, B objected to the shift pattern proposed by S because it included some night working with a 4 am finishing time and some work on weekends. Her objections to the proposed shift pattern were threefold: lack of family time, fatigue and not being with her children if they woke in the middle of the night. Rather than apply to the panel to have her proposed working pattern reconsidered, B resigned and claimed indirect sex discrimination.

13.99 The employment tribunal found that the police force was intending to impose a PCP – i.e. the new shift pattern – that would put women at a particular disadvantage within the meaning of S.19(2)(b) in that women would find it more difficult to look after their children and/or meet their childcare commitments as a result of the application of the PCP. However, it rejected B's argument that she herself had been put at '*that* disadvantage' (our stress) as required by S.19(2)(c). The pattern proposed for B meant that either she or her husband would have been with the children at all times when they were not at school. It did not necessitate any third-party assistance to help look after the children. Nor did the proposal afford substantially less time with the children. It could not therefore be said that B would suffer the disadvantage of it being more difficult for her to look after her children or to meet childcare commitments. The disadvantages that B complained of were fatigue, lack of family time and the possibility of the children waking in the night. None of these related to childcare commitments and, except for the night-time issue, were suffered by most, if not all, officers (male and female), irrespective of childcare commitments. They also could have been ameliorated or eradicated if B had engaged in discussions with the force. Moreover, the issue regarding the possible waking and settling of the children at night was a personal choice for B – she wished to be the one present if they woke in the night. According to the tribunal, B's preference to settle the children could not reasonably be categorised as being the same disadvantage as the identified and accepted group disadvantage. It followed that the individual disadvantage relied upon by B was not the same as the group disadvantage identified in the claim: B would not find it more difficult to look after her children or meet childcare commitments as a result of the new shift pattern. In actual fact, the tribunal accepted that the proposed work pattern was in some respects better than her current childcare arrangement – for instance, B would no longer have to rely on her mother to look after the children from time to time. Her claim accordingly failed.

As noted under 'Group disadvantage' above, the EAT's decision in Hacking and Paterson and anor v Wilson (above) left the distinct impression that it may be more difficult in future to establish either group or individual disadvantage in flexible working cases. However, it remains to be seen whether tribunals will start to pay closer attention to the reasons put forward as to why work and childcare commitments may not be reconcilable, and whether it is reasonable for the claimant to feel disadvantaged by a rejection of a flexible working request. In Cooper v House of Fraser (Stores) Ltd (above) the employment tribunal noted that the EAT's controversial view in that case that it would be difficult to regard a woman as personally disadvantaged by a refusal to allow her to work flexibly where she chose to work part time raised a number of questions. For instance, at what point can it be said that part-time working is a matter of choice rather than a necessity? How much effort should women be expected to make to ensure alternative childcare arrangements? Should a woman's partner who works from home, for example, be expected to provide the childcare? What if full-time childcare is expensive or the woman considers it would not be in her child's best interests? The tribunal assumed that it was *possible* for the employee in the instant case, whose flexible working request had been turned down, to work full time in the sense that she could either afford to pay for childcare or her partner could have assisted with childcare. However, the employee felt that it was not appropriate for her young daughter to spend ten to 11 hours a day, five days a week, in a nursery or with other carers. According to the tribunal, that was a reasonable position to take. Having regard to the House of Lords' decision in Shamoon v Chief Constable of the Royal Ulster Constabulary (see 'Defining "disadvantage"' above), it concluded that she had a justified sense of grievance, and was therefore disadvantaged within the meaning of S.19, when the employer required her to work full time. The claim of indirect sex discrimination therefore succeeded.

A different question on individual disadvantage arose in Little v Richmond **13.100** Pharmacology Ltd 2014 ICR 85, EAT: namely, whether a successful internal appeal, which reversed the employer's initial decision to refuse a part-time working request and allowed the employee to work reduced hours on a trial basis, meant that the employee was no longer personally disadvantaged by the application of the PCP. During her maternity leave, L had requested part-time working on her return to work. R Ltd turned this application down on the basis that it was not feasible for its sales executives to work part time. L brought an internal appeal against this decision but then resigned before a hearing could be arranged. R asked L to reconsider her decision to resign and arranged an appeal hearing which she attended. At this hearing, R agreed to L's part-time working arrangement on a three-month trial basis, to begin following her return from maternity leave. However, L did not accept this offer and instead confirmed her resignation. An employment tribunal dismissed L's claim of indirect sex discrimination holding that, in light of R's decision at the appeal hearing, she had not suffered a disadvantage.

615

In upholding the tribunal's decision, the EAT rejected L's contention that she implicitly withdrew her appeal when she resigned; as the tribunal had pointed out, L had attended the appeal hearing. The EAT held that 'an internal appeal process, consensually pursued, forms part and parcel of the employer's decision-making process', and further noted that R's initial decision to reject L's request for part-time working was expressed to be subject to her right of appeal and, to that extent, the decision was conditional. L exercised her right of appeal and her flexible working request was allowed. This meant that L did not suffer any disadvantage or detriment as the PCP – namely, full-time working – would not be applied to her until she had completed her maternity leave. The EAT was at pains to point out that this case was particularly fact- and claim-sensitive. L had not claimed constructive dismissal as a result of indirect sex discrimination. Her claim was that she had been subjected to a detriment when her application to work part time was initially rejected by R. A key factor which led to the conclusion that L did not suffer any form of personal disadvantage or detriment was that she was still on maternity leave and had not returned to work when the decision was made at the appeal hearing to allow her to work part time. The EAT also emphasised that L had attended the appeal hearing. It remains to be seen, therefore, whether a claimant who opts to entirely disengage from the appeal process, but nevertheless has the rejection of her flexible working application overturned on appeal, will similarly be held not to have suffered a personal disadvantage.

13.101 Justification

In many cases, a finding of indirect discrimination will hinge on whether or not an employer can show a PCP to be justified. The justification defence is found in S.19(2)(d) EqA, which requires the employer to show that the PCP was a 'proportionate means of achieving a legitimate aim'. So far as the wording goes, this is a substantial departure from the pre-2005 approach, which required the employer to show that the PCP was 'justifiable irrespective of sex'. In practice, however, the current definition of justification is consistent with the approach that has been taken by courts and tribunals ever since the ECJ's decision in Bilka-Kaufhaus GmbH v Weber von Hartz 1987 ICR 110, ECJ (an equal pay case), and cases determined under the old test which took into account the ECJ's decision will continue to be relevant under the current formula.

As the test for justification has its origins in European law, it should be noted that the actual wording used in S.19(2)(d) differs from that now found in Article 2(1) of the recast EU Equal Treatment Directive in that the word 'proportionate' replaces the stipulation that the measure be 'appropriate and necessary'.

13.102 Case law has established that in order to successfully defend a claim of indirect discrimination, the employer must show that it has carried out a balancing exercise, weighing the business's need to impose the PCP against the discriminatory effect of that PCP, and, in doing so, must put forward cogent evidence tipping the scales in favour of its argument: generalisations will not be acceptable. This process requires the employer critically and objectively to evaluate its business decisions where discrimination is obvious or likely. Having an apparently sound business reason for denying a female employee's application to work part time, for example, is not sufficient in itself – the employer must also consider whether the reasons for insisting on full-time work are strong enough to overcome any indirectly discriminatory impact. In particular, an employer should consider whether there are any alternatives that would achieve the same aim without being as disadvantageous to an individual. Two examples of the above principles in practice:

- **Savva v Hillgate Travel Ltd** ET Case No.2200525/06: in upholding S's claim that her employer's decision to dismiss her because she could not work a flexible shift amounted to indirect sex discrimination, an employment tribunal found that the employer had failed to put forward sufficient evidence that it had carried out any research or made any enquiries as to the need to abandon the fixed shift that had fitted in with S's childcare needs. The tribunal also took account of the fact that current social policy – underpinned by the right to request flexible working in the ERA – is to provide for working arrangements that assist those with caring responsibilities

- **Chandler v American Airlines Inc** ET Case No.2329478/10: C was employed as a lead agent at the time she made an application for flexible working following the birth of her second child. Her application was refused, but AA agreed to a reduction in her working hours on her return in April 2009. AA carried out a review of its passenger services in July 2009 and as a result the post of lead agent was abolished and post-holders were invited to apply to become operational coordinators or team leaders. C applied for a post as team leader and was successful, but AA informed her that the post was full time and although it would honour her hours and roster pattern for a trial period of four months it would expect her to increase her hours to full time at the end of that period. She told AA that she was not in a position to work full time and at the end of the trial period she was given a choice: she could work full time, consider a job-share as an operational coordinator, consider suitable alternative employment or accept a redundancy package. She accepted redundancy under duress and brought a claim of sex discrimination. On the basis of its recognition that significantly more women than men have primary responsibility for childcare, the employment tribunal found that a requirement to work full time was to the detriment of women and was not a proportionate means of achieving AA's legitimate aim of improving management. AA had accepted before the tribunal that the post could have been undertaken other than on a full-time basis, although not on the hours that C had been working. It

617

followed that there was a less discriminatory alternative to the requirement to work full time, which could not therefore be justified.

13.103 To succeed in the defence of justification, an employer must first establish that the PCP was applied in pursuit of a legitimate aim. If the aim behind a PCP is itself discriminatory then it can never be justified – see R v Secretary of State for Employment ex parte EOC and anor 1994 ICR 317, HL, and Allonby v Accrington and Rossendale College and ors 2001 ICR 1189, CA.

13.104 **Grounds of justification.** In the context of maternity and parental rights, the question of justification should be considered in tandem with the permitted grounds for refusing a flexible working request under S.80G(1)(b) ERA. Those grounds are: the burden of additional costs; the detrimental effect on ability to meet customer demand; the inability to reorganise work among existing staff; the inability to recruit additional staff; a detrimental impact on quality; a detrimental impact on performance; insufficiency of work during the periods the employee proposes to work; planned structural changes; and any other ground the Secretary of State may specify by regulations – for further details see IDS Employment Law Handbook, 'Atypical and Flexible Working' (2014), Chapter 4, 'Flexible working', under 'Handling flexible working requests – grounds upon which employer can refuse request'. This list is by no means definitive when it comes to justification under the EqA. However, since flexible working requests and sex discrimination are so closely linked, the list provides some guidance as to the matters that may constitute justification with respect to indirect sex discrimination claims.

While the test for justification has always been set out by statute, it is largely a question of fact for tribunals to determine whether the employer has satisfied the statutory test. Unlike in unfair dismissal cases, there is no 'room for manoeuvre' for employers or, to put it another way, no range of reasonable responses. An employment tribunal should make its own judgment, upon a fair and detailed analysis of the working practices and business considerations involved, as to whether the PCP at issue is justified – Hardys and Hansons plc v Lax 2005 ICR 1565, CA. This has the effect of restricting the ability to challenge a tribunal's conclusion on appeal, and also means that it would be unwise to regard the outcome of cases that turn largely on their own facts as constituting precedents of any sort. Nevertheless, the following are useful illustrations of the grounds on which tribunals have found justification.

13.105 *Role not suitable for job-sharing.* Women returning from maternity leave often ask to reduce their hours, a request that may entail some form of job-sharing. In Eley v Huntleigh Diagnostics Ltd EAT 1441/96 an employer's refusal to allow E to job-share her receptionist role was held to be justifiable as the expense of training someone else to 'fill in' for her for a few hours a week was prohibitive, and the nature of the business demanded a full-time receptionist. Similarly, in Burston v Superior Creative Services Ltd ET Case No.72892/95 a refusal by the employer to allow B to work three days a week was found to be justified. B had wanted to reduce her role from five to three days a week by carrying out sales work only while a part-time replacement was employed to carry out the general administration duties that had previously taken up two days of her working week. However, sales had been poor before B's maternity leave and the employer was entitled to demand that she spend more than three days a week on sales in future.

However, the onus of establishing justification is on the employer, who will be expected to put forward evidence of why the role is not suitable for job-sharing. In Funge v Ravensbourne College of Design and Communication ET Case No.1101233/07 an employment tribunal found that there was an opposition to job-sharing in general on the part of the employer, and that it had failed to show that the PCP that all staff work full time was justified.

Costs. It is open to an employment tribunal to find that cost is a factor justifying **13.106** indirect discrimination, provided it is combined with other factors – Cross and ors v British Airways plc 2005 IRLR 423, EAT. In that case the female claimants complained about a retirement policy allowing employees recruited before 1971 to retire at 60 instead of 55 – the age applied to most of the workforce. The claimants pointed out that in a workforce of 13,127 in 2002, there remained only 536 employees with a contractual retirement age of 60, the vast majority of whom – 436 – were male, whereas the workforce as a whole was predominantly female. In holding that the policy was justified, an employment tribunal found that the discriminatory impact of the policy weighed lightly, given the small number of individuals affected. With this in mind, the tribunal took into account the cost implications for BA of altering the retirement age and the knock-on detrimental impact the change would have for the majority of the cabin crew whose pension benefits would be reduced if they sought to retire at 55 instead of 60.

On appeal to the EAT, the claimants argued that the employment tribunal had erred in taking into account the issue of cost. They relied on a number of decisions of the ECJ, culminating in Schönheit v Stadt Frankfurt am Main and another case 2004 IRLR 983, ECJ, which appeared to confirm that budgetary considerations can never justify sex discrimination. In the EAT's view, the ECJ decisions had established that an EU Member State, with its notionally bottomless purse, cannot rely on budgetary considerations to justify a discriminatory social policy. On the other hand, an employer seeking to justify a discriminatory PCP is entitled to put cost into the balance along with other justifications if there are any, even though considerations of cost cannot be the sole basis for justification. However, the EAT did add that when it comes to the weighing exercise, costs justifications may be less highly valued where the discrimination is substantial, obvious and even deliberate. (Note that the Cross

619

case was appealed to the Court of Appeal – 2006 ICR 1239, CA – but on different points from the one discussed above.)

13.107 This 'cost plus' approach has since been doubted, albeit in the different context of age discrimination and only in obiter (i.e. non-binding) remarks. In Woodcock v Cumbria Primary Care Trust 2011 ICR 143, EAT, the Appeal Tribunal upheld an employment tribunal's decision that the redundancy dismissal of an employee approaching his 50th birthday – at which point he would be entitled to termination payments and pension enhancements worth between £500,000 and £1,000,000 – was justified age discrimination. (Direct age discrimination, unlike most other forms of direct discrimination, can be objectively justified in the same way as indirect discrimination.) The EAT held that the tribunal had properly applied the 'cost plus' approach endorsed in Cross and ors v British Airways plc (above). It noted that while the fear of the potential costs consequences of the claimant remaining in employment on his 50th birthday had motivated the choice of date for his redundancy dismissal, it would be artificial to regard that factor in isolation as having been the reason for his dismissal. On this analysis, objective justification was made out.

That conclusion therefore disposed of the appeal. However, the then President of the EAT, Mr Justice Underhill, went on to cast doubt over the correctness of the 'cost plus' orthodoxy. He accepted that as a matter both of principle and of common sense, considerations of cost must be admissible in considering whether a *prima facie* discriminatory PCP may nevertheless be justified. But he saw no principled basis for a rule that such considerations can never by themselves constitute sufficient justification. The adoption of such a rule would tend to involve parties and tribunals in an artificial game of 'find the other factor', producing arbitrary and complicated reasoning. Underhill P also noted that deciding where 'cost' stops and other factors start is not always straightforward.

13.108 The Court of Appeal rejected the claimant's further appeal in Woodcock v Cumbria Primary Care Trust 2012 ICR 1126, CA, and expressed its own doubts on the continued correctness of the 'cost plus' orthodoxy. The Court noted that there is 'some degree of artificiality' in an approach to justification that renders cost inadmissible as a factor on its own, but admissible if linked to a non-cost factor. The Court observed that every decision an employer takes is likely to involve the question of cost in some way, and that the wording of the discrimination legislation then in force did not exclude cost considerations – it merely required that the treatment be a 'proportionate means of achieving a legitimate aim', as S.19 EqA does now. However, the Court summarised the effect of ECJ case law as being that 'an employer cannot justify discriminatory treatment "solely" because the elimination of such treatment would involve increased costs'. Accordingly, while the wider implications of Cross and ors v British Airways plc (above) have now been doubted at a higher level, its general principle survives.

620

The fact that these comments were made with regard to age discrimination should not diminish their potential importance to sex discrimination. Underhill P in Woodcock v Cumbria Primary Care Trust (above) referred to Cross and ors v British Airways plc (above), the leading case, and did not expressly confine his views to cost as a justification for age discrimination. An employer defending an indirect sex discrimination claim based on a refusal to allow family-friendly working may find these comments particularly useful. It is worth noting that the burden of additional costs is, on its own, enough to justify an employer's refusing a flexible working request under S.80G(1)(b)(i) ERA. So, for as long as Cross remains the leading authority, it is entirely possible for an employer to find itself in the peculiar position of losing an indirect sex discrimination claim while successfully defending a claim under the ERA. A departure from the 'cost plus' orthodoxy might mean that that result is less likely to occur.

Organisational and administrative efficiency. A common reason cited as **13.109** justification in indirect discrimination cases is that the PCP is necessary for the operational or administrative efficiency of the organisation. In Greater Glasgow Health Board v Carey 1987 IRLR 484, EAT, C was a health visitor who wanted to work part time after maternity leave. The employer agreed but only on the basis that C spread her hours over five days a week. She, however, wanted to work either two and a half or three days a week. An employment tribunal found the employer's requirement to be unjustified but the EAT disagreed. It said that the tribunal had disregarded the factor of the efficiency of the service and that there was substantial evidence that people needed their health visitor to be available five days a week. Similarly, in Nelson v Chesterfield Law Centre EAT 1359/96 the EAT upheld a tribunal's decision that a requirement to work full time was justified since the post for which the complainant had applied involved close collaboration with an existing worker at the law centre so that further subdivision by way of job sharing was undesirable.

In Bradley v West Midlands Fire and Rescue Authority ET Case No.1304700/06 B was a single parent mother who worked as a firefighter. Her employer introduced a new shift pattern to ensure that firefighting crew cover was available when required. WMF's aim had two elements: to comply with a mandatory requirement of central government to devise an integrated risk management plan, and to ensure the most efficient deployment of the Fire Service's resources in the interests of public safety and well-being. Although an employment tribunal accepted that the new arrangements were to the disadvantage of B, it held that WMF had demonstrated that they were a proportionate means of achieving a legitimate aim. In reaching this conclusion, the tribunal took account of the fact that the attitude of WMF to the implementation of the new shift system had not been inflexible. At a strategic level it had amended the system once evidence based on the experience of its operation had become available. In addition, as far as B was concerned, WMF had put forward a number of alternatives that she had declined for reasons that were less than convincing. Furthermore, because B would only have been required to work late shifts for six consecutive nights three or four times a year, the tribunal felt that she would have been able to accommodate these shifts by a combination of paid childcare and family support.

13.110 These cases can be contrasted with the employment tribunal's decision in Henery v Quoteline Insurance Services Ltd t/a Sureplan Insurance ET Case No.2502542/13, where H was employed as a 'controller', which meant that she could arrange insurance policies without obtaining prior approval. Due to childcare commitments, H worked two full days a week. A number of other staff also worked part time. When the employer became concerned about the number of employees working part time, it decided that experienced staff, such as H, had to work a minimum of three full days a week. H was unable to arrange childcare for three full days and refused to increase her number of days. She did, however, offer to increase her hours by an additional half day, which was rejected by the employer. In due course, H was dismissed and offered re-engagement on the new terms. An employment tribunal upheld her claims for unfair dismissal and indirect sex discrimination. With regard to the S.19 claim, the tribunal accepted that the employer's PCP pursued a legitimate aim: it wanted to ensure that suitably qualified staff were available during office hours to serve its clients' business needs. However, the employer failed to show why that aim could only be achieved by implementation of a PCP of having experienced staff work a minimum of three full days in the office. This had never previously been a requirement. Nor had the employer made any reasonable attempts to investigate or consider alternatives. The fact that other female employees had agreed to increase their working hours did not make the claimant's refusal so unreasonable as to make her dismissal proportionate in all the circumstances.

In some organisations, it may be more difficult for higher grade managers than lower grade workers to work part time. In Ogilvie v Ross and anor t/a Braid Veterinary Hospital EAT 1115/99 the EAT upheld an employment tribunal's decision that the veterinary hospital was justified in refusing to let O, the head nurse, work part time. When she returned from her maternity leave, O worked part time for nine months but problems arose in her absence, which she often had to resolve the following morning at work. She maintained that if the deputy head nurse had pulled her weight the problems would not have arisen, but the tribunal found that the deputy's job specification was very different to O's, as O had a much higher level of management input. The employer had explored all reasonable options and, while part-time working could be tolerated for a while with the cooperation of other employees, the employer was not required to restructure and reorganise arrangements with other employees to suit O's childcare needs. The position of head nurse was a senior one which, bearing in mind the size and resources of the business, required a full-time employee.

Security. A requirement that a web editor be office-based and work normal **13.111** office hours (namely 9/9.30 am – 5/5.30 pm) was found to be justified for a number of reasons in Legall v Governing Body of Lewisham College ET Case No.2306039/04, including the fact that the security and integrity of the College's network could be compromised by remote working. Similarly, in McKinnon v Automated Control Services Ltd ET Case No.3104607/08 the tribunal accepted that the employer had been justified in refusing an office manager's request to work from home for reasons of security, confidentiality and cost.

Client needs. In Sullivan v John S Braid and Co Ltd ET Case No.2302098/03 **13.112** the claimant had specifically been recruited to work as a shipping coordinator on a contract that her employer had with a cruise line company. This company was responsible for 75 per cent of the employer's revenue, and the employer had contracted with the cruise line to provide a full-time coordinator to work exclusively on that contract. An employment tribunal found that the employer was justified in dismissing the claimant, who, having agreed to work full time, then announced that she could only work part time. The requirement that the position be full time was necessary to meet the specific needs of the contract, which was to have a dedicated shipping coordinator assigned to it, and to meet the needs of the employer's clients generally, as the coordinator had to be available for work at a time that coincided with various time zones. In reaching this conclusion, the employment tribunal noted that the employer had considered whether it was possible for the claimant to work at home, but had rejected the idea because she was still being trained. It also took account of the significant value of the main contract to the employer's business.

Client needs were also successfully relied upon as a basis for justifying indirect discrimination by a marketing/design agency in Edgley v Oliver and Graimes Design Associates Ltd ET Case No.3101782/05. In that case the employer refused to allow E – a senior account manager – to return to work three days a week following her maternity leave. An employment tribunal was satisfied that there was a legitimate ethos, essential to the survival of the business, whereby an immediate and personal service was provided by employees to clients, and that this required E's post to be full time. The delegation of urgent client enquiries to other employees and the need to resort to returning calls by mobile telephone were all anathema to the service ethos on which the employer depended. Those reasons outweighed the discriminatory effect on E of refusing to allow her to return on a part-time basis.

Harassment

13.113

As we noted at the beginning of this chapter, the EqA contains a specific provision outlawing harassment. S.26(1) provides that an employer harasses a person if it engages in unwanted conduct 'related to a relevant protected

623

characteristic' *and* the conduct has the purpose or effect of violating that person's dignity, or of creating an intimidating, hostile, degrading, humiliating or offensive environment for that person. Although 'pregnancy and maternity' is a protected characteristic under the Act, it is not included in the list of 'relevant' protected characteristics in relation to harassment in S.26(5), and so there is no specific protection against pregnancy or maternity harassment. However, any harassment relating to pregnancy or maternity would inevitably amount to harassment related to sex.

In practice, claimants often add a claim of harassment to a claim of pregnancy or maternity discrimination, particularly where there has been a breakdown in the employer/employee relationship. Two examples:

- **Hildreth v Collingwood Street Ltd and ors** ET Case No.2504768/06: the employer, upon being notified of the employee's pregnancy, suspended her with immediate effect; informed her that, if she continued with the pregnancy, she would be dismissed; and refused to allow her to return to work until she had decided whether she would be having a termination. An employment tribunal found that comments to the effect of 'keep the baby or the job' were offensive and upsetting to the claimant and amounted to harassment

- **Gardner v BBT Thermotechnology UK Ltd** ET Case No.1307647/07: during her maternity leave, G's manager had repeatedly sent her letters enquiring as to whether she was going to return from maternity leave, and if so, when. The letters threatened disciplinary action if she failed to respond. An employment tribunal found that the letters amounted to harassment on the ground of her pregnancy, and therefore her sex.

13.114 There is no requirement that the alleged harasser be of the same or different sex to the complainant in order for a claim to be well founded. It is perfectly possible, for example, for a woman to be guilty of sex-related harassment towards another woman. For example, in Gashi v European Pensions Management Ltd ET Case No.3100490/10 the employer became increasingly exasperated by the employee's persistent requests to leave work early to care for her children. On one occasion the company's female Chief Executive, M, said to G, 'I'm very disappointed. You are playing the childcare thing, fine, I'm a woman too... please just stick up for the sex and do the job.' Later in the conversation M said, 'I think you remain restricted by your kids; you need to bend a bit further, get half an hour more childcare; I want you to tell me you have found someone else, employ a nanny.' The conversation ended with M asking, 'How do we get around the baby?' The tribunal found that this amounted to harassment related to sex (although it found that the company's requirement that G remain in the office until after 5 pm in order to supervise her staff effectively was a proportionate means of achieving a legitimate aim and so did not amount to indirect discrimination).

624

Derogatory remarks about a female employee formed the basis of a claim for harassment in Haynes v Neon Digital (Document Solutions) Ltd and ors ET Case No.1501563/10. In that case H argued that the following behaviour of S, ND Ltd's owner and managing director, amounted to harassment under S.4A SDA (the precursor to S.26 EqA): after she suffered a miscarriage, he had expressed his annoyance to another employee that he had not known that H was pregnant; he had told H to 'grow a pair of balls' in a meeting; and he had said to a colleague, 'Is Kate fucking pregnant? Her boobs are massive.' The tribunal found that these comments were offensive and clearly related to her sex, and although two of them were not made to H directly, S must have known that in such a small organisation it was very likely that they would get back to her. The tribunal accordingly found that harassment was made out. In so finding, it also took into account S's attitude towards women, and towards pregnant women in particular, and the atmosphere that this created at work. For instance, S handed out a 'cock of the week' award to the employee with the lowest weekly sales; S believed that women were only good at sales if they 'flashed their tits'; upon hearing that a female employee was pregnant, S enquired whether it might be possible for her to accidentally fall down the stairs; and S told H that he wanted an employee who had recently married dismissed before she got pregnant.

In Nixon v Ross Coates Solicitors and anor EAT 0108/10 office gossip about **13.115** the paternity of the employee's unborn child was held to constitute harassment. N was employed by RCS at its Ipswich office for over ten years to bring in clients and assist with corporate hospitality. She was in a relationship with one of the firm's solicitors. However, at the staff Christmas party she ended up publicly kissing the IT manager. They spent the night together in a room charged to the firm's account. Following the party, N took annual leave and then sick leave, during which she informed the firm's managing director that she was eight weeks' pregnant but did not want this disclosed until she had crossed the 12-week threshold. However, the HR manager, O, found out and started gossiping about who the father might be. A tribunal dismissed N's claim for harassment. While conceding that O had been 'indiscreet', the tribunal did not consider that her behaviour could be regarded as 'intimidating, hostile, degrading or humiliating'. The EAT allowed N's appeal. The harassment claim was based on the fact that O was spreading gossip about the paternity of N's child. This gossip was connected with N's pregnancy, which in turn related to her sex, and constituted a course of unwanted conduct meeting the definition of harassment. The fact that N's behaviour at the Christmas party was public and so would inevitably give rise to comment did not mean that confidential information about her pregnancy could be disclosed and in a derogatory manner.

A decision that appears to depart from well-established principles is Warby v Wunda Group plc EAT 0434/11, where the EAT upheld an employment tribunal's decision that there was no harassment on the ground of an employee's pregnancy, and therefore her sex, when the employee was accused of lying about her pregnancy and miscarriage. W was employed as a sales consultant by WG plc. There was disagreement between her and her manager, P, as to what had been agreed at a meeting in 2009 with regard to her entitlement to wage increases. They met to discuss this in early 2010 and during the course of the meeting both P and W became convinced the other was lying. At an acrimonious meeting in March 2010, W asserted that her wages were being changed to her detriment because she was pregnant. P denied this, but then asked her why she had lied about having a miscarriage. The accusation was based on anomalies over dates that W had posted on Facebook, which suggested that her ongoing pregnancy commenced before her alleged miscarriage. On the basis of that meeting, W brought a complaint of harassment under S.4A SDA. The tribunal found that P's accusation that W had lied about her pregnancy and miscarriage created an intimidating, hostile, degrading, humiliating or offensive environment for her. However, it considered that the accusation was not made on the ground of her pregnancy but in relation to her lying more generally. While such an accusation may be unreasonable, it was not harassment on the ground of her pregnancy.

13.116 On appeal, the EAT concurred. Mr Justice Langstaff, President of the EAT, agreed with the tribunal that P's comments created an intimidating, hostile, degrading, humiliating or offensive environment for W. The critical question was therefore whether P's accusation 'related to her sex' within the meaning of S.4A(1) SDA. Langstaff P noted that, in setting out this issue, the tribunal incorrectly had regard to the statutory definition of harassment in force prior to April 2008, which prohibited unwanted conduct meted out 'on the ground of' a woman's sex. However, the definition in force at the time of W's complaint required the unwanted conduct to be 'related to' her sex or the sex of another person. While there was clearly a distinction between the terms 'on the ground of' and 'related to', the parties did not consider it to be a material distinction in the circumstances of the case. Langstaff P accordingly proceeded on the basis that the tribunal had not made an error of law in having regard to the outdated version of S.4A.

After dealing with this preliminary point, the EAT proceeded to hold that the tribunal's overall conclusion had been permissible on the facts. Langstaff P held that the context in which the words were spoken was important, and that the tribunal had been entitled to find that the accusation was made in the context of a dispute over a work matter, about which the employer believed that the employee was lying. Thus, the conduct at issue was an emphatic complaint about alleged lying; it was not made because of the employee's sex, because she was pregnant, or because she had had a miscarriage. The tribunal was therefore entitled to find that the remark, however unpleasant and unacceptable, was made in a particular context in which the words did not relate to the employee's pregnancy but to lying generally, and so were not inherently discriminatory. W's claim was dismissed.

The EAT's acquiescence in the parties' view that there is no material distinction **13.117** between the terms 'on the ground of' and 'related to' is surprising, given the High Court's decision in R (Equal Opportunities Commission) v Secretary of State for Trade and Industry 2007 ICR 1234, QBD, that the former formulation was too narrow to implement correctly the recast EU Equal Treatment Directive (No.2006/54). It was this decision that resulted in the SDA being amended in 2008. As the High Court accepted in that case, 'related to' is clearly wider than 'on the ground of'. On this analysis, it is strongly arguable that a reference to an employee's alleged miscarriage is indeed 'related to' her sex, given that pregnancy can only affect women.

The EAT may well have complicated matters for itself by considering the harassment issue alongside one of W's other grounds of appeal – namely, her appeal against the tribunal's finding that there was no direct sex discrimination, which it also dismissed. Many of the authorities cited by the EAT in support of its conclusion on harassment are, in fact, direct discrimination cases. These cases make it clear that a direct sex discrimination claim will succeed only where the treatment complained of was done 'because of', 'on the ground of' or 'by reason of' sex. Context is indeed highly relevant in such cases, in that the tribunal must establish the reason why the employer acted in the way complained of. But it is strongly arguable that conduct can be 'related to' sex even if sex is not the reason for it, and so it does not follow that a harassment claim stands or falls with a direct discrimination claim on the same facts.

It is also worth noting that the EAT considered that a finding in the claimant's **13.118** favour would have far-reaching – and unwelcome – consequences. The lay members, in particular, stressed the fact that many comments made in heated discussions between employers and employees would amount to harassment if a mere reference to miscarriage and pregnancy would suffice for the purposes of S.4A(1) SDA. However, the EAT seems to have overlooked the fact that a tribunal must make two positive findings before concluding that an act of harassment has taken place. In addition to the conduct being related to sex, it must also find that the conduct had the purpose or effect of creating an intimidating and offensive environment for the employee. S.4A(2) SDA specifically provided that conduct would only be regarded as having this effect on the employee if, having regard to all the circumstances, including in particular the perception of the woman, it should reasonably be considered as having that effect. This provision acted as a safeguard against unmeritorious claims brought in response to conduct that, although unpleasant, could not be considered sufficient to amount to harassment under the SDA. A similar provision is now contained in S.26(4) EqA. Thus, even if the merest reference to pregnancy must be considered to be 'related to' sex, tribunals can still avoid

627

a finding of harassment where the context would make such a finding unreasonable. But even applying that test, it is questionable whether the correct result had been reached here. Where, as here, the tribunal had found that there was 'no good reason' why the manager chose to raise the subject of the miscarriage and do something which was 'so obviously offensive and upsetting', it seems arguable that the manager's conduct was not simply unacceptable but amounted to an act of harassment.

13.119 Marital and civil partnership discrimination

The EqA makes it unlawful to discriminate, either directly or indirectly, against married persons and civil partners on the ground of their marital/civil partnership status – Ss.8, 13 and 19. Since the legalisation of same-sex marriage (in England and Wales in March 2014 and in Scotland in December 2014), marriage covers those who are married to someone of the opposite or the same sex.

Unfavourable treatment of those with young children may be directly discriminatory under S.13 if the employer is simply treating, for example, a married woman (or man) differently from the way it would treat an unmarried woman (or man). Equally, adopting a different attitude towards civil partners with young children would amount to direct discrimination. Any less favourable treatment of same-sex couples who are married or in a civil partnership is also likely to found a claim for sexual orientation discrimination.

13.120 It is important to stress that only someone who is married or in a civil partnership can complain of direct marital or civil partnership discrimination under S.13 – see S.8(1). The Act does not prohibit less favourable treatment of someone on the ground that he or she is not married or has not entered into a civil partnership. Furthermore, S.13(4) provides that an individual may only claim direct discrimination in employment on the basis of marriage or civil partnership if the treatment is because the claimant him or herself is married or is a civil partner. Accordingly, the claimant's association with someone who has married or civil partnership status will not suffice, and nor will treatment on the basis that the claimant is single.

Apart from direct discrimination, treatment may be indirectly discriminatory under S.19 (see 'Indirect sex discrimination' above) if it amounts to a 'provision, criterion or practice' that puts married persons or civil partners at a particular disadvantage compared with unmarried persons or those who are not in a civil partnership. In Hurley v Mustoe 1981 ICR 490, EAT, the Appeal Tribunal held that H had been indirectly discriminated against on the ground of her marital status when she was dismissed as soon as she started work as a waitress because M considered women with children to be 'unreliable'. (The EAT also decided that H had been directly discriminated against on the ground of her sex.) Note,

628

however, that this case is over 30 years old and the increasing trend for unmarried couples to have children may mean that the gap between the proportion of married people of working age with children and the proportion of unmarried people of working age with children has shrunk to such an extent that the disproportionate impact has ceased to be large enough to support an indirect discrimination claim.

Again, this type of claim is only available to someone who is married or a civil **13.121** partner – S.8(1). A single person cannot, therefore, bring him or herself within S.19. However, any policy that treats unmarried employees with children less favourably than married employees with children may still be unlawful, as it could constitute indirect sex discrimination against women if it put women at a particular disadvantage and cannot be objectively justified.

For further details, see IDS Employment Law Handbook, 'Discrimination at Work' (2012), Chapter 8, 'Marriage and civil partnership'.

Discrimination against men   **13.122**

As we have seen throughout this chapter, women who are pregnant or on maternity leave are in a unique position that requires special protection under the law. However, they are not the only ones who benefit from wide-reaching protection against discrimination. Men enjoy a number of family-friendly rights – ranging from paternity leave and pay to the right to request flexible working – that enable them to take an active role in looking after their children and the EqA protects them from suffering less favourable treatment as a result of exercising these rights. This protection is only likely to increase in importance as the Government legislates to move away from traditional gender roles – where women are assumed to be the primary carers – towards a more balanced division of childcaring responsibilities. The new shared parental leave scheme, which allows parents to share leave periods in the first year of their child's life, is a paradigm example of this and we discuss the potential discrimination issues that may arise under the new scheme under 'Shared parental leave and pay' below.

In this section, we consider the protection available to men under the EqA and the potential claims they may bring to enforce their family-friendly rights. However, it is worth noting at the outset that in some circumstances the protection will be limited. As we have seen under 'Indirect sex discrimination' above, the law of indirect discrimination provides protection for female employees seeking to work family-friendly working hours, on the basis that women are more likely than men to have primary responsibility for childcare and so an employer's failure to accommodate the childcare needs of its employees will put women at a particular disadvantage compared with men. This argument does not embrace men who have primary responsibility for a child, or who wish to share more responsibility with the child's mother.

629

Furthermore, the law on direct discrimination recognises that women may require special protection during pregnancy and childbirth – see S.13(6)(b) EqA. However, this special protection does not extend to favouring women beyond what is reasonably necessary to compensate them for the disadvantages occasioned by their condition so where an employer takes a blanket approach and automatically favours the female employee above others, the 'special treatment' may amount to sex discrimination against a male colleague – see 'Direct discrimination' below.

13.123 Direct discrimination

Where a man's request for family-friendly hours has been turned down, he may be able to show that the employer would have allowed a woman in the same position to change her hours. Sometimes the man will be able to point to an actual female employee who has been allowed to work family-friendly hours. He would then have to show that her circumstances were the same or not materially different from his. Even if the male employee cannot point to an actual female employee with whom to compare himself, he may be able to succeed in arguing that a 'hypothetical female' in comparable circumstances would have been more successful in her request for a change in working hours. If the employer cannot show that there was a reason – unconnected with sex – why the man's request was turned down, then a tribunal may infer that the difference in treatment was due to the difference in sex.

Some employers make the assumption, based on a stereotypical view of gender roles in society, that only female employees need to work family-friendly hours, or that male employees have a lesser need because they have a wife or partner whose working life can (or even should) be rearranged in order to cope with children. A decision influenced in whole or in part by such gender bias can in itself amount to direct discrimination. In Walkingshaw v John Martin Group Ltd ET Case No.S/401126/00, for example, W was a senior technician at JMG Ltd's garage. After W's wife finished her maternity leave, they decided that she would return to work as her employment benefits were greater than his. He suggested to his employer that he could work two weekdays a week, plus Saturday mornings, and do extra work in the evenings if needed. He also suggested a job-share arrangement. The employer dismissed his ideas as too complicated and messy. However, the tribunal found that the employer had given 'no meaningful consideration' to W's suggestions, whereas similar requests from a number of female employees had been granted in the past. The employer argued that since none of the female employees worked in the mechanics department they could not be used as a basis for comparison, but the tribunal held that the fact that employees worked in different departments did not of itself mean that the relevant circumstances were materially different. The tribunal could find no material differences between W's case and those of the female employees and inferred that W had been discriminated against due to his sex.

Similarly, in Pietzka v PricewaterhouseCoopers LLP ET Case No.1603520/12 **13.124**
P was employed by PwC to work a five-day week. He was promoted to manager in July 2010. Later that year he raised the issue of flexible working, asking if he could work a four-day week for childcare reasons. However, he was told that, given his role in the business and the level of work he carried out, it was not possible for him to be allowed to work flexibly. He raised the issue again in August 2011, this time asking to reduce his working week by 50 per cent. His request was not agreed but he was told that a formal application to work 75 per cent of his contractual hours would be supported. An employment tribunal accepted P's evidence that his manager's attitude towards him changed after he began requesting flexible working. In particular, he spoke of flexible working harming P's career prospects. He found it difficult to accept that P would wish to put family issues above work. There was no evidence that such harm had been caused to the prospects of women who had taken up flexible working at PwC. Indeed P's manager had been supportive of flexible working requests from female colleagues. P's path to flexible working was more difficult than it had been for female employees. Furthermore, once P's request was granted PwC wished to exercise greater control over whether the flexibility arrangement would continue than in other cases. On the basis of these facts the tribunal upheld P's direct discrimination claim.

'Special treatment' defence. Section 11 EqA makes it clear that the principle **13.125**
of equal treatment applies to both men and women. However, as noted above, S.13(6)(b) EqA goes on to provide that in determining whether a man has suffered sex discrimination, 'no account is to be taken of special treatment afforded to a woman in connection with pregnancy or childbirth'. This 'special treatment' defence, which was previously contained in S.2(2) SDA, has long been used to justify a woman's more favourable treatment when she is pregnant or on maternity leave. However, in Eversheds Legal Services Ltd v De Belin 2011 ICR 1137, EAT, the Appeal Tribunal held that S.13(6) cannot be used to favour such women beyond what is *reasonably necessary* to compensate them for the disadvantages occasioned by their condition. In that case B, a man, scored lower in a redundancy exercise than a colleague on maternity leave, R, who was given the maximum notional score for a criterion measuring the period between work being done for clients and receipt of payment. As a result, B scored lower overall and was made redundant. When B claimed sex discrimination, the employer argued that the 'special treatment' defence in S.2(2) SDA defeated his claim because it provided that no account shall be taken of special treatment afforded to women in connection with pregnancy or childbirth. An employment tribunal interpreted 'special treatment' as including only 'those rights where statutory provision has been made for pregnant women and those on maternity leave'. In its view, S.2(2) could not have been intended to give employers blanket protection against sex discrimination claims by men, and did not protect a woman on maternity leave in a redundancy scoring

631

exercise where she received an unfairly inflated score. The tribunal therefore upheld B's sex discrimination and unfair dismissal claims and awarded him £123,053 in compensation.

On appeal, the EAT agreed with the tribunal, noting that ECJ decisions such as Johnston v Chief Constable of the Royal Ulster Constabulary 1987 ICR 83, ECJ, indicate that the principle of proportionality applies to the right to 'special treatment'. Consequently, S.2(2) should be construed so as only to refer to treatment which is 'a proportionate means of achieving the legitimate aim of compensating [a woman] for the disadvantages occasioned by her pregnancy' or maternity leave. As a result, where a maternity or pregnancy benefit is disproportionate, a disadvantaged colleague should be able to claim sex discrimination. In the EAT's view, giving legislation protecting pregnant women and those on maternity leave an excessively wide interpretation would bring it into disrepute. Applying this reasoning to the instant case, the EAT concluded that the employer's approach to scoring R in the redundancy selection exercise was not proportionate and went beyond what was reasonably necessary, especially since there were alternative ways of dealing with the situation without disproportionately disadvantaging B. The appeal was therefore rejected.

13.126 Indirect discrimination
A man who has been refused paternity leave, or who has suffered a detriment or been dismissed because he took, or sought to take, paternity leave, is unlikely to succeed with a claim of direct sex discrimination. This is because the employer would most likely have reacted in the same way if the request for paternity leave had come from the mother's female spouse or partner. He may, however, have a better chance of success with a claim for indirect sex discrimination, on the basis that men are more likely than women to take paternity leave and will therefore be disproportionately affected by a refusal or other detriment. An example:

- **Jackson v Instant Installations Ltd** ET Case No.2801865/07: J asked for two weeks' paternity leave, which was refused by the employer. The tribunal found that the employer would have reacted the same way if a woman had requested paternity leave and J was therefore unable to show that he had suffered direct discrimination. However, his indirect discrimination claim succeeded before the tribunal, as the employer's refusal would have a greater impact on men. As the employer failed to justify its actions, the claim was upheld.

13.127 Marital discrimination
A married man whose request for family-friendly working hours is refused may be able to argue that he has been indirectly discriminated against on the ground of his marital status. He would have to show that married employees were (or would be) put at a particular disadvantage by the employer's requirements

compared with unmarried employees. In Hurley v Mustoe 1981 ICR 490, EAT, the Appeal Tribunal decided that a married woman who was dismissed because she had young children had been indirectly discriminated against on the ground of marital status. However, it should be noted that this case is over 30 years old and the increasing trend for unmarried couples to have children may mean that the gap between the proportion of married people of working age with children and the proportion of unmarried people of working age with children has shrunk to such an extent that the disproportionate impact has ceased to be large enough to support an indirect discrimination claim.

Harassment   13.128
The provisions relating to harassment in the EqA apply equally to men and women. S.26 EqA defines harassment as unwanted conduct 'related to a relevant protected characteristic' that has the proscribed effect. There is no requirement that the harassment relate to a protected characteristic of the victim him or herself, so that harassment because of the victim's association with someone of another sex would fall within the prohibition. However, neither pregnancy or maternity, nor marital status or civil partnership, are protected characteristics for the purpose of harassment – S.26(5). So if a man were to be harassed on the basis of his association with a pregnant woman, he would need to claim harassment related to the protected characteristic of sex, or alternatively to claim direct discrimination under S.13, in respect of which pregnancy and maternity is a protected characteristic – see the discussion under 'Discrimination by association' below.

Shared parental leave and pay   13.129
In Chapter 8, 'Shared parental leave and pay', we discuss the nuts and bolts of the detailed and complex shared parental leave scheme, which came into force in December 2014. Suffice it to say here that under the scheme, which applies in respect of children born on or after 5 April 2015, a woman who is eligible for statutory maternity leave and pay can choose to bring both to an early end and share the remaining balance with the father (or partner) of her child. It is up to the parents to decide whether to take a period of shared parental leave (SPL) at the same time or whether to take it in turns to look after the child. Although the first two weeks following the birth remain reserved for the mother, the remaining 50 weeks' leave may be shared, subject to various notification and eligibility requirements. The maximum amount of statutory shared parental pay (SSPP) available is 37 weeks. Any leave (and pay) must be taken before the child's first birthday. A similar right also applies to adoptive parents and to intended parents through a surrogacy arrangement.

The new scheme raises a number of potentially discriminatory issues in relation to the pay aspect of the scheme. An employee who is entitled to pay under the scheme is paid SSPP at the flat rate of £138.18 a week. This is much

633

lower than the amount many employers offer under enhanced schemes for those on maternity leave. Does this mean that employers will leave themselves open to claims of discrimination if they fail to replicate these enhanced benefits for employees who take periods of family leave under the SPL scheme? Offering enhanced benefits under the scheme could prove costly, since potentially any employee (i.e. including men) can make use of SPL, provided the mother is willing to curtail her SML. The Government's view on this is clear: there is no legal requirement for employers to an create occupational shared parental pay scheme and it is entirely at their discretion whether or not they do so – see the 'Employer's Technical Guide to Shared Parental Leave and Pay' (September 2014).

13.130 However, things may not be quite so simple. Certainly there is no legal obligation on employers in the SPL legislation to match enhanced maternity pay. But the question remains whether they might be obliged to do so under the EqA in order to avoid discrimination claims – either direct or indirect – from men on SPL receiving less pay than women on maternity leave.

13.131 **Direct discrimination.** It is not the first time that employers have had to review their family-friendly policies in order to ensure that they are not leaving themselves open to complaints of discrimination. When additional paternity leave (APL) was introduced in 2011, many employers were considering the same question: should they offer an occupational scheme to ensure that a man on APL received the same benefits as a woman on maternity leave? The position taken by the previous Government was that employers were not required to offer an enhanced paternity pay scheme, as there would be no risk of this amounting to direct sex discrimination. The thinking behind this was as follows: since APL could be taken by employees of either sex, so long as a man taking APL was in the same position as a woman taking APL – for example, the same-sex partner of a birth mother – there was no less favourable treatment.

The approach advocated by the Government was adopted by an employment tribunal in Shuter v Ford Motor Co Ltd ET Case No.3203504/13. FMC Ltd operated a non-contractual maternity policy that gave women on maternity leave full pay for up to 52 weeks. Its policy on APL was to pay only the statutory rate. S took 20 weeks of APL and was paid accordingly. While on leave, he brought claims of direct and indirect sex discrimination, arguing that the difference in treatment between him and a mother on maternity leave meant that he was paid around £18,000 less for an equivalent period of leave. For the purpose of his direct discrimination claim, S sought to compare himself with a female employee on maternity leave, who would have been entitled to full pay throughout. The tribunal considered that this was not a valid comparison: the correct comparator was a woman who had also applied for APL (such as a female spouse or civil partner). As such a woman would have been treated no differently, his direct discrimination claim failed.

The Shuter decision gives some indication as to how a direct discrimination **13.132** claim under the SPL scheme might be decided. Assuming the same logic prevails, the correct comparator would be a woman on SPL (such as a mother, female spouse or female partner), who would also be treated no differently. If tribunals follow this approach, a man on SPL would struggle to win a direct sex discrimination claim in these circumstances.

The more interesting question, however, is whether there is a viable argument that, rather than compare himself with a woman on SPL, a man could compare himself with a woman on maternity leave who is paid more than him. The ECJ's decision in Roca Álvarez v Sesa Start España ETT SA 2011 1 CMLR 28, ECJ, could possibly be used to support such a line of argument. There, the European Court held that a Spanish law that gave women a right to time off for breastfeeding was discriminatory. The law was originally introduced to promote breastfeeding but was later extended to bottle-feeding. It expressly stated that the right applied to both mothers and fathers, but fathers were only entitled where both mother and father were employees, whereas mothers were entitled regardless of the father's employment status. The ECJ held that linking the father's entitlement to the employment status of his partner – when no such restriction applied to female employees – amounted to sex discrimination contrary to the Equal Treatment Directive. Although Article 2(3) of the Directive allows national law to protect a woman's biological condition during and after pregnancy, and protect the special relationship between a woman and her child following childbirth, the right to time off was designed to ease the burden of taking care of the child and not to protect a woman's biological condition.

Furthermore, in Markin v Russia 56 EHRR 8, ECtHR, the European Court of **13.133** Human Rights stressed that parental leave was intended to enable the parent concerned to stay at home to look after the child, and that men and women were similarly placed to take on that role. In contrast with maternity leave, which was intended to enable women to recover from childbirth and to breastfeed, men and women were in an analogous situation in so far as parental leave was concerned. The difference in treatment could not therefore be justified by reference to the special role of women in raising children.

On the basis of these decisions, it could be argued that there comes a point in time when maternity leave is no longer designed to protect a woman's biological condition following pregnancy, or the special relationship between mother and baby. Instead, it becomes more akin to parental leave, in that the woman is taking leave to look after the child – something that, according to the ECtHR in Markin, men are similarly well placed to do. As a result, the situation of a man on SPL may be comparable to that of a woman on maternity leave, especially once she has entered the latter stages of the maternity leave period.

In actual fact, an argument along these lines was run by the claimant in Shuter **13.134** v Ford Motor Co Ltd (above), and rejected by the tribunal. S argued that he could compare himself with a mother on maternity leave 20 weeks after the birth of the child. He submitted that the introduction of APL reflected Parliament's view that, after 20 weeks, maternity leave is no longer aimed at protecting the mother but at facilitating childcare, which can be undertaken by either parent. The tribunal disagreed. It could not accept that Parliament intended to change the character of maternity leave in this way. In its view, the father's right to APL was dependent on the mother choosing to return to work, which was a decision personal to her. Thus, there was a material difference in circumstances between the mother and the father even at this late stage. The tribunal also rejected S's argument that the ECJ's decision in Roca Álvarez v Sesa Start España ETT SA (above) supported his interpretation of the purpose of maternity leave.

Shuter is only a decision at first instance and is not binding on other tribunals. It therefore remains to be seen if other tribunals – and the EAT – take the same approach. The tribunal in Shuter considered that the purpose of maternity leave did not change until such point as the woman decided to transfer any 'unused' portion to the father. Only then could it be said that the nature of the leave changed. However, it could similarly be said that the fact that the woman is allowed to transfer leave to the father in the first place means that the leave is no longer aimed at protecting her health and safety after childbirth. In respect of SPL, this would be the case in respect of the whole period of maternity leave other than the first two weeks after childbirth. It seems clear, however, that women must be granted a minimum period of maternity leave of at least 14 weeks under Article 8 of the Pregnant Workers Directive. Still, it is difficult to regard the whole of the woman's maternity leave period as designed to protect a woman's biological condition or the special relationship she has with the child, given that the leave can be allocated to the father. It seems almost inevitable that before long an argument along these lines will be tested before the courts. As traditional gender roles continue to be challenged and case law in this area continues to evolve, the prospect of success must be a real possibility.

13.135 **Indirect discrimination.** The second – and perhaps more compelling – route by which a male employee may be able to claim enhanced pay during SPL is via an indirect sex discrimination claim. An indirect discrimination claim was also put forward by the claimant in Shuter v Ford Motor Co Ltd (see 'Direct discrimination' above). The tribunal accepted that the relevant 'provision, criterion or practice' for the purpose of S.19 EqA was FMC Ltd's policy of paying full pay to women on maternity leave beyond 20 weeks after the birth of the child. FMC Ltd conceded that, on this formulation, men as a group, and S as an individual, were placed at a disadvantage. The tribunal therefore moved directly to consider the question of objective justification.

The tribunal accepted that FMC Ltd's objective in paying full pay throughout maternity leave was to recruit and retain women, which was clearly legitimate.

As for the means employed to further that objective, the tribunal agreed with S that it was relevant that FMC Ltd had not come anywhere near reaching its target of a 25% female workforce, but did not consider that this proved that FMC Ltd's approach was disproportionate. It noted that there had been an increase in the number of female employees overall, against a background of a shrinking workforce, and an increase in women in professional and senior management grades. In addition, the substantial majority of women who took maternity leave returned to work and stayed for more than a year. The tribunal was thus prepared to accept that the enhanced maternity pay policy had been effective at promoting the recruitment and retention of women.

Having regard to the principle that the greater a disadvantageous effect, the **13.136** more cogent the justification for it must be, the tribunal observed that men were wholly excluded from receiving full pay while caring for a child from 20 weeks after birth, whereas only a small proportion of women would be. However, in its judgment, this disadvantage arose from the fact that men cannot qualify for maternity leave and that women are treated more favourably in connection with pregnancy and childbirth. Thus, it arose from treatment that was lawful irrespective of the legitimate aim. In the tribunal's view, this meant that the extent of male disadvantage could not be a factor capable of rendering FMC Ltd's pursuit of its legitimate aim disproportionate. It accordingly rejected S's claim of indirect sex discrimination.

As we have seen, the employer in Shuter conceded that the application of the PCP put men at a particular disadvantage compared with women. A failure to offer enhanced SPL is also likely to have a disparate impact on men on the basis that they are more likely than women to make use of SPL. However, this is open to debate. On the one hand, it is arguable that, although mothers are entitled to take SPL, whereas they were not eligible for APL, it is still likely that more men than women will make use of SPL – meaning that men should still be able to establish a particular disadvantage for the purpose of bringing an indirect sex discrimination claim. On the other hand, it is fair to say that overall take-up of SPL is expected to be low. And of course, SPL is available to both men and women. Therefore a male employee might struggle to show that, in a pool that is likely to be small, men as a group suffer a particular disadvantage as a result of the denial of the enhanced benefits.

Assuming, however, that group disadvantage is established, the next step for a **13.137** tribunal is to consider the question of objective justification – was the employer's failure to match enhanced maternity benefits for men on SPL justified? Employers must put forward cogent reasons for the maternity pay policy and detailed evidence to show how the policy's aim is being achieved. It is worth remembering in this context that costs alone will not be sufficient to justify indirect discrimination – see the section 'Indirect sex discrimination' above, under 'Justification – grounds of justification'. In Shuter, the employer was able to show that the policy achieved its objective of recruiting and retaining women in a male-dominated sector. In workplaces where there is a more even male-to-female split, an indirect sex discrimination claim is likely to stand a greater chance of success.

13.138 **Enhanced pay for mothers only.** Mothers who receive enhanced maternity pay will understandably be reluctant to opt into SPL if it means losing out on enhanced maternity pay. However, employers who offer enhanced SSPP to mothers to match their maternity pay without enhancing shared parental pay for fathers would run into difficulties. If the scheme is discretionary, men taking SPL would have strong grounds on which to argue that they are the victims of direct sex discrimination because they are suffering less favourable treatment compared to female colleagues on SPL.

Employers defending such claims would need to rely upon the exemption in S.13(6) EqA, which affords female employees special treatment in connection with pregnancy or childbirth. However, as the EAT emphasised in Eversheds Legal Services Ltd v De Belin 2011 ICR 1137, EAT (see 'Direct discrimination' above), the obligation to protect such employees does not extend to favouring them beyond what is reasonably necessary to compensate them for the disadvantages occasioned by their condition. In addition, the EAT in De Belin suggested that 'special treatment' includes only 'those rights where statutory provision has been made for pregnant women and those on maternity leave'. On this logic, since SPL applies to men and women alike and is aimed at equalising parents' access to leave, it is arguable that the special treatment exemption would not apply at all, in which case any direct discrimination claim brought by a man would be almost bound to succeed. However, given that the De Belin case was not addressing the issue of SPL (which can be taken by mothers *instead* of maternity leave), it is by no means certain that this is the case.

13.139 Note that if the employer offers enhanced pay to mothers on a *contractual* basis, the father's claim would instead be one of equal pay. However, a similar 'special treatment exemption' applies under para 2, Sch 7 EqA. This exemption is discussed under 'Equal Pay – equal pay claims by male employees' below.

13.140 ## Discrimination by association

As we explain in IDS Employment Law Handbook, 'Atypical and Flexible Working' (2014), Chapter 4, 'Flexible working', the beneficiaries of the right to request flexible working were for many years parents of children under the age of 17 and disabled children under the age of 18, and carers of adult dependants. Although the right has now been extended to all employees, it remains particularly useful for those with parental or caring responsibilities. While the right in respect of young children dovetails with the provisions relating to indirect sex discrimination – see 'Indirect sex discrimination' above – there is also the possibility that a request by the parent of a disabled child or the carer of a disabled adult can be backed up by a claim for disability discrimination, due to what is known as 'discrimination by association', or 'associative discrimination'.

Such a claim works thus. If an employer refuses a flexible working request from a person seeking to care for a disabled child, that may amount to direct disability discrimination if it can be shown that the reason for the refusal was in some way motivated by the fact of disability. The European Court of Justice in Coleman v Attridge Law and anor 2008 ICR 1128, ECJ, established that such treatment is covered by the EU Equal Treatment Framework Directive (No.2000/78). It held that the principle of equal treatment enshrined in the Directive does not apply to particular types of person, but to the particular grounds of discrimination set out in Article 1 – disability, age, religion or belief and sexual orientation. Thus, in so far as disability is the ground for the treatment complained of, that treatment will be unlawful under the Directive. It is possible to interpret the EqA as permitting such a claim – direct discrimination in S.13 is defined as less favourable treatment 'because of a protected characteristic', and so does not require that the complainant actually have the protected characteristic at issue. (For a fuller explanation of this rationale, see IDS Employment Law Handbook, 'Discrimination at Work' (2012), Chapter 15, 'Direct discrimination', under 'Discrimination by association'.)

13.141 This analysis does not, however, support a right not to be discriminated against because a person has caring responsibilities *per se*. To establish discrimination by association with a disabled person, a comparison would have to be made between the treatment of an employee requesting flexible working to care for someone with a disability, and the treatment of an employee seeking flexible working to care for someone who does not have a disability, e.g. a non-disabled child. Only if the employer is more sympathetic to those with childcare responsibilities than to those who had to care for someone with a disability would direct discrimination arise.

Note, also, that there is no possibility of a claim for indirect discrimination by association. S.19 EqA is clearly worded to require that the complainant have the protected characteristic at issue. For this reason, discrimination by association is thought of solely in terms of direct discrimination.

13.142 **Discrimination by association with a pregnant woman?** While the ECJ's decision in Coleman v Attridge Law and anor (above) concerned the Equal Treatment Framework Directive (which covers disability, age, religion and philosophical belief and sexual orientation, but not sex and race) it is arguable that much of the reasoning could apply equally to pregnancy under the recast Equal Treatment Directive, which deals with gender discrimination. The ECJ observed that the dignity and autonomy of people who belong to a certain group can be undermined if third persons closely associated with them, but

639

who do not themselves belong to the group, are targeted for discrimination. It was therefore necessary, in the ECJ's view, that the Directive be interpreted not only as protecting the disabled but also those closely associated with them who are subjected to less favourable treatment on the ground of that disability. That rationale would equally support a case for EU law outlawing discrimination by association with a pregnant woman. After all, detrimental treatment of a pregnant woman's spouse or partner on the ground of her pregnancy has the effect of undermining her autonomy and dignity and excludes her from the full range of possibilities that would otherwise be open to her.

The issue arose under UK law in Kulikaoskas v MacDuff Shellfish and anor 2011 ICR 48, EAT, where the Appeal Tribunal held that an employee allegedly dismissed because of his partner's pregnancy could not bring a claim of pregnancy discrimination by association. The case was decided on the basis of the interpretation of S.3A SDA then in force (discrimination on the ground of pregnancy and maternity). The EAT held that the ECJ's decision establishing disability discrimination by association in Coleman v Attridge Law and anor (above) could be distinguished as, among other things, it did not apply to the Pregnant Workers Directive or the recast Equal Treatment Directive. Thus, the EAT did not feel bound to interpret the SDA so as to allow such a claim. It also declined to make a reference to the ECJ, holding that the law is sufficiently clear. On further appeal, however, the Court of Session took a different view and decided to make a reference to the ECJ for a preliminary ruling, asking whether the recast Directive prohibits less favourable treatment of a person on the ground of a woman's pregnancy generally, or on the ground of his partner's pregnancy or that of a woman otherwise associated with him. But before the ECJ was able to give its preliminary ruling, the case was settled and the reference withdrawn.

13.143 The EAT's reasoning for rejecting the claim in the Kulikaoskas case was that, *prima facie*, S.3A SDA, which prohibited pregnancy discrimination, clearly related to discrimination against 'a woman' on the ground of 'the woman's pregnancy'. In the EAT's view, the text of the recast Directive did not support associative discrimination on the ground of pregnancy. While the Directive protects a 'person' treated less favourably on the ground of sex, it specifically limits protection to 'a woman' in relation to pregnancy discrimination. Although Article 2(2)(c) of the recast Directive prohibits less favourable treatment of a woman 'related to pregnancy', the EAT did not consider that – hypothetically – this would protect the lesbian partner of a pregnant woman. Protection could not, therefore, be extended to men either. Finally, the recast Directive did not call for Member States to go any further than ensuring that women continue to receive special protection while pregnant. The EAT did consider, in passing, whether the situation would have been any different under the EqA, but its thinking was inconclusive, observing that it was 'not entirely clear' whether the Act would have rendered K's dismissal unlawful.

In our view, although the protection against pregnancy discrimination in S.18 clearly applies only to a woman 'in relation to a pregnancy of hers', and so does not cover those associated with that woman, the prohibition on direct discrimination in S.13 potentially applies to pregnancy and maternity cases that fall outside the scope of S.18 – see 'Direct discrimination' above for a full explanation of this rationale. If that is the case, associative pregnancy discrimination along the lines of the facts in Kulikaoskas is potentially covered under the EqA.

It is also possible that an employee may claim discrimination because of sex **13.144** (as opposed to pregnancy or maternity) under S.13 because of his or her association with a pregnant woman. The EHRC's Code of Practice on Employment states that 'a worker treated less favourably because of association with a pregnant woman, or a woman who has recently given birth, may have a claim for sex discrimination' (para 8.16). Arguably, then, if a man were dismissed or treated less favourably at work because of his partner's pregnancy, he could claim direct associative sex discrimination under S.13. In Kulikaoskas v MacDuff Shellfish and anor (above), the EAT commented that its interpretation of S.3A SDA meant that a priest dismissed for getting a nun pregnant, or a teacher dismissed for getting a pupil pregnant, could not bring claims of unlawful discrimination. If S.13 EqA does indeed have the wide application we suggest, then such circumstances would also, on the face of them, now be covered by discrimination law.

As it happens, a Scottish employment tribunal has recently concluded that S.13 is wide enough to cover discrimination by association with a pregnant woman. In Gyenes and anor v Highland Welcome (UK) Ltd t/a The Star Hotel ET Case No.S/4112392/12 G worked as a waitress at the employer's hotel. Her husband, V, was employed as a kitchen porter. They lived in a room at the hotel for which they paid £15 each per week. In early October 2012 G told her manager, M, that she was pregnant. In mid-October, M approached G and asked her what plans she and V had, as they could not raise a baby in a hotel room. G told her that they were intending to look for alternative accommodation. On 22 October G and V were called to separate meetings and informed that they were dismissed with one week's notice. A letter was sent the following day, confirming that their employment was terminated due to 'lack of work'. No other employees were dismissed and no redundancy payments were made. G and V brought various claims before an employment tribunal, including a claim by G for pregnancy discrimination under S.18 and a claim by V for associative sex discrimination under S.13. V maintained that his less favourable treatment – i.e. his dismissal – was because of his association with his pregnant wife.

The tribunal found in the claimants' favour in respect of all of their claims. It **13.145** rejected the employer's central submission that there was a genuine redundancy situation. The proper inference to be drawn from the facts was that the effective

641

cause of G's dismissal was her pregnancy. In reaching this conclusion, the tribunal took into account the fact that G had an exemplary work record and that she was dismissed within a matter of weeks of the employer becoming aware of her pregnancy. Furthermore, M had expressed concerns prior to her dismissal as to how G and V would be able to look after a baby in the one-room accommodation. The tribunal also had regard to the peremptory manner of G's dismissal, without any advance warning, and of the employer's insistence that G and V move out of their hotel accommodation immediately. Thus G's pregnancy discrimination claim under S.18 succeeded.

Turning to V, the tribunal noted that S.18 was not available to him: a claim under that section could only be brought by a woman complaining of unfavourable treatment related to her own pregnancy. The wording of S.18 therefore precluded a pregnancy-by-association claim. However, the tribunal went on to consider whether V had a claim for associative discrimination under S.13. It noted that S.13(1) prohibits less favourable treatment because of 'a' protected characteristic – it does not state that it has to be the complainant's own protected characteristic. The wording was therefore wide enough to cover a claim of direct sex discrimination because of association with a pregnant woman. The tribunal noted that this was also the view taken in the EHRC Employment Code of Practice at para 8.16. Furthermore, the tribunal observed that the instant case had striking similarities with the facts in Coleman v Attridge Law and anor (above) – V maintained that his less favourable treatment was by association not with a disabled person, but with his pregnant wife. While the ECJ's decision in Coleman was concerned with the provisions of the Equal Treatment Framework Directive, the tribunal took the view that much of its reasoning – such as the need to protect not only someone who has the protected characteristic (in that case, disability) but also those closely associated with that person – could apply equally to gender discrimination under the recast Equal Treatment Directive. Furthermore, the recast Directive could be interpreted as allowing for such a type of claim. Pregnancy discrimination was one aspect of direct discrimination on the ground of sex. Article 2(1)(a), which defines direct sex discrimination, was wide enough to include claims relating to treatment on the ground of another person's sex. And the tribunal took the view that Article 2(2)(c) – which explains that 'discrimination' includes 'any less favourable treatment of a woman related to pregnancy or maternity leave' – did not restrict pregnancy claims to women or preclude claims of sex discrimination by association.

13.146 Having found that V was able to bring a claim of associative sex discrimination under S.13, the tribunal considered how a comparator would have been treated in the same (or not materially different) circumstances. It concluded that a hypothetical comparator – i.e. a kitchen porter employed at the hotel who was not associated with a pregnant woman – would not have been dismissed. Accordingly, V's claim under S.13 succeeded. In assessing compensation, the tribunal awarded £10,000 each to G and V in respect of injury to feelings.

Although only a decision at first instance, and therefore not binding on other tribunals, the Gyenes decision nonetheless confirms that discrimination suffered as a result of association with a pregnant woman is actionable under S.13 as a claim for direct associative sex discrimination. The more interesting question, which has not (as far as we are aware) yet been adjudicated on, is whether a claimant in the same situation as the husband in Gyenes would be able to claim direct discrimination by association under S.13 because of the protected characteristic of pregnancy or maternity (as opposed to sex). No doubt this question will come before a tribunal in due course.

Discrimination by perception
13.147

Section 18 protects a woman throughout the protected period against any unfavourable treatment suffered because of her pregnancy. The requirement in S.18(2) that the unfavourable treatment must relate to a 'pregnancy of hers' means that the treatment must be related to the woman's own pregnancy. Furthermore, the special protection afforded by S.18 only applies during the protected period – i.e. while she is pregnant or on maternity leave. This means that a woman who is discriminated against because she is perceived to be pregnant cannot rely on S.18 because she is not actually pregnant. However, a woman in these circumstances could fall back on S.13. That section – which prohibits less favourable treatment 'because of a protected characteristic' – is wide enough to encompass discrimination because of a person's perceived characteristic. The Explanatory Notes to the EqA make this clear by stating that S.13 is 'broad enough to cover cases where the less favourable treatment is because… the victim is wrongly thought to have a protected characteristic'. It goes on to state that this approach applies to all the protected characteristics except for marriage and civil partnership (which requires the victim him or herself to have the protected characteristic – S.13(4)). It therefore appears that a woman who is wrongly perceived to be pregnant, and suffers less favourable treatment as a result, is able to complain of discrimination by perception under S.13.

Discrimination against part-time workers
13.148

Having granted an employee's request to go part time in order to look after his or her children, an employer must take care not to discriminate in respect of the terms and conditions of employment and other treatment that it applies to the employee. This is because part-time workers enjoy special protection from discrimination under the Part-time Workers (Prevention of Less Favourable Treatment) Regulations 2000 SI 2000/1551 ('the Part-time Workers Regulations'). This protection exists in addition to, and separate from, any right a part-time female employee may have to claim indirect sex discrimination

643

where she has been subjected to detrimental treatment on the ground of her part-time status – see 'Indirect sex discrimination' above.

Note that the Part-time Workers Regulations apply only to workers who already work part time. They do not provide a right to change from full-time to part-time work (or vice versa) and a woman whose request to return to work on a part-time basis following maternity leave is refused will have to rely on the EqA's protection from sex discrimination. An employee of either sex whose request to work part time is turned down may also have a claim under the 'flexible working' provisions contained in Part 8A ERA – see IDS Employment Law Handbook, 'Atypical and Flexible Working' (2014), Chapter 4, 'Flexible working'.

13.149 **Part-time Workers Regulations**
Regulation 5(1) of the Part-time Workers Regulations states that a part-time worker has the right not to be treated by his or her employer less favourably than the employer treats a comparable full-time worker as regards the terms of his or her contract of employment, or by being subjected to any other detriment by any act, or deliberate failure to act, of his or her employer. This right only applies where the reason for the treatment is that the worker is a part-time worker and the treatment is not justified on objective grounds – Reg 5(2). Here we give a brief outline of the main points. For a full discussion of the protection afforded by the Part-time Workers Regulations, see IDS Employment Law Handbook, 'Atypical and Flexible Working' (2014), Chapter 3, 'Part-time workers'.

13.150 **Less favourable treatment.** Examples of less favourable treatment include a lower hourly rate of pay; exclusion from training or promotional opportunities; failure to offer similar entitlements to annual leave, sick pay, maternity pay and pensions (on a *pro rata* basis where appropriate); and selection of part-time workers for redundancy in preference to full-time workers.

By virtue of Reg 5(4), a part-time worker must be paid the same overtime rates as a full-time worker, but he or she does not become entitled to overtime pay until he or she has worked the same number of hours that a full-time worker must work in order to become so entitled. Note, however, that a practice of only offering available overtime to full-time workers may be discrimination against part-time workers under the general principle in Reg 5(1).

13.151 It used to be the case that a person complaining of discrimination on the ground of his or her part-time status would have to show that his or her status was the sole reason for the treatment complained of. This was the view taken by the Scottish EAT in Gibson v Scottish Ambulance Service EATS 0052/04, where it held that a worker had not been unlawfully subjected to a detriment on the ground of his part-time status because there were other business reasons for the treatment. It reached this conclusion on the basis of Clause 4 of the Framework Agreement on Part-time work, which is annexed to the EU

Part-time Work Directive (No.97/81) (implemented in the UK by the Part-time Workers Regulations), which prohibits part-time workers being less favourably treated 'solely because they work part time'. However, the Appeal Tribunal in a later case – Sharma v Manchester City Council 2008 ICR 623, EAT – took a different view. It disapproved Gibson and held that, if it is established that a part-timer is treated less favourably than a comparator full-timer, and that being part time is one of the reasons for that treatment, then there is unlawful less favourable treatment under the Regulations. The reference to 'solely' in the Part-time Work Directive is simply intended to focus upon the fact that the discrimination against a part-timer must be because he or she is a part-timer and not for some other independent reason. The same reasoning was adopted and applied by the EAT in the subsequent case of Carl v University of Sheffield 2009 ICR 1286, EAT.

Comparators. By virtue of Reg 2(4), a part-time worker can compare his or **13.152** her position with that of a full-time worker employed by the same employer under the same type of contract and engaged in the same or broadly similar work, having regard – where relevant – to whether they have a similar level of qualification, skills and experience. In Matthews and ors v Kent and Medway Towns Fire Authority and ors 2006 ICR 365, HL, the House of Lords stated that in assessing the question of 'same or broadly similar' work, particular weight should be given to the extent to which the work of the two groups is in fact the same and the importance of that work to the enterprise as a whole. Otherwise there is a risk of giving too much weight to differences that are the almost inevitable result of one worker being full time and another working less than full time.

The full-time worker must work or be based at the same establishment as the part-time worker, but if there is no one at the same establishment who satisfies the relevant criteria a worker based at a different establishment (working for the same employer) can be used.

Where a full-time worker becomes a part-time worker, either seamlessly or **13.153** following a period of absence (which could include periods of family leave) not exceeding 12 months, he or she has an additional right to compare his or her treatment with the way in which he or she was treated as a full-time worker – Regs 3 and 4.

Note that the worker must be employed by the same employer as his or her comparator. There is no provision for comparison with a worker employed by an associated employer. Furthermore, unlike in claims under discrimination law, there is no provision for a comparison to be made with a hypothetical comparator.

Pro rata principle. Regulation 5(3) of the Part-time Workers Regulations **13.154** provides that, in determining whether a worker has been treated less favourably on account of his or her part-time status, the *pro rata* principle must be applied

645

unless it is inappropriate to do so. Therefore, where a comparable full-time worker receives a particular level of pay or any other benefit, a part-time worker is entitled to receive the proportion of that pay or other benefit which reflects the number of hours that he or she works – Reg 1(2).

Equal entitlements to, for example, pay, bonuses, bank holidays and annual leave are clearly susceptible to a pro rata calculation. Other benefits – for example, health insurance, subsidised mortgages, staff discounts and company cars – should where possible be provided to part-time workers pro rata. Where this is not possible, part-time workers may have to be given the full benefit or the pro rata financial equivalent.

13.155 **Justification.** Neither the Part-time Work Directive nor the Part-time Workers Regulations give any guidance as to what might amount to objective justification of a provision that discriminates against part-time workers. The Government's online guide to 'Part-time workers' rights' suggests that objective justification involves an employer showing that there is 'a good reason' to treat part-time workers differently, such as not providing health insurance for part-time employees because the costs involved are disproportionate to the benefits to which part-timers are entitled. More helpfully, the archived 2008 BERR guide, 'Part-time workers: The law and best practice – a detailed guide for employers and part-timers' (URN 02/1710), states that less favourable treatment will only be justified on objective grounds if it can be shown that the treatment is:

- to achieve a legitimate business objective

- necessary to achieve that objective, and

- an appropriate way of achieving that objective.

It is therefore likely that cases on objective justification in the context of indirect sex discrimination are relevant in relation to assessing justification under the Part-time Workers Regulations – see 'Indirect sex discrimination' above.

13.156 **Remedies.** A part-time worker who believes he or she is being discriminated against has the right under Reg 6 to request a written statement of the employer's reasons for the treatment, which must then be given within 21 days. The worker can also complain to an employment tribunal under Reg 8. However, although the tribunal can award compensation, it cannot make an award for injury to feelings, and so a woman who has been discriminated against would be well advised to bring a complaint of indirect sex discrimination as well (see 'Indirect sex discrimination' above).

A part-time worker also has the right not to be dismissed or subjected to any detriment because he or she has made a complaint or taken any other action under the Part-time Workers Regulations – Reg 7.

Equal pay

As noted at the beginning of this chapter, UK law has historically distinguished between sex discrimination in employment generally and sex discrimination in contractual matters – see 'Preliminary matters – overview of relevant UK and European law' above.

The Equal Pay Act 1970 (EqPA) operated by implying an 'equality clause' into contracts of employment where men and women were employed on equal work, so that any less favourable terms in the woman's contract were modified to be no less favourable than those enjoyed by the man, and *vice versa*. Following amendments introduced in 2005, the EqPA was amended to include specific provisions relating to maternity leave in S.1(2)(d)–(f). These provisions were added to the EqPA to ensure compliance with Article 157 of the Treaty on the Functioning of the European Union (TFEU) (previously Article 141, and before that Article 119, of the EC Treaty) following the ECJ's decision in Alabaster v Woolwich plc 2005 ICR 695, ECJ (a case dealing with non-backdated pay rises which is considered under 'Pay rises during maternity leave' below). The effect of these amendments was to:

- confirm that a woman is entitled to any pay rise awarded during her maternity leave period, or which would have been awarded had she not been on maternity leave, irrespective of whether or not it is backdated, and

- establish the circumstances under which a woman will be entitled to a bonus that is awarded while she is on maternity leave, or would have been awarded to her had she not been on maternity leave.

As the provisions in S.1(2)(d)–(f) EqPA related exclusively to maternity leave, the statutory wording was such that there was no need for a woman to identify a male comparator.

Employers became obliged to maintain a woman's contractual benefits (except **13.158** remuneration) during both the ordinary and additional maternity leave period – see Ss.71(4)(a) and 73(4)(a) ERA and Reg 9 MPL Regulations (discussed in Chapter 3, 'Maternity leave', under 'Terms and conditions during maternity leave'). This change was brought about by the Sex Discrimination Act (Amendment) Regulations 2008 SI 2008/656, following the High Court's decision in R (Equal Opportunities Commission) v Secretary of State for Trade and Industry 2007 ICR 1234, QBD, that the distinction between contractual rights during ordinary maternity leave and additional maternity leave was contrary to EU law (see 'Direct discrimination – pregnancy and maternity discrimination' above).

The EqPA was, of course, repealed and replaced by the EqA on 1 October 2010. The EqA maintains the distinction between sex discrimination in matters of contract (including pay) and other forms of sex discrimination in employment. It also replicates the special treatment in respect of equal pay during maternity leave by implying a 'maternity equality clause' into a woman's contract of employment, enshrining a right to equal treatment – see Ss.72–74. This has the same effect as the provisions noted above.

13.159 ## No entitlement to full pay during maternity leave

Applying the analysis used by the ECJ in Webb v EMO Air Cargo (UK) Ltd 1994 ICR 770, ECJ (see 'Direct discrimination – pregnancy and maternity discrimination' above), to an equal pay context appeared to open up the possibility of a woman making a claim of automatic direct sex discrimination where she received a lower rate of pay or other benefits during maternity leave compared with the benefits she would have received had she remained at work. However, in Gillespie and ors v Northern Health and Social Services Board and ors 1996 ICR 498, ECJ, the European Court rejected that proposition. The case was brought by several women employed by the Board who had taken maternity leave during 1988. In accordance with the terms of a relevant collective agreement, all the women were on half-pay for most of that period. They argued that this constituted discrimination on the ground of their sex because, during their maternity leave, they had effectively suffered a reduction in pay compared with their normal weekly wage. Another feature of the women's case was that, as a result of the method of calculating the benefits they were entitled to during maternity leave, they had not received the benefit of a pay rise agreed when they were on maternity leave (this aspect of their claim is discussed under 'Pay rises during maternity leave' below). The Northern Ireland Court of Appeal referred a number of questions to the ECJ for a preliminary ruling.

On the principal question – whether European anti-discrimination law required that women be paid full pay during maternity leave – the ECJ's decision was unequivocal. The essence of discrimination, it said, was 'the application of different rules to comparable situations or the application of the same rule to different situations'. However, the present case did not fall within either of these scenarios since, according to the ECJ, women taking maternity leave are 'in a special position which requires them to be afforded special protection, but which is not comparable either with that of a man or with that of a woman actually at work'. Consequently, neither Article 157 TFEU nor the recast EU Equal Treatment Directive (No.2006/54) could be relied upon to give women the right to continue to receive full pay during maternity leave. Nor did those provisions lay down any specific criteria for determining the amount of benefit to be paid to women during that period, except that the amount payable should not be 'so low as to undermine the purpose of maternity leave, namely the protection of women before and after giving birth'. The process of assessing the adequacy of the amount payable was a matter for national courts but, the ECJ

648

added, this assessment should take account not only of the length of maternity leave but also of 'the other forms of social protection afforded by national law in the case of justified absence from work'.

What is an 'adequate' level of maternity pay?   13.160

The ECJ's reference to the 'adequacy' of the amount payable seemed to leave open the possibility that a woman could claim the same level of pay as a man who is absent from work for a similar period on sick leave but who is paid at a more generous rate than a woman receiving maternity pay. However, this was rejected by the Northern Ireland Court of Appeal when the Gillespie case returned there for determination of the outstanding issue of whether the claimants' maternity pay was, in fact, adequate – see Gillespie and ors v Northern Health and Social Services Board and ors (No.2) 1997 IRLR 410, NICA. The Court interpreted the ECJ's reference to 'social protection afforded by national law' to mean a reference to *statutory* rather than contractual benefits and the Court noted that, on the particular facts, all the claimants had received maternity pay at a rate that exceeded the statutory levels of maternity pay and sickness benefit. The Court of Appeal also took note of the fact that Article 11(3) of the Pregnant Workers Directive (which did not apply to Gillespie as it had not yet come into force) stipulates that maternity pay 'shall be deemed adequate if it guarantees income at least equivalent to that which the worker concerned would receive in the event of a break in her activities on grounds connected with her state of health, subject to any ceiling laid down under national legislation'. The Court was of the firm opinion that this provision was also intended to refer to statutory sickness benefit and not contractual sick pay. On this basis, the Court concluded that maternity pay could not be said to be inadequate if it was higher than statutory sickness benefit. This leads to the inevitable conclusion that if a woman is paid statutory maternity pay – the lower rate of which is the same as statutory sick pay – that will not amount to unfavourable treatment contrary to European law.

Practical importance of Gillespie. The effect of the ECJ's decision in Gillespie 13.161 and ors v Northern Health and Social Services Board and ors (see 'No entitlement to full pay during maternity leave' above) was to narrow drastically the scope for women on maternity leave to claim equality of entitlement with male and female colleagues who are at work or absent from work for some reason other than maternity leave. In most circumstances, women on maternity leave are to be treated as being in a 'special position', effectively barring them from seeking to compare their benefits with those of their colleagues for the purposes of establishing an equal pay claim. The fact that they are on maternity leave constitutes a 'genuine material factor' under the EqA distinguishing their situation from that of any male comparator. And so long as the benefits she receives are not inferior to comparable statutory entitlements, such as statutory sick leave, a woman on maternity leave is unlikely to have any alternative equal pay claim directly based on Article 157 TFEU either.

The repercussions of the Gillespie decision can sometimes appear a little harsh. For instance, in Clark v Secretary of State for Employment 1997 ICR 64, CA, the Court of Appeal relied on Gillespie to reject a claim that the exclusion of women absent from work owing to pregnancy from the statutory right to claim a payment in lieu of notice from the Secretary of State on the insolvency of the employer was incompatible with Article 157. The provisions that each EU Member State makes in respect of women on maternity leave, the Court said, form a separate code that provides them with special protection, but the position of women in receipt of benefits under that code cannot be compared with that of a man or with that of a woman at work as the basis of a discrimination claim.

13.162 In the remainder of this chapter we examine a number of cases decided since Gillespie where the courts have adjudicated on the nature and extent of the benefits to which a woman is entitled while on maternity leave. As we shall see, on most occasions the effect of these cases has been to confirm that those benefits can be restricted, relative to the entitlements of employees still at work or absent from work for some reason other than maternity leave.

13.163 ## Conditions on entitlement to maternity pay
As explained in Chapter 5, 'Statutory maternity pay', under 'Normal weekly earnings', entitlement to statutory maternity pay (SMP) is conditional on a woman's average earnings being at or above the lower earnings limit for the payment of national insurance contributions (£111 a week for the 2014/15 tax year) during the eight weeks ending with the qualifying week – which is the 15th week before the expected week of childbirth. The question of whether this condition is compatible with the principle of equal pay in Article 157 TFEU was considered by the EAT in Banks v Tesco Stores Ltd and anor 1999 ICR 1141, EAT.

The employee in Banks – whose average earnings fell below the lower earnings limit current at the time – cited the ECJ's statement in Gillespie and ors v Northern Health and Social Services Board and ors (see 'No entitlement to full pay during maternity leave' above) that the amount of benefit payable during maternity leave must not be 'so low as to undermine the purpose of maternity leave, namely, the protection of women before and after giving birth'. Relying on this, she argued that to deprive her of any entitlement to SMP simply because she earned less than the lower earnings limit would defeat the purpose of maternity leave. The EAT was not persuaded. It pointed out that the Pregnant Workers Directive envisages that in certain circumstances a woman may receive no payment at all during maternity leave. This conclusion was drawn from Article 11(3), which provides that an allowance is deemed to be adequate if it guarantees income 'at least equivalent to that which the worker concerned would receive in the event of a break in her activities on grounds connected with her state of health, subject to any ceiling laid down under national legislation'. An examination of the provisions of the statutory sick pay (SSP) legislation revealed that if B had been absent on sick leave, as opposed to maternity leave, she would not have qualified for SSP either. This was because SSP is subject to the same lower earnings limit as SMP. The EAT also thought that the application of the lower earnings limit was permitted by virtue of Article 11(4) of the Directive, which provides that an allowance may be made subject to certain conditions of eligibility by the Member State.

The case therefore turned on the ECJ's decision in Gillespie. If the proper **13.164** interpretation of the ECJ's judgment was that Article 157 required every woman on maternity leave to receive some payment, then there would be an apparent conflict between that Article and the Pregnant Workers Directive. However, the EAT thought such an interpretation inherently unlikely. In its view, the ruling in Gillespie was to be interpreted as meaning that, where a woman otherwise qualifies for maternity pay, the level at which the pay is set must be sufficient to satisfy the overriding requirement that maternity leave should not be undermined. If, however, a woman falls within an exception contemplated by Article 11(4) of the Directive, she cannot rely on Article 157 to claim a right to maternity pay.

(Note that women who do not qualify for SMP may be entitled to state Maternity Allowance – see Chapter 5, 'Statutory maternity pay', under 'Maternity Allowance'.)

Pay rises during maternity leave   13.165

Although the ECJ in Gillespie and ors v Northern Health and Social Services Board and ors (see 'No entitlement to full pay during maternity leave' above) rejected the contention that women on maternity leave are entitled to receive the same rate of pay as they would have received if they were still at work, there was one aspect of the claimants' claim that the Court was prepared to accept. The employers, who were health authorities in Northern Ireland, had awarded all relevant employees a pay rise in November 1988, backdated to April 1988. However, as a result of a collective agreement governing the calculation of maternity pay in the health service, the pay increase was not taken into account for calculating the maternity pay for certain employees who had taken maternity leave and whose reference period for calculating earnings for maternity pay purposes ended after the date in April when the pay rise was deemed to take effect. The employees claimed that this constituted discrimination, since they would have benefited from the pay rise from April onwards had they not taken maternity leave. The ECJ agreed, stating that 'the principle of non-discrimination... requires that a woman who is still linked to her employer by a contract of employment or by an employment relationship during maternity

651

leave must, like any other worker, benefit from any pay rise, even if backdated, which is awarded between the beginning of the period covered by reference pay [i.e. the pay with regard to which maternity pay is calculated] and the end of maternity leave'. The Court went on to hold that 'to the extent that [maternity pay] is calculated on the basis of pay received by a woman before the commencement of maternity leave, the amount of benefit must include pay rises awarded between the beginning of the period covered by reference pay and the end of maternity leave, as from the date on which they take effect'.

In light of the ruling in Gillespie, the UK Government amended the Statutory Maternity Pay (General) Regulations 1986 SI 1986/1960 by adding a new provision – Reg 21(7) – requiring that a woman's normal weekly earnings must be recalculated to include any pay rise that is awarded after the relevant period for calculating her normal weekly earnings for SMP has passed, provided the pay rise is *backdated* to a date prior to the end of that period. In these circumstances, the woman's SMP is adjusted and any shortfall is made up by the employer. Where a woman who was not previously in receipt of SMP qualifies for SMP as a consequence of a backdated pay rise, the employer must pay the difference between any Maternity Allowance already paid and the SMP due – see further Chapter 5, 'Statutory maternity pay', under 'Normal weekly earnings'.

13.166 Following this legislative change, employees who found themselves in the same situation as the claimants in Gillespie were able to rely on Reg 21(7) to take any backdated pay rises into account when determining the amount of SMP payable to them. But what about women in respect of whom a pay rise was effective after the qualifying week and before the end of paid maternity leave but was *not* backdated? On the face of it, Reg 21(7) (as originally drafted) did not provide redress in this situation. The question therefore arose as to whether the provision properly implemented the decision in Gillespie and ors v Northern Health and Social Services Board and ors (above): it only allowed for a recalculation of SMP where the pay rise was actually backdated to the period used for calculating maternity pay, whereas the ECJ had clearly stated that a woman is entitled to benefit from any pay rise awarded to her before the end of her maternity leave.

This question was addressed by the EAT in Alabaster v Woolwich plc 2000 ICR 1037, EAT. In that case, the employee received a pay rise after the qualifying week but before she started her maternity leave. Under Reg 21(7) her normal weekly earnings did not have to be recalculated because the pay rise was not backdated. However, she argued that, following the ECJ's decision in Gillespie, all pay rises, not just those that were backdated, should be taken into account in calculating maternity pay and that Reg 21(7) had not properly implemented the requirements of EU law. Both the employment tribunal and the EAT upheld her claim on the basis that the Gillespie decision covered any pay increase between the beginning of the 'relevant period' and the end of maternity leave, and not just a backdated increase. The ECJ in Gillespie had not, in the EAT's view, tied in the pay increase to the 'relevant period' for calculating earnings in Reg 21(3). On a further appeal by the employer, the Court of Appeal made a reference to the ECJ, which determined that a woman must benefit from any pay rise that is awarded between the beginning of the period used to calculate statutory maternity pay and the end of maternity leave – Alabaster v Woolwich plc 2005 ICR 695, ECJ. This requirement is not limited to cases where the employer agrees to backdate a pay award to a date within the calculation period (i.e. the period specified under domestic law for determining the amount of maternity pay payable). To deny such an increase to a woman on maternity leave would discriminate against her since, had she not been pregnant, she would have received the pay rise.

On remission, the Court of Appeal held that, in the light of the ECJ's ruling, the **13.167** appropriate course was to disapply those parts of S.1 EqPA which prevented the claimant succeeding in her equal pay claim – Alabaster v Barclays Bank plc (formerly Woolwich plc) and anor 2005 ICR 1246, CA. Furthermore, Reg 21(7) of the 1986 Regulations was amended to provide that any pay rise awarded after the beginning of the period used to calculate SMP and before the end of the maternity leave period must be taken into account when calculating the amount of SMP payable.

The ECJ's decision in Alabaster also led to changes to the EqPA and these are now reflected in the EqA. S.74(1) and (2) EqA provides that where a term of the woman's work provides for maternity-related pay to be calculated by reference to her pay at a particular time and after that time (but before the end of the protected period) her pay increases, or would have increased had she not been on maternity leave, the 'maternity equality clause' implied into her contract will operate to modify her contract so as to provide for the increase to be taken into account for maternity pay purposes. The only occasions when this provision will not apply are where the maternity-related pay is what her pay would have been had she not been on statutory maternity leave, where the maternity-related pay is the difference between what her pay would have been had she not been on statutory maternity leave and any statutory maternity pay to which she is entitled, and where the terms of her work already provide for any increase to be taken into account – S.74(3) and (4) EqA. It would seem that these exclusions simply reflect the fact that, in such circumstances, pay rises during maternity leave would be taken into account in any event.

It is important to note that 'maternity-related pay' for these purposes means **13.168** the pay that a woman is entitled to as a result of being pregnant or in respect of times when she is on maternity leave, *other than statutory maternity pay* – S.74(9). The definition of 'maternity-related pay' that used to apply under S.1(2) EqPA expressly included pay by way of bonus but this has been left out

653

of the definition in the EqA. However, nothing in the consultation on the Act, the Explanatory Notes to the Act or the EHRC's 'Code of Practice on Equal Pay' (2010) suggests that any narrowing of the definition of 'pay' was intended. Indeed, the Explanatory Notes state that S.74 is designed to replicate the effect of provisions previously found in the EqPA – para 256. In any event, European and domestic case law indicating that bonuses amount to 'pay' continue to apply.

13.169 Pay during a period of maternity suspension

In British Airways (European Operation) Gatwick Ltd v Moore and anor 2000 ICR 678, EAT, the Appeal Tribunal confirmed that the reasoning used in Gillespie and ors v Northern Health and Social Services Board and ors 1996 ICR 498, ECJ – i.e. that a woman on maternity leave is not entitled to her full remunerative benefits because she is in a special position that is not comparable to that of a man or a woman working normally – also applies to situations where a woman is suspended from work on maternity grounds in accordance with Ss.66–70A ERA. The two claimants in Moore were female cabin crew who were removed from flying duties after their 16th week of pregnancy in accordance with the terms of a relevant collective agreement. Both women continued to work on other duties but lost a proportion of their pay because, as grounded crew, they were no longer entitled to the special 'flying allowances' paid to staff engaged on flying duties.

Despite this shortfall in pay, the EAT accepted the employer's argument that the claimants had no right to equal pay in respect of the flying allowances. The EAT took the view that a woman suspended from her normal work on maternity grounds is, like a woman on maternity leave, in a special position. Although this requires her to be accorded special protection, it is not comparable with either that of a man or that of a woman engaged on normal duties. Just as a woman will have no equal pay claim in respect of a period of maternity leave where 'adequate allowance' is made under national legislation, so she can have no claim during a period of suspension from normal work on maternity grounds where she is entitled to 'adequate allowance' in the form of remuneration under Ss.66–70A. Adopting the same approach as the Northern Ireland Court of Appeal in Gillespie (No.2) 1997 IRLR 410, NICA (discussed under 'What is an "adequate" level of maternity pay?' above), the EAT stated that there could be no question about the adequacy of the remuneration received in the present case because the employer was required by S.69 to pay women on maternity suspension at least as much as their statutory sick pay entitlement, and had, in fact, paid the claimants a lot more than this. The EAT was also satisfied that these arrangements were entirely compatible with the terms of the Pregnant Workers Directive. Accordingly, the EAT concluded that where a woman is suspended on maternity grounds, her position is governed by Ss.66–70A ERA, and no separate equal pay claim will arise under either the EqA or Article 157 TFEU in relation to alternative work performed by that worker.

It appears that this decision may in fact offer women more protection than is **13.170** required by EU law. In Parviainen v Finnair Oyj 2011 ICR 99, ECJ, a Finnish stewardess was transferred to ground duties during her pregnancy. As a result, she lost various supplementary allowances, amounting to around 40 per cent of her normal pay. The ECJ ruled that this did not amount to a breach of the Pregnant Workers Directive. A pregnant woman who is transferred to alternative duties is not entitled to receive the same average pay that she received before the transfer, where some of that pay depends on the performance of specific functions. Where a pregnant worker is temporarily transferred to another job, she remains entitled to the pay components or supplementary allowances which relate to her professional status, such as seniority, length of service, and professional qualifications, but not supplementary allowances dependent on the performance of specific functions.

Similarly, in Gassmayr v Bundesminster für Wissenschaft und Forschung 2011 1 CMLR 7, ECJ, the European Court held that a pregnant doctor who was suspended on health grounds was not entitled to continue receiving an on-call allowance during her suspension. The allowance was paid in accordance with the length of time the worker was on call and as the worker was prohibited from working, she could not perform the duties entitling her to payment of the allowance. However, the ECJ noted that the Pregnant Workers Directive only provided for *minimum* protection with regard to pay, and that there was nothing to prevent Member States from introducing legislation providing for the maintenance of all pay components during transfer or suspension.

Note that the right to suspend a pregnant woman from work is discussed **13.171** in Chapter 2, 'Health and safety protection', under 'Suspension on maternity grounds'.

Holidays
13.172

In Edwards v Derby City Council 1999 ICR 114, EAT, the Appeal Tribunal was asked to consider the implications of the decision in Gillespie and ors v Northern Health and Social Services Board and ors 1996 ICR 498, ECJ (discussed under 'Pay rises during maternity leave' above), for women who are on maternity leave during a holiday period. E, who was employed as a primary school teacher, took 18 weeks' contractual maternity leave during the late summer and autumn of 1997. For most of this period she received half-pay in accordance with the School Teachers' Pay and Conditions of Service. These arrangements meant that E received half-pay during the half-term, which fell from 24 October to 3 November, while the other teachers who were not working received full pay. In other words, but for the maternity provisions, E would also have been entitled to full pay during the ten days of the half-term holiday.

E asked an employment tribunal to make a declaration to the effect that the payment of half-pay during the half-term was discriminatory and breached the principle of equal pay set out in Article 157 TFEU. She argued that, when looking at a question of discrimination, it was necessary to ask whether an employee not actually at work because of maternity leave was treated less favourably than a male employee not actually at work because he was on holiday. The tribunal rejected her claim on the basis of the principles established in the Gillespie case. It stated that the proper approach was not to compare E with employees who were away from work for a non-pregnancy reason but to accept that pregnant workers are in a special position, which cannot be directly compared in that way. Since there was no doubt that a half-salary in E's case qualified as an 'adequate allowance' as defined in Gillespie (see 'What is an "adequate" level of maternity pay?' above), E could not be said to have been discriminated against contrary to Article 157.

13.173 The EAT upheld the tribunal's decision, applying much the same reasoning. In particular, it criticised E's contention that it was appropriate, for the purposes of claiming equal pay, to ask whether an employee not actually at work because of maternity leave was treated less favourably than a male employee not actually at work because he was on holiday. If that contention were correct, then she was to be treated for pay purposes as only on maternity leave when the school was open. The leave would not apply when the school was closed for the holiday, but would apply again when the school reopened. Such a situation was in stark contrast with the collectively agreed terms as to maternity pay applicable to teachers. The proper approach was not to look at a specific period of school closure in isolation but to look at the contractual provisions as a whole. The Gillespie case was authority for the proposition that women taking maternity leave provided by national legislation are in a special position. The EAT confirmed that there are no criteria for determining the amount of maternity pay, provided that it is not so low as to jeopardise the purpose of maternity leave. It was implicit that, subject to that proviso, arrangements for maternity pay are a matter for Member States and such arrangements as provide for maternity pay at a rate less than full pay do not, for that reason, fall foul of Article 157.

As a result of this decision, employees in similar circumstances who find that a large part of a low-paid maternity leave period falls during the long summer vacation might be better off financially by terminating their leave and returning to work 'normally' (and then possibly use the remainder of their leave as shared parental leave later in the year). In this situation they would have the benefit of the long vacation on full pay. In some respects, of course, the position of schoolteachers is unusual in that they cannot take holidays when they want, but only in accordance with the school calendar. However, the EAT's decision may also have implications for other types of employee. For example, some companies – usually factories – have an annual shutdown during which the staff have to take holiday. Women whose maternity leave overlaps with such a period might find themselves forced to accept lower-paid maternity pay, missing out on the normal salary that would be paid if they were to take holiday in the usual way. The same goes for employees whose contracts of employment require them to treat bank holidays as part of their annual leave entitlement.

Accrual of leave during maternity leave. In Boyle and ors v Equal Opportunities **13.174** Commission 1999 ICR 360, ECJ, the European Court held that a rule whereby holiday entitlement ceased to accrue during any period of unpaid leave, although ostensibly gender neutral, affected a substantially greater proportion of women than men. However, the fact that the rule disproportionately affected women resulted from the exercise by them of their right to unpaid contractual maternity leave. Since such leave was a special advantage over and above the protection afforded by the Pregnant Workers Directive and was available only to women, the fact that annual leave ceased to accrue during that period of leave could not amount to less favourable treatment of women contrary to the Equal Treatment Directive.

It should be noted, however, that under Reg 9 of the Maternity and Parental Leave etc Regulations 1999 SI 1999/3312, contractual holiday entitlement accrues as normal during both ordinary and additional maternity leave. Similarly, statutory annual leave accrues under Reg 13 of the Working Time Regulations 1998 SI 1998/1833 during both ordinary and additional maternity leave. For full details on the relationship between maternity leave and annual leave, see Chapter 3, 'Maternity leave', under 'Terms and conditions during ordinary maternity leave – annual leave'.

Bonuses   13.175

An issue notorious for its complexity concerns employees' entitlement to bonuses during maternity leave. A bonus – whether contractual or discretionary – can constitute 'pay' within the meaning of Article 157 TFEU, even if paid as an incentive for future performance or loyalty – Lewen v Denda 2000 ICR 648, ECJ.

An important point to note is that the nature of the bonus will normally determine the type of claim that should be brought in the event that a bonus is refused (or reduced) for maternity-related reasons. Contractual bonuses will fall within the remit of the equal pay provisions of the EqA (Ss.64–80) while non-contractual (i.e. discretionary) bonuses are more likely (but not certain) to be protected from less favourable treatment on the ground of sex under S.13, or unfavourable treatment with regard to pregnancy or maternity under S.18. As all those familiar with employment law know, there is no easy distinction between contractual and discretionary bonuses. If there is any doubt as to which type of claim applies, it would be sensible for a claimant to plead sex discrimination and equal pay in the alternative.

Below we outline the key legal principles that apply in respect of contractual and non-contractual bonuses.

13.176 **Contractual bonuses.** Section 74(6) and (7) EqA provides that a woman shall receive the following contractual payments if they would, aside from her maternity leave, have been paid:

- pay (including pay by way of bonus) in respect of times before she begins her statutory maternity leave

- pay by way of bonus in respect of times when she is on the period of two weeks' compulsory maternity leave

- pay by way of bonus in respect of times after she returns to work after the end of the protected period.

A woman will not, therefore, lose entitlement to a bonus in respect of work already done simply due to her being on maternity leave on the date the bonus is paid. This reflects the reasoning in Lewen v Denda (above), a case concerning a German parental leave law that has nevertheless been influential in relation to maternity leave. The meaning of 'bonus in respect of times after she returns to work' is open to debate, but could be interpreted as referring to bonuses that are an incentive for future performance or loyalty. In Lewen, the ECJ held that it was not a breach of duty to deny such a bonus to a woman who was absent from work on parental leave in circumstances where the sole qualifying condition for the bonus was that the employee was in active employment on the date when it was awarded. If the above interpretation of S.74(7) is correct, this means that the protection it offers is wider than that established in Lewen.

13.177 An entitlement to a bonus will not continue to accrue during ordinary or additional maternity leave in the same way that, for example, statutory and contractual holiday entitlement will. So, an employer can pro-rate a bonus that is awarded for a period during part of which the employee was on maternity leave, so long as the bonus is paid in respect of the time when the employee actually worked and for the two weeks' compulsory maternity leave period.

Where a woman is entitled to a bonus by virtue of S.74(6) and (7), the law requires the bonus to be paid at the time it would have been paid had she not been on maternity leave. It is therefore not open to the employer to defer payment of the bonus until a later date; for example, to a date after she returns to work from maternity leave. The EHRC's 'Code of Practice on Equal Pay' (2010) states that where, for example, a woman goes on maternity leave on 1 June and a contractual bonus for the year ending 30 April is payable on 1 July, the bonus must be paid to her on 1 July without delay (para 97).

13.178 *Enforcement.* With regard to enforcement, the EqA replicates the pre-October 2010 position whereby claims of sex, pregnancy and maternity discrimination relating to contractual terms were enforced differently to claims of non-contractual discrimination. It does so by providing that the 'equal pay' provisions (i.e. Ss.64–80) are the exclusive avenue of redress for sex, pregnancy and maternity discrimination in contractual matters. S.70(1) provides that the relevant sex discrimination provision – in this case, S.13 read with S.39 – has no effect in relation to a term 'that is modified by, or included by virtue of, a sex equality clause'. Furthermore, under S.71, any term that relates to pay, but in respect of which the equality clause has no effect, may not be the subject of a sex discrimination claim under S.39, except in limited circumstances. S.76(1) goes on to provide that the relevant pregnancy and maternity discrimination provision – in this case, S.18 read with S.39 – has no effect 'in relation to a term of the woman's work that is modified by a maternity equality clause'. And S.76(1A) stipulates that a term that relates to pay, but in respect of which a maternity clause has no effect, may not be the subject of a pregnancy or maternity discrimination claim. The effect of Ss.70 and 76(1) is that where a claim of sex or pregnancy/maternity discrimination can be brought under the 'equality clause' mechanism, it must be brought that way. The effect of Ss.71 and 76(1A) is that no contractual term that relates to pay can be made the subject of a sex or pregnancy/maternity discrimination claim. Thus, any claim in respect of a contractual bonus must be brought under Ss.64–80.

For details of the enforcement mechanism for equal pay claims, see IDS Employment Law Handbook, 'Equal Pay' (2011), Chapter 1, 'Law in context', under 'UK gender equality legislation – equal pay or sex discrimination?', and Chapter 2, 'Right to equal pay', under 'The sex equality clause – effect of the sex equality clause'.

Discretionary bonuses. The position with regard to discretionary (i.e. non-contractual) bonuses is less clear cut than that regarding contractual bonuses. As outlined earlier in this chapter, S.18(3) and (4) EqA provides that an employer discriminates against a woman if it treats her unfavourably because she exercised or sought to exercise her rights to ordinary or additional maternity leave, or because she is on compulsory maternity leave. No comparator is required to establish such unfavourable treatment – so, for example, there is no need to show that a person absent from work on a different type of leave would have been treated more favourably. Thus, on a strict reading of these provisions, failing to pay a discretionary bonus to an employee who is on any form of statutory maternity leave would amount to discrimination. **13.179**

This view accords with the EAT's decision in GUS Home Shopping Ltd v (1) Green (2) McLaughlin 2001 IRLR 75, EAT, decided as a sex discrimination claim at a time before the SDA included specific maternity and pregnancy protection. The employer in that case decided to move its marketing department from Worcester to Manchester and introduced a discretionary loyalty bonus contingent on three things: an orderly and effective transfer; cooperation and goodwill of the individual employee; and the employee remaining in post until the transfer date. M was on maternity leave throughout the whole period covered by the bonus and received no bonus. The employer's reasoning was that she had not been present during the transfer period to demonstrate commitment. G had been present for part of the period, had then taken sick leave for a pregnancy-related illness, and had subsequently taken maternity leave for the remainder of the period. She received only a part-payment of the bonus. An employment tribunal decided that the employees had been discriminated against on the ground of sex: the only reason for non-payment had been the employees' absence, which was due to pregnancy. The failure to recognise the protected status of pregnant employees amounted to an act of sex discrimination, based on the ECJ's decision in Webb v EMO Air Cargo (UK) Ltd 1994 ICR 770, ECJ. The EAT agreed.

13.180 There are, however, major problems with the EAT's decision and the view that non-payment of a discretionary bonus during maternity leave will be in breach of S.18 EqA (formerly S.3A SDA). First, the EAT did not refer to the ECJ's decisions in either Gillespie and ors v Northern Health and Social Services Board and ors (see 'No entitlement to full pay during maternity leave' above) or Lewen v Denda (above) and therefore seemed oblivious to the European Court's view that the principle in Webb does not extend to pay and bonuses. But more importantly, the decision does not appear to survive later legislative developments. When S.3A was inserted into the SDA in 2005 to provide specific protection from pregnancy and maternity discrimination, a further crucial amendment was made in the form of a new S.6A. This provided that S.3A did not extend to non-contractual remuneration by way of wages or salary, which included bonuses, unless the remuneration in question was either:

- maternity-related remuneration (i.e. pay to which a woman was entitled as a result of being pregnant or in respect of times when she was on maternity leave)

- remuneration in respect of times when the woman was not on maternity leave (such as a bonus or commission for work done before the commencement of such leave), or

- remuneration by way of bonus in respect of times when a woman was on compulsory maternity leave.

Similar provision is now made at para 17 of Schedule 9 to the EqA. As the EHRC Code of Practice on Employment notes, at paras 8.39–40: 'There is no obligation on an employer to extend to a woman on maternity leave any noncontractual benefit relating to pay, such as a discretionary bonus. For the purposes of this exception, "pay" means a payment of money by way of wages or salary. However, this exception does not apply to any maternity-related pay (whether statutory or contractual), to which a woman is entitled as a result of being pregnant or on maternity leave. Nor does it apply to any maternity-related

660

pay arising from an increase that the woman would have received had she not been on maternity leave.'

It seems, therefore, that the scope to claim pregnancy and maternity **13.181** discrimination under S.18 EqA in relation to bonuses is limited to claims for a pro rata 'discretionary' bonus that takes into account any period the employee actually worked, plus the two weeks' compulsory maternity leave period; or a full bonus that is regulated neither by the contract of employment, nor by way of wages or salary. The latter of these two categories would seem to be extremely narrow but could, for example, incorporate circumstances where a non-monetary bonus is awarded to all staff as a goodwill gesture.

Repayment of maternity pay

13.182

Some employers who offer maternity pay over and above the statutory minimum rate qualify this by requiring their employees to recompense the employer if they do not return to work (often for a minimum period) when maternity leave ends. The question has arisen as to whether such a requirement breaches equal pay principles. In Boyle and ors v Equal Opportunities Commission 1999 ICR 360, ECJ, the EOC operated a contractual maternity scheme which provided that women who had been employed for at least a year were entitled to maternity leave of three months and one week on full pay if they stated that they intended to return to work after maternity leave and agreed to be liable to repay their contractual maternity pay if they did not return for at least one month after their leave ended. Several women employed by the EOC applied to an employment tribunal for a declaration that the repayment clause was discriminatory. In support of their claim, they pointed to the fact that, by contrast, EOC employees on sick leave, who were entitled to their full salary for a maximum of six months in any 12-month period, were not required to repay their contractual sick pay if they did not return to work.

Once again, the application of the principle established in Gillespie and ors v Northern Health and Social Services Board and ors 1996 ICR 498, ECJ, had the effect of preventing the employees from pursuing a claim for equal pay in these circumstances. The ECJ repeated its view that the position of women on maternity leave cannot be compared with that of a man or a woman on sick leave. Article 157 TFEU and the recast Equal Treatment Directive therefore did not preclude a clause in a contract of employment whereby a woman who did not return to work after maternity leave would be required to repay the difference between the contractual maternity pay that she had received and the statutory maternity pay to which she was entitled, notwithstanding that workers who were absent on sick leave were not required to repay any part of their contractual sick pay if they did not return to work. The ECJ also added that there was nothing in the repayment clause that was contrary to the Pregnant Workers Directive. It explained that Article 11(2)(b) and (3) of that Directive is intended to ensure that, during the minimum period of at least 14 weeks'

661

maternity leave referred to in Article 8, a woman receives an income at least equivalent to the sickness allowance provided for by national social security legislation. There is no intention to guarantee a woman a higher income equivalent to contractual sick pay.

13.183 Sick leave

Another provision of the contractual maternity scheme considered in Boyle and ors v Equal Opportunities Commission (see 'Repayment of maternity pay' above) was a clause which stated that a woman who became ill during her maternity leave could not take advantage of the contractual sick leave arrangements – which in certain respects were more favourable than the arrangements for contractual maternity leave – unless she elected to 'return' to work and terminate her maternity leave. The ECJ ruled that the recast Equal Treatment Directive does not require a woman to be able to exercise simultaneously both the right to supplementary maternity leave granted to her by the employer and the right to sick leave. Consequently, in order for a woman on maternity leave to qualify for sick leave, it was open to an employer to require her to terminate a period of supplementary maternity leave granted to her by her contract.

13.184 Pensions

In addition to being entitled to certain protections in relation to pay while absent from work, a woman on maternity leave also benefits from protection in relation to her rights under an occupational pension scheme. This is the effect of S.75 EqA, which provides for the deemed inclusion of a 'maternity equality rule' in an occupational pension scheme. In brief, the rule has the effect that any term of the scheme, or any discretion capable of being exercised under it, that purports to treat a woman differently in respect of time when she is on maternity leave compared with time when she is not, is modified so that both periods fall to be treated in the same way – S.75(3) and (4). Any term or discretion relating to membership of the scheme, accrual of rights or determination of benefits payable under the scheme falls within the scope of the maternity equality rule – S.75(5) and (6). The maternity equality rule is discussed in IDS Employment Law Handbook, 'Equal Pay' (2011), Chapter 2, 'Right to equal pay', under 'Maternity – maternity and pensions'.

13.185 Equal pay claims by male employees

The ECJ's decision in Abdoulaye v Régie Nationale des Usines Renault SA 2001 ICR 527, ECJ, shows that the reasoning underpinning Gillespie and ors v Northern Health and Social Services Board and ors (see 'No entitlement to full pay during maternity leave' above) can cut both ways. In Abdoulaye several male employees claimed equal pay with women who received a lump-sum maternity allowance. They complained that their employer's refusal to pay an equivalent allowance to fathers was contrary to Article 157. The employer, relying on Gillespie, responded that the male and female employees were not in a comparable position. The lump-sum payments were designed to offset the occupational disadvantages, inherent in maternity leave, that affect female workers. The ECJ agreed that, in circumstances where one-off maternity payments were, in fact, designed for such a purpose, men were not in a comparable position and therefore could not claim entitlement under Article 157 to an equivalent lump-sum allowance. It accepted the employer's premise that women who take maternity leave may, in practice, face disadvantages in the workplace, including non-promotion and denial of performance-related salary increases either during the leave period or on their return to work (although it is important to note that treatment of this nature may be discriminatory if it is connected with pregnancy or maternity – see, for example, Thibault v Caisse Nationale d'Assurance Vieillesse des Travailleurs Salariés (CNAVTS) 1999 ICR 160, ECJ, referred to under 'Direct discrimination – pregnancy and maternity discrimination' above).

The decision in Abdoulaye v Régie Nationale des Usines Renault SA (above) accords with the thrust of para 2 of Schedule 7 to the EqA, which allows an employer to discriminate between men and women with regard to maternity pay without breaking the law. Para 2 provides that 'a sex equality clause does not have effect in relation to terms of work affording special treatment to women in connection with pregnancy or childbirth'. This prevents men bringing claims for special treatment to which only women are entitled in connection with their pregnancy. This would appear to preclude, for example, a claim by a man receiving the flat rate statutory shared parental pay trying to claim equal pay with a woman who is receiving enhanced contractual pay during her maternity leave. The potential for discrimination claims by men in respect of the shared parental leave scheme is discussed under 'Discrimination against men – shared parental leave and pay' above.

14 Replacement employees

Less favourable treatment

Dismissal of replacement

Retention of replacement

An employer may need to engage a temporary replacement for an employee **14.1** who takes a period of family leave, or who is suspended from work on medical or maternity grounds. However, this can lead to problems when the original employee returns to work. This chapter considers two scenarios: the first is where the employer dismisses the replacement employee at the end of the leave period; and the second is where the employer retains the replacement employee in preference to the returning employee.

However, before examining the legal implications of these scenarios, it is first important to mention the impact of the Fixed-term Employees (Prevention of Less Favourable Treatment) Regulations 2002 SI 2002/2034 ('the Fixed-term Work Regulations'), which came into force on 1 October 2002. This is because many replacement employees are employed on fixed-term contracts covering the specific period for which the permanent employee is due to be absent on statutory leave. What follows is a brief explanation of the relevant provisions of the Regulations. For a detailed discussion on the full scope of the Regulations, see IDS Employment Law Handbook, 'Atypical and Flexible Working' (2014), Chapter 2, 'Fixed-term employees'.

Less favourable treatment
14.2

When considering the position of replacement employees it should be borne in mind that most such employees are employed on fixed-term contracts. They are therefore protected under the Fixed-term Work Regulations, which provide that a fixed-term employee has the right not to be treated less favourably by his or her employer than the employer treats a comparable permanent employee:

- as regards the terms of his or her contract, or

- by being subjected to any other detriment by any act, or deliberate failure to act, of the employer – Reg 3(1).

Reg 3(2) adds that the right not to be less favourably treated includes in particular the right not to be treated less favourably in relation to:

- any period of service qualification relating to any particular condition of service

---
665

- the opportunity to receive training, or

- the opportunity to secure any permanent position in the establishment.

14.3 This principle of equal treatment applies only if the treatment in question is on the ground that the employee is a fixed-term employee and the treatment cannot be objectively justified – Reg 3(3).

In effect this means that an employer cannot treat a replacement employee less favourably than it treats comparable permanent employees on the ground that the replacement employee is employed under a fixed-term contract, unless the employer can objectively justify the difference in treatment. So, for example, it would be unlawful for an employer to give permanent employees a bonus or make training available to them without providing these benefits to the replacement employee unless the employer can show a good reason for this difference in treatment.

14.4 Right to be informed of available vacancies

In addition to the right not to be treated less favourably, fixed-term employees have the right to be informed of any available vacancies in the establishment by the employer – Reg 3(6). This is a free-standing right, so even if the replacement employee has not been treated less favourably in the selection procedure for a permanent post, the fact that he or she was not informed of it could give rise to a claim – Reg 7(1).

14.5 Successive fixed-term contracts

Regulation 8 is aimed at preventing abuse arising from the use of successive fixed-term contracts. It provides that an employee on a fixed-term contract will be regarded as a permanent employee if all the following circumstances apply:

- the employee is currently employed under a fixed-term contract and that contract has previously been renewed, or the employee has previously been employed on a fixed-term contract before the start of the current contract

- the employee has been continuously employed under fixed-term contracts for four years or more

- at the time of the most recent renewal – or, where the contract has not been renewed, at the time that the contract was entered into – employment under a fixed-term contract was not justified on objective grounds.

This provision is unlikely to apply in the majority of cases where a fixed-term employee is taken on as a replacement for an employee who is on family leave or has been suspended on medical or maternity grounds, given the limited amount of time involved. However, it may be relevant in a large organisation where an employee is employed on a series of fixed-term contracts to provide temporary cover on an ongoing basis. In these circumstances, the need to cover staff shortages may constitute an objective reason justifying the continued use of fixed-term contracts.

This was confirmed by the ECJ in Kücük v Land Nordrhein-Westfalen 2012 **14.6** ICR 682, ECJ, which observed that where an employer has a large workforce, it is inevitable that temporary replacements will frequently be necessary due to employees being on sick, parental, maternity or other leave. In these circumstances the temporary replacement of employees could constitute an objective reason under Clause 5(1)(a) of the EU Fixed-term Work Directive (No.99/70) (implemented in the UK by Reg 8) justifying the use of successive fixed-term contracts. According to the Court, this conclusion was all the more compelling where, as in the case before it, national legislation justifying the renewal of fixed-term contracts also pursued recognised social policy objectives. Indeed, previous ECJ case law had held that the concept of 'objective reason' in Clause 5(1)(a) encompasses the pursuance of social policy objectives, which include pregnancy and maternity protection and reconciling professional and family obligations – objectives met by using successive fixed-term contracts to provide temporary cover.

However, the ECJ also emphasised that the renewal of successive fixed-term contracts must be intended to cover temporary, as opposed to permanent, needs. But it stressed that the mere fact that the need to cover temporary personnel shortages could be met by hiring permanent staff – even where those shortages are recurring or even permanent – did not mean that an employer who uses successive fixed-term contracts is acting in an abusive manner contrary to Clause 5(1). To hold that that provision requires the moving of a fixed-term worker onto a permanent contract where an employer has a permanent need for replacement staff would go beyond the objectives of the Directive and would disregard the discretion left to Member States in implementing it into national law.

Dismissal of replacement   14.7

Section 106(1) of the Employment Rights Act 1996 (ERA) provides that the dismissal of a replacement employee will, in certain circumstances, be treated for the purposes of S.98(1)(b) – dismissal for 'some other substantial reason' (SOSR) – as being for a substantial reason of a kind such as to justify the dismissal of an employee holding the position which that employee held. In other words, the dismissal will be a potentially fair dismissal for a substantial reason. This provision applies where:

- the employer informs the temporary employee in writing at the time of recruitment that his or her employment will be terminated on the resumption of work by another employee who is, or will be, absent wholly or partly because of pregnancy or childbirth, or on adoption leave or shared parental leave – S.106(2)(a), and

- the dismissal takes place in order to make it possible to give work to the returning employee – S.106(2)(b).

'Dismissal' for these purposes includes the expiry of a fixed-term contract which is not then renewed – S.95(1)(b) ERA.

These requirements are cumulative, meaning that both must be observed by an employer seeking to rely on S.106(1) when dismissing the replacement employee. We examine each in more detail under 'The S.106(2) requirements' below.

14.8 Section 106(3) ERA makes similar provision where a replacement employee is recruited to cover for an employee who is suspended from work on maternity grounds (see Chapter 2, 'Health and safety protection', under 'Suspension on maternity grounds'), or on 'medical grounds' in compliance with a statutory enactment or the provisions of an approved Code of Practice within the terms of S.64. If the replacement employee is informed in writing at the time of recruitment that he or she will be dismissed when the suspension comes to an end, and if the dismissal takes place in order to allow the suspended employee to resume her work, then the dismissal of the replacement is for a substantial reason under S.98(1)(b).

So summarising the above, the special provision regarding the dismissal of replacement employees in S.106 applies whenever that employee has been engaged to cover for another employee who is, or will be, absent because of pregnancy, childbirth, adoption leave, shared parental leave, or maternity or medical suspension. It should be noted, however, that even if the dismissal of a temporary replacement employee is deemed to be potentially fair under S.106, tribunals must still consider the reasonableness of such a dismissal under S.98(4) – S.106(4) (see 'Effect of S.106(1) and question of reasonableness' below).

14.9 **Two-year qualifying period for unfair dismissal claims.** Before looking at the S.106(2) requirements, it should perhaps be pointed out that the usefulness of the provision has diminished considerably since the qualifying period for claiming unfair dismissal was increased from one year to two years in 2012 – see S.108. Given that statutory maternity/adoption/shared parental leave is for a maximum of 52 weeks, few replacement employees will be able to satisfy this qualifying condition, rendering S.106 effectively otiose. Of course, this would not necessarily be true of a replacement employee who is already employed by the employer but, as Victoria and Albert Museum v Durrant 2011 IRLR 290, EAT, shows, an employer would need to proceed with caution before treating such an employee as a 'replacement' for the purposes of S.106 – see 'The S.106(2) requirements' below.

The S.106(2) requirements

14.10

As stated previously, the provision governing the dismissal of a replacement employee in S.106(1) is only triggered if the employer has satisfied the two requirements spelled out in S.106(2). Both of these were separately scrutinised by the Appeal Tribunal in Victoria and Albert Museum v Durrant (above). With regard to the first requirement – that the employer, on engaging the employee, must inform the replacement employee 'in writing that his [or her] employment will be terminated on the resumption of work' of the employee whom he or she is replacing – the EAT held that this should be interpreted strictly. In its view, the provisions of S.106(1) will only apply where the employer informed the employee on his or her engagement, in clear and unambiguous language, that the employment would be terminated on the return of the permanent employee.

In the Durrant case the claimant was already a permanent employee of the employer but, owing to long-term absence caused by illness, had been subject to a capability procedure during which other permanent positions were being sought by the employer to avoid the necessity of dismissing him on capability grounds. However, as no suitable position was found, the claimant was given notice of dismissal. While he was on notice, the employer offered him a fixed-term contract of six months' duration as a replacement for a permanent employee on maternity leave. The offer letter noted that this contract was being provided to 'facilitate' a further search for other work in the museum which the employer ran. Later, he received a written offer of a further six-month fixed-term contract when the employee on maternity leave extended her leave. An employment tribunal found that neither letter satisfied the requirements of S.106(2)(a) because they had not unambiguously stated that the claimant's employment would be terminated on the resumption of work by the permanent employee. Upholding this decision on appeal, the EAT ruled that it was not possible to accept the employer's contention that a combination of the factual matrix and the text of the letters was sufficient compliance with S.106(2)(a) in that the non-renewal of the fixed-term contract was timed to coincide with the return to work of the permanent post-holder, the claimant knew that to be the case, and the non-renewal of the contract did enable the permanent post-holder to return. The EAT was adamant that the statutory requirement envisages a clear notice being given at the outset so as to leave no doubt on the part of the employee as to the circumstances in which the contract will end. If the language of the written information does not convey the simple message required by the subsection, there was nothing in the statute to suggest that the information can instead be conveyed by a combination of the text of the written document and inferences drawn from the surrounding circumstances.

If an employer fails to give the written notice required by S.106(2)(a) to a 14.11 replacement employee this does not mean that a subsequent dismissal will be automatically unfair, however. In Hayes v South Glamorgan County Council

EAT 702/84 H was engaged as a temporary library assistant to cover for an employee's maternity leave. His appointment was extended to cover for a second employee's maternity leave until eventually the last of a series of fixed-term contracts under which he had worked was not renewed. He was never given the statutory notification set out in S.106(2) and claimed that this made his dismissal automatically unfair. The EAT held that 'the fact that the prudent employer will follow the [S.106] procedure does not mean, however, that employers who act outside it will automatically stumble into statutory unfairness... the issue of general fairness still remains wholly at large for the tribunal to decide'. The employer has to show the reason for dismissal and the tribunal must then decide the issue of fairness under S.98(4).

Turning to the second requirement of S.106(2) – that the employer must have dismissed the replacement employee 'in order to make it possible to give work' to the returning employee – the EAT in Victoria and Albert Museum v Durrant (above) emphasised that, unlike S.106(2)(a), it is critical to consider the factual matrix when determining whether the requirement in S.106(2)(b) has been met. In its view, this was precisely what the tribunal had done when reaching its conclusion that the claimant had not been dismissed to facilitate the return of his absent colleague. He was not a temporary employee engaged as a stopgap measure because of the permanent employee's maternity leave, but rather a permanent employee who had been moved into whatever temporary post was available and suitable. The reason for his dismissal was that there was no alternative work for him to do, and not the return of the post-holder from maternity leave. According to the EAT, the tribunal could not be criticised for looking at a broader horizon than just the last 12 months or so of the claimant's employment. When looked at in the broader perspective, it had been open to the tribunal to conclude that the letters were ambiguous and that the claimant had not been dismissed in order to allow the resumption of work by the other employee.

14.12 Effect of S.106(1) and question of reasonableness

Assuming that the two requirements specified in S.106(2) are met, what is the legal effect of S.106(1) vis-à-vis the dismissal of the replacement employee? S.106(1) stipulates that, where it applies, the replacement employee 'shall be regarded for the purposes of S.98(1)(b) as having been dismissed for a substantial reason of a kind such as to justify the dismissal of an employee holding the position which the employee held'. On the face of it, this would seem to specify that any replacement employee dismissed in circumstances where the requirements of subsection (2)(a) and (b) have been met will be deemed to be dismissed for 'some other substantial reason justifying dismissal' (SOSR) in accordance with S.98(1)(b). But according to obiter observations of the EAT in Victoria and Albert Museum v Durrant (above), this is not necessarily so. In that case the Appeal Tribunal (presided over by His Honour Judge Hand QC) opined that S.106(1) does not mean, in all conceivable circumstances, that the reason for dismissal must be deemed to be SOSR. There may be cases where, even though S.106 might otherwise be engaged because the employee has been dismissed in order to facilitate the return of the permanent employee from maternity or applicable leave, the reason for dismissal might still be redundancy – particularly bearing in mind the impact of the presumption of redundancy in S.163(2) ERA. One example might be where there has been a 'bumping' of an employee out of a post to accommodate somebody whose post had disappeared and the 'bumped' employee is then given work covering for an employee on maternity leave and is subsequently dismissed on her return. S.106 does not displace all other reasons for dismissal by deeming the reason to be some other substantial reason. Where another reason for dismissal exists (and realistically that is only likely to occur in a redundancy situation), S.106 will not deem the dismissal to be for some other substantial reason; this will only happen where there is no reason for dismissal other than the need to facilitate the return of the woman from maternity leave. In effect, SOSR is the default reason if no other reason applies.

Reasonableness. Turning from the reason for dismissal to the fairness of **14.13** dismissal, it is important to note that the fact that a dismissal under S.106 is deemed – at least in cases where no other reason applies – to be for SOSR does not automatically mean that the dismissal is fair. This is made clear by S.106(4), which states that: 'Subsection (1) does not affect the operation of S.98(4) in a case to which this section applies.' So although the employer will have cleared the first obstacle of showing the reason for dismissal, the question of whether the dismissal was fair still falls to be considered under the reasonableness test set out in S.98(4). In practice, it is unlikely that a tribunal would find the dismissal of a replacement employee to make way for a returning permanent employee to be unfair since tribunals are generally very reluctant to accept a preference for a replacement employee as overriding the absent employee's express statutory right to return to his or her old job. However, if, for example, there are other positions that the temporary replacement employee could fill, the employer may have acted unreasonably in dismissing without at least considering the possibility of retaining the replacement employee in one of those positions. For further discussion on the retention of replacement employees, see 'Retention of replacement' below.

Replacement employees who fall pregnant **14.14**

Problems may arise where the replacement employee is herself pregnant at the time of her dismissal. In Webb v EMO Air Cargo (UK) Ltd 1994 ICR 770, ECJ, a replacement employee was recruited for an unlimited term with a view, initially, to covering for another employee taking maternity leave. However, when the employer discovered that she too was pregnant, she was dismissed on the ground that she would be unavailable for work during the crucial period of the other employee's maternity leave. The European Court of Justice ruled that dismissal in those circumstances was contrary to the EC Equal Treatment Directive (No.76/207) – now repealed and replaced by the recast EU Equal Treatment Directive (No.2006/54). This case is discussed in Chapter 13, 'Discrimination and equal pay', under 'Direct discrimination – pregnancy and maternity discrimination'. Note, however, that the employee in the Webb case, although recruited for the purpose of providing maternity cover, was engaged on a contract of indefinite duration with the expectation that she would continue to be employed after the other employee returned from maternity leave. It should also be noted that an employee in Ms Webb's position would probably now be able to claim that she was automatically unfairly dismissed for a reason connected with her pregnancy under S.99 ERA, for which there is no minimum period of qualifying service – see Chapter 12, 'Detriment and unfair dismissal', under 'Automatically unfair dismissal'.

14.15 Employees who delay their return or who do not return at all

It is not immediately clear whether S.106 ERA applies where a permanent employee does not return from a period of maternity/adoption/shared parental leave immediately but instead goes on some other form of leave (such as holiday or sickness leave). Take the example of a woman who is ill and may not be in a position to return from additional maternity leave on the expected date. If the replacement employee is kept on until the permanent employee does return, would the employer be able to rely on S.106 when dismissing the replacement at that point? This is not an issue that appears to have been considered by the courts, but, in our view, the employer would still be entitled to rely on S.106 in these circumstances. The rationale for this lies in the wording of S.106(2), which states: 'This section applies to an employee where (a) *on engaging him* the employer informs him in writing that his employment will be terminated on the resumption of work by another employee who is, or will be, absent wholly or partly because of pregnancy or childbirth, or on adoption leave or shared parental leave' (our stress). The italicised words lend support to the view that what actually triggers S.106 are the circumstances that obtain at the time the replacement employee is engaged. Provided that the employer's actions are directed at temporarily replacing an employee whose absence, wholly or partly, falls into one of the categories of leave (or grounds of suspension) caught by S.106, then the provisions of the section can be relied on. This is so provided that the other requirement of S.106(2) is met; namely, that the replacement employee is dismissed in order to make it possible to give work to the returning employee.

In practice, employees often have a right to tack a period of annual leave or unpaid parental leave onto the end of maternity, adoption or shared parental leave, so may be away for longer than the specific period covered by the relevant type of statutory leave. When the qualifying limit for claiming unfair dismissal was just one year, this could present the unwary employer with a problem, as any replacement employee who was kept on might clock up continuous service of more than a year and so be eligible to claim unfair dismissal. Similarly, a replacement employee who was recruited to cover for an employee suspended on maternity or medical grounds and who remained in the job once the suspended employee started maternity leave, or whose contract was extended to cover for an employee who was unable to return to work after maternity, adoption or shared parental leave on health grounds (i.e. went on sick leave), might well have ended up meeting the one-year continuous service requirement. But now that the continuous service requirement to claim unfair dismissal has been extended to two years (from 6 April 2012), employers are much less likely to face this risk. However, if they do it is likely that S.106 would apply (for the reasons mentioned above).

Employees on maternity or adoption leave sometimes change their minds about **14.16** returning to work at all. In these circumstances, S.106 would not apply to the dismissal of the replacement employee. That is because the employer would be unable to satisfy the requirement in S.106(2)(b) that the dismissal be 'in order to make it possible to give work to the other employee'.

So what are the rights of the replacement employee in this position? First and foremost, the employer is under a duty to inform the employee of the vacancy (and of any other permanent vacancies) under the Fixed-term Work Regulations – see 'Less favourable treatment – right to be informed of available vacancies' above. But this does not mean that the replacement employee has any prescriptive right to have his or her appointment made permanent. As for claiming unfair dismissal, the employee would be able to do this only if he or she has sufficient continuous service. And, for the reasons previously mentioned, this is unlikely now that the qualifying period for claiming unfair dismissal has been increased to two years. Should the employee be eligible, however, his or her dismissal would be judged according to ordinary unfair dismissal principles. The employer would therefore do well to give serious consideration to any suitable alternative employment as a way of demonstrating that the dismissal was fair and reasonable for the purposes of S.98(4) ERA. Two contrasting examples, both of which were decided when the qualifying period for claiming unfair dismissal was just one year:

- **Webster v Chester Health Authority** ET Case No.30300/82: W was taken on as a temporary replacement for a secretary, who eventually decided not to return from maternity leave. The employer required secretaries to have minimum typing speeds. W's speed was adequate for a temporary post but not for a permanent one, so she was considered unsuitable and dismissed. The employment tribunal held that this was a fair dismissal for SOSR

- **Darbyshire v Governing Body of All Saints Church of England Primary School** ET Case No.2405746/05: D was employed as a full-time teacher on a temporary fixed-term contract from 1 September 2004 to 31 August 2005

673

'or on the return of the post-holder from maternity leave, whichever was the sooner'. She had made it clear on a number of occasions that she would be interested in remaining at the school should the teacher on maternity leave decide not to return. Early in July 2005 a teaching assistant in the school told the head that she would like to apply for the post if the teacher did not return. The head teacher approached the governing body, which agreed the appointment. D was informed of the appointment on 12 July and she resigned on 21 July 2005. She subsequently brought a claim for unfair dismissal against the school. The employment tribunal agreed that D had been unfairly dismissed. It had been unreasonable for the head not to have given her an opportunity to be considered for the post and to have taken no steps to consult her before giving the post to another person. Had the governing body been made aware of D's wish to remain at the school, it was likely that it would have appointed her, given that she was more suitably qualified than the teaching assistant who was in fact appointed to the role.

The law on unfair dismissal is discussed in depth in IDS Employment Law Handbook, 'Unfair Dismissal' (2010).

14.17 Retention of replacement

In practice, employers are more likely to run into trouble if they decide to keep the replacement employee on – and either offer the returning employee a different job or refuse to have him or her back at all – than if they simply dismiss the replacement on the permanent employee's return. In Berry v BP International Ltd ET Case No.19359/82, for example, the employer felt an obligation to a replacement employee taken on to fill a high-level secretarial position. The employment tribunal pointed out that the employer had a statutory obligation to allow the returner to return to her old job and that this must override any assumed obligation to her replacement. It made a reinstatement order in favour of the returning employee.

The statutory obligation to allow an employee to return to his or her old job applies even if the replacement employee is actually better qualified or generally more satisfactory. The relative merits of the replacement will not outweigh the statutory right to return, even though the return of the employee on leave will necessitate the dismissal of the replacement employee. In McLean v William Hill Organisation Ltd ET Case No.3800/90, for example, the replacement improved the turnover of the employer's shop while M was absent on maternity leave. The employment tribunal held, however, that this was no excuse for denying M her statutory right to return.

14.18 In Rees v Apollo Watch Repairs plc 1996 ICR 466, EAT – a sex discrimination case – the Appeal Tribunal held that an employer had unlawfully discriminated against an employee on the ground of her sex when refusing to take her back from maternity leave because the replacement was more efficient. Although the immediate cause of the employee's dismissal was gender neutral, the effective and underlying cause was her absence on maternity leave.

Similar reasoning would almost certainly apply in an unfair dismissal case to render the dismissal of the original employee automatically unfair for a reason connected with his or her taking maternity, adoption or shared parental leave. Tribunals are very unlikely in these circumstances to accept the argument that the dismissal was for some other substantial reason justifying dismissal (SOSR), since the dismissal was intrinsically linked with the employee's reason for being absent – see further Chapter 12, 'Detriment and unfair dismissal', under 'Automatically unfair dismissal'.

Redundancy and reorganisation. In a redundancy situation employers must **14.19** be very wary of retaining the replacement employee in preference to the returner. In Lane v Pickfords Travel Service Ltd ET Case No.20607/84, for example, the tribunal found that even if L was redundant, it would have been unreasonable to select her for redundancy because she had much longer service, backed up by her statutory right to return, than the employee who was retained.

Tribunals will not find that the returner was redundant if the job is still there but being done by somebody else. In Mundie v Drysdale Brothers ET Case No.100586/04 the employer felt that M's maternity replacement was efficient and hard-working and as a result decided to make M redundant and to retain her replacement instead. An employment tribunal held that M had been unlawfully discriminated against on the ground of her sex and unfairly dismissed. If she had not been pregnant and on maternity leave, the temporary appointment would not have been made; the comparison of M with her replacement would not have occurred; and the dismissal would not have come about. Therefore the underlying reason for her dismissal was her absence on maternity leave. It was clear that there was no genuine redundancy and that M's role still existed.

Similar considerations are taken into account where an employer claims that **14.20** the returner is disentitled to her job for SOSR because a reorganisation has taken place – see, for example, Hill v Supasnaps Ltd ET Case No.13110/87. The facts of that case can be found in Chapter 4, 'Returning to work after maternity leave', under 'Redundancy during maternity leave – meaning of "suitable available vacancy"'.

In Victoria and Albert Museum v Durrant 2011 IRLR 290, EAT, the Appeal Tribunal cautioned against the assumption that an employee who is 'surplus to requirements' is thereby redundant within the meaning of the statutory definition of redundancy in S.139(1) ERA. That case concerned a replacement employee who was dismissed, ostensibly under S.106(1), following the return of a colleague who had been on maternity leave. However, the EAT's

675

observations would apply with equal force to an employee on statutory leave who has no job to return to. The EAT asserted that the finding of the employment tribunal that the claimant was 'surplus to requirements' was not part of the statutory concept of redundancy, nor even an analogue of the concept. The question posed by the definition of redundancy in S.139(1)(b) ERA is not whether the need for employees on certain terms and conditions to carry out work had ceased or diminished, but whether the need of the employer to carry out work of a particular kind had ceased or diminished. The issue was thus not whether there was less need for those on the claimant's grade to carry out the work, but whether there was less need for such work to be carried out at all. A similar interpretation of S.139(1)(b) was adopted by the President of the EAT, Mr Justice Langstaff, in Packman (t/a Packman Lucas Associates) v Fauchon 2012 ICR 1362, EAT.

Case list

(Note that employment tribunal cases are not included in this list.)

677

L

Land Brandenburg v Sass 2005 IRLR 147, ECJ	3.59, 3.102, 13.29
Lavery v Plessey Telecommunications Ltd 1983 ICR 534, CA	3.118
Lewen v Denda 2000 ICR 648, ECJ	3.68, 10.59, 10.105,
	13.175, 13.176, 13.180
Little v Richmond Pharmacology Ltd 2014 ICR 85, EAT	13.100
Lyons v DWP Jobcentre Plus 2014 ICR 668, EAT	4.39, 12.43, 13.56

M

McGuigan v TG Baynes and Sons EAT 1114/97	4.68
MacCulloch and Wallis Ltd v Moore EAT 51/02	11.18, 11.22, 11.31, 11.45
Madarassy v Nomura International plc 2007 ICR 867, CA	2.78
Mahlburg v Land Mecklenburg-Vorpommern 2001 ICR 1032, ECJ	2.82, 13.31, 13.65
Maksymiuk v Bar Roma EATS 0017/12	13.40
Markin v Russia 56 EHRR 8, ECtHR	13.19, 13.133
Matthews and ors v Kent and Medway Towns Fire Authority and ors 2006 ICR 365, HL	13.152
Mayr v Bäckerei und Konditorei Gerhard Flöckner OHG 2008 IRLR 387, ECJ	1.16, 3.14, 8.15, 12.16, 12.17, 12.49, 13.48, 13.68
Meade-Hill and anor v British Council 1995 ICR 847, CA	13.87
Meerts v Proost NV 2010 All ER (EC) 1085, ECJ	10.51, 10.52
Merino Gómez v Continental Industrias del Caucho SA 2005 ICR 1040, ECJ	3.81, 3.85, 3.86, 6.97, 6.98
Miles v Gilbank and anor 2006 ICR 1297, CA	13.80
Ministry of Defence v Jeremiah 1980 ICR 13, CA	12.7
Ministry of Defence v Williams EAT 0833/02	4.22
Mitchell v David Evans Agricultural Ltd EAT 0083/06	13.87
Murray and anor v Foyle Meats Ltd 1999 ICR 827, HL	4.67

N

Napoli v Ministero della Giustizia, Dipartimento dell'Amministrazione Penitenziaria 2014 ICR 486, ECJ	13.29
Nelson v Chesterfield Law Centre EAT 1359/96	13.109
New Southern Railway Ltd (formerly South Central Trains Ltd) v Rodway 2005 ICR 1162, CA	10.37, 10.87, 10.97, 12.19
New Southern Railway Ltd v Quinn 2006 ICR 761, EAT	2.34
Nixon v Ross Coates Solicitors and anor EAT 0108/10	13.115

O

O'Neill v Buckinghamshire County Council 2010 IRLR 384, EAT	2.23, 2.79
O'Neill v Governors of St Thomas More Roman Catholic Voluntarily Aided Upper School and anor 1997 ICR 33, EAT	12.39, 13.63
Ogilvie v Ross and anor t/a Braid Veterinary Hospital EAT 1115/99	13.110
Onu v Akwiwu and anor; Taiwo v Olaigbe and anor 2014 ICR 571, CA	13.38
Oxford Health NHS Foundation Trust v Laakkonen and ors EAT 0536/12	13.87

P

P and O European Ferries (Dover) Ltd and anor v Iverson 1999 ICR 1088, EAT	2.82
Packman (t/a Packman Lucas Associates) v Fauchon 2012 ICR 1362, EAT	14.20

681

Index

713

If Cresswell plc had any growth prospects shareholders may be willing to pay more than £2.07, because Cresswell's potential profit growth would increase after returning the cash to shareholders, which was providing no more than average returns.

However, in practice, as a mature company, investors are unlikely to see Cresswell plc as having any growth prospects – it had not been able to invest its £20m surplus cash in new value-adding projects. Therefore, it is likely that investors may not even be willing to pay £2.07 per share.

E15.10 Cresswell plc

Using the information from E15.9 we can see what would happen if the original share price had been higher than £2 at £3.

> Cresswell's current eps are £30m/100m = 30p
> and its P/E ratio is £2.0/30p = 6.67 times

If the original share price had been higher than £2 at £3, then

> £20m cash would have bought 6.67m shares (£20m/£3)
> eps would have remained at the original 30p (£28m/93.34m)
> P/E ratio would have been 10 times (£3/30p)

The share price of £3 is the 'equilibrium' price, which equals the original earnings level of 30p multiplied by the £20m cash divided by the annual interest of £2m. At any share price above £3 eps will fall, and the P/E ratio will increase. The company should therefore buy back its shares when its P/E ratio is at a relatively low level.

E16.1 Pitch plc

$$\text{number of Perfecto ordinary shares in issue} = \frac{\text{balance sheet value of ordinary shares}}{\text{nominal value of each ordinary share}}$$

$$= £600,000/£1$$

$$= 0.6\text{m shares}$$

stock market valuation of Perfecto plc   = number of ordinary shares in issue × market price

$$= 0.6\text{m} × £1.84$$

$$= £1,104,000$$

	£000
Total assets less current liabilities	1,625
less	
Intangible non-current assets	(203)
	1,422
less	
Long-term debt	(85)
	1,337

Net asset value (NAV)	£1,337,000
Number of ordinary shares	0.6m
Value per ordinary share	= £1,337,000/600,000
	= £2.23 per share

It can be see from the above calculation that the valuation of the company based on the historical costs of its book assets is around 21% more than the market value.

E16.2 Pitch plc

The costs of acquiring the separate assets of a target company may be determined on an open market basis. These are the costs to replace the assets, rather than what they could be sold for. The advantage of this method is that replacement cost valuations are more relevant than historical cost book valuations or current realisable valuations.

Disadvantages are that this method ignores goodwill, and it is usually difficult to identify separate assets, like separate individual factories, machinery, etc., and determine their replacement cost. Assets may also be complementary and therefore their separate valuation may not be totally realistic. There is no data available to value Perfecto plc in this way.

E16.3 Pitch plc

Using the data from E16.1 the directors of Pitch plc may calculate a capitalised earnings valuation of Perfecto plc.

$$\text{capitalised earnings value} = \frac{\text{annual maintainable expected earnings}}{\text{required earnings yield}}$$

required earnings yield	= eps/share price
Perfecto plc required earnings yield	= the reciprocal of its P/E ratio
	= $1 \times 100/7.36$ = 13.587%
Perfecto plc's capitalised earnings value	= £150,000/0.13587 (assuming that current earnings are equal to its maintainable expected earnings)
	= £1,104,000 (rounded up)

E16.4 Pitch plc

Using the data from E16.1 the directors of Pitch plc may calculate a price/earnings ratio valuation of Perfecto plc. Pitch plc must decide on a suitable P/E ratio and then multiply this by Perfecto plc's eps. Perfecto plc's eps may be its historical eps or its expected future eps.

Pitch may use one of a number of P/E ratios: Pitch plc's P/E ratio; Perfecto plc's P/E ratio; the weighted average of the P/E ratios of the two companies. We will consider valuations of Perfecto plc using its historical (2012) eps and the three different P/E ratios.

Pitch plc P/E ratio

$$\text{Market value of Perfecto plc} = \text{Perfecto 2012 eps} \times \text{Pitch P/E} \times \text{number of Perfecto ordinary shares}$$

$$= £0.25 \times 9 \times 600,000$$
$$= £1,350,000$$

Perfecto plc P/E ratio

$$\text{Market value of Perfecto plc} = \text{Perfecto 2012 eps} \times \text{Perfecto P/E} \times \text{number of Perfecto ordinary shares}$$

$$= £0.25 \times 7.36 \times 600,000$$
$$= £1,104,000 \text{ (equal to the capitalised earnings valuation)}$$

Weighted average P/E ratio

The combined earnings (profit on ordinary activities after tax)
$$= £150,000 + £800,000$$
$$= £950,000$$

Perfecto plc P/E ratio weighted by combined earnings
$$= \frac{7.36 \times £150,000}{£950,000} = 1.16$$

Pitch plc P/E ratio weighted by combined earnings
$$= \frac{9 \times £800,000}{£950,000} = 7.58$$

$$\text{Weighted average P/E ratio} = 1.16 + 7.58$$
$$= 8.74$$
$$\text{Market value of Perfecto plc} = £0.25 \times 8.74 \times 600,000$$
$$= £1,311,000$$

E16.5 Pitch plc

Using the data from E16.1 the directors of Pitch plc may use the DCF method to compare the present value of the future cash flows of the combined entity with the present values of its future cash flows if the acquisition did not go ahead.

Using distributable earnings (profit on ordinary activities after tax) as an approximation of cash flows:

Present value of future cash flows – no acquisition

$$\text{Pitch plc current distributable earnings} = £800,000$$
$$\text{Discount factor} = \text{Pitch plc WACC} = 6\%$$
$$\text{Present value of future expected cash flows} = \frac{£800,000}{0.06}$$
$$= £13,333,333$$

Present value of future cash flows – with acquisition

Pitch plc post-acquisition distributable earnings = £130,000 + £800,000

The present values of future cash flows can then be calculated using Pitch plc's WACC, applied to distributable earnings, plus the estimated additional cash flows for 2013 to 2017.

Present value of post-acquisition cash flows

$$= \frac{£930,000}{0.06} + \frac{£130,000}{1.06} + \frac{£130,000}{1.06^2} + \frac{£150,000}{1.06^3} + \frac{£100,000}{1.06^4} + \frac{£130,000}{1.06^5}$$

$$= £16,040,638$$

The difference between the present values of the future cash flows assuming acquisition and no acquisition are:

	£16,040,638
	less £13,333,333
Maximum price that should be paid by Pitch plc for Perfecto plc	£2,707,305

E16.6 Pitch plc

Using the data from E16.1 the directors of Pitch plc may use the CAPM to value Perfecto plc. The risk-free rate of return R_f is 1% per annum and the market rate of return R_m is 6.5% per annum. Perfecto plc's beta factor $\beta = 1.20$.

Using $K_e = R_f + \beta \times (R_m - R_f)$

Perfecto plc cost of equity = 1% + 1.20 × (6.5% − 1%)

= 7.6%

Perfecto plc market value, assuming a 4% p.a. increase in future dividends:

$$= \frac{£40,000 \times 1.04}{(0.076 - 0.04)}$$

$$= £1,155,556$$

It should be noted that this valuation is lower than Perfecto plc's book value of its net assets valuation of £1,337,000 at 30 September 2012, but higher than the valuation based on its share price 30 September 2012 of £1.84 × 600,000 = £1,104,000.

E16.7 Horse and Cart

(i)

PV of gain = £2.5m/0.10 − £2m = £23m

(ii)   If £70m offer is accepted the gain for Horse plc shareholders would be:

	£
Net acquisition cost (£70m − £50m)	20m
PV of gain	23m
Gain for Horse plc shareholders	3m

E16.10 Porgy plc

(i)
Value created by merger
£158m − (£90m + £40m + £20m + £5m) = £3m
Present value £3.0m/0.10 = £30.0m

(ii)
Cash price
(£40m + £20m)/20m = £3.00 per share

(iii)
Value = (2/3 × £158m) − £90m = £15.3m

(iv)
Gain = (£158 − £90m − £60) = £8m

(**v**)   A target company may contest an offer on several grounds:
- offer is unacceptable because insufficient additional value will be created
- merger or acquisition has no obvious advantage
- employees may be strongly opposed.

(**vi**) Defensive tactics:
- publicly refute profit forecasts
- lobby the Office of Fair Trading (OFT) or department of Business, Innovation and Skills (BIS)
- refer offer to Monopoly and Mergers Commission
- refer offer to the European Union
- find a 'white knight' company as an alternative buyer
- make a counter bid for the predator company
- arrange an MBO or MBI.

E16.11 Black Ltd

Alternative valuation models:

- Dividend model
- Dividend model (with growth)
- Assets-based valuation
- Earnings-based valuation – current
- Earnings-based valuation – future
- Accounting rate of return (ARR).

Dividend model

(£45,000/0.12)/300,000 = £1.25 per share

Dividend model (with growth)

(£45,000(1.04)/(0.12 − 0.04))/300,000 = £1.95 per share

Assets-based valuation

Net assets £1,060,000 − non-current assets £1,305,000 + re-valued non-current assets
(£1,075,000 + £480,000 + £45,000) = £1,355,000/300,000 = £4.52 per share

Earnings-based valuation – current

P/E = MV/earnings
Average earnings over the last 5 years
= (£90,000 + £80,000 + £105,000 + £90,000 + £100,000)/5
= £93,000
Average most recent market P/Es

(8.5 + 9.0 + 10.0)/3 = 9.167

Using an unadjusted P/E ratio

(9.167 × £93,000)/300,000 = £2.84 per share

Adjusted P/E ratio (say reduced by 30% because Black is not a plc)
Say 9.167 × 70% = 6.42

(6.42 × £93,000)/300,000 = £1.99 per share

Earnings based valuation – future

Say over five years increase at 4% per annum

Year 1	£100,000
Year 2	£104,000
Year 3	£108,160
Year 4	£112,486
Year 5	£116,985

Average = £541,631/5 = £108,326

Average most recent market P/Es

(8.5 + 9.0 + 10.0)/3 = 9.167

Using an unadjusted P/E ratio

(9.167 × £108,326)/300,000 = £3.31 per share

Adjusted P/E ratio (say reduced by 30% because Black is not a plc)
Say 9.167 × 70% = 6.42

(6.42 × £108,326)/300,000 = £2.32 per share

Accounting rate of return

Assume ROCE = 18%

$$\frac{\text{average profit over next five years/ROCE}}{\text{number of issued shares}} = \frac{£108,326/0.18}{300,000} = £2.01 \text{ per share}$$

E17.8 Blue Sky plc

(i)

Reasons for mergers and acquisitions would include:

- operating economies of scale
- economies of vertical and horizontal integration
- combining complementary resource structures
- utilisation of surplus funds
- utilisation of tax shields
- strategic growth
- diversification
- asset backing
- increasing quality of earnings.

(ii)

PV of gain

$$(£2.75\text{m}/0.10) - £5\text{m} = £22.5\text{m}$$

(iii)

If £65m offer is accepted, the gain for Blue Sky plc shareholders would be:

Net cost (£65m − £50m)	15.0m
PV of gain	22.5m
Gain for Blue Sky plc shareholders	7.5m

(iv)

Value of 70% for Blue Sky plc of the merged company

70% × (£80m + £50m + £22.5m) = £106.75m

Value created for Blue Sky plc shareholders

£106.75m − £80m = £26.75m

(v)

Defensive tactics would include:

- publicly refute profit forecasts
- lobby the OFT or BIS
- refer offer to Monopoly and Mergers Commission
- refer offer to the European Union
- find a 'white knight' company
- make a counter bid for the predator company
- arrange an MBO or MBI.

E17.9 Arkwright plc

(i)

	£
Current profits	3,600,000
Increase	
(£2m − extra interest 8% × £10,000,000)	1,200,000
New profits after acquisition	4,800,000
New cost of equity	15%
New market value (£4.8m/0.15)	32,000,000
Old market value (£3.6m/0.12)	30,000,000
Increase in shareholders' wealth	2,000,000

(ii)

NPV of the acquisition

$$(£2m/0.10) − £10m = £10m$$

Therefore impact of financing the acquisition = £10m − £2m = £8m

Change in the value of the company

	£
NPV of acquisition	10,000,000
Loss due to increase in cost of equity	(8,000,000)
Increase in shareholders' wealth	2,000,000

(iii) Reasons for an increase in cost of equity may include:
- greater perceived financial risk from an increase in debt and gearing
- reduced chance of dividend payments.

E18.7 Pomfrit Ltd

£m	Year 1	Year 2	Year 3	Year 4
Earnings	10.0000	11.8000	13.1275	14.6043
Dividends	(4.0000)	(2.9500)	(3.2819)	(7.3022)
Retained earnings	6.0000	8.8500	9.8456	7.3021
New equity	6.0000			
Funds invested	12.0000	8.8500	9.8456	
ROI (15%)	1.8000	1.3275	1.4768	
(add to next year's earnings)				

The growth rate G can be estimated assuming the expected long-term retention rate of 50%, and future return of 10%.

$$G = \text{retention rate} \times \text{expected future returns} = 50\% \times 10\% = 5\%$$

The value in Year 3 would be £7.3022m/(0.10 − 0.05) = £146.044m
The value of the company today would therefore be:

$$£4m/1.10 + £2.95m/(1.10)^2 + £3.2819m/(1.10)^3 + £146.044m/(1.10)^3 = £118.265m$$

and the value of a share would be:

$$£118.265m/1.5m = £78.84 \text{ per share}$$

E18.8 Gillie plc

Current market value			**Current returns**
£			£
Debt	2,000,000	£2m debt × 10%	200,000
Equity	6,000,000	3m shares × 40p	1,200,000
	8,000,000		1,400,000

Cost of equity using the dividend growth model and assuming zero dividend growth:

$$K_e = \frac{v}{S} = \frac{40p}{£2.00} = 20\%$$

$$\text{WACC} = \frac{£1,400,000}{£8,000,000} \times 100 = 17.5\%$$

$$\text{Reorganisation evaluation NPV} = \frac{£525,000}{0.175} - £2,000,000 = +£1,000,000$$

	£	
Current dividend	1,200,000	
Current interest	200,000	
	1,400,000	
Additional income	525,000	
	1,925,000	
New total interest	(400,000)	(£2m + £2m) debt × 10%
	1,525,000	

New cost of equity 20% + 5% = 25%

Therefore, new value of equity = £1,525,000/0.25	=	£6,100,000
Current value of equity	=	£6,000,000
Increase in value of equity	=	£100,000

New value of company at WACC = £1,925,000/0.175	=	£11,000,000
Current value of company = £4,000,000 + £6,100,000	=	£10,100,000
Increase in value		£900,000
NPV of project		£100,000
Increase in value of equity		£100,000

Although the reorganisation is viable, the method of financing has considerably reduced the net benefit.

Index

Definitions may be found in the Glossary for key terms that have page numbers in **bold** type.

The names of companies mentioned in the book are in **bold** type.